HOW
GOVERNMENTS
WORK

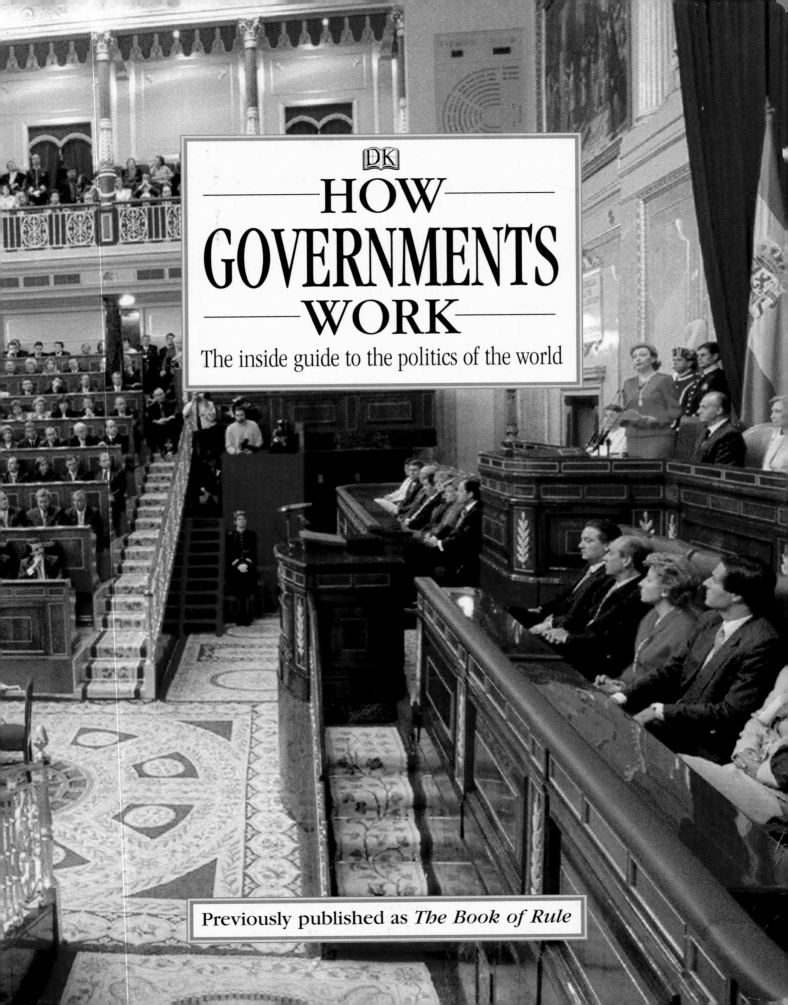

HOW GOVERNMENTS WORK

The inside guide to the politics of the world

Previously published as *The Book of Rule*

LONDON, NEW YORK, MELBOURNE,
MUNICH AND DELHI

Conceived and produced for
Dorling Kindersley by

NEWEARTHMEDIA

EDITORIAL PRODUCER Timothy M. Cain
PROJECT MANAGER Natalie C. Dippenaar
MANAGING EDITOR Elaine Hanson Cardenas
POLITICAL CONSULTANT Danielle Pletka
WRITERS Kenneth Minogue, David E. Roach,
Elaine Hanson Cardenas, Albert R. Karr,
Gerald M. Bastarache, Rebecca Frey, Rory G. Lukins,
Natalie C. Dippenaar, Peter M. Schwartz, Janet Wagner,
Emilie Bahr, Elahe Parsa, Chris Delboni,
Eiman Hajabbasi, Fiona J. Mackintosh
COPY EDITORS Dina C. Hernandez, James K. Bock,
Bob Guldin
DESIGNERS Jo Scraba, Anne L. Dougherty,
Katharine Doret, Rashida Kopti, Chuck Bussenger
GRAPHICS Rob Cady
IMAGE RESEARCHERS Nicole E. Schofer, Alexa Keefe,
Meaghan Curry, Brenda Andrews, PhotoAssist
EDITORIAL RESEARCH Heather L. Dresser, Laurie Burkitt,
Molly K. McKew, Alan Ingle

Dorling Kindersley Limited

DTP DESIGNER John Goldsmid
MAPS Julie Turner, David Roberts, Philip Rowles
DATA Circa International
PICTURE RESEARCH Carolyn Clerkin, Samantha Nunn,
Anna Grapes, Juliet Duff
DK PICTURE LIBRARY Claire Bowers, Lucy Claxton,
Hayley Smith, Romaine Werblow
PRODUCTION Rita Sinha

Published in Great Britain in 2006 by
Dorling Kindersley Limited
80 Strand, London WC2R 0RL
Copyright © 2004, 2006
Dorling Kindersley Limited
A Penguin Company

First published in 2004 as
The Book of Rule: How the World is Governed

A CIP catalogue record for this book is available
from the British Library
ISBN: 1 4053 1453 2

Colour reproduction by Colourscan, Singapore
Printed and bound in China by Toppan

For our complete catalogue visit
www.dk.com

PUBLISHER'S NOTE

TODAY, AS THE WORLD'S POPULATION HAS REACHED SIX BILLION, every one of us lives, willingly or otherwise, as part of a political state of one sort or another; even the nomadic peoples of Central Asia or the bedou of Arabia and the Sahara, the tribal peoples of Amazonia, sub-Saharan Africa and the Arctic north exist as citizens of their respective nation states; they appear on national censuses and are dependent upon their governments for economic and social support, and for protection of their traditional lifestyles.

With the exception of Antarctica (itself subject to international treaty arrangements to protect it as a global wilderness and site of scientific interest), the Earth's surface is entirely divided, controlled and administered by 193 states, with a handful of dependent (often unpopulated) territories. Even offshore sea areas are claimed as part of national territories, some nations exceeding the generally accepted 22-mile (35-km) territorial limit, in order to secure mineral or fishery resources.

20TH CENTURY TRANSFORMATIONS

At the beginning of the last century, the world was very different. The world map comprised less than 80 countries, and less than one third of the global population lived in what we would recognize as independent states. Most of the peoples of Europe, Asia, and Africa were subjects of less than a dozen imperial powers: France, Spain, Portugal, Great Britain, the Netherlands, Turkey, Russia, China, and Japan. Great Britain also ruled all of Australasia and the largest country in the Americas—Canada. But is was here, in the western hemisphere, that European notions of anti-imperial, national self-determination had flourished with the Declaration of Independence, from British rule, of the United States in 1776, and the struggle for the liberation of Latin America from Spanish and Portuguese rule which took place over the next century.

Furthermore, that small minority of the world's population who had the right to vote to determine their manner of governance were for the most part defined by sex and wealth—they were male, and they were property owners.

The great political achievement of the 20th century was the progress toward universal suffrage, the enfranchisement of both sexes and all classes, and the right, in principle, of every adult to participate in the government of themselves and their fellow citizens.

COMMUNISM AND FASCISM

However, this was bought at an enormous cost: the first half of the 20th century was dominated by two ideological political experiments—the doctrine of communism, and the nationalist creed of fascism. Both sought to replace the dominance of the deep-rooted imperial powers with radical, "modern" political systems.

Communism set out to liberate the urban, and later the rural, proletariat from the economic burdens of capitalism, through the demolition of the class structure, the forcible redistribution of wealth and property, and the introduction of communal ownership and equality before the law. Evolving from the ideas of two middle-class 19th-century German radicals, Karl Marx and Frederic Engels, communism was first implemented in Russia in 1917 as the imperial government crumbled during World War I (itself the product of a struggle for supremacy between the imperial Great Powers). The practical problems of implementing such a doctrine were harshly imposed by Trotsky, Lenin and Stalin in the formation of the Soviet Union, a coda adapted in the wake of the Chinese civil war, in 1949, by Mao Zedong. It may be said that the various doctrinal "-isms" which communism spawned—Leninism, Trotskyism, Stalinism, Maoism—sought at root to provide a solution to a single issue: how to feed, clothe and house a rapidly expanding population on an equable basis. The solutions proved fundamentally flawed, however, in that they involved the inevitable creation of a governing elite, the imposition of political ideology at any price, and social and economic engineering on a scale which ignored the cost in human lives.

Fascism, as exemplified by Benito's Mussolini's Italy, General Franco's Spain and Aldof Hitler's Nazi Party in Germany, emerged in the wake of World War I as a creed of national unification and self-determination, and involved social engineering of a different sort—racial, ethnic and political "cleansing" through repression and, ultimately, mass murder.

Communism and Fascism defined the extremes of modern political nom-enclature, the Left and the Right respectively. While communism and fascism were in principle antithetical—in World War II both Hitler and Stalin saw themselves as fighting an ideological war against each other - they both adopted totalitarian methods to impose political ideas, rode roughshod over any sense of political accountability, and rapidly evolved versions of the very imperialism they sought to supplant.

While fascism on a global scale was eradicated by World War II, through the temporary alliance of the Soviet Union and the democratic governments of Britain and the USA, the consequence of the Allied victory was the persistence of communist governments in the Soviet Union and China, and the evolution of a new global political dynamic—the "Cold War"—dominated by "superpowers," between the (liberal, largely democratic) West under the aegis of America and the North Atlantic Treaty Organization (NATO), and the (communist) East under the Soviet Union's Warsaw Pact and, from 1961, a separate communist sphere of influence radiating from the People's Republic of China.

DECOLONIZATION
The third great struggle of the twentieth century saw the demolition of the remaining European colonial empires in the wake of World War II. This began with the independence of British South Asia—formerly British Queen Victoria's "Jewel in the Crown"—to form the world's largest democracy in India and, significantly, the partition of the territory into Hindu India and Muslim Pakistan, in 1947. Between 1950 and 1976 a further 100 or so colonies achieved independence, largely from Britain, France, Portugal, and the Netherlands and, by the end of the 1990s, the collapse of Soviet communism saw the electoral process introduced in the 12 Soviet republics, and restored throughout the Warsaw Pact countries of eastern Europe and the Baltic States.

The last decade of the century witnessed the emergence of two slumb-ering political problems which had largely been held in check during the Cold War: on a national level, tensions between centralized political control and various urges toward devolution; on an international scale, a new conflict between the developed world, and the developing world (variously termed First and Third worlds, North and South). These were often manifested in terrorism.

GOVERNING OURSELVES
Suffrage still remains far from universal, and while concerns about a new sort of economic and cultural imperialism, stemming largely from the growing power and influence of the "developed" world—dubbed globalization—dominate the political agenda, in proportional terms the world may safely be said to be a better and fairer place today than in 1900. A glance at the world map showing the systems of rule operating in the world today (page 28-29) illustrates that the greater majority of us live in democracies of one sort or another—some admittedly in name only—certainly many in societies in which freedom of speech, open debate and universal representation lie at the core of the national ethos. Unfortunately, even today, not many "democracies" recognize the double-edged meaning of the term—that the will of the majority is only granted by their acknowledgement of the rights and concerns of the minority.

And yet, how many of us really understand how we are governed? How many truly and fully exercise the political, social, ethical and moral rights which form part of the legacy won by the blood and determination of our forebears? In what way did our systems of government evolve? How are those who rule us selected and elected? How is political power checked and balanced, and indeed what are the limits of political power?

This remarkable book, conceived and created by Washington-based NEWEARTH MEDIA, seeks to provide an introduction to our political birthright. Drawing upon the expertise of a wide range of writers, journalists, political analysts, and consultants, this remains the first attempt to provide a political guide to the world. It inevitably suffers from all the flaws of such a ground-breaking enterprise.

The book is organized by style of government, or rule, and provides a succinct overview of the political structure and system of every country in the world. A carefully constructed fact panel provides an instant assessment of the political values and status of each nation and, where appropriate, an issues panel focuses on the key challenges confronted by the nation state.

A selection of countries are afforded a larger, more detailed treatment; the criteria for selection has been based on their uniqueness or influence in terms of providing eminent models of various styles of governance, models often emulated (as in the case of say France, Spain, or the United Kingdom) widely among their former colonies. The introductory pages, in the Global Matrix section, provide an overview of the major factors which have molded and continue to affect the political map of the world.

Any attempt to paint a portrait of the contemporary world is beset by the problem that the world changes, often dramatically and unpredictably, on a daily basis. Thus, this is not intended to be a book of current affairs, but rather an assessment of how the political jigsaw of the world has evolved, its general characteristics and, hopefully, it may suggest ways in which we can evolve fairer and more just methods of conducting our affairs.

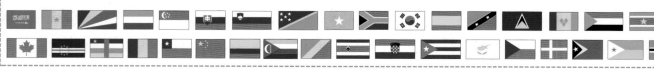

CONTENTS

HOW TO USE THE BOOK

THE *BOOK OF RULE* IS ORGANIZED IN THREE SECTIONS. The book opens with a brief, illustrated Chronology of Rule which charts the development of political thought and the emergence of systems of rule, from around 8000 B.C. to the present day. The second section is The Global Matrix—an overview of the world's international networks, which influence and determine the nature of politics in every country around the globe. The book's third section, the Systems of Rule, clearly explains the six basic systems of rule in operation in the world today and offers a detailed profile of each of the world's 193 nations. The nations in each subsection are presented in order of size of population.

COUNTRY PROFILES
Each of the world's nations is allocated one or more pages. Key nations, which include the US, the UK, France, Spain, Russia, Germany, Canada, Japan, Australia, and Iraq are profiled in greater depth with between two and 12 pages each. This is on the basis of their size, GNP, ranking in world affairs or current issues.

Seat of Government
Capital icon pinpoints and labels the location where the highest-level legislative body of the country meets on a regular basis.

Country Map
Full-color maps of the country depict major geographical features, while the locator globe shows the nation's location in the world.

Type of Rule
Nations are categorized, in descending order of population, under six systems of governance: Monarchal Rule, Theocratic Rule, Military Rule, Democratic Rule, Single Party Rule, and Transitional Rule.

Official Country Name

Vital Statistics
Displays the country's population, total area, date of independence and the date of the original constitution.

Official Country Seal
Displays the national coat of arms, symbol, or seal.

Country Flag

Country Factfile
At-a-glance, up-to-date political and social information on each country.

Economics Score Cards
A broad picture of the country's economy. Gross National Product (GNP) includes income from investments held abroad. Balance of payments (Balance of trade) is the difference between the funds received by a country and those that the country pays.

Government Spending
The percentage of the country's Gross Domestic Product (GDP) that is spent on defense, education and health.

Global Conflicts Chart
The incidence of national and international conflict over the past 25 years, and key military or defense issues.

Political Overviews
The text provides a brief history of the country's origins, focusing on the most important political events that have occurred, key related developments and current events, in order to provide an overview of how the nation has evolved politically into the government and policies it has today.

Issues and Challenges
The panel provides an insight into the most pressing issues and challenges facing the nation today, or in recent history.

Notes of Distinction
These highlight a unique aspect of the nation.

How the Government Works Chart
This diagram provides a breakdown of the current structure of the nation's government as stipulated by the most recent draft of the constitution. It also details the roles and responsibilities of the highest-ranking and most important components of the executive, legislative, and judicial branches.

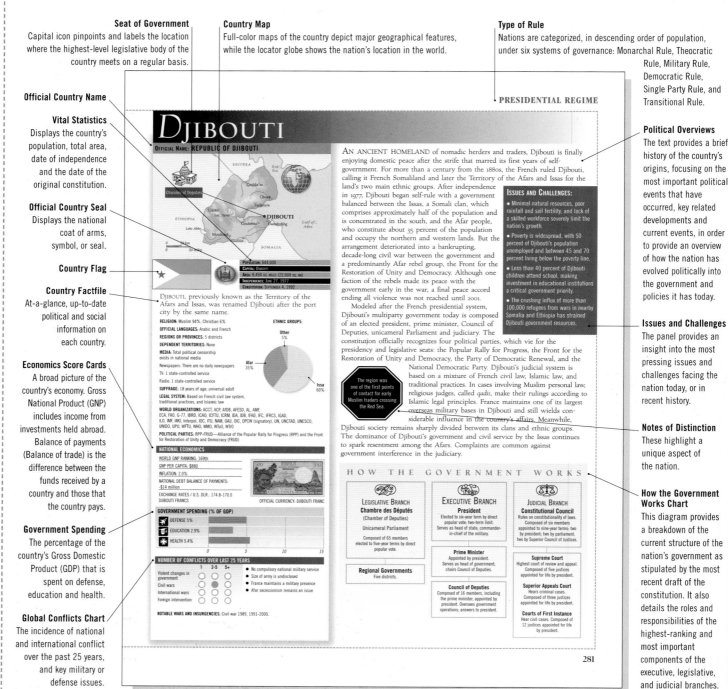

Historical and Political Overview
The main text on introductory pages outlines significant events in the political history of the nation that have influenced its formation and development. There is also a spotlight on a key figure in the development or governance of the nation.

How the Government Works
This layers the hierarchy of the executive, legislative and judicial branches of the nation. An expanded version similar to those of the one-page countries (shown opposite page), these go into more detail on the key roles and responsibilities of the various components.

Regional and Local Governments
This highlights provincial and regional-level administrative structures reporting to the national-level government.

Primary Coverage
The larger and often more politically dominant nations of the world are given extended coverage. These vary in length to include the origins of the body politic and a detailed description of the current executive, legislative and judicial systems.

Key Political Figure
Although many people contribute to the formation of or play an important role in events in a nation, often one person stands out as significant or key. This offers a brief bio of such individuals and their contribution to the nation as a whole.

Electoral System
This box highlights key aspects or components of the electoral system of the country.

Overview of Executive Branch
The executive pages outline the roles and responsibilities of the highest-level decision makers of the executive branch of the nation. Major leaders from the country's modern history are shown with brief outlines of their time in office and key administrative buildings are also featured.

Overview of Legislative Branch
The legislative pages outline the roles and responsibilities of the principal components of the legislative branch of the nation.

Cabinet Ministries
The various departments represented in the Cabinet are described here.

Key Heads of State
Brief biographies and dates in office of the key movers and shakers of the nation's political history.

Powers and Procedures
Legislative bodies have significant powers that they are constitutionally allowed to exercise, while limited by certain procedures, both of which are briefly introduced in this section.

Overview of Judicial Branch
The judicial pages outline the highest decision-making bodies in the judicial system, as well as an introduction to the workings of lower level courts. (Country factfiles appear on these pages when a nation has more than four pages of display.)

Landmark Supreme Court Cases
This section presents key court decisions that have been made at the highest-levels of the judicial system, either the Supreme Court or Constitutional Court.

CHRONOLOG

C. 8000 B.C. ◀◀ ▶▶ 0

PEOPLE SETTLE DOWN...TO THE BUSINESS OF GOVERNMENT

Until around 8000 B.C., human beings lived as hunter-gatherers. As the ice caps receded and climate changes encouraged the domestication of livestock and the growing of crops, roamers became settlers. The first farmers located themselves in fertile river basins in Mesopotamia, and in the Indus and Yangtse valleys in India and China. These newly-settled farmers developed into communities and began to articulate themselves into herders, tillers of the soil, craftsmen, warriors, priests and, over time, scribes, the precursors of bureaucracy. But settled peoples became prey to marauders eager to enjoy the harvest without the labor of sowing. The earliest settlers needed protection and thus primitive governments arose to provide a common defense. So communities became larger, absorbing more and diverse peoples with differing customs, all of which required a ruling hand and laws to provide order. States superseded wandering clans, and growing states found they needed to record their affairs—resources, inventories, beliefs, and customs—which led to the invention of writing, in turn promoting the capacity to think in abstract terms. They found that expansion and consolidation improved security against invaders, which led to states expanding by conquest and alliance, by trade and treaty, to form empires, which began to appear from around 3000 B.C.

THE PYRAMIDS OF POWER

The classic form of rule in early states and empires was absolute monarchy, and the ruler, at the apex of society, had total power over his subjects. The ruler—king, emperor or pharaoh by title—was a usually a high priest, chief judge, commander-in-chief and very likely a worshiped deity as well, all rolled into one. Property was held at the mercy of the ruler. The ruler was, however, by no means omnipotent, and was bound by custom and influenced by scribes, advisers, priests,

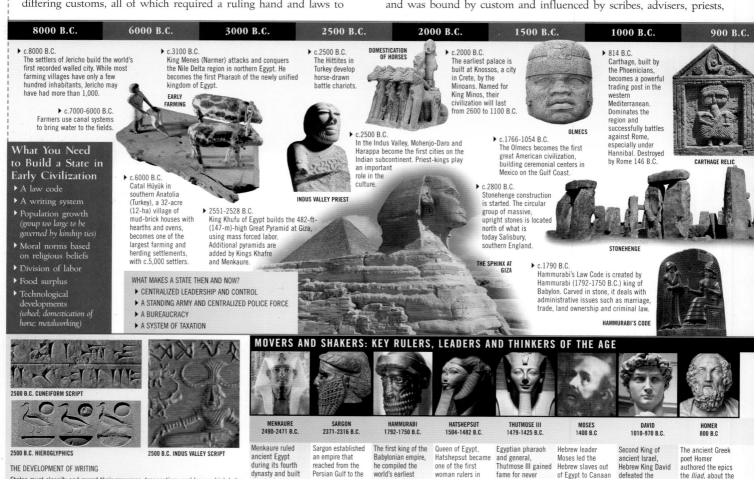

8000 B.C.	6000 B.C.	3000 B.C.	2500 B.C.	2000 B.C.	1500 B.C.	1000 B.C.	900 B.C.

▶ c.8000 B.C.
The settlers of Jericho build the world's first recorded walled city. While most farming villages have only a few hundred inhabitants, Jericho may have had more than 1,000.

▶ c.7000–6000 B.C.
Farmers use canal systems to bring water to the fields.

▶ c.3100 B.C.
King Menes (Narmer) attacks and conquers the Nile Delta region in northern Egypt. He becomes the first Pharaoh of the newly unified kingdom of Egypt.

EARLY FARMING

▶ c.2500 B.C.
The Hittites in Turkey develop horse-drawn battle chariots.

DOMESTICATION OF HORSES

▶ c.2000 B.C.
The earliest palace is built at Knossos, a city in Crete, by the Minoans. Named for King Minos, their civilization will last from 2600 to 1100 B.C.

▶ 814 B.C.
Carthage, built by the Phoenicians, becomes a powerful trading post in the western Mediterranean. Dominates the region and successfully battles against Rome, especially under Hannibal. Destroyed by Rome 146 B.C.

CARTHAGE RELIC

▶ c.2500 B.C.
In the Indus Valley, Mohenjo-Daro and Harappa become the first cities on the Indian subcontinent. Priest-kings play an important role in the culture.

INDUS VALLEY PRIEST

OLMECS

▶ c.1766-1054 B.C.
The Olmecs becomes the first great American civilization, building ceremonial centers in Mexico on the Gulf Coast.

▶ c.6000 B.C.
Catal Hüyük in southern Anatolia (Turkey), a 32-acre (12-ha) village of mud-brick houses with hearths and ovens, becomes one of the largest farming and herding settlements, with c.5,000 settlers.

▶ 2551-2528 B.C.
King Khufu of Egypt builds the 482-ft-(147-m)-high Great Pyramid at Giza, using mass forced labor. Additional pyramids are added by Kings Khafre and Menkaure.

▶ c.2800 B.C.
Stonehenge construction is started. The circular group of massive, upright stones is located north of what is today Salisbury, southern England.

STONEHENGE

THE SPHINX AT GIZA

▶ c.1790 B.C.
Hammurabi's Law Code is created by Hammurabi (1792-1750 B.C.) king of Babylon. Carved in stone, it deals with administrative issues such as marriage, trade, land ownership and criminal law.

HAMMURABI'S CODE

What You Need to Build a State in Early Civilization

▶ A law code
▶ A writing system
▶ Population growth *(group too large to be governed by kinship ties)*
▶ Moral norms based on religious beliefs
▶ Division of labor
▶ Food surplus
▶ Technological developments *(wheel; domestication of horse; metalworking)*

WHAT MAKES A STATE THEN AND NOW?

▶ CENTRALIZED LEADERSHIP AND CONTROL
▶ A STANDING ARMY AND CENTRALIZED POLICE FORCE
▶ A BUREAUCRACY
▶ A SYSTEM OF TAXATION

2500 B.C. CUNEIFORM SCRIPT

2500 B.C. HIEROGLYPHICS

2500 B.C. INDUS VALLEY SCRIPT

THE DEVELOPMENT OF WRITING

States must classify and record their resources, transactions and laws, which helps bring writing into existence as early as the middle of the fourth millennium B.C. Before alphabets are developed, scribes record daily life with pictograms on clay tablets and on papyrus. The first picture- and word-writing express only basic ideas.

MOVERS AND SHAKERS: KEY RULERS, LEADERS AND THINKERS OF THE AGE

MENKAURE 2490-2471 B.C.	SARGON 2371-2316 B.C.	HAMMURABI 1792-1750 B.C.	HATSHEPSUT 1504-1482 B.C.	THUTMOSE III 1479-1425 B.C.	MOSES 1400 B.C	DAVID 1010-970 B.C.	HOMER 800 B.C
Menkaure ruled ancient Egypt during its fourth dynasty and built the third and smallest pyramid at Giza—finished in mud and brick.	Sargon established an empire that reached from the Persian Gulf to the Mediterranean. The first Mesopotamian king to declare himself divine.	The first king of the Babylonian empire, he compiled the world's earliest known code of laws, which he carved on stone and used to rule his people.	Queen of Egypt, Hatshepsut became one of the first woman rulers in history but often disguised herself as a man, wearing a false beard.	Egyptian pharaoh and general, Thutmose III gained fame for never losing a battle in 17 campaigns across Nubia, Palestine and Syria.	Hebrew leader Moses led the Hebrew slaves out of Egypt to Canaan and received the Ten Commandments at Mount Sinai from his God (Yaweh).	Second King of ancient Israel, Hebrew King David defeated the Philistines, captured Jerusalem and established it as the nation's capital.	The ancient Greek poet Homer authored the epics the *Iliad*, about the Trojan War, and the *Odyssey*, which recorded many basic Greek myths.

Y OF RULE

and wives. The life of the humble peasant was subject to many types of calamity—famine, disease, flood, forced labor, and invasion—but day-to-day work and family life changed little from generation to generation. Why did these early states take this form? Part of the answer may be that they grew up around river valleys whose fertility could be harnessed only by irrigation works and channels for flood control. This required the use of mass forced labor, a system of control that could be adapted to other projects, such as building pyramids, and which further enhanced the god-like powers of the rulers.

THE BEGINNING OF POLITICS

Politics in the strict Greek sense—the activity of generating public decisions among free men—emerged outside the perimeters of the early empires, first in ancient Greek cities from about 700 to 500 B.C. The word "politics" comes from the Greek *polis* meaning a city, or city-state, which was often centered on a strong, defensible location (such as the

Acropolis in Athens), and which could also serve as a place of worship and a market. City dwellers, often from different tribes, came together to manage their common business and build defenses for their protection. As a result, territorial loyalty slowly supplanted tribal ties. In 594 B.C. the lawgiver Solon reorganized the government of Athens on territorial, not clan, lines, allowing its peoples to create the brave new world of the equal citizen and direct democracy, (albeit for less than 4,000 citizens and excluding women and slaves). The head of each household (*oikos*) was a citizen (*polites*), with a vote and, in this role, he was the equal of others. Decisions in the new politics were made through discussion rather than command, and discussion could be swayed through the new art of using language for persuasion, called rhetoric. Plato's *Republic* and Aristotle's *Politics* reflected on the new Greek model, and helped to create political science. Aristotle recognized the three basic forms of politics: rule by one (monarchy); by few (aristocracy or oligarchy); and by many (democracy).

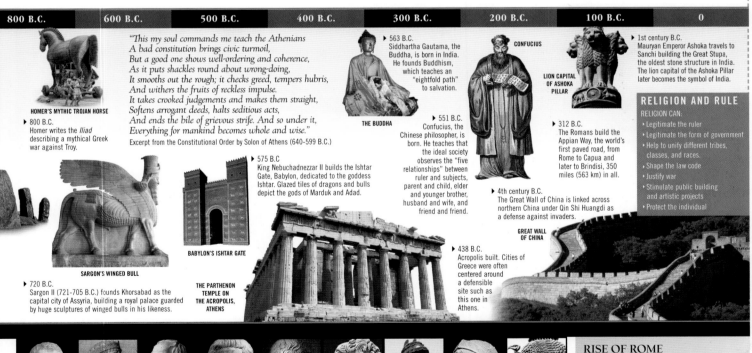

800 B.C.	600 B.C.	500 B.C.	400 B.C.	300 B.C.	200 B.C.	100 B.C.	0

HOMER'S MYTHIC TROJAN HORSE

▶ 800 B.C.
Homer writes the *Iliad* describing a mythical Greek war against Troy.

"*This my soul commands me teach the Athenians
A bad constitution brings civic turmoil,
But a good one shows well-ordering and coherence,
As it puts shackles round about wrong-doing,
It smooths out the rough; it checks greed, tempers hubris,
And withers the fruits of reckless impulse,
It takes crooked judgements and makes them straight,
Softens arrogant deeds, halts seditious acts,
And ends the bile of grievous strife. And so under it,
Everything for mankind becomes whole and wise.*"
Excerpt from the Constitutional Order by Solon of Athens (640-599 B.C.)

▶ 575 B.C
King Nebuchadnezzar II builds the Ishtar Gate, Babylon, dedicated to the goddess Ishtar. Glazed tiles of dragons and bulls depict the gods of Marduk and Adad.

BABYLON'S ISHTAR GATE

SARGON'S WINGED BULL

▶ 720 B.C.
Sargon II (721-705 B.C.) founds Khorsabad as the capital city of Assyria, building a royal palace guarded by huge sculptures of winged bulls in his likeness.

THE PARTHENON TEMPLE ON THE ACROPOLIS, ATHENS

▶ 563 B.C.
Siddhartha Gautama, the Buddha, is born in India. He founds Buddhism, which teaches an "eightfold path" to salvation.

THE BUDDHA

▶ 551 B.C.
Confucius, the Chinese philosopher, is born. He teaches that the ideal society observes the "five relationships" between ruler and subjects, parent and child, elder and younger brother, husband and wife, and friend and friend.

▶ 438 B.C.
Acropolis built. Cities of Greece were often centered around a defensible site such as this one in Athens.

CONFUCIUS

LION CAPITAL OF ASHOKA PILLAR

▶ 312 B.C.
The Romans build the Appian Way, the world's first paved road, from Rome to Capua and later to Brindisi, 350 miles (563 km) in all.

▶ 4th century B.C.
The Great Wall of China is linked across northern China under Qin Shi Huangdi as a defense against invaders.

GREAT WALL OF CHINA

▶ 1st century B.C.
Mauryan Emperor Ashoka travels to Sanchi building the Great Stupa, the oldest stone structure in India. The lion capital of the Ashoka Pillar later becomes the symbol of India.

RELIGION AND RULE

RELIGION CAN:
- Legitimate the ruler
- Legitimate the form of government
- Help to unify different tribes, classes, and races
- Shape the law code
- Justify war
- Stimulate public building and artistic projects
- Protect the individual

SOLON 639-559 B.C.	DARIUS 550-486 B.C.	SOCRATES 470-399 B.C.	PLATO 427-347 B.C.	ARISTOTLE 384-322 B.C.	ALEXANDER THE GREAT 356-323 B.C.	QIN SHI HUANGDI 259-210 B.C.	HANNIBAL 247-182 B.C.	CLEOPATRA VII 69-30 B.C.
Leader of Athens, Solon enacted democratic reforms and established courts to allow Greek citizens to appeal against government decisions.	Darius ruled the Persian Empire and extended its territory to Pakistan and southeastern Europe, but failed in his attempt to conquer Greece.	The Greek philosopher, Socrates taught the importance of moral character and the search for truth through discussion and argument.	Plato founded the Academy, ancient Greece's most important school of philosophy. He wrote *The Republic* about an ideal state based on justice.	Aristotle tutored Alexander the Great, established Greece's Lyceum philosophy school, and wrote on politics, ethics, the use of logic and rhetoric.	In just 13 years the king of Macedon, Alexander the Great, conquered the Persian Empire and helped spread Greek culture and ideas from Egypt to India.	Qin Shi Huangdi founded the Qin dynasty, created the first united Chinese empire and oversaw the completion of the Great Wall of China.	The Carthaginian, Hannibal, led his army across the Alps to invade Italy and win many battles; but he failed to topple the Roman Empire.	Restored to Egypt's throne by Rome's Julius Caesar, Cleopatra married Mark Antony. Their armies lost the battle of Actium to Octavian (later Augustus).

RISE OF ROME

Greek domination of the eastern Mediterranean after the conquests of Alexander the Great gave way in the second century to the rise of Rome. A city-state, or *civitas*, Rome had been founded in 753 B.C. as a monarchy, only to expel its kings and establish what we now call a republic in 509 B.C.

Kings were replaced by two consuls, elected for one-year terms (to prevent one elected leader becoming too powerful). Provision was also made for a dictator accorded the power in emergencies to give Rome the central direction it might temporarily need.

A class struggle between patricians and plebeians (a recurring form of political conflict) was settled by establishing a new kind of magistrate called a "tribune". The concept of "veto" (literally "I forbid it") to block measures by the government was born here.

CHRONOLOGY OF RULE

0 ◀◀ ▶▶ A.D. 1500

THE RISE AND DECLINE OF ROME

After the Romans had defeated Hannibal and destroyed Carthaginian power, they went on to conquer the whole of the Mediterranean area. However, Rome was becoming a state so spread out, and with populated with such disparate peoples that republican institutions could no longer govern it. City republics like Athens and Rome could be ruled by popular decision because they were small and homogeneous, but larger and more heterogeneous states, it was believed, must be governed from on high. After the assassination of the Roman emperor Julius Caesar in Rome in 44 B.C., his nephew Octavius Caesar eventually became emperor. He was given the title Augustus ("revered") by the senate and the Roman people in 29 B.C. and effectively the powers of an absolute monarch. However, Augustus chose to present himself as the preserver of republican traditions and revived the Republic by establishing a new government system called the Principate. Nevertheless, after a century and a half of the Pax Romana, the once austere values of republican Rome were dissipated by greed, hedonism and self destruction.

CHINESE CIVILIZATION

Not long before Rome's defeat of Hannibal, the warring states of China were being unified in 221 B.C. under the Ch'in emperor Zheng. Here was a civilization quite different from that of Greece or Rome. It was based on the idea of a perfect form of order to which everyone must fit. The emperor was at the top of a hierarchy of officials; scholars or mandarins were in the top rank and warriors much lower down. The "rules" for this form of life had been given by the philosopher Confucius, who turned submission to superiors into a supreme ethical ideal. But other schools of thought in China saw the establishment of order in far more brutally self-interested terms.

CHRISTIANITY AND THE MEDIEVAL WORLD

Rule in Western Europe was transformed under the Roman Empire by the coming of Christianity. Jesus had at first seemed to be a purely Jewish Messiah, but St. Paul spread his message of salvation as being

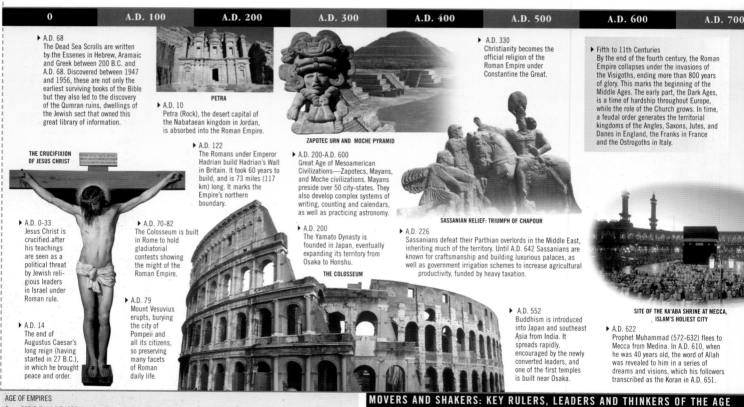

0	A.D. 100	A.D. 200	A.D. 300	A.D. 400	A.D. 500	A.D. 600	A.D. 700

▶ A.D. 68
The Dead Sea Scrolls are written by the Essenes in Hebrew, Aramaic and Greek between 200 B.C. and A.D. 68. Discovered between 1947 and 1956, these are not only the earliest surviving books of the Bible but they also led to the discovery of the Qumran ruins, dwellings of the Jewish sect that owned this great library of information.

PETRA

▶ A.D. 10
Petra (Rock), the desert capital of the Nabataean kingdom in Jordan, is absorbed into the Roman Empire.

ZAPOTEC URN AND MOCHE PYRAMID

THE CRUCIFIXION OF JESUS CHRIST

▶ A.D. 122
The Romans under Emperor Hadrian build Hadrian's Wall in Britain. It took 60 years to build, and is 73 miles (117 km) long. It marks the Empire's northern boundary.

▶ A.D. 200-A.D. 600
Great Age of Mesoamerican Civilizations—Zapotecs, Mayans, and Moche civilizations. Mayans preside over 50 city-states. They also develop complex systems of writing, counting and calendars, as well as practicing astronomy.

SASSANIAN RELIEF: TRIUMPH OF CHAPOUR

▶ A.D. 330
Christianity becomes the official religion of the Roman Empire under Constantine the Great.

▶ Fifth to 11th Centuries
By the end of the fourth century, the Roman Empire collapses under the invasions of the Visigoths, ending more than 800 years of glory. This marks the beginning of the Middle Ages. The early part, the Dark Ages, is a time of hardship throughout Europe, while the role of the Church grows. In time, a feudal order generates the territorial kingdoms of the Angles, Saxons, Jutes, and Danes in England, the Franks in France and the Ostrogoths in Italy.

▶ A.D. 0-33
Jesus Christ is crucified after his teachings are seen as a political threat by Jewish religious leaders in Israel under Roman rule.

▶ A.D. 70-82
The Colosseum is built in Rome to hold gladiatorial contests showing the might of the Roman Empire.

▶ A.D. 200
The Yamato Dynasty is founded in Japan, eventually expanding its territory from Osaka to Honshu.

THE COLOSSEUM

▶ A.D. 226
Sassanians defeat their Parthian overlords in the Middle East, inheriting much of the territory. Until A.D. 642 Sassanians are known for craftsmanship and building luxurious palaces, as well as government irrigation schemes to increase agricultural productivity, funded by heavy taxation.

▶ A.D. 14
The end of Augustus Caesar's long reign (having started in 27 B.C.), in which he brought peace and order.

▶ A.D. 79
Mount Vesuvius erupts, burying the city of Pompeii and all its citizens, so preserving many facets of Roman daily life.

▶ A.D. 552
Buddhism is introduced into Japan and southeast Asia from India. It spreads rapidly, encouraged by the newly converted leaders, and one of the first temples is built near Osaka.

SITE OF THE KA'ABA SHRINE AT MECCA, ISLAM'S HOLIEST CITY

▶ A.D. 622
Prophet Muhammad (572-632) flees to Mecca from Medina. In A.D. 610, when he was 40 years old, the word of Allah was revealed to him in a series of dreams and visions, which his followers transcribed as the Koran in A.D. 651.

AGE OF EMPIRES

From 200 B.C. to A.D. 200 three great empires dominated the world, containing half of the world's population. Land and sea routes connected these empires. After conquering much of Central Asia in the 1st century B.C., the Chinese opened the Silk Roads— trading routes—connecting them to Persia and the Middle East. In 106 B.C. the first trading caravan traveled between the Parthian Empire and China.

Western Europe ROMANS—By 100 B.C. Rome dominated the Mediterranean and North Africa, including Egypt. By the 2nd century A.D. the Roman Empire stretched from Armenia to the Atlantic. Forts and walls protected frontiers, while highly trained legionary soldiers formed the backbone of the army. Wearing body armor and a helmet, the weapons of choice were the short sword and javelin. Extensive road networks were built, enabling the movement of troops and supplies across the empire. By the third century the Persians had begun invading in the east, and the Roman capital moved to Constantinople. Roman rule collapsed in the 5th century A.D. when Germanic invaders, including Goths (Italy and Iberia), Franks (Gaul), and Anglo-Saxons (Britain), occupied former Roman provinces.

Middle East PARTHIANS—The inheritors of the eastern territories of the Seluccids, the Parthians dominated Persia and Mesopotamia, and Northern India and traded with the Chinese and Roman empires.

China HAN DYNASTY—From 206 B.C. to A.D. 220 the Han Empire encompassed the area that is now modern China, and also Korea, and Vietnam. Centrally administered from Chang'an, and later Luoyang, the empire was divided into 1,500 administrative districts, each centered in a walled town. The Great Wall of China provided a stable and secure frontier. Trade and agriculture were the predominant activities and cities were connected by roads and canals. Eventually, the Han Dynasty fragmented into independent states in A.D. 220

MOVERS AND SHAKERS: KEY RULERS, LEADERS AND THINKERS OF THE AGE

CAESAR AUGUSTUS 63 B.C.-A.D. 14	CONSTANTINE A.D. 275-337	JUSTINIAN I A.D. 483-565	CHARLEMAGNE A.D. 742-814	MINAMOTO A.D. 1147-1199	GENGHIS KHAN A.D. 1162-1227
Caesar Augustus ended decades of civil war and then ruled as Rome's first emperor. He greatly expanded the empire and was declared a god one month after his death.	The first Christian Roman emperor, Constantine accepted the faith and moved the empire's power east to Byzantium, setting the stage for the Byzantine Empire.	Byzantine Emperor Justinian I compiled Roman laws into one far-reaching code called the Corpus Juris Civilis. He tried to reunite the split Christian church.	King of the Franks, Charles I was crowned Holy Roman Emperor and named Charlemagne. He created the political foundation for Western feudalism.	Minamoto Yoritomo defeated a rival clan and in 1192 A.D. founded Japan's first "shogunate" warrior government based on a network of fiefdoms.	Chieftain of the Mongols (central Asian nomads), Genghis Khan ruled a vast empire from China to Europe and established the first Mongol code of laws.

one for Jew and Gentile alike. Christian doctrine during the long period in which the religion was persecuted, until Constantine accepted Christianity in A.D. 313, emphasized a basic division between the sacred and the secular, between religion and politics. This was a distinction unique to Christianity and absolutely fundamental to the development of Western politics and liberal democracy.

In the fourth and fifth centuries *anno Domini* (A.D. or after Christ), the Western Roman Empire began to collapse under successive waves of barbarian incursion, leading to what is sometimes called "the Dark Ages" until the 8th century and the coronation of Charlemagne. But the unity of Western Europe after this king's death began to break down and violence and instability were endemic. Fierce invaders like the Vikings and Magyars wreaked havoc, and only the Church sustained a certain stability and culture as peoples were converted to Christianity and monasteries spread.

A feudal order arose–a system by which land was filtered down by the king to his lords in return for their own and their subjects' service and fealty–and by the 12th century, a new and confident civilization had emerged in Western Europe. Kings were ruling law-governed societies in consultation with new institutions called "parliaments." A new kind of

political player called a "representative" was emerging into the political spotlight. Authority was widely dispersed between religious and civil institutions and among the variety of kingdoms, duchies, free cities, palatinates, and so on into which Europe was divided.

PROPHETS, CALIPHS, SULTANS, AND CZARS

Meanwhile in Arabia, the Prophet Muhammad had declared the principles of the Muslim submission to God, and some 100 years after his famous flight (the *hegira*) from Mecca to Medina in A.D. 622, Arab rule had spread all around the southern Mediterranean and into Spain, and had advanced to China and the borders of the Byzantine or Eastern Roman Empire, which had survived the Roman collapse in the West.

Absolute monarchs ruled the Muslim world. In the 11th century, the Ottoman Turks came to dominate Muslim lands, and in 1453 they conquered Byzantium and established the Ottoman Sultanate. But to the north, the ruler of Muscovy—the czar—was claiming to be the founder of the "third Rome" and building the beginnings of the Russian state. Indeed, in 1462 Ivan III declared himself the "Czar of all the Russias"— the title "Czar" being a reference to the days of the Roman Empire since it was derived from the Latin "Caesar".

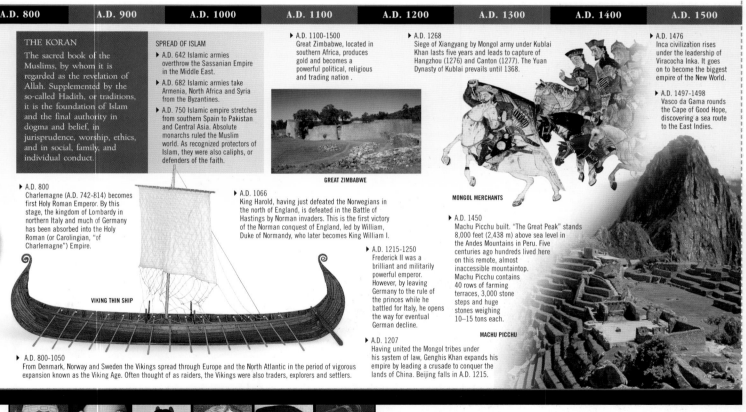

A.D. 800	A.D. 900	A.D. 1000	A.D. 1100	A.D. 1200	A.D. 1300	A.D. 1400	A.D. 1500

THE KORAN

The sacred book of the Muslims, by whom it is regarded as the revelation of Allah. Supplemented by the so-called Hadith, or traditions, it is the foundation of Islam and the final authority in dogma and belief, in jurisprudence, worship, ethics, and in social, family, and individual conduct.

SPREAD OF ISLAM

▶ A.D. 642 Islamic armies overthrow the Sassanian Empire in the Middle East.

▶ A.D. 682 Islamic armies take Armenia, North Africa and Syria from the Byzantines.

▶ A.D. 750 Islamic empire stretches from southern Spain to Pakistan and Central Asia. Absolute monarchs ruled the Muslim world. As recognized protectors of Islam, they were also caliphs, or defenders of the faith.

▶ A.D. 1100-1500 Great Zimbabwe, located in southern Africa, produces gold and becomes a powerful political, religious and trading nation.

GREAT ZIMBABWE

▶ A.D. 1268 Siege of Xiangyang by Mongol army under Kublai Khan lasts five years and leads to capture of Hangzhou (1276) and Canton (1277). The Yuan Dynasty of Kublai prevails until 1368.

▶ A.D. 1476 Inca civilization rises under the leadership of Viracocha Inka. It goes on to become the biggest empire of the New World.

▶ A.D. 1497-1498 Vasco da Gama rounds the Cape of Good Hope, discovering a sea route to the East Indies.

MONGOL MERCHANTS

▶ A.D. 800 Charlemagne (A.D. 742-814) becomes first Holy Roman Emperor. By this stage, the kingdom of Lombardy in northern Italy and much of Germany has been absorbed into the Holy Roman (or Carolingian, "of Charlemagne") Empire.

▶ A.D. 1066 King Harold, having just defeated the Norwegians in the north of England, is defeated in the Battle of Hastings by Norman invaders. This is the first victory of the Norman conquest of England, led by William, Duke of Normandy, who later becomes King William I.

▶ A.D. 1450 Machu Picchu built. "The Great Peak" stands 8,000 feet (2,438 m) above sea level in the Andes Mountains in Peru. Five centuries ago hundreds lived here on this remote, almost inaccessible mountaintop. Machu Picchu contains 40 rows of farming terraces, 3,000 stone steps and huge stones weighing 10–15 tons each.

MACHU PICCHU

VIKING THIN SHIP

▶ A.D. 1215-1250 Frederick II was a brilliant and militarily powerful emperor. However, by leaving Germany to the rule of the princes while he battled for Italy, he opens the way for eventual German decline.

▶ A.D. 1207 Having united the Mongol tribes under his system of law, Genghis Khan expands his empire by leading a crusade to conquer the lands of China. Beijing falls in A.D. 1215.

▶ A.D. 800-1050 From Denmark, Norway and Sweden the Vikings spread through Europe and the North Atlantic in the period of vigorous expansion known as the Viking Age. Often thought of as raiders, the Vikings were also traders, explorers and settlers.

INNOCENT III A.D. 1198-1216	OSMAN I A.D. 1258-1324	ZHU YUANZHANG A.D. 1328-1398	IVAN THE GREAT A.D. 1462-1505	MARTIN LUTHER A.D. 1483-1546	CHARLES V A.D. 1500-1558
Pope who launched the failed Fourth Crusade to free Jerusalem from Islamic rule and created the doctrine of papal control over the monarchs.	Turkish leader Osman I conquered the Byzantine Empire in the Battle of Baphaeon and later established the Ottoman Empire in Asia Minor.	A Buddhist monk, Zhu Yuanzhang led the Red Scarves band of revolutionaries to overthrow the Mongols and found China's Ming Dynasty.	Ivan III freed Russia from Mongol control, united the country, extended its territory to Siberia, and declared himself czar of all the Russias.	Martin Luther sparked the Protestant Reformation by teaching that the Bible instead of the papacy is the sole authority of the Christian church.	The most powerful of the Habsburgs, as Holy Roman Emperor from 1519, he ruled Austria, the Netherlands, the Kingdom of Naples, and Spain and its own empire.

"One of the penalties for refusing to participate in politics is that you end up being governed by your inferiors."
—Plato, Greek philosopher, *"The Republic"*

Genghis Khan (1162-1227), reputed to have killed his own brother for stealing, had a reputation of fearlessness and courage. By 17, he had united Mongols and led them to defeat their enemies. Genghis is credited with the creation of the Ih Zasag ("the Great Law"), a codified set of laws. By 1206 Genghis was named Khan of Khans.

"With Heaven's aid I have conquered for you a huge empire. But my life was too short to achieve the conquest of the world. That is left for you."—Genghis Khan to his sons at the end of his life.

CHRONOLOGY OF RULE

1500 ◀◀ ▶▶ PRESENT DAY

THE MODERN EUROPEAN STATE

In Europe the rebirth in interest in the arts, architecture, and learning—the Renaissance—also encouraged new thoughts and ideas about the art and science of politics. The study of statecraft became part of that Western search for knowledge. In 1513 Florentine diplomat and political philosopher Niccolo Machiavelli wrote *Il Principe* ("The Prince".) His famous and influential treatise set out his beliefs on how a state should be run. Regarded by many as the founder of modern political science, Machiavelli has left his legacy in the English lexicon by expounding the principle of statecraft that any political means, however unscrupulous ("Machiavellian",) are justified if they strengthen the power of a state. In the meantime, feudal monarchs consolidated their power by centralizing functions previously carried out locally. They gained power at the expense of barons and the Church. Sovereignty emerged, which allowed rulers to make the law (and especially to unmake it.) Religious dissension among Christian believers during the Protestant Reformation split Europe into hostile camps and was manipulated by rulers to increase absolute power. Religious conflict often nearly destroyed European societies during the 16th and early 17th centuries. Germany was ravaged by the Thirty Years' War until the peace of Westphalia in 1648 established a new international order of sovereign states. Absolute rulers used their growing resources to centralize their realms ever further and expand their territories by conquest.

REVOLUTIONARY CHANGES

Following on the developments of the Renaissance and Reformation, the 18th century was a time of great change—scientific and political. At the end of the century, the German philosopher Immanuel Kant argued that the secret of peace was the abolition of monarchy. Who but kings, it was argued, benefited from the death and destruction of war? Certainly the rejection of monarchy, or at least of specific monarchs, became the next move in the evolution of rule. The Americans rejected George III in 1776, and the French rejected Louis XVI after 1789. These were the first significant drumbeats of the

1500–1600	1625	1650	1700	1725	1750	1800	1825

The Age of Reason and the Enlightenment

Following the "darkness" of the Middle Ages, the 18th century is a period of mathematical and scientific discovery. Mankind begins to change its perceptions of authority and religion. Reasoning provides the mechanism and this is reflected in literature, art, family life, agriculture and manufacturing. Thinkers and philosophers question rule and the monarchy, as people struggle for individuality and freedom in this Age of Reason.

▶ 1642
The English Civil War begins. In 1648, Oliver Cromwell (1599-1658), Lord General of the Army, reduces the Long Parliament to a "Rump" Parliament that rules to execute Charles I, and abolish the monarchy and House of Lords. Cromwell is appointed the Lord Protector of the Realm in 1653, which he remains until his death in 1658. The monarchy is reinstated within two years.

TREATY OF WESTPHALIA

▶ 1648
Peace Treaty of Westphalia is signed ending the Thirty Years' War that has ravaged Europe from 1618, and establishing a new international order of sovereign states.

OLIVER CROMWELL

▶ 1701-1714
The War of the Spanish Succession is fought. Rooted in King Louis XIV's desire to extend French territory. It ends with the signing of the Treaty of Utrecht.

▶ 1707
The third Act of Union is signed, uniting England and Scotland as the United Kingdom of Great Britain. Ruled by the British monarch from 1603, this act joined them in a single parliament, abolishing the Scottish parliament.

▶ 1700-1721 .
The Northern War begins between Charles XII of Sweden and Peter I of Russia. Sweden, dominating the Baltic, sought to prevent Russia's sea link with Europe, but failed against Russian forces.

▶ 1724
The German Immanuel Kant is born. He writes *Critique of Pure Reason* in 1781 and *Perpetual Peace* in 1795. A philosopher, he questions the role of the monarchy and argues that a political system should maximize individual freedoms.

US SIGNING OF THE DECLARATION OF INDEPENDENCE

▶ 1776
On July 2nd, the Continental Congress carries a motion for the independence of the 13 states on the East Coast of America. Two days later the Declaration of Independence is adopted and democracy is born.

GEORGE WASHINGTON

▶ 1789
George Washington (1732-1799) becomes the first president of the newly independent United States of America.

▶ 1789
The French Revolution begins with the storming of the Bastille in July. It is followed in August by the declaration of equality for all, bringing an end to feudalism and the monarchy in France. The French revolutionary spirit continued in 1830 and 1848.

REVOLUTION OF 1830 IN FRANCE

SHOGUNATE OF TOKUGAWA

▶ 1603-1867
While the Manchus in China forge a vigorous new power that rules for 300 years, Japan begins its Tokugawa, or Edo, period after a series of civil wars. Tokugawa Ieyasu (1543-1616) is named shogun by the emperor. The family hold the shogunate, ruling nearly one quarter of Japan as a peaceful and centralized feudalism (until 1867). Land is redistributed to the most loyal barons under new strict laws that moderated their power.

▶ 1837
Queen Victoria ascends to the throne, aged barely eighteen. Her 64-year reign witnesses Britain's great age of industrial expansion, economic progress, and especially, empire.

QUEEN VICTORIA

MOVERS AND SHAKERS: KEY RULERS, LEADERS AND THINKERS OF THE AGE

RENÉ DESCARTES 1596-1650	JOHN LOCKE 1632-1704	PETER THE GREAT 1672-1725	CHARLES MONTESQUIEU 1689-1755	BENJAMIN FRANKLIN 1706-1790	JEAN-JACQUES ROUSSEAU 1712-1778	ADAM SMITH 1723-1790	THOMAS PAINE 1737-1809	WILLIAM WILBERFORCE 1759-1833	NAPOLEON BONAPARTE 1808-1873	ABRAHAM LINCOLN 1809-1865	KARL MARX 1818-1883
A French mathematician, Descartes invented analytic geometry and founded the notion of modern philosophy with his theories of mind and matter.	English philosopher Locke taught that the government's duty is to protect the natural rights of its citizens to life, liberty and property. He had great influence.	Czar of Russia, Peter centralized its government and "Westernized" the nation, transforming it into a modern European power. He founded a navy and St. Petersburg.	Inspiring the US Constitution, the French philosopher Montesquieu championed individual rights and liberty through separating branches of government.	An American statesman, Franklin helped draft the Declaration of Independence and persuade France to support the colonies in their revolution against England.	Philosopher Jean-Jacques Rousseau inspired the French Revolution with his writings advocating that legitimate governments must operate with the people's consent.	Father of modern economics, Adam Smith wrote in *The Wealth of Nations* (1776) that social progress is fostered by free trade and self-regulating capital markets.	With attacks on the English monarchy and calls for independence , Paine's Common Sense and Rights of Man stirred American colonists to revolution.	Liberal William Wilberforce led the successful campaign to abolish slavery in the British colonies and to open India to Christian missionaries.	Through military conquests, Napoleon Bonaparte created a French empire that spanned most of Europe and then crowned himself its emperor.	Abraham Lincoln ended slavery and kept the American states "United" in spite of the Civil War between the North and South. First US president to be assassinated.	German historian Karl Marx championed the rights of workers and inspired the socialist movement with his attacks on private enterprise capitalism.

coming era of rights, democracy, and socialism. "Life, Liberty, and the Pursuit of Happiness" and "*Liberté, Fraternité, Egalité*" became the common parlance—the political slogans of the time—as a new national ideology emerged. Here was a desire for a state governed for the people by the people without bowing to king, queen or emperor. It was revolutionary in concept and in practise. The French Revolution of 1789 was particularly influential in spreading the idea that a modern state was an association of equal human beings with some claim to influence how they might improve themselves. At the same time the growing philosophy of liberalism (freedom of the individual) also influenced the abolition of slavery in 1806 and was part of this democratization process.

WORKERS OF THE WORLD

The Industrial Revolution spread prosperity and discontent in equal measure, and in 19th-century Europe the problem of the poor began to dominate political discussion. In 1848 Marx and Engels published the *Communist Manifesto*, the springboard for communist states. Before that, the steady growth of representative institutions and broader suffrage throughout Europe during the 19th century, culminated in the vote for women in the 20th. The need to appeal to this rising democratic constituency accounted for the development of the welfare state. To be the citizen of a European state came to mean not only benefiting from protection and a system of justice, but also enjoying subsidised healthcare and support in times of unemployment.

Though Western empires declined, Western political institutions were everywhere imitated. The newly independent states of South America already had an apparatus of presidents and parliaments, courts and bureaucracies, but now these institutions spread to Japan, China, Thailand, and, after 1945, to all the post-colonial states.

The history of government remains what it has always been: a "dialogue" between centralized control on the one hand and individual freedom on the other. After the Cold War stalemate between communism and democracies, the balance began to swing in favor of democratic rule of law, especially in the 1990s as formerly totalitarian regimes toppled much the same way as the Berlin Wall, the defining post-war symbol of a lack of "dialogue." Today, in our highly interconnected but splintered world, the idea of politics, of attaining power and holding on to it by governing the common affairs of a people (whether benignly or duplicitiously, with or without their interests at heart), remains ever-evolving.

1850	1875	1900	1925–1940	1940–1955	1955–1970	1970–1990	1990–PRESENT

1851-1864
Under Hong Xiuquan (1812-1864), the Taiping Rebellion is a revolt against the Qing dynasty of China. Beginning in southern China, Xiuquan's new political system derives elements from Protestantism. The rebellion results in more than 20 million deaths.

1848
The *Communist Manifesto* is written by Karl Marx and Frederick Engels. It proposes government by the working class.

LENIN, ENGELS AND MARX

WORLD WAR I

1914-1918
World War I fought after the assassination of Archduke Ferdinand visiting Sarajevo in Bosnia.

1917
The Bolsheviks under Lenin revolt against the rule of Czar Nicolas II in the Russian Revolution, leading to the formation of the communist United Soviet Socialist Republic (USSR)

1939-1945
World War II fought after Germany under Adolf Hitler invades Poland. Hitler was appointed Chancellor of Germany in 1933.

US CIVIL WAR

1861
The Civil War breaks out between the United States of America and the eleven states of the Confederate States of America. The Confederates surrender in 1865, after more than 600,000 Americans have died.

1863
The Emancipation Proclamation is issued by US President Abraham Lincoln, declaring freedom for black slaves in the Confederate States of America.

1870
Otto von Bismarck (1815-1898) founds the German Empire following the formation of the North German Alliance between Prussia and northern Germany.

New York World-Telegram
1500 DEAD IN HAWAII
Congress Votes War on Japan; Manila Bases Bombed Again

PEARL HARBOR

1941
Japan attacks US troops at Pearl Harbor, killing thousands and bringing America into World War II.

ATOM BOMB

1945
The US drops atomic bombs on Hiroshima and Nagasaki, killing 210,000 people and forcing Japan's surrender.

1947
Mohandas Gandhi's passive resistance movement leads India to independence from Great Britain.

1948
Israel becomes an independent Jewish state in Palestine, recognized by the United Nations. That same day, it is invaded by Egypt, Lebanon, Iraq, and Syria.

1949
The North Atlantic Treaty (NATO) is signed. Its purpose is to safeguard and promote freedom in the North Atlantic.

1949
Mao Zedong leads the Chinese Communist Party to victory, proclaiming the People's Republic of China.

BENITO MUSSOLINI AND ADOLF HITLER

1963
Martin Luther King leads a civil rights march on Washington D.C. delivering his famous "I have a dream" speech. His assassination in 1968 sparks mass riots across the US.

MARTIN LUTHER KING JR.

1963
John F. Kennedy, 35th president of the United States is assassinated, devastating the nation.

FIDEL CASTRO

1959
Fidel Castro leads the Cuban Communist Revolution against the Batista government. Joining forces with the USSR, Castro implements Marxist-Leninist principles.

1965-1973
Vietnam War spans the reign of two US presidents and ends with US troop withdrawal after more than 58,000 have died.

VIETNAM WAR

1979
The Shah of Iran is overthrown, replacing the absolute monarchy with an Islamic Republic under the Ayatollah Khomeini.

1989
Students in China hold pro-democracy demonstrations which turn deadly as the military attempts to subdue the crowds with force.

1990
Apartheid is dismantled in South Africa, opening the way for the first multiracial and democratic elections and a black president, Nelson Mandela, to be elected in 1994.

1989
The fall of the Berlin Wall allows for East and West Germany to be reunited as one nation in 1990.

1990
Iraq invades Kuwait. Iraqis defeated in the Persian Gulf War of 1991 by a US-led coalition.

RUSSIAN COUP

1991
Russian coup results in the collapse of the Soviet Union.

1992
The European Union is established to integrate the economies of member states.

1997
Hong Kong reverts to the People's Republic of China, following 156 years of democratic rule as a colony of the United Kingdom.

9/11 NEW YORK'S WORLD TRADE CENTER

SEPTEMBER 11, 2001
The terrorists attacks on the World Trade Center in New York and other attacks in Pennsylvania and on the US Pentagon in Washington D.C. kill thousands and lead to a global war on terrorism.

2003
US President George Bush orders war on Iraq, ending Saddam Hussein's 24-year Iraqi regime.

LEO TOLSTOY 1828-1910	**SIGMUND FREUD** 1856-1939	**MOHANDAS GANDHI** 1869-1948	**VLADIMIR LENIN** 1870-1924	**FRANKLIN ROOSEVELT** 1882-1945	**ADOLF HITLER** 1889-1945	**SIR WINSTON CHURCHILL** 1874-1965	**DAVID BEN-GURION** 1886-1973	**MAO ZEDONG** 1893-1976	**JOHN F. KENNEDY** 1917-1963	**MIKHAIL GORBACHEV** 1931-	**NELSON MANDELA** 1918-

Russian author Leo Tolstoy gained acclaim for his epic novels War and Peace and Anna Karenina and preached non-violent resistance to aggression.

Austrian physician Sigmund Freud revolutionized psychiatry and psychology with his theories that unconscious impulses motivate human behavior.

Influenced by the writings of Tolstoy, Gandhi used non-violent resistance to lead the nationalist movement that secured India's independence from British colonial rule.

Lenin founded the Communist Party in Russia, and led the October Revolution of 1917, later becoming the USSR's first leader. He lies embalmed in the Moscow Kremlin.

As president, "FDR" led the United States through the Great Depression and enlarged the federal government with his proposed "New Deal for workers' welfare."

German dictator Adolf Hitler promoted the supremacy of Aryan people, sparked off World War II, overran Europe, and ordered the deaths of millions of Jews.

Led Britain as prime minister through World War II with stirring oratory about loyalty to country, "Blood, Sweat and Tears" and resistance to surrender.

David Ben-Gurion helped lead the Zionist movement to create a Jewish state in Palestine and became first prime minister of Israel after its creation in 1948.

Founder of the Chinese Communist Party, Mao Zedong (Mao Tse Tung) led the struggle to expel Japan's occupation forces. Became first ruler of People's Republic of China.

First Catholic and youngest candidate elected American president, John F. Kennedy avoided nuclear war in the Cuban missile crisis and pioneered the US space program.

The seventh leader of the Soviet Union, Mikhail Gorbachev pursued political restructuring that ultimately led to the breakup of the communist superpower in 1991.

After 27 years as a political prisoner, Mandela, the anti-apartheid leader, was released from jail in South Africa and became its first elected black president.

THE GLOBAL

FOR MANY OF US, THE ENDURING LEGACY of the twentieth century was the way in which the Earth got smaller. Over the previous two thousand years, the world comprised largely separate regions linked by trade and by the infrastructure of successive colonial empires, but equally kept apart by distance and the arduousness of travel. In the last, brief, 125 years, all this has changed.

THE COMMUNICATIONS REVOLUTION

Railroads, telegraphs, the telephone, the internal combustion engine, radio and the discovery of powered flight were all technologies which began the process of linking and shrinking our planet. In the last fifty years, television, jet travel, satellites, the microcomputer and the internet have made the world a single, unified global domain, demolishing time lapse and collapsing distance.

It has been said that television defeated the American forces in Vietnam, by beaming images of warfare into stateside living rooms nightly, thereby eroding domestic support for the war. Today, the amount of information about our world is unstoppable, and indigestible. Telecommunications can span the greatest distances in fractions of a second, while our multi-media environment hurls uninterrupted streams of data at us, on the printed page, through the airwaves, across our television and computer screens. Events from all corners of the globe reach us instantaneously, and are witnessed as they unfold. Our sense of stability and certainty is diminished as we become more aware that the world is in constant state of flux and change.

A consequence of this eruption in communication, and of mass tourism, is the increasing flow and exchange of ideas and cultural values. Repressive states normally shield their populations from information, by limiting access to the media and by censorship, only releasing selective information in the form of propaganda. As mass communication grows, so it has become more difficult to sustain such regimes. Glasnost in the USSR was partly a product of popular yearnings for the liberalism, goods, services, commodities and lifestyles enjoyed in the West, a yearning made acute by access to information.

Conversely new technologies are widely used by modern terrorists; the success of the al-Qaeda network relies on a lack of one to one communication, and its operations upon the internet, cellular phones and credit cards —ironically products of the developed, capitalist world it seeks to destroy.

A sense of proportion however should not be forgotten; there are approximately 1.8 billion televisions in the world today—one for every three people; 962 million telephone land lines— less than one for every six; 760 million cellular phones—one for every eight; and less than 100 million internet host computers, around one in sixty of the world's population having access. Thus, despite the evident impact of the revolution in communications, access to information and to power remains in the hands of a small minority.

THE CHALLENGE OF GLOBALIZATION

When the Berlin Wall was torn down in 1989, signaling the end of the Cold War, it was symbolic of an end to barriers dividing the world—physical, cultural, and commercial. The old trade links have been gradually replaced by a new network of commerce

EUROPE
POPULATION: 701.9 MILLION
AREA: (3,837,081 SQ MILES/9,938,000 SQ KM —6.7% OF EARTH)
NUMBER OF COUNTRIES: 46
LARGEST COUNTRY: EUROPEAN RUSSIA
LARGEST CITY: MOSCOW, RUSSIA—9.3 MILLION
COUNTRY WITH HIGHEST GDP: GERMANY
HIGHEST MILITARY EXPENDITURE: FRANCE
COUNTRY WITH HIGHEST DEBT: RUSSIA
DOMINANT RELIGION: CHRISTIANITY
MAIN LANGUAGES: ENGLISH, FRENCH, GERMAN, RUSSIAN, SPANISH

ASIA
POPULATION: 3,755.3 MILLION
AREA: 17,212,000 SQ MILES/44,579,000 SQ KM —30% OF THE EARTH)
NUMBER OF COUNTRIES: 45
LARGEST COUNTRY: ASIATIC RUSSIA
LARGEST CITY: TOKYO, JAPAN—26.4 MILLION
COUNTRY WITH HIGHEST GDP: CHINA
HIGHEST MILITARY EXPENDITURE: CHINA
COUNTRY WITH HIGHEST DEBT: CHINA
DOMINANT RELIGION: ISLAM
MAIN LANGUAGES: BENGALI, CHINESE, HINDI, JAPANESE, JAVANESE, KOREAN

AFRICA
POPULATION: 811.6 MILLION
AREA: 11,608,000 SQ MILES/30,065,000 SQ KM —20.2% OF THE EARTH)
NUMBER OF COUNTRIES: 53
LARGEST COUNTRY: SUDAN
LARGEST CITY: LAGOS, NIGERIA—13.4 MILLION
COUNTRY WITH HIGHEST GDP: SOUTH AFRICA
HIGHEST MILITARY EXPENDITURE: EGYPT
COUNTRY WITH HIGHEST DEBT: EGYPT
DOMINANT RELIGION: CHRISTIANITY
MAIN LANGUAGES: ARABIC, HAUSA, KISWAHILI, SWAHILI, YORUBA, ZULU

MATRIX

> *"Humankind has not woven the web of life.*
> *We are but one thread within it. Whatever we do to the web, we do to ourselves.*
> *All things are bound together. All things connect"*
> — *Chief Seattle, Chief of the Suquamish Tribe, Washington State, 1854*

wherein corporations increasingly view the world as a single market place, and the world's resources in terms of labor and materials as a set of variables which, if exploited efficiently, can maximize margins and profits. And those who have developed the communications technology to shrink the world, are the very ones poised to take advantage of this new scenario, a process known as globalization.

When a manufacturing company scatters its operations around the world to take advantage of tax breaks, cheaper raw materials and lower-wage workers, what happens to the domestic workers who lose those jobs? To the foreign workers who gain those jobs? And to the environment, when more manufacturing is performed in countries with looser pollution standards? Do lower prices offset the cost of lost jobs and more pollution? And for whom? Do the lower wage workers regard these jobs as

opportunities or oppression? Often, the consequences of this transformation are very difficult to predict or control.

When the developed world exports its goods and culture to the Middle East, Africa and Asia, will it return in the form of idealistic graduate students seeking the tools of development, or as a jet plane aimed at the epitome of Western financial power? Will military power projected around the world make one's own country safer or more vulnerable to attacks incubated in the caves or schools of distant lands? These are the sorts of questions raised by the new global matrix.

An economic crisis in a small, isolated Asian country can trigger a chain reaction that cripples the economies of the whole region, ruins the Russian bond market, sparks a fire sale of Brazilian stocks, and provokes a stampede into United States Treasury bonds and out of corporate bonds. Financial troubles can spread from one continent to another like

viruses, indeed, very much like real viruses, such as SARS and AIDS, that spread worldwide via modern communications.

Even the book you're holding now is a product of our inter-connected world. The publishers are based in London; the book was written and designed in the US; the book was created entirely digitally, research was made much easier using the internet, and files were circulated across the globe daily and nightly. Editions printed in Europe and the Far East. You're reading it in your language; people in numerous different countries around the world are reading it in theirs.

This level of exposure to information, communication, and commerce means that new strategies need to be developed between governments and industry, between the great and the small, the developed and the developing, to meet the needs of the mosaic of nations, peoples and individuals which make up our world.

OCEANIA
POPULATION: 30.4 MILLION
AREA: 3,132,059 SQ MILES/7,687,000 SQ KM—5.3% OF THE EARTH)
NUMBER OF COUNTRIES: 14
LARGEST COUNTRY: AUSTRALIA
LARGEST CITY: SYDNEY, AUSTRALIA—3.6 MILLION
COUNTRY WITH HIGHEST GDP: AUSTRALIA
HIGHEST MILITARY EXPENDITURE: AUSTRALIA
COUNTRY WITH HIGHEST DEBT: AUSTRALIA
DOMINANT RELIGION: CHRISTIANITY
MAIN LANGUAGES: ENGLISH

SOUTH AMERICA
POPULATION: 350.6 MILLION
AREA: 6,879,000 SQ MILES/17,819,000 SQ KM—12% OF THE EARTH)
NUMBER OF COUNTRIES: 12
LARGEST COUNTRY: BRAZIL
LARGEST CITY: SÃO PAULO, BRAZIL—17.8 MILLION
COUNTRY WITH HIGHEST GDP: BRAZIL
HIGHEST MILITARY EXPENDITURE: BRAZIL
COUNTRY WITH HIGHEST DEBT: BRAZIL
DOMINANT RELIGION: CHRISTIANITY
MAIN LANGUAGES: PORTUGUESE, SPANISH

NORTH AMERICA
POPULATION: 482.9 MILLION
AREA: 9,449,460 SQ MILES/24,256,000 SQ KM—16.5% OF THE EARTH)
NUMBER OF COUNTRIES: 23
LARGEST COUNTRY: CANADA
LARGEST CITY: MEXICO CITY, MEXICO—18.1 MILLION
COUNTRY WITH HIGHEST GDP: USA
HIGHEST MILITARY EXPENDITURE: USA
COUNTRY WITH HIGHEST DEBT: USA
DOMINANT RELIGION: CHRISTIANITY 83.9%
MAIN LANGUAGES: ENGLISH, SPANISH

SUPRANATIONAL

THE HISTORY OF THE UNITED NATIONS can be traced back more than 100 years to the International Peace Conference convened in 1899 at The Hague by Czar Nicholas II of Russia. Ironically, the idea of an organization to promote international peace and justice was delayed by World War I and by the Russian Revolution, in which the czar and his family were brutally murdered. The League of Nations, a precursor to the UN, was created in 1919 by the Treaty of Versailles. Unfortunately, the League of Nations proved ineffective in preventing World War II, so it was replaced in 1946 when representatives of 50 nations met in San Francisco to draft the charter for the UN. Headquartered in New York City,

Secretariat Building, 39 stories

General Assembly Hall, seats 1,800

Security Council

Trusteeship Council

Economic and Social Council

UN WORLD HEADQUARTERS
The New York complex was designed by Wallace Harrison and an international board of design consultants. The 18 acres (74,843 sq m) were purchased for $8.5 million with a donation by John D. Rockefeller.

MAJOR BODIES OF THE

GENERAL ASSEMBLY

As the main deliberative body of the United Nations, the General Assembly is made up of representatives of member nations. The Assembly votes on such matters as the admission of new members, issues relating to peace and security and the budget, all of which require a two-thirds majority. Other matters can be decided with a simple majority. Although the decisions of the General Assembly are only recommendations and have no binding legal authority whatsoever, they do carry the weight of world opinion. The General Assembly meets annually in the Autumn, beginning with the election of a new president, 21 vice-presidents and chairs of its six main committees. The presidency rotates among regions of the world. The six standing committees of the General Assembly are the Disarmament and International Security Committee, the Economic and Finance Committee, the Social, Humanitarian and Cultural Committee, the Special Political and Decolonization Committee, the Administration and Budgeting Committee, and a General Committee composed of the president, vice-presidents and the committee chairs. The General Assembly may call special sessions. With the Security Council, the General Assembly elects judges to the International Court of Justice. It also controls the UN's finances and decides on the contribution to be made by each member state to the UN budget.

SECURITY COUNCIL

Charged with responsibility for maintaining peace and security, the Security Council manages the principal functions of the UN and is the most powerful organ of the United Nations—one of the most powerful organizations in the world. Located at the headquarters in New York City, it is required to operate continuously, with one representative of each member nation present at all times. It is responsible for responding to threats presented to the Council and for seeking peaceful resolution of potential problems. The Council has historically taken such steps as taking military action against aggressors, as it did when North Korea invaded South Korea in the early 1950s; sending peace keeping forces to troubled areas, as it has done recently in several African countries; and imposing sanctions, as it did in South Africa in protest against apartheid. It may also conduct investigations, as it has done in sending arms inspectors to Iraq. There are 15 members on the Security Council. Five are permanent: Great Britain, Russia, France, China, and the United States. Each of these can veto a decision in the Council. The other ten members, who are elected by the General Assembly, serve two-year terms. Non-member nations can participate in debates if they are a party to a dispute, but cannot vote. The presidency of the Security Council rotates monthly, alphabetically by nation.

UNITED NATIONS KEY EVENTS TIMELINE

1899
Twenty-six nations convene for International Peace Conference at The Hague to establish conventions for peaceful settlement of disputes and rules of

1919
Treaty of Versailles includes covenant for League of Nations

1920
League of Nations convenes for the first time

1937
Japan withdraws from the League of Nations

1941
Atlantic Charter includes set of principles for international collaboration in maintaining peace and security

1942
Representatives of 26 nations fighting Axis Powers pledge support for Atlantic Charter, signing "Declaration by United Nations"

1944
At Dumbarton Oaks in Washington, D.C., the US, the UK, the USSR and China reach agreement on purpose and structure of world organization

1945

At Yalta, Roosevelt, Churchill, and Stalin resolve to establish an international organization to maintain peace and security

In San Francisco, 50 nations draw up charter for United Nations

1960
Security Council calls for member states to assist South Korea in repelling invasion from the north

1967
Following Six-Day War, the Security Council adopts a resolution as basis for achieving peace in the Middle East

POWERS

United Nations flag

the UN comprises six organizational units: the General Assembly, the Security Council, the Economic and Social Council, the Trusteeship Council, the International Court of Justice, and the Secretariat. Nations can only be admitted to membership by a two-thirds vote of the General Assembly, following recommendation by the Security Council. The annual budget, which was approximately $2.5 billion in 2001, comes from contributions of the member states, which are assessed on a sliding scale based on share of the total Gross National Product, adjusted for other factors, such as per capita income. The US is the single largest donor, contributing 22 percent of the annual budget.

THE UN CHARTER
The United Nations was officially founded on October 24, 1945 when the Charter—drawn up by a conference in San Francisco—was ratified by China, France, the USSR, the UK, and the US.

UNITED NATIONS ORGANIZATION

INTERNATIONAL COURT OF JUSTICE

The International Court of Justice, the principal judicial body of the UN, is responsible for settling international legal disputes and for advising the UN on legal questions. Since 1946, the court has issued 76 judgments spanning such issues as land frontiers, maritime boundaries, territorial sovereignty, hostage-taking, and the right of asylum. The court has given 24 opinions to other UN organizations on such matters as admission to UN membership, reparation for injuries sustained in the services of the UN, and the legality of threats to use nuclear weapons. Determinations are made on the basis of treaties and conventions. The court may accept a case only if the states concerned accept its jurisdiction. If there is no judge with the nationality of a case, then a judge may be appointed to sit for the case on an ad hoc basis.

TRUSTEESHIP COUNCIL

The Trusteeship Council, which was established in the original UN charter to promote self-governance, has been inactive since 1994, when Palau, the last of the UN trust territories, became independent. It can be reconstituted at the request of the General Assembly or the Security Council.

In addition to the six main organizational units, the United Nations also has numerous agencies, programs and funds, including the UN Children's Fund (UNESCO) and the UN Development Program (UNDP). The UN administers the largest humanitarian aid program in world history—the Oil for Food Program for Iraq—which resumed operations in the Spring of 2003 after sanctions were lifted following the US invasion. There are currently 170 member nations. The authority of the UN derives solely from the voluntary compliance of its members with decisions and recommendations of the General Assembly and Security Council.

ECONOMIC AND SOCIAL COUNCIL

The Economic and Social Council, which has control of 70 percent of the human and financial resources of the UN, coordinates the work of 14 special agencies, ten functional commissions and five regional commissions. It is responsible for promoting the economic and social advancement of member nations and facilitating international cultural and educational cooperation. It accomplishes all of this by issuing policy recommendations developed in consultation with academicians and some 2,100 non-governmental organizations (NGOs). Key policy areas have been poverty and African development. Starting in 1998, the ECOSOC has been meeting each April with financial ministers who head the Bretton Woods institutions (the World Bank and the International Monetary Fund) to address global financial issues such as financial flows.

SECRETARIAT

The Secretariat is in effect the administrative unit of the United Nations and is located in the 39-story tower of the UN complex in New York City. It staffs the services of the other organizations and administers the policies and programs they establish. It is headed by the secretary-general, who is usually from a small neutral country, and is appointed by the General Assembly on the recommendation of the Security Council for a five-year term, which is renewable. There are 8,900 staff members, who perform such varied duties as conducting surveys of economic and social trends, convening conferences on issues of international concern, administering peacekeeping operations, and interacting with the international media.

The UN complex is situated on international territory in Manhattan—it has its own post office and stamps

---

1968

General Assembly approves Treaty on the Non-Proliferation of Nuclear Weapons, a commitment to the goal of disarmament by the nuclear-weapon states

1971

General Assembly votes to seat representatives of the People's Republic of China

1972

The first UN Environment Conference is held in Stockholm, Sweden, leading to the establishment of the UN Environment Program (UNEP), headquartered in Nairobi

1980

The World Health Organization declares smallpox eradicated

1981

Office of the UN High Commissioner for Refugees awarded Nobel Peace Prize for assistance to Asian refugees

1984

General Assembly adopts the Convention Against Torture and Other Cruel, Inhuman or Degrading Treatment or Punishment

1990

Convention on the Rights of the Child comes in force

UNICEF convenes the World Summit for Children, attended by 71 heads of state and government—a plan for action is adopted

UN imposes economic sanctions on Iraq following invasion of Kuwait

1992

UN Conference on Environment and Development—the Earth Summit—held in Rio de Janeiro, is the largest intergovernmental gathering in history

1994

Elections are held in South Africa, arms embargo lifted, South Africa is re-admitted to the UN General Assembly

1996

General Assembly adopts Comprehensive Nuclear Test-Ban Treaty

1997

Media titan Ted Turner gives $1 billion donation to UN

2002

Security Council passes resolution 1441 that returns UN inspectors to Iraq in search of weapons of mass destruction

2003

Security Council votes to lift sanctions on Iraq. Peacekeeping activities continue in various trouble spots around the world

UNITED NATIONS GENERAL ASSEMBLY
The General Assembly in session. An average of 5,000 official meetings are held at the UN headquarters every year.

THE NEW SUPRANATIONALISM

A NEW TYPE OF ORGANIZATION EMERGED in the late 20th century: the suprapowers—international coalitions of nations, civil societies, and multinational organizations joined together to address problems that transcend national boundaries, including human rights violations, international trade, disease, natural disasters, civil war, terrorism, and threats to the environment.

Previously, world powers vied for control, usually over natural resources, markets, or trade routes. In the 16th century, for example, there was an explosion of competition between world powers—England, France, Holland, Portugal, and Spain—following the discovery of the New World in 1492 by Christopher Columbus, who was employed by the Spanish government. A period of land-grabbing and colonization ensued in which Spain laid claim to large areas of the Americas and Caribbean; Britain and France claimed holdings in North America; Portugal took Brazil, and Holland claimed some of the Caribbean islands. The Portuguese and the Dutch also took the East Indies. A similar flurry of colonization occurred following the 1878 Congress of Berlin, in which the German leader, Bismarck, set out guidelines for the colonization of Africa. Although territorial lines shifted slightly over the years as a result of conflicts between these superstates, the power remained concentrated in a few European nations up until the 20th century.

By 1900, European nations controlled 90 percent of the African continent, 99 percent of Polynesia, 57 percent of Asia, 100 percent of Australia, and 27 percent of the Americas. The United States, which won its independence from British colonial rule in 1776, lay dormant, in part because of its youth and in part because of a policy of isolationism that endured until World War I.

The collapse of the Ottoman Empire, the Austro-Hungarian Empire and the German Empire at the end of World War I heralded the end of the era of the superstate. A new era emerged at the end of World War II, with the convergence of several historical events. Throughout the 1940s, 1950s and 1960s, the United Kingdom and France, among others, shed their colonies with increasing rapidity. African and Middle Eastern states once controlled by European powers suddenly gained independence. At the same time, in the immediate aftermath of World War II, the nations of the world agreed to establish the United Nations to provide a forum for the peaceful resolution of disagreements among nations and to establish a dialogue on political, economic, social, and cultural issues. Both the United States and the Union of Soviet Socialist Republics (USSR)—post-czarist Russia—emerged as new world leaders, roughly equal in power and influence. Accordingly, the world divided into

SUPRANATIONAL POWERS

EUROPEAN UNION

In 1952, six countries—Belgium, Germany, France, Italy, Luxembourg, and the Netherlands—joined together to form the European Coal and Steel Community. Its success encouraged the member states to pursue greater economic integration and create a customs union and common market—the European Economic Community (EEC). This grew into the European Union (EU) in which, by 2004, the original six nations were joined by nineteen other European states including Denmark, Ireland, the United Kingdom, Greece, Spain, Portugal, Austria, Poland, Hungary and Sweden. On topics of joint interest, member states delegate authority to the Union, which makes decisions on the basis of treaties ratified by the member states.

Five institutions govern the European Union: (1) the European Parliament, which is elected by the people of the member states but, despite its name, has few legislative powers;

(2) the Council of the Union, made up of member states; (3) the European Commission, the executive body of the EU; (4) the Court of Justice, which ensures compliance with the law; and (5) the Court of Auditors, which oversees management of the European Union budget. In addition to numerous lesser agencies, five organizations have responsibility for specific concerns: the European Economic and Social Committee, the Committee of the Regions, the European Ombudsman, the European Investment Bank, and the European Central Bank.

OBJECTIVE: The Union promotes peace in Europe through economic interdependence. It aims to assure fundamental rights for European citizens; ensure freedom, security, and justice; promote economic and social progress; and promote Europe's interests in the world.

WORLD TRADE ORGANIZATION

The World Trade Organization (WTO), which is a permanent organization with its own staff, located in Geneva, Switzerland, establishes and monitors rules of trade between nations. It replaced the General Agreement on Tariffs and Trade (GATT) in 1995. The WTO administers agreements negotiated by trading nations and ratified by their legislatures, handles disputes, monitors trade policies, and provides technical assistance and training to developing countries. Unlike the GATT, the dispute resolution system is much less susceptible to the blocking power of individual members. Member nations make all decisions and negotiate the rules among themselves. The WTO has 146 members, who hold summit meetings to discuss issues such as how to hasten the process of globalization and establish tighter controls on trading policies.

OBJECTIVE: The purpose of the WTO is to support business.

INTERNATIONAL AND REGIONAL ORGANIZATIONS

ACC Arab Cooperation Council. Promotes Arab Economic Cooperation

ACP African, Caribbean, and Pacific Countries. Preferential economic and aid relationship with the EU under the Lomé convention

ACS Association of Caribbean States. Promotes economic, scientific, and cultural cooperation in the region

ADB Asian Development Bank. Encourages regional development

AfDB African Development Bank. Encourages African economic and social development

AFESD Arab Fund for Economic and Social Development. Promotes social and economic development in Arab states

AL League of Arab States. Forum to promote Arab cooperation on social, political, and military issues

ALADI Latin American Integration Association. trade and regional integration

AMCC Amazonian Cooperation Council. Promotes the harmonious development of the Amazon region

AMF Arab Monetary Fund. Promotes monetary and economic cooperation

AMU Arab Maghreb Union. Promotes integration and economic cooperation among North African Arab states

ANZUS Australia-New Zealand-United States Security Treaty. Trilateral security agreement. Security relations between the US and New Zealand were suspended in 1984 over the issue of US nuclear-powered or potentially nuclear-armed naval vessels visiting New Zealand ports. High-level contacts between the US and New Zealand were resumed in 1994

AP Andean Pact (Acuerdo de Cartagena), also known as Andean Community. Promotes development through integration

APEC Asia-Pacific Economic Cooperation. Promotes regional economic cooperation

ASEAN Association of Southeast Asian Nations. Promotes economic, social, and cultural cooperation

AU African Union. Promotes Unity and cooperation in Africa. (The African Union was, until 2002, the Organization for African Unity)

BADEA Arab Bank for Economic Development in Africa. Established as an agency of the Arab League to promote economic development in Africa

BDEAC Central African States Development Bank. Furthers economic development

Benelux Benelux Economic Union. Develops economic ties between member countries

BOAD West African Development Bank. Promotes economic development and integration in West Africa

BSEC Organization of the Black Sea Economic Cooperation. Furthers regional stability through economic cooperation

CAEU Council of Arab Economic Unity. Encourages economic integration

Caricom Caribbean community and Common Market. Fosters economic ties in the Caribbean

CBSS Council of the Baltic Sea States. Promotes cooperation among Baltic States

CDB Caribbean Development Bank. Promotes regional development

CE Council of Europe. Promotes unity and quality of life in Europe

CEFTA Central European Free Trade Agreement. Promotes trade and cooperation

CEMAC Central African Economic and Monetary Community. Aims to promote

subregional integration by economic and monetary union (replaced UDEAC)

CEPGL Economic Community of the Great Lake Countries. Promotes regional economic cooperation

CERN European Organization for Nuclear Research. Provides for collaboration in nuclear research for peaceful purposes

CILSS Permanent Interstate Committee for Drought Control in the Sahel. Promotes the prevention of drought and crop failure in the region

CIS Commonwealth of Independent States. Promotes interstate relationships among former republics of the Soviet Union

CMCA Central American Monetary Council. Now a subsystem of SICA. Furthers economic ties between members

COI Indian Ocean Commission. Promotes regional cooperation

COMESA Common Market for Eastern and Southern Africa. Promotes Economic Development and cooperation (replaced PTA)

Comm Commonwealth. Develops relationships and contacts between members

CP Colombo Plan. Encourages economic and social development in the Asia-Pacific region

CPLP Community of Portuguese-speaking countries. To promote political and diplomatic links between member states on economic, social, cultural, judicial, and scientific issues among Portuguese-speaking countries

Damasc Damascus Declaration. A loose association formed after the Gulf War, which aims to secure the stability of the region

EAC East African Community. Promotes economic cooperation

EAPC Euro-Atlantic Partnership Council. Forum for Cooperation on political and security issues (successor to NACC, North Atlantic Cooperation Council)

EBRD European Bank for Reconstruction and Development. Helps transition of former communist European states to market economies

ECO Economic Cooperation Organization. Aims at cooperation in economic, social and cultural affairs

ECOWAS Economic Community of West African States. Promotes regional economic development

EEA European Economic Area. Aims to include EFTA members in the EU single market

EEC Eurasian Economic Community. Coordinates regional trade

EFTA European Free Trade Association. Promotes economic cooperation

ESA European Space Agency. Promotes cooperation in space research for peaceful purposes

Franc Zone Aims to form monetary union among countries whose currencies are linked to that of France

G3 Group of 3. Aims to ease trade restrictions

G7 Group of 7. Summit meetings of the seven major industrialized countries, originally for economic purposes. For political purposes summit meetings are now held as the G8, including Russia.

G8 Group of 8. Global forum for world's major powers, which holds regular summit meetings.

G10 Group of 10. Ministers meet to discuss monetary issues

G15 Group of 15. Meets annually to further cooperation among developing countries

THE EUROPEAN UNION ASSEMBLY
Members of the EU gather in the Hemicycle of the European Parliament in Strasbourg, France.

BRUSSELS EU HEADQUARTERS
Flags of the members of the European Union can be seen outside the EU headquarters in Brussels, Belgium.

CHINA AND THE WTO
China has opened to foreign banks. Its WTO membership since 2001 provides what could be the world's largest consumer market to foreign businesses.

other undeveloped areas in South America and elsewhere in the world. The term "domino effect," coined by the American president Dwight Eisenhower, was a metaphor for the US fear that the USSR would gain world domination by toppling small, vulnerable nations, eventually capturing control of the world. It was this opposition that created the Cold War—a non-military era of hostility and competition.

The collapse of the Soviet Union in 1991 ended the Cold War, and left the United States as the world's only superpower—not only an economic, but also a military and cultural superpower. Viewed one way, the emerging suprapowers offer bargaining power, resources, and protection to smaller nations, much as labor unions support the interests of the workers against management. Seen in this light, what larger nations lose is their independence. If they accede to the collective will, they voluntarily relinquish some of their power and autonomy, in addition to economic benefits. Viewed another way, the suprapowers offer a mechanism for achieving consensus on how to resolve issues of

two competing camps, both founded on deep ideological beliefs about the nature of human rights and the best way to achieve prosperity. The Soviet camp represented communism, the US capitalism and individual freedoms. The Soviet influence extended to North Korea, China, Vietnam, Cuba, and some African nations, and threatened to spread to

common concern effectively as we become increasingly interdependent and interconnected globally. Theoretically, everyone should benefit. What remains to be seen is how this unipolar world will evolve. Could this infringe on individual freedoms? Will it give rise to more and more suprapowers whose aim, at least in part, will be to counter US influence?

INTERNATIONAL CRIMINAL COURT

In March 2003, the International Criminal Court (ICC) came into existence officially after five years of planning, which began with a UN Conference held in Rome in 1998. The court, which is located in The Hague, was established to try serious crimes committed by individuals, such as genocide, war crimes or aggression initiated by heads of state. Eighty-nine countries and more than 2,000 civil and non-governmental organizations worldwide have endorsed the court. A prosecutor was appointed and 11 men and women sworn in as the first judges of the court in March 2003. The ICC sets a precedent by being the first suprapower to attempt to exercise authority over non-member nations.

OBJECTIVE: The ICC will investigate and bring to justice individuals who violate international humanitarian law.

KYOTO PROTOCOL

In 1997, participants in the Framework Convention on Climate Change adopted the Kyoto Protocol in response to increasing evidence of global warming. The Protocol establishes binding emission targets for developed countries, a system for financing energy-efficient projects in less-developed countries, clean-development mechanisms, and emissions trading. Clean-development mechanisms entail capacity-building and technology transfer aimed at controlling emissions, while emissions trading allows countries to trade emissions allowances to achieve a balance and maintain the current climatic conditions. Although the United States signed the protocol, it has since announced it will not abide by the emissions targets set.

OBJECTIVE: The purpose of the Kyoto Protocol is to protect the climate, while also promoting sustainable development.

ORGANIZATION FOR THE PROHIBITION OF CHEMICAL WEAPONS

The Organization for the Prohibition of Chemical Weapons (OPCW) promotes international security and stability through disarmament. The organization, which has 152 member states, works for the peaceful application of chemistry and a world free of chemical weapons. The OPCW provides capacity-building assistance to developing nations that are member states to promote economic development through peaceful uses of chemistry.

OBJECTIVE: The OPCW has four objectives: (1) the destruction of chemical weapons in member states; (2) the protection of member nations from chemical weapons; (3) the promotion of peaceful uses of chemicals; and (4) universal membership in the OPCW.

G24 Group of 24. Promotes the interests of developing countries on monetary issues

GCC Gulf Cooperation Council. Promotes cooperation on social, economic and political matters

GEPLACEA Latin American and Caribbean Sugar Exporting Countries

GGC Gulf of Guinea Commission. Promotes regional cooperation

IAEA International Atomic Energy Agency. Promotes and monitors use of atomic energy

IBRD International Bank for Reconstruction and Development

ICRC International Committee of the Red Cross. Coordinates all international humanitarian activities of the International Red Cross and Red Crescent Movement. Gives legal and practical assistance to the victims of wars and disasters. Works through national committees of Red Cross and Red Crescent societies.

IDB Inter-American Development Bank. Promotes development in Latin America and the Caribbean through the financing of economic and social development projects and the provision of technical assistance

IGAD Intergovernmental Authority on Development. Promotes cooperation of food security, infrastructures, and other development issues (supercedes IGAAD, to promote cooperation on drought-related matters)

IMF International Monetary Fund. Promotes international monetary cooperation, the balanced growth of trade, and exchange rate stability; provides credit resources to members experiencing balance-of-trade difficulties

ISDB Islamic Development Bank. Promotes economic development on Islamic principles among Muslim communities (agency of OIC)

IWC International Whaling Commission. Reviews conduct of whaling throughout the world. Coordinates and funds whale research

LCBC Lake Chad Basin Commission. Encourages economic and environmental development in Lake Chad region

Mekong River Mekong River Commission. Accord on the sustainable development of Mekong River basin

Mercosur Southern Common Market. Promotes economic integration, free trade, and common external tariffs

MRU Mano River Union. Aims to create customs and economic union in order to promote development

NAFTA North American Free Trade Agreement. Free trade zone

NAM Non-Aligned Movement. Fosters political and military cooperation away from traditional Eastern or Western blocs

NATO North Atlantic Treaty Organization. Promotes mutual defense cooperation. Since January 1994 NATO's Partnership for Peace programs have provided a loose framework for cooperation with former members of the Warsaw Pact and the ex-Soviet republics. A historic Founding Act signed between Russia and NATO in May 1997 allowed for the organization's eastward expansion

NC Nordic Council. Promotes cultural and environmental cooperation in Scandinavia

OAPEC Organization of Arab Petroleum Exporting Countries. Aims to promote the interests of member countries and increase cooperation in the petroleum industry

OAS Organization of American States. Promotes security, economic, and social development in the Americas

OAU Organization of African Unity. Predecessor of the AU

OECD Organization for Economic Cooperation and Development. Forum for coordinating economic policies among industrialized countries

OECS Organization of Eastern Caribbean States. Promotes political, economic, and defense cooperation

OIC Organization for the Islamic Conference. Furthers Islamic solidarity and cooperation

OIF International Organization of Francophony. To promote cooperation and cultural and technical links among French-speaking countries and communities

OMVG Gambia River Development Organization. Promotes integrated development of the Gambia River basin

Opanal Agency for the prohibition of Nuclear Weapons in Latin America and the Caribbean. Aims to ensure compliance with the Treaty of Tlatelolco (banning nuclear weapons from the region)

OPEC Organization of the Petroleum Exporting Countries. Aims to coordinate oil policies to ensure fair and stable price

OSCE Organization for Security and Cooperation in Europe. Aims to strengthen democracy and human rights, and settle disputes peacefully (formerly CSCE, renamed 1994)

Partnership for Peace (PfP) See NATO

PC Pacific Community (formerly South Pacific Commission). A forum for dialogue between Pacific countries and powers administering Pacific territories

PIF Pacific Island Forum (formerly the South Pacific Forum). Develops regional political cooperation

RG Rio Group. Forum for Latin American and Caribbean issues (evolved from Contadora Group, established 1948)

SAARC South Asian Association for Regional Cooperation. Encourages economic, social, and cultural cooperation

SACU Southern African Customs Union. Promotes cooperation in trade and customs matters among Southern African states

SADC Southern African Development Community. Promotes economic integration and aims to lessen poverty

San José Group A "complementary, voluntary, and gradual" economic union

SCO Shanghai Cooperation Organization. Promotes regional security and cooperation

SELA Latin American Economic System. Promotes economic and social development through regional cooperation

SICA Central American Integration System. Coordinates the political, economic, social, and environmental integration of the region

UEMOA West African Economic and Monetary Union. Aims for convergence of monetary policies and economic union

UN United Nations. Aims to maintain international peace and security and to promote cooperation over economic, social, cultural, and humanitarian problems

WEU Western European Union. A forum for European military cooperation

INTERNATIONAL

As NATIONS DEVELOPED, THEY RELIED on their own laws and courts to resolve legal disputes that transcended national borders. With state self-interest being paramount this was, perhaps, not surprising. However, in 1625, Dutch scholar and statesman, Hugo Grotius, published *De Jure Belli ac Pacis* ("On the Law of War and Peace") which set down the notion of a natural law more important than the sovereignty, or independence, of any state, as well as the need to regulate and humanize the conduct war. Grotius today is considered the father of international law.

In 1864, the first Geneva Convention provided protection for those wounded in war. Subsequent conventions have prohibited torture and the taking of hostages while assuring war prisoners the right to medical care and guaranteeing humanitarian organizations, such as the Red Cross, safe passage across the lines of battle. There have also been various attempts to set up international courts to settle disputes between nations. The Hague Peace Conference of 1899 planned the Permanent Court of International Arbitration. This was superseded to some extent by the Permanent

JUDGEMENT AT NUREMBERG
Many of Germany's Nazi leaders, military leaders, and local functionaries faced prosecution and sentence in Nuremberg before the International Military Tribunal for atrocities committed during World War II.

Court of International Justice in 1922 which was taken over the by United Nations in 1946. Prior to that there had been no established legal remedy for crimes committed by the leader of another country unless the country was defeated in war. Such was the case when the Allied Powers defeated the Axis Powers in World War II. The International Military Tribunal at Nuremberg in Germany in 1945–1946 was set up by the allies—the United States, the United Kingdom, and Russia—to try German war criminals, from Nazi leaders to local functionaries. Concurrently, the Allied Powers tried Japanese war criminals, including premier Heideke Tojo, in the International Military Tribunal for the Far East.

PURSUING THE PERPETRATORS

Bringing the perpetrators of international crimes from another country to justice may have been established in international law by 1946 but many countries have still sought a unilateral resolution to a transnational dispute. In a stark example, the United States in 1989 invaded the Central American country of Panama to capture and later convict its military leader General Manuel Noriega in American courts for drug trafficking. Similarly,

THE GENEVA CONVENTIONS
Gathering in Lausanne, Switzerland, in 1949 for the fourth Geneva Convention, diplomats from around the world responded to Nazi atrocities during World War II by ratifying new protections for the sick and wounded, shipwrecked sailors, prisoners of war, and civilians in occupied territory.

POST WAR INTERNATIONAL TRIBUNALS

1945–1946
INTERNATIONAL MILITARY TRIBUNAL AT NUREMBERG
Created by the four victorious allied powers — France, Great Britain, the Soviet Union, and the United States— the tribunal prosecuted 21 of Germany's Nazi leaders for planning and waging World War II in violation of international treaties and for war crimes against humanity. Eleven were sentenced to death by hanging; 7 were given long prison terms; 3 were acquitted.

1946
INTERNATIONAL MILITARY TRIBUNAL FOR THE FAR EAST
Established by the United States and allied nations, this brought to trial 28 Japanese military and government leaders for initiating and waging WWII in Asia and for crimes against humanity. Seven were sentenced to death by hanging; 16 received life terms in prison; 2 were given prison terms; 2 died during trial; one was sent to a psychiatric ward.

1993–present
INTERNATIONAL CRIMINAL TRIBUNAL FOR THE FORMER YUGOSLAVIA (ICTY)
The ICTY was created by the U.N. Security Council to prosecute war crimes, genocide and violations of the Geneva Convention, committed during the ethnic warfare from 1991 in Bosnia, Croatia, Kosovo, and Macedonia. Over 80 individuals are under indictment; 14 are serving sentences; many indictees remain at large.

1994–present
INTERNATIONAL CRIMINAL TRIBUNAL FOR RWANDA (ICTR)
Created by the UN Security Council, the tribunal is charged with prosecuting perpetrators of genocide and flagrant breeches of international humanitarian law during the conflict between Hutus and Tutsis that left more than 500,000 dead. Of 73 individuals indicted; 8 have been sentenced to prison; one acquitted; 12 suspects are at-large; 8 trials are in progress.

1998
THE ROME STATUTE
Delegates from nearly 150 nations gathered for a United Nations conference in Rome to adopt a convention for the creation of the world's first international criminal court to try cases of genocide and other grave human-rights violations. Called the Rome Statute, the treaty for the court won the support of 120 nations; 21 abstained; and 7 voted "no," including China, Israel, and the United States.

LAW

Spain in the 1990s sought to extradite and prosecute the onetime dictator Augusto Pinochet for human rights violations against the Spanish population in Chile during his 17-year rule. Although the case never came to trial, it set an important precedent. for pursuing those accused of war crimes.

INTERNATIONAL CRIMINAL COURTS

Since the war-crime tribunals of World War II, new international legal forums to settle transnational issues have proliferated. And, increasingly, they are supplanting the historical inclination of nations to act alone. In general, international legal issues have been handled on a case-by-case basis. For example, the Lockerbie case, in which terrorists were charged with the explosion of an airplane over Lockerbie, Scotland, was finally tried in The Hague by Scottish lawyers under Scottish law, because Libya, where the suspected terrorists were living, would not release the terrorists under any other arrangement. The archetype for many of the recent legal venues is the United Nation's International Court of Justice.

Located in The Hague, the court has jurisdiction over numerous disputes between nations, including land and marine boundaries and political asylum. However, it has no authority over cases of individual criminal acts. Instead, war crimes, massacres and other violations of human rights have been pursued by special international courts established by the United Nations independent of its Court of Justice (*see boxes below*).

Although these international tribunals rely partly on the legal foundation of the Geneva Conventions, questions have been raised about their effectiveness and legitimacy. The criticism helped propel a movement by many nations for a permanent court to try international criminals, including heads of state accused of human rights violations. At a UN-sponsored conference in 1998 in Rome, 160 nations endorsed plans for such a tribunal. In March 2003, 89 UN member nations voted to create the International Criminal Court and give it jurisdiction over the perpetrators of war crimes, genocide and aggression against sovereign states. "There can be no justice unless the worse of crimes—crimes against humanity—are subject to the law," said UN Secretary Kofi Annan in support of this new international court, which may prove to be the missing link in the international legal system.

THE PEACE PALACE
Built in the early 1900s in The Hague, Netherlands, the Peace Palace houses the UN's International Court of Justice and the recently established International Criminal Court.

EMBLEM OF THE COURT OF INTERNATIONAL JUSTICE

U.N. WAR CRIMES JUSTICES
The 13 justices of the UN War Crimes Tribunal in 1999 each represent a different nation, the president being from France, and vice president from Zambia.

2000–2001	2002–present	2002–present	2003–present	2003–present
THE WOMEN'S INTERNATIONAL WAR CRIMES TRIBUNAL	**AD HOC HUMAN RIGHTS COURT FOR EAST TIMOR**	**SPECIAL COURT FOR SIERRA LEONE**	**INTERNATIONAL CRIMINAL COURT**	**SPECIAL COURT FOR CAMBODIA**
Human rights and Asian women's groups established the tribunal to compel Japan to acknowledge sex crimes perpetrated during WWII by its military against nearly 250,000 Korean, Malaysian, Indonesian, Chinese, Filipino and Taiwanese women. Although lacking legal powers, the tribunal found the State of Japan and Emperor Hirohito responsible.	The UN Transitional Administration for East Timor established the court to prosecute acts of genocide, murder, sexual offenses, torture and war crimes committed during Indonesia's control and amid the violence that erupted when East Timor broke free in 1999. More than 80 individuals have been indicted; 21 have been convicted and sentenced to prison.	Authorized by the UN Security Council, the court is a joint enterprise between the UN and the Sierra Leone government. It is charged with prosecuting massacres, mutilations and sex crimes committed during the decade-long conflict that began in 1991. The special court includes judges appointed by the Sierra Leone government. Eight individuals have been indicted and face trial.	Headquartered in The Hague, this court is an independent organization that coordinates its activities with the UN. Its jurisdiction includes acts of genocide, crimes against humanity and war crimes committed in countries that cannot or will not prosecute the crimes. China, Russia, the US, and many smaller nations do not support it because of perceived threats to national sovereignty.	The court is a joint endeavor between the UN and the government of Cambodia for prosecuting war crimes committed by leaders of the Khmer Rouge, which controlled the country between 1975 and 1979. An estimated 1.7 million Cambodian were executed or died of disease, starvation, and forced labor. The Extraordinary Chambers of Cambodia's court system will conduct trials.

COURTROOM SCENE
International Military Tribunal for the Far East 1946

INTERNATIONAL

THE ATTACKS ON AMERICA on September 11, 2001, by Al-Qaeda terrorists changed the network of international security worldwide. Previously insulated from terrorist incidents that were commonplace elsewhere, the US acted swiftly in what became a global effort to reduce terrorism. In fact, terrorism had been on the rise since the end of WWII, as increasing numbers of people, disenfranchised or ignored by those that governed them, took up arms to achieve their aims.

The risk of global conflict fueled by terrorism became real when US forces attacked the Taliban in Afghanistan after 9/11. After the Iraqi regime was accused of terrorist links and harboring weapons of mass destruction, a US coalition invaded Iraq in 2003. Significantly, the conflict was pursued without the full endorsement of the UN Security Council—the executive organ responsible for maintaining world peace and security. Its five permanent members (France, China, the UK, US, and Russia) have veto powers over the other temporary members. The 1945 United Nations Charter limits war to self-defense and restricts UN actions to "peace-keeping." While this worked in a world where the balance of two nuclear superpowers produced a "Cold War" stalemate in international relations, the UN has shown itself less effective in a world splintered and de-stabilized by many dozens of localized conflicts. Indeed conflict is just as likely within states as between states, variously fueled by ethnic tensions, religious division and state-sponsored terrorism.

KEY ZONES OF CONFLICT

- **MYANMAR** (Burma) Military junta wages war against its own people, one million flee. Ethnic conflict from 1948 onwards, latest conflict began 1988.

- **CHECHNYA** Separatist movement leads to Russian crackdown, retaliation by Chechens. Begins 1994, ongoing.

- **COLOMBIA** Long guerrilla war fueled by drug money kills 35,000 civilians. Begins early 1960s, ongoing.

- **INDONESIA** Sectarian and ethnic violence. Terrorist bombings in Bali kill 202; 36 killed in Jakarta. Bombing 2002, ongoing.

- **ISRAEL** Palestinian militants resist Israeli clampdown, cycle of retaliation continues. Wars in 1948, 1956, 1967, 1967-1970, 1973, 1982. Latest conflict began in 1987, ongoing.

- **IRAQ** US-led coalition repel invasion of Kuwait, 1991. Invasion by US coalition in 2003 leads to guerrilla warfare. .

- **KOSOVO** "Ethnic cleansing" 1998-99 results in trial of Serbian leader Slobodan Milosevic for genocide. Under UN auspices, KFOR troops from 30 NATO and non-NATO nations enter to establish and maintain security.

- **LIBERIA** Fifteen years of civil war kills 100,000, UN. enforces truce.

- **NORTHERN IRELAND** 3,228 killed. Irish Republican Army/Unionist sectarian conflict and occupation by British troops. Tentative peace from 1997.

- **RWANDA** International court investigating the 1994 murder of almost one million Tutsis by Hutus. Since 1962, latest conflict began 1994.

LARGEST ACTIVE MILITARY FORCES

(In descending order according to number of active personnel)

1. **CHINA** 2,310,000 active personnel, 8,000 tanks, 62 warships, 0 carriers, 69 submarines, 2,900 aircraft, 400 nuclear weapons

2. **UNITED STATES** 1,367,700 active personnel, 7,620 tanks, 116 warships, 12 carriers, 73 submarines, 4,147 aircraft, 10,656 nuclear weapons plus 150 in Europe

3. **INDIA** 1,263,000 active personnel, 3,414 tanks, 26 62 warships, 1 carrier, 16 submarines, 738 aircraft, more than 60 nuclear weapons

4. **NORTH KOREA** 1,082,000 active personnel, 3,500 tanks, 3 warships, 0 carriers, 26 submarines, 621 aircraft, unknown number of nuclear weapons

5. **RUSSIA** 977,100 active personnel, 21,820 tanks , 34 warships, 1 carrier, 56 submarines, 4,380 aircraft, over 10,000 nuclear weapons

6. **SOUTH KOREA** 683,000 active personnel, 2,330 tanks, 39 warships, 0 carriers, 19 submarines, 555 aircraft, no nuclear weapon

7. **PAKISTAN** 620,000 active personnel, 2,300 tanks, 8 warships, 10 submarines, 353 aircraft, upwards of 24-48 nuclear weapons

8. **TURKEY** 515,100 active personnel, 4,205 tanks, 23 warships, 13 submarines, 505 aircraft, no nuclear weapons

9. **IRAN** - 513,000 active personnel, 1,565 tanks, 3 warships, 6 submarines, 283 aircraft, rumored to have nuclear weapons

10. **VIETNAM** - 484,000 active personnel, 1,315 tanks, 6 warships, 2 submarines, 189 aircraft, no nuclear weapons

KEY STRATEGIC MILITARY BASES

- **US EUROPEAN COMMAND,** Stuttgart, Germany

- **ALLIED COMMAND EUROPE RAPID REACTION CORPS,** Monchengladbach, Germany

- **US JOINT FORCES COMMAND,** NATO Supreme Allied Commander, Atlantic, Norfolk, Va.

- **US STRATEGIC COMMAND,** Offut Air Force Base, Nebraska

- **US NORTHERN COMMAND,** Peterson Air Force Base, Colorado

- **US CENTRAL COMMAND,** MacDill Air Force Base, Florida

- **US SOUTHERN COMMAND,** Miami, Florida

- **GUANTANAMO NAVAL BASE,** Cuba (US Navy/Marines)

- **CAMP DOHA,** Kuwait (US Army)

- **HQNI** (Headquarters Northern Ireland), Lisburn, Northern Ireland (UK Army)

- **XV CORPS,** Srinagar, Kashmir (Indian Army)

- **MUSADAN-RI LAUNCH FACILITY,** North Korea (ballistic missile site)

SECURITY

A FRACTURED WORLD ORDER

Since the UN was formed, nearly all of the world's 193 nations have been involved in more than one conflict. The UN reported that 43% of Middle East nations were at war after 2000. and more than a quarter of all African nations were at war in 2003. In Asia, Pakistan has had three wars with India, and split with Bangladesh; India clashed with China, annexed Kashmir, and had conflicts with Sri Lanka. The UN tries to fill the role of global peacemaker, yet it cannot become involved in military action. It has the bark but not the bite, and powerful nations don't always listen.

The need for collective security is not new: The League of Nations was set up in 1920 for this role well before the UN took over. But as terrorist strikes intensify globally, other institutions are relied on such as Interpol, the International Criminal Police Organization and world's largest police agency in 177 countries. On a more covert level, security and intelligence-gathering organizations such as MI5 and the CIA and "special operations" are in the frontline of anti-terrorist surveillance and engagement using satellite tracking and other new technologies.

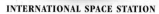

INTERNATIONAL SPACE STATION
The International Space Station and other technologies are used for surveillance; "Echelon" (bottom left in photo gallery) intercepts satellite telephone calls.

TERRORISTS NETWORKS

- **ABU NIDAL ORGANIZATION** (ANO) —also called the Fatah Revolutionary Council, the Arab Revolutionary Brigades, or the Revolutionary Organization of Socialist Muslims. Splinter group of PLO operating in Middle East, Asia, and Europe to eliminate Israel.

- **AL-QAEDA** International network led by Osama bin Laden. Seeks to rid Islamic nations of what it sees as the profane influence of the West and replace home governments with fundamentalist Islamic regimes. Also networked with the Egyptian Islamic Jihad, Jamaat Islamiyya (Egypt), The Libyan Islamic Fighting Group, Islamic Army of Aden (Yemen), Lashkar-e-Taiba and Jaish-e-Muhammad (Kashmir), Islamic Movement of Uzbekistan, Salafist Group for Call and Combat and the Armed Islamic Group (Algeria), Abu Sayyaf Group (Malaysia, Philippines)—all terrorist networks.

- **ETA** (Euskadi Ta Askatasuna)—Separatist movement in northern Spain and southwestern France to establish independent Basque state.

- **HAMAS** Middle East-based Islamic resistance movement to eliminate Israel, form independent Palestinian state.

- **SHINING PATH** (Sendero Luminoso)—Peruvian movement to replace current government with communist state opposed to foreign influences.

- **REAL IRA** (True IRA)—splinter group of Irish Republican Army dedicated to removing British control from Northern Ireland and unification of Ireland.

- **REVOLUTIONARY ARMED FORCES OF COLOMBIA** (FARC)— Operating in Colombia, Venezuela, Panama and Ecuador to replace ruling government with Marxist state.

PHOTO GALLERY OF INTERNATIONAL SECURITY AND SURVEILLANCE

Clockwise from top left: *World Trade Center in New York attacked by terrorists (9/11/01); UN Peacekeepers' regulation helmets; UN Security Council holds a minute of silence following September 11, 2001; People flee collapsing World Trade Center; UN Peacekeeper ("Blue Helmet") on border patrol; Israeli soldiers mourning the death of a fellow soldier killed in terrorist bombing; Saudi dissident and Al-Qaeda mastermind, Osama bin Laden; Palestinian soldier celebrating the September 11, 2001 attacks; Palestinian militant; Fighter jets flying in formation; US troops in Iraq; Echelon surveillance ball tower observes all of Europe; Satellite photograph of Washington DC (US bill passed in 1994 making space cameras available to the private sector); Sniper security at international summit; Iraqis gather to rally national support of Saddam Hussein (2003); British soldiers in Iraq; Gas masks in event of chemical warfare; Menwith Hill surveillance center (UK), capable of two million intercepts per hour.*

SUMMIT SECURITY
An armed guard at a G7 (the 7 major industrial powers) summit in Naples, Italy.

THE GLOBAL ECC

In 1899, Charles H. Duell, Commissioner of the United States Office of Patents, said, "Everything that can be invented has been invented." But 20th century technological advances fueled an unprecedented internationalization of economic activity. Air travel made virtually all parts of the globe accessible in just a matter of hours. Advanced telecommunications and the Internet shortened that time to minutes and seconds. Yet it must be recognized that economic globalization began long before the 20th century.

ROOTS OF GLOBAL COMMERCE

For centuries, trade between China and Europe flourished along the ancient Silk Road. By 1600, the British East India Company began establishing its trading posts in India. The Hudson's Bay Company was an economic force in Canada from the 1670s onwards, while the Dutch East India Company led the Dutch commercial empire to colonize the islands of Indonesia. By 1900, most of the world's economy was controlled by just a few European nations. The trade between empires and colonies provided the origins for today's division of a developed, prosperous "north," and under-developed, dependent "south." And things haven't got better in the post-colonial era. Since 1950, the gap between the average income in the richest and poorest country had doubled. The wealthy countries dominate the world economic infrastructure–with aggressive market-led economies and access to productive new technologies. A quarter of the world's population has 80 percent of the world's manufacturing income. The influence of multinational corporations from these countries also adds to this dominance. Globalization critics warn that international corporations now wield more power than democratically elected governments and put shareholder profits above the interests of workers, and the environment, in developing countries. The cycle of debt that pervades many developing nations is now recognized as a major issue of global commerce.

TRADING BLOCS AND COMMON MARKETS

Global trade has undoubtedly been stimulated since the signing of the General Agreement on Tariffs and Trade (GATT) in 1947 by many countries wanting to see trade barriers come down. At the same time new trading blocs, groups of nations that want to stimulate trade with each other, emerged. Powerful trade blocs include the European Union (EU), the North American Free Trade Agreement (NAFTA), and the Association of South-East

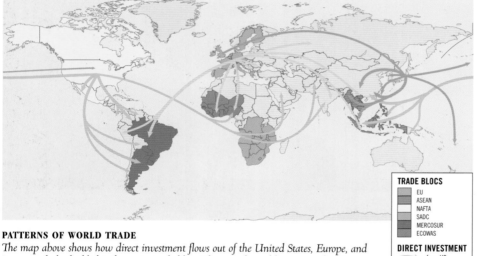

TRADE BLOCS
- EU
- ASEAN
- NAFTA
- SADC
- MERCOSUR
- ECOWAS

DIRECT INVESTMENT
- from US
- from Europe
- from Japan

PATTERNS OF WORLD TRADE

The map above shows how direct investment flows out of the United States, Europe, and Japan, and also highlights the major trade blocs. These are formed by groups of nations with similar political and economic interests, wishing to reduce the barriers to trade between members. The three main blocs are the EU, NAFTA and ASEAN (see right).

Ordered by geographic location, East to West; in Greenwich Mean Time   MAJOR STOCK EXCHANGE

| TOKYO | HONG KONG | FRANKFURT | ZURICH |

Although Japan first began trading in the 1870s, the Tokyo stock exchange was founded in 1949. It is the first market to open each day at midnight (GMT). The 2.3 million issued shares are valued at 11.5 billion yen. Major Index: NIKKEI 225.

First trading in 1891, the Hong Kong Stock exchange completed a merger with three Asian stock exchanges in 2000. It opens at 2am (GMT) and 812 companies are listed with a value of over HK$3,559 billion. Major Index: HANG SENG.

Tracing its history to 1585 when merchants met to discuss currency issues, the Frankfurt Stock Exchange was established in 1682, and the first exchange built in 1843. It opens at 8am (GMT) with 5,768 companies listed on the Deutsche Börse. Major Index: DAX.

Trading from 1852, the Stock Exchange Association was formed in 1873. It was renamed the SWX Swiss Exchange in 1995, when the three exchanges in Geneva, Basle and Zurich merged. Zurich opens at 8am (GMT) for trading. Major Index: SNMI.

NOMY

Asian Nations (ASEAN). In South America, Mercosur, a common market/customs union was created in 1991 by Argentina, Brazil, Paraguay, and Uruguay (Chile and Bolivia joined later). The EU and Mercosur began negotiations on areas of cooperation in 1999. But Argentina's economic crisis in 2002 (*see right*) triggered financial turmoil within Mercosur. The EU reconfirmed its supportive commitment to Mercosur countries and their economic integration efforts.

More economically influential than the trading blocs are the many agencies of the United Nations that can impose sanctions and restrictions or distribute aid. The International Monetary Fund (IMF) and the World Bank have become critical in sustaining faltering national economies. Both financial institutions extend loans to struggling countries but require internal and often austere economic and governmental reforms. The World Trade Organization (WTO) established in 1995, in Geneva, Switzerland, is a global international organization dealing with the rules of trade between nations. It also monitors all stock market indexes. The WTO recommends checks and balances to the ebb and flow of global trade, especially in money transactions and also monitors all stock marked indexes.

THE STOCK EXCHANGES

To follow those indexes, investors can access major stock exchanges around the world. A stock exchange, or bourse, is a market in which businesses and governments seek to raise fresh capital from investors looking for profit. Its performance is shown in an index

GOVERNMENT BANKRUPTS ECONOMY
Protesters in Argentina demanded the return of their bank deposits, which were seized by the government in December 2001. Because of hyperinflation, Argentina's government had gone into debt and borrowed heavily, making credit more expensive for business and forcing many companies to close. Believing their pesos would be devalued, Argentines rushed to the banks to convert them to dollars, but the government limited withdrawals, sparking riots in the streets. Argentina's economic crisis reverberated throughout the international financial system.

which summarizes the ups and downs of a number of top companies. Stock exchanges operate across continents and time zones. Thus, the global economy never sleeps. Yet, despite its benefits, the integration of national economies and the powers of intervention granted to the IMF, the World Bank, and the WTO have provoked growing disaffection. The organizations are often regarded as the servants of supranational economic interests. The disparity of the world's wealth and the perceived exploitation of that imbalance has led to marches, and protests now regularly accompany gatherings of the WTO and IMF.

F THE GLOBAL ECONOMY

PARIS	LONDON	BUENOS AIRES	NEW YORK

With 1,484 listed companies, the Paris stock exchange market capitalization value is 1,477 billion euros. Formed in 2000, when the stock exchanges of Brussels, Amsterdam and Paris were merged, Euronext Paris opens at 8am (GMT). Major Index: CAC40.

One of the world's oldest trading organizations in the world, London has traded since 1698, with formal trading beginning in 1801. Some 2,700 companies are listed worth 3,375.8 billion pound sterling. London opens at 8am (GMT). Major Index: FTSE, ("Footsie") 100.

One of the oldest and most important trading markets in Latin America, the Buenos Aires exchange was established in 1854. The market opens at 2pm (GMT) with a total trading value of approximately 213.4 billion pesos. Major Index: MERVAL.

Founded by 24 businesses in 1792, the New York stock exchange was registered in 1934. The Wall Street premises have been in use since 1922. Opening at 2.30pm (GMT), New York is the last of these eight markets to open daily. Major Index: DOW JONES AVERAGES.

THE SYSTEM

WHY DO PEOPLE FORM GOVERNMENTS? Plato pointed out that citizens "chafe impatiently at the least touch of authority," but become lawless and insecure when given unlimited freedom. Nevertheless, since prehistoric times, some rules have been seen as necessary for the survival and welfare of the group, even at the basic family and clan level.

As clans joined into tribes, organization and cooperation were required, especially for defense. Tribes then formed themselves into nations of ethnic communities with deep historical roots, and shared cultural values, such as religion, tradition, and language. From them, the world's nation-states evolved, combining nations (ethnic groups), states (governments), and territories (boundaries) into what became the political map of the entire world. Centuries of colonization, conquest, and treaties have created today's patchwork world map of 193 nations.

POLITICAL SYSTEMS

The modern world map reveals the five principal systems of rule extant in the world today, and highlights those nations in a state of transition from one style of rule to another.

Theocratic rule (government in the name of religion) and non-parliamentary, or absolute, monarchies tend to persist where the force of tradition outweighs the desire among the citizens for change—although change can and does occur: the kingdom of Bahrein, for example, is gradually introducing elections to form a democratic government. By contrast, Iran saw the introduction of Islamic government only after the overthrow of the monarchy in 1979. There are many countries in which both religion and the monarchy continue to play an important part in the government of a country, but where their powers are limited by the instruments of government. Conversely, there are many countries which are entirely secular (indeed most communist states outlawed religious practice), and many which abolished or

rejected their traditional monarchal rule—often centuries ago—such as France and the USA.

Military rule tends to exist as a legacy of some form of national emergency—riots, civil war or a coup— whereby control of the country was assumed by the armed forces, often for viable reasons of stability and security. Frequently, a return to free elections is assured—in time. Today, military regimes rarely outlast their leaders.

Single-party rule tends today to be associated with various forms of communist government, although in Libya, Syria and, until 2003, Iraq, it was the product of a ruthless individual or dynasty. Elections of a sort may be held, but merely in order to endorse the existing status quo. Here again, as the ruling generation passes, so frequently the pressure for change and liberalizaton proves irresistable.

DEFINING DEMOCRACY

The predominant system of rule today is democracy, which takes a wide variety of forms. This prevalence is a relatively recent development; a mere 50 years ago over three quarters of the world's population did not

have the right to vote to determine their manner of government.

Anthropologists have shown than democratic principles—inclusive argument, discussion and consensus—are widely used as a basis for organization among primitive tribal peoples. Democracy as we understand it has its roots in the city states of Ancient Greece and the republican system of Ancient Rome, at a time when other political entities around the world were chiefdoms, monarchies, or empires. Greek ideas were preserved in the writings of Socrates, Plato, and Aristotle. Rome regarded governing as a *res publica*, a "public thing" (republic), in which consuls, the Senate,

"The ills of the human race will never disappear until by God's gift those who are sincere and true lovers of wisdom attain political power."
—Plato, Athenian philosopher

S OF RULE

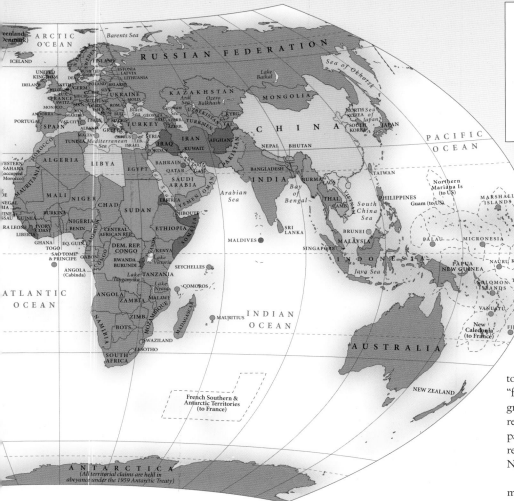

REGIONS OF RULE

The map demonstrates the various systems of rule worldwide at the time of this book's printing. For further information on each type of rule, please refer to the opening to each system section. Democratic Rule is subdived into five subsets within its section.

- Monarchal Rule
- Theocratic Rule
- Military Rule
- Democratic Rule
- Single-party Rule
- Transitional Rule

THE POLITICAL PUZZLE

The world map here demonstrates not only the divisions of rule around the world, but also the concentrations of certain types of rule. For instance, some of the oldest forms of rule remain assembled in areas of earliest civilization, while the Americas, developed much later, are almost entirely under democratic rule.

elected members from minority parties who are said to be in "opposition". The electoral process might be based on proportional representation, whereby the seats in parliament are allocated according to the total number of votes for each party, or by a "first past the post" system, in which the greatest number of votes in each voting region wins the day. A traditional, non-partisan monarch may possibly still be regarded as a symbolic head of state, as in Norway, the Netherlands, and the UK.

Multiparty republics operate in a similar manner, but a presidential head of state is elected by parliamentary representatives.

In a presidential democracy, again parliamentary representatives are elected by voting regions, but a separate election is held by popular vote to select a presidential head of state; thus, in principle, it is possible to have a head of state who is from a party which is in minoriy in parliament, or indeed who has no party allegiance whatsoever.

and the aristocracy shared power with the people through elections, proving the Athenian theory that democracy could work, ideas codified in Roman law. The Middle Ages saw these principles largely disappear with a return to kingdoms and empires, but also heralded the world's first parliament, the Althing, founded in Iceland in A.D. 930. In England, the rise of a strong parliament led to the development of a constitutional monarchy, and in 1789, the United States became the world's first constitutional republic. The post-Renaissance Enlightenment provoked a reassessment of the legacy of Classical concepts of government, and democratic ideas once more took root.

Parliamentary democracy relies upon the election of representatives from each voting region to form a governing body. These representatives may be from different political parties, but that party which holds the majority in parliament is held to be in control, and its leader becomes the prime minister, but it is checked and countered by

"What luck for rulers that men do not think."
—Adolf Hitler, *Nazi leader*

"The price of freedom is eternal vigilance."
—Thomas Jefferson, *US statesman and president*

"Many forms of government have been tried, and will be tried in this world of sin and woe. No-one pretends that democracy is perfect or all-wise. Indeed, it has been said that democracy is the worst form of government except all those other forms that have been tried from time to time."

—Winston Churchill (November 11, 1947)

Non-party democracies, which tend to occur in states that have small populations, see individuals voted into parliament without specific party allegiances.

The process of liberal democracy has seen the erosion of extremes of left and right and an increasing centralism, often expressed in coalition governments, where members from opposing political parties collaborate to form an administration.

Following the end of World War II, some former colonies formed their own systems of rule based on that of their former colonizers, while others followed internal influences, often leading to civil war, successive coups, and military or single-party regimes. Some nations were split between types of rule: Germany, Vietnam, and Korea were divided between communist and democratic rule.

NAMING NAMES

The name of some nations' governments may be misleading. The Democratic People's Republic of Korea has only one legal political party, the Korean Workers' Party. Is the nation democratic, or a genuine republic? In reality, it is the world's last Stalinist communist dictatorship. Its nomenclature should not lead it to be confused with the Republic of South Africa, for example, which is, indeed, a democracy. The Republic of Liberia, founded in 1847 as a constitutional republic for freed slaves, has been a military dictatorship beset by civil war in recent years. Is it a true republic?

Some governments and leaders have been elected democratically, but have effectively suspended the democratic process in order to retain power. Democracies in name only, these are termed presidential regimes.

World Trade Organization, the Kyoto Protocol, the International Criminal Court, the World Bank, the International Monetary Fund, and human rights groups such as Amnesty International. The emerging suprapowers provide a way for the former colonies and their colonizers to meet the challenges of the 21st century.

"Globalization," meantime, has become a unifying influence. While generally referring to international trade, globalization also encompasses culture and technology. For most of human history, people saw the governments of different states as essentially competitive rather than cooperative: one empire's power depended on the decline or defeat of others. But with the development of nuclear weapons, high-speed communications, environmental sciences, and the emergence of globalization in the late 20th century, people everywhere are increasingly aware of the need for peaceful cooperation. Whether or not the new "supranational" alliances (see The Global Matrix, page 16) herald a new system of rule is an open question.

NATIONS WITHOUT A STATE

As globalization breaks down barriers between countries, the world has seen a resurgence of nationalism—the desire for cultural, political, and economic autonomy—among cultural groups, in other words "nations" with no recognized country of their own. These "stateless nations" have identities built on their history (sometimes reaching back to Antiquity, often shared across modern state boundaries,) a distinct culture and often also a distinct language, and their own political institutions, whether traditional, or modern regional in nature. Some stateless nations are explosive, pushing violently for autonomy such as the Palestinians or the Chechens; others have channeled their nationalistic aspirations through orderly political processes, such as the Scots in the UK or the Catalans in Spain; and still others are politically quiescent with little hope for self-rule.

Because stateless nations claim territory within states or crossing state borders, they can act as powerful and often destabilizing political forces within those countries. It is estimated that there are about 1,600 to 2,000 stateless nations today (as opposed to 193 states).

JUNE 2, 2003—MEETING OF THE G8
World leaders attend the Group of 8 Summit in Evian, France, to address challenges of international growth: (left-right) Romano Prodi (President of the EU Commission), Junishiro Koizumi (Japan), Gerhard Schröder (Germany), Jean Chrétien (Canada), Vladimir Putin (Russia), Jacques Chirac (France), George W. Bush (US), Tony Blair (UK), Silvio Berlusconi (Italy), and Kostas Simitis (Greek prime minister, President of EU Council).

Vietnam was reunited under a communist government in 1975 after a long war. As a result of Glasnost and the disintegration of the Soviet Union, Germany was peacefully reunited in 1990 as a federal republic, and the countries of Eastern Europe were freed from Soviet domination. The former Soviet Union fragmented into 15 independent nations that each chose different types of rule, from communist control in Mongolia to democratic coalition government in Estonia.

SUPRAPOWERS AND GLOBALIZATION

Supranational power is the phenomenon of international coalitions of nations and multinational organizations that address problems that transcend the era of the individual nation state (see pp 20-21). The collapse of the Soviet Union in 1991 made the US the sole surviving superpower. Concerns about possible US hegemony led to increasing reliance on suprapowers such as the United Nations with its agencies and programs, the

MONARCHAL
RULE

KINGDOMS AND DYNASTIES

MONARCHAL RULE MEANS ONE PERSON RULES FOR LIFE, usually inheriting the title. Monarchs go under a great variety of titles: king, queen, prince, emperor, czar, sultan, and many more. In early history, hereditary monarchs were the norm, with all power vested in them until death. Pepi II of the "Old Kingdom" reportedly had the longest reign in Ancient Egyptian history, 2278 to 2184 B.C. The longest reigning European was King Louis XIV of France (the "Sun King"), who ruled from 1643 to 1715. An absolute monarch rules alone, or with advisers of his choosing, but in constitutional monarchies, elected officials make policy decisions. In Europe absolute monarchy thrived into the 17th century, when England replaced absolute rule with parliamentary governance, with France following a century later. Some eras are named after monarchs: Queen Victoria's 1837-1901 reign is known as the Victorian Age. The rise of the middle class, the tide of democratic liberalism, and World War I sounded the death knell for many monarchies. The Russian empire fell in 1917, followed by the German and Austro-Hungarian empires in 1918. Even so, as the 20th century advanced, monarchs continued to draw world attention through marriage. King Edward VIII abdicated the British throne in 1936 to marry an American divorcee, Wallis Simpson. In 1956, Prince Rainier III of Monaco married the actress Grace Kelly. And in 1978, King Hussein of Jordan married American-born Lisa Halaby, who took the name Queen Noor.

MONARCHS PAST AND PRESENT

Clockwise from top left: Sultan Mohammed VI, the last Ottoman sultan, deposed in 1922; King Faisal, king of Saudi Arabia (reigned 1964-1975); Charlemagne, King of the the Franks and the first Holy Roman Emperor, crowned by the pope in 800; King Hussein of Jordan (reigned 1953-1999), who steered his country through the crises of the Arab-Israeli wars; Queen Victoria, queen of the United Kingdom of Great Britain and Ireland, crowned Empress of India in 1876; King Rama V, king of Siam (reigned 1868-1910), who modernized his country along western lines; King Rudolf I (1218-1291), who by his death ruled the duchies of Austria, Styria and Carinthia, the nucleus of the Habsburg empire; Wilhelm I, king of Prussia and the first emperor (kaiser) of a united Germany; Jigme Singye Wangchuk, ruler of Bhutan, crowned "Dragon King" in 1974; Queen Elizabeth I of England, who ruled through a turbulent period of the Reformation from 1558 to 1603; Queen Isabella of Castile, whose marriage to Ferdinand of Aragon in 1469 was the foundation of a united Spain; Emperor Selim II, Ottoman emperor (1566-1574), son of Suleyman the Magnificent; Prince Galenga, present-day Zulu chieftain, a member of the family of the great 19th-century Zulu king Shaka; Emperor Charles V, Holy Roman Emperor, king of Spain, and ruler of the Low Countries, whose vast empire was divided in two when he abdicated in 1555.

MOROCCO

OFFICIAL NAME: KINGDOM OF MOROCCO

PORTUGAL
SPAIN
Mediterranean Sea
ATLANTIC OCEAN
Tanger • Ceuta (to Spain) • Melilla (to Spain)
Tétouan
Oujda
RABAT • Fès
Casablanca
Safi • Khouribga
Marrakech • Beni Mellal
Essaouira
Agadir • Ouarzazate
ALGERIA
WESTERN SAHARA (Occupied by Morocco)

Parliament

0   100 km
0   100 miles

POPULATION: 30.4 MILLION
CAPITAL: RABAT
AREA: 172,316 SQ. MILES (446,298 SQ. KM)
INDEPENDENCE: 1956
CONSTITUTION: 1972

MOROCCO is a European rendition of the original Arab name "Maghrib el Aksa", meaning "the far west".

RELIGION: Muslim (mainly Sunni) 99%, Other (mostly Christian) 1%

OFFICIAL LANGUAGE: Arabic

REGIONS OR PROVINCES: 16 regions

DEPENDENT TERRITORIES: None

MEDIA: Newspapers: There are 22 daily newspapers

TV: 2 services: 1 state-owned, 1 independent

Radio: 3 services: 1 state-owned, 2 independent

SUFFRAGE: 21 years of age; universal

LEGAL SYSTEM: Shari'a (Islamic), French and Spanish law; no ICJ jurisdiction

WORLD ORGANIZATIONS: ABEDA, ACCT, AfDB, AFESD, AL, AMF, AMU, CCC, EBRD, ECA, FAO, G-77, IAEA, IBRD, ICAO, ICC, ICFTU, ICRM, IDA, IDB, IFAD, IFC, IFRCS, IHO, ILO, IMF, IMO, Interpol, IOC, IOM, ISO, ITU, MONUC, NAM, OAS (observer), OIC, OPCW, OSCE (partner), PCA, UN, UNCTAD, UNESCO, UNHCR, UNIDO, UPU, WCL, WHO, WIPO, WMO, WToO, WTrO

POLITICAL PARTIES: K—Koatla bloc (includes Socialist Union of Popular Forces and Istiqal), W—Wifaq bloc (includes Constitutional Union & Popular Movement), C—Center bloc (includes National Rally of Independents and Democratic Popular Movement), MPCD—Constitutional and Democratic Popular Movement, FDD—Democratic Forces Front, PSD—Democratic Socialist Party

ETHNIC GROUPS:
European 1%
Berber 29%
Arab 70%

NATIONAL ECONOMICS

WORLD GNP RANKING: 56th

GNP PER CAPITA: $1,180

INFLATION: 1.9%

BALANCE OF PAYMENTS (BALANCE OF TRADE): -$475 million

EXCHANGE RATES / U.S. DLR.: 10.563-11.519 MOROCCAN DIRHAMS

OFFICIAL CURRENCY: MOROCCAN DIRHAM

GOVERNMENT SPENDING (% OF GDP)

✈ DEFENSE 5.1%	
🎓 EDUCATION 5%	
✚ HEALTH 1.2%	

0   5   10   15

NUMBER OF CONFLICTS OVER LAST 25 YEARS

	1	2-5	5+
Violent changes in government	○	○	○
Civil wars	◐	○	○
International wars	○	○	○
Foreign intervention	◐	○	○

- Polisario Front guerrillas have pursued independence for Western Sahara since 1983. A UN-brokered peace plan failed to end the dispute in 1991.
- Disputes with Spain over enclaves of Ceuta and Melilla, and Mediterranean islands.

NOTABLE WARS AND INSURGENCIES: War against Saharan secessionists 1975-1991. UN intervention (MINURSO)

ANCIENT MOROCCO WAS RULED by Romans, Vandals, Visigoths, and Greeks before an Arab invasion in the 7th century brought Islam to the land. Morocco later governed itself briefly as an independent monarchy before Arab-Berber civil warfare divided the kingdom. In the 1400s, Portugal and Spain took control of Morocco's port cities until the 1600s, and in the 18th and 19th centuries, pirates used Morocco as an outpost from which to attack trading ships in the Mediterranean. Between 1904 and 1923, Morocco was divided between France and Spain. Under the French protectorate, Moroccans used the British-US Atlantic Charter, which declared the right of people to choose their government, to bolster their call for independence. Despite quelling a revolt for self-rule by young Moroccans, banning the leading independence party, Istiqlal, and exiling Sultan Mohammed V, demands for independence intensified after World War II, and in 1956 France was compelled to grant Morocco its sovereignty and restore the monarchy.

Mohammed V, believed by Moroccans to be a descendant of the Prophet Muhammad, was named king and religious leader. His family, the Alaoui dynasty, has now provided Morocco's indigenous rulers for three centuries, making Morocco the oldest kingdom in the Arab world. After his death in 1961, his son Hassan II took the throne and established a constitution creating a bicameral Parliament. Faced with in-fighting between many political factions, Hassan reimposed royal authority. Hassan survived an assassination attempt in 1972, and in 1977 Morocco returned to parliamentary democracy.

Although constitutional reforms in the 1990s expanded the Parliament's powers, the king retained substantial control by reserving the right to make appointments and preside over the judiciary's supervisory body. With Hassan's death in 1999, his son Mohammed VI became king and has since advocated social and economic reforms.

LEGISLATIVE ELECTIONS
On September 27, 2002, the first elections were held for Parliament's lower house since King Mohammed VI took the throne in July 1999. A man holds a poster of one of the 26 parties registered to take part in the elections.

HOW THE GOVERNMENT WORKS

LEGISLATIVE BRANCH
Parlement (Parliament) Bicameral Parliament

Majlis al-Mustasharin (Chamber of Councilors)
Composed of 270 members who serve nine-year terms: 162 elected by regional, local, and professional councils; 108 elected by direct popular vote.

Majlis al-Nuwab (Chamber of Representatives)
Composed of 325 members elected to six-year terms by direct popular vote. May dissolve government with no-confidence vote.

Regional Governments
Sixteen administrative regions overseen by locally elected assemblies and governors appointed by the monarch.

EXECUTIVE BRANCH
Monarch
Position is hereditary. Serves as head of state, nation's religious leader and commander-in-chief of armed services. May dissolve Parliament; call new elections; rule by decree.

Prime Minister
Appointed by monarch following elections. Serves as head of government and presents administration's program to Parliament.

Council of Ministers
Appointed by monarch on advice of prime minister. Meetings chaired by monarch.

JUDICIAL BRANCH
Constitutional Council
Rules on elections, referenda, constitutionality of laws. Composed of 12 members who serve single nine-year terms: six appointed by monarch, six by parliamentary leaders.

Supreme Court
Highest court of appeal. Judges appointed by monarch on advice of Supreme Council of the Judiciary.

Appellate Court
Primarily handles crimes punishable by five or more years in prison.

Courts of First Instance
Rule on minor criminal and civil cases.

NEPAL

OFFICIAL NAME: KINGDOM OF NEPAL

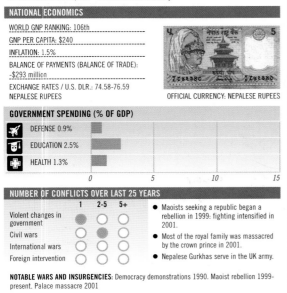

POPULATION: 23.6 MILLION	
CAPITAL: KATHMANDU	
AREA: 52,818 SQ. MILES (136,800 SQ. KM)	
INDEPENDENCE: 1769	
CONSTITUTION: 1990	

NEPAL is mentioned in the context of the Nepal Valley in Buddhist texts at least two millennia old.

RELIGION: Hindu 90%, Buddhist 4%, Muslim 3%, Christian 1%, Other 2%

OFFICIAL LANGUAGE: Nepali

REGIONS OR PROVINCES: 14 zones

DEPENDENT TERRITORIES: None

MEDIA: Total political censorship exists in national media

Newspapers: There are 29 daily newspapers, including the leading Gorkhapatra, Nepali Hindi Daily, and Rising Nepal

TV: 1 limited state-owned service

Radio: 2 services: 1 state-owned, 1 independent

ETHNIC GROUPS:
Bhojpuri 8%
Tibeto-Burmese 10%
Nepalese 52%
Maithili 11%
Other 19%

SUFFRAGE: 18 years of age; universal

LEGAL SYSTEM: English common law; Hindu legal traditions; no ICJ jurisdiction

WORLD ORGANIZATIONS: AsDB, CCC, CP, ESCAP, FAO, G-77, IBRD, ICAO, ICC, ICFTU, ICRM, IDA, IFAD, IFC, IFRCS, ILO, IMF, IMO, Interpol, IOC, IOM (observer), ISO (correspondent), ITU, MONUC, NAM, OPCW, SAARC, UN, UNAMSIL, UNCTAD, UNESCO, UNFICYP, UNIDO, UNIFIL, UNMEE, UNMIBH, UNMIK, UNMOP, UNMOT, UNTAET, UPU, WFTU, WHO, WIPO, WMO, WToO, WTrO (observer)

POLITICAL PARTIES: NCP—Nepali Congress Party, CPN-UML—Communist Party of Nepal-United Marxist-Leninist, NDP—National Democratic Party

NATIONAL ECONOMICS

WORLD GNP RANKING: 106th

GNP PER CAPITA: $240

INFLATION: 1.5%

BALANCE OF PAYMENTS (BALANCE OF TRADE): -$293 million

EXCHANGE RATES / U.S. DLR.: 74.58-76.59 NEPALESE RUPEES

OFFICIAL CURRENCY: NEPALESE RUPEES

GOVERNMENT SPENDING (% OF GDP)

✈	DEFENSE 0.9%	
🎓	EDUCATION 2.5%	
✚	HEALTH 1.3%	

0   5   10   15

NUMBER OF CONFLICTS OVER LAST 25 YEARS

	1	2-5	5+
Violent changes in government		○	○
Civil wars	○	○	○
International wars	○	○	○
Foreign intervention	○	○	○

- Maoists seeking a republic began a rebellion in 1999; fighting intensified in 2001.
- Most of the royal family was massacred by the crown prince in 2001.
- Nepalese Gurkhas serve in the UK army.

NOTABLE WARS AND INSURGENCIES: Democracy demonstrations 1990. Maoist rebellion 1999-present. Palace massacre 2001

THE ANCIENT BIRTHPLACE OF BUDDHA, Nepal succeeded for centuries in avoiding occupation by outside powers. Today, the remote Himalayan nation is struggling to make its troubled government work amid internal discord.

For generations, dozens of small kingdoms occupied Nepal's valleys and hills. By the end of the 18th century, the legendary ruler Prithvi Narayan Shah and his kingdom of Gorkha united Nepal as a single nation. Heirs of Shah ruled until the mid-1800s, when quarrels inside the monarchy erupted in a violent fight in which scores of Nepal's leading nobles were killed. The infamous Kot Massacre launched the century-long dictatorship of Jang Bahadur and his Ranas family. Taking over as prime minister, Bahadur usurped the king's powers and established a hereditary succession that guaranteed the premiership to his descendents.

The Ranas family ruled until internal opposition and pressure by Nepalese exiles culminated in an armed insurrection in 1951. A cease-fire returned King Mahendra to power and ushered in the first-ever national elections and multiparty rule. Mahendra, however, viewed the reforms as a threat to the throne. He dissolved the government, abolished political parties and imposed a regime based on local councils, or "panchayats", with the king as pre-eminent ruler. But by 1990, public agitation for democracy compelled Mahendra's successor, King Birendra, to establish a parliamentary democracy under a constitutional monarch. Elections in 1994, though, produced a hung parliament and minority government led by the United Marxist and Leninist Party. Subsequent elections returned power to the mainstream Nepali Congress party. In 2001, Birendra, the Queen and other royal family members were slain by Crown Prince Dipendra, who later died of self-inflicted wounds. The late King's brother, Gyanendra, was proclaimed king. In 2005, faced with a renewal of a decade-long Maoist revolt, Gyanendra dismissed his government and assumed direct power, promising to restore democracy within three years.

KING GYANENDRA'S BIRTHDAY
Thousands of Nepalese people gather outside Narayanhiti Royal Palace in Kathmandu to celebrate the King's birthday. The monarch came to the throne after the tragic deaths of King Birenda and Queen Aiswarya in 2001.

HOW THE GOVERNMENT WORKS

LEGISLATIVE BRANCH

Parliament
Bicameral Parliament

Rashtriya Sabha
(House of States)
Composed of 60 members who serve six-year terms: 35 appointed by House of Representatives; 10 named by monarch; 15 elected by an electoral college. One third of members selected every two years.

Pratinidhi Sabha
(House of Representatives)
Composed of 205 members elected to five-year terms by direct popular vote.

Regional Governments
Fourteen zones, divided into 75 districts, administered by commissioners appointed by monarch.

EXECUTIVE BRANCH

Monarch
Position is hereditary.
Serves as head of state; may dissolve or summon Parliament into session; call new elections; grant pardons; commute sentences.

Prime Minister
Traditionally the leader of House of Representatives' majority party or coalition. Appointed by monarch following elections. Serves as head of state; chairs Council of Ministers.

Council of Ministers
Appointed by monarch on advice of prime minister.
Oversees government operations.

JUDICIAL BRANCH

Supreme Court
Highest court of appeal.
Chief justice appointed to seven-year term by monarch on advice of Constitutional Council; 14 other judges appointed by monarch on advice of Judicial Council.

Appellate Courts
Eleven courts hear lower-level appeals.
Judges appointed by monarch on advice of Judicial Council.

District Courts
Seventy-five courts.
Judges appointed by monarch on advice of Judicial Council.

SAUDI ARABIA

OFFICIAL NAME: KINGDOM OF SAUDI ARABIA

POPULATION: 21 MILLION
CAPITAL: RIYADH; JIDDAH (ADMINISTRATIVE)
AREA: 756,981 SQ. MILES (1,960,580 SQ. KM)
INDEPENDENCE: 1932
CONSTITUTION: 1993

SAUDI ARABIA is named after the house of Sa'ud and is ruled by the lineage of Muhammad ibn Sa'ud.

RELIGION: Sunni Muslim 85%, Shi'a Muslim 15%

OFFICIAL LANGUAGE: Arabic

REGIONS OR PROVINCES: 13 provinces

DEPENDENT TERRITORIES: None

MEDIA: Total political censorship exists in national media

NEWSPAPERS: There are 13 daily newspapers, in Arabic and English. The leading papers are *Ar-Riyadh, Sharq Al Awsat, Al-Jazirah,* and *Riyadh Daily.* The government imposes total press censorship.

TV: 2 state-owned services

RADIO: 2 services: 1 state-owned, 1 owned by a private oil company

SUFFRAGE: None

LEGAL SYSTEM: Shari'a (Islamic) law; no ICJ jurisdiction

WORLD ORGANIZATIONS: ABEDA, AfDB, AFESD, AL, AMF, BIS, CCC, ESCWA, FAO, G-19, G-77, GCC, IAEA, IBRD, ICAO, ICC, ICRM, IDA, IDB, IFAD, IFC, IFRCS, ILO, IMF, IMO, Interpol, IOC, ISO, ITU, NAM, OAPEC, OAS (observer), OIC, OPCW, OPEC, PCA, UN, UNCTAD, UNESCO, UNIDO, UPU, WFTU, WHO, WIPO, WMO, WTrO (observer)

POLITICAL PARTIES: None

ETHNIC GROUPS:
Afro-Asian 10%
Arab 90%

NATIONAL ECONOMICS

WORLD GNP RANKING: 27th

GNP PER CAPITA: $7,230

INFLATION: -0.8%

BALANCE OF PAYMENTS (BALANCE OF TRADE): $15.6 billion

EXCHANGE RATES / U.S. DLR.: 3.7505-3.7504 SAUDI RIYALS

OFFICIAL CURRENCY: SAUDI RIYAL

GOVERNMENT SPENDING (% OF GDP)

	%
✈ DEFENSE	10.1%
🎓 EDUCATION	7.5%
✚ HEALTH	6.4%

0   5   10   15

NUMBER OF CONFLICTS OVER LAST 25 YEARS

	1	2-5	5+
Violent changes in government	○	○	○
Civil wars	◐	○	○
International wars	◐	○	○
Foreign intervention	○	○	○

- Skilled foreign personnel operate much of the modern military hardware.
- The paramilitary National Guard is drawn from tribal supporters of the al-Sa'ud regime.
- No compulsory military service.

NOTABLE WARS AND INSURGENCIES: Grand Mosque violence 1987

THE KINGDOM OF SAUDI ARABIA was founded as a unified state in 1932 by King Abd al-Aziz. He solidified his power through marriage and family alliances, and his more than 40 sons became the dominant force behind the Saudi kingdom. Saudi Arabia long remained isolated from Western values. However, sitting atop the world's largest oil reserves as economic globalization takes hold, the Saudi monarchy, at present an absolute monarchy, has felt pressure to modernize its political structure and international relations.

Only when the current king, Fahd ibn Abd al-Aziz, succeeded his brother Khalid, after his death in 1982, did Saudi Arabia begin to see profound changes. The most significant was the creation in 1993 of a Consultative Council, or Majlis ash-Shoura, with legislative functions. The country also adopted the Basic Law, which defines Saudi Arabia as an Islamic state whose constitution is based on the Koran and the Sunna, a supplement to the Muslim holy book that is accepted by members of the Sunni sect.

The first Consultative Council had 60 members, appointed by King Fahd, and its primary function was advisory. Although the Council has since doubled in size, power is still vested completely in the House of Sa'ud. The Council's proposals are subject to royal approval, and members of the royal family hold key government positions at all levels. Crown Prince Abdullah is largely responsible for the day-to-day running of the country.

As of April 2001, King Fahd ibn Abd al-Aziz al-Sa'ud is the world's richest monarch, estimated to be worth $30 bn

After Iraq's invasion of Kuwait in 1990, Saudi Arabia received the Kuwaiti royal family and 400,000 refugees within its borders. Western and Arab troops were permitted to deploy on its soil for the liberation of Kuwait. Since the terrorist attacks against the United States of September 11, 2001, in which 15 of 19 hijackers were Saudis, the nation has condemned extremism. In 2003, King Fahd promised to broaden participation in the political process. Yet reports of Saudi backing for Islamist militants have put the regime on the defensive in its relations with the West.

ISSUES AND CHALLENGES:

- Saudi exile Osama bin Laden, head of the al-Qaeda terrorist network, has vowed to overthrow the House of Sa'ud. While Saudi Arabia is accused of fomenting Islamist movements abroad, its royal family could be undermined by the same radicalism at home.

- Saudi Arabia's great oil wealth has left it highly dependent on foreign workers and imported goods. Meanwhile, many young Saudis are unemployed.

- Punishments based on Islamic law, including stoning, amputation, and beheading, have spurred growing criticism by international human-rights groups.

HOW THE GOVERNMENT WORKS

LEGISLATIVE BRANCH
**Majlis ash-Shoura
(Consultative Council)
Unicameral Parliament**
Composed of 120 members appointed by monarch to four-year terms.
Acts as advisory body; all legislation must be approved by monarch.

Regional governments
Thirteen provinces governed by princes and other royal family members who are appointed by monarch.

EXECUTIVE BRANCH
Monarch
Position is hereditary.
Serves as head of state and government and supreme religious leader.
Must observe Shari'a law and Saudi traditions.

Council of Ministers
Composed of 29-plus ministers, mostly royal family members. Appointed to four-year terms by monarch. Formulates policy and oversees government operations.

Royal Council
Composed of leading princes; meets in secret on royal family matters, such as succession and stipends.

JUDICIAL BRANCH
Supreme Judicial Council
Composed of 12 justices appointed by Justice Ministry and confirmed by Royal Court. Oversees judiciary; serves as final court of appeal for some Shari'a Court verdicts.

Shari'a Courts
Adjudicate criminal cases and civil suits, including divorce, child custody, and inheritance. Jurisdiction includes non-Muslims. Judges appointed by monarch and rule by the Koran and Sunna.

CAMBODIA

OFFICIAL NAME: KINGDOM OF CAMBODIA

POPULATION: 13.4 MILLION	
CAPITAL: PHNOM PENH	
AREA: 69,900 SQ. MILES (181,041 SQ. KM)	
INDEPENDENCE: 1953	
CONSTITUTION: 1993	

CAMBODIA's name derives from Kambuja, "descendants of Kambu", a mythological Indian king.

RELIGION: Buddhist 93%, Muslim 6%, Christian 1%

OFFICIAL LANGUAGE: Khmer

REGIONS OR PROVINCES: 20 provinces

DEPENDENT TERRITORIES: None

MEDIA: Total political censorship exists in national media

NEWSPAPERS: There are 2 daily newspapers. The government has used a 1995 press law to prosecute the nations's newspapers for defamation and disinformation.

TV: 6 services: 1 state-run, 5 independent.

RADIO: 10 services; 2 state-run, 8 independent

SUFFRAGE: 18 years of age; universal

LEGAL SYSTEM: Customary and civil law; including UN Transitional Authority legal codes; accepts ICJ jurisdiction

WORLD ORGANIZATIONS: ACCT, ARF, AsDB, ASEAN, CCC, CP, ESCAP, FAO, G-77, IAEA, IBRD, ICAO, ICRM, IDA, IFAD, IFC, IFRCS, ILO, IMF, IMO, Interpol, IOC, IOM (observer), ISO (subscriber), ITU, NAM, OPCW (signatory), PCA, UN, UNCTAD, UNESCO, UNIDO, UPU, WFTU, WHO, WIPO, WMO, WToO, WTrO (observer)

POLITICAL PARTIES: CPP—Cambodian People's Party, Funcinpec—United National Front for an Independent Neutral Peaceful and Cooperative Cambodia, SRP—Sam Rainsy Party

ETHNIC GROUPS:

Vietnamese 4%
Chinese 1%
Other 5%
Khmer 90%

NATIONAL ECONOMICS

WORLD GNP RANKING: 130th

GNP PER CAPITA: $260

INFLATION: -0.8%

BALANCE OF PAYMENTS (BALANCE OF TRADE) -$19 million

EXCHANGE RATES / U.S. DLR.: 3835 CAMBODIAN RIELS

OFFICIAL CURRENCY: CAMBODIAN RIEL

GOVERNMENT SPENDING (% OF GDP)

✈ DEFENSE 6.1%	
🎓 EDUCATION 5.5%	
✚ HEALTH 0.6%	

0 — 5 — 10 — 15

NUMBER OF CONFLICTS OVER LAST 25 YEARS

	1	2-5	5+
Violent changes in government			
Civil wars			
International wars			
Foreign intervention			

● Under a nominal overall structure, there remain three main armies—the Cambodian People's Armed Forces, the Armé Nationale Sihanoukiste, and the Khmer People's National Liberation Armed Forces.

NOTABLE WARS AND INSURGENCIES: The Killing Fields of Pol Pot 1975-1979. Vietnamese invasion 1978-1991. Khmer Rouge insurgency 1992-1998. UN intervention (UNAMIC)

CAMBODIA IS COUNTING ON its reestablished constitutional monarchy to revive some of the majesty of its past and repair a society shattered by years of civil war and one of history's most horrific episodes of genocide.

Starting in about A.D. 600, Cambodia was the flourishing center of the Khmer Empire that spanned Southeast Asia and built some of the world's most elaborate religious temples. But after devastating attacks by Thai and Vietnamese invaders, by the mid-1800s Cambodia teetered on the edge of collapse and turned for protection to France. For the next seven decades, France ruled Cambodia as a colony, stripping its longtime monarchy of most of its authority.

Cambodia secured independence in 1953, but ultimately fell victim to the turmoil of the escalating war in Vietnam. By 1975, the communist Khmer Rouge insurgency overwhelmed the US-backed regime of General Lon Nol, which earlier had abolished Cambodia's monarchy and taken charge of its government. Once in power, the Khmer Rouge and its leader, Pol Pot, abolished money and private property, and commenced a murderous campaign to cleanse Cambodian society of all "bourgeois" influences. Hundreds of thousands of people fled the country, starved, died of disease, or were executed as Pol Pot evacuated cities and towns, sending entire urban populations into the countryside to be re-educated with revolutionary ideology.

> Between 1975 and 1979, 1.7m men, women, and children lost their lives in Cambodia's "killing fields"

Occupation by Vietnam ended the brutal reign in 1979 but spawned a costly guerrilla war with ousted Khmer forces that lasted through the 1980s. A UN-monitored cease-fire led to peace accords that established, within the framework of a constitutional monarchy, a new multiparty parliamentary democracy and elevated Prince Norodom Sihanouk to the throne as king. Cambodia's legislature holds two sessions each year and is responsible for approving the national budget, ratifying treaties, and declaring states of war, but substantial powers remain vested in the executive branch. Cambodia's critical test remains resolving rivalries in the government and rebuilding its war-torn economy.

ISSUES AND CHALLENGES

● Building a modern infrastructure —especially in the countryside—of roads, electricity, and water, and providing education and job skills remain the most daunting challenges.

● Illegal logging annually costs the government millions of dollars in badly needed revenue.

● HIV and AIDS spread by a booming sex industry are outpacing government resources to care for afflicted citizens.

● Years of war have left Cambodia's population with a very high proportion of orphans and widows.

HOW THE GOVERNMENT WORKS

LEGISLATIVE BRANCH

Parliament
Unicameral Parliament

National Assembly
Composed of 122 members, elected by popular vote to five-year terms.

Senate
Composed of 61 members who serve five-year terms. Two members appointed by the monarch, 59 elected by the National Assembly.

Regional Governments
Twenty provinces and four municipalities with leaders appointed by the national government and split between Cambodia's two coalition parties.

EXECUTIVE BRANCH

Monarch
Chosen by Royal Throne Council. Serves as head of state and commander-in-chief of armed forces. Appoints ambassadors and government officials; declares states of emergency; grants amnesty.

Prime Minister
Majority party leader, named by National Assembly chairman and appointed by monarch. Serves as head of government and leads the Council of Ministers.

Council of Ministers
Composed of 24 members appointed by monarch. Oversees government operations.

JUDICIAL BRANCH

Constitutional Council
Rules on constitutionality of laws. Composed of nine members holding staggered, nine-year terms. Three appointed by monarch, three by National Assembly, and three by Supreme of Magistracy (which oversees the judiciary).

Supreme Court
Highest court of review and appeal. Composed of five justices appointed by monarch.

Appeals Court
Hears appeals from lower courts. Composed of three justices appointed by monarch.

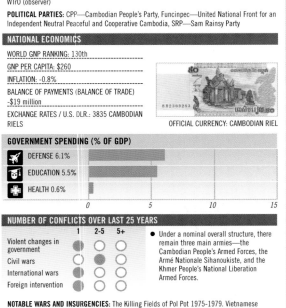

JORDAN

OFFICIAL NAME: HASHEMITE KINGDOM OF JORDAN

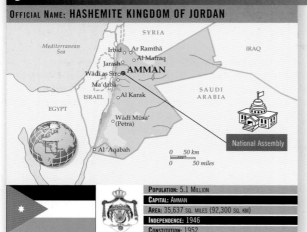

POPULATION: 5.1 MILLION	
CAPITAL: AMMAN	
AREA: 35,637 SQ. MILES (92,300 SQ. KM)	
INDEPENDENCE: 1946	
CONSTITUTION: 1952	

JORDAN is named for the River Jordan on its western border. In 1099 the Crusaders formed the principality of Oultre Jourdain, a name anglicized to Transjordan in 1921 when Britain gained control.

RELIGION: Sunni Muslim 92%, Christian 6%, Other 2%

OFFICIAL LANGUAGE: Arabic

REGIONS OR PROVINCES: 12 governorates

DEPENDENT TERRITORIES: None

MEDIA: Partial political censorship exists in national media

Newspapers: There are 8 daily newspapers

TV: 1 state-controlled service

Radio: 1 state-controlled service

SUFFRAGE: 20 years of age; universal

LEGAL SYSTEM: Shari'a (Islamic) and French law; no ICJ jurisdiction

ETHNIC GROUPS:

Armenian 1%
Circassian 1%
Arab 98%

WORLD ORGANIZATIONS: ABEDA, ACC, AFESD, AL, AMF, CAEU, CCC, ESCWA, FAO, G-77, IAEA, IBRD, ICAO, ICC, ICFTU, ICRM, IDA, IDB, IFAD, IFC, IFRCS, ILO, IMF, IMO, Interpol, IOC, IOM, ISO, ITU, MONUC, NAM, OIC, OPCW, OSCE (partner), PCA, UN, UNAMSIL, UNCTAD, UNESCO, UNIDO, UNMEE, UNMIBH, UNMIK, UNMOP, UNMOT, UNOMIG, UNRWA, UNTAET, UPU, WFTU, WHO, WIPO, WMO, WToO, WTrO

POLITICAL PARTIES: Ind—Independents, IAF—Islamic Action Front, AAP—Al-Ahd Party

NATIONAL ECONOMICS

WORLD GNP RANKING: 92nd

GNP PER CAPITA: $1,710

INFLATION: 0.7%

BALANCE OF PAYMENTS (BALANCE OF TRADE): $59 million

EXCHANGE RATES / U.S. DLR.: 0.7100-0.7088 JORDANIAN DINARS

OFFICIAL CURRENCY: JORDANIAN DINAR

GOVERNMENT SPENDING (% OF GDP)

✈ DEFENSE	6.9%	
🎓 EDUCATION	6.8%	
✚ HEALTH	3.6%	

0   5   10   15

NUMBER OF CONFLICTS OVER LAST 25 YEARS

	1	2-5	5+
Violent changes in government	○	○	○
Civil wars	○	○	○
International wars	○	○	○
Foreign intervention	○	○	○

- The well-trained and professional military is loyal to the monarchy.
- Jordan is dependent on Western support for credit for purchasing advanced arms and equipment.

NOTABLE WARS AND INSURGENCIES: None

LIKE MANY YOUNG COUNTRIES in the Middle East, Jordan was assigned its borders by European powers after the collapse of the Ottoman Empire following World War I. Owing to its location, Jordan has played a significant role in the history of the Arab-Israeli conflict. In 1967, Jordan lost the West Bank territory and East Jerusalem to Israel in the Six-Day War. It also has received an influx of Palestinian refugees, and half of its current population is of Palestinian descent. In 1994, Jordan signed a peace treaty with Israel, marking the beginning of improved relations. King Abdullah II, who came to power on the death of his father, King Hussein, in 1999 has continued the peace established by his father.

As formalized in the constitution of 1952, executive authority is held by the king, who controls the armed forces and appoints the prime minister and Cabinet, though prime ministers customarily have chosen their Cabinets with the king's approval. The king also has veto power. However, a two-thirds vote in the National Assembly's House of Deputies and House of Notables can override his veto. While political parties were legalized in 1992 and the country's first multiparty elections held in 1993, pro-government parties remain strong, in spite of considerable Islamist opposition.

In the face of widespread criticism, the government passed a restrictive press and publications law in 1998, undoing reforms that had made Jordan one of the most open societies in the region. Additionally, National Assembly elections have been postponed a number of times, causing public dissatisfaction with the system. While political liberalization remains an area of weakness for the kingdom, King Abdullah II focuses much of his attention on economic reform. In 2000 Jordan became a member of the World Trade Organization, and signed a free trade agreement with the United States. It also signed an agreement with the European Free Trade Association in 2001.

Jordan ceded its claim to the West Bank to the Palestine Liberation Organization in 1988

ISSUES AND CHALLENGES:

- Jordan has inadequate supplies of water and other natural resources, including oil.
- Debt, poverty, and unemployment are fundamental problems.
- In 2003, the US-led war in Iraq dealt an economic blow to Jordan, dependent on Iraq for discounted oil. How Jordan will finance energy imports in the absence of such a deal remains to be seen.
- The signature of international trade agreements has liberalized trade, improving productivity and putting Jordan on the foreign investment map.
- Further challenges include fiscal adjustment to reduce the budget deficit and broader investment incentives to promote job-creating ventures.

HOW THE GOVERNMENT WORKS

LEGISLATIVE BRANCH

Majlis al-'Umma
(National Assembly)
Bicameral Parliament

Majlis al-Ayyan
(House of Notables)
Composed of 40 members appointed to four-year terms by the monarch.

Majlis al-Nuwaab
(House of Deputies)
Composed of 80 members elected to four-year terms by direct universal vote. May override, with approval of the House of Notables, monarch's vetoes of legislation.

Regional Governments
Twelve governorates headed by governors appointed by the monarch. Oversee government departments and development projects in their areas.

EXECUTIVE BRANCH

Monarch
Position is hereditary.
Serves as chief of state, head of the government and commander-in-chief of the armed forces. Powers include vetoing legislation, dissolving National Assembly, and calling new elections.

Prime Minister
Appointed by the monarch.
Oversees government operations.

Cabinet
Appointed by the prime minister with the approval of the monarch. Responsible to House of Deputies on matters of general policy and can be forced to resign by a two-thirds vote of "no confidence."

JUDICIAL BRANCH

High Court of Justice
Highest court of review and appeal. Judges are appointed by the Ministry of Justice.

Court of Appeal
Decides appeals from decisions of Courts of First Instance and Religious Courts.

Courts of First Instance
Seven tribunals hear all criminal and civil matters not expressly granted to lower magistrates courts.

Religious Courts
Divided into Shari'a Courts for Muslims and Ecclesiastical Courts for Christians. Jurisdiction includes matters of marriage, divorce, inheritance and alimony.

UNITED ARAB EMIRATES

OFFICIAL NAME: UNITED ARAB EMIRATES

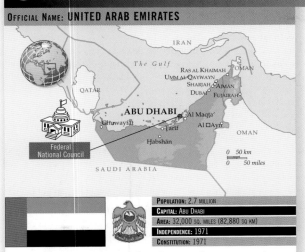

POPULATION: 2.7 MILLION
CAPITAL: ABU DHABI
AREA: 32,000 SQ. MILES (82,880 SQ KM)
INDEPENDENCE: 1971
CONSTITUTION: 1971

UNITED ARAB EMIRATES (UAE), created in 1971, is the Arab world's only working federation.

RELIGION: Shi'a Muslim 16%, Other Muslim 80%, Christian, Hindu, and Other 4%

OFFICIAL LANGUAGE: Arabic

REGIONS OR PROVINCES: 7 emirates

DEPENDENT TERRITORIES: None

MEDIA: Total political censorship exists in the national media.

Newspapers: There are 7 daily newspapers

TV: 4 state-owned services, satellite unrestricted, Dubai Media City, opened in 2001, promotes greater press freedoms.

Radio: 7 state-owned services

SUFFRAGE: None

LEGAL SYSTEM: Shari'a (Islamic) and civil law; no ICJ jurisdiction

WORLD ORGANIZATIONS: ABEDA, AFESD, AL, AMF, CAEU, CCC, ESCWA, FAO, G-77, GCC, IAEA, IBRD, ICAO, ICRM, IDA, IDB, IFAD, IFC, IFRCS, IHO, ILO, IMF, IMO, Intelsat, Interpol, IOC, ISO, ITU, NAM, OAPEC, OIC, OPCW, OPEC, UN, UNCTAD, UNESCO, UNIDO, UPU, WHO, WIPO, WMO, WTrO

POLITICAL PARTIES: None

ETHNIC GROUPS:

- European 3%
- Other Arab 12%
- Emirian 25%
- Asian 60%

NATIONAL ECONOMICS

WORLD GNP RANKING: 49th

GNP PER CAPITA: $17,870

INFLATION: 4.5%

BALANCE OF PAYMENTS (BALANCE OF TRADE): $24.6 billion

EXCHANGE RATES / U.S. DLR.: 3.6730-3.6729 UAE DIRHAMS

OFFICIAL CURRENCY: UAE DIRHAM

GOVERNMENT SPENDING (% OF GDP)

✈ DEFENSE 5.9%			
🎓 EDUCATION 1.9%			
✚ HEALTH 0.8%			

0   5   10   15

NUMBER OF CONFLICTS OVER LAST 25 YEARS

	1	2-5	5+
Violent changes in government	○	○	○
Civil wars	○	○	○
International wars	○	○	○
Foreign intervention	○	○	○

- Army personnel are mainly drawn from other Arab states and the Indian subcontinent.
- US air bases in the UAE have been used consistently in regional conflicts.
- No compulsory military service.

NOTABLE WARS AND INSURGENCIES: None

THE UNITED ARAB EMIRATES IS A FEDERATION of seven emirates: Abu Dhabi, Ajman, Dubai, Fujairah, Sharjah, Ras al Khaimah, and Umm al Qaywayn. Each member state is dominated by its respective ruling family. UAE nationals enjoy free education, free primary health care, one of the highest per-capita incomes in the Arab world, and no income tax. The 1970s oil boom brought an influx of foreign workers, who today outnumber UAE nationals. Most foreign workers are from Asia, drawn by the UAE's considerable oil and gas reserves—the third-largest in OPEC.

Executive power in the federation is held by the Supreme Council of the Union, the president and vice-president, and a Council of Ministers. Rulers of the seven member states make up the Supreme Council of the Union. Its powers include proposing federal legislation, selecting federal officials, and electing the president and vice-president. Abu Dhabi's ruler, Shaikh Zayed, is the only UAE president to date, having served since the federation was founded in 1971. Dubai's ruler, Shaikh Maktoum al-Maktoum, serves as vice-president and prime minister.

EID PRAYER
On December 5, 2002, UAE prime minister Sheikh Maktoum al-Maktoum and his brothers joined the dawn Eid al-Fitr prayer in Dubai, marking the end of the holy fasting month of Ramadan.

In 1993 President Zayed reinstalled the Federal National Council in response to criticisms regarding the UAE's lack of democracy. This advisory body has representatives appointed by each state's emir for a two-year renewable term. The Federal National Council does not have authority to enact legislation on its own, and both the Council of Ministers and the Supreme Council of the Union can overrule any Federal National Council proposals. While the authoritarian nature of the UAE government may not be welcome among all of its citizens, there are few calls for popular participation in the political system. The federation's strong economy makes it unlikely that the rulers will face any pressure to liberalize.

HOW THE GOVERNMENT WORKS

LEGISLATIVE BRANCH
Majlis al-Ittihad al-Watani
(Federal National Council)

Unicameral Parliament
Composed of 40 members appointed to two-year terms by rulers of member emirates. Constitutionally fixed quota allots more members to wealthiest and most populous emirates. Consults and reviews legislation, but cannot change or veto laws.

Regional Governments
Seven emirates with local rulers and control over their mineral rights and revenues.

EXECUTIVE BRANCH
Supreme Council of the Union
Composed of rulers of seven member emirates. Highest constitutional authority. Establishes federal policies and legislation; meets four times a year; Abu Dhabi and Dubai rulers have effective veto power.

President and Vice-president
Elected to five-year terms by Supreme Council of the Union. President serves as head of state; chairs Supreme Council of the Union; supervises armed forces.

Prime Minister
Appointed by president; serves as head of government.

Council of Ministers
Appointed by president.

JUDICIAL BRANCH
Union Supreme Court
Adjudicates disputes among emirates and between emirates and federal government; rules on constitutionality of laws. Composed of five judges appointed by president.

Lower Federal Courts
Hear civil and commercial cases that involve the federal government.

Local Courts
Justice administered by federal Ministry of Justice in Abu Dhabi, Fujairah, and Sharjah, and by local rulers in Ajman, Dubai, Ras al Khaimah, and Umm al-Qaywayn.

ROYAL MOTORCADE
King Abdullah of Jordan with his wife, Queen Rania, in Amman upon his succession in 1999.

OMAN

POPULATION: 2.6 MILLION	
CAPITAL: MUSCAT	
AREA: 82,031 SQ. MILES (212,460 SQ. KM)	
INDEPENDENCE: 1951	
CONSTITUTION: 1996	

OMAN is thought to be derived from the Arabic word *aamen* meaning "a settled man".

RELIGION: Ibadi Muslim 75%, Other Muslim and Hindu 25%

OFFICIAL LANGUAGE: Arabic

REGIONS OR PROVINCES: 6 regions and 2 governorates

DEPENDENT TERRITORIES: None

MEDIA: Total political censorship exists in national media

NEWSPAPERS: There are 5 daily newspapers

TV: 1 state-controlled service

RADIO: 2 state-controlled services

SUFFRAGE: In Oman's most recent elections in 2000, limited to approximately 175,000 Omanis chosen by the government to vote in elections for the Majlis ash-Shoura

LEGAL SYSTEM: Shari'a (Islamic) and English common law; no ICJ jurisdiction

WORLD ORGANIZATIONS: ABEDA, AFESD, AL, AMF, CCC, ESCWA, FAO, G-77, GCC, IBRD, ICAO, IDA, IDB, IFAD, IFC, IHO, ILO, IMF, IMO, Interpol, IOC, ISO (correspondent), ITU, NAM, OIC, OPCW, UN, UNCTAD, UNESCO, UNIDO, UPU, WFTU, WHO, WIPO, WMO, WTrO

POLITICAL PARTIES: None

ETHNIC GROUPS:

- Indian and Pakistani 3%
- Persian 3%
- African 2%
- Baluch 4%
- Arab 88%

NATIONAL ECONOMICS

WORLD GNP RANKING: 80th

GNP PER CAPITA: $4,778

INFLATION: -1.1%

BALANCE OF PAYMENTS (BALANCE OF TRADE): $3.35 billion

EXCHANGE RATES / U.S. DLR.: 0.3851 OMANI RIALS

OFFICIAL CURRENCY: OMANI RIALS

GOVERNMENT SPENDING (% OF GDP)

✈	DEFENSE	10%
🎓	EDUCATION	3.9%
✚	HEALTH	2.9%

0   5   10   15

NUMBER OF CONFLICTS OVER LAST 25 YEARS

	1	2-5	5+
Violent changes in government	○	○	○
Civil wars	○	○	○
International wars	○	○	○
Foreign intervention	○	○	○

- The Defense Council was established in 1996 and has upgraded the armed forces.
- Baluchi mercenaries supplement army strength.
- Border disputes with the UAE were resolved in 1999.

NOTABLE WARS AND INSURGENCIES: None

LOCATED ON THE EASTERNMOST POINT of the Arabian Peninsula at the entrance to the Persian Gulf, Oman is considered to be the least developed of the Arab states. The majority of the population belongs to the Ibadi branch of Islam, which is considered moderately liberal and follows an elected leader, the imam. Oman has been independent for much of its history, but its coast was controlled by the Portuguese for most of the 16th century, and in 1737 it fell briefly under Persian rule. In 1749 Ahmed ibn Sa'id was elected imam and political power shifted from the imam to the hereditary dynasty he founded, the Albusaidi. His descendents have ruled the country to this day. A powerful nation throughout the 19th century, Oman signed a number of friendship treaties with the United Kingdom, including one in 1951 in which the UK formally accepted Oman's independent status.

Oman is ruled by Sultan Qaboos ibn Sa'id, an authoritarian leader who serves as prime minister as well as minister of foreign affairs, defense, and finance. Oman became an oil exporter two years before Qaboos seized power in a coup against his father, Sa'id ibn Taymur, in 1970. A Marxist-led insurgency originating in the province of Dhofar in 1964 was finally defeated in 1975, with Qaboos using oil revenue to finance social and economic reform. In 1996, the sultan developed Oman's first written constitution, called the "Basic Statutes of the State," which guaranteed the rights of the people and established the laws of succession.

The sultan or a representative chairs all policy-making bodies: the Council of Ministers, and Specialize Councils for Economic Development, Finance, and Defense. The legislative Majlis Oman (Council of Oman), comprises the appointed Majlis ad-Dawla (State Council) and the elected Majlis ash-Shoura (Consultative Council). The legislative branch emerged only in 1991 when an indirectly elected Consultative Council was set up to review the budget and prepare legislation. In 2002, the sultan provided for its direct election by extending voting rights to all citizens aged 21 and over. The development of oil and gas fields has strengthened Oman's economy and spurred an influx of some 450,000 foreign workers. To curb oil dependence, the government is trying to boost the service sector and educate young Omanis to replace migrant workers.

ISSUES AND CHALLENGES:

- Contributing 90 percent of the GNP, much of Oman's revenue comes from oil exports. Yet with reserves projected to last less than 20 years, reducing dependence remains a high priority. Opportunities do exist to develop the service and tourism industries, although Oman is largely dependent on foreign workers.

- With nearly half of Oman's population under 15 years of age, education of the country's youth is rapidly becoming an important issue. Rural illiteracy also remains high.

- Over-pumping of groundwater has led to seepage of seawater into irrigation areas.

HOW THE GOVERNMENT WORKS

LEGISLATIVE BRANCH

Majlis Oman
(Council of Oman)
Bicameral Parliament

Majlis ad-Dawla
(State Council)
Comprises 48 members, mostly former ministers and military officers, appointed by sultan.

Majlis ash-Shoura
(Consultative Council)
Comprises 83 members nominated by provincial committees and appointed by sultan. Has only advisory authority; reviews legislation on economic development and social services; may summon ministers for questioning.

Regional Governments
Fifty-nine districts headed by governors who settle local disputes, collect taxes and maintain peace.

EXECUTIVE BRANCH

Sultan
Position is hereditary.
Serves as sole executive authority with no formal checks on power. Acts as head of state, commander-in-chief of armed forces, prime minister, minister of foreign affairs and finance.

Council of Ministers
Composed of 26 members, appointed by sultan. Chaired by sultan; oversees government operations.

JUDICIAL BRANCH

Magistrates' Courts
Established by royal decree to adjudicate misdemeanors and serious criminal matters. Court president reports directly to sultan, who also appoints judges.

Shari'a Courts
Rule on minor criminal offenses and civil cases, including deportation, divorce, inheritance and wrongful injury. Judges appointed by sultan.

Commercial Courts
Hear cases involving bankruptcy, contracts, construction, insurance, shipping, and trademarks. Judges appointed by sultan.

LESOTHO

OFFICIAL NAME: KINGDOM OF LESOTHO

Parliament

MASERU

Hlotse

Teyateyaneng

Mokhotlong

Morija · Mantsonyane

Mafeteng

Mohales Hoek

SOUTH AFRICA

SOUTH AFRICA

0   50 km
0   50 miles

POPULATION: 2.1 MILLION
CAPITAL: MASERU
AREA: 11,720 SQ. MILES (30,355 SQ. KM)
INDEPENDENCE: 1966
CONSTITUTION: 1993

LESOTHO was named after the predominant ethnic group in the country, the Sotho people.

RELIGION: Christian 80%, Indigenous beliefs 20%

OFFICIAL LANGUAGES: English and Sesotho

REGIONS OR PROVINCES: 10 districts

DEPENDENT TERRITORIES: None

MEDIA: Partial political censorship exists in the national media.

Newspapers: There are 2 daily newspapers, only the *Mirror* is independent. *Leselinyana la Lesotho* is a popular religious periodical

TV: 1 state-owned service

Radio: 1 state-owned service

SUFFRAGE: 18 years of age; universal

LEGAL SYSTEM: Roman-Dutch and English common law; no ICJ jurisdiction

WORLD ORGANIZATIONS: ACP, AfDB, C, CCC, ECA, FAO, G-77, IBRD, ICAO, ICRM, IDA, IFAD, IFC, IFRCS, ILO, IMF, Interpol, IOC, ISO (subscriber), ITU, NAM, OAU, OPCW, SACU, SADC, UN, UNCTAD, UNESCO, UNHCR, UNIDO, UPU, WCL, WFTU, WHO, WIPO, WMO, WToO, WTrO

POLITICAL PARTIES: LCD—Lesotho Congress for Democracy Party, BNP—Basotho National Party, NIP—National Independent Party, LPC—Lesotho People's Congress

ETHNIC GROUPS:

European and Asian 3%

Sotho 97%

NATIONAL ECONOMICS

WORLD GNP RANKING: 150th

GNP PER CAPITA: $580

INFLATION: 6.1%

BALANCE OF PAYMENTS (BALANCE OF TRADE): -$151 million

EXCHANGE RATES / U.S. DLR.: 7.570-11.995 MALOTI

CENTRAL BANK OF LESOTHO

OFFICIAL CURRENCY: MALOTI

GOVERNMENT SPENDING (% OF GDP)

DEFENSE 4%		
EDUCATION 13%		
HEALTH 4%		

0   5   10   15

NUMBER OF CONFLICTS OVER LAST 25 YEARS

	1	2-5	5+
Violent changes in government		●	
Civil wars	○	○	○
International wars	○	○	○
Foreign intervention	●	○	○

● South African assistance was called in to quell political violence in 1998.

● Foreign policy is dominated by the nature of Lesotho's dependent relationship with South Africa.

NOTABLE WARS AND INSURGENCIES: Civil conflict. South Africa intervenes to restore order

---

LESOTHO IS ENTIRELY BORDERED BY SOUTH AFRICA. As it is dependent on its neighbor for security and jobs, many of the male population work as migrant laborers in South African mines. In spite of this, 90 percent of the population lives below the poverty line. Formerly a British territory, Lesotho was known as Basutoland until independence in 1966.

Each of the three major powers—the monarch, the army and the government—has at various junctures thrown the country into political turmoil. Rather than lose the 1970 elections, the ruling Basotho National Party (BNP) led by Prime Minister Chief Leabua Jonathan declared the elections irregular, suspended the constitution and dissolved Parliament. The government's harboring of African National Congress members from South African resulted in South Africa closing its borders. These two events ultimately spurred the military coup of 1986, handing executive and legislative authority to King Moshoeshoe II in conjunction with the Military Council that appointed him. His subsequent over-involvement in government activities led to his exile. Seemingly less interested in politics, his son King Letsie III was appointed. However, ignoring a constitutional change in 1993 that stripped him of executive authority, the new king took power one year later and suspended Parliament. With the assistance of neighboring countries Letsie was overthrown in favor of his father and a new government elected. He resumed the throne on his father's death in 1996 and despite numerous coup attempts, has disregarded the constitution and continued to perform an active, albeit contentious, role in politics.

South Africa and Botswana have quelled ongoing violence and demonstrations that arose from irregularities in elections, and an Interim Political Authority has begun the task of reviewing the electoral process. Amongst other things this has resulted in the addition of 40 new members to the National Assembly elected by proportional representation. Elections in May 2002 were unanimously declared free and fair, and the Lesotho Congress for Democracy Party (LCD) took 77 of the 80 directly elected seats, while nine of the 19 parties taking part in the elections divided the new proportional seats.

ISSUES AND CHALLENGES:

● Lesotho's unstable political climate continues unabated, and has made it largely dependent on South Africa for security, as well as employment and trade. The Lesotho Highlands Water Project has provided water and jobs, as well as providing revenue from South Africa, but new solutions are required.

● Unemployment is rife and life expectancy is falling as a quarter of the population is infected with the HIV virus. It is anticipated that average life expectancy will be only 37 years by 2017.

HOW THE GOVERNMENT WORKS

LEGISLATIVE BRANCH
Parliament
Bicameral Parliament

Senate
Composed of 33 members who serve five-year terms: 11 appointed by ruling party; 22 by principal chiefs. Senate president elected by secret-ballot vote of members.

National Assembly
Composed of 120 members who serve five-year terms: 80 elected by direct popular vote; 40 by proportional vote.

Regional Governments
Ten districts each headed by secretary appointed by central government and military officer appointed by Lesotho Defense Force.

EXECUTIVE BRANCH
Monarch
Position is hereditary. College of chiefs determines successor and may depose monarch. Serves as ceremonial head of state with no executive or legislative authority. Prohibited from engaging in politics.

Prime Minister
Leader of National Assembly's majority party automatically assumes post. Serves as head of government; chairs Cabinet.

Cabinet
Composed of 17 members, including the prime minister and deputy prime minister.

JUDICIAL BRANCH
High Court
Highest court of appeal with power to review legislative decisions. Chief justice appointed by monarch.

Court of Appeal
Rules on appeals from lower courts.

Magistrates' Courts
Judges, not juries, conduct trials. In criminal cases, two judges act as observers.

Traditional Courts
Located in rural areas.

BHUTAN

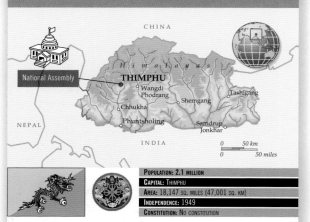

National Assembly

CHINA

Himalayas

THIMPHU
Wangdi
Phodrang
Shemgang
Tashigang
Chhukha
Phuntsholing
Samdrup
Jonkhar

NEPAL

INDIA

0   50 km
0   50 miles

POPULATION: 2.1 MILLION	
CAPITAL: THIMPHU	
AREA: 18,147 SQ. MILES (47,001 SQ. KM)	
INDEPENDENCE: 1949	
CONSTITUTION: NO CONSTITUTION	

BHUTAN is named after the Bhotia people who arrived there from Tibet in the 10th century.

RELIGION: Mahayana Buddhism 70%, Hindu 24%, Other 6%

OFFICIAL LANGUAGE: Dzongkha

REGIONS OR PROVINCES: 18 districts

DEPENDENT TERRITORIES: None

MEDIA: Total political censorship exists in national media

Newspapers: There are no daily newspapers

TV: 1 state-owned service. Until 1999 television was banned, in order to protect cultural values.

Radio: 1 state-owned service

SUFFRAGE: Each family has one vote in village-level elections

LEGAL SYSTEM: Indian and English common law; no ICJ jurisdiction

WORLD ORGANIZATIONS: AsDB, CP, ESCAP, FAO, G-77, IBRD, ICAO, IDA, IFAD, IMF, IOC, IOM (observer), ITU, NAM, OPCW (signatory), SAARC, UN, UNCTAD, UNESCO, UNIDO, UPU, WHO, WIPO, WTrO (observer)

POLITICAL PARTIES: There are no legal political parties; members are elected individually to the National Assembly, to advise the king who rules as absolute monarch.

ETHNIC GROUPS:

Indigenous or migrant tribes 15%

Bhote 50%

Ethnic Nepalese 35%

NATIONAL ECONOMICS

WORLD GNP RANKING: 171st

GNP PER CAPITA: $590

INFLATION: 6.8%

BALANCE OF PAYMENTS (BALANCE OF TRADE): -$87 million

EXCHANGE RATES / U.S. DLR.: 46.68-48.22 NGULTRUM

OFFICIAL CURRENCY: NGULTRUM

GOVERNMENT SPENDING (% OF GDP)

✈	DEFENSE	5.6%
	EDUCATION	4.1%
✚	HEALTH	3.2%

0   5   10   15

NUMBER OF CONFLICTS OVER LAST 25 YEARS

	1	2-5	5+
Violent changes in government	○	○	○
Civil wars	○	○	○
International wars	○	○	○
Foreign intervention	○	○	○

- The army is commanded by the king.
- India is obliged to defend Bhutan.
- There is tension with Nepal over the treatment of ethnic Nepalese.

NOTABLE WARS AND INSURGENCIES: None

BHUTAN IS LOCATED between India and China, with much of its northern half dominated by the high peaks of the Himalayas. First united as a Buddhist theocracy under the Drukpa people of Tibet in 1656, Bhutan came under British influence and formed a hereditary monarchy, the Wangchuk dynasty, in 1907. A 1910 treaty provided for Bhutanese independence in internal matters and British guidance on foreign affairs. In 1947, this task was handed to India. The Indo-Bhutanese accord granted complete independence from India in 1949.

The Druk Gyalpo (literally "dragon king") controls nearly every facet of political life, from commanding the army to nominating judges and members of the Council of Ministers. Bhutan has no constitution or bill of rights. Since independence, however, the monarch has increasingly moved toward decentralization and national representation. Before the early 1980s, the kingdom's 18 *dzongkhag* (districts) were under central control. Since then, a decentralization program, instituted by King Jigme Singye Wangchuk (in power since 1972), has ceded considerable administrative power to local and district officials and allowed them a greater voice on government policy.

In 1998 the king decreed reforms granting legislative powers to the National Assembly and allowing its partial election. Village councils choose representatives in 105 constituencies, with elections being held when there is not a clear initial consensus. Only the head of each "family" in the village is allowed to vote. In practice, the king retains absolute power, and though his parliamentary veto has gone, his word carries great weight.

There is serious tension between the government and the ethnic Nepalese community in the south (Lhotshampa, literally "southerners"). State support for the majority Drukpa culture and language has angered Nepalese. Political reforms were introduced in part to address these concerns through representation, though the state continues to repress dissent. Dissidents continue to suffer human rights abuses at the hands of security forces and monarchal control of the judiciary limits their access to a fair trial.

ISSUES AND CHALLENGES:

- Serious ethnic conflict exists in southern Bhutan, where Lhotshampa (Nepali Bhutanese) communities make up the vast majority of the country's population.

- The government has labeled Nepalese Bhutanese (Lhotshampa) dissidents *ngolops*, or traitors, and commonly refers to Lhotshampa resistance groups as terrorists.

- Some 100,000 Bhutanese refugees now reside in UN-sponsored refugee camps in southeastern Nepal.

Bhutan is the world's only Buddhist kingdom

HOW THE GOVERNMENT WORKS

LEGISLATIVE BRANCH

Tshogdu
(National Assembly)
Unicameral Parliament
Composed of 154 members who serve three-year terms: 105 elected from village constituencies; 12 monastic representatives appointed by Buddhist monk bodies; 37 civil servants appointed by monarch. Enacts civil, criminal, and property laws; may remove monarch and ministers; controls auditor general.

Regional Governments
Four administrative zones; 20 districts.

EXECUTIVE BRANCH

Druk Gyalpos
(Dragon King)
Position is hereditary.
Serves as head of state and government. May send bills back to parliament for reconsideration but has no veto.

Royal Advisory Council
Composed of National Assembly members. Serves as liaison between monarch and parliament.

Cabinet
Council of Ministers
Composed of 15 members nominated by monarch with parliament's approval to five-year terms. Chaired by monarch; oversees government operations.

JUDICIAL BRANCH

Supreme Court of Appeal
Highest court of appeal.
Sole member is monarch.

High Court
(judges appointed by the monarch)
Hears lower-court appeals.
Composed of six justices who serve five-year terms: two elected by parliament; four appointed by monarch.

District Courts

KUWAIT

OFFICIAL NAME: STATE OF KUWAIT

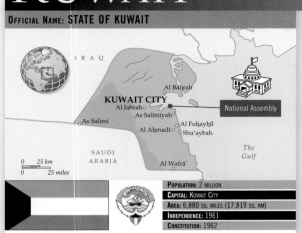

POPULATION: 2 MILLION
CAPITAL: KUWAIT CITY
AREA: 6,880 SQ. MILES (17,819 SQ. KM)
INDEPENDENCE: 1961
CONSTITUTION: 1962

KUWAIT's first city, named Kuwait, was founded in the 18th century by the Anaiza tribe from Qatar.

RELIGION: Sunni Muslim 60%, Shi'a Muslim 25%, Christian, Hindu, Parsi, and Other 15%

OFFICIAL LANGUAGE: Arabic

REGIONS OR PROVINCES: 5 governorates

DEPENDENT TERRITORIES: None

MEDIA: Partial political censorship exists in national media

NEWSPAPERS: There are 7 daily newspapers

TV: 1 state-controlled service

RADIO: 1 state-controlled service

SUFFRAGE: Adult males who have been naturalized for 30 years or more or have resided in Kuwait since before 1920 and their male descendants at age 21

LEGAL SYSTEM: Shari'a (Islamic) and civil law; no ICJ jurisdiction

WORLD ORGANIZATIONS: ABEDA, AfDB, AFESD, AL, AMF, BDEAC, CAEU, CCC, ESCWA, FAO, G-77, GCC, IAEA, IBRD, ICAO, ICC, ICRM, IDA, IDB, IFAD, IFC, IFRCS, ILO, IMF, IMO, Interpol, IOC, ISO, ITU, NAM, OAPEC, OIC, OPCW, OPEC, UN, UNCTAD, UNESCO, UNIDO, UNITAR, UPU, WFTU, WHO, WIPO, WMO, WTrO

POLITICAL PARTIES: Formation of political parties is illegal. Islamists, liberals and government supporters make up National Assembly

ETHNIC GROUPS:

Other 7%
Iranian 4%
South Asian 9%
Kuwaiti 45%
Other Arab 35%

NATIONAL ECONOMICS

WORLD GNP RANKING: 54th

GNP PER CAPITA: $18,030

INFLATION: 1.8%

BALANCE OF PAYMENTS (BALANCE OF TRADE): $14.9 billion

EXCHANGE RATES / U.S. DLR.: 0.3055-0.3071 KUWAITI DINARS

GOVERNMENT SPENDING (% OF GDP)

0   5   10   15

NUMBER OF CONFLICTS OVER LAST 25 YEARS

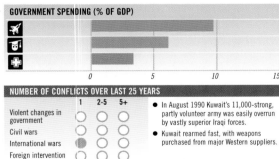

	1	2-5	5+
Violent changes in government	○	○	○
Civil wars	○	○	○
International wars	●	○	○
Foreign intervention	○	○	○

- In August 1990 Kuwait's 11,000-strong, partly volunteer army was easily overrun by vastly superior Iraqi forces.
- Kuwait rearmed fast, with weapons purchased from major Western suppliers.

NOTABLE WARS AND INSURGENCIES: Iraqi invasion leading to Gulf War 1990-1991

LOCATED AT THE NORTHWESTERN CORNER of the Persian Gulf, Kuwait lives handsomely from oil production, which accounts for more than 80 percent of export earnings. After the 1940s, Arabs from neighboring nations moved to Kuwait seeking the prosperity gained through oil production. Since then, Kuwait has faced territorial claims from Iraq, its northern neighbor. These culminated in Iraq's invasion of Kuwait in 1990, which sparked off the Gulf War. The US-led a UN coalition in several weeks of aerial attack, followed by a ground assault against Iraqi forces. Four days later on February 23, 1991, Kuwait was liberated.

Kuwait is a constitutional monarchy. It is among the most politically open states in the Arab world, even though the al-Sabah dynasty has ruled since the mid-1700s. In 1899, Shaikh Mubarak negotiated Kuwait's independence from the Ottoman Empire by signing a treaty that gave control of foreign affairs to Britain. This lasted until full independence in 1961. A year later, Kuwait's new constitution granted the highest power to an amir, a chief executive selected from Shaikh Mubarak's male descendants. Since 1915, virtually all amirs have come from the heirs of Mubarak's sons, Salim and Jabir. Family consensus still reigns in Kuwait, although the amir has the greatest influence. If the amir dies, the crown prince takes over, but a member of the Sabah family who is a direct descendant of Shaikh Mubarak names the new leader. The National Assembly must confirm the nomination, providing a check on the monarchy's power.

> Native Kuwaitis are outnumbered by resident foreign nationals, who make up more than half of the population

Although the amir decreed in 1999 that women be given the vote, the National Assembly rejected the move, and in 2003 women were still disenfranchised. The National Assembly, first elected in 1963 and dissolved several since, can write and veto legislation, as well as challenge members of the Council of Ministers. No bill can become law without parliamentary approval. The 1999 elections strengthened the Islamists' and liberals' parliamentary position.

ISSUES AND CHALLENGES:

- Kuwait is overly dependent on its oil reserves.
- The instability of the region has limited tourism, even from neighboring states.
- Landmines are an ever-present danger in border regions.
- The Iraqi invasion caused untold damage to the environment—destroying marine life and polluting much land under cultivation.
- Kuwait's postwar foreign policy acknowledges that security—especially with regard to Iraq—is its primary concern. It is clear that Kuwait alone, or even Kuwait with the support of the Gulf Cooperation Council (GCC) and other Arab members of the Gulf War coalition, cannot provide for its own defense needs. Security ultimately can be guaranteed only by the United States.

HOW THE GOVERNMENT WORKS

LEGISLATIVE BRANCH

Majlis al-Umma
(National Assembly)
Unicameral Parliament
Composed of 50 members elected to four-year terms by direct vote. Twenty-five districts are each represented by two members.
Powers include initiating legislation, approving decrees, questioning government ministers, expressing lack of confidence in individual ministers.

Regional Governments
Five provincial governorates are administered by governors and municipal councils appointed by amir.

EXECUTIVE BRANCH

Amir
Position is hereditary.
Monarch serves as head of state and commander-in-chief of armed forces; initiates laws; issues decrees; appoints and dismisses civil, military, and diplomatic officials; grants pardons; commutes sentences.

Prime Minister
By tradition, the crown prince; appointed by amir.
Serves as head of government.

Council of Ministers
Composed of 16 members.
Appointed by prime minister with amir's approval.

JUDICIAL BRANCH

Constitutional Council
Rules on electoral disputes and constitutionality of laws.
Composed of six judges: and five chosen by Judicial Council, one appointed by amir.

Court of Cassation
Highest court of appeal.
Judges appointed by amir, serve to age 65.

High Court of Appeal
Hears lower court appeals.
Judges appointed by amir, serve to age 65.

Courts of First Instance
Hears civil and criminal cases.
Judges appointed by amir, serve to age 65.

SWAZILAND

OFFICIAL NAME: PEOPLE'S KINGDOM OF SWAZILAND

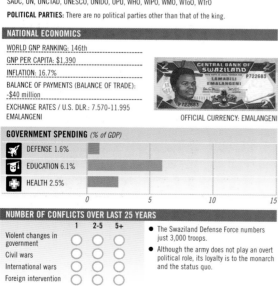

Parliament

Piggs Peak
Tshaneni
MBABANE
Manzini
Siteki
Bhunya
Sidvokodvo
MOZAMBIQUE

SOUTH AFRICA

Hlathikulu
SOUTH
Nhlangano
AFRICA

0   25 km
0   25 miles

POPULATION: 938,000
CAPITAL: Mbabane
AREA: 6,704 SQ. MILES (17,363 SQ. KM)
INDEPENDENCE: 1968
CONSTITUTION: 1968

SWAZILAND means the land of the people of Mswati (Mswazi), the first king of a land defined thus in 1839.

RELIGION: Christian 60%, Traditional beliefs 40%

OFFICIAL LANGUAGES: English and siSwati

REGIONS OR PROVINCES: 4 districts

DEPENDENT TERRITORIES: None

MEDIA: Total political censorship exists in national media. The king, responding to pressure, rapidly reversed his 2001 decree which had ensured the continued closure of the independent *Swaziland Observer*.

Newspapers: There is currently only one daily newspaper

TV: One state-owned service

Radio: Three services: one state-owned, two independent

SUFFRAGE: 18 years of age

LEGAL SYSTEM: Swazi traditional law; South African Roman-Dutch law; no ICJ jurisdiction

WORLD ORGANIZATIONS: ACP, AfDB, C, CCC, ECA, FAO, G-77, IBRD, ICAO, ICFTU, ICRM, IDA, IFAD, IFC, IFRCS, ILO, IMF, Interpol, IOC, ISO (correspondent), ITU, NAM, OAU, OPCW, PCA, SACU, SADC, UN, UNCTAD, UNESCO, UNIDO, UPU, WHO, WIPO, WMO, WToO, WTrO

POLITICAL PARTIES: There are no political parties other than that of the king.

ETHNIC GROUPS:
European 3%
African 97%

NATIONAL ECONOMICS

WORLD GNP RANKING: 146th

GNP PER CAPITA: $1,390

INFLATION: 16.7%

BALANCE OF PAYMENTS (BALANCE OF TRADE): -$40 million

EXCHANGE RATES / U.S. DLR.: 7.570-11.995 EMALANGENI

CENTRAL BANK OF SWAZILAND
P722683
LAMABILI EMALANGENI
P722683

OFFICIAL CURRENCY: EMALANGENI

GOVERNMENT SPENDING (% of GDP)

DEFENSE	1.6%
EDUCATION	6.1%
HEALTH	2.5%

0   5   10   15

NUMBER OF CONFLICTS OVER LAST 25 YEARS

	1	2-5	5+
Violent changes in government	○	○	○
Civil wars	○	○	○
International wars	○	○	○
Foreign intervention	○	○	○

- The Swaziland Defense Force numbers just 3,000 troops.
- Although the army does not play an overt political role, its loyalty is to the monarch and the status quo.

NOTABLE WARS AND INSURGENCIES: None

ONE OF THE MOST PROSPEROUS southern African countries, Swaziland faces an uncertain future as internal and international pressure to modernize challenges the country's monarch. The Nkosi Dlamini dynasty has ruled the Swazi people continuously, since the Ndwandwe people migrated south and joined other tribes in a territory governed by King Mswati (or Mswazi), bequeathed to him by his father, King Sobhuza of the Ndwandwe. Prior to the country's independence in 1968, Swaziland was administered first by South Africa, from 1894, and then by Britain as a protectorate from 1903 until independence. Much of the country's political structure has its origins in 1921, which saw the establishment of the first legislative body, an advisory council to the British commission, and the crowning of a new monarch, King Sobhuza II. The king gradually extended his powers from the people to the land and economy until, by the early 1960s, local pressure for an independent, party-ruled state could no longer be resisted. To retain control, the king formed a party, the Imbokodvo National Movement (INM).

KING MSWATI III

In Swaziland, succession to the throne is passed to the youngest son to ensure a long reign. King Mswati III was crowned in 1986, at the age of 18 making him the world's youngest ruling monarch. He is seen with some of his wives and his fiancé at a trade fair in Manzini, Swaziland on November 1, 2002.

In 1968, Swaziland won independence, combining an elected parliament with a traditional, tribal system of rule headed by the king and his advisors, who oversee the chiefs of 55 *Tinkhundla* (subregions). (Before independence, Britain's plan had been to incorporate Swaziland into South Africa.) Although the INM won the first election, it lost seats in the 1972 election to a party that proposed the limitation of absolute royal power.

Swaziland has been without a constitution since 1973

The king responded by dissolving parliament, banning political parties, and abandoning the constitution. After the king's death in 1986, his son Mswati III claimed the throne, permitting the election of a new parliament and cabinet. He has promised reform and a new constitution, but has been slow to deliver on his promises, maintaining his grip on every aspect of government.

HOW THE GOVERNMENT WORKS

LEGISLATIVE BRANCH

Libandla
(Parliament)
Bicameral Parliament

Senate
Composed of 30 members who serve five-year terms: 20 appointed by monarch; ten by the House of Assembly.

House of Assembly
Composed of 65 members who serve five-year terms; ten appointed by monarch; 55 directly elected by popular vote. Authority limited to debating government proposals and advising monarch

Regional Governments
Four regions with monarch-appointed administrators; 55 traditional "tinkhundla," units overseen by chiefs.

EXECUTIVE BRANCH

Monarch
Position is hereditary. Serves as head of state; approves legislation passed by parliament before it becomes law; broad appointment powers.

Prime minister
Appointed by monarch. Serves as head of government; chairs cabinet.

Cabinet
Council of Ministers
Composed of 16 members, including the prime minister and deputy pm. Appointed by monarch on advice of prime minister

JUDICIAL BRANCH

High Court
Highest court of appeal. Chief Justice and judges appointed by monarch.

Court of Appeal
Hears appeals from lower courts. Judges appointed by monarch.

Lower Courts
Traditional Swazi law administered by clan chiefs.

QATAR

OFFICIAL NAME: STATE OF QATAR

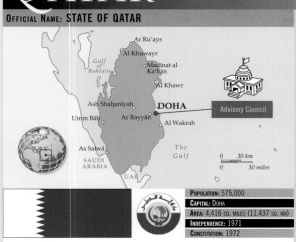

POPULATION: 575,000
CAPITAL: Doha
AREA: 4,416 SQ. MILES (11,437 SQ. KM)
INDEPENDENCE: 1971
CONSTITUTION: 1972

QATAR, inhabited since 4000 BC, was first referred to as "Qatara" by Ptolemy in the second century A.D.

RELIGION: Muslim 95%, Other 5%.

OFFICIAL LANGUAGE: Arabic

REGIONS OR PROVINCES: Nine municipalities

DEPENDENT TERRITORIES: None

MEDIA: Partial political censorship exists in national media

Newspapers: There are six daily newspapers.

TV: Two services: one state-controlled. Qatari TV is the most independent in the region; Al-Jazeera offers the leading Arab perspective internationally.

Radio: One state-controlled service

SUFFRAGE: Limited to municipal elections

LEGAL SYSTEM: Shari'a (Islamic) law; legal decisions by emir; no ICJ jurisdiction

WORLD ORGANIZATIONS: ABEDA, AFESD, AL, AMF, CCC, ESCWA, FAO, G-77, GCC, IAEA, IBRD, ICAO, ICC, ICRM, IDB, IFAD, IFRCS, IHO (pending member), ILO, IMF, IMO, Interpol, IOC, ISO (correspondent), ITU, NAM, OAPEC, OIC, OPCW, OPEC, UN, UNCTAD, UNESCO, UNIDO, UPU, WHO, WIPO, WMO, WToO, WTrO

POLITICAL PARTIES: Qatar is an absolute monarchy, but engaged in partial democratic reform

ETHNIC GROUPS:

- Iranian 10%
- Other 14%
- Arab 40%
- Indian 18%
- Pakistani 18%

NATIONAL ECONOMICS

WORLD GNP RANKING: 96th

GNP PER CAPITA: $11,570

INFLATION: -1.0%

BALANCE OF PAYMENTS (BALANCE OF TRADE): -$1.66 billion

EXCHANGE RATES / U.S. DLR.: 3.6393-3.6395 QATAR RIYALS

OFFICIAL CURRENCY: QATAR RIYAL

GOVERNMENT SPENDING (% OF GDP)

✈ DEFENSE 11.7%		
📖 EDUCATION 3.4%		
✚ HEALTH 2.9%		

0   5   10   15

NUMBER OF CONFLICTS OVER LAST 25 YEARS

	1	2-5	5+
Violent changes in government	○	○	○
Civil wars	○	○	○
International wars	○	○	○
Foreign intervention	○	○	○

- Defense agreement with the US: joint exercises, stockpiling of US equipment, US access to bases.
- Hawar Islands awarded to Bahrain in 2001.

NOTABLE WARS AND INSURGENCIES: None

THE AL-THANI FAMILY HAS LED this semiarid desert kingdom since the 18th century, including during periods of Turkish and then British control. Like other Gulf states, Qatar came under Great Britain's authority by negotiating for its protection, promising in exchange not to strike foreign deals without British consent. Qatar declared independence in 1971. Now, as then, the internal power disputes of the al-Thani family dominate national politics. Shaikh Ahmad bin Ali al-Thani, amir upon independence, was deposed in 1972 by his cousin, Shaikh Khalifa bin Hamad al-Thani. Amir Khalifa lost power in 1995 to his son, Shaikh Hamad bin Khalifa al-Thani. In 1996, Shaikh Hamad named his son, Jassim, crown prince.

The monarchy has reformed under Amir Hamad's leadership, making moves toward a semi-democratic electoral system. In 1999, the amir formed a committee to draw up a permanent constitution—initially drafted in 1972—in which the people would be better represented in the political system. That year also saw Qatar's first-ever elections, with voters—men and women—choosing members of a new municipal council for the capital city, Doha. This was no small concession: the capital and surrounding areas house nearly 90 percent of the population, a result of oil wealth which has left the landscape dotted with deserted

Qatar is dominated by the Persian Gulf's largest ruling family, the al-Thani.

villages. Employment opportunities have drawn large numbers of workers from nearby nations; only one in five of the country's inhabitants is native-born.

In April 2003, Qataris voted to endorse the constitution, which keeps power with the amir, but calls for direct, popular election of two-thirds of the Advisory Council, which acts as the legislative branch of the government. Elections to the council are expected to occur in 2004, which should see the number of members increase from 35 to 45. The new constitution also recognizes women's suffrage and right to hold office. Again, this move toward increased democratization and liberation was substantiated when Amir Hamad appointed Qatar's first female cabinet member, Minister of Education and Teaching Shaikha bint Ahmed Al-Mahmud, in May 2003.

ISSUES AND CHALLENGES:

- Even though elections to the Advisory Council are anticipated in 2004, there is no guarantee that they will take place, as al-Thani power struggles have defined Qatari politics for hundreds of years. Twice in the recent history of Qatar, amirs have been overthrown by one of their own. However, the current amir seems to enjoy strong popular support, but his moves toward a more democratic, liberated political system could still be undermined either internally, or by instability in the Gulf region.

HOW THE GOVERNMENT WORKS

LEGISLATIVE BRANCH
Majlis al-Shura
(Advisory Council)
Unicameral Parliament
Composed of 35 members elected by property-owning citizens in ten voting districts and appointed by amir. Has only advisory authority; debates draft legislation before it becomes law; may summon ministers to answer questions on proposed bills. Voter-approved new constitution in 2003 expands Council to 45 members: 30 to be elected by direct popular vote; 15 appointed by amir.

Regional Governments
Ten municipalities.

EXECUTIVE BRANCH
Amir
Position is hereditary.
Acts as sole executive authority with few checks on power. Serves as head of state, commander-in-chief of the armed forces; legislates by decree; appoints and dismisses civil servants and military officers.

Prime minister
Often a royal family member; appointed by amir. Serves as head of government; formulates government programs; supervises government finances.

Cabinet
Council of ministers
Appointed by amir. Drafts legislation; oversees government operations.

JUDICIAL BRANCH
Court of Appeal
Highest judicial authority.
Judges are usually selected and promoted by the Ministry of Justice from amongst graduates of recognized law or Shariah colleges.

Higher Criminal Courts
Lower Criminal Courts
Commercial Contract Courts
Labor Courts
Shari'a Courts
Personal Status Matters.

BRUNEI

POPULATION: 335,000
CAPITAL: Bandar Seri Begawan
AREA: 2,228 SQ. MILES (5,770 SQ. KM)
INDEPENDENCE: 1984
CONSTITUTION: 1959

BRUNEI is said to have developed from Po-ni, an ancient trading nation situated on the Brunei River.

RELIGION: Muslim (official) 67%, Buddhist 13%, Christian 10%, Indigenous beliefs and Other 10%

OFFICIAL LANGUAGE: Malay

REGIONS OR PROVINCES: 4 districts

DEPENDENT TERRITORIES: None

MEDIA: Total political censorship exists in national media

NEWSPAPERS: There are 3 daily newspapers, the Borneo Bulletin, the Daily News Digest, and the News Express

TV: 1 state-owned service

RADIO: 1 state-owned service

SUFFRAGE: None

LEGAL SYSTEM: Shari'a (Islamic) and English common law; no ICJ jurisdiction

WORLD ORGANIZATIONS: APEC, ARF, ASEAN, C, CCC, ESCAP, G-77, IBRD, ICAO, ICRM, IDB, IFRCS, IMF, IMO, Interpol, IOC, ISO (correspondent), ITU, NAM, OIC, OPCW, UN, UNCTAD, UPU, WHO, WIPO, WMO, WTrO

POLITICAL PARTIES: Political parties banned since 1988

ETHNIC GROUPS:

- Indigenous 6%
- Other 11%
- Chinese 16%
- Malay 67%

NATIONAL ECONOMICS

WORLD GNP RANKING: 95th

GNP PER CAPITA: $24,762

INFLATION: 1.0%

BALANCE OF PAYMENTS (BALANCE OF TRADE): $2.09 billion

EXCHANGE RATES / U.S. DLR.: 1.734-1.847 BRUNEI DOLLARS

OFFICIAL CURRENCY: BRUNEI DOLLAR

GOVERNMENT SPENDING (% OF GDP)

- DEFENSE 5.8%
- EDUCATION 3.1%
- HEALTH 5.7%

0   5   10   15

NUMBER OF CONFLICTS OVER LAST 25 YEARS

	1	2-5	5+
Violent changes in government	○	○	○
Civil wars	○	○	○
International wars	○	○	○
Foreign intervention	○	○	○

- As well as being head of the armed forces, the sultan has a personal bodyguard of 2000 UK-trained Gurkhas.
- The UK and Singapore are close defense allies.

NOTABLE WARS AND INSURGENCIES: None

THE SULTANATE OF BRUNEI IS A MUSLIM MONARCHY with no democratic checks on the sultan's power. Located on the island of Borneo in Southeast Asia, the nation is divided geographically by a strip of Malaysian territory. For centuries, Brunei was a native-ruled monarchy; its control extended over northwestern Borneo and the southern Philippines. In the late 19th century, European expansion and internal conflict over royal succession led to Brunei becoming a British colony. A 1959 constitution made the colony self-governing, and Brunei gained full independence in 1984. For the past 600 years, descendants of one family have ruled Brunei. Rich oil reserves have given Brunei a high standard of living.

Since a failed rebellion in 1962, the nation has been ruled under a state of emergency. Political parties were banned in 1988, and no elections are now held. Nonetheless, the government has enjoyed strong support from its citizens, as the economy allows for many benefits, such as free health care and education as well as inexpensive housing, food, and fuel. These privileges do not extend to the Chinese population, who are either stateless or holders of British passports designating them as protected persons. The "Malay Muslim Monarchy" was introduced in 1990 to promote Islamic values. Although the Asian financial crisis of the 1990s created instability, Brunei's oil revenues permitted it to weather the storm.

WEALTH DISPARITY
Brunei's oil wealth is clearly shown by the Sultan Omar Ali Saifuddien Mosque, a stark contrast to the stilt-homes on the Brunei River in which one quarter of the population live. Insert: Prince Hadji al-Muhtadee Billan of Brunei.

The sultan is chief of state, head of government and since 1967, prime minister. He acts as minister of both defense and finance. Members of the royal family occupy most seats in the cabinet.

HOW THE GOVERNMENT WORKS

LEGISLATIVE BRANCH
Majlis Masyuarat Megeri
(Legislative Council)
Unicameral Parliament
Composed of 20 members appointed by sultan. Serves only as consultative body for sultan.

Regional Governments
Four districts, Belait, Brunei-Muara, Temburong, Tutong, each headed by a district officer.

EXECUTIVE BRANCH
Sultan
Position is hereditary.
Serves as head of state and government, commander-in-chief of armed forces, religious leader, and prime minister.
Enacts legislation by decree.

Privy Council
Appointed by sultan.
Advises on pardons, constitutional matters; bestows honors and titles.

Council of Succession
Appointed by sultan; determines succession to throne.

Religious Council
Appointed by sultan; advises on Shari'a (Islamic) law.

JUDICIAL BRANCH
Supreme Court
Divided into Court of Appeal for civil disputes and High Court for criminal cases and legal interpretations.
Judges are from United Kingdom. Final appeals in civil, but not criminal, cases may be made to Privy Council in London.

Magistrates' Courts
Rule on minor cases.
Judges appointed by sultan.

Islamic Courts
Rule on cases involving Muslims.

TONGA

OFFICIAL NAME: KINGDOM OF TONGA

Niuatoputapu
Tafahi

PACIFIC OCEAN

Vava'u Group
'Uta Vava'u
Neiafu

PACIFIC OCEAN

Tofua
Ha'apai Group
Kotu Group
Pangai
Nomuka Group
Otu Tolu Group

NUKU'ALOFA
Tongatapu
Legislative Assembly
Ohonua
Tongatapu Group

0 100 km
0 100 miles

POPULATION: 102,200	
CAPITAL: NUKU'ALOFA	
AREA: 289 SQ. MILES (720 SQ. KM)	
INDEPENDENCE: 1970	
CONSTITUTION: 1875	

TONGA means "south" in many of the Polynesian languages, appropriate for its location.

RELIGION: Free Wesleyan 64%, Roman Catholic 15%, Other 21%

OFFICIAL LANGUAGES: English and Tongan

REGIONS OR PROVINCES: 3 island groups; Ha'apai, Tongatapu, Vava'u

DEPENDENT TERRITORIES: None

MEDIA: Partial political censorship exists in national media

NEWSPAPERS: There is 1 daily newspaper. Weeklies include the Conch Shell and the Tonga Chronicle

TV: 1 service relaying US programs

RADIO: 4 independent services

In 2000 Cable and Wireless relinquished control of Tonga's telecommunications services, which it had run since 1978, to a local company

SUFFRAGE: 21 years of age; universal

LEGAL SYSTEM: English common law; no ICJ jurisdiction

WORLD ORGANIZATIONS: ACP, AsDB, C, ESCAP, FAO, G-77, IBRD, ICAO, ICFTU, ICRM, IDA, IFAD, IFC, IFRCS, IHO, IMF, IMO, Interpol, IOC, ITU, Sparteca, SPC, SPF, UN, UNCTAD, UNESCO, UNIDO, UPU, WHO, WIPO, WMO, WTrO (observer)

POLITICAL PARTIES: There are no political parties.

ETHNIC GROUPS:

Other 1%

Polynesian 99%

NATIONAL ECONOMICS

WORLD GNP RANKING: 186th

GNP PER CAPITA: $1,660

INFLATION: 5.9%

BALANCE OF PAYMENTS (BALANCE OF TRADE): Zero

EXCHANGE RATES / U.S. DLR.: 1.7997-1.9535 PA'ANGA

OFFICIAL CURRENCY: PA'ANGA

GOVERNMENT SPENDING (% OF GDP)

✈ DEFENSE (N/A)		
📖 EDUCATION 4.3%		
✚ HEALTH 7.8%		

0   5   10   15

NUMBER OF CONFLICTS OVER LAST 25 YEARS

	1	2-5	5+
Violent changes in government	○	○	○
Civil wars	○	○	○
International wars	○	○	○
Foreign intervention	○	○	○

- Tongan police assisted in the Solomon Islands in 2000.
- Arms bound for Palestine were discovered aboard a Tongan-registered vessel in 2002, raising concern over the flag-of-convenience fleet.

NOTABLE WARS AND INSURGENCIES: None

TONGA, AN ARCHIPELAGO OF 169 RAISED CORAL and volcanic islands, is located in the South Pacific. British explorer Captain James Cook visited the islands twice in the 1770s, naming them the Friendly Islands because he thought the people were so amiable. Cook was blissfully unaware of the fiery debate among Tongan nobles, who were vying for the honor of attacking his ships and killing everyone aboard. Now the only monarchy in the Pacific, Tonga was co-ruled by three kings from the 14th century until the late 18th century, when the three royal lines fought for dominance.

Taufa'ahau emerged as the sole monarch and in the following years united the Tongan islands for the first time in recorded history. Taufa'ahau took the name George to honor Britain's King George III when he converted to Christianity (the missionaries were British), and was proclaimed King George Tupou I in 1845. He established a constitution that was ratified in 1875 and a parliamentary government that was based loosely on the British system but incorporated Tongan traditions and social structure. Anxiety over Germany's purchase of large tracts of western Samoa prompted Tonga to become a British protectorate in 1900. Tonga relinquished its protectorate status on June 4, 1970, and a new constitution was promulgated that is based on the 1875 document.

Although in theory Tonga is a constitutional monarchy, the king is chief of state and essentially controls politics. He appoints the prime minister and the cabinet, he initiates development projects without consulting the government, and he is deferred to by the Legislative Assembly. There are no political parties, but a harbinger of change may be the March 2002 election to the Legislative Assembly of seven members associated with the Tongan Human Rights and Democracy Movement, a reformist pro-democracy group.

ISSUES AND CHALLENGES:

- Tonga has traditionally been a net importer of food causing a balance of payment deficit. With growing emphasis on tourism this has slowly been improving, but remains an important issue for the government.

- The aid-dependent nation's economy has a large non-monetary sector and high external debt. With unemployment above 13 percent, emigration is high. Remittances from Tongans living abroad are the nation's primary source of hard currency.

- Unrest in Fiji and the Solomon Islands has brought a rise in tourism despite the country's location off major shipping routes. The increased exposure to Western influences intensifies the problem of how to preserve Tongan culture and traditions while becoming less isolated and more modern.

- The sovereign continues to exert control over all branches of the government. Growing demands for democracy will be a challenge for a society based on traditional respect for the nobility.

HOW THE GOVERNMENT WORKS

LEGISLATIVE BRANCH

Fale Alea
(Legislative Assembly)
Unicameral Parliament
Composed of 30 members: nine elected by direct popular vote; nine selected by Tonga's 33 hereditary nobles; 12 cabinet ministers appointed by monarch. Terms of service are three years, except for ministers who retain their seats until retirement. Assembly sits four to five months a year.

Regional Governments
Twenty-three districts overseen by officers popularly elected to three-year terms.

EXECUTIVE BRANCH

Monarch
Position is hereditary.
Serves as head of state.

Prime Minister
Appointed for life by monarch.
Serves as head of government.

Cabinet
Composed of 12 ministers appointed by monarch.

Privy Council
Composed of monarch, cabinet ministers, governors of Vava'u and Ha'apai. Issues ordinances that became law when confirmed by Legislative Assembly. May act as final court of appeal except in criminal cases.

JUDICIAL BRANCH

Supreme Court
Highest court of appeal.
Judges appointed by monarch.

Court of Appeal
Hears cases from lower courts.
Judges appointed by monarch.

Magistrates' Court
Sits in nine locations and adjudicates most disputes. Composed of ten magistrates appointed by prime minister with cabinet approval.

Land Court
Rules on land ownership disputes. Cases heard by Supreme Court justice appointed by Privy Council.

MONACO

OFFICIAL NAME: PRINCIPALITY OF MONACO

F R A N C E

0   1000 m
0   1500 yds

Lycée L'Annonciade
Musée Nation
Larvotto
Centre de la
Culture et
d'Expositions
Monte-Carlo
Sporting
Club d'Été
Hospitalier
Grace
La Condamine
Grand Prix
Circuit
Casino
Centre de Congrès
Railway
Station
Palais du Prince
Port de Monaco
Stade Louis II
Ministère d'État
Fontvieille
Cathédrale
Musée Océanographique

Côte d'Azur

Mediterranean Sea

National Council

POPULATION: 31,700
CAPITAL: Monaco
AREA: 0.75 SQ. MILES (1.95 SQ. KM)
INDEPENDENCE: 1861
CONSTITUTION: 1962

MONACO'S name may come from a reference to the Greek hero, Hercules, who was associated with the main port of Monaco, known as Port Hercules. He was often referred to as Herakles Monoikos meaning "Hercules alone".

RELIGION: Roman Catholic 89%, Protestant 6%, Other 5%

OFFICIAL LANGUAGE: French

REGIONS OR PROVINCES: None; there are four quarters

DEPENDENT TERRITORIES: None

MEDIA: No political censorship exists in national media

Newspapers: There is 1 daily newspaper

TV: 2 services

Radio: 4 services: 1 part owned by French state, 3 independent

SUFFRAGE: 21 years of age; universal

LEGAL SYSTEM: French law; no ICJ jurisdiction

WORLD ORGANIZATIONS: ACCT, ECE, FAO, IAEA, ICAO, ICC, ICRM, IFRCS, IHO, IMO, Interpol, IOC, ITU, OPCW, OSCE, UN, UNCTAD, UNESCO, UPU, WHO, WIPO, WMO, WToO

POLITICAL PARTIES: UND—National and Democratic Union, UPM—Union for Monaco

ETHNIC GROUPS:

Monegasque 16%
French 47%
Italian 16%
Other 21%

NATIONAL ECONOMICS

WORLD GNP RANKING: 158th

GNP PER CAPITA: $25,000

INFLATION: Included in French total

BALANCE OF PAYMENTS (BALANCE OF TRADE): Included in French total

EXCHANGE RATES / U.S. DLR: 1.0651-1.1231 EUROS

5 EURO

OFFICIAL CURRENCY: EURO

GOVERNMENT SPENDING (% OF GDP)

DEFENSE (N/A)		
EDUCATION (N/A)		
HEALTH 8%		

0   5   10   15

NUMBER OF CONFLICTS OVER LAST 25 YEARS

	1	2-5	5+
Violent changes in government	○	○	○
Civil wars	○	○	○
International wars	○	○	○
Foreign intervention	○	○	○

- Monaco has no armed forces and no defense budget.
- France is responsible for defense.
- A 24-hour video surveillance system covers the entire principality.

NOTABLE WARS AND INSURGENCIES: None

LARGER ONLY THAN the Vatican City, Monaco is the world's second smallest independent state. Its only land border is with France, which surrounds Monaco on all sides but for its Mediterranean coastline. France also provides protection under a treaty signed in 1918, which required that all Monaco's political, economic, and military policies should be aligned with those of France. The treaty, as it currently stands, is being revised to provide greater autonomy. Tax haven status has made Monaco one of the most desirable countries of residence for the world's rich and famous. Tourism provides more than 25 percent of the annual revenue, much of this coming from casinos. Additionally, Monaco is recognized in the scientific world for work in the field of marine sciences.

Originally the site of a Genoese fortress, Monaco was a colony of Genoa from 1215 to 1297 when the Grimaldi family established it as a state under their rule. With the exception of the period between 1789 and 1861, their reign has continued to the present day. Falling under French rule for the 25 years until 1814, it was designated a protectorate of Sardinia by the Treaty of Vienna. In 1848 France annexed it from Sardinia, restoring the Grimaldi princes as absolute monarchs in 1860. Independence followed in 1861.

In 1911, under the direction of Prince Albert I, Monaco became a constitutional monarchy, with the Prince the head of State. Prince Rainier III ruled the Principality for more than five decades from 1949, doing much to transform it into a prosperous modern state. On his death in 2005, he was succeeded by his son Prince Albert.

In 1962, the monarchy gave up some of its powers in favor of a more democratic constitution, although the prince remains head of state. The chief minister, the minister of state, is required to be a French citizen, and is selected by the prince from a list of suitable candidates supplied by France. All power vested in the legislature and judiciary is derived from the prince.

MONACO'S ROYAL DYNASTY
National day celebrations in 1998 were overseen by three generations of Grimaldis. From left to right, Prince Albert, Charlotte, Princess Caroline, Pierre, Prince Rainier, and Princess Stephanie.

HOW THE GOVERNMENT WORKS

LEGISLATIVE BRANCH

Conseil National
(National Council)
Unicameral Parliament
Composed of 24 members who serve five-year terms: 16 elected by direct popular vote; 8 elected by proportional representation. Debates and passes bills and budget proposed by monarch; amends constitution jointly with monarch.

Regional governments
Four quarters administered by mayor and elected, 15-member Communal Council.

EXECUTIVE BRANCH

Monarch
Position is hereditary.
Serves as head of state. Proposes and vetoes bills; signs and ratifies treaties.

Minister of State
French citizen appointed by monarch from three-candidate list presented by French government. Head of government. Answers to monarch; presides over cabinet; foreign affairs; commands police.

Cabinet
Council of Government
Minister of state and 3 councilors: finance and the economy; interior; public works and social affairs. Appointed by and answers to monarch.

Council of the Crown
7 members appointed to three-year terms by monarch, including 3 with parliament's consent. Advises monarch on constitutionally specified matters.

JUDICIAL BRANCH

Supreme Court
Highest court of review and appeal. Rules on constitutionality of laws. Composed of 7 judges nominated by parliament, appointed by monarch.

Higher Court of Appeal

Court of Appeal

Criminal Court
(Assize Court)

Court of First Instance

THEOCRATIC
RULE

RULING IN THE NAME OF GOD

MANY RULERS THROUGHOUT HISTORY have claimed a divine mandate. A true theocracy, however, is a system of government where the roles of priest and ruler are combined. There is evidence that the ancient Hebrews, Egyptians, and Tibetans lived under theocracies, as did early American civilizations such as the Mayans, Aztecs, and Incas. Augustus Caesar used religion to legitimize his rule and later Roman emperors proclaimed their own divinity. In China during the Middle Ages, every dynasty would bring a new "Son of Heaven" to restore order. Today, only the 100-acre Vatican may be technically considered a Christian theocracy because of the pope's authority both in the temporal affairs of the city-state and in matters of morals for all Roman Catholics. In 1943, when Allied leaders tried to convince Joseph Stalin (1879-1953) of the Pope's worldwide influence, he allegedly asked, "How many divisions has the Pope?" In the past popes had maintained a standing army and in the early 16th century, Pope Julius II led his troops into battle. From 622-632, the prophet Muhammad ruled Medina as an Islamic theocracy. After Muhammad's death, the Islamic Caliphate rapidly spread to Iraq, Syria, Iran, Egypt, Morocco, and Spain. Today—following the defeat of the Taliban in Afghanistan in 2001—only Iran can be considered an Islamic theocracy where the clergy have ultimate political authority. However, fundamentalists in other Muslim nations from Indonesia to Algeria are urging theocratic forms of government.

THEOCRATIC RULERS, SELF-STYLED DIVINE RULERS, AND RULERS BY DIVINE RIGHT

Clockwise from top left: Ramses II, Egyptian pharaoh, who filled his empire with colossal statues of himself; Montezuma II, Aztec ruler, whose semi-divine status was shattered by the arrival of the Spanish; Pope John Paul II, who was spiritual leader of the world's Catholics and temporal ruler of the Vatican City 1978–2005; Louis XIV, absolute monarch of France, the "Sun King", who believed that he was God's representative on earth; Augustus, the first emperor of Rome, who was worshipped as a god throughout his empire; Charles I of England, whose insistence on his divine right to rule led to civil war and his execution; Solomon, the biblical King of Judaea, son of King David and builder of the Temple; Moses, spiritual and political leader of the people of Israel on their journey from Egypt to the "promised land"; Henry VIII of England, founder of the Church of England with himself as its head; Ayatollah Khomeini, ruler of the Islamic Republic of Iran after the revolution of 1979; Julius II, Renaissance pope, who was prince, politician, and soldier, as well as man of God; Xerxes, all-powerful king of Persia in the 5th century BC ; King David, who established Jerusalem as the spiritual centre of the Israelites; Shah Jehan, Mughal emperor of India, builder of the Taj Mahal.

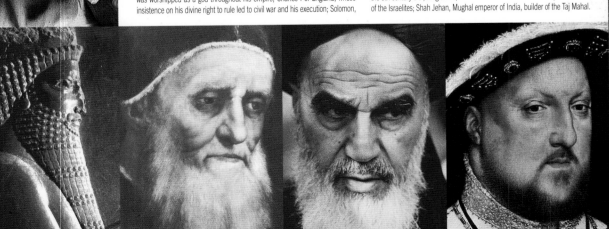

IRAN

IRAN IS A STRATEGICALLY IMPORTANT COUNTRY, situated in the midst of tumultuous states, with Iraq to the west, Afghanistan and Pakistan to the east, and the republics of the former Soviet Union to the north. While most Iranians are ethnically Persian there are many other ethnic groups in Iran, including the Kurds, Azeris, Lurs, and Bakhtiaris.

IRANIAN FLAG
Adopted on July 29, 1980, it shows Islam (green), peace (white), and courage (red), with four crescents symbolizing Allah.

SHAHYAD MONUMENT
This spectacular gateway to Tehran was built in 1971 to commemorate the 2,500th anniversary of Persia.

Largest number of world's refugees: between one and two million, chiefly from Afghanistan.

Iran was ruled by a monarchy until the Islamic Revolution of 1979. That year, the Shah was overthrown and forced into exile, while the masses ushered Ayatollah Khomeini back from France, where he had been in exile. The revolution he led was fueled by widespread resentment towards the Shah's corrupt and repressive regime. Shortly after the revolution, the broad coalition made up of clergy, merchants, students, liberal reformists, and leftists fell apart, and the clergy consolidated power under Ayatollah Khomeini. After a national referendum in March 1979, Iran became an Islamic Republic, putting into practice Ayatollah Khomeini's ideas of Islamic government and *velayat-e faqih*, or "leadership of the Islamic jurist," which called upon the clergy to establish and lead a just political system based on Islamic law (shari'a). While Shi'a Islam is a significant force, Khomeini's interpretation and application of *velayat-e faqih* and the political hierarchy outlined in Iran's modern theocracy remain controversial, even among devout Shi'a Muslims, especially since the second *vali-e faqih* or Supreme Leader, Ayatollah Ali Khamenei, does not possess the popularity or

AYATOLLAH RUHOLLAH KHOMEINI
Declared a grand ayatollah in the early 1960s, Khomeini was a Shi'ite supreme leader, when he began the revolution that led to the overthrow of Shah Pahlavi in 1979. The new constitution made Iran an Islamic republic and the Khomeini became Iran's political and religious leader for life. A position he held until his death in 1989.

HOW THE GOVERNM

SUPREME LEADER
Sits at the top of the structure as the chief of state. He appoints the head of the judiciary, six out of the twelve members on the Council of Guardians, and is commander of the armed forces; appointed by the Assembly of Experts.

THE SUPREME LEADER
Ayatollah Ali Khamenei addressing a crowd in Tehran.

COUNCIL OF GUARDIANS
Most influential body in Iran, it is made up of twelve jurists, six of whom are chosen by the Supreme Leader. The head of the judiciary recommends the remaining six, who are then appointed by Parliament. This influential oversight body examines whether the laws passed by Parliament are in accord with Islamic law, and has veto power. Also oversees presidential and parliamentary candidates, and candidates for the Assembly of Experts.

LEGISLATIVE BRANCH

CONSULTATIVE COUNCIL
The 290-seat unicameral Consultative Council (Majlis) members are elected every four years, with seats allotted for minorities. It drafts legislation—reviewed by the Council of Guardians, ratifies treaties, and approves the budget. It may impeach the president with a two-thirds majority vote.

EXECUTIVE BRANCH

PRESIDENT
Four-year term by a majority vote. Second highest ranking official; head of the executive; appoints and dismisses ministers; heads Cabinet; selects policies before legislature. Responsible to Supreme Leader and Majlis.

▶ **VICE-PRESIDENTS**
Eight vice-presidents in the executive.

▶ **CABINET**
Composed of 22 ministries.

MAJLIS
The Consultative Council in session in its new building, which opened on March 13, 2001.

REGIONAL GOVERNMENTS
▶ Provinces (ostans) led by governor-general
▶ Counties led by clerical imam jomehs
▶ Districts (bakhshs), subdistricts, villages

> "In Islam, the legislative power and competence to establish laws belong exclusively to God Almighty."
> —Ayatollah Khomeini (1900-1989)

legitimacy Khomeini enjoyed. While the ulama (Islamic clergy) have always played a significant role, providing guidance in spiritual and other matters, the extent of their direct involvement in the political system has become a source of contention. Furthermore, the ill-defined division of power between church and state has led to friction between the two. Many Iranians, including the liberal-religious camp, argue that such things as the restriction of freedoms and the extensive powers vested in the Supreme Leader simply don't have any basis in Islam, and call for political reform. Demands for reform have been met with stiff resistance from the conservatives, who feel reforms would weaken their grip on power. When President Khatami ran on a platform of reform in 1997 and in 2001, an overwhelming majority rallied behind him, indicating the prevalent enthusiasm of the populace toward reforms.

OFFICIAL NAME: ISLAMIC REPUBLIC OF IRAN

Islamic Consultative Assembly

POPULATION: 71.4 MILLION
CAPITAL: TEHRAN
AREA: 636,293 SQ. MILES (1,647,999 SQ. KM)
INDEPENDENCE: 1979
CONSTITUTION: 1979

IRAN is a Persian name given to the country, which means "land of the Arayans" or "land of the free", where "Arya" means "free or noble".

RELIGION: Shi'a Muslim 95%, Sunni Muslim 4%, Other 1%

OFFICIAL LANGUAGE: Farsi

REGIONS OR PROVINCES: 28 provinces

DEPENDENT TERRITORIES: None

MEDIA: Total political censorship exists in national media

Newspapers: 5 of the 33 daily newspapers are national

TV: 1 state-controlled service

Radio: 1 state-controlled service

SUFFRAGE: 15 years of age; universal

LEGAL SYSTEM: Shari'a (Islamic) law; no ICJ jurisdiction

WORLD ORGANIZATIONS: CCC, CP, ECO, ESCAP, FAO, G-19, G-24, G-77, IAEA, IBRD, ICAO, ICC, ICRM, IDA, IDB, IFAD, IFC, IFRCS, IHO, ILO, IMF, IMO, Interpol, IOC, IOM, ISO, ITU, NAM, OIC, OPCW, OPEC, PCA, UN, UNCTAD, UNESCO, UNHCR, UNIDO, UPU, WCL, WFTU, WHO, WIPO, WMO, WToO

POLITICAL PARTIES: IIPF—Islamic Iran Participation Front (reformists), C—Coalition of Followers of the Line of Imam (conservatives), Ind—Independents

ETHNIC GROUPS:
- Persian 50%
- Azeri 24%
- Other 10%
- Lur and Bakahtiari 8%
- Kurd 8%

NATIONAL ECONOMICS

WORLD GNP RANKING: 34th

GNP PER CAPITA: $1,680

INFLATION: 14.5%

BALANCE OF PAYMENTS (BALANCE OF TRADE): $12.6 billion

EXCHANGE RATES / U.S. DLR.: 1747.5-1750.0 IRANIAN RIALS

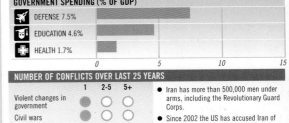

OFFICIAL CURRENCY: IRANIAN RIAL

GOVERNMENT SPENDING (% OF GDP)

DEFENSE	7.5%
EDUCATION	4.6%
HEALTH	1.7%

0   5   10   15

NUMBER OF CONFLICTS OVER LAST 25 YEARS

	1	2-5	5+
Violent changes in government	●	○	○
Civil wars	●	○	○
International wars	●	○	○
Foreign intervention	●	○	○

- Iran has more than 500,000 men under arms, including the Revolutionary Guard Corps.
- Since 2002 the US has accused Iran of covertly seeking to develop nuclear weapons.

NOTABLE WARS AND INSURGENCIES: Islamic Revolution 1979. Iran-Iraq War 1980-1988

...NT WORKS

ASSEMBLY OF EXPERTS

Made up of 96 clerics, this assembly is directly elected by the public every eight years, and its functions are to appoint and oversee the Supreme Leader, whose appointment is for life. The Assembly of Experts is often compared to the College of Cardinals, which chooses the Pope for the Roman Catholic church.

EXPEDIENCY COUNCIL

This 34-member council advises the Supreme Leader on matters of national policy; created to resolve disputes over legislation between Parliament and the Council of Guardians. Includes heads of branches of government, Council of Guardians members, and members appointed by Supreme Leader.

⚖ JUDICIAL BRANCH

The Supreme Leader appoints the head of the judiciary to a five-year term. Public courts deal with civil and criminal cases, revolutionary courts deal with acts that undermine the Islamic Republic.

SUPREME COURT

Enforces and establishes legal policies and supervises the correct implementation of the laws by the courts. Chief of Supreme Court is a Mujtahid (muslim divine of the highest degree) specialized in Islamic law, nominated by head of judiciary in consultation with the judges of the Supreme Court to a five-year term.

HIGH COUNCIL OF THE JUDICIARY

Consists of the head of the Supreme Court, the attorney general, and three judges; five-year terms, limited to two terms. Appointed and dismissed by the Supreme Leader. Responsibilities overlap with Supreme Court.

ELECTORAL SYSTEM
Iran's electoral system allows for the Council of Guardians to approve all who wish to run for office; no standard criterion has been established for approving or rejecting candidates. While the constitution allows for multiple parties, there were no officially recognized parties until recently, when two new parties were formed.

A PAPAL BLESSING
From 1978 until his death in 2005, Pope John Paul II turned the papacy into a highly influential global voice, in political as well as religious matters. He attracted admirers from around the world, as seen at this Christmas Day blessing in St. Peter's Square.

VATICAN CITY

OFFICIAL NAME: STATE OF THE VATICAN CITY

POPULATION: 1,000	
CAPITAL: VATICAN CITY	
AREA: 0.17 SQ. MILES (0.44 SQ. KM)	
INDEPENDENCE: 1929	
CONSTITUTION: APOSTOLIC CONSTITUTION OF 1967	

VATICAN as a word is derived from an ancient Latin root "vates" which means "tellers of the future" or "prophecy." The entire Vatican City is built on Vaticanus Mons (the prophetic hill), so named in Roman times for the fortune-tellers who worked there.

RELIGION: Roman Catholic 100%

OFFICIAL LANGUAGES: Italian and Latin

REGIONS OR PROVINCES: None

DEPENDENT TERRITORIES: None

MEDIA: No political censorship exists in national media

NEWSPAPERS: There is 1 daily newspaper

TV: 1 state-owned service

RADIO: 1 state-owned service

SUFFRAGE: Limited to cardinals less than 80 years old

LEGAL SYSTEM: Italian law; Roman Catholic Church decrees; no ICJ jurisdiction

WORLD ORGANIZATIONS: CE (observer), IAEA, ICFTU, IOM (observer), ITU, NAM (guest), OAS (observer), OPCW, OSCE, UN (observer), UNCTAD, UNHCR, UPU, WHO (observer), WIPO, WToO (observer), WTrO (observer)

POLITICAL PARTIES: None

NATIONAL ECONOMICS

WORLD GNP RANKING: N/A

GNP PER CAPITA: N/A

INFLATION: N/A

BALANCE OF PAYMENTS (BALANCE OF TRADE): N/A

EXCHANGE RATES / U.S. DLR: 1.0651-1.1231 EUROS

OFFICIAL CURRENCY: EURO

GOVERNMENT SPENDING (% OF GDP)

		0	5	10	15
✈	DEFENSE (N/A)				
	EDUCATION (N/A)				
✚	HEALTH (N/A)				

NUMBER OF CONFLICTS OVER LAST 25 YEARS

Years	1	2-5	5+
Violent changes in government	○	○	○
Civil wars	○	○	○
International wars	○	○	○
Foreign intervention	○	○	○

- The Vatican is strictly neutral territory.
- The famous Swiss guards provide security: to qualify, applicants must be Catholic, Swiss, and over 5 ft 8 in (173 cm) tall.

NOTABLE WARS AND INSURGENCIES: None

THE VATICAN CITY, LOCATED WITHIN ROME, Italy, is the governmental and spiritual capital of the Roman Catholic Church. For more than 1,000 years, the temporal powers of the pope included control of Papal States, which at one time extended across a large swath of central Italy. By the mid-19th century most of the Papal States had been lost, and in 1870 the new Kingdom of Italy annexed Rome. The pope and his successors, questioning the annexation, declared themselves prisoners in the Vatican. The dispute was resolved with three agreements signed by the Italian government and the Holy See in 1929. The agreements recognized the sovereignty and independence of the Holy See and created the State of the Vatican City, defined the relationship between the government and the church, and provided compensation for land seized in 1870.

The Holy See is recognized by international law and enters into treaties and sends and receives diplomatic envoys. It enjoys diplomatic relations with 173 states. The government of the Vatican City is ecclesiastical, with a constitution and a legal system based on canon law. The pope holds ultimate executive, legislative, and judicial power, but he delegates administration to a number of officials and bodies. The secretary of state, a cardinal appointed by the pope, acts much like a prime minister. He oversees the Roman Curia, a body that includes the Secretariat of State and various congregations, commissions, councils, and tribunals that assist in the administration of the Holy See and the Vatican.

ECUMENICAL COUNCIL
Pope John XXIII's ecumenical council meets in St. Peter's Basilica in the Vatican City in September 1962.

The only election is that of the pope himself; the election is held 18 days after a pope's death, and suffrage is limited to cardinals under the age of 80. The 1978 election of the Polish Karol Wojtyla as John Paul II, the first non-Italian pope in nearly 500 years, set a precedent—he was succeeded in 2005 by the German Joseph Ratzinger as Benedict XVI, and a Latin American or African pope is a distinct possibility in the future.

HOW THE GOVERNMENT WORKS

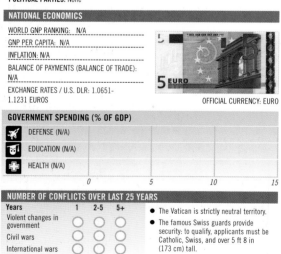

⚙ EXECUTIVE BRANCH

Pope
Head of executive. Elected for life by Roman Catholic Church's Sacred College of Cardinals. He is assisted by the bodies that make up the Roman Curia.

Secretary of State
Cardinal appointed by the pope. Presides over the Secretariat of State; often represents the pope.

Secretariat of State
Most important body within Roman Curia. Consists of a General Section and a Section for Relations with States.

Congregations
Bodies that oversee theological and spiritual matters, including the appointment of bishops.

Pontifical Councils
Bodies covering wide range of concerns, including family issues, youth activities, charities, and canon law.

Pontifical Commissions
These include a commission of cardinals to assist the pope in the economic management of the Vatican.

⚖ JUDICIAL BRANCH

Pope
Head of judiciary, which consists of three tribunals.

Supreme Tribunal of the Apostolic Signature
Highest court of appeal, ensures Church justice is correctly administered. All members are appointed by the pope; responsible to Roman Curia.

Apostolic Penitentiary
Tribunal responsible for handling matters of conscience. All members are appointed by the pope and are responsible to Roman Curia.

Roman Rota
Tribunal responsible for judging appeals on ecclesiastical cases, particularly those concerning marriage annulments. Promotes unity of jurisprudence.

MILITARY
RULE

ENFORCERS OF LAW AND ORDER

RULE BY A MILITARY STRONGMAN OR JUNTA has occurred periodically throughout history. Military rule is often associated with single-party rule, as with the Axis Powers in World War II, or transitional rule, where a military force exercises temporary control until government can be restored, as in present-day Iraq. Military rule should not be confused with militarism, where a nation emphasizes military power and the use of military force to resolve disputes even though it may not be ruled by the military. A 1989 analysis of the tendency of Third World military elites to overthrow civilian governments showed that of a total of 120 Third World countries, 64 were ruled by military-controlled governments where senior officers held key positions and order was maintained by martial law. It also found that these forces were often aided by the intelligence agencies or military of one of the two Cold War superpowers. After overthrowing the democratically-elected government of Salvador Allende in 1973, General Augusto Pinochet was military ruler of Chile until 1989 when his rule was rejected by popular referendum. Support from a superpower did not always last. Panamanian strongman General Manuel Noriega, a one-time US intelligence operative, was captured by US troops in 1989 and convicted of drug-trafficking and other crimes.

MILITARY RULERS AND LEADERS OF MILITARIST REGIMES

Clockwise from top left: Genghis Khan, Mongol conqueror of much of Asia in the 13th century; Manuel Noriega, Panamanian dictator removed by US troops in 1989; Yuan Shi-Kai, Chinese general who proclaimed himself emperor in 1915; Frederick the Great, king of Prussia (1740-1786), who made his country into a significant power by means of a large, well-trained, modern army; Julius Caesar (c.100-44 B.C.), who used his legions to defeat all rivals in his rise to power in Rome; Abdul Hamid II, Ottoman emperor, forced to abdicate in 1909 after military revolution by the Young Turks; Josef Broz Tito, commander of Yugoslavian partisans in World War II, who became communist premier in 1945; Attila the Hun, the "Scourge of God", leader of nomadic tribe which attacked the Roman Empire in the 5th century A.D.; Otto von Bismarck, chancellor of Prussia from 1862 and then of the German empire (1871-1890), who used his country's military might to impose his will on Europe; Marcus Aurelius, Roman emperor (A.D. 161-180), who spent most of his reign campaigning against Germanic invaders; Chiang Kai-Shek, leader of the Chinese nationalists from 1928, defeated by the communists, then ruler of Taiwan from 1949 until his death in 1975; Than Shwe, general and leader of ruling military junta in present-day Burma (Myanmar); Augusto Pinochet, architect of military coup in Chile in 1973, which overthrew left-wing Allende government; Alexander the Great, King of Macedonia, conqueror of the mighty Persian Empire and much of the known world in the 4th century B.C.

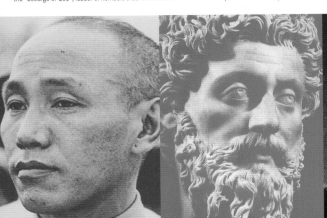

PAKISTAN

FOUNDED IN 1947, Pakistan is the world's second largest Muslim country, after Indonesia. Given its geopolitical position, with India to the east, Iran and Afghanistan to the west, and China to the North, Pakistan has been and remains a crossroads connecting South and Central Asia and the Middle East. One man was instrumental in the formation of Pakistan: Mohammed Ali Jinnah.

FLAG OF PAKISTAN
Adopted on August 14, 1947, the flag shows the star of light and crescent of progress.

TOMB OF BIBI JAWINDI
Built in 1494, the ornate tomb is located in Uch, Pakistan, once the center of Sufism.

Born in India, Jinnah firmly believed that Hindus and Muslims would work together for an India independent of Britain. With the breakdown of relations between the Hindu majority and the Muslim minority in the 1940s, Jinnah's ideals seemed unobtainable. Subsequently he became the main driving force behind a separate Islamic state. Pakistan emerged on August 15, 1947 as a new state with Jinnah as its first governor-general.

In its relatively short history, the country has undergone three wars with India, and one civil war which resulted in the secession of what was then East Pakistan—founding Bangladesh in 1971.

Pakistan's army often intervened in politics, first seizing power in 1958. Following a military coup in 1999, General Pervez Musharraf assumed the position of chief executive, while suspending the Constitution, dissolving Parliament, and putting multiparty democracy on hold. The coup was initially welcomed, which indicated widespread dissatisfaction with the abuse of democratic institutions at the hands of corrupt politicians. Soon afterwards, General Musharraf appointed himself president in 2001, and extended his term for another five years following a controversial referendum in 2002.

HOW THE GOVERNM

🏛 LEGISLATIVE BRANCH

MAJLIS-E-SHOORA

In 2003, the role of the bicameral Parliament was limited by the powers the president awarded himself in 2002 to sack Parliament.

▶ **NATIONAL ASSEMBLY**
Dissolved after the military coup of October 12, 1999, elections were held in October 2002 for the new National Assembly, which consists of 342 members. Sixty seats are reserved for women, ten for minorities. All members are elected by popular vote to serve a four-year term.

▶ **SENATE**
The Senate consists of 100 seats. All members are indirectly elected by provincial assemblies to serve a four-year term. As of the last elections in February 2003, the Pakistan Muslim League holds the majority of seats.

PROVINCIAL GOVERNMENT
▶ Four provinces
▶ Appointed governor
▶ Appointed Cabinet

PARLIAMENT HOUSE INTERIOR
After a three-year hiatus resulting from the coup of 1999, this chamber is once again home to Pakistan's National Assembly.

🚗 EXECUTIVE BRANCH

PRESIDENT
▶ Chief of State.
▶ Usually indirectly elected by an electoral college made up of the National Assembly, Senate, and the provincial assemblies. In 2001, however, the president appointed himself.
▶ Serves a five-year term, with possibility for renewal.

LEGISLATIVE BUILDING
Military installations were added to the Parliament House (right) in 2001 following outbreaks of anti-US violence.

PRIME MINISTER
▶ Head of the government.
▶ Presides over the Cabinet of Ministers, which he appoints.
▶ Elected by members of the National Assembly for a four-year term.
▶ Usually the head of the largest party .
▶ His power is checked by both the president and by the courts' power of judicial review.

"The foundations of your State have been laid and it is now for you to build as quickly and as well as you can."
–Ali Jinnah, August 1948 in his last speech

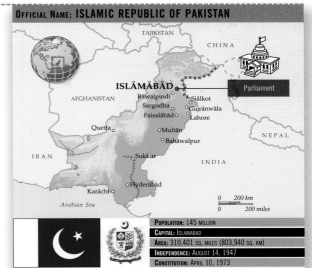

Parliament

POPULATION: 145 MILLION
CAPITAL: ISLAMABAD
AREA: 310,401 SQ. MILES (803,940 SQ. KM)
INDEPENDENCE: AUGUST 14, 1947
CONSTITUTION: APRIL 10, 1973

Pakistan's main political parties include the Pakistan Muslim League (PML) and the Pakistan People's Party (PPP). While the support base for the PML is in Punjab, the PPP has a strong following in Sind, as well as in parts of Punjab and the North-West Frontier Province. Ethnic and religious (Islamic) groups comprise the remaining political parties. There has been a marked increase in Islamic fundamentalist militancy in recent years, and the regime has been careful to avoid conflict with the militants, especially over issues such as foreign policy and the implementation of Islamic law (shari'a).

MOHAMMED ALI JINNAH

Jinnah was the main force behind the move for a separate Islamic State. Considered the founder of Pakistan, Jinnah became the first governor-general in 1947, and remained in power until his death in 1948.

In response to India's six nuclear tests in May of 1998, Pakistan carried out seven tests later that same month, emerging as the world's seventh nuclear power. In late 2001–early 2002, the conflict over Kashmir almost led to war between India and Pakistan causing much concern over the threat of a nuclear war in the region.

While Pakistan has profited economically from its strategic and diplomatic standing following the September 11, 2001 attacks, this poor and underdeveloped nation is struggling with a lack of foreign investment and a weak infrastructure which has made it heavily dependent on aid. Corruption is prevalent at all levels of government, though the regime's efforts to confront corruption and poverty were praised by the World Bank in 2001. In addition to these and other economic problems, present concerns are to reduce internal tensions and restore democracy.

PAKISTAN is derived from the Persian words "pak", meaning holy or pure, and "istan" meaning homeland, literally the "homeland of the holy people".

RELIGION: Sunni Muslim 77%, Shi'a Muslim 20%, Hindu 2%, Christian 2%

OFFICIAL LANGUAGE: Urdu

REGIONS OR PROVINCES: 4 provinces, 1 territory, and 1 capital territory

DEPENDENT TERRITORIES: None

MEDIA: Partial political censorship
Newspapers: There are 264 daily newspapers
TV: 2 services: 1 state-owned
Radio: 3 services: 2 state-owned

SUFFRAGE: 21 years of age; universal; separate electorates and reserved parliamentary seats for non-Muslims

LEGAL SYSTEM: Shari'a (Islamic) and English common law; accepts ICJ jurisdiction

WORLD ORGANIZATIONS: AsDB, ASEAN (dialogue partner), C (suspended), CCC, CP, ECO, ESCAP, FAO, G-19, G-24, G-77, IAEA, IBRD, ICAO, ICC, ICFTU, ICRM, IDA, IDB, IFAD, IFC, IFRCS, IHO, ILO, IMF, IMO, Interpol, IOC, IOM, ISO, ITU, MINURSO, MONUC, NAM, OAS (observer), OIC, OPCW, PCA, SAARC, UN, UNAMSIL, UNCTAD, UNESCO, UNHCR, UNIDO, UNIKOM, UNMIBH, UNMIK, UNMOP, UNOMIG, UNTAET, UPU, WCL, WFTU, WHO, WIPO, WMO, WToO, WTrO

POLITICAL PARTIES: PML—Pakistan Muslim League, W—Women, PPP—Pakistan People's Party, MQM(A)—Mohajir Quami Movement (A) Haq Parast Group, ANP—Awami National Party, N-M—Non-Muslim Minorities, Balichistan National Party, Jamiat-Ulema-e-Pakistan, Pakistan People's Party, Jamhoori Watan Party, National People's Party, Independents

ETHNIC GROUPS

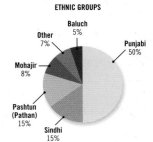

Baluch 5%
Punjabi 50%
Other 7%
Mohajir 8%
Pashtun (Pathan) 15%
Sindhi 15%

N T   W O R K S

⚖ JUDICIAL BRANCH

SUPREME COURT

The Supreme Court is the highest court in Pakistan's four-tier court system. The chief justice and other justices are appointed by the president in conjunction with the chief executive. Rules on civil and criminal matters.

▶ **FEDERAL COURT**
The Federal Islamic Court, or Shari'a Court, rules on matters related to Islamic law and enforces the 1979 Hudood Ordinances, but not Koranic punishments such as stoning.

HIGH COURT OF LAHORE, PAKISTAN
Serving Punjab province, the High Court in Lahore is one of four in Pakistan.

▶ **HIGH COURTS**
Each province has one High Court, whose justices are appointed by the president in consultation with the chief justice of the Supreme Court and the provincial chief justice.

▶ **LOWER COURTS**
Pakistan's District Courts rule on civil matters, while Session Courts rule on criminal matters.

NATIONAL ECONOMICS

WORLD GNP RANKING: 45th
GNP PER CAPITA: $440
INFLATION: 4.4%
BALANCE OF PAYMENTS (BALANCE OF TRADE): -$2.21 billion
EXCHANGE RATES / U.S. DLR.: 57.6-59.9 PAKISTANI RUPEES

OFFICIAL CURRENCY: PAKISTANI RUPEE

GOVERNMENT SPENDING (% OF GDP)

		0	5	10	15
✈	DEFENSE 5.8%				
📚	EDUCATION 2.7%				
✚	HEALTH 0.7%				

NUMBER OF CONFLICTS OVER LAST 25 YEARS

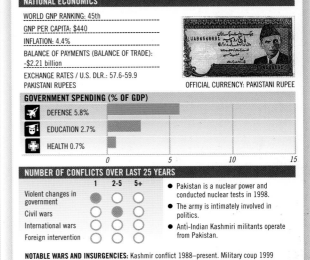

	1	2-5	5+
Violent changes in government			
Civil wars			
International wars			
Foreign intervention			

- Pakistan is a nuclear power and conducted nuclear tests in 1998.
- The army is intimately involved in politics.
- Anti-Indian Kashmiri militants operate from Pakistan.

NOTABLE WARS AND INSURGENCIES: Kashmir conflict 1988–present. Military coup 1999

⊞ ELECTORAL SYSTEM
The Election Commission of Pakistan is an independent and autonomous constitutional body responsible for conducting free and impartial elections to the National and Provincial Assemblies. However, elections to the office of the president and the senate are solely the functions of the chief election commissioner (chairman of the Election Commission) as are local government elections.

CONGO (DEMOCRATIC REPUBLIC)

OFFICIAL NAME: DEMOCRATIC REPUBLIC OF THE CONGO

POPULATION: 52.5 MILLION
CAPITAL: KINSHASA
AREA: 905,563 SQ. MILES (2,345,408 SQ. KM)
INDEPENDENCE: 1960
CONSTITUTION: 1967

THE DEMOCRATIC REPUBLIC OF CONGO's name is derived from "Kong" meaning "mountainous" in Bantu.

RELIGION: Roman Catholic 50%, Protestant 20%, Kimbanguist 10%, Muslim 10%, Other syncretic sects and indigenous beliefs 10%

OFFICIAL LANGUAGE: French

REGIONS OR PROVINCES: 10 provinces

DEPENDENT TERRITORIES: None

MEDIA: Only press is privately owned

Newspapers: There are 9 daily newspapers

TV: 1 state-controlled service, independent services

Radio: 2 state-controlled services, independent services

SUFFRAGE: 18 years of age; universal and compulsory

LEGAL SYSTEM: Tribal and Belgian law; no ICJ jurisdiction

WORLD ORGANIZATIONS: ACCT, ACP, AfDB, CCC, CEEAC, CEPGL, ECA, FAO, G-19, G-24, G-77, IAEA, IBRD, ICAO, ICFTU, ICRM, IDA, IFAD, IFC, IFRCS, IHO, ILO, IMF, IMO, Interpol, IOC, IOM, ISO (correspondent), ITU, NAM, OAU, OPCW (signatory), PCA, SADC, UN, UNCTAD, UNESCO, UNHCR, UNIDO, UPU, WCL, WFTU, WHO, WIPO, WMO, WToO, WTrO

POLITICAL PARTIES: PDSC—Democratic Social Christian Party, FONUS—Forces for Renovation for Union and Solidarity, MNC—National Congolese Lumumbist Movement, MPR—Popular Movement of the Revolution, PALU—Unified Lumumbast Party, UDPS—Union for Democracy and Social Progress, UFERI—Union of Federalists and Independent Republicans

NATIONAL ECONOMICS

WORLD GNP RANKING: 108th

GNP PER CAPITA: $110

INFLATION: 540%

BALANCE OF PAYMENTS (BALANCE OF TRADE):
-$798 million

EXCHANGE RATES / U.S. DLR.: 4.5-313
CONGOLESE FRANCS

OFFICIAL CURRENCY: CONGOLESE FRANC

GOVERNMENT SPENDING (% OF GDP)

DEFENSE	8.4%
EDUCATION	0.1%
HEALTH	1.7%

0   5   10   15

NUMBER OF CONFLICTS OVER LAST 25 YEARS

	1	2-5	5+
Violent changes in government	○	●	○
Civil wars	○	●	○
International wars	○	○	○
Foreign intervention	○	●	○

● No compulsory national military service.
● Ongoing violence undermines UN peacekeeping operations.
● Boundary dispute with Congo.

NOTABLE WARS AND INSURGENCIES: Coups in 1997 and 2001. Internal conflicts in 1986 and 1990. Civil War 1996–2003. UN intervention, peacekeeping force (MONUC)

ONCE THE PERSONAL FIEF OF BELGIUM'S King Leopold II, the Democratic Republic of the Congo (DRC) is one of the largest countries in Africa and home to more than 200 ethnic groups. Thanks to a wealth of natural resources, the DRC, unlike most of Africa, has the potential to become a very rich nation. International outcry over Leopold's ownership of what was called the Congo Free State prompted Belgium to assume control in 1908, renaming the country the Belgian Congo. Independence in 1960 brought the country's current name, as well as political instability, social upheaval, and ethnic violence that continue today.

ISSUES AND CHALLENGES:

● Ethnic differences pose a seemingly insurmountable obstacle to national unity.

● Continuing civil war and a corrupt leadership that robbed the country of its wealth have resulted in a crumbling infrastructure and dwindling social services.

● The high number of people infected with HIV/AIDS is a growing health crisis.

● Chaotic internal politics makes the international community and businesses reluctant to become involved with the DRC.

● The DRC's agriculture and mining industries continue to operate well below their potential, and the country is unable to produce enough food.

Joseph Mobutu seized control in November 1965, promising eventual democracy but ruling as an autocratic dictator for 32 years. Mobutu fomented ethnic strife to achieve his own ends. In 1971, to underscore ethnic identity, he changed his name to Mobutu Sese-Seko and the country's name to Zaire while requiring citizens to take African names. Laurent-Désiré Kabila, with help from Rwanda and Uganda, toppled Mobutu's corrupt 32-year regime in May 1997. Mobutu fled to Morocco, where he died in September. Naming himself president and returning the country's name to the Democratic Republic of the Congo, Kabila promised transition to a pluralist democracy but dissolved the legislature and abandoned the constitution. Rwanda and Uganda supported an ethnic Tutsi uprising against Kabila in 1998, which plunged the country into chaos, preventing the 1999 elections. Ten days after Kabila's assassination in January 2001, his son Joseph Kabila was appointed president. Talks between the various factions in 2001, and again in 2002, resolved little save Rwanda agreeing to withdraw some of its troops from the DRC.

Joseph Kabila inherited a presidency in which all power is vested. While he speaks of moving toward democracy and economic liberalism, Kabila also rules as a dictator. Though often promised, elections have not been held since the 1980s, and the country remains without a constitution. The country's legal system is a mix of tribal and Belgian civil law. The judiciary lacks autonomy, and military leaders serve as adjudicators in some areas.

HOW THE GOVERNMENT WORKS

LEGISLATIVE BRANCH
Parliament
Unicameral Parliament
Transitional Constituent Assembly.
Composed of 300 members appointed by president.

Regional Governments
Ten provinces administered by governors appointed by president.

EXECUTIVE BRANCH
The President
Elected to seven-year term by direct popular vote. Serves as head of state and government; commander-in-chief of armed forces. Rules by decree with few checks on power.

National Executive Council
Composed of 25 members appointed by president. Presided over by president; oversees government operations.

JUDICIAL BRANCH
Military Tribunals
Rule on civilian and military cases; no appeal of verdicts is allowed. Presided over by a military judge.

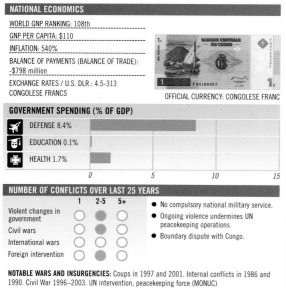

MYANMAR

OFFICIAL NAME: UNION OF MYANMAR

POPULATION: 48.4 MILLION
CAPITAL: RANGOON (YANGON)
AREA: 261,969 SQ. MILES (678,500 SQ. KM)
INDEPENDENCE: 1948
CONSTITUTION: 1974

MYANMAR'S name comes from the Burmese words "mein" meaning strong and "ma" meaning honorable.

RELIGION: Buddhist 87%, Christian 6%, Muslim 4%, Hindu 1%, Other 2%

OFFICIAL LANGUAGE: Burmese (Myanmar)

REGIONS OR PROVINCES: 7 states and 7 divisions

DEPENDENT TERRITORIES: None

MEDIA: Total political censorship exists in national media

NEWSPAPERS: There are 5 daily newspapers

TV: 1 state-controlled service;

RADIO: 1 state-controlled service

SUFFRAGE: 18 years of age; universal

LEGAL SYSTEM: Judiciary controlled by military regime; vestiges of English common law; no ICJ jurisdiction

WORLD ORGANIZATIONS: ARF, AsDB, ASEAN, CCC, CP, ESCAP, FAO, G-77, IAEA, IBRD, ICAO, ICRM, IDA, IFAD, IFC, IFRCS, ILO, IMF, IMO, Interpol, IOC, ITU, NAM, OPCW (signatory), UN, UNCTAD, UNESCO, UNIDO, UPU, WHO, WIPO, WMO, WToO, WTrO

POLITICAL PARTIES: NLD—National League for Democracy, SNLD—Shan National League for Democracy, NUP—National Unity Party, RDL—Rakhine Democracy League, MNDF—Mon National Democratic Front, NDP—National Democratic Party for Human Rights

ETHNIC GROUPS:

- Rakhine 4%
- Karen 6%
- Shan 9%
- Other 13%
- Burman (Bamah) 68%

NATIONAL ECONOMICS

WORLD GNP RANKING: 43rd

GNP PER CAPITA: $1,500

INFLATION: -0.1%

BALANCE OF PAYMENTS (BALANCE OF TRADE): -$293 million

EXCHANGE RATES / U.S. DLR.: 6.526-6.771 KYATS

OFFICIAL CURRENCY: KYAT

GOVERNMENT SPENDING (% OF GDP)

✈	DEFENSE 2.1%	
🎓	EDUCATION 1.2%	
✚	HEALTH 0.2%	

0   5   10   15

NUMBER OF CONFLICTS OVER LAST 25 YEARS

	1	2-5	5+
Violent changes in government	●	○	○
Civil wars	○	●	○
International wars	○	○	○
Foreign intervention	○	○	○

- The junta has doubled the size of the army.
- China has supplied over $1 billion in arms since 1989.
- The army is accused of human rights abuses.

NOTABLE WARS AND INSURGENCIES: Intense student and worker protests followed by coup 1988. Various regional insurrections

AFTER YEARS OF WARFARE, Britain gained control of Burma in 1885, governing the ancient Buddhist kingdom as part of India for the next six decades. Upon its independence, Burma's attempt at self-rule was shattered with the assassinations of its top leaders and the government subsequently fell under military control. Today, a military junta, which has renamed the nation "Myanmar," still rules despite international condemnation of its brutal treatment of the people.

A Burmese kingdom was established in the 11th century under the Pagan Dynasty, which constructed thousands of elaborate pagodas and monasteries, many still standing today. Succeeding dynasties ruled until the country became a British colony in 1886. During World War II, Burmese nationalists led by General Aung San fought with Japan and drove out the British, then later switched sides and aided British and American troops. At the war's end, Britain consented to Aung San's demand for Burma's independence, but his murder, along with those of most of his Cabinet, plunged Burma into turmoil. In 1962, the military seized control of the government and installed a Leninist-style regime. Anger at years of repression and a failing economy erupted in 1988 in mass student protests. In reaction, the military declared martial law and ordered the army into the streets, killing several thousand demonstrators.

National elections in 1990 gave eight of every ten seats in the People's Assembly to the National League for Democracy, the pro-democracy party led by Aung San Suu Kyi, daughter of the country's assassinated first leader. However, the military-controlled government refused to let the People's Assembly meet and draw up a new constitution as intended. It also imprisoned Suu Kyi and other political activists. Power in Myanmar continues to be strictly centered in the hands of the junta, the so-called State Peace and Development Council, which rules by decree without a constitution or legislature. The regime continues to severely restrict freedom of speech and press, ban unions, imprison political reformers, and operate forced labor camps.

OPPOSITION LEADER
Protesters condemn the placing of opposition leader Aung San Suu Kyi under house arrest in 1998. Below: Aung San Suu Kyi addresses a gathering on January 4, 1997—the 49th anniversary of independence.

HOW THE GOVERNMENT WORKS

LEGISLATIVE BRANCH
Pyithu Hluttaw
(People's Assembly)
Unicameral Parliament
Composed of 485 members elected to four-year terms by direct popular vote. Has not convened since 1990 election.

Regional Governments
Seven ethnic-minority states and seven ethnic Burmese divisions; all governed by military-controlled State Peace and Development Council.

EXECUTIVE BRANCH
Prime Minister
Chairman of military-controlled State Peace and Development Council. Serves as head of state and government; commander-in-chief of armed forces. Rules by decree with no checks on power.

Cabinet
Composed of 35 members: 27 military officers, eight civilians. All appointed by State Peace and Development Council.

JUDICIAL BRANCH
Supreme Court
Justices appointed by military-controlled State Peace and Development Council.

Lower Courts
Judges appointed by Supreme Court with approval of military-controlled State Peace and Development Council.

SUDAN

OFFICIAL NAME: REPUBLIC OF THE SUDAN

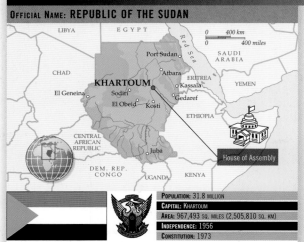

POPULATION: 31.8 MILLION
CAPITAL: KHARTOUM
AREA: 967,493 SQ. MILES (2,505,810 SQ. KM)
INDEPENDENCE: 1956
CONSTITUTION: 1973

SUDAN is derived from an Arabic phrase "bilad as-sudan" which means "land of the blacks."

RELIGION: Muslim (mainly Sunni) 70%, Traditional beliefs 20%, Christian 9%, Other 1%

OFFICIAL LANGUAGE: Arabic

REGIONS OR PROVINCES: 26 states

DEPENDENT TERRITORIES: None

MEDIA: Total political censorship

Newspapers: There are 7 daily newspapers

TV: 1 state-controlled service

Radio: 2 services: 1 state-controlled, 1 rebel-controlled

SUFFRAGE: 17 years of age; universal, but non-compulsory

LEGAL SYSTEM: Shari'a (Islamic) and English common law; accepts ICJ jurisdiction

WORLD ORGANIZATIONS: ABEDA, ACP, AfDB, AFESD, AL, AMF, CAEU, CCC, ECA, FAO, G-77, IAEA, IBRD, ICAO, ICRM, IDA, IDB, IFAD, IFC, IFRCS, IGAD, ILO, IMF, IMO, Interpol, IOC, IOM, ISO (correspondent), ITU, NAM, OAU, OIC, OPCW, PCA, UN, UNCTAD, UNESCO, UNHCR, UNIDO, UNU, UPU, WFTU, WHO, WIPO, WMO, WToO, WTrO (observer)

POLITICAL PARTIES: NC—National Congress supporters, Ind–Independents

ETHNIC GROUPS:

- Foreigners 2%
- Beja 6%
- Other 1%
- Arab 39%
- Black 52%

NATIONAL ECONOMICS

WORLD GNP RANKING: 84th

GNP PER CAPITA: $310

INFLATION: 16%

BALANCE OF PAYMENTS (BALANCE OF TRADE): -$557m

EXCHANGE RATES / U.S. DLR: 258.70 SUDANESE DINARS

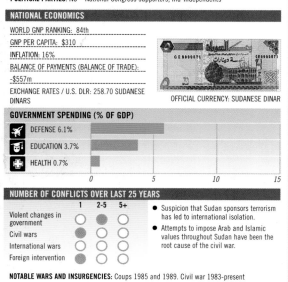

OFFICIAL CURRENCY: SUDANESE DINAR

GOVERNMENT SPENDING (% OF GDP)

- DEFENSE 6.1%
- EDUCATION 3.7%
- HEALTH 0.7%

0   5   10   15

NUMBER OF CONFLICTS OVER LAST 25 YEARS

	1	2-5	5+
Violent changes in government	○	○	○
Civil wars	●	○	○
International wars	○	○	○
Foreign intervention	●	○	○

- Suspicion that Sudan sponsors terrorism has led to international isolation.
- Attempts to impose Arab and Islamic values throughout Sudan have been the root cause of the civil war.

NOTABLE WARS AND INSURGENCIES: Coups 1985 and 1989. Civil war 1983–present

---

SUDAN IS THE LARGEST COUNTRY IN AFRICA, stretching more than 1,200 miles (1,900 km) from north to south. Between the dominant Arab Muslims in the north, who run the Sudanese government, and the black African animist or Christian population in the south there is a seemingly unbridgeable gap. Religious, cultural, racial, and political differences between these two groups account for the bloody turmoil and failed attempts to establish democracy since Sudan gained independence from a British-Egyptian "condominium" in 1956.

Sudan's politics have followed a similar course to those of other late 20th-century African nations—military coups and suspended constitutions, with occasional periods of parliamentary rule. But Sudan has gone further—imposing military rule and Islamic law, amid accusations of religious persecution and slavery. Civil war in the south between government forces and the Sudanese People's Liberation Army (SPLA) has killed over 2 million people and displaced 4 million more.

In 1985 Col. Jafar Numeiry's attempt to introduce shari'a, or Islamic law, sparked off a military coup and suspension of the constitution, followed by an experiment in democracy. That failed, and in 1989 Gen. Omar Bashir, an Islamist ideologue, seized power. He dismantled much of the civilian government and promoted supporters in the National Islamic Front to key posts. His regime imposed a shari'a-based penal code, including punishment by amputation and stoning, in northern Sudan in 1991.

Bashir was eventually elected to power in 1996, but in 1999 he disbanded parliament, suspended the constitution, and declared a national emergency. Parliament resumed in 2001 after December 2000 elections, but major parties boycotted the vote and joined southerners in rebelling against the government. Since 2003, a major revolt among non-Arab Sudanese in the western region of Darfur has sparked a humanitarian crisis, with the government's treatment of civilians in the area attracting international condemnation.

ISSUES AND CHALLENGES:

- Ongoing violence has forced more than four million people to flee to neighboring countries including Ethiopia, Kenya, Uganda, and Egypt.

- Human rights abuses, pro-Iraq sentiment and suspicion of terrorist support resulted in the suspension of IMF funding in 1990.

- Severe drought has exacerbated the critical food shortage, leaving many facing starvation. The US is amongst the many countries that have had to provide food aid to avert a disaster.

- The war prevents Sudan taking full advantage of the significant oil reserves discovered in the 1980s.

- In spite of turning a corner through solid economic policies and investments, the nation still faces looming economic problems.

HOW THE GOVERNMENT WORKS

LEGISLATIVE BRANCH
House of Assembly
Unicameral Parliament
Composed of 360 members who serve four-year terms: 270 elected by direct popular vote; 90 by National Congress, an assembly of interest groups.

Regional Governments
Twenty-six states each administered by governor, local cabinet and regional ministers, all appointed by president.

EXECUTIVE BRANCH
President
Elected to five-year term by direct popular vote. Serves as head of state and government; commander-in-chief of armed forces. Dissolves parliament; suspends constitution; rules by decree.

Two Vice-presidents
Appointed by president.

Council of Ministers
Appointed by president.

JUDICIAL BRANCH
Supreme Court
Constitutional Court

Civil and Special Tribunals
Sudan's judicial system has two major branches, a civil branch overseeing most cases and an Islamic branch handling personal and family matters.

Tribal Courts

DEMOCRATIC
RULE

GOVERNMENT BY THE PEOPLE

DEMOCRACY MEANS RULE BY THE PEOPLE. It developed in Athens in the 5th century B.C., but critics even then questioned what constitutes "the people" (the Athenians excluded slaves and women from citizenship) and considered that democracy differed little from mob rule. But the ideals of both democratic Athens and republican Rome, where citizenship, justice, equality among citizens, and a sense of public duty were prized, have helped shape political thinking ever since. During the Renaissance (c.1300–c.1600), the highest political ideal was an independent, self-governing republic, where citizens participated in their own governance within a constitutional framework. Self-government was regarded as the basis of liberty, an idea which carried through to the American Revolution and the many independence movements in the colonial empires of the 19th and 20th centuries. Modern democratic rule takes several forms: parliamentary democracy, where the chief executive is the prime minister who relies on the support of an elected parliament (e.g. the United Kingdom); presidential democracy, where the president is directly elected (e.g. the United States); or multiparty democracy, a mix where the presidential role is often balanced by a prime minister (e.g. France). There are also non-party democracies, where democratic elections occur on individual merits, not party platforms (e.g. Peru). In some regimes a president may be elected democratically, but then assumes dictatorial powers.

DEMOCRATIC RULERS AND THEORISTS

Clockwise from top left: Mahatma Gandhi, charismatic leader of nonviolent movement for Indian self-rule; Jawaharlal Nehru, India's first prime minister after independence in 1947; Plato (c. 428-348 B.C.), author of "The Republic," vision of an ideal state; Thomas Jefferson, who drafted the declaration of Independence and became the third president of the USA (1801-1809); John F. Kennedy, US president (1961-1963); Margaret Thatcher, British prime minister (1979-1990); Abraham Lincoln, US president during the Civil War, who emancipated the southern slaves; Oliver Cromwell, parliamentary leader and Lord Protector of England, Ireland, and Scotland under Britain's Commonwealth (1649-1658); Boris Yeltsin, first elected president of Russia following the collapse of communism; Pericles, ruler of Athens in the golden age of Athens (443-429 B.C.); George Washington, first president of the USA; Nelson Mandela, elected first president of a democratic South Africa in 1994; Jean-Jacques Rousseau, 18th-century French philosopher, whose ideas on individual liberty inspired the leaders of the French Revolution; Golda Meir, Israeli prime minister (1969-1974).

INDIA

INDIAN FLAG
Adopted on July 22, 1947, the Indian flag shows the Ashoka Chakra or "wheel of law" at its center.

INDIA, WITH MORE THAN A BILLION PEOPLE, is the world's largest democracy. Since independence from Britain in 1947, it has preserved the liberties enshrined in its constitution and achieved huge increases in economic investment and output, but given the country's sheer size and complexity, this has not been easy. India teems with one third of the world's poor.

TAJ MAHAL
One of the emblems of India, built between 1632 and 1647 by the Mughal emperor Shah Jahan, the Taj Mahal was a tribute to his wife who died in childbirth.

Before the British began their conquest in the 18th and 19th centuries, India had been a mosaic of states, large and small, some ruled by Hindu princes, others by Muslims. It was not until 1858, after the great revolt of 1856-1857, that the government of India came under the British crown. Up until then it had been controlled by the British East India Company.

Organized nationwide opposition to British rule began in 1885, with the founding of the Indian National Congress. The dominant figure in India's quest for independence was Mahatma ("great soul") Mohandas K. Gandhi. Gandhi took the helm of the Congress party in 1920 and started his first campaign of civil disobedience against British rule. Gandhi's

belief in nonviolent disobedience was grounded in his fervent devotion to truth, freedom, and God. His example became an inspiration for other leaders such as Martin Luther King and union leader Cesar Chavez, in the United States.

Sadly, when India achieved independence after World War II, it was an event marked by bloody Hindu-Muslim riots and massacres. Despite Gandhi's dream of a united independent India, the country was

GANDHI AND THE SPINNING WHEEL
Gandhi spun daily, referring to the spinning wheel as a symbol of India's struggle for independence—providing an industry that would make India self-reliant.

HOW THE GOVE

LEGISLATIVE BRANCH

PARLIAMENT

Bicameral Parliament. The House of the People is the more powerful of the two houses. All financial legislation has to be introduced there, but bills have to be passed in both houses.

▶ **RAJYA SABHA**

Council of States, the upper house; 245 seats; 233 indirectly elected by state legislatures and territorial assemblies; 12 seats reserved for distinguished citizens nominated by president; members serve six-year terms; one-third retire every two years.

▶ **LOK SABHA**

House of the People, the lower house; 545 seats, of which 543 are directly elected by popular vote and two appointed by the president from Anglo-Indian community; members serve five-year terms; 79 seats are reserved for representatives of scheduled castes (untouchables) and 40 for scheduled tribes.

PARLIAMENT HOUSE
Located in New Delhi, this wheel-shaped building is home to both the Council of States and the House of the People.

EXECUTIVE BRANCH

PRESIDENT

Elected by an electoral college comprising members of both houses of parliament and the state legislatures; serves terms of five years; acts as head of state, largely ceremonial role.

▶ **VICE-PRESIDENT**

Elected by electoral college; serves five-year term—staggered from the president's term; ex-officio chairman of the upper house.

STATE AND LOCAL GOVERNMENTS
▶ 28 states, seven administered union territories
▶ State chief minister responsible to state legislature
▶ State governor appointed by president

*"An eye for an eye only
ends up making the whole world blind."*
—Mohandas K. Gandhi

partitioned with the creation of the Muslim state of Pakistan. Against a background of economic chaos provoked by partition and problems posed by refugees and continuing communal violence, India set about devising a constitution. Gandhi, who refused office, was assassinated by a Hindu fanatic in 1948.

In its 1950 constitution, India based its central government on British parliamentary democracy, with two houses: a directly elected lower house, the Lok Sabha, and an upper house, the Rajya Sabha. The members of the latter are indirectly elected by the legislatures of India's states and territories. In establishing the framework of a federal republic, India drew on the federal systems of the United States, Canada, and Australia.

For the first four decades after independence, politics was dominated by the Congress party. Jawaharlal Nehru, India's first prime minister, served for 17 years—his daughter Indira Gandhi and his grandson Rajiv Gandhi also later occupied the office. Congress

REPUBLIC DAY
Every year on January 26, the day the constitution of India came into force in 1950, India celebrates its independence with a national holiday. The date was chosen to commemorate a vow made at the Indian National Congress meeting in Lahore in 1929-1930. In New Delhi, the festivities include military parades.

suffered a humiliating election defeat in 1989 and had to give way to other parties, most notably the Bharatiya Janata Party, or BJP, which appealed to rising Hindu nationalism.

The original Congress party espoused moderate socialism and a planned, mixed, self-sufficient economy. Its spin-off and successor, Congress (I)—"I" in honor of Indira Gandhi—now supports deregulation, privatization, and foreign investment. The BJP also moved away from Gandhian socialism in the 1990s becoming a critic of state intervention in the economy.

RNMENT WORKS

PRIME MINISTER
Head of government; appointed by the president on nomination of the majority party in the Lok Sabha after legislative elections; communicates all decisions of Council of Ministers to president.

▶ **COUNCIL OF MINISTERS**
Appointed by the president on the recommendation of the prime minister who leads the Council, responsible to the Lok Sabha; comprises cabinet ministers, ministers of state, and deputy ministers.

⚖ JUDICIAL BRANCH

SUPREME COURT
Highest judicial authority in civil, criminal, and constitutional cases; consist of up to 26 judges, including the Chief Justice of India. All judges are appointed by the president on the recommendation of the prime minister and serve until the age of 65. Jurisdiction includes appellate cases and original cases between the government and one or more states or between states; has power to transfer civil and criminal cases between high courts.

▶ **HIGH COURTS**
Eighteen courts, of which three have jurisdiction over more than one state; chief justices are appointed by the president in consultation with Chief Justice of India and state governor. Number of sitting judges varies from court to court; all judges retire at 62.

▶ **DISTRICT COURTS**
Judges are appointed by state governor in consultation with state's high court. Each district (zilla) has a judge who hears civil cases. A sessions judge presides over criminal cases.

RASHTRAPATI BHAWAN
The official residence of the president of India in Delhi is a 340-room palace, built during British rule.

 ELECTORAL SYSTEM
Lok Sabha members are directly elected from single-member constituencies using the first-past-the-post system. There are certain constituencies where only candidates from scheduled castes and scheduled tribes are allowed to stand. Most Rajya Sabha members are elected by the state legislatures.

INDIA

OFFICIAL NAME: REPUBLIC OF INDIA

PAKISTAN · Chandigarh · CHINA
NEW DELHI · Delhi · NEPAL · BHUTAN
Parliament · Agra · Patna · Shiliguri · Imphāl
Jodhpur · Kānpur · Dhanbād · BANGLADESH
Bhopāl · Jabālpur · MYANMAR (BURMA)
Rajkot · Vadodara · Nāgpur · Kolkata (Calcutta)
Mumbai (Bombay) · Surat · Nānded · Cuttack
· Pune · Visākhapatnam · Bay of Bengal
Arabian Sea · Hyderābād
Pānāji · Chennai (Madras) · Andaman Is.
Bangalore · INDIAN OCEAN
Lakshadweep (Laccadive Is.) · Salem · Nicobar Is.
Cochin · Madurai
SRI LANKA

0 400 km
0 400 miles

POPULATION:	1.03 BILLION
CAPITAL:	NEW DELHI
AREA:	1,269,338 SQ. MILES (3,287,585 SQ. KM)
INDEPENDENCE:	1947
CONSTITUTION:	1950

INDIA'S name comes from the Sanskrit *sundhu* meaning the "great river".

RELIGION: Hindu 83%, Muslim 11%, Other 6%

OFFICIAL LANGUAGES: Hindi and English

REGIONS OR PROVINCES: 28 states and 7 union territories

DEPENDENT TERRITORIES: None

MEDIA: Partial political censorship exists in national media

Newspapers: There are 5157 daily newspapers, TV: 1 state-owned service, Radio: 1 state-owned service

SUFFRAGE: 18 years of age; universal

LEGAL SYSTEM: English common law; accepts ICJ jurisdiction

WORLD ORGANIZATIONS: AfDB, ARF (dialogue partner), AsDB, ASEAN (dialogue partner), BIS, C, CCC, CP, ESCAP, FAO, G-6, G-15, G-19, G-24, G-77, IAEA, IBRD, ICAO, ICC, ICFTU, ICRM, IDA, IEA (observer), IFAD, IFC, IFRCS, IHO, ILO, IMF, IMO, Interpol, IOC, IOM (observer), ISO, ITU, MIPONUH, MONUC, NAM, OAS (observer), OPCW, PCA, SAARC, UN, UNCTAD, UNESCO, UNHCR, UNIDO, UNIFIL, UNIKOM, UNMEE, UNMIBH, UNMIK, UNMOVIC, UNU, UPU, WCL, WFTU, WHO, WIPO, WMO, WToO, WTrO

POLITICAL PARTIES: BJP—Bharatiya Janata Party and Allies (including the All-India Anna Dravida Munnetra Kazhagam, C(I)-Congress (I) and Allies, UF—United Front and Allies (including the Communist Party of India (Marxist)—CPI(M)

ETHNIC GROUPS:

Mongoloid and Other 3%
Dravidian 25%
Indo-Aryan 72%

NATIONAL ECONOMICS

WORLD GNP RANKING: 12th

GNP PER CAPITA: $450

INFLATION: 4%

BALANCE OF PAYMENTS (BALANCE OF TRADE): -$4.2 billion

EXCHANGE RATES / U.S. DLR.: 46.68-48.22 INDIAN RUPEES

OFFICIAL CURRENCY: INDIAN RUPEE

GOVERNMENT SPENDING (% OF GDP)

✈	DEFENSE 3.1%	
🎓	EDUCATION 3.3%	
✚	HEALTH 5.1%	

0 5 10 15

NUMBER OF CONFLICTS OVER LAST 25 YEARS

	1	2-5	5+
Violent changes in government	○	○	○
Civil wars	○	○	●
International wars	○	○	○
Foreign intervention	○	○	○

- India has the world's third-largest military, and produces its own hardware.
- A nuclear deterrent is considered vital.
- There is serious tension with Pakistan over Kashmir.

NOTABLE WARS AND INSURGENCIES: Sectarian clashes. Various separatist struggles. Conflict in Kashmir 1947-present

---

*"Democracy is good.
I say this because other systems are worse."*
—*Jawaharlal Nehru,
first prime minister of India*

India has evolved from a highly centralized state dominated by one political party to an increasingly fragmented one, controlled by unstable multiparty alliances and influenced more and more by regional parties. Groups such as the Dalits, the lowest Hindu caste, and tribal peoples have also demanded a greater voice in government.

Lacking majority support, the country's prime minister and Council of Ministers can be forced to resign by the Lok Sabha (House of the People) as has happened frequently since 1979. Coalitions form and collapse rapidly, resulting in hung parliaments, and cabinets are frequently reshuffled, with ministers resigning amid corruption charges.

GUARDING AGAINST FURTHER VIOLENCE
People attend a prayer meeting on September 29, 2002 at the Swaminarayan Hindu temple in Gandhinagar in the state of Gujarat, where 28 worshippers were gunned down a week earlier.

While the Indian constitution has been praised as a model for seeking to end social inequality, it is also one of the most amended national documents in the world, with more than 80 changes since 1950. A focus of many such amendments has been a long-running dispute involving the Parliament and the Supreme Court, over the rights of parliamentary sovereignty as they clash with those of judicial review of laws and constitutional amendments.

RELIGIOUS CONTROVERSY AND POLITICAL UNREST

Bitter Hindu-Muslim relations have been an ongoing challenge for India, on both the foreign and home fronts. A centuries-old rivalry between the two religious populations led to partition on independence from Britain. The Muslim state of Pakistan consisted of two widely separated regions—West Pakistan and East Pakistan—on opposite sides of northern India. An Indian invasion in 1971 allowed East Pakistan to become the separate nation of Bangladesh. A main source of dispute was and still is the status of the Muslim-dominated region of Kashmir, on the border with Pakistan. Other issues have also strained relations, and both India and Pakistan conducting nuclear weapons tests in the late 1990s despite international condemnation. However, relations between the neighbouring powers have recently undergone a remarkable improvement, despite continued tension in the region and occasional attacks by militants across Kashmir's so-called "Line of Control".

Domestically, the Muslim population has tended to rely on the Congress party for protection from the vast Hindu majority, but the rise of the BJP in the late 1990s gave vigor to the idea of Hindutva, or Hindu-based national identity. When the BJP gained power, prime minister Atal Bihari Vajpayee attempted to keep that ideology in the background, despite pressure from the militant Hindu Sangh movement. One particular flashpoint has been Ayodhya in Uttar Pradesh, where the 1992 destruction of a Muslim mosque by Hindu activists set off communal riots that killed 1,200 people. In 2002, Hindu pilgrims returning from Ayodhya were massacred on a train, setting off a wave of revenge attacks in Gujarat that led to 2,000 more deaths. However, the surprise return of the Congress party to power in 2004, coupled with the growing rapprochement with Pakistan, may help to ease such tensions.

BANGLADESH

OFFICIAL NAME: PEOPLE'S REPUBLIC OF BANGLADESH

India
Saidpur
Dinajpur
Rangpur
Jamalpur
Sylhet
Mymensingh
Rajshahi
Shirajganj Ghat
Pabna
Brahmanbaria
DHAKA
Comilla
Jessore
Khulna
Barisal
INDIA
Chittagong
MYANMAR (BURMA)
Bay of Bengal

National Parliament

0 100 km
0 100 miles

POPULATION: 140.4 MILLION	
CAPITAL: DHAKA	
AREA: 55,598 SQ. MILES (144,000 SQ. KM)	
INDEPENDENCE: 1971	
CONSTITUTION: 1972	

BANGLADESH literally translated means "the Bengal nation" or land of the Bengali people.

RELIGION: Muslim (mainly Sunni) 87%, Hindu 12%, Other 1%

OFFICIAL LANGUAGE: Bengali

REGIONS OR PROVINCES: 6 divisions

DEPENDENT TERRITORIES: None

MEDIA: Partial political censorship exists in the national media

Newspapers: There are 37 daily newspapers

TV: 1 state-controlled service, 1 independent service

Radio: 1 state-controlled service

SUFFRAGE: 18 years of age; universal

LEGAL SYSTEM: English common law; no ICJ jurisdiction

WORLD ORGANIZATIONS: AsDB, C, CCC, CP, ESCAP, FAO, G-77, IAEA, IBRD, ICAO, ICC, ICFTU, ICRM, IDA, IDB, IFAD, IFC, IFRCS, IHO, ILO, IMF, IMO, Interpol, IOC, IOM, ISO, ITU, MINURSO, MONUC, NAM, OIC, OPCW, SAARC, UN, UNAMSIL, UNCTAD, UNESCO, UNHCR, UNIDO, UNIKOM, UNMEE, UNMIBH, UNMIK, UNMOP, UNMOT. UNOMIG, UNTAET, UNU, UPU, WCL, WFTU, WHO, WIPO, WMO, WToO, WTrO

POLITICAL PARTIES: BNP—Bangladesh Nationalist Party and allies AL—Awami League, JI—Jamaat-e-Islami, JD—Jatiya Dal (Ershad), Ind—Independents

ETHNIC GROUPS:

Other 2%

Bengali 98%

NATIONAL ECONOMICS

WORLD GNP RANKING: 51st

GNP PER CAPITA: $370

INFLATION: 2.3%

BALANCE OF PAYMENTS (BALANCE OF TRADE): -$306 million

EXCHANGE RATES / U.S. DLR.: 54.1-56.95 TAKA

OFFICIAL CURRENCY: TAKA

GOVERNMENT SPENDING (% OF GDP)

✈ DEFENSE 1.8%

📚 EDUCATION 2.2%

✚ HEALTH 1.7%

0   5   10   15

NUMBER OF CONFLICTS OVER LAST 25 YEARS

	1	2-5	5+
Violent changes in government	○	○	○
Civil wars	○	●	○
International wars	○	○	○
Foreign intervention	○	○	○

- The military dominated politics from 1975 to 1990 and remains influential.
- Tensions persist over the illegal emigration of Bangladeshis to India.
- The army has been mobilized to fight crime.

NOTABLE WARS AND INSURGENCIES: Coup 1982. Regional insurgencies

HISTORICALLY, POLITICALLY, CULTURALLY, and geographically, Bangladesh abounds with challenges. Previously known as East Pakistan, the country was renamed following a brutal war for independence from Pakistan in 1971. Since independence, Bangladesh has suffered periods of great political instability, resulting in a rapid succession of changes in the way the country is ruled. Systems of rule have included a presidential system, a military regime from 1975 to 1990, and the current parliamentary system.

Under the current constitution, the prime minister wields most of the political power in Bangladesh. The country's first woman prime minister, Begum Khaleda Zia, was elected in 1991. Shaikh Hasina Wajed took power in 1996 and became Bangladesh's first prime minister to serve an entire term. Khaleda Zia returned to power in 2001. Although these elections were declared the fairest in the history of Bangladesh, Shaikh Hasina, who has subsequently called for new elections, contested them. The constitution grants the president special, expanded powers should the political environment necessitate a caretaker government. The military remains influential in executive decision-making.

Like neighboring India, Bangladesh suffers from sustained and sometimes violent religious tensions. The central government fights an ongoing though low-level guerrilla war with indigenous Buddhist tribespeople in the Chittagong Hill Tracts. Violent clashes between Muslims and Hindus are also common. The country's Hindu minority feels especially threatened as all the most influential political parties—the Bangladesh Nationalist Party, the Awami League, the Jatiya Dal, and the Islamic Assembly have Islamic roots and loyalties.

Many economic and political challenges derive, at least in part, from Bangladesh's geographic location at the confluence of two enormous rivers: the Ganges and the Jamuna. While these rivers deposit rich soil for agriculture, the delta is prone to severe flooding and cyclones that destroy entire crops, severely damage infrastructure, and kill hundreds of thousands of people.

ISSUES AND CHALLENGES:

- Border disputes continue to frustrate relations with India.
- Bangladesh remains an important transit country for illicit drugs produced in the region.
- A significant portion of Bangladesh's economy comes from international aid, which is greater than direct foreign investment.
- Freedom of the press continues to be eroded under civilian government.
- A sharp increase in violent crime—abduction, rape, and murder—against women.
- The educational system in the country is poor, and the universities often come under political attack.

HOW THE GOVERNMENT WORKS

LEGISLATIVE BRANCH

Jatiya Sangsad (National Parliament) Unicameral Parliament
Composed of 300 members elected to five-year terms by direct popular vote from single-member districts. Meets at least twice annually. Debates and passes bills; approves or rejects budget; impeaches president; declares war.

Regional Governments
6 divisions headed by civil-servant commissioners; 64 districts overseen by elected councils and deputy commissioners; 486 subdistricts headed by executive officer and elected council. 4,405 local councils with elected and appointed members.

EXECUTIVE BRANCH

President
Elected to five-year term by parliament. Serves as head of state; commander-in-chief of armed forces. Summons and dissolves parliament; grants pardons; commutes sentences; appoints attorney general.

Prime Minister
Leader of parliament's majority party or coalition. Serves as head of government.

Cabinet
Composed of parliament members and non-members; appointed by president on advice of prime minister. Oversees government operations; chaired by prime minister; answers to parliament.

JUDICIAL BRANCH

Supreme Court
Highest court of review and appeal. Divided into court of last appeal and high court chambers. Judges appointed by president.

District Courts
Hear civil and criminal cases at local level. Judges appointed by president.

JAPAN

ACCORDING TO LEGEND, the Japanese empire was founded in 660 B.C. by the emperor, Jimmu, a descendant of the Shinto sun goddess, Amaterasu. Jimmu is said to be the ancestor of the present emperor—giving Japan the longest unbroken hereditary line of rulers in the world.

FLAG OF JAPAN
Adopted on January 27, 1870, the Japanese flag shows the red disk of the rising sun (Hinomaru) at its center.

MOUNT FUJI
The sacred Mount Fuji is a potent national symbol. It is Japan's highest mountain, rising 12,388 feet (3,776 m) above sea level.

By the 9th century, a strong system of imperial rule was established in Japan, with its capital in Kyoto, but in the 12th century, a new type of leader emerged—the shogun, a powerful military dictator. As rival families fought for control of the country, the emperor's authority was gradually eroded and real power passed to the shogun.

The 16th century saw the arrival of European traders and Christian missionaries in Japan, but contact was short-lived. The Tokugawa Shogunate, founded in 1603, won control of the country, which was now administered from Edo (Tokyo). From the 1630s foreigners were

effectively excluded from Japan. This isolation lasted until 1853, when an American naval squadron under Commodore Matthew Perry sailed into Edo harbor. Perry forced the Japanese government to sign the Treaty of Kanagawa allowing foreign merchants to enter the country and granting privileges to the US.

Under foreign and domestic pressure, the Shogunate was overthrown in 1867, and the following year the young emperor Meiji was restored to absolute authority. A modern government, army and navy were established and industrial development

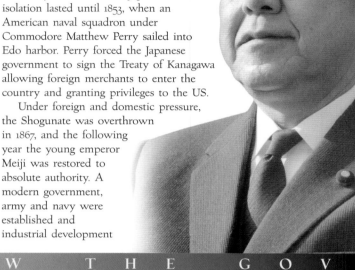

LEGISLATIVE BRANCH

DIET
The Kokkai (Diet) of Japan is a bicameral Parliament. In the event of disgreement between the houses, the House of Representatives prevails.

▶ **THE HOUSE OF COUNCILLORS**
The upper house; consists of 252 members, 100 elected by proportional representation at national level, 152 directly elected at local prefecture level, to terms of six years; elections are staggered with half the members elected every three years. Serves as check on House of Representatives.

▶ **THE HOUSE OF REPRESENTATIVES**
The lower house; consists of 480 members elected to a four-year term, although this is often cut short when the House is dissolved. 300 are elected from single-seat constituencies; 180 are elected by proportional representation from 11 regions on a party-list system.

EXECUTIVE BRANCH

THE EMPEROR
A hereditary position, the emperor is the ceremonial head of state with no governing powers. Most of his limited powers require the approval of either the Diet or Cabinet. These include appointing the prime minister, the chief justice and ministers of state; promulgating constitutional amendments, dissolving the House of Representatives and convoking the Diet.

THE NATIONAL DIET
The legislative building is home to the chambers of the House of Councillors (Sangi-in) and the House of Representatives (Shugi-in).

STATE AND LOCAL GOVERNMENTS
▶ 47 prefectures
▶ Elected governors and mayors
▶ Local governments have own assemblies

INTERIOR OF THE HOUSE OF COUNCILLORS
US president, George W. Bush, addresses Japan's upper house on February 19, 2002.

"Unite your total strength, to be devoted to construction for the future...so that you may enhance the innate glory of the Imperial state and keep pace with the progress of the world."
— Emperor Hirohito, in his surrender speech, August 15, 1945

BUDDHA
Thought to have spread from China in the 6th century A.D., Buddhism is practiced alongside the traditional religion of Japan—Shinto.

and education for the masses were promoted. In 1889 a new constitution was introduced, with a bicameral Parliament, called the Diet (Kokkai). At the same time, the glorification of the emperor helped create a new, vigorous form of Japanese nationalism.

By the 1890s, Japan had the military strength to begin a period of imperial expansion. In 1894-1895, Japan fought and won a war with China, gaining control of Formosa (Taiwan). Japan established itself as a major world power with the Russo-Japanese War of 1904-1905. To the amazement of the West, Japan defeated the huge Russian empire, winning territories in northern China. It annexed Korea in 1910 and won concessions from China in 1915. In 1931, Japan invaded and

GENERAL MACARTHUR
The US general responsible for supervising Japan after World War II. Here MacArthur meets with Emperor Hirohito.

EISAKU SATO (1901-1975)
Japan's longest-serving prime minister since the new constitution was introduced after World War II, Sato held office for eight years.

annexed the Chinese province of Manchuria. Following League of Nations objections, Japan withdrew from the League. In 1937, Japan went to war for total control of China.

With the start of World War II in 1939, Japan expanded further and allied with the Axis powers, Germany and Italy. In 1941, the US declared a full trade embargo and froze Japanese assets in protest at the seizure of French Indochina. Japan's prime minister, Hideki Tojo, ordered the bombing of the US naval fleet in Pearl Harbor on December 7, 1941, thereby triggering war with the United States. After an extended war in the Pacific, the United States dropped atomic bombs on

two Japanese cities—Hiroshima and Nagasaki —in August 1945. The only nuclear weapons ever used in war, they created unprecedented destruction, killing more than 200,000 people. On August 15 of that year, Emperor Hirohito announced Japan's unconditional surrender, and a new age for Japan had begun.

The emperor was allowed to remain on the throne, but only in a ceremonial role, while US General Douglas MacArthur was put in charge of leading Japan through the transition to democracy. The new constitution created a bicameral parliament, and eliminated the armed forces, although a limited self-defense force was later permitted. By the 1970s Japan's economy was very prosperous—the second largest in the world, after America's. Because of its anti-militarist constitution, which continues to enjoy popular support, Japan plays a restrained role on the world stage. Although Japan is an economic powerhouse with trade connections worldwide and gives substantial foreign aid, it does not engage in military activities overseas.

...RNMENT WORKS

PRIME MINISTER
Chosen by the Diet from among its members; usually the leader of the majority party or the majority coalition in House of Representatives; must be elected by a parliamentary majority on a single signed ballot. Appointed by the emperor to a four-year term; immediately following his selection, the prime minister chooses the ministers of state who will form his cabinet.

▶ **CABINET SECRETARIAT**
Headed by chief cabinet secretary; reports to prime minister; coordinates cabinet meetings; assists cabinet.

  ▶ **THE CABINET**
  Headed by the prime minister; limited by the constitution to an additional 14 regular members, with the possibility of three special members. Nominated by the prime minister; half must be members of the Diet.

⚖ JUDICIAL BRANCH

SUPREME COURT
The highest court in Japan; chief justice is appointed by the emperor following selection by the Cabinet; 14 other judges selected and appointed by Cabinet; rules on the constitutionality of laws and executive orders; right of judicial review; court of final appeal if constitutionality is in question; decisions are binding on lower courts.

▶ **HIGH COURTS**
Eight courts; judges appointed by Cabinet from nominations by the Supreme Court; handles appeals from lower courts.

▶ **DISTRICT AND FAMILY COURTS**
50 district courts; 50 family courts; all judges appointed by Cabinet from nominations by the Supreme Court; together they handle civil or criminal cases involving small claims or offenses punishable with light penalties.

▶ **SUMMARY COURTS**
438 courts; judges appointed by Cabinet from nominations by the Supreme Court.

THE SUPREME COURT
Built in 1974, the granite building is home to the court's Grand Bench and three Petty Benches.

ELECTORAL SYSTEM
The public elects representatives to the House of Councillors every three years and to the House of Representatives whenever an election is held. Voters cast two votes by secret ballot, one for the candidate directly and the other for a political party.

最 髙 裁 判 所

EXECUTIVE BRANCH

EISAKU SATO (1901-1975)
Prime Minister Sato became the first Asian to win the Nobel Peace Prize in 1974—for promoting cooperation with foreign nations.

HIROBUMI ITO (1841-1909)
A Choshu Samurai, Hirobumi was the first prime minister of modern Japan and drafted the Meiji Constitution of 1889. He was assassinated in 1909.

EMPEROR HIROHITO (1901-1989)
Succeeding his father, Yoshihito, in 1926, Hirohito reigned for 19 years virtually as a god, but after World War II renounced all claim to divine status.

HIDEKI TOJO (1884-1948)
Tojo was the prime minister who ordered the attack on Pearl Harbor in December 1941. Also Japan's minister for war, he was tried and executed for war crimes.

THE EMPEROR

Having little political power, the Japanese emperor is seen more as the symbol of the state and the unity of the people. This was not always the case. The former emperor, Hirohito, was the longest-reigning emperor, serving 62 years, as well as the longest-living at 87 years, in Japanese history. Although stripped of his power following World War II, he was permitted to remain emperor as a figurehead, denied the sovereignty enjoyed by Japan's imperial family for so long. Before the surrender in August 1945, the Japanese people were forbidden to look at the emperor, who was believed to be divine, but following the armistice, leaders of the occupation forces paraded Hirohito in front of his people, ordering them to raise their eyes and look at the emperor for the first time, reinforcing the message that the emperor was now to be treated as a man, not a god. As a consequence of the surrender and under the new democratic constitution, the emperor now serves a strictly ceremonial role.

He is responsible for appointing the prime minister and the chief justice of the Supreme Court, but only after their selection by the Diet. He holds state dinners for visiting dignitaries, convokes the Diet, and awards honors on the advice of the Diet.

The current emperor, Akihito, took the throne on the death of his father, Hirohito in 1989. He was crowned in traditional fashion in a short silent ceremony, during which he was handed the mirror, sword, and jewel of the throne. Akihito's oldest child, Crown Prince Naruhito, is first in line to succeed as emperor. Current Imperial House law permits only the succession of the male offspring of the emperor, preventing Crown Prince Naruhito's eldest child, a daughter, from taking the throne.

THE CABINET OF JAPAN

The Cabinet originally consisted of 10 ministers of state, including the prime minister. With the new constitution and Cabinet Law of 1947, the number was increased to 16 excluding the prime minister. By 1974, amendments permitted a maximum of 20 ministers, but in 2001, this was reduced to a maximum of 14 ministers with provision for three more in circumstances of special need.

FINANCE
Responsible for implementing and monitoring the Japanese government's budget, setting and collecting tariffs and duties with regards trade, issuing new currency, determining income tax levels, monitoring the domestic economy, securities, and exchanges.

JUSTICE
Deals with all legal matters, civil and criminal, from the prosecution of cases to the correction and rehabilitation of criminals. Additional responsibilities include immigration and naturalization laws, and laws relating to real estate and e-commerce.

HEALTH, LABOR, & WELFARE
Concerned with all health- and labor-related issues, including food safety and inspection standards, hospitals, pharmaceuticals, labor standards, workers' compensation, employment security, pensions, social welfare, war victims, the elderly, and people with disabilities.

ECONOMY, TRADE, & INDUSTRY
Oversees economic and industrial policy, concentrates on structural reform and economic growth, promotes entrepreneurship, responsible for manufacturing, trade, natural resources and energy, nuclear safety, and mine safety. Implements information policies.

KEY EMPERORS OF JAPAN

Since Jimmu, the first emperor, who ruled from 660 to 582 B.C., there have been 125 emperors. Of these, eight have been women. The last empress permitted to rule held the throne from 592-628 A.D. The throne is now only handed from father to son.

EMPEROR KOMEI
1847-1866 (not pictured)
The 121st emperor and the last to rule Japan before the beginning of the modern era, Komei was a virtually powerless leader while Japan was dominated by the Shogunate of the Tokugawa family, which had ruled since 1603. It was during Komei's rule, in 1854, that Commander Perry forced Japan to sign the Treaty of Kanagawa, finally opening Japan's borders to the outside world.

EMPEROR MEIJI 1866-1912
Crowned in 1868, Prince Mutsuhito called himself Meiji meaning "enlightened ruler". He was the 122nd emperor and first to gain full sovereignty, after the last Shogunate.

EMPEROR HIROHITO
1926-1989
Hirohito, whose reign was called "Showa" or period of enlightened peace, assumed his duties in 1926, and was crowned the 124th emperor in 1928. He is said to have straddled two eras—the first as a sovereign ruler, the second as a mortal ruler stripped of his sovereignty following the Japanese surrender in 1945. Although opposed to war with China in 1937 and later with the Allies, he was required by the Tojo government to declare war and give ritual sanction to it.

EMPEROR AKIHITO 1989-
Akihito's reign as the 125th emperor is called "Heisei", meaning "the achievement of complete peace." In 1959, he became the first heir to the throne to marry a commoner.

JAPAN

PRIME MINISTER'S KANTEI
The official residence and office of the prime minister is located in Tokyo near the former residence used by 42 prime ministers during its 73-year history. The new building was constructed with traditional Japanese materials: paper, wood, stone, glass and clay, and contains reception rooms, the cabinet meeting room, a crisis management center, and two helipads. It was opened on April 22, 2002.

VISITING HEADS OF STATE
Members of the G7 meet at Akasaka Palace in July 1993.

AKASAKA PALACE
Originally built in 1909 as the residence of the crown prince, Akasaka Palace is now the official guesthouse of visiting dignitaries and the venue for meetings with heads of state.

"Each and every politician for his or her part must enhance their awareness in order to gain the trust and confidence of the people." — Prime Minister Koizumi, October 2003

THE PRIME MINISTER

The Japanese prime minister is a member of the Diet and usually the leader of the majority party or a majority coalition. To date, the position has always been held by a male, selected by a resolution of the Diet and officially appointed by the emperor. If the two houses cannot reach agreement on a single candidate, the decision of the House of Representatives always prevails. In practice, the prime minister has almost always been the leader of the Liberal Democratic Party—between 1955 and 1993 all prime ministers selected were members of the party—a conservative party formed in 1955 that maintained control of the House of Representatives throughout that period of time.

The prime minister heads the Cabinet and appoints the ministers, who may be replaced at any time. He represents the Cabinet, submitting bills to the Diet, reporting on national affairs and foreign relations and supervising the administration of the government. He can theoretically have a term of four years, because the House of Representatives is officially elected for a four-year term. In fact, most prime ministers have served much shorter terms—their terms cut short by discontent with their leadership or by a government scandal. Early termination occurs when the House forces a vote of no confidence, requiring the prime minister's resignation, or when the prime minister dissolves the House and calls new elections. Such events occur frequently.

OVERLEAF: THE EMPEROR'S BIRTHDAY
Tenno Tanjobi, the emperor's birthday (December 23), is a national holiday in Japan. The public are allowed to enter the grounds of the Imperial Palace and the emperor and empress appear on a balcony (behind bulletproof glass) to greet the crowds.

ENVIRONMENT
Responsible for all environmental issues including water, noise pollution, energy efficiency, waste, soil preservation, biodiversity, and the country's national parks; also commissions studies on major concerns such as the ozone layer and climate change.

PUBLIC MANAGEMENT, HOME AFFAIRS, POSTS & TELECOMMUNICATIONS
Has responsibility for local administration structures, local elections, fire and disaster prevention, the civil service, and the postal and telecommunications service.

FOREIGN AFFAIRS
Charged with diplomatic and foreign policy including human rights and terrorism prevention, consular and migration affairs; overseas public relations and foreign aid, economic affairs including commerce and navigation; treaties and the arrangement of cultural exchanges.

AGRICULTURE, FORESTRY, & FISHERIES
Responsible for all legislation regarding food and agriculture, including food-labeling, whaling, paddy-field farming, and rural development initiatives; funds recreation and protection of cultural heritage; encourages biotechnology.

LAND, INFRASTRUCTURE, & TRANSPORTATION
Development of public works infrastructure; meteorology, transportation-related departments, including civil aviation, ports and harbors, department of motor vehicles and road development, government buildings.

EDUCATION, CULTURE, SPORTS, SCIENCE & TECHNOLOGY
Responsible for elementary and secondary education, higher education and lifelong learning, and sports and youth affairs; promotes the learning of English; encourages scientific and technological research and development.

KEY PRIME MINISTERS
From the establishment of the position of prime minister in 1885—and the appointment of Hirobumi Ito as the first prime minister—to the present day, there have been 69 prime ministers of Japan. Of these, 28 have held office since World War II.

SHIGERU YOSHIDA
1946-1947, 1948-1949, 1949-1952, 1952-1953, 1953-1954

Appointed as Japan's 45th prime minister in 1946, Yoshida served four further terms in the office. He was the founder of the Liberal Party. It was Yoshida who signed the first postwar treaties with the United States regarding security

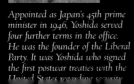

ICHIRO HATOYAMA
1954-1955, 1955-1955, 1955-1956

Serving as the 52nd through 54th prime minister, Hatoyama founded the Liberal Democratic Party, which has provided the majority of postwar prime ministers. He led Japan to becoming a member of the United

EISAKU SATO
1964-1967, 1967-1970, 1970-1972

Nobel Peace Prize winner and 61st through 63rd prime minister, Sato focused on Japan's foreign policy. He was known and admired for his opposition to nuclear war and for his participation in the nonproliferation

TAKEO FUKUDA
1976-1978

During his two-year tenure as the 67th prime minister, Fukuda signed a friendship treaty with China. His administration imposed aggressive fiscal policies to stimulate the economy

LEGISLATIVE BRANCH

Aerial view of the Diet building

QUESTION-TIME DEBATE
Keizo Obuchi (prime minister from 1998 to 2000) in debate with the leader of the SDPJ in the House of Councillors, November 1999.

CHAMBER OF THE HOUSE OF COUNCILLORS
Members enter the house through an entrance in the north wing of the Diet building. The Imperial Throne of Japan's emperor sits in the center of the dais at the front of the chamber.

THE DIET

Japan has a bicameral legislature, called the Kokkai or Diet. Its right to select the prime minister makes it the most powerful arm of government, establishing its supremacy over the various agencies of the executive branch. Government officials, from the prime minister and cabinet members downwards, must appear when summoned by the Diet and answer questions from its investigative committees. The Diet is responsible for lawmaking and approval of the budget as well as having the right to impeach judges and amend the constitution. Generally, decisions are made by a majority vote, although a two-thirds majority is required in special cases.

THE HOUSE OF COUNCILLORS

The Diet's upper chamber is called the House of Councillors. Known as the "house of wisdom" and the "house of careful consideration," it is supposed to reflect the views of Japan's citizens. Unlike the House of Representatives, the lower house, it cannot be dissolved by the prime minister, but when the House of Representatives is dissolved, the House of Councillors closes its session at the same time. By influencing or delaying the legislative process, it serves as a check on the lower chamber, but otherwise it has

HOUSE OF COUNCILLORS ADDRESS
Prime Minister Koizumi delivers a speech in February 2002, in which he promised to deliver economic reforms in the hope of avoiding a recession.

limited powers. It may not hold a vote of no confidence in the cabinet.

During the decades prior to World War II, the upper chamber of the Imperial Diet was called the House of Peers and modeled after the British parliament's House of Lords. Its members included appointed relatives of the imperial family and descendants of lords.

Under the post-war constitution, the upper chamber is composed of 252 members who serve fixed terms of six years, with

elections for half of the members every three years. One hundred members are elected by proportional representation in a single nationwide ballot. Instituted in 1982, this proportional representation system was the first major electoral reform under the 1947 constitution. It was intended to reduce the enormous amounts of money candidates were spending on their election campaigns. The change in the electoral system may have achieved its goal, but proportional representation also had the effect of favoring Japan's larger political parties. The other 152 members of the House of Councillors are directly elected from small local districts.

LEGISLATIVE POWERS AND PROCEDURES

APPOINT THE PRIME MINISTER

The prime minister is chosen from among the Diet members by a resolution passed in both houses of the Diet. If the two houses choose different candidates and no compromise can be reached by a conference committee, the House of Representatives' selection becomes prime minister. This occurred for the first time in 1989. The same happens if the House of Councillors fails to make a choice within 10 days (excluding recesses) of the House of Representatives making its choice.

INTRODUCE, DEBATE, AND PASS BILLS

Bills may be introduced by the Cabinet or by either of the houses of the Diet. Important bills are first discussed in a plenary session, then referred to a committee, where they are examined, issues are debated, and amendments are drafted, before taking a vote. Approved bills are presented in a plenary session, debated and voted on, then passed to the other house for approval. The Cabinet presents the bill to the emperor before implementation.

AMEND THE CONSTITUTION

Amendments to the Japanese constitution of 1947 can only be initiated by the Diet. They must receive the support of at least two-thirds of all the members of each house. Once amendments have been proposed, debated, finalized, and voted on in the Diet, they are subsequently submitted to the people in a national referendum. Final ratification of constitutional amendments requires a simple majority of all the votes cast in the referendum.

APPROVE THE BUDGET

The Cabinet first submits the annual budget to the House of Representatives, then to the House of Councillors. When the House of Councillors makes a decision on the budget different from that of the House of Representatives, and when no compromise can be reached by a joint committee of both houses, or when the House of Councillors fails to come to a decision within 30 days, the decision of the House of Representatives becomes the decision of the Diet.

OPENING THE DIET
Emperor Akihito delivers the opening oath for a special session of the Diet in July 2000.

THE HOUSE OF REPRESENTATIVES

The constitution gives the House of Representatives "preeminence over the House of Councillors." Its powers include enacting laws, passing the budget, approving treaties, and designating the prime minister. In prewar Japan, the emperor selected the prime minister, making the cabinet responsible to the monarchy. With the power of choosing the prime minister now in the hands of the Diet, the government answers today to the legislative branch. If the Diet's two chambers disagree on the selection of a prime minister, the choice of the House of Representatives prevails. Bills passed by the House of Representatives but rejected by the House of Councillors within the 60 days allowed may still become law if the House of Representatives passes them a second time by a two-thirds majority.

The ability to hold a vote of no confidence in the cabinet is one of the House of Representatives' most significant powers. The cabinet is required to resign as a bloc if it receives a vote of no confidence, unless the prime minister dissolves the House of Representatives and asks Japanese voters to

express their faith in the government in a new election of the lower chamber.

The 480 members of the House of Representatives are elected from the nation's 47 local prefectures. Three hundred are elected from single-seat constituencies; the other 180 are elected on the basis of proportional representation from 11 large electoral regions. Theoretically, members are elected to a four-year term. However, the members of the legislative body have served only one full term since the establishment of the modern-day Diet. The average duration for the terms of representatives in postwar Japan is about two and a half years.

Early elections are common because the prime minister has the power to call them at any time, in a fashion similar to the British parliamentary system. Under certain circumstances, the prime minister is constitutionally required to call elections. Typically, if public opinion polls indicate that the majority party in the lower house has high approval ratings, the prime minister will call for "snap elections" in order to increase the party's majority in the House. This often-used tactic was one of the chief reasons the Liberal Democratic Party managed to remain in control of Japan's parliament for 38 years.

The Diet convenes in January each year in an ordinary session for 150 days to vote on the annual budget and other bills. The Diet may also meet in extraordinary sessions, special sessions, and emergency sessions depending on the circumstances. The Japanese emperor delivers the oath at the opening of all types of official parliamentary sessions.

OPENING OF THE FIRST DIET
The first meeting of the Japanese parliament was held in 1890—Emperor Meiji is shown presiding over the occasion.

THE DIET BUILDING
Located in Tokyo, the four-story structure with its 215-foot (65.45-meter) tower, took 16 years to build—from 1920 to 1936. It holds the house chambers, committee rooms, cabinet rooms, and a room used exclusively by the emperor when he is in attendance.

CHAMBER OF THE HOUSE OF REPRESENTATIVES
The speaker of the House has center stage facing the members' seats. Alongside his chair is a row reserved for the ministers of state. Members sit in blocks representing their political parties.

IMPEACH JUDGES

If a judge stands accused of negligence, corruption, or any other crime, the Diet establishes a special court of impeachment from among the members of the House of Representatives and the House of Councillors. In practice such a court is hardly ever required because the Japanese judicial system is sufficiently transparent and the public have faith in the integrity of judges. Corruption charges against members of the Diet and government officials are far more common.

FORCE RE-ELECTION OF THE CABINET THROUGH A VOTE OF NO CONFIDENCE

If the House of Representatives passes a resolution of no confidence or rejects a confidence resolution, the Cabinet must resign unless the prime minister dissolves the House of Representatives within 10 days. A member of the house initiates a vote of no confidence by drafting a resolution with the reasons for it attached, securing the signatures of at least 50 supporters, and submitting it to the speaker.

DECIDE ON TREATIES

Treaties are considered first by the House of Representatives. When the House of Councillors differs on the decision reached by the House of Representatives, a joint committee on both houses will attempt to seek a compromise. If this committee cannot reach an agreement on the treaty, or if the House of Councillors does not act within thirty days of receiving the treaty from the other body, the House of Representatives' position prevails.

RESEARCH AND INVESTIGATIONS

The Lower House Legislative Bureau and the National Diet Library Research and Legislation office assist members in conducting research. Each house may hold investigations of government operations and demand the presence and testimony of witnesses and the production of records. Investigations are normally conducted in committee meetings. Both a standing committee and a special committee may investigate government-related matters under their jurisdiction.

JUDICIAL BRANCH

"We believe that no nation is responsible to itself alone, but that laws of political morality are universal; and that obedience to such laws is incumbent upon all nations..." — Preamble from the constitution of Japan

THE SUPREME COURT

Japan's judicial system is based on customary law, civil law, and Anglo-American common law. The constitution of 1947 establishes the Supreme Court as the court of last resort for determining the "constitutionality of any law, order, regulation, or official act" including legislation passed by the Diet. The Supreme Court also has the right of judicial review, but rarely exercises it. The Court consists of 15 justices—14 are selected and appointed by the Cabinet, while the emperor himself appoints the chief justice on the advice of the Cabinet. Every ten years a justice's tenure has to be confirmed by referendum. In practice, the justices are almost always reselected and are allowed to serve until the age of 70. Historically, the Supreme Court has played a very low-key role, generally maintaining the status quo, avoiding controversy or politically loaded issues, and supporting the government. As a result, individual members of the Supreme Court are virtually unknown to the general public.

There is no witness stand in the Grand Bench courtroom of the Supreme Court.

Appeal cases are first heard at one of the three Petty Benches—these are courts presided over by a maximum of five justices. Where an issue of constitutionality or precedent is raised, the case will usually be transferred to the Grand Bench, where it is heard by all 15 justices of the Supreme Court.

DEDICATION OF TOKYO'S NEW SUPREME COURT BUILDING
In November 1949, the Supreme Court building was dedicated in a grand ceremony attended by nearly 1,200 guests. The Chief Justice, Tadahiko Mibuchi, delivered an address.

REGIONAL COURTS

Eight high courts, located in Tokyo, Osaka, Nagoya, Hiroshima, Fukuoka, Sendai, Sapporo, and Takamatsu, handle appeals filed against judgments made in lower courts. There are also district courts and family courts in 50 locations throughout Japan.

Trials normally begin in the district court, but may be appealed to a high court. Decisions are made on the basis of legal statutes. Unlike the United States, where precedent is an important factor, only Supreme Court decisions influence later interpretation of the law. In the high courts and district courts most cases are heard by three judges—or one judge and two subordinates with legal expertise. Summary courts, of which there are 438, are presided over by a single judge. These courts handle civil cases involving claims of up to 900,000 yen, civil conciliations, and minor criminal cases.

For at least two reasons, there are far fewer civil proceedings in Japan than in other democratic countries. Many matters that would typically be resolved in court are settled out of court in Japan through mediation to avoid the embarrassment of airing personal business in public. In addition, the judicial system is inaccessible to most Japanese citizens. The Civil Proceedings Law, which is very antiquated and difficult to understand because of the classical, literary language in which it is written, has been unchanged for 70 years.

Public prosecutors investigate crimes, initiate prosecutions, conduct hearings, and supervise the enforcement of adjudication. There are four types of public prosecutor's offices: Supreme, High, District, and Local Public Prosecutor's Offices, corresponding to the different levels of court. District prosecutors handle cases in both district courts and family courts. The principle of discretionary prosecution gives the prosecutor the sole authority to initiate prosecution. Consequently, the prosecutor may decline to prosecute, even when there is ample evidence of a crime. Members of the public, however, have the right to challenge a public prosecutor's decision not to prosecute. The district courts and their branches throughout the country have Committees for the Inquest of Prosecution. Members of these committees are selected randomly from the electoral register. Each committee has 11 members who are commissioned to determine whether or

LANDMARK CASES	1954	1997		2000

WAR CRIMES
Following World War II, Japanese leaders were tried before the International War Crimes Tribunal in Tokyo. Hideki Tojo, the former prime minister, was among those tried and executed.

ON TRIAL
Defendants facing charges of war crimes stand before the International Bar of Justice.

A VICTORY FOR TRUTH
Historian Saburo Ienaga is shown on August 29, 1997 after winning his case over government censorship.

CENSORSHIP
The Supreme Court awarded damages to Saburo Ienaga, the author of a history textbook, whose description of Japanese involvement in World War II was altered by the government to remove mention of Japanese atrocities.

APPEAL DISMISSED
Tomasa Salinog, 71, one of the appellants in the sex slavery case awaits the verdict of the court.

SEX SLAVERY
In 2000, eighty Filipino women appealed a court ruling absolving the government of any obligation to women forced into sex slavery by the Japanese army during World War II. The court up-held the initial ruling, rejecting their appeal and refusing damages of $9 million.

JAPAN

SUPREME COURT JUSTICES
In the Grand Bench courtroom 15 justices sit facing the defendants, plaintiffs, and prosecutors. The Nishijin tapestries and slits in the granite walls prevent echoing.

not a public prosecutor's decision not to prosecute is appropriate. The committee is empowered to review records and call witnesses. If non-prosecution is determined to be inappropriate, the prosecutor may issue an indictment, based on the committee's report.

There are no jury trials in Japan, but there is another way in which citizens participate in judicial proceedings. Individuals selected for their reputation, good character, knowledge, and experience, serve as members of civil and family affairs conciliation boards. Their role is to work with judges to resolve civil and family disputes. In addition to drawing up settlement proposals, a large part of the role of these individuals is to persuade the parties to disputes to agree to the proposed settlement terms. There are at least two citizens and one judge involved in conciliation cases.

EXTERIOR OF SUPREME COURT
The white exterior walls of the building are made of granite.

OFFICIAL NAME: JAPAN

Diet

POPULATION: 127.3 MILLION	
CAPITAL: TOKYO	
AREA: 145,882 SQ. MILES (377,835 SQ. KM)	
INDEPENDENCE: 660 B.C.	
CONSTITUTION: 1947	

JAPAN is derived from a Chinese phrase meaning "land of the rising sun", because it lay east of China.

RELIGION: Shinto and Buddhist 76%, Buddhist 16%, Other (including Christian) 8%

OFFICIAL LANGUAGE: Japanese

REGIONS OR PROVINCES: 47 prefectures

DEPENDENT TERRITORIES: None

MEDIA: No political censorship exists in national media

Newspapers: There are 122 daily newspapers

TV: 128 services: 1 publicly owned, 127 commercial

Radio: 100 services: 1 publicly owned, 99 commercial

SUFFRAGE: 20 years of age; universal

LEGAL SYSTEM: American-European legal traditions; accepts ICJ jurisdiction

ETHNIC GROUPS:
Other (mainly Korean) 1%
Japanese 99%

WORLD ORGANIZATIONS: AfDB, APEC, ARF (dialogue partner), AsDB, ASEAN (dialogue partner), Australia Group, BIS, CCC, CE (observer), CERN (observer), CP, EBRD, ESCAP, FAO, G- 5, G- 7, G-8, G-10, IADB, IAEA, IBRD, ICAO, ICC, ICFTU, ICRM, IDA, IEA, IFAD, IFC, IFRCS, IHO, ILO, IMF, IMO, Interpol, IOC, IOM, ISO, ITU, NAM (guest), NEA, NSG, OAS (observer), OECD, OPCW, OSCE (partner), PCA, UN, UNCTAD, UNDOF, UNESCO, UNHCR, UNIDO, UNITAR, UNMOVIC, UNRWA, UNU, UPU, WCL, WFTU, WHO, WIPO, WMO, WToO, WTrO, ZC

POLITICAL PARTIES: LDP—Liberal Democratic Party, DPJ—Democratic Party of Japan, NK—New Komeito, LP—Liberal Party, JPC—Japan Communist Party, SDPJ—Social Democratic Party of Japan

NATIONAL ECONOMICS

WORLD GNP RANKING: 2nd

GNP PER CAPITA: $35,620

INFLATION: -0.6%

BALANCE OF PAYMENTS (BALANCE OF TRADE): $117 billion

EXCHANGE RATES / U.S. DLR.: U.S. DLR: 114.20-131.06 YEN

OFFICIAL CURRENCY: YEN

GOVERNMENT SPENDING (% OF GDP)

DEFENSE 1%	
EDUCATION 3.5%	
HEALTH 5.7%	

0   5   10   15

AERIAL VIEW OF THE SUPREME COURT
Completed in 1974, Japan's Supreme Court building in Tokyo was the work of 17 architects headed by Shinichi Okada.

2002

1996-2003

ELECTRONIC I.D. CARDS
The court heard lawsuits against the government's computerized national registry called Juki Net, which it was feared would infringe privacy rights.

LAND LEASES
In a 1996 decision, the court upheld a lower court ruling forcing Okinawa landowners to lease land to the US military. Refusals to comply with the ruling have led to further cases.

PROTESTS AGAINST JUKI NET
Rallies were held throughout the hearings, but despite its unpopularity, the system is now up and running.

OKINAWA PROTEST
A protesting landowner wears a headband with the motto "Life is a treasure."

NUMBER OF CONFLICTS OVER LAST 25 YEARS

	1	2-5	5+
Violent changes in government	○	○	○
Civil wars	○	○	○
International wars	○	○	○
Foreign intervention	○	○	○

NOTABLE WARS AND INSURGENCIES: None

- Article 9 of the constitution renounces war.
- Self-Defense Forces are increasingly active: North Korean naval incursions are violently repelled, and parliament has discussed how to respond to attack.

GERMANY

AT THE TIME OF THE ROMAN EMPIRE the German-speaking tribes inhabited an area similar to that of present-day Germany. In the Middle Ages, however, this was divided into many small principalities and it was not until 1871 that the dominant kingdom of Prussia was able to create a united Germany.

GERMAN FLAG
Adopted on May 9, 1949 the German flag is known as the "Schwarz-Rot-Gold", (Black-Red-Gold).

As the power of Rome waned, Germanic tribes, such as the Goths, Franks, Lombards and Saxons took control of large portions of its crumbling empire. In the early 9th century the Franks under Charlemagne carved out an empire that stretched from the Pyrenees to the North Sea and the Baltic to northern Italy. Following Charlemagne's death, his empire was divided, but the small states of the German part continued to owe feudal allegiance to a

BRANDENBURG GATE STATUE
The gate, crowned by a statue of the Goddess of Peace, stood close to the old dividing line between East and West Berlin. It is now a symbol of reunification.

German king. A number of dynasties vied for control of Germany, but they in turn had to contend with the power of the medieval popes, who claimed ultimate authority over the so-called Holy Roman Empire. The reign of Frederick Barbarossa, who died in 1190 while leading the Third Crusade, was one of almost continuous conflict with the papacy.

German territory meanwhile expanded to the east, as German settlers took over Slav and Baltic lands, and the empire evolved a system of Electors, German princes and bishops, who chose their "emperor". In time the Austrian Hapsburgs became hereditary holders of the title, but their authority was limited outside their own lands. Following the Reformation, sparked off by Martin Luther in 1517, most of northern Germany

HOW THE GOVE

✦ LEGISLATIVE BRANCH

PARLIAMENT

The two houses of parliament have very different functions. The Bundestag is a national legislative assembly, while the Bundesrat represents the interests of Germany's federal states.

▸ **BUNDESRAT**
The upper house of Germany's parliament is the Bundesrat (Federal Council). Its 69 representatives are nominated by the governments of the 16 states (Länder), each Land being represented by between 3 and 6 members.

BUNDESRAT
The former Reichstag building in Berlin is now home to the Bundesrat.

▸ **BUNDESTAG**
The lower house of the German parliament is the Bundestag (Federal Diet or Assembly), with approximately 662 members elected (some directly, some by proportional representation) to a term of four years. The lower house is the main legislative body, responsible for establishing and amending the laws. It also elects the chancellor for a four-year term.

✦ EXECUTIVE BRANCH

CHANCELLOR

The chancellor serves as the head of government and is the most powerful official in Germany. Elected by the members of the Bundestag for a term of four years, he functions as prime minister in the cabinet, makes recommendations to the president on the appointment and dismissal of ministers, determines number of ministers and structure of the cabinet, and carries out domestic policy. The Federal Chancellery supports the chancellor in the performance of his duties, keeping him informed of current issues concerning politics in general and the work of the individual Federal Ministries.

OFFICIAL PRESIDENTIAL RESIDENCE
The Schloss Bellevue, home of the German president, is located in the center of Berlin.

⚖ **REGIONAL GOVERNMENTS**
▸ 16 states or Länder
▸ Each state has an elected legislature (Landtag)
▸ Legislature responsible for education and policing

SIEGESSÄULE
The gold statue atop Berlin's victory column faces France, rather insensitively commemorating Prussia's victory in the Franco-Prussian War of 1870.

"I have been underestimated for decades. I've done very well that way."
— Helmut Kohl, German Chancellor (January 1987)

HELMUT KOHL
Elected West German chancellor in 1982, Kohl presided over the fall of the Berlin Wall in November 1989 and German reunification in 1990. He served until 1998.

became Protestant. The devastating Thirty Years' War (1618-48) pitted Catholic and Protestant Germans against each other.

In the mid-19th century two states dominated the German-speaking world—Austria in the south and Prussia in the north. By the 1860s Prussia was the greatest military power in Europe, its foreign policy skillfully directed by Otto von Bismarck, the "iron chancellor." After defeating Austria in 1866, then France in 1870, Prussia persuaded the smaller German states to become part of Prussian-led German Empire.

The new Germany's militarism led it into the disastrous World War of 1914-1918. The Treaty of Versailles in 1919 imposed harsh terms on the defeated Germany, causing a severe economic crisis. The Weimar Republic, which replaced the German Empire, proved ineffective and disaffected Germans embraced the fanaticism of Adolf Hitler, who became chancellor in 1933. Parliamentary rule was abandoned for a single-party Nazi state and

in 1939, Hitler plunged Germany into another war that would end in humiliating defeat. At the end of World War II the victorious Allies divided Germany and Berlin into four zones of occupation—American, British, French, and Soviet. In 1949, the United States, Britain, and France consolidated their zones into the free and autonomous Federal Republic of Germany (West Germany), while the Soviet zone became the German Democratic Republic (East Germany) under communist rule.

In 1961, the Berlin Wall was built, separating the eastern and western sectors of the city. It came to symbolize the Cold War and the division of Germany. In the late 1980s, the Soviet Union under Mikhail Gorbachev began a new period of "glasnost" (openness) and Soviet influence in East Germany waned. In 1989, the East Germans peacefully ousted the communist government and the Berlin Wall came down. On October 3, 1990, East and West Germany were reunited as the Federal Republic of Germany.

...NMENT WORKS

PRESIDENT

Serving as the chief of state, the president is elected to a five-year term by the Federal Convention and may be re-elected once. The Federal Convention consists of all members of the Bundestag and an equal number of members from the Landtage (state legislatures). The president's duties are largely ceremonial—they include signing all treaties and bills and representing the country abroad.

▶ **CABINET**
Composed of the chancellor and federal ministers who are appointed by the president. Ministers operate autonomously within prescribed guidelines; chancellor and ministers decide jointly on matters of state.

⚖️ JUDICIAL BRANCH

SUPREME COURT

The Federal Constitutional Court is Germany's Supreme Court. Its role is essentially "Guardian of the Constitution." There are 16 judges divided between two Senates, each holding office for a non-renewable period of 12 years. Half the judges are elected by the Bundestag and half by the Bundesrat, in both cases by a two-thirds majority.

HIGH COURT BUILDING
The Constitutional Court meets in the High Court, located in Karlsruhe.

▶ **CONSTITUTIONAL COURT**
Cases coming before the Constitutional Court may be heard by one of its two Senates, or for important cases, by the Court in plenary session. Its main jurisdictional areas include disputes between federal agencies, between the states and federation, the verifying of the constitutionality of laws and regulations, hearing complaints of unconstitutionality and indictments against the president or judges.

ELECTORAL SYSTEM FOR THE BUNDESTAG
Roughly half the delegates are directly elected to represent a particular district, the other half are elected by proportional representation. Each voter casts two ballots: the first for a candidate for the district, the second for a political party. Each party's share of these second votes determines how many seats it is awarded by proportional representation.

EXECUTIVE BRANCH

GUSTAV HEINEMANN (1899-1976)
Heinemann succeeded Heinrich Lübke as president of the Federal Republic of Germany from 1969 to 1974 and led Germany to membership of the United Nations. In 1972, East and West Germany signed the Basic Treaty, regularizing relations.

ADOLF HITLER (1889-1945)
Hitler, founder of the Nazi party and chancellor from 1933, later taking the title Führer (leader). His invasion of Poland in 1939 started World War II.

KONRAD ADENAUER (1876-1967)
Adenauer was Christian Democrat chancellor from 1949 to 1963. He led postwar rebuilding of West Germany and was a strong supporter of US anti-communist policies.

HELMUT KOHL (1930-)
Kohl is considered by many to be the founding father of modern Germany. Chancellor from 1982 to 1998, he launched a new era with reunification in 1990.

THE CHANCELLOR

Although a dual executive exists, it is the powerful position of federal chancellor (Bundeskanzler)—in his capacity as head of the government—that directs the executive branch and determines the general guidelines of government policy. Usually the leader of the majority party (sometimes a coalition), he is nominated by the president. His authority, although bestowed by the Basic Law, also derives from his election by the majority of all elected members in the Bundestag. He in turn decides the number and composition of his ministers, and their duties. Subsequently,

all ministers in the cabinet report directly to him. Most significantly, the chancellor cannot be dismissed by a vote of no confidence.

During the German Empire of 1871, an Imperial Chancellor (Reichskanzler) was appointed by the Emperor to lead the government, but was not considered responsible to the elected Parliament. By 1918, the constitution had been amended and with the implementation of the Weimar Republic, the Imperial Chancellor became both elected by and responsible to the Parliament itself. During the Nazi era, Adolf Hitler transformed the office into one that

combined the duties of the president and the chancellor, so it was only after World War II with the development of the 1949 Grundgesetz (Basic Law) that the position of chancellor took its current form.

Before East and West Germany were unified in 1990, the chancellor resided in Bonn. But the unification treaty moved the national capital back to Berlin, where it had been before the nation was divided at the end of World War II. Today, the chancellor lives in the Bundeskanzleramt (chancellor residency), located in the heart of Berlin next to the Reichstag in the Tiergarten park.

THE CABINET

While the largest cabinet was that of Ludwig Erhard in the 1960s with 22 members, the current cabinet consists of 13 federal ministers. All ministers and the president of the German Federal Bank are appointed by and responsible to the chancellor.

TRANSPORT, BUILDING, & HOUSING
Germany maintains an extensive network of highways and a rail network providing all major cities with a high-speed service. There is also a network of inland waterways.

INTERIOR
Forests cover almost 30 percent of Germany's land, supporting a strong timber industry. Mines yield coal, potash, quartz, clays, and iron ore. Limited amounts of natural gas and petroleum are produced.

HEALTH & SOCIAL SECURITY
Germany's health and sanitary conditions are among the world's best, with a life expectancy of 75 years. Its social welfare system covers almost the entire national population.

FINANCE
Germany, which adopted the Euro as its currency in 2002, maintains a positive trade balance, exporting motor vehicles and parts, industrial machinery, electronics, chemicals, and iron and steel products.

ECONOMICS & LABOR
Germany has a free-market economy based largely on manufacturing and services. Labor is fully unionized with special courts settling employer-employee and disputes among unions.

EDUCATION & RESEARCH
Education is free and compulsory for all Germans six to 18 years old. Germany's many universities include Heidelberg, founded in 1386, and Cologne, founded in 1388.

KEY FEDERAL CHANCELLORS OF GERMANY

Germany's postwar chancellors steered the country through the reconstruction from the rubble of war to the 1990 reunification of Germany as a single nation with a respected place among the world's democracies.

KONRAD ADENAUER
1949-1963
Elected chancellor at age 73, served 14 years; rebuilt Germany after World War II.

LUDWIG ERHARD
1963-1966
Economics minister under Adenauer; helped create Germany's postwar "economic miracle."

KURT GEORGE KIESINGER
1966-1969
Created "grand coalition" government of Christian Democrats and Social Democrats.

WILLY BRANDT
1969-1974
Won the Nobel Peace Prize in 1971 for his "Ostpolitik," relaxing tensions between East and West Germany.

HELMUT SCHMIDT
1974-1982
Continued Brandt's policies; signatory of the Helsinki Accords on security and human rights in 1975.

HELMUT KOHL
1982-1998
Presided over the reunification of Germany in 1990. Leader of center-right CDU party.

GERHARD SCHRÖDER
1998-
Chairman of the SPD, re-elected in 2002 after victory of the Red-Green coalition.

GERMANY

ENTRANCE OF THE CHANCELLERY
The central structure of the chancellery is nine stories high, flanked by two five-story administrative wings.

GERMAN CABINET
The chancellor acts as "prime minister" in cabinet meetings. Key areas of concern are foreign policy, finance, defense, internal affairs, justice, and the economy. Cabinet concerns also include the telephone and postal services.

FEDERAL CHANCELLERY
Designed by Berlin architects Axel Schulte and Charlotte Frank in 1991, the Chancellery is part of a "ribbon" of new government buildings forming a symbolic link between East and West.

"I want a modernized society, but also one in which everyone has the same chances."
— Gerhard Schröder, Chancellor of Germany

EAGLE CREST OF THE EXECUTIVE OFFICE

THE PRESIDENT

The president is elected for a maximum of two five-year terms by an electoral college, which consists of members of the Bundestag and representatives of the state legislatures.

The Basic Law devotes an entire chapter to the role of the president, the "first man of the state" both at home and abroad. The titles "supreme federal notary," "first representative of the state," and "figure of integration" all describe aspects of the role of the president. Although chief of state, the position is considered to be largely ceremonial with duties that include representing Germany in international diplomatic functions, signing treaties and laws, and inviting and receiving foreign diplomats and politicians. As there is no office of vice-president stipulated in the Basic Law, the president of the Bundesrat fills the post in the president's absence.

The president is assisted in his duties by the Office of the Federal President. The Office advises the president on all issues relating to his position, informs him of all problems, whether relating to home or foreign affairs, the economy, society, or culture. It completes preparatory work for decisions by the president and carries out his instructions or forwards them to the appropriate ministry or authority. The Office of the Federal President is divided into three directorates-general: the Central Directorate General with five divisions; the Home Affairs Directorate General with six divisions, and the Foreign Affairs Directorate General with three divisions. Since 1998, the Office of the Federal President has been located near the main official residence of the president in a newly erected administration building at the edge of the English Garden in Berlin.

CONSUMER PROTECTION AND AGRICULTURE
Agriculture is responsible for only about two percent of Germany's gross domestic product but employs about six percent of the labor force.

JUSTICE
All trial and appellate courts in Germany are state courts, while courts of last resort are federal. These include special courts that decide on administrative, labor, social security, and tax matters.

FAMILY AFFAIRS, SENIOR CITIZENS, WOMEN, AND YOUTH
Germany provides benefits to nearly all of its citizens for old age, disability, widowhood, maternity, sickness, work injury, and unemployment.

FOREIGN OFFICE
Since unification in 1990, the country has emerged as a leader among democratic nations not only in Western Europe, but on the world stage through the United Nations and North American Trade Organization.

ENVIRONMENT, NATURE CONSERVATION, AND NUCLEAR SAFETY
The Germans are among the world's most environmentally conscious people with strict anti-pollution controls. Since the environmentalist Green Party became a member of the ruling coalition in 1998, it has influenced governmental decisions: a gradual program of closing existing nuclear power plants was approved in 2001, although waste disposal is still an issue.

DEFENSE
Germany's military consists of an Army, Navy, Air Force, Medical Corps, and Joint Support Service. The Constitutional Court ruled in 1994 that army units could take part in collective defense activities abroad.

ECONOMIC CO-OPERATION AND DEVELOPMENT
Germany is Europe's major industrial power with the world's third strongest economy, but struggles with high welfare costs and rising unemployment.

KEY PRESIDENTS OF THE GERMAN REPUBLIC

There have been 12 presidents in the history of Germany, although only eight of these have been since the development of the Federal Republic. Two people have served as both chancellor and president, and only Adolf Hitler did so concurrently. Representing Germany internationally, the president's powers are limited by the Basic Law.

THEODOR HEUSS
1949-1959
Elected the first president of the German Federal Republic (West Germany), as the nation was rebuilt post WWII.

WALTER SCHEEL
1974-1979
Previously vice-chancellor and foreign minister where he practiced the diplomacy of "rapprochement" with the Soviet Bloc.

KARL CARSTENS
1979-1984
German representative in the Council of Europe. He helped draft the Treaty of Rome (1957), first step on road to European Union.

RICHARD VON WEIZSÄCKER
1984-1994
First to acknowledge the responsibility of the German people for the Holocaust and led reunification.

ROMAN HERZOG
1994-1999
Gave up all claims to territory in Eastern Europe. Proposed amnesty for crimes committed under communist regime in East Germany.

LEGISLATIVE BRANCH

Aerial view of the Reichstag

**EAGLE CREST OF
THE BUNDESTAG**

THE BUNDESTAG

The Bundestag forms
the basis of the country's
democratic government.
It is the lower house of
the bicameral Federal
Assembly; the Bundesrat
is the upper house. The
Bundestag consists of 662 delegates who are
chosen every four years in general elections
or in special by-elections. Of these delegates,
328 are directly elected from individual
constituencies, and 334 are elected through
party lists in each of the 16 states (Länder)
to obtain proportional representation.
Political parties must win at least five
percent of the national vote, or three
constituency seats, to earn representation.
Because of this system, the total number of
seats in the Bundestag may vary slightly.

At its first meeting of each legislative
term, the Bundestag elects a chancellor on
the nomination of the president to head the
national government. The Bundestag also
participates every five years in an electoral
college with representatives of the state
(Länder) legislatures to elect the president,
who serves as head of state.

The Bundestag originates all federal
legislation affecting such areas as foreign
affairs, defense, international trade, customs,
currency, citizenship, postal service and
telecommunications. But its power is checked
by the state parliaments (Landtage), which

THE NEW REICHSTAG DOME
*Recreated after reunification,
the dome is second only to the
Brandenburg Gate as a symbol
a reunited Berlin.*

REICHSTAG
*The Reichstag in Berlin, which houses the German
legislature, was reopened in 1999 after a four-year
renovation by the British architect Sir Norman Foster.
For more than 50 years the seat of the federal
parliament had been in Bonn.*

may pass legislation in response to the
needs of the individual states and may act
in legislative areas not reserved for the
Bundestag by the Basic Law. In addition, the
Bundestag and the state parliaments may pass
concurrent legislation on which they agree.

Each political party in the Bundestag is
organized as a party group (Fraktion). The
size of a Fraktion determines the number of
places its members are assigned on the
various parliamentary standing committees.
The head of the largest Fraktion is named
president of the Bundestag. The four vice-
presidents usually come from the majority

BUNDESTAG
*The Bundestag is Germany's lower house of parliament.
It consists of 662 members elected from all 16 states.*

coalition. This group, along with 23 members
selected according to the size of the party
groups, make up the Council of Elders
(Ältestenrat). This council sets the agenda for
business in the Bundestag and appoints the
chairs of some 20 special committees.

GERMAN POWERS AND PROCEDURES

NATIONAL MANDATE
The Basic Law (Grundgesetz), the Federal
Republic of Germany's constitution, called
upon the people to "achieve in free self-
determination the unity and freedom of
Germany." First adopted in 1949, it mandated
a new and independent democratic system.
With the 1990 Unification Treaty, the German
people were finally reunited in the single state
that had been denied them after World War II.

CONSTITUTIONAL MATTERS
The Bundesrat is responsible for the election of many senior posts,
including half of the members of the Constitutional Court and the
Federal Prosecutor. The Bundesrat has the right to initiate
proceedings in the Constitutional Court and may even state its
view on current proceedings before the court.

OLD IMPERIAL PARLIAMENT BUILDING
*Members attending a Reichstag meeting in
1889. The new Reichstag building was not
completed until 1894, 23 years after the
birth of the German Empire in 1871.*

GERMANY

ADDRESS TO BUNDESTAG
The German flag and eagle adorn the chamber of the Bundestag, which assembles in the Reichstag for legislative sessions.

power to veto legislation that affects the powers of the states. All constitutional changes must be approved by a two-thirds majority in both houses.

The Bundesrat has a total of 69 seats, six each from Bavaria, Baden-Württemberg, Lower Saxony, and North Rhine-Westphalia. Four seats each are from Berlin, Brandenburg, Hesse, Rhineland-Palatinate, Saxony, Saxony-Anhalt, Schleswig-Holstein, and Thuringia. Three seats each are held by the smallest states, Bremen, Hamburg, Mecklenburg-West Pomerania, and the Saarland. Votes of all the delegates from any one state must be cast en bloc.

The consent of the Bundesrat is necessary for certain legislative matters coming from the Bundestag, in particular bills that affect finance and administration or in which questions of the Basic Law are involved. While it may reject legislation proposed by the Bundestag, about 90 percent of all federal legislation is passed without opposition from the Bundesrat. To resolve differences that do arise between the two houses, compromises are reached in a conciliation committee made up of equal numbers of members from both houses.

THE BUNDESRAT

The upper house of the Federal Assembly is the Bundesrat (Federal Council). Its members are appointed by the governments of the 16 states (Länder), each state sending from three to six

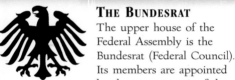

EAGLE CREST OF THE BUNDESRAT

members, depending on the size of its population. The delegations are required to follow the instructions of their state governments; thus, it is in the Bundesrat that the states exercise authority to protect their rights and prerogatives. The Bundesrat has the

BUNDESRAT
Germany's upper legislative house has 69 delegates representing all 16 of the state governments, or Landtage.

THE REICHSTAG UNDER THE NAZIS
Shortly after the Reichstag fire in 1933, the Nazis passed legislation outlawing all other political parties and the Reichstag was used for Nazi rallies.

The Reichstag Then and Now

Near Berlin's Tiergarten Park and the famous Brandenburg Gate, the Reichstag was built to plans by Paul Wallot and opened in 1894 as the Parliament building for a united Germany. On November 9, 1918, Phillip Scheidemann proclaimed a new republic from the ledge of a window in the Reichstag.

The Nazis are thought to have set fire to the building in February 1933 and subsequently blamed the fire on the communists. This gave the Nazis an excuse to accuse the communists of trying to overthrow the government and start a nationwide crackdown. The dome of the building was badly damaged by a bomb in 1945 and was removed in 1954.

After the war, Germany was divided into East and West Germany with two capitals and the West German parliament was moved to Bonn. With reunification in 1990 however, it was proposed that parliament be moved back to Berlin and the Reichstag once again adopted as the Parliament building. This was not a universally accepted decision as the name Reichstag is often associated with Hitler's Third Reich, but following reunification it was a place where people gathered to celebrate and it was recognized central to the spirit of the newly united Germany.

Remodeled in 1994-99 to a design by the British architect, Sir Norman Foster, the Reichstag has been the seat of the Bundestag since 1999 and has become a symbol of the new federal capital.

FOREIGN POLICY
When any international treaties are proposed that will affect Germany's system of government, especially the powers of the individual federal states, they require the consent of the Bundesrat. This is especially true of EU treaties, such as the Maastricht Treaty of 1992, which propose greater political and economic integration of the member states.

HISTORIC ADDRESS TO THE BUNDESTAG
French President Jacques Chirac delivers a speech to the Bundestag on June 27, 2000 proposing the strengthening of European Union ties.

BUNDESTAG DEBATES
Plenary sittings consist of a series of debates on political decisions that have been prepared in the parliamentary groups. Debates on these decisions form the core of the sittings, but in the case of undisputed decisions the Council of Elders may choose not to debate the resolution but to take a vote immediately. These decisions once adopted form the basis of federal laws.

INITIATION OF LEGISLATION
The Federal Government, the Bundesrat and members of the Bundestag can all initiate legislation. In practice, it is the Federal Government that introduces nearly two-thirds of all bills. Since the government is elected by the the majority in the Bundestag, it is generally unnecessary for individual members to initiate legislation directly. Even so, this does not ensure that the majority in the Bundestag automatically approves all legislation proposed by the government.

JUDICIAL BRANCH

"The Basic Law has proved its worth. It is the most liberal constitution the Germans have ever had..." — Roman Herzog, president 1994-1999

SYMBOL OF JUSTICE
This bronze figure of Blind Justice with scales and sword adorns Frankfurt's Fountain of Justice.

EAGLE CREST OF JUDICIAL BRANCH

THE FEDERAL CONSTITUTIONAL COURT

The Basic Law of 1949 established the Federal Constitutional Court (Bundesvefassungsgericht) as the highest court in Germany's judicial system. It consists of 16 judges, eight of whom are appointed by the lower house of the Federal Assembly, the Bundestag, and eight by the upper house, the Bundesrat. Each judge serves a term of 12 years, which may not be renewed. Once appointed, a judge may be removed only by the court itself. The seat of the court is in Karlsruhe in the state of Baden-Württemberg.

Two panels, called "senates," of eight judges each have their own chief justice. One senate reviews federal legislation to make sure it is constitutional and does not infringe on basic rights. The other settles disagreements among government agencies over interpretation of the constitution. All of its decisions require a two-thirds majority of participating judges. The Constitutional Court hears only cases involving questions of constitutionality and its rulings are final. A separate court, the Federal Court of Justice is responsible for hearing final appeals not related to constitutional issues.

While lower courts in Germany are responsible for seeing that legislation in their jurisdictions is constitutional,

THE FEDERAL CONSTITUTIONAL COURT
The Federal Constitutional Court in Karlsruhe is Germany's Supreme Court, hearing complaints about breaches of the constitution.

only the Constitutional Court has the ultimate task of constitutional oversight for the entire country. Because of this role, and because it hears complaints from citizens nationwide who believe their rights under the Basic Law may have been violated, the Constitutional Court is regarded as the chief bulwark of the rule of law in Germany.

THE FEDERAL COURT OF JUSTICE

Germany's highest court of appeal is the Federal Court of Justice (Bundesgerichtshof), also located in Karlsruhe. It hears appeals against findings in the state courts, but deals only with points of law and procedure; it does not hear any new evidence. German law is based on Roman Law and is contained in a series of detailed codes, the principal ones being the Civil Code, the Code of Civil Procedure, the Commercial Code, the Penal Code, and the Code of Criminal Procedure.

The Federal Court of Justice makes sure that the law is being applied correctly and consistently throughout the sixteen states of the Federal Republic.

OTHER FEDERAL COURTS

A number of specialized courts exist for citizens seeking redress for government actions they consider unfair or harmful in cases involving administrative, labor, social, and financial law. These issues are normally dealt with at local or state level, but it is possible to appeal to the higher authority of a Federal Court. These courts are located in various cities around Germany: the Federal Administrative Court is in Berlin, the Federal Labor Court has seats in Kassel and Erfurt, the Federal Social Court is in Kassel, and the Federal Financial Court in Munich. Each court is designed to give specialized

---

LANDMARK CASES

THE CREATION OF A STATE

In a 1951 referendum the three southwestern states of Württemberg-Baden, Württemberg-Hohenzollern, and Baden chose to unite to form Baden-Württemberg. The new state was constituted on April 25, 1952.

1982 DISSOLUTION
Kohl forced premature dissolution of the Bundestag in 1982.

PARLIAMENTARY DISSOLUTION

The Basic Law allows for the dissolution of parliament in exceptional cases. In 1972, Chancellor Willy Brandt forced a premature dissolution of the Bundestag, as did Chancellor Kohl in December 1982. Kohl lost a no-confidence vote, thus forcing elections, in which his coalition won a larger majority.

THE FEDERAL CONSTITUTIONAL COURT
Judges discuss the participation of German troops in the conflict in Somalia in the late 1990s.

TROOPS IN SOMALIA

The Federal Constitutional Court ruled that Germany could participate militarily as NATO units carrying out a UN Security Council resolution, and could be present on a UN peacekeeping mission. However, such missions still need to be approved by the Bundestag.

DECKERT CASE

The Supreme Court declared denial of the historical facts of the Holocaust to be a serious crime, when it found the extremist Günter Deckert guilty of the charges brought against him. It also found that political conviction was not a mitigating circumstance in such court cases.

GERMANY

OFFICIAL NAME: FEDERAL REPUBLIC OF GERMANY

attention to complaints in its specific area of law. For example, complaints about the safety of nuclear power plants are heard by the administrative courts, while disputes over working conditions will be heard by the labor courts. Matters relating to unemployment and social security payments go before the social courts, while complaints about tax and related issues are heard by the financial courts. There is also a Federal Patents Court located in Munich.

STATE AND LOCAL COURTS

Even though it is federal law that establishes the court system nationwide, it is one of the principles of the Basic Law that the federal government does not intrude unnecessarily on the rights of the states and the citizenry.

Most German courts fall under the jurisdiction of the states, with only the highest courts operating at the federal level. Minor criminal and civil cases are heard by local courts, which generally have just a single judge. At the next level up is the state court (Landesgericht), in which judges who specialize in different areas of the law, hear major civil and criminal cases. At the third level are the state appellate courts. These are the final courts of appeal for cases originally heard in the local courts. These courts, like the state courts, have panels of judges specialized in specific areas of the law.

In Germany, those who embark on a legal career must decide if they want to be a lawyer or a judge. Both aspiring lawyers and judges must first go to law school, pass an examination, then serve several years in legal training. After that training period, they must pass another examination, and at this point decide whether to become a lawyer or a judge. Those who choose to be a judge then undergo a considerable period of further training before they are fully qualified.

THE JUSTICES
Sixteen justices make up the Federal Constitutional Court, Germany's highest and most important judicial body. They are chosen by the Bundestag and Bundesrat and serve 12-year terms. Decisions require a two-thirds majority.

NEO-NAZI NPD RULING
In March 2003, the Federal Constitutional Court ruled not to uphold the government's request to outlaw the extreme right-wing National Democratic Party. The reason given was that government informants planted inside the party had acted as agents provocateurs in order to discredit it.

OPPOSITION TO THE NPD
Anti-NPD demonstrators protest as the court grapples with the issue.

POPULATION: 82 MILLION	
CAPITAL: BERLIN	
AREA: 137,846 SQ. MILES (357,021 SQ. KM)	
INDEPENDENCE: 1871	
CONSTITUTION: 1949	

GERMANY was called Germania by the Romans. Deutschland (the Germans' own word for the country) derives from an old Teutonic word for "people."

RELIGION: Protestant 34%, Roman Catholic 33%, Muslim 3%, Other and non-religious 30%

OFFICIAL LANGUAGE: German

REGIONS OR PROVINCES: 16 states

DEPENDENT TERRITORIES: None

MEDIA: No political censorship exists

NEWSPAPERS: There are 375 daily newspapers

TV: 3 public service and several independent commercial channels. TV is supervised by the political parties to ensure a balance of views

RADIO: 13 public and several independent networks

SUFFRAGE: 18 years of age; universal

LEGAL SYSTEM: Civil law; no ICJ jurisdiction

ETHNIC GROUPS:
- German 92%
- Other European 3%
- Turkish 2%
- Other 3%

WORLD ORGANIZATIONS: AfDB, AsDB, Australia Group, BDEAC, BIS, CBSS, CCC, CDB, CE, CERN, EAPC, EBRD, ECE, EIB, EMU, ESA, EU, FAO, G- 5, G- 7, G- 8, G-10, IADB, IAEA, IBRD, ICAO, ICC, ICFTU, ICRM, IDA, IEA, IFAD, IFC, IFRCS, IHO, ILO, IMF, IMO, Interpol, IOC, IOM, ISO, ITU, MONUC, NAM (guest), NATO, NEA, NSG, OAS (observer), OECD, OPCW, OSCE, PCA, UN, UNCTAD, UNESCO, UNHCR, UNIDO, UNIKOM, UNMIBH, UNMIK, UNMOVIC, UNOMIG, UPU, WADB (nonregional), WEU, WHO, WIPO, WMO, WToO, WTrO, ZC

POLITICAL PARTIES: SDP—Social Democratic Party of Germany, CDU/CSU—Christian Democratic Union/Christian Social Union, A/G—Alliance 90/Greens, FDP—Free Democratic Party, PDS—Party of Democratic Socialism

NATIONAL ECONOMICS

WORLD GNP RANKING: 3rd

GNP PER CAPITA: $25,120

INFLATION: 1.9%

BALANCE OF PAYMENTS (BALANCE OF TRADE): -$18.7 billion

EXCHANGE RATES / U.S. DLR.: 1.0651-1.1231 EUROS

OFFICIAL CURRENCY: EURO

GOVERNMENT SPENDING (% OF GDP)

✈ DEFENSE 1.6%	
🎓 EDUCATION 4.6%	
✚ HEALTH 7.9%	

(scale: 0 5 10 15)

NUMBER OF CONFLICTS OVER LAST 25 YEARS

	1	2-5	5+
Violent changes in government	○	○	○
Civil wars	●	○	○
International wars	○	○	○
Foreign intervention	○	○	○

- In 1994 the Constitutional Court ruled that military units could participate in collective defense activities abroad.
- The 1999 action against Serbia (over Kosovo) was a landmark.
- Compulsory military service.

NOTABLE WARS AND INSURGENCIES: Baader-Meinhof Gang/Red Army Faction violence 1970-1992

TURKEY

OFFICIAL NAME: REPUBLIC OF TURKEY

POPULATION: 67.6 MILLION
CAPITAL: ANKARA
AREA: 301,382 SQ. MILES (780,579 SQ. KM)
INDEPENDENCE: 1923
CONSTITUTION: 1982

TURKEY is strategically located in both Europe and Asia, dominating the entrance to the Black Sea.

RELIGION: Muslim (mainly Sunni) 99%, Other 1%

OFFICIAL LANGUAGE: Turkish

REGIONS OR PROVINCES: 81 provinces

DEPENDENT TERRITORIES: None

MEDIA: Partial political censorship exists in national media

Newspapers: There are 57 daily newspapers.

TV: 1 state-controlled service with 5 national channels

Radio: 1 state-controlled national service and over 50 local stations

SUFFRAGE: 18 years of age; universal

LEGAL SYSTEM: European continental legal traditions; accepts ICJ jurisdiction

ETHNIC GROUPS:
- Arab 2%
- Other 8%
- Kurdish 20%
- Turkish 70%

WORLD ORGANIZATIONS: AsDB, Australia Group, BIS, BSEC, CCC, CE, CERN (observer), EAPC, EBRD, ECE, ECO, ESCAP, EU (applicant), FAO, IAEA, IBRD, ICAO, ICC, ICFTU, ICRM, IDA, IDB, IEA, IFAD, IFC, IFRCS, IHO, ILO, IMF, IMO, Interpol, IOC, IOM (observer), ISO, ITU, NATO, NEA, NSG, OAS (observer), OECD, OIC, OPCW, OSCE, PCA, UN, UNCTAD, UNESCO, UNHCR, UNIDO, UNIKOM, UNMIBH, UNMIK, UNOMIG, UNRWA, UNTAET, UPU, WEU (associate), WFTU, WHO, WIPO, WMO, WToO, WTrO, ZC

POLITICAL PARTIES: DSP—Democratic Left Party, MHP—Nationalist Action Party, Virtue Party, ANAP—Motherland Party, DYP—True Path Party, Ind—Independents

NATIONAL ECONOMICS

WORLD GNP RANKING: 23rd

GNP PER CAPITA: $3,100

INFLATION: 54.9%

BALANCE OF PAYMENTS (BALANCE OF TRADE): -$9.77 billion

EXCHANGE RATES / U.S. DLR.: 670,300-1,455,000 TURKISH LIRA

OFFICIAL CURRENCY: TURKISH LIRA

GOVERNMENT SPENDING (% OF GDP)

		0	5	10	15
✈	DEFENSE 5.2%				
📖	EDUCATION 2.2%				
✚	HEALTH 3.3%				

NUMBER OF CONFLICTS OVER LAST 25 YEARS

	1	2-5	5+
Violent changes in government	○	○	○
Civil wars	◐	○	○
International wars	○	○	○
Foreign intervention	○	○	○

- Turkey's armed forces are the second-largest in NATO. The great majority of personnel are conscripts.
- Kurdish autonomy movement has led to years of violence and instability.

NOTABLE WARS AND INSURGENCIES: Kurdistan movement 1979-1995

MODERN TURKEY CAME INTO BEING IN 1923, when World War I hero and leader of the Turks in their war against Greece, Mustafa Kemal—known as "the father of the Turks," or Atatürk—established the republic. A year later, the first constitution determined a democratic and secular system of government in which the president was a member of the majority party. Since then, however, power struggles among ethnic and religious groups have been the major source of instability.

In 1961, after the first serious military intervention, a new constitution established that the president would be elected by and from the Grand National Assembly and that the term of office would be limited to seven years. At that time, the advisory Milli Guvenlik Konseyi, or National Security Council (NSC), dissolved the parliament and nominated a new Council of Ministers. Political activities were forbidden during the period of NSC rule, and military officers took over most of the government functions, all in the name of a process of economic liberalization. That lasted until 1982, when another new constitution was drafted. By then, some democratic changes had occurred, and the NSC once again allowed the creation of political parties and popular participation in the electoral process. Equilibrium and political balance remain elusive, however, among the different religious groups and their beliefs. These differences are the major cause—as well as the consequence—of economic turmoil in Turkey,

75TH ANNIVERSARY OF INDEPENDENCE
In front of a banner depicting Mustafa Kemal Atatürk, founder of the Turkish Republic, a boy raises the flag among thousands of celebrants on Cummhurriyet Day (Nation Day) in 1998, the anniversary of the birth of the nation.

which has worked through many reforms and negotiations with the International Monetary Fund (IMF) in the past few years. Economic growth had returned by 2002.

By 2002, a new prime minister, Abdullah Gul, promised economic modernization and a solid secular democratic system. Despite Gul's handover to Recep Tayyip Erdogan, who initially had been banned from the office because of past involvement in Islamist sedition, Turkey has seen rapid change in the past few years, and has even begun tentative and controversial negotiations to join the European Union.

HOW THE GOVERNMENT WORKS

LEGISLATIVE BRANCH

Turkiye Buyuk Millet Meclisi
(Grand National Assembly of Turkey)
Unicameral Parliament
Composed of 550 members directly elected to five-year terms by proportional representation. Votes approval or rejection following each election of new government program presented by prime minister-designate.

Regional Governments
Eighty-one provinces headed by governors, appointed by the president and responsible to the Ministry of the Interior.

EXECUTIVE BRANCH

President
Elected to single seven-year term by parliament. Serves as head of state; ratifies international treaties; grants pardons; can dissolve parliament.

Prime Minister
Traditionally the leader of parliament's majority party. Appointed by president. Serves as head of government and administers government operations.

Council of Ministers
Composed of 20 to 24 members, including the prime minister.
Nominated by prime minister and appointed by president.

JUDICIAL BRANCH

Constitutional Court
Rules on constitutionality of laws. Composed of 11 judges and four alternates appointed by president to serve until age 65.

Court of Cassation
Highest court of appeal. Comprises 20 civil and 10 penal chambers; each composed of five judges. Judges elected by Supreme Council of Judges and Prosecutors.

Council of State
Highest court for cases involving government actions or disputes.

THAILAND

OFFICIAL NAME: KINGDOM OF THAILAND

POPULATION: 63.6 Million	
CAPITAL: Bangkok	
AREA: 198,455 SQ. MILES (513,998 SQ KM)	
INDEPENDENCE: 1238	
CONSTITUTION: 1997	

THAILAND takes its name from "Thai" meaning "free", hence "Land of the Free".

RELIGION: Buddhist 95%, Muslim 3%, Christian 1%, Other 1%

OFFICIAL LANGUAGE: Thai

REGIONS OR PROVINCES: 76 provinces

DEPENDENT TERRITORIES: None

MEDIA: No political censorship exists in national media. Newspapers enjoy a high level of freedom in political reporting.

Newspapers: There are 30 daily newspapers

TV: 9 services, two are military-run

Radio: 4 state-controlled services

SUFFRAGE: 18 years of age; universal and compulsory

LEGAL SYSTEM: Civil and common law; no ICJ jurisdiction

WORLD ORGANIZATIONS: APEC, ARF, AsDB, ASEAN, BIS, CCC, CP, ESCAP, FAO, G-77, IAEA, IBRD, ICAO, ICC, ICFTU, ICRM, IDA, IFAD, IFC, IFRCS, IHO, ILO, IMF, IMO, Interpol, IOC, IOM, ISO, ITU, NAM, OAS (observer), OIC (observer), OPCW (signatory), OSCE (partner), PCA, UN, UNAMSIL, UNCTAD, UNESCO, UNHCR, UNIDO, UNIKOM, UNITAR, UNMIBH, UNTAET, UNU, UPU, WCL, WFTU, WHO, WIPO, WMO, WToO, WTrO

POLITICAL PARTIES: TRT—Thais Love Thais, DP—Democrat Party, CT—Thai Nation, NAP—New Aspiration Party, CP—New Development

ETHNIC GROUPS:

- Malay 3%
- Chinese 12%
- Khmer and Other 2%
- Thai 83%

NATIONAL ECONOMICS

WORLD GNP RANKING: 31st

GNP PER CAPITA: $2,000

INFLATION: 1.5%

BALANCE OF PAYMENTS (BALANCE OF TRADE): $9.2 billion

EXCHANGE RATES / U.S. DLR.: 43.38-44.23 BAHT

OFFICIAL CURRENCY: BAHT

GOVERNMENT SPENDING (% OF GDP)

✈ DEFENSE 2%	
🎓 EDUCATION 4.7%	
✚ HEALTH 1.9%	

0   5   10   15

NUMBER OF CONFLICTS OVER LAST 25 YEARS

	1	2-5	5+
Violent changes in government	○	○	○
Civil wars	●	○	○
International wars	○	●	○
Foreign intervention	○	○	○

- Military either ruled, or played a prominent role, for over 50 years from 1932.
- The main concerns are fishing rights in the South China Sea, border disputes, and piracy.

NOTABLE WARS AND INSURGENCIES: Khmer Rouge raids 1975-1979. Vietnamese border raids 1979-1988. Thai-Laotian border clash 1987-1988

THAI POLITICS ARE OFTEN PERSONAL. For many years they seemingly consisted of a perpetual cycle of coup, military rule, constitutional reform, general elections, parliamentary governance, political crisis, and coup. Between 1932 and 1998 there were 10 successful and seven attempted coups. But since the 1992 elections and a new constitution in 1997, the country has settled down into a solid parliamentary democracy, though still troubled by frequent cabinet reshuffles, government collapses, and snap elections.

The constant has been the monarchy. The Chakri dynasty has ruled Siam, as Thailand was known until 1939, from the 18th century to the present. King Bhumibol Adulyadej has occupied the throne since 1946. The country's political culture of kingship and independence allied to the Thais' very strong Buddhism has produced a lasting reverence for the monarch even after revolutionaries challenged the absolute monarchy in a 1932 coup, replacing it with a constitutional monarchy. The monarch still grants others their authority and commands the military, resolving civilian-military clashes and coping with natural disasters.

THAILAND ELECTION
Monks parade a poster depicting Thaksin Shinawatra, the controversial billionaire elected premier in 2001.

However, the king's total power has declined, giving way in particular to an increasingly powerful Council of Ministers. The nature of Thai government is that its National Assemblies are large and politically weak, lawmaking is slow, and Council ministers' personal policy-making is swift. Political parties are largely built around individuals, not policy platforms, so they typically lack a leadership succession. Parties try to woo experienced politicians from rival parties with money and promises of Council appointments. The prime minister heads the government, but has less influence these days, facing pressures from frequently elected coalitions and trying to avoid offending Council allies or risking government collapse.

HOW THE GOVERNMENT WORKS

LEGISLATIVE BRANCH

Rathasapha
(National Assembly)
Bicameral Parliament

Wuthisapha
(Senate)
Composed of 200 members elected to four-year terms by direct popular vote.

Sapha Phuthaen Ratsadon
(House of Representatives)
Composed of 500 members elected to four-year terms: 100 from party lists, 400 from single-member districts.

Regional Governments
Seventy-six provinces overseen by career civil-servant governors appointed by Ministry of the Interior, except for Bangkok's popularly elected governor.

EXECUTIVE BRANCH

Monarch
Position is hereditary.
Parliament must approve succession to throne. Serves as head of state and symbol of national unity.

Prime Minister
Leader of majority coalition, appointed by monarch.
Serves as head of government; chairs the Council of Ministers.

Council of Ministers
Composed of 25 members, including prime minister and five deputy prime ministers.
Determines government policy and distribution of resources.

JUDICIAL BRANCH

Constitutional Tribunal
Rules on legality of bills passed by parliament. Decisions are final and cannot be appealed.

Supreme Court
Highest court of appeal.
Judges appointed by monarch with Judicial Service Commission approval and serve to age 60.

Courts of Appeal
Four courts. Rule on lower-level appeals. Judges appointed by monarch.

Courts of First Instance
135 courts.
Hear civil and criminal cases.
Judges appointed by monarch.

UNITED KING

UNITED KINGDOM FLAG
Combines the crosses of St Andrew of Scotland, St Patrick of Ireland, and St George of England.

THE ROOTS OF BRITISH PARLIAMENTARY DEMOCRACY go back to the 13th century, when the English king was forced to acknowledge the rights of his most important subjects. The bicameral Parliament that evolved in the following century was to serve as a model for others throughout the world.

ROYAL FOOT GUARD
Serving the monarchy for hundreds of years, this symbol of the United Kingdom has changed little and is nearly identical to the Royal Foot Guard of 150 years ago during the reign of Queen Victoria.

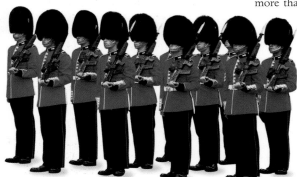

Around 2,000 years ago the British Isles were populated by numerous tribal communities. The first step toward the unification of the country came in A.D. 43, with the capture of the south by the Romans. They ruled for more than 350 years before being forced to withdraw as Angle, Saxon, and Jute raiders began to build settlements. A number of small Anglo-Saxon kingdoms were formed, of which Wessex became the most important under King Alfred in the 9th century. He prevented the Danes from conquering the whole country, confining them to an area in the north, and laid the foundations of a united English kingdom.

The conquest of England in 1066 by William of Normandy (William I of England) changed the course of British history. Under William, strong central government and feudalism—an economic and social system under which land was held in return for homage, military service, or labor—were established. In 1215 King John was forced to sign the Magna Carta, a charter defining the feudal rights of the king while protecting those of the barons, merchants, and town boroughs. Although often ignored by later kings, today the Magna Carta is celebrated as a precursor to modern democracy, influencing documents such as the American Bill of Rights.

When the Magna Carta was signed, Parliament was simply an assembly of great landholders who met only when summoned

HOW THE GOVE

LEGISLATIVE BRANCH

PARLIAMENT

The bicameral structure of the British Parliament emerged in the 14th century, and has served as a model to many other parliamentary systems.

▶ **HOUSE OF LORDS**
Comprises around 670 members: 92 hereditary peers, 26 senior bishops, and around 550 life peers. Questions and debates government's activities; may initiate legislation (not money bills); power limited to delaying legislation for one year. Essentially subordinate to House of Commons.

▶ **HOUSE OF COMMONS**
Comprises 659 members: 529 from England, 72 from Scotland, 40 from Wales, 18 from Northern Ireland; elected by popular vote to five-year term. May initiate bills; sole right to introduce tax and public expenditure bills; discusses and votes on intended government legislation; questions ministers.

THE HOUSE OF COMMONS
The lower house of Parliament shown in session.

EXECUTIVE BRANCH

MONARCH

Chief of state; commander-in-chief of the armed forces; head of the Church of England; hereditary, largely ceremonial position. While in theory the monarch has executive authority, in practice this is exercised by the Cabinet. Duties include signing treaties, hosting visiting heads of state, appointing a number of posts in the judicial system and Parliament and a weekly meeting with the prime minister; has the power to dissolve Parliament.

PALACE OF WESTMINSTER
Home to the Houses of Parliament and the famous clock tower, Big Ben, the Palace was rebuilt in 1870 after a fire destroyed it in 1834.

REGIONAL ASSEMBLIES
▶ Scottish Parliament: 129 members
▶ Northern Ireland Assembly: 108 members
▶ Welsh Assembly: 60 members

DOM

"The House of Commons is absolute. It is the state."
—Benjamin Disraeli (1844), British Tory statesman and prime minister

SIR WINSTON CHURCHILL

Referred to as "The Last Lion," Churchill was a man of exceptional achievement—journalist, member of parliament, prime minister, and Nobel Prize winner. Articulate and fearless, he led the British effort to secure victory against the Axis Powers during World War II.

by the king. In the 14th century it developed into a bicameral body, consisting of the Lords and Commons, whose consent to taxation by the crown was required. While, in the following centuries, other European Parliaments disappeared, the joint English and Welsh Parliament survived. The 1707 Act of Union between England and Scotland converted it into a British Parliament, for which the franchise was gradually extended to all adults between 1832 and 1928.

During the late 18th and 19th centuries, Britain was the world's leading imperial power, acquiring an empire that by 1900 comprised over one fifth of the world's land surface. It was also at the forefront of the Industrial Revolution that was to transform the world, and for many decades it was the world's leading industrial nation.

In the 20th century the position of the UK in the global arena, like that of many European powers, was drastically affected by World Wars I and II. It gradually lost its empire, with Canada, Australia, New Zealand, and South Africa becoming independent states in the 1930s, and the majority of colonies in Asia, Africa, the Caribbean, and the Pacific gaining their independence between the late 1940s and 1980. The UK, however, did not suffer the same degree of destruction—at least in terms of political and economic infrastructure—as continental Europe. Its major role in the victorious Allied coalition during World War II earned it a privileged position in the post-war global order: a permanent seat in the UN Security Council, a place in the G8, and an influential position in the European Union.

NMENT WORKS

PRIME MINISTER

Leader of the majority party or majority coalition of Parliament; acts as head of government; responsible for decisions of government; appoints the Cabinet and oversees the civil service.

▶ **CABINET**

Consists of roughly 20 senior members, most of whom are heads of government departments. Appointed by prime minister, their exact number varies. Must be members of Parliament.

▶ **GOVERNMENT**

Comprises about 100 members of the majority party; includes Cabinet members, ministers, undersecretaries, the chief whip, assistant whips, and a few peers.

 JUDICIAL BRANCH

DEPARTMENT FOR CONSTITUTIONAL AFFAIRS

This recently developed executive department replaces the Lord Chancellor's Department as the head of the British judiciary; aims to reform the UK's archaic judicial system; provides for the establishment of a Supreme Court, as well as single National Courts for Scotland, Wales, and Northern Ireland.

▶ **COURT OF APPEAL**

Hears appeals on criminal matters from the Crown Court and on civil matters from the High Court, County Courts, and Tribunals.

▶ **HIGH COURT**

Hears civil cases, including contractual, commercial, family, and patent matters.

▶ **REGIONAL AND DISTRICT COURTS**

The Crown, County, and Magistrates' Courts administer justice locally. Tribunals hear appeals from decisions on immigration, social security, pensions, tax, and lands. Judges are appointed by the Judicial Appointments Committee. Wales, Northern Ireland, and Scotland have separate judicial systems.

ELECTORAL SYSTEM

The United Kingdom is divided into 659 constituencies. General elections are held at least once every five years to elect one person per constituency—in a "first past the post" system—to serve as a member of Parliament (MP) in the House of Commons.

EXECUTIVE BRANCH

HAROLD WILSON (1916-1995)
Under his leadership, the Labour government ended capital punishment, liberalized the laws on homosexuality, and dealt with an economic recession, the devaluation of the currency, and troubled negotiations for the UK's entry to the EU.

BENJAMIN DISRAELI (1804-1881)
Disraeli began by writing political novels, but, changing career, he rose quickly in politics to serve twice as the UK's only Jewish prime minister.

DAVID LLOYD GEORGE (1863-1945)
He led the UK through part of World War I and the turbulent postwar years. His work in establishing the Irish state lost him his prime ministership.

MARGARET THATCHER (1925-)
The UK's first female prime minister and the longest serving of the 20th century, her political philosophies dominated the 1980s.

THE MONARCH

The history of the executive office in the United Kingdom is inseparably intertwined with the tradition of monarchy, which can be traced back to the early medieval kings of England, Scotland, and Wales. Since then, monarchy in Britain has been abolished only once: during the English Civil War, when rebel parliamentarian forces under Oliver Cromwell overthrew Charles I. Cromwell was installed as head of a republican "commonwealth" in 1649, but the experiment effectively ended in 1653 when Cromwell refused the crown and became Lord Protector of the Realm—a monarch in all

but name, even designating his son his successor. Two years after Cromwell's death in 1658, general consensus restored the monarchy.

England's line of hereditary monarchs stretches from the post-Roman Houses of Cerdic and Denmark, through the French Houses of Normandy, Blois, and Anjou, to the Welsh House of Tudor. Great Britain's subsequent rulers were of the Houses of Stuart (Scottish), Orange (Dutch), and Hanover and Saxe-Coburg-

CORONATION THRONE
Monarchs have been crowned on this throne for more that 700 years.

Gotha (German). The present queen, Elizabeth II, who inherited the throne in 1952, belongs to the House of Windsor.

As head of state and head of the British Commonwealth, the British monarch is nominally vested with a tremendous degree of official power—from the appointment and removal of all government personnel to negotiation of treaties and implementation of foreign policy. In practice, the monarch today has a largely ceremonial role, acting as the emblematic figurehead of the nation and hosting visiting heads of state.

THE CABINET OF THE UNITED KINGDOM

First developed in the 18th century to wield executive power on behalf of Hanoverian kings, the Cabinet developed over two centuries into an integral component of the executive branch. The secretaries of state each preside over one of the 15 executive ministries that comprise the British civil service.

CABINET OFFICE
Supports the prime minister in implementing executive policy and leading the government; primarily responsible for the administration of the Cabinet and government; coordinates disaster and intelligence initiatives.

H.M. TREASURY
Monitors, formulates, and implements the United Kingdom's financial policy, including maintaining low inflation; aims to raise sustainable growth, improve economic prosperity and productivity, and provide employment opportunities.

HOME OFFICE
Responsible for domestic affairs within England and Wales; works to reduce crime and to stimulate a safe, tolerant society.

TRANSPORTATION
Monitors and maintains the domestic transportation

system including road and rail; implements the government's far-reaching transportation policy.

EDUCATION AND SKILLS
Monitors and maintains the English education system; aims to provide training and skills development.

HEALTH
Responsible for improving the health and well-being of the British public; establishes overall direction for the National Health Service and social care organizations; sets and monitors national standards for health and social care.

DEFENSE
Ensures the defense and security of the UK, its overseas territories and citizens; responsible for the Armed Forces, including Royal Navy, Air Force and Army; administers programs for veterans; works toward international peace.

KEY RULERS

The foundation of both England and Scotland as kingdoms dates back to the 9th century A.D.

ALFRED THE GREAT
871-899
Defeated Danes in the Battle of Eddington. Father of the English navy.

WILLIAM I THE CONQUEROR
1066-1087
Led the Norman conquest of England, winning the crown at the Battle of Hastings.

KING JOHN
1199-1216
Lost French territory. Highly unpopular, he was forced into signing the Magna Carta by his barons.

HENRY V
1413-1422
Led an English army to victory against France and briefly recognized as heir to French throne.

HENRY VIII
1509-1547
Renewed English claims to Scotland and established the Church of England.

GALLERY OF PRIME MINISTERS

Since the first PM. in 1721, the importance of the office has steadily increased, making it the most important political role in the UK. To the right are ten of the most influential PM's who have served in the last 300 years.

ROBERT WALPOLE, EARL OF ORFORD
1721-1742
[Whig]

WILLIAM PITT, EARL OF CHATHAM (PITT THE ELDER)
1766-1768
[Whig]

WILLIAM PITT (PITT THE YOUNGER)
1783-1801, 1804-1806
[Tory]

HENRY JOHN TEMPLE, VISCOUNT PALMERSTON
1855-1858, 1859-1865
[Whig]

UNITED KINGDOM

10 DOWNING STREET
The prime minister's office and official residence in London.

IMPERIAL STATE CROWN
Encrusted with over 3,000 precious stones, including the 3,174-carat "Cullinan II," the world's second largest diamond, the crown was designed in 1838 for Queen Victoria, and has been worn by four British monarchs.

BUCKINGHAM PALACE
Originally a townhouse of the Dukes of Buckingham, the palace has been the monarch's official residence since the accession of Victoria to the throne in 1837.

QUEEN ELIZABETH II
Fourth monarch of the House of Windsor, the Queen has reigned since 1952.

"[The British Constitution] presumes more boldly than any other the good sense and the good faith of those who work it."—William Gladstone, 19th-century Liberal Party statesman

PRIME MINISTER

First introduced in 1721 with the appointment of Robert Walpole, the office of prime minister of the United Kingdom has since always been the country's most influential political position.

Under the current political system, the prime minister wields most of the power in the executive branch, acting as the head of government. Following national parliamentary elections, the leader of the majority party becomes prime minister. The monarch officially confirms the appointment and asks the prime minister to form a government. The prime minister's position has become so

important in contemporary British politics that many voters in the United Kingdom select which candidate they will vote for as their local member of parliament based on their preference for prime minister.

The prime minister's political strength essentially derives from his or her position as leader of the Cabinet, which is the primary decision-making body in the executive. In this function, the prime minister selects the composition and size of the Cabinet (usually 20 or so members), and may invite the attendance of non-Cabinet members to official meetings. The prime minister also schedules

Cabinet meetings, sets the agenda, directs its discussions and oversees the implementation of its decisions. Currently, the Cabinet usually meets once a week. The prime minister also has the ability to take important actions without first referring to the Cabinet or Parliament, if he or she so chooses. The prime minister is assisted by the Prime Minister's Office, which is staffed by civil servants and special advisers.

The prime minister has become the most important and high-profile representative of British policy in the global arena, attracting a large degree of national and international attention to that role in British politics.

DEPARTMENT FOR CONSTITUTIONAL AFFAIRS
Responsible for the administration and modernization of the justice system; incorporates the former Lord Chancellor's Department. Works closely with Home Office.

OFFICE OF THE DEPUTY PRIME MINISTER
Responsible for executive policy promoting social inclusion, neighborhood renewal, and regional prosperity; monitors the policy of local and regional governments and the fire service; sets housing policy.

FOREIGN AND COMMONWEALTH
Promotes British interests abroad; works with international agencies to strengthen world community; maintains the UK's foreign embassies and consulates; responsible for business with other governments.

INTERNATIONAL DEVELOPMENT
Works with foreign countries and international organizations to promote sustainable economic development and reduce levels of poverty in economically depressed countries around the world.

TRADE AND INDUSTRY
Encourages advanced sustainable growth through scientific and technological innovation, research and development; provides support and advice for startup ventures in the UK and promotes prosperity through productivity.

ENVIRONMENT, FOOD, RURAL AFFAIRS
Monitors, protects, and ensures the quality of the nation's food supply; develops protection policies to ensure the integrity of the environment; responsible for animal welfare, rural development, and wildlife.

CULTURE, MEDIA, SPORT
Provides for the support of the the nation's cultural heritage; maintains museums, libraries, and other historical venues; supports the creative arts; responsible for quality of life through culture and sport; encourages tourism.

WORK AND PENSIONS
Assists the population in becoming financially independent and endeavors to reduce child poverty; operates Jobcentre Plus and the Pension Service; and provides support to employers, pensioners, and disabled people.

ELIZABETH I
1558–1603
Ambitious and skilled in power politics, her reign initiated England's ascent to global power.

JAMES I
1603–1625
Also James VI of Scotland. United Scotland and England as the latter's first Stuart monarch.

OLIVER CROMWELL
1649–1658
Led armed revolution, deposed the monarchy, and established a brief republic.

GEORGE I
1714–1727
A Hanoverian king. Allowed England to rule itself, which led to establishment of an office of prime minister.

VICTORIA
1837–1901
The figurehead of British industrialism and the British Empire, which grew under her to be the world's largest ever.

WILLIAM EWART GLADSTONE
1868–1874,
1880–1885,
Feb–July 1886,
1892–1894
[Liberal]

HERBERT HENRY ASQUITH
1908–1916
[Liberal]

STANLEY BALDWIN
1923,
1924–1929,
1935–1937
[Conservative]

WINSTON CHURCHILL
1940–1945,
1951–1955
[Conservative]

HAROLD MACMILLAN
1957–1963
[Conservative]

TONY BLAIR
1997–
[Labour]

LEGISLATIVE BRANCH

Aerial View of the Palace of Westminster

HOUSE OF COMMONS
The Commons' chamber is quite small, with room for only 427 of the body's 659 members to sit. There is a public gallery, and debates are broadcast live on the internet.

Central Lobby

THE HOUSES OF PARLIAMENT

The British Parliament is considered to be one of the oldest parliamentary bodies in the world. At the beginning of the 13th century it was the preserve of great landholders. However, it also included knights and representatives of the boroughs when, in 1265, it was summoned by Simon de Montfort, Earl of Leicester, after he had effectively dethroned King Henry III. By the 1330s two separate bodies had emerged—the Lords and the Commons.

The word "parliament" is derived from a Latin word for "discussion," and so it is that Parliament meets for sessions typically lasting one year to discuss legislation, taxation, government policies, and major public issues. The absence of a written constitution in the UK means that Parliament is not limited by legal restraints, apart from those related to membership of the European Union. It can make or change any legislation, although in practice it usually follows precedent.

THE PALACE OF WESTMINSTER
On the River Thames and formerly the home of the British monarch, the palace has been the seat of both Houses of Parliament since 1547. The only surviving medieval part is Westminster Hall.

Big Ben

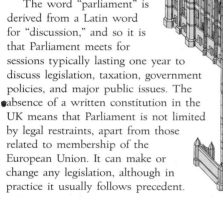

A THWARTED CONSPIRACY
The Gunpowder Plot of November 5, 1605, was the first major act of terrorism aimed at the British government. Guy Fawkes was part of a conspiracy to blow up King James I and the House of Lords during the State Opening of Parliament.

DEVOLUTION

England and Wales were united in 1536, and were joined in 1707 by Scotland. Ireland joined the trio in 1801, to form the United Kingdom. By the 1970s, Welsh and Scottish nationalist movements prompted an unsuccessful initiative to devolve power to regional governments. Devolution was revived under the Labour government in the late 1990s and elected assemblies were created in Northern Ireland, Scotland, and Wales.

Westminster Hall

LEGISLATIVE POWERS AND PROCEDURES

MAKING OF LAWS IN THE UK

Parliament is the law-making body, but the government has enormous control over what legislation is enacted. The large majority of bills introduced in Parliament are sponsored by the government. Bills must be agreed to by both Houses and receive royal assent from the monarch to become law. Government-backed bills are rarely defeated.

QUESTION TIME
Each Wednesday the British prime minister (here Tony Blair, standing at bottom left) responds to members of the House of Commons, answering questions regarding the activities of the government, and hearing any issues they might wish to raise.

DISCUSSING GOVERNMENT POLICIES

Parliament routinely discusses government policies during Question Time (see photograph at left), a formal period for querying government ministers. In the House of Commons, Question Time lasts for an hour four days each week. In the House of Lords up to four questions may be asked of the government at the start of each day. The prime minister answers questions in the House of Commons for a half hour every Wednesday which is broadcast live on the internet. During this time only the Leader of the Opposition (the leader of the Labour or Conservative Party) and the Liberal Democrat leader are allowed to ask follow-up questions.

UNITED KINGDOM

Victoria Tower

Each member of parliament (MP) is elected by a particular constituency in the UK to represent it in the House of Commons. Since 1997, there have been 659 constituencies electing MPs—529 from England, 72 from Scotland, 40 from Wales, and 18 from Northern Ireland.

House of Lords portcullis emblem

The speaker is the Commons' presiding officer. Unlike the speaker of the US House of Representatives, the post is non-political.

The government of the UK has in practice worked as a two-party system since the 18th century. The party that wins the majority of seats in the Commons in general elections forms the Government. The second largest party becomes the "official opposition," with the other parties forming the rest of the opposition. As well as a party leader, each party also has one or more "whips" —officials who keep members of Parliament apprised of party opinion and ensure their presence at debates and votes in the House of Commons. The speaker ensures the orderly conduct of debates.

The Commons also has Select Committees— teams of MPs from all parties which each specialize in examining the work of specific government departments, and in the running of Parliament in general. In addition, the Scottish, Welsh, and Northern Ireland Grand Committees, comprising in the main the MPs from these regions, examine bills that relate to their regions. The parliamentary commissioner for administration looks at public complaints of government maladministration.

THE QUEEN'S SPEECH
Delivered during the State opening of Parliament (see image below), the speech is written by the Government and approved by the Cabinet.

HOUSE OF LORDS
The ornate Neogothic chamber is bedecked with frescos representing religion, justice and chivalry. A gallery is open for the general public to observe live sessions.

St. Stephen's Entrance

THE HOUSE OF COMMONS
This is the most important political institution in the UK. Though called the lower house, it is where the government sits and the peoples' representatives fight political battles. The Acts of Parliament of 1911 and 1949 ensure that the Commons has overriding authority over the House of Lords on any bill that is introduced. The lower house scrutinizes and approves all legislation.

House of Commons portcullis emblem

THE HOUSE OF LORDS
Throughout its history, the House of Lords, consisted of Lords Spiritual (members of the clergy), and Lords Temporal (nobles and judges). In 1958 a reforming Act of Parliament allowed for the creation of life peers. In 1999 another Act reduced the hereditary membership to a minority of just 92, so that now the vast majority are life peers. Peerages, normally for life, are conferred by the Queen on the advice of the prime minister in recognition of the recipient's service to the nation. The House of Lords also includes 26 senior bishops of the Church of England. At the end of 2001 it was proposed that the House of Lords should be replaced by a largely appointed upper house, with 120 elected members.

The functions of the Lords include revision of legislation. It may reject legislation passed by the Commons, but so doing will only delay it for one year, after which the Commons may reintroduce it, unhindered, for royal assent. The Lords also provides independent expertise on public policy. It is currently the highest Court of Appeal of the British Commonwealth. The "law lords" deal only with the meaning of the law, rather than with case evidence.

STATE OPENING OF PARLIAMENT
Usually held in November, this ceremony is attended by the entire Parliament, including peers and judges in traditional dress.

OVERLEAF: QUEEN'S GOLDEN JUBILEE
On June 4, 2002, Queen Elizabeth II celebrated the 50th anniversary of her reign. The occasion was marked by a ceremonial procession in the Gold Coach from Buckingham Palace to St. Paul's Cathedral.

LEVYING TAXES
The finance bill sets out the chancellor of the exchequer's budget proposals for taxation. It is presented to Parliament each year and must begin in the House of Commons' Committee on Ways and Means. The speaker of the House of Commons signs a certificate indicating it is a money bill involving taxes. The House of Lords has no power over taxation or other money bills. Otherwise, a tax bill advances through Parliament in the same way as any other measure and becomes law with the monarch's assent.

THE WOOLSACK
In the 14th century, the woolsack symbolized the wealth that England had gained from wool. Today, the wool used in the woolsack is from all the countries of the Commonwealth and the lord chancellor sits on the woolsack in the House of Lords.

DEBATING MAJOR PUBLIC ISSUES
A debate is a formal discussion on a specific topic in the House of Commons or House of Lords. Members speak in turn on the topic at issue. Debate in the House of Commons is strictly controlled by a set of rules and presided over by the speaker. In the House of Lords, members control the debate themselves. A member in the House of Commons may raise a motion for closure to end debate. The motion is accepted if the majority of MPs present vote for it and at least 100 MPs vote.

JUDICIAL BRANCH

*"Laws and institutions must
go hand in hand with the progress of the human mind."*
—Sir Francis Bacon, lord chancellor (1618-1621) and philosopher

**ROYAL COURTS
OF JUSTICE**
*Located on The Strand,
London, the Royal Court
houses the High Court
and the Court of Appeal.*

DEPARTMENT OF CONSTITUTIONAL AFFAIRS
Although the United Kingdom recently began an ambitious program to reform its judicial system, the British judicial branch remains extremely complex. Unlike most countries, which generally employ one national system, the United Kingdom operates three separate legal systems: one for England and Wales, one for Scotland, and one for Northern Ireland. Although bound by similar principles, these systems differ in form

**ROYAL COURT OF
JUSTICE FACADE**
*Opened in 1882 by Queen
Victoria, the Gothic-style
building consists of more
than 1,000 rooms, of
which, 88 are
courtrooms.*

and the manner of operation. Furthermore, on top of these three systems, all judicial decisions must accord with the statutes of the European Court of Justice, with which the United Kingdom—as a member of the European Union— is obligated to comply. Given the convoluted nature of this system, the British government has recently undertaken significant reforms to modernize the judiciary. In June 2003, the United Kingdom announced the abolition of the lord chancellor's position and department,

**VISITING
HEAD OF STATE**
*(above) On a state visit
in 1996, the South
African president Nelson
Mandela meets with the
then-lord chancellor,
Lord Mackay
of Clashfern.*

which had—for 1,400 years—maintained the judiciary in England and the UK.

In an effort to further separate the three branches of government, the executive established the Department for Constitutional Affairs to replace the former Lord Chancellor's Department, which was widely considered too arcane and ineffective for a modern democratic state. The lord chancellor was appointed as the secretary of state of the new department. Like the lord chancellor's former ministry, the Department for Constitutional Affairs is charged with the efficient, impartial, and unbiased administration of the court system, including the Court of Appeal, the High Court, the Crown, County and Magistrates' Courts, and Tribunals. A Judicial Appointments Commission is to be set up to advise the secretary of state on the appoint-ment of new judges—an important role, considering such appointments are made until retirement age. Local advisory committees presently recommend the people to be appointed as magistrates.

LANDMARK CASES

1996

DEPORTATION
Despite a long residency in the UK, the High Court controversially found in favor of deportation of Nigerian asylum-seeker, Abdul Onibiyo.

PROTESTERS
A crowd gathered outside the High Court carring anti-deportation placards.

2000

PINOCHET
Following the home secretary's decision to release the former leader of Chile, Augusto Pinochet, from custody on the grounds of his failing health, six organizations filed suits to prevent his release.

CANDLELIT VIGIL
Protesters against Pinochet's release held a peaceful vigil outside the Houses of Parliament.

2001

EUTHANASIA
The High Court heard a case brought by a terminally ill woman seeking to overturn the Director of Public Prosecutions' anti-euthanasia decision as inhuman and contrary to the Human Rights Act.

THE RIGHT TO DIE
Diane Petty, suffering from motor-neurone disease, sought the right to end her own life.

UNITED KINGDOM

"A government above the law is a menace to be defeated."
—Lord Scarman, British judge

The department also has the duty of establishing policy for the Magistrates' Courts, and providing legal aid to the population, in order to secure equal access to justice throughout England and Wales. Reforming and modernizing the British judiciary is an important task for the new executive department, whose two main goals are the establishment of a Supreme Court with the powers of judicial and constitutional review—currently lacking in the system, as the highest court of appeal is the House of Lords—and the formation of national courts for Wales and Northern Ireland. Finally, the department has the duty of promoting and enforcing changes in English civil law. Given the global influence of England's system of civil law, this role is of great importance.

REGIONAL COURTS

Most civil cases in England and Wales are dealt with by over 230 County Courts, while most criminal cases are dealt with by Magistrates' Courts. Above them is the Crown Court, which deals with all serious offences that must be tried before a judge and jury. There are over 90 Crown Court centers which are divided into six "circuits." While the judicial system of Northern Ireland is quite similar to this, the Scottish system is unique. Whereas in most of the United Kingdom, the Department for Constitutional Affairs is responsible for the administration of the legal system, in Scotland this role is performed by the Scottish Executive Justice Department, which ultimately falls under the jurisdiction of the Scottish Parliament.

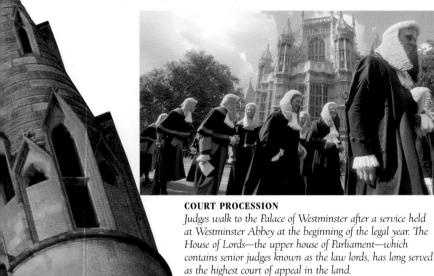

COURT PROCESSION
Judges walk to the Palace of Westminster after a service held at Westminster Abbey at the beginning of the legal year. The House of Lords—the upper house of Parliament—which contains senior judges known as the law lords, has long served as the highest court of appeal in the land.

2003

OFFICIAL SECRETS ACT
A former spy convicted in November 2002 for deliberately leaking government secrets in 1996 lost his case in the Court of Appeal, in which he sought to clear his name on the grounds that his original trial was not conducted freely or fairly.

SPY TRIAL
David Shayler, former MI5 officer, was accused of disclosing state secrets.

OFFICIAL NAME:
UNITED KINGDOM OF GREAT BRITAIN AND NORTHERN IRELAND

POPULATION: 59.5 MILLION	
CAPITAL: LONDON	
AREA: 94,525 SQ. MILES (244,820 SQ. KM)	
INDEPENDENCE: 1707	
CONSTITUTION: UNWRITTEN	

THE UNITED KINGDOM derives its name from the uniting of England, Scotland, Wales, and Ireland in 1801.

RELIGION: Anglican 47%, Roman Catholic 9%, Presbyterian 4%, Muslim 3%, Methodist 1%, Other 36%

OFFICIAL LANGUAGE: English, Welsh (in Wales)

REGIONS OR PROVINCES: England—47 boroughs; Northern Ireland—24 districts; Scotland—32 council areas; Wales—11 county boroughs

DEPENDENT TERRITORIES: 15 territories

MEDIA: No political censorship

Newspapers: 99 daily newspapers

TV: 5 networks: 2 public, 3 independent

Radio: 5 public networks, many independent

SUFFRAGE: 18 years of age; universal

LEGAL SYSTEM: English common law; accepts ICJ jurisdiction

ETHNIC GROUPS:

- West Indian, Asian, and Other 5%
- Northern Irish 3%
- Welsh 3%
- Scottish 9%
- English 80%

WORLD ORGANIZATIONS: AfDB, AsDB, Australia Group, BIS, C, CDB, CE, CERN, EAPC, EBRD, ECA (associate), ECE, ECLAC, EIB, ESA, ESCAP, EU, FAO, G- 5, G- 7, G- 8, G-10, IADB, IAEA, IBRD, ICAO, ICC, ICCt, ICFTU, ICRM, IDA, IEA, IFAD, IFC, IFRCS, IHO, ILO, IMF, IMO, Interpol, IOC, IOM, ISO, ITU, MONUC, NAM (guest), NATO, NEA, NSG, OAS (observer), OECD, OPCW, OSCE, PCA, SPC, UN, UN Security Council, UNAMSIL, UNCTAD, UNESCO, UNFICYP, UNHCR, UNIDO, UNIKOM, UNITAR, UNMIBH, UNMIK, UNMOVIC, UNOMIG, UNRWA, UNU, UPU, WCL, WCO, WEU, WHO, WIPO, WMO, WTrO, ZC

POLITICAL PARTIES: Lab—Labour Party, Con—Conservative and Unionist Party, LD—Liberal Democrats, UU—Ulster Unionist Parties (official)—Ulster Unionist Party, Democratic Unionist Party, UK Unionist, SNP—Scottish Nationalist Party, PC—Plaid Cymru

NATIONAL ECONOMICS

WORLD GNP RANKING: 4th

GNP PER CAPITA: $24,430

INFLATION: 2.9%

BALANCE OF PAYMENTS (BALANCE OF TRADE): -$24.5 billion

EXCHANGE RATES / U.S. DLR.: 0.6694-0.6871 POUNDS STERLING

OFFICIAL CURRENCY: POUND STERLING

GOVERNMENT SPENDING (% OF GDP)

DEFENSE	2.4%
EDUCATION	4.7%
HEALTH	5.8%

0   5   10   15

NUMBER OF CONFLICTS OVER LAST 25 YEARS

	1	2-5	5+
Violent changes in government	○	○	○
Civil wars	●	○	○
International wars	○	●	○
Foreign intervention	○	○	○

- Leading arms exporter.
- A founder member of NATO, the UK holds a permanent seat on the UN Security Council.
- 2003 Iraq war aroused strong public opposition.

NOTABLE WARS AND INSURGENCIES: Northern Ireland Troubles 1968-1998. Falkland Islands War 1982. Gulf War 1991. Intervention over Kosovo 1999. War on terrorism in Afghanistan 2001. Invasion of Iraq 2003

ITALY

AFTER THE FALL OF ROME, Italy did not become a nation state again until the 19th century, when it was reunited under the royal house of Savoy. The monarchy survived only until 1946, when the Italians, disillusioned by Fascism and war, voted for a republic instead. But, plagued by a succession of short-lived governments, Italy remains in pursuit of a stable political system.

ITALIAN FLAG
Adopted on June 19, 1946 the Italian flag is known as the Tricolore.

COLOSSEUM
Built between 70 and 82 A.D., the Colosseum in Rome was used for gladiatorial combat, with up to 50,000 spectators.

Ancient Italy formed the core of the Roman Empire, but after the empire's collapse, Italy split into rival kingdoms often warring among themselves or subjugated by foreign powers. Rome itself remained a center of Christianity, the city and surrounding lands ruled by the pope. By the 11th century, many small, independent city-states had also emerged, dominated by a wealthy burgher class. These flourished as centers of banking and commerce and—in the Renaissance—of the arts. By the 1500s, frequent wars left the city-states vulnerable and the peninsula fell under French and then Spanish and Austrian control. Napoleon's invasion at the turn of the 19th century briefly restored French domination, but also helped ignite a nationalist movement, the Risorgimento. By 1861 the movement had united most of Italy under a constitutional monarchy and an elected parliament.

Yet, at the close of World War I, rising nationalism and

GIUSEPPE GARIBALDI (1807-1882)
Garibaldi, the most famous Italian patriot, conquered Sicily and Naples in 1860 with his army of "red shirts". Although a republican, Garibaldi presented his conquests to Vittorio Emanuele, who was proclaimed king of a united Italy on March 17, 1861.

HOW THE GOVERNM

LEGISLATIVE BRANCH

PARLAMENTO

The two houses of the bicameral parliament are of equal status and all bills must be passed in both houses before becoming law.

▶ **SENATO DELLA REPUBBLICA**
(Senate)
The upper house has 324 seats, 232 directly elected, including six by Italians living abroad, 83 elected by regional proportional representation. Members serve five-year terms. Also nine senators, including former presidents, appointed for life.

▶ **CAMERA DEI DEPUTATI**
(Chamber of Deputies)
The lower house of Parliament; 630 seats; 475 are directly elected, including 12 by Italians living abroad, 155 are elected by regional proportional representation; members serve terms of five years.

EXECUTIVE BRANCH

PRESIDENT
Elected by two-thirds majority vote of parliament sitting jointly with 58 regional delegates; seven-year term; chief of state; commander-in-chief of armed forces; can send legislation back for reconsideration; can dissolve parliament after consultation with leaders of both chambers.

PRIME MINISTER
President of the Council of Ministers; nominated by the president and confirmed by parliament; head of government; responsible for general policy of the government, coordinates activities of the ministers.

▶ **COUNCIL OF MINISTERS**
Nominated by president on the advice of the prime minister and confirmed by parliament; oversees the state bureaucracy.

 REGIONS
▶ 20 regions (5 with limited autonomy)
▶ Elected regional councils
▶ 105 provinces, also with elected councils

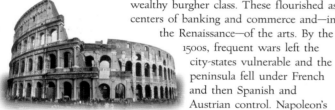

PARLIAMENT BUILDING
Palazzo Montecitorio houses the Camera dei Deputati, the lower house of the Italian Parliament.

> *"The Liberal State is a mask behind which there is no face; it is a scaffolding behind which there is no building."*
> — Benito Mussolini, Italian dictator (1883–1945)

BENITO MUSSOLINI
Founder of Fascism, the Italian dictator was ruler of Italy from 1922 to 1943.

rampant unemployment threatened the the country's stability. Followers of the new Fascist movement marched on Rome and persuaded Italy's king to name its leader, Benito Mussolini, prime minister. Mussolini quickly imposed dictatorial rule, outlawing rival political parties and terrorizing opponents with his squads of "blackshirt" thugs.

In 1940 Italy entered World War II as an ally of Nazi Germany, but suffered disastrous military defeats. Driven from power, Mussolini was captured and executed by anti-Fascist partisans.

At the end of the war, Italians abolished the monarchy and established a democratic republic. But, with dozens of political parties vying for power, Italy found it hard to establish stable government. More than 40 coalition governments have

ruled Italy since the war, most of them very briefly. Either parliamentary deadlocks forced new elections or governments were brought down by revelations of corruption. Reforms enacted in the 1990s aimed at winnowing out marginal parties through minimum vote requirements to secure seats in parliament. Italy's political parties have undergone a radical realignment, but the old problems still dominate political life. Ruling coalitions find it hard to agree and financial scandals continue to haunt individual politicians. Silvio Berlusconi, prime minister since 2001, faces corruption charges dating from the 1980s. He brazenly introduced a bill granting himself immunity from prosecution.

IT WORKS

 **JUDICIAL BRANCH**

SUPREME COURT

Italy's highest court of judicial review. Has the power in civil and criminal cases to re-examine decisions or orders from lower courts, but only on points of law. For ordinary cases, divides into ten separate panels: six criminal, three civil, and one for employment disputes.

▶ **CONSTITUTIONAL COURT**

Composed of 15 judges appointed to nine-year terms; one-third appointed by president, one-third elected by Parliament, one-third elected by courts. Ensures that all laws comply with the constitution; conducts presidential impeachment proceedings.

▶ **THE LOWER COURTS**

Justice, in ordinary civil and criminal cases, is administered by professional career magistrates who are selected through competitive exams and in general advance through seniority.

ELECTORAL SYSTEM

Seventy-five percent of the members of the Chamber of Deputies and the Senate are elected by simple majority vote in single-member districts. Twenty-five percent are elected by proportional regional representation. All voters therefore cast two ballots. Parties must receive at least four percent of the national vote to receive seats via proportional representation.

PARLIAMENT IN SESSION

Far left: Italy's Chamber of Deputies in session.
Left: On November 14, 2002, Pope John Paul II addressed a joint session of the Italian parliament in Rome for the first time in Italy's history.

OFFICIAL NAME: ITALIAN REPUBLIC

POPULATION: 57.5 MILLION	
CAPITAL: ROME	
AREA: 116,305 SQ. MILES (301,230 SQ. KM)	
INDEPENDENCE: MARCH 17, 1861	
CONSTITUTION: JANUARY 1, 1948	

ITALY was called "Italia" by the Romans. The name, probably Greek or Etruscan in origin, meant "land of the grazing calves."

RELIGION: Roman Catholic 83%, Other and non-religious 17%

OFFICIAL LANGUAGE: Italian

REGIONS OR PROVINCES: 20 regions

DEPENDENT TERRITORIES: None

MEDIA: No political censorship exists in national media

Newspapers: There are 78 daily newspapers

TV: 1 publicly owned service, 16 independent national networks, over 900 independent stations

Radio: 1 publicly owned service, over 2100 independent stations

SUFFRAGE: 18 years of age; universal (except in senatorial elections, where minimum age is 25)

LEGAL SYSTEM: Civil law; no ICJ jurisdiction

WORLD ORGANIZATIONS: AfDB, AsDB, Australia Group, BIS, BSEC (observer), CCC, CDB, CE, CEI, CERN, EAPC, EBRD, ECE, ECLAC, EIB, EMU, ESA, EU, FAO, G-7, G-8, G-10, IADB, IAEA, IBRD, ICAO, ICC, ICFTU, ICRM, IDA, IEA, IFAD, IFC, IFRCS, IHO, ILO, IMF, IMO, Interpol, IOC, IOM, ISO, ITU, LAIA (observer), MINURSO, MONUC, NAM (guest), NATO, NEA, NSG, OAS (observer), OECD, OPCW, OSCE, PCA, UN, UNCTAD, UNESCO, UNHCR, UNIDO, UNIFIL, UNIKOM, UNMEE, UNMIBH, UNMIK, UNMOGIP, UNTSO, UPU, WCL, WEU, WHO, WIPO, WMO, WToO, WTrO, ZC

POLITICAL PARTIES: PdL—Freedom Alliance (includes Forza Italia, National Alliance-AN, and Northern League-LN), U—Olive Tree Alliance (includes Democrats of the Left-DS and Party of Italian Communists-PdCI) PRC—Communist Refoundation Party, U-SVP—Olive Tree-South Tyrolese People's Party

ETHNIC GROUPS:
Other 4%
Sardinian 2%
Italian 94%

NATIONAL ECONOMICS

WORLD GNP RANKING: 6th

GNP PER CAPITA: $20,160

INFLATION: 2.5%

BALANCE OF PAYMENTS (BALANCE OF TRADE): -$5.67billion

EXCHANGE RATES / U.S. DLR.: 1.0651-1.1231 EUROS

OFFICIAL CURRENCY: EURO

GOVERNMENT SPENDING (% OF GDP)

✈ DEFENSE 1.9%	
🎓 EDUCATION 4.7%	
✚ HEALTH 5.6%	

0   5   10   15

NUMBER OF CONFLICTS OVER LAST 25 YEARS

	1	2-5	5+
Violent changes in government	○	○	○
Civil wars	○	○	○
International wars	○	○	○
Foreign intervention	○	○	○

● Compulsory national military service to be stopped by 2005.

● "New Model Defense" was introduced in 1992 permitting women soldiers.

● Soldiers were deployed in UN peace-keeping missions in Somalia, Mozambique and East Timor and in "war on terrorism" in Afghanistan.

NOTABLE WARS AND INSURGENCIES: None

SOUTH AFRICA

EMBRACING DIVERSITY, SOUTH AFRICA has come to be known as the Rainbow Nation. A multiracial democracy, it has 11 official languages, recognizing the many cultural groups within its territory. However this transformation has been recent, as ethnic clashes had long been a part of South Africa's history.

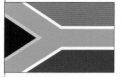

SOUTH AFRICAN FLAG
Adopted on April 27, 1994, the "Y" shape symbolizes convergence of the people.

TABLE MOUNTAIN
This huge sandstone outcrop towers over the city of Cape Town.

Driven by English domination of the Cape, the Afrikaners—descendants of the Dutch explorers who landed in 1652—migrated inland on the Great Trek. From the skirmishes with the Xhosa at the Great Fish River to the Battle of Blood River with the Zulus, Afrikaners struggled to maintain control of their new land. Finally settling in the north they formed two independent Boer Republics. Tensions with the British resulted in the Anglo-Boer Wars beginning in 1880.

British victory ensured that by 1910 the republics were absorbed into the self-governing Union of South Africa, a dominion of the British Empire. They remained so until 1961 when South Africa became an independent republic.

Attempting to gain rights and representation under a white-dominated British system, the South African Native National Council was formed in 1912, later becoming the African National Congress (ANC). From 1948 to 1989 the Afrikaner National Party (NP) won the all-white elections and enforced strict apartheid laws. These divided

HOW THE GOVERNM

LEGISLATIVE BRANCH

PARLIAMENT
South Africa has a bicameral Parliament. All seats in both houses are held by political parties; they may not be held by individuals on their own account.

▶ **NATIONAL COUNCIL OF PROVINCES**
Consists of 90 seats, ten for each of nine provinces (54 permanent, 36 special or floating); members elected to five-year term to represent provincial interests, including ethnic cultural differences, in Parliament. Introduces laws on provincial matters, which must be approved by the National Assembly; approves National Assembly bills and has control of bills relating to monetary matters.

▶ **NATIONAL ASSEMBLY**
Comprises 400 members elected by popular vote through proportional representation to a five-year term. Elects president, passes laws and monitors executive branch. All laws except those relating to provincial matters can be introduced and passed with the approval of the National Council of Provinces.

 PROVINCES
▶ Nine regional provinces
▶ Elected provincial legislatures
▶ Municipalities

EXECUTIVE BRANCH

PRESIDENT
Chief of state and head of government; leader of the largest party in the National Assembly; limited to two five-year terms; serves as leader of the Cabinet; has broad executive powers including assigning Cabinet portfolios and signing bills into law. Can be removed by a vote of no confidence or by impeachment.

▶ **DEPUTY PRESIDENT**
Appointed by the president, assists in executing government functions.

UNION BUILDINGS
The seat of the presidency, these government offices are located in the administrative capital, Pretoria.

 LOWER HOUSE
The National Assembly in session at the Parliament building located in the legislative capital of Cape Town.

> *"I have cherished the ideal of a democratic and free society in which all persons live together in harmony with equal opportunities. It is an ideal which I hope to live for.... an ideal for which I am prepared to die."* —*Nelson Mandela*

South Africans by race into whites, and three black groups: "colored" (people whose descent was deemed mixed), Asians, and Africans. Each category had different political, economic, and social rights, with black Africans being the most severely isolated and discriminated against.

Banned as political organizations in 1960, the Pan African Congress (PAC) and ANC became armed liberation movements, receiving aid from Cuba and Russia. After their leaders in South Africa were jailed, including Nelson Mandela in 1962, new leaders operated from neighboring countries. With the intensification of the black struggle for freedom, the government imposed a state of emergency in 1985. International sanctions on South Africa were applied in response. In 1989 the

NELSON ROLIHLAHLA MANDELA *(1918-)*
Imprisoned for 28 years under apartheid, Mandela became president of South Africa in 1994 and served until 1999.

National Party elected a new leader, F. W. De Klerk. Recognizing the potential for full-scale civil war, his government began to dismantle the apartheid system. The ANC and PAC were legalized, and Mandela released from prison in 1990.

In 1994 the first democratic elections permitting all races to vote were held and Mandela was elected the first president of the new South Africa. Mandela and De Klerk were jointly awarded the Nobel Peace Prize in 1993 for their efforts in bringing about the changes. In 1999 Mandela stepped down, handing the leadership of the ANC and South Africa to his deputy, Thabo Mbeki.

Today, South Africa is a country of sharp contrasts—offering world-class infrastructure and a growing economy, while dealing with the issues of high unemployment, rampant crime and a growing HIV/AIDS epidemic, which affects nearly six million South Africans.

OFFICIAL NAME: REPUBLIC OF SOUTH AFRICA

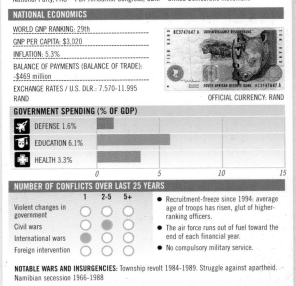

POPULATION: 43.8 MILLION	
CAPITAL: PRETORIA (ADMIN), CAPE TOWN (LEGIS), BLOEMFONTEIN (JUD)	
AREA: 471,008 SQ. MILES (1,219,911 SQ. KM)	
INDEPENDENCE: 1910	
CONSTITUTION: 1996	

SOUTH AFRICA derives its name from its southern location, with Africa thought to be rooted in the Latin *aprica* ("sunny"), the Greek *aphrike* ("without cold"), or the Phoenician *afri* ("black men").

RELIGION: Christian 68%, Muslim 2%, Hindu 1.5% (60% of Indians), indigenous beliefs and animist 28.5%

OFFICIAL LANGUAGES: Afrikaans, English, and 9 African languages

REGIONS OR PROVINCES: 9 provinces

DEPENDENT TERRITORIES: None

MEDIA: No political censorship exists in national media

Newspapers: There are 20 daily newspapers

TV: 1 state-owned service

Radio: 1 state-owned service

SUFFRAGE: 18 years of age; universal

LEGAL SYSTEM: English common law; Roman-Dutch legal traditions; accepts ICJ jurisdiction

WORLD ORGANIZATIONS: ACP, AfDB, BIS, C, CCC, ECA, FAO, G-24, G-77, IAEA, IBRD, ICAO, ICC, ICFTU, ICRM, IDA, IFAD, IFC, IFRCS, IHO, ILO, IMF, IMO, Interpol, IOC, IOM, ISO, ITU, MONUC, NAM, NSG, OAU, OPCW, PCA, SACU, SADC, UN, UNCTAD, UNESCO, UNHCR, UNIDO, UNITAR, UNMEE, UPU, WCL, WFTU, WHO, WIPO, WMO, WToO, WTrO, ZC

POLITICAL PARTIES: ACDP—African Christian Democratic Party, ANC—African National Congress, DA—Democratic Alliance (formed from the merger of the Democratic Party, or DP, and the New National Party, or NP), FF—Freedom Front, IFP—Inkatha Freedom Party, NP—New National Party, PAC—Pan-Africanist Congress, UDM—United Democratic Movement

ETHNIC GROUPS:

- Other 4%
- Xhosa 9%
- Mixed 10%
- White 16%
- Other Black 38%
- Zulu 23%

NATIONAL ECONOMICS

WORLD GNP RANKING: 29th

GNP PER CAPITA: $3,020

INFLATION: 5.3%

BALANCE OF PAYMENTS (BALANCE OF TRADE): -$469 million

EXCHANGE RATES / U.S. DLR.: 7.570-11.995 RAND

OFFICIAL CURRENCY: RAND

GOVERNMENT SPENDING (% OF GDP)

		0	5	10	15
✈ DEFENSE 1.6%					
📖 EDUCATION 6.1%					
✚ HEALTH 3.3%					

NUMBER OF CONFLICTS OVER LAST 25 YEARS

	1	2-5	5+
Violent changes in government	○	○	○
Civil wars	○	●	○
International wars	●	○	○
Foreign intervention	○	○	○

- Recruitment-freeze since 1994: average age of troops has risen, glut of higher-ranking officers.
- The air force runs out of fuel toward the end of each financial year.
- No compulsory military service.

NOTABLE WARS AND INSURGENCIES: Township revolt 1984-1989. Struggle against apartheid. Namibian secession 1966-1988

⚖ JUDICIAL BRANCH

SUPREME COURT OF APPEAL

Situated in the judicial capital, Bloemfontein; composed of a president and other appeal judges appointed by the president; the highest court for all non-constitutional matters and court of final appeal; can determine appeals against High Court decisions; decisions are binding on all lower courts.

▶ CONSTITUTIONAL COURT

Composed of chief justice chosen by the president, and ten other judges chosen by president and Cabinet; all serve a non-renewable 12-year term; must retire at 70. Certifies constitution when amended; rules on constitutional matters; can determine acts of Parliament and conduct of president and executive unconstitutional. A matter before the court must be heard by at least eight judges; generally all 11 preside.

▶ HIGH COURTS

Operate in ten provincial court divisions; decisions are binding on all Magistrates' Courts within their areas of jurisdiction; all but one have a judge president and as many other judges as the president determines appropriate. Also three local divisions presided over by provincial court judges.

ELECTORAL SYSTEM

According to the constitution, elections and referendums fall under the control of the Independent Electoral Commission (IEC) which is headed by five commissioners including a chairperson. Elections are held at the national, provincial and local levels.

SPAIN

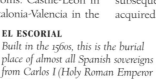

SPANISH FLAG
Adopted on December 19, 1981, the Spanish flag is known as the Rojigualda (the "Red-and-Yellow.")

SPAIN HAS ITS ORIGIN AS A NATION STATE in the marriage of Ferdinand II of Aragon and Isabella I of Castile in 1469 and reached its present boundaries with their capture of Granada from the Moors in 1492. It has remained a monarchy ever since except for brief interludes from 1873 and 1931 as a republic, and from 1939 as a fascist dictatorship.

Spain's initial experience of unified rule was as the Roman province of Hispania, although the Basque and other northern regions remained less romanized than the rest of Iberia. The Romans were followed by Visigoths then, in 711, by Muslim Berbers from North Africa. Soon, small Christian kingdoms emerged in the north to begin almost six centuries of reconquest. Forming dynastic and military alliances, they eventually crystallized into two main groupings of kingdoms: Castile-León in the west, and Aragón-Catalonia-Valencia in the east. Though united in cause, they maintained their own *cortes*, the fore-runners of today's Parliament. These had their origin in a council called in 1188 by Alfonso X of León, in which town representatives were given a vote—an essential concession as the Crown raised its taxes from the merchant classes.

As a uified nation, Spain passed into Habsburg hands in 1516, and subsequently acquired a

EL ESCORIAL
Built in the 1560s, this is the burial place of almost all Spanish sovereigns from Carlos I (Holy Roman Emperor Charles V) onward.

HOW THE GOVE

🏛 LEGISLATIVE BRANCH

CORTES GENERALES

Spain is governed by a bicameral parliament. Bills become law if passed by a majority in both chambers or, in the case of non-agreement, by an absolute majority vote in Congress.

▶ **SENADO**
(Senate)
Composed of 208 members directly elected from the provinces for four years by simple vote, and 51 appointed by the Parliaments of the autonomous communities. Has no authority to introduce bills, but may veto or amend them. Has a maximum of eight weeks in which to complete deliberations.

▶ **CONGRESO DE LOS DIPUTADOS**
(Congress of Deputies)
The more powerful chamber of the Cortes Generales. Composed of 350 members elected for four years by proportional representation. Initiates all legislation; may override Senate vetoes; ratifies monarch's nomination of the prime minister. Prime minister, vice-presidents and Council of Ministers all responsible to Congress.

AUTONOMOUS COMMUNITIES
▶ 19 communities subdivided into provinces
▶ Each has elected president and unicameral assembly
▶ Supreme Court in each community

CONGRESS OF DEPUTIES
Right: The Lower Chamber's mid-19th century seat in Madrid. Right: The royal opening of Parliament on May 3, 2000.

🏛 EXECUTIVE BRANCH

MONARCH

Hereditary position; represents the unity of Spain; head of state and commander-in-chief of armed forces. Appoints Spain's president of the government on recommendation of the Congress of Deputies, and vice-presidents on recommendation of the president. May promulgate or sanction legislation.

▶ **COUNCIL OF STATE**
Purely advisory body composed of eminent figures in the law, the armed forces, the civil service, and other walks of life. Its president is appointed by Council of Ministers.

CONGRESO DE L

"I am responsible only to God and history."
— Francisco Franco, "El Caudillo" (The Leader),
Spanish soldier and political leader 1892-1975

vast New World empire. Its monarchs gradually imposed Castilian values and institutions throughout their possessions, dispensing with the medieval *cortes*, and centralizing power until Spain, under a new Bourbon dynasty installed in 1700, was ruled as an absolute monarchy. This lasted through the 18th century—though with control often wielded by royal favorites.

The 19th century was a disastrous time in Spanish politics. After a period of French Napoleonic rule (1808-1814), Spain was torn apart by civil wars between absolutists and liberals. It experienced its first liberal consitution in 1814 and First Republic in 1873, and lost most of its empire in Central and South America. The birth of socialism, anarchism, and Catalan and Basque regionalism culminated in the

JUAN CARLOS DE BORBÓN Y BORBÓN
(1938-) Coming to the throne just two days after Francisco Franco's death, Juan Carlos has led Spain towards democracy. He was the first Spanish king to visit the Americas and the first king to visit communist China.

Second Republic in 1931. Reactionary nationalists under Franco fomented the catastrophic Spanish Civil War in 1936, and in 1939 overcame the last strongholds of republicanism in the Basque Country, Barcelona, and Madrid.

Franco established dictatorial rule, heading the Movimiento Nacional as the sole political party and instituting total state control of the economy. He kept the military at the center of government, relegated the Cortes to a passive role, and stamped on any form of separatism. Spain was in effect isolated from the outside world until he was forced to accept World Bank intervention in the 1960s to bring Spain out of serious economic collapse. In 1969 he named the Bourbon heir, Juan Carlos, as his successor. Although Franco also declared Spain to be a representative monarchy with himself as regent, this was but a front—he kept total, authoritarian control until his death in 1975.

King Juan Carlos played a key personal role in speeding the transition to democracy by sacking Franco's last prime minister, and

GENERAL FRANCO
As military dictator from 1939, Francisco Franco isolated Spain from the rest of Europe and the world for two thirds of his 36 years in power.

appointing Adolfo Suárez to steer bills for a bicameral parliamentary system through the Cortes. Suárez's centrist party won the first elections in 1977, and in 1978 a new constitution provided for unprecedented autonomy in every region of Spain. Heady with new-found democratic freedoms, Spaniards voted in a socialist administration in the following four elections. However, a series of governmental financial and police scandals tipped the balance of power back to the center right in 1996 under José María Aznar. Whatever the color of the central government, devolution of further powers to the regions remains in progress.

...NMENT WORKS

PRIME MINISTER

President of the Government and usually head of dominant party in Parliament; not directy elected by popular vote but appointed by monarch subject to vote of confidence by Congress of Deputies; nominates candidates for the two vice-presidencies for appointment by monarch

▸ **COUNCIL OF MINISTERS**
Headed by the prime minister and his deputies; determines government policy.

⚖ JUDICIAL BRANCH

SUPREME COURT

Heads Spain's judicial system. Divided into five chambers: civil, criminal, administrative, social, and military. Its 95 judges are led by a president, who is appointed by the monarch after nomination by a 20-member Council of the Judiciary (8 appointed by Parliament, 12 by judges). The Council serves an administrative function, appointing judges and maintaining legal standards.

▸ **CONSTITUTIONAL COURT**
Ensures all laws comply with the constitution and international treaties signed by Spain; 12 judges appointed for nine-year terms by government, Judicial Council and Cortes. Citizens may appeal to it for protection against government violations of civil rights.

▸ **LOWER COURTS**
Regional Courts, one Supreme Court in each autonomous community, Provincial Courts, Courts of First Instance and Municipal Courts. A new, totally separate court hears cases relating to terrorism, drugs, and money laundering.

TRIBUNAL SUPREMO
The Spanish Supreme Court in Madrid.

⊞ ELECTORAL SYSTEM
The chambers of Parliament are elected by different systems. The Congress has a system of proportional representation in which voters in each province are presented with a list of parties among which to make a single choice. For the elected seats in the Senate, voting is by simple majority for candidates standing in 208 constituencies (four in each mainland province, with the rest apportioned among the islands, and Ceuta and Melilla).

...PUTADOS

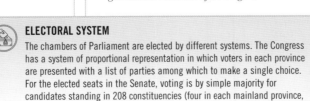

SPAIN

OFFICIAL NAME: KINGDOM OF SPAIN

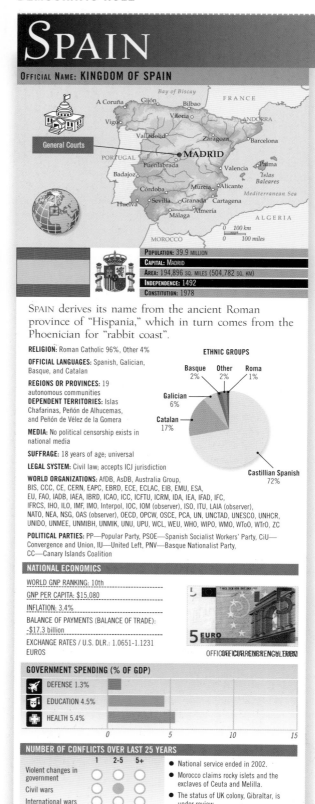

POPULATION: 39.9 MILLION	
CAPITAL: MADRID	
AREA: 194,896 SQ. MILES (504,782 SQ. KM)	
INDEPENDENCE: 1492	
CONSTITUTION: 1978	

SPAIN derives its name from the ancient Roman province of "Hispania," which in turn comes from the Phoenician for "rabbit coast".

RELIGION: Roman Catholic 96%, Other 4%

OFFICIAL LANGUAGES: Spanish, Galician, Basque, and Catalan

REGIONS OR PROVINCES: 19 autonomous communities

DEPENDENT TERRITORIES: Islas Chafarinas, Peñón de Alhucemas, and Peñón de Vélez de la Gomera

MEDIA: No political censorship exists in national media

SUFFRAGE: 18 years of age; universal

LEGAL SYSTEM: Civil law; accepts ICJ jurisdiction

WORLD ORGANIZATIONS: AfDB, AsDB, Australia Group, BIS, CCC, CE, CERN, EAPC, EBRD, ECE, ECLAC, EIB, EMU, ESA, EU, FAO, IADB, IAEA, IBRD, ICAO, ICC, ICFTU, ICRM, IDA, IEA, IFAD, IFC, IFRCS, IHO, ILO, IMF, IMO, Interpol, IOC, IOM (observer), ISO, ITU, LAIA (observer), NATO, NEA, NSG, OAS (observer), OECD, OPCW, OSCE, PCA, UN, UNCTAD, UNESCO, UNHCR, UNIDO, UNMEE, UNMIBH, UNMIK, UNU, UPU, WCL, WEU, WHO, WIPO, WMO, WToO, WTrO, ZC

POLITICAL PARTIES: PP—Popular Party, PSOE—Spanish Socialist Workers' Party, CiU—Convergence and Union, IU—United Left, PNV—Basque Nationalist Party, CC—Canary Islands Coalition

ETHNIC GROUPS

- Castillian Spanish 72%
- Catalan 17%
- Galician 6%
- Basque 2%
- Other 2%
- Roma 1%

NATIONAL ECONOMICS

WORLD GNP RANKING: 10th

GNP PER CAPITA: $15,080

INFLATION: 3.4%

BALANCE OF PAYMENTS (BALANCE OF TRADE): -$17.3 billion

EXCHANGE RATES / U.S. DLR.: 1.0651-1.1231 EUROS

OFFICIAL CURRENCY: EURO

GOVERNMENT SPENDING (% OF GDP)

- DEFENSE 1.3%
- EDUCATION 4.5%
- HEALTH 5.4%

NUMBER OF CONFLICTS OVER LAST 25 YEARS

	1	2-5	5+
Violent changes in government	○	○	○
Civil wars	○	●	○
International wars	○	○	○
Foreign intervention	○	○	○

- National service ended in 2002.
- Morocco claims rocky islets and the exclaves of Ceuta and Melilla.
- The status of UK colony, Gibraltar, is under review.

NOTABLE WARS AND INSURGENCIES: Basque separatist terrorism 1968-present. Catalan terrorism 1980-1987

"The singular remarkable fact about the Basques is that they still exist."
—Mark Kurlansky, The Basque History of the World (1999)

AUTONOMOUS COMMUNITIES

A key feature of Spanish government is the devolution of wide-ranging powers to the nation's 19 constituent "autonomous communities". These function as microcosms of the central government, having their own elected presidents, unicameral parliaments elected by direct popular vote, cabinets, supreme courts, capital cities and flags.

Catalonia, the Basque Country (Euskadi), and Galicia each have their own language and culture and began their modern struggle for autonomy in the 1930s. In 1932 the central government recognized a Catalan statute of autonomy, and in 1936 plebiscites in the Basque country and Galicia showed majority support in favor. However, the 1936-1939 Spanish Civil War intervened. Galicia soon fell to Franco's nationalists, but the Basque Country and Catalonia remained republican until the final stages. Franco's fascist, Madrid-centered regime then quashed all vestiges of political (and cultural) autonomy.

The post-Franco Spanish Constitution of 1978 provided for regional autonomy throughout Spain, granting the Basque Country, Catalonia and Galicia special recognition as "historic nationalities" because of their long-standing claims. It also provided for a special fast-track process which meant that these were able to elect their own parliaments, following confirmatory regional referenda, in 1980-1981. The other "communities" followed in 1982 and 1983, with the Spain's North African possessions of Ceuta and Melilla gaining "autonomous city" status in 1995.

The autonomous communities receive their funding from the central government, which raises the money through a combination of taxes and surpluses from the social security system. Communities may also collect local taxes and borrow money. The "historic nationalities" have greater autonomy than the other communities, including responsibility for economic development, education, health, environment, tourism, and social security, but all communities will eventually have equal autonomy. The communities are accountable to the Senate. Spain's central government has a delegate in each community appointed by the Spanish Council of Ministers. Each community has a Supreme Court responsible to the state's Supreme Court in Madrid. The central Constitutional Court decides questions over the constitutionality of regional legislation.

Despite the transfer of power and the unusual degree of regional autonomy in Spain, separatism continues to be one of the most serious problems confronting it. The Basque separatist paramilitary organization, Euskadi Ta Askatasuna (ETA—Basque Homeland and Freedom), founded in 1959, has been responsible for more than 800 deaths in the past 30 years. The Basque desire for complete separation from Spain arises from deep ethnic, cultural, and linguistic differences between it and the rest of Spain—its language, Euskera (Basque), is unrelated to any Indo-European language. The Basque community wants unification with the historically related province of Navarre, while more extreme elements also demand historical Basque lands in southern France. In 2002, ETA has abandoned a 1999 cease-fire, provoking public anti-violence demonstrations right across Spain. However the most traumatic events of recent times have been the Madrid train bombings of 11 March 2004, carried out by Islamic militants, which led to the government's downfall at the general election.

SPANISH ROYAL FAMILY
King Juan Carlos, surrounded by his family, delivers a speech on May, 3, 2000 at the official opening of the Spanish Parliament in the seventh post-Franco legislature.

POLAND

OFFICIAL NAME: REPUBLIC OF POLAND

POPULATION: 38.6 million
CAPITAL: Warsaw
AREA: 120,728 SQ. MILES (312,685 SQ. KM)
INDEPENDENCE: 1918
CONSTITUTION: 1997

POLAND comes from the Slavic *polanie*, which means "field," referring to the flat plains that cover the country.

RELIGION: Roman Catholic 93%, Eastern Orthodox 2%, Other and non-religious 5%

OFFICIAL LANGUAGE: Polish

REGIONS OR PROVINCES: 16 provinces

DEPENDENT TERRITORIES: None

MEDIA: No political censorship exists in national media

NEWSPAPERS: There are 52 daily newspapers

TV: 3 independent services

RADIO: 6 independent services

SUFFRAGE: 18 years of age; universal

LEGAL SYSTEM: French law; Communist legal traditions; accepts ICJ jurisdiction

ETHNIC GROUPS:
Other 1%
German 1%
Polish 98%

WORLD ORGANIZATIONS: ACCT (observer), Australia Group, BIS, BSEC (observer), CBSS, CCC, CE, CEI, CERN, EAPC, EBRD, ECE, EU, FAO, IAEA, IBRD, ICAO, ICC, ICFTU, ICRM, IDA, IEA (observer), IFC, IFRCS, IHO, ILO, IMF, IMO, Interpol, IOC, IOM, ISO, ITU, MINURSO, MONUC, NAM (guest), NATO, NSG, OAS (observer), OECD, OPCW, OSCE, PCA, PFP, UN, UNCTAD, UNDOF, UNESCO, UNHCR, UNIDO, UNIFIL, UNIKOM, UNMEE, UNMIBH, UNMIK, UNMOP, UNMOT, UNOMIG, UPU, WCL, WEU (associate), WFTU, WHO, WIPO, WMO, WToO, WTrO, ZC

POLITICAL PARTIES: SLD-UP—Democratic Left Alliance-Labor Union, PO—Civic Platform, S—Self Defense, PIS—Law and Justice, PSL—Polish Peasant Party, LPR—League of Polish Families, GM—German Minority of Lower Silesia, Bloc—Senate 2001 Bloc, Ind—Independents

NATIONAL ECONOMICS

WORLD GNP RANKING: 25th

GNP PER CAPITA: $4,190

INFLATION: 10.1%

BALANCE OF PAYMENTS (BALANCE OF TRADE): -$10.0 billion

EXCHANGE RATES / U.S. DLR.: 4.133-3.952 ZLOTYS

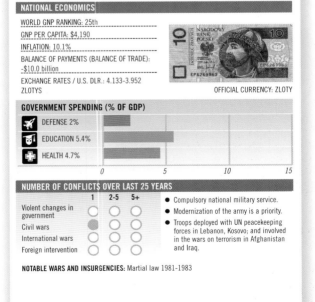

OFFICIAL CURRENCY: ZLOTY

GOVERNMENT SPENDING (% OF GDP)

- DEFENSE 2%
- EDUCATION 5.4%
- HEALTH 4.7%

0   5   10   15

NUMBER OF CONFLICTS OVER LAST 25 YEARS

	1	2-5	5+
Violent changes in government	○	○	○
Civil wars	◐	○	○
International wars	○	○	○
Foreign intervention	○	○	○

- Compulsory national military service.
- Modernization of the army is a priority.
- Troops deployed with UN peacekeeping forces in Lebanon, Kosovo; and involved in the wars on terrorism in Afghanistan and Iraq.

NOTABLE WARS AND INSURGENCIES: Martial law 1981-1983

POLAND'S BOUNDARIES WERE ALREADY DEFINED much as they are in the present day by the early 11th century. However, the country endured long periods of occupation, and was completely partitioned between Russia, Prussia and Austria in 1772, 1792 and 1795. It regained nation status in 1918, but Nazi Germany invaded in 1939 and divided it with the Stalinist Soviet Union, leaving a broken state. Following World War II, the electorate voted in favor of communism, whose remnants have carried over to today's socialist-leaning government.

The faltering Soviet-modeled economy of the 1970s enabled the 1980 rise of Solidarity, a trade union headed by electrician Lech Walesa. Solidarity pushed for socioeconomic reforms, particularly a market economy. The 1990 resignation of President Wojciech Jaruzelski prompted the Sejm, or Lower House—the more powerful of Poland's two legislative bodies, to pass a constitutional amendment establishing direct election of the president. Walesa was subsequently elected, but adopted an increasingly dictatorial stance which distanced him from the Solidarity Party he had helped to found. In 1995, Aleksander Kwasniewski of the Democratic Left Alliance (SLD), a reformed communist party with a social democrat stance, was elected president with 51.7 percent of the vote, as voters cast aside Walesa's tough anti-communist ideology. Kwasniewski's party, the SLD, won the parliamentary elections of 2001, forming a coalition with the Polish Peasant Party (PSL) and Union of Labor (UP), although by March 2003, only the SLD and UP remained.

ELECTIONS—OCTOBER 27, 2002
Former President Lech Walesa casts his vote in local elections in Gdansk, Poland.

Poland's rocky transition to democracy began to stabilize in the late 1990s. A referendum in 1997 finally approved a new post-communist constitution formalizing free presidential and parliamentary elections. Civil rights in place since 1989 include freedom of speech, public assembly (except for "totalitarian" organizations), and the press. Poland joined NATO in 1999 and is in line for EU accession in 2004. A superfluity of political factions makes building coalitions difficult. Parties need at least 8 percent of the vote to be eligible to join a coalition government.

HOW THE GOVERNMENT WORKS

LEGISLATIVE BRANCH

Zgromadzenie Narodowe (National Assembly) Bicameral Parliament

Senat (Senate)
Composed of 100 members elected to four-year terms by direct popular vote.

Sejm (Lower House)
460 members directly elected to four-year terms by proportional representation. Initiates and passes bills; overrides vetoes by three-fifths majority vote; dissolves itself by two-thirds majority vote; removes prime minister and Council of Ministers with no-confidence vote.

Regional Governments
49 provinces administered by locally elected executives and legislatures.

EXECUTIVE BRANCH

President
Elected to five-year term by direct popular vote; two-term limit. Serves as head of state; commander-in-chief of armed forces. Directs international affairs; dissolves Parliament; sets legislative elections.

Prime Minister
Member of majority party in Lower House. Appointed by president, confirmed by Lower House. Serves as head of government. Directs domestic affairs; chairs Council of Ministers.

Deputy Prime Ministers
Appointed by president, confirmed by Lower House.

Council of Ministers
Appointed by president on advice of prime minister, confirmed by Lower House. Oversees government operations.

JUDICIAL BRANCH

Constitutional Tribunal
Rules on constitutionality of laws; decides election disputes. Judges appointed to nine-year terms by Lower House.

Constitutional Tribunal
Rules on constitutionality of laws; decides election disputes. Judges appointed to nine-year terms by Lower House.

Supreme Court
Highest court of review and appeal for civil and criminal cases. Judges appointed for life by president on advice of National Council of the Judiciary.

Provincial Courts

Local Courts

CANADA

CANADA enjoys the status of a highly developed, modern, wealthy, and industrialized nation, but the history of its development since the 18th century is nonetheless marked by distinct—often turbulent—political divides based on language and culture.

CANADIAN FLAG
Adopted on February 15, 1965 the Canadian flag, known as the "maple-leaf flag", shows the national colors, proclaimed by King George V in 1921.

CANADIAN MOUNTIES
The Royal Canadian Mounted Police, commonly known as Mounties, were established in 1873 to maintain order in the western territories.

Modern Canada—its national identity, its borders, and its political system—was forged over three centuries of political friction between the Francophone Quebecois and Anglophone settlers.

Inhabited for millennia by indigenous Algonquin, Blackfoot, Iroquois, and Inuit peoples, Canada first attracted the attention of Europeans when ships began exploring the Hudson Bay area in search of the "Northwest Passage."

The first European commercial ventures in Canada were predominantly French, and based upon the fur trade. In fact, the French population in Canada grew rapidly after 1600, and the eastern regions soon

became known as *Nouvelle France* (New France), which encompassed the important colonies of Quebec and Acadia. The French monarch retained considerable control and influence over the area until France's defeat by the British in 1763 in the Seven Years' War. Control of the Canadian colonies subsequently passed to the British, an event that would forever alter the sociopolitical composition of the Canadian homeland.

Over the next three decades Canada received roughly 40,000 United Empire Loyalists from the USA, creating both a substantial English-speaking population and sharp ethnic tensions between the Anglophones and the Francophones. To

HOW THE GOVE

LEGISLATIVE BRANCH

PARLIAMENT

Bicameral Parliament. All bills must be passed by both houses before becoming law. The Senate can amend or reject bills, and return them to the Commons for reconsideration.

▶ **SENATE**

The upper house of Parliament; 105 senators appointed by the governor-general to serve until the age of 75. Intended to be a place of "sober second thought," the Senate was created to protect the interests of smaller provinces and discuss major issues in open hearings. Although it possesses the same legislative powers as the lower house, the Senate rarely addresses matters of day-to-day government.

▶ **HOUSE OF COMMONS**

The lower house of Parliament: 301 members elected by popular vote term of five years. Unless the government is defeated or resigns, the prime minister requests dissolution from governor-general every five years. The House of Commons is responsible for the daily business of legislature and for overseeing government.

EXECUTIVE BRANCH

MONARCH

The king or queen of the United Kingdom; sovereign of the Commonwealth; head of state; his or her official role is formal and largely ceremonial.

▶ **GOVERNOR-GENERAL**

Appointed by the monarch to serve as his or her representative; serves a minimum of five years. Appoints prime minister, summons and dissolves the Parliament.

PROVINCIAL LEGISLATURE
The impressive façade of the provincial parliament building in Victoria, British Columbia.

PROVINCES & TERRITORIES
▶ 10 provinces and 3 territories
▶ Provincial legislative assemblies
▶ Lieutenant-governors represent the Queen

THE SENATE
The interior of the Senate Chamber in the Canadian Parliament building, Ottawa, Ontario.

"I believe a constitution can permit the co-existence of several cultures and ethnic groups within a single state."
— *Pierre Trudeau, September 30, 1965*

PIERRE TRUDEAU
A popular and influential Prime Minister, Trudeau was a strong advocate of bilingualism, ethnic tolerance, and a unified Canada.

ease tensions, the British crown implemented the Constitutional Act of 1791, designed to placate both English- and French-speakers. It created the colonies of Upper and Lower Canada, each of which enjoyed limited autonomy.

With the Union Act of 1840, the British crown attempted to loosen political control over the colonies, but re-established the notion of a unified Canadian political entity, which it had abandoned in 1791. In 1867, the crown created the Dominion of Canada through the union of Ontario, Quebec, Nova Scotia, and New Brunswick.

In 1931 the Statute of Westminster established Canada as an independent sovereign state, with Quebec maintaining an unusual degree of autonomy. At this time Canada comprised nine provinces and two territories. Newfoundland joined later, in 1949, and the Inuit territory of Nunavut was formed in 1999.

...RNMENT WORKS

PRIME MINISTER

Serves as the head of government; generally the leader of the majority party in the House of Commons occupies this office.

▶ **PRIVY COUNCIL**
The monarch's ceremonial advisory council; members appointed by governor-general on advice of prime minister.

  ▶ **CABINET**
Members are appointed by the prime minister primarily from the majority party in Parliament with at least one minister per province; must be or become a member of the Privy Council and of the House of Commons within a reasonable time, or resign from the Cabinet.

JUDICIAL BRANCH

SUPREME COURT

The country's highest judicial authority in civil, criminal, and constitutional cases; nine judges nominated by the prime minister and appointed by the governor-general to serve until the age of 75.

▶ **FEDERAL COURT**
The only fully integrated judicial branch in any modern federation; administers justice throughout most of Canada; court of justice in all criminal cases.

▶ **PROVINCIAL COURTS**
Each province operates an individual court system—complete with appellate courts and a provincial superior court—with federally appointed judges.

▶ **TAX COURT**
A subdivision of the Federal Court, the Tax Court oversees cases involving violations of Canada's federal tax codes and regulations.

SUPREME COURT JUDGES
The judges of Canada's Supreme Court represent the highest judicial authority. In recent years, attempts have been made to make the country's Supreme Court a geographically representative body.

 ELECTORAL SYSTEM
Members of Canada's House of Commons are elected from single-seat parliamentary districts. The districts are commonly referred to as "ridings." The first-past-the-post system is also used for elections to provincial legislatures.

EXECUTIVE / LEGISLATIVE / JUDICIAL BRANCHES

*"It is what we prevent, rather than what we do
that counts most in government"*
— Prime Minister William Mackenzie King, August 26, 1936

EXECUTIVE BRANCH

At the apex of the Canadian executive and legislative branches is the British monarch. As a constitutional monarchy and member of the Commonwealth, Canada acknowledges the Queen as head of state. Her position within Canadian politics is insignificant, however, in terms of influence and power. Her role—just as it has become in the UK—is emblematic: the symbolic figurehead of the kingdom and the Commonwealth. As in many countries of the British Commonwealth, the monarch appoints a governor-general to represent her as the titular head of Canada's federal government, but this is always done on the recommendation of the prime minister. Due to the large cultural cleavage in Canada between Francophone and Anglophone peoples, the position of governor-general is alternately assigned to a French-speaker and an English-speaker. The appointment is deliberately apolitical—for example in 1999, noted journalist and broadcaster Adrienne Clarkson was appointed. Only the second female governor-general, she is also the first to have immigrated to Canada. While the governor-general's position is vested with power to make royal appointments and approve legislation on behalf of the monarch, the duties of governor-general are also largely ceremonial, as the British crown rarely interferes with domestic politics. The same applies to the Queen's Privy Council, which—in theory—serves as the chief advisory council for the head of state. Again, its role is symbolic, serving only in a ceremonial capacity.

The majority of political power in the executive is wielded by the prime minister, who is generally the leader of the majority party in Parliament and therefore elected at the annual national party leadership convention. The prime minister forms the cabinet, outlines the government's agenda and establishes the government's policy on all issues of domestic politics and foreign affairs.

The cabinet is the most important political group in the executive. Appointed by the prime minister following parliamentary elections, each member of the cabinet is assigned one—or sometimes more than one—"portfolio," or government ministry. Several factors influence cabinet appointments. Talent and experience aside, the cabinet is generally constructed on a principle of fair representation for all the country's provinces. Furthermore, certain posts are usually assigned to representatives from particular parts of Canada. For instance, the Department of Agriculture is generally assigned to a cabinet member from the prairie provinces. In other words, the prime minister attempts to create a cabinet—and a government—from across the country in order to attend to the interests of the country as a whole.

ISSUES AND CHALLENGES

A deep cultural divide exists between the Francophone province of Quebec and the rest of Canada, which is Anglophone. This cultural distinction manifests itself in Canadian national politics in the form of a Québécois separatist movement, which ultimately seeks to establish an autonomous nation for Quebec and maintain only economic ties with Canada.

The character of the movement changed in 1963 with the formation of the Front de Libération du Québec. This violent faction carried out several waves of terrorist attacks in Canada throughout the following decade, eventually provoking the October Crisis of 1970, when they kidnapped a British trade official and kidnapped and murdered Pierre Laporte, labor minister of Quebec. The government suspended normal civil liberties in order to round up suspected members of the movement. The Front de Libération du Québec never gained popular support, however, and more liberal groups emerged to spearhead the movement. The most important of these was the Parti Québécois, formed in 1968, which has continued to play a significant role in Canadian politics.

QUEBEC SEPARATIST MOVEMENT
The separatist movement, part of Canada's national identity for some 35 years, suffered a setback with the defeat of the Parti Québécois in the 2003 provincial elections.

BRIEF CHRONOLOGY OF CANADA'S PARLIAMENT

1867 *British North America Act (also known in Canada as the Constitution Act) unites four colonies— Ontario, Quebec, Nova Scotia, and New Brunswick—to form the Dominion of Canada. By the constitution, power is vested in the Sovereign, the House of Commons, and the Senate.*

1869 *The first Great Seal of Canada is minted.*

1870 *Manitoba Act creates the province of Manitoba, following opposition from settlers and Métis (descendants of the children of fur-traders and native women) in the Red River region.*

1871 *British Columbia (including the colony of Vancouver Island) joins Canada. Parliament restructures to accommodate new representatives.*

1873 *Prince Edward Island joins Canada. Parliament is again restructured accordingly.*

1905 *The provinces of Alberta and Saskatchewan are created. Their natural resources remain under the control of the federal government until the 1920s.*

1916 *Large parts of the parliamentary building in Ottawa are destroyed by fire. It is rebuilt in 1917–1927.*

GALLERY OF PRIME MINISTERS

Since 1867, the office of prime minister has played an important role in the nation's political life—as both head of government and as the liaison between the executive branch, its policy, and Parliament. To the right are some of the Canadians who have held the office of prime minister.

SIR JOHN ALEXANDER MACDONALD
July 1, 1867– Nov 5, 1873 and Oct 17, 1878 – June 6, 1891

- An early leader of the Conservative Party.
- Influential in the formation of Canada.
- Formed the new Dominion's first government in 1867

SIR WILFRID LAURIER
July 11, 1896 – Oct 6, 1911

- First French Canadian to become Prime Minister of Canada.
- A strong advocate of North American free-trade.
- Served 44 years, 11 months as a member of parliament.

WILLIAM LYON MACKENZIE KING
Dec 1921 – June 1926; Sep 1926 – Aug 1930; Oct 1935 – Nov 1948

- A popular politician, King served as prime minister for nearly twenty-five years.
- A passionate advocate of Canadian autonomy, he was a catalyst for the Statute of Westminster.

JOHN DIEFENBAKER
June 21, 1957 – April 21, 1963

- His administration marked a conservative shift in Canadian politics after 22 years of liberal rule.
- Introduced agricultural reforms in the 1960s and extended federal citizenship to indigenous population

CANADA

SUPREME COURT
The building of the Canadian Supreme Court stands on Parliament Hill, Ottawa, Ontario.

STATE FUNERAL
A detachment of Mounties carries the flag-draped coffin of Pierre Trudeau, one of Canada's most popular (and controversial) prime ministers.

LEGISLATIVE BRANCH

In the Canadian political system, the legislative branch encompasses nearly the entire government, making it the paramount governing body in Canada. Whereas in many countries, the executive holds the majority of political power, Canadian politics mandate that the executive branch and the federal bureaucracy are but a branch of parliamentary rule. The prime minister is almost always a member of the majority party in the House of Commons and most cabinet ministers also hail from the majority party of the lower house. The executive government then—along with its policies, procedures, and mandates—is inevitably responsible to Parliament.

The principal body of Parliament is the 301-member House of Commons, whose members are popularly elected to represent single-seat constituencies. As the only elected body in the federal political system, the House of Commons represents the political will of the population, and therefore monitors the daily activity of the government as well as matters of legislation. Most important legislation originates in the House, and all of the financial legislation is created there. Furthermore, the House of Commons has the ability to declare the government incompetent and effectively dissolve it should it so choose.

According to Canadian political tradition, all remarks in the House must be directed to the Speaker, who controls the daily debate in the House. Members of the House of Commons are not allowed to address one another on the Floor of the House, and must refer to each other by their titles—i.e. the honorable member, the leader of the opposition—a measure designed to promote democratic integrity.

In many ways, the Canadian Senate resembles the British House of Lords rather than its American counterpart. Senators are nominated by the prime minister and appointed by the governor-general. Most serve until the mandatory retirement age of 75. Senate seats are allotted by province, and the system is weighted to balance representation in the House, which favors the two most populous provinces: Ontario and Quebec. These receive 24 Senate seats each. The four western provinces receive 24 seats between them, as do the maritime provinces of the eastern seaboard. The province of Newfoundland and Labrador receives six seats, while each of the three territories is represented by a single senator.

OVERLEAF: PARLIAMENT HILL, OTTAWA
Guards perform the Changing of the Guard in front of the Centre Block on Parliament Hill. Rebuilt in 1920, this is home to the Senate, the House of Commons, the Prime Minister's Office, and the Office of the Leader of the Opposition.

1931 *The United Kingdom passes the Statute of Westminster, which recognizes the independence and sovereignty of Canada.*

1939 *Canadian prime minister, William Lyon Mackenzie King, declares war on Germany, in the House of Commons.*

1940 *The controversial National Resources Mobilization Act passes, which legalizes forced conscription for the Canadian Armed Forces.*

1949 *Newfoundland, Canada's newest province, votes to join Canada.*

1960 *Parliament adopts the Canadian Bill of Rights, assuring the civil liberties of all Canadian citizens.*

1977 *The first live telecast from the floor of the House of Commons—making Canada the first country to broadcast its legislative proceedings.*

1982 *New Constitution Act, which includes the Canadian Charter of Rights and Freedoms (Canada Act): an amendment of the Constitution of 1867, which asserts Canadian separation from the United Kingdom and dispenses with the need for British approval of parliamentary acts.*

LESTER B. PEARSON
April 22, 1963 – April 19, 1968

- President of the UN General Assembly in 1952-1953.
- Nobel Peace Prize (1957).
- Instituted a comprehensive pension plan, socialized medicine, and introduced the maple-leaf flag.

PIERRE ELLIOTT TRUDEAU
April 4, 1968 – June 3, 1979
March 3, 1980 – June 29, 1984

- Pursued a policy of preserving Quebec's heritage while maintaining a unified Canada. A critic of Quebecois separatism, he worked to defeat Quebec independence during the Quebec Referendum (1980).

KIM (AVRIL PHAEDRA) CAMPBELL
June 25, 1993 – Nov 3, 1993

- Canada's first female prime minister and the first from British Columbia.
- Held the office for just over four months before she and the Progressive Conservative Party were defeated in national elections in 1993.

JEAN CHRÉTIEN
November 4, 1993 – December 12, 2003

- A popular politician and an influential force in the administrations of Pearson and Trudeau. Won three consecutive general elections as leader of the Liberal Party.

CANADA

OFFICIAL NAME: CANADA

POPULATION: 31.6 MILLION
CAPITAL: OTTAWA
AREA: 3,855,081 SQ. MILES (9,984,670 SQ. KM)
INDEPENDENCE: 1867
CONSTITUTION: 1867

CANADA is derived from "Kanata", an Algonquian word, meaning "community" or "little settlement."

RELIGION: Roman Catholic 44%, Protestant 29%, Other and non-religious 27%

OFFICIAL LANGUAGES: English and French

REGIONS OR PROVINCES: 10 provinces; 3 territories

DEPENDENT TERRITORIES: None

MEDIA: No political censorship exists

SUFFRAGE: 18 years of age; universal

LEGAL SYSTEM: English common law; French legal traditions in Quebec; accepts ICJ jurisdiction

WORLD ORGANIZATIONS: ACCT, AfDB, APEC, ARF (dialogue partner), AsDB, ASEAN (dialogue partner), Australia Group, BIS, C, CCC, CDB, CE (observer), EAPC, EBRD, ECE, ECLAC, ESA (cooperating state), FAO, G- 7, G- 8, G-10, IADB, IAEA, IBRD, ICAO, ICC, ICFTU, ICRM, IDA, IEA, IFAD, IFC, IFRCS, IHO, ILO, IMF, IMO, Interpol, IOC, IOM, ISO, ITU, MINURCA, MIPONUH, MONUC, NAM (guest), NATO, NEA, NSG, OAS, OECD, OPCW, OSCE, PCA, UN, UNAMSIL, UNCTAD, UNDOF, UNESCO, UNFICYP, UNHCR, UNMEE, UNMIBH, UNMIK, UNMOP, UNMOVIC, UNTSO, UNU, UPU, WCL, WFTU, WHO, WIPO, WMO, WToO, WTrO, ZC

POLITICAL PARTIES: LP—Liberal Party, CA—Canadian Reform Conservative Alliance, BQ—Bloc Québécois, NDP—New Democratic Party, PCP—Progressive Conservative Party, Ind—Independents

ETHNIC GROUPS

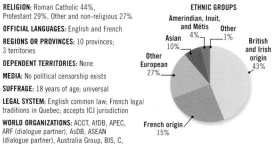

- British and Irish origin 43%
- French origin 15%
- Other European 27%
- Asian 10%
- Amerindian, Inuit, and Métis 4%
- Other 1%

NATIONAL ECONOMICS

WORLD GNP RANKING: 8th

GNP PER CAPITA: $21,130

INFLATION: 2.2%

BALANCE OF PAYMENTS (BALANCE OF TRADE): $12.7 billion

EXCHANGE RATES / U.S. DLR.: 1.311-1.313 CANADIAN DOLLARS

OFFICIAL CURRENCY: CANADIAN DOLLAR

GOVERNMENT SPENDING (% OF GDP)

DEFENSE	1.2%	
EDUCATION	5.6%	
HEALTH	6.6%	

0   5   10   15

NUMBER OF CONFLICTS OVER LAST 25 YEARS

	1	2-5	5+
Violent changes in government	○	○	○
Civil wars	○	○	○
International wars	○	○	○
Foreign intervention	○	○	○

- The focus of defense planning is now the creation of rapid reaction forces.
- Over 125,000 Canadian personnel have served in peacekeeping operations for UN—more than any other country.

NOTABLE WARS AND INSURGENCIES: None

"Politics is the skilled use of blunt objects."
— *Lester B. Pearson, Prime Minister (1963-1968)*

THE SENATE

Unlike the House of Commons, Canada's Senate rarely involves itself with the daily affairs of state and government, but rather spends its time debating and questioning the larger political and social phenomena occurring in Canada. The Senate is intended to be the philosophical forum for political issues, and its decisions—in theory—are made in the best interests of the nation, rather than motivated by local or party politics.

Although the two houses of Parliament diverge in form and scope, each are vested with equal powers in the legislature. Any legislation derived from the House of Commons or the government must pass the Senate in order to become law. The conceptual disparities between the two houses serve as an effective system of checks and balances rather than a hindrance to public policy.

JUDICIAL BRANCH

Like the Canadian nation itself, the judiciary in Canada preserves both English and French influences and traditions. Thus, the country's legal system is based

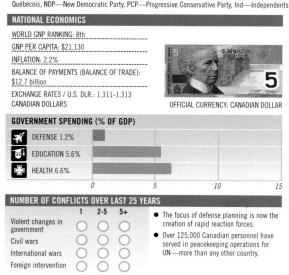

43RD PREMIERS' CONFERENCE – 2002
The 10 provincial and three territorial premiers met in August 2002 to discuss the Kyoto Protocol. Left to right: Paul Okalik (Nunavut), Pat Duncan (Yukon), Ralph Klein (Alberta), Pat Binns (Prince Edward Island) and Gary Doer (Manitoba).

principally on English common law except in the Francophone province of Quebec, where it is modeled on French civil law. Of paramount importance to the judiciary is its independence—the "rule of law" which considers no person or body above the law. Generally, the initial trial of any case in the provincial courts, which handle the vast majority of cases, is heard by a single judge. In a federal or appellate case it is heard by three judges.

Established by an Act of Parliament in 1875, the highest court in the nation is the Supreme Court of Canada. This is composed of nine judges: one Chief Justice and eight other judges, chosen not only for their political persuasions but also for geographic reasons. Canada is thoroughly committed to equal geographical representation, which means that three of the judges must be from Quebec, three traditionally come from Ontario, two from western Canada, and one from the Atlantic provinces. Sitting in Ottawa, it is the final court of appeal for all civil, criminal, and constitutional cases. The scope of the Supreme Court, however, extends beyond judicial review, as the judges also provide the philosophical and ethical anchor for the national legal system. While executing this role, the Court often reviews legislation, both proposed and existing, to assure its accordance with the Canadian constitution. By deciding constitutional matters, the Supreme Court defines the limits of both federal and provincial powers.

Operating under the Supreme Court is the Canadian Federal Court, or the national court system. This tribunal consists of two main divisions: the trial court and the appellate court. It does, however, operate certain specialty courts to deal specifically with cases of national importance—such as immigration, administrative law, and taxation.

The country's ten provinces and three territories also operate their own legal system: the Provincial Courts. Though the systems and names of the courts do vary somewhat, each province generally operates a three-tiered court system to deal with civil and criminal cases within its jurisdiction.

MALAYSIA

OFFICIAL NAME: FEDERATION OF MALAYSIA

POPULATION: 22.6 MILLION	
CAPITAL: KUALA LUMPUR; PUTRAJAYA (ADMINISTRATIVE)	
AREA: 127,316 SQ. MILES (329,748 SQ. KM)	
INDEPENDENCE: 1963	
CONSTITUTION: 1957	

MALAYSIA literally means the land of the Malays and came into being in 1963.

RELIGION: Muslim (mainly Sunni) 53%, Buddhist 19%, Chinese faiths 12%, Christian 7%, Traditional beliefs 2%, Other 7%

OFFICIAL LANGUAGE: Bahasa Malaysia

REGIONS OR PROVINCES: 13 states

DEPENDENT TERRITORIES: None

MEDIA: Total political censorship exists in national media

NEWSPAPERS: There are 42 daily newspapers

TV: 7 services: 3 state-controlled broadcasting to Peninsular Malaysia, Sarawak, and Sabah

RADIO: 5 services: 3 state-controlled broadcasting to Peninsular Malaysia, Sarawak, and Sabah

SUFFRAGE: 21 years of age; universal

LEGAL SYSTEM: English common law; no ICJ jurisdiction

WORLD ORGANIZATIONS: APEC, ARF, AsDB, ASEAN, BIS, C, CCC, CP, ESCAP, FAO, G-15, G-77, IAEA, IBRD, ICAO, ICFTU, ICRM, IDA, IDB, IFAD, IFC, IFRCS, IHO, ILO, IMF, IMO, Interpol, IOC, ISO, ITU, MINURSO, MONUC, NAM, OIC, OPCW, UN, UNAMSIL, UNCTAD, UNESCO, UNIDO, UNIKOM, UNMEE, UNMIBH, UNMIK, UNTAET, UPU, WCL, WFTU, WHO, WIPO, WMO, WToO, WTrO

POLITICAL PARTIES: BN—National Front (dominated by the United Malays National Organization—UMNO), PAS—Pan-Malaysian Islamic Party, DAP—Democratic Action Party, PKN—National Justice Party (Kaedilan), PBS—United Sabah Party

ETHNIC GROUPS:

Indian 6%
Other 5%
Indigenous tribes 12%
Malay 48%
Chinese 29%

NATIONAL ECONOMICS

WORLD GNP RANKING: 42nd

GNP PER CAPITA: $3,380

INFLATION: 1.5%

BALANCE OF PAYMENTS (BALANCE OF TRADE): $12.6 million

EXCHANGE RATES / U.S. DLR.: 3.8 RINGGITS

OFFICIAL CURRENCY: RINGGIT

GOVERNMENT SPENDING (% OF GDP)

✈ DEFENSE 3.1%		
🎓 EDUCATION 4.9%		
✚ HEALTH 1.4%		

0   5   10   15

NUMBER OF CONFLICTS OVER LAST 25 YEARS

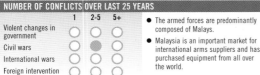

	1	2–5	5+
Violent changes in government	○	○	○
Civil wars	○	●	○
International wars	○	○	○
Foreign intervention	○	○	○

● The armed forces are predominantly composed of Malays.

● Malaysia is an important market for international arms suppliers and has purchased equipment from all over the world.

NOTABLE WARS AND INSURGENCIES: Sporadic communist insurgency: on mainland to 1989, on Sarawak to 1990

THE STATES OF THE MALAYAN PENINSULA formally gained independence from Britain in 1957 as the Federation of Malaya. Singapore, Sarawak, and Sabah joined the mainland states in 1963, creating the Federatation of Malaysia. Two years later, Singapore withdrew and formed an independent republic. The creation of Malaysia was not welcomed by neighboring Indonesia, which subjected the new state to a program of economic, political, and military confrontation. This continued until the fall of Indonesia's president, Dr. Achmad Sukarno, in 1966. Malaysia also had to face internal threats. Throughout the 1950s communist factions, predominantly Chinese, had waged guerrilla warfare against the British. Communist insurgency remained a problem after independence and continued to flare up in Sarawak until 1990. Ethnic tension, especially between the Malay majority and the Chinese business elite, has also been a source of conflict in post-independence Malaysia. Attempting to ease tension between the two groups, prime minister Mahathir Mohamad in 2003 revoked Malaysia's positive discrimination policy that benefited Malay over Chinese students in college admissions.

The United Malays National Organization (UMNO) has dominated politics since 1957. However, its authority has been weakened by recent economic crises. Most notably, the economic crisis of 1997 spurred dissent against UMNO leader Prime Minister Mahathir Mohamad and his economic policy. Deputy Prime Minister and Finance Minister Anwar Ibrahim led the opposition and was dismissed by Mahathir in 1998. Domestic and international observers declared that Anwar's trials and convictions for corruption and sodomy were unfair and politically motivated. Anwar's wife, Wan Azizah, formed a new opposition party called the National Justice Party (PKN). In October 2003, Mahathir Mohamad finally retired from office, handing over to his deputy, Abdullah Ahmad Badawi.

OPENING OF PARLIAMENT, 2003
King Tuanku Syed Sirajuddin Syed Putra Jamalullail arrives at the opening of the fifth session of the 10th parliament at Parliament House in Kuala Lumpur.

HOW THE GOVERNMENT WORKS

LEGISLATIVE BRANCH

Parliament
Bicameral Parliament

Dewan Negara
(Senate)
69 members serve three-year terms: 43 appointed by monarch on advice of prime minister, two each appointed by 13 state legislatures.

Dewan Rakyat
(House of Representatives)
Composed of 193 members elected to five-year terms by direct popular vote.

Majlis Raja Raja
(Conference of Rulers)
Nine hereditary sultans; four governors. Serves as "third house" of parliament.

Regional Governments
Thirteen states administered by elected unicameral legislatures and hereditary sultans or appointed governors.

EXECUTIVE BRANCH

Yang di-Pertuan Agong
(Paramount Ruler or Monarch)
Elected to five-year term by nine hereditary sultans from among their members. Head of state; leader of Islamic faith in Malaysia. Dissolves Parliament on advice of prime minister.

Prime Minister
Leader of majority party in Parliament's lower house, appointed by monarch. Serves as head of government.

Cabinet
Composed of Parliament members, appointed by monarch on advice of prime minister. Oversees government operations; answers to Parliament.

JUDICIAL BRANCH

Supreme Court
Highest court of review and appeal in criminal cases; rules on constitutionality of laws; decides intergovernmental disputes. Judges appointed by monarch on advice of prime minister and Conference of Rulers.

High Court for West Malaysia and High Court for East Malaysia
Civil and criminal cases; hear appeals from lower courts.

Lower Courts

AUSTRALIA

AUSTRALIAN FLAG
Adopted on May 22, 1909, the flag shows the Union flag, the Star of Federation, and the Southern Cross constellation.

SYDNEY OPERA HOUSE
Opened in 1973, the building has become a symbol of Australia's confidence as a modern independent nation.

WHEN DUTCH SAILORS FIRST SIGHTED AUSTRALIA at the start of the 17th century, perhaps a third of a million aboriginal natives—belonging to hundreds of tribes with their own languages and lifestyles—inhabited the land that their ancestors had first reached 60,000 years before.

Colonial rule by Great Britain opened the continent to European settlers and brought British customs and law to Australia. Today, the nation is a parliamentary democracy that borrows from the political traditions of both Britain and the United States.

William Dampier became the first British explorer to set foot on Australia's shores in 1688. But Britain's long relationship with Australia started in earnest in 1770 when Captain James Cook, on a scientific voyage to the South Pacific, mapped its coastlines and those of nearby New Zealand. After Cook had claimed Australia for the crown, Britain, in need of a place to

hold convicts, began using the new territory as a penal colony. During eight decades, more than 160,000 prisoners were shipped to the continent. But drawn by the prosperous wool industry and the discovery of gold, free settlers soon greatly outnumbered convicts. By the mid-1800s, Britain established the six colonies—New South Wales, Queensland, South Australia, Tasmania, Western Australia and Victoria—that now are the states of the same names. With labor scarce, government policies emancipated convicts and promoted the immigration of free

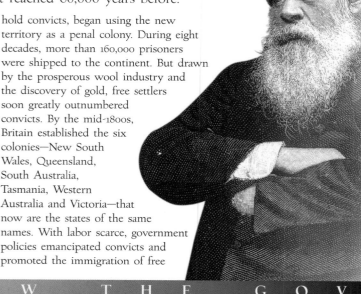

HOW THE GOVE...

🕸 LEGISLATIVE BRANCH

CONGRESS

The assent of both houses of the bicameral Parliament is required for a bill to become law. If agreement cannot be reached, both bodies may be dissolved and new elections called.

▶ **SENATE**
The upper house, composed of 76 seats, with 12 allocated to the six states and 2 each to the two territories. Senators from states are elected by direct popular vote for six-year terms, with half elected every 3 years. Senators from territories are elected for three-year terms. With law-making powers almost equal to those of the House of Representatives, the Senate is a very powerful legislative body.

▶ **HOUSE OF REPRESENTATIVES**
The lower house, required by the constitution to have "as nearly as practicable" double the number of members as the Senate. Its 150 seats are allocated among states and territories in proportion to their population, although each state must have at least five members. Members elected by direct popular vote to three-year terms.

🕸 EXECUTIVE BRANCH

MONARCH

The king or queen of the United Kingdom; sovereign of the Commonwealth; head of state; his or her official role is formal and largely ceremonial.

▶ **GOVERNOR-GENERAL**
Appointed by the British monarch on advice of prime minister. Powers include calling Parliament into session or dissolving it, assenting to legislation. Serves until resignation or replacement by the monarch.

⚖ PROVINCES & TERRITORIES
▶ 6 states and 2 territories
▶ Bicameral legislatures
▶ Premiers are majority party leaders of lower houses

THE LOWER HOUSE
Australia's House of Representatives in seen here in session at Parliament House in Canberra.

"The lesson of the Federation should be that the lesson is over. Australia must have a new idea of itself. We have to strike out in a new direction, in a new way, armed with our own self-regard, our own confidence and fully appreciating our own uniqueness. All other roads will lead us into the shadow of great powers." — Paul Keating, former prime minister, May 2001

people. However, as in New Zealand and the US, new Australian settlements soon drove indigenous tribes from their ancient homelands. The treatment of aboriginal peoples during the settlement era left a legacy of discrimination that Australia still struggles to overcome. Indeed, a "White Australia" policy, not abolished until the 1970s, barred for decades almost all except Europeans from immigrating to Australia.

By the turn of the 20th century, Australia had matured into an open and largely democratic society unconstrained by the entrenched aristocracies of the European world. A long-building popular movement, led by Sir Henry Parkes, to unite the colonies into an independent nation culminated in 1901 with the adoption of Australia's constitution. The document, mirroring

SIR HENRY PARKES
(1815-1896) Leader of the movement toward a federal state, which resulted in self-rule for the nation in 1901, Henry Parkes served as prime minister of New South Wales for five terms, and by 1880 he was referred to as the "Grand Old Man" of Australian politics.

the federalism of the US constitution, defines the powers of the national government and reserves other powers for its states. Each former colony, already ruled by its own elected Parliament and independent judiciary, retained its government institutions and authority, save for explicit national powers vested in the new Commonwealth of Australia. These powers include currency, foreign affairs, immigration, international trade, national defense, and postal services. Rivalry between the various states led to the creation of a new capital at Canberra, where the national parliament was eventually transferred from Melbourne in 1927.

Three political parties dominate in Australia: the Liberal Party representing urban and business interests, the National Party reflecting rural concerns, and the Australian Labor Party traditionally speaking for trade unions and liberal groups. Voters in 1996 ended 13 years of Labor rule by electing a Liberal/National coalition government that after two succeeding election victories continues to hold power.

CENTENARY OF AUSTRALIA
A service was held at Westminster Abbey in London to mark the 100th anniversary of the Commonwealth of Australia in July 2000, attended by the Archbishop of Brisbane, Peter Hollingworth, and, representing the indigenous people, an aborigine from the Nyoongar tribe of south Western Australia, Richard Walley.

N M E N T   W O R K S

PRIME MINISTER

Chairs the Cabinet and serves as head of government; traditionally is the leader of the majority party or governing coalition of the House of Representatives. Tenure lasts as long as party or coalition retains control of House.

▶ **FEDERAL EXECUTIVE COUNCIL**
Comprises all ministers; presided over by governor-general, who, in practice, always acts on advice of council; approves signing of formal documents.

▶ **CABINET**
Sixteen ministers who are members of parliament and appointed by the governor-general on the advice of the prime minister.

⚖ JUDICIAL BRANCH

HIGH COURT

The country's highest judicial authority in criminal and civil cases, constitutionality of law, treaty issues and disputes between states; 7 justices appointed by the governor-general to serve until the age of 70.

▶ **FEDERAL COURT**
Administers cases involving civil and criminal law, native issues, bankruptcy, and corporate practices; 45 justices appointed by the governor-general to serve until the age of 70.

▶ **FAMILY COURT**
Administers cases involving matrimonial, divorce and child-custody matters. Judges appointed by the governor-general.

HIGH COURT
The highest court of Australia is the High Court in Canberra. The building was completed in 1980.

▶ **FEDERAL MAGISTRATES SERVICE**
Provides a speedy, inexpensive and informal alternative to other courts on cases involving bankruptcy, trade practices and family law. Magistrates appointed by the governor-general.

PARLIAMENT HOUSE
Located on Capital Hill, the Australian parliamentary buildings were completed for the country's bicentennial in 1988.

 ELECTORAL SYSTEM
Australia pioneered the printed secret ballot, now used for elections around the world, in the colony of Victoria in 1855. The nation has universal suffrage, starting at age 18, and compulsory voting, although the penalty for noncompliance is only a minor fine. Turnouts of more than 90 percent for national and state elections are routine.

EXECUTIVE / LEGISLATIVE / JUDICIAL BRANCHES

*"The Labor Party is a party of conviction.
The Liberal Party is a party of convenience."* — Paul Keating

EXECUTIVE BRANCH

Australia's head of state remains, at least technically, the British monarch through the appointment of a governor-general. However, as with the governor-generals of Canada and other former British colonies, holders of the office in Australia carry out their duties only on the advice of the government and especially the prime minister.

Actual government power is wielded by the prime minister and Cabinet. The prime minister, by tradition, is the leader of the majority party or coalition in the House of Representatives and chairs the Cabinet. The Cabinet ministers decide the government's legislative programs and policies. The Cabinet meets in private, with no public record of its deliberations, except for subsequent announcements of its decisions. Cabinet ministers are selected from both the Senate and the House of Representatives. Numbering 16 in the current Cabinet, they are the most senior of the 28 ministers who comprise the federal government's larger policy-making "Ministry."

LEGISLATIVE BRANCH

Australia's bicameral Parliament is required to meet at least once each year. A candidate for Parliament must be at least 21 years of age and either a natural-born citizen or naturalized for at least five years. Bills imposing taxes or appropriating revenue must begin in the House of Representatives. Proposed laws are presented to the governor-general, who can give his assent or send them back to Parliament for amendments. After receiving a bill from Parliament, the governor-general may also "reserve" the measure and delay its enactment for a period of two years. However, in theory,

PARLIAMENT HOUSE, CANBERRA

Opened by Queen Elizabeth II in 1988, Australia's Parliament House is one of the largest buildings in the southern hemisphere and houses both the Senate and the House of Representatives.

the British monarch may disallow any law within a year of the governor-general's assent. To settle prolonged legislative disagreements between the Senate and House, the governor-general may dissolve both bodies simultaneously and force their re-election. If the deadlock persists after an election, the governor-general may convene a joint sitting of the Senate and the House to deliberate and vote together on the disputed measure. Only six "double dissolutions" of Parliament and just one joint sitting have been used in the history of the nation.

RESIGNATION
Governor-general Peter Hollingworth resigned in May 2003 after allegations of a cover-up while he was archbishop of Brisbane.

ISSUES AND CHALLENGES

Since gaining the right to vote in 1962, Aborigines have been fighting for their land rights and an apology for discriminatory policies. Although land councils were established in 1976, not all states recognized Aboriginal ownership. The first nationwide act, the Native Title Act, was passed in 1993 specifying that native title existed for all Crown land held by federal and state governments. Much of this land is leased to farmers and mining concerns, and a new ruling in 1998, the Native Title Amendment Bill, restricted the rights of Aborigines somewhat, in order to protect the rights of these leaseholders. Another controversial government policy was the so-called "stolen generation" which permitted Aboriginal children to be forcibly removed from their parents in order to assimilate them into white families. To date, the government has expressed regret, but not given a formal apology for these and other actions. For 30 years, Aborigines have camped within full view of parliament, hoping to receive such an apology.

ABORIGINES
Aboriginal protester watches question time at Parliament.

BRIEF CHRONOLOGY OF AUSTRALIA'S PARLIAMENT

1901 The first Commonwealth Parliament opens in Melbourne. "White Australia" laws are enacted, barring non-European immigrants and deporting people from the Pacific islands.

1902 Women granted the vote in federal elections. Aboriginals barred from voting.

1924 In order to counter voter apathy, voting is made compulsory and penalties established for violations. Before 1924 the vote in Australian elections had fallen as low as 47 percent.

1927 Federal Parliament transferred to new national capital of Canberra.

1942 Parliament adopts Statute of Westminster declaring Australia free and equal in relation to the British government.

1949 End of the status of Australians, including indigenous people, as subjects under the British Commonwealth.

1962 Federal voting rights extended to adult Aboriginal people.

1966 Immigration reforms allow entry of non-Europeans and end decades-old "White Australia" policy. For the first time, aboriginal land rights are recognized by Australian government.

KEY PRIME MINISTERS

The office of prime minister plays the key role in setting the strategic direction of the government. The position has been held by 25 people since Federation. Key Australian prime ministers are shown to the right.

SIR EDMUND BARTON
Jan 1, 1901–
Sept 24, 1903

- One of the fathers of confederation.
- First prime minister.
- Resigned office of prime minister to become a High Court judge

ALFRED DEAKIN
Sept 24, 1903–
April 27, 1904
July 5, 1905–Nov 13, 1908
June 2, 1909–Apr 29, 1910

- Three terms as prime minister.
- Championed old-age pensions and the "White Australia" policy.
- Only prime minister to reject the title "Right Honorable."

ANDREW FISHER
Nov 13, 1908–June 2, 1909
Apr. 29, 1910–June 24, 1913
Sept. 17, 1914–Oct. 27, 1915

- Three terms as prime minister.
- Passed laws for Commonwealth Bank, worker's compensation, and Australian bank notes.
- Initiated transcontinental railroad

JOHN JOSEPH AMBROSE CURTIN
Oct. 7, 1941–July 5, 1945

- Led Australia through World War II.
- Championed employment for all who wanted to work.
- One of three prime ministers in Australia's history to die in office

AUSTRALIA

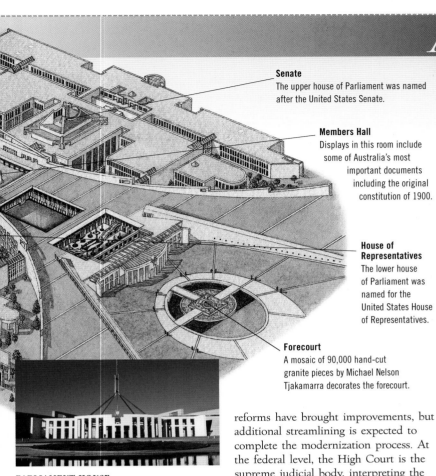

Senate
The upper house of Parliament was named after the United States Senate.

Members Hall
Displays in this room include some of Australia's most important documents including the original constitution of 1900.

House of Representatives
The lower house of Parliament was named for the United States House of Representatives.

Forecourt
A mosaic of 90,000 hand-cut granite pieces by Michael Nelson Tjakamarra decorates the forecourt.

OFFICIAL NAME: COMMONWEALTH OF AUSTRALIA

POPULATION:	19.3 MILLION
CAPITAL:	CANBERRA
AREA:	2,941,283 SQ. MILES (7,617,930 SQ. KM)
INDEPENDENCE:	JANUARY 1, 1901
CONSTITUTION:	JULY 9, 1900

AUSTRALIA is derived from the Latin word "australis," which means "southern".

RELIGION: Roman Catholic 26%, Anglican 26%, Other Christian 23%, Non-religious 13%, Other 13%

OFFICIAL LANGUAGE: English

REGIONS OR PROVINCES: 6 states and 2 territories

DEPENDENT TERRITORIES: Ashmore and Cartier Islands, Christmas Island, Cocos (Keeling) Islands, Coral Sea Islands, Heard Island and McDonald Islands, Norfolk Island

MEDIA: No political censorship exists in the media

Newspapers: There are 65 daily newspapers, mostly state circulation

TV: 1 state-owned service, 44 independent stations

Radio: 6 state-owned networks, 166 independent stations

SUFFRAGE: 18 years of age; universal and compulsory

LEGAL SYSTEM: English common law; accepts ICJ jurisdiction

WORLD ORGANIZATIONS: ANZUS, APEC, ARF (dialogue partner), AsDB, ASEAN (dialogue partner), Australia Group, BIS, C, CCC, CP, EBRD, ESCAP, FAO, IAEA, IBRD, ICAO, ICC, ICFTU, ICRM, IDA, IEA, IFAD, IFC, IFRCS, IHO, ILO, IMF, IMO, Interpol, IOC, IOM, ISO, ITU, NAM (guest), NEA, NSG, OECD, OPCW, PCA, Sparteca, SPC, SPF, UN, UNCTAD, UNESCO, UNHCR, UNMEE, UNTAET, UNTSO, UNU, UPU, WFTU, WHO, WIPO, WMO, WTrO, ZC

POLITICAL PARTIES: LP—Liberal Party, ALP—Australian Labor Party, NP—National Party, Ind—Independents, CLP—County-Liberal Party, AD—Australian Democrats, G—Greens

ETHNIC GROUPS:
Asian 5%
Aboriginal and Other 3%
European 92%

PARLIAMENT HOUSE
The 266-ft (81-meter) flag mast that rises above Parliament House in Canberra is one of the largest stainless steel structures in the world.

JUDICIAL BRANCH

Australia's judicial system is based on English legal traditions. But duplications have plagued the system for decades, due largely to the already established courts of the six colonies when the Commonwealth was founded. Recent reforms have brought improvements, but additional streamlining is expected to complete the modernization process. At the federal level, the High Court is the supreme judicial body, interpreting the constitution and ruling on appeals. The second-highest court, called the Federal Court, was established in 1976, and its broad jurisdiction covers almost all civil and some criminal matters arising under Australian federal law.

The nation's Federal Court shares partial jurisdiction with two other recently created national judicial bodies, the Family Court of Australia and the Federal Magistrates Service.

NATIONAL ECONOMICS

WORLD GNP RANKING:	15th
GNP PER CAPITA:	US$20,240
INFLATION:	4.5%
BALANCE OF PAYMENTS (BALANCE OF TRADE):	-US $15.5 billion
EXCHANGE RATES / U.S. DLR.:	1.7997-1.9535 AUSTRALIAN DOLLARS

OFFICIAL CURRENCY: AUSTRALIAN DOLLAR

GOVERNMENT SPENDING (% OF GDP)

- ✈ DEFENSE 1.9%
- 🎓 EDUCATION 4.8%
- ✚ HEALTH 6%

0   5   10   15

NUMBER OF CONFLICTS OVER LAST 25 YEARS

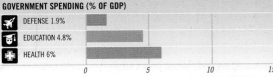

	1	2-5	5+
Violent changes in government	○	○	○
Civil wars	○	○	○
International wars	●	○	○
Foreign intervention	○	○	○

- 2000 Australian troops joined the 2003 Iraq invasion, the largest deployment since the Vietnam War.
- Terrorism has become a major priority; a special antiterrorist unit was created in 2002.

NOTABLE WARS AND INSURGENCIES: Invasion of Iraq 2003

1975 *Northern Territory and Australian Capital Territory granted two senators and one member each in the House of Representatives. Senate refuses to approve revenue supply of Gough Whitlam's Labor government. Governor-general, Sir John Kerr, intervenes, dismissing Whitlam and appointing opposition leader John Malcolm Fraser interim prime minister.*

1986 *Australia Act confirms full sovereignty and independence from British parliament and courts and ends appeals from Australian courts to Privy Council in London.*

1999 *Parliament expresses regret for harm government policies have caused in the past to indigenous Australians.*

SIR ROBERT GORDON MENZIES
April 26, 1939–
Aug 29, 1941
Dec 19, 1949–
Jan 26, 1966

- *The longest-serving prime minister.*
- *Completed plans for Canberra, Australia's federal capital.*
- *In 1941, became the first prime minister to fly overseas.*

JOHN MALCOLM FRASER
Nov 11, 1975 –
Mar 11, 1983

- *At the age 25, became youngest member of Parliament in 1955.*
- *Won largest-ever landslide victory in 1975 in the nation's most controversial federal election.*

PAUL JOHN KEATING
Dec 20, 1991–
Mar 11, 1996

- *Championed the land rights of indigenous people.*
- *Proposed making Australia a republic*
- *Deregulated airlines and banks.*

NETHERLANDS

OFFICIAL NAME: KINGDOM OF THE NETHERLANDS

POPULATION: 16.2 MILLION
CAPITALS: AMSTERDAM; THE HAGUE (ADMINISTRATIVE)
AREA: 16,033 SQ. MILES (41,525 SQ. KM)
INDEPENDENCE: 1815
CONSTITUTION: 1814

THE NETHERLAND'S byname, Holland ("Wooded Land") was originally given to one of the medieval cores of what later became the modern state.

RELIGION: Roman Catholic 36%, Protestant 27%, Muslim 3%, Other 34%

OFFICIAL LANGUAGE: Dutch

REGIONS OR PROVINCES: 12 provinces

DEPENDENT TERRITORIES: Aruba, Netherlands Antilles

MEDIA: No political censorship exists in national media

NEWSPAPERS: There are 38 national dailies

TV: 3 services: 1 public, 2 independent

RADIO: 5 privately owned national stations

SUFFRAGE: 18 years of age; universal

LEGAL SYSTEM: Civil law with French legal influences; accepts ICJ jurisdiction

WORLD ORGANIZATIONS: AfDB, AsDB, Australia Group, Benelux, BIS, CCC, CE, CERN, EAPC, EBRD, ECE, ECLAC, EIB, EMU, ESA, ESCAP, EU, FAO, G-10, IADB, IAEA, IBRD, ICAO, ICC, ICFTU, ICRM, IDA, IEA, IFAD, IFC, IFRCS, IHO, ILO, IMF, IMO, Interpol, IOC, IOM, ISO, ITU, NAM (guest), NATO, NEA, NSG, OAS (observer), OECD, OPCW, OSCE, PCA, UN, UNCTAD, UNESCO, UNHCR, UNIDO, UNITAR, UNMEE, UNMIBH, UNTSO, UNU, UPU, WCL, WEU, WHO, WIPO, WMO, WToO, WTrO, ZC

POLITICAL PARTIES: CDA—Christian Democratic Appeal, LPF—List Pim Fortuyn, VVD—People's Party for Freedom and Democracy, PvdA—Labor Party, GL—Green Left, SP—Socialist Party, D66—Democrats 66

ETHNIC GROUPS:

- Turkish 2%
- Surinamese 2%
- Moroccan 2%
- Other 12%
- Dutch 82%

NATIONAL ECONOMICS

WORLD GNP RANKING: 14th

GNP PER CAPITA: $24,970

INFLATION: 2.5%

BALANCE OF PAYMENTS (BALANCE OF TRADE): $16.3 billion

EXCHANGE RATES / U.S. DLR.: 1.0651-1.1231 EUROS

OFFICIAL CURRENCY: EURO

GOVERNMENT SPENDING (% OF GDP)

DEFENSE	1.9%
EDUCATION	4.9%
HEALTH	6%

0 — 5 — 10 — 15

NUMBER OF CONFLICTS OVER LAST 25 YEARS

	1	2-5	5+
Violent changes in government	○	○	○
Civil wars	○	○	○
International wars	○	○	○
Foreign intervention	○	○	○

● The Netherlands has a large defense industry specializing in submarines, weapons systems, and aircraft.

NOTABLE WARS AND INSURGENCIES: None

THE NETHERLANDS IS A PARLIAMENTARY DEMOCRACY with some trappings of a constitutional monarchy. It has enjoyed matriarchal rule for more than a century—with the accession to the throne by Queen Wilhelmina in 1898, Queen Juliana in 1948, and Queen Beatrix in 1980. The Netherlands is also a highly tolerant nation, where immigrants and refugees are welcome and where, within certain limitations, prostitution, same-sex marriage, and euthanasia are legal.

Founded in 1579, the Kingdom of the Netherlands freed itself from 18 years of French rule in 1813 and adopted a new constitution, formally declaring independence in 1815 under the restored House of Orange. Active royal intervention has decreased since 1849, when constitutional amendments transferred real power from the monarch to parliament. Today, although an integral part of the government, the monarch's functions are largely ceremonial. Duties include announcing the government's plans in an annual speech, and naming a *formateur* to form a Council of Ministers after an election. In the latter function, the present Queen does have some personal influence.

Most executive authority is exercised by the prime minister—it is usually the *formateur* who is chosen—and his Council of Ministers. The main lawmaking body is the the Second Chamber of States General. The First Chamber may approve or object to laws but may not propose or amend any. Members of the States General are directly elected by proportional representation. Any party gaining at least 0.66 percent of the vote is guaranteed at least one seat. In consequence, political parties are numerous—no party has ever held a majority in a coalition government. New elections are held when a government falls, lacking the States General's confidence. The Council of State is the government's chief advisory body, composed of the monarch, heir apparent, and councilors. Its advice is required on proposed legislation before laws are sumitted to Parliament.

ASSASSINATED POLITICIAN
People pay their last respects to the ultra-nationalist leader, Pim Fortuyn, assassinated in 2002. His party, opposed to liberal policies on multiculturalism and immigration, won a large sympathy vote in the 2002 elections.

HOW THE GOVERNMENT WORKS

LEGISLATIVE BRANCH

Staten Generaal
(States General)
Bicameral Parliament

Eerste Kamer
(First Chamber)
Composed of 75 members elected to four-year terms by country's 12 provincial councils. Primarily reviews bills for constitutionality.

Tweede Kamer
(Second Chamber)
Composed of 150 members directly elected to four-year terms by proportional representation. Exercises administrative oversight; initiates legislation; amends bills submitted by Council of Ministers.

Regional Governments
Twelve provinces governed by locally elected councils and headed by commissioner appointed by monarch.

EXECUTIVE BRANCH

Monarch
Position is hereditary. Serves as head of state; appoints formateur following elections to forge governing coalition in Second Chamber and determine government policy program.

Prime Minister
Traditionally the leader of States General's majority party or coalition. Appointed by monarch. Serves as head of government and coordinates activities of Council of Ministers.

Council of Ministers
Appointed by monarch; ministers cannot simultaneously serve in States General. Plans and implements government policy.

JUDICIAL BRANCH

Supreme Court
Highest court of appeal. Rules on application of law but not facts of case or constitutionality of law. Composed of president, six vice-presidents, and 35 justices. Members appointed by monarch to serve until age 70.

Courts of Appeal
Five courts; hear appeals from lower courts.

District Courts
Nineteen courts. Hear civil and criminal cases.

Sub-District Courts
Sixty-one courts.

BELGIUM

OFFICIAL NAME: KINGDOM OF BELGIUM

POPULATION: 10.3 MILLION	
CAPITAL: BRUSSELS	
AREA: 11,780 SQ. MILES (30,510 SQ. KM)	
INDEPENDENCE: 1830	
CONSTITUTION: 1831	

BELGIUM derives it name from Gallia Belgica, established by the Romans as a province of Gaul in 27 B.C.

RELIGION: Roman Catholic 88%, Muslim 2%, Other 10%

OFFICIAL LANGUAGES: Dutch (Flemish), French, and German

REGIONS OR PROVINCES: 10 provinces and 1 region

DEPENDENT TERRITORIES: None

MEDIA: No political censorship in the national media

Newspapers: There are 30 daily newspapers

TV: 3 state-owned services, 5 independent services

Radio: 3 state-owned services

SUFFRAGE: 18 years of age; universal and compulsory

LEGAL SYSTEM: Civil law based on English legal traditions; accepts ICJ jurisdiction

ETHNIC GROUPS:

- Other 6%
- Italian 2%
- Moroccan 1%
- Walloon 33%
- Fleming 58%

WORLD ORGANIZATIONS: ACCT, AfDB, AsDB, Australia Group, Benelux, BIS, CCC, CE, CERN, EAPC, EBRD, ECE, EIB, EMU, ESA, EU, FAO, G- 9, G-10, IADB, IAEA, IBRD, ICAO, ICC, ICFTU, ICRM, IDA, IEA, IFAD, IFC, IFRCS, IHO, ILO, IMF, IMO, Interpol, IOC, IOM, ISO, ITU, MINURSO, MONUC, NATO, NEA, NSG, OAS (observer), OECD, OPCW, OSCE, PCA, UN, UNCTAD, UNESCO, UNHCR, UNIDO, UNMIK, UNMOGIP, UNMOP, UNRWA, UNTSO, UPU, WADB (nonregional), WCL, WEU, WHO, WIPO, WMO, WTrO, ZC

POLITICAL PARTIES: VLD/PRL—Flemish Liberals Party/Liberal Reform Party (Walloon), SP/PS—Socialist Party (Flemish)/Socialist Party (Walloon), CVP/PCS—Christian People's Party (Flemish)/Christian Social Party (Walloon), VB—Vlaams Blok, Ecolo—French Greens, Agalev—Flemish Ecologists, Co-op—Co-opted members

NATIONAL ECONOMICS

WORLD GNP RANKING: 19th

GNP PER CAPITA: $24,540

INFLATION: 2.5%

BALANCE OF PAYMENTS: (BALANCE OF TRADE): $11.9 billion

EXCHANGE RATES / U.S. DLR.: 1.0651-1.1231 EUROS

OFFICIAL CURRENCY: EURO

GOVERNMENT SPENDING (% OF GDP)

- ✈ DEFENSE 1.4%
- 🎓 EDUCATION 5.6%
- ✚ HEALTH 6.3%

0   5   10   15

NUMBER OF CONFLICTS OVER LAST 25 YEARS

	1	2-5	5+
Violent changes in government	○	○	○
Civil wars	○	○	○
International wars	○	○	○
Foreign intervention	○	○	○

- Since 1996, the Belgian and Dutch navies have been under a joint operational command.
- Tensions between Flanders and Wallonia are dissipated by the federalist structure of government.

NOTABLE WARS AND INSURGENCIES: None

BELGIUM IS LINGUISTICALLY DIVIDED between Dutch-speaking Flanders in the north, French-speaking Wallonia in the south, a bilingual Brussels, which, in practice, is 85 percent French-speaking, and a small German-speaking community in the east of the country. Historically part of the Low Countries, Belgium came under Spanish Habsburg, Austrian Habsburg, French and then Dutch rule before gaining independence from the Netherlands in a revolution in 1830. It became a constitutional monarchy, with the monarch chosen from the German House of Saxe-Coburg Gotha. Belgium was occupied by Germany through both world wars.

Tensions between the two main linguistic communities were kept alive by the French-speaking community's greater wealth, and the greater political power given to it by the constitution. However, since the 1970s, changes in industry have made Flanders the wealthier region. Between 1980 and 1993, sweeping constitutional changes were made to minimize linguistic and cultural conflicts. Belgium was reorganized from a highly centralized state into a federal monarchy and, in practice, became the most federal state in Europe. Cultural tensions are also kept at bay by national consensus on the benefits of European Union membership—Belgium was an EU founder member, and Brussels hosts the EU and NATO headquarters.

The federal authority controls defense, internal security, the budget, monetary policy, and some matters of foreign policy and social welfare. Three "community" governments (Dutch, French, and German) based on the concept of language and culture govern education, culture, and other aspects of social welfare. Regional governments (Flanders, Wallonia and the Brussels capital region) have jurisdiction over transportation, public works, the environment, and the economy and employment. The Flanders and Flemish-community are covered by a single administration. There are no "national" parties that function on both sides of the linguistic border. There are both French and Flemish right-liberal, socialist, Christian democrat and green parties. As a result, elections in Belgium are a competition between Flemish parties on one side and Francophone parties on the other.

ISSUES AND CHALLENGES:

- Belgium has become a center for the production of synthetic illegal drugs, supplying precursor chemicals to South American cocaine processors. It is a major transit point for US-bound ecstasy and also for cocaine, heroin, hashish, and marijuana entering Western Europe. Money laundering results from the trafficking of drugs, automobiles, alcohol, and tobacco.

HOW THE GOVERNMENT WORKS

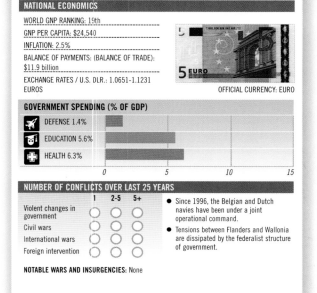

LEGISLATIVE BRANCH

Parlement
Bicameral Parliament

Senaat or **Senat**
(Senate)
Seventy-one members, reflecting the ethnic distribution: 41 elected or appointed by the Flemish; 29 by the Walloons; one by the Germans. All four-year terms. Monarch's heirs are also senators by right.

Kamer van Volksvertegenwoordigers or **Chambre des Représentants**
(Chamber of Representatives)
One hundred and fifty members directly elected to four-year terms by proportional representation for 20 districts.

Regional and Community Governments
Elected to five-year terms.
Communes
Elected by proportional representation.

EXECUTIVE BRANCH

Monarch
Serves as head of state, selects the prime minister and may dissolve Parliament.

Prime Minister
Appointed by the monarch from the Chamber of Representatives. Serves as head of government and selects the Cabinet.

Cabinet
Chosen from members of the Chamber of Representatives and includes the prime minister. Once appointed, ministers lose their seat in Parliament and may not return until re-elected.

JUDICIAL BRANCH

High Council for Justice
Supervises appointment of judges and hears complaints about miscarriages of justice. Set up as a judicial watchdog in the late 1990s after the Dutroux paedophile scandal.

Court of Cassation
Highest court of appeal, but may not review constitutionality of legislation. Justices appointed for life by the Cabinet from nominations submitted by the Court and the Parliament.

Courts of Appeal
Courts of the Provinces and Brussels
District Courts
Canton Courts

CZECH REPUBLIC

OFFICIAL NAME: CZECH REPUBLIC

POPULATION: 10.3 MILLION	
CAPITAL: PRAGUE	
AREA: 30,450 SQ. MILES (78,866 SQ. KM)	
INDEPENDENCE: 1993	
CONSTITUTION: 1992	

THE CZECH REPUBLIC is named after the Czech people dominant in the "Czech lands" of Bohemia and Moravia.

RELIGION: Roman Catholic 39%, Protestant 3%, Hussites 2%, Other 18%, Atheist 38%

OFFICIAL LANGUAGE: Czech

REGIONS OR PROVINCES: 13 regions and 1 capital city

DEPENDENT TERRITORIES: None

MEDIA: No political censorship exists in national media

NEWSPAPERS: There are 21 daily newspapers

TV: 5 services: 2 state-owned, 3 independent

RADIO: 1 state-owned service, independent services

SUFFRAGE: 18 years of age; universal

LEGAL SYSTEM: Civil law system based on Austro-Hungarian legal traditions; no ICJ jurisdiction

WORLD ORGANIZATIONS: ACCT (observer), Australia Group, BIS, CCC, CE, CEI, CERN, EAPC, EBRD, ECE, EU, FAO, IAEA, IBRD, ICAO, ICC, ICFTU, ICRM, IDA, IEA, IFC, IFRCS, ILO, IMF, IMO, Interpol, IOC, IOM, ISO, ITU, MONUC, NATO, NEA, NSG, OAS (observer), OECD, OPCW, OSCE, PCA, PFP, UN, UNAMSIL, UNCTAD, UNESCO, UNIDO, UNMEE, UNMIBH, UNMIK, UNMOP, UNMOT, UNOMIG, UPU, WCL, WEU (associate), WFTU, WHO, WIPO, WMO, WToO, WTrO, ZC

POLITICAL PARTIES: CSDD—Czech Social Democratic Party, ODS—Civic Democratic Party, KSCM—Communist Party of Bohemia and Moravia, K—Coalition of the Christian Democratic Union-Czech People's Party (KDU-CSL) and the Freedom Union (US), QC—Quad Coalition, comprising the KDU-CSL, the US, the Civic Democratic Alliance (ODA) and the Democratic Union (DEU), Ind—Independents

ETHNIC GROUPS:

Slovak 6%
Moravian 13%
Czech 81%

NATIONAL ECONOMICS

WORLD GNP RANKING: 46th

GNP PER CAPITA: $5,250

INFLATION: 3.9%

BALANCE OF PAYMENTS (BALANCE OF TRADE): -$2.34 billion

EXCHANGE RATES / U.S. DLR.: 37.63-35.56 CZECH KORUNY

OFFICIAL CURRENCY: CZECH KORUNA

GOVERNMENT SPENDING (% OF GDP)

DEFENSE 2.2%
EDUCATION 4.2%
HEALTH 6.6%

0   5   10   15

NUMBER OF CONFLICTS OVER LAST 25 YEARS

	1	2-5	5+
Violent changes in government	○	○	○
Civil wars	○	○	○
International wars	○	○	○
Foreign intervention	○	○	○

- The Czech Republic is among the world's 20 largest arms exporters.
- Professional soldiers with a communist past were the first to be demobilized after 1993.
- Phasing out conscription.

NOTABLE WARS AND INSURGENCIES: None

THE CZECH REPUBLIC IS A SMALL, landlocked country in central Europe which only came into being as an independent nation in 1993. From the 16th century the Czech territories of Bohemia and Moravia formed part of the Habsburg and then the Austro-Hungarian Empire. In 1918, they were joined with the adjacent Slovak territories to form the new state of Czechoslovakia. Following 20 years of independence, Czechoslovakia was occupied by Germany and became part of the Third Reich under Adolf Hitler.

After World War II, Czechoslovakia became part of the Soviet Communist bloc. Czech resistance to communist domination flared up in 1968 during an uprising called the "Prague spring", when reformers tried to establish a liberal "socialism with a human face". But the brief experiment was soon crushed by Soviet and other Soviet bloc troops, after which Czechoslovakia endured another 20 years of Soviet dictatorship. Liberation finally came in 1989 when, in response to new reform policies in the Soviet Union under Mikhail Gorbachev, Czechoslovakia was permitted to carry out the so-called "Velvet Revolution"—the peaceful transformation from communism to democracy.

The first president of democratic Czechoslovakia was poet and playwright Vaclav Havel, who became a worldwide spokesman for human rights. In the early 1990s, pro-independence sentiment grew in Slovakia, and it was agreed that Slovakia and the Czech Republic would go their separate ways. This became known as the "Velvet Divorce". In January 1993, they became two independent nations, which now enjoy peaceful and cooperative relations.

The Czech parliamentary system consists of a president and a prime minister, a bicameral legislature, an independent judiciary, and a spectrum of political parties ranging from far-left communists to right-wing nationalists.

Since their overthrow of communism, the Czechs have made strong economic progress, and have received a great deal of foreign investment. The Czech Republic was expected to join the European Union in 2004.

ISSUES AND CHALLENGES:

- The Czech Republic handled the transition from communism to capitalism skillfully, and became the first post-communist country to receive an investment-grade credit rating by international credit institutions. However, it still faces serious challenges in completing the transition to a modern capitalist economy, such as restructuring outmoded industries, increasing transparency in its capital markets, and transforming the housing sector, and pension and health care systems.

- The government faces pressure to cut expenditure in order to reduce a serious budget deficit.

- Pollution from power, chemical, and cement industries along with the newly-created Temelin nuclear plant, pose environmental concerns.

HOW THE GOVERNMENT WORKS

LEGISLATIVE BRANCH

Parlament
(Parliament)
Bicameral Parliament

Senat
(Senate)
Composed of 81 members directly elected to six-year terms. One-third of members elected every two years. Senate may not be dissolved.

Poslanecka Snemovna
(Chamber of Deputies)
Composed of 200 members elected to four-year terms by proportional representation from 14 regions.

Regional Governments
Fourteen regions, including one for the capital Prague, are governed by presidents elected (with consent of the Senate) to ten-year terms.

EXECUTIVE BRANCH

President
Elected to five-year term by a simple majority of deputies and senators in joint parliamentary session. Serves as chief of state; dissolves Chamber of Deputies; calls legislative elections; vetoes legislation.

Prime Minister
Appointed by president. Serves as head of government and sets agenda for foreign and domestic policies.

Council of Ministers
Appointed by president on advice of prime minister. Oversees government operations.

JUDICIAL BRANCH

Supreme Court
Highest court of review and appeal. Composed of three judges appointed for life by president on advice of the prime minister.

Constitutional Court
Final authority on constitutional issues and election laws. Composed of 15 judges appointed to ten-year terms by president with consent of the Senate.

Supreme Administrative Court
Rules on administrative regulations and mediates jurisdictional conflicts.

Chief Courts

Regional Courts

District Courts

PORTUGAL

OFFICIAL NAME: REPUBLIC OF PORTUGAL

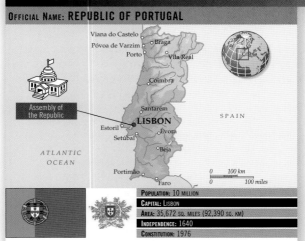

Viana do Castelo
Póvoa de Varzim • Braga
Porto • Vila Real
Coimbra
Santarém
Estoril LISBON SPAIN
Setúbal • Évora
• Beja
Portimão
Faro

ATLANTIC OCEAN

Assembly of the Republic

0   100 km
0   100 miles

POPULATION: 10 MILLION	
CAPITAL: LISBON	
AREA: 35,672 SQ. MILES (92,390 SQ. KM)	
INDEPENDENCE: 1640	
CONSTITUTION: 1976	

PORTUGAL derives its name from the Roman port of Portus Cale, today's city of Porto.

RELIGION: Roman Catholic 97%, Protestant 1%, Other 2%

OFFICIAL LANGUAGE: Portuguese

REGIONS OR PROVINCES: 18 districts and 2 autonomous regions

DEPENDENT TERRITORIES: None

MEDIA: No political censorship exists in national media

NEWSPAPERS: There are 31 daily newspapers

TV: 1 state-owned service, several independent services

RADIO: 1 state-owned service, several independent national and regional services

SUFFRAGE: 18 years of age; universal

LEGAL SYSTEM: Civil law; accepts ICJ jurisdiction

WORLD ORGANIZATIONS: AfDB, Australia Group, BIS, CCC, CE, CERN, EAPC, EBRD, ECE, ECLAC, EIB, EMU, ESA, EU, FAO, IADB, IAEA, IBRD, ICAO, ICC, ICFTU, ICRM, IDA, IEA, IFAD, IFC, IFRCS, IHO, ILO, IMF, IMO, Interpol. IOC, IOM, ISO, ITU, LAIA (observer), MINURSO, NAM (guest), NATO, NEA, NSG, OAS (observer), OECD, OPCW, OSCE, PCA, UN, UNCTAD, UNESCO, UNIDO, UNMIBH, UNMIK, UNMOP, UNTAET, UPU, WCL, WEU, WFTU, WHO, WIPO, WMO, WToO, WTrO, ZC

POLITICAL PARTIES: PSD—Social Democratic Party, PS—Socialist Party, PP—People's Party, CDU—United Democratic Coalition, BE—Left Bloc

ETHNIC GROUPS:

African and Other 2%

Portuguese 98%

NATIONAL ECONOMICS

WORLD GNP RANKING: 33rd

GNP PER CAPITA: $11,120

INFLATION: 2.9%

BALANCE OF PAYMENTS (BALANCE OF TRADE): -$10.6 billion

EXCHANGE RATES / U.S. DLR.: 1.0651-1.1231 EUROS

OFFICIAL CURRENCY: EURO

5 EURO

GOVERNMENT SPENDING (% OF GDP)

DEFENSE 2.2%	
EDUCATION 5.7%	
HEALTH 5.1%	

0   5   10   15

NUMBER OF CONFLICTS OVER LAST 25 YEARS

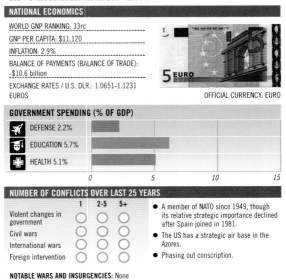

	1	2-5	5+
Violent changes in government	○	○	○
Civil wars	○	○	○
International wars	○	○	○
Foreign intervention	○	○	○

• A member of NATO since 1949, though its relative strategic importance declined after Spain joined in 1981.
• The US has a strategic air base in the Azores.
• Phasing out conscription.

NOTABLE WARS AND INSURGENCIES: None

PORTUGAL, ONE OF EUROPE'S oldest nations, has existed since becoming an independent kingdom in 1139. During the 15th and 16th centuries it built a large empire, but fell under the rule its more powerful neighbour, Spain, in 1580. On regaining its independence in 1640, Portugal remained a kingdom until the 1910 revolution toppled the monarchy and established a republic.

More than four decades of right-wing dictatorship started in 1932 with António Salazar and ended in 1974 with the overthrow of Marcelo Caetano in a coup known as the "Carnation Revolution". This was led by military officers of the left-wing Armed Forces Movement (MFA) and initiated Portugal's passage to parliamentary democracy. The movement's leader, General António de Spínola released political prisoners, and abolished censorship and the secret police. However, more radical members of the MFA and communist civilians soon gained control. During two years of revolution, Portugal suffered political chaos, enduring six provisional governments and two coup attempts.

In 1976 a new constitution was promulgated, a parliament was elected, and General António Eanes became president. Since the first draft of the constitution, subsequent revisions have placed the military under civilian control, while limiting the power of the president and moving Portugal toward greater democracy, including privatization of the media—previously government-owned. Political and economic integration with Europe has been a key issue since Portugal joined the EU in 1986.

ANNIVERSARY CELEBRATIONS
Young people riding a 1970s armored car celebrate the 25th anniversary of the 1974 Carnation Revolution—a bloodless coup led by the army that did away with almost 50 years of dictatorship.

The controversial Council of the Revolution was abolished under the 1982 constitution which curtailed the powers of the president, partly through the creation of the advisory Council of State. Several political parties vie for control of the Assembly of the Republic; the largest are the Socialists and the Social Democrats.

HOW THE GOVERNMENT WORKS

LEGISLATIVE BRANCH

Assembleia da Republica (Assembly of the Republic) Unicameral Parliament
Composed of 230 members directly elected to four-year terms. Has sole jurisdiction over civil rights, liberties and citizenship; political parties and elections; creation of taxes and revenue; national and regional planning; agrarian reforms.

Regional Government
Eighteen regional districts administered by assemblies of municipal authorities and governors appointed by national government. Autonomous regions (the Azores and Madeira) each have their own government and president.

EXECUTIVE BRANCH

President
Elected to five-year term by direct vote; limited to two consecutive terms. Serves as head of state and commander-in-chief of armed forces, heads Council of State; appoints ambassadors; declares war; and grants pardons.

Prime Minister
Appointed by president following elections and after consultation with Assembly of the Republic. Serves as head of government.

Council of Ministers
Composed of 15 to 18 ministers appointed by president on advice of prime minister. Sets government policy.

JUDICIAL BRANCH

Constitutional Court
Rules on constitutionality of laws and treaties. Ten of its 13 judges are selected by the Assembly of the Republic

Supreme Court of Justice
Highest court of appeal; may serve sometimes as court of first or second instance. Judges appointed for life by Superior Council of Magistracy.

Courts of Second Instance
Four courts; hear lower-level appeals.

Courts of First Instance
Municipal and district courts; hear civil and criminal cases.

HUNGARY

OFFICIAL NAME: REPUBLIC OF HUNGARY

POPULATION: 9.9 MILLION	
CAPITAL: BUDAPEST	
AREA: 35,919 SQ. MILES (93,303 SQ. KM)	
INDEPENDENCE: 1918	
CONSTITUTION: 1949	

HUNGARY derives from "Hun," earlier nomads than the Magyars, or from the Bulgarian "ungur," ("ten tribes").

RELIGION: Roman Catholic 64%, Calvinist 20%, Nonreligious 7%, Lutheran 4%, Greek Orthodox 3%, Other 2%

OFFICIAL LANGUAGE: Hungarian

REGIONS OR PROVINCES: 19 counties, 20 urban counties and 1 capital city

DEPENDENT TERRITORIES: None

MEDIA: No political censorship exists in national media

Newspapers: There are 40 daily newspapers

TV: 2 services: 1 state-owned, 1 independent

Radio: 4 services: 1 state-owned, 3 independent

SUFFRAGE: 18 years of age; universal

LEGAL SYSTEM: Western legal traditions; accepts ICJ jurisdiction

ETHNIC GROUPS:

- German 2%
- Roma 1%
- Slovak 1%
- Other 6%
- Magyar 90%

WORLD ORGANIZATIONS: ABEDA, Australia Group, BIS, CCC, CE, CEI, CERN, EAPC, EBRD, ECE, EU, FAO, G- 9, IAEA, IBRD, ICAO, ICC, ICFTU, ICRM, IDA, IEA, IFC, IFRCS, ILO, IMF, IMO, Interpol, IOC, IOM, ISO, ITU, MINURSO, NAM (guest), NATO, NEA, NSG, OAS (observer), OECD, OPCW, OSCE, PCA, PFP, UN, UNCTAD, UNESCO, UNFICYP, UNHCR, UNIDO, UNIKOM, UNMIBH, UNMIK, UNOMIG, UNU, UPU, WCL, WEU (associate), WFTU, WHO, WIPO, WMO, WToO, WTrO, ZC

POLITICAL PARTIES: Fidesz-MPP—Young Democrats-Hungarian Civic Party, MSzP—Hungarian Socialist Party, SzDSz—Alliance of Free Democrats

NATIONAL ECONOMICS

WORLD GNP RANKING: 52nd

GNP PER CAPITA: $4,710

INFLATION: 9.8%

BALANCE OF PAYMENTS (BALANCE OF TRADE): - $1.49 billion

EXCHANGE RATES / U.S. DLR.: 282.3-274.8 FORINT

OFFICIAL CURRENCY: FORINT

GOVERNMENT SPENDING (% OF GDP)

- ✈ DEFENSE 1.7%
- 🎓 EDUCATION 4.6%
- ✚ HEALTH 5.2%

0   5   10   15

NUMBER OF CONFLICTS OVER LAST 25 YEARS

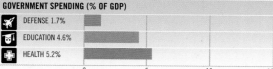

	1	2-5	5+
Violent changes in government	○	○	○
Civil wars	○	○	○
International wars	○	○	○
Foreign intervention	○	○	○

- The military was streamlined in advance of NATO membership in 1999.
- Relations with neighboring countries are troubled by government efforts to provide benefits to ethnic Hungarian communities.
- Phasing out conscription.

NOTABLE WARS AND INSURGENCIES: None

FOR MORE THAN 400 YEARS, great powers—from the Ottomans and Hapsburgs to Nazi Germany and then the Soviet Union—dominated Hungary. But with the thawing of the Cold War Eastern Bloc, Hungary became the first Soviet satellite to throw off communist rule and embrace Western-style democracy. Today, Hungary rules itself under the multiparty parliamentary government that first took root in the late 1980s, while building a free-market, capitalist economy.

As part of the Austro-Hungarian Empire, Hungary lost two-thirds of its land and population at the end of World War I. It fought reluctantly with Germany during the early years of World War II, losing 40,000 troops in the disastrous Axis invasion of Stalingrad. Wary that Hungary would strike a separate peace with the Allies, Hitler sent German troops to occupy the country near the war's end.

ISSUES AND CHALLENGES:

- With one of Europe's fastest-growing and most open economies, Hungary hopes to join the European Union as early as 2004.

- Issues pertaining to ethnic Hungarian minorities in neighboring countries cause bilateral tension.

- Salaries in the public sector fall short of the cost of living, which has created a widening income gap between young skilled workers and those in education, health and other state sectors.

- Organized crime and illegal immigration is rising.

In 1949, Hungary in adopted a Soviet-style constitution and launched a Marxist economic plan, including nationalization of private industries and land collectivization. In 1955, Hungary joined the Warsaw Pact, but government repression and a faltering economy provoked student demonstrations and mass public protests. In response, Hungary's communist government relented, promised free elections, sought to withdraw from the pact, declared its neutrality, and appealed to the Western powers for protection. When the West failed to respond, Soviets troops invaded, installed a new communist regime, and imprisoned or executed thousands of dissidents. By the 1960s, the regime curbed some police-state abuses and for the next two decades steered a gradually more liberal cultural and economic course.

Hungary expects to join the European Union as early as 2006.

By 1988, Hungary's government relaxed restrictions on speech, the press, and labor unions. A national roundtable of Communist Party leaders and reformers drafted constitutional revisions for free elections and a new multiparty government. The reforms established an elected president, prime minister, cabinet, elected unicameral legislature, and independent judiciary. Hungary held its first free elections in 1990. Since then, power has been peacefully transferred in four elections between four different coalition governments.

HOW THE GOVERNMENT WORKS

LEGISLATIVE BRANCH

Orszaggyules
(National Assembly)
Unicameral Parliament
Composed of 386 members elected to four-year terms under a system of direct popular vote and proportional representation. Passes legislation; approves budget and government program; declares war and states of emergency; oversees local assemblies; may dismiss prime minister.

Regional Governments
Thirty-eight counties, including capital of Budapest, administered by mayors and legislative assemblies elected to four-year terms.

EXECUTIVE BRANCH

President
Elected to five-year term by parliament with two-term limit. Serves as head of state; represents nation in international forums; initiates referenda; returns bills to parliament for reconsideration.

Prime minister
Member of largest legislative party; appointed by president, approved by parliament. Serves as head of government; runs domestic affairs; sponsors legislation; dismisses cabinet ministers.

Cabinet
Members appointed by prime minister, approved by parliament.

JUDICIAL BRANCH

Constitutional Court of Hungary
Rules on constitutionality of laws and government actions. Composed of 11 justices elected to nine-year terms by two-thirds majority vote of parliament.

Supreme Court
Highest court of appeal for civil and criminal cases.

Courts of Appeals
Hears appeals from lower courts.

County Tribunals
and Local Courts

SWEDEN

OFFICIAL NAME: KINGDOM OF SWEDEN

POPULATION: 8.8 MILLION
CAPITAL: STOCKHOLM
AREA: 173,731 SQ. MILES (449,963 SQ. KM)
INDEPENDENCE: 1523
CONSTITUTION: 1975

SWEDEN's name originates from "Sverige," or "Svea Rike," meaning "realm of the Svea people."

RELIGION: Evangelical Lutheran 89%, Roman Catholic 2%, Other Protestant 1%, Russian Orthodox 1%, Muslim 1%, Other 6%

OFFICIAL LANGUAGE: Swedish

REGIONS OR PROVINCES: 21 counties

DEPENDENT TERRITORIES: None

MEDIA: No political censorship exists in national media

SUFFRAGE: 18 years of age; universal

LEGAL SYSTEM: Civil and customary law; accepts ICJ jurisdiction

WORLD ORGANIZATIONS: AfDB, AsDB, Australia Group, BIS, CBSS, CCC, CE, CERN, EAPC, EBRD, ECE, EIB, ESA, EU, FAO, G- 6, G- 9, G-10, IADB, IAEA, IBRD, ICAO, ICC, ICFTU, ICRM, IDA, IEA, IFAD, IFC, IFRCS, IHO, ILO, IMF, IMO, Interpol, IOC, IOM, ISO, ITU, MONUC, NAM (guest), NC, NEA, NIB, NSG, OAS (observer), OECD, OPCW, OSCE, PCA, PFP, UN, UNAMSIL, UNCTAD, UNDOF, UNESCO, UNHCR, UNIDO, UNIKOM, UNITAR, UNMEE, UNMIBH, UNMIK, UNMOGIP, UNMOP, UNOMIG, UNTAET, UNTSO, UPU, WEU (observer), WFTU, WHO, WIPO, WMO, WTrO, ZC

POLITICAL PARTIES: SAP—Social Democratic Labor Party, M—Moderate Party, FP—Liberal Party, Kd—Christian Democratic Party, VP—Left Party, CP—Center Party, MpG—Green Party

ETHNIC GROUPS:

Other European 6%
Finnish and Sami 3%
Swedish 91%

NATIONAL ECONOMICS

WORLD GNP RANKING: 21st

GNP PER CAPITA: $27,140

INFLATION: 1.0%

BALANCE OF PAYMENTS (BALANCE OF TRADE): $6.62 billion

EXCHANGE RATES / U.S. DLR.: 9.436-10.490 KRONOR

OFFICIAL CURRENCY: SWEDISH KRONA

GOVERNMENT SPENDING(% OF GDP)

✈ DEFENSE 2.2%

🎓 EDUCATION 8%

✚ HEALTH 6.6%

0   5   10   15

NUMBER OF CONFLICTS OVER LAST 25 YEARS

	1	2-5	5+
Violent changes in government	○	○	○
Civil wars	○	○	○
International wars	○	○	○
Foreign intervention	○	○	○

- Advanced defense industry includes Saab jets.
- Traditional neutrality is giving way to cooperation with NATO.
- Defense reforms introduced regular office hours and canceled large-scale exercises from 2001.

NOTABLE WARS AND INSURGENCIES: None

ONE OF THE WORLD'S MOST LIBERAL NATIONS, Sweden is 80 percent unionized, with an advanced social welfare state, high taxes, and also a burgeoning high-tech industrial base. Unlike its neighbor, Norway, Sweden is also a member of the European Union, having joined in 1995. The country has a penchant for stable parliamentary democracy and, for nearly two centuries, armed neutrality in military conflicts (despite supplying Germany during World War I). The *Riksdag* (Parliament) became a permanent institution as early as the 15th century. Executive power was vested in the monarch until 1917, when the principles of cabinet and prime ministerial authority and responsibility to Parliament were accepted. Universal suffrage was introduced in 1919, and by 1974, a new constitution had reduced the monarch's role to a purely ceremonial one, completing the metamorphosis from monarchal rule to a liberal democratic structure in little over half a century.

Since the 1930s, the Social Democratic Labor Party (SAP) has rarely been out of (often coalition) government. In 2002, it gained 41 percent of parliamentary seats. The SAP has long been at the forefront of Sweden's prominent liberal policy, the concomitant of which were the high labor costs and escalating budget deficits of the late 1980s to 1990s. Another cornerstone of Sweden's liberal regime is a progressive environmental policy: the government plans to shut down all nuclear reactors by 2010. However, political stability did not prevent the 1986 assassination of Prime Minister Olof Palme, nor has it prevented governments from resigning. In 1914 the first liberal administration left office over defense policy, and in 1978 the non-socialist government resigned over nuclear-power. Today, the Green party and the left often hold the balance of power.

The unicameral parliament is a model of liberal democratic principles: nearly half of its 349 members are women, and all members are elected by proportional representation. There are 21 regional authorities under its control.

Over 45% of the Swedish Parliament is women, the highest in the world

ISSUES AND CHALLENGES:

- Sweden's indecision over what its role should be in the political and economic integration of Europe delayed its entry into the EU until 1995, and caused it to forego introduction of the euro into the Swedish economy in 1999. On September 14 2003, Swedish voters turned down entry into the Euro system, concerned about the impact on democracy and sovereignty.

- Sweden is in the tier of countries with a 99 percent literacy rate for persons age 15 and over.

- In 1979, the Act of Succession was amended to allow a female first-born child of the monarch, such as Crown Princess Victoria, to ascend to the throne.

HOW THE GOVERNMENT WORKS

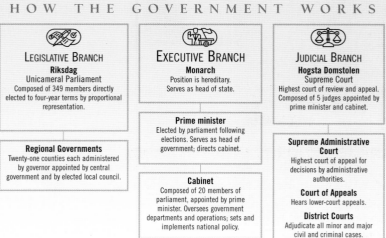

LEGISLATIVE BRANCH
Riksdag
Unicameral Parliament
Composed of 349 members directly elected to four-year terms by proportional representation.

Regional Governments
Twenty-one counties each administered by governor appointed by central government and by elected local council.

EXECUTIVE BRANCH
Monarch
Position is hereditary. Serves as head of state.

Prime minister
Elected by parliament following elections. Serves as head of government; directs cabinet.

Cabinet
Composed of 20 members of parliament, appointed by prime minister. Oversees government departments and operations; sets and implements national policy.

JUDICIAL BRANCH
Hogsta Domstolen
Supreme Court
Highest court of review and appeal. Composed of 5 judges appointed by prime minister and cabinet.

Supreme Administrative Court
Highest court of appeal for decisions by administrative authorities.

Court of Appeals
Hears lower-court appeals.

District Courts
Adjudicate all minor and major civil and criminal cases.

AUSTRIA

OFFICIAL NAME: REPUBLIC OF AUSTRIA

POPULATION: 8.1 MILLION
CAPITAL: VIENNA
AREA: 32,378 SQ. MILES (83,859 SQ. KM)
INDEPENDENCE: 1918
CONSTITUTION: 1920

AUSTRIA is derived from the German word, "Österreich", which means "eastern kingdom".

RELIGION: Roman Catholic 78%, Non-religious 9%, Protestant 5%, Other (including Jewish and Muslim) 8%

OFFICIAL LANGUAGE: German

REGIONS OR PROVINCES: 9 states

DEPENDENT TERRITORIES: None

MEDIA: No political censorship exists in the national media

NEWSPAPERS: There are 17 daily newspapers

TV: 2 state-owned channels

RADIO: 1 state-owned service

SUFFRAGE: 18 years of age; universal; compulsory for presidential elections

LEGAL SYSTEM: Civil law based on Roman legal traditions; accepts ICJ jurisdiction

WORLD ORGANIZATIONS: AfDB, AsDB, Australia Group, BIS, BSEC (observer), CCC, CE, CEI, CERN, EAPC, EBRD, ECE, EIB, EMU, ESA, EU, FAO, G- 9, IADB, IAEA, IBRD, ICAO, ICC, ICFTU, ICRM, IDA, IEA, IFAD, IFC, IFRCS, ILO, IMF, IMO, Interpol, IOC, IOM, ISO, ITU, MINURSO, NAM (guest), NEA, NSG, OAS (observer), OECD, OPCW, OSCE, PCA, PFP, UN, UNCTAD, UNDOF, UNESCO, UNFICYP, UNHCR, UNIDO, UNIKOM, UNITAR, UNMEE, UNMIBH, UNMIK, UNMOGIP, UNMOT, UNOMIG, UNTSO, UPU, WCL, WEU (observer), WFTU, WHO, WIPO, WMO, WToO, WTrO, ZC

POLITICAL PARTIES: SPÖ—Social Democratic Party of Austria, FPÖ—Freedom Party of Austria, ÖVP—Austrian People's Party, GA—Green Alternative

ETHNIC GROUPS:

- Croat, Slovene, Hungarian 6%
- Other 1%
- German 93%

NATIONAL ECONOMICS

WORLD GNP RANKING: 22nd

GNP PER CAPITA: $25,220

INFLATION: 2.4%

BALANCE OF PAYMENTS (BALANCE OF TRADE): -$5.21 billion

EXCHANGE RATES / U.S. DLR.: 1.0651-1.1231 EUROS

OFFICIAL CURRENCY: EURO

GOVERNMENT SPENDING (% OF GDP)

- ✈ DEFENSE 0.8%
- 📚 EDUCATION 6.3%
- ✚ HEALTH 5.9%

0   5   10   15

NUMBER OF CONFLICTS OVER LAST 25 YEARS

	1	2-5	5+
Violent changes in government	○	○	○
Civil wars	○	○	○
International wars	○	○	○
Foreign intervention	○	○	○

- The 1955 State Treaty, which restored Austria's independence, enshrined the country's neutrality.
- Despite the small size of Austria's armed forces, its arms industry is strong.
- Compulsory military service.

NOTABLE WARS AND INSURGENCIES: None

ONCE THE HEART OF THE POWERFUL Austro-Hungarian Empire, Austria became a separate republic following the break-up of the empire after World War I. However, the Nazi German army marched in to annex the country in 1938 in accordance with Adolf Hitler's desire to create a unified state of German-speaking peoples. Following World War II, elections were held splitting the vote between three parties: the conservative Austrian People's Party (ÖVP), the Socialists – now the Social Democratic Party of Austria (SPÖ) – and the communists. By 1947, the communists had abandoned the government, and the remaining two parties formed a coalition that remained in power until 1966.

The devastation of World War II had left Austria in ruins. Occupation by US, British, French, and Soviet forces continued until 1955, when Austria regained its sovereignty. The Allied Occupation Force took great care to install a strong form of democratic government to ensure lasting stability and independence in Austria. Subsequently, the Austrian State Treaty of 1955 declared independence and neutrality, and created a unique form of government based on a combination of parliamentary and presidential systems. While the president is democratically elected by popular vote, the office is mostly ceremonial. Nearly every decision the president makes must be co-signed by the chancellor—who wields the majority of executive power—or the appropriate member of the Council of Ministers. Moreover, most of the important decisions of the executive branch are made by the Council of Ministers, which is led by the chancellor. Fundamental political power in the country is vested in the Bundesversammlung, or Federal Assembly, and its main chamber, the Nationalrat (National Council). The health and stability of the multiparty system is most visible in this body: rarely does any one of the four major parties—the SPÖ, the Freedom Party of Austria (FPÖ), the ÖVP and the Green Alternative (GA)—hold a majority in the Assembly.

The social and political consequences of World War II still linger in contemporary Austrian society, most visibly in Austria's forceful insistence on cultural, political, and economic independence from Germany.

ISSUES AND CHALLENGES:

- Austria's membership in the European Union is a volatile issue among the population. Many fear that membership will compromise a national Austrian identity.

- Ethnic tensions have increased recently between the far right and migrants from Eastern Europe and the Caucasus, who comprise Austria's poorest social class.

- As a small, mountainous country, Austria has few natural resources. Its economy is dependent on imported fuel resources and energy.

- Tourism is an important component of the economy, which has experienced a slump in recent years.

HOW THE GOVERNMENT WORKS

LEGISLATIVE BRANCH

Bundesversammlung
(Federal Assembly)
Bicameral Parliament

Bundesrat
(Federal Council)
64 members elected to six-year terms by nine state legislatures. Reviews and delays but cannot veto bills.

Nationalrat
(National Council)
83 members elected to four-year terms by direct popular vote. Initiates and passes bills; amends constitution with two-thirds majority vote. Removes Council of Ministers members with no-confidence vote.

Regional Governments
Nine states administered by elected legislatures that select governors.

EXECUTIVE BRANCH

President
Elected to six-year term by direct popular vote; limit of two consecutive terms. Serves as head of state; commander-in-chief of armed forces. Appoints government officials; signs bills and treaties; convenes and dissolves parliament.

Chancellor
Leader of parliament's majority party or coalition; appointed by president. Serves as head of government. Controls civil servant promotions.

Council of Ministers
Appointed by president on advice of chancellor. Oversees government operations; chaired by chancellor.

JUDICIAL BRANCH

Constitutional Court
Rules on constitutionality of laws. Composed of 14 judges, six alternates appointed by president on advice of Council of Ministers and parliament.

Supreme Judicial Court
Highest court of review and appeal. Judges appointed by president on advice of Council of Ministers.

Administrative Court
Rules on cases involving administrative agencies. Judges appointed by president on advice of Council of Ministers.

High Provincial Courts
Four courts.

Provincial and District Courts
17 courts

Local Courts

SWITZERLAND

OFFICIAL NAME: SWISS CONFEDERATION

POPULATION: 7.2 MILLION	
CAPITAL: BERN	
AREA: 15,942 SQ. MILES (41,290 SQ. KM)	
INDEPENDENCE: 1291	
CONSTITUTION: 1874	

SWITZERLAND is named for one of its founding cantons, "Schwyz," which derives from "schweitz," or swamp.

RELIGION: Roman Catholic 46%, Protestant 40%, Muslim 2%, Other and non-religious 12%

OFFICIAL LANGUAGES: French, German, and Italian

REGIONS OR PROVINCES: 26 cantons

DEPENDENT TERRITORIES: None

MEDIA: No political censorship exists in national media

Newspapers: There are 84 daily newspapers

TV: 3 independent services broadcasting in German, Romansch, French, and Italian

Radio: 3 independent services broadcasting in German, Romansch, French, and Italian

ETHNIC GROUPS:
- Other 6%
- Romansch 1%
- Italian 10%
- French 18%
- German 65%

SUFFRAGE: 18 years of age; universal

LEGAL SYSTEM: Civil and customary law; accepts ICJ jurisdiction

WORLD ORGANIZATIONS: ACCT, AfDB, AsDB, Australia Group, BIS, CCC, CE, CERN, EAPC, EBRD, ECE, EFTA, ESA, FAO, G-10, IADB, IAEA, IBRD, ICAO, ICC, ICFTU, ICRM, IDA, IEA, IFAD, IFC, IFRCS, ILO, IMF, IMO, Interpol, IOC, IOM, ISO, ITU, LAIA (observer), MONUC, NAM (guest), NEA, NSG, OAS (observer), OECD, OPCW, OSCE, PCA, PFP, UN (observer), UNCTAD, UNESCO, UNHCR, UNIDO, UNITAR, UNMEE, UNMIBH, UNMIK, UNMOP, UNOMIG, UNTSO, UNU, UPU, WCL, WHO, WIPO, WMO, WToO, WTrO, ZC

POLITICAL PARTIES: SP/PS—Social Democratic Party, SVP/UDC—Swiss People's Party, FDP/PDR—Radical Democratic Party, CVP/PDC—Christian Democratic People's Party, GPS/PES—Green Party of Switzerland

NATIONAL ECONOMICS

WORLD GNP RANKING: 18th

GNP PER CAPITA: $38,140

INFLATION: 1.6%

BALANCE OF PAYMENTS (BALANCE OF TRADE): $32.5 billion

EXCHANGE RATES / U.S. DLR.: 1.6205-1.6603 SWISS FRANCS

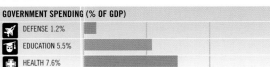

OFFICIAL CURRENCY: SWISS FRANC

GOVERNMENT SPENDING (% OF GDP)

- ✈ DEFENSE 1.2%
- 📖 EDUCATION 5.5%
- ➕ HEALTH 7.6%

| 0 | 5 | 10 | 15 |

NUMBER OF CONFLICTS OVER LAST 25 YEARS

	1	2-5	5+
Violent changes in government	○	○	○
Civil wars	○	○	○
International wars	○	○	○
Foreign intervention	○	○	○

- Switzerland is a neutral country.
- Almost 400,000 conscripts can be called up and armed in a few hours.
- Bridges and tunnels are still mined in accordance with early 1900s defense strategy.

NOTABLE WARS AND INSURGENCIES: None

THE ORIGIN OF THE SWISS CONFEDERATION was the defensive alliance signed by the cantons of Uri, Schwyz and Unterwalden in 1291. The cornerstone of the modern Swiss Confederation has been its centuries-old policy of neutrality. Since the country first gained recognition as an independent state following the Peace of Westphalia in 1648, it has not actively participated in any European wars or military engagements. Recently, though, Switzerland has faced international criticism for having allowing its renowned banking sector to finance the Nazi military and hide substantial assets stolen from Jewish victims of the Holocaust during World War II. The country has also stood apart from political and economic integration in Europe; the Swiss have consistently refused to join the European Union.

Unlike that of any other European nation, Switzerland's executive branch is directed by a Federal Council rather than a president or a prime minister. All executive decisions are made by this council, none of whose seven members holds more authority than another. The leadership positions rotate on an annual basis with the vice-president of one year becoming the president of the next. The seven members are elected according to a specified formula—two from each of the Christian Democrats, Social Democrats, Free Democrats, and one from the Swiss People's Party (SVP). However, with the SVP taking a larger percentage of the vote with each election, it is quite possible that it might gain a second member on the Council. While the country does have a president and vice-president, these offices do not exercise a great deal of power, but serve to organize and coordinate council meetings and agendas.

Supreme political power in Switzerland is vested in the Bundesversammlung, or Federal Assembly. Conflicts between members of the legislature's two houses are rare. Virtually the same coalition has retained power in the assembly since 1959, and the country's political climate has remained stable. Yet political tensions have heightened over such issues as immigration, integration into the EU, increasing drug abuse in Swiss society, and the World War II banking scandal.

ISSUES AND CHALLENGES:

- Swiss voters are divided on the issue of whether to join the European Union or even the European Economic Area. Although the advantages to business would be plentiful, there is the fear of an influx of immigrants who would lower the standard of living, and of losing the decentralized system of rule that currently exists.

- In common with many other European countries, Switzerland faces the problem of an ageing population.

- While Switzerland has few natural resources, it is self-sufficient in its energy needs and has a highly diversified economy.

HOW THE GOVERNMENT WORKS

LEGISLATIVE BRANCH

Bundesversammlung
(Federal Assembly)
Bicameral Parliament

Ständerat
(Council of States)
Composed of 46 members elected to four-year terms by direct popular vote: two each from 20 "full" cantons, 1 each from 6 "half" cantons.

Nationalrat
(National Council)
Composed of 200 members directly elected to four-year terms by proportional representation.

Regional Governments
Twenty-six cantons administered by elected unicameral legislatures and appointed executives.

EXECUTIVE BRANCH

Federal Council
7 parliament members elected to four-year terms by parliament; 2 Christian Democrats, 2 Social Democrats, 2 Free Democrats, 1 from Swiss People's Party. Sets national policy; oversees government operations. Councilors constitutionally act collectively in all matters, not as individual ministers.

President
Elected annually by parliament from members of Federal Council; Head of state and government. Organizes and coordinates the Federal Council.

Vice-president
Elected annually by parliament from members of Federal Council. Assists president; acts as president during president's absence.

JUDICIAL BRANCH

Federal Tribunal
Highest court of review and appeal of civil and criminal cases. No power to rule on constitutionality of laws. Composed of 30 full-time and 30 part-time judges elected to six-year terms by parliament.

Canton-level Courts

ISRAEL

OFFICIAL NAME: STATE OF ISRAEL

POPULATION: 6.2 MILLION	
CAPITAL: JERUSALEM	
AREA: 8,019 SQ. MILES (20,770 SQ. KM)	
INDEPENDENCE: 1948	
CONSTITUTION: 1948	

ISRAEL was named after Jacob, whom the Biblical God renamed "Israel" in Genesis 32:28.

RELIGION: Jewish 82%, Muslim (mainly Sunni) 14%, Druze and Other 2%, Christian 2%

OFFICIAL LANGUAGES: Hebrew and Arabic

REGIONS OR PROVINCES: Six districts

DEPENDENT TERRITORIES: None

MEDIA: Partial political censorship exists in national media

Newspapers: There are 34 daily newspapers

TV: Two services: one state-owned, one independent

Radio: Two state-owned services, many independent stations. The number of private radio stations, many right-wing, is rising.

SUFFRAGE: 18 years of age; universal

LEGAL SYSTEM: English common law; Jewish, Christian, Muslim legal traditions; no ICJ jurisdiction

WORLD ORGANIZATIONS: BSEC (observer), CCC, CE (observer), CERN (observer), EBRD, ECE, FAO, IADB, IAEA, IBRD, ICAO, ICC, ICFTU, IDA, IFAD, IFC, IFRCS (associate), ILO, IMF, IMO, Interpol, IOC, IOM, ISO, ITU, OAS (observer), OPCW (signatory), OSCE (partner), PCA, UN, UNCTAD, UNESCO, UNHCR, UNIDO, UPU, WHO, WIPO, WMO, WToO, WTrO

POLITICAL PARTIES: One Isr—One Israel (comprising Labor, Gesher and Meymad), Li—Likud, Sh—Shas, M—Maretz-Democratic Israel, YB—Yisrael Ba'aliya, NRP—National Religious Party

ETHNIC GROUPS:

Other (mostly Arab) 18%

Jewish 82%

NATIONAL ECONOMICS

WORLD GNP RANKING: 35th

GNP PER CAPITA: $16,710

INFLATION: 1.1%

BALANCE OF PAYMENTS (BALANCE OF TRADE): -$1.42 billion

EXCHANGE RATES / U.S. DLR.: 4.044-4.412 SHEQALIM

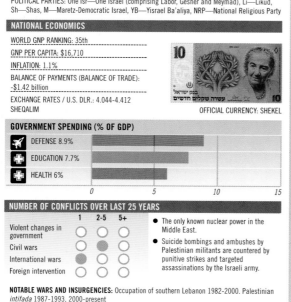

OFFICIAL CURRENCY: SHEKEL

GOVERNMENT SPENDING (% OF GDP)

✈ DEFENSE 8.9%

➕ EDUCATION 7.7%

➕ HEALTH 6%

0   5   10   15

NUMBER OF CONFLICTS OVER LAST 25 YEARS

	1	2-5	5+
Violent changes in government	○	○	○
Civil wars	○	●	○
International wars	●	○	○
Foreign intervention	○	○	○

- The only known nuclear power in the Middle East.
- Suicide bombings and ambushes by Palestinian militants are countered by punitive strikes and targeted assassinations by the Israeli army.

NOTABLE WARS AND INSURGENCIES: Occupation of southern Lebanon 1982-2000. Palestinian *intifada* 1987-1993, 2000-present

---

WHEN THE OTTOMAN EMPIRE CRUMBLED after World War I, the League of Nations awarded Great Britain a mandate to govern Palestine. Drawn by a traditional desire to return to their ancestral homeland, Jews had emigrated to Palestine before the mandate was passed, but intense persecution in Europe swelled their numbers. The resulting conflict between Palestinian Arabs and Jews prompted the newly formed United Nations to pass a plan to partition Palestine into Jewish and Arab states. The State of Israel was proclaimed in 1948. The neighboring Arab states, having rejected partition, attacked the nascent state and were defeated. Israel's victory brought it 50% more territory. Subsequent wars in 1956, 1967, and 1973 led to Israel's control over additional lands, e.g., the Sinai Desert, West Bank, and Gaza Strip. Egypt regained the Sinai Desert in 1977 under the Camp David peace accords. However, Israelis, many with strong religious views about Israel's right to these lands, established settlements on the West Bank and Gaza Strip and resisted moving. During the 1990s, "land for peace" proposals, (the Oslo Accords), attempted to provide Israel security and the Palestinians independence. These proposals foundered on escalating violence with Palestinian suicide bombers killing Israeli civilians and Israel's army attacking and clamping down on Palestinians. Extremists on both sides derailed peace talks and polarized public opinion.

Israel's fractious politics originate in its cultural diversity (émigrés come from more than 100 countries and five continents) and in the intensity and multiplicity of Israelis' religious and political views. Since no single party has ever won a majority, every government has been a coalition of multiple parties. Even small parties wield great decision-making power, and ministerships are distributed through intense bargaining. Irreconcilable differences among religious parties blocked the adoption of a constitution at independence, and a set of basic laws serves this function instead. No issue polarizes Israeli politics more than the Israeli-Palestinian conflict. Israeli elections increasingly turn on a party's ability to convince the electorate that it can deliver security and peace.

ISSUES AND CHALLENGES:

- Both Palestinians and Jews have ancient attachments to the same land and desire their own states. Israel's violent birth displaced many Arabs living within its borders. Of the 1.3 million Arabs living in pre-war Palestine, 150,000 remained after independence. Others fled to the West Bank, the Gaza Strip, and neighboring Arab countries. As citizens, Israeli Arabs are guaranteed equal religious and civil rights, but have always suffered social, economic, and political discrimination. Once apolitical and isolated, Israeli Arabs were politicized after 1967 through contact with "diaspora" Palestinians in the West Bank and Gaza Strip and have become increasingly active proponents of an independent Palestinian state.

HOW THE GOVERNMENT WORKS

LEGISLATIVE BRANCH

Knesset (Parliament) Unicameral Parliament
Composed of 120 members elected to four-year terms on party lists of candidates by proportional representation. Approves budget and taxes; passes bills introduced by executive branch; removes prime minister and cabinet with no-confidence vote.

Regional Governments
Six districts administered by elected local councils and commissioners appointed by Ministry of Interior.

EXECUTIVE BRANCH

President
Elected to single five-year term by parliament. Serves as head of state. Signs laws; appoints diplomats and judges; grants pardons; commutes sentences.

Prime minister
Leader of parliament's largest party; appointed by president. Serves as head of government. Sets cabinet's policy agenda; dissolves parliament.

Cabinet
Members appointed by prime minister, approved by parliament. Oversees government operations; presents legislation to parliament.

JUDICIAL BRANCH

Supreme Court
Highest court of review and appeal in civil and criminal cases. Judges appointed for life by president on advice of nominating committee chaired by prime minister.

Military Court of Appeal
Hears cases from lower military courts; responsible to Supreme Court. Judges appointed by president on advice of nominating committee chaired by prime minister.

District Courts

Magistrates Courts

Religious Courts
Jewish, Muslim, and Christian; hear marriage, divorce, alimony and inheritance cases.

SLOVAKIA

OFFICIAL NAME: SLOVAK REPUBLIC

National Council of
the Slovak Republic

POPULATION: 5.4 MILLION
CAPITAL: BRATISLAVA
AREA: 18,859 SQ. MILES (48,845 SQ. KM)
INDEPENDENCE: 1993
CONSTITUTION: 1992

SLOVAKIA, the land of the Slovaks, is derived from a local word that means "glory" or "the word".

RELIGION: Roman Catholic 60%, Atheist 10%, Protestant 8%, Orthodox 4%, Other 18%

OFFICIAL LANGUAGE: Slovak

REGIONS OR PROVINCES: Eight regions

DEPENDENT TERRITORIES: None

MEDIA: No political censorship exists in national media

Newspapers: There are 17 daily newspapers. The state news agency has been accused of lacking objectivity and depending on government funding

TV: Three services: one state-controlled, two independent

Radio: One state-controlled service and many privately owned stations

SUFFRAGE: 18 years of age; universal

LEGAL SYSTEM: Civil law; Austro-Hungarian legal traditions; no ICJ jurisdiction

WORLD ORGANIZATIONS: Australia Group, BIS, BSEC (observer), CCC, CE, CEI, CERN, EAPC, EBRD, ECE, EU, FAO, IAEA, IBRD, ICAO, ICC, ICFTU, ICRM, IDA, IFC, IFRCS, ILO, IMF, IMO, Interpol, IOC, IOM, ISO, ITU, NAM (guest), NSG, OECD, OPCW, OSCE, PCA, PFP, UN, UNAMSIL, UNCTAD, UNDOF, UNESCO, UNFICYP, UNIDO, UNMEE, UNTAET, UNTSO, UPU, WCL, WEU (associate partner), WFTU, WHO, WIPO, WMO, WToO, WTrO, ZC

POLITICAL PARTIES: HZDS—Movement for a Democratic Slovakia, SDKU—Slovak Democratic and Christian Union, Smer—Direction, SMK—Hungarian Coalition Party, KDH—Christian Democratic Movement, ANO—New Civic Alliance, KSS—Slovak Communist Party

ETHNIC GROUPS:

Other 2%
Czech 1%
Roma 1%
Magyar 11%
Slovak 85%

NATIONAL ECONOMICS

WORLD GNP RANKING: 66th

GNP PER CAPITA: $3,700

INFLATION: 12.0%

BALANCE OF PAYMENTS (BALANCE OF TRADE): -$694 million

EXCHANGE RATES / U.S. DLR.: 46.88-48.01 SLOVAK KORUNY

OFFICIAL CURRENCY: SLOVAK KORUNA

GOVERNMENT SPENDING (% OF GDP)

✈	DEFENSE	1.8%
✚	EDUCATION	4.3%
✚	HEALTH	5.7%

0   5   10   15

NUMBER OF CONFLICTS OVER LAST 25 YEARS

	1	2-5	5+
Violent changes in government	○	○	○
Civil wars	○	○	○
International wars	○	○	○
Foreign intervention	○	○	○

- The armed forces include some 13,600 conscripts at any one time.
- Membership of the EU and NATO are due in 2004.
- There is no navy.

NOTABLE WARS AND INSURGENCIES: None

SLOVAKIA MAY BE A PARLIAMENTARY DEMOCRACY, but it has little experience of being either independent or democratic. The country was under Hungarian rule for 900 years, then spent the years up until the outbreak of World War II as part of a democratic Czechoslovakia. In 1939, a separate Slovak state was declared under a pro-Nazi puppet government, before the Czechoslovak state was restored under communist rule in 1947. In 1968 the "Prague Spring" was ended by the Warsaw Pact invasion. A bloodless "Velvet Revolution" occurred in 1989, leading to the 1993 formation of separate Slovak and Czech states. Throughout this long and complex history, the recurring theme was a Slovakian desire for independence and democracy. Uprisings were frequent—from nationalist revivals in the late 18th and 19th centuries, to a 1944 revolt against Hitler, to the formation of the first government of Slovakia headed by Vladimir Meciar, to later political rebuffs of Meciar himself.

Now, the Slovakian presidency has become potentially powerful. Initially, the president was elected by the unicameral parliament, the National Council of the Slovak Republic, but the constitution was changed in 1998 to provide for the president's direct popular election. The president holds veto power and can dissolve the National Council if it repeatedly fails to pass the government's program. The president also appoints and dismisses the prime minister, who is usually the leader of a majority coalition, and names the cabinet on the prime minister's recommendation. The National Council of the Slovak Republic is a true multiparty parliament, with seven parties winning seats in the 2002 election. Four- and five-party ruling coalitions are commonplace.

Slovakia is one of ten European countries that completed negotiations in 2002 to join the European Union. The new prospects were scheduled to join the EU in mid-2004, pending ratification of an Accession Treaty by EU members and each candidate country. The other countries are the Czech Republic, Estonia, Hungary, Latvia, Lithuania, Poland, Slovenia, and the islands of Cyprus and Malta.

ISSUES AND CHALLENGES:

- A broad coalition led by center-right politician Mikulas Dzurinda won power in 1998, ending Meciar's domination of Slovak politics and reversing his pro-Russian policies.

- Historical, political, and geographical factors have caused Slovakia to experience more difficulty in moving from a centrally planned economy to a modern market economy than some of its Central European neighbors, but the Dzurinda government made great strides in 2001 and 2002.

- Dual Czech-Slovak citizenship is allowed. A former Czech living in Slovakia can retain Czech status when becoming a Slovak citizen, and a Slovak moving to the Czech republic has a similar dual-citizenship right.

HOW THE GOVERNMENT WORKS

LEGISLATIVE BRANCH

Narodna Rada Slovenskej Republiky
(National Council of the Slovak Republic)
Unicameral Parliament
Composed of 150 members directly elected to four-year terms by proportional representation. Passes laws; adopts budget; overrides vetoes with simple majority vote; removes prime minister and cabinet with no-confidence vote.

Regional Governments
Eight regions and 88 districts overseen by administrators appointed to four-year terms by prime minister.

EXECUTIVE BRANCH

President
Elected to five-year term by direct popular vote; limit of two consecutive terms. Serves as head of state; commander-in-chief of armed forces. Vetoes bills; dissolves parliament; grants pardons.

Prime minister
Leader of parliament's majority party or coalition, appointed by president. Serves as head of government.

Cabinet
Members appointed by president on advice of prime minister. Oversees government operations.

JUDICIAL BRANCH

Constitutional Court
Rules on constitutionality of laws. Composed of 13 judges nominated by parliament, appointed by president.

Supreme Court
Highest court of review and appeal. Composed of 80 judges appointed by president on advice of Judicial Council.

Regional Courts

District Courts

DENMARK

OFFICIAL NAME: KINGDOM OF DENMARK

POPULATION: 5.3 MILLION
CAPITAL: COPENHAGEN
AREA: 16,639 SQ. MILES (43,095 SQ. KM)
INDEPENDENCE: 950
CONSTITUTION: 1849

DENMARK was founded around 980 A.D. The origin is not clear, but it may come from "denbera" (a clearing).

RELIGION: Evangelical Lutheran 89%, Roman Catholic 1%, Other 10%

OFFICIAL LANGUAGE: Danish

REGIONS OR PROVINCES: 14 counties and two *kommunes*

DEPENDENT TERRITORIES: None—Faroe Islands and Greenland are self-governing overseas territories

MEDIA: No political censorship exists in national media

SUFFRAGE: 18 years of age; universal

LEGAL SYSTEM: Civil law; accepts ICJ jurisdiction

WORLD ORGANIZATIONS: AfDB, AsDB, Australia Group, BIS, CBSS, CCC, CE, CERN, EAPC, EBRD, ECE, EIB, ESA, EU, FAO, G- 9, IADB, IAEA, IBRD, ICAO, ICC, ICFTU, ICRM, IDA, IEA, IFAD, IFC, IFRCS, IHO, ILO, IMF, IMO, Interpol, IOC, IOM, ISO, ITU, MONUC, NATO, NC, NEA, NIB, NSG, OAS (observer), OECD, OPCW, OSCE, PCA, UN, UNAMSIL, UNCTAD, UNESCO, UNHCR, UNIDO, UNIKOM, UNMEE, UNMIBH, UNMIK, UNMOGIP, UNMOP, UNMOT, UNOMIG, UNTAET, UNTSO, UPU, WEU (observer), WHO, WIPO, WMO, WTrO, ZC

POLITICAL PARTIES: V—Liberal Party (Venstre), SD—Social Democrats, DFP—Danish People's Party, KF—Conservative People's Party, SF—Socialist People's Party

ETHNIC GROUPS:

Other (including Scandinavian and Turkish) 3%
Faeroe and Inuit 1%
Danish 96%

NATIONAL ECONOMICS

WORLD GNP RANKING: 24th

GNP PER CAPITA: $32,280

INFLATION: 2.9%

BALANCE OF PAYMENTS (BALANCE OF TRADE): $3.35 billion

EXCHANGE RATES / U.S. DLR.: 7.9499-8.3504 DANISH KRONER

OFFICIAL CURRENCY: DANISH KRONE

GOVERNMENT SPENDING (% OF GDP)

✈ DEFENSE	1.5%	
🎓 EDUCATION	8.2%	
✚ HEALTH	6.9%	

0   5   10   15

NUMBER OF CONFLICTS OVER LAST 25 YEARS

	1	2-5	5+
Violent changes in government	○	○	○
Civil wars	○	○	○
International wars	○	○	○
Foreign intervention	○	○	○

- Denmark was neutral until 1945.
- A quarter of the Danish armed forces are conscripts.
- Defense spending is low—less than 2% of GDP.

NOTABLE WARS AND INSURGENCIES: None

BASED ON LIBERAL POLITICAL PHILOSOPHIES, modern Denmark has a 100-plus year history of governmental stability, and the oldest monarchy in Europe. The current political system, a combination of parliamentary democracy and constitutional monarchy, was established in 1901. It survived the internal unrest of the Easter Crisis of 1920 (when the government refused the king's call for new elections,) and the overwhelming threat of Nazi occupation between 1940 and 1945. Further-more, the postwar constitution remains unchanged since its inception in 1953. Absolute political authority traditionally rests in the hereditary monarch, currently Queen Margrethe II, who succeeded her father in 1972. However, her power is largely ceremonial, and the majority of executive decisions are made by the appropriate cabinet ministers and the prime minister, who are responsible to Parliament.

Vital to Denmark's political stability is its complex legislative system. In order to assure accurate reflection of voter preferences and inclinations, the country established an intricate system of proportional representation. While the model fosters a stable electoral system, it has also produced numerous minority governments over the past 100 years. However, the national political system remains strong and the multiparty system of government is vibrant.

The strongest of the country's many political parties are the Venstre (V), Danish Liberal Party, and Social Democrats (SD). There are few disparities in major policy issues between the Venstre and the Social Democrats, though immigration and fiscal policy are sometimes points of contention. Danes are proud of the social benefits of such political stability and liberalism. A national healthcare system provides free coverage for nearly every medical necessity. Per capita income is among the highest in the world, as is average life expectancy.

ISSUES AND CHALLENGES:

- Immigration is a controversial topic in Danish politics. A recent rise in far-right parties based on anti-immigration—especially from Turkey and external Turkish communities—now challenges the traditional liberal philosophy of open immigration and is creating political tensions throughout the country.

- Although Denmark's fiscal and economic characteristics far exceed the EU's qualifications for monetary integration, the Danish population consistently rejects the 1992 Maastricht Treaty in favor of a national monetary policy, which underscores the skepticism of the EU among Denmark's population.

- High government spending has kept taxation levels excessive. The largest benefactors are public sector employees—encompassing nearly one quarter of the employable population and the more than 800,000 people who receive welfare. This has affected other government-funded services including health care.

HOW THE GOVERNMENT WORKS

LEGISLATIVE BRANCH

Folketing
(Parliament)
Unicameral Parliament
Composed of 179 members directly elected to four-year terms by proportional representation; includes 2 members from Greenland, 2 two from Faroe Islands. May vote no confidence in individual ministers or cabinet.

Regional Governments
Fourteen counties and two boroughs administered by mayors elected by local councils.

EXECUTIVE BRANCH

Monarch
Position is hereditary. Serves as largely ceremonial head of state.

Prime minister
Leader of parliament's majority party or coalition appointed following elections by monarch. Serves as head of government; may dissolve parliament and call new elections.

Cabinet
Composed of 20 members appointed by monarch on advice of prime minister, approved by parliament.

JUDICIAL BRANCH

Supreme Court
Highest court of review and appeal. Composed of 15 justices appointed for life by monarch on the governments recommendation.

High Courts
Hear civil and criminal case appeals from lower courts.

Local Courts

FINLAND

OFFICIAL NAME: REPUBLIC OF FINLAND

POPULATION: 5.2 MILLION
CAPITAL: HELSINKI
AREA: 130,127 SQ. MILES (337,029 SQ. KM)
INDEPENDENCE: DECEMBER 6, 1917
CONSTITUTION: JULY 17, 1919

FINLAND is first alluded to (as "fenni") by Tacitus in 98 A.D. It derives from local words meaning "wanderers".

RELIGION: Evangelical Lutheran 89%, Finnish Orthodox 1%, Roman Catholic 1%, Other 9%

OFFICIAL LANGUAGES: Finnish and Swedish

REGIONS OR PROVINCES: 6 provinces

DEPENDENT TERRITORIES: None

MEDIA: No political censorship exists in national media

SUFFRAGE: 18 years of age; universal

LEGAL SYSTEM: Civil law; Swedish legal traditions; accepts ICJ jurisdiction

WORLD ORGANIZATIONS: AfDB, AsDB, Australia Group, BIS, CBSS, CCC, CE, CERN, EAPC, EBRD, ECE, EIB, EMU, ESA, EU, FAO, G- 9, IADB, IAEA, IBRD, ICAO, ICC, ICFTU, ICRM, IDA, IEA, IFAD, IFC, IFRCS, IHO, ILO, IMF, IMO, Interpol, IOC, IOM, ISO, ITU, NAM (guest), NC, NEA, NIB, NSG, OAS (observer), OECD, OPCW, OSCE, PCA, PFP, UN, UNCTAD, UNESCO, UNFICYP, UNHCR, UNIDO, UNIFIL, UNIKOM, UNMEE, UNMIBH, UNMIK, UNMOGIP, UNMOP, UNMOVIC, UNTSO, UPU, WEU (observer), WFTU, WHO, WIPO, WMO, WTrO, ZC

POLITICAL PARTIES: SDP—Social Democratic Party, KESK—Center Party, KOK—National Coalition Party, VL—Left-wing Alliance, SFP—Swedish People's Party, G—Greens

ETHNIC GROUPS:

Other (including Sami) 7%

Finnish 93%

NATIONAL ECONOMICS

WORLD GNP RANKING: 28th

GNP PER CAPITA: $25,130

INFLATION: 3.4%

BALANCE OF PAYMENTS (BALANCE OF TRADE): $8.89 billion

EXCHANGE RATES / U.S. DLR.: 1.0651-1.1231 EUROS

OFFICIAL CURRENCY: EURO

5 EURO

GOVERNMENT SPENDING (% OF GDP)

		0	5	10	15
✈	DEFENSE 1.3%				
	EDUCATION 7.5%				
⚕	HEALTH 5.2%				

NUMBER OF CONFLICTS OVER LAST 25 YEARS

	1	2-5	5+
Violent changes in government	○	○	○
Civil wars	○	○	○
International wars	○	○	○
Foreign intervention	○	○	○

- Finland is a neutral country.
- Government policy focuses on ties to western Europe, but maintains special relationship with Russia.
- The majority of the armed forces are conscripts.

NOTABLE WARS AND INSURGENCIES: None

FINLAND'S HISTORY HAS BEEN intertwined with Sweden's. Incorporated into Sweden in the 12th century, it was conquered by Czar Alexander I in 1809. Gaining independence from Russia in 1917, Finland did not establish an autonomous nation-state until relatively late in comparison with its European neighbors. Prior to its allegiance to Russia, Finland was a colony of its western neighbor, Sweden, for nearly 500 years. In spite of a bloody, class-based civil war and attempted invasions by the USSR and Germany in World War II, Finland nonetheless has developed into a politically stable country founded on a prosperous open-market economy. It joined the EU in 1995 and in 1999 became the only Nordic country to join the Euro monetary system.

The majority of political power in the country is vested in the president, making it unique among parliamentary democracies. Most notably, the Finnish president has the power to appoint or dismiss governments without the approval of the parliament, or *Eduskunta*. The president can—and occasionally does—appoint to influential positions candidates who enjoy the confidence of neither the parliament nor the electorate. Subsequently, executive decisions are not bound to electoral patterns or prevailing political philosophies. However, the constitution does place checks on presidential power: The cabinet, called the State Council—*Valtioneuvosto*—plays an important and influential role in presidential policy decisions, and decisions are rarely made that contradict its advice. Moreover, the parliament can overturn presidential decisions with a simple majority vote.

Much like its Northern European neighbors, Finland has an active multiparty system. While this often results in high political participation among the electorate, it also fosters fractious minority coalition governments. Currently, the Finnish Social Democratic Party (SDP), Center Party (KESK), National Coalition Party (KOK), and Left-Wing Alliance (VL) dominate the political environment. However, several smaller parties maintain a substantial voter base and command popular attention in national politics.

ISSUES AND CHALLENGES:

- Finland suffered a severe economic recession between 1991 and 1993, when real GDP dropped by 15%. Remnants of the economic downturn are still present in the country, most visibly in the high unemployment rate, which consistently hovers around ten percent.

- Over half of the population inhabits the southernmost region of the country. The arctic north is sparsely populated by ethnically and linguistically distinct groups.

- The relative instability of Russia creates tensions along the shared border, which subsequently creates Finland's only viable defense concern.

HOW THE GOVERNMENT WORKS

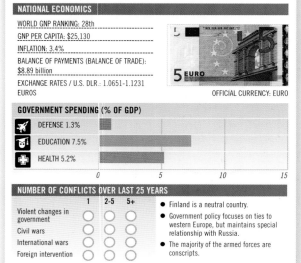

LEGISLATIVE BRANCH
Eduskunta
(Parliament)
Unicameral Parliament
Composed of 200 members directly elected to four-year terms by proportional representation. May alter constitution; force resignation of cabinet; override presidential vetoes and decrees; its acts are not subject to judicial review.

Regional Governments
Six provinces administered by boards of civil servants headed by a governor; provincial self-rule for Aland Islands.

EXECUTIVE BRANCH
President
Elected to six-year term by direct popular vote. Serves as head of state; commander-in-chief of armed forces; initiates or pocket vetoes legislation; dissolves parliament; calls special sessions.

Prime minister
Appointed following elections by president from parliament's majority party. Serves as head of government; leads cabinet.

Cabinet
Council of State
Composed of 15 members appointed by president. Drafts bills; oversees civil service; responsible to parliament.

JUDICIAL BRANCH
The Supreme Court
Highest court of appeal. Composed of 24 justices appointed for life by president.

The Court of Appeal
Composed of six courts that hear appeals from lower courts.

District Courts

PAPUA NEW GUINEA

OFFICIAL NAME: INDEPENDENT STATE OF PAPUA NEW GUINEA

POPULATION: 5.2 MILLION	
CAPITAL: PORT MORESBY	
AREA: 174,849 SQ. MILES (452,860 SQ. KM)	
INDEPENDENCE: 1975	
CONSTITUTION: 1975	

PAPUA is the Malay word for frizzled Melanesian hair, while "New Guinea" was added for the similarity between the inhabitants and those of African Guinea.

RELIGION: Protestant 60%, Roman Catholic 37%, Other 3%

OFFICIAL LANGUAGE: English

REGIONS OR PROVINCES: 20 provinces

DEPENDENT TERRITORIES: None

MEDIA: No political censorship exists in national media.

NEWSPAPERS: There are 3 daily newspapers

TV: 2 independent services. The dismissal of the head of the National Broadcasting Commission in 2001 raised concerns over the freedom of the media.

RADIO: 3 services: 1 state-owned, 2 independent

SUFFRAGE: 18 years of age; universal

LEGAL SYSTEM: English common law; no ICJ jurisdiction

WORLD ORGANIZATIONS: ACP, APEC, ARF (dialogue partner), AsDB, ASEAN (associate member), C, CP, ESCAP, FAO, G-77, IBRD, ICAO, ICFTU, ICRM, IDA, IFAD, IFC, IFRCS, IHO, ILO, IMF, IMO, Interpol, IOC, IOM (observer), ISO (correspondent), ITU, NAM, OPCW, Sparteca, SPC, SPF, UN, UNCTAD, UNESCO, UNIDO, UPU, WFTU, WHO, WIPO, WMO, WTrO

POLITICAL PARTIES: NAP—National Alliance Party, Ind—Independents, PDM—People's Democratic Movement, PPP—People's Progress Party, PP—Pangu Pati, PAP—People's Action Party

ETHNIC GROUPS:

Melanesian, Papuan, Negrito, Micronesian, Polynesian 100%

NATIONAL ECONOMICS

WORLD GNP RANKING: 125th

GNP PER CAPITA: $700

INFLATION: 15.6%

BALANCE OF PAYMENTS (BALANCE OF TRADE): -$8 million

EXCHANGE RATES / U.S. DLR.: 3.035- 3.767 KINA

OFFICIAL CURRENCY: KINA

GOVERNMENT SPENDING (% of GDP)

		0	5	10	15
✈	DEFENSE 1.2%				
🎓	EDUCATION 4.7%				
✚	HEALTH 2.5%				

NUMBER OF CONFLICTS OVER LAST 25 YEARS

	1	2-5	5+
Violent changes in government	○	○	○
Civil wars	○	○	○
International wars	○	○	○
Foreign intervention	●	○	○

- Disgruntled soldiers have staged mutinies, most recently in 2001.
- Relations with Indonesia are strained by separatists in neighboring Papua.
- Australian police boosted internal security from 2003.

NOTABLE WARS AND INSURGENCIES: Bougainville secessionist struggle 1988-2001

THE INDIGENOUS POPULATION of Papua New Guinea is so diverse that the folk saying is "For each village, there is a different culture." The citizens of Papua New Guinea speak more than 750 different languages in some 1,000 separate communities, many of them islands. Such diversity makes achieving political order and cohesion a considerable challenge.

Papua New Guinea became independent from Australia in 1975 after passing through the hands of several powers. In 1884, Germany annexed the northeast of the island of New Guinea. In 1914, Australia occupied the German sector, and after World War I it retained control under a League of Nations mandate. Meanwhile, the southeast portion (Papua) of the island had been claimed by Britain in 1884 and administered by Australia since 1906. Japan occupied parts of New Guinea during World War II. After the Japanese surrender in 1945, Papua and New Guinea joined to form one unit that was administered by Australia as a UN trust territory. A House of Assembly replaced the Legislative Council in 1963, and in 1971 the the Territory of Papua and New Guinea changed its name to Papua New Guinea. It achieved independence under Michael Somare, who was confirmed as prime minister in 1977.

In 1988 an insurrection broke out on the island of Bougainville with a demand that the island should receive a greater share of the profits from its mineral assets. In 1990 the Bougainville Revolutionary Army proclaimed the island's independence. The government launched a series of offensives against the rebels until a ceasefire was agreed in 1998. A peace agreement granting the island autonomy was signed in 2001.

Papua New Guinea has many political parties, making it extremely difficult for one party to secure an outright majority in elections. Party allegiances are not strong, and pressure is put on individuals to change parties and form coalitions. As a result, coalition changes between elections have played a key role in the country's political history. The government is protected from a vote of no confidence in the 18 months following elections and the 12 months preceding the next elections.

ISSUES AND CHALLENGES:

- Urbanization and overpopulation of some areas have led to high levels of unemployment and social problems.

- Government coalitions can be corrupt, as political parties are based more on patronage than on ideology. The nation's tribal differences make centralization difficult and political stability elusive.

- The Bougainville Island insurgency resulted in government pledges in 2001 of autonomy and eventual independence, but armed rebels could decide to press the issue.

- Although natural resources are plentiful, mountainous terrain and inadequate capital to improve the infrastructure limit development.

HOW THE GOVERNMENT WORKS

LEGISLATIVE BRANCH

House of Assembly
Unicameral Parliament
Composed of 109 members who serve five-year terms: 89 elected to single-member districts by direct popular vote; 20 elected from provinces and capital district. May dismiss prime minister with no-confidence vote.

Regional Governments
Twenty provinces and national capital district of Port Moresby; regional Parliament members are appointed as provincial governors.

EXECUTIVE BRANCH

British monarch
Head of state. Ceremonial role.

Governor-general
Appointed by National Executive Council to represent British monarch.

Prime Minister
Leader of Parliament's majority party or coalition; appointed by governor-general following elections. Head of government; may ask governor-general to dissolve Parliament and call new elections.

National Executive Council
Prime minister and 27 members of Parliament's majority party or coalition; appointed by governor-general on advice of prime minister

JUDICIAL BRANCH

Supreme Court
Highest court of review and appeal; rules on lower-court decisions and constitutionality of laws. At least three judges preside; chief justice appointed by governor-general on advice of cabinet and justice minister; other judges appointed by Judicial and Legal Services Commission.

National Court
Hears lower-court appeals. Single judge presides.

Local Courts

Village Courts

CROATIA

OFFICIAL NAME: REPUBLIC OF CROATIA

POPULATION: 4.7 MILLION	
CAPITAL: ZAGREB	
AREA: 21,831 SQ. MILES (56,542 SQ. KM)	
INDEPENDENCE: 1991	
CONSTITUTION: 1990	

CROATIA means "Land of the Croats", the south Slavic people dominant there since the 7th century A.D.

RELIGION: Roman Catholic 76%, Orthodox 11%, Muslim 1%, Other 12%

OFFICIAL LANGUAGE: Croatian

REGIONS OR PROVINCES: 20 counties and 1 city

DEPENDENT TERRITORIES: None

MEDIA: No political censorship exists in national media

NEWSPAPERS: There are 12 daily newspapers

TV: 1 state-controlled service, three channels state-owned

RADIO: 4 stations: 1 state-controlled, 3 independent

SUFFRAGE: 18 years of age; universal (16 years of age, if employed)

LEGAL SYSTEM: Civil law; no ICJ jurisdiction

WORLD ORGANIZATIONS: BIS, CCC, CE, CEI, EAPC, EBRD, ECE, FAO, IADB, IAEA, IBRD, ICAO, ICFTU, ICRM, IDA, IFAD, IFC, IFRCS, IHO, ILO, IMF, IMO, Interpol, IOC, IOM, ISO, ITU, NAM (observer), OAS (observer), OPCW, OSCE, PCA, PFP, UN, UNAMSIL, UNCTAD, UNESCO, UNIDO, UNMEE, UPU, WHO, WIPO, WMO, WToO, WTrO

POLITICAL PARTIES: SDP-HSLS—SDP-Social Democratic Party, HSLS-Croatian Social Liberal Party, HDZ—Croatian Democratic Union, All—Alliance (HSS-Croatian Peasant Part, IDS—Istrian Democratic Assembly, HNS—Croatian People's Party, LS—Liberal Party, ASH—Croatian Social Democrats' Action) HSP-HKDU—HSP-Croatian Party of Rights, HKDU—Croatian Christian Democratic Union

ETHNIC GROUPS:
- Other Slav 1%
- Other 5%
- Serb 4%
- Croat 90%

NATIONAL ECONOMICS

WORLD GNP RANKING: 61st

GNP PER CAPITA: $4,620

INFLATION: 5.4%

BALANCE OF PAYMENTS (BALANCE OF TRADE): -$399 million

EXCHANGE RATES / U.S. DLR.: 8.087-8.254 KUNA

OFFICIAL CURRENCY: KUNA

GOVERNMENT SPENDING (% OF GDP)

- ✈ DEFENSE 2.7%
- 🎓 EDUCATION 5.3%
- ✚ HEALTH 9.5%

0 — 5 — 10 — 15

NUMBER OF CONFLICTS OVER LAST 25 YEARS

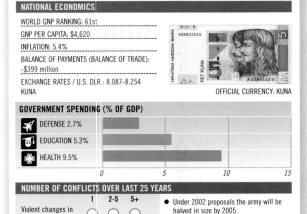

	1	2-5	5+
Violent changes in government	○	○	○
Civil wars	●	○	○
International wars	●	○	○
Foreign intervention	●	○	○

- Under 2002 proposals the army will be halved in size by 2005.
- A dispute with Montenegro over the Prevlaka Peninsula was resolved in 2002.
- Extradition of war criminals is a major issue.

NOTABLE WARS AND INSURGENCIES: Croatian war of independence 1991-1995. Involved in Bosnian Civil War

---

CROATIA only emerged as a sovereign and independent state in 1991. It had been an independent kingdom in the 10th and 11th centuries, but in 1102 it united with Hungary and from the 16th century it was part of the Habsburg and then the Austro-Hungarian Empire. After this empire disintegrated during World War I, Croatia became part of the new kingdom of the Serbs, Croats and Slovenes, renamed Yugoslvia in 1929. Following World War II, Croatia came under the communist regime in Yugoslavia, headed by Josip Broz Tito. Tito's death in 1980, and the fall of communism in Eastern Europe in 1989, weakened Yugoslavia's hold on Croatia, which held multi-party elections for the first time in 1990. Under newly-elected President Franjo Tudjman, a strong, right-wing Croatian nationalist, the nation declared independence in 1991 following a referendum that was overwhelmingly in favor of such a course.

Within a month of Croatia's declaration, the Yugoslav National Army attacked Croatia with the support of Serbs within Croatia. This was the first stage of a long civil war that racked Yugoslavia throughout the 1990s. At first, Croatia lost more than a third of its territory. But by 1995, Croatia had strengthened its armed forces and was able to recapture all of its national territory, in the process driving large numbers of Serbs out of Croatia. In 1993 it had also attacked Bosnia, which had a significant Croat population. The fighting ended over a year later with the creation of a Croat-Bosniac federation in Bosnia, and Croatian forces subsequently fought with the Bosnian army against the Serbs fighting in Bosnia. The war in Bosnia ended with the signing of the Dayton Peace Agreement in 1995.

After the death of President Tudjman in 1999, his Croatian Democratic Union was defeated in a general election in January 2000 by a more liberal and westward-leaning alliance of Social Democrats and Social Liberals. Presidential powers were curtailed, and the government has since made significant progress toward peace and reconciliation with Croatia's neighbors.

ISSUES AND CHALLENGES:

- There are nearly one million landmines scattered across Croatia, which the government plans to remove by 2010.

- Although agreement has been reached regarding land boundaries with Serbia and Montenegro, there are outstanding negotiations underway with Bosnia and Herzegovina, Slovenia, and Italy regarding boundary-related issues.

- Initiatives to privatize state-subsidized industries are ongoing. This, together with a growing economy, should result in increasing foreign investment and further reduce unemployment, a serious concern for Croatia. Tourism is considered to be a major area of growth.

- Croatia is seeking to further improve relations with Europe through the EU and NATO.

HOW THE GOVERNMENT WORKS

LEGISLATIVE BRANCH

Sabor
(House of Representatives)
Unicameral Parliament
Composed of 151 members elected to four-year terms by direct popular vote; several seats reserved for minority representation. Meets twice a year; passes laws; amends constitution; adopts state budget; declares war; may vote no confidence in individual ministers or cabinet.

Regional Governments
Twenty counties governed by prefect and council; city of Zagreb governed by mayor and council.

EXECUTIVE BRANCH

President
Elected to five-year term by direct popular vote with two-term limit. Serves as head of state and commander-in-chief of armed forces; rules by decree during emergencies.

Prime Minister
Appointed by president, approved by Parliament. Serves as head of government; proposes budget; executes laws; guides foreign and domestic policies.

Council of Ministers
Members appointed by president on advice of prime minister, approved by Parliament. Chaired by president.

JUDICIAL BRANCH

Constitutional Court
Rules on constitutionality of laws; decide disputes between government branches; oversees electoral process; protects individual rights. Composed of 13 judges appointed to eight-year terms by Parliament.

Supreme Court of Republic
Highest court of appeal; reviews and interprets law. Justices appointed for life by National Judicial Council

County Courts

Municipal Courts

NORWAY

OFFICIAL NAME: KINGDOM OF NORWAY

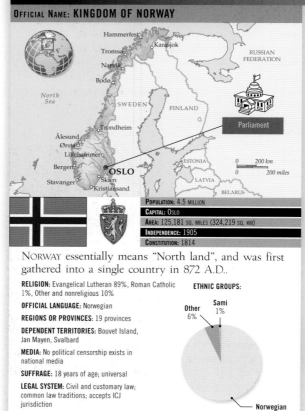

Parliament

POPULATION: 4.5 MILLION
CAPITAL: OSLO
AREA: 125,181 SQ. MILES (324,219 SQ. KM)
INDEPENDENCE: 1905
CONSTITUTION: 1814

NORWAY essentially means "North land", and was first gathered into a single country in 872 A.D..

RELIGION: Evangelical Lutheran 89%, Roman Catholic 1%, Other and nonreligious 10%

OFFICIAL LANGUAGE: Norwegian

REGIONS OR PROVINCES: 19 provinces

DEPENDENT TERRITORIES: Bouvet Island, Jan Mayen, Svalbard

MEDIA: No political censorship exists in national media

SUFFRAGE: 18 years of age; universal

LEGAL SYSTEM: Civil and customary law; common law traditions; accepts ICJ jurisdiction

WORLD ORGANIZATIONS: AfDB, AsDB, Australia Group, BIS, CBSS, CCC, CE, CERN, EAPC, EBRD, ECE, EFTA, ESA, FAO, IADB, IAEA, IBRD, ICAO, ICC, ICFTU, ICRM, IDA, IEA, IFAD, IFC, IFRCS, IHO, ILO, IMF, IMO, Interpol, IOC, IOM, ISO, ITU, NAM (guest), NATO, NC, NEA, NIB, NSG, OAS (observer), OECD, OPCW, OSCE, PCA, UN, UN Security Council (temporary), UNCTAD, UNESCO, UNHCR, UNIDO, UNMEE, UNMIBH, UNMIK, UNMOP, UNTAET, UNTSO, UPU, WEU (associate), WHO, WIPO, WMO, WTrO, ZC

POLITICAL PARTIES: DNA—Norwegian Labor Party, H—Hoeyre (Conservative Party), FrP—Progress Party, SV—Socialist Left Party, KrF—Christian Democracy Party, SP—Center Party, V—Venstre (Liberal Party)

ETHNIC GROUPS:

Other 6%
Sami 1%
Norwegian 93%

NATIONAL ECONOMICS

WORLD GNP RANKING: 26th

GNP PER CAPITA: $34,530

INFLATION: 3.1%

BALANCE OF PAYMENTS (BALANCE OF TRADE): $23 billion

EXCHANGE RATES / U.S. DLR.: 8.819-8.969 NORWEGIAN KRONER

7303011216
50 NORGES BANK
FEMTI KRONER

OFFICIAL CURRENCY: NORWEGIAN KRONE

GOVERNMENT SPENDING (% OF GDP)

- DEFENSE 1.8%
- EDUCATION 7.7%
- HEALTH 0.8%

0   5   10   15

NUMBER OF CONFLICTS OVER LAST 25 YEARS

	1	2-5	5+
Violent changes in government	○	○	○
Civil wars	○	○	○
International wars	○	○	○
Foreign intervention	○	○	○

- Norway joined NATO in 1949.
- Norway has played peacemaker in a number of major conflicts, notably the Israeli–Palestinian conflict and in Sri Lanka.
- Compulsory military service.

NOTABLE WARS AND INSURGENCIES: None

THE NORWEGIANS' ANCESTORS WERE the Viking warriors who conducted raids throughout Europe in the Middle Ages. Norway was later ruled by Denmark for hundreds of years, and then became a dependency of Sweden in the 19th century. Norway gained full independence in 1905, and remains a parliamentary democracy headed by a constitutional monarch. The monarchy is mainly ceremonial, but the king has great importance as a symbol of national unity, and has a role in government as well.

Political parties are central to Norway's political process, which is strongly based on negotiation and consensus. Since the industrial revolution, the Labor Party, founded in 1887, has been a major force in the parliament, or Storting, due to a strong association with trade unions that developed before World War I. From 1935 to 1981, Labor governments ruled Norway almost continuously. Since 1981, however, power has frequently shifted between Labor and more conservative parties. The Labor Party itself has undergone power struggles and internal splits between moderate and more radical elements.

Women comprise 40 percent of the members of the government.

From 1990 to 1996, the Labor Party's Gro Harlem Brundtland became the first woman to serve as prime minister, and has become a recognized leader on international issues. Norway's political history is so steadfast that its constitution, adopted on May 17, 1814, remains in force to this day, making it the oldest in Europe.

Norway was a founding member of NATO, but never joined the European Union—even though all other Scandinavian countries have. As a member of the European Economic Area, Norway has relatively free trade with the EU, except in agriculture and fish. Norway has also played the role of peacemaker in several international conflicts, most notably in getting the "Oslo peace process" started between Israelis and Palestinians in the early 1990s.

ISSUES AND CHALLENGES:

- In the 1970s, Norway began exploiting its large offshore deposits of oil and natural gas. It is now the world's third largest oil exporter. The over-dependence on oil revenue prompted the government to create a special fund that would help finance the government when oil and gas are depleted. By 2001, the fund held $67 billion in reserves.

- In recent decades, tens of thousands of immigrants have entered Norway, which has aroused hostility, especially from right-wing groups. In the 2001 elections, 26 seats in the 165-seat Storting were captured by the anti-immigrant populist Progress Party.

- Rejecting membership in 1972, 52% of Norwegians again voted against joining the EU in a 1994 referendum, though more recent polling data indicate that a majority now favors membership.

HOW THE GOVERNMENT WORKS

LEGISLATIVE BRANCH

Storting
(Parliament)
Bicameral Parliament
Composed of 165 members who serve four-year terms: 157 directly elected from 19 counties by proportional representation; eight popularly elected at large. Parliament is elected as single body, but divided after elections by its members into two chambers: Lagting, or upper division—42 members, and Odelsting, or lower division—23 members.

Regional Governments
Nineteen counties governed by elected councils.

EXECUTIVE BRANCH

Monarch
Position is hereditary. Serves as head of state; commander-in-chief of armed forces; head of Church of Norway. Responsible for collecting taxes and duties.

Prime minister
Leader of parliament's majority party or coalition; appointed by monarch with parliament's approval. Serves as head of government.

Council of State
Composed of members appointed by monarch with parliament's approval.

JUDICIAL BRANCH

High Court of the Realm
Hears impeachment cases. Judges appointed by Supreme Court.

Hoyesterett
(Supreme Court)
Highest court of review and appeal. Composed of president and 17 judges nominated by Ministry of Justice and appointed by monarch.

Court of Appeal

City and County Courts

MOLDOVA

OFFICIAL NAME: REPUBLIC OF MOLDOVA

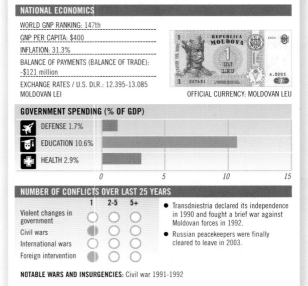

POPULATION: 4.3 MILLION
CAPITAL: CHISINAU
AREA: 13,067 SQ. MILES (33,844 SQ. KM)
INDEPENDENCE: 1991
CONSTITUTION: 1994

MOLDOVA is thought to derive from the Dacian words "molta" (many) and "dava" (fortress, or city).

RELIGION: Eastern Orthodox 98%, Jewish 1.5%, Baptist and other 0.5%

OFFICIAL LANGUAGE: Moldovan

REGIONS OR PROVINCES: Nine counties, one municipality, one autonomous territorial unit, and one territorial unit

DEPENDENT TERRITORIES: None

MEDIA: Partial political censorship exists in national media

NEWSPAPERS: There are four daily newspapers

TV: One state-controlled service

RADIO: One state-controlled service

SUFFRAGE: 18 years of age; universal

LEGAL SYSTEM: Civil law; no ICJ jurisdiction

WORLD ORGANIZATIONS: ACCT, BIS, BSEC, CCC, CE, CEI, CIS, EAPC, EBRD, ECE, FAO, IAEA, IBRD, ICAO, ICFTU, IDA, IFAD, IFC, IFRCS, ILO, IMF, IMO, Interpol, IOC, IOM (observer), ISO (correspondent), ITU, OPCW, OSCE, PFP, UN, UNCTAD, UNESCO, UNIDO, UPU, WHO, WIPO, WMO, WToO, WTrO

POLITICAL PARTIES: CPM—Communist Party of Moldova, BEAB—Electoral Bloc Braghis Alliance, PPCD—Christian Democratic People's Party

ETHNIC GROUPS:

- Moldovan 65%
- Ukrainian 14%
- Russian 13%
- Other 4%
- Gagauz 4%

NATIONAL ECONOMICS

WORLD GNP RANKING: 147th

GNP PER CAPITA: $400

INFLATION: 31.3%

BALANCE OF PAYMENTS (BALANCE OF TRADE): ~$121 million

EXCHANGE RATES / U.S. DLR.: 12.395-13.085 MOLDOVAN LEI

OFFICIAL CURRENCY: MOLDOVAN LEU

GOVERNMENT SPENDING (% OF GDP)

- ✈ DEFENSE 1.7%
- 📖 EDUCATION 10.6%
- ✚ HEALTH 2.9%

(scale: 0, 5, 10, 15)

NUMBER OF CONFLICTS OVER LAST 25 YEARS

	1	2-5	5+
Violent changes in government	○	○	○
Civil wars	◐	○	○
International wars	○	○	○
Foreign intervention	◐	○	○

- Transdniestria declared its independence in 1990 and fought a brief war against Moldovan forces in 1992.
- Russian peacekeepers were finally cleared to leave in 2003.

NOTABLE WARS AND INSURGENCIES: Civil war 1991-1992

MODERN-DAY MOLDOVA CORRESPONDS roughly to the eastern part of the Romanian principality of Moldavia, much of which was annexed by Russia in 1812 as Bessarabia. Today, Moldova is finally charting its own course as a multiparty parliamentary democracy after centuries of being at the centre of claims and conquests by the Greeks, Romans, Huns, Bulgars, and Mongols. In the 1500s, the Ottoman Empire seized and ruled Moldova, but later ceded its eastern half to Russia. Romania took over after the turn of the 20th century, but in the tumult of World War II the Soviet Union gained control.

With the Soviet Union breaking apart, Moldova seized its chance for sovereignty in 1991 and declared independence, adopting its first post-Soviet constitution and holding parliamentary elections three years later. Moldova's government now is composed of a president, who serves as the head of state; a prime minister who functions as the head of the government; and a cabinet (confusingly, called the Government). The unicameral parliament meets for four-month sessions twice a year and has the power to pass laws, call for referenda, ratify treaties, approve and control the national budget, and declare states of emergency, martial law, and war. Moldova's judiciary is independent from the executive and legislative branches and relies on a blend of Soviet and continental legal traditions. Despite the new democracy, longtime tensions still simmer between the ethnic Romanian majority and non-Romanian minorities. In a hotly contested plebiscite held after independence, voters rejected a bid to reunite the country with Romania. Unrest continues in the Trans-Dniester region along Moldova's eastern border, where the rebellious majority population of mostly Russians and Ukrainians are seeking an independent state. Chronic deadlocks also have plagued Moldova's government, while broad public dissatisfaction with the struggling economy led to a surprise and overwhelming victory in 2001 by the Communist Party, which swept two-thirds of Parliament's seats and claimed the presidency.

First former Soviet republic to reinstall a communist government after 2001 elections

ISSUES AND CHALLENGES:

- Reducing Moldova's massive debt to foreign creditors, the service of which accounts for more than a third of the government's budgetary revenues, is an ongoing, looming national problem.

- Smuggling, tax evasion, and corruption by poorly paid civil servants continue to plague Moldova's plans for moving from its old Soviet-based command economy to a modern free-market economy.

- Government investments in health-care, education, and pensions are a pressing priority for Moldova, one of Europe's poorest nations.

HOW THE GOVERNMENT WORKS

LEGISLATIVE BRANCH

Parlamentul Moldovei (Parliament)
Unicameral Parliament
Composed of 101 members directly elected to four-year terms by proportional representation.
Votes on confidence in government program submitted by prime minister following elections; passes laws; may call for referenda.

Regional Governments
Forty districts administered by locally elected councils.

EXECUTIVE BRANCH

President
Elected to four-year term by direct popular vote; limit of two consecutive terms. Serves as head of state; commander-in-chief of armed forces; negotiates treaties; participates in parliament's debates.

Prime minister
Appointed by president, approved by parliament. Serves as head of government; chairs cabinet; crafts program for operating government.

Government (Cabinet)
Composed of 21 members nominated by president on advice of prime minister, confirmed by parliament.

JUDICIAL BRANCH

Supreme Council of the Magistrature
Nominates, promotes and disciplines judges. Composed of 11 magistrates who serve five-year-terms.

Constitutional Court
Rules on constitutionality of laws. Six justices who serve six-year terms; two appointed by president, two by parliament, two by Supreme Council of the Magistrature.

Supreme Court of Justice
Highest court of appeal. Composed of 49 magistrates appointed by parliament to serve until age 65.

Courts of Appeal
Lower-court appeals. Six districts; 87 magistrates appointed by president serve until age 65.

SINGAPORE

OFFICIAL NAME: REPUBLIC OF SINGAPORE

LARGELY UNINHABITED UNTIL THE 19TH CENTURY, the island of Singapore is now one of the world's most densely populated countries. It was founded as a British trading outpost in 1819. Since then, it has been a prosperous trading nation, and the opening of the Suez Canal in 1869 provided additional transit trade. The island was captured by the Japanese in 1942, but Britain regained control at the end of World War II. After achieving independence from Britain in 1963, Singapore briefly became part of Malaysia until friction with the central government in Kuala Lumpur caused it to separate and become a republic in 1965. Singapore is now a parliamentary democracy. The president was largely a ceremonial head of state until the role became directly elected, with significant discretionary powers, under 1991 constitutional amendments.

The president's powers include naming the prime minister, naming the cabinet—on advice of the prime minister—and withholding consent to any bill. For the most part, however, the president must act under the authority of the cabinet, and after the first direct vote for the president in 1993, the first major new amendment to the constitution eliminated presidential power to veto defense and security measures. The main source of executive power remains with the prime minister and the cabinet. Lee Kuan Yew served as prime minister from 1959 to 1990, providing unusual continuity in leadership and policy.

> Most densely populated country in Asia with 17,408 people per square mile

Until 1981, the unicameral Parliament consisted only of elected representatives from the People's Action Party (PAP). To inject some opposition and debate into the political process, the constitution was changed to provide Parliament with one or more "non-constituency members," who had been electoral losers, and some "nominated" government appointees, but both lack the ability to vote on certain measures. The government can politically co-opt distinguished citizens in the fields of arts, academia, public service, or industry as nominated appointees. The PAP still won 87 percent of legislative seats in 2001.

ISSUES AND CHALLENGES:

- Limited availability of land makes waste disposal an ongoing problem, while rapidly expanding urban development has forced the acceleration of deforestation and land reclamation.

- An over dependence on the export of electronic and other manufactured goods, makes the economy susceptible to global recession and market changes in the technology sector, as was experienced in 2001-2002. The government is seeking to reduce this dependence on exports while maintaining and growing Singapore as a technology center.

- Limited fresh water resources make Singapore dependent on Malaysia for its water supply, and disputes have disrupted deliveries.

POPULATION: 4.1 MILLION	
CAPITAL: SINGAPORE	
AREA: 236 SQ. MILES (611 SQ. KM)	
INDEPENDENCE: 1965	
CONSTITUTION: 1959	

SINGAPORE means City of Lions from the Sanskrit words, "singha" meaning lion and "pore" meaning city.

RELIGION: Buddhist (Chinese), Muslim (Malays), Christian, Hindu, Sikh, Taoist, Confucianist

OFFICIAL LANGUAGES: Malay, English, Mandarin, and Tamil

REGIONS OR PROVINCES: None

DEPENDENT TERRITORIES: None

MEDIA: Total political censorship exists in national media

Newspapers: Eight daily newspapers

TV: Five services: four independent, one US-controlled

Radio: Six privately owned services

SUFFRAGE: 21 years of age; universal, compulsory

LEGAL SYSTEM: English common law; no ICJ jurisdiction

WORLD ORGANIZATIONS: APEC, ARF, AsDB, ASEAN, BIS, C, CCC, CP, ESCAP, G-77, IAEA, IBRD, ICAO, ICC, ICFTU, ICRM, IFC, IFRCS, IHO, ILO, IMF, IMO, Interpol, IOC, ISO, ITU, NAM, OPCW, PCA, UN, UN Security Council (temporary), UNCTAD, UNIKOM, UNMEE, UNTAET, UPU, WCL, WHO, WIPO, WMO, WTrO

POLITICAL PARTIES: PAP—People's Action Party, Nom—Nominated, SPP—Singapore People's Party, NC—Non-constituency member, WP—Worker's Party

ETHNIC GROUPS:

Indian 8%
Other 1%
Malay 14%
Chinese 77%

NATIONAL ECONOMICS

WORLD GNP RANKING: 37th

GNP PER CAPITA: $24,740

INFLATION: 1.4%

BALANCE OF PAYMENTS (BALANCE OF TRADE): $21.8 billion

EXCHANGE RATES / U.S. DLR.: 1.734-1.847 SINGAPORE DOLLARS

OFFICIAL CURRENCY: SINGAPORE DOLLAR

GOVERNMENT SPENDING (% OF GDP)

✈ DEFENSE 4.9%		
🎓 EDUCATION 3%		
⚕ HEALTH 1.2%		

0   5   10   15

NUMBER OF CONFLICTS OVER LAST 25 YEARS

	1	2-5	5+
Violent changes in government	○	○	○
Civil wars	○	○	○
International wars	○	○	○
Foreign intervention	○	○	○

- Despite Singapore's small size, its armed forces have a total strength of over 60,000.
- Military service is compulsory.
- About 300,000 reserves can be called up; they undergo annual training.

NOTABLE WARS AND INSURGENCIES: None

HOW THE GOVERNMENT WORKS

LEGISLATIVE BRANCH

Parliament
Unicameral Parliament
Composed of 84 members elected to five-year terms by direct popular vote. Besides elected members, up to six "non-constituency" seats may be added for the top voting-getting but losing opposition candidates and up to nine "nominated" seats for government appointees. Before enactment, bills are reviewed by presidential council for sensitivity to minorities.

EXECUTIVE BRANCH

President
Elected to six-year term by direct popular vote. Serves as head of state; oversees nation's financial reserves; acts as watchdog against executive abuse; may veto bills.

Prime minister
Leader of parliament's majority party or coalition; appointed by president. Serves as head of government; has sole authority to summon cabinet.

Cabinet
Composed of members of parliament; appointed by president on advice of prime minister.

JUDICIAL BRANCH

Supreme Court
Divided into two branches: High Court and Court of Appeal. Composed of chief justice and other judges appointed by president to serve to age 65.

Court of Appeal
Hears only civil and criminal appeals from High Court

High Court
Rules on serious criminal and civil cases; hears appeals from lower courts.

District Courts

Magistrates Courts

IRELAND

OFFICIAL NAME: IRELAND

POPULATION: 3.8 MILLION	
CAPITAL: DUBLIN	
AREA: 27,135 SQ. MILES (70,279 SQ. KM)	
INDEPENDENCE: 1922	
CONSTITUTION: 1937	

IRELAND, or Eire, may derive from Eire, wife of MacColl, a legendary king. It may also be a derived from the Latin "Iberio" (or Hibernia), meaning the "winter land".

RELIGION: Roman Catholic 88%, Anglican 3%, Jewish 1%, Other and non-religious 8%

OFFICIAL LANGUAGES: Irish and English

REGIONS OR PROVINCES: 26 counties

DEPENDENT TERRITORIES: None

MEDIA: No political censorship exists in national media

Newspapers: There are six daily newspapers

TV: Two services: one state-owned, one independent

Radio: Three services: one state-owned, two independent

SUFFRAGE: 18 years of age; universal

LEGAL SYSTEM: Local legal traditions; English common law; no ICJ jurisdiction

WORLD ORGANIZATIONS: Australia Group, BIS, CCC, CE, EAPC, EBRD, ECE, EIB, EMU, ESA, EU, FAO, IAEA, IBRD, ICAO, ICC, ICFTU, ICRM, IDA, IEA, IFAD, IFC, IFRCS, ILO, IMF, IMO, Interpol, IOC, IOM (observer), ISO, ITU, MINURSO, MONUC, NAM (guest), NEA, NSG, OAS (observer), OECD, OPCW, OSCE, PFP, UN, UN Security Council (temporary), UNCTAD, UNESCO, UNFICYP, UNHCR, UNIDO, UNIFIL, UNIKOM, UNITAR, UNMEE, UNMIBH, UNMIK, UNMOP, UNTAET, UNTSO, UPU, WEU (observer), WHO, WIPO, WMO, WTrO, ZC

POLITICAL PARTIES: FF—Fianna Fail, FG—Fine Gael, LP—Labour Party, PD—Progressive Democrats, GP—Green Party, SF—Sinn Fein

ETHNIC GROUPS:

Other 5%

Irish 95%

NATIONAL ECONOMIC$

WORLD GNP RANKING: 39th

GNP PER CAPITA: $22,660

INFLATION: 5.6%

BALANCE OF PAYMENTS (BALANCE OF TRADE): -$593 million

EXCHANGE RATES / U.S. DLR.: 1.0651-1.1231 EUROS

OFFICIAL CURRENCY: EURO

GOVERNMENT SPENDING (% OF GDP)

DEFENSE 0.7%	
EDUCATION 4.5%	
HEALTH 5.2%	

0   5   10   15

NUMBER OF CONFLICTS OVER LAST 25 YEARS

	1	2-5	5+
Violent changes in government	○	○	○
Civil wars	○	○	○
International wars	○	○	○
Foreign intervention	○	○	○

- Ireland is determined to maintain its neutrality.
- It has observer status at the WEU.
- The issue of Northern Ireland dominates relations with the UK.

NOTABLE WARS AND INSURGENCIES: None

REUNIFICATION WITH NORTHERN IRELAND has been the overriding political issue facing Ireland since independence from the United Kingdom in 1922 left it partitioned from the six northern counties known as Ulster, which remain part of the UK. United States-brokered efforts to achieve a compromise and end anti-British violence by the pro-unification Irish Republican Army (IRA) in Northern Ireland met with some success in the 1998 Good Friday Agreement, which is still being implemented. This involves nationalists sharing governing power in Northern Ireland with the pro-British unionists. Terrorist attacks and the threat of violence have since diminished.

Since 1932, politics have been largely dominated by two main parties' fight over reunification—the Fianna Fail (FF), which favors reunification and which governed alone or by coalition until 1973; and the Fine Gael, (FG), which formed some governments after 1973, favoring Northern Ireland's continued unity with the UK. Back in power in 2002, the FF won 49 percent of seats in the Dail Eireann, or House of Representatives, and 50 percent of seats in the Seanad Eireann, or Senate. FF candidate Mary McAleese became Ireland's first president from Northern Ireland in 1997. But the real power to govern is held by the prime minister and cabinet. The Irish president must seek the advice of the Council of State, made up of other high officials, before exercising most powers.

EU TREATY PLACARDS
Like many EU members, Ireland has mixed feelings about the European Union. In 2002, it needed two referenda before ratifying the Nice expansion treaty.

Other political parties have played a role in Irish affairs, but the reunification issue is so pervasive as to crowd out significant divisions of economic class and religion. Ireland has one of the lowest levels of support for left-wing parties of any European nation, helped by its small industrial working class, the dominant Roman Catholic Church's hostility to socialism, and the presence in of one of the healthiest economies in Europe thanks to massive inward investment in the 1990s.

HOW THE GOVERNMENT WORKS

LEGISLATIVE BRANCH

Oireachtas
Bicameral Parliament

Seanad Eireann
(Senate)
60 members who serve five-year terms: 43 elected from vocational-based panels; 6 elected by universities; 11 nominated by prime minister. May amend or delay bills from House.

Dail Eireann
(House of Representatives)
166 members directly elected to five-year terms by proportional representation. Handles bills for taxes, appropriations, public loans.

Regional Governments
Twenty-six counties administered by elected councils.

EXECUTIVE BRANCH

President
Elected to seven-year term by direct popular vote, with two-term limit. Serves as head of state; assents to bills; dissolves parliament on advice of prime minister.

Prime minister
Leader of majority legislative party or coalition; elected by House, appointed by the president. Serves as head of government.

Cabinet
Government
Composed of 15 members nominated by prime minister, confirmed by House. Oversees government operations.

JUDICIAL BRANCH

Supreme Court
Highest court of appeal. Composed of six justices appointed by president on advice of prime minister and cabinet.

High Court
Hears most serious crimes and civil case appeals. Composed of 17 judges appointed by president.

Circuit Courts
Eight courts hear serious cases.

District Courts
Twenty-three courts hear minor civil and criminal cases.

NEW ZEALAND

OFFICIAL NAME: NEW ZEALAND

POPULATION: 3.8 MILLION
CAPITAL: WELLINGTON
AREA: 103,733 SQ. MILES (268,668 SQ. KM)
INDEPENDENCE: 1947
CONSTITUTION: 1986

NEW ZEALAND's first Maori settlers called their land "Aotearoa" meaning "land of the long white cloud".

RELIGION: Anglican 24%, Presbyterian 18%, Roman Catholic 15%, Methodist 5%, Other 22%, Non-religious 16%

OFFICIAL LANGUAGES: English and Maori

REGIONS OR PROVINCES: 16 regions

DEPENDENT TERRITORIES: Cook Islands, Niue, Tokelau

MEDIA: No political censorship exists in national media

Newspapers: There are 29 daily newspapers.

TV: One state-owned, six independent services

Radio: Three services: one state-owned, 2 independent

SUFFRAGE: 18 years of age; universal

LEGAL SYSTEM: English common law; accepts ICJ jurisdiction

WORLD ORGANIZATIONS: ABEDA, ANZUS (US suspended security obligations to NZ on 11 August 1986), APEC, ARF (dialogue partner), AsDB, ASEAN (dialogue partner), Australia Group, C, CCC, CP, EBRD, ESCAP, FAO, IAEA, IBRD, ICAO, ICC, ICFTU, ICRM, IDA, IEA, IFAD, IFC, IFRCS, IHO, ILO, IMF, IMO, Interpol, IOC, IOM (observer), ISO, ITU, NAM (guest), NSG, OECD, OPCW, PCA, Sparteca, SPC, SPF, UN, UNAMSIL, UNCTAD, UNESCO, UNIDO, UNMOP, UNTAET, UNTSO, UPU, WFTU, WHO, WIPO, WMO, WTrO

POLITICAL PARTIES: LP—Labour Party, NP—National Party, NZF—New Zealand First Party, ACT—ACT New Zealand (Association of Consumers and Taxpayers), GP—Green Party, UFNZ—United Future, PC—Progressive Coalition

ETHNIC GROUPS:

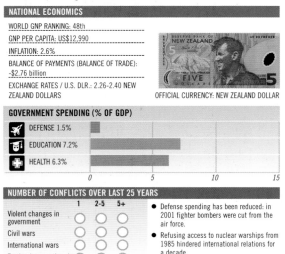

Other immigrant 6%
Pacific islander 5%
Maori 12%
Europea 77%

NATIONAL ECONOMICS

WORLD GNP RANKING: 48th

GNP PER CAPITA: US$12,990

INFLATION: 2.6%

BALANCE OF PAYMENTS (BALANCE OF TRADE): -$2.76 billion

EXCHANGE RATES / U.S. DLR.: 2.26-2.40 NEW ZEALAND DOLLARS

OFFICIAL CURRENCY: NEW ZEALAND DOLLAR

GOVERNMENT SPENDING (% OF GDP)

DEFENSE 1.5%
EDUCATION 7.2%
HEALTH 6.3%

0   5   10   15

NUMBER OF CONFLICTS OVER LAST 25 YEARS

	1	2-5	5+
Violent changes in government	○	○	○
Civil wars	○	○	○
International wars	○	○	○
Foreign intervention	○	○	○

- Defense spending has been reduced: in 2001 fighter bombers were cut from the air force.
- Refusing access to nuclear warships from 1985 hindered international relations for a decade.

NOTABLE WARS AND INSURGENCIES: None

FOR A CENTURY, NEW ZEALAND LIVED UNDER British colonial rule. It secured full independence in 1947, but had already established a parliament in 1850, become a semi-autonomous dominion in 1907 and fully self-governing in 1926. During that half-century march toward self determination, the New Zealand government became the first country in the world to grant women the vote (in 1893), and also the first to establish a full welfare state. These were the foundations of its progressive modern-day social programs.

A people of Polynesian ancestry, the Maori populated New Zealand in the mid-1600s. A century later, English Captain James Cook charted the coastlines of New Zealand and nearby Australia. Cook's maps opened New Zealand to an era of lumbering, seal hunting, and whaling by generations of European settlers. Britain's rule began in 1840 under a treaty with the Maori, but the push of settlements into tribal lands soon sparked fierce wars before the people were finally subdued. Britain's declaration of New Zealand as a dominion began the process that led to independence and membership of the Commonwealth.

Based on the British model, the government has an executive branch with a governor-general, prime minister and cabinet; unicameral parliament; and an independent judiciary that interprets English Common Law. Parliament is headed by a non-partisan speaker of the house and reserves seven seats for the Maori. Like Britain, New Zealand has no written constitution.

ISSUES AND CHALLENGES:

- Tense relations between the Maori minority and the European-descended majority result from a wide gap in living standards and employment rates.

- New Zealand has expanded its foreign trade with Pacific Rim countries, following the United Kingdom's participation in the European Union.

- Major environmental issues include deforestation, depletion of the ozone layer over Antarctica, and protecting native flora and fauna.

Parliamentary control alternates between two major political parties: the liberal Labour Party and conservative National Party. Under early Labour administrations, the government adopted sweeping social legislation, including social security, a 40-hour working week, a minimum wage, and compulsory unionism. But new market-oriented economic policies and cuts in welfare since the 1980s have been unpopular with the public. In 1995, a referendum mandated increased minority party representation in parliament through a new system of proportional representation. Since then, coalition governments have controlled parliament.

New Zealand was the first country to give women the right to vote.

HOW THE GOVERNMENT WORKS

LEGISLATIVE BRANCH
Parliament
(House of Representatives)
Unicameral Parliament
Composed of 120 members who serve three-year terms: 67 elected by direct popular vote from single-member districts; 53 elected from party lists by proportional representation. Seven single-member districts reserved for Maori minority. Must meet within six weeks of elections.

Regional Governments
Twelve regions administered by locally elected councils. Responsibilities include environmental management, civil defense, transportation planning.

EXECUTIVE BRANCH
Governor General
Appointed by British monarch following elections. Serves as head of government; assents to bills; may dissolve parliament.

Prime minister
Leader of parliament's majority party or coalition; appointed by governor-general following elections. Serves as head of government; may call snap election of parliament at any time.

Cabinet
Composed of 15-20 members of parliament; appointed by governor-general on advice of prime minister.

JUDICIAL BRANCH
Privy Council in London
Highest tribunal for appeals.

Court of Appeal
Hears appeals from High Court. Composed of president and six judges appointed by governor-general.

High Court
Hears appeals from District Courts and more serious cases. Composed of chief justice and 36 judges who travel on circuit; appointed by governor-general.

District Courts

Courts of First Instance

LITHUANIA

OFFICIAL NAME: REPUBLIC OF LITHUANIA

POPULATION: 3.7 Million
CAPITAL: VILNIUS
AREA: 25,174 SQ. MILES (65,201 SQ. KM)
INDEPENDENCE: 1990
CONSTITUTION: 1992

LITHUANIA as a name is thought to come from "litus" (tubes), referring to the trumpets tribesmen played.

RELIGION: Roman Catholic (primarily), Lutheran, Russian Orthodox, Protestant, Evangelical Christian Baptist, Muslim, Jewish

OFFICIAL LANGUAGE: Lithuanian

REGIONS OR PROVINCES: 10 counties

DEPENDENT TERRITORIES: None

MEDIA: No political censorship exists in national media

Newspapers:There are 19 daily newspapers. The mainstream media, Russian under communism, now publish and broadcast mainly in Lithuanian.

TV: 10 services: one state-owned, nine independent

Radio: 24 services: one state-owned, 23 independent

SUFFRAGE: 18 years of age; universal

LEGAL SYSTEM: Civil law; no ICJ jurisdiction

WORLD ORGANIZATIONS: ACCT (observer), BIS, CBSS, CCC, CE, EAPC, EBRD, ECE, EU, FAO, IAEA, IBRD, ICAO, ICC, ICFTU, ICRM, IFC, IFRCS, ILO, IMF, IMO, Interpol, IOC, IOM, ISO (correspondent), ITU, OPCW, OSCE, PFP, UN, UNCTAD, UNESCO, UNIDO, UNMIK, UPU, WCL, WEU (associate partner), WHO, WIPO, WMO, WTrO

POLITICAL PARTIES: ABSD—A. Brazauskas Social Democratic Coalition, LLS—Lithuanian Liberal Union, NS(SL)—New Union (Social Liberals), TS(LK)—Homeland Union (Lithuanian Conservatives)

ETHNIC GROUPS:
- Belarussian 2%
- Polish 7%
- Other 2%
- Russian 9%
- Lithuanian 80%

NATIONAL ECONOMICS

WORLD GNP RANKING: 81st

GNP PER CAPITA: $2,930

INFLATION: 1.0%

BALANCE OF PAYMENTS (BALANCE OF TRADE): -$675 million

EXCHANGE RATES / U.S. DLR.: 3.9990-3.9984 LITAI

OFFICIAL CURRENCY: LITA

GOVERNMENT SPENDING (% OF GDP)

- ✈ DEFENSE 1.8%
- 🎓 EDUCATION 6.4%
- ✚ HEALTH 5.7%

0   5   10   15

NUMBER OF CONFLICTS OVER LAST 25 YEARS

	1	2-5	5+
Violent changes in government	○	○	○
Civil wars	○	○	○
International wars	○	○	○
Foreign intervention	○	○	○

- A large National Guard patrols the country's frontiers.
- Legislation was passed in 2003 to cut active troop numbers from 22,000 to 17,000 by 2008.
- Compulsory military service.

NOTABLE WARS AND INSURGENCIES: None

ONCE A THRIVING MEDIEVAL KINGDOM, Lithuania spent most of the 20th century under military or communist rule. In both world wars, German troops occupied the Baltic nation. Throughout the decades of the Cold War, it was governed as part of the Union of Soviet Socialist Republics (USSR). Today, Lithuania is a parliamentary democracy.

The Grand Duchy of Lithuania was created in the 1200s to defend against invasions by Germanic monastic military orders. During the next three centuries, the kingdom united with Poland, doubling in size. But weakened by repeated wars, it had fragmented by the end of the 18th century. Lithuania was taken over and ruled by the Russian Empire until World War I. It subsequently overcame the Bolshevik Red Army and German and Polish troops to secure its independence. However, the newly established parliamentary republic ended in 1926 with a military coup and the formation of a one-party autocratic regime. On the eve of World War II, the Soviet Union annexed Lithuania by force. Later, Nazi troops terrorized the country until the end of the war, when the Red Army reoccupied it and ushered in decades of totalitarian rule by the Lithuania Communist Party.

By the late 1980s, the liberalization initiatives of the Soviet Union's Mikhail Gorbachev drew broad support in Lithuania, where a growing reform movement called the "Sajudis" was already demanding democratic and national rights. In response, Lithuania's communist government declared the country sovereign in 1990, legalized a multi-party system and set the stage for free elections and the withdrawal of Soviet troops. Under its new constitution, Lithuania's parliamentary government is composed of an elected president, appointed prime minister, a unicameral legislature and an independent judiciary. Control of parliament alternated between the conservative Union of the Fatherland party and the formerly communist Democratic Labor Party until the 2000 election, when voters gave the majority to a new centrist coalition party.

ISSUES AND CHALLENGES:

- Because teaching is in Lithuanian, minority access to education is difficult.

- Out of concern for radioactive leaks and accidents, the European Union has been pressuring for decommission of Lithuania's Chernobyl-type nuclear plant at Ignalina. The government has agreed to decommission it by 2009.

- Soil and groundwater contamination from military bases is an environmental concern.

- Since independence, Lithuania has experienced a widening income gap between the rich and poor.

- Lithuania has poor raw material resources and must import oil and gas from Russia.

- Unhappy with Lithuania's taxing and funding system which gives a large portion to Vilnius, the capital, local authorities have called for more autonomy in decision-making.

HOW THE GOVERNMENT WORKS

LEGISLATIVE BRANCH

Seimas
Unicameral Parliament
Composed of 141 members who serve four-year terms: 70 elected from party lists by proportional representation; 71 by direct popular vote from single-member districts. Wields final authority on legislative matters.

Regional Governments
Ten counties administered by local councils elected to two-year terms.

EXECUTIVE BRANCH

President
Elected to five-year term by direct popular vote with two-term limit. Serves as head of state; commander in chief; may dissolve parliament and return bills to legislators for reconsideration.

Prime Minister
Nominated by president, approved by parliament. Serves as head of government.

Cabinet
Council of Ministers
Composed of members nominated by prime minister, appointed by president.

JUDICIAL BRANCH

Constitutional Court
Rules on constitutionality of laws; protects individual rights; only court with authority to review legislation. Composed of 9 judges nominated to nine-year terms by president, confirmed by parliament.

Supreme Court
Highest court of appeal for lower-court decisions. Judges nominated by president, confirmed by parliament.

Appellate Courts

Local Courts

JAMAICA

OFFICIAL NAME: **JAMAICA**

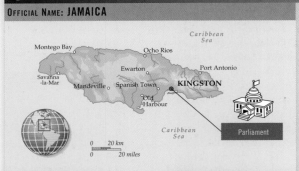

Caribbean Sea

Montego Bay · Ocho Rios · Port Antonio · Ewarton · Savanna-la-Mar · Mandeville · Spanish Town · **KINGSTON** · Old Harbour

Caribbean Sea

Parliament

0   20 km
0   20 miles

POPULATION:	2.6 MILLION
CAPITAL:	KINGSTON
AREA:	4,243 SQ. MILES (10,990 SQ. KM)
INDEPENDENCE:	1962
CONSTITUTION:	1962

JAMAICA means "the island of water springs" in Arawak, the language of the indigenous people.

RELIGION: Church of God 21%, Baptist 10%, Anglican 7%, Other Protestant 23%, Catholic 4%, Other and non-religious 35%

OFFICIAL LANGUAGE: English

REGIONS OR PROVINCES: 14 parishes

DEPENDENT TERRITORIES: None

MEDIA: No political censorship exists in national media

NEWSPAPERS: There are 4 daily newspapers. The Jamaican press is one of the most influential in the Caribbean.

TV: 3 independent services. The government has loosened its hold on broadcasting.

RADIO: 7services: 1 public-service, 6 independent

SUFFRAGE: 18 years of age; universal

LEGAL SYSTEM: English common law; no ICJ jurisdiction

WORLD ORGANIZATIONS: ACP, C, Caricom, CCC, CDB, ECLAC, FAO, G-15, G-19, G-77, IADB, IAEA, IBRD, ICAO, ICFTU, ICRM, IFAD, IFC, IFRCS, IHO, ILO, IMF, IMO, Interpol, IOC, IOM (observer), ISO, ITU, LAES, NAM, OAS, OPANAL, OPCW, UN, UNCTAD, UNESCO, UNIDO, UPU, WFTU, WHO, WIPO, WMO, WToO, WTrO

POLITICAL PARTIES: PNP—People's National Party, JLP—Jamaica Labour Party

ETHNIC GROUPS:

East Indian 1.3%
Mixed 7.3%
Other (including white and Chinese) 0.5%
Black 90.9%

NATIONAL ECONOMICS

WORLD GNP RANKING:	98th
GNP PER CAPITA:	$2,610
INFLATION:	8.2%
BALANCE OF PAYMENTS (BALANCE OF TRADE):	-$275 million
EXCHANGE RATES / U.S. DLR.:	45.10-47.05 JAMAICAN DOLLARS

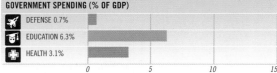

OFFICIAL CURRENCY: JAMAICAN DOLLAR

GOVERNMENT SPENDING (% OF GDP)

- DEFENSE 0.7%
- EDUCATION 6.3%
- HEALTH 3.1%

0   5   10   15

NUMBER OF CONFLICTS OVER LAST 25 YEARS

	1	2-5	5+
Violent changes in government	○	○	○
Civil wars	○	○	○
International wars	○	○	○
Foreign intervention	○	○	○

- The army's main role is combating narcotics smuggling and assisting the police in breaking up unrest, as in 1999 and 2001.
- The army is trained by the US, the UK, and Canada.

NOTABLE WARS AND INSURGENCIES: None

SHEDDING NEARLY 300 YEARS of British rule, Jamaica in 1962 became the first Caribbean colony to gain independence after World War II. In the years since, its parliamentary democracy has been buffeted by dramatic changes in political ideologies, and the effects of wide disparities in wealth and periodic civil unrest.

Arawak Indians from South America had begun to inhabit Jamaica long before Christopher Columbus landed on the island's shores in 1494 and claimed it for Spain. However, disease, slavery, and war during Spain's occupation quickly resulted in the extermination of the Arawak. The British seized Jamaica by force in 1655 and turned the island into a crown colony in 1670. With its bountiful sugar production on plantations worked by African slaves, the island became the most prized possession in the West Indies.

Jamaicans secured limited political rights and held their first local elections in the 1940s. Pressure for self-rule continued to mount and culminated in the 1961 rejection by Jamaica voters of membership in the British West Indies federation of colonial territories, which they had joined in 1958 along with nine other British territories. A year later, Jamaica enjoyed independence under a new constitution that established a British-style government with a governor-general, prime minister, Cabinet, bicameral Parliament, and an independent judiciary modeled after the British legal system.

Although Jamaica's lively political system is open, few minority or independent parties have made headway. Legalized by London prior to independence, Jamaica's labor unions soon formed alliances with political parties: the National Workers Union with the traditionally socialist People's National Party (PNP), and the Bustamante Industrial Trade Union with the conservative Jamaica Labor Party (JLP). Both parties, however, moderated their ideologies in the 1980s and shifted toward centrist, free-market economic policies. The PNP dominated Jamaican politics in the 1990s, and with its election victories in 2002 it became the first political party in the island's history to win four consecutive general elections.

ISSUES AND CHALLENGES:

- Competition for territory between narcotics gangs in the slums of Kingston results in armed crime.

- Agreement to the creation of the Caribbean Court of Justice raises the likelihood of hangings, on which there has been a moratorium since 1988.

- Acidic dust from bauxite production, Jamaica's most abundant natural resource, poses an environmental hazard.

- High unemployment and poverty continue to be major problems.

- Jamaica is a transit point for South American cocaine en route to USA and is a major exporter of marijuana.

- Government initiatives in 1998 and 1999 to combat economic recession and a large fiscal deficit sparked violence and unrest.

HOW THE GOVERNMENT WORKS

LEGISLATIVE BRANCH

Parliament
Bicameral Parliament

Senate
Composed of 21 members appointed to five-year terms by governor-general: 13 allocated to ruling party; eight to opposition. May submit bills and review or delay legislation from House; must approve constitutional amendments.

House of Representative
Composed of 60 members elected to five-year terms by direct popular vote. Originates all money bills.

Regional Governments
Fourteen parishes administered by elected local councils.

EXECUTIVE BRANCH

British Monarch
Head of state. Ceremonial role.

Governor-general
Appointed by monarch to represent him or her following elections on advice of prime minister.

Prime Minister
Leader of Parliament's majority party or coalition; appointed by governor-general following elections. Serves as head of government; answers to House.

Cabinet
Composed of members of Parliament, including at least two but not more than four senators; appointed by prime minister. Oversees government.

JUDICIAL BRANCH

Privy Council in London
Final tribunal for appeals.

Court of Appeals
Highest Jamaican court of appeal.

Supreme Court
Hears lower-court appeals. Chief justice appointed by governor-general on advice of prime minister and opposition leader; other judges appointed by governor-general on advice of Judicial Service Commission.

Lower Courts

LATVIA

OFFICIAL NAME: REPUBLIC OF LATVIA

ESTONIA

Gulf
of Riga

Valmiera
Cēsis

Baltic
Sea

Ventspils

RIGA

Tukums

Jelgava

Saldus

Jēkabpils

RUSSIAN
FEDERATION

Liepāja

Parliament

Daugavpils

LITHUANIA

BELARUS

0   50 km
0   50 miles

POPULATION: 2.4 MILLION	
CAPITAL: RIGA	
AREA: 24,938 SQ. MILES (64,589 SQ. KM)	
INDEPENDENCE: 1991	
CONSTITUTION: 1991	

LATVIA as a name first came into use in the 19th century. It was derived from the people's old name for themselves—the Latviji.

RELIGION: Lutheran, Roman Catholic, Russian Orthodox

OFFICIAL LANGUAGE: Latvian

REGIONS OR PROVINCES: 26 counties and 7 municipalities

DEPENDENT TERRITORIES: None

MEDIA: No political censorship exists in national media

NEWSPAPERS: There are 23 daily newspapers

TV: 2 services: 1 state-owned, 1 independent

RADIO: 16 services: 1 state-owned, 15 independent

SUFFRAGE: 18 years of age; universal for Latvian citizens

LEGAL SYSTEM: Civil law; no ICJ jurisdiction

WORLD ORGANIZATIONS: BIS, CBSS, CCC, CE, EAPC, EBRD, ECE, EU, FAO, IAEA, IBRD, ICAO, ICFTU, ICRM, IDA, IFC, IFRCS, ILO, IMF, IMO, Interpol, IOC, IOM, ISO (correspondent), ITU, NSG, OAS (observer), OPCW, OSCE, PCA, PFP, UN, UNCTAD, UNESCO, UPU, WEU (associate partner), WHO, WIPO, WMO, WTrO

POLITICAL PARTIES: TP—People's Party, LC—Latvia's Way, TB/LNNK—Fatherland and Freedom, TSP—National Harmony Party, LSDA—Social Democratic Party, JL—New Era Party

ETHNIC GROUPS:

- Polish 2%
- Ukrainian 3%
- Other 2%
- Belarussian 4%
- Russian 32%
- Latvian 57%

NATIONAL ECONOMICS

WORLD GNP RANKING: 97th

GNP PER CAPITA: $2,920

INFLATION: 2.7%

BALANCE OF PAYMENTS (BALANCE OF TRADE): -$485 million

EXCHANGE RATES / U.S. DLR.: 0.6178-0.6292 LATS

LATVIJAS BANKAS NAUDAS ZĪME
PIECI LATI
OFFICIAL CURRENCY: LATS

GOVERNMENT SPENDING (% OF GDP)

- ✈ DEFENSE 1%
- 📖 EDUCATION 6.8%
- ✚ HEALTH 4%

0   5   10   15

NUMBER OF CONFLICTS OVER LAST 25 YEARS

	1	2-5	5+
Violent changes in government	○	○	○
Civil wars	○	○	○
International wars	○	○	○
Foreign intervention	●	○	○

- Compulsory national military service.
- Participates in NATO's Partnership for Peace program.
- Plans to build military based on a rapid response force.
- Russia completed withdrawal of its military bases in 2000.

NOTABLE WARS AND INSURGENCIES: Attack on the Latvian Ministry of the Interior in Riga by Soviet units 1991

LATVIA WAS ONE OF THREE BALTIC STATES, along with Lithuania and Estonia, to gain independence from the Soviet Union in 1991 and undergo the institutionalization of democratic ideals in a relatively smooth and successful manner. With 57 percent of the population defined as ethnic Latvians, the country is home to a variety of cultures, including Russians, Belarussians, and other ethnic groups. In March 1991, the Supreme Council declared "equal rights to all nationalities and ethnic groups." However, Latvia has faced challenges resulting from stringent naturalization laws (conditions for which have since been eased), and a language law that was passed in December 1999, which appeared to favor ethnic Latvians, alienating the large minority population of ethnic Russians and preventing them running for political office. The EU and NATO demanded the language law be dropped, and the parliament voted in favor of doing so in May 2002.

ISSUES AND CHALLENGES:

- Latvia has limited natural resources, making it dependent on imports, particularly of oil and natural gas—many of which come from Russia.

- The language law proclaiming Latvian the official language of the public sector, prevented most Russians from running for political office. Although it was withdrawn, Russians still feel under-represented.

- Collective farming has left a legacy of outdated farms that desperately need new technology to become productive.

Political parties have remained fairly fluid in Latvia. From 1995 to 1997, Andris Skele—a populist—served as premier, paving the way toward economic reforms. In 1998 elections, his newly formed People's Party won 24 seats, more than any other party, in the Saeima, Latvia's parliament. Skele became prime minister again in 1999, but his coalition collapsed in less than a year and he was replaced by Andris Berzins, the mayor of Riga. Berzins, of Latvia's Way, a pro-market, pro-democracy, center-right party in favor of Latvia's accession to the EU, was able to organize a seemingly stable, four-party coalition government. The latest legislative elections, in October 2002, brought the New Era party (JL) to the fore, as the largest party in the parliament, taking 26 of the 100 seats. Leader of the party, Einars Repse, became prime minister and formed a new coalition led by the JL.

Latvia began negotiations to join the EU in 2000, signing the Treaty of Accession on April 16, 2003. It has US backing for entry to NATO, which it will join in 2004. Virtually all control of Latvia's government resides in the parliament, which co-signs bills into law, selects the president, and whose members are immune from criminal prosecution. While the prime minister has the greatest executive authority, the president serves primarily as a ceremonial head.

HOW THE GOVERNMENT WORKS

LEGISLATIVE BRANCH
Saeima
(Parliament)
Unicameral Parliament
Composed of 100 members elected to three-year terms by direct popular vote. Initiates legislation; approves bills sponsored by prime minister; overrides presidential vetoes by simple majority vote; removes prime minister with no-confidence vote; amends constitution with two-thirds majority vote.

Regional Governments
33 districts administered by elected local councils.

EXECUTIVE BRANCH
President
Elected to three-year term by parliament; limit of two consecutive terms. Serves as head of state. Represents nation in international arena; co-signs bills with prime minister; dissolves parliament with approval of national referendum.

Prime Minister
Appointed by president, confirmed by parliament. Serves as head of government; chairs cabinet; answers to parliament.

Council of Ministers
Members nominated by prime minister, appointed by parliament. Oversees government operations.

JUDICIAL BRANCH
Constitutional Court
Rules on constitutionality of laws. Composed of seven judges.

Supreme Court
Highest court of review and appeal for civil and criminal cases. Parliament appoints court president to seven-year term, other justices for life.

Regional Courts

District Courts

SLOVENIA

OFFICIAL NAME: REPUBLIC OF SLOVENIA

POPULATION: 2 MILLION	
CAPITAL: LJUBLJANA	
AREA: 7,820 SQ. MILES (20,253 SQ. KM)	
INDEPENDENCE: 1991	
CONSTITUTION: 1991	

SLOVENIA is named after the Slovene people dominant in the country since the 6th century A.D.

RELIGION: Roman Catholic (Uniate 2%) 70.8%, Lutheran 1%, Muslim 1%, Atheist 4.3%, Other 22.9%

OFFICIAL LANGUAGE: Slovene

REGIONS OR PROVINCES: 182 municipalities and 11 urban municipalities

DEPENDENT TERRITORIES: None

MEDIA: No political censorship exists in national media

NEWSPAPERS: There are 7 daily newspapers

TV: 4 services: 1 state-controlled, 3 independent

RADIO: 4 services and many regional stations

SUFFRAGE: 18 years of age; universal (16 years of age, if employed)

LEGAL SYSTEM: Civil law; no ICJ jurisdiction

WORLD ORGANIZATIONS: ABEDA, ACCT (observer), BIS, CCC, CE, CEI, EAPC, EBRD, ECE, EU, FAO, IADB, IAEA, IBRD, ICAO, ICC, ICRM, IDA, IFC, IFRCS, ILO, IMF, IMO, Interpol, IOC, IOM, ISO, ITU, NAM (guest), NSG, OPCW, OSCE, PCA, PFP, UN, UNCTAD, UNESCO, UNIDO, UNMIK, UNTSO, UPU, WEU (associate partner), WHO, WIPO, WMO, WToO, WTrO, ZC

POLITICAL PARTIES: LDS—Liberal Democracy of Slovenia, SDS—Social Democratic Party of Slovenia, ZLSD—United List of Social Democrats, SLS/SKD—Slovene People's Party/Christian Democrats of Slovenia, Nsi—New Slovenia-Christian People's Party, MR—Two Seats are reserved for Italian and Hungarian minority representatives.

ETHNIC GROUPS:

Croat 3%
Serb 2%
Muslim 1%
Other 6%
Slovene 88%

NATIONAL ECONOMICS

WORLD GNP RANKING: 65th

GNP PER CAPITA: $10,050

INFLATION: 10.8%

BALANCE OF PAYMENTS (BALANCE OF TRADE): -$594 million

EXCHANGE RATES / U.S. DLR.: 227.5–245.6 TOLARS

OFFICIAL CURRENCY: SLOVENIAN TOLAR

GOVERNMENT SPENDING (% OF GDP)

- DEFENSE 1.2%
- EDUCATION 5.8%
- HEALTH 6.7%

0   5   10   15

NUMBER OF CONFLICTS OVER LAST 25 YEARS

	1	2-5	5+
Violent changes in government	○	○	○
Civil wars	◐	○	○
International wars	○	○	○
Foreign intervention	○	○	○

- Slovene troops staved off Yugoslav forces after secession in 1991.
- Compulsory military service was phased out in 2003, and replaced with a voluntary service option.

NOTABLE WARS AND INSURGENCIES: Independence conflict 1991

THE REPUBLIC OF SLOVENIA is a robust parliamentary democracy. It has become the most prosperous of all the former communist Eastern Europe countries and now has a stable and politically open government.

In 1918, Slovenia joined with other southern Slavic states to form what was later named Yugoslavia. Following the death of Yugoslavia's leader, Tito, in 1980, Serbian communist leaders tried to concentrate power further in their own hands. This was resisted by the Slovenes, who held elections after the collapse of communism throughout Eastern Europe in 1989. A non-communist coalition government was formed and the country's independence was declared in 1991. There was some fighting between Slovenes and the soldiers in the Yugoslav army, but it was short-lived, and Slovenia's independence was internationally recognized in 1992.

Today, the country has a dual executive—a president, who is chief of state, and a prime minister, who is head of the political party or coalition that controls the Drzavni Zbor (National Assembly), the lower and main house of the legislative body. The president nominates a candidate for prime minister, calls National Assembly elections, and acts as commander-in-chief. Unlike their counterparts in Serbia and Croatia, two other former Yugoslav republics, Slovenia's presidents and prime ministers have not used their offices to expand control and have worked within constitutional limits.

The constitution gives the National Assembly the greatest legislative authority, but most legislation is proposed by the executive. The lower house also has the power to call ministers to account. An upper house, the Drzavni Svet, or National Council, is an advisory body. Its members are elected to represent local, professional, and socioeconomic interests. The council may propose laws and ask to review National Assembly decisions. In the 2000 elections the center-left Liberal Democracy of Slovenia (LDS) won 38 percent of the assembly's seats. Coalitions are usually necessary for governing. A Constitutional Court seeks to ensure that laws and regulations conform with the constitution. It also settles disputes between government branches and between national and local authorities.

Slovenia is the most prosperous of the former Eastern European communist states

ISSUES AND CHALLENGES:

- Slovenia, with already close ties to Western Europe, has been at the forefront of nations on a "fast track" to join both the European Union and the North Atlantic Treaty Organization.
- Slovenia is a focus nation for the United States' southeast European policy of reinforcing regional stability.
- Upon gaining independence, Slovenia offered citizenship to all residents, avoiding a sectarian trap.

HOW THE GOVERNMENT WORKS

LEGISLATIVE BRANCH

Parlamenta
(Parliament)
Bicameral

Drzavni Svet
(National Council)
Forty members elected to five-year terms by professional and occupational interest groups. Advisory body; proposes laws; reviews Parliament's decisions.

Drzavni Zbor
(National Assembly)
Composed of 90 members who serve four-year terms: 40 elected by direct popular vote; 50 directly elected by proportional representation. Enacts laws; initiates referenda; ratifies treaties; may vote no-confidence in ministers.

Regional Governments
There are 147 municipalities with elected mayors and councils.

EXECUTIVE BRANCH

President
Elected to five-year term by direct popular vote, limit of two consecutive terms. Serves as head of state; commander-in-chief of armed forces.

Prime Minister
Leader of Parliament's majority party or coalition; nominated by president following legislative elections, approved by Parliament. Serves as head of government; sets national policies with Cabinet.

Council of Ministers
Composed of members nominated by prime minister, elected by Parliament.

JUDICIAL BRANCH

Constitutional Court
Rules on constitutionality of laws; decides disputes between government branches. Composed of nine judges nominated by National Assembly, elected by Parliament to nine-year terms.

Supreme Court
Highest court of appeal. Composed of 37 judges nominated by Judicial Council, elected by Parliament to life terms.

Court of Appeals
Four courts

Regional Courts
11 courts

District Courts
44 courts

ESTONIA

OFFICIAL NAME: REPUBLIC OF ESTONIA

POPULATION: 1.4 MILLION	
CAPITAL: TALLINN	
AREA: 17,462 SQ. MILES (45,226 SQ. KM)	
INDEPENDENCE: 1991	
CONSTITUTION: 1992	

ESTONIA is derived from the word "Aestii" used to describe the people living east of the Germanic people along the Baltic shore.

RELIGION: Evangelical Lutheran 56%, Russian Orthodox 25%, Other, including Estonian Orthodox, Baptist, Methodist, Seventh-Day Adventist, Roman Catholic, Pentecostal, Word of Life, Jewish 19%

OFFICIAL LANGUAGE: Estonian

REGIONS OR PROVINCES: 15 counties

DEPENDENT TERRITORIES: None

MEDIA: No political censorship exists in national media

NEWSPAPERS: There are 17 daily newspapers

TV: 3 services: 1 state-owned, 2 independent

RADIO: 30 services: 1 state-owned, 29 independent

SUFFRAGE: 18 years of age; universal for all Estonian citizens

LEGAL SYSTEM: Civil law; accepts ICJ jurisdiction

WORLD ORGANIZATIONS: BIS, CBSS, CCC, CE, EAPC, EBRD, ECE, EU, FAO, IAEA, IBRD, ICAO, ICFTU, ICRM, IFC, IFRCS, IHO, ILO, IMF, IMO, Interpol, IOC, IOM (observer), ISO (correspondent), ITU, OPCW, OSCE, PFP, UN, UNCTAD, UNESCO, UNMIBH, UNMIK, UNTSO, UPU, WEU (associate partner), WHO, WIPO, WMO, WTrO

POLITICAL PARTIES: K—Center Party, PPU—Pro Patria Union, R—Reform Party, M—Moderates, CPP—Rural People's Party, KMU—Coalition Party, UPP—United People's Party

ETHNIC GROUPS:

Other 8%
Russian 30%
Estonian 62%

NATIONAL ECONOMICS

WORLD GNP RANKING: 112th

GNP PER CAPITA: $3580

INFLATION: 4%

BALANCE OF PAYMENTS (BALANCE OF TRADE): -$315 million

EXCHANGE RATES / U.S. DLR.: 16.675-17.577 KROONI

OFFICIAL CURRENCY: KROON

GOVERNMENT SPENDING (% OF GDP)

✈ DEFENSE 1.4%.
⚕ HEALTH 5.1%
➕ EDUCATION 6.8%

0 — 5 — 10 — 15

NUMBER OF CONFLICTS OVER LAST 25 YEARS

	1	2-5	5+
Violent changes in government	○	○	○
Civil wars	○	○	○
International wars	○	○	○
Foreign intervention	○	○	○

- The US now supports Estonia's application for full membership of NATO.
- Estonia has accepted its eastern border; it effectively ceded a portion of its territory during the Soviet period.
- Compulsory military service.

NOTABLE WARS AND INSURGENCIES: None

ESTONIA'S POLITICAL LIFE is best viewed through the lens of its centuries-old struggle for cultural and political independence. Dominated by Danish, Swedish, German, Imperial Russian, and, most significantly and recently, Soviet rule, Estonia first gained independence in 1918. Its first constitution, adopted in 1920, established parliamentary rule, and the popularly elected government effected sweeping land reform and protection for minorities. Estonian-language schools were established, and cultural life flourished. Independence, however, lasted only 22 years. In 1940, Estonia, along with Lithuania and Latvia, was forcibly incorporated into the Soviet Union, as had been agreed in a secret German-Soviet pact before the outbreak of World War II. The following year the occupying Soviet forces were driven out by the Germans, but Soviet troops returned in 1944 and Estonia became one of the 15 socialist republics of the Soviet Union.

The Estonians strongly opposed Soviet rule, and in 1990, following the collapse of communism in Eastern Europe, they declared their country's independence. A new constitution was adopted in 1992 which is imbued with the democratic spirit of the 1920 document. A "weak" president and a strong prime minister share the executive branch. The president represents Estonia at international forums, appoints diplomatic personnel, and nominates the prime minister. Presidents can introduce and veto legislation, ask the National Court to rule on its constitutionality, dissolve Parliament after a vote of no-confidence, and issue decrees with the force of law when Parliament cannot convene—powers balanced by Parliament's power to elect the president. The prime minister is the chief executive and runs the government, implementing policy with the Council of Ministers. The unicameral Parliament passes all laws and approves and controls the budget. Estonia's three levels of courts decide cases based on the law and a conflict's context without recourse to earlier court decisions.

Many wars have been fought on the soil of Estonia, whose strategic location has precipitated battles between rival powers at its own expense. In 1944 the USSR granted Russia the trans-Narva and Petseri regions located on Estonia's eastern frontier. Estonia only relinquished its claims in the region in 1995.

ISSUES AND CHALLENGES:

- Soviet domination of Estonia brought a huge influx of ethnic Russians, many of whom still live there. Estonia's desire to protect and preserve Estonian culture and language has inevitably created tensions between the two groups. The government has acted to provide equal civil protection to "resident aliens" by renewing its liberal 1938 citizenship law.

- All agree that Estonia should enact economic reform and become a fully-fledged member of the European Union, but there are disagreements on how to accomplish this.

HOW THE GOVERNMENT WORKS

LEGISLATIVE BRANCH
Riigikogu (Parliament) Unicameral
Composed of 101 members elected to four-year terms by direct popular vote. Initiates and approves legislation sponsored by prime minister; passes bills and budget; may be dissolved by president when deadlocked.

Regional Governments
Fifteen counties administered by councils elected to three-year terms.

EXECUTIVE BRANCH
President
Elected to five-year term by Parliament. Serves as head of state; appoints diplomats; represents nation in international forums; may send bills back to Parliament for reconsideration.

Prime Minister
Nominated by president, confirmed by Parliament. Serves as head of government; implements policy; oversees government operations.

Council of Ministers
Appointed by prime minister, approved by Parliament. Chaired by prime minister; answers to Parliament for its actions.

JUDICIAL BRANCH
National Court
Highest court of appeal. Reviews lower-court rulings; decides constitutional issues. Chairman appointed for life by Parliament.

District Courts
Hear appeals from local courts.

Local Courts

TRINIDAD & TOBAGO

OFFICIAL NAME: REPUBLIC OF TRINIDAD AND TOBAGO

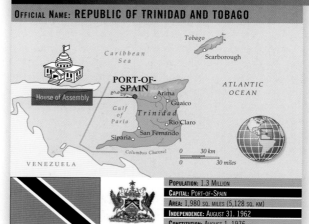

POPULATION: 1.3 Million
CAPITAL: PORT-OF-SPAIN
AREA: 1,980 SQ. MILES (5,128 SQ. KM)
INDEPENDENCE: AUGUST 31, 1962
CONSTITUTION: AUGUST 1, 1976

TRINIDAD, Spanish for "trinity", comes from the island's three prominent peaks. Tobago comes from "tavaco", the pipe tht natives used for smoking tobacco leaves.

RELIGION: Roman Catholic 29.4%, Hindu 23.8%, Anglican 10.9%, Muslim 5.8%, Presbyterian 3.4%, Other 26.7%

OFFICIAL LANGUAGE: English

REGIONS OR PROVINCES: 8 counties, 3 municipalities, and 1 ward

DEPENDENT TERRITORIES: None

MEDIA: No political censorship exists in national media

NEWSPAPERS: There are 4 daily newspapers

TV: 2 services: 1 state-owned, 1 independent

RADIO: 7 services: 1 state-owned, 6 independent

SUFFRAGE: 18 years of age; universal

LEGAL SYSTEM: English common law; no ICJ jurisdiction

WORLD ORGANIZATIONS: ACP, C, Caricom, CCC, CDB, ECLAC, FAO, G-24, G-77, IADB, IBRD, ICAO, ICFTU, ICRM, IDA, IFAD, IFC, IFRCS, IHO, ILO, IMF, IMO, Interpol, IOC, ISO, ITU, LAES, NAM, OAS, OPANAL, OPCW, UN, UNCTAD, UNESCO, UNIDO, UNU, UPU, WCL, WFTU, WHO, WIPO, WMO, WTrO

POLITICAL PARTIES: PNM—People's National Movement, UNC—United National Congress

ETHNIC GROUPS:
- White and Chinese 1%
- Mixed 19%
- South Asian 40%
- Black 40%

NATIONAL ECONOMICS

WORLD GNP RANKING: 103rd

GNP PER CAPITA: $4,930

INFLATION: 3.6%

BALANCE OF PAYMENTS (BALANCE OF TRADE): -$644 million

EXCHANGE RATES / U.S. DLR.: 6.240-6.115 TRINIDAD AND TOBAGO DOLLARS

OFFICIAL CURRENCY: TRINIDAD & TOBAGO DOLLAR

GOVERNMENT SPENDING (% OF GDP)

- DEFENSE 0.5%
- EDUCATION 3.6%
- HEALTH 2.5%

0   5   10   15

NUMBER OF CONFLICTS OVER LAST 25 YEARS

	1	2-5	5+
Violent changes in government	○	○	○
Civil wars	○	○	○
International wars	○	○	○
Foreign intervention	○	○	○

- Defense forces comprise a land army and coast guard (with air wing), used to patrol fishing grounds.
- Sea border disputes with Venezuela relate to fishing and marine oil rights.

NOTABLE WARS AND INSURGENCIES: None

UNITED AS A PARLIAMENTARY DEMOCRACY, the islands of Trinidad and Tobago have strikingly different histories. Trinidad was explored by Christopher Columbus in 1498 and settled by the Spanish in the late 16th century. The island remained in Spanish hands until Britain seized control in 1797. By that time many of the indigenous Arawak and Carib inhabitants had been eradicated. Dutch, French, and British forces fought for control of Tobago, and possession of the island changed 22 times during the colonial period—more than any other West Indian island. Ceded to Britain in 1814, Tobago was incorporated with Trinidad in 1886; the islands became independent in 1962.

British governmental structure and common law served as patterns for the nation's government and legal system. A republican constitution, adopted in 1976, provides for a president who is elected by Parliament to be head of state, a prime minister who is head of government and presides over a Cabinet that directs the government, and a bicameral Parliament. Both chambers of Parliament can introduce bills, but bills regarding money must arise in the House of Representatives. Amendments to the constitution and bills regarding money must be passed by both the House and the Senate. Elections may be called by the president, either at the request of the prime minister or after a vote of no confidence by the House of Representatives. The judiciary branch enjoys autonomy.

In 1980, the creation of the Tobago House of Assembly gave Tobago a measure of self-government; legislation passed by Parliament in 1996 granted the island further self-determination. Trinidad and Tobago's complex ethnic and cultural mix makes government a challenge. In July 1990, the extremist black Muslim group Jamaat al Muslimeen, angered by unresolved land claims, attempted to overthrow the government. The group held the prime minister and members of Parliament hostage for five days before surrendering to police.

ISSUES AND CHALLENGES:

- By regional standards, Trinidad and Tobago has an adequate infrastructure, but in some areas water shortages, power failures, and drainage problems are common. Concern over the government's ability to ensure adequate water supply to industrial plants under construction in central Trinidad prompted plans for a large desalination plant. A significant portion of the national budget will be spent on upgrading the infrastructure in rural areas to accommodate increasing industrialization.

- In the 1990s, marine boundary disputes that affect oil and fishing rights erupted with Venezuela.

- The sharp disparity between the oil-rich elite who are often expatriates and the farm laborers and tourism industry workers who struggle to make a living on low wages exacerbates existing tensions.

HOW THE GOVERNMENT WORKS

LEGISLATIVE BRANCH
House of Assembly
Bicameral Parliament

Senate
Composed of 31 members appointed to five-year terms by president: 16 on advice of prime minister; six on advice of opposition leader; nine chosen from outstanding community leaders.

House of Representatives
Composed of 36 members elected to five-year terms by direct popular vote. Two seats are assigned to Tobago.

Regional Governments
Seven counties administered by local councils. Tobago governed by elected 15-member assembly.

EXECUTIVE BRANCH
President
Elected to five-year term by joint session of Parliament following general elections. Serves as head of state. May call early elections at request of prime minister.

Prime Minister
Leader of House's majority party or coalition; appointed by president. Serves as head of government; chairs Cabinet.

Cabinet
Composed of members of Parliament, appointed by prime minister. Oversees government operations; answers to Parliament.

JUDICIAL BRANCH
Privy Council in London
Final court of appeal.

Supreme Court of Judicature
Divided into two courts: High Court of Justice and Court of Appeal.

Court of Appeal
Highest island court of appeal. Composed of chief justice and three other judges.

High Court of Justice
Hears civil and criminal cases. Chief justice appointed by president on advice of prime minister and opposition leader; ten judges appointed by prime minister on advice of Judicial Service Commission.

MAURITIUS

OFFICIAL NAME: REPUBLIC OF MAURITIUS

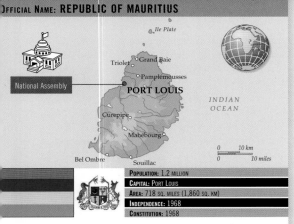

POPULATION: 1.2 MILLION	
CAPITAL: PORT LOUIS	
AREA: 718 SQ. MILES (1,860 SQ. KM)	
INDEPENDENCE: 1968	
CONSTITUTION: 1968	

MAURITIUS was named after Prince Maurice of Nassau by Dutch explorers in the 17th century.

RELIGION: Hindu 52%, Roman Catholic 26%, Muslim 17%, Protestant 2%, Other 3%

OFFICIAL LANGUAGE: English

REGIONS OR PROVINCES: 9 districts and 3 dependencies

DEPENDENT TERRITORIES: Agalega Islands, Cargados Carajos Shoals, Rodrigues (all Indian Ocean islands)

MEDIA: No political censorship exists in national media

NEWSPAPERS: There are 10 daily newspapers

TV: 1 independent service

RADIO: 1 independent service

SUFFRAGE: 18 years of age; universal

LEGAL SYSTEM: French and English common law; accepts ICJ jurisdiction

WORLD ORGANIZATIONS: ACCT, ACP, AfDB, C, CCC, ECA, FAO, G-77, IAEA, IBRD, ICAO, ICFTU, ICRM, IDA, IFAD, IFC, IFRCS, ILO, IMF, IMO, InOC, Interpol, IOC, ISO, ITU, NAM, OAU, OPCW, PCA, SADC, UN, UN Security Council (temporary), UNCTAD, UNESCO, UNIDO, UPU, WCL, WFTU, WHO, WIPO, WMO, WToO, WTrO

POLITICAL PARTIES: MSM/MMM—Mauritian Socialist Movement/Mauritian Militant Movement, PTr/PMXD—Labour Party/Mauritian Social Democratic Party of Xavier Duval, OPR—Organization of the People of Rodrigues, MR—Mouvement Rodriguais

ETHNIC GROUPS:

- Sino-Mauritian 3%
- Franco-Mauritian 2%
- Creole 27%
- Indo-Mauritian 68%

NATIONAL ECONOMICS

WORLD GNP RANKING: 116th

GNP PER CAPITA: $3,750

INFLATION: 4.2%

BALANCE OF PAYMENTS (BALANCE OF TRADE): -$33.0 million

EXCHANGE RATES / U.S. DLR.: 27.82-30.25 MAURITIAN RUPEES

OFFICIAL CURRENCY: MAURITIAN RUPEE

GOVERNMENT SPENDING (% OF GDP)

- DEFENSE 1.8%
- EDUCATION 4.3%
- HEALTH 1.8%

0   5   10   15

NUMBER OF CONFLICTS OVER LAST 25 YEARS

	1	2-5	5+
Violent changes in government	○	○	○
Civil wars	○	○	○
International wars	○	○	○
Foreign intervention	○	○	○

- Mauritius has no standing defense forces.
- A special police mobile unit ensures internal security.
- Disputes persist over French-ruled island of Tromelin and UK-administered Diego Garcia island (a US-UK military base in the British Indian Ocean Territory).

NOTABLE WARS AND INSURGENCIES: None

THE ECONOMIC AND POLITICAL PROSPERITY enjoyed by Mauritius is rivaled by few post-colonial African states. Known to Arab and Malay sailors in the 10th century, the islands were a colonial possession from Portugal's initial claim in 1505 to its independence from Britain in 1968. That period also included separate eras of rule by the Dutch and the French, all of which accounts for the vibrant, multi-cultural society present in one of the world's most densely populated nations.

Mauritius has had a stable democratic political system since independence. Elections and transfers of power on the islands have been consistently peaceful and orderly. The national press is relatively active, seldom subject to governmental regulations and has a wide readership. Opposition groups are free to congregate, disseminate information, and run freely in elections. Furthermore, the national judiciary has remained an independent, stable, and respected institution. All this continues despite the ethnically diverse nature of the population, which can occasionally result in friction between the numerous political parties in the parliamentary system.

The stability of Mauritius's political system derives in large part from the its prosperous economy, a result of recent industrial divers-ification and the expansion of tourism. For the last twenty years, annual growth has been nearly six percent. As a colonial possession, Mauritius was a large producer of sugar. Though sugar remains an important export crop the country has wisely developed a diverse economic base, focusing mainly on the financial, textile, and tourism industries. Its successful development draws attention and investment from foreign sources, which further supports it as one of Africa's most competitive economies.

Sir Anerood Jugnauth of the Mauritian Socialist Movement (MSM) had been prime minister for 13 years before losing elections in 1995 to the Labour Party (PTr). He was returned to power when corruption scandals led to early elections in 2000; under the coalition deal that he made with the Mauritian Militant Movement (MMM), Jugnauth stepped aside in favor of MMM leader Paul Bérenger in late 2003, halfway through the government's term in office.

ISSUES AND CHALLENGES:

- Current disputes over the ownership of the Chagos Archipelago affect relations with the UK, and similarly over Tromelin with France.
- Mauritius is a minor transport hub for heroin from South Asia.
- The economic stability of the islands is subject to fluctuations in the world price of sugar.
- Rapid industrialization as well as unchecked hotel building have caused environmental problems.
- Mauritius is far from self-sufficient in food—it has to import 75 percent of its needs.

HOW THE GOVERNMENT WORKS

LEGISLATIVE BRANCH

National Assembly
Unicameral Parliament
Composed of up to 70 members who serve five-year terms: 62 directly elected by popular vote; up to eight additional members appointed by elections commission from the unsuccessful candidates who received the most votes, to give representation to ethnic minorities. Ordinary legislation requires majority vote for passage; constitutional amendments a three-quarters majority.

Regional Governments
Nine districts and three dependencies.

EXECUTIVE BRANCH

President
Elected to five-year term by simple majority vote of National Assembly. Serves as chief of state.

Vice-president
Elected to five-year term by majority vote of National Assembly.

Prime Minister
Leader of National Assembly's majority party or coalition leader; appointed by president. Serves as head of government; answers to National Assembly.

Council of Ministers
Twenty-plus members, prime minister; appointed by president on advice of prime minister. Directs government operations.

JUDICIAL BRANCH

Privy Council in London
Final tribunal for appeals.

Supreme Court
Highest Mauritius court of review and appeal; rules on lower-court appeals and constitutionality of laws. Composed of nine judges who also preside in lower courts.

Lower Courts

SOLOMON ISLANDS

OFFICIAL NAME: SOLOMON ISLANDS

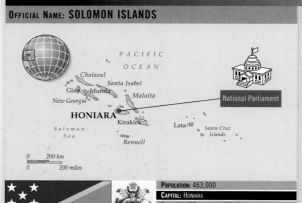

POPULATION: 463,000	
CAPITAL: HONIARA	
AREA: 10,985 SQ. MILES (28,451 SQ. KM)	
INDEPENDENCE: 1978	
CONSTITUTION: 1978	

THE SOLOMON ISLANDS were so named by the Spanish because they thought King Solomon had financed his temple in Jerusalem with gold from there.

RELIGION: Anglican 34%, Roman Catholic 19%, South Seas Evangelical Church 17%, Methodist 11%, Seventh-day Adventist 10%, Other 9%

OFFICIAL LANGUAGE: English

REGIONS OR PROVINCES: 9 provinces and 1 capital territory

DEPENDENT TERRITORIES: None

MEDIA: No political censorship exists in national media

NEWSPAPERS: There are two daily newspapers

TV: 1 US-based Christian service

RADIO: 1 independent service

SUFFRAGE: 21 years of age; universal

LEGAL SYSTEM: English common law; no ICJ jurisdiction

WORLD ORGANIZATIONS: ACP, AsDB, C, ESCAP, FAO, G-77, IBRD, ICAO, ICRM, IDA, IFAD, IFC, IFRCS, ILO, IMF, IMO, IOC, ITU, Sparteca, SPC, SPF, UN, UNCTAD, UNESCO, UPU, WFTU, WHO, WMO, WTrO

POLITICAL PARTIES: PAP—People's Alliance Party, Ind—Independents, SIACC—Solomon Islands Alliance for Change Coalition, PPP—People's Progressive Party, LP—Labour Party

ETHNIC GROUPS:

Micronesian 1.5%
Other (including European and Chinese) 1.5%
Polynesian 4%
Melanesian 93%

NATIONAL ECONOMICS

WORLD GNP RANKING: 177th

GNP PER CAPITA: $620

INFLATION: 8.3%

BALANCE OF PAYMENTS (BALANCE OF TRADE): $21 million

EXCHANGE RATES / U.S. DLR.: 5.163-5.640 SOLOMON ISLANDS DOLLARS

OFFICIAL CURRENCY: SOLOMON ISLANDS DOLLAR

GOVERNMENT SPENDING (% OF GDP)

		0	5	10	15
✈	DEFENSE (N/A)				
	EDUCATION 4.2%				
✚	HEALTH 4.2%				

NUMBER OF CONFLICTS OVER LAST 25 YEARS

	1	2-5	5+
Violent changes in government	●	○	○
Civil wars	●	○	○
International wars	○	○	○
Foreign intervention	○	●	○

- The Peace Plan 2000 includes the creation of a panethnic security force.
- In 2003, Australia agreed to lead a regional peacekeeping force, the Regional Assistance Mission.

NOTABLE WARS AND INSURGENCIES: Civil war 1998-2000. Australian-led regional peacekeeping force in 2003

THE SOLOMON ISLANDS FORM the southerly portion of the archipelago which begins with Bougainville, in Papua New Guinea. European adventurers came into contact with the local Melanesian tribal communities in the 19th century. Determined to regulate the islands' potential, the UK established a protectorate in the south in 1893. It acquired other islands later in the decade, and the German-administered northern islands in 1900.

Local autonomy was granted in stages in the later 20th century until full independence as a parliamentary democracy was achieved in 1978. The Queen of England remains titular head of state, with a governor-general acting in her stead. The prime minister, who is elected by the National Parliament from among their number, wields executive powers as head of government. The cabinet is formally appointed by the governor-general (who is elected by Parliament) on the recommendation of the prime minister. The 50 members of the National Parliament are directly elected. The government of the islands is highly centralized, prompting resentment from outlying districts. The party system is weak, and prominent local figures—known as "big men"—are often elected by rural communities.

Tensions on the main island, Guadalcanal (Isatabu) between locals and migrant workers, principally from neighboring Malaita, erupted into open conflict between the Malaita Eagle Force (MEF) and the Isatabu Freedom Movement in 1998. The rule of law broke down on the main island, paralyzing the government. In 2000 the MEF kidnapped the then prime minister.

Australia led reconciliation efforts and the Townsend Peace Accord was signed on October 15, 2000. A succession of new governments have proposed reconstruction schemes, including a more federalized structure to appease growing separatist sentiment in the outlying districts. None have yet been implemented. Compensation claims from the conflict had bankrupted the government by the end of 2002 and violence inten-sified once again. An Australian-led Regional Assistance Mission (Ramsi) arrived in July 2003. Peace has since been restored, and the country's finances are now in the hands of Ramsi.

ISSUES AND CHALLENGES:

- The recent civil conflict has destroyed the economy. Infrastructure was directly damaged, peacetime compensation claims quickly outstripped government funds, and international investors and tourists have lost confidence in the islands

- The potential for future conflict remains. Gang violence has become commonplace, and local warlords are reluctant to relinquish their influence

- Natural resources are limited, and their exploitation poses serious dangers to the local ecology.

HOW THE GOVERNMENT WORKS

LEGISLATIVE BRANCH

National Parliament
Unicameral Parliament
Composed of 50 members elected to four-year terms by direct popular vote from single-member districts. May be dissolved by absolute majority vote of its members before completion of its term; new elections must be held within four months.

Regional Governments
Nine provinces administered by elected local assemblies; capital of Honiara governed by elected town council.

EXECUTIVE BRANCH

British Monarch
Head of state. Ceremonial role.

Governor-general
Appointed to five-year term by National Parliament to represent British monarch; limit of two terms.

Prime Minister
Leader of National Parliament's majority party or coalition; appointed by governor-general, elected by National Parliament to five-year term. Serves as head of government.

Cabinet
Composed of 20 members of National Parliament appointed by prime minister.

JUDICIAL BRANCH

High Court
Highest court with unlimited jurisdiction throughout country. Composed of chief justice and judges appointed by governor-general on advice of prime minister and Judicial Service.

Court of Appeal

Magistrates' Courts

Customary Land Appeal Courts

LUXEMBOURG

OFFICIAL NAME: GRAND DUCHY OF LUXEMBOURG

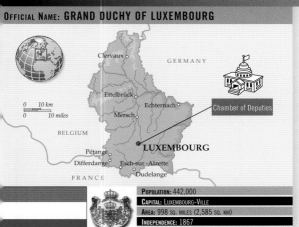

POPULATION: 442,000
CAPITAL: LUXEMBOURG-VILLE
AREA: 998 SQ. MILES (2,585 SQ. KM)
INDEPENDENCE: 1867
CONSTITUTION: 1868

LUXEMBOURG derives its name from Lucilinburhuc meaning "little fortress," the Saxon name for its capital.

RELIGION: Roman Catholic 97%, Protestant, Greek Orthodox, and Jewish 3%

OFFICIAL LANGUAGES: French, German, and Letzeburgish

REGIONS OR PROVINCES: 3 districts

DEPENDENT TERRITORIES: None

MEDIA: No political censorship exists in national media

NEWSPAPERS: There are 5 daily newspapers

TV: 2 independent services

RADIO: 11 independent services

SUFFRAGE: 18 years of age; universal and compulsory

LEGAL SYSTEM: Civil law; accepts ICJ jurisdiction

WORLD ORGANIZATIONS: ACCT, Australia Group, Benelux, CCC, CE, EAPC, EBRD, ECE, EIB, EMU, EU, FAO, IAEA, IBRD, ICAO, ICC, ICFTU, ICRM, IDA, IEA, IFAD, IFC, IFRCS, ILO, IMF, IMO, Interpol, IOC, IOM, ISO, ITU, NATO, NEA, NSG, OECD, OPCW, OSCE, PCA, UN, UNCTAD, UNESCO, UNIDO, UPU, WCL, WEU, WHO, WIPO, WMO, WTrO, ZC

POLITICAL PARTIES: CSV / PCS—Christian Social Party, DP/PD—Democratic Party, LSAP/POSL—Luxembourg Socialist Workers' Party, ACDJ—Action Committee for Democracy and Justice, G—Greens, L—The Left

ETHNIC GROUPS:

Foreign residents 27%

Luxembourger 73%

NATIONAL ECONOMICS

WORLD GNP RANKING: 69th

GNP PER CAPITA: $42,060

INFLATION: 3.1%

BALANCE OF PAYMENTS (BALANCE OF TRADE): $1.59 billion

EXCHANGE RATES / U.S. DLR.: 1.0651-1.1231 EURO

OFFICIAL CURRENCY: EURO

GOVERNMENT SPENDING (% OF GDP)

✈	DEFENSE	0.8%
🎓	EDUCATION	4%
✚	HEALTH	5.7%

0   5   10   15

NUMBER OF CONFLICTS OVER LAST 25 YEARS

	1	2-5	5+
Violent changes in government	○	○	○
Civil wars	○	○	○
International wars	○	○	○
Foreign intervention	○	○	○

- A few members of the 900-strong army assist in international peacekeeping missions.
- There is no navy or air force.
- Member of NATO.

NOTABLE WARS AND INSURGENCIES: None

THE GRAND DUCHY OF LUXEMBOURG has maintained its separate political status since the 10th century and has been a duchy since 1364, despite coming at various times in its history under the control of surrounding states—today's France, Germany, and the Netherlands. Full independence came in 1867. For many years Luxembourg was neutral, but after World War II it joined the NATO alliance. Luxembourg was one of the founding members of the European Union, and is one of the most prosperous countries in the world.

Luxembourg is a parliamentary democracy and a constitutional monarchy. The head of state is the grand duke, whose position is hereditary. Grand Duke Henri came to power after his father, Grand Duke Jean, abdicated following 35 years of rule. He has considerable power and also performs ceremonial roles, while the Council of Government or Cabinet—which includes the prime minister— exercises the government's main executive power. The prime minister is the leader of the political party or coalition with the majority of seats in the parliament. Legislative power is vested in the Chamber of Deputies, elected directly to five-year terms. A second body, the Council of State, composed of 21 ordinary citizens appointed by the grand duke, advises the Chamber of Deputies in the drafting of legislation. Under the constitution, the Chamber of Deputies is required to reaffirm legislation after three months unless the Council of State waives that rule. Luxembourg law is a composite of local practice, legal tradition, and French, Belgian, and German systems.

Since the end of the World War II, the Christian Social party (CSV) has been the dominant political force. However, in the past few years the Liberal Democratic Party (DP) has drawn strong support from the professional and urban middle class. Mainstream parties all back Luxembourg's central role in the European Union. The nation is home to key EU institutions, including the Secretariat of the European Parliament and the Court of Justice.

Luxembourg has the highest per capita income in the EU

ISSUES AND CHALLENGES:

- International service industries account for 65% of Luxembourg's GDP, making it vulnerable to changing conditions oversees.

- The majority of the country's energy needs have to be imported.

- The growing number of old people and the lack of population growth have the potential to slow economic growth, and have spurred an increase in immigrant workers (nearly half of its workers are foreigners).

- The country's banking secrecy rules have provoked international criticism, as they can provide a cover for both tax evasion and fraud.

HOW THE GOVERNMENT WORKS

LEGISLATIVE BRANCH

Chambre des Députés
(Chamber of Deputies)
Unicameral Parliament
Composed of 60 members elected to five-year terms by direct popular vote in proportional representation in four multi-seat constituencies; legislative power vested in this body.

Regional Governments
Three districts.

EXECUTIVE BRANCH

Grand Duke
Position is hereditary. Serves as head of state. Mostly Ceremonial role. Maintains power to dissolve Chamber of Deputies.

Prime Minister
Leader of parliament's majority party or coalition; appointed by monarch following elections. Serves as head of government; answers to Chamber of Deputies.

Deputy Prime Minister
Appointed by the monarch.

Council of Ministers
Members appointed by monarch on advice of prime minister.

Council of State
Twenty-one members appointed for life by monarch on advice of prime minister. Issues advisory opinions on draft bills before introduction in Chamber of Deputies.

JUDICIAL BRANCH

Superior Court of Justice
Highest court of review and appeal. Composed of 16 judges appointed for life by monarch on advice of the court itself.

District Courts

Justices of Peace

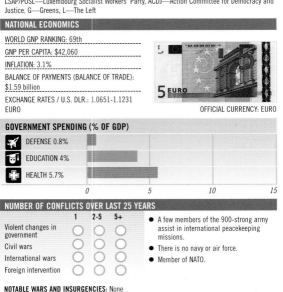

MALTA

OFFICIAL NAME: REPUBLIC OF MALTA

Ghawdex (Gozo)
Victoria
Kemmuna
Mellieħa
Bugibba
St Julian's
Mosta
Malta
Ħamrun **VALLETTA**
Qormi
Rabat
Marsaxlokk
Birzebbuga

House of Representatives

Mediterranean Sea

0   5 km
0   5 miles

  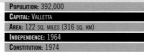

POPULATION:	392,000
CAPITAL:	VALLETTA
AREA:	122 SQ. MILES (316 SQ. KM)
INDEPENDENCE:	1964
CONSTITUTION:	1974

MALTA was named either after the Latin and Greek words for "honey" (for which it is famous), or the Pheonician word for "safe harbor".

RELIGION: Roman Catholic 98%, Other and non-religious 2%

OFFICIAL LANGUAGES: English and Maltese

REGIONS OR PROVINCES: None (administered directly from Valletta)

DEPENDENT TERRITORIES: None

MEDIA: No political censorship exists in national media

NEWSPAPERS: There are 4 daily newspapers

The Malta press is largely party politically orientated with two of the three main press groups affiliated to the NP or MLP; one is independent

TV: 7 services: 1 state-owned, 6 independent

RADIO: 2 services: 1 state-owned, 11 independent

SUFFRAGE: 18 years of age; universal

LEGAL SYSTEM: Roman and English common law; accepts ICJ jurisdiction

WORLD ORGANIZATIONS: C, CCC, CE, EBRD, ECE, EU, FAO, G-77, IAEA, IBRD, ICAO, ICFTU, ICRM, IFAD, IFRCS, ILO, IMF, IMO, Interpol, IOC, IOM (observer), ISO, ITU, NAM, OPCW, OSCE, PCA, UN, UNCTAD, UNESCO, UNIDO, UPU, WCL, WHO, WIPO, WMO, WToO, WTrO

POLITICAL PARTIES: NP—Nationalist Party, MLP—Malta Labour Party

ETHNIC GROUPS:

Other 4%

Maltese 96%

NATIONAL ECONOMICS

WORLD GNP RANKING: 127th

GNP PER CAPITA: $9,120

INFLATION: 2.4%

BALANCE OF PAYMENTS (BALANCE OF TRADE): -$515 million

EXCHANGE RATES / U.S. DLR.: 0.4357-0.4503 MALTESE LIRI

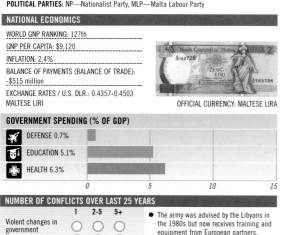

OFFICIAL CURRENCY: MALTESE LIRA

GOVERNMENT SPENDING (% OF GDP)

DEFENSE 0.7%

EDUCATION 5.1%

HEALTH 6.3%

0   5   10   15

NUMBER OF CONFLICTS OVER LAST 25 YEARS

	1	2-5	5+
Violent changes in government	○	○	○
Civil wars	○	○	○
International wars	○	○	○
Foreign intervention	○	○	○

- The army was advised by the Libyans in the 1980s but now receives training and equipment from European partners.
- Staunchly non-aligned foreign policy is threatened by EU membership.

NOTABLE WARS AND INSURGENCIES: None

MALTA CURRENTLY ENJOYS SELF-RULE as a parliamentary democracy. However, for most of the past 3,000 years, the island endured domination by a succession of foreign powers. Colonized by the Phoenicians perhaps as early as the 16th century B.C., the Maltese archipelago—in which just Malta, Ghawdex, and Kemmuna are inhabited—was subsequently conquered by the Romans and the Byzantine Empire. From the 9th century, it fell under the control of the Arabs, Normans, and Spanish before becoming a possession of the Holy Roman Emperor, who in 1530 granted it to the military religious order of the Knights Hospitaller. The French took control of the fortresses in 1798, but in 1814 Malta became a British crown colony. This long and constant struggle for control of Malta derived from the island's strategic, and highly desirable, location between Europe and north Africa. Malta gained independence from the United Kingdom in 1964, and became a republic in 1974.

The government is based on the British system. The president is head of state with the power to assent to bills and dissolve the House of Representatives, Malta's Parliament. The prime minister functions as Malta's chief executive officer, selecting House members for the Cabinet and overseeing government operations. The constitution grants the House broad powers to "make laws for the peace, order, and good government of Malta". The House meets at least once every 12 months, and bills imposing or increasing taxes must be recommended by the president before they are considered. House members are elected by popular vote on the basis of proportional representation every five years. There are usually 65 seats, but under a system in which additional seats are given to the party with the largest vote in order to ensure a working majority in the House, there may be more. The 1998 elections, for example, resulted in 69 seats.

The country's judiciary is headed by a Constitutional Court, which rules on human rights cases and constitutional and House-election disputes; a Court of Appeal, which hears appeals of civil cases; and a Court of Criminal Appeal, which decides appeals of criminal verdicts.

ISSUES AND CHALLENGES:

- Tourism accounts for half of the economy, with the population outnumbered three to one by tourists. Malta hopes its new international airport and a half-dozen new four-star hotels will create jobs by attracting even more vacationers.

- To reduce its public debt, Malta has partially privatized the formerly government-owned tele-communications company and is considering the sale of other state-controlled properties.

- With few natural resources to develop, Malta aims to attract high-tech companies, in part with its recently installed national fiber-optics telecommunications system.

HOW THE GOVERNMENT WORKS

LEGISLATIVE BRANCH

House of Representatives
Unicameral Parliament
Composed of members—usually 65—directly elected to five-year terms by proportional representation. Meets once annually; proposes and passes laws; adopts budget; may remove prime minister and cabinet with no-confidence vote.

Regional Governments
Sixty-seven elected municipal councils oversee local government services, including police, post offices, and medical facilities.

EXECUTIVE BRANCH

President
Elected to five-year term by Parliament. Serves as head of state; assents to bills; dissolves Parliament; grants pardons.

Prime Minister
Leader of Parliament's majority party or coalition; appointed to five-year term by president. Serves as head of government; presides over cabinet.

Cabinet
Composed of Parliament members appointed by president on advice of prime minister. Oversees government operations; answers to Parliament.

JUDICIAL BRANCH

Constitutional Court
Highest court of appeal.
Rules on constitutionality of laws; election disputes; human-rights cases. Composed of nine justices appointed by president on advice of prime minister to serve until age 65.

Court of Appeals
Hears civil case appeals.
Three justices appointed by president to serve until age 65.

Court of Criminal Appeals
Hears criminal case appeals.
Three justices appointed by president to serve until age 65.

Lower Courts

BAHAMAS

OFFICIAL NAME: COMMONWEALTH OF THE BAHAMAS

POPULATION: 308,000
CAPITAL: NASSAU
AREA: 3,864 SQ. MILES (10,010 SQ. KM)
INDEPENDENCE: 1973
CONSTITUTION: 1973

THE BAHAMAS is named after the Spanish for "shallow sea"—*baja mar*.

RELIGION: Baptist 32%, Anglican 20%, Roman Catholic 19%, Church of God 6%, Methodist 6%, Other 17%

OFFICIAL LANGUAGE: English

REGIONS OR PROVINCES: 21 districts

DEPENDENT TERRITORIES: None

MEDIA: No political censorship exists in national media

NEWSPAPERS: There are 4 daily newspapers

TV: 1 state-owned service

RADIO: 5 services: 1 state-owned, 4 independent

SUFFRAGE: 18 years of age; universal

LEGAL SYSTEM: English common law; no ICJ jurisdiction

WORLD ORGANIZATIONS: ACP, C, Caricom, CCC, CDB, ECLAC, FAO, G-77, IADB, IBRD, ICAO, ICFTU, ICRM, IFC, IFRCS, ILO, IMF, IMO, Interpol, IOC, ITU, LAES, NAM, OAS, OPANAL, OPCW (signatory), UN, UNCTAD, UNESCO, UNIDO, UPU, WHO, WIPO, WMO, WTrO (observer)

POLITICAL PARTIES: PLP—Progressive Liberal Party, FNM—Free National Movement, Ind—Independents

ETHNIC GROUPS:

- Asian and Hispanic 3%
- White 12%
- Black 85%

NATIONAL ECONOMICS

WORLD GNP RANKING: 115th

GNP PER CAPITA: $14,960

INFLATION: 1.6%

BALANCE OF PAYMENTS (BALANCE OF TRADE): -$438 million

EXCHANGE RATES / U.S. DLR.: 1 BAHAMIAN DOLLAR

OFFICIAL CURRENCY: BAHAMIAN DOLLAR

GOVERNMENT SPENDING (% OF GDP)

- DEFENSE 0.6%
- EDUCATION 3.6%
- HEALTH 2.5%

0   5   10   15

NUMBER OF CONFLICTS OVER LAST 25 YEARS

	1	2-5	5+
Violent changes in government	○	○	○
Civil wars	○	○	○
International wars	○	○	○
Foreign intervention	○	○	○

- The Bahamas has no land army.
- The small navy is armed and trained by the UK.
- Main priorities are the interception of narcotics and illegal immigrants.

NOTABLE WARS AND INSURGENCIES: None

AN ARCHIPELAGO OF MORE THAN 700 ISLANDS, the Bahamas has served as a haven for Caribbean pirates, an outpost for slave traders, a new home during the American Revolution for fleeing colonists loyal to Britain, and a base for rum runners during Prohibition in the United States.

British settlers from Bermuda founded the Bahamas' first permanent European settlements in the mid-1600s before the British government claimed the islands and ruled them as a colony for nearly three centuries. Today the Bahamas is an independent parliamentary democracy and a mecca for tourists and offshore banking. A member of the British Commonwealth of Nations, the island nation enjoys political and legal customs that closely mirror those of the United Kingdom.

> The Bahamas were the first landfall in the Americas on Christopher Columbus's voyage of 1492.

The country's 1973 constitution established an executive branch, a bicameral Parliament, an independent judiciary, and three civil service commissions to oversee the police, government workers, and the courts. Constitutional amendments require both an act of Parliament and a popular referendum. Heading the executive branch is a governor-general, appointed by the British monarch following each election of Parliament. However, the actual power to run the government is vested in the Cabinet and prime minister. Together, they decide government policies and set the country's legislative agenda.

In Parliament, House of Assembly members are elected every five years. Senators are appointed by the governor-general after each House election. The House has oversight of the Cabinet and responsibility for money bills in Parliament. The Senate has the power to consent to or reject bills after House passage, but the House can override Senate rejection by passing the bill in two successive sessions. The Bahamian legal system follows English common law. The country's highest court of law is the Judicial Committee of Her Majesty's Privy Council in England.

ISSUES AND CHALLENGES:

- Combating money laundering in the burgeoning offshore banking industry is an ongoing government challenge.

- With more than 60 percent of the economy based on tourism, slowdowns in the travel and recreation industry dramatically affect the island nation.

- The Bahamas has been a key transport point for smuggling cocaine, marijuana, and illegal migrants to Europe and the United States.

- Per capita income ranks among the world's top 30, but most of the wealth is concentrated among affluent professionals in the islands' banking and commercial centers.

HOW THE GOVERNMENT WORKS

LEGISLATIVE BRANCH
National Parliament
Bicameral Parliament

Senate
Composed of 16 members appointed for five-years by governor-general: nine on advice of prime minister; four on advice of opposition leader; three on advice of prime minister and opposition leader.

House of Assembly
Composed of 40 members elected to five-year terms from single-member districts by direct popular vote. Holds power of the purse.

Regional Governments
Eighteen districts administered by appointed commissioners.

EXECUTIVE BRANCH
British Monarch
Head of state. Ceremonial role.

Governor-general
Appointed by British monarch to represent him or her after elections.

Prime Minister
Leader of House's majority party or coalition; appointed by governor-general following elections. Serves as head of government; presides over cabinet.

Cabinet
At least nine members of Parliament, including prime minister; appointed by governor-general on advice of prime minister. Oversees government operations; drafts legislation.

JUDICIAL BRANCH
Privy Council in London
Final tribunal for appeals.

Court of Appeal
Highest Bahamian court of appeal. Composed of president and two judges, all appointed by governor-general.

Supreme Court
Hears cases from lower courts. Composed of chief justice and 11 judges, all appointed by governor-general.

Magistrates' Courts
Adjudicates civil and minor criminal cases.

ICELAND

OFFICIAL NAME: REPUBLIC OF ICELAND

Parliament

Akureyri   Húsavík

Akranes   ATLANTIC
REYKJAVÍK   OCEAN

Hafnarfjördhur
Selfoss   Egilsstadhir

Vestmannaeyjar

Norwegian Sea

0   50 km
0   50 miles

POPULATION: 281,000
CAPITAL: REYKJAVIK
AREA: 39,768 SQ. MILES (102,999 SQ. KM)
INDEPENDENCE: 1944
CONSTITUTION: 1944

ICELAND, "land of ice" was settled in the 9th century by Norse voyagers and ruled by Denmark from 1380 to 1944.

RELIGION: Evangelical Lutheran 93%, Other Christian 1%, Nonreligious 6%

OFFICIAL LANGUAGE: Icelandic

REGIONS OR PROVINCES: 8 regions; divided into 23 counties, 15 independent towns and 4 districts.

DEPENDENT TERRITORIES: None

MEDIA: No political censorship exists in national media

NEWSPAPERS: There are 4 daily newspapers— Iceland has one of the highest per capita newspaper circulations in the world

TV: 11 services: 1 state-owned, 10 independent

RADIO: 17 services: 1 state-owned, 16 independent

SUFFRAGE: 18 years of age; universal

LEGAL SYSTEM: Civil law based on Danish legal traditions; no ICJ jurisdiction

WORLD ORGANIZATIONS: Australia Group, BIS, CBSS, CCC, CE, EAPC, EBRD, ECE, EFTA, FAO, IAEA, IBRD, ICAO, ICC, ICFTU, ICRM, IDA, IEA (observer), IFAD, IFC, IFRCS, IHO, ILO, IMF, IMO, Interpol, IOC, ISO, ITU, NATO, NC, NEA, NIB, OECD, OPCW, OSCE, PCA, UN, UNCTAD, UNESCO, UNMIBH, UNMIK, UNU, UPU, WEU (associate), WHO, WIPO, WMO, WTrO

POLITICAL PARTIES: IP—Independence Party, ULP—United Left Party, PP—Progressive Party, L-GA—Left-Green Alliance, LP—Liberal Party

ETHNIC GROUPS:

Other 5%   Danish 1%

Icelandic 94%

NATIONAL ECONOMICS

WORLD GNP RANKING: 91st

GNP PER CAPITA: $30,390

INFLATION: 5.2%

BALANCE OF PAYMENTS (BALANCE OF TRADE): -$851 million

EXCHANGE RATES / U.S. DLR.: 84.7-102.9 ICELANDIC KRONUR

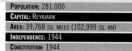

500   FIMM HUNDRUD KRONUR
SEÐLABANKI ÍSLANDS

OFFICIAL CURRENCY: ICELANDIC KRONA

GOVERNMENT SPENDING (% OF GDP)

DEFENSE (N/A)

EDUCATION 5.4%

HEALTH 7.4%

0   5   10   15

NUMBER OF CONFLICTS OVER LAST 25 YEARS

	1	2-5	5+
Violent changes in government	○	○	○
Civil wars	○	○	○
International wars	○	○	○
Foreign intervention	○	○	○

● Despite being a member of NATO, Iceland has no armed forces.

NOTABLE WARS AND INSURGENCIES: None

AFTER THEY SETTLED ON ICELAND in the 9th century, the Norse established a parliament, the Althing in 930, and Iceland then remained an independent republic until forming a union with Norway in 1262. Norway's union with Denmark in 1380 made Iceland a Danish dependency, until the 1918 Act of Union recognized it as a sovereign state represented by the Danish crown in foreign affairs and defense. German occupation of Denmark in 1940 dissolved the union between the two countries and left Iceland without defense. The United States of America assumed responsibility for Iceland's defense and, upon the creation of NATO, entered a bilateral defense agreement. Under this, the US maintains a military presence in Iceland in exchange for access to the NATO Naval Air Station in Keflavik.

> Iceland has the oldest parliament in the world, established in 930.

Executive duties are divided between two officials: the president and the prime minister. Icelandic presidents, who run as individuals without ties to political parties, are often re-elected for several terms. They mainly perform ceremonial functions previously carried out by the Danish king. Presidential powers are limited to appointing the prime minister and veto power—refusal to sign a proposed law forces a referendum on the proposal. The prime minister and Cabinet carry out most executive functions. Iceland's unicameral Parliament is the most powerful and influential of the three branches of government. It can make law on any subject within constitutional boundaries, dissolve and establish governments, and alter budgets.

Much of Iceland's political history has been dominated by its coalition governments. During 1992 the main issue under national discussion was whether or not to join the EU. A compromise was reached giving Iceland access to EU markets through the EEA (European Economic Area). Since 1995, a coalition of the conservative Independence Party and the rural-based Progressive Party has held a comfortable majority in the Parliament. Left-wing attempts at establishing coalitions to win a majority in the Parliament have been hindered by differing views on foreign policy.

ISSUES AND CHALLENGES:

● International disputes with nearby maritime countries center around fishing rights that are vitally important to Iceland. These include a dispute with Denmark and Britain regarding the boundary agreement of the Rockall continental shelf, and a dispute with Denmark over the Faroe Islands' fisheries' median line boundary.

● With over 70 percent of export earnings derived from fishing, Iceland must diversify economically.

● Iceland has few social problems. It has the world's highest literacy rate (99.9 percent) and the world's lowest infant mortality rate.

HOW THE GOVERNMENT WORKS

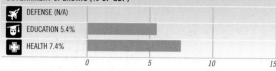

LEGISLATIVE BRANCH

Althing
(Parliament)
Unicameral Parliament
Composed of 63 members directly elected to four-year terms by proportional representation from eight districts. Amends and enacts budget; makes laws on topics it chooses; elects members of national boards and committees; may remove prime minister and Cabinet with no-confidence vote.

Regional Governments
Twenty-three counties, 15 towns and 4 districts; subdivided into 105 municipalities.

EXECUTIVE BRANCH

President
Elected to four-year term by direct popular vote. Serves as head of state. May dissolve Parliament on advice of prime minister.

Prime Minister
Appointed by president following elections. Serves as head of government; presides over Cabinet.

Cabinet
Composed of 12 members appointed by prime minister, approved by Parliament. Oversees government; drafts bills.

JUDICIAL BRANCH

Supreme Court
Hears civil and criminal cases. Rules on constitutionality of laws. Composed of judges appointed for life by president on advice of minister of justice.

District Courts
Eight courts; hear civil and criminal cases.

High Court of State
Holds impeachment proceedings for Cabinet ministers; has never convened.

Labor Court
Tries cases involving trade unions and employer associations.

BARBADOS

OFFICIAL NAME: BARBADOS

Map showing: Speightstown, Bathsheba, Holetown, Marchfield, BRIDGETOWN, Hastings, Oistins, Parliament. Atlantic Ocean. 0–5 km / 0–5 miles.

POPULATION: 268,000
CAPITAL: Bridgetown
AREA: 166 sq. miles (430 sq. km)
INDEPENDENCE: 1966
CONSTITUTION: 1966

BARBADOS'S NAME comes from the Portuguese for "bearded ones", given by explorer Pedro a Campos on seeing the island's fig trees.

RELIGION: Anglican 40%, Pentecostal 8%, Methodist 7%, Roman Catholic 4%, Other 24%, Non-religious 17%

OFFICIAL LANGUAGE: English

REGIONS OR PROVINCES: 11 parishes and 1 city.

DEPENDENT TERRITORIES: None

MEDIA: No political censorship exists in the national media

NEWSPAPERS: There are 2 daily newspapers, both privately owned

TV: 1 state-owned service with subscription option

RADIO: 3 services: 1 state-owned, 2 independent

SUFFRAGE: 18 years of age; universal

LEGAL SYSTEM: English common law; accepts ICJ jurisdiction

WORLD ORGANIZATIONS: ACP, C, Caricom, CCC, CDB, ECLAC, FAO, G-77, IADB, IBRD, ICAO, ICFTU, ICRM, IDA, IFAD, IFC, IFRCS, ILO, IMF, IMO, Interpol, IOC, ISO, ITU, LAES, NAM, OAS, OPANAL, UN, UNCTAD, UNESCO, UNIDO, UPU, WFTU, WHO, WIPO, WMO, WTrO

POLITICAL PARTIES: BLP—Barbados Labour Party, DLP—Democratic Labour Party

ETHNIC GROUPS:
Asian and mixed 6%
White 4%
Black 90%

NATIONAL ECONOMICS

WORLD GNP RANKING: 133rd

GNP PER CAPITA: $9,250

INFLATION: 2.4%

BALANCE OF PAYMENTS (BALANCE OF TRADE): -$126 million

EXCHANGE RATES / U.S. DLR.: 1.99 BARBADOS DOLLARS

OFFICIAL CURRENCY: BARBADOS DOLLAR

GOVERNMENT SPENDING (% OF GDP)

✈	DEFENSE	0.5%
🎓	EDUCATION	7.2%
✚	HEALTH	4.5%

0   5   10   15

NUMBER OF CONFLICTS OVER LAST 25 YEARS

	1	2-5	5+
Violent changes in government	○	○	○
Civil wars	○	○	○
International wars	○	○	○
Foreign intervention	○	○	○

● Barbados hosts the Regional Security System, established in 1982, which acts as a multinational security force for its Caribbean members.

NOTABLE WARS AND INSURGENCIES: None

GREAT BRITAIN RULED BARBADOS FROM 1627, when British settlers discovered the uninhabited island and populated it with slaves to work the sugar crop they then introduced. In 1966, Barbados negotiated its independence at a constitutional conference. It has the third-oldest legislative body in the Western Hemisphere and is one of the world's best-governed countries. Britain's abolition of slavery emancipated Barbados' slaves early in the 19th century, and political, social, and labor unrest in the early 20th century led to social and political reforms supported by the British government. Further emancipation took place in 1951, when universal suffrage was adopted. Today, despite racial and class stratification—most economic and political power is still held by whites— Barbados' racial and class tensions seldom turn violent, and many blacks have become professionals and civil servants. The political parties have few ideological disagreements, and elections turn on personal, rather than political, differences among candidates.

Located northeast of Trinidad in the Atlantic Ocean, Barbados is the most easterly of the West Indian Windward Islands. From its centuries-long association with Great Britain and its maintenance of that country's traditions and institutions, it is probably the most English of the Caribbean countries and is often referred to as "little England" by its neighbors. Barbados' parliamentary democracy is based on that of the United Kingdom, and the British monarch is the head of state. The monarch's island representative, the governor-general, appoints as prime minister the leader of the ruling political party in the House of Assembly. The governor-general also appoints the 21 members of the Senate. House of Assembly members are popularly elected by 28 constituencies every five years.

Barbados' independent judicial system is based on Great Britain's, and the court of final appeal is the Judicial Committee of Her Majesty's Privy Council in London whose decisions are binding on all parties. The country's supreme court is composed of the High Court and the Court of Appeal. Barbados' history of enlightened, democratically oriented rule has helped give it one of the highest standards of living in the Caribbean. There is a push to transform it into a republic while retaining its membership of the Commonwealth.

ISSUES AND CHALLENGES:

● The country's biggest challenge is how to promote economic growth through agricultural diversification, light industry (especially software and computer services), and tourism. In the 1990s, tourism and manufacturing outpaced the sugar industry. An emphasis on manufacturing has made Barbados one of the world's most economically successful new countries.

HOW THE GOVERNMENT WORKS

LEGISLATIVE BRANCH
Parliament
Bicameral Parliament

Senate
Composed of 21 members appointed to five-year terms by governor-general: 12 on advice of prime minister; two on advice of opposition leader; seven at governor-general's discretion.

House of Assembly
Composed of 28 members directly elected to five-year terms by proportional representation.

Regional Governments
Eleven parishes and 1 city administered by central government.

EXECUTIVE BRANCH
British Monarch
Head of state. Ceremonial role.

Governor-general
Appointed by British monarch to represent him or her following elections.

Prime Minister
Leader of House's majority party or coalition; appointed by governor-general following elections. Serves as head of government; presides over Cabinet.

Cabinet
Composed of members appointed by governor-general on advice of prime minister. Oversees government operations.

JUDICIAL BRANCH
Privy Council in London
Final tribunal for appeals.

Supreme Court of the Judicature
Divided into two courts: High Court and Court of Appeal. Judges appointed by governor-general on advice of Service Commissions for the Judicial and Legal Services.

Court of Appeal
Hears appeals of High Court decisions. Composed of four judges.

High Court
Hears civil and criminal cases. Composed of four judges.

Magistrates' Courts
Adjudicates civil and minor criminal cases.

BELIZE

OFFICIAL NAME: BELIZE

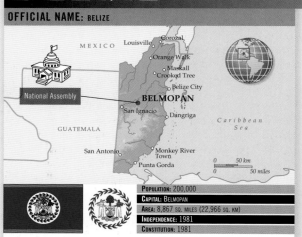

POPULATION: 200,000
CAPITAL: Belmopan
AREA: 8,867 SQ. MILES (22,966 SQ. KM)
INDEPENDENCE: 1981
CONSTITUTION: 1981

BELIZE'S name is probably derived from the Mayan word *beliz*, meaning "muddy water".

RELIGION: Roman Catholic 49.6%, Protestant 27% (Anglican 5.3%, Methodist 3.5%, Mennonite 4.1%, Seventh-Day Adventist 5.2%, Pentecostal 7.4%, Jehovah's Witnesses 1.5%), None 9.4%, Other 14%

OFFICIAL LANGUAGE: English

REGIONS OR PROVINCES: 6 districts

DEPENDENT TERRITORIES: None

MEDIA: No political censorship exists in national media

NEWSPAPERS: There are no daily newspapers

TV: 9 services: 1 state-owned and 8 independent

RADIO: 6 services: 1 state-owned and 5 independent

SUFFRAGE: 18 years of age; universal

LEGAL SYSTEM: English common law; no ICJ jurisdiction

WORLD ORGANIZATIONS: ACP, C, Caricom, CDB, ECLAC, FAO, G-77, IADB, IBRD, ICAO, ICFTU, ICRM, IDA, IFAD, IFC, IFRCS, ILO, IMF, IMO, Interpol, IOC, IOM, ITU, LAES, NAM, OAS, OPANAL, UN, UNCTAD, UNESCO, UNIDO, UPU, WCL, WHO, WIPO, WMO, WTrO

POLITICAL PARTIES: PUP—People's United Party, UDP—United Democratic Party

ETHNIC GROUPS:

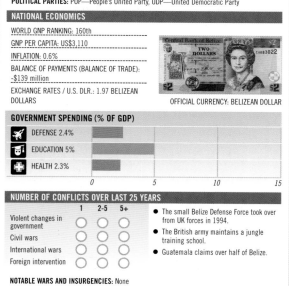

- Asian Indian 4%
- Other 4%
- Garifuna 7%
- Maya 11%
- Mestizo 44%
- Creole 30%

NATIONAL ECONOMICS

WORLD GNP RANKING: 160th

GNP PER CAPITA: US$3,110

INFLATION: 0.6%

BALANCE OF PAYMENTS (BALANCE OF TRADE): -$139 million

EXCHANGE RATES / U.S. DLR.: 1.97 BELIZEAN DOLLARS

OFFICIAL CURRENCY: BELIZEAN DOLLAR

GOVERNMENT SPENDING (% OF GDP)

- ✈ DEFENSE 2.4%
- 🎓 EDUCATION 5%
- ✚ HEALTH 2.3%

0   5   10   15

NUMBER OF CONFLICTS OVER LAST 25 YEARS

	1	2-5	5+
Violent changes in government	○	○	○
Civil wars	○	○	○
International wars	○	○	○
Foreign intervention	○	○	○

- The small Belize Defense Force took over from UK forces in 1994.
- The British army maintains a jungle training school.
- Guatemala claims over half of Belize.

NOTABLE WARS AND INSURGENCIES: None

ANCIENT RUINS MARK THE LANDSCAPE of Belize, indicating a past in which the advanced Mayan civilization flourished. Spain lay claim to the area in the 16th century, but the first Europeans to settle here were the British in the 17th century. Spain made several attempts to reclaim the area before it became a full British colony—called the British Honduras—in 1862. It became a self-governing nation with the name Belize in 1973, and won full independence from the UK in 1981. A member of the Commonwealth of Nations, Belize is a parliamentary democracy with a well-developed two-party system. The People's United Party (PUP) dominated politics from the 1950s until 1984, when the more conservative, opposition United Democratic Party (UDP) won elections and came to power. National power and leadership alternated between the two parties every five years until 2003, when Belizeans returned the PUP to power for a second consecutive term.

Historically, a major issue for both parties has been the often heated territorial dispute with Guatemala, which borders Belize on the south and west. Since the 19th century Guatemala has claimed ownership of more than half of Belize and it refused to recognize Belize as an independent and sovereign nation until 1991. The issue returned to the forefront in 2000. A draft resolution to end the dispute was announced in September 2002, with final acceptance required of voters in both countries via referenda.

Belize was the last Central American country to gain independence.

The economy, immigration policies, charges of government corruption, and taxes are also prominent issues. The PUP's 1998 victory in the 29-member House of Representatives grew out of voters' dissatisfaction with the UDP government's tax policies. Belize's parliament, or National Assembly, also includes a 12-member appointed Senate, which is considered the weaker house.

ISSUES AND CHALLENGES:

- The population is racially and ethnically very diverse, and the granting of citizenship to foreigners is one of the main political issues often in debate. The dominant ethnic group in the country is Mestizo, of mixed Mayan and European descent, followed by Creole, of Afro-European ancestry and Mayan with the remainder coming from Europe, China, East India, the Middle East, and North America.

- Protecting natural resources is an issue that unites Belizeans, who have set aside more than 40 percent of their country as parks and preserves.

- The logging industry and tourist developments have resulted in deforestation of the tropical forests. Mahogany is now considered endangered and requires a certificate of origin before it may be exported.

- An international dispute with Guatemala over the southern half of Belize is ongoing. Guatemalan squatters continue to settle along the border despite an agreement in 2000.

HOW THE GOVERNMENT WORKS

LEGISLATIVE BRANCH
House of Assembly
Bicameral Parliament

Senate
Composed of eight members appointed to five-year terms by governor-general: five on advice of prime minister; two on advice of opposition leader; one on advice of Belize Advisory Council.

House of Representatives
Composed of 29 members directly elected to five-year terms from single-member districts. Initiates all money bills.

Regional Governments
Six towns governed by elected boards; Belize City administered by elected council.

EXECUTIVE BRANCH
British Monarch
Head of state. Ceremonial role.

Governor-general
Appointed by British monarch to represent him or her following elections.

Prime Minister
Leader of House's largest party; appointed by governor-general following elections. Serves as head of government; presides over cabinet.

Cabinet
Composed of 13 majority-party members of Parliament appointed by governor-general on advice of prime minister. Oversees government operations; formulates national policy.

JUDICIAL BRANCH
Privy Council in London
Final tribunal for appeals.

Supreme Court
Hears appeals and original cases. Chief justice appointed by governor-general on advice of prime minister and opposition leader; two judges appointed by governor-general on advice of Public Service Commission.

Court of Appeal
Lower-court appeals. Four judges appointed by governor-general on advice of prime minister and opposition leader.

Summary Court
Hears criminal cases.

District Court
Hears civil cases.

Magistrates' Courts

VANUATU

OFFICIAL NAME: REPUBLIC OF VANUATU

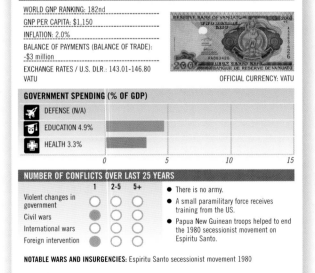

POPULATION: 200,000
CAPITAL: Port Vila
AREA: 4,710 SQ. MILES (12,200 SQ. KM)
INDEPENDENCE: 1980
CONSTITUTION: 1980

VANUATU, originally named the New Hebrides by Captain Cook in 1774, was renamed on independence in 1980.

RELIGION: Presbyterian 37%, Anglican 15%, Roman Catholic 15%, Indigenous beliefs 8%, Seventh-day Adventist 6%, Other 19%

OFFICIAL LANGUAGES: Bislama, English, and French

REGIONS OR PROVINCES: 6 provinces

DEPENDENT TERRITORIES: None

MEDIA: No political censorship exists in national media

NEWSPAPERS: There is one daily newspaper, the *Port Vila Presse*, published in French and English.

TV: 1 state-owned limited service

RADIO: 1 state-owned service

SUFFRAGE: 18 years of age; universal

LEGAL SYSTEM: French and English common law; no ICJ jurisdiction

WORLD ORGANIZATIONS: ACCT, ACP, AsDB, C, ESCAP, FAO, G-77, IBRD, ICAO, ICFTU, ICRM, IDA, IFC, IFRCS, IMF, IMO, IOC, ITU, NAM, Sparteca, SPC, SPF, UN, UNCTAD, UNESCO, UNIDO, UNMIBH, UPU, WFTU, WHO, WMO, WTrO (observer)

POLITICAL PARTIES: UMP—Union of Moderate Parties, VP—Vanua'aku Pati, NUP—National United Party, Ind—Independents, MPP—Melanesian Progressive Party

ETHNIC GROUPS:

Polynesian 3%
Other 3%
Melanesian 94%

NATIONAL ECONOMICS

WORLD GNP RANKING: 182nd

GNP PER CAPITA: $1,150

INFLATION: 2.0%

BALANCE OF PAYMENTS (BALANCE OF TRADE): -$3 million

EXCHANGE RATES / U.S. DLR.: 143.01-146.80 VATU

OFFICIAL CURRENCY: VATU

GOVERNMENT SPENDING (% OF GDP)

✈ DEFENSE (N/A)			
🎓 EDUCATION 4.9%			
➕ HEALTH 3.3%			

0   5   10   15

NUMBER OF CONFLICTS OVER LAST 25 YEARS

	1	2-5	5+
Violent changes in government	○	○	○
Civil wars	●	○	○
International wars	○	○	○
Foreign intervention	●	○	○

- There is no army.
- A small paramilitary force receives training from the US.
- Papua New Guinean troops helped to end the 1980 secessionist movement on Espiritu Santo.

NOTABLE WARS AND INSURGENCIES: Espiritu Santo secessionist movement 1980

LOCATED IN THE SOUTH PACIFIC, Vanuatu is spread over 800 miles (1,300 km) and consists of 82 mostly mountainous and volcanic islands. Although 67 of the islands are inhabited, recent urbanization has resulted in 80 percent of the population living on the 12 main islands.

Vanuatu has a unique history as a colony of two nations. France and the United Kingdom came to an agreement early on to administer the islands jointly as a condominium government, the British-French Condominium, a clumsy structure, in which the French and British commissioners were responsible for their own nationals and exercised joint authority over the islanders. It was only in the 1970s that Vanuatu saw the formation of the first political party. This marked the beginning of the process toward independence, especially after the Vanua'aku Pati (VP), originally formed as the New Hebrides National Party, came into existence. The condominium arrangement lasted until 1980, when Vanuatu became an independent state some 40 years after the nationals had began to challenge the current order and foreign domination.

Vanuatu's modern political system operates under a parliamentary democracy. However, due to its complicated dual colony history, many observers describe its current politics as chaotic. The country's political struggles, which are endemic both between and within party alliances, reflect the divisions between the English speakers, who are in the minority, and the French speakers. In the 1970s, for example, English-speaking leaders such as Walter Lini, the charismatic man who founded the VP, traditionally favored independence, while French-speaking leaders favored the annexation of the entire country by France. In fact, real power does not lie in the institutions of government but in the hands of those elected with the personal skills necessary to build coalitions and create a consensus. When Lini's party leadership collapsed in 1991, after 11 years as prime minister, he formed another alliance between the Union of Moderate Parties (UMP) and the National United Party (NUP). Lini is recognized as one of the most important names in Vanuatu's politics to this day. Lini died in 1999, just one year after new coalitions were established.

ISSUES AND CHALLENGES:

- Vanuatu's main challenge to this day is its history and dual colony tradition. The condominium system created by the French and the British lasted so long and left such strong roots that the current structure, struggling to find a balance, is still very volatile, and unstable. In 2001, Prime Minister Barak Sope, who led an anti-VP coalition, was ousted by the Parliament who voted in a VP leader, Edward Natapei, and a new coalition with the UMP.

- Classified by the UN as the least developed country in the world, Vanuatu is heavily dependent on financial aid.

HOW THE GOVERNMENT WORKS

LEGISLATIVE BRANCH

Parlement/Parliament
Unicameral Parliament
Composed of 52 members elected to four-year terms by popular vote. May remove prime minister and cabinet with no-confidence vote.

National Council of Chiefs
Composed of traditional chiefs elected by district councils of chiefs. Meets at least once a year; no legislative powers; advises government on matters concerning ni-Vanuatu culture and language.

EXECUTIVE BRANCH

President
Elected to four-year term by electoral college of Parliament and elected regional councils. Serves as head of state. May dissolve Parliament on advice of prime minister.

Prime Minister
Leader of Parliament's majority party or coalition; elected by Parliament following elections. Serves as head of government; presides over cabinet.

Council of Ministers
Limited to 13 members of Parliament; appointed by prime minister.

JUDICIAL BRANCH

Supreme Court
Highest court with unlimited jurisdiction in civil and criminal cases. Composed of chief justice and three judges appointed by president on advice of prime minister, opposition leader and Judicial Service Commission.

Court of Appeal
Hears lower-court appeals; rulings are final. Composed of two or more Supreme Court judges.

Magistrates' Courts
Try routine cases.

Village Courts
Hear customary law cases; chiefs preside as judges.

SAMOA

OFFICIAL NAME: INDEPENDENT STATE OF SAMOA

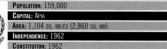

POPULATION: 159,000	
CAPITAL: APIA	
AREA: 1,104 SQ. MILES (2,860 SQ. KM)	
INDEPENDENCE: 1962	
CONSTITUTION: 1962	

SAMOA'S name is derived from the Samoan words *sa* (meaning "sacred") and *moa* (the meaning of which varies according to tribal legends; usually accepted as "center").

RELIGION: Christian 99.7% (about one-half of population associated with the London Missionary Society; includes Congregational, Roman Catholic, Methodist, Latter-Day Saints, Seventh-Day Adventist), 0.3% Other.

OFFICIAL LANGUAGES: English and Samoan

REGIONS OR PROVINCES: 11 districts

DEPENDENT TERRITORIES: None

MEDIA: No political censorship exists in the national media

NEWSPAPERS: There are no daily newspapers

TV: 1 state-owned service

RADIO: 3 services: 1 state-owned, 2 independent

SUFFRAGE: 21 years of age; universal

LEGAL SYSTEM: Customary and English common law; no ICJ jurisdiction

WORLD ORGANIZATIONS: ACP, AsDB, C, ESCAP, FAO, G-77, IBRD, ICAO, ICFTU, ICRM, IDA, IFAD, IFC, IFRCS, IMF, IMO, IOC, ITU, OPCW (signatory), Sparteca, SPC, SPF, UN, UNCTAD, UNESCO, UPU, WHO, WIPO, WMO, WTrO (observer)

POLITICAL PARTIES: HRPP—Human Rights Protection Party, SNDP—Samoan National Development Party, Ind—Independents

ETHNIC GROUPS:

Euronesian 9%
Other 1%
Polynesian 90%

NATIONAL ECONOMICS

WORLD GNP RANKING: 180th

GNP PER CAPITA: $1,450

INFLATION: 1%

BALANCE OF PAYMENTS (BALANCE OF TRADE): -$19 million

EXCHANGE RATES / U.S. DLR.: 3.339–3.558 TALA

OFFICIAL CURRENCY: TALA

GOVERNMENT SPENDING (% of GDP)

✈ DEFENSE 0%		
🏛 EDUCATION 4.2%		
✚ HEALTH 4.8%		

0   5   10   15

NUMBER OF CONFLICTS OVER LAST 25 YEARS

	1	2-5	5+
Violent changes in government	○	○ ○ ○	○ ○
Civil wars	○	○ ○ ○	○ ○
International wars	○	○ ○ ○	○ ○
Foreign intervention	○	○ ○ ○	○ ○

- No compulsory national military service.
- No armed forces; New Zealand provides defense.
- The chiefs provide internal security.

NOTABLE WARS AND INSURGENCIES: None

LONG KNOWN AS WESTERN SAMOA, in 1997 the nine sister isles that comprise this Polynesian nation dropped "Western" from their name to become simply Samoa and distinguish themselves from the neighboring United States territory of American Samoa. Ruled for decades by New Zealand, in 1962 Samoa became the first Pacific island country to gain its independence. Its parliamentary government blends British practices with Samoan tribal customs.

The islands of Samoa were first settled by Polynesians about 3,000 years ago. Dutch and French expeditions arrived from the early 1700s and were followed in the 19th century by English, American, and German missionaries and merchants. In 1899 the islands were divided into two territories: American Samoa and German-controlled Western Samoa. Following World War I, Germany relinquished its islands to New Zealand, which administered them under the League of Nations and later as a United Nations trusteeship. Samoa now maintains an alliance with New Zealand under the Treaty of Friendship, which also provides for Samoa's defense. Ethnic Samoans belong to the second largest Polynesian group, after the Maoris. The Samoan way of life, *fa'a Samoa*, is based on the extended family structure.

The constitution fuses democratic ideals with the traditional system of chiefs, or *matai*. Upon independence, Samoa appointed its two highest-ranking *matai* as lifetime heads of state. One died the following year. Upon the death of the surviving *matai*, Malietoa Tanumafili II, a successor will be named to a five-year term by Samoa's Legislative Assembly. The constitution also establishes a prime minister, cabinet, and the elected unicameral Legislative Assembly, or Fono a Faipule.

Disputes over the legitimacy of the traditional *matai* system gave rise in the 1970s to political parties. Lacking clearly defined ideologies, these parties garner allegiance mainly through personalities, political pragmatism, and patronage. The Human Rights Protection Party (HRPP) has held the majority in the Legislative Assembly since 1982, though its autocratic style and restrictions on the press have provoked periodic outbursts of civil protest.

ISSUES AND CHALLENGES:

- The constitutional requirement that the next head of state be among the highest ranking *matai* in the country is a topic of regular dispute. Also, of over 25,000 *matai* in Samoa, only 5 percent are women; so limiting the role of women in Samoan politics.

- There is a need to reduce poverty and improve the quality of education and health care.

- Many young people are rebelling against the traditional *fa'a Samoa*, preferring instead a modern Western lifestyle. There is a high rate of suicide among the young.

- A lack of jobs has resulted in high emigration to New Zealand and the United States.

HOW THE GOVERNMENT WORKS

LEGISLATIVE BRANCH

Fono a Faipule
(Legislative Assembly)
Unicameral Parliament
Composed of 49 members elected to five-year terms by direct popular vote; 47 by Samoans; two by descendants of Europeans. Only matai (chiefs) may run for Samoan seats.

Regional Governments
11 districts
360 village councils (fonos) main authority in rural areas.

EXECUTIVE BRANCH

Chief of State
Position held by *matai*; appointed for life. Parliament elects successor.

Prime Minister
Parliament member supported by majority of legislative colleagues; appointed to five-year term by chief of state. Serves as head of government.

Cabinet
Composed of 12 Parliament members; appointed by chief of state on advice of prime minister, approved by Parliament. Oversees government operations.

JUDICIAL BRANCH

Supreme Court
Highest court; hears civil and criminal cases; rules on constitutionality of laws. Chief justice appointed by chief of state with approval of prime minister.

Court of Appeal
Rules on lower-court appeals. Composed of judges appointed by Judicial Service Commission.

Magistrates' Courts
Adjudicate most civil and criminal cases.

Land and Titles Court
Hears disputes over land tenure and Samoan names and titles.

Village Courts
Resolve village disputes; *matai* preside as judges.

ST. LUCIA

OFFICIAL NAME: SAINT LUCIA

Gros Islet
CASTRIES
Parliament
Canaries · *The Pitons* · Praslin · ATLANTIC OCEAN
Soufrière
Caribbean Sea
Micoud
Vieux Fort
0 5 km
0 5 miles

POPULATION: 156,300	
CAPITAL: CASTRIES	
AREA: 239 SQ. MILES (620 SQ. KM)	
INDEPENDENCE: 1979	
CONSTITUTION: 1979	

ST. LUCIA is so called as the island was first sighted by Columbus on St. Lucia's Day (December 22) 1502.

RELIGION: Roman Catholic 90%, Other 10%

OFFICIAL LANGUAGE: English

REGIONS OR PROVINCES: 11 quarters

DEPENDENT TERRITORIES: None

MEDIA: No political censorship exists in national media

NEWSPAPERS: There are no daily newspapers

TV: 4 independent services

RADIO: 4 services: 1 state-owned, 3 independent

SUFFRAGE: 18 years of age; universal

LEGAL SYSTEM: English common law; no ICJ jurisdiction

WORLD ORGANIZATIONS: ACCT, ACP, C, Caricom, CDB, ECLAC, FAO, G-77, IBRD, ICAO, ICFTU, ICRM, IDA, IFAD, IFC, IFRCS, ILO, IMF, IMO, Interpol, IOC, ISO (correspondent), ITU, NAM, OAS, OECS, OPANAL, OPCW, UN, UNCTAD, UNESCO, UNIDO, UPU, WCL, WFTU, WHO, WIPO, WMO, WTrO

POLITICAL PARTIES: SLP—St Lucia Labour Party, UWP—United Workers' Party

ETHNIC GROUPS:

East Indian 3%
White 1%
Mixed 6%
Black 90%

NATIONAL ECONOMICS

WORLD GNP RANKING: 165th

GNP PER CAPITA: $4,120

INFLATION: 5.4%

BALANCE OF PAYMENTS (BALANCE OF TRADE): -$80 million

EXCHANGE RATES / U.S. DLR.: 2.7 EASTERN CARIBBEAN DOLLARS

OFFICIAL CURRENCY: E. CARIB. DOLLAR

GOVERNMENT SPENDING (% of GDP)

✈ DEFENSE (N/A)	
🎓 EDUCATION 9.8%	
✚ HEALTH 2.4%	

0   5   10   15

NUMBER OF CONFLICTS OVER LAST 25 YEARS

	1	2-5	5+
Violent changes in government	○	○	○
Civil wars	○	○	○
International wars	○	○	○
Foreign intervention	○	○	

- The police force is supported by a small paramilitary unit.
- Training is provided by the US and the UK.
- No compulsory military service.

NOTABLE WARS AND INSURGENCIES: None

SPANISH EXPLORERS NEAR the beginning of the 16th century were the first Europeans to set foot on St. Lucia's shores. However, later it was the British and French, lured by a lucrative sugar industry, who competed relentlessly for ownership of the island. Fourteen times the two powers exchanged control of St. Lucia before Britain took possession in 1814 and ruled the island until it gained independence in 1979. With a population descended from a mixture of Africans, Caribs and Europeans, St. Lucia has not suffered the racial tensions encountered by so many other nations. St. Lucians today enjoy self-government under a Westminster-style parliamentary democracy.

Although still under British colonial governance, St. Lucia gradually advanced toward self-rule throughout the 20th century, beginning with a 1924 constitution granting election to a minority of seats in the previously all-appointed legislative council. In 1951, islanders won universal adult suffrage and the right to elect a majority of the council. Soon after, a ministerial government was established, and St. Lucia became a member of the West Indies Federation, a semi-autonomous dependency of the UK. After the federation collapsed in 1962, St. Lucia became an associated state of the UK, handling its own internal government operations but leaving its external affairs and defense to Britain.

With full independence, St. Lucians ratified a constitution establishing an executive branch composed of a governor-general, prime minister, and cabinet, and a legislative branch consisting of the bicameral Parliament. St. Lucia's independent judiciary is composed of district courts and a High Court with appeals decided by the Eastern Caribbean Court of Appeals and ultimately the Privy Council in London. Lacking a standing military force, St. Lucia relies on its police force and coast guard for defense.

Until recently, the United Workers Party (UWP) dominated politics. From independence until 1997, it governed for all but a three-year period. The St. Lucia Labor Party (SLP) has controlled Parliament and the prime minister's office since 1997. A new bill passed in 1998 allows the occasional use of Creole in Parliament.

ISSUES AND CHALLENGES:

- Following the successful US-led campaign to end preferential access for Caribbean bananas to EU markets, many fear that St. Lucia will be unable to compete with South and Central American banana producers.

- Business pressures to bolster tourism outweigh environmental concerns, as was evidenced by the building of a luxury hotel on an ecologically important site.

- Like most other Caribbean nations, St. Lucia agreed to cut ties with the UK and plans to replace the London Privy Council with the Caribbean Court of Justice.

HOW THE GOVERNMENT WORKS

LEGISLATIVE BRANCH

Parliament
Bicameral Parliament

Senate
Composed of eleven members appointed to five-year terms by governor-general: six on advice of prime minister; three on advice of opposition leader; two on advice of religious, economic and social groups.

House of Assembly
Composed of 17 members elected to five-year terms by direct popular vote from single-member districts. May remove prime minister and cabinet with no-confidence vote.

Regional Governments
Elected town and village councils.

EXECUTIVE BRANCH

British Monarch
Head of state. Ceremonial role.

Governor-general
Appointed by British monarch to represent him or her following elections. May dissolve Parliament on request of prime minister or following no-confidence vote by House.

Prime Minister
Leader of Parliament's majority party or coalition; appointed by governor-general following elections. Head of government; oversees cabinet.

Vice-president
Appointed by prime minister

Cabinet
Composed of House members; appointed by prime minister.

JUDICIAL BRANCH

Privy Council in London
Final tribunal for appeals.

Eastern Caribbean Supreme Court
Highest court with unlimited jurisdiction. Based in St. Lucia; hears cases from nine Caribbean states.

High Court of St. Lucia

District Courts

St. Vincent & the Grenadines

Official Name: SAINT VINCENT AND THE GRENADINES

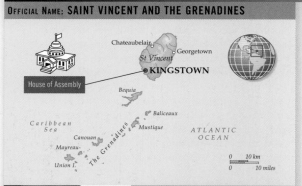

Population: 115,500	
Capital: Kingstown	
Area: 150 sq. miles (389 sq. km)	
Independence: 1979	
Constitution: 1979	

St. Vincent was sighted by Christopher Columbus on January 22, 1498. He named it after the Catholic saint whose feast falls on that day.

RELIGION: Anglican 42%, Methodist 20%, Roman Catholic 19%, Other 19%

OFFICIAL LANGUAGE: English

REGIONS OR PROVINCES: 6 parishes

DEPENDENT TERRITORIES: None

MEDIA: No political censorship exists in national media—freedom of the press is written into the constitution

NEWSPAPERS: There is one daily newspaper

TV: 1 state-owned service

RADIO: 1 state-owned service

SUFFRAGE: 18 years of age; universal

LEGAL SYSTEM: English common law; no ICJ jurisdiction

WORLD ORGANIZATIONS: ACP, C, Caricom, CDB, ECLAC, FAO, G-77, IBRD, ICAO, ICFTU, ICRM, IDA, IFAD, IFRCS, ILO, IMF, IMO, Interpol, IOC, ITU, OAS, OECS, OPANAL, OPCW (signatory), UN, UNCTAD, UNESCO, UNIDO, UPU, WCL, WFTU, WHO, WIPO, WTrO

POLITICAL PARTIES: ULP—Unity Labour Party, NDP—New Democratic Party

ETHNIC GROUPS:

- East Indian 6%
- Carib Amerindian 2%
- Other 7%
- Mixed 19%
- Black 66%

NATIONAL ECONOMICS

WORLD GNP RANKING: 176th

GNP PER CAPITA: $2,720

INFLATION: 0.2%

BALANCE OF PAYMENTS (BALANCE OF TRADE): -$66 million

EXCHANGE RATES / U.S. DLR.: 2.7 EASTERN CARIBBEAN DOLLARS

OFFICIAL CURRENCY: E. CARIB. DOLLAR

GOVERNMENT SPENDING (% OF GDP)

✈ DEFENSE (N/A)		
📚 EDUCATION 6.7%		
✚ HEALTH 4.2%		

0 — 5 — 10 — 15

NUMBER OF CONFLICTS OVER LAST 25 YEARS

	1	2-5	5+
Violent changes in government	○	○	○
Civil wars	○	○	○
International wars	○	○	○
Foreign intervention	○	○	○

- St. Vincent and the Grenadines has no army.
- A small police force, trained by the US and the UK, is part of the Regional Security System.

NOTABLE WARS AND INSURGENCIES: None

With its Carib Amerindian inhabitants aggressively fighting intrusion by outsiders, St. Vincent staved off European settlement until the 18th century. It also became the last of the Windward Islands to gain independence, casting off nearly three centuries of British colonial rule in 1979. Today, St. Vincent and its Grenadines sister isles together are a British-style parliamentary democracy with a society reliant on agriculture and up-market tourism.

The French were the first Europeans to occupy St. Vincent, harvesting coffee, tobacco, indigo, cotton, and sugar on plantations worked by African slaves. The French ceded the island to Great Britain in 1763 under the Treaty of Paris, took it back briefly, and then lost it permanently to the British in 1783. The new owners, however, were greeted by a fierce uprising by the island's "black Caribs"—descendants of unions between the original native inhabitants and escaped slaves. The British finally extinguished the revolt by deporting thousands of the resisters to the Honduran island of Roatan. Beginning with the establishment of a representative assembly in 1776, St. Vincent passed through various types of British governance, including a crown colony government installed in 1877, a legislative council created in 1925, and universal adult suffrage granted in 1951. Internal self-government emerged in 1969, as the country became a self-governing state under the British monarch. Full independence came in October 1979 A member today of the Commonwealth of Nations, St. Vincent now rules itself under a constitution that provides for a governor-general, prime minister, cabinet, unicameral legislature, and a judiciary rooted in British common law.

Backed by the island's black middle class, the St. Vincent Labor Party dominated politics through the mid-1980s with a conservative law-and-order agenda and pro-western foreign policy. Power subsequently shifted to the upstart New Democratic Party as it won four straight election victories. However, its control of the government ended with a crushing defeat in 2001, after St. Vincent voters gave 12 of the Parliament's 15 seats to the Unity Labor Party, a coalition composed of supporters of the St. Vincent Labor Party and the Movement for National Unity.

HOW THE GOVERNMENT WORKS

LEGISLATIVE BRANCH

House of Assembly
Unicameral Parliament
Composed of 21 members who serve five-year terms: 15 elected by direct popular vote; six appointed by governor-general, four on advice of prime minister, two on advice of opposition leader.

Regional Governments
Six parishes administered by central government.

EXECUTIVE BRANCH

British Monarch
Head of government. Ceremonial role.

Governor-general
Appointed by British monarch following elections.

Prime Minister
Leader of Parliament's majority party or coalition; appointed by governor-general following elections. Head of government; oversees cabinet; may call elections at any time.

Deputy Prime Minister
Appointed by governor-general on advice of prime minister.

Cabinet
Appointed by governor-general on advice of prime minister. Oversees government operations.

JUDICIAL BRANCH

Privy Council in London
Final tribunal for appeal.

Eastern Caribbean Supreme Court
Highest court with unlimited jurisdiction. Based in St. Lucia; hears cases from nine Caribbean states; one of court's judges sits in St. Vincent.

Magistrates' Courts
Eleven courts in three magisterial districts; adjudicate civil and minor criminal cases.

GRENADA

OFFICIAL NAME: GRENADA

POPULATION: 98,000	
CAPITAL: ST. GEORGE'S	
AREA: 131 SQ. MILES (340 SQ. KM)	
INDEPENDENCE: 1974	
CONSTITUTION: 1973	

GRENADA may have been named by Spanish sailors after the Spanish city Granada.

RELIGION: Roman Catholic 68%, Anglican 17%, Other 15%

OFFICIAL LANGUAGE: English

REGIONS OR PROVINCES: 6 parishes

DEPENDENT TERRITORIES: 1
(Carriacou and Petite Martinique)

MEDIA: No political censorship exists in national media

Newspapers: There are no daily newspapers

TV: 1 state-owned service

Radio: 3 services: 1 partly state-owned, 2 independent

SUFFRAGE: 18 years of age; universal

LEGAL SYSTEM: English common law; no ICJ jurisdiction

WORLD ORGANIZATIONS: ACP, C, Caricom, CDB, ECLAC, FAO, G-77, IBRD, ICAO, ICFTU, ICRM, IDA, IFAD, IFC, IFRCS, ILO, IMF, IMO, Interpol, IOC, ISO (subscriber), ITU, LAES, NAM, OAS, OECS, OPANAL, OPCW (signatory), UN, UNCTAD, UNESCO, UNIDO, UPU, WHO, WIPO, WTrO

POLITICAL PARTIES: NNP—New National Party, NDC—National Democratic Congress, GULP—Grenada United Labor Party

ETHNIC GROUPS:

Mixed black and European 13%

European and East Indian 5%

Black 82%

NATIONAL ECONOMICS

WORLD GNP RANKING: 174th

GNP PER CAPITA: $3,770

INFLATION: 0.2%

BALANCE OF PAYMENTS (BALANCE OF TRADE): -$79 million

EXCHANGE RATES / U.S. DLR.: 2.7 EASTERN CARIBBEAN DOLLARS

OFFICIAL CURRENCY: E. CARIB. DOLLAR

GOVERNMENT SPENDING (% OF GDP)

		0	5	10	15
✈	DEFENSE(N/A)				
🎓	EDUCATION 4.7%				
✚	HEALTH 2.9%				

NUMBER OF CONFLICTS OVER LAST 25 YEARS

	1	2-5	5+
Violent changes in government	○	◑	○
Civil wars	○	○	○
International wars	●	○	○
Foreign intervention	○	○	○

- The People's Revolutionary Army was replaced in 1983 by a paramilitary defense unit.
- Since 1983, Grenada has supported United States policy, but restored links with Cuba in 2002.

NOTABLE WARS AND INSURGENCIES: Coups 1979 and 1983. US invasion 1983

WITH ITS TUMULTUOUS FIRST YEARS of nationhood behind it, Grenada today counts on its nutmeg and other spice exports, tourism, and a revived democracy for a calmer, more prosperous future.

A British colony for more than two centuries, Grenada secured independence in 1974 and established a parliamentary constitution. However, its initial attempt at democratic rule ended abruptly with a coup by the Marxist-leaning New Jewel Movement (NJM) in 1979. The NJM and its leader, Maurice Bishop, wielded power until NJM hard-liners executed Bishop in 1983. The United States promptly sent in troops to quell the revolt. Grenada's constitution was restored a year later with parliamentary elections.

Grenada's government is composed of a governor-general, a prime minister, a cabinet, and a bicameral Parliament. The executive branch is headed by the governor-general, who is appointed by the British monarch. The office's powers include approving or rejecting bills passed by Parliament, pardoning criminals, and declaring states of emergency. The governor-general also appoints the cabinet, members of the Senate, and the prime minister, who traditionally is the leader of the majority party of the House of Representatives. The prime minister advises the governor-general on appointments, oversees the cabinet, and can call for the meeting or dissolution of Parliament.

Parliament meets at least once each year, with a maximum interval of six months between sessions. The 15 members of the House of Representatives are directly elected every five years from single districts. The 13 members of the Senate are appointed after each parliamentary election. All bills involving taxes, public debt, and grants of public funds must begin in the House.

The judicial system for Grenada and eight other West Indies island nations is administered by the Eastern Caribbean Supreme Court, which is composed of a High Court of Justice and a Court of Appeal. Final appeals of some verdicts may be made to the Privy Council in London.

ISSUES AND CHALLENGES:

- Sagging prices for Grenada's spice and fruit exports and a weak tourism industry pose major challenges to the government's effort to fund improvements in schools, roads, housing, and health care.

- Despite new hotel and resort construction, falling cruise ship business and post-September 11 air travel jitters have caused a worrying decline in tourism dollars.

- Falling prices for nutmeg, the mainstay of Grenada's dominant spice and fruit industry, are increasing the urgency for new on-island secondary and tertiary processing businesses.

- Worsening poverty during the 1990s and growing crime by young Grenadians mean that there is a pressing need for the government to invest more in education, housing, and health initiatives.

HOW THE GOVERNMENT WORKS

LEGISLATIVE BRANCH
National Parliament
Bicameral Parliament

Senate
Composed of 13 members appointed to five-year terms by governor-general: 10 on advice of prime minister; 3 on advice of opposition leader.

House of Representatives
Composed of 15 members elected to five-year terms by direct popular vote.

Regional Governments
Six parishes and one dependency: Carriacou and Petite Martinique.

EXECUTIVE BRANCH
British Monarch
Head of state. Ceremonial role.

Governor-general
Appointed by British monarch following elections.

Prime Minister
Leader of Parliament's majority party; appointed by governor-general following elections. Serves as head of government; presides over Cabinet.

Cabinet
Composed of members of Parliament; appointed by governor-general on advice of prime minister.

JUDICIAL BRANCH
Privy Council in London
Final tribunal for appeals.

Eastern Caribbean Supreme Court
Highest court with unlimited jurisdiction. Based in St. Lucia; hears cases from nine Caribbean states; one of court's nine judges sits in Grenada.

Magistrates' Courts
Adjudicate civil and minor criminal cases.

DOMINICA

OFFICIAL NAME: COMMONWEALTH OF DOMINICA

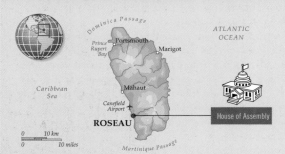

POPULATION: 73,000	
CAPITAL: ROSEAU	
AREA: 291 SQ. MILES (753 SQ. KM)	
INDEPENDENCE: 1978	
CONSTITUTION: 1978	

DOMINICA was named by Christopher Columbus on November 3, 1493 with the Latin word for Sunday, the day he discovered it.

RELIGION: Roman Catholic 77%, Protestant 15%, Other 8%

OFFICIAL LANGUAGE: English

REGIONS OR PROVINCES: 10 parishes

DEPENDENT TERRITORIES: None

MEDIA: No political censorship exists in national media

NEWSPAPERS: There are no daily newspapers

TV: No TV service

RADIO: 3 services: 1 state-owned, 2 independent

SUFFRAGE: 18 years of age; universal

LEGAL SYSTEM: English common law; no ICJ jurisdiction

WORLD ORGANIZATIONS: ACCT, ACP, C, Caricom, CDB, ECLAC, FAO, G-77, IBRD, ICFTU, ICRM, IDA, IFAD, IFC, IFRCS, ILO, IMF, IMO, Interpol, IOC, ISO (subscriber), ITU, NAM (observer), OAS, OECS, OPANAL, OPCW, UN, UNCTAD, UNESCO, UNIDO, UPU, WCL, WHO, WIPO, WMO, WTrO

POLITICAL PARTIES: DLP—Dominica Labour Party, DUWP—Dominica United Workers' Party, DFP—Dominica Freedom Party

ETHNIC GROUPS:
- Mixed 6%
- Carib 2%
- Other 1%
- Black 91%

NATIONAL ECONOMICS

WORLD GNP RANKING: 181st

GNP PER CAPITA: $3,260

INFLATION: 0.8%

BALANCE OF PAYMENTS (BALANCE OF TRADE): -$69 million

EXCHANGE RATES / U.S. DLR.: 2.7 EASTERN CARIBBEAN DOLLARS

OFFICIAL CURRENCY: EAST CARIBBEAN DOLLAR

GOVERNMENT SPENDING (% OF GDP)

✈ DEFENSE (N/A)				
🎓 EDUCATION 5.8%				
✚ HEALTH 3.8%				
0	5	10	15	

NUMBER OF CONFLICTS OVER LAST 25 YEARS

	1	2-5	5+
Violent changes in government	○	○	○
Civil wars	○	○	○
International wars	○	○	○
Foreign intervention	○	○	○

- Dominica has no armed forces.
- It participates in the US-sponsored Regional Security System.
- The police force includes a special service unit and a coast guard.

NOTABLE WARS AND INSURGENCIES: None

THOUGH ONE OF THE WORLD'S SMALLEST COUNTRIES, Dominica is distinguished by a number of exceptional historical facts. It was the last Caribbean island to be colonized by Europeans. Although Spanish ships, including that of Columbus, frequently landed there in the 16th century, they were repelled by fierce resistance from the Carib Indians. Today, Dominica is the only island with an extant pre-Columbian population: 3,400 people of Carib descent live on its east coast. Europeans first settled in the early 1700s, after which rule passed between France and Britain. However, control of the island passed definitively back to Britain under American, British and French agreements in the 1783 Treaty of Paris that ended the American Revolutionary War. The first legislature represented only the white population, but in 1831 a Brown Privilege Law gave rights to free non-white residents, and three non-whites were appointed to the legislature in 1832.

Dominica was the first—and only—British Caribbean colony to have a black-controlled legislature in the 19th century, just four years after the abolition of slavery in 1834. The priorities of the black merchants differed from those of the white planters, and after much lobbying by the planters, the legislative assembly was replaced by one composed of half appointed and half elected members. This gave much power back into the hands of the white minority, and with the establishment of a Crown Colony government in 1896, the majority were further disenfranchised. Political instability just after independence in 1978 was worsened by problems brought by years of underdevelopment. However, by 1979, an interim government was in place. Dominica became the first Caribbean country to elect a female prime minister: Eugenia Charles' government replaced a corrupt and tyrannical administration in 1980, two years after independence, and ruled for 15 years.

Not surprisingly, Dominica's parliamentary government and judicial system are based on Great Britain's. The president's powers are largely formal, while the real executive power resides with the prime minister. The unicameral Parliament, the House of Assembly, is composed of elected regional representatives and senators. The former determine whether the latter will be appointed or elected.

ISSUES AND CHALLENGES:

● Impoverished and dependent on the vicissitudes of its banana crop and foreign trade, Dominica continues to debate how best to improve the country's economy.

● Uncertainties over the North American Free Trade Agreement (NAFTA) have discouraged foreign investment, and the banana trade has been threatened by pressures to end privileges for West Indian bananas imported into Europe.

● The lack of a well-developed network of roads and a modern airport has stunted the growth of a competitive tourism industry, the backbone of so many other Caribbean countries.

HOW THE GOVERNMENT WORKS

LEGISLATIVE BRANCH

House of Assembly
Unicameral Parliament
Composed of 30 members who serve five-year terms: 21 regional representatives elected by direct popular vote; nine senators. Representatives decide whether senators are appointed or elected. If appointed, president chooses five on advice of prime minister, four on advice of opposition leader. If elected, representatives vote for senators. Assembly may remove prime minister and Cabinet with no-confidence vote.

Regional governments
Towns and villages administered by elected councils.

EXECUTIVE BRANCH

President
Jointly nominated by leaders of majority and opposition party; elected to five-year term by House of Assembly. Serves as head of state.

Prime Minister
Leader of House of Assembly's majority party or coalition; appointed by president following elections. Serves as head of government; presides over Cabinet; may call elections at any time.

Cabinet
Composed of ruling party members in House of Asembly; appointed by president on advice of prime minister.

JUDICIAL BRANCH

Privy Council of London
Final tribunal for appeals.

Eastern Caribbean Supreme Court
Highest court with unlimited jurisdiction. Based in St. Lucia; hears cases from nine Caribbean states; one of court's judges sits in Dominica.

Magistrates' Courts
Three courts.

MARSHALL ISLANDS

OFFICIAL NAME: REPUBLIC OF THE MARSHALL ISLANDS

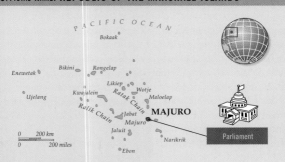

POPULATION: 68,100
CAPITAL: MAJURO
AREA: 70 SQ. MILES (181 SQ. KM)
INDEPENDENCE: 1986
CONSTITUTION: 1979

THE MARSHALL ISLANDS were named after Captain John Marshall, whose ship visited the islands in 1788 en route to China from Botany Bay.

RELIGION: Christian (mostly Protestant)

OFFICIAL LANGUAGES: English and Marshallese

REGIONS OR PROVINCES: 33 municipalities

DEPENDENT TERRITORIES: None

MEDIA: No political censorship exists in national media

NEWSPAPERS: There are no daily newspapers

TV: 2 independent services

RADIO: 2 services: 1 state-owned, 1 independent—radio is the major source of information

SUFFRAGE: 18 years of age; universal

LEGAL SYSTEM: Customary and Trust Territory laws; no ICJ jurisdiction

WORLD ORGANIZATIONS: ACP, AsDB, ESCAP, FAO, G-77, IAEA, IBRD, ICAO, IDA, IFC, IMF, IMO, Interpol, ITU, OPCW (signatory), Sparteca, SPC, SPF, UN, UNCTAD, UNESCO, WHO

POLITICAL PARTIES: UDP—United Democratic Party, K—Pro-Kabua Grouping

ETHNIC GROUPS:

Other 3%

Micronesian 97%

NATIONAL ECONOMICS

WORLD GNP RANKING: 187th

GNP PER CAPITA: $1,970

INFLATION: 5.0%

BALANCE OF PAYMENTS (BALANCE OF TRADE): $21 million

EXCHANGE RATES / U.S. DLR.: CURRENCY IS US DOLLAR

OFFICIAL CURRENCY: US DOLLAR

GOVERNMENT SPENDING (% OF GDP)

✈ DEFENSE (N/A)		
🎓 EDUCATION (N/A)		
✚ HEALTH 9%		

0   5   10   15

NUMBER OF CONFLICTS OVER LAST 25 YEARS

	1	2-5	5+
Violent changes in government	○	○	○
Civil wars	○	○	○
International wars	○	○	○
Foreign intervention	○	○	○

- There is no defense force.
- Defense is guaranteed by the US: the navy patrols regularly.
- The US paid US$1 billion for the use of Kwajalein Atoll as a missile range.

NOTABLE WARS AND INSURGENCIES: None

TWO PARALLEL STRINGS OF ATOLLS AND ISLANDS in the western Pacific known as the Ratak or "sunrise" chain, and the Ralik or "sunset" chain compose the Marshall Islands. They were first claimed by Spain in 1874, were made a German protectorate in 1885, and ruled by Japan from the start of World War I until United States troops took control in 1944. In 1946, the US and the United Nations Security Council entered into an agreement authorizing the US to administer Micronesia, which includes the Marshall Islands, as the Trust Territory of the Pacific Islands. In 1979, the Marshall Islands gained independence when the United States recognized the nation's constitution, a mix of American and British concepts.

The Nitijela, or Parliament, wields significant power, both directly and indirectly. It elects the president from among its members. The Cabinet, which holds most executive powers, is selected from and answers to the Nitijela. The advisory Council of Iroij (Council of High Chiefs) reflects traditional Marshallese life, which revolves around chiefs and clans. The president serves as chief of state for a four-year term and also selects members of the Cabinet.

Although there are two political groups that participate in the legislative process, both are considered factions rather than political parties, and have no formal structure or headquarters. The legal system is an amalgamation of Trust Territory laws, parliamentary acts, municipal and common law, and custom. The Marshall Islands' autonomous judiciary has four divisions, one of which adjudicates only traditional rights matters. After more than a decade of negotiation a Compact of Free Association was signed with the United States in 1983. It was approved by the Marshallese people that year, and signed into US law in 1986. The Compact of Free Association recognizes the Marshall Islands as a sovereign nation in free association with the US, which has full authority and responsibility for the security of the islands. A new 20-year Compact was signed in 2003, setting up a trust fund to provide aid after 2003.

ISSUES AND CHALLENGES:

- Environmental concerns include an inadequate supply of potable water and rising sea levels.

- The aid-dependent nation derives 55 percent of its gross domestic product from US payments made under the Compact of Free Association.

- Having few natural resources, the nation must import most of what it needs, including food, fuel, and consumer goods.

- Government subsidies are necessary to support copra (dried coconut meat) production, the largest commercial activity over the past century, and prevent migration from the outer atolls.

HOW THE GOVERNMENT WORKS

LEGISLATIVE BRANCH

Nitijela
(Parliament)
Unicameral Parliament
Composed of 33 members elected to four-year terms by direct vote. Proposes and passes laws; adopts budget.

Council of Iroij
(Council of High Chiefs)
Composed of 12 high chiefs. Serves as advisory body; reviews bills passed by Nitijela; has no veto.

EXECUTIVE BRANCH

President
Nitijela member elected to four-year term by Nitijela; must relinquish legislative seat. Serves as head of state; has no legislative veto; may dissolve Nitijela.

Cabinet
Composed of six to ten Nitijela members appointed by president. Oversees government operations.

JUDICIAL BRANCH

Supreme Court
Highest court; rules on High Court appeals. Composed of judges appointed by Cabinet with approval of Nitijela.

High Court
Tries civil and criminal cases; hears lower-court appeals.

District and Community Courts
Hear civil and criminal cases.

Traditional Rights Court
Hear customary law and tradition cases and land-rights disputes.

ANDORRA

OFFICIAL NAME: PRINCIPALITY OF ANDORRA

POPULATION: 66,800	
CAPITAL: Andorra la Vella	
AREA: 181 sq. miles (468 sq. km)	
INDEPENDENCE: 1278	
CONSTITUTION: 1993	

ANDORRA'S name is of unknown origin but may have come from the Basque people who now live to the west.

RELIGION: Roman Catholic 94%, Other 6%

OFFICIAL LANGUAGE: Catalan

REGIONS OR PROVINCES: 7 parishes

DEPENDENT TERRITORIES: None

MEDIA: No political censorship exists in the national media

NEWSPAPERS: There are 2 daily newspapers

TV: 1 independent commercial channel. Also receives French and Spanish television channels.

RADIO: 6 independent commercial stations

SUFFRAGE: 18 years of age; universal

LEGAL SYSTEM: French and Spanish law; no ICJ jurisdiction

WORLD ORGANIZATIONS: CCC, CE, ECE, ICAO, ICRM, IFRCS, Interpol, IOC, ITU, OSCE, UN, UNESCO, WHO, WIPO, WToO, WTrO (observer)

POLITICAL PARTIES: PLA—Liberal Party of Andorra, PSD—Social Democratic Party, PD—Democratic Party, UL—Unió Laurediana

ETHNIC GROUPS:

- Spanish 43%
- Andorran 33%
- Portuguese 11%
- French 7%
- Other 6%

NATIONAL ECONOMICS

WORLD GNP RANKING: 154th

GNP PER CAPITA: $15,600

INFLATION: 1.62%

BALANCE OF PAYMENTS (BALANCE OF TRADE): Included in Spanish total

EXCHANGE RATES / U.S. DLR.: 1.0651-1.1231 EUROS

OFFICIAL CURRENCY: EURO.

GOVERNMENT SPENDING (% OF GDP)

✈	DEFENSE 0%	
🎓	EDUCATION (N/A)	
⚕	HEALTH 10.6%	

0 — 5 — 10 — 15

NUMBER OF CONFLICTS OVER LAST 25 YEARS

	1	2-5	5+
Violent changes in government	○	○	○
Civil wars	○	○	○
International wars	○	○	○
Foreign intervention	○	○	○

- Andorra has no defense budget; France and Spain provide protection.
- The last military action was intervention by French gendarmes to restore order after a royalist coup in 1933.

NOTABLE WARS AND INSURGENCIES: None

NESTLED HIGH IN A POCKET of the eastern Pyrenees mountains between Spain and France, Andorra is one of Europe's smallest countries in both population and size. Created by Charlemagne as a state in order to halt the advance of Muslim Moors into France, Andorra has been a co-principality ruled since 1278 by twin heads of state referred to as co-princes. The Spanish co-prince is the Roman Catholic Bishop of Urgell, whose diocese is the nearby Spanish town of La Seu d'Urgell. The French co-prince originally was the Count of Foix, whose rights passed later to the French crown, then to the head of state, currently the president of France. This unusual arrangement grew out of a sovereignty-sharing agreement that settled a conflict between the Bishop of Urgell and the Count of Foix over who owned the land. The co-princes shared the revenues of Andorra for centuries.

In 1993, after 715 years as a co-principality, popular vote established a parliamentary democracy, which created Andorra's own constitution and reduced the role of the co-princes, who now function largely as figureheads. This change came about mainly as a result of the European Union's recommendation that full integration could only be achieved with the development of a constitution that guaranteed the rights of citizens. The new constitution gave the power of the co-princes to veto legislation to the new head of government—the president. The president is elected from Andorra's legislative body, the General Council of the Valleys, and is confirmed by the co-princes. The president selects members of the cabinet, or Executive Council. The co-princes' overview of the General Council is perfunctory and primarily involves formalizing decisions of the president: calling elections, sanctioning bills, and dissolving the Council.

The unicameral General Council is elected by direct popular vote and is responsible for legislation, budget, treaties, and constitutional amendments. The 1993 referendum legalized political parties. In the 2001 election, the Liberal Party of Andorra (PLA) received 54 percent of the vote. Five separate courts make up the Andorran judicial system. There is no judicial review of legislative acts.

ISSUES AND CHALLENGES:

- France and Spain provide military defense of Andorra and effectively decide its economic policy.
- Strict banking secrecy laws make Andorra an important tax haven, for which it has been criticized by the Organization for Economic Cooperation and Development.
- Immigration is limited to French and Spanish nationals intending to work in Andorra.
- Andorra depends on tourism, which accounts for 80 percent of the GDP.
- Most food has to be imported, as agriculture is limited due to the mountainous nature of the land.

HOW THE GOVERNMENT WORKS

LEGISLATIVE BRANCH

Consell General de las Valls
(General Council of the Valleys)
Unicameral Parliament
Composed of 28 members who serve four-year terms: 14 selected from a single national constituency, 14 elected at large; two each elected from seven parishes. Members are elected in the general elections held every four years. Sindic (president) and subsindic chosen by General Council to implement its decisions. Responsible for budget, international treaties, constitutional amendments. Elects head of government.

Regional
Seven parishes (parroquies) make up the districts represented in the General Council.

EXECUTIVE BRANCH

Co-Princes
President of France and Spain's Bishop of Urgell automatically hold office jointly. Serve as head of state.

President
Member of Parliament; elected by Parliament and appointed by co-princes. Serves as head of government; countersigns acts by co-princes; may veto legislation.

Executive Council
Composed of members elected by Parliament. Oversees government operations.

JUDICIAL BRANCH

Higher Council of Justice
Responsible for general administration of courts. Composed of five members who serve six-year terms.

Constitutional Court
Can assess constitutionality of laws. Composed of four judges who serve eight-year terms.

Tribunal
Divided into three courts: High Court of Justice, Criminal Courts, Magistrates' Courts.

High Court of Justice
Hear appeals from lower courts.

Criminal Courts
Hear criminal cases.

Magistrates' Courts
Hear civil cases.

ANTIGUA & BARBUDA

OFFICIAL NAME: ANTIGUA AND BARBUDA

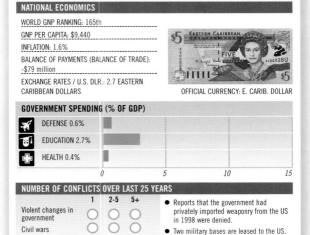

POPULATION: 66,400
CAPITAL: St. John's
AREA: 170 SQ. MILES (440 SQ. KM)
INDEPENDENCE: 1981
CONSTITUTION: 1981

ANTIGUA was named by Columbus in 1493, after the church of Santa María de la Antigua in Seville, Spain.

RELIGION: Anglican 45%, Other Protestant 42%, Roman Catholic 10%, Rastafarian 1%, Other 2%

OFFICIAL LANGUAGE: English

REGIONS OR PROVINCES: 6 parishes

DEPENDENT TERRITORIES: 2 (Barbuda and Redonda)

MEDIA: Partial political censorship exists in the national media

NEWSPAPERS: There is 1 daily newspaper

TV: 1 state-owned, 1 independent

RADIO: 5 services: 1 state-owned, 4 independent

SUFFRAGE: 18 years of age: universal

LEGAL SYSTEM: English common law. No ICJ jurisdiction

WORLD ORGANIZATIONS: ACP, C, Caricom, CDB, ECLAC, FAO, G-77, IBRD, ICAO, ICFTU, ICRM, IFAD, IFC, IFRCS, ILO, IMF, IMO, Interpol, IOC, ISO (subscriber), ITU, NAM (observer), OAS, OECS, OPANAL, UN, UNCTAD, UNESCO, UPU, WCL, WFTU, WHO, WIPO, WMO, WTrO

POLITICAL PARTIES: ALP—Antigua Labour Party, UUP—United Progressive Party, BPM—Barbuda People's Movement

ETHNIC GROUPS:

Other 5%

Black African 95%

NATIONAL ECONOMICS

WORLD GNP RANKING: 165th

GNP PER CAPITA: $9,440

INFLATION: 1.6%

BALANCE OF PAYMENTS (BALANCE OF TRADE): -$79 million

EXCHANGE RATES / U.S. DLR.: 2.7 EASTERN CARIBBEAN DOLLARS

OFFICIAL CURRENCY: E. CARIB. DOLLAR

GOVERNMENT SPENDING (% OF GDP)

✈ DEFENSE 0.6%		
🏫 EDUCATION 2.7%		
✚ HEALTH 0.4%		

0   5   10   15

NUMBER OF CONFLICTS OVER LAST 25 YEARS

	1	2-5	5+
Violent changes in government	○	○	○
Civil wars	○	○	○
International wars	○	○	○
Foreign intervention	○	○	○

- Reports that the government had privately imported weaponry from the US in 1998 were denied.
- Two military bases are leased to the US.

NOTABLE WARS AND INSURGENCIES: None

THE WEST INDIAN ISLAND OF ANTIGUA was named by Christopher Columbus in 1493, but the island was not successfully colonized by Europeans until 1632, when a British settlement was established. The British also colonized the nearby island of Barbuda in 1678. In the 16th century the indigenous population consisted of Arawak and Carib Indians, but today the population is mainly descended from the African slaves who were brought to the islands to work on the sugar plantations. Even though Antigua has been a parliamentary democracy since it gained its independence from the UK in 1981, the British influence still lingers. Antiguans chose to retain the British monarch as their head of state, as did several other former British dominions. The monarch is represented by the governor-general, who appoints the prime minister, invariably the leader of the majority party or majority coalition in the House of Representatives. The governor-general also appoints a Council of Ministers on the advice of the prime minister.

The prime minister and the Council of Ministers are responsible to Parliament, which consists of an elected House of Representatives and an appointed Senate. All legislation is introduced in the House, and the Senate then reviews each measure and passes it to the governor-general for official approval. An election must be held at least every five years, but the prime minister may call an election at any time within that period.

For many years, the politics of Antigua and Barbuda have been dominated by the Bird family and their Antigua Labor Party (ALP). First serving as the president of the Antigua Trades and Labor Union, formed to improve the labor conditions of the freed slaves, Vere Bird founded the ALP, spearheaded the movement for independence, and served as the first post-independence prime minister. His son, Lester Bird, succeeded him in 1994. The family has been plagued by accusations of abuse of authority, and by scandals such as the 1995 conviction of one of Lester Bird's brothers for cocaine smuggling.

Within Antigua and Barbuda, a system of magistrates' courts and a High Court of Justice deal with both civil and criminal matters.

ISSUES AND CHALLENGES:

- Given its lack of mineral resources and limited agricultural production, Antigua and Barbuda is dependent on tourism, making it vulnerable to fluctuations in the world tourism market and to damage caused by seasonal hurricanes. Hurricane Luis in 1995 is said to have set back the country's development by ten years.

- Evidence that drug traffickers and criminal gangs may be using the country for offshore money laundering has damaged Antigua's international reputation.

- Antigua has to import almost all of its energy requirements, due to lack of resources.

HOW THE GOVERNMENT WORKS

LEGISLATIVE BRANCH
Parliament
Bicameral Parliament

Senate
Composed 17 members appointed to five-year terms by governor-general: 11 on advice of prime minister; four on advice of opposition leader; one on advice of Barbuda Council; one by governor-general alone.

House of Representatives
Composed of 17 members directly elected to five-year terms from single-member districts by proportional representation.

Regional Governments
Six parishes and two dependencies: Barbuda and Redonda.

EXECUTIVE BRANCH
British Monarch
Head of state. Ceremonial role.

Governor-general
Appointed by British monarch on advice of prime minister following elections.

Prime Minister
Leader of House's majority party or coalition; appointed by governor-general following elections. Head of government; oversees Council of Ministers.

Council of Ministers
Members appointed by governor-general on advice of prime minister. Oversees government operations; answers to Parliament.

JUDICIAL BRANCH
Privy Council in London
Final tribunal for appeal.

Eastern Caribbean Supreme Court
Hears lower-court appeals. Based in St. Lucia; hears cases from nine Caribbean states.

High Court of Justice
Hears major civil and criminal cases within Antigua and Barbuda.

Magistrates' Courts
Adjudicate civil and minor criminal cases.

ST. KITTS & NEVIS

OFFICIAL NAME: FEDERATION OF SAINT CHRISTOPHER AND NEVIS

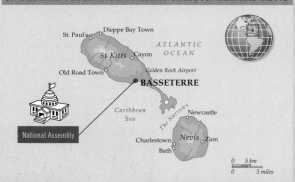

POPULATION:	41,000
CAPITAL:	BASSETERRE
AREA:	139 SQ. MILES (360 SQ. KM)
INDEPENDENCE:	1983
CONSTITUTION:	1983

ST. KITTS & NEVIS was named by Christopher Columbus after his patron saint. The English shortened it to St. Kitts.

RELIGION: Anglican 33%, Methodist 29%, Moravian 9%, Roman Catholic 7%, Other 22%

OFFICIAL LANGUAGE: English

REGIONS OR PROVINCES: 14 parishes

DEPENDENT TERRITORIES: None

MEDIA: No political censorship exists in national media

Newspapers: There are no daily newspapers

TV: 1 state-owned service

Radio: 4 services: 1 state-owned, 3 independent

SUFFRAGE: 18 years of age; universal

LEGAL SYSTEM: English common law; no ICJ jurisdiction

WORLD ORGANIZATIONS: ACP, C, Caricom, CDB, ECLAC, FAO, G-77, IBRD, ICFTU, ICRM, IDA, IFAD, IFC, IFRCS, ILO, IMF, IMO, Interpol, IOC, OAS, OECS, OPANAL, OPCW (signatory), UN, UNCTAD, UNESCO, UNIDO, UPU, WCL, WHO, WIPO, WTrO

POLITICAL PARTIES: SKLP—St Kitts Labor Party, CCM—Concerned Citizens' Movement, NRP—Nevis Reformation Party

ETHNIC GROUPS:
- Other and Amerindian 2%
- Mixed 3%
- White 1%
- Black 94%

NATIONAL ECONOMICS

WORLD GNP RANKING: 178th

GNP PER CAPITA: $6,570

INFLATION: 3.9%

BALANCE OF PAYMENTS (BALANCE OF TRADE): $267 million

EXCHANGE RATES / U.S. DLR.: 2.7 EASTERN CARIBBEAN DOLLARS

OFFICIAL CURRENCY: E. CARIB. DOLLAR

GOVERNMENT SPENDING (% OF GDP)

- DEFENSE (N/A)
- EDUCATION 3.8%
- HEALTH 3.1%

NUMBER OF CONFLICTS OVER LAST 25 YEARS

	1	2-5	5+
Violent changes in government	○	○	○
Civil wars	○	○	○
International wars	○	○	○
Foreign intervention	○	○	○

- First army disbanded to cut government spending in 1981.
- A small full-time defense force was re-established in 1997.
- The secessionist movement on Nevis remains an issue.

NOTABLE WARS AND INSURGENCIES: None

CARIB INDIANS INHABITED ST. KITTS AND NEVIS when Christopher Columbus discovered the islands on his second voyage to the New World. European colonization began in the 1600s, with Great Britain claiming Nevis and developing settlements. Through most of the 17th and 18th centuries, British and French settlers vied for control of St. Kitts. This protracted battle over it was not decided until the Treaty of Paris in 1783 gave Britain permanent ownership of both islands. Britain maintained colonial rule of the islands until 1983, when St. Kitts and Nevis secured independence.

First West Indian islands to be colonized by Britain, in 1623 and 1628 respectively.

Today, St. Kitts and its sister isle Nevis rule themselves as a federation of two Caribbean islands in the Leeward Islands group under a parliamentary democracy with a lengthy and peaceful history of free elections.

The executive branch is composed of a governor-general appointed by the monarch and a prime minister and cabinet to oversee a wide range of government operations. Failure to reach unanimous agreement by cabinet ministers on government policy results in the resignation of the disagreeing minister or ministers.

During the country's first years of independence, the conservative People's Action Movement, founded by Dr. Kennedy Simmonds, maintained a majority in the National Assembly. Simmonds' tenure as prime minister, however, ended in 1995 amid revelations of corruption. Elections that year gave the center-left St. Kitts and Nevis Labor Party control of the National Assembly and the prime minister's post. Labor maintained its majority in the 2000 elections. Meanwhile, the possibility of Nevis' withdrawal from the federation remains a lively topic despite rejection by Nevis voters in a 1998 secession referendum. In 1996, Nevis had announced a desire to seek independence from St. Kitts, claiming that is was dissatisfied with the relationship between the two islands. By virtue of its constitution, Nevis could have withdrawn from the federation if two-thirds of the voters had approved.

ISSUES AND CHALLENGES:

- Its proximity to Puerto Rico and the US Virgin Islands makes St. Kitts and Nevis a convenient drug trafficking post. In an effort to combat drug trafficking, the federation has signed a Maritime Law Enforcement Treaty and an Extradition Treaty with the United States.

- A secession movement simmers on Nevis, led by the island's pro-independence Concerned Citizens' Movement, which is gaining dominance in the Nevis Island Administration.

- St. Kitts and Nevis, like many other Caribbean states, opposes Venezuela's claim to a 200-mile economic exclusion zone around the Aves Islands.

HOW THE GOVERNMENT WORKS

LEGISLATIVE BRANCH

National Assembly
Unicameral Parliament
Composed of 14 members who serve five-year terms: 11 elected by direct popular vote from single-member districts, including three from Nevis; three appointed by governor-general with consent of prime minister.

Nevis Island Administration
Nevis National Assembly
Composed of eight members: five elected; three appointed by governor-general. Reserves right to secede with two-thirds assembly vote and two-third referendum vote by islanders.

EXECUTIVE BRANCH

National Assembly
The British Monarch. Chief of State. Ceremonial role.

Governor-general
Appointed by British monarch following elections. Serves as head of state.

Prime Minister
Leader of parliament's majority party of coalition; appointed by governor-general. Head of government; answers to parliament; may call early elections.

Deputy Prime Minister
Appointed by governor-general.

Cabinet
Prime minister, attorney general, members of parliament; appointed by governor-general on advice of prime minister. Oversees government operations.

JUDICIAL BRANCH

Privy Council in London
Final tribunal for appeals.

Eastern Caribbean Supreme Court
Highest court with unlimited jurisdiction. Based in St. Lucia; hears cases from nine Caribbean states; one of court's judges sits in St. Kitts.

Magistrates' Courts

LIECHTENSTEIN

OFFICIAL NAME: PRINCIPALITY OF LIECHTENSTEIN

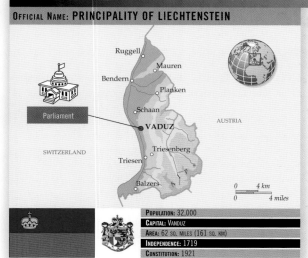

- Ruggell
- Mauren
- Bendern
- Planken
- Parliament
- Schaan
- VADUZ
- AUSTRIA
- Triesenberg
- SWITZERLAND
- Triesen
- Balzers

0   4 km
0   4 miles

POPULATION: 32,000
CAPITAL: Vaduz
AREA: 62 SQ. MILES (161 SQ. KM)
INDEPENDENCE: 1719
CONSTITUTION: 1921

LIECHTENSTEIN, named after the family that bought Vaduz in 1699, became an independent principality of the Holy Roman Empire in 1719.

RELIGION: Roman Catholic 81%, Protestant 7%, Other 12%

OFFICIAL LANGUAGE: German

REGIONS OR PROVINCES: 11 communes

DEPENDENT TERRITORIES: None

MEDIA: No political censorship exists in national media

Newspapers: There are 2 daily newspapers

TV: No TV service

Radio: 1 radio service

SUFFRAGE: 18 years of age; universal

LEGAL SYSTEM: Civil law; accepts ICJ jurisdiction

WORLD ORGANIZATIONS: CE, EBRD, ECE, EFTA, IAEA, ICRM, IFRCS, Interpol, IOC, ITU, OPCW, OSCE, PCA, UN, UNCTAD, UPU, WIPO, WTrO

POLITICAL PARTIES: FBP—Progressive Citizens' Party, VU—Fatherland Union, FL—Freelist

ETHNIC GROUPS:

Italian, Turkish, and other 13%

Alemannic 87%

NATIONAL ECONOMICS

WORLD GNP RANKING: 142nd

GNP PER CAPITA: $50,0000

INFLATION: 0.5%

BALANCE OF PAYMENTS (BALANCE OF TRADE): Included in Swiss total

EXCHANGE RATES / U.S. DLR.: 1.6205–1.6603 Swiss francs

OFFICIAL CURRENCY: SWISS FRANC

GOVERNMENT SPENDING (% OF GDP)

✈ DEFENSE N/A			
📖 EDUCATION N/A			
✚ HEALTH N/A			

0   5   10   15

NUMBER OF CONFLICTS OVER LAST 25 YEARS

	1	2-5	5+
Violent changes in government	○	○	○
Civil wars	○	○	○
International wars	○	○	○
Foreign intervention	○	○	○

- There has been no standing army since 1868.
- De facto protection is provided by Switzerland.
- In theory any male under 60 is liable for military service.

NOTABLE WARS AND INSURGENCIES: None

LIECHTENSTEIN IS THE THIRD SMALLEST COUNTRY IN EUROPE after Monaco and the Vatican City. In 1699, the Liechtenstein family of Austria purchased the fiefdom of Vaduz, followed by that of Schellenberg in 1713. Within six years Emperor Charles VI declared these two counties the Imperial Principality of Liechtenstein. Until gaining independence as a sovereign state in 1806, the Principality remained part of the Holy Roman Empire. The princes of the House of Liechtenstein have ruled since independence, making them one of the oldest existing royal families. Napoleon seized power briefly during his reign as Emperor of France, but independence was regained by 1815 when Liechtenstein became part of the then German Confederation. When the Confederation was dissolved over a half-century later in 1868 Liechtenstein declared its neutrality, disbanding its army. In 1924, Liechtenstein adopted the Swiss currency and joined Switzerland to form a customs union, making the two countries one economic area. As part of this arrangement, Switzerland handles all Liechtenstein's external relations, including security. Like Switzerland, Liechtenstein remained neutral in both world wars and has become an important banking center. Prince Hans Adam II assumed his executive powers in 1984, succeeding his father, Prince Franz Joseph II on his death in 1989. Prince Joseph had been the first prince to break tradition and set up residence in Liechtenstein, rather than the customary Vienna or Moravia, a part of the Czech Republic.

Liechtenstein is governed by the principle of collegiality, or colleagues working together toward a common goal. Two political parties—the Fatherland Union (VU) and the Progressive Citizens' Party (FBP)—shared the rule of the country as a coalition government from 1938 to 1997. Since that time, political power has shifted between the two parties.

After legislative elections, the Prince appoints the leader of the majority party as the head of government and the leader of the largest minority party as the deputy head of government. Constitutional changes, once drafted and approved by the Prince, go before voters in a referendum to obtain their approval.

ISSUES AND CHALLENGES:

- Few challenges exist due to a high standard of living, uniform wealth distribution, low inflation and low unemployment. Thriving banking and manufacturing industry give it the highest GNP per capita in the world.

- Integration with surrounding countries has been challenging, as Liechtenstein struggles to maintain its independence economically.

- As a result of its low taxes and financial secrecy, money laundering has been a problem. After international criticism, controls were tightened in 2000 prohibiting anonymous accounts to avoid major scandals.

HOW THE GOVERNMENT WORKS

LEGISLATIVE BRANCH

Landtag
Unicameral Parliament
Composed of 25 members directly elected to four-year terms by proportional representation: 15 from highland, 10 from lowland. Adopts budget; drafts and passes laws; ratifies treaties; commutes sentences.

Regional Governments
Eleven communes overseen by independent administrative bodies.

EXECUTIVE BRANCH

Monarch
Position is hereditary position. Serves as head of state; convenes and dissolves parliament; issues decrees; vetoes legislation; grants pardons.

Head of Government
Leader of parliament's majority party or coalition; appointed by monarch following elections.

Deputy Head of Government
Leader of parliament's largest minority party; appointed by monarch following elections.

Cabinet
Composed of six members; elected by parliament, appointed by monarch. Oversees government operations.

JUDICIAL BRANCH

State Court
Rules on constitutionality of laws. Judges recommended by parliament, appointed by monarch.

Supreme Court
Highest court for civil and criminal appeals. Judges recommended by parliament, appointed by monarch.

Superior Court
Hears civil and criminal cases. Judges recommended by parliament, appointed by monarch.

Administrative Court of Appeals
Hears complaints against government actions. Judges recommended by parliament, appointed by monarch.

SAN MARINO

OFFICIAL NAME: REPUBLIC OF SAN MARINO

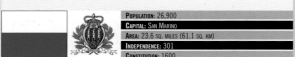

POPULATION: 26,900
CAPITAL: SAN MARINO
AREA: 23.6 SQ. MILES (61.1 SQ. KM)
INDEPENDENCE: 301
CONSTITUTION: 1600

SAN MARINO was named in A.D. 301 for stonemason Marinus the Dalmation when he fled there to escape the Christian persecutions of Roman emperor Diocletian.

RELIGION: Roman Catholic 93%, Other and non-religious 7%

OFFICIAL LANGUAGE: Italian

REGIONS OR PROVINCES: 9 municipalities

DEPENDENT TERRITORIES: None

MEDIA: No political censorship exists in national media

NEWSPAPERS: There are 4 daily newspapers

TV: 1 independent service

RADIO: 2 independent services

SUFFRAGE: 18 years of age; universal

LEGAL SYSTEM: Civil law with Italian legal traditions; no ICJ jurisdiction

WORLD ORGANIZATIONS: CE, ECE, FAO, IBRD, ICAO, ICFTU, ICRM, IFRCS, ILO, IMF, IOC, IOM (observer), ITU, OPCW, OSCE, UN, UNCTAD, UNESCO, UPU, WHO, WIPO, WToO

POLITICAL PARTIES: PDCS—San Marino Christian Democratic Party, PSS—Socialist Party of San Marino, PPDS—Progressive Democratic Party, APDS—Popular Democratic Alliance, RC—Communist Refoundation, AN—National Alliance

ETHNIC GROUPS:

Other 1%

Italian 19%

Sammarinese 80%

NATIONAL ECONOMICS

WORLD GNP RANKING: 185th

GNP PER CAPITA: $7,830

INFLATION: 2.2%

BALANCE OF PAYMENTS (BALANCE OF TRADE): $11 million

EXCHANGE RATES / U.S. DLR.: 1.0651-1.1231 EUROS

OFFICIAL CURRENCY: EURO

GOVERNMENT SPENDING (% OF GDP)

✈ DEFENSE (N/A)		
🎓 EDUCATION (N/A)		
✚ HEALTH 7.5%		

0   5   10   15

NUMBER OF CONFLICTS OVER LAST 25 YEARS

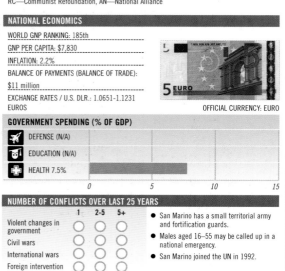

	1	2-5	5+
Violent changes in government	○	○	○
Civil wars	○	○	○
International wars	○	○	○
Foreign intervention	○	○	○

- San Marino has a small territorial army and fortification guards.
- Males aged 16–55 may be called up in a national emergency.
- San Marino joined the UN in 1992.

NOTABLE WARS AND INSURGENCIES: None

APPROXIMATELY ONE TENTH the size of New York City, San Marino was founded, according to legend, on September 3, A.D. 301. San Marino's political system has traditionally been based on family alliances and consensus. The first political structure was the Arengo, an assembly run by the heads of elite families. By 1243, the families decided to elect two men as co-captains of the government, which marked the beginning of the executive power of the *capitani reggenti*, or captains regent, that continues to operate to this day. Until 1483 San Marino consisted of only the area known as Mount Titano. At that time, Pope Pius II Piccolomini gave it three additional towns. After the addition later that year of Faetano, San Marino was established as it stands today. The constitution dates to the early 1600s, and in 1631 the country was recognized by the Pope. The Arengo has given way to the Great and General Council, the legislative branch of today's San Marino.

During World War II the nation was under Fascist rule, and was afterwards governed by a Communist-Socialist coalition from 1945 to 1957. A coalition of Christian Democrats and Social Democrats then came to power. By 1960, women had gained the right to vote, but were not allowed to hold public office until 1973.

Today, the country is a parliamentary democracy with three main political parties: the San Marino Christian Democratic Party (PDCS), the Socialist Party of San Marino (PSS), and the Progressive Democratic Party of San Marino (PPDS). It is seldom that one party holds the majority of the seats in the Great and General Council. Like the family alliances of San Marino's early days, frequently shifting party coalitions are the norm in government.

The atypical executive post is held by two co-chiefs of state, the captains regent, who are invested each year on April 1 and October 1 for six-month terms. The captains regent are from opposing parties to ensure a balance of political power. To keep a check on abuses of power, San Marino's citizens are granted a period of three days following each captain regent's tenure of office in which to lodge complaints against the captain regent that might require further action or even prosecution. As the country is an enclave in the heart of Italy, in practice most of its affairs depend on and are controlled by Italy.

ISSUES AND CHALLENGES:

- Lack of natural resources means that San Marino has to import all of its raw material and energy needs.
- Although not a recipient of aid, San Marino is dependent on annual subsidies from Italy and preferential access to its markets. Italy is also responsible for foreign affairs.

San Marino claims to be the oldest republic in the world

HOW THE GOVERNMENT WORKS

LEGISLATIVE BRANCH
Consiglio Grande e Generale
(Great and General Council)
Unicameral Parliament
Composed of 60 members
directly elected to five-year terms by
proportional representation.
Approves budget; proposes and passes
legislation by majority vote.

Regional Governments
Nine municipalities administered
by elected local councils.

EXECUTIVE BRANCH
Captains Regent
Parliament members of opposing parties.
Two "captains" elected to six-month
terms by Parliament twice annually.
Serve jointly as heads of state.

State Congress
Composed of 10 members of
Parliament elected by Parliament to head
state ministries for five-year terms.
Proposes and implements policies
and laws. Secretary of State for
Foreign and Political Affairs serves as
head of government.

JUDICIAL BRANCH
Council of Twelve
Highest judicial authority.
Interprets law;
hears lower-court appeals.
Composed of judges elected to
five-year terms by Parliament.
Justices are hired foreigners
to ensure neutrality.

Justices of Peace

INDONESIA

OFFICIAL NAME: REPUBLIC OF INDONESIA

POPULATION: 214 MILLION	
CAPITAL: JAKARTA	
AREA: 741,096 SQ. MILES (1,919,439 SQ. KM)	
INDEPENDENCE: 1949	
CONSTITUTION: 1959	

INDONESIA, whose name derives from the Greek words Idos (Indian) and nesos (island), is the world's largest archipelago, crossing three time zones.

RELIGION: Sunni Muslim 87%, Protestant 6%, Roman Catholic 3%, Hindu 2%, Buddhist 1%, Other 1%

OFFICIAL LANGUAGE: Bahasa Indonesia

REGIONS OR PROVINCES: 30 provinces

DEPENDENT TERRITORIES: None

MEDIA: Partial political censorship exists in national media

NEWSPAPERS: There are 69 daily newspapers

TV: 6 services: 1 state-owned, 5 independent

RADIO: 1 state-owned service, 1 independent station

SUFFRAGE: 17 years of age and married persons regardless of age; universal

LEGAL SYSTEM: Roman-Dutch law; local legal traditions; no ICJ jurisdiction

WORLD ORGANIZATIONS: APEC, ARF, AsDB, ASEAN, CCC, CP, ESCAP, FAO, G-15, G-19, G-77, IAEA, IBRD, ICAO, ICC, ICFTU, ICRM, IDA, IDB, IFAD, IFC, IFRCS, IHO, ILO, IMF, IMO, Interpol, IOC, IOM (observer), ISO, ITU, MONUC, NAM, OIC, OPCW, OPEC, UN, UNAMSIL, UNCTAD, UNESCO, UNIDO, UNIKOM, UNMIBH, UNMOP, UNMOT, UNOMIG, UPU, WCL, WFTU, WHO, WIPO, WMO, WToO, WTrO

POLITICAL PARTIES: PDI-P—Indonesian Democratic Party of Struggle, Gol—Golkar, PPP—United Development Party, PKB—National Awakening Party, PAN—National Mandate Party

ETHNIC GROUPS:

- Javanese 45%
- Other 25%
- Sundanese 14%
- Madurese 8%
- Coastal Malays 8%

NATIONAL ECONOMICS

WORLD GNP RANKING: 32nd

GNP PER CAPITA: $570

INFLATION: 3.7%

BALANCE OF PAYMENTS (BALANCE OF TRADE): $7.99 billion

EXCHANGE RATES / U.S. DLR.: 9675-10,400 RUPIAHS

OFFICIAL CURRENCY: RUPIAH

GOVERNMENT SPENDING (% OF GDP)

- DEFENSE 1%
- EDUCATION 1.4%
- HEALTH 0.8%

0   5   10   15

NUMBER OF CONFLICTS OVER LAST 25 YEARS

	1	2-5	5+
Violent changes in government	○	○	○
Civil wars	○	○	●
International wars	○	○	○
Foreign intervention	○	○	○

- The constitution enshrines the military's political role.
- The army is accused of human rights abuses.
- There are tensions between the army and non-military security forces.

NOTABLE WARS AND INSURGENCIES: Separatist struggles; Aceh, East Timor (to 2002), Papua (formerly Irian Jaya). Sectarian violence

COMPRISING MORE THAN 13,000 ISLANDS, Indonesia is the world's fourth most populous nation. From independence from the Dutch in 1949 until the resignation of President Mohamed Suharto in 1998 the military dominated political life. Today a multiparty democracy, Indonesia faces the huge challenge of holding together its diverse population. More than 1.3 million people have been displaced by ethnic, religious, and separatist violence in recent years. In 2002, the government granted East Timor independence, but harshly suppresses secessionist movements in Aceh in northern Sumatra and in Irian Jaya. The daughter of Indonesia's first president, Megawati Sukarnoputri, led the opposition Indonesian Democratic Party of Struggle (PDI-P) to win the first post-Suharto legislative elections in June 1999. After becoming president in 2001, Megawati chose a Cabinet that represents every major political party and interest group.

The president is both head of government and chief of state and has executive and legislative powers. The People's Consultative Assembly (MPR) elected the president and vice-president up until recently, but a constitutional amendment adopted in 2001 mandated direct election of the president and vice-president from 2004 onward. The MPR also approves the broad outlines of national policy and amends the constitution. The unicameral House of Representatives (DPR) has become a fully functioning, independent legislature since the end of the Suharto regime. The legislature became bicameral in 2004 with the creation of the Regional Representative Council (DPD).

In 1999, the government passed an ambitious devolution law making Indonesia's districts responsible for important public services such as health care and education. Local control over a quarter of the public-sector budget has led to reckless extravagance and misuse of funds in many districts. Another area of government in need of significant reform is the judiciary, which is widely considered to be corrupt and arbitrary.

REBEL NATION
East Timorese students shouting pro-independence slogans hold the rebel Fretilin flag in a demonstration before their homeland's independence in 2002.

HOW THE GOVERNMENT WORKS

LEGISLATIVE BRANCH

Majilis Permusyarawatan Rakyat (People's Consultative Assembly)
Composed of 695 members: 500 People's Representative Council members; 130 elected by provincial legislatures; 65 appointed by community groups. Amends constitution; issues decrees; elects (until 2004) and may remove the president.

Dewan Perwakilan Raakyat (People's Representative Council) Unicameral Parliament
Composed of 500 members; five-year terms: 462 elected by popular vote; 38 military appointees (until 2004).

Regional Government
Thirty provinces, over 300 districts which provide most government services.

EXECUTIVE BRANCH

President
Elected to five-year term by People's Consultative Assembly. (Elected by popular vote after 2004.) Serves as head of state and government; commander-in-chief of armed forces. Issues regulations; declares war; negotiates treaties.

Vice-President
Elected to five-year term by People's Consultative Assembly. (Elected by popular vote after 2004.)

Cabinet
Appointed by president; oversees government operations.

JUDICIAL BRANCH

Supreme Court
Highest court; hears original cases and lower-court appeals. Composed of justices nominated by Parliament, appointed by president.

General Courts
Military Courts
Administrative Courts
Religious Courts
Commercial Courts

NIGERIA

OFFICIAL NAME: FEDERAL REPUBLIC OF NIGERIA

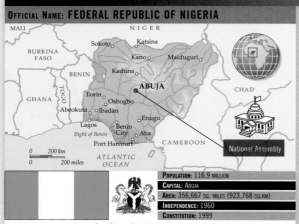

POPULATION: 116.9 MILLION	
CAPITAL: ABUJA	
AREA: 356,667 SQ. MILES (923,768 SQ.KM)	
INDEPENDENCE: 1960	
CONSTITUTION: 1999	

Nigeria is named after the Niger River, the country's principal river.

RELIGION: Muslim 50%, Christian 40%, Traditional beliefs 10%

OFFICIAL LANGUAGE: English

REGIONS OR PROVINCES: 36 states and 1 territory

DEPENDENT TERRITORIES: None

MEDIA: Partial political censorship exists in national media

NEWSPAPERS: There are 25 daily newspapers

TV: 1 state-controlled service, about 60 private stations

RADIO: 4 services: 2 state-controlled, 2 independent

SUFFRAGE: 18 years of age; universal

LEGAL SYSTEM: Shari'a (Islamic) and English common law; accepts ICJ jurisdiction

WORLD ORGANIZATIONS: ACP, AfDB, C, CCC, ECA, ECOWAS, FAO, G-19, G-24, G-77, IAEA, IBRD, ICAO, ICC, ICFTU, ICRM, IDA, IFAD, IFC, IFRCS, IHO, ILO, IMF, IMO, Interpol, IOC, ISO, ITU, MINURSO, MONUC, NAM, OAU, OIC, OPCW, OPEC, PCA, UN, UNAMSIL, UNCTAD, UNESCO, UNHCR, UNIDO, UNIKOM, UNITAR, UNMEE, UNMIK, UNMOP, UNMOT, UNMOVIC, UNU, UPU, WFTU, WHO, WIPO, WMO, WToO, WTrO

POLITICAL PARTIES: PDP—People's Democratic Party, APP—All People's Party, AD—Alliance for Democracy

ETHNIC GROUPS:

Kanuri 4%
Ibibio 3%
Tiv 3%
Hausa and Fulani 29%
Ijaw 10%
Other (more than 250 small ethnic groups)
Ibo 18%
Yoruba 21%

NATIONAL ECONOMICS

WORLD GNP RANKING: 57th

GNP PER CAPITA: $260

INFLATION: 6.9%

BALANCE OF PAYMENTS (BALANCE OF TRADE): $6.98 billion

EXCHANGE RATES / U.S. DLR.: 110-120 NIGERIAN NAIRA

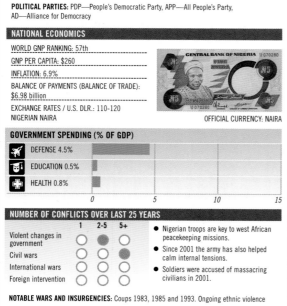

OFFICIAL CURRENCY: NAIRA

GOVERNMENT SPENDING (% OF GDP)

		0	5	10	15
✈	DEFENSE 4.5%				
	EDUCATION 0.5%				
✚	HEALTH 0.8%				

NUMBER OF CONFLICTS OVER LAST 25 YEARS

	1	2-5	5+	
Violent changes in government	○	●	○	• Nigerian troops are key to west African peacekeeping missions.
Civil wars	○	○	●	• Since 2001 the army has also helped calm internal tensions.
International wars	○	○	○	• Soldiers were accused of massacring civilians in 2001.
Foreign intervention	○	○	○	

NOTABLE WARS AND INSURGENCIES: Coups 1983, 1985 and 1993. Ongoing ethnic violence

---

NIGERIA GAINED INDEPENDENCE from the UK on October 1, 1960 as a three-region federation and, in 1963, became a federal republic with a new constitution. The most populous country in Africa with over 200 ethnic groups (the three major ones are Hausa/Fulani, Yoruba, and Ibo), Nigeria has been torn by ethnic, religious, and regional divisions in its struggle to become a democracy. Mostly corrupt military rule, interrupted by coups and brief, unsuccessful civilian governments, has dominated. In 1999, Nigeria became a multiparty democracy with the election of President Olusegun Obasanjo and a revised constitution. Corruption and unrest, however, have marred subsequent elections, and Nigeria has yet to make a successful transition from one civilian government to another.

Since independence, ethnic struggles have dominated Nigeria's politics and government. Religious differences, inequalities in oil resources among regions, and pervasive corruption and poverty have intensified strife. To counteract these divisive forces, Nigeria split its original three regions into 36 autonomous states so diluting the power of the large ethnic groups and enabling a wider distribution of government jobs. It moved its capital from the southern, Christian, Yoruba-dominated city of Lagos to the centrally located, ethnically mixed Federal Capital Territory of Abuja. It distributed revenues more equitably to states to compensate for unequal populations and oil reserves. Nevertheless, ethnic, religious, and geographic conflicts have continually turned deadly. In 1967, the Eastern Ibo region seceded, leading to the 30-month Biafran War and 600,000 deaths. In 1995, the execution of Ogoni activist Ken Saro-Wiwo led to Nigeria's expulsion from the Commonwealth of Nations. The introduction of shari'a law in some northern states has sparked violence, as was seen in 2000 in Kaduna. In 2002, Muslims and Christians again clashed over strict Islamic punishments, leaving 500 dead.

Under the constitution, both the president and the National Assembly members are elected by popular vote. The president appoints most of the federal judiciary (Supreme Court and Federal Court of Appeal) with advice from the Advisory Judicial Committee. The Nigerian legal and judicial system operates according to Nigerian statute, customary, and shari'a, or Islamic law.

ISSUES AND CHALLENGES:

• Reconciling antagonistic Muslim Hausa/Fulanis in the north (the majority), Christian Yorubas in the south, and Christian Ibos in the east.

• Equitable distribution of revenues from oil reserves among all the states and local governments.

• Halting corruption in the public sector which threatens loss of public confidence in government. Private sector corruption has lined the pockets of a few, while leaving the country's major public construction projects unfinished.

HOW THE GOVERNMENT WORKS

LEGISLATIVE BRANCH
National Assembly
Bicameral Parliament

Senate
Composed of 109 members elected to four-year terms by direct popular vote: three from each state; one from Federal Capital Territory Abuja.

House of Representatives
Composed of 360 members elected to four-year terms by direct popular vote: ten from each state.

Regional Governments
Thirty-six states plus Federal Capital Territory of Abuja; administered by governors and vice-governors elected to four-year terms, and elected legislatures.

EXECUTIVE BRANCH
President
Elected to four-year term by direct popular vote, two-term limit. Serves as head of state and government; commander-in-chief of armed forces.

Federal Executive Council
Composed of military officers, ethnic leaders and chiefs, academics. Appointed by president; oversees government operations.

JUDICIAL BRANCH
Supreme Court
Highest court of review and appeals; hears disputes between federal and state governments. Composed of up to 15 justices appointed to serve to age 70 by president on advice of Judicial Service Commission.

Court of Appeal
Hears state and federal lower-court appeals. Composed of up to 50 justices appointed to serve to age 70 by president on advice of Judicial Service Commission.

Federal Courts

State Courts

Shari'a Courts

Customary Courts

ETHIOPIA

OFFICIAL NAME: FEDERAL DEMOCRATIC REPUBLIC OF ETHIOPIA

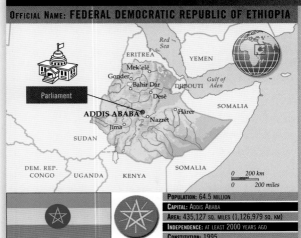

POPULATION: 64.5 MILLION
CAPITAL: ADDIS ABABA
AREA: 435,127 SQ. MILES (1,126,979 SQ. KM)
INDEPENDENCE: AT LEAST 2000 YEARS AGO
CONSTITUTION: 1995

ETHIOPIA means "burned faces," from the Greek, referring to dark skins.

RELIGION: Muslim 40%, Ethiopian Orthodox 40%, Traditional beliefs 15%, Other 5%

OFFICIAL LANGUAGE: Amharic

REGIONS OR PROVINCES: 9 ethnically-based states

DEPENDENT TERRITORIES: None

MEDIA: Partial political censorship exists in national media

NEWSPAPERS: There are 3 daily newspapers

TV: 1 state-owned service

RADIO: 4 services: 1 state-owned, 3 independent

SUFFRAGE: 18 years of age; universal

LEGAL SYSTEM: In transition; regional and national courts; no ICJ jurisdiction

WORLD ORGANIZATIONS: ACP, AfDB, CCC, ECA, FAO, G-24, G-77, IAEA, IBRD, ICAO, ICRM, IDA, IFAD, IFC, IFRCS, IGAD, ILO, IMF, IMO, Interpol, IOC, IOM (observer), ISO, ITU, NAM, OAU, OPCW, UN, UNCTAD, UNESCO, UNHCR, UNIDO, UNU, UPU, WFTU, WHO, WIPO, WMO, WToO, WTrO (observer)

POLITICAL PARTIES: OPDO—Oromo People's Democratic Coalition, ANDM—Amhara National Democratic Movement, TPLF—Tigre People's Liberation Front, Ind—Independents

ETHNIC GROUPS:

- Oromo 40%
- Amhara 25%
- Other 14%
- Sidamo 9%
- Somali 6%
- Berta 6%

NATIONAL ECONOMICS

WORLD GNP RANKING: 99th

GNP PER CAPITA: $100

INFLATION: 5.9%

BALANCE OF PAYMENTS (BALANCE OF TRADE): $16 million

EXCHANGE RATES / U.S. DLR.: 8.225-8.450 ETHIOPIAN BIRR

OFFICIAL CURRENCY: ETHIOPIAN BIRR

GOVERNMENT SPENDING (% OF GDP)

- DEFENSE 6.8%
- EDUCATION 4.3%
- HEALTH 1.3%

| | 0 | 5 | 10 | 15 |

NUMBER OF CONFLICTS OVER LAST 25 YEARS

	1	2-5	5+
Violent changes in government	○	○	○
Civil wars	○	○	○
International wars	●	○	○
Foreign intervention	●	○	○

- One of the most militarized states in Africa.
- Border disputes led to war with Eritrea in 1998–2000.
- Clan-based militias battle against government control throughout the country.

NOTABLE WARS AND INSURGENCIES: Eritrea war of secession 1961-1993. Civil war 1974-1991. Border war with Eritrea 1998-2000. UN intervention (UNMEE)

ETHIOPIA IS ONE OF the oldest countries in existence, dating back to around 1,000 B.C. It abandoned imperial rule in September 1974, when military rebels under the leadership of Mengistu Haile Mariam overthrew the government of Emperor Haile Selassie. The Derg, a military council, implemented a Soviet-based policy of collectivizing agriculture, and initiated a "red terror" in which political opponents were tortured and executed. In 1984, the policy of collectivization coupled with drought produced a terrible famine that led to a massive international relief effort. The country has since suffered further famine. In May 1991 Mengistu fled into exile as rebel forces of the Ethiopian People's Revolutionary Democratic Front (EPRDF), an ethnic alliance dominated by Tigreans, took control. After a four-year transitional government led by the EPRDF, the Federal Democratic Republic of Ethiopia (FDRE) emerged in 1995. Meanwhile, in 1993 Eritrea gained the independence for which it had been fighting for over 30 years, after being annexed by Ethiopia. In 1998 a two-year war broke out between the two countries.

Ethiopia has a parliamentary system with periodic elections. Executive power rests with the prime minister, who is also the chairman of the EPRDF, which includes all the main parties. The prime minister has the authority to appoint and remove members of the judiciary and the legislature, and can overrule the Council of Ministers. The legislature consists of the 550-member House of People's Representatives and the House of Federation. This secondary chamber has 108 seats filled by ethnic minorities, serves a ceremonial function, and has no law-making authority. Many opposition parties declined to participate in the 1995 national elections, leveling accusations of government interference with the outcome, but 49 parties took part in the elections of 2000.

The constitution devolves power to nine ethnically-based states, giving them autonomy to raise and spend their own revenues and even to secede.

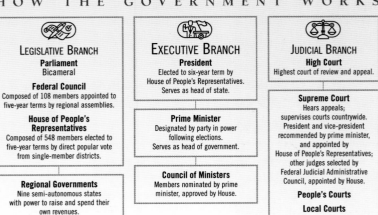

FOOD DISTRIBUTION
Ethiopian women wait for a food in Imi, a village in drought-ridden western Ethiopia, April 20, 2000. The country is prone to devastating famine and drought.

HOW THE GOVERNMENT WORKS

LEGISLATIVE BRANCH

Parliament
Bicameral

Federal Council
Composed of 108 members appointed to five-year terms by regional assemblies.

House of People's Representatives
Composed of 548 members elected to five-year terms by direct popular vote from single-member districts.

Regional Governments
Nine semi-autonomous states with power to raise and spend their own revenues.

EXECUTIVE BRANCH

President
Elected to six-year term by House of People's Representatives. Serves as head of state.

Prime Minister
Designated by party in power following elections. Serves as head of government.

Council of Ministers
Members nominated by prime minister, approved by House.

JUDICIAL BRANCH

High Court
Highest court of review and appeal.

Supreme Court
Hears appeals; supervises courts countrywide. President and vice-president recommended by prime minister, and appointed by House of People's Representatives; other judges selected by Federal Judicial Administrative Council, appointed by House.

People's Courts

Local Courts

Military Tribunals

FRANCE

FRENCH FLAG
Adopted on February 15, 1794 the French flag, known as the "Tricolore", was used until the fall of Napoleon in 1814-15. It was revived under the Second Republic in 1848.

EIFFEL TOWER
Considered by many to be a monstrosity when it was completed in 1889, the tower is now a well-loved emblem both of Paris and of France.

AFTER JULIUS CAESAR CONQUERED THE AREA known as Gaul in 58-50 B.C., almost five centuries of Roman rule imposed laws and a common language that unified the Gallic tribes, giving them a common identity and an enduring notion of the geographical boundaries of their realm.

The people who gave their name to the country, however, were the Franks, Germanic invaders who crossed into Gaul at the fall of the Western Roman Empire. Under Clovis (ruled A.D. 481-511), they won control of almost all of modern France. Clovis's Merovingian dynasty was succeeded in the 8th century by the Carolingians, whose greatest king, Charlemagne (ruled 768-814), established a vast empire extending far into Germany. On Charlemagne's death, the empire was divided and the French part became a loose collection of feudal fiefdoms owing allegiance to the French king, but these vassals were often more powerful than their nominal overlord. The French crown also had to face prolonged wars with England, culminating in the Hundred Years' War (1337-1453).

The French kings gradually reasserted their authority and created a powerful absolute monarchy, its zenith coming in the 17th century in the reign of the "Sun King," Louis XIV (1643-1715). The king's palace at Versailles was the most magnificent court in Europe, and the country became the dominant force in European politics.

After Louis' death in 1715, France's political hegemony declined, but its cultural influence remained strong. French writers were the leading figures of the Enlightenment, a philosophical movement that questioned the traditional authority of the church and the monarchy. It influenced Americans such as Thomas Jefferson and Benjamin Franklin, who were involved in fashioning a new democratic state in North America. It also fomented the

HOW THE GOV

⚖ LEGISLATIVE BRANCH

PARLIAMENT

The Senate tends to specialize in constitutional matters and foreign affairs, the Assembly in the scrutiny of day-to-day government business.

▶ **SENATE**
The upper house has 321 seats: 296 representing France, 13 France's overseas territories, and 12 French nationals abroad; indirectly elected by electoral college for nine-year terms; one-third of seats come up for election every three years.

▶ **NATIONAL ASSEMBLY**
The lower house of Congress consists of 577 seats; members elected by popular vote to five-year terms. As the principal legislative body, the National Assembly can overrule the Senate in the case of a disagreement.

SENATE INTERIOR
Senate Chamber in Luxembourg Palace, the interior of which was decorated by Poussin, Philippe de Champaigne, and Rubens.

EXECUTIVE BRANCH

THE PRESIDENT

Chief of state, popularly elected to seven-year term. Must be French citizen over 23 years who has satisfied French legal requirements for military service, and obtain 500 sponsoring signatures of elected officials from at least 30 departments or overseas territories. Duties include negotiation of treaties and appointment of prime minister; has power to dismiss National Assembly; chairs Council of Ministers and Higher Council of the Judiciary. Highest office in France, but all domestic decisions must be approved by the prime minister.

ASSEMBLÉE NATIONALE
Detail of the frieze by Jean-Pierre Cortot placed on the National Assembly building in 1842. It shows the personification of France, flanked by various allegorical figures.

REGIONAL GOVERNMENTS
▶ 22 Administrative regions
▶ 96 Administrative departments
▶ Overseas departments, territories, collectivities

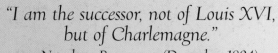

> *"I am the successor, not of Louis XVI,*
> *but of Charlemagne."*
> — *Napoleon Bonaparte (December 1804)*
> *to Pope Pius VII*

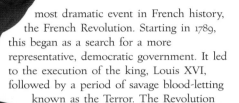

most dramatic event in French history, the French Revolution. Starting in 1789, this began as a search for a more representative, democratic government. It led to the execution of the king, Louis XVI, followed by a period of savage blood-letting known as the Terror. The Revolution failed to establish democratic rule, giving rise instead to the reign of Napoleon (1799-1815), under whose leadership France briefly regained its military and political pre-eminence.

In the course of the 19th century France experienced two further revolutions—in 1830 and 1848. The latter gave rise to a short-lived republic, then to the Second Empire under Napoleon's nephew, who ruled as Napoleon III. After his defeat in the Franco-Prussian War (1870-71), France returned to republican rule.

The Third Republic lasted until 1940, when France was conquered by Nazi Germany. The Fourth Republic, established at the end of the war, proved unworkable. In 1958, with a crisis looming over France's colonial war in Algeria, Charles de Gaulle took power under a new constitution, the Fifth Republic, which gave the president new executive powers. This system of government, in which a president sometimes has to work with an opposition majority in the National Assembly, has survived to the present. A newly confident France has repaired relations with Germany, forging a partnership instrumental in the creation of the European Union and the Euro monetary zone.

MARIANNE
This young woman has been a symbol of the French people and the Republic since the Revolution.

NAPOLEON BONAPARTE
Having risen to power as a successful general in the wars that followed the French Revolution, Napoleon created an empire that dominated Europe at the beginning of the 19th century. He crowned himself emperor in 1804.

N M E N T   W O R K S

THE PRIME MINISTER

Head of government; nominated by majority party or coalition in parliament; appointed by president for an indefinite term. Manages daily affairs of government, answers to the government; leader of the cabinet, recommends ministers to the president and sets their duties and responsibilities; issues decrees; responsible for national defense.

▶ **THE CABINET**
Chaired by the president, the Council of Ministers is headed by the prime minister; it consists of the ministers of the 15 executive agencies.

⚖ JUDICIAL BRANCH

SUPREME COURT OF APPEALS

France's highest appellate court; members are appointed by the president; divided into six chambers responsible for civil, criminal, social, commercial, economic, and financial law and decides only on matters of law not questions of fact when reviewing lower court decisions.

▶ **CONSTITUTIONAL COUNCIL**
Nine members; one appointment made by each of the president, the president of the Senate, and the president of the National Assembly every three years; vested with the power of constitutional review over government and electoral procedures.

PALAIS DE JUSTICE
Located on the Île de la Cité, Paris, the Hall of Justice contains the Supreme Court and Paris Court of Appeal as well as other lesser courts of Paris.

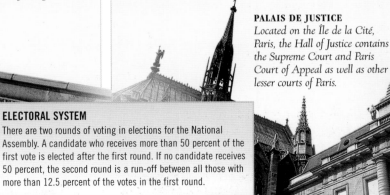

ELECTORAL SYSTEM
There are two rounds of voting in elections for the National Assembly. A candidate who receives more than 50 percent of the first vote is elected after the first round. If no candidate receives 50 percent, the second round is a run-off between all those with more than 12.5 percent of the votes in the first round.

EXECUTIVE BRANCH

GEORGES POMPIDOU (1911-1974)
Pompidou (right) helped draft the 1958 constitution and negotiated a secret treaty with Algeria in 1961. He served as prime minister in the de Gaulle administration between 1962 and 1968, then succeeded de Gaulle as president in 1969.

CHARLES DE GAULLE (1890-1970)
Leader of the Free French forces in World War II, de Gaulle led a provisional government after the war, but resigned because he thought the constitution unworkable. He returned to power during the Algeria crisis of 1958 and became the first president under the Fifth Republic.

FRANÇOIS MITTERRAND (1916-1996)
The first Socialist president of the Fifth Republic, Mitterrand served two terms from 1981 to 1995. He twice had to share power with a prime minister of the center-right.

THE PRESIDENCY

Under the constitution of 1958, the president of the Fifth Republic is endowed with more political responsibilities than any other single member of the French system of rule.

Elected by popular vote to a renewable term of five years, the president is the highest political authority in the country, and has special individual powers in certain matters of state: defense, national territories and institutions, and foreign affairs. The president may also dissolve the National Assembly, call new elections, or declare popular referenda should he or she believe that the current political environment impedes the successful execution of presidential duties.

However, while the president is also vested with all the usual powers of a democratic president—ultimate control of the military as commander-in-chief of the armed forces, reception of diplomatic envoys, high-level government appointments including that of the prime minister, treaty negotiation, and pardon rights—his domestic policy decisions must be approved and cosigned by the prime minister. Despite possessing extraordinary powers, the French president is not, therefore, the ultimate political authority in the country, but the key partner in a form of cooperative government.

CARDINAL RICHELIEU (1585-1642)
A brilliant statesman, Richelieu became chief minister to Louis XIII in 1624, serving him for 18 years until his death in 1642. Richelieu's opportunistic diplomacy helped make France the leading power in Europe.

THE CABINET

Officially titled the Council of Ministers; the prime minister and the senior member from each of the government's 15 ministries comprise the cabinet. Responsible to the president; transacts official government business; advises the president; implements executive policy.

INTERIOR & DOMESTIC SECURITY
Administers national territory and provides the population with domestic security; protects the integrity of public institutions and guarantees universal suffrage; oversees decentralization policies.

SOCIAL AFFAIRS & EMPLOYMENT
Monitors and maintains citizens' rights in the public sphere; provides employment information at local, regional, and national levels; administers state social security, pensions, disability, and migrant workers' funds.

JUSTICE & KEEPER OF THE SEALS
Monitors and assures the integrity of the French judicial system; monitors application of EU and international law in France; works to maximize transparency and efficiency in the judicial system.

FOREIGN AFFAIRS
Primary intelligence agency: provides policy-makers with accurate information on external states and non-governmental organizations.

OVERSEAS TERRITORIES
Administers France's overseas possessions.

DEFENSE AND VETERANS
Administers the French armed forces (army, navy, air force and armed police force) and assures national security; implements defense policy; provides benefit programs for French veterans.

YOUTH, EDUCATION & RESEARCH
Administers the French education system; ensures the integrity of education; oversees teaching standards and recruitment; promotes the use of new technology; promotes research and doctoral studies.

HALL OF RULERS

Matters of state in France were conducted by the monarch and his personally chosen ministers until the Revolution in 1789.

 CHARLEMAGNE 768-814 Consolidated the kingdom and created an extensive empire.

PHILIP I 1060-1108 Ruler when the kingdom was eclipsed by Duchy of Normandy.

LOUIS VII 1137-1180 Led troops to the Holy Land during the Second Crusade.

 CHARLES VII 1422-1461 Reigned during the life of Joan d'Arc.

 HENRY I 1589-1610 The first Bourbon monarch.

HALL OF PRESIDENTS

The French presidency dates back to 1848, when popular uprisings demanded democratic rule and toppled King Louis-Philippe. The first president, Louis-Napoléon, staged a coup in 1852 to

LOUIS-NAPOLEON BONAPARTE 1848-1852

LOUIS ADOLPHE THIERS 1871-1873

MARIE E. PATRICE MAURICE MACMAHON

FRANÇOIS PAUL JULES GRÉVY 1879-1887

MARIE FRANÇOIS SADI CARNOT

JEAN PAUL PIERRE CASIMIR-PÉRIER

FRANÇOIS FELIX FAURE 1895-1899

ÉMILE FRANÇOIS LOUBET 1899-1906

CLÉMENT ARMAND FALLIÈRES 1906-1913

RAYMOND POINCARÉ 1913-1920

PAUL EUGENE LOUIS DESCHAN

FRANCE

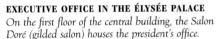

EXECUTIVE OFFICE IN THE ÉLYSÉE PALACE
On the first floor of the central building, the Salon Doré (gilded salon) houses the president's office.

THE FRENCH PRESIDENT'S PALACE
Built during the reign of Louis XV, the Elysée Palace was used as a private residence by Napoleon. The palace became the official residence of the president of France during the Second Republic (1848-1852).

HÔTEL MATIGNON
This French nobleman's house, completed in 1725, is now the official residence of the prime minister. It is located near the Elysée Palace.

REPUBLICAN GUARD
These soldiers protect government officials throughout Paris.

"I have come to the conclusion that politics are too serious a matter to be left to the politicians."
— Charles de Gaulle

THE PRIME MINISTER

The second highest political authority in the French government is the prime minister. Appointed by the president to an indefinite term, the prime minister shares a large degree of political responsibility and authority with the president.

As all of the president's domestic policy decisions require approval by the prime minister, the relationship between the two offices is integral, perhaps even paramount, to a successful government. Aside from that relationship, however, the prime minister also has a number of individual duties, including managing the government's daily affairs, acting as the liaison between the National Assembly and the *pouvoir exécutif* (executive branch), and overseeing the parliamentary majority. He is responsible for national defense, appoints members of the government, and, as head of the government, is considered the person most embodying the will of the government.

Therefore, the confidence of the president and of the legislative body are essential to the effectiveness of a prime minister, whose term in office depends largely on their continuing support. With regard to this, the president is well-advised to choose a prime minister who has the political support of the majority in the National Assembly. Should the majority not be of the same political persuasion as the president, the executive branch requires the "cohabitation" of these two opposed figures of authority. This has occurred three times, first in 1986, and again in 1993 and 1997.

Broadly speaking the constitution requires the president to preserve national interests, while the prime minister and the government define and implement national policy. The prime minister may go on to occupy the office of president, as is the current case.

ECONOMY, FINANCE & INDUSTRY	TRANSPORT, HOUSING, TOURISM & THE SEA	ENVIRONMENT & SUSTAINABLE DEVELOPMENT	HEALTH, FAMILY & DISABILITY	AGRICULTURE, FOOD, FISHERIES & RURAL AFFAIRS	CULTURE & COMMUNICATION	CIVIL SERVICE & ADMINISTRATIVE REFORM	SPORT
Monitors markets; influences economic policy; administers the French treasury and postal service; collects taxes; controls fraud; regulates trade and industry, and information technology standards; oversees nuclear safety.	Maintains France's sea, river, air, rail and road transportation infrastructure; assures housing standards; administers state housing; safeguards France's tourism sites and promotes tourism.	Protects nature and endangered species; prevents pollution; protects and develops national water supply; develops environmental research; promotes eco-industries.	Maintains the integrity of the French healthcare system; oversees standards in hospitals; provides benefit programs for the disabled; implements family planning and drug rehabilitation programs.	Controls the quality and hygiene of French food supplies; monitors the agricultural sectors of the economy; controls rural development and aspects of nature conservation.	Preserves and protects French culture and France's cultural institutions; assures access to French cultural objects for all French people; promotes understanding of French culture abroad.	Monitors the integrity of France's governmental administration; provides advice to increase administrative efficiency and integrity; develops electronic methods of administration.	Promotes interactive community lifestyles in France; provides continuing education; promotes programs to help provide youth and disabled persons' access to sport; maintains integrity of sports activities, including drug control.

LOUIS XIV
1643-1715
"The Sun King"– commissioned royal palace at Versailles.

LOUIS XVI
1774-1792
His reign fomented the French Revolution and the collapse of the monarchy.

ROBESPIERRE
1793-1794
One of the leaders of the French Revolution during the Reign of Terror.

NAPOLEON
1799-1814
Ruled initially with the title of First Consul; subsequently crowned emperor.

LOUIS XVIII
1814-1815, 1815-1824
Restored to the throne following Napoleon's defeat at Waterloo.

ALEXANDRE MILLERAND
1920-1924

GASTON DOUMERGUE
1924-1931

PAUL DOUMER
1931-1932

ALBERT LEBRUN
1932-1940

Between 1940 and 1947, there was no president. The 3rd Republic was replaced by a French state under Marshal Pétain, and after the war by the governments of General de Gaulle, Felix Gouin and finally Georges Bidault.

VINCENT AURIOL
1947-1954

RENÉ COTY
1954-1959

CHARLES DE GAULLE
1959-1969

GEORGES POMPIDOU
1969-1974

VALÉRY GISCARD D'ESTAING
1974-1981

FRANÇOIS MITTERRAND
1981-1995

JACQUES RENÉ CHIRAC
1995-present

LEGISLATIVE BRANCH

CHAMBER OF THE NATIONAL ASSEMBLY
The interior of the National Assembly chamber, distinguished by its red décor and neoclassical architecture. At the front sits the president of the National Assembly— surrounded by the Steering Committee—who moderate legislative sessions.

Detail of insignia on National Assembly desk

National Assembly with Palais Bourbon in the foreground

THE NATIONAL ASSEMBLY

The origins of France's National Assembly are rooted in the democratic fervor of the French Revolution. On June 17, 1789, members of the Third Estate (the Commons) declared themselves the representative, and thus legitimate, ruling body in France. Naming themselves the National Assembly, they spent two years drawing up a new constitution for France. When this was completed in 1791, the National Assembly was dissolved to make way for the new Legislative Assembly. This soon lost control of events and the Revolution degenerated into the 'Terror'. Napoleon's rise to power curtailed democratic representation in France, and the National Assembly was—for all intents and purposes— replaced by the Imperial Senate.

The composition and political influence of France's legislative body fluctuated throughout the 19th century. By the constitution of 1875, the Third Republic established a Senate and a Chamber of Deputies. It was not until the aftermath of World War II that the National Assembly regained its name. The 1946 constitution placed the National Assembly at the apex of government, a position it enjoyed until the constitution of 1958 equalized power

THE NATIONAL ASSEMBLY
The imposing façade of the Palais Bourbon, built between 1722 and 1728 for Louise Françoise de Bourbon, houses the National Assembly.

among the three branches of government and restored the Senate to its position of prominence in the legislative system.

The scope of the National Assembly differs from that of the Senate in several important ways. The National Assembly, elected from single-member constituencies throughout the French state, lacks the specific territorial concerns of the Senate. Secondly, the primary political concern of

the National Assembly is the passage of statutes. Subsequently, the National Assembly concerns itself primarily with legislating domestic matters such as public liberties, crime, taxation, education, law, the budget and national defense. Lastly, the National Assembly is also charged

LEGISLATIVE POWERS AND PROCEDURES

GOVERNMENT OVERSIGHT
Most oversight responsibilities fall on the Assembly, which can pass votes of "no confidence" and censure government officials. Questions can be put to ministers or the government on the floor on certain specified days, or in writing when clarification of government policy is required.

DEBATE IN THE NATIONAL ASSEMBLY
The Assembly debates the implications of further European integration.

DEBATING TREATIES AND INTERNATIONAL AFFAIRS
Both chambers of Parliament have the right to examine treaties or international agreements negotiated by the president, especially those affecting domestic politics, namely commercial, trade, or financial treaties. Should there be disagreement as to the constitutionality of the bill, 60 deputies or senators can request the Constitutional Council's ruling. Treaties are not approved until passed by a ratification statute.

EUROPEAN INTEGRATION
Integration into the European Union is a controversial issue in most European countries. In order to monitor French integration into the European Union, Parliament established special delegations from the National Assembly and from the Senate to keep the two houses informed of European Union legislation and how it will affect France. There is also a special office of the Senate in Brussels, charged with monitoring the European Union.

FRANCE

THE SENATE CHAMBER
A privileged view of the Senate's ornate interior: the president of the Senate presides over the daily business of the house from his lofted position.

with the important task of governmental oversight. It therefore devotes a vast amount of its resources to reviewing and monitoring the actions of the executive branch. The lower house maintains a distant, yet cooperative, relationship with the government—allowing special sessions for debate and questioning government officials, and maintaining special committees for supervising the policies of the executive.

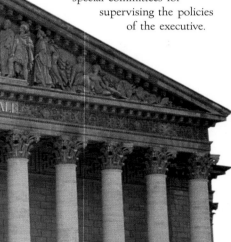

THE SENATE

The history of the French Senate begins with the establishment of the Council of Elders (le Conseil des Anciens) in the constitution of 1795. After seizing power, Napoleon Bonaparte drastically altered the Council of Elders in 1799, renaming it the Conservative, or Imperial Senate (1799-1814) and changing the format to resemble the ancient Roman Senate. Such a transformation was indicative of the way the upper house of the country's legislature was to be treated throughout its history. It has altered formats several times over the course of the past two centuries, changing with roughly every new regime: it became the Chambre des Pairs during the Restoration (1814-30) and the July Monarchy (1830-48), the Senate of the Second Empire (1851-70), and the Council of the Republic (1946-58) following World War II. Much like the rest of the Fifth Republic, however, the current senatorial system is a product of the Constitution of 1958, which drastically restructured the French political system.

In France's parliamentary system, the legislative functions of the Senate vary from those of the National Assembly in several ways. The foremost of these differences are the Senate's commitment to geographic representation—many French senators are also high-level local officials—and representation of French expatriates, which requires an alternate electoral process and therefore different political strategies. These differences, however, also extend to matters of policy and procedure. In the current legislative system, only senators and executive officials have the legal right to introduce potential amendments to the constitution.

The Senate is also given authority to monitor and control the country's foreign affairs and, perhaps even more importantly, European integration. To that end, the Senate is provided with special resources not allocated to the National Assembly: a "listening post" in Brussels—the headquarters of the European Union—and special relations with the Executive to continuously update integration policy. The upper house also has the power to ratify treaties and modify statutory provisions that may alter the size and shape of French territory.

INTERIOR OF THE FRENCH SENATE
Built in 1615, the Luxembourg Palace has been substantially remodeled over the last two centuries to accommodate the upper house of the French parliament.

LEGISLATIVE INITIATIVE
Deputies and the government are entitled to initiate legislation: either a new bill or the amendment of an existing one. If it is in accordance with Article 40 of the constitution, it proceeds to debate. During this process, the Constitutional Council or either chamber of parliament may amend the bill.

VOTING
Deputies of the National Assembly show their support for a bill.

CONSTITUTIONAL AMENDMENT
A change to the constitution is initiated by passing the identical bill in both chambers. It does not come into effect until approved by referendum or by a special joint session of the Senate and National Assembly at Versailles. This requires a three-fifths majority vote.

CONSTITUTIONAL REVIEW
There are periodic reviews of the constitution, such as this one held at the Palace of Versailles in 1995.

JUDICIAL BRANCH

"Terrorism takes us back to ages we thought were long gone if we allow it a free hand to corrupt democratic societies and destroy the basic rules of international life."
— *Jacques Chirac, president of France*

CONSTITUTIONAL COUNCIL

Much like other modern European nations, France's legal and judicial system consists of an intricate web of traditional national law and developing European judicial practices. As a sovereign nation, France operates its own national judiciary, with laws that pertain solely to French territories. As a member of European Union, however, France is obligated to enforce the legal statutes developed by the European Union, which are applied in all the member states. France's judiciary does have some unusual features. The French Supreme Court (Cour de Cassation) does not—like Supreme Courts in other nations—have the power of judicial review. Such power is vested in the Constitutional Council (Conseil Constitutionnel), a judicial body that meets infrequently, only upon referral.

Only legislation referred by the president, prime minister and Parliament may be reviewed by France's Constitutional Court

A unique creation of the Constitution of the Fifth Republic, the Constitutional Council has no institutional precedent in France. The establishment of the Council was advocated by Charles de Gaulle in the late 1950s in order to diminish the excessive powers enjoyed by the legislature in the Fourth Republic and provide for equality of power between the three branches of government.

Prior to 1974, the Council considered only the constitutionality of cases that were referred to it by the president, the prime minister, or the leaders of the two houses of Parliament. A constitutional amendment in 1974, however, granted referral rights to legislative coalitions consisting of 60 or more members from either chamber. The caseload of the Council increased annually, to the point at which it now considers the constitutionality of nearly every new piece of legislation. Since that amendment, the Council's influence over French politics has drastically increased, leading some to criticize the overly judicial emphasis on political procedures. In reality, the Constitutional Council rarely rejects legislation or annuls it for reasons of constitutionality. Rather, its role consists of reviewing legislation and suggesting changes to ensure its legality. Some of its key findings are detailed in the "Landmark Cases" below.

The Council comprises nine judges, a third of whom are appointed every three years by the president, the prime minister, and the president of the National Assembly. Members serve nine-year, non-renewable terms. In order to maintain a degree of political distance, the judges are not overtly political appointments—they cannot hold positions in the government, the legislature, the European Parliament, or the Economic and Social Council during their tenure. All ex-presidents of the Republic are also de jure members of the Council, provided they do not hold any of the aforementioned positions.

PALAIS DE JUSTICE
The Palais de Justice is home to the highest law courts of Paris. The palace was the seat of the French monarchy until 1358, when it was attacked during a popular uprising against the crown and the nobility.

COUR DE CASSATION
President Jacques Chirac is seen with the state prosecutor Jean-Francois Burgelin, first president Guy Canivet and other presidents of the Supreme Court chambers during the opening ceremony in 2001.

LANDMARK CASES

PÉTAIN TRIAL, 1945
Pétain, a national hero of World War I, was found guilty of collaborating with the Nazis.

COLLABORATION
After World War II, the leader of the Vichy government, Marshal Philippe Pétain, was tried for collaborating with the Nazis and sentenced to death (later commuted to life imprisonment.

STANDING ORDERS OF THE NATIONAL ASSEMBLY
In June 1959, Major Decision no. 3 of the Constitutional Council declared a number of provisions of the first National Assembly of the Fifth Republic unconstitutional and forced changes in legislative policy. As a result parliamentary standing orders had to be submitted for review by the Constitutional Council.

PROTECTION OF BEAUTY SPOTS AND MONUMENTS
On June 26, 1969, Major Decision no. 18 established guidelines for the protection and preservation of the country's cultural monuments and other national treasures. Research and preservation of historical monuments are the sole responsiblity of the Ministry for Culture and Communication.

SECURITY AND LIBERTY
Major Decision no. 30, January 20, 1981, was an important piece of legislation on the rights of persons accused of serious crimes. One of the Constitutional Council's guidelines is the safeguarding of the liberties of individuals. The court's finding issued directives on how to judge unconstitutional infringements of the law.

FRANCE

OFFICIAL NAME: FRENCH REPUBLIC

POPULATION: 59.9 MILLION	
CAPITAL: PARIS	
AREA: 211,208 SQ. MILES (547,030 SQ. KM)	
INDEPENDENCE: 486	
CONSTITUTION: 1958	

FRANCE is named for the Germanic conquerors of the 400s, the Franks, meaning "free men".

RELIGION: Roman Catholic 88%, Muslim 8%, Protestant 2%, Buddhist 1%, Jewish 1%

OFFICIAL LANGUAGE: French

REGIONS OR PROVINCES: 22 regions

DEPENDENT TERRITORIES: 4 overseas departments, 4 overseas territories, 2 special status territories

MEDIA: No political censorship exists in the national media

SUFFRAGE: 18 years of age; universal

LEGAL SYSTEM: Civil law; no ICJ jurisdiction

WORLD ORGANIZATIONS: ACCT, AfDB, AsDB, Australia Group, BDEAC, BIS, CCC, CDB (non-regional), CE, CERN, EAPC, EBRD, ECA (associate), ECE, ECLAC, EIB, EMU, ESA, ESCAP, EU, FAO, FZ, G- 5, G- 7, G- 8, G-10, IADB, IAEA, IBRD, ICAO, ICC, ICFTU, ICRM, IDA, IEA, IFAD, IFC, IFRCS, IHO, ILO, IMF, IMO, InOC, Interpol, IOC, IOM, ISO, ITU, MINURSO, MIPONUH, MONUC, NAM (guest), NATO, NEA, NSG, OAS (observer), OECD, OPCW, OSCE, PCA, SPC, UN, UN Security Council, UNAMSIL, UNCTAD, UNESCO, UNHCR, UNIDO, UNIFIL, UNIKOM, UNITAR, UNMEE, UNMIBH, UNMIK, UNMOVIC, UNOMIG, UNRWA, UNTSO, UNU, UPU, WADB (nonregional), WCL, WEU, WFTU, WHO, WIPO, WMO, WToO, WTrO, ZC

POLITICAL PARTIES: UMP—Union for a Presidential Rally (Rally for the Republic—RPR and the Liberal Democracy—DL), PS—Socialist Party, UDF—Union for French Democracy, PCF— Communist Party of France, UC—Centrist Union, Rep—Republican and Independents, RCC—Republicans, Communists, and Citizens, ROSE—European Democratic and Social Rally, Ind—Independents, G—Greens

ETHNIC GROUPS:

- German (Alsace) 2%
- Other (including Corsicans) 1%
- Breton 1%
- North African (mainly Algerian) 6%
- French 90%

NATIONAL ECONOMICS

WORLD GNP RANKING: 5th

GNP PER CAPITA: $24,090

INFLATION: 1.7%

BALANCE OF PAYMENTS (BALANCE OF TRADE): $20.4 billion

EXCHANGE RATES / U.S. DLR.: U.S. DLR: 1.0651- 1.1231 euros

OFFICIAL CURRENCY: EURO

GOVERNMENT SPENDING (% OF GDP)

✈ DEFENSE 2.6%	
🎓 EDUCATION 5.9%	
✚ HEALTH 7.3%	

0   5   10   15

NUMBER OF CONFLICTS OVER LAST 25 YEARS

	1	2-5	5+
Violent changes in government	○	○	○
Civil wars	○	○	○
International wars	○	○	○
Foreign intervention	○	○	○

NOTABLE WARS AND INSURGENCIES: None

- France left the NATO military command in 1966 in opposition to US domination.
- It maintains an independent nuclear deterrent.
- France has a large, export-oriented defense industry.

CRIMINAL CHAMBER
Of the six chambers comprising the Cour de Cassation, the Criminal Chamber is the only one devoted to hearing criminal cases and reviewing matters related to penal law.

COUR DE CASSATION

Formerly known as the Tribunal de Cassation, the Cour de Cassation was established by the Assemblée Constituante in 1790, following the French Revolution. Although it lacks constitutional review, the Cour de Cassation is nonetheless France's highest appellate court, exercising judicial review over the departmental and local court systems. Consisting of six chief judges (présidents), 85 judges (conseillers), and 43 assistant judges (conseillers référendaires), the court is divided into six separate chambers—five civil and one criminal—each headed by a president. The highest authority is the first president of the Cour de Cassation, who presides over special sessions, and oversees discipline of French judges through the Conseil supérieur de la Magistrature.

The court's first three chambers consider civil cases—each chamber having specific areas of legal specialization. The fourth chamber, the Criminal Chamber considers all matters of penal law. The fifth chamber of the Cour de Cassation, the Commercial, Economic, and Financial Law Chamber, deals primarily with cases pertaining to economic and financial policy: bankruptcy, corporations, business contracts, commerce, banking, and patents. The Social Law Chamber, deals specifically with civil cases involving labor, social security, and worker-compensation. Generally, the highest ranking prosecutor, the Procureur Général, or an assistant prosecutor, presents the cases before a panel of three judges, who hear the case and subsequently pass judgment.

Gate of the Palais de Justice

TERRORISM LAW

On September 3, 1986, the Constitutional Council rejected a proposal to create a separate criminal procedure for prosecuting terrorism cases. Such cases continue to be tried in the criminal courts.

TERRORISM IN FRANCE

The scene of one of a series of terrorist attacks on the Paris Metro in 1995. In 2001 two Algerian men were charged with the crime.

ALGERIA

OFFICIAL NAME: PEOPLE'S DEMOCRATIC REPUBLIC OF ALGERIA

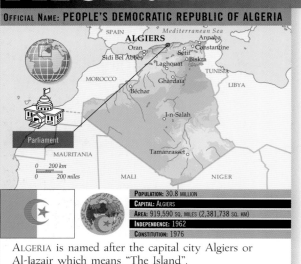

Parliament

POPULATION: 30.8 MILLION
CAPITAL: ALGIERS
AREA: 919,590 SQ. MILES (2,381,738 SQ. KM)
INDEPENDENCE: 1962
CONSTITUTION: 1976

ALGERIA is named after the capital city Algiers or Al-Jazair which means "The Island".

RELIGION: Sunni Muslim 99%, Christian and Jewish 1%

OFFICIAL LANGUAGES: Arabic and Tamazight

REGIONS OR PROVINCES: 48 provinces

DEPENDENT TERRITORIES: None

MEDIA: Total political censorship exists in national media

NEWSPAPERS: There are 23 daily newspapers, most of which are state-owned

TV: 1 state-run service

RADIO: 4 state-run networks

SUFFRAGE: 18 years of age; universal

LEGAL SYSTEM: French and Shari'a (Islamic) law; no ICJ jurisdiction

WORLD ORGANIZATIONS: ABEDA, AfDB, AFESD, AL, AMF, AMU, CCC, ECA, FAO, G-15, G-19, G-24, G-77, IAEA, IBRD, ICAO, ICC, ICFTU, ICRM, IDA, IDB, IFAD, IFC, IFRCS, IHO, ILO, IMF, IMO, Interpol, IOC, IOM, ISO, ITU, MONUC, NAM, OAPEC, OAS (observer), OAU, OIC, OPCW, OPEC, OSCE (partner), UN, UNCTAD, UNESCO, UNHCR, UNIDO, UNMEE, UPU, WHO, WIPO, WMO, WToO, WTrO (observer)

POLITICAL PARTIES: FLN—National Liberation Front, RND—National Democratic Rally, MRN—Movement for National Reform, MSP—Movement for Peaceful Society, Ind—Independents, PT—Workers' Party, FFS—Front of Socialist Forces

ETHNIC GROUPS:

European 1%

Berber 24%

Arab 75%

NATIONAL ECONOMICS

WORLD GNP RANKING: 50th

GNP PER CAPITA: $1,580

INFLATION: 2.6%

BALANCE OF PAYMENTS (BALANCE OF TRADE): $8.9 billion

EXCHANGE RATES / U.S. DLR.: 73.42-76.86 ALGERIAN DINARS

OFFICIAL CURRENCY: ALGERIAN DINAR

GOVERNMENT SPENDING (% OF GDP)

✈ DEFENSE 6.8%		
📖 EDUCATION 6%		
✚ HEALTH 2.6%		

0   5   10   15

NUMBER OF CONFLICTS OVER LAST 25 YEARS

	1	2-5	5+
Violent changes in government	●	○	○
Civil wars	●	○	○
International wars	○	○	○
Foreign intervention	○	○	○

- National Liberation Army is dominant power in politics.
- Islamist militants want Algeria to become a theocracy.
- July 2002 terrorist attacks killing 49, and another 58 in January 2003 were blamed on Islamic fundamentalist rebels.
- Military suspected of reprisal killings of Islamists.

NOTABLE WARS AND INSURGENCIES: Civil conflict waged by Islamic Salvation Front (FIS) and splinters

AFTER AN EIGHT-YEAR WAR WITH FRANCE, Algeria gained independence in 1962 and functioned as a single-party socialist state for over two decades. Under the system of "Islamic Socialism" and the National Liberation Front (FLN) party, the country enjoyed a period of relative prosperity and popularity in the international community, especially in the United Nations and the Arab League. However, Algeria was not spared the collapse of socialist governments throughout the world in the late 1980s. Spurred by rapidly deteriorating economic and social conditions, riots erupted in October 1988 that forced the FLN to draft several unprecedented constitutional amendments, the most important of which removed the FLN as the official state apparatus and established the legality of a multiparty system. Algeria in effect abandoned its commitment to socialism.

The 1989 amendments did not, however, remove the traditional political elite from authority, and in 1991 the military intervened in an election that would have granted power to the fundamentalist Islamic Salvation Front (FIS). There followed a period of extreme political tension. The outlawing of the FIS sparked a violent civil war with social and political consequences that still haunt Algeria. A 1996 "Declaration of Understanding" was intended to unite the nation and end the conflict. Instead, it essentially legitimized the state's brutal crackdown on Islamic fundamentalists and Berber separatists, extending aggressions and prolonging the war. Elected in April 1999, President Abdelaziz Bouteflika held a referendum to obtain approval for an amnesty program for all surrendering FIS soldiers. By this time, an estimated 100,000 people had been killed in the violence since 1992. Soon afterwards in June 1999, the FIS armed wing disbanded. Nearly 80 percent of their soldiers took advantage of the program, and violence has reduced in all but the most rural areas where militants persist with sporadic terrorist attacks.

The prolonged violence and unrest have contributed to recent social fragmentation and economic decline. Direct foreign investment and other aid dwindle as international pressure increases against the repression of political dissent and deteriorating human rights conditions.

ISSUES AND CHALLENGES:

- Perhaps the most pressing political issue, both domestically and internationally, is residual government violence and guerrilla warfare against Islamic fundamentalists and radicals, who remain a volatile force regardless of government crackdowns.

- Diplomatic relations with France remain fragile, yet nonetheless important, as the government has sought to eradicate French cultural influences. Algerian emmigration to France, Italy and Spain is a major political concern for western European governments. In particular, France has been the target of Algerian terrorist attacks in recent years.

HOW THE GOVERNMENT WORKS

LEGISLATIVE BRANCH

Parlement
(Parliament)
Bicameral Parliament

Conseil de la Nation
(Council of the Nation)
Composed of 144 members appointed to six-year terms: 96 elected by local councils; 48 appointed by president.

Assemblée Populaire Nationale
(National People's Assembly)
Composed of 389 members elected to five-year terms by direct popular vote.

Regional Governments
Forty-eight provinces administered by governors appointed by president.

EXECUTIVE BRANCH

President
Elected to five-year terms by direct popular vote; limit of two consecutive terms. Serves as head of state; commander-in-chief of armed forces; initiates legislation; dissolves Parliament; calls early elections.

Prime Minister
Appointed by president following elections. Serves as head of government.

Council of Ministers
Appointed by prime minister; president presides. Oversees government operations.

JUDICIAL BRANCH

Supreme Court
Highest court of review and appeal.

Council of State
Protects citizens from official abuses; advises on legislation.

Supreme Council of Magistracy
Appoints all judges. Members include president, justice minister.

Tribunal of Conflicts
Determines jurisdiction of Supreme Court and Council of State.

State High Court
Tries president for high crimes.

Provincial Courts

Courts of First Instance

TAIWAN

OFFICIAL NAME: REPUBLIC OF CHINA (ROC)

CHINA
TAIPEI
Hsinchuang
Hsinchu Pate
T'aichung
Yüanlin Hualien
Chiai
South China Sea
PACIFIC OCEAN
T'ainan
T'aitung
Kaohsiung P'ingtung

Legislative Yuan

0 40 km
0 40 miles

POPULATION: 22.2 MILLION	
CAPITAL: TAIPEI	
AREA: 13,892 SQ. MILES (35,980 SQ. KM)	
INDEPENDENCE: 1949	
CONSTITUTION: 1947	

TAIWAN, means "terraced bay" taken from where the Chinese landed in 1644. Portuguese sailors had called the island "Ilha Formosa" (beautiful island).

RELIGION: Buddhist, Confucian, Taoist 93%, Christian 5%, Other 2%

OFFICIAL LANGUAGE: Mandarin

REGIONS OR PROVINCES: 18 counties, 5 municipalities, and 2 special municipalities

DEPENDENT TERRITORIES: None

MEDIA: No political censorship exists in national media

NEWSPAPERS: There are 35 daily newspapers

TV: 1 public-service station, 64 cable companies, and 129 satellite broadcasting channels

RADIO: 110 independent corporations

SUFFRAGE: 20 years of age; universal

LEGAL SYSTEM: Civil law; accepts ICJ jurisdiction

WORLD ORGANIZATIONS: APEC, AsDB, BCIE, ICC, ICFTU, IFRCS, IOC, WCL, WTrO

POLITICAL PARTIES: DPP—Democratic Progressive Party, KMT—National Party of China (Kuomintang), PFP—People First Party, TSU—Taiwan Solidarity Union, Ind—Independents

ETHNIC GROUPS:

Aborigine 2%
Mainland Chinese 14%
Indigenous Chinese 84%

NATIONAL ECONOMICS

WORLD GNP RANKING: 16th

GNP PER CAPITA: $13,450

INFLATION: 1.3%

BALANCE OF PAYMENTS (BALANCE OF TRADE): $9.32 billion

EXCHANGE RATES / U.S. DLR.: 33.08-34.99 TAIWAN DOLLARS

OFFICIAL CURRENCY: TAIWAN DOLLAR

GOVERNMENT SPENDING (% OF GDP)

✈	DEFENSE	5.6%
📖	EDUCATION	3.6%
✚	HEALTH	(N/A)

0 5 10 15

NUMBER OF CONFLICTS OVER LAST 25 YEARS

	1	2-5	5+
Violent changes in government	○	○	○
Civil wars	○	○	○
International wars	○	○	○
Foreign intervention	○	○	

- Compulsory national military service.
- China is greatest defense threat.
- 5th largest navy in world.
- More than 1.5 million reservists.

NOTABLE WARS AND INSURGENCIES: None

TAIWAN'S CURRENT SOCIO-POLITICAL FRAMEWORK is rooted in two mass migrations from mainland China. The first occurred in 1644, when the Ming dynasty was transplanted to the island. The Han Chinese descendants of those migrants now constitute nearly 85 percent of Taiwan's population. The second and most politically significant migration occurred in 1949, when hundreds of thousands of Nationalists fled the Communist revolution in mainland China, seeking refuge in the island province of Taiwan just off the southeast coast.

Following this migration, the exiled Republic of China (ROC) established itself as the island's governing body, led by President Chiang Kai-shek and his Nationalist Party (KMT). Although the KMT was essentially a de facto military regime, the party made several strides toward democratization in its nearly 50 years of rule. The most significant occurred in 1986, when Chiang Kai-shek's son and successor, General Chiang Ching-kuo, allowed the first free multiparty elections. The political environment became increasingly open to dissent and opposition, culminating in 2000 with the election of Chen Shui-bian, the first non-KMT president since 1949, whose party, the Democratic Progressive Party became the largest in the Parliament, or Lifa Yuan.

Under the current constitution, the president retains a large degree of power and influence over the political system. However, recent constitutional reforms aim to cede more executive power to the premier and give greater influence to the legislature in order to stabilize a political system that only recently emerged from single-party rule.

The overwhelming political concern on the island is its relationship with the People's Republic of China (PRC) on the mainland. The PRC still asserts territorial claims over Taiwan and insists that the island is part of the Chinese nation. In reality, several crucial factors separate the two. Primarily, Taiwan's nascent multiparty democracy is in stark contrast to the single-party rule of the PRC, as is the island's aggressive capitalist economy compared with the PRC's controlled economy. Living standards are also much higher in Taiwan than on the mainland.

ISSUES AND CHALLENGES:

- Recent debates regarding Taiwanese independence have complicated diplomatic relations with China and other nations. The People's Republic of China vigorously opposes independence, and has threatened military action to prevent it. Concerns over the threat of military interference in Taiwan have spread to many of its neighbors, creating a political situation that could destabilize regional and international diplomacy.

- Taiwan's efficient, export-based economy—it is known as one of the "Asian Tigers"—wins it wide-ranging support from Western nations, and further complicates relations with China.

HOW THE GOVERNMENT WORKS

LEGISLATIVE BRANCH
Lifa Yuan
(Legislative body)
Unicameral Parliament
Composed of 225 members who serve three-year terms: 168 elected by direct popular vote; 41 by proportional representation; eight from overseas; eight by aboriginal population. Initiates legislation; amends constitution, recalls or impeaches president and vice-president; removes premier and Cabinet with no-confidence vote; ratifies senior-level presidential appointments.

Regional Governments
Eighteen counties and 5 municipalities administered by elected magistrates; 2 special municipalities directly administered by the central government.

EXECUTIVE BRANCH
President
Four-year term by direct popular vote. Serves as head of state; commander-in-chief of armed forces. May dissolve Parliament after no-confidence vote in premier and Cabinet.

Vice-president
Elected on same ballot with president; assists with presidential duties.

Premier
Appointed by president. Serves as head of government.

Executive Yuan
Cabinet
Appointed by president. Chaired by premier; oversees government; may grant emergency powers to president.

JUDICIAL BRANCH
Judicial Yuan
(Judicial body)
Rules on constitutionality of laws; administers lower courts. Composed of 15 justices appointed to eight-year non-consecutive terms by president, approved by Parliament.

Supreme Court
High Court
District Courts

ROMANIA

OFFICIAL NAME: ROMANIA

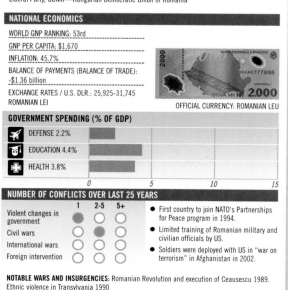

POPULATION: 21.7 MILLION	
CAPITAL: BUCHAREST	
AREA: 91,669 SQ. MILES (237,500 SQ. KM)	
INDEPENDENCE: 1877	
CONSTITUTION: 1991	

ROMANIA, which has a Latin-based language, means "land of the Romans" from its era as part of the Roman empire.

RELIGION: Romanian Orthodox 87%, Roman Catholic 5%, Protestant 4%, Greek Catholic (Uniate) 1%, Greek Orthodox 1%, Other 2%

OFFICIAL LANGUAGE: Romanian

REGIONS OR PROVINCES: 41 counties and 1 municipality

DEPENDENT TERRITORIES: None

MEDIA: Partial political censorship exists in national media

NEWSPAPERS: There are 106 daily newspapers

TV: 5 services: 2 state-owned, 3 independent

RADIO: 4 services: 3 state-owned, 1 independent

SUFFRAGE: 18 years of age; universal

LEGAL SYSTEM: French law; no ICJ jurisdiction

ETHNIC GROUPS:

- Magyar 9%
- Roma 1%
- Other 1%
- Romanian 89%

WORLD ORGANIZATIONS: ACCT, Australia Group, BIS, BSEC, CCC, CE, CEI, EAPC, EBRD, ECE, EU (applicant), FAO, G-9, G-77, IAEA, IBRD, ICAO, ICC, ICFTU, ICRM, IFAD, IFC, IFRCS, ILO, IMF, IMO, Interpol, IOC, IOM, ISO, ITU, LAIA (observer), MONUC, NAM (guest), NSG, OAS (observer), OPCW, OSCE, PCA, PFP, UN, UNCTAD, UNESCO, UNIDO, UNIKOM, UNMEE, UNMIBH, UNMIK, UPU, WCL, WEU (associate partner), WFTU, WHO, WIPO, WMO, WToO, WTrO, ZC

POLITICAL PARTIES: PDSR—Social Democratic Pole of Romania, (led by the Social Democracy Party of Romania), PRM—Greater Romania Party, PD—Democratic Party, PNL—National Liberal Party, UDMR—Hungarian Democratic Union of Romania

NATIONAL ECONOMICS

WORLD GNP RANKING: 53rd

GNP PER CAPITA: $1,670

INFLATION: 45.7%

BALANCE OF PAYMENTS (BALANCE OF TRADE): -$1.36 billion

EXCHANGE RATES / U.S. DLR.: 25,925-31,745 ROMANIAN LEI

OFFICIAL CURRENCY: ROMANIAN LEU

GOVERNMENT SPENDING (% OF GDP)

✈ DEFENSE	2.2%
📚 EDUCATION	4.4%
✚ HEALTH	3.8%

0 5 10 15

NUMBER OF CONFLICTS OVER LAST 25 YEARS

	1	2-5	5+
Violent changes in government	●	○	○
Civil wars	○	●	○
International wars	○	○	○
Foreign intervention	○	○	○

- First country to join NATO's Partnerships for Peace program in 1994.
- Limited training of Romanian military and civilian officials by US.
- Soldiers were deployed with US in "war on terrorism" in Afghanistan in 2002.

NOTABLE WARS AND INSURGENCIES: Romanian Revolution and execution of Ceausescu 1989. Ethnic violence in Transylvania 1990

ROMANIA GAINED STATEHOOD as an independent monarchy in 1878 after years of domination by Poland, Hungary and the Ottomans. When it became a communist People's Republic in 1947, Romania presented a more liberal image to the West than other Soviet satellites. The liberal façade was kept up by Nicolae Ceausescu, who became president in 1967, but his regime was one of harsh repression enforced by the Securitate secret police. The last member of the former Warsaw Pact to overthrow its Communist-era dictator and begin a transition to democracy and a market system, Romania has experienced enormous difficulty in initiating economic and political reforms. A poor economy, combined with frequent border disputes and Romanian political parties' long reliance on nationalism for political gain, has exacerbated ethnic tensions and violence targeted at minority Roma and Hungarians.

A 1989 "revolution" ousted Ceausescu, but was limited in scope. Ion Iliescu (a former Communist Party official) and the conservative National Salvation Front then took control. They outlawed the Communist Party, declared a return to democratic ideals, and repealed some

HUMAN CHAIN PROTEST—MARCH 11, 2003
An estimated 3,000 Romanians formed a chain nearly two miles long around the presidential palace, demanding the release of secret information regarding the names of informers and officers of the Securitate.

of Ceausescu's most unpopular social measures, including bans on abortion and contraception. A 1991 referendum approved a new Parliament-drafted constitution that established a bicameral legislature and affirmed civil rights and political pluralism, while proclaiming Romania a democracy and market economy. The regime's make-up of former communists made significant political reorganization doubtful.

Iliescu was returned to the presidency through subsequent national elections. His renamed Social Democratic Pole of Romania (PDSR) maintained control until 1996, when coalition center-right parties took over the presidency and Parliament. Treaties signed with the EU in 1993, Hungary in 1996, and Ukraine in 1997 show Romania's commitment to building closer ties with western Europe. Iliescu, now a social democrat, regained control in the 2000 elections, boosted by support from conservative miners and rural workers. In 2001 the PDSR electoral coalition merged its two main constituent parties to form the Social Democrat Party (PSD).

HOW THE GOVERNMENT WORKS

LEGISLATIVE BRANCH

Parlament
(Parliament)
Bicameral Parliament

Senat
(Senate)
Composed of 140 members elected to four-year terms by proportional representation.

Adunarea Deputatilor
(Chamber of Deputies)
Composed of 328 members elected to four-year terms by proportional representation; 15 seats reserved for ethnic minority parties.

Regional Governments
Forty-one counties governed by elected councils and prefects appointed by central government.

EXECUTIVE BRANCH

President
Elected to four-year term by direct popular vote; two-term limit. Severs political ties when assumes office. Serves as head of state; commander-in-chief of armed forces. May return bills to Parliament; calls for referenda; dissolves Parliament; issue decrees co-signed by prime minister.

Prime Minister
Nominated by president, appointed by both chambers of Parliament. Serves as head of government; presides over Council of Ministers.

Council of Ministers
Members appointed by prime minister. Oversees government operations; answers to Parliament.

JUDICIAL BRANCH

Constitutional Court
Rules on constitutionality of laws. Nine judges appointed to nine-year terms: three by Chamber of Deputies; three by Senate; three by president.

Superior Council of Magistracy
Ensures independence of justice. Fifteen judges or prosecutors appointed by Parliament to four-year terms.

Supreme Court of Justice
Highest court of review and appeal. Forty justices appointed to six-year terms by president.

Courts of Appeal

Tribunals

Courts of First Instance

YEMEN

OFFICIAL NAME: REPUBLIC OF YEMEN

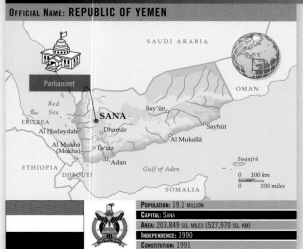

POPULATION: 19.1 MILLION
CAPITAL: SANA
AREA: 203,849 SQ. MILES (527,970 SQ. KM)
INDEPENDENCE: 1990
CONSTITUTION: 1991

YEMEN's name means "to the south" or "to the right" in Arabic, indicating its location on the southern tip of the Arabian peninsula.

RELIGION: Muslim including Shaf'i (Sunni) and Zaydi (Shi'a), small numbers of Jewish, Christian, and Hindu

OFFICIAL LANGUAGE: Arabic

REGIONS OR PROVINCES: 19 governorates

DEPENDENT TERRITORIES: None

MEDIA: Government keeps tight control on the media

NEWSPAPERS: There are 4 daily newspapers

TV: 1 state-controlled service

RADIO: 1 state-controlled service

SUFFRAGE: 18 years of age; universal

LEGAL SYSTEM: Tribal customary laws; Shari'a (Islamic) law, Turkish and English common law; no ICJ jurisdiction

WORLD ORGANIZATIONS: ACC, AFESD, AL, AMF, CAEU, CCC, ESCWA, FAO, G-77, IAEA, IBRD, ICAO, ICFTU, ICRM, IDA, IDB, IFAD, IFC, IFRCS, ILO, IMF, IMO, Interpol, IOC, IOM, ITU, NAM, OAS (observer), OIC, OPCW, UN, UNCTAD, UNESCO, UNIDO, UPU, WFTU, WHO, WIPO, WMO, WToO, WTrO (observer)

POLITICAL PARTIES: There are over 12 political parties active in Yemen, some of the more prominent are: GPC—General People's Congress, Ind—Independents, YAR—Yemeni Alliance for Reform (al-Islah), NUPO—Nasserite Unionist Party, Ba'ath—Arab Socialist Ba'ath Party

ETHNIC GROUPS:

Indian, Somali, European 2%
Afro-Arab 3%
Arab 95%

NATIONAL ECONOMICS

WORLD GNP RANKING: 102nd

GNP PER CAPITA: $370

INFLATION: 7.9%

BALANCE OF PAYMENTS (BALANCE OF TRADE): $2.06 billion

EXCHANGE RATES / U.S. DLR.: 164.39-170.70 YEMENI RIALS

OFFICIAL CURRENCY: YEMENI RIAL

GOVERNMENT SPENDING (% OF GDP)

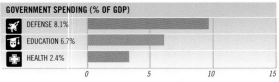

DEFENSE 8.1%
EDUCATION 6.7%
HEALTH 2.4%

0   5   10   15

NUMBER OF CONFLICTS OVER LAST 25 YEARS

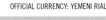

	1	2-5	5+
Violent changes in government	○	○	○
Civil wars	○	●	○
International wars	○	○	○
Foreign intervention	○	○	○

- Biggest threats are insurgent tribesmen and anti-Western terrorism.
- Difficulty in bringing the two defense forces of YAR and PDRY together since unification.
- Top al-Qaida terrorism suspects have been arrested in Yemen.

NOTABLE WARS AND INSURGENCIES: North-South war 1979. Southern civil wars 1986 and 1994. Border clashes with Saudi Arabia 1998-1999.

ONE OF THE WORLD'S MOST ANCIENT centers of civilization and home of the legendary Queen of Sheba, the Republic of Yemen is situated on the southern border of Saudi Arabia. The country, known to Romans as "Arabia Felix" which referred to the fertile lands and frankincense trade for which it was famous, was ruled by the Zaydi dynasty from the 9th century until its defeat by the Ottoman Turks in 1517.

Modern Yemen was born of a merger in 1990 between two, sometimes warring, neighbors: the Yemen Arab Republic (YAR), or North Yemen, and the Marxist People's Democratic Republic of Yemen (PDRY), or South Yemen. While the YAR had been ruled by a succession of military regimes, the PDRY had been the only Arab Marxist state. Ali Saleh, former president of the YAR, became president of Yemen, uniting it for the first time since 1735. In 1994, after civil war erupted, a secessionist movement was formed in the former PDRY under ex-vice president, Ali Salem al-Baidh. It was defeated, and the constitution was amended to strengthen the central government. In the 1997 elections Saleh's party—the GPC—won the absolute majority, although the victory was somewhat diminished by the boycott of the southern Yemeni Socialist Party. In 1999, Saleh was elected president in the first direct vote since unification. Though Yemen's leadership has received much praise for its attempts at a multiparty democracy in the face of a monarchical trend in the region, there is growing frustration within the country due to the social and economic problems, especially in the south, where the civil war had a devastating effect.

Yemen's considerable oil reserves only entered production in 1987. Unemployment reached catastrophic levels when Saudi Arabia expelled over a million Yemeni workers in 1991 because of Yemen's support for Iraq in the Gulf War. Relations with the Saudis remain strained over border disputes, oil exportation rights, and charges that Saudi cash bankrolls Yemeni insurgent tribesmen. A terrorist bomb attack in 2000 on the destroyer USS *Cole* in the Yemeni port of Aden, killing 17 US sailors, and repeated kidnappings of foreigners have damaged Yemen's relations with the West.

ISSUES AND CHALLENGES:

- Strained relations over oil exploration rights and an ongoing border dispute with neighbor Saudi Arabia, as well as rising tribal insurgencies threaten the stability of Yemen.

- Tourism has decreased and foreign investment has remained low owing to internal instability and terrorist acts against foreigners.

- There has been heavy economic damage caused by the civil war.

- Unemployment is rising owing to population growth.

- A poorly educated populace and high illiteracy rates, particularly amongst women, are a concern.

HOW THE GOVERNMENT WORKS

LEGISLATIVE BRANCH

Parliament
Bicameral Parliament

Shura
(Council)

Composed of 111 members appointed to six-year terms by president.

Majlis al-Nuwaab
(House of Representatives)

Composed of 301 members elected to six-year terms by direct popular vote. Enacts laws; approves state budget; ratifies international treaties and agreements.

Regional Governments
Nineteen governorates.

EXECUTIVE BRANCH

President
Elected to seven-year term by direct popular vote; two-term limit. Serves as head of state; commander-in-chief of armed forces. Promulgates laws; calls referenda; appoints senior civilian and military officials; grants political asylum.

Vice-president
Appointed by president.

Prime Minister
Appointed by president. Serves as head of government; presides over Council of Ministers.

Council of Ministers
Appointed by president on advice of prime minister. Oversees government operations; prepares state budget.

JUDICIAL BRANCH

The Supreme Court of the Republic
Highest court of review and appeal; rules on constitutionality of laws; tries top government officials; decides jurisdiction disputes between courts.

Criminal Courts
Civil Courts
Commercial Courts
Courts Martial

MOZAMBIQUE

OFFICIAL NAME: REPUBLIC OF MOZAMBIQUE

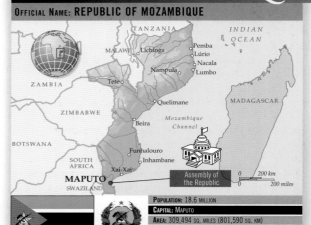

POPULATION: 18.6 MILLION	
CAPITAL: Maputo	
AREA: 309,494 SQ. MILES (801,590 SQ. KM)	
INDEPENDENCE: 1975	
CONSTITUTION: 1990	

MOZAMBIQUE is named, according to legend, after the local leader Mussa Mbiki, who controlled islands in the area when Portuguese explorers arrived in the 15th century.

RELIGION: Traditional beliefs 60%, Christian 30%, Muslim 10%

OFFICIAL LANGUAGE: Portuguese

REGIONS OR PROVINCES: 10 provinces, 1 city

DEPENDENT TERRITORIES: None

MEDIA: Partial political censorship exists in national media

NEWSPAPERS: There are 6 daily newspapers

TV: 2 services: 1 state-owned, 1 independent

RADIO: 3 services: 1 state-owned, 2 independent

SUFFRAGE: 18 years of age; universal

LEGAL SYSTEM: Customary and Portuguese law; no ICJ jurisdiction

WORLD ORGANIZATIONS: ACP, AfDB, C, CCC, ECA, FAO, G-77, IBRD, ICAO, ICFTU, ICRM, IDA, IDB, IFAD, IFC, IFRCS, IHO, ILO, IMF, IMO, Interpol, IOC, IOM (observer), ISO (correspondent), ITU, MONUC, NAM, OAU, OIC, OPCW, SADC, UN, UNCTAD, UNESCO, UNHCR, UNIDO, UNTAET, UPU, WFTU, WHO, WIPO, WMO, WToO, WTrO

POLITICAL PARTIES: FRELIMO—Front for the Liberation of Mozambique, RENAMO—Mozambique National Resistance

ETHNIC GROUPS:

Makua Lomwe 47%
Tsonga 23%
Malawi 12%
Shona 11%
Yao 4%
Other 3%

NATIONAL ECONOMICS

WORLD GNP RANKING: 123rd

GNP PER CAPITA: $210

INFLATION: 2.0%

BALANCE OF PAYMENTS (BALANCE OF TRADE): -$764 million

EXCHANGE RATES / U.S. DLR.: 17.175-22.885 METICAIS

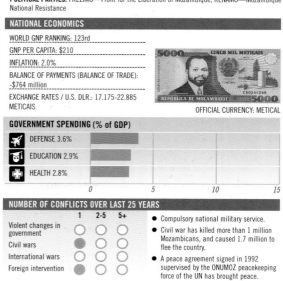

OFFICIAL CURRENCY: METICAL

GOVERNMENT SPENDING (% of GDP)

DEFENSE 3.6%
EDUCATION 2.9%
HEALTH 2.8%

	0	5	10	15

NUMBER OF CONFLICTS OVER LAST 25 YEARS

	1	2-5	5+
Violent changes in government	○	○	○
Civil wars	●	○	○
International wars	◐	○	○
Foreign intervention	●	○	○

- Compulsory national military service.
- Civil war has killed more than 1 million Mozambicans, and caused 1.7 million to flee the country.
- A peace agreement signed in 1992 supervised by the ONUMOZ peacekeeping force of the UN has brought peace.
- Difficulty retraining demobilized soldiers.

NOTABLE WARS AND INSURGENCIES: RENAMO Insurgency 1976-1992. UN intervention (ONUMOZ)

JUST AS IT WAS FINDING its way out of the catastrophic legacy of civil war and poverty, Mozambique was devastated in 2000 and 2001 by floods that displaced tens of thousands of people and further damaged a weak infrastructure.

Led by the Front for the Liberation of Mozambique (FRELIMO), Mozambique won independence from Portugal in 1975, concluding a ten-year war. The new Soviet-backed Marxist-Leninist regime faced immediate opposition from the anti-Marxist Mozambique National Resistance Movement (RENAMO), supported by Southern Rhodesia (now Zimbabwe) and South Africa. Sixteen years of brutal conflict followed. United Nations-aided attempts at peace in the 1980s failed, including the Nkomati Accord. In 1990, the government created a new constitution establishing a market economy, a multiparty system, and free elections, replacing the Marxist government with a social democracy. The UN General Peace Agreement (GPA) in 1992 ended the civil war, though the country remains polarised by the ruling FRELIMO party and the opposition RENAMO. In a very close and contested race, FRELIMO won multiparty elections in 1994. It again narrowly won in the 1999 elections, though RENAMO alleged electoral fraud.

Although it was never a British colony, Mozambique joined the Commonwealth of Nations in 1995, securing additional aid. Mozambique is one of the world's poorest nations, and the second-most dependent on foreign aid. At the head of the government is the president, elected for up to three five-year terms and backed by the prime minister. President Joaquim Chissano has been in office since 1986. The president can dissolve the unicameral legislature, the Assembly of the Republic. Until the 1990 constitution established an independent judiciary, the Assembly controlled the judicial system. The constitutional court required by the constitution has yet to be established, so the Supreme Court serves as the highest court. The understaffed, antiquated judicial system is frequently criticized for corruption and inefficiency.

ISSUES AND CHALLENGES:

- Mozambique has been ravaged by AIDS, poverty, years of civil war, bureaucratic corruption and—most recently—devastating floods.

- The country is one of the poorest in the world, and one of the countries most dependent on foreign aid.

- Efforts to revitalize the tourism industry, one of the most promising options for economic development, are hindered by a lack of transportation within the country, the prevalence of land mines, and disease, including cholera.

- Allegations of election fraud from RENAMO, walk-outs by RENAMO members of the legislature, and threats by the northern and central provinces to form a separate government have contributed to the polarisation of Mozambique's political environment.

HOW THE GOVERNMENT WORKS

LEGISLATIVE BRANCH
Assembleia da República
(Assembly of the Republic)
Unicameral Parliament
Composed of 250 members directly elected to five-year terms by proportional representation. Meets twice annually.

Regional Governments
Ten provinces overseen by governor appointed by president.
Capital Maputo governed by elected city council and chairman.

EXECUTIVE BRANCH
President
Elected to five-year term by direct popular vote; limit of three terms.
Serves as head of state and government; commander-in-chief of armed forces.
May dissolve Assembly of the Republic.

Prime Minister
Appointed by president. Presides over Council of Ministers; presents budget and government programs to Assembly of the Republic.

Council of Ministers
Appointed by president.

JUDICIAL BRANCH
Supreme Court
Highest court for civil and criminal appeals; rules on constitutionality of laws; hears charges against members of Assembly of the Republic. Court president and vice-president appointed by president.

Provincial Courts
District Courts
Military Courts

IVORY COAST

OFFICIAL NAME: REPUBLIC OF CÔTE D'IVOIRE

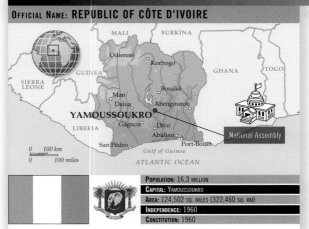

POPULATION: 16.3 MILLION
CAPITAL: YAMOUSSOUKRO
AREA: 124,502 SQ. MILES (322,460 SQ. KM)
INDEPENDENCE: 1960
CONSTITUTION: 1960

IVORY COAST was so-named because of the abundance of ivory exported from the area by Europeans.

RELIGION: Muslim 25%, Roman Catholic 23%, Traditional beliefs 23%, Protestant 6%, Other 23%

OFFICIAL LANGUAGE: French

REGIONS OR PROVINCES: 58 departments

DEPENDENT TERRITORIES: None

MEDIA: Total political censorship exists in national media

Newspapers: There are 16 daily newspapers

TV: 2 services: 1 state-owned, 1 independent

Radio: 8 services: 1 state-owned, 7 independent

SUFFRAGE: 18 years of age; universal

LEGAL SYSTEM: Customary and French law; no ICJ jurisdiction

WORLD ORGANIZATIONS: ACP, AfDB, CCC, ECA, ECOWAS, Entente, FAO, FZ, G-24, G-77, IAEA, IBRD, ICAO, ICFTU, ICRM, IDA, IFAD, IFC, IFRCS, ILO, IMF, IMO, Interpol, IOC, IOM, ISO (correspondent), ITU, NAM, OAU, OIC, OPCW, UN, UNCTAD, UNESCO, UNHCR, UNIDO, UPU, WADB (regional), WAEMU, WCL, WFTU, WHO, WIPO, WMO, WToO, WTrO

POLITICAL PARTIES: FPI—Ivorian Popular Front, PDCI—Democratic Party of Ivory Coast, Ind—Independent, RDR—Rally of the Republicans, PIT—Ivorian Labor Party

ETHNIC GROUPS:

- Other 3%
- Southern Mandes 10%
- Krous 11%
- Northern Mandes 16%
- Voltaiques or Gur 18%
- Akan 42%

NATIONAL ECONOMICS

WORLD GNP RANKING: 85th

GNP PER CAPITA: $600

INFLATION: 2.5%

BALANCE OF PAYMENTS (BALANCE OF TRADE): -$13.0 million

EXCHANGE RATES / U.S. DLR.: 698.7-736.7 CFA FRANCS

OFFICIAL CURRENCY: CFA FRANC

GOVERNMENT SPENDING (% of GDP)

- ✈ DEFENSE 0.9%
- 🎓 EDUCATION 4.2%
- ✚ HEALTH 1.2%

0   5   10   15

NUMBER OF CONFLICTS OVER LAST 25 YEARS

	1	2-5	5+
Violent changes in government		●	
Civil wars		●	
International wars		●	
Foreign intervention	●		

- Compulsory national military service.
- France is major supplier of weapons and training for armed forces.
- French and West African troops maintain peace following peace accords, although tensions remain between rebel-dominated north and government-controlled south.

NOTABLE WARS AND INSURGENCIES: Coup 1999. Popular uprising 2000. Civil war 2002-2003

WHEN EUROPEANS, mainly French and Portuguese, started trading ivory and slaves on the coast of today's Côte d'Ivoire, or Ivory Coast, in the 18th century, the interior was divided into several kingdoms, including those of Islamic culture in the north and Akan culture in the forested interior. Treaties signed with indigenous kings made the area a French colony in 1893. Since its independence from France in 1960, Ivory Coast has, until recently, been one of the most prosperous and politically stable countries in West Africa. Its success is due in large part to its position as the world's largest producer of cocoa, which has served as its cornerstone industry. Consequently, urban living standards are higher than in most African countries.

The economic stability of the country allowed the author of the 1960 constitution, Félix Houphouët-Boigny, to serve peacefully as president from independence until his death in 1993. Not surprisingly, the 1960 constitution grants most political power to the president, who has the ability to initiate legislation in the National Assembly as well as submit bills to national referendum. The president also has complete control over the Cabinet. Houphouët-Boigny's death initiated a period of political instability from which the country is still recovering. The speaker of the National Assembly became president, as law mandates. Subsequent elections were marred by accusations of the president's tampering with votes to ensure re-election. The challenges to political legitimacy, coupled with falling cocoa prices, culminated in the country's first military coup in 1999.

The military regime of General Robert Guei was ousted after Guei ran for president in October 2000, excluding opposition-party candidates from the ballot and falsely pronouncing himself the winner. Violent popular protests followed, and Guei left the country. Laurent Gbagbo, the actual winner of the election, took office after skirmishes among the opposition parties. His Ivorian Popular Front (FPI) party dominated legislative elections, held two months, later by a slim margin.

Electoral fraud and political rifts are not the only challenges. Inadequate investment in education and professional training has produced a lack of skilled labor. It is rumored that unskilled labor on cocoa plantations is undertaken by slaves.

ISSUES AND CHALLENGES:

- An overdependence on cocoa and coffee makes Ivory Coast susceptible to fluctuations in the world market.
- The incidence of HIV and AIDS is high, affecting approximately 10 percent of the population. In 2001, suppliers agreed to cut the prices of drugs to make treatment affordable.
- Instability in Liberia is a cause of much concern for the government, as is the reported support of local rebel fighters by Liberia and Burkina Faso.
- Crime and corruption are prevalent.

HOW THE GOVERNMENT WORKS

LEGISLATIVE BRANCH
Assemblée Nationale
(National Assembly)
Unicameral Parliament
Composed of 225 members elected to five-year terms by direct popular vote. Meets twice annually; Ratifies presidential decisions; powers limited to voting laws and authorizing taxes.

Regional Governments
Fifty departments, each governed by prefect appointed by president.

EXECUTIVE BRANCH
President
Elected to five-year term by direct popular vote. Serves as head of state; commander-in-chief of armed forces. Initiates legislation; calls referenda; appoints high-ranking civil and military leaders; negotiates treaties.

Prime Minister
Appointed by president. Serves as head of government.

Cabinet
Members appointed by president. Presided over by president.

JUDICIAL BRANCH
Supreme Court
Consists of four chambers: Judicial Chamber, Audit Chamber, Constitutional Chamber, and Administrative Chamber.

High Court of Justice
Rules on charges of treason and criminal cases involving National Assembly members. National Assembly members serve as judges.

The Court of Appeals

Lower Courts

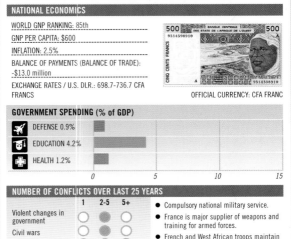

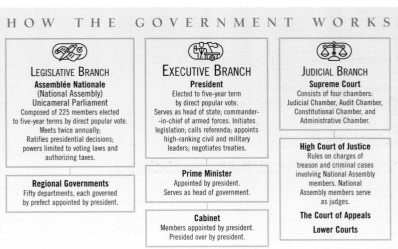

179

BURKINA FASO

OFFICIAL NAME: BURKINA FASO

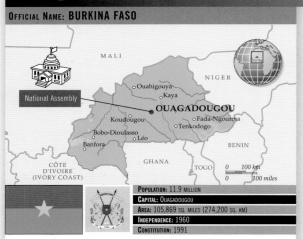

MALI
NIGER
Ouahigouya
Kaya
OUAGADOUGOU
Koudougou
Fada-Ngourma
Tenkodogo
Bobo-Dioulasso
Léo
Banfora
BENIN
National Assembly
CÔTE
D'IVOIRE
(IVORY COAST)
GHANA
TOGO
0   100 km
0   100 miles

POPULATION: 11.9 million
CAPITAL: OUAGADOUGOU
AREA: 105,869 SQ. MILES (274,200 SQ. KM)
INDEPENDENCE: 1960
CONSTITUTION: 1991

BURKINA FASO means "the country of honorable people" and was adopted as the new name in 1984.

RELIGION: Traditional beliefs 55%, Muslim 35%, Roman Catholic 9%, Other Christian 1%

OFFICIAL LANGUAGE: French

REGIONS OR PROVINCES: 45 provinces

DEPENDENT TERRITORIES: None

MEDIA: Partial political censorship exists in the national media

NEWSPAPERS: There are 6 daily newspapers

TV: 4 services: 1 state-owned, 3 independent

RADIO: 1 state-owned service, 46 independent stations

SUFFRAGE: Universal

LEGAL SYSTEM: Customary and French law; no ICJ jurisdiction

WORLD ORGANIZATIONS: ACCT, ACP, AfDB, CCC, ECA, ECOWAS, Entente, FAO, FZ, G-77, IAEA, IBRD, ICAO, ICC, ICFTU, ICRM, IDA, IDB, IFAD, IFC, IFRCS, ILO, IMF, Interpol, IOC, IOM, ISO (subscriber), ITU, MONUC, NAM, OAU, OIC, OPCW, PCA, UN, UNCTAD, UNESCO, UNIDO, UPU, WADB (regional), WAEMU, WCL, WFTU, WHO, WIPO, WMO, WToO, WTrO

POLITICAL PARTIES: CDP—Congress for Democracy and Progress, ADF-RDA—Alliance for Democracy and Federation-African Democratic Rally, PDP—Party for Democracy and Progress, PAREN—Party for National Renewal

ETHNIC GROUPS:

Mossi 50% — Other 50%

NATIONAL ECONOMICS

WORLD GNP RANKING: 134th

GNP PER CAPITA: $210

INFLATION: -0.3%

BALANCE OF PAYMENTS (BALANCE OF TRADE): -$65m

EXCHANGE RATES / U.S. DLR.: 698.7–736.7 CFA FRANCS

OFFICIAL CURRENCY: CFA FRANC

GOVERNMENT SPENDING (% OF GDP)

		0	5	10	15
DEFENSE 1.8%					
EDUCATION 3%					
HEALTH 1.5%					

NUMBER OF CONFLICTS OVER LAST 25 YEARS

	1	2-5	5+
Violent changes in government	○	●	○
Civil wars	○	○	○
International wars	○	○	○
Foreign intervention	○	●	○

- No compulsory national military service.
- France is major supplier of weapons and training for armed forces.
- Border areas are home to Liberian and Côte d'Ivoire rebels and refugees.

NOTABLE WARS AND INSURGENCIES: Coups 1980, 1983 and 1987. Border conflicts with Mali in 1985

KNOWN AS UPPER VOLTA when it gained independence from France in 1960, Burkina Faso was governed largely by its military in the three decades after independence, with succession by coup as the rule. Political parties were repeatedly banned during this period, but resistance and opposition to the central government could not be suppressed. Captain Thomas Sankara, appointed prime minister in 1983, vowed to democratize the country. Despite his initial popularity, Sankara was assassinated in a popularly supported coup that brought to power former associate Captain Blaise Compaoré. A democratic constitution was approved by referendum in 1991, and Compaoré was elected president the following year. As many as 46 registered political parties sprang up. Multiparty municipal elections were held twice, and Compaoré was elected for a second term in 1998, with almost 90 percent of the vote.

The constitution calls for a strong president, a prime minister, a Council of Ministers, and an independent bicameral legislature and judiciary. Although the document's intent is to create a multiparty representative government, democratic institutions are fragile. The legislative and judicial branches are easily bullied by the strong president, and constitutional checks and balances are seldom effective. Though the 36-member Council of Ministers includes members of opposition parties and non-political ministers, it is still dominated by Compaoré and his ruling party, the Congress for Democracy and Progress (CDP). Assassinations of Compaoré's close military colleagues and journalist Norbert Zongo (who was investigating the death of Compaoré's brother's chauffeur) are reminiscent of the methods of the country's previous military dictatorships and have fueled opposition. One group, Collective Against Impunity, have challenged Compaoré to bring the murderers to justice, while making political reforms.

The CDP has won all its elections convincingly with an increasing percentage of the electorate voting, but critics question the legitimacy of the results. Strong political divisions, rampant corruption, and a weak economy hamper the country's full transition to democracy.

ISSUES AND CHALLENGES:

- Though Burkina Faso is a multi-party democracy on paper and, to some degree, in practice, it suffers from authoritarian rule and has yet to hold elections that are generally perceived to be fair. Fueling the problem of legitimacy is the problem of being a former European colony. As with many other African countries, Europeans carved out Burkina Faso without regard to the location of diverse tribal groups. National boundaries do not necessarily reflect local allegiances, and ethnic institutions remain trusted alternatives to the central government. Within this context, popular attitudes toward even the ideal of a central representative government remain unclear.

HOW THE GOVERNMENT WORKS

LEGISLATIVE BRANCH

Assemblée Nationale
(National Assembly)
Bicameral Parliament

Assemblée des Députés Populaires
(Assembly of Popular Deputies)
Composed of 111 members elected to five-year terms by direct popular vote.
Introduces and passes legislation.

Chambre des Représentants
(Chamber of Representatives)
Composed of 178 members appointed to three-year terms on non-party basis by provincial councils.
Serves as consultative body.

Regional Governments
Forty-five provinces governed by elected local councils.

EXECUTIVE BRANCH

President
Elected to five-year terms by direct popular vote, with two-term limit.
Serves as head of state.
May introduce bills in Parliament.

Prime Minister
Appointed by president, approved by Parliament.
Serves as head of government.

Council of Ministers
Composed of 36 members, including opposition party members and non-political ministers appointed by president on advice of prime minister. Oversees government operations.

JUDICIAL BRANCH

Supreme Court
Highest court of review and appeal.
Divided into four chambers specializing in the resolution of constitutional, administrative, judicial, and financial disputes.

Courts of Appeal
Two courts; hear civil, criminal, and commercial case appeals.

Tribunals of First Instance
Ten courts; hear civil and criminal cases.

MALI

OFFICIAL NAME: REPUBLIC OF MALI

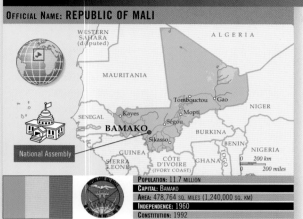

POPULATION: 11.7 MILLION
CAPITAL: BAMAKO
AREA: 478,764 SQ. MILES (1,240,000 SQ. KM)
INDEPENDENCE: 1960
CONSTITUTION: 1992

MALI was named after the ancient African kingdom of Mali, the second Sahelian kingdom.

RELIGION: Muslim (mainly Sunni) 80%, Traditional beliefs 18%, Christian 1%, Other 1%

OFFICIAL LANGUAGE: French

REGIONS OR PROVINCES: 8 regions, 1capital district

DEPENDENT TERRITORIES: None

MEDIA: No political censorship

NEWSPAPERS: There are 5 daily newspapers

TV: 3 services: 1 state-owned, 2 independent

RADIO: 15 services: 1 state-owned, 14 independent

SUFFRAGE: 18 years of age; universal

LEGAL SYSTEM: Customary and French law; no ICJ jurisdiction

WORLD ORGANIZATIONS: ACCT, ACP, AfDB, CCC, ECA, ECOWAS, FAO, FZ, G-77, IAEA, IBRD, ICAO, ICFTU, ICRM, IDA, IDB, IFAD, IFC, IFRCS, ILO, IMF, Interpol, IOC, IOM, ISO (subscriber), ITU, MIPONUH, NAM, OAU, OIC, OPCW, UN, UNAMSIL, UNCTAD, UNESCO, UNIDO, UPU, WADB (regional), WAEMU, WFTU, WHO, WIPO, WMO, WToO, WTrO

POLITICAL PARTIES: Espoir 2002—Hope 2002 (led by the Rally for Mali-RPM), ARD—Alliance for the Republic and Democracy, (led by the Alliance for Democracy in Mali-ADEMA), ACC—Convergence for Rotation and Change, Ind—Independents, SADI—Party for African Solidarity, Democracy and Integration

ETHNIC GROUPS:

- Songhai 6%
- Other 5%
- Tuareg and Moor 10%
- Voltaic 12%
- Mande 50%
- Peul 17%

NATIONAL ECONOMICS

WORLD GNP RANKING: 132nd

GNP PER CAPITA: $240

INFLATION: -0.7%

BALANCE OF PAYMENTS (BALANCE OF TRADE): -$178 million

EXCHANGE RATES / U.S. DLR.: 698.7-736.7 CFA FRANCS

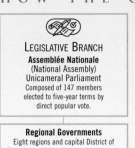

OFFICIAL CURRENCY: CFA FRANC

GOVERNMENT SPENDING (% OF GDP)

- ✈ DEFENSE 1%
- 🎓 EDUCATION 3%
- ✚ HEALTH 2.1%

0   5   10   15

NUMBER OF CONFLICTS OVER LAST 25 YEARS

	1	2-5	5+
Violent changes in government	●	○	○
Civil wars		○	○
International wars	●	○	○
Foreign intervention	○	○	○

- Compulsory national military service.
- As part of ECOWAS, armed forces assisted ECOMIL in Liberia in 2003.
- The US provides military equipment to help in the fight against cross-border terrorism.
- Bandits from Mali often attack towns across the border in Algeria.

NOTABLE WARS AND INSURGENCIES: Agacher Strip War with Burkina Faso 1985. Tuareg separatism 1990-1995

AFTER GENERATIONS OF COLONIAL RULE, Mali secured independence in 1960, then spent the next three decades under first a Marxist president and then the lengthy dictatorship of General Moussa Traoré. Traoré's own military toppled his rule, ushering in a new constitution and elections in 1992, and the multiparty democratic government that rules today.

Historically, Mali was the ancient homeland of a centuries-long succession of powerful African empires—the Ghana starting around A.D. 700, followed by the Malinké and the Songhai. Later, in the European scramble to claim African territory, France overcame stiff armed resistance by Malian warriors, established the colony of French Soudan before the close of the 19th century, and governed the land for nearly seven decades. Traoré's long military rule after independence survived several failed coups, sporadic student-led protests, and a chronically sagging economy until the early 1990s. Renewed student demonstrations then drew support from trade unionists and government workers, erupting into anti-government riots and the dictator's removal from power. He was replaced by an interim president and later by President Alpha Oumar Konaré.

Mali's young parliamentary democracy provides for a popularly elected president who serves as the head of state, an appointed prime minister and Council of Ministers, an independent judiciary that relies significantly on French legal codes, and a unicameral legislature that meets for two sessions each year.

While at least eight political parties vie for power inside the Assemblée Nationale, or National Assembly, Mali's activist student groups remain a potent outside force in pressuring the government and influencing election outcomes. Rural residents angered by the lack of basic services, and government workers irked by lagging salaries exert considerable clout as well. After economic reforms failed to revive the country's flagging economy, voters in the 2002 elections—with the support of opposition parties—chose Amadou Toumai Touré as president, the retired military officer who had led the coup against Traoré and helped return the country to civilian rule.

ISSUES AND CHALLENGES:

- Mali remains one of the world's ten poorest countries, with six of every ten citizens living below the poverty line.
- With some 70 percent of its people occupied in farming and fishing, Mali struggles with a chronic shortage of educated and skilled workers.
- Heavily dependent on foreign aid, Mali's economy is also especially vulnerable to fluctuations in world prices for cotton, gold and livestock, its main exports.
- Female genital mutilation is widespread among Malian women, especially in rural areas where the practice follows traditional customs.

HOW THE GOVERNMENT WORKS

LEGISLATIVE BRANCH

Assemblée Nationale
(National Assembly)
Unicameral Parliament
Composed of 147 members elected to five-year terms by direct popular vote.

Regional Governments
Eight regions and capital District of Bamako, each overseen by governor who reports to minister of territorial administration and internal security.

EXECUTIVE BRANCH

President
Elected to five-year term by direct popular vote. Serves as head of state; commander-in-chief of armed forces. Vetoes legislation; calls for referenda; dissolves National Assembly; grants pardons and amnesty; declares states of emergency.

Prime Minister
Appointed by president. Coordinates Council of Ministers.

Council of Ministers
Composed of 22 members appointed by president on advice of prime minister.

JUDICIAL BRANCH

Constitutional Court
Rules on constitutionality of laws. Composed of nine members who serve seven-year terms with two-term limit: three named by president; three by president of National Assembly; three by Superior Council of the Magistracy.

High Court of Justice
Hears charges of crimes or treason by president and government ministers. Composed of members named by National Assembly.

Supreme Court
Highest court for civil and criminal appeals.

Court of Appeals

Lower Courts

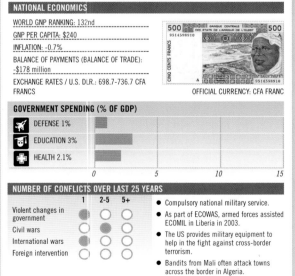

NIGER

OFFICIAL NAME: REPUBLIC OF NIGER

POPULATION: 11.2 MILLION
CAPITAL: NIAMEY
AREA: 489,188 SQ. MILES (1,267,000 SQ. KM)
INDEPENDENCE: 1960
CONSTITUTION: 1999

NIGER is thought to be derived from the word for "river" in Songhai or from the Latin for "black".

RELIGION: Muslim 80%, Indigenous beliefs and Christian 20%

OFFICIAL LANGUAGE: French

REGIONS OR PROVINCES: 7 departments, 1 capital district

DEPENDENT TERRITORIES: None

MEDIA: Partial political censorship exists in national media

NEWSPAPERS: There is 1 daily newspaper

TV: 3 services: 2 state-owned, 1 independent

RADIO: 3 services: 1 state-owned, 2 independent

SUFFRAGE: 18 years of age; universal

LEGAL SYSTEM: Customary and French law; no ICJ jurisdiction

WORLD ORGANIZATIONS: ACCT, ACP, AfDB, CCC, ECA, ECOWAS, Entente, FAO, FZ, G-77, IAEA, IBRD, ICAO, ICFTU, ICRM, IDA, IDB, IFAD, IFC, IFRCS, ILO, IMF, Interpol, IOC, ITU, MIPONUH, MONUC, NAM, OAU, OIC, OPCW, UN, UNCTAD, UNESCO, UNIDO, UNMIK, UPU, WADB (regional), WAEMU, WCL, WFTU, WHO, WIPO, WMO, WToO, WTrO

POLITICAL PARTIES: MNSD—National Movement for the Development of Society, CDS—Democratic and Social Convention, PNDS—Niger Democracy and Progress, ANDP—Niger Alliance for Democracy and Progress

ETHNIC GROUPS:

- Other 6%
- Tuareg 9%
- Fulani 10%
- Djerma and Songhai 21%
- Hausa 54%

NATIONAL ECONOMICS

WORLD GNP RANKING: 139th

GNP PER CAPITA: $180

INFLATION: 2.9%

BALANCE OF PAYMENTS (BALANCE OF TRADE): -$168 million

EXCHANGE RATES / U.S. DLR.: 698.7–736.7 CFA FRANCS

OFFICIAL CURRENCY: CFA FRANC

GOVERNMENT SPENDING (% OF GDP)

✈ DEFENSE 1.5%		
🎓 EDUCATION 2.7%		
✚ HEALTH 1.2%		

0   5   10   15

NUMBER OF CONFLICTS OVER LAST 25 YEARS

	1	2-5	5+
Violent changes in government	○	●	○
Civil wars	○	●	○
International wars	○	○	○
Foreign intervention	○	○	○

- Compulsory national military service.
- Military dominate political arena.
- As part of ECOWAS, armed forces assisted ECOMIL in Côte d'Ivoire in 2003.
- France is the primary provider of military aid, providing both training in France and equipment.

NOTABLE WARS AND INSURGENCIES: Tuareg separatism 1990-1995. Coups and army mutinies

ONCE AN IMPORTANT CROSSROADS of transafrican trade, Niger is today one of the poorest nations in the world. The largest country in West Africa, Niger is located along the southern edge of the Sahara Desert. Landlocked between seven other African countries, Niger's only access to the sea is along the Niger River. A majority of its people are farmers; many others in the arid and semi-arid regions are nomads and herders. While much of its economy is based on subsistence agriculture, Niger has some of the world's largest uranium deposits, which have helped its export picture. From the early 20th century to 1960, Niger was a French colony. Since gaining independence from France, the country has had a number of different governments, including one-party and military rule.

For 14 years, a single-party civilian regime ran Niger under President Hamani Diori, who was overthrown in 1974 on charges of corruption and as a result of public desperation over severe food shortages caused by the worst drought in 15 years. A military coup was led by General Seyni Kountche, who remained in power until his death in 1987. In the early 1990s, Niger developed a multiparty democratic regime, which held several free elections. After five years, divisions within the ruling coalition led to a military coup by General Ibrahim Baré Mainassara. Mainassara's government fell three years later, when he was assassinated by his own national guard. In 1999, a new military regime established a transitional National Reconciliation Council that drafted a new constitution with a semi-presidential system, as had been the case in the 1992 constitution of the Third Republic. The constitution was approved in a popular vote that was considered free and fair. Mamadou Tandja led a coalition of the National Movement for the Development of Society (MNSD) and the Democratic and Social Convention (CDS) parties, and won the presidency.

Currently a multiparty republic, Niger has executive power mostly in the hands of its president who is both of chief of state and head of government, although the prime minister's duties involve the implementation of the president's agenda.

ISSUES AND CHALLENGES:

- Niger's foremost challenge is its enduring poverty. The French did little to develop the economy, and economic progress has been sporadic since independence. The country has a high fertility rate and a very high rate of child mortality. Only 34 percent of children attend school. In 2000, Niger's newly elected government embarked upon an ambitious program of economic reform. Twelve large companies were to be privatized, and the government was taking action to reduce corruption and increase free and fair competition among businesses.

- A dependence on uranium reserves makes Niger susceptible to low world market prices, as was the case in the 1980s.

- Ongoing tensions between the various ethnic groups, Tuareg, Toubou, Djerma and Hausa, and the government.

HOW THE GOVERNMENT WORKS

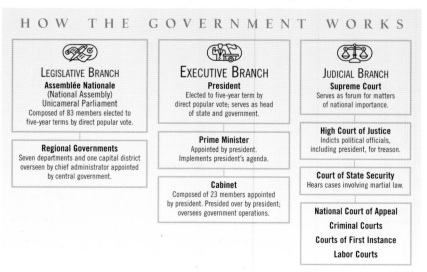

LEGISLATIVE BRANCH

Assemblée Nationale (National Assembly) Unicameral Parliament
Composed of 83 members elected to five-year terms by direct popular vote.

Regional Governments
Seven departments and one capital district overseen by chief administrator appointed by central government.

EXECUTIVE BRANCH

President
Elected to five-year term by direct popular vote; serves as head of state and government.

Prime Minister
Appointed by president. Implements president's agenda.

Cabinet
Composed of 23 members appointed by president. Presided over by president; oversees government operations.

JUDICIAL BRANCH

Supreme Court
Serves as forum for matters of national importance.

High Court of Justice
Indicts political officials, including president, for treason.

Court of State Security
Hears cases involving martial law.

National Court of Appeal

Criminal Courts

Courts of First Instance

Labor Courts

SERBIA & MONTENEGRO

OFFICIAL NAME: SERBIA AND MONTENEGRO

POPULATION: 10.5 MILLION
CAPITAL: BELGRADE
AREA: 39,517 SQ. MILES (102,350 SQ. KM)
INDEPENDENCE: 1992
CONSTITUTION: 2003

SERBIA AND MONTENEGRO derives from *serbi* meaning "men", and *montenegro* meaning "black mountain" referring to the mountains that cover much of Montenegro.

RELIGION: Orthodox 65%, Muslim 19%, Roman Catholic 4%, Protestant 1%, Other 11%

OFFICIAL LANGUAGE: Serbo-croat

REGIONS OR PROVINCES: 2 republics, Serbia contains 2 autonomous provinces

DEPENDENT TERRITORIES: None

MEDIA: Free media is flourishing

NEWSPAPERS: There are 18 daily newspapers

TV: 2 state-controlled, several independent services

RADIO: 3 state-controlled, several independent services

SUFFRAGE: 16 years of age, if employed; 18 years of age, universal

LEGAL SYSTEM: Civil law; no ICJ jurisdiction

WORLD ORGANIZATIONS: ABEDA, BIS, CCC, CE (guest), CEI, EBRD, FAO, G- 9, G-77, IAEA, IBRD, ICAO, ICC, ICFTU, ICRM, IDA, IFAD, IFC, IFRCS, IHO, ILO, IMF, IMO, Interpol, IOC, IOM, ISO, ITU, NAM, OPCW, OSCE, PCA, UN, UNCTAD, UNESCO, UNIDO, UPU, WHO, WIPO, WMO, WToO, WTrO (observer)

POLITICAL PARTIES: DOS—Democratic Opposition of Serbia, SVM—Alliance of Vojvodina Hungarians, LDK—Democratic League of Kosovo, DLECG—Democratic List for European Montenegro, DS—Democratic Party, DSS—Democratic Party of Serbia, DPS—Democratic Party of Socialists of Montenegro, SSJ—Party of Serb Unity, SRS—Serbian Radical Party, SPS—Serbian Socialist Party, SDP—Social Democratic Party, ZP—Together for Changes

ETHNIC GROUPS:
- Magyar 3%
- Montenegrin 5%
- Bosniak 3%
- Other 10%
- Albanian 17%
- Serb 62%

NATIONAL ECONOMICS

WORLD GNP RANKING: 83rd

GNP PER CAPITA: $940

INFLATION: 42%

BALANCE OF PAYMENTS (BALANCE OF TRADE): -$1.42 billion

EXCHANGE RATES / U.S. DLR.: 13.65-66.48 DINARS

CURRENCY: DINAR (EURO IN MONTENEGRO)

GOVERNMENT SPENDING (% OF GDP)

- ✈ DEFENSE 10%
- 📖 EDUCATION 4.2%
- ✚ HEALTH 4.5%

	0	5	10	15

NUMBER OF CONFLICTS OVER LAST 25 YEARS

	1	2-5	5+
Violent changes in government	●	○	○
Civil wars	●	○	○
International wars	●	○	○
Foreign intervention	●	○	○

- Compulsory national military service.
- Military targeted by NATO in the air strikes of 1999, following the role of the Serbian military in the conflict in Yugoslavia.
- Soldiers were deployed for the first time in a UN peacekeeping mission in East Timor in 2002.

NOTABLE WARS AND INSURGENCIES: Wars of the Yugoslav Succession 1991-1995. Kosovo conflict 1998-1999. NATO intervention (K-For). Assassination of Prime Minister Zoran Djindjic 2003

FOR THE PEOPLE OF SERBIA AND MONTENEGRO, ethnic ties are stronger than national boundaries. Throughout decades of being grouped and regrouped with other Slavic peoples, autonomy remained an abiding goal. In 1918, Serbia, Montenegro, and other Slavic states were united under the Serbian monarch as the Kingdom of Serbs, Croats, and Slovenes; in 1929, it took the name Yugoslavia, meaning "union of south Slavs". Almost immediately the Croats chafed at control from the capital, Belgrade. The country reacted to division among the Axis powers and their allies during World War II by forming resistance groups that battled occupying forces and each other. The communist resistance leader Josip Broz (Tito) emerged on top; during his 35-year rule, a personality cult developed around him that helped coalesce the disparate ethnic groups. He served as prime minister from 1945, and as president from 1953.

After Tito's death in 1980, the country began to fall apart. In 1992, after Slovenia, Croatia, Bosnia and Herzegovina, and Macedonia had declared their independence, Serbia and Montenegro reconstituted as the Federal Republic of Yugoslavia. Slobodan Milosevic, who had been elected president of Serbia in 1989, became president of Yugoslavia in 1997. His campaign of brutality, terror and oppression of the Serbian province of Kosovo begun in 1998 forced thousands of ethnic Albanians to flee their homes. NATO responded with aerial bombings that lasted from March through June of 1999. Milosevic was defeated in the presidential elections of 2000 by Vojislav Kostunica and in April 2001 was arrested for crimes against humanity and extradited to face charges in The Hague. In 2002, talks began that culminated in February 2003 with the two republics signing an agreement creating a loose federation called Serbia and Montenegro under a new constitution and with Svetozar Marovic as president. Popular calls for Montenegrin independence are subdued under the new structure. Both republics will have the option for independence in 2006. Kosovo remains part of Serbia, but is in practice still under UN protection.

Each republic has executive, legislative, and judicial branches that handle its economy and local matters. At the union level, a president, elected by the unicameral Assembly for a four-year term, serves as chief of state.

HOW THE GOVERNMENT WORKS

LEGISLATIVE BRANCH

Skupstina Srbije i Crne Gore
(Assembly of Serbia & Montenegro)
Unicameral Parliament
126 members, 91 from Serbia and 35 from Montenegro, elected in the first instance by the republican assemblies and in future by direct election, for a two-year term.

Republican Assemblies
Elect prime minister and ministers, oversee internal affairs of republic.

Narodna Skupstina Srbije
(Serbian National Assembly)

Skupstina Republike Crne Gore
(Assembly of Republic of Montenegro)

Regional Governments
Two nominally autonomous provinces, with an elected president and Assembly.

EXECUTIVE BRANCH

President of Serbia & Montenegro
Elected for a four-year term by the Assembly of Serbia and Montenegro. Serves as head of state, chairs the Council of Ministers.

Council of Ministers of Serbia & Montenegro
Five members, two from the same republic as the president and three from the other republic, for four-year term.

Republican Presidents
Each elected for a five-year term, serves as head of republic.

Republican Governments
Each comprises a prime minister, deputy prime minister and ministers, elected by the Republican Assembly.

JUDICIAL BRANCH

Court of Serbia & Montenegro
Composed of equal number of judges from both member states appointed to serve six-year terms by Assembly of Serbia & Montenegro.

Constitutional Courts
Serbia: Composed of nine judges, elected by Assembly for life. Montenegro: Composed of five judges, elected by Assembly for nine-year terms. Oversees republic's constitution and its compliance with the Serbia and Montenegro constitution.

Supreme Courts
Highest court of law in each republic.

Courts of Law

GUINEA

OFFICIAL NAME: REPUBLIC OF GUINEA

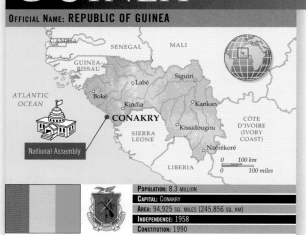

POPULATION: 8.3 MILLION
CAPITAL: CONAKRY
AREA: 94,925 SQ. MILES (245,856 SQ. KM)
INDEPENDENCE: 1958
CONSTITUTION: 1990

GUINEA derives from the Berber word *aguinaw* or *gnawa*, which means "black man".

RELIGION: Muslim 85%, Christian 8%, Indigenous beliefs 7%

OFFICIAL LANGUAGE: French

REGIONS OR PROVINCES: 33 prefectures and 1 special zone

DEPENDENT TERRITORIES: None

MEDIA: Total political censorship exists in national media

Newspapers: There is 1 daily newspaper

TV: 1 state-owned service

Radio: 1 state-owned service

SUFFRAGE: 18 years of age; universal

LEGAL SYSTEM: Customary and French law; no ICJ jurisdiction

WORLD ORGANIZATIONS: ACCT, ACP, AfDB, CCC, ECA, ECOWAS, FAO, G-77, IBRD, ICAO, ICFTU, ICRM, IDA, IDB, IFAD, IFC, IFRCS, ILO, IMF, IMO, Interpol, IOC, IOM, ISO (correspondent), ITU, MINURSO, NAM, OAU, OIC, OPCW, UN, UN Security Council (temporary), UNAMSIL, UNCTAD, UNESCO, UNIDO, UPU, WCL, WFTU, WHO, WIPO, WMO, WToO, WTrO

POLITICAL PARTIES: PUP—Party of Union and Progress, UPR—Union for Progress and Renewal, UPG—Union for the Progress of Guinea, PDG—Democratic Party of Guinea

ETHNIC GROUPS:

- Kissi 10%
- Other 5%
- Malinke 30%
- Other tribes 10%
- Soussou 15%
- Fila (Fulani) 30%

NATIONAL ECONOMICS

WORLD GNP RANKING: 128th

GNP PER CAPITA: $450

INFLATION: 6.0%

BALANCE OF PAYMENTS (BALANCE OF TRADE): -$165 million

EXCHANGE RATES / U.S. DLR.: 1880-1970 GUINEA FRANCS

OFFICIAL CURRENCY: GUINEA FRANC

GOVERNMENT SPENDING (% OF GDP)

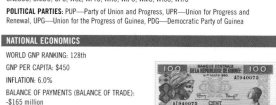

- ✈ DEFENSE 1.5%
- 📖 EDUCATION 1.8%
- ✚ HEALTH 2.3%

0   5   10   15

NUMBER OF CONFLICTS OVER LAST 25 YEARS

	1	2-5	5+
Violent changes in government	●	○	○
Civil wars	●	○	○
International wars	○	●	○
Foreign intervention	○	○	○

- As part of ECOWAS, armed forces participated with ECOMOG in Liberia, Sierra Leone and Guinea-Bissau.
- Liberia and Sierra Leone have both supported dissidents attacking Guinea.
- Military equipment supplied by France and the US.

NOTABLE WARS AND INSURGENCIES: Coup 1984. Conflict across southern borders 2000

GUINEA'S MODERN POLITICAL HISTORY has been tumultuous, marked by dictatorship, an army coup, disputed elections, and violence that escalated into a civil war in 2000. Upon gaining independence from France in 1958, Guinea was ruled by a single Marxist party: the Democratic Party of Guinea (PDG), under the dictatorship of President Sekou Touré. The military seized power upon Touré's death in 1984. A 1990 referendum overwhelmingly approved democratic changes, but the military regime of President Lansana Conté delayed elections until 1993. Under its 1990 constitution, the country is now a multiparty democracy, but General Conté and his Party of Unity and Progress (PUP) continue to dominate the nation's politics.

Guinea recently became important to US foreign policy, first, as a cornerstone of stability in the greatly unstable West Africa sub-region, but also, with its temporary admission to the United Nations Security Council, for its potential role as a moderate Muslim country in the war against terrorism. Guinea was center stage when, by rotation, it chaired the Security Council in March 2003 as the United States was seeking a second Council resolution for war with Iraq. Guinea would have been a swing vote, but the war began with no vote taken.

The constitution already gives the president strong executive powers, but General Conté has made the office even stronger, ruling with an iron fist. The president, elected by an absolute majority of the voters, appoints all ministers, including the prime minister. The president chairs meetings of the Council of Ministers, or cabinet, can propose laws, and can dissolve the National People's Assembly once during a term. The president's tenure was limited to two terms, but constitutional changes in 2001 threatened to reverse a trend toward decentralization and greater democracy and included a revision allowing the president to run for a third term. Two-thirds of the single-chamber Assemblée Nationale Populaire, or People's National Assembly, are elected by proportional representation from a national list of candidates presented by political parties, and one-third are elected from electoral districts. The PUP won 74 percent of the National Assembly seats in a delayed election in 2002. The judiciary includes the Supreme Court, or Cour d'Appel, which acts as the court of final appeal, and two lower appeal courts, in Kankan and in the capital, Conakry.

ISSUES AND CHALLENGES:

- The civil war that began in 2000 was fueled by cross-border incursions by rebels based in Liberia and Sierra Leone supporting internal Guinean rebels.

- Some 300,000 refugees from a civil war in Sierra Leone overwhelmed Guinea's weak economy.

- Following his 1998 re-election, Conté reversed direction, making regressive changes to his cabinet and other changes in the bureaucracy that led to increased cronyism, corruption and a retrenchment of political reform.

HOW THE GOVERNMENT WORKS

LEGISLATIVE BRANCH

Assemblée Nationale Populaire
(National People's Assembly)
Unicameral Parliament
Composed of 114 members who serve five-year terms: 76 directly elected from national candidate lists by proportional representation; 38 elected by direct popular vote by districts. Initiates legislation; adopts budget.

Regional Governments
Eight administrative regions governed by officials appointed by president.

EXECUTIVE BRANCH

President
Elected to five-year terms by direct popular vote. Serves as head of state; commander-in-chief of armed forces. Issues decrees and ordinances; initiates legislation; appoints civil servants; may dissolve National People's Assembly.

Prime Minister
Appointed by president. Serves as head of government.

Council of Ministers
Composed of 25 members appointed by president. Presided over by president; oversees government operations.

JUDICIAL BRANCH

Supreme Court
Highest court of review and appeal. Judges appointed by president.

Courts of Appeal
Two courts; hear lower-court appeals. Judges appointed by president.

Courts of First Instance
Hear civil and criminal cases. Judges appointed by president.

HAITI

OFFICIAL NAME: REPUBLIC OF HAITI

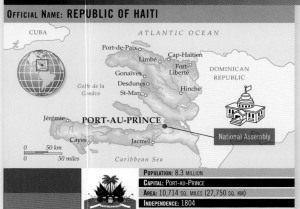

POPULATION: 8.3 MILLION	
CAPITAL: PORT-AU-PRINCE	
AREA: 10,714 SQ. MILES (27,750 SQ. KM)	
INDEPENDENCE: 1804	
CONSTITUTION: 1987	

HAITI is derived from the Taino Indian word *hayiti*, which means "high ground" or "tall mountain".

RELIGION: Roman Catholic 80%, Protestant 16%, Other 3%, Non-religious 1%

OFFICIAL LANGUAGES: French and French Creole

REGIONS OR PROVINCES: 9 departments

DEPENDENT TERRITORIES: None

MEDIA: Partial political censorship exists in national media

NEWSPAPERS: There are 2 daily newspapers

TV: 5 services: 1 state-owned, 4 independent

Radio: 18 services: 1 state-owned, 17 independent

SUFFRAGE: 18 years of age; universal

LEGAL SYSTEM: Roman law; accepts ICJ jurisdiction

ETHNIC GROUPS:

Mulato and White 5%

Black 95%

WORLD ORGANIZATIONS: ACCT, ACP, Caricom, CCC, ECLAC, FAO, G-77, IADB, IAEA, IBRD, ICAO, ICRM, IDA, IFAD, IFC, IFRCS, ILO, IMF, IMO, Interpol, IOC, IOM, ITU, LAES, OAS, OPANAL, OPCW (signatory), PCA, UN, UNCTAD, UNESCO, UNIDO, UPU, WCL, WFTU, WHO, WIPO, WMO, WToO, WTrO

POLITICAL PARTIES: ALAH—Alliance for the Liberation and Advancement of Haiti, RDNP—Assembly of Progressive National Democrats, Convergence, ESPACE—Democratic Consultation Group coalition, PDCH—Haitian Christian Democratic Party, PADEM—Haitian Democratic Party, FL—Lavalas Family, MDN—Mobilization for National Development, MRN—Movement for National Reconstruction, MIDH—Movement for the Installation of Democracy in Haiti, MOP—Movement for the Organization of the Country, MKN—National Cooperative Action Movement, FNCD—National Front for Change and Democracy, MOCHRENA—New Christian Movement for a New Haiti, PLB—Open the Gate, OPL—Struggling People's Organization

NATIONAL ECONOMICS

WORLD GNP RANKING: 117th

GNP PER CAPITA: $510

INFLATION: 13.7%

BALANCE OF PAYMENTS (BALANCE OF TRADE): -$38 million

EXCHANGE RATES / U.S. DLR.: 21.00-25.74 GOURDES

OFFICIAL CURRENCY: GOURDE

GOVERNMENT SPENDING (% OF GDP)

✈	DEFENSE	1.5%
🎓	EDUCATION	1.8%
✚	HEALTH	1.4%

0   5   10   15

NUMBER OF CONFLICTS OVER LAST 25 YEARS

	1	2-5	5+
Violent changes in government	○	○	○
Civil wars	○	◐	○
International wars	○	○	○
Foreign intervention	◐	○	○

- No compulsory national military service.
- Armed forces and police were disbanded after military ousted in 1994 by a multinational force consisting of 31 countries.
- The new national police force was created and trained by the US.

NOTABLE WARS AND INSURGENCIES: Haitian revolution 1985-1986. Coups 1988, 1991-1994. US and UN intervention (UNMIH)

A HISTORIC SLAVE REBELLION IN 1804 transformed Haiti into the world's first black republic and the first Caribbean nation to gain independence, but failed to create a stable government. Instead, strife and economic despair have dominated the island's decades of self-rule. Present-day Haiti's constitutional democracy, restored in 1995 after a military coup, still struggles with chronic social and political divisions that have plagued the nation's years of independence.

For nearly two centuries, Spain used the country as an outpost for exploring the Western Hemisphere before eventually ceding it to France in 1697. African slaves imported by France worked the island's plantations until their rebellion in 1791 overwhelmed French troops. The newly independent Haiti, however, endured decades of political infighting until, in 1915, the unrest prompted a 19-year-long US occupation of the island. Haiti later struggled for three decades under the brutal dictatorship of the Duvalier family until it was finally ousted in 1986.

The constitution Haitians subsequently ratified created a three-branch government with an elected president who serves as head of state, a prime minister and Cabinet, a bicameral Parliament, and a Supreme Court. In 1990, Haitians elected as president a charismatic Roman Catholic priest, Jean-Bertrand Aristide, but within months a military clique seized the government. Thousands of Haitians were killed under the new regime and many more fled in boats before the US, with the blessing of the United Nations, forced the military from power under the threat of an armed invasion and restored Aristide to the presidency. The pro-Aristide Lavalas party won the 1995 elections with overwhelming support, but Haiti's government within a few short years came under public fire for its austerity policies and fell into gridlock between the legislative and executive branches. In the highly disputed elections of 2000, Aristide won the presidency and Lavalas the majority of parliamentary seats. Haiti's major opposition coalition boycotted the elections and afterwards announced its own symbolic "alternative government." Despite efforts by the Organization of American States to bring the sides together, Haiti's government remains at political stalemate.

ISSUES AND CHALLENGES:

- With 80 percent of its population living in slums without running water or sanitation, Haiti is considered the poorest country in the Americas.
- Political instability has deterred much-needed foreign aid and investment.
- Corruption in the judicial system and police force leads to brutality.

Haiti is the world's oldest black republic.

HOW THE GOVERNMENT WORKS

LEGISLATIVE BRANCH

Assemblée Nationale
(National Assembly)
Bicameral Parliament

Sénat
(Senate)
Composed of 27 members elected to six-year terms by direct popular vote. Permanently in session. Recommends Supreme Court candidates to president.

Chambre des Députés
(House of Representatives)
Composed of 83 members elected to four-year terms by direct popular vote. Holds two sessions annually. May initiate impeachment proceedings for government officials with two-thirds majority vote.

Regional Governments
Nine departments administered by three-member council elected to four-year terms.

EXECUTIVE BRANCH

President
Elected to five-year term by direct popular vote; may be re-elected after five-year interim; two-term limit. Head of state. Promulgates laws; enforces judicial decisions; appoints ambassadors; grants pardons.

Prime Minister
Leader of majority party in National Assembly; appointed by president following elections, confirmed by parliament. Head of government. Appoints and dismisses government officials.

Council of Ministers
Appointed by prime minister on advice of president. Presided over by president; oversees government operations.

JUDICIAL BRANCH

Supreme Court
Highest court of review and appeal. Judges appointed to ten-year terms by president.

Courts of Appeal
Hears lower-court appeals; judges appointed to ten-year terms by president.

Courts of First Instance
Fifteen courts; judges appointed to seven-year terms by president.

Justices of the Peace
Judges appointed to seven-year terms by president on advice of community assemblies.

AZERBAIJAN

OFFICIAL NAME: REPUBLIC OF AZERBAIJAN

POPULATION: 8.1 MILLION
CAPITAL: BAKU
AREA: 33,436 SQ. MILES (86,600 SQ. KM)
INDEPENDENCE: 1991
CONSTITUTION: 1995

AZERBAIJAN's name is thought to come from the Persian for "land of fire"—a reference to the fire temples of its fervent Zoroastrians.

RELIGION: Muslim 93.4%, Russian Orthodox 2.5%, Armenian Orthodox 2.3%, Other 1.8%

OFFICIAL LANGUAGE: Azerbaijani

REGIONS OR PROVINCES: 59 rayons, 11 cities, 1 autonomous republic

DEPENDENT TERRITORIES: None

MEDIA: Total political censorship exists in the national media

NEWSPAPERS: There are 6 daily newspapers

TV: 1 state-controlled service, 1 independent station

RADIO: 1 state-controlled service

SUFFRAGE: 18 years of age; universal

LEGAL SYSTEM: Civil law; no ICJ jurisdiction

WORLD ORGANIZATIONS: AsDB, BSEC, CCC, CE, CIS, EAPC, EBRD, ECE, ECO, ESCAP, FAO, IAEA, IBRD, ICAO, ICFTU, ICRM, IDA, IDB, IFAD, IFC, IFRCS, ILO, IMF, IMO, Interpol, IOC, IOM, ISO (correspondent), ITU, NAM (observer), OAS (observer), OIC, OPCW, OSCE, PFP, UN, UNCTAD, UNESCO, UNIDO, UPU, WFTU, WHO, WIPO, WMO, WToO, WTrO (observer)

POLITICAL PARTIES: YAP—New Azerbaijan Party, Ind—Independents, AKC—Azerbaijan Popular Front, VBP—Civic Solidarity Party

ETHNIC GROUPS:

Russian 3%
Armenian 2%
Other 2%
Dagestani 3%
Azeri 90%

NATIONAL ECONOMICS

WORLD GNP RANKING: 113th

GNP PER CAPITA: $600

INFLATION: 1.8%

BALANCE OF PAYMENTS (BALANCE OF TRADE): -$168 million

EXCHANGE RATES / U.S. DLR.: 4456-4475 MANATS

OFFICIAL CURRENCY: MANAT

GOVERNMENT SPENDING (% OF GDP)

✈ DEFENSE 4.5%		
🎓 EDUCATION 3.4%		
✚ HEALTH 1%		

0   5   10   15

NUMBER OF CONFLICTS OVER LAST 25 YEARS

	1	2-5	5+
Violent changes in government	○	○	○
Civil wars	○	○	○
International wars	◐	○	○
Foreign intervention	◐	○	○

- Compulsory national military service.
- Member of NATO's Partnership for Peace program since 1994.
- Despite 1994 ceasefire in Nagorno Karabakh, ongoing sporadic violence undermines peace process and negotiations.

NOTABLE WARS AND INSURGENCIES: Nagorno-Karabakh War 1988-1994

FIRST CONQUERED BY THE ARABS IN 642, Azerbaijan was invaded by the Mongols in the 13th century, and later by Persians, Russians and Ottomans. One of their main objectives was to gain control of the major trade routes that ran through Azerbaijan between Asia and Europe. Azerbaijan became part of the Czarist Russian Empire in the 19th century, and briefly achieved independence in 1918 when the empire fell. Two years later the Soviet Union invaded the country, and it remained part of the communist state until 1991. Despite its considerable oil wealth—it was one of the world's first big oil-producing regions in the 1870s—economic progress has been difficult to attain since its independence.

Azerbaijan has operated as a multiparty republic since independence. However, international observers consider the elections held so far to have been unfair and manipulated. Ayaz Mutalibov, appointed president on independence, resigned in March 1992 after the loss of Nagorno-Karabakh to Armenian insurgents. He was reappointed in May, but within one week had been ousted by the Popular Front Party (PFP) for his efforts to prevent the next elections. The first non-communist president elected, Abulfaz Elchibey of the PFP, took office in June 1992. He was overthrown after just one year. The Milli Majlis replaced him with Heydar Aliyev, formerly Azerbaijan's Communist Party leader and Soviet deputy prime minister. Four months later, the country held a new election, which Aliyev claimed to have won with 98 percent of the vote. The results were not endorsed by the international community. Aliyev won another five-year term in 1998 in an election marred by serious irregularities. The 1995 constitution places no limit on the president's number of terms in office.

The first directly elected Azerbaijani National Assembly was elected in 1995. Twenty-five of the 125 members were elected by proportional representation. As from the 2005 parliamentary elections, all 125 members have been elected from single-member constituencies.

> Azerbaijan was the first Soviet republic to declare its independence from Moscow

ISSUES AND CHALLENGES:

- A large section of Azerbaijan, Nagorno-Karabakh, is occupied by Armenian insurgents who defeated the Azerbaijani army in a conflict between 1988 and 1994. A cease-fire has held, but no peace agreement has been reached. The conflict has burdened Azerbaijan with many thousands of refugees, requires the maintenance of a large army, and discourages foreign investment and the development of oil pipelines.

- Women, who were once prominent in the ruling party, have lost their political status and their general status is declining.

- Relations between Azerbaijan and Armenia remain a central issue for the government.

HOW THE GOVERNMENT WORKS

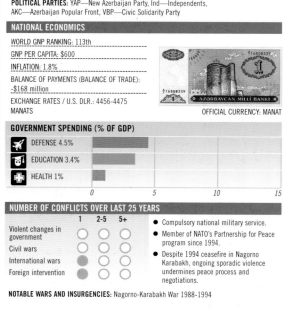

LEGISLATIVE BRANCH

Milli Mejlis (National Assembly)
Composed of 125 members elected to five-year terms: 100 from single-member districts by direct popular vote; 25 by proportional representation.

Regional Governments
Fifty-nine provinces administered by governors appointed by president.

EXECUTIVE BRANCH

President
Elected to five-year term by direct popular vote. Serves as head of state; commander-in-chief of armed forces.

Prime Minister
Appointed by president, confirmed by Milli Mejlis. Serves as head of government; presides over Council of Ministers.

Council of Ministers
Composed of eight members appointed by president, confirmed by National Assembly.

JUDICIAL BRANCH

Constitutional Court
Rules on constitutionality of laws. Composed of nine judges nominated by president, appointed by National Assembly.

Supreme Court
Highest court of review and appeal; exclusive jurisdiction over national security cases. Judges nominated by president, appointed by National Assembly.

Courts of Appeal
Hears lower-court appeals. Judges nominated by president, appointed by National Assembly.

BULGARIA

OFFICIAL NAME: REPUBLIC OF BULGARIA

POPULATION: 7.9 MILLION	
CAPITAL: SOFIA	
AREA: 42,822 SQ. MILES (110,910 SQ. KM)	
INDEPENDENCE: 1908	
CONSTITUTION: 1991	

BULGARIA derives its name from the Bulgars, a nomadic Asian people who migrated to the area in A.D. 600.

RELIGION: Bulgarian Orthodox 84%, Muslim 13%, Jewish 1%, Roman Catholic 1%, Other 1%

OFFICIAL LANGUAGE: Bulgarian

REGIONS OR PROVINCES: 28 regions

DEPENDENT TERRITORIES: None

MEDIA: Partial political censorship exists in national media

NEWSPAPERS: There are 21 daily newspapers

TV: 3 services: 2 state-owned, 1 independent

RADIO: 10 services: 1 state-owned service, 9 independent

SUFFRAGE: 18 years of age; universal

LEGAL SYSTEM: Civil law and Roman legal traditions; accepts ICJ jurisdiction

WORLD ORGANIZATIONS: ACCT, Australia Group, BIS, BSEC, CCC, CE, CEI, CERN, EAPC, EBRD, ECE, EU (applicant), FAO, G- 9, IAEA, IBRD, ICAO, ICFTU, ICRM, IFC, IFRCS, IHO (pending member), ILO, IMF, IMO, Interpol, IOC, IOM, ISO, ITU, NAM (guest), NSG, OAS (observer), OPCW, OSCE, PCA, PFP, UN, UN Security Council (temporary), UNCTAD, UNESCO, UNIDO, UNMEE, UNMIBH, UNMIK, UNMOP, UPU, WCL, WEU (associate partner), WFTU, WHO, WIPO, WMO, WToO, WTrO, ZC

POLITICAL PARTIES: NMS II—National Movement Simeon II, UDF—Union of Democratic Forces, BSP—Bulgarian Socialist Party, MRF—Movement for Rights and Freedoms

ETHNIC GROUPS:

- Macedonian 3%
- Roma 3%
- Turkish 9%
- Bulgarian 85%

NATIONAL ECONOMICS

WORLD GNP RANKING: 79th	
GNP PER CAPITA: $1,520	
INFLATION: 10.3%	
BALANCE OF PAYMENTS (BALANCE OF TRADE): -$701 million	
EXCHANGE RATES / U.S. DLR.: 2.084-2.187 LEVA	

OFFICIAL CURRENCY: LEV

GOVERNMENT SPENDING (% OF GDP)

✈	DEFENSE	2.8%
📖	EDUCATION	3.4%
✚	HEALTH	3.9%

0   5   10   15

NUMBER OF CONFLICTS OVER LAST 25 YEARS

	1	2-5	5+
Violent changes in government	○	○	○
Civil wars	○	○	○
International wars	○	○	○
Foreign intervention	○	○	○

- Plan 2004 required a major restructuring of the armed forces, reducing personnel and cutting costs.
- Invited to join NATO in 2004.
- Plays important role in resolution of interethnic conflict in Balkan Peninsula.
- Troops are deployed in Bosnia and Herzegovina, Kosovo and Afghanistan.

NOTABLE WARS AND INSURGENCIES: Turkish assimilation campaign 1984-1985

BULGARIA IS ONE OF THE WORLD'S youngest multiparty democracies. During its early history it had brief periods of self-rule. The first Kingdom of Bulgaria was established in A.D. 681, culminating in the reign of Czar Simeon I (893-927), a period known as the country's "Golden Age." After both Byzantine rule and a second period of self-rule, Bulgaria was absorbed into the Ottoman Empire in 1396, where it remained for the next five centuries. Official and lasting independence from the Ottomans finally came in 1908 when a monarchy was established under King Ferdinand. Years of war and political turmoil followed independence, and after a World War II alliance with Germany, Bulgaria became a communist-controlled satellite of the Soviet Union. Todor Zhivkov's dictatorship, from 1954 to his dismissal in 1989, led to state control of industry and religion. His departure marked the beginning of Bulgaria's transformation to democracy, with the first multiparty elections being held the following year. The 1990s were marred by social and political conflict, and a succession of ineffective governments dismissed by no-confidence votes. Prime Minister Ivan Kostov of the Union of Democratic Forces (UDF) came to power in 1997 and initiated a series of economic reforms that stabilized the country.

Under the 1991 constitution, the appointed prime minister leads the government, while the elected president serves as head of state. Mindful of the legacy of Stalinism, Bulgarians created a weak presidency. The president cannot initiate legislation, but can return a bill to the unicameral National Assembly for further debate. The Assembly can overturn the president's objection by a simple majority vote.

The pro-monarchy National Movement Simeon II (NMS II) party unexpectedly took 50 percent of the Assembly seats in the 2001 elections. The former king, Simeon II, who acceded as a child in 1943 and was exiled in 1946, became prime minister and head of a coalition government that also included the Movement for Rights and Freedoms (MRF) party. Sixty-three of the 240 members elected to the Assembly were women.

ISSUES AND CHALLENGES:

- Outdated infrastructure and equipment is slowing the pace of economic reform. Trade with Romania is mostly conducted by ferries that cross the Danube River, but an agreement is in place to build a second bridge between two countries.

- Concerns about the safety of the Kozloduy nuclear power plant are delaying Bulgaria's admission to the European Union. EU assistance with upgrades has been conditional on the closure of other reactors.

- The weak judiciary has been unable to curb the widespread corruption among government and law enforcement officials.

- The Gypsy or Roma minority—constituting three percent of the population—is discriminated against at all levels of society.

HOW THE GOVERNMENT WORKS

LEGISLATIVE BRANCH

Narodno Sobranie (National Assembly) Unicameral Parliament
Composed of 240 members directly elected to four-year terms by proportional representation from 28 districts. Enacts laws, approves budget, schedules presidential elections, may dismiss prime minister and other ministers, override presidential vetoes, declare war, deploy troops outside Bulgaria, ratify treaties.

Regional Governments
28 regions headed by governors appointed by the Council of Ministers; harmonize regional and state laws.

EXECUTIVE BRANCH

President
Elected to five-year term, two-term limit. Serves as head of state; commander-in-chief of armed forces. May return bills to National Assembly, negotiates treaties, appoints diplomats, issues pardons.

Prime Minister
Leader of the largest party or coalition in National Assembly; appointed by president following elections. Serves as head of government; chairs Council of Ministers.

Council of Ministers
Members appointed by prime minister, approved by National Assembly. Oversees government operations, national budget.

JUDICIAL BRANCH

Supreme Judicial Council
Appoints, transfers, and replaces judges, prosecutors, investigating magistrates. Composed of 25 jurists nominated by judicial bodies and elected by National Assembly.

Constitutional Court
Rules on the constitutionality of laws and treaties; hears disputes between government branches. Composed of 12 justices who serve nine-year terms: four appointed by president; four by National Assembly; four by Supreme Court of Administration and Supreme Court of Cassation.

Supreme Court of Cassation
Highest court of review and appeal. Justices appointed for life.

Appeal Courts

District Courts

SIERRA LEONE

OFFICIAL NAME: REPUBLIC OF SIERRA LEONE

GUINEA

Kabala

Lunsar • Makeni
FREETOWN • Njaiama
• Boajibu
Bo • Kenema
LIBERIA
Zimmi

ATLANTIC
OCEAN

House of
Representatives

0   50 km
0   50 miles

POPULATION: 4.6 MILLION
CAPITAL: FREETOWN
AREA: 27,698 SQ. MILES (71,740 SQ. KM)
INDEPENDENCE: 1961
CONSTITUTION: 1991

SIERRA LEONE was named by a Portuguese sailor in 1462 who saw the mountains of Freetown Peninsula, which looked like *serra lyoa* or "lion mountains".

RELIGION: Muslim 60%, Indigenous beliefs 30%, Christian 10%

OFFICIAL LANGUAGE: English

REGIONS OR PROVINCES: 3 provinces and 1 area

DEPENDENT TERRITORIES: None

MEDIA: Total political censorship exists in national media

NEWSPAPERS: There is 1 daily newspaper

TV: 1 state-controlled service

RADIO: 1 state-controlled service

SUFFRAGE: 18 years of age; universal

LEGAL SYSTEM: Tribal laws; English common law; no ICJ jurisdiction

WORLD ORGANIZATIONS: ACP, AfDB, C, CCC, ECA, ECOWAS, FAO, G-77, IAEA, IBRD, ICAO, ICFTU, ICRM, IDA, IDB, IFAD, IFC, IFRCS, ILO, IMF, IMO, Interpol, IOC, IOM, ITU, NAM, OAU, OIC, OPCW (signatory), UN, UNCTAD, UNESCO, UNIDO, UPU, WCL, WFTU, WHO, WIPO, WMO, WToO, WTrO

POLITICAL PARTIES: SLPP—Sierra Leone People's Party, APC—All People's Congress, App—Appointed: 12 paramount chiefs are indirectly elected to represent each province, PLP—Peace and Liberation Party

ETHNIC GROUPS:

Kuranko 4%
Limba 8%
Mende 35%
Other 21%
Temne 32%

NATIONAL ECONOMICS

WORLD GNP RANKING: 164th

GNP PER CAPITA: $130

INFLATION: -0.8%

BALANCE OF PAYMENTS (BALANCE OF TRADE): -$127 million

EXCHANGE RATES / U.S. DLR.: 1899-2091 LEONES

BANK OF SIERRA LEONE
A076851
ONE LEONE
OFFICIAL CURRENCY: LEONE

GOVERNMENT SPENDING (% of GDP)

✈ DEFENSE 1.2%			
EDUCATION 1%			
✚ HEALTH 0.9%			

0   5   10   15

NUMBER OF CONFLICTS OVER LAST 25 YEARS

	1	2-5	5+
Violent changes in government	○	○	○
Civil wars	○	●	○
International wars	○	○	○
Foreign intervention	○	●	○

- No compulsory national military service.
- Exploitation of child soldiers during civil war.
- Assistance from UN peacekeepers and UK forces during 2000.
- UN tribunal, Special Court for Sierra Leone, to try war crimes found seven people guilty in March 2003.

NOTABLE WARS AND INSURGENCIES: Civil war 1991-2001. Coups 1992, 1996 and 1997. Intervention by ECOMOG (ECOWAS—Economic Community of West African States—Armed Monitoring Group) 1998 onwards, UN 1999 onwards, UK 2000-2002

THROUGHOUT THE 1700S inhabitants of the area of Sierra Leone were taken as slaves to the east coast of America. In 1787 Great Britain established Freetown, as a refuge for freed African slaves, and Sierra Leone became the first British colony in West Africa in 1792. The ethnic diversity of the population comes from these returning slaves, who came to be known as the "Krio" people. The period under colonial rule saw many revolts by the local population, but by 1961 peaceful independence had been attained.

The form of the current government dates to 1991, when a constitution was ratified that intended to transform the West African country into a functioning constitutional democracy. That same year, the rebel group Revolutionary United Front (RUF) contested the new government's legitimacy and began a bloody civil war of extraordinary savagery. The conflict inhibited the function and performance of the official government, as large portions of the country were outside the control of the executive authority, and political representation in the parliament became geographically disproportional throughout the country. Military officers overthrew the civilian government in 1992. President Ahmad Tejan Kabbah was popularly elected in 1996, ousted in 1997, and reinstated in 1998. A 1999 attempt by the RUF to overthrow Kabbah's government failed.

Since 1999 and the Lomé Peace Accord, fighting has been less frequent owing to several fragile cease-fire agreements brokered by the United Nations and supported by United Nations and British forces. The original cease-fire of 1999 crumbled early in 2000, but international pressure helped to re-establish delicate yet sporadic peace in the country. The RUF has transformed itself into a political party in an effort to gain post-war legitimacy. However, it failed to take any seats in parliament in the 2002 elections, a convincing defeat that restored a great deal of power and legitimacy to the dominant Sierra Leone People's Party (SLPP) and President Kabbah. Although sporadic fighting persists in isolated areas throughout the country, the SLPP victory in the elections and an increased international presence offer a beacon of hope to a population in desperate need of peace and normalcy.

ISSUES AND CHALLENGES:

- Sierra Leone suffers severe economic depression; persisting conflicts inhibit development and investment.

- The civil war in Liberia —Sierra Leone's neighbor to the southeast—displaced a large portion of its population, and the sheer volume of displaced persons and refugees moving through Sierra Leone continues to be a strain on political and economic resources.

- The WHO places Sierra Leone's health care system last in the world rankings, which reflects the dire situation of many of its citizens; life expectancy is only 39 years.

HOW THE GOVERNMENT WORKS

LEGISLATIVE BRANCH

House of Representatives
Unicameral Parliament
Composed of 124 members who serve five-year terms: 112 elected by direct popular vote; 12 appointed by president from paramount chiefs of each province.

Regional Governments
Three provinces administered by governing ministers appointed by president and part-elected, part-appointed local councils.

EXECUTIVE BRANCH

President
Elected to five-year term by direct popular vote; two-term limit. Serves as head of state and government; commander-in-chief of armed forces. May dissolve House of Representatives; calls new elections.

Vice-president
Member of House of Representatives appointed by president.

Ministers of State
Composed of 17 members of House of Resrpesentatives appointed by president, approved by House. Oversees government operations; answers to president.

JUDICIAL BRANCH

Supreme Court,
Highest court of review and appeal. Judges appointed by president on advice of Judicial and Legal Service Commission, approved by House of Representatives.

Court of Appeal
Hears lower-court appeals. Judges appointed by president on advice of Judicial and Legal Service Commission, approved by House of Representatives.

High Court
Hears civil and criminal cases.

Magistrates' Court

Local Traditional Courts

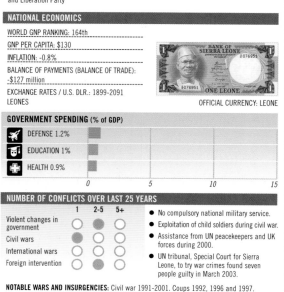

BOSNIA & HERZEGOVINA

OFFICIAL NAME: BOSNIA AND HERZEGOVINA

CROATIA

Prijedor · Modriča
Bihać · *Republica Srpska*
Banja Luka · Doboj
SERBIA &
MONTENEGRO
Tuzla
Travnik · Zenica · Zvornik
Srebrenica
CROATIA · Bugojno
Federacija
Bosna i · **SARAJEVO**
Hercegovina
Mostar

Adriatic
Sea
0   50 km
0   50 miles

Parliamentary
Assembly

POPULATION: 4.1 MILLION
CAPITAL: SARAJEVO
AREA: 19,741 SQ. MILES (51,129 SQ. KM)
INDEPENDENCE: 1992
CONSTITUTION: 1995

BOSNIA & HERZEGOVINA are named after the Bosna River and Herceg (Duke) Stefan Vukcic respectively. The latter made himself ruler of Herzegovina in the mid-15th century.

RELIGION: Muslim (mainly Sunni) 40%, Serbian Orthodox 31%, Roman Catholic 15%, Protestant 4%, Other 10%

OFFICIAL LANGUAGE: Serbo-Croat

REGIONS OR PROVINCES: 2 first-order administrative divisions and 1 internationally supervised district

DEPENDENT TERRITORIES: None

MEDIA: Partial political censorship exists in the national media.

NEWSPAPERS: There are 6 daily newspapers

TV: 8 independent services

RADIO: 10 independent services

SUFFRAGE: 16 years of age, if employed; 18 years of age, universal

LEGAL SYSTEM: Civil law system; no ICJ jurisdiction

WORLD ORGANIZATIONS: BIS, CE (guest), CEI, EBRD, ECE, FAO, G-77, IAEA, IBRD, ICAO, IDA, IFAD, IFC, IFRCS, ILO, IMF, IMO, Interpol, IOC, IOM (observer), ISO, ITU, NAM (guest), OAS (observer), OIC (observer), OPCW, OSCE, UN, UNCTAD, UNESCO, UNIDO, UNMEE, UPU, WHO, WIPO, WMO, WToO, WTrO (observer)

POLITICAL PARTIES: SDP—Social Democratic Party, SDA—Party of Democratic Action, SDS—Serb Democratic Party, SbiH—Party for Bosnia and Herzegovina, HDZ—Croatian Democratic Union

ETHNIC GROUPS:

Yugoslav 5.5%
Other 2.5%
Croat 17%
Serb 31%
Bosniak 44%

NATIONAL ECONOMICS

WORLD GNP RANKING: 111th

GNP PER CAPITA: $1,230

INFLATION: 8%

BALANCE OF PAYMENTS (BALANCE OF TRADE):
-$565 million

EXCHANGE RATES / U.S. DLR.: 2.083-2.197 MARKAS

OFFICIAL CURRENCY: MARKA

GOVERNMENT SPENDING (% OF GDP)

DEFENSE 3.7%
EDUCATION (N/A)
HEALTH 8%

0   5   10   15

NUMBER OF CONFLICTS OVER LAST 25 YEARS

	1	2-5	5+	
Violent changes in government	○	○	○	● Compulsory national military service.
Civil wars	◐	○	○	● Bosnian and Croat forces merged under Dayton Accord by 1997.
International wars	○	○	○	● UN peacekeeping forces remained for three years, followed by NATO troops.
Foreign intervention	◐	○	○	

NOTABLE WARS AND INSURGENCIES: Bosnian Civil War 1992-1995. UN and NATO intervention (UNMIBH, S-FOR)

UNDER THE IRON RULE OF Marshal Tito (1945-1980), Yugoslavia's republic of Bosnia and Herzegovina enjoyed a period of peace, despite its diverse Croatian, Bosniak-Muslim, and Serbian population. But following the collapse of communism in 1989, coexistence disintegrated into a brutal civil war. Today, with NATO troops guarding a delicate peace, Bosnia and Herzegovina struggles to mend a fractured society with a complicated power-sharing government.

Religious divisions stem from Christian rule under the Roman Empire and conquest by the Ottoman Turks in the 1400s, when many Bosnians converted to Islam. After World War I, Bosnia became part of Yugoslavia. In 1992, Bosnia and Herzegovina held a successful referendum for independence, with Muslims and Croats voting strongly for the measure. But Bosnian Serbs, backed by Serbia, responded with armed resistance. Their goal was to divide the republic along ethnic lines and unit the Serbian portion with other Serb-controlled areas. By 1995, when US-led negotiations brought together the warring sides under the Dayton Accords, ethnic cleansing had displaced more than half the population.

The multiparty democracy established by the Accords divides Bosnia into two entities: the largely Bosniak-Muslim Federation of Bosnia and Herzegovina and the primarily Serb Republic of Srpska. Each elects its regional government and maintains an army. Both are united under a central government with a shared presidency, Council of Ministers, constitutional court, central bank, and bicameral legislature, the Skupstina. The Skupstina approves the national budget, ratifies treaties, and carries out other functions set out in the Dayton Accords. Overseeing the accords is the Office of the High Representative, a UN body with the power to impose legislation and remove officials who obstruct the pact's implementation.

CIVIL WAR
A man grieves during a funeral in Sarajevo. Between 1992 and 1996 death became a daily occurrence in the lives of Bosnians, with the Serbians' siege of Sarajevo resulting in the deaths of nearly 12,000 people.

HOW THE GOVERNMENT WORKS

LEGISLATIVE BRANCH

Skupstina
Bicameral Parliament

Predstavnicki Dom
(National House of Representatives)
Composed of 42 members elected to four-year terms by direct popular vote: 14 Serb; 14 Croat; 14 Bosniak-Muslim.

Dom Naroda
(House of Peoples)
Fifteen members (five Bosniak-Muslim, five Croat, five Serb) elected to four-year terms by Bosniak/Croat Federation's House of Representatives and Republika Srpska's National Assembly.

Regional
Two administrative divisions
– Muslim/Croat Federation of Bosnia and Herzegovina (divided into 10 cantons)
– Republika Srpska; one internationally-supervised district: Brcko district.

EXECUTIVE BRANCH

Tripartite Presidency
Composed of one Bosniak, one Croat, one Serb; each elected to four-year terms by direct popular vote from their ethnic groups. Chair of the presidency rotates among the three every eight months. Powers include conducting foreign affairs, naming ambassadors; overseeing militaries of both entities; executing decisions of parliament.

Council of Ministers
Members approved by National House of Representatives. Chairman nominated by presidency, confirmed by National House.

JUDICIAL BRANCH

Constitutional Court
Appeals from courts in both entities; rules on constitutionality of laws. nine judges who serve until age 70: four selected by Bosniak/Croat Federation's House of Representatives, two by Republika Srpska's National Assembly; three non-Bosnian judges by president of European Court of Human Rights.

State Court
Nine judges, three divisions—Administrative, Appellate, Criminal; jurisdiction over state-level law.

Supreme Court
One per entity.

Lower courts
Federation has ten cantonal courts, plus a number of lower courts. Republika Srpska government has five municipal courts.

ARMENIA

OFFICIAL NAME: REPUBLIC OF ARMENIA

POPULATION: 3.8 MILLION	
CAPITAL: YEREVAN	
AREA: 11,506 SQ. MILES (29,800 SQ. KM)	
INDEPENDENCE: 1991	
CONSTITUTION: 1995	

ARMENIA was perhaps named by 6th-century B.C. Greeks or Persians who confused its inhabitants with Aramaeans.

RELIGION: Armenian Apostolic 94%, Other Christian 4%, Yezidi (Zoroastrian/Animist) 2%

OFFICIAL LANGUAGE: Armenian

REGIONS OR PROVINCES: 11 provinces

DEPENDENT TERRITORIES: None

MEDIA: Partial political censorship exists in the national media

NEWSPAPERS: There are 11 daily newspapers

TV: 1 state-controlled service, several independent stations

RADIO: 1 state-controlled service, several independent stations

SUFFRAGE: 18 years of age; universal

LEGAL SYSTEM: Civil law; no ICJ jurisdiction

WORLD ORGANIZATIONS: BSEC, CCC, CE, CIS, EAPC, EBRD, ECE, ESCAP, FAO, IAEA, IBRD, ICAO, ICRM, IDA, IFAD, IFC, IFRCS, ILO, IMF, Interpol, IOC, IOM, ISO, ITU, NAM (observer), OAS (observer), OPCW, OSCE, PFP, UN, UNCTAD, UNESCO, UNIDO, UPU, WFTU, WHO, WIPO, WMO, WToO, WTrO (observer)

POLITICAL PARTIES: UB—Unity Bloc (alliance of the republican party of Armenia-RPA and the People's Party of Armenia—PPA) Ind—Independents, CP—Communist Party, LUB—Law and Unity Bloc, ARF-D—Armenian Revolutionary Federation-Dashnaktsutyun

ETHNIC GROUPS:

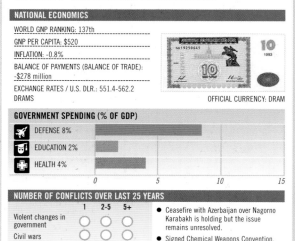

Other 2%
Russian 2%
Azeri 3%
Armenian 93%

NATIONAL ECONOMICS

WORLD GNP RANKING: 137th

GNP PER CAPITA: $520

INFLATION: -0.8%

BALANCE OF PAYMENTS (BALANCE OF TRADE): -$278 million

EXCHANGE RATES / U.S. DLR.: 551.4-562.2 DRAMS

OFFICIAL CURRENCY: DRAM

GOVERNMENT SPENDING (% OF GDP)

✈	DEFENSE	8%
📖	EDUCATION	2%
✚	HEALTH	4%

0   5   10   15

NUMBER OF CONFLICTS OVER LAST 25 YEARS

	1	2-5	5+
Violent changes in government	○	○	○
Civil wars	○	○	○
International wars	◑	○	○
Foreign intervention	◑	○	○

- Ceasefire with Azerbaijan over Nagorno Karabakh is holding but the issue remains unresolved.
- Signed Chemical Weapons Convention, requiring the elimination of chemical weapons in 1993, quickly acceded to the nuclear Non-Proliferation Treaty.
- Police brutality and human rights violations are issues.

NOTABLE WARS AND INSURGENCIES: Nagorno-Karabakh War 1988-1994. Soviet troops deployed in 1990.

A FIERCE DESIRE FOR INDEPENDENCE has driven Armenian politics for centuries. The history of the Armenian people dates back to about 800 B.C. The ancient kingdoms of Armenia covered a far larger area than the present-day republic, at times occupying much of modern Turkey and stretching as far east as Iran. Over the centuries, Armenians have been overwhelmed by the Roman, Byzantine, Arab, Persian, Ottoman, and Soviet empires. Large portions of the original Armenia have been annexed by its neighbors. Armenians have been severely persecuted, most notably by Turkey at the start of World War I, when up to 1.5 million Armenians died in the 20th century's first genocide.

Armenia was the first nation to adopt Christianity as a state religion, A.D. 301

Swallowed up by the Soviet Union in 1920, Armenia—the smallest former Soviet state—was one of the first republics to declare independence after communism's fall. But trouble had long been brewing with neighboring Azerbaijan. Ethnic Armenians of Azerbaijan's Nagorno-Karabakh region had agitated for years for union with Armenia. Nagorno-Karabakh declared independence from Azerbaijan in 1992, and war broke out. Armenia supplied the insurgent government with troops, money, and supplies. By the time a cease-fire was brokered in 1994, 50,000 people were dead, and Azerbaijan had lost control of the territory. The cease-fire has yet to progress to a comprehensive settlement.

Armenia's 1995 constitution shifted much power from the legislature, the National Assembly, to the presidency, leaving the Assembly with few checks on presidential power. The president may dissolve parliament, appoint and dismiss the prime minister, appoint almost half of the judges of the highest court, appoint or remove prosecutors, and declare martial law and rule by decree. Parliamentary elections have improved in fairness and efficiency but still don't meet international standards. The judiciary is corrupt, serving the state in all politically sensitive matters. Armenians typically settle disputes privately rather than resort to the courts.

ISSUES AND CHALLENGES:

- Dependent on outside energy sources and raw materials and suffering economically from the USSR's dissolution. Armenia has faced increased hardships as Turkey, in support of Azerbaijan, has closed its border with Armenia since 1993.

- In a seismic zone, Mezamor nuclear power station, that reopened in 1995 after being declared unsafe in 1988, has caused international concern.

- The country has nothing to attract outside investors, and massive emigration has crippled the economy.

- Dishonest elections and heavy-handed repression have eroded the government's legitimacy.

- As the Caucasian oil boom transforms the Azerbaijani and Georgian economies, Armenia seems likely to miss out.

HOW THE GOVERNMENT WORKS

LEGISLATIVE BRANCH

Azgayin Zhoghov (National Assembly) Unicameral Parliament
Composed of 131 members elected to four-year terms by direct popular vote from single-member districts. Approves or rejects government program of prime minister and Council of Ministers.

Regional Governments
Eleven provinces administered by governors appointed by president, elected local councils.

EXECUTIVE BRANCH

President
Elected to five-year term by direct popular vote; limit of two consecutive terms. Serves as head of state; may dissolve National Assembly, declare martial law, rule by decree.

Prime Minister
May not be member of National Assembly; appointed by president. Serves as head of government; presides over Council of Ministers.

Council of Ministers
Not members of National Assembly; appointed by prime minister. Oversees government operations.

JUDICIAL BRANCH

Council of Justice
Evaluates, nominates, disciplines judges; chaired by president.

Constitutional Court
Rules on constitutionality of laws. Composed of four judges appointed by president; five by National Assembly.

Court of Appeals

Review Courts

Lower Courts

Courts of First Instance

CENTRAL AFRICAN REPUBLIC

OFFICIAL NAME: CENTRAL AFRICAN REPUBLIC

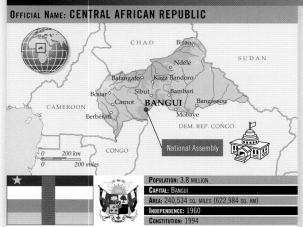

POPULATION:	3.8 MILLION
CAPITAL:	BANGUI
AREA:	240,534 SQ. MILES (622,984 SQ. KM)
INDEPENDENCE:	1960
CONSTITUTION:	1994

CENTRAL AFRICAN REPUBLIC was established by the French as the colony of Oubangui-Chari in 1905.

RELIGION: Indigenous Beliefs 35%, Protestant 25%, Roman Catholic 25%, Muslim 15%

OFFICIAL LANGUAGE: French

REGIONS OR PROVINCES: 14 prefectures, 2 economic prefectures and 1 commune

DEPENDENT TERRITORIES: None

MEDIA: Total political censorship exists in national media

NEWSPAPERS: There are 3 daily newspapers

TV: 1 state-owned service

RADIO: 1 state-owned service

SUFFRAGE: 21 years of age; universal

LEGAL SYSTEM: French law; no ICJ jurisdiction

WORLD ORGANIZATIONS: ACCT, ACP, AfDB, BDEAC, CCC, CEEAC, CEMAC, ECA, FAO, FZ, G-77, IAEA, IBRD, ICAO, ICFTU, ICRM, IDA, IFAD, IFC, IFRCS, ILO, IMF, Interpol, IOC, ITU, NAM, OAU, OIC (observer), OPCW (signatory), UN, UNCTAD, UNESCO, UNIDO, UPU, WCL, WHO, WIPO, WMO, WToO, WTrO

POLITICAL PARTIES: MLPC—Central African People's Liberation Movement, RDC—Central African Democratic Rally, MDD—Movement for Democracy and Development, Ind—Independents, PSD—Social Democratic Party, FPP—Patriotic Front for Progress, ADP—Alliance for Democracy and Progress, PUN—National Unity Party, PLD—Liberal Democratic Party

ETHNIC GROUPS:

- Baya 34%
- Banda 27%
- Mandjia 21%
- Sara 10%
- Other 8%

NATIONAL ECONOMICS

WORLD GNP RANKING: 152nd

GNP PER CAPITA: $280

INFLATION: -1.5%

BALANCE OF PAYMENTS: (BALANCE OF TRADE) Zero

EXCHANGE RATES / U.S. DLR.: 698.7-736.7 CFA FRANCS

OFFICIAL CURRENCY: CFA FRANC

GOVERNMENT SPENDING (% OF GDP)

- ✈ DEFENSE 3.7%
- 🎓 EDUCATION 1.9%
- ✚ HEALTH 2%

0   5   10   15

NUMBER OF CONFLICTS OVER LAST 25 YEARS

	1	2-5	5+
Violent changes in government	○	●	○
Civil wars	○	●	○
International wars	○	○	○
Foreign intervention	○	○	○

- Compulsory national military service.
- French officers hold most senior army posts.
- The UN peacekeeping mission that replaced the African peacekeeping forces in 1998, stayed for two years.

NOTABLE WARS AND INSURGENCIES: Coups 1979, 1981, 1986, 2003. Interspersed with civil conflict. French withdraw 1997. Intervention by Libyan, Chadian & Congolese forces 2001; by Libyan forces 2002

THE CENTRAL AFRICAN REPUBLIC, OR CAR, has for the most part been a multiparty democracy since 1993. But its political history since the country gained independence from France in 1960 has been stormy, involving numerous successful and failed coups; armed military rebellions; a president who declared himself emperor; interventions by French, Libyan, and United Nations forces; voting and other scandals surrounding political leaders; and economic unrest.

The CAR in 1993 made a peaceful transition from an earlier military regime to the most democratically chosen government, at least in theory, that the country has had. Ange-Félix Patassé was elected president and, even though economic pressures continued to be an issue, was re-elected in 1999. An attempted military coup by the former president, General André Kolingba in 2000 was contained by loyalists and troops from Libya, Chad and the Congo. However, on March 15, 2003, General François Bozize led a successful coup, suspending the constitution, dissolving the cabinet of President Ange-Félix Patassé, and promising a return to the CAR's democratic institutions within 30 months. Bozize formed a 28-member transitional government, representing all political parties, to help write legislation, draft a new constitution, and plan new elections. Under the current suspended constitution, the government combines features of presidential and parliamentary systems. The president is elected by popular vote in two rounds of voting, involving a runoff between the most successful candidates in the first round. The president names a prime minister and other members of the Council of Ministers, which initiates legislation.

The single-chamber National Assembly acts on legislation or questions submitted by its executive committee, one-third of its deputies, or the president. The president summons the legislature for two sessions a year, each lasting no more than 60 days. A dozen political parties vied for seats in 1998, with Patassé's Central African People's Liberation Movement (MLPC), a religious center-right party, gaining 43 percent of the vote and the right-wing Central African Democratic Rally (RDC) getting 18 percent.

ISSUES AND CHALLENGES:

- Strapped for funds, the CAR continues to rely heavily on financial help, particularly from France.
- Two-thirds of the country's population lives below the poverty line, according to 2002 data.
- Persistent political instability deters foreign investment and hinders aid programs.
- Although the official language is French, most of the more than 80 ethnic groups—each with their own language—speak a local language called Sangho and have limited knowledge of French.

HOW THE GOVERNMENT WORKS

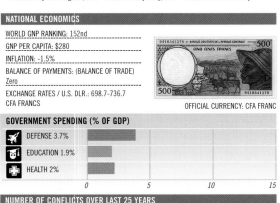

LEGISLATIVE BRANCH

Assemblee Nationale (National Assembly) Unicameral Parliament
Composed 109 members elected to five-year terms by direct popular vote. Meets twice annually.

Regional Governments
Sixteen prefectures and the federal district, administered by central government.

EXECUTIVE BRANCH

President
Elected to six-year term by direct popular vote. Serves as head of state; calls National Assembly into session; appoints top military officials.

Prime Minister
Appointed by president. Serves as head of government.

Council of Ministers
Appointed by president. Presided over by president; oversees government operations; initiates laws.

JUDICIAL BRANCH

Constitutional Court
Rules on constitutionality of laws. Composed of nine members appointed to single nine-year term: three by president; three by president of National Assembly; three by fellow judges.

Supreme Court
Highest court of review and appeal. Judges appointed by president.

Court of Appeal

Criminal Courts

Civil Courts

Labor Courts

LEBANON

OFFICIAL NAME: REPUBLIC OF LEBANON

POPULATION: 3.6 MILLION
CAPITAL: BEIRUT
AREA: 4,015 SQ. MILES (10,400 SQ. KM)
INDEPENDENCE: 1941
CONSTITUTION: 1926

LEBANON derives its name from the Mount Lebanon mountain range that runs parallel to the coast.

RELIGION: Muslim—mainly Shi'a, Sunni and Druze 70%, Christian—mainly Maronite, Greek Orthodox and Greek Catholic 30%

OFFICIAL LANGUAGE: Arabic

REGIONS OR PROVINCES: 6 governorates

DEPENDENT TERRITORIES: None

MEDIA: Total political censorship exists in national media

NEWSPAPERS: There are 41 daily newspapers

TV: 5 services: 1 state-controlled, 4 independent

RADIO: 1 state-owned service

SUFFRAGE: 21 years of age; compulsory for all males; authorized for women at age 21 with elementary education

LEGAL SYSTEM: Civil law; French and Ottoman legal traditions; no ICJ jurisdiction

WORLD ORGANIZATIONS: ABEDA, ACCT, AFESD, AL, AMF, CCC, ESCWA, FAO, G-24, G-77, IAEA, IBRD, ICAO, ICC, ICFTU, ICRM, IDA, IDB, IFAD, IFC, IFRCS, ILO, IMF, IMO, Interpol, IOC, ISO (correspondent), ITU, NAM, OAS (observer), OIC, PCA, UN, UNCTAD, UNESCO, UNHCR, UNIDO, UNRWA, UPU, WFTU, WHO, WIPO, WMO, WToO, WTrO (observer)

POLITICAL PARTIES: RD—Resistance and Development List, Ind—Independents, D—Dignity, BH—Baalbek-Hermel List, NS—National Struggle List, MLU—Mount Lebanon Party

ETHNIC GROUPS:

Armenian 4%
Other 1%
Arab 95%

NATIONAL ECONOMICS

WORLD GNP RANKING: 72nd

GNP PER CAPITA: $4,010

INFLATION: 0%

BALANCE OF PAYMENTS (BALANCE OF TRADE): -$3.07 billion

EXCHANGE RATES / U.S. DLR.: 1507.0-1513.8 LEBANESE POUNDS

OFFICIAL CURRENCY: LEBANESE POUND

GOVERNMENT SPENDING (% OF GDP)

✈ DEFENSE	3.5%	
🎓 EDUCATION	2.1%	
✚ HEALTH	2.2%	

0   5   10   15

NUMBER OF CONFLICTS OVER LAST 25 YEARS

	1	2-5	5+
Violent changes in government	○	○	○
Civil wars	●	○	○
International wars	●	○	○
Foreign intervention	●	○	○

- Compulsory national military service.
- A UN peacekeeping force maintains the border with Israel.
- Hezbollah guerrilla troops control southern Lebanon after the Israeli withdrawal of 2000.

NOTABLE WARS AND INSURGENCIES: Lebanese civil war 1975-1989. UN intervention (UNIFIL). Israeli occupation of southern Lebanon 1982-2000

LEBANON'S POLITICAL HISTORY HAS BEEN MARKED by religious differences that led to periods of turmoil and more recently to a violent civil war. The first constitution of 1926 established a balance of power among the many religious groups, but many amendments later, this has still not been fully accomplished. The dispute started when the Ottoman Empire collapsed after World War I, and the League of Nations mandated that the territory of current Lebanon would go to France, which then dominated the country, with Christians as major power players, until the withdrawal of its forces in 1946.

Lebanon had declared independence in 1941, but the year 1943 marked a major development in the country's political system: the concluding of an unwritten agreement known as the National Pact. This determined that the presidency would always be held by a maronite Christian, that the post of speaker of the National Assembly would go to a Shi'a Muslim, and that the prime minister would be a Sunni Muslim. This arrangement lasted until 1975, when civil war broke out, which would last more than a decade. Once again, the war came as a result of political power struggles between Muslims and Christians as well as strong discontent with socioeconomic injustices. This long civil war disrupted both the economic and the political semi-stability in Lebanon.

In 1982, the situation in Lebanon was further complicated by an invasion by Israel, in reaction to renewed Palestinian Liberation Organization (PLO) activity across the border. Only in 1989, after years of violence had killed more than 100,000 people, was the Ta'if Accord signed, guaranteeing the evacuation of Syrian troops, equal representation of Christians and Muslims in the National Assembly, and the shifting of some of the president's powers to the Council of Ministers. The constitution calls for parliamentary elections every four years, and the president is elected by Parliament every six years. In 1992 the first postwar elections were held, and a new Parliament elected. However Syria still held the reins of power, and it was only a surge of popular protest in 2005 that finally led to a full withdrawal.

ISSUES AND CHALLENGES:

- The main challenge to this day remains the old disagreements among religious groups, as the Ta'if Accord's practical resolution to this problem is still questioned by many segments of the population. Even though, in theory, a balance of power is maintained by leadership of the executive and legislative being shared among religious factions, Christians and Muslims continue to struggle over a series of political issues, such as the decentralization of the government.

- Sunni Muslim extremists and groups linked with terrorist organizations still provide a challenge to the government. In January 2002, Elie Hobeika, a former Parliament and three-times Council of Ministers member was assassinated.

- The majority of the population is poor, mainly Shi'a Muslims.

HOW THE GOVERNMENT WORKS

LEGISLATIVE BRANCH

Majlis Alnuwab
Assemblée Nationale
(National Assembly)
Unicameral Parliament
Composed of 128 members directly elected to four-year terms by sectarian proportional representation. Parliament's speaker traditionally a Shi'a Muslim. Meets twice annually. Levies taxes; approves budget; removes ministers with no-confidence vote.

Regional Governments
Six governorates administered by governors appointed by Council of Ministers.

EXECUTIVE BRANCH

President
Elected to single six-year term by two-thirds majority vote of National Assembly. Traditionally a Maronite Christian. Serves as head of state; commander-in-chief of armed forces. Promulgates laws; vetoes bills; issues regulations; negotiates treaties; dissolves National Assembly.

Prime Minister
Appointed by president on advice of National Assembly. Traditionally a Sunni Muslim.

Council of Ministers
Members appointed by president on advice of prime minister. Presided over by prime minister; oversees government operations.

JUDICIAL BRANCH

Constitutional Council
Rules on constitutionality of laws.

Supreme Council
Hears charges against the president and prime minister.

Courts of Cassation
Three courts for civil and commercial cases; one for criminal cases. Each court composed of three judges.

Courts of Appeal
Eleven courts, each composed of three judges.

Courts of First Instance
Fifty-six courts.

ALBANIA

OFFICIAL NAME: REPUBLIC OF ALBANIA

- POPULATION: 3.1 MILLION
- CAPITAL: TIRANA
- AREA: 11,100 SQ. MILES (28,748 SQ. KM)
- INDEPENDENCE: 1912
- CONSTITUTION: 1998

ALBANIA means "white land", being derived from the Latin *albus* meaning "white".

RELIGION: Sunni Muslim 70%, Orthodox Christian 20%, Roman Catholic 10%

OFFICIAL LANGUAGE: Albanian

REGIONS OR PROVINCES: 36 districts and 1 municipality

DEPENDENT TERRITORIES: None

MEDIA: Partial political censorship exists in the national media

NEWSPAPERS: There are 4 daily newspapers

TV: 1 state-run service, 75 private stations

RADIO: 1 state-run service, 30 private stations

SUFFRAGE: 18 years of age; universal and compulsory

LEGAL SYSTEM: No ICJ jurisdiction

WORLD ORGANIZATIONS: ACCT, BSEC, CCC, CE, CEI, EAPC, EBRD, ECE, FAO, IAEA, IBRD, ICAO, ICRM, IDA, IDB, IFAD, IFC, IFRCS, ILO, IMF, IMO, Interpol, IOC, IOM, ISO (correspondent), ITU, OIC, OPCW, OSCE, PFP, UN, UNCTAD, UNESCO, UNIDO, UNOMIG, UPU, WFTU, WHO, WIPO, WMO, WToO, WTrO

POLITICAL PARTIES: PSS—Socialist Party of Albania, BF—Union for Victory led by the Democratic Party—PD, DP—Democratic Party (splinter from PD), PDS—Social Democratic Party

ETHNIC GROUPS:

- Greek 3%
- Other (Vlach, Gypsy, Serb, and Bulgarian) 2%
- Albanian 95%

NATIONAL ECONOMICS

WORLD GNP RANKING:	122nd
GNP PER CAPITA:	$1,120
INFLATION:	0.1%
BALANCE OF PAYMENTS (BALANCE OF TRADE):	-$156 million
EXCHANGE RATES / U.S. DLR.:	142.75–136.80 LEKE

OFFICIAL CURRENCY: LEK

GOVERNMENT SPENDING (% OF GDP)

- DEFENSE 3%
- EDUCATION 3.1%
- HEALTH 2%

0   5   10   15

NUMBER OF CONFLICTS OVER LAST 25 YEARS

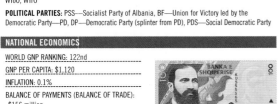

	1	2-5	5+
Violent changes in government		○	○
Civil wars	○	○	○
International wars	○	○	○
Foreign intervention	●	○	○

- Compulsory national military service.
- In 2000, a 10-year program of reconstruction began.
- Belongs to International Strategic Force (SFOR).

NOTABLE WARS AND INSURGENCIES: Civil conflict 1997. UN-backed peacekeeping mission.

AN OUTPOST OF THE OTTOMAN EMPIRE FOR FIVE CENTURIES, Albania finally secured independence in 1912. During the Cold War the country endured decades of communist rule, then in the years after the collapse of the Eastern Bloc, it struggled through economic calamity and outbreaks of anarchy. Albania now is taking its first strides as a multiparty democracy.

Scholars trace the ancestry of the Albanian people to the Illyrians, a group of tribes which first appeared in the Balkans around 2000 B.C. and later fell under the rule of the Romans. In subsequent centuries, its people were controlled by the Byzantine Empire and then the Ottomans.

For a few brief decades in the 15th century, Albanians threw off Turkish control when their legendary military leader, Gjergj Kastrioti, also known as Skanderbeg, united them in a temporarily successful revolt. Albanian nationalism finally resurfaced at the turn of the 20th century, and this time Turkey could not suppress it. However, after World War II, Albania adopted a harsh brand of Stalinist communism. With government and society under the strict rule of leader Enver Hoxha, Albania became increasingly isolated from the world.

PROTESTS OVER ALBANIAN ELECTIONS
The elections of October 2000, marred by accusations of irregularities and intimidation, did nothing to solve Albania's poverty and instability.

Hoxha's death in 1985 unleashed a turbulent decade of reform that saw multiparty elections in 1991—the first in almost 50 years—and culminated in the 1998 ratification of a new democratic constitution. The document made provision for a president, prime minister, Council of Ministers, and the unicameral People's Assembly, or Kuvendi Popullor. The new government faces the daunting task of resurrecting a struggling economy stifled by decades of communist rule and battered by the collapse in the 1990s of "pyramid" financial schemes that cost millions of Albanians their life savings. Other issues include modernizing outdated and dilapidated infrastructure and solving the frequent electrical outages that plague the economy.

HOW THE GOVERNMENT WORKS

LEGISLATIVE BRANCH

Kuvendi Popullor
(People's Assembly)
Unicameral Parliament
Composed of 140 members elected to four-year terms: 100 by direct popular vote to single-district seats; 40 by proportional representation. Enacts laws; amends constitution; adopts budget; ratifies treaties.

Regional Governments
Twenty-seven districts; 43 municipalities; 310 counties administered by elected mayors and councils.

EXECUTIVE BRANCH

President
Elected to five-year term by secret ballot by three-fifths majority of People's Assembly, two-term limit. Head of state. May return bills to Parliament; issue pardons, bestow decorations and honors, sign treaties; sets referenda and election dates.

Prime Minister
Leader of People's Assembly majority party, appointed by president, approved by Assembly. Head of government. Drafts budget.

Council of Ministers
Members nominated by prime minister, approved by president. Chaired by prime minister; oversees government operations.

JUDICIAL BRANCH

High Court of Justice
Appoints, transfers, disciplines lower-level judges. Composed of president, High Court chairman, minister of justice, three members elected by parliament, nine judges of all levels elected by National Judicial Conference.

Constitutional Court
Rules on constitutionality of laws; decides federal-local government disputes. Composed of nine justices appointed to single nine-year terms by president with consent of People's Assembly.

High Court
Highest court for civil and criminal appeals. Composed of 17 justices appointed to single nine-year terms by president with consent of People's Assembly.

MAURITANIA

OFFICIAL NAME: ISLAMIC REPUBLIC OF MAURITANIA

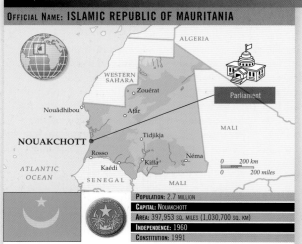

POPULATION: 2.7 MILLION
CAPITAL: NOUAKCHOTT
AREA: 397,953 SQ. MILES (1,030,700 SQ. KM)
INDEPENDENCE: 1960
CONSTITUTION: 1991

MAURITANIA is derived from the Spanish for "land of the Moors," the Arab rulers of southern Spain.

RELIGION: Muslim (Sunni) 100%

OFFICIAL LANGUAGE: Arabic

REGIONS OR PROVINCES: 12 regions and 1 capital district

DEPENDENT TERRITORIES: None

MEDIA: Total political censorship exists in national media

NEWSPAPERS: There are 3 daily newspapers

TV: 1 state-owned service

RADIO: 1 state-owned service

SUFFRAGE: 18 years of age; universal

LEGAL SYSTEM: Shari'a (Islamic) and French law; no ICJ jurisdiction

WORLD ORGANIZATIONS: ABEDA, ACCT, ACP, AfDB, AFESD, AL, AMF, AMU, CAEU, CCC, ECA, FAO, G-77, IBRD, ICAO, ICFTU, ICRM, IDA, IDB, IFAD, IFC, IFRCS, IHO (pending member), ILO, IMF, IMO, Interpol, IOC, ITU, NAM, OAU, OIC, OPCW, UN, UNCTAD, UNESCO, UNIDO, UPU, WCL, WHO, WIPO, WMO, WToO, WTrO

POLITICAL PARTIES: PRDS—Democracy and Social Republican Party, AC—Action for Change, Rep—Representatives for Mauritanians living abroad, Ind—Independents

ETHNIC GROUPS:

Black 30%
Mixed Maur/Black
Maur 30%

NATIONAL ECONOMICS

WORLD GNP RANKING: 155th

GNP PER CAPITA: $370

INFLATION: 3.3%

BALANCE OF PAYMENTS (BALANCE OF TRADE): $90 million

EXCHANGE RATES / U.S. DLR.: 250.97-264.01 OUGUIYAS

OFFICIAL CURRENCY: OUGUIYA

GOVERNMENT SPENDING (% OF GDP)

DEFENSE 2.8%
EDUCATION 4.3%
HEALTH 1.4%

0   5   10   15

NUMBER OF CONFLICTS OVER LAST 25 YEARS

	1	2-5	5+
Violent changes in government			
Civil wars			
International wars			
Foreign intervention			

- Compulsory national military service.
- France is the major supplier of military equipment.
- Troops, a strain on the budget, are often used for government projects.

NOTABLE WARS AND INSURGENCIES: Coup 1984. Senegal-Mauritania Border War 1989-1991 as a result of ethnic violence. Mauritanian nationals in Senegal, and Black Mauritanians and Senegalese nationals in Mauritania attacked and displaced

AFTER IT GAINED INDEPENDENCE FROM FRANCE IN 1960, northwest African Mauritania underwent rapid transformation into an Arab, Islamic state. Once rid of French cultural ties, the country embraced Islamic governing principles. In 1964, all political parties merged to form the Party of the People of Mauritania (PPM), beginning a period of single-party Islamic military rule that still influences contemporary politics.

Though Mauritania officially declared itself a multiparty republic in 1991, the Social and Democratic Republican Party (PRDS) dominates national politics, and the most recent elections merely reinstated incumbent military leader President Maaouya ould Sid'Ahmed Taya and his ministers, all PRDS members. Taya has led the country since seizing power in 1984. Most tensions in Mauritania are deeply rooted in its ethnic diversity. Moors (Maures), people of Arab and Berber descent, dominate the PRDS and opposition parties, while the black population, comprising several ethnic groups living mainly in the south, has been subject to oppression and human rights violations.

Another remnant of the single-party rule, most political power is wielded by the president, who by law must be Muslim. With the advice of the High Council of Islam—a group of imams who advise the government—the president appoints the prime minister and members of the Council of Ministers. No presidential appointment requires the approval of the legislature. With presidential authority, the ministers direct and implement national policy throughout the country's 12 regions. The PRDS also controls a significant portion of the legislative branch, roughly 80 percent of the National Assembly, and over 90 percent of the Senate, an obvious indication of the party's dominance.

Officially, the legal system is Shari'a (Islamic law), introduced in 1980 to certain judicial divisions and extended to the entire legal system in 1983. However, in 1985, the military Special Court of Justice adopted aspects of French civil law for civilian magistrates. These allow the right of appeal in certain commercial and civil cases.

ISSUES AND CHALLENGES:

- Only one percent of the land is arable, and the ever-encroaching Sahara desert constantly threatens to consume precious farmland.

- The black population is severely oppressed by the Moorish majority; there are estimated to be tens of thousands of blacks in slavery despite the outlawing of slavery in Mauritani in 1980.

- Transportation infrastructure is underdeveloped; Mauritania has two main roads.

- Caught between the Arab north and sub-Saharan Africa, the country has experienced political tensions with all of its neighbors. The large army strains the country's fiscal and economic resources.

- Half the population is illiterate.

> Mauritania was the last nation in the world to outlaw slavery, though it still continues today

HOW THE GOVERNMENT WORKS

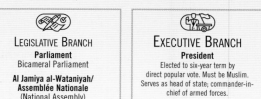

LEGISLATIVE BRANCH

Parliament
Bicameral Parliament

Al Jamiya al-Wataniyah/ Assemblée Nationale
(National Assembly)
Composed of 79 members elected to five-year terms by direct popular vote from single-member districts.

Majlis al-Shuyukh/ Sénat
(Senate)
Composed of 56 members elected to six-year terms by direct popular vote: 53 elected by municipal leaders; three elected by Mauritanian expatriates.

Regional Governments
Twelve regions administered by appointees of central government.

EXECUTIVE BRANCH

President
Elected to six-year term by direct popular vote. Must be Muslim. Serves as head of state; commander-in-chief of armed forces.

Prime Minister
Appointed by president. Serves as head of government. Defines and directs governmental policy; delegates tasks among members of Council of Ministers.

Council of Ministers
Appointed by president on advice of prime minister. Presided over by president.

High Islamic Council
Five Islamic leaders appointed by president. Advises president.

JUDICIAL BRANCH

Islamic Court of Justice
Tries crimes against people and property; adjudicates family matters.

Special Military Court of Justice
Tries national security cases.

Appellate Courts

Labor Tribunals

Civil Courts

Revenue Court

MONGOLIA

OFFICIAL NAME: MONGOLIA

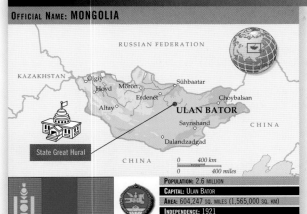

POPULATION: 2.6 MILLION	
CAPITAL: ULAN BATOR	
AREA: 604,247 SQ. MILES (1,565,000 SQ. KM)	
INDEPENDENCE: 1921	
CONSTITUTION: 1992	

MONGOLIA means "land of the Mongols". The powerful ancient Mongol empire reached as far as Europe.

RELIGION: Tibetan Buddhist Lamaism 96%, Muslim, Shamanism, and Christian 4%

OFFICIAL LANGUAGE: Khalka Mongol

REGIONS OR PROVINCES: 21 provinces and 1 municipality

DEPENDENT TERRITORIES: None

MEDIA: No political censorship exists in national media. Slander and libel laws were abolished in 1990, and legislation enacted in 1999 eased curbs on the media.

Newspapers: There are 3 daily newspapers.

TV: 5 services: 1 state-owned, 4 independent

Radio: 9 services: 1 state-owned, 8 independent

SUFFRAGE: 18 years of age; universal

LEGAL SYSTEM: German, Soviet and American legal traditions; no ICJ jurisdiction

WORLD ORGANIZATIONS: ARF (dialogue partner), AsDB, ASEAN (observer), CCC, CP (provisional), EBRD, ESCAP, FAO, G-77, IAEA, IBRD, ICAO, ICFTU, ICRM, IDA, IFAD, IFC, IFRCS, ILO, IMF, IMO, Interpol, IOC, ISO, ITU, NAM, OPCW, UN, UNCTAD, UNESCO, UNIDO, UPU, WHO, WIPO, WMO, WToO, WTrO

POLITICAL PARTIES: MPRP—Mongolian People's Revolutionary Party, Ind—Independents, MNDP—Mongolian National Democratic Party

ETHNIC GROUPS:
Mongol 90%, Kazakh 4%, Chinese 2%, Russian 2%, Other 2%

NATIONAL ECONOMICS

WORLD GNP RANKING: 156th

GNP PER CAPITA: $390

INFLATION: 7.6%

BALANCE OF PAYMENTS (BALANCE OF TRADE): -$112 million

EXCHANGE RATES / U.S. DLR.: 1097–1102 TUGRIKS

OFFICIAL CURRENCY: TUGRIK

GOVERNMENT SPENDING (% OF GDP)
- DEFENSE 2%
- EDUCATION 5.7%
- HEALTH 4.3%

0　5　10　15

NUMBER OF CONFLICTS OVER LAST 25 YEARS

	1	2-5	5+
Violent changes in government	○	○	○
Civil wars	○	○	○
International wars	○	○	○
Foreign intervention	○	○	○

- Compulsory national military service.
- Russian Federation provides assistance to Mongolian forces.
- India and Mongolia have signed agreements pledging defense cooperation.

NOTABLE WARS AND INSURGENCIES: None

THE WARLORD GENGHIS KHAN UNIFIED the nomadic tribes of Mongolia at the start of the 13th century into a formidable state that over the next 200 years conquered Russia and China and extended its power into Europe and Southeast Asia. But once its short-lived empire collapsed, Mongolia fell to the Manchus, remaining under Chinese rule until the early 20th century, when it gained independence, installed a communist government, and operated for decades as a satellite country of the Soviet Union.

By 1990, with the Soviet Union disintegrating and amid large street protests for reform, Mongolia's ruling communist politburo resigned. The country rapidly fashioned a new constitution, established a multiparty parliamentary government, and held its first democratic elections. Democracy was not an easily accepted alternative for most Mongolians, who had enjoyed the sense of stability under communism, and in the elections of 1992 the communist party—reformed as the Mongolian National Democratic Party (MPRP)—won the vote. By 1996 many had realized that the communist party was unable to address the severe economic issues that faced Mongolia, and a democratic coalition took power, although the presidency was held by the MPRP. By 2000, the MPRP had once again taken complete control of the government.

VOTING MONK
At 90 years of age, Shagdarsuren, a Buddhist monk, exercises his right to vote in the July 2000 parliamentary elections—the third elections since communism was abandoned in 1990.

Although Mongolia is seeking to reform its economic situation and improve its infrastructure, change has been slow in coming. Relations with China are tense as the majority of Mongolians live in Inner Mongolia, a province of China.

Mongolia's parliament, the State Great Hural, meets at least twice annually and has the power to enact or amend laws, override presidential vetoes, ratify international treaties, declare a state of war, and set domestic and foreign policies. The independent judiciary is headed by a Supreme Court, which hears appeals from lower civil and criminal trial courts. Disputes over the constitutionality of all laws are heard exclusively by the Tsets, a separate constitutional court.

HOW THE GOVERNMENT WORKS

LEGISLATIVE BRANCH

State Great Hural
Unicameral Parliament
Composed of 76 members elected to four-year terms by direct popular vote. Meets twice annually. Enacts and amends laws; determines domestic and foreign policy; ratifies treaties; declares states of emergency; overrides presidential vetoes.

Regional
Local hurals elected by 21 provinces and the capital, Ulan Bator.

EXECUTIVE BRANCH

President
Nominated by Parliament, elected to four-year term by direct popular vote, two-term limit. Serves as head of state; commander-in-chief of armed forces. Directs foreign policy; grants pardons; vetoes legislation; dissolves Parliament.

Prime Minister
Leader of Parliament's majority party or coalition, nominated to four-year term by president, confirmed by Parliament. Serves as head of government.

Cabinet
Members appointed by prime minister, approved by Parliament. Oversees government operations.

JUDICIAL BRANCH

Constitutional Court
Rules on constitutionality of laws. Composed of nine judges appointed to six-year terms by Parliament.

Supreme Court
Highest court for civil and criminal appeals. Composed of chief justice and ten justices appointed by president, confirmed by Parliament.

Lower Courts
Civil, criminal, and administrative courts are specialized and exist at all levels. Not subject to Supreme Court supervision. Local authorities—district and city governors—ensure courts abide by presidential decrees and State Great Hural decisions.

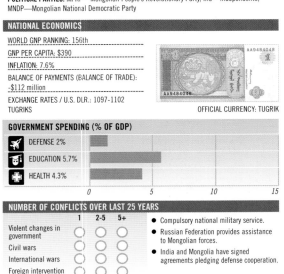

MACEDONIA

Official Name: FORMER YUGOSLAV REPUBLIC OF MACEDONIA

POPULATION: 2 Million
CAPITAL: Skopje
AREA: 9,781 SQ. MILES (25,333 SQ. KM)
INDEPENDENCE: 1991
CONSTITUTION: 1991

MACEDONIA is derived from the Greek for "high" used to describe the Macedonians, who came from the highlands.

RELIGION: Macedonian Orthodox 67%, Muslim 30%, Other 3%

OFFICIAL LANGUAGES: Macedonian and Albanian

REGIONS OR PROVINCES: 123 municipalities

DEPENDENT TERRITORIES: None

MEDIA: Partial political censorship exists in national media

Newspapers: There are 4 daily newspapers

TV: 3 services: 1 state-owned, 2 independent

Radio: 1 state-owned, also independent services

SUFFRAGE: 18 years of age; universal

LEGAL SYSTEM: Civil law; no ICJ jurisdiction

WORLD ORGANIZATIONS: ACCT, BIS, CCC, CE, CEI, EAPC, EBRD, ECE, FAO, IAEA, IBRD, ICAO, ICRM, IDA, IFAD, IFC, IFRCS, ILO, IMF, IMO, Interpol, IOC, IOM (observer), ISO, ITU, OPCW, OSCE, PCA, PFP, UN, UNCTAD, UNESCO, UNIDO, UPU, WCL, WHO, WIPO, WMO, WToO, WTrO (observer)

POLITICAL PARTIES: ZMZ—Together for Macedonia, headed by the Social Democratic Alliance of Macedonia (SDSM), VMRO-DPMNE—International Macedonian Revolutionary Organization-Democratic Party for Macedonian National Unity, BDI—Democratic Party of Albanians, PPD—Party of Democratic Prosperity, PDK—National Democratic Party, SPM—Socialist Party of Macedonia

ETHNIC GROUPS:

- Serb 2%
- Roma 2%
- Other 2%
- Turkish 4%
- Albanian 23%
- Macedonian 67%

NATIONAL ECONOMICS

WORLD GNP RANKING: 124th

GNP PER CAPITA: $1,820

INFLATION: -1.3%

BALANCE OF PAYMENTS (BALANCE OF TRADE): -$107 million

EXCHANGE RATES / U.S. DLR.: 66.26-69.17 MACEDONIAN DENARI

OFFICIAL CURRENCY: MACEDONIAN DENAR

GOVERNMENT SPENDING (% OF GDP)

✈ DEFENSE	2.1%	
📖 EDUCATION	5.1%	
✚ HEALTH	5.3%	

0   5   10   15

NUMBER OF CONFLICTS OVER LAST 25 YEARS

	1	2-5	5+
Violent changes in government	○	○	○
Civil wars	◉	○	○
International wars	○	○	○
Foreign intervention	◉	○	○

- Compulsory national military service.
- NATO intervention in 2001 resulted in a peace agreement between ethnic Albanian militants.
- Officers are trained in NATO countries.

NOTABLE WARS AND INSURGENCIES: Ethnic Albanian insurgency 2001

DURING THE BALKAN WARS OF 1912-13, Macedonia passed out of the control of the disintegrating Ottoman Empire and was incorporated in the new state of Yugoslavia after World War I. In 1991, as Yugoslavia began to fall apart, Macedonia declared its independence. The Greeks, whose northern province is also called Macedonia, objected to the use of this Hellenistic name for the new state. They felt this implied a claim to the whole historical region of Macedonia. International recognition of Macedonia was delayed until an agreement was reached between the two countries in 1995. The accord formally named the country the Former Yugoslav Republic of Macedonia (FYRM) and confirmed as inviolable the existing shared frontier between Macedonia and Greece.

Upon declaring independence, Macedonia adopted a constitution establishing a dual executive parliamentary democracy. The president, popularly elected to a five-year term, was to be head of state and represent the country in foreign affairs. However, Kiro Gligorov, Macedonia's first elected president, expanded the role by actively leading the country and government.

With the dawn of the 21st century, the country chose to end its one-party communist monopoly by amending the constitution and holding multiparty elections, resulting in the emergence of three major parties: the Internal Macedonian Revolutionary Organization-Democratic Party for Macedonian National Unity (VMRO-DPMNE) and the Social Democratic Alliance of Macedonia (SDSM), both largely Slavic parties; and the Party of Democratic Prosperity (PPD), primarily supported by ethnic Albanians. A 1995 law requiring a minimum membership of 500 citizens before party registration is permitted has decreased the number of proclaimed minority parties, which usually form coalitions with the major parties.

Although constitutionally mandated democratic provisions are in place, insurgencies by ethnic minorities coupled with mounting pressure from neighboring countries threaten Macedonian national and democratic stability.

KOSOVAN REFUGEES
In March 1999, the NATO bombing campaign against Serbia over the Serbians' treatment of ethnic Albanians in Kosovo led to an exodus of Kosovan refugees, many fleeing on foot into Macedonia.

HOW THE GOVERNMENT WORKS

LEGISLATIVE BRANCH

Sobranje (Assembly) Unicameral Parliament
Composed of 120 members elected to four-year terms; 85 by direct popular vote; 35 by proportional representation. Enacts laws; overrides presidential vetoes; adopts budget, elects government officials, ratifies treaties; declares war.

Regional Governments
123 municipalities governed by elected mayors and councils.

EXECUTIVE BRANCH

President
Elected to five-year term by direct popular vote. Serves as head of state; commander-in-chief of armed forces. Represents nation in foreign affairs; signs or vetoes bills; bestows honors and decorations.

Prime Minister
Leader of Assembly's majority party or coalition; nominated by president, approved by Assembly. Serves as head of government.

Cabinet
Members elected by Assembly. Oversees government operations; proposes budget.

JUDICIAL BRANCH

Constitutional Court
Rules on constitutionality of laws, individual rights, jurisdictional disputes, inter-governmental disputes. Composed of nine judges elected to single nine-year terms by Assembly.

Supreme Court
Highest court of review and appeal. Judges nominated for life by Republican Judicial Council, confirmed by Assembly.

Appellate Courts
Three courts; hear appeals from lower court.

Court of First Instance
Twenty-seven courts; adjudicate civil and criminal cases.

THE GAMBIA

OFFICIAL NAME: REPUBLIC OF THE GAMBIA

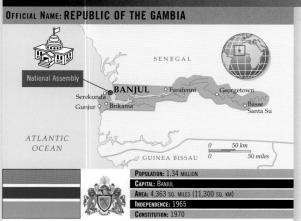

POPULATION: 1.34 million	
CAPITAL: BANJUL	
AREA: 4,363 SQ. MILES (11,300 SQ. KM)	
INDEPENDENCE: 1965	
CONSTITUTION: 1970	

THE GAMBIA is named after the local word for river, "ba-dimma", which refers to the Gambia River itself.

RELIGION: Muslim 90%, Christian 9%, Indigenous beliefs 1%

OFFICIAL LANGUAGE: English

REGIONS OR PROVINCES: 8 local government areas, including Banjul.

DEPENDENT TERRITORIES: None

MEDIA: Total political censorship exists in national media

NEWSPAPERS: There are 2 daily newspapers

TV: 1 state-owned service

RADIO: 9 services: 1 state-owned, 8 independent

SUFFRAGE: 18 years of age; universal

LEGAL SYSTEM: Customary, Shari'a (Islamic) and English common law; accepts ICJ jurisdiction

WORLD ORGANIZATIONS: ACP, AfDB, C, CCC, ECA, ECOWAS, FAO, G-77, IBRD, ICAO, ICFTU, ICRM, IDA, IDB, IFAD, IFC, IFRCS, ILO, IMF, IMO, Interpol, IOC, IOM, ITU, NAM, OAU, OIC, OPCW, UN, UNAMSIL, UNCTAD, UNESCO, UNIDO, UNMEE, UNMIK, UPU, WCL, WFTU, WHO, WIPO, WMO, WToO, WTrO

POLITICAL PARTIES: APRC—Alliance for Patriotic Reorientation and Construction, PDOIS—People's Democratic Organization for Independence and Socialism, NRP—National Reconciliation Party

ETHNIC GROUPS:

Mandinka 42%
Fulani 18%
Wolof 16%
Jolo 10%
Serahuli 9%
Other 5%

NATIONAL ECONOMICS

WORLD GNP RANKING: 172nd

GNP PER CAPITA: $340

INFLATION: 0.8%

BALANCE OF PAYMENTS (BALANCE OF TRADE): -$48 million

EXCHANGE RATES / U.S. DLR.: 15.28-17.54 DALASIS

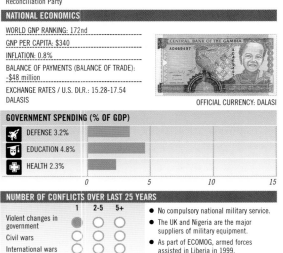

OFFICIAL CURRENCY: DALASI

GOVERNMENT SPENDING (% OF GDP)

DEFENSE 3.2%
EDUCATION 4.8%
HEALTH 2.3%

0   5   10   15

NUMBER OF CONFLICTS OVER LAST 25 YEARS

	1	2-5	5+
Violent changes in government	●	○	○
Civil wars	○	○	○
International wars	○	○	○
Foreign intervention	○	○	○

- No compulsory national military service.
- The UK and Nigeria are the major suppliers of military equipment.
- As part of ECOMOG, armed forces assisted in Liberia in 1999.
- Internal security and law enforcement are the responsibility of the police force.

NOTABLE WARS AND INSURGENCIES: Coup 1994

UNTIL THE FINAL 20 YEARS of the 20th century, The Gambia was most remarkable for its stability and peaceful rule. In 1965 it gained independence from Britain, but remained within the British Commonwealth. Though the government failed early on to win support for conversion to a republic with an elected president, The Gambia won international praise for its democratic election processes and civil-liberties record.

The country became a republic in 1970 through a referendum in which then Prime Minister Dawda Jawara was elected president. Jawara and his People's Progressive Party (PPP) were re-elected five times and dominated Gambian politics, maintaining one of few African democracies, until a violent but unsuccessful coup in 1981. The coup was led by Kukoi Samba Sanyang, who had failed to win election to parliament on two occasions. Senegalese forces subdued the rebellion at Jawara's request, and The Gambia and Senegal entered into a confederation—sharing security, communications, and monetary and economic systems, and coordinating foreign policy—until 1989, when the arrangement was discontinued. The PPP remained in government throughout, however, until Lieutenant Yaya Jammeh staged a successful coup in 1994 and instituted military rule, claiming a moral mandate to rid the country of corruption and sex tourism. When political activity was allowed to resume in 2001, the country elected Jammeh president and adopted a rewritten constitution, under which presidential and legislative elections took place in 2001 and 2002.

In many ways, the Gambia is a model democracy, with a constitution that protects civil liberties, guarantees an independent judiciary, and provides for three political parties and representative government. Its Constitutional Review Commission makes the constitution responsive to the needs of the people. However, The Gambia has often purchased peace and stability at the price of having an executive with enormous power. Balancing the need to rid the country of corruption, vice, and debt and to rebuild its infrastructure against the need to protect the nation's political freedoms is one of its biggest challenges.

ISSUES AND CHALLENGES:

- One of the government's biggest challenges is encouraging greater political freedom and participation in the election process.

- With few natural resources and most Gambians practicing subsistence farming, the government needs to grow its revenue base.

- Fostering market-driven economic growth is necessary, to overcome the dependence on foreign aid.

- The Gambia is overly dependent on its one main agricultural crop—groundnuts.

- The River Gambia provides an excellent opportunity to conduct trade, but is underutilized.

HOW THE GOVERNMENT WORKS

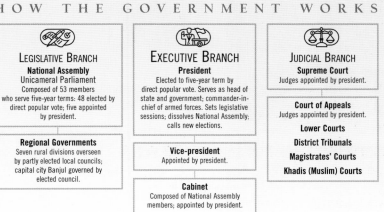

LEGISLATIVE BRANCH

National Assembly
Unicameral Parliament
Composed of 53 members who serve five-year terms: 48 elected by direct popular vote; five appointed by president.

Regional Governments
Seven rural divisions overseen by partly elected local councils; capital city Banjul governed by elected council.

EXECUTIVE BRANCH

President
Elected to five-year term by direct popular vote. Serves as head of state and government; commander-in-chief of armed forces. Sets legislative sessions; dissolves National Assembly; calls new elections.

Vice-president
Appointed by president.

Cabinet
Composed of National Assembly members; appointed by president.

JUDICIAL BRANCH

Supreme Court
Judges appointed by president.

Court of Appeals
Judges appointed by president.

Lower Courts

District Tribunals

Magistrates' Courts

Khadis (Muslim) Courts

GABON

OFFICIAL NAME: GABONESE REPUBLIC

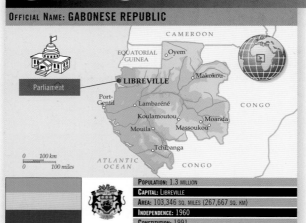

POPULATION: 1.3 MILLION	
CAPITAL: LIBREVILLE	
AREA: 103,346 SQ. MILES (267,667 SQ. KM)	
INDEPENDENCE: 1960	
CONSTITUTION: 1991	

GABON is derived from the Portuguese word "gabão", which is a coat with sleeves and a hood thought by sailors to resemble the shape of the Como River estuary.

RELIGION: Christian 55%-75%, Animist 24%-44%, Muslim less than 1%

OFFICIAL LANGUAGE: French

REGIONS OR PROVINCES: 17 districts

DEPENDENT TERRITORIES: None

MEDIA: Partial political censorship exists in national media

NEWSPAPERS: There are 2 daily newspapers. There was a crackdown in the late 1990s on independent media

TV: 3 services: 1 state-owned, 2 independent

RADIO: 7 services: 2 state-controlled, 5 independent

LEGAL SYSTEM: Customary and French law; no ICJ jurisdiction

WORLD ORGANIZATIONS: ACCT, ACP, AfDB, BDEAC, CCC, CEEAC, CEMAC, ECA, FAO, FZ, G-24, G-77, IAEA, IBRD, ICAO, ICFTU, IDA, IDB, IFAD, IFC, IFRCS, ILO, IMF, IMO, Interpol, IOC, ITU, NAM, OAU, OIC, OPCW, UN, UNCTAD, UNESCO, UNIDO, UPU, WCL, WHO, WIPO, WMO, WToO, WTrO

POLITICAL PARTIES: PDG—Gabonese Democratic Party, RNB—National Rally of Woodcutters, PGP—Gabonese Progressive Party

ETHNIC GROUPS:

- French 2%
- European and other African 9%
- Fang 35%
- Eshira 25%
- Other Bantu 29%

NATIONAL ECONOMICS

WORLD GNP RANKING: 118th

GNP PER CAPITA: $3,190

INFLATION: 1.5%

BALANCE OF PAYMENTS (BALANCE OF TRADE): $385 million

EXCHANGE RATES / U.S. DLR.: 698.7-736.7 CFA FRANCS

OFFICIAL CURRENCY: CFA FRANC

GOVERNMENT SPENDING (% OF GDP)

- DEFENSE 2.2%
- EDUCATION 3.3%
- HEALTH 2.1%

(scale: 0, 5, 10, 15)

NUMBER OF CONFLICTS OVER LAST 25 YEARS

	1	2-5	5+
Violent changes in government	○	○	○
Civil wars	○	○	○
International wars	○	○	○
Foreign intervention	○	○	○

- No compulsory national military service.
- France is a major supplier of security, maintaining defense forces.
- A plan to recruit 1500 new soldiers by 2006 began in 2001.

NOTABLE WARS AND INSURGENCIES: None

LIKE FREETOWN IN SIERRA LEONE named by slaves liberated by the British, Gabon's Libreville or "free town" was so called by slaves establishing a new home there after being rescued by the French. A French colony from 1886, Gabon was administered as part of French Equatorial Africa until 1960. Since independence from France, the country's most powerful political office has been the presidency, which from 1967 has been held by one man, Omar Bongo. When then Vice-president Bongo came to power after the death of President Léon M'ba, he tried to suppress political rivalries by abolishing all political parties except the Gabonese Democratic Party (PDG), eliminating the vice-presidency and the automatic right to succession that had given him the presidency, and creating an appointed prime minister post. Pushed, however, by political unrest throughout the 1970s and 1980s and two failed coups, Bongo presided over a national conference in 1990 that led to Gabon's first multiparty elections in 1991 and sweeping political reforms. These included a rewritten constitution, a bill of rights, freedom of assembly and of the press, and legalization of opposition political parties.

Charges of fraud have tainted elections since then, but have also led to further reforms, such as the inclusion of opposition leaders in national unity governments. The transformation to a multiparty democracy has thus been largely, if imperfectly, accomplished. Amendments to the constitution in 1997 extended the president's term of office to seven years, created a vice-presidency, and provided for a national Senate. Bongo's party, the PDG, won the national parliamentary elections in 2001 and established a majority.

Despite Gabon's democratic process and institutions, the president retains powers far stronger than in most other countries, including the authority to dissolve the National Assembly, declare a state of siege, initiate and delay legislation, conduct referenda, and appoint and dismiss the prime minister and Cabinet members. The National Assembly's role is to make laws, approve taxes, and censure and withdraw its confidence from the government, an act that precipitates the prime minister's resignation. The independence of the judiciary is guaranteed by the constitution and maintained by the president.

ISSUES AND CHALLENGES:

- While much reform has taken place, further progress toward free and fair elections is necessary.
- Equitable distribution of the wealth generated by Gabon's petroleum reserves is a concern, with most low-income jobs being done by immigrants.
- Ethnic conflict is an ongoing issue that needs to be resolved.
- There is an overdependence on France for both financial aid and technical assistance, although much of the aid received goes towards the debt incurred in the 1970s.

HOW THE GOVERNMENT WORKS

LEGISLATIVE BRANCH

Parliament
Bicameral Parliament

Senat
(Senate)
Composed of 91 members elected to six-year terms by municipal councils and departmental assemblies. Initiates local government bills.

Assemblée Nationale
(National Assembly)
Composed of 120 members who serve five-year terms: 111 elected by direct popular vote; nine appointed by president. Initiates finance bills and constitutional amendments.

Regional Governments
Nine provinces administered by governors appointed by president.

EXECUTIVE BRANCH

President
Elected to seven-year term by direct popular vote. Serves as head of state; commander-in-chief of armed forces. Dissolves National Assembly; declares states of siege; proposes or delays legislation; calls for referenda.

Prime Minister
Appointed by president. Serves as head of government.

Cabinet
Composed of 39 members, many from National Assembly; appointed by president on advice of prime minister. Oversees government operations.

JUDICIAL BRANCH

Constitutional Court
Rules on constitutionality of laws; oversees elections. Composed of nine judges; president appoints three.

Judicial Court
Hears civil, criminal and commercial cases. Judges appointed by president.

Administrative Courts
Hear administrative cases.

Court of Accounts
Hear cases involving public funds.

High Court of Justice
Convenes by two-thirds majority vote of parliament to hear charges against president.

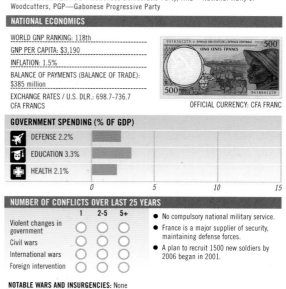

EAST TIMOR

OFFICIAL NAME: EAST TIMOR

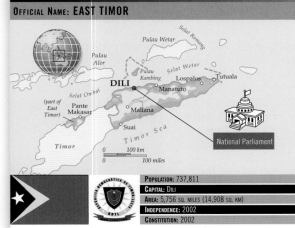

POPULATION: 737,811
CAPITAL: DILI
AREA: 5,756 SQ. MILES (14,908 SQ. KM)
INDEPENDENCE: 2002
CONSTITUTION: 2002

EAST TIMOR is derived from the Malay word "Timur" meaning "east" or "Orient". The Timorese call their country Timor Lorosae and the Indonesians call it Timor Timur, both of which mean "eastern east".

RELIGION: Roman Catholic 95%, Other (including Muslim and Protestant) 5%

OFFICIAL LANGUAGE: Tetum (Portuguese/Austronesian) and Portuguese

REGIONS OR PROVINCES: 13 administrative districts

DEPENDENT TERRITORIES: None

MEDIA: No political censorship exists in national media

Newspapers: There are 2 daily newspapers

TV: 1 state-owned service

Radio: 3 stations: 1 state-owned, 1 run by the Catholic Church, 1 community

SUFFRAGE: 17 years of age; universal

LEGAL SYSTEM: In transition; no ICJ jurisdiction

WORLD ORGANIZATIONS: IBRD, IMF, UN

POLITICAL PARTIES: Fretilin—Revolutionary Front for an Independent East Timor, PD—Democratic Party, PSD—Social Democratic Party, ASDT—Timorese Social-Democratic Association

NATIONAL ECONOMICS

WORLD GNP RANKING: 172nd

GNP PER CAPITA: $458

INFLATION: 0%

BALANCE OF PAYMENTS (BALANCE OF TRADE): $8 million

EXCHANGE RATES / U.S. DLR.: Currency is US DOLLAR

OFFICIAL CURRENCY: US DOLLAR

GOVERNMENT SPENDING (% OF GDP)

	0	5	10	15
DEFENSE (N/A)				
EDUCATION (N/A)				
HEALTH (N/A)				

NUMBER OF CONFLICTS OVER LAST 25 YEARS

	1	2-5	5+
Violent changes in government	◑	○	○
Civil wars	◑	○	○
International wars	○	○	○
Foreign intervention	◑	○	○

- No compulsory national military service.
- A defense force, which acts mainly as a police force, was established in 2001.
- UN soldiers provide most external defense.

NOTABLE WARS AND INSURGENCIES: Pre-independence violence 1999. UN intervention (UNMISET)

EAST TIMOR IS THE NEWEST DEMOCRACY IN THE WORLD. In 2002, after more than 450 years of rule by Portugal and later by Indonesia which occupied the country in 1975, East Timor elected its first president and now operates as a multiparty republic. José Alexandre (Xanana) Gusmão, who had been the leader of the Fretilin independence movement since 1979, was inaugurated in May 2002.

Portugal withdrew from East Timor in 1975, alleging that it was too costly to maintain. Fretilin declared independence, but that lasted only nine days as Indonesian forces occupied the territory, annexing it in 1976 amid violence in which it is estimated that about a third of the Timorese population was killed. Indonesia controlled the country for more than 20 years by intimidation and violence, resulting in human-rights violations that drew international condemnation until, in 1999, a UN mission was allowed full operational power to re-establish order. Indonesia then conceded a referendum on East Timor's future. Following the ballot in which 80 percent of voters called for independence, pro-Indonesian militias went on the rampage, murdering hundreds and causing enormous damage to public buildings, and transportation and utilities infrastructure. The UN reimposed order and set up a transitional administration (UNTAET). In 2002, the UN secretary general, Kofi Annan, symbolically handed over political power to the new president. The UN, however, maintains a peacekeeping mission of troops and police officers.

INDEPENDENCE CELEBRATIONS
May 19, 2002 was a night of much celebration in East Timor. The next day marked the independence of the nation that had long been occupied by Indonesia and had seen much violence.

In 1996, East Timor independence activists José Ramos Horta and Bishop Carlos Belo won the Nobel Peace Prize.

East Timor's greatest challenges arise from the violence that has beset it. During 1999, some 260,000 people fled East Timor, but by 2002, 80 percent of the refugees had returned. The government is now faced with rebuilding the devastated infrastructure, developing the economy, which so far has consisted of little more than subsistence farming, and providing education and welfare for the many thousands of homeless.

HOW THE GOVERNMENT WORKS

LEGISLATIVE BRANCH

National Parliament
Unicameral Parliament
Composed of a minimum of 52 seats and a maximum of 65 seats; members elected to five-year terms by direct popular vote. For its first term of office the National Parliament exceptionally has 88 members.

Regional
13 administrative districts.

EXECUTIVE BRANCH

President
Elected to five-year term by direct popular vote. Serves as head of state.

Prime Minister
Leader of Parliament's majority party or coalition, appointed by president. Serves as head of government.

Council of State.
Composed of nine ministers and eight secretaries selected in consultation with UNTAET and Parliament.

JUDICIAL BRANCH

Court of Appeal
Highest court of review and appeal. Composed of three judges who serve for life: one appointed by parliament; two by Superior Council for the Judiciary. Court president appointed to four-year term by president from among presiding judges.

District Courts
First judges selected by UNTAET. Future appointments made by government on advice of Superior Council for the Judiciary.

Superior Council for the Judiciary
Appoints and disciplines judges.

FIJI

OFFICIAL NAME: REPUBLIC OF THE FIJI ISLANDS

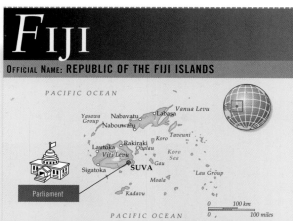

FIJI'S name is a Tongan corruption of the indigenous word "Viti".

POPULATION: 823,000
CAPITAL: SUVA
AREA: 7,054 SQ. MILES (18,270 SQ. KM)
INDEPENDENCE: 1970
CONSTITUTION: 1990

RELIGION: Hindu 38%, Methodist 37%, Roman Catholic 9%, Muslim 8%, Other 8%

OFFICIAL LANGUAGE: English

REGIONS OR PROVINCES: 4 divisions

DEPENDENT TERRITORIES: 1 dependency

MEDIA: No political censorship exists in national media

NEWSPAPERS: There are 2 English-language dailies

TV: 2 services: 1 state-owned, 1 independent

RADIO: 4 services: 1 state-controlled, 3 independent

SUFFRAGE: 21 years of age; universal

LEGAL SYSTEM: English common law; no ICJ jurisdiction

WORLD ORGANIZATIONS: ACP, AsDB, C, CCC, CP, ESCAP, FAO, G-77, IBRD, ICAO, ICFTU, ICRM, IDA, IFAD, IFC, IFRCS, IHO, ILO, IMF, IMO, Interpol, IOC, ISO (subscriber), ITU, OPCW, PCA, Sparteca, SPC, SPF, UN, UNCTAD, UNESCO, UNIDO, UNIFIL, UNIKOM, UNMIBH, UNMIK, UNTAET, UPU, WFTU, WHO, WIPO, WMO, WToO, WTrO

POLITICAL PARTIES: SDL—Fijian People's Party, FLP—Fiji Labor Party, MV—Conservative Alliance (Mantinatu Vanau), NLUP—New Labor Unity Party, Ind—Independents

ETHNIC GROUPS:

European, other Pacific Islanders, overseas Chinese, and Other 5%

Indian 44%

Fijian 51%

NATIONAL ECONOMICS

WORLD GNP RANKING: 145th

GNP PER CAPITA: $1,820

INFLATION: 1.1%

BALANCE OF PAYMENTS (BALANCE OF TRADE): $13 million

EXCHANGE RATES / U.S. DLR.: 2.176-2.298 FIJI DOLLARS

OFFICIAL CURRENCY: FIJI DOLLAR

GOVERNMENT SPENDING (% OF GDP)

✈ DEFENSE 2.1%		
🎓 EDUCATION 5.4%		
✚ HEALTH 2.9%		

0   5   10   15

NUMBER OF CONFLICTS OVER LAST 25 YEARS

	1	2-5	5+
Violent changes in government	○	●	○
Civil wars	○	○	○
International wars	○	○	○
Foreign intervention	○	○	○

● No compulsory national military service.
● Troops participate in UN initiatives, including Lebanon, Egypt, East Timor and the Middle East.
● Most of the military are ethnic Fijian.

NOTABLE WARS AND INSURGENCIES: Coups 1987, 2000

FIJI COMPRISES TWO MAIN ISLANDS and some 750 other islands and islets, one of which, Rotuma, lies 400 miles (640 km) north of the main group. The dominant issue of Fijian politics and government—ethnic conflict between indigenous Fijians and Indo-Fijians—originated in the mid-1800s, when British colonialists imported Indians to work their sugar plantations. By the mid-20th century, Indo-Fijians outnumbered indigenous Fijians. When Fiji won independence in 1970, indigenous fears of Indian dominance were beginning to boil.

The first of two military coups by indigenous forces in 1987 sparked a mass exodus by Indo-Fijians and returned indigenous Fijians to the majority. The second coup, in which the constitution was revoked and Fiji declared a republic, provoked protests from India, expulsion from the British Commonwealth, and official nonrecognition from Australia and New Zealand. In 1990, the indigenous Fijian-controlled government drafted a new constitution that reserved majorities in both legislative houses for indigenous Fijians, discriminating against the Indo-Fijians.

Much of the conflict centers on land rights. Indo-Fijian farmers produce most of the sugar crop, but by law must lease land from indigenous Fijians. In 1997, tensions over leases led to a new constitution that expanded Parliament, reduced its reserved seats, and opened the post of prime minister to all ethnic groups. In 1999, Fiji's first Indo-Fijian prime minister was elected but in 2000 was taken hostage, along with much of Parliament, by indigenous supremacists. The Supreme Court reaffirmed the 1997 constitution and returned the government to power. Nevertheless, troubles continue. In 2001, the indigenous Fiji Labor Party (SDL) won power but excluded the Indo-Fijian FLP party from the government on a technicality.

As written, the country's constitution balances power and fosters multiparty democracy. But its most distinctive feature, the Council of Chiefs, is made up of indigenous Fijians, protects their interests, and appoints the president, vice-president, and most of the Senate. The president appoints Supreme Court justices, and the prime minister, who must come from the elected House of Representatives. All legislation originates in the House.

ISSUES AND CHALLENGES:

● The coups have damaged Fiji's reputation globally, raising awareness of the Fijian government's discrimination against Indo-Fijians.

● There is a high level of immigration of Indo-Fijian professionals, leaving a shortage of highly-skilled workers.

● All major exports are subject to world market price fluctuations, while the main crop, sugar cane, is highly vulnerable to drought.

● Many environmental issues are a concern, including the damage tourists have caused to the coral reefs, and the lingering effect of nuclear tests performed in the Pacific by France.

HOW THE GOVERNMENT WORKS

LEGISLATIVE BRANCH

Parliament
Bicameral Parliament

Senate
Composed of 34 members who serve five-year terms: 24 appointed by Council of Chiefs; nine appointed by president; one appointed by Council of Rotuma.

House of Representatives
Composed of 71 members elected to five-year terms by direct popular vote. 25 open seats; 23 reserved for Fijians; 19 for Indo-Fijians; three for other ethnic groups; one for Council of Rotuma. Originates all legislation.

EXECUTIVE BRANCH

President
Five-year term by Great Council of Chiefs, two-term limit. Must be indigenous Fijian. Serves as head of state; commander-in-chief of armed forces. May dissolve parliament on advice of prime minister.

Vice-president
Elected to five-year term by Great Council of Chiefs; two-term limit. Must be from non-Fijian ethnic group.

Prime Minister
Member of House of Representatives, appointed by president, approved by Parliament. Head of government.

Cabinet
Up to 15 parliament members, appointed by president on advice of prime minister. Oversees government operations.

Great Council of Chiefs
Composed of 46 elected and appointed members. Advises on Fijian heritage.

JUDICIAL BRANCH

Supreme Court
Highest court of review and appeal. Judges appointed to serve to age 70 by president on advice of Judicial Services Commission, minister for justice.

Court of Appeals
Hears appeals from High Court.

High Court
Hears civil or criminal cases.

Magistrates' Court

CAPE VERDE

OFFICIAL NAME: REPUBLIC OF CAPE VERDE

POPULATION: 437,000	
CAPITAL: PRAIA	
AREA: 1,557 SQ. MILES (4,033 SQ. KM)	
INDEPENDENCE: 1975	
CONSTITUTION: 1992	

CAPE VERDE is named after the closest point to it on the African continent, Cap Vert in Senegal.

RELIGION: Roman Catholic (infused with indigenous beliefs); Protestant (mostly Church of the Nazarene)

OFFICIAL LANGUAGE: Portuguese

REGIONS OR PROVINCES: 17 districts

DEPENDENT TERRITORIES: None

MEDIA: No political censorship exists in national media

Newspapers: There are no daily newspapers

TV: 1 state-controlled service

Radio: 1 state-controlled service

SUFFRAGE: 18 years of age; universal

LEGAL SYSTEM: Portuguese law; no ICJ jurisdiction

WORLD ORGANIZATIONS: ACCT, ACP, AfDB, CCC, ECA, ECOWAS, FAO, G-77, IBRD, ICAO, ICFTU, ICRM, IDA, IFAD, IFC, IFRCS, ILO, IMF, IMO, Interpol, IOC, IOM, IOM (observer), ITU, NAM, OAU, OPCW (signatory), UN, UNCTAD, UNESCO, UNIDO, UPU, WHO, WIPO, WMO, WTrO (observer)

POLITICAL PARTIES: PIACV—African Party for Independence of Cape Verde, MPD—Movement for Democracy, ADM—Democratic Alliance for Change

ETHNIC GROUPS:

- Other 10%
- African 30%
- Mestico 60%

NATIONAL ECONOMICS

WORLD GNP RANKING: 167th

GNP PER CAPITA: $1,330

INFLATION: 4.4%

BALANCE OF PAYMENTS (BALANCE OF TRADE):- $67 million

EXCHANGE RATES / U.S. DLR.: 118.2–119.8 CAPE VERDE ESCUDOS

OFFICIAL CURRENCY: CAPE VERDE ESCUDO

GOVERNMENT SPENDING (% OF GDP)

✈	DEFENSE	2.7%
🎓	EDUCATION	4.2%
✚	HEALTH	1.8%

0   5   10   15

NUMBER OF CONFLICTS OVER LAST 25 YEARS

	1	2-5	5+
Violent changes in government	○	○	○
Civil wars	○	○	○
International wars	○	○	○
Foreign intervention	○	○	○

- Compulsory national military service.
- Armed forces are limited to a small army, air force and a coastguard.
- Greatest threats are smuggling and illegal fishing.

NOTABLE WARS AND INSURGENCIES: None

THE CAPE VERDE archipelago consists of ten volcanic islands and five islets located just off the westernmost coast of Africa. Discovered and colonized by the Portuguese in 1456, the islands played an integral role in the slave trade between the 16th and the 19th centuries. Situated on the shipping routes, Cape Verde became the ideal stopping point to trade and restock supplies. As a result, the population today is largely of Portuguese and African descent.

From independence in 1975 to 1991, the African Party for the Independence of Cape Verde (PAICV) ruled Cape Verde. Formed in 1956 as the African Party for the Independence of Guinea and Cape Verde (PAIGC), the party organized an underground movement aimed at consolidating resistance to Portugal's control of Guinea-Bissau and Cape Verde. Unlike Guinea-Bissau, which expressed its resistance through a guerrilla war, Cape Verde pursued an extended campaign of unrest, protests and strikes, which, in 1975, led Portugal to permit the first elections for a National Assembly. Although the PAIGC won these elections and Cape Verde's independence was granted five days later, plans for a united country of Guinea-Bissau and Cape Verde were abandoned in 1980 after a coup in Guinea-Bissau resulted in a party split. Changes to the constitution in 1991 led to the first multiparty elections. Cape Verde thus became the first single-party state in sub-Saharan Africa to hold multiparty democratic elections. A new party, the Movement for Democracy (MPD) won the majority of seats in the National Assembly and a new constitution was adopted in 1992. In 2001, the PAICV regained control, with the candidate, Pedro Pires, winning by a narrow margin.

Limited job opportunities in the country have caused many Cape Verdeans to move to Europe, the United States, and West Africa. Diaspora residents in each of these regions form overseas electoral districts and each elect two deputies to the unicameral National Assembly.

ALBERTO WAHON MEETS OTHER WORLD LEADERS
On April 10, 2000 the Group of 77 South Summit was held in Havana. Cuban President Fidel Castro greets UN Secretary-General Kofi Annan and prime minister of Cape Verde, Alberto Wahnon.

HOW THE GOVERNMENT WORKS

LEGISLATIVE BRANCH
National Assembly
Unicameral Parliament
Composed of 72 members elected to five-year terms by direct popular vote: 66 from 17 island districts; two each from three overseas districts of Africa, America and Europe.

Regional Governments
Seventeen municipalities administered by elected mayors and local councils.

EXECUTIVE BRANCH
President
Elected to five-year term by direct popular vote. If no outright winner, two leading candidates vie in runoff election. Serves as head of state.

Prime Minister
Nominated by parliament, appointed by president. Serves as head of government.

Council of Ministers
Members appointed by prime minister. Oversees government operations.

JUDICIAL BRANCH
Supreme Court of Justice
Highest court of review and appeals. Composed of five or more judges appointed to five-year terms: one by president; one by parliament; remainder by Supreme Council of Magistrates.

Civil Courts
Criminal Courts

SÃO TOMÉ & PRÍNCIPE

OFFICIAL NAME: DEMOCRATIC REPUBLIC OF SÃO TOMÉ AND PRÍNCIPE

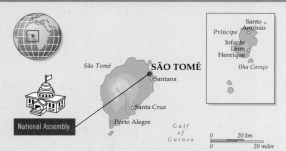

POPULATION: 159,900
CAPITAL: São Tomé
AREA: 386 SQ. MILES (1,001 SQ. KM)
INDEPENDENCE: 1975
CONSTITUTION: 1990

SÃO TOMÉ & PRÍNCIPE is Portuguese for St. Thomas and Prince, although the origin of the names is unknown.

RELIGION: Christian 80% (Roman Catholic, Evangelical Protestant, Seventh-Day Adventist), Other 20%

OFFICIAL LANGUAGE: Portuguese

REGIONS OR PROVINCES: 2 provinces

DEPENDENT TERRITORIES: None

MEDIA: No political censorship exists in national media

NEWSPAPERS: There are no daily newspapers

TV: 1 state-controlled service

RADIO: 1 state-controlled service

SUFFRAGE: 18 years of age; universal

LEGAL SYSTEM: Customary and Portuguese law; no ICJ jurisdiction

WORLD ORGANIZATIONS: ACCT, ACP, AfDB, CEEAC, CEMAC, ECA, FAO, G-77, IBRD, ICAO, ICRM, IDA, IFAD, IFRCS, ILO, IMF, IMO, Interpol, IOC, IOM (observer), ITU, NAM, OAU, UN, UNCTAD, UNESCO, UNIDO, UPU, WCL, WHO, WIPO, WMO, WToO, WTrO (observer)

POLITICAL PARTIES: MLSTP-PSD— São Tomé and Príncipe Liberation Movement-Social Democratic Party, MDFM-PCD—Force for Change Democratic Movement-Democratic Convergence Party, UK—Ue Kedadji coalition

ETHNIC GROUPS:

Portuguese and Creole 10%

Black 90%

NATIONAL ECONOMICS

WORLD GNP RANKING: 191st

GNP PER CAPITA: $290

INFLATION: 5.0%

BALANCE OF PAYMENTS (BALANCE OF TRADE): -$9 million

EXCHANGE RATES / U.S. DLR.: 2390-8937 DOBRAS

OFFICIAL CURRENCY: DOBRA

GOVERNMENT SPENDING (% OF GDP)

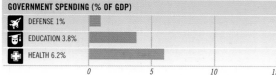

- DEFENSE 1%
- EDUCATION 3.8%
- HEALTH 6.2%

0   5   10   15

NUMBER OF CONFLICTS OVER LAST 25 YEARS

	1	2-5	5+
Violent changes in government			
Civil wars		●	
International wars			
Foreign intervention			

- No compulsory national military service.
- The armed forces have been used extensively to prevent coups.
- Military and police fall under the Minister of National Defense, Security, and Internal Order.

NOTABLE WARS AND INSURGENCIES: Popular unrest in 1992 and 1996-1997. Brief coups

SÃO TOMÉ AND PRÍNCIPE, a group of volcanic islands, is located approximately 200 miles (320 km) off the northwest coast of Gabon. The culture is a mix of African and Portuguese. Almost all the population belongs to one of six groups of people: Portuguese, *mestiços* (mixed race), *angolares* (descendents of Angolan slaves shipwrecked on São Tomé in the 16th century), *forros* (descendents of freed slaves), *serviçais* (descendents of contract laborers brought from other Portuguese colonies after the abolition of slavery), and *tongas* (children of *serviçais* who were indented laborers from other colonies).

Discovered by the Portuguese in the late 1400s, the islands were a colony administered by Portugal from 1522 and became an important exporter of sugar cane. In the early 1800s, two more lucrative crops were planted—coffee and cocoa—and São Tomé became the world's largest producer of cocoa. Even after slavery was abolished, simmering tensions between rich land owners and their laborers remained, and led in 1953 to the riots known as the Batepa Massacre, in which many hundreds were killed.

São Tomé began the road to independence in the 1960s with the formation of the São Tomé and Príncipe Liberation Movement (MLSTP). After the overthrow in 1974 of Portuguese dictator Marcelo Caetano, the new government in Lisbon immediately relinquished control of its overseas colonies, and São Tomé gained independence in 1975. MLSTP leader Manuel Pinto da Costa became president of a one-party, Marxist regime. In 1985, with the country facing economic collapse, da Costa was forced to pursue a series of westernizing economic changes.

In 1990, São Tomé and Príncipe began moving toward democracy, after a referendum showed 75 percent of voters favored such a change. A new constitution allowed for multiparty elections. Miguel Trovoada, a former prime minister, returned from exile to win the presidency as an independent in 1991 and was re-elected in 1996. The MLSTP, renamed the MLSTP-PSD, holds a parliamentary plurality. Businessman Fradique de Menezes ran in 2001 in place of Trovoada, who had served the maximum two terms, and defeated da Costa. He formed a coalition government with the MLSTP-PSD.

ISSUES AND CHALLENGES:

- Mismanagement and corruption have left São Tomé and Príncipe with severe debts, despite the high level of international aid received.

- Though significant offshore oil revenues are et to come on stream, the islands themselves lack mineral resources.

- Although education is compulsory to age 14, all of the staff at the one technical and three secondary schools are foreigners.

- The country is highly dependent on cocoa exports that account for 90 percent of export earnings, diversification is necessary.

HOW THE GOVERNMENT WORKS

LEGISLATIVE BRANCH

Assembleia Nacional (National Assembly) Unicameral Parliament
Composed of 55 members elected to four-year terms by direct popular vote. Amends constitution with two-thirds majority vote.

Regional Governments
Two provinces; seven counties administered by elected local councils.

EXECUTIVE BRANCH

President
Elected to five-year term by direct popular vote; two-term limit. Serves as head of state; commander-in-chief of armed forces. Answers to National Assembly.

Prime Minister
Appointed by president, approved by National Assembly. Serves as head of government.

Council of Ministers
Composed of 14 members appointed by president on advice of prime minister. Chaired by prime minister. Oversees government operations; answers to president and National Assembly.

JUDICIAL BRANCH

Supreme Court
Judges appointed by National Assembly.

SEYCHELLES

OFFICIAL NAME: REPUBLIC OF THE SEYCHELLES

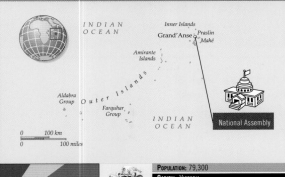

INDIAN OCEAN

Inner Islands
Grand'Anse • Praslin
• Mahé

Amirante Islands

Aldabra Group — Outer Islands

Farquhar Group

INDIAN OCEAN

National Assembly

| 0 | 100 km |
| 0 | 100 miles |

POPULATION: 79,300
CAPITAL: Victoria
AREA: 176 SQ. MILES (455 SQ. KM)
INDEPENDENCE: 1976
CONSTITUTION: 1993

THE SEYCHELLES were named after Moreau de Séchelles, who was the finance minister under King Louis XV.

RELIGION: Roman Catholic 90%, Anglican 8%, Other (including Muslim) 2%

OFFICIAL LANGUAGES: Seselwa (French Creole)

REGIONS OR PROVINCES: 23 administrative districts

DEPENDENT TERRITORIES: None

MEDIA: Partial political censorship exists in national media

NEWSPAPERS: There is 1 daily newspaper

TV: 2 independent services

RADIO: 3 independent services

SUFFRAGE: 17 years of age; universal

LEGAL SYSTEM: Customary and French law; English common law; no ICJ jurisdiction

WORLD ORGANIZATIONS: ACCT, ACP, AfDB, C, CCC, ECA, FAO, G-77, IBRD, ICAO, ICFTU, ICRM, IFAD, IFC, IFRCS, ILO, IMF, IMO, InOC, Interpol, IOC, ISO (correspondent), ITU, NAM, OAU, OPCW, SADC, UN, UNCTAD, UNESCO, UNIDO, UPU, WHO, WIPO, WMO, WToO, WTrO (observer)

POLITICAL PARTIES: SPPF—Seychelles People's Progressive Party, UO—United Opposition, DP—Democratic Party

ETHNIC GROUPS:

Other 4%
Indian 5%
Chinese 2%
Creole 89%

NATIONAL ECONOMICS

WORLD GNP RANKING: 168th

GNP PER CAPITA: $7,050

INFLATION: 6.3%

BALANCE OF PAYMENTS (BALANCE OF TRADE): -$114 million

EXCHANGE RATES / U.S. DLR.: 6.261-5.618 SEYCHELLES RUPEES

OFFICIAL CURRENCY: SEYCHELLES RUPEE

GOVERNMENT SPENDING (% OF GDP)

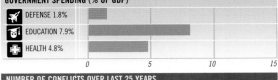

✈ DEFENSE 1.8%
📖 EDUCATION 7.9%
➕ HEALTH 4.8%

| 0 | 5 | 10 | 15 |

NUMBER OF CONFLICTS OVER LAST 25 YEARS

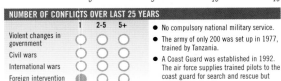

	1	2-5	5+
Violent changes in government	○	○	○
Civil wars	○	○	○
International wars	○	○	○
Foreign intervention	◐	○	○

- No compulsory national military service.
- The army of only 200 was set up in 1977, trained by Tanzania.
- A Coast Guard was established in 1992. The air force supplies trained pilots to the coast guard for search and rescue but does not assist in missions.

NOTABLE WARS AND INSURGENCIES: Tanzanian forces helped prevent coup in 1981

COMPRISING 115 ISLANDS OFF THE EASTERN COAST of Africa, the Republic of the Seychelles is populated mainly by Creoles of mixed European and African descent, many of whom are descended from slaves freed by the British in the 19th century. Possession of the Seychelles alternated between France and Britain throughout the French Revolution and Napoleonic Wars. The islands were first claimed by France in 1756, and eventually ceded to Britain in 1814, becoming an independent nation in 1976.

James Mancham, leader of the conservative Seychelles Democratic Party (SDP), became the nation's first president and France Albert René, leader of the socialist Seychelles People's Unity Party (SPUP), became prime minister (a post that no longer exists). As leaders of their respective parties, these two men had formed a coalition government in June 1975 with the intention of leading the Seychelles to independence, so it was only fitting that they should take leadership positions in the newly independent Seychelles.

In 1977, with irreconcilable political divisions between the two parties, René usurped control through a coup, forcing Mancham into exile. He dismissed Parliament and suspended the constitution, ruling by decree until 1979 when a new constitution was adopted establishing a single-party, socialist state. Bowing to mounting international pressures, René returned the Seychelles to a multiparty government in 1991, and in 1992 Mancham returned from exile. René's popular social welfare system, his successful development of a mixed economy, and a fractious opposition enabled him to retain the presidency in free elections held under the new constitution of 1993. With its victory in the 1998 elections, René's party abandoned much of its socialist rhetoric and adopted westernizing economic reforms. These included plans to open the Seychelles to international trade and to attract foreign industry by the development of an International Trading Zone.

According to the 1993 constitution, the president is elected by popular vote to a five-year term and serves as both chief of state and head of government. The president appoints the Council of Ministers, an advisory body.

ISSUES AND CHALLENGES:

- The country's economy relies heavily on tourism, which can experience sudden downturns when terrorism makes people reluctant to fly.

- Tuna fishing has the potential to diversify the economy, but huge foreign fleets are already active around the Seychelles in the Indian Ocean, and the government must negotiate agreements to protect its fishing grounds.

- No higher education is available on the islands, and a lack of skilled labor inhibits economic growth. Young people who do venture abroad to study often do not return because of limited opportunities.

HOW THE GOVERNMENT WORKS

LEGISLATIVE BRANCH

Assemblée Nationale (National Assembly) Unicameral Parliament
Composed of 34 members elected to five-year terms: 25 by direct popular vote; nine by proportional representation. Passes laws; adopts budget; confirms presidential appointments; ratifies treaties; censures ministers.

Regional Governments
Twenty-three administrative districts overseen by elected councils.

EXECUTIVE BRANCH

President
Elected to five-year term by direct popular vote; three consecutive term limit. Serves as head of state and government; commander-in-chief of armed forces. Grants pardons; creates and abolishes government offices; appoints ambassadors; negotiates treaties; dissolves National Assembly.

Council of Ministers
Appointed by president. Presided over by president; oversees government operations.

JUDICIAL BRANCH

Court of Appeal
Hears appeals of Supreme Court decisions. Judges appointed to serve to age 75 by president on advice of Constitutional Appointments Authority.

Supreme Court
Hears appeals and original civil and criminal cases; rules on constitutionality of laws. Judges appointed to serve to age 75 by president on advice of Constitutional Appointments Authority.

Magistrates' Courts

UNITED STATE

AT THE START OF THE 21ST CENTURY, the United States remains the world's only superpower as a result of the collapse of communism in the former Soviet Union, and also the single most influential political entity in the United Nations and North Atlantic Treaty Organization.

OLD GLORY
Created by Betsy Ross in 1776, the stars and stripes symbolize the unity of the USA. The stripes represent the 13 original colonies, and the stars today's 50 independent states.

The area which today comprises the United States was inhabited for thousands of years by the descendants of Asiatic peoples who crossed the land-bridge between Asia and present-day Alaska during the last Ice Age. Norseman Leif Eriksson was probably the first European to set foot in North America around the year 1000. Not until Christopher Columbus landed in the West Indies in 1492 did European powers begin full-scale occupation of the Western Hemisphere. The 13 original English colonies formed the core of the present-day US. Aspirations of religious freedom and a mercantile economy dominated the northern Puritan colonies. By the mid-1700s, disenchantment simmered in the colonies under the English crown. On

July 4, 1776, colonial leaders adopted the Declaration of Independence, penned by Thomas Jefferson, which asserted the political self-determination of the colonies and has become the definitive statement of democratic principles worldwide. England's King George III responded by dispatching British troops, so unleashing the American Revolutionary War (1776-1783). Colonial forces, under General George Washington's command—with the assistance of France—

GEORGE WASHINGTON
Considered the founder of the United States, George Washington was the general of the American forces during the Revolutionary War and later the country's first president.

HOW THE GOV

LEGISLATIVE BRANCH

CONGRESS

A bicameral legislative body; constitutionally vested with powers equal to those of the executive branch; serves as the primary source of new legislation and executive oversight.

▶ **SENATE**
The upper house of Congress; 100 members elected by popular vote to terms of six years; one-third of the seats come up for election every two years; two senators represent each state; 16 standing committees focus on issues ranging from education to foreign affairs.

▶ **HOUSE OF REPRESENTATIVES**
The lower house of Congress; 435 members elected by popular vote to terms of two years; arranged into 21 specialized committees.

EXECUTIVE BRANCH

PRESIDENT

Elected by Electoral College, members of which are directly elected by the voters in each state; serves a term of four years, which may be repeated once; acts as head of state, head of government, and commander-in-chief of the armed forces.

▶ **VICE-PRESIDENT**
Elected on the same ticket as the president, to a term of four years; assists the president in implementing executive policy.

STATE AND LOCAL GOVERNMENTS
▶ 50 states, 1 district, and 14 overseas territories
▶ Popularly elected bicameral legislatures
▶ Executive branches led by state governors

THE HOUSE OF REPRESENTATIVES
An important part of legislature, the lower house of Congress meets in the House Chamber in the Capitol building.

"Liberty, when it begins to take root,
is a plant of rapid growth."
—John F. Kennedy (1917-1963)

ABRAHAM LINCOLN
Lincoln delivered the Emancipation Proclamation—effectively freeing southern slaves—and guided the country through the Civil War.

won independence. Following victory, a new constitution was drawn up in 1787—which still exists today—uniting the colonies as states in the new nation while restraining the powers of the federal government. American voters elected Washington as their first president.

The nation doubled in size in 1803 with the purchase of France's vast Louisiana territory. Westward expansion was a brutal affair, with the deaths of thousands of settlers and the eradication or subjugation of Native Americans. Dispute over whether or not slavery would be permitted in the new lands widened the rift between the North and the slave-owning South.

Southern states seceded from the Union and, in 1861, ignited the Civil War. When the last shot was fired in 1865, slavery was ended and the nation was reunited.

By the start of the 20th century a huge gap between the wealth of industrial titans and the near-poverty of many workers prompted an era of protests and reforms. Constitutional amendments gave women suffrage and voters the right to elect US senators directly. But the prosperity of the "Roaring Twenties" collapsed with the 1929 Wall Street crash and Great Depression of the 1930s. Voters turned to Franklin Delano Roosevelt for an activist federal government. The Democratic president crafted an unprecedented array of "New Deal" programs which put millions of jobless Americans to work. Following the bombing of Pearl Harbor, the US entered World War II in 1941. By 1945 Japan was defeated and the US had helped liberate Europe from the Nazis. Victory catapulted the US into the role of global superpower and leader of the democratic world in the Cold War against the Soviet Union.

Domestically, beset by stagflation and high unemployment, American voters twice in the 1980s sent the conservative Republican Ronald Reagan to the White House, launching the era of "Reaganomics." The nation in the 1990s took a turn toward more liberal politics under William J. Clinton, the first Democratic president since Franklin D. Roosevelt to be elected to a second term of office.

In 2001, following the September 11 terrorist attacks in New York, George W. Bush traced the footsteps of his father George H. Bush back to the White House and the Middle East, where a US-led coalition toppled the regime of Saddam Hussein—his father's nemesis in the Gulf War of 1991.

THE STATUE OF LIBERTY
Originally a gift from France, the Statue of Liberty is perhaps the most internationally recognizable symbol of American liberties.

...NMENT WORKS

▸ **CABINET**
Comprises 15 members appointed by the president with approval of the Senate; each member represents one of the executive agencies; part of the president's network of advisors and councilors.

▸ **EXECUTIVE AGENCIES**
Essentially subdivisions of the vast executive bureaucracy; charged with implementing executive policy nationwide.

CAPITOL HILL
The Capitol building is the seat of legislative government in the US.

⚖ JUDICIAL BRANCH

SUPREME COURT
Composed of nine judges appointed for life by the president and approved by the Senate; exercises judicial review over federal and state judiciaries and serves as the final court of appeal; rules on matters of constitutionality and is involved, to a certain degree, in policy making.

▸ **UNITED STATES COURTS OF APPEAL**
Located regionally, these courts serve as the federal appellate court.

▸ **UNITED STATES DISTRICT COURTS**
The lowest level of federal courts.

▸ **STATES COURTS**
Administer justice at the state level according to each state's constitution.

▸ **COUNTY COURTS**
Administer state law locally.

ELECTORAL SYSTEM
The United States has universal suffrage. Generally, all federal, state, and local elections are decided by a simple plurality. The president, however, is chosen by an electoral college, in which state voters elect a representative to vote on their behalf (see The Party System, pages 214-215). Each state's electoral representation is determined by its population.

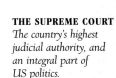

THE SUPREME COURT
The country's highest judicial authority, and an integral part of US politics.

EXECUTIVE BRANCH

RONALD REAGAN (1911-2004)
Reagan promoted four "Pillars of Freedom": individual liberty, economic opportunity, global democracy, and national pride.

JOHN F. KENNEDY (1917-1963)
Kennedy was the first Roman Catholic and youngest president ever elected. A popular head of state, the nation was devastated when he was assassinated in 1963.

FRANKLIN DELANO ROOSEVELT (1882-1945)
Elected to four consecutive terms, Roosevelt was best known for the "New Deal" that helped address the effect of the Depression, and his "fireside chats."

ABRAHAM LINCOLN (1809-1865)
Lincoln led the US through the Civil War of 1861-1865, and was the driving force behind the Emancipation Proclamation of January 1, 1863 that liberated slaves.

THE PRESIDENCY

At the head of the vast executive branch sits the president, who acts as the head of the government and is generally the most powerful and influential political figure in the United States. The president's prominent position as chief of state and head of government also makes him or her the emblematic figurehead of the nation to the world. Consequently, the president's personal ideas and aspirations play an important part in shaping national policy, and are closely watched by interest and pressure groups at home as well as by foreign governments. Almost every facet of the

president's life also becomes the subject of intense scrutiny by the media.

In the official structure of the executive branch, the vice-president is second in command, though in reality the roles of that office are vague. The only official duties given to the vice-president are as a member of the National Security Council (NSC), and the president's Cabinet; as the ex-officio president of the Senate, and the Board of Regents of the Smithsonian Institution; and as the executive assistant to the president. These positions are generally ceremonial, and are consequently vested with little actual power.

This office is of national importance, however, as the vice-president must be prepared to assume the office of president should the incumbent become incapacitated.

Upon inauguration, the president makes an array of political appointments—which can range into the thousands—to high-ranking positions in 15 executive departments nationwide in order to ensure that presidential policy is carried out on a daily basis. The most notable of these appointments are the members of the president's Cabinet, who not only act as political advisors, but also individually serve as the highest-ranking official for each of the

THE CABINET OF THE UNITED STATES

Comprising the 15 highest-ranking members of the executive departments, the Cabinet dates back to 1789—as old as the presidency itself. Members advise the president on policy matters specific to their respective departments and assist with shaping executive policy.

STATE
Manages diplomatic relations with foreign countries; promotes stability in regions vital to foreign policy; monitors and protects American interests abroad. The secretary of state is the president's main foreign policy adviser.

TREASURY
Monitors the country's monetary and financial systems, including taxes, budgets, currency production and circulation; also provides federal finance for combating terrorism and money-laundering by criminals.

DEFENSE
Formulates national security and defense policy; responsible for the army, navy, marine corps, air force, and coast guard; administers military recruitment. Maintains safety of US citizens at home and abroad.

JUSTICE
Represents the USA in the federal judiciary; enforces federal criminal and civil law; administers the major law enforcement agencies; also the immigration and naturalization service, and the national drug intelligence center.

INTERIOR
Promotes the sound use of natural and cultural resources; encourages and conducts scientific, especially environmental, research; works to protect the rights and improve the quality of life of the Native American communities.

AGRICULTURE
Responsible for the safety and inspection of the food supply from agricultural sources; promotes research; provides food aid both domestically and internationally. Also conserves and protects national forests and nature preserves.

HALL OF PRESIDENTS

The men who have worn the mantle of the nation's highest office.

GEORGE WASHINGTON 1789-1797	
JOHN ADAMS 1797-1801	
THOMAS JEFFERSON 1801-1809	
JAMES MADISON 1809-1817	
JAMES MONROE 1817-1825	
JOHN QUINCY ADAMS 1825-1829	
ANDREW JACKSON 1829-1837	
MARTIN VAN BUREN 1837-1841	
WILLIAM H. HARRISON 1841	
JOHN TYLER 1841-1845	

GROVER CLEVELAND 1885-1889
BENJAMIN HARRISON 1889-1893
GROVER CLEVELAND 1893-1897
WILLIAM McKINLEY 1897-1901
THEODORE ROOSEVELT 1901-1909
WILLIAM H. TAFT 1909-1913
WOODROW WILSON 1913-1921
WARREN G. HARDING 1921-1923
CALVIN COOLIDGE 1923-1929
HERBERT C. HOOVER 1929-1933
FRANKLIN D. ROOSEVELT 1933-1945

UNITED STATES

THE BUSH DYNASTY
The 41st and 43rd presidents. George W. Bush, appointed in 2001 (left), with father George H. W. Bush, president from 1989 to 1993.

THE BUCK STOPS HERE
A sign from the desk of President Truman indicating responsibility for the final decision.

WHITE HOUSE CABINET ROOM
Located in the West Wing, the Cabinet Room is where the president listens to his advisors on matters from the budget to national security.

1600 PENNSYLVANIA AVENUE
The address synonymous with ultimate authority, the White House is the official residence and office of the president and first lady.

Presidential seal

"The presidency is not merely an administrative office. That's the least of it... It is preeminently a place of moral leadership."—Franklin Delano Roosevelt (September 1932)

executive departments, therefore overseeing nearly three million federal employees in the implementation of executive policy.

The president also has a vast network of staff and advisors, who are separate from the Cabinet departments, to facilitate the operation of the executive branch. The most important of these are the Executive Office of Management and Budget (OMB), which reviews budget proposals and congressional legislation submitted by executive agencies, and the National Security Council (NSC), which is the primary source of counsel to the President on matters of foreign policy and

national defense. In fact, the national security advisor, who briefs the president daily, is often the most influential executive aid in matters of foreign policy.

The White House also has a staff of nearly 400 people to assist the President with matters of national policy, foreign affairs, and relations with the media.

Aside from the organizations that directly advise the president, the executive branch oversees 133 independent government agencies. These specialize in a wide range of political issues: from collecting foreign intelligence, such as the Central Intelligence Agency (CIA) and

the National Security Agency (NSA), or dealing with criminal activity at home, such as the FBI, to scientific research and exploration of global importance such as the Environmental Protection Agency (EPA), and the National Aeronautics and Space Administration (NASA).

OVERLEAF: OVAL OFFICE, WASHINGTON D.C.
Located in the West Wing of the White House, the oval-shaped room is the official office of the president. Conceived by George Washington, it was thought that the shape would allow Washington to look everyone in the eye during meetings. To this day, meetings between the highest officials of the world are held in this office.

ENERGY
Promotes the development and diversification of energy supply to meet national needs; applies advanced science and nuclear technology to defense; ensures the safe disposal of radioactive waste; provides specialized scientific research capacity.

LABOR
Monitors and maintains the labor environment by promoting safe and healthy working conditions, minimum wage laws, free collective bargaining and retirement benefits; helps job-seekers find placements, and employers find workers.

COMMERCE
Works to promote and stimulate economic growth and free trade; monitors economic systems and maintains human resources; provides up-to-date statistics on the economy; promotes technological innovations.

HOUSING & URBAN DEVELOPMENT
Promotes home ownership; provides housing assistance to low-income communities; assists the homeless; encourages the development of community organizations; enforces fair-housing laws nationwide.

TRANSPORTATION
Monitors and maintains the enormous US land, sea and air transportation infrastructure; advises the federal government on transportation policy; and negotiates and administers international transportation agreements.

HEALTH & HUMAN SERVICES
Protects all aspects of the population's health; provides financial and human resources to maintain food and drug safety; prevents outbreaks of infectious diseases; promotes medical and social research.

EDUCATION
Supports state and local education systems with research, information-sharing, and other federal resources; works to assure equal access to education; encourages public, parent, and student participation in education programs.

HOMELAND SECURITY
Protects the nation from terrorist threats, both domestic and international.

VETERAN AFFAIRS
Provides compensation, education, training, and medical care to the nation's military veterans.

JAMES KNOX POLK
1845-1849

ZACHARY TAYLOR
1849-1850

MILLARD FILLMORE
1850-1853

FRANKLIN PIERCE
1853-1857

JAMES BUCHANAN
1857-1861

ABRAHAM LINCOLN
1861-1865

ANDREW JOHNSON
1865-1869

ULYSSES S. GRANT
1869-1877

RUTHERFORD B. HAYES
1877-1881

JAMES A. GARFIELD
1881

CHESTER A. ARTHUR
1881-1885

HARRY S. TRUMAN
1945-1953

DWIGHT D. EISENHOWER
1953-1961

JOHN F. KENNEDY
1961-1963

LYNDON B. JOHNSON
1963-1969

RICHARD M. NIXON
1969-1974

GERALD R. FORD
1974-1977

JAMES E. CARTER
1977-1981

RONALD W. REAGAN
1981-1989

GEORGE H. W. BUSH
1989-1993

WILLIAM J. CLINTON
1993-2001

GEORGE W. BUSH
2001-

LEGISLATIVE BRANCH

Aerial view of the United States Capitol

THE CAPITOL
The Capitol building has been the center of the US legislative process for over 200 years. Its Neoclassical architecture reflects the principles of Ancient Greece and Rome that influenced the development of America's political system.

THE HOUSE OF REPRESENTATIVES
The compact seating of the House Chamber offers an "intimate" environment for the lower house's Congressional debates.

The National Statuary Hall
In 1864 Congress invited each state to contribute statues of two prominent citizens to stand here.

THE HOUSE OF REPRESENTATIVES

Upon its inception in 1787, the House of Representatives was intended to be the most popular and politically dominant entity in the

Federal system. Truly representative of the people, members are elected from carefully delineated districts in each state. In the late 18th and early 19th centuries, the House served as the primary forum for popular discussions on national issues following independence. The severe ideological rifts among its members between 1829 and 1861 were the most visible symptoms of the national divide in political agendas before the Civil War. In the 20th century, however, the workload delegated to the House increased rapidly, forcing it to adopt a variety of restrictive and cumbersome rules, and its national prominence vis-à-vis the Senate diminished. However, it still exerts a great deal of power and is tremendously influential in domestic spending policies, having the exclusive right to initiate revenue and appropriation bills. Its large number of members (435) compared with the Senate (100) requires it to be highly regulated. Consequently, since 1822,

STATE OF THE UNION
Flanked by the vice-president (center) and Speaker of the House, President George W. Bush gives his annual address in the House Chamber in January 2003.

The House Chamber
This is the debating place of the House of Representatives

The Hall of Columns
It is lined with statues of notable Americans.

Rotunda
The architectural center of the building is also the geographic center of Washington, D.C.

it has depended heavily on standing committees to transact its business. Owing to its decentralized nature, it functions according to many institutionalized procedures to which the Senate is not subject—floor debate in the House is strictly limited, virtually eliminating the possibility of a filibuster, whereas in the Senate it is an influential threat. The two houses nonetheless share equal importance in the legislative procedure. The Speaker, who leads the House, exerts much influence over legislation and, in turn, national politics. Having a majority in the House is vitally important for a party, as it invariably furthers its party agenda and ensures its political influence in law-making.

POWERS AND PROCEDURES

IMPEACHMENT
The House of Representatives has the power to impeach, but it is the Senate that conducts impeachment trials, convicting with a two-thirds majority. Since 1789, 17 federal officials, including two presidents, Andrew Johnson and Bill Clinton, have been impeached. President Nixon resigned rather than face charges.

NOMINATIONS
The president may nominate candidates for executive and judicial posts, but the Senate has the power to review and reject presidential appointees.

IMPEACHMENT COMMITTEE
The House of Representatives Judiciary Committee discusses whether or not to impeach President Clinton in 1998.

TREATIES
The Senate has the power to approve—by a two-thirds vote—or amend treaties made by the executive branch. The Senate has rejected relatively few of the hundreds of treaties it has considered, although many have died in committee or been withdrawn by the president. The president may enter into executive agreements with foreign nations that are not subject to Senate approval.

UNITED STATES

The Senate Chamber
This famous room has been occupied by the upper house of Congress since 1859.

The Old Senate Chamber
Seat of the Senate until 1859.

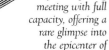

THE SENATE
The 107th Senate convenes for its opening meeting with full capacity, offering a rare glimpse into the epicenter of senatorial politics.

THE SENATE

The Senate today is perhaps the most powerful upper house of any legislative body in the world. However, the original intention of the authors of the US Constitution was that the Senate should be a regulatory group serving as a liberal, intellectual forum for debate on national policy, while the House of Representatives was the politically dominant arm of government. As senators were elected by the state legislatures until 1922 and were not therefore directly responsible to their state's population, it was believed that they would be able to debate political matters with a more philosophical approach, unburdened by the exigencies of state politics. Consequently, any legislation passed by Congress requires the approval of both houses—allowing the Senate regulatory rights over the House without disrupting the equal distribution of power between the two chambers. The Senate has authority over national politics not granted to the House. Most notably, it is vested with executive branch oversight, and the power to approve or reject presidential appointments to the Cabinet, the executive departments, and the Supreme Court, as well as treaties brokered by staff of the executive. Significantly smaller than the House, the Senate has only 100 members— two elected from each state for six-year terms, as compared with the two-year terms of the members of the House. As a result, political power in the US Senate tends to be distributed differently. With no limit to the number of terms a senator may serve, the Senate operates on a system of seniority, in which senators with the longest tenure of office acquire the most power. Long-standing senators are more likely to obtain politically influential positions in one of the 16 standing committees, and also have the ability to wield that power effectively. Senators generally acquire a degree of political power that is rare in the House, making them important politicians on the national scene. The senatorial system functions more rapidly and with greater efficiency than the House: rather than the complicated pattern of official channels through which members of the House must work, the Senate runs on a system of interpersonal relationships based on knowledge of one another's working methods and politics. In cases of stalemate, the deciding vote is cast by the ex-officio president of the Senate, the vice-president. Vice-presidential intervention is rare, however. The role of day-to-day leadership of the Senate is enacted by its president, who ensures the smooth operation of floor sessions and senatorial votes, but otherwise has no other special powers.

So You Want to Run for Senate?

Well, your chances are much better than you may imagine! Unlike many countries around the world, the American legislative system has remarkably few prerequisites for its elected representatives. As long as you're over 30 years of age, a resident of the state from which you are elected, and have been a citizen of the USA for nine years, you're qualified. No formal education, training, or technical skills are required. You don't even have to have been born in the USA,

HILLARY RODHAM CLINTON
Senator Clinton, former first lady, debates with President Bush in the same Oval Office her husband once occupied.

which means virtually anyone across the globe has the potential to serve in the Senate. A keen interest in American politics would obviously be an advantage. However, other than that, any career path can lead to the Senate. Throughout its history the Senate has been composed of people with very diverse occupations: lawyers, doctors, soldiers, writers, farmers, teachers, and business leaders, to name just a few.

Senator Kennedy

Even first ladies are not excluded, as shown by Hillary Clinton, who was elected in 1999. Of course, sometimes it helps to come from a family with a rich political history—just ask Edward "Ted" Kennedy, who has been a senator since 1962.

FILIBUSTER AND CLOTURE
The Senate has a long history of using the filibuster—a term from the 1850s meaning to delay debate or block legislation by obstructive tactics like making excessively long speeches. Unlimited debate was permitted in the Senate until 1917, when the Senate adopted Rule 22 allowing it to end a debate with a two-thirds majority vote—a tactic known as "cloture." In 1975, the Senate reduced the number of votes required from two-thirds to three-fifths.

MR. SMITH GOES TO WASHINGTON
Once criticized as naïve and overly optimistic, the film Mr. Smith Goes to Washington has become a classic American cultural representation of the power of democratic idealism. In the climactic scene, Smith uses the filibuster to stop an ethically questionable bill.

EXPULSION AND CENSURE
Article I, Section 5, of the US Constitution provides that each house of Congress may "...punish its members for disorderly behavior, and, with the concurrence of two-thirds, expel a member." Since 1789, the Senate has expelled only 15 of its entire membership and censured nine. A censure is a formal statement of disapproval, made without removing a senator from office.

JUDICIAL BRANCH

"I have always found that mercy bears richer fruits than strict justice."
—Abraham Lincoln (1809-1865), speech in Washington D.C., 1865

SUPREME SEAL
This official seal of the judiciary depicts an eagle soaring above one star, symbolizing the Constitution's creation of one Supreme Court.

THE SUPREME COURT

At the apex of the country's comprehensive judicial system resides the Supreme Court. Originally created by the Judiciary Act of September 24, 1789 in the first legislation to pass before the Senate, the Supreme Court was inaugurated on February 2, 1790 and delivered its initial judicial decision two years later. Ironically, the court's most important and celebrated function, judicial review, was not a function granted it under the Judiciary Act. Rather, the Court—under the influence of Chief Justice John Marshall—asserted that role in the landmark decision, Marbury v. Madison, in 1803. Since that date, the Supreme Court has been vested with the power of judicial review for all judicial decisions throughout the country, and in doing so, is charged with guaranteeing equality under the law

> William H. Taft is the only US president ever to also serve as Supreme Court Chief Justice

to all citizens of the United States. The Supreme Court therefore wields the power to declare legislation, law, or judicial decisions unconstitutional, and thus illegal and obsolete. This particular aspect of the judiciary is uniquely American, as no other high court in the world is vested with the scope of power and influence that the US Supreme Court has.

Terms for the Supreme Court begin in October and run continuously until late June or July. These terms are intense and involve an immense case load, as 7,000 cases are submitted for review each session. During this period, the Court operates on a cyclic system of sessions and recesses, each lasting roughly two weeks. While in session, the court hears up to 24

THE SUPREME COURT FRIEZE

The relief sculpture by Robert Aitken, represents Liberty Enthroned guarded by Order and Authority. On either side are groups of three figures depicting Council and Research.

SUPREME COURT BRONZE DOORS
The door panels (detail), sculpted by John Donnelly, Jr., depict historic scenes in the development of law.

cases, with each side in the case allotted one half-hour to present its argument before the court. During recess, the justices consider other matters of the court, consulting one another regarding cases they have heard throughout the preceding court session.

The American constitution provides for many special measures in order to assure the separation of the judicial branch from the other branches of government. Most notable among these is the fact that the justices of the Supreme Court are appointed for life—what the USA calls a term of "good behavior"—and their salaries cannot be decreased during their tenure. Nominated by the president, all appointments require the approval of the Senate before justices can take their seat in the Supreme Court.

EQUAL JUSTICE UNDE

LANDMARK CASES

1954

BROWN V. BOARD OF EDUCATORS
This declared that racially segregated education was unconstitutional, leading to the civil rights reforms of the 1950s and 1960s.

SEGREGATION
Racial segregation on public transit was banned in 1956.

1962

ENGEL V. VITALE
In this controversial decision the Court declared the practice of daily prayer in New York's public schools unconstitutional in order to preserve the separation of church and state.

1966

MIRANDA V. ARIZONA
This upheld the Fifth Amendment of the Constitution by declaring all confessions obtained by improper means unconstitutional. Suspects must be advised of their right to remain silent during arrest.

ERNESTO MIRANDA
Forced to confess, Miranda's (right) conviction was overturned, but he was later reconvicted on new evidence.

1973

ROE V. WADE
Easily the most controversial decision made by the Supreme Court, it declared the practice of abortion legal.

HARRY BLACKMUN
An associate Justice, Blackmun ruled for the legalization of abortions.

SUPREME COURT
The Neoclassical Corinthian style of the Supreme Court building was chosen to symbolize the Court's position of "dignity and importance" in government.

REGIONAL COURT SYSTEMS

Under the Supreme Court operates a complex system of appellate, district, regional, state, and local courts. The federal judiciary is divided into 94 separate judicial districts—with each state containing at least one district, as do the territories of Guam, the US Virgin Islands, and the Northern Mariana Islands—which have jurisdiction over all federal cases, civil or criminal. These districts are divided into 12 regional circuits, each of which contains an appellate court with jurisdiction over the district courts in its particular region. A Court of Appeals for the federal circuit has national jurisdiction in matters that involve patent laws, and cases tried by the Court of International Trade (which hears international trade and customs cases) and the Court of Federal Claims

(which hears primarily money claims against the state involving areas such as tax, contract, pay, Native American rights, and intellectual property issues).

As each state in the union is a separate entity, each contains a judicial system of varying complexity. Most American states operate their own system of regional and local courts, as well as a supreme court: all of which ultimately fall under the jurisdiction of the Supreme Court of the United States.

SUPREME COURT JUSTICES
Originally six, the number of Supreme Court judges fluctuated for most of the 19th century, arriving at the current nine in 1869. This picture shows the 2004 line-up of justices, headed by Chief Justice William H. Rehnquist (front center). By that time, there had been no vacancies on the bench for more than ten years.

OFFICIAL NAME: UNITED STATES OF AMERICA

POPULATION: 281.4 MILLION	
CAPITAL: WASHINGTON, D.C.	
AREA: 3,717,792 SQ. MILES (9,626,091 SQ. KM)	
INDEPENDENCE: 1776	
CONSTITUTION: 1787	

THE USA derives its name from the states that united to form the American nation, named for Florentine navigator Amerigo Vespucci, who reached the South American mainland in 1499.

RELIGION: Protestant 61%, Roman Catholic 25%, Jewish 2%, Other and non-religious 12%

OFFICIAL LANGUAGE: English

REGIONS OR PROVINCES: 50 states and 1 district

DEPENDENT TERRITORIES: American Samoa, Baker Island, Guam, Howland Island, Jarvis Island, Johnston Atoll, Kingman Reef, Midway Islands, Navassa Island, Northern Mariana Islands, Palmyra Atoll, Puerto Rico, Virgin Islands, Wake Island

MEDIA: No political censorship exists in national media

SUFFRAGE: 18 years of age; universal

LEGAL SYSTEM: English common law; accepts ICJ jurisdiction

WORLD ORGANIZATIONS: AfDB, ANZUS, APEC, ARF (dialogue partner), AsDB, ASEAN (dialogue partner), Australia Group, BIS, CCC, CE (observer), CERN (observer), CP, EAPC, EBRD, ECE, ECLAC, ESCAP, FAO, G- 8, G-5, G-7, G-10, IADB, IAEA, IBRD, ICAO, ICC, ICFTU, ICRM, IDA, IEA, IFAD, IFC, IFRCS, IHO, ILO, IMF, IMO, Interpol, IOC, IOM, ISO, ITU, MINURSO, MIPONUH, NAM (guest), NATO, NEA, NSG, OAS, OECD, OPCW, OSCE, PCA, SPC, UN, UN Security Council, UNCTAD, UNHCR, UNIKOM, UNITAR, UNMEE, UNMIBH, UNMIK, UNMOVIC, UNOMIG, UNRWA, UNTAET, UNTSO, UNU, UPU, WCL, WHO, WIPO, WMO, WTrO, ZC

POLITICAL PARTIES: Rep—Republican Party, Dem—Democratic Party, Ind—Independents

ETHNIC GROUPS:

- Asian 4%
- Native American 2%
- Hispanic 12%
- Black American/African 13%
- White 69%

NATIONAL ECONOMICS

WORLD GNP RANKING: 1st

GNP PER CAPITA: $34,100

INFLATION: 3.4%

BALANCE OF PAYMENTS (BALANCE OF TRADE): -$445 billion

EXCHANGE RATES / U.S. DLR.: Currency is US dollar

OFFICIAL CURRENCY: US DOLLAR

GOVERNMENT SPENDING (% OF GDP)

- ✈ DEFENSE 3%
- 🎓 EDUCATION 5%
- ✚ HEALTH 5.7%

(0, 5, 10, 15)

NUMBER OF CONFLICTS OVER LAST 25 YEARS

	1	2-5	5+
Violent changes in government	○	○	○
Civil wars	○	○	○
International wars	○	●	○
Foreign intervention	○	○	○

- No compulsory military service.
- Sole global superpower.
- Defense spending equivalent to about one third of world expenditure.
- US military led anti-terrorism war against Afghanistan and Iraq.

NOTABLE WARS AND INSURGENCIES: Invasion of Grenada 1982, Panama 1989. Gulf War 1991. Intervention over Kosovo 1999. War on terrorism in Afghanistan 2001. Invasion of Iraq 2003

1976

CAPITAL PUNISHMENT
Beginning with Gregg v. Georgia, the Supreme Court heard a number of cases on the constitutionality of capital punishment, eventually declaring it not necessarily cruel and inhumane.

ELECTRIC CHAIR
One of the methods used to carry out the death penalty.

1989

TEXAS V. JOHNSON
The court struck down a Texan law forbidding the desecration of the American flag—declaring it an act of free speech.

BURNING THE FLAG
A man burns the flag in protest against the ban on such actions.

THE PARTY SYSTEM

"I hold that this elevation of politics to the plane of undiluted comedy is peculiarly American."
—H. L. Mencken, 1880-1956

Election symbols have been popular since the 1830s.

In the 1930s, Parker Brothers Inc. mirrored American presidential elections with the "Game of Politics."

"Give 'em Hell" Harry

The 1948 election was the biggest upset in American history; Truman overcame two splits within his own party as well as pollsters' predictions of his defeat. The comic book below produced by the Democratic National Committee was intended to portray the President as a "grassroots" hero; apparently this "fun" approach made him more appealing to voters than Thomas Dewey.

THOSE FELLOWS SEEM MORE CONCERNED WITH BEATING **ME** THAN **DEWEY**!

HARRY TRUMAN FOR PRESIDENT

The Story of HARRY S. TRUMAN

PARTY ORGANIZATION

Political parties in the United States represent the "cadre" type of party, in contrast to a mass-membership party like the Chinese Communist Party. The word "cadre" refers to the small group of active members of the party who do most of the work of getting out the vote for elections. This description does not mean that party participation and leadership are limited to a small exclusive group; in America anyone can get involved in a party and seek to represent that party at the local, state, or national level. The two major American parties are decentralized, with separate Democratic and Republican parties in each of the 50 states. The permanent national committees coordinate the activities of the

TEDDY ROOSEVELT
In the Clifford K. Berryman cartoon (right), Teddy Roosevelt holds the railroad rebate bill in front of a hemming-and-hawing elephant, while the donkey in the background says, "That's a good thing!"

DEMOCRATS
The donkey has been associated with the Democratic Party since 1837, when Andrew Jackson was labeled a "jackass" for his stubbornly-held political views. As a result, Jackson began using the donkey on his campaign posters. Political cartoonist Thomas Nast elevated the donkey to the status of party icon in his political illustrations in Harper's Weekly.

PARTIES AND ELECTIONS

THE EMERGENCE OF POLITICAL PARTIES IN THE US
The Constitution of the United States, written in 1778, makes no mention of political parties as such. Several of the Founding Fathers disapproved of "party spirit" because they feared that such divisions would weaken the new nation. Despite this, the first parties surfaced during George Washington's second administration in the 1790s, although the factors that caused them existed earlier. Delegates to the Constitutional Convention of 1787 had already disagreed on slavery, the public debt, and the proper balance between federal and state powers—all issues related to the different economies of the northern and southern states, and reflected by the first major parties, the Federalists and the Antifederalists. These were not party organizations in the modern sense, but different sets of beliefs about the proper role of government. American political parties encouraged popular participation from their beginnings, unlike the early parties in Great Britain.

A TWO-PARTY SYSTEM
The US has had a two-party system for most of its history. The Democratic Republicans of Jackson's day evolved into the modern Democratic Party, while the Republican Party developed during the 1850s in opposition to both the Democrats and the Whigs. (The Whig Party had existed briefly between 1834 and 1852 as a loose alliance of groups opposed to the increasingly strong powers that President Jackson assumed over the legislature.) The differences between Republicans and Democrats have blurred since the 1960s. Many voters now identify themselves as independents, while others may identify with a party but not vote that ticket consistently. One explanation for the durability of the two major parties is that they are not tight ideological organizations, but loose alliances of state and local parties that come together every four years for the presidential election. Although Republicans are generally more conservative than Democrats, both parties contain left- and right-wing groups that compete for influence.

NATIONAL CONVENTIONS
The first national convention of a major party took place in 1832. The convention system extended popular participation in the electoral process and gave both major parties an opportunity to unify their internal divisions. At present, the tasks of the national convention include the following:

UNITED STATES

In 1952, Dwight Eisenhower's "man from Abilene" television commercials helped him defeat Adlai Stevenson by a landslide.

state parties. This decentralized structure results in a lack of connection between the executive and legislative branches of the federal government. While the national parties nominate candidates for the presidency and vice-presidency, the state parties nominate members of Congress with little reference to the national party. As a result, the Democrats and Republicans do not control the votes of legislators to the extent that political parties do in Great Britain, where members of Parliament must vote according to "party line."

Florida Fiasco

The longest election dispute in American history began in the small hours of November 8, 2000. Democratic candidate Al Gore had initially conceded defeat, but changed his mind when he was told that results in the key state of Florida were much closer than earlier reports had indicated. A large number of improperly filled-out "butterfly" ballots in one Florida county triggered a month-long argument between teams of lawyers on both sides, as the closeness of the outcome required an automatic recount under Florida law. The results of both hand and machine recounts taught Americans more than they really wanted to know about the fine distinctions between "hanging chads" and "dimpled chads," a chad being the piece of paper that is punched out of a "butterfly" ballot paper when it is correctly marked. The nation watched a three-ring legal circus that moved from the Supreme Court of Florida to the United States Supreme Court, and waited until December 11 to find out who would be its 43rd president.

The media frenzy kept voters tuned in for the final result.

REPUBLICANS
Thomas Nast first represented the GOP (Grand Old Party) as an elephant in 1874, when the Democrats were trying to panic Republican voters by suggesting that President Grant would seek a third term. Nast portrayed the party thus because elephants are steadfast and controlled when calm, yet unmanageable when frightened. This remains the party symbol today.

COLLEGE BOUND?
Everything you ever wanted to know about the Electoral College system—and even how to ask

Official Florida Presidential Ballot
Follow the arrow and Punch the appropriate dot.

Bush
Buchanan
Gore
Nader

A political parody packs a punch.

Nominating the candidates for office. At the state and local level, voters registered with a major party vote in a primary election for delegates to the national convention. Those delegates then nominate their party's presidential candidate, known as the "standard-bearer."

Conducting internal party business. Examples of internal business include such matters as settling questions of rules and credentials. The Republican nomination of Eisenhower in 1952, for example, depended on the acceptance of his credentials as a member of the GOP (Grand Old Party).

Adopting a party platform. The platform is a statement of the party's principles and often a forecast of the legislative agenda of the party that wins the election. Parties have sometimes split over platform issues of major national

importance—examples being the Democrats in 1860 (slavery), the Republicans in 1964 (civil rights), and the Democrats in 1968 (the Vietnam War).

Gearing up for the election campaign. These activities include raising and spending money to support the candidates and encouraging voters to go to the polls. This is accomplished through media such as television, radio, print advertising, and cross-country tours.

Third Parties and Independent Candidates. The American electoral system has built-in features that discourage the formation of third parties: single-member districting; campaign financing rules; automatic ballot access for major party candidates; and the Electoral College (see below). Third parties rarely last longer than one election because the issues or ideas that they represent are

absorbed by one or both of the major parties. Some third-party challenges in American elections include the Anti-Masonic Party of 1832; the Progressive Republicans of 1912; and the States' Rights Party of 1948.

THE ELECTORAL COLLEGE

This is the system used for electing the US president and vice-president. The two major parties in each state nominate a set number ("slate") of individuals equal to the numbers of representatives that state sends to Congress. These pledge to vote for their party's candidate for each of the two posts. The slate winning the greatest popular vote becomes that state's electors. Each of these then casts two votes—one for president and one for vice-president. Successful candidates are decided by absolute majority.

BRAZIL

BRAZILIAN FLAG
Adopted on May 11, 1992, each star represents a state.

AFTER MANY YEARS AS A PORTUGUESE COLONY and a long period of military rule that intensified in the 1960s, Brazil today is a presidential democracy. It has come so far that in the 2002 presidential elections, the vote was fully automated for the first time and results were available within just a few hours.

Brazil proclaimed its independence from Portugal in 1822 under Emperor Pedro I. The empire was brought to an end in 1889 by a bloodless military coup, and a constitutional democracy known as the "First Republic" was established. This lasted until 1930, when a revolt brought Getulio Vargas to power. Vargas ruled by decree for four years, until a new constitution was completed. The military supported his

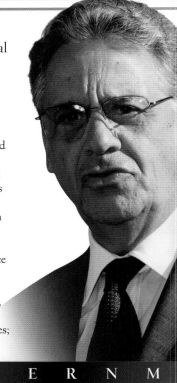

"New State" dictatorship until forcing him to leave office in 1945. Brazil then enjoyed a more democratic 15-year period of elected presidents—including Vargas, who was returned to office in 1950 until his death in 1954. In 1960, Janio Quadros won the presidential vote by a huge popular majority, but he resigned within seven months to be replaced by Vice-president João Goulart. Known for his leftist politics, Goulart refused to distance himself from the Communist Party and was ousted by the military in 1964. The next 21 years were marked by autocratic, military-controlled governments; human rights violations; frequent economic crises; and violent student demonstrations.

CHRIST STATUE ON MOUNT CORVOCADO
A symbol of Brazil, more than 300,000 people visit the famous Christ the Redeemer Statue annually. Built in 1931, the statue stands 98.5 feet (38 m) tall.

HOW THE GOVERNM

LEGISLATIVE BRANCH

CONGRESS

A bicameral National Congress, comprising the Chamber of Deputies and the Federal Senate, meets every year for two sessions of four and a half months.

▶ **CHAMBER OF DEPUTIES**

513 seats; members elected by direct popular vote on a secret ballot, in proportion to the population of each state and the Federal District, to terms of four years. Each state cannot have less than eight, or more than 60, representatives.

▶ **FEDERAL SENATE**

81 seats; three members elected by popular vote from each of the 26 states and the Federal District; members serve eight-year terms although elections are held every four years at the same time as those for the lower house.

REGIONAL GOVERNMENTS
▶ State Assemblies and governors
▶ City mayors
▶ Municipal city councils

THE INTERIOR OF THE SENATE
Senators discuss legislature in the Senate Chamber of the Brazilian National Congress. The building was designed by architect Oscar Niemeyer.

EXECUTIVE BRANCH

THE PRESIDENT

Acts as head of state and head of government. Elected by popular vote to a renewable term of four years, limited to two consecutive terms; must be a native Brazilian over 35 years of age.. Has power to appoint nearly 48,000 positions, although ambassadors, higher-court judges, solicitor-general, and Central Bank directors must be approved by the Senate; issues decrees, initiates legislation, enacts laws.

BRAZILIAN PALACE OF NATIONAL CONGRESS
The National Congress building in Brasília contains both the Federal Senate and the Chamber of Deputies. The Senate is located in the upturned "bowl," with the Chamber in the "dome."

> "Brazil does not belong to Lula; it is Lula that belongs to Brazil."
> —Luiz Inácio Lula da Silva

VANISHING INDIGENOUS PEOPLE

With over an acre of rainforest lost every second, the number of indigenous people has shrunk from an estimated six to nine million in 1500 to less than 250,000 today. In September 2003, a new chief was appointed to the National Indian Foundation, pledging the new government's intention to demarcate additional ancestral lands, for conversion to Indian reserves.

By 1985, a move toward the creation of a more open and democratic government had begun, and Brazil returned to civilian rule under President José Sarney. A new constitution was approved in 1988, and a year later Brazilian citizens elected their president for the first time since 1960. President Fernando Collor de Mello resigned in 1992 over charges of corruption and was replaced by Vice-president Itamar Franco. Fernando Henrique Cardoso came to prominence as Franco's finance minister and was elected president in 1994. Cardo's "Real

FERNANDO HENRIQUE CARDOSO

Cardoso's "Real Plan", which he introduced when finance minister, was the beginning of a successful economic program in Brazil. As president from 1995 to 2003, he introduced major financial and administrative reforms that helped to make the democratic system of government more secure, thus bringing to Brazil's citizens a greater sense of political responsibility.

Plan" helped to stabilize the currency and keep inflation under control. He was re-elected as president in 1998.

Economic woes, corruption, and an energy crisis plagued Cardoso's second term. In 2002, the fourth presidential campaign of the former union leader Luis Inácio Lula da Silva's was rewarded when the Brazilians elected him to power. In spite of his left-wing history, "Lula" commenced his presidency with fiscally conservative policies, returning Brazil to a period of sustained growth and economic recovery.

OFFICIAL NAME: FEDERATIVE REPUBLIC OF BRAZIL

POPULATION: 172.6 MILLION	
CAPITAL: BRASÍLIA	
AREA: 3,265,059 SQ. MILES (8,456,503 SQ. KM)	
INDEPENDENCE: 1822	
CONSTITUTION: 1988	

BRAZIL was named by the Portuguese after the large amounts of brazilwood (*pau-brasil*) in the country.

RELIGION: Roman Catholic 70%, Protestant 15%, Atheist 7%, Afro-American Spiritist 1%, Other 3%

OFFICIAL LANGUAGE: Portuguese

REGIONS OR PROVINCES: 26 states and 1 federal district

DEPENDENT TERRITORIES: None

MEDIA: No political censorship exists in national media

Newspapers: There are 380 daily newspapers

TV: 19 state-owned services, 237 independent

Radio: 1 state-owned service, more than 2,900 independent services

SUFFRAGE: Voluntary between 16 and 18 years of age and over 70; compulsory over 18 and under 70 years of age

LEGAL SYSTEM: Roman legal traditions; no compulsory ICJ jurisdiction

WORLD ORGANIZATIONS: AfDB, BIS, CCC, ECLAC, FAO, G-15, G-19, G-24, G-77, IADB, IAEA, IBRD, ICAO, ICC, ICFTU, ICRM, IDA, IFAD, IFC, IFRCS, IHO, ILO, IMF, IMO, Interpol, IOC, IOM (observer), ISO, ITU, LAES, LAIA, Mercosur, NAM (observer), NSG, OAS, OPANAL, OPCW, PCA, RG, UN, UNCTAD, UNESCO, UNHCR, UNIDO, UNITAR, UNMOP, UNMOVIC, UNTAET, UNU, UPU, WCL, WFTU, WHO, WIPO, WMO, WToO, WTrO

POLITICAL PARTIES: PFL—Liberal Front Party, PT—PT Leftist Coalition (Includes the Workers' Party-PT, the Democratic Labor Party-PDT), PSDB—Brazilian Social Democratic Party, PMBD—Brazilian Democratic Movement Party, PPB—Brazilian Progressive Party, PTB—Brazilian Labor Party, PPS—the Popular Socialist Party

ETHNIC GROUPS:

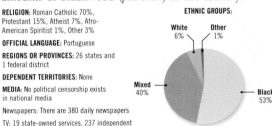

- White 6%
- Other 1%
- Mixed 40%
- Black 53%

NATIONAL ECONOMICS

WORLD GNP RANKING: 9th

GNP PER CAPITA: $3,580

INFLATION: 7%

BALANCE OF PAYMENTS (BALANCE OF TRADE): -$24.6 billion

EXCHANGE RATES / U.S. DLR.: 1.950-2.311 REAIS

OFFICIAL CURRENCY: REAL

GOVERNMENT SPENDING (% of GDP)

- DEFENSE 2.8%
- EDUCATION 4.6%
- HEALTH 2.9%

(scale: 0, 5, 10, 15)

NUMBER OF CONFLICTS OVER LAST 25 YEARS

	1	2-5	5+
Violent changes in government	○	○	○
Civil wars	○	○	○
International wars	○	○	○
Foreign intervention	○	○	○

NOTABLE WARS AND INSURGENCIES: None

- Compulsory national military service.
- Military has an important internal security role.
- Large arms industry.
- Increased military cooperation with Argentina, Paraguay and Uruguay.
- Soldiers have been deployed in UN peacekeeping missions, including in East Timor.

N T   W O R K S

▶ **THE VICE-PRESIDENT**

Elected on the same ticket as president, by popular vote, also for a maximum of two four-year terms. Assists the president with the executive administration.

▶ **CABINET**

The number of ministers varies. Appointed and dismissed by the president.

ELECTORAL SYSTEM

Voting is mandatory over the age of 18, and every four years all Brazilian citizens, home or abroad, cast their vote to elect a new president. Women won the right to vote in 1932. Citizens residing in Brazil additionally vote for governors, senators, federal deputies and state legislators every four years.

⚖ JUDICIAL BRANCH

SUPREME FEDERAL TRIBUNAL

The highest judicial authority consists of 11 justices of proven legal and constitutional training and experience; appointed for life by the president after their nomination is approved by the absolute majority of the Senate.

▶ **SUPREME COURT OF JUSTICE**

An appellate court with primary jurisdiction over crimes and injunctions against the government; composed of 33 judges who are appointed by the president with the Senate's approval.

▶ **REGIONAL FEDERAL COURTS**

Located in each state capital and the Federal District; administers justice at the regional level and oversees the local courts; must have at least seven judges sitting at each court.

RUSSIAN FEDE

SPANNING EIGHT TIME ZONES, Russia is the world's largest country and one of the most sparsely populated. Its size and ethnic diversity have made ruling post-Soviet Russia a daunting challenge.

By A.D. 862, the state known as Kievan Rus was established in what is now Ukraine. In the 10th century, the ruler Vladimir had embraced Greek Orthodox Christianity and made it the state religion. Assailed by many would-be conquerors, the Kievan state fell in 1223 to the Mongols. When the Russians threw off the Mongol yoke in the late 15th century, Muscovy emerged as the dominant principality, gaining suzerainty over its neighbors by a combination of diplomacy and conquest. The coronation of Czar Mikhail in 1613 established the Romanov dynasty, which would rule Russia until 1917, building it into a great empire stretching half way around the Northern Hemisphere.

The foundations of modern Russia were laid by Czar Peter the Great (1689-1725), who referred to the country as the "Empire of All the Russias." Peter was the first czar to travel to western Europe. His conquests in the Baltic region provided coveted sea access and he built up a navy, organizing it and the army after European models. He also required the

RUSSIAN FLAG
The flag was adopted on August 22, 1991, replacing the old Soviet red flag.

ST BASIL'S CATHEDRAL
Built to commemorate victory over the Mongol armies in 1552.

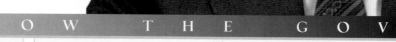
HOW THE GOV

LEGISLATIVE BRANCH

FEDERAL ASSEMBLY

The Federation Council may reject a bill passed in the Duma, but this can be overridden if a second vote in the Duma obtains a two-thirds majority.

▶ **FEDERATION COUNCIL**

The upper house: 178 members appointed to four-year terms by top regional officials. Appoints country's highest judges and prosecutor-general, calls presidential elections, approves border changes, can impeach president, adopts or rejects bills from Duma.

FEDERATION COUNCIL
The upper house of Russia's Federal Assembly.

▶ **STATE DUMA**

The lower house: 450 members elected to four-year terms: half from single-member districts, half by proportional representation from party lists. Passes laws, adopts national budget, approves ministers and Central Bank head, oversees government operations.

EXECUTIVE BRANCH

PRESIDENT

Elected by direct vote to no more than two consecutive four-year terms, the president is head of state and also head of the armed forces and National Security Council. Sets general policy for country, acts as final arbiter between executive and legislative branches, represents nation abroad, issues decrees and edicts, declares states of emergency, nominates high government officials, dismisses ministers, may dissolve parliament and call new elections.

▶ **PRESIDENTIAL ADMINISTRATION**

Includes the Security Council, the Defense Council, and the Administration of Affairs; supports the president by drafting decrees and manages the implementation of government policy.

STATE AND LOCAL GOVERNMENTS
▶ 21 ethnic republics, 68 provinces and regions
▶ Elected provincial governors
▶ Elected regional councils and presidents

RATION

nobility to wear Western clothing and adopt Western habits and subordinated the church's power to that of the czar.

By the 19th century, the Russian economy, lacking an industrial base, lagged behind the west, and the gulf between the wealthy elite and the impoverished masses grew wider. Russia expanded across Siberia to open the port of Vladivostok in 1860; the Trans-Siberian Railroad, the world's longest railroad, was begun in 1891 and completed in 1917, making vast territories more accessible.

In the wake of Russia's humiliating defeat in the Russo-Japanese War (1904-1905), civil

> *"Without glasnost there is not, and there cannot be, democratism, the political creativity of the masses and their participation in management." — Mikhail Gorbachev*

MIKHAIL SERGEYEVICH GORBACHEV (1931-)
Elevated in 1985 to general secretary, Gorbachev pursued cooperation with the West instead of military confrontation. His reforms, glasnost (openness) and perestroika (economic restructuring), led to the breakup of the Soviet Union.

unrest grew, and Czar Nicholas II was forced to allow a constitution and limited democratic reforms. Economic conditions exacerbated by involvement in World War I and internal pressures ignited a revolution in 1917. On March 15, 1917, Czar Nicholas was forced to abdicate. The following year the czar and his family were executed.

On November 7, 1917, Lenin's Bolshevik (Communist) Party staged a second revolution, overthrowing the provisional government. Civil war ensued and the Bolsheviks prevailed. After conquering most of the old Russian Empire, they established the Union of Soviet Socialist Republics (USSR) in 1922.

The USSR lasted 69 years. All economic activity was subjected to the demands of the centralized state. Agriculture was collectivized and the country was industrialized, but at a terrible price. Countless citizens died in political purges or famines. The eventual collapse of the Soviet Union came as a result of the cost of maintaining its position as a military superpower. From 1985 Mikhail Gorbachev introduced liberal reforms. An attempted coup by the communist old guard in 1991 was resisted by Russian president Boris Yeltsin, who emerged as president of a new state, the Commonwealth of Independent States (CIS), later renamed the Russian Federation. Political and economic reforms caused enormous upheaval in the new Russia, but Vladimir Putin, elected president in 2000, has restored aspects of authoritarian communist rule.

N M E N T   W O R K S

PRIME MINISTER

Nominated by the president and confirmed by the Duma, the prime minister is the chairman of government and serves at the president's pleasure. He is assisted by four deputy prime ministers, nominates cabinet ministers, oversees daily workings of the executive branch, and carries out presidential decrees.

▶ **COUNCIL OF MINISTERS**
Composed of 23 ministry and agency heads, the prime minister, and the deputy prime ministers; the prime minister nominates ministers who must then be appointed by the president.

⚖️ JUDICIAL BRANCH

CONSTITUTIONAL COURT

Composed of 19 justices nominated by the president and appointed for life by the Federation Council; adjudicates in matters relating to the constitution; rules on the constitutionality of federal laws, presidential decrees and directives, and local constitutions, charters, and laws; resolves jurisdictional disputes between federal and local authorities.

▶ **SUPREME COURT**
Highest court for civil and criminal appeals. Comprises 20 justices nominated by president and appointed for life by Federation Council.

▶ **COURT OF ARBITRATION**
Handles economic matters, especially contract disputes and hears lower-court appeals; comprises 70 justices; cases are decided by justices, not juries.

THE KREMLIN
The word "kremlin" means "citadel." Moscow's kremlin was the czar's residence until 1712, when it became a seat of civil government. Today it is the official residence of the president and seat of the executive.

🗳️ ELECTORAL SYSTEM
Voters elect president by popular vote. Duma members directly elected from districts or from party lists. Federal Council members appointed by regional officials. Approximately 150 political parties, blocs, and movements compete for elected offices.

EXECUTIVE BRANCH

JOSEPH STALIN (1875-1953)
Stalin ran a centrally planned economy, employing purges, mass starvation, and prison camps to instill fear and maintain control. In keeping with his personality, he chose the name Stalin, meaning "man of steel."

VLADIMIR ILICH LENIN (1870-1924)
Lenin believed that all power should be given to the Communist Party, which would understand needs of the proletariat and act on its behalf; he ruled as a dictator and censored all media.

LEONID BREZHNEV (1906-1982)
A time of conservative policies and party retrenchment, Brezhnev's rule repressed individual expression and persecuted political dissidents.

BORIS YELTSIN (1931-)
Striving to revive the flagging Russian economy, Yeltsin pushed radical reforms to move the country from central planning to a market-based economy.

THE PRESIDENT

The figure of the president dominates the government of post-Soviet Russia. The Soviet constitution intended the Congress of the People's Deputies to be the ultimate arbiter, but under Yeltsin's influence, the 1993 constitution gave the president significantly greater powers, far more than most of his Western counterparts. This was intended to avoid the constant clashes between the executive and legislative branches that plagued the first two years of Yeltsin's presidency. The president now has the right to use military force without the approval of the legislature, as well as the power to dismiss ministers and to dissolve the legislature. The president essentially dictates the government's program, determining foreign and domestic policy, negotiating with foreign powers, and signing treaties. He controls not only the armed forces but also the Ministry of Internal Affairs. He fills many high offices and appoints judges (with the approval of the Duma), but can pass decrees that become law without the input of the Duma. Candidates for the presidency must be citizens of the Federation and at least 35 years old, and must have been permanent residents for ten years.

THE END OF AN ERA
Gorbachev delivers a speech standing in front of a statue of Lenin. Gorbachev's policies brought about the fall of the USSR, originally created by Lenin.

THE CABINET OF THE RUSSIAN FEDERATION

The Cabinet, or Council of Ministers, formulates government policy and manages the day-to-day activities of departments of the executive branch. The size of the cabinet and number of ministries varied enormously under Boris Yeltsin in the 1990s, but in the more settled period since Vladimir Putin took over the presidency, the number has levelled out at 23 or 24.

FOREIGN AFFAIRS
Carries out government policy with foreign states and international organizations; maintains Russian diplomatic relations worldwide.

DEFENSE
Responsible for national defense, armed forces and protecting nuclear arsenal.

CIVIL DEFENSE, EMERGENCIES, AND DISASTER MANAGEMENT
Develops policy and implements programs on protecting population and territories from natural and man-made disasters; supervises civil defense. One of the "presidential bloc" of ministries directly responsible to president.

INTERNAL AFFAIRS
Investigates crimes and carries out criminal penalties; supervises internal security forces.

JUSTICE
Carries out judicial policy; maintains courts; protects intellectual property and citizens' rights; coordinates federal judicial authorities.

FINANCE
Implements financial policy; maintains budget; disseminates information on key economic indicators, external and domestic debt.

TAXATION
Enforces legislation on taxes in federation republics, provinces, autonomous areas, cities, and towns.

ECONOMIC DEVELOPMENT AND TRADE
Promotes growth of the economy at all levels and stimulates trade.

PROPERTY RELATIONS
Carries out state policy for privatization and management of state property and land resources.

ANTIMONOPOLY POLICY AND BUSINESS SUPPORT
Enforces laws against monopolistic activities and unfair competition.

NATURAL RESOURCES
Carries out government policy and enforces laws on the use, protection, and study of natural resources and the environment.

KEY LEADERS OF RUSSIA

Before the 1917 revolution, Russia was an empire ruled by the czar. The USSR was controlled by the Communist Party, the most powerful position being General Secretary of the Central Committee. Today's democratic Russia is led by an elected president.

CZAR NICHOLAS II
1894-1917
The last czar of Russia, who tried to rule in the autocratic style of his forebears. During World War I he was forced to abdicate by the Duma and later executed.

VLADIMIR ILICH LENIN
1917-1924
The first leader of the USSR, Lenin was exiled from Russia for his revolutionary activities in 1907. He returned in 1917 and in November of that year launched the coup that brought Russia under communist rule. After victory in the Civil War of 1918-1920, he laid the foundations of the all-powerful Soviet state.

JOSEF VISSARYONOVICH STALIN
1922-1953
General Secretary of the Central Committee, Stalin ruled the USSR as a brutal dictator. He led his country to victory over Nazi Germany in World War II and transformed the USSR into an industrialized nation and global superpower, but these achievements were made possible only by completely ignoring the rights of the individual.

NIKITA KHRUSHCHEV
1953-1964
Krushchev began a policy of de-Stalinization and worked with the US to develop nuclear testing procedures.

RUSSIAN FEDERATION

PRESIDENT PUTIN MEETS WITH US PRESIDENT BUSH
On May 24, 2002 the leaders of the two nuclear superpowers met to sign a treaty that would dramatically reduce their nuclear capabilities over the course of the next decade.

GRAND KREMLIN PALACE
Standing on Borovitsky Hill in the Kremlin, the palace was originally decorated with eagles and the coat of arms of Russia, but these were replaced in the Soviet era with the letters CCCP (USSR in Russian), or Union of Soviet Socialist Republics.

Head of state's entrance to Kremlin

THE PRESIDENT AND THE GOVERNMENT
President Putin presides over a meeting with government ministers in March 2003.

> *"You can build a throne with bayonets, but you can't sit on it for long."*
> — Boris Yeltsin

Boris Yeltsin was elected deputy for Moscow in 1989 with a majority of 4,726,112 votes—the highest ever majority in an election.

THE PRIME MINISTER

Called the "chairman of the government," the prime minister is responsible for the day-to-day administration of the executive branch, with the assistance of four deputy prime ministers. The prime minister heads the cabinet, which is responsible for formulating government policy and managing the activities of the various departments and agencies. Within one week of his confirmation in office, the prime minister must submit nominations for Cabinet ministers to be appointed by the president and approved by the Duma.

If the president cannot continue in office because of ill health, impeachment, or resignation, the prime minister serves as acting president until a new president is elected. However, the Russian constitution does not specify how it is to be decided that the president is incapable of fulfilling the duties of the office because of ill health. Similarly, it provides no guidance on what would happen if the Duma were to pass a vote of no-confidence in a prime minister serving as acting president. On the other hand, the constitution does set certain limits

to the powers of the prime minister when acting as head of state. He or she may not dissolve the Duma, call a referendum, or make any proposals to amend or revise the constitution.

OVERLEAF: INTERIOR OF THE KREMLIN
President Putin walks through his offices at the Kremlin in Moscow, December 9, 2002. A statue of Peter the Great (1672-1725) can be seen on the right. Peter transferred Russia's capital from Moscow to St Petersburg in 1712, but it returned to Moscow in 1918.

AGRICULTURE
Provides information on commodity prices; sets standards for food industry; operates advisory service on latest developments for crops and stock-breeding; draws up initiatives for foreign investment and expertise in developing agricultural methods and productivity.

ENERGY
Formulates and carries out policy on fuel and power resources; promotes international energy cooperation.

ATOMIC ENERGY
Regulates Russia's nuclear energy program; oversees storage and disposal of radioactive materials.

INDUSTRY, SCIENCE, AND TECHNOLOGY
Regulates industry, controls scientific resources, and encourages technological innovation.

HEALTH
Develops initiatives to protect health of population and to train healthcare personnel; promotes research.

LABOR AND SOCIAL DEVELOPMENT
Promotes improvements in labor conditions and increases in incomes; seeks to raise the standard of living evenly over all regions; oversees pension and unemployment programs; provides services for veterans, invalids, women and children.

EDUCATION
Responsible for implementing the country's education policies.

CULTURE
Promotes the arts and educational programs through museums, galleries, and libraries; also cultural links between Russia and other nations.

TRANSPORTATION
Coordinates development of transportation infrastructure; provides assistance to increase efficiency of export-import transport operations.

RAIL TRANSPORTATION
Regulates rail industry and manages construction and repair of rail infrastructure.

FEDERATION AND ETHNIC MATTERS
Deals with issues relating to national migratory policy, including refugees.

PRESS, TV, RADIO BROADCASTING, AND MASS MEDIA
Concerned with the regulation of state-controlled mass media.

COMMUNICATIONS AND INFORMATION
Sets and implements policies, standards, and regulation for the postal service, the telecommunications industry, and commercial satellite communication systems; manages allocation of frequencies for electronic communications devices.

LEONID BREZHNEV
1964-1982
General Secretary from 1966, Brezhnev ordered the Soviet invasions of Czechoslovakia in 1968 and Afghanistan in 1979.

YURI ANDROPOV
1982-1984
Head of the KGB at the time of his appointment, he worked towards reducing corruption in the party.

KONSTANTIN CHERNENKO
1984-1985
General Secretary of the Central Committee, he suffered from ill-health through much of his brief tenure of power.

MIKHAIL GORBACHEV
1985-1991
Gorbachev was awarded the Nobel Peace Prize in 1990 for his part in ending the Cold War.

BORIS YELTSIN
1991-1999
Negotiated independence for many Soviet Republics; liberalized economy; behaved erratically at end of rule.

VLADIMIR PUTIN
1999-
Named as successor by Yeltsin, then elected in 2000, Putin has attempted to reimpose law and order.

LEGISLATIVE BRANCH

EXTERIOR OF THE STATE DUMA
Originally built to house the Sovnarkom (Council of People's Commissars) in the 1930s, the building was later used by the Soviet state planning agency. Today it houses the meeting rooms and offices of the State Duma.

INTERIOR OF THE STATE DUMA
Representatives gather for session. The first State Duma was elected in 1906, following its creation by Czar Nicholas II. Elections for the new State Duma, the first since 1917, were held on December 12, 1993.

THE RUSSIAN FEDERATION COAT OF ARMS

THE DUMA

The lower house, the State Duma, has a complicated election process. Half of the 450 members are directly elected by the regions; as in elections to the House of Representatives in the United States, the number of seats a region has is determined by the region's population. The remaining 225 members are elected through balloting based on party lists. Citizens vote for a political party, and parties that collect at least five percent of the total votes receive a number of seats determined by their percentage of the total number of ballots cast.

Legislation is initiated in the Duma. It may be introduced by members of the Duma or by the president or the prime minister. Bills are required to pass two separate votes, three if they relate to the budget, and then must be sent to the Federation Council within five days. The Council has fourteen days to approve or reject a bill; if there is no action, the bill goes to the president for review and signature. If the Council rejects a bill, it returns to the Duma, and if two-thirds of the house support the bill, the Council's rejection is waived. If the bill lacks the support of two-thirds of the Duma, the two houses can form a committee to generate a compromise bill that both houses would pass. If the Duma objects to the Federation Council's proposals during conciliation, it may send by a two-thirds majority vote its version to the president for signature. When a bill reaches the president, he may sign it into law or veto it within 14 days of receiving it. After veto, the bill can begin the legislative process anew, or, If the State Duma and Federation Council again pass the bill by a two-thirds majority of their total memberships, the president must sign it into law within seven days. The president can

SWEARING IN OF THE PRESIDENT
On August 9, 1996 at the Kremlin, Boris Yeltsin took the oath of office as the first President of the Russian Federation, promising to uphold the new democracy. Joining the ceremony is Patriarch Alexei II (robed on right), head of the Russian Orthodox Church.

A New System of Rule

When Mikhail Gorbachev became president in 1985, he launched three programs, perestroika (restructuring), glasnost (openness), and demokratizatsiya (democratization), to pull the USSR up to the economic level of the West. Citizens began questioning the Communist Party's hold over Russia while party members plotted a return to a centrally controlled state. When a coup in August 1991 failed, Boris Yeltsin, president of the Soviet Republic of Russia, saw an opportunity to promote himself and Russia. On December 25, 1991, Gorbachev, undone by forces his reforms had unleashed, resigned, and the USSR was dissolved the following day by agreement between Yeltsin and the leaders of Belarus and Ukraine.

risk conflict with the legislature and resist signing the bill into law.

Although its effectiveness is limited by the extensive powers enjoyed by the president, the legislature can still check executive power because it holds the purse strings. It can also be a forum for criticism of the government. The Duma has the right to confirm or reject the president's candidate for prime minister and it can initiate impeachment proceedings against the president, as it did in 1999 against Boris Yeltsin, although it was unable to muster enough votes to proceed with the action.

LEGISLATIVE POWERS AND PROCEDURES

NOMINATIONS

After the president has nominated a candidate for the position of prime minister, the Duma has the power to refuse or ratify the nomination. This effectively gives the Duma the right to select the prime minister.

RATIFYING NOMINATIONS
The Duma ratifies President Yeltsin's choice of Yevgeny Primakov as prime minister in 1998.

LEGISLATIVE INITIATIVE

Although the Federation Council is largely responsible for reviewing legislation proposed by the State Duma, it has the right to initiate legislation independently. It may draft and review federal-level legislation and has the right to approve some presidential decrees. Non-constitutional federal legislation requires the approval of half the Federal Council members in order to be passed.

NO CONFIDENCE

If a simple majority of the State Duma votes no confidence in the government twice within three months, the president must announce the resignation of the government or dissolve the Duma.

IMPEACHMENT HEARING
Members of the State Duma discuss the impeachment of President Yeltsin in 1999.

RUSSIAN FEDERATION

"Only Jesus Christ could take a few loaves of bread and feed the thousands ... Only Jesus Christ could solve problems such as these."
— Mikhail Gorbachev

THE FEDERATION COUNCIL

The upper chamber, the Federation Council, has two representatives from each region, much like the US Senate. However, there are no elections to the Council; instead, the deputies are nominees sent by the legislative assemblies of the region.

The Federation Council has authority over internal border adjustments and presidential decrees declaring martial law or states of emergency. It confirms and may remove

State Armory

Considered the oldest museum in Russia, the Armory contains artifacts dating back to the 12th century. The building itself was completed in the 1840s under Czar Nicholas I.

the procurator general and confirms, on the president's recommendation, justices of the Constitutional Court, Supreme Court, and Superior Court of Arbitration. In addition, the Council makes the final decision to remove the president from office once the Duma has voted impeachment charges.

THE KREMLIN

Home to churches, palaces and towers, the Kremlin has served as a fortress and a royal residence. After the revolution, it became the seat of the communist government, which it remained until 1991 when it became the executive residence and headquarters of the president.

State Kremlin Palace

Also known as the Palace of Congresses, the glass and concrete building was built between 1959 and 1961 to host Communist Party congresses.

Great Kremlin Palace

The yellow and white Russo-Byzantine palace was built for Czar Nicholas I in 1837. The west wing houses the czar's private apartments. During the Soviet era, one chamber was used for meetings of the Supreme Soviet. Today, the palace's magnificent halls are used for state receptions.

On legislative matters, the Federation Council has less power than the State Duma and acts largely as a reviewing and consulting chamber. The Council examines bills passed by the Duma concerning budgetary, tax, and other fiscal matters as well as issues dealing with war and peace and treaty ratification.

After receiving legislation adopted by the Duma, the Federation Council has just 14 days to approve or reject the measure. If the Council has not acted within that time period, the legislation is automatically considered approved and legally binding. If the Council rejects a bill that has been passed by the Duma, the two chambers empanel a conciliation commission to try to forge a compromise bill acceptable to both houses.

INTERIOR OF THE FEDERATION COUNCIL

The original Council of the Federation established in 1991 consisted of the chairmen of the Supreme Soviets of the Republics, all regions, and the Moscow and Leningrad City Councils. In 1993 with the new constitution, the Council took its current form with two deputies nominated by each region.

FEDERATION COUNCIL BUILDING, MOSCOW
The Federation Council, or Soviet Federatsii, is the upper house of the Russian Federal Assembly. Under Putin it has lost much of the influence it enjoyed under Yeltsin.

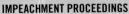

IMPEACHMENT PROCEEDINGS

The president may be removed from office for high treason and grave crimes. The State Duma votes to bring impeachment charges. The charges are presented to both the Supreme Court, which must confirm the presence of an impeachable crime, and the Constitutional Court, which must confirm that proper procedures are observed in bringing charges. The Federal Council then votes to accept the charges and ultimately to remove the president.

APPROVING THE BUDGET

The government submits the state budget to the State Duma. The Duma must muster three separate majority votes to approve the budget. If the budget is rejected, it is submitted to a conciliation commission of legislative and executive branch members. The commission can approve the bill or suggest amendments.

BUDGET APPROVAL

The cabinet presents the budget to the State Duma for approval.

AMENDING THE CONSTITUTION

Amendments to the constitution are adopted only by a majority vote of at least three-quarters of the total number of Federal Council deputies and at least two-thirds of the total number of State Duma deputies. To formally take effect, all amendments must be approved by at least two-thirds of the citizens of the Russian Federation.

JUDICIAL BRANCH

"I am, of course, opposed to arm-twisting and jail cells."
— Vladimir Putin, on dealing with economic crimes

RUSSIAN COURTS

Under both the czars and the Soviet-era communist state, the judiciary in Russia was subject to manipulation by forces outside the legal system. Today, the judiciary is an independent third branch of government, but is plagued by inefficiency and underfunded courts. Critics also contend that it is still prey to political interference and corruption.

The Russian judiciary consists of three branches: the Constitutional Court, courts of general jurisdiction, and courts of arbitration. Courts of general jurisdiction include the Supreme Court of the Russian Federation, 89 regional courts, and approximately 2,000 district courts. Judges for all federal high courts are selected by the president and appointed for life by the Federation Council. The judiciary is administered by the Ministry of Justice. Its responsibilities include the establishment of lower courts and appointment of judges at levels below the federal district courts. It also gathers forensic statistics and sponsors crime-prevention research programs.

THE CONSTITUTIONAL COURT

The constitution empowers the Constitutional Court to arbitrate in disputes between the executive and legislative branches and between Moscow and regional and local governments. The court's 19 justices also rule on violations of constitutional rights, examine appeals from various bodies, and participate in presidential impeachment proceedings. However, the court is prohibited from examining cases on its own initiative. Former President Yeltsin suspended the court in 1993 during a political showdown with parliament, but it was re-established in 1995 and since then has played an active role in the judicial system.

THE SUPREME COURT

The Supreme Court is divided into three chambers, one each for civil, criminal, and military matters. Criminal appeals and complaints of civil rights violations and abuses by the state may be advanced from lower courts to the Supreme Court for a hearing and final decision. The high court is staffed by 20 justices and more than 40 assessors. Cases before the court typically are heard by three judges or one judge and two assessors.

COURTS OF ARBITRATION

The Superior Court of Arbitration is the highest court for economic disputes. Courts of arbitration also exist at lower jurisdictional levels. The Superior Court of Arbitration is staffed by 70 justices and hears matters in four major categories: economic disputes, economic administration problems, review of decisions by lower arbitration courts that have legally binding force, and review of

SUPREME COURT BUILDING

The plotters of the 1991 coup went on trial at the Supreme Court in 1993. Outside, pro-communist demonstrators wave old Soviet flags in support of the accused.

LANDMARK CASES

1992
DECISION ON POLICE MERGER
Shortly after the creation of the Constitutional Court, it overturned a Yeltsin decree to combine the state police and other internal security forces into one agency under his command. Liberal Russian deputies in parliament vigorously protested and accused Yeltsin of seeking to recreate the Soviet-era KGB that Stalin had used to terrorize his opponents. Forcefully exercising its authority in a landmark decision, the court declared the presidential merger order unconstitutional and advised Yeltsin to abandon it.

1998
DECISION ON COURT FINANCING
After the Russian federal government cut funding for the judiciary, the Constitutional Court ruled that the spending reductions violated the Russian constitution and the European Convention for the Protection of Human Rights and Fundamental Freedoms. By reducing funding, the court ruled, the government failed to assure the complete and independent administration of justice, jeopardizing the right to judicial protection guaranteed by the constitution. It ordered the government to maintain its commitment to the judiciary and fully fund the courts.

1999
DECISION ON CAPITAL PUNISHMENT
The Constitutional Court declared capital punishment unconstitutional and outlawed it. The Russian constitution says trials of crimes that carry the death penalty should be heard by juries, but only nine out of Russia's 89 regions have such a system. The court ruled that Russia's courts had no right to impose the death penalty unless citizens facing execution are tried by a jury and not just a judge.

LIFE IMPRISONMENT
Those convicted of serious crimes in Russia are now sentenced to life imprisonment rather than death. Here a life prisoner waits for permission to eat his lunch.

RUSSIAN FEDERATION

non-binding lower court rulings. Courts of arbitration rarely employ juries; instead litigants appear before judges.

THE LEGAL SYSTEM

Russia follows the traditional continental legal system in which precedent plays no part and judges act as interpreters of the law. However, large case backlogs, poorly paid court personnel, trial delays, and lengthy pretrial detentions continue to plague the judicial system. With

SUPREME COURT IN SESSION
In this case, Vladimir Zhirinovsky, leader of the Russian Liberal-Democratic party, sued the Electoral Commission following his suspension from the 2000 elections.

enforcement of court decisions not always reliable, some people ignore the judiciary and turn to crime bosses to resolve disputes. Many Russian judges have been on the bench since the Soviet era, when they were used to handing down verdicts that would please local Communist Party leaders.

Critics say the appointment process for Russian judges leaves the courts open to political interference. Few judges have worked as lawyers at the

private bar. Instead, most are appointed early in their legal careers after working for a law-enforcement arm of the state, such as a prosecutor's office or police investigations office. At the same time inadequate salaries make judges susceptible to bribery. Partly because of low wages, many judicial positions remain vacant, exacerbating case backlogs and trial delays. Chronic underfunding leaves many courts in jeopardy of improper influence by local authorities, on which they depend for basic necessities such as stationery, heating, and photocopies.

These persistent problems have compelled President Putin to make judicial reform a priority of his government. In 2000, the institution of the Justice of the Peace was re-established and some 1,000 justices of the peace were appointed in 33 regions throughout the country to handle family law and minor criminal cases. Because many judges have tended to favor the prosecution, trial by jury is also slowly being incorporated into the judicial system. Typically, the acquittal rate for defendants by Russian juries is 20 percent, compared to less than one percent under judges.

After several years of intense lobbying, the State Duma in 2001 passed a major package of additional Putin-backed reforms, including a new criminal procedures code for greater protection of the defendant's rights, a substantial budget increase for the courts, and a number of disciplinary and administrative measures to increase the accountability of judges.

OFFICIAL NAME: RUSSIAN FEDERATION

POPULATION: 144.7 MILLION
CAPITAL: Moscow.
AREA: 6,592,735 SQ. MILES (17,075,184 SQ. KM)
INDEPENDENCE: 1991
CONSTITUTION: 1993

RUSSIA means "land of the Rus", a reference to the kingdom founded by Vikings in Ukraine in the 9th century. "Rus" derives from a Swedish word for "tribe."

RELIGION: Russian Orthodox 75%, Other and non-religious 25%

OFFICIAL LANGUAGE: Russian

REGIONS OR PROVINCES: 21 republics, 68 other administrative divisions

DEPENDENT TERRITORIES: None

MEDIA: Partial political censorship exists in national media

Newspapers: There are 285 daily newspapers

TV: 2 main partly state-owned services, several independent channels

Radio: 1 main state-run service, 1 foreign broadcasting service, several independents

SUFFRAGE: 18 years of age; universal

LEGAL SYSTEM: Civil law; no ICJ jurisdiction

WORLD ORGANIZATIONS: APEC, ARF (dialogue partner), ASEAN (dialogue partner), BIS, BSEC, CBSS, CCC, CE, CERN (observer), CIS, EAPC, EBRD, ECE, ESCAP, G-8, GEF, IAEA, IBRD, ICAO, ICC, ICFTU, ICRM, IDA, IFC, IFRCS, IHO, ILO, IMF, IMO, Interpol, IOC, IOM (observer), ISO, ITU, LAIA (observer), MINURSO, MONUC, NAM (guest), NSG, OAS (observer), OPCW, OSCE, PCA, PFP, UN, UN Security Council, UNAMSIL, UNCTAD, UNDP, UNHCR, UNIDO, UNIKOM, UNITAR, UNMEE, UNMIBH, UNMIK, UNMOP, UNMOVIC, UNOMIG, UNTAET, UNTSO, UPU, WFTU, WHO, WIPO, WMO, WToO, WTrO (observer), ZC

POLITICAL PARTIES: CP—Communist Party, Ind—Independents, U—Unity, FAR—Fatherland-All Russia, UFR—Union of the Right Forces, Y—Yabloko, Z—Zhirinovsky

ETHNIC GROUPS:
Tatar 4%
Ukrainian 3%
Chavash 1%
Other 10%
Russian 82%

NATIONAL ECONOMICS

WORLD GNP RANKING: 20th

GNP PER CAPITA: $1,660

INFLATION: 20.8%

BALANCE OF PAYMENTS (BALANCE OF TRADE): $46.3 billion

EXCHANGE RATES / U.S. DLR.: 28.65-30.50 RUSSIAN ROUBLES

OFFICIAL CURRENCY: RUSSIAN ROUBLE

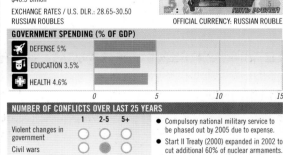

GOVERNMENT SPENDING (% OF GDP)

✈ DEFENSE 5%

📖 EDUCATION 3.5%

✚ HEALTH 4.6%

0   5   10   15

NUMBER OF CONFLICTS OVER LAST 25 YEARS

	1	2-5	5+
Violent changes in government	○	○	○
Civil wars	○	○	○
International wars	●	○	○
Foreign intervention	○	○	○

• Compulsory national military service to be phased out by 2005 due to expense.
• Start II Treaty (2000) expanded in 2002 to cut additional 60% of nuclear armaments.
• State-owned weapons manufacturers facing bankruptcy are privatizing and forming international partnerships.

NOTABLE WARS AND INSURGENCIES: Occupation of Afghanistan 1979-1988. Attempted coups 1991 and 1993. Chechen Wars 1994-1996 and 1999-present

1999

DECISION ON CRIMINAL INVESTIGATIONS
The Constitutional Court ruled that it is unconstitutional to prevent citizens from appealing preliminary investigations or searches and seizure of assets by law-enforcement authorities that may violate their rights. Citizens must be able to lodge complaints with the court immediately during the investigation phase and not be required to wait until the trial stage of a prosecution, the court said. Deferring complaints until the trial stage may cause irreparable damage, it ruled.

MEXICO

RELICS OF THE MAYAN AND AZTEC past abound in Mexico. Spain's 300-year rule also left a powerful legacy. Today, Mexico is the world's most populous Spanish-speaking country. Since independence, it has experienced civil wars, but since the revolution of 1910–1917 has known comparative stability. In modern Mexico's democratic system the president enjoys sweeping powers.

MEXICAN FLAG
Adopted on September 16, 1968 the flag shows the colors of hope (green), unity and peace (white) and the blood of heroes (red).

Mexico fell to Spain in 1521 after Hernán Cortés vanquished the Aztec and their emperor, Montezuma. Heavily taxed by Spain and dominated by the Catholic Church, the colony became a caste state. Enslaved at the bottom, Mexico's Indians labored in mines and vast plantation fields. Rebellion finally freed Mexico in 1821. Its first constitution, based on the US model, established a government with shared powers to avoid executive

PYRAMID OF KUKULKAN
Located in Chichén Itzá, the pyramid (left) was constructed in 1050 during the late Mayan period.

abuse. But its provisions soon were ignored. Once in the presidency, General Antonio López de Santa Ana ruled as a dictator until 1855. During his three-decade tenure, Mexico lost to the United States Texas and its lands in America's far southwest.

Later, President Benito Juárez instituted land reforms and restrictions on the military and church. The measures enraged conservatives and clerics and ignited the "War of Reform." Although reformers prevailed, by 1861 the government was bankrupt. Backed by Mexico's aristocracy,

HOW THE GOVERNM

LEGISLATIVE BRANCH

CONGRESS

Bicameral parliament, whose upper house is focused primarily on international policy issues, and the lower on domestic financial management.

▶ **SENATE**
The upper house; 128 seats, 96 elected by direct popular vote, 32 allotted to most popular candidates in each party. Members serve six-year terms with no consecutive re-election. Addresses foreign policy, approves international agreements, and presidential appointments.

▶ **CHAMBER OF DEPUTIES**
500 seats, 300 elected by direct popular vote to single-member districts, 200 allotted in five electoral regions to each party's most popular candidates; members serve three-year terms with no consecutive re-election. Initiates bills concerning loans, taxes, and troops.

THE CHAMBER OF DEPUTIES
The lower house is focused on a practical, domestic agenda.

 REGIONAL POWERS
▶ Thirty-one states or "estados"
▶ Popularly elected governors
▶ Unicameral legislatures

EXECUTIVE BRANCH

THE PRESIDENT

Elected by direct popular vote to a non-renewable term of six years; serves as head of state and government and commander-in-chief of the armed forces; directly introduces legislation in Congress and may veto bills and issue broad presidential decrees; must be native-born Mexican of native-born parents.

▶ **THE CABINET**
Appointed by the president; confirmed by the Senate. Oversees and sets policy for government operations.

▶ **EXECUTIVE AGENCIES**
Appointed by the president; the appointment of the attorney general requires congressional approval.

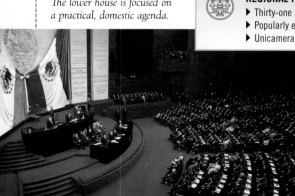

> *"Poor Mexico, so far from God and*
> *so close to the United States."*
> —*Porfirio Díaz*

France invaded and installed the Austrian archduke Maximilian as emperor. Reform forces later retook the government and executed him.

Mexico slipped again under despotic rule when General Porfirio Díaz in 1876 seized and kept power for the next 35 years. The wealthy prospered, but Mexico's masses plunged deeper into poverty. Shortly after the publication of a book by Francisco Madero that protested the Díaz regime, peasant anger erupted in the bloody 1910 revolution and civil war between rival rebel forces before the uprising was crushed. Emerging from the strife came the new 1917 constitution. It established a federal government divided

METROPOLIAN CATHEDRAL, MEXICO CITY
Despite a history of anticlerical regimes, Roman Catholicism is still a powerful force in Mexico.

FRANCISCO INDALECIO MADERO *(1873-1913)*
Madero was a Mexican revolutionist and politician who opposed President Porfirio Díaz and was elected president from 1911 to 1913 following a military campaign, which culminated in the resignation of Díaz.

into independent executive, legislative, and judicial branches. Mexico's presidency, which is sometimes called the "six-year monarchy," dominates the government. Founded in 1929, the National Revolutionary Party—later renamed the Institutional Revolutionary Party—joined political bosses, military leaders, labor unions, peasant groups, and regional parties in a coalition that controlled the country's government until 2000. That year, Mexican voters elected as president Vicente Fox of the conservative National Action Party.

T   W   O   R   K   S

⚖ JUDICIAL BRANCH

SUPREME COURT

Mexico's highest court of review and appeal, with jurisdiction over all state and federal courts. Eleven justices are nominated by the president and confirmed with a two-thirds majority vote by the Senate. If the Senate fails to act within 30 days, the appointment becomes automatic. Justices serve until age 65 but may be removed by the president with the approval of the Congress.

▶ THE FEDERAL COURTS

Administers justice in civil cases and major felonies. In most criminal cases there is trial by judge, not jury, with an initial presumption of guilt.

▶ THE STATE COURTS

Administers justice locally. Justices of state Superior Courts of Justice appointed by governors with approval of state legislatures.

ELECTORAL SYSTEM

Voting is compulsory, but penalties for noncompliance are rarely enforced. Voters elect by a simple majority the president and members of Congress, except for 32 senators and 200 deputies who are selected by proportional representation. For each senator and deputy, a substitute is also elected.

NATIONAL PALACE
The seat of Mexico's government stands on the Zócola, Mexico City's main square. It was formerly the Spanish Viceroy's palace.

OFFICIAL NAME: UNITED MEXICAN STATES

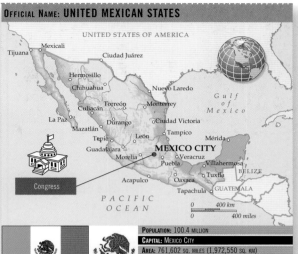

| POPULATION: 100.4 MILLION |
| CAPITAL: MEXICO CITY |
| AREA: 761,602 SQ. MILES (1,972,550 SQ. KM) |
| INDEPENDENCE: 1836 |
| CONSTITUTION: 1917 |

MEXICO is thought to have been named after Mexitl, the Aztec god of war and storms.

RELIGION: Roman Catholic 95%, Protestant 1%, Other 4%

OFFICIAL LANGUAGE: Spanish

REGIONS OR PROVINCES: 31 states and one federal district

DEPENDENT TERRITORIES: None

MEDIA: Partial political censorship exists in national media

NEWSPAPERS: There are 295 daily newspapers

TV: Many state-owned and independent services

RADIO: Many state-owned and independent services

ETHNIC GROUPS:
- Other 9%
- European 16%
- Mestizo 55%
- Indigenous Amerindian 20%

SUFFRAGE: 18 years of age; universal and compulsory (but not enforced)

LEGAL SYSTEM: Civil law; American legal traditions; accepts ICJ jurisdiction

WORLD ORGANIZATIONS: APEC, BCIE, BIS, Caricom (observer), CCC, CDB, CE (observer), EBRD, ECLAC, FAO, G-3, G-6, G-15, G-19, G-24, IADB, IAEA, IBRD, ICAO, ICC, ICFTU, ICRM, IDA, IEA (observer), IFAD, IFC, IFRCS, ILO, IMF, IMO, Interpol, IOC, IOM (observer), ISO, ITU, LAES, LAIA, NAM (observer), NEA, OAS, OECD, OPANAL, OPCW, PCA, RG, UN, UN Security Council (temporary), UNCTAD, UNESCO, UNHCR, UNIDO, UNITAR, UNU, UPU, WCL, WFTU, WHO, WIPO, WMO, WToO, WTrO

POLITICAL PARTIES: PAN-PVEM—Alliance for Change (National Action Party and Green Party), PRI—Institutional Revolutionary Party, PRD-PT—Alliance for Mexico (Party of the Democratic Revolution and Labor Party)

NATIONAL ECONOMICS

WORLD GNP RANKING: 11th

GNP PER CAPITA: $5,070

INFLATION: 9.5%

BALANCE OF PAYMENTS (BALANCE OF TRADE): -$17.8 billion

EXCHANGE RATES / U.S. DLR.: 9.609-9.169 MEXICAN PESOS

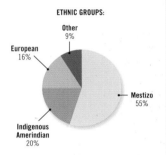

OFFICIAL CURRENCY: MEXICAN PESO

GOVERNMENT SPENDING (% OF GDP)

✈ DEFENSE 1%	
🐾 EDUCATION 4.9%	
✚ HEALTH 2.6%	

0   5   10   15

NUMBER OF CONFLICTS OVER LAST 25 YEARS

	1	2-5	5+
Violent changes in government	○	○	○
Civil wars	○	●	○
International wars	○	○	○
Foreign intervention	○	○	○

- Compulsory national military service.
- Army acts to defend internal security.
- Weapons are obtained mainly from United States and France.
- Increasing militarization since 1994.

NOTABLE WARS AND INSURGENCIES: Zapatista rebellion 1994-1995. EPR revolt 1996

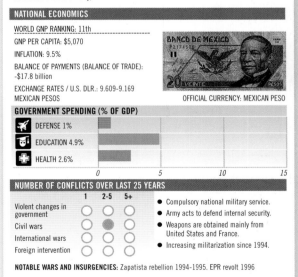

PHILIPPINES

OFFICIAL NAME: REPUBLIC OF THE PHILIPPINES

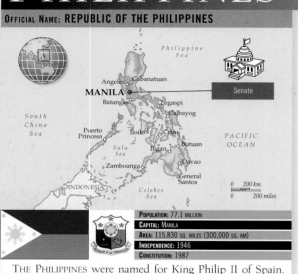

POPULATION: 77.1 MILLION	
CAPITAL: MANILA	
AREA: 115,830 SQ. MILES (300,000 SQ. KM)	
INDEPENDENCE: 1946	
CONSTITUTION: 1987	

THE PHILIPPINES were named for King Philip II of Spain.

RELIGION: Roman Catholic 83%, Protestant 9%, Muslim 5%, Other (including Buddhist) 3%

OFFICIAL LANGUAGES: English and Filipino

REGIONS OR PROVINCES: 73 provinces, 61 chartered cities

DEPENDENT TERRITORIES: None

MEDIA: No political censorship exists in national media

SUFFRAGE: 18 years of age; universal

LEGAL SYSTEM: American and Spanish law; accepts ICJ jurisdiction

WORLD ORGANIZATIONS: APEC, ARF, AsDB, ASEAN, CCC, CP, ESCAP, FAO, G-24, G-77, IAEA, IBRD, ICAO, ICC, ICFTU, ICRM, IDA, IFAD, IFC, IFRCS, IHO, ILO, IMF, IMO, Interpol, IOC, IOM, ISO, ITU, NAM, OAS (observer), OPCW, UN, UNCTAD, UNESCO, UNHCR, UNIDO, UNMIK, UNTAET, UNU, UPU, WCL, WFTU, WHO, WIPO, WMO, WToO, WTrO

ETHNIC GROUPS:
- Filipino 50%
- Indonesian and Polynesian 30%
- Chinese 10%
- Indian 5%
- Other 5%

POLITICAL PARTIES: Lakas-NUCD—Lakas-National Union of Christian Democrats, LAMP—Party of the Filipino Masses, LDP—Fight of Democratic Filipinos, LP—Liberal Party, Ind—Independents, PP—People's Power (coalition led by Lakas-NUCD and including LP) PnM—Strength of the Masses (coalition of LAMP and LDP)

NATIONAL ECONOMICS

WORLD GNP RANKING: 41st

GNP PER CAPITA: $1,040

INFLATION: 4.4%

BALANCE OF PAYMENTS (BALANCE OF TRADE): $9.08 billion

EXCHANGE RATES / U.S. DLR.: 50.0-51.6 PHILIPPINE PESOS

OFFICIAL CURRENCY: PHILIPPINE PESO

GOVERNMENT SPENDING (% OF GDP)

- ✈ DEFENSE 1.9%
- 📖 EDUCATION 3.2%
- ✚ HEALTH 1.6%

(scale 0 to 15)

NUMBER OF CONFLICTS OVER LAST 25 YEARS

	1	2-5	5+
Violent changes in government	○	○	○
Civil wars	○	○	●
International wars	○	○	○
Foreign intervention	○	○	○

- No compulsory national military service.
- Rebel separatists are an ongoing threat.
- US are providing assistance with modernization of armed forces and, since 2001 logistical support, against separatists.

NOTABLE WARS AND INSURGENCIES: Regional rebellions. Popular uprisings 1986 and 2001

FIRST CLAIMED BY MAGELLAN for King Charles I, the Philippines were ruled by the Spanish for 377 years before being ceded to the United States in 1898 following the Spanish-American War. The purpose of the US occupation was to assist in establishing a free and democratic government, which despite initial resistance began to take shape by 1907. In 1935, the country became a self-governing commonwealth, but during World War II, the Japanese gained control of the islands until the surrender of 1945. The Philippines became an independent republic in the following year.

Since then, the country's political history has been marked by conflict and corruption, with its system of presidential democracy set back many times, first by the communist Huk Rebellion, and later by the dictatorial rule of Ferdinand Marcos. For 21 years from 1965, he presided over a disastrous decline in economic growth which, combined with an appalling human rights record, contributed to ongoing political instability.

Opposition leader, Benigno Aquino, was assassinated in 1983 after returning from exile, an event which saw the groundswell of hatred towards Marcos finally overflow, forcing a presidential election three years later under pressure from the US. Aquino's widow, Corazon, headed the opposition

PRE-TRIAL—MARCH 15, 1999
Supporters surround Imelda Marcos before her pre-trial. Some 9,539 Filipinos won a class action suit against the Marcos estate for the execution and disappearance of dissidents during Ferdinand Marcos' rule.

under the United Nationalist Democratic Organization party (UNIDO), and became president. She revitalized democratic institutions and civil liberties, but undermined by military coups her government lost power after its first term. National reconciliation became the dominant focus of the Fidel Ramos, who took office from 1992 until 1998. During his term, he legalized the Communist Party, brokered talks with the rebels, Muslim separatists, and the military, and brought an end to the military insurgency. The former vice-president, Joseph Ejercito Estrada, won the 1998 presidential elections, but three years later was replaced by his vice-president Gloria Macapagal-Arroyo, after his impeachment trial on corruption charges broke down. The negotiation of peace talks with Muslim separatist groups and communist insurgents remains an issue.

HOW THE GOVERNMENT WORKS

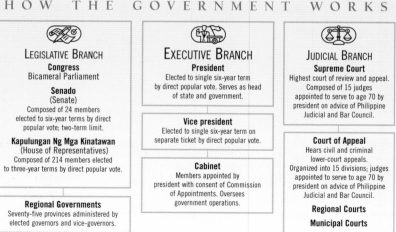

LEGISLATIVE BRANCH

Congress
Bicameral Parliament

Senado
(Senate)
Composed of 24 members elected to six-year terms by direct popular vote; two-term limit.

Kapulungan Ng Mga Kinatawan
(House of Representatives)
Composed of 214 members elected to three-year terms by direct popular vote.

Regional Governments
Seventy-five provinces administered by elected governors and vice-governors.

EXECUTIVE BRANCH

President
Elected to single six-year term by direct popular vote. Serves as head of state and government.

Vice president
Elected to single six-year term on separate ticket by direct popular vote.

Cabinet
Members appointed by president with consent of Commission of Appointments. Oversees government operations.

JUDICIAL BRANCH

Supreme Court
Highest court of review and appeal. Composed of 15 judges appointed to serve to age 70 by president on advice of Philippine Judicial and Bar Council.

Court of Appeal
Hears civil and criminal lower-court appeals. Organized into 15 divisions; judges appointed to serve to age 70 by president on advice of Philippine Judicial and Bar Council.

Regional Courts

Municipal Courts

EGYPT

OFFICIAL NAME: ARAB REPUBLIC OF EGYPT

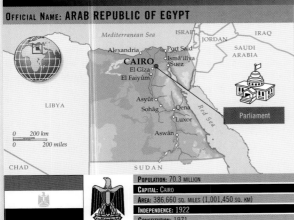

POPULATION: 70.3 MILLION	
CAPITAL: CAIRO	
AREA: 386,660 SQ. MILES (1,001,450 SQ. KM)	
INDEPENDENCE: 1922	
CONSTITUTION: 1971	

EGYPT means "temple of the soul of Ptah," after the Egyptian god Ptah, patron deity of Memphis, Egypt.

RELIGION: Muslim (mainly Sunni) 94%, Coptic Christian and other 6%

OFFICIAL LANGUAGE: Arabic

REGIONS OR PROVINCES: 26 governorates

DEPENDENT TERRITORIES: None

MEDIA: Total political censorship exists in national media

Newspapers: There are 17 daily papers

TV: One state-owned service

Radio: Two services: one state-owned, one independent

SUFFRAGE: 18 years of age; universal and compulsory

LEGAL SYSTEM: Shari'a (Islamic), English and French law; accepts ICJ jurisdiction

ETHNIC GROUPS:

Other (Nubian, Armenian, Greek) 10%

Eastern Hamitic 90%

WORLD ORGANIZATIONS: ABEDA, ACC, ACCT, AfDB, AFESD, AL, AMF, BSEC (observer), CAEU, CCC, EBRD, ECA, ESCWA, FAO, G-15, G-19, G-24, G-77, IAEA, IBRD, ICAO, ICC, ICRM, IDA, IDB, IFAD, IFC, IFRCS, IHO, ILO, IMF, IMO, Interpol, IOC, IOM, ISO, ITU, MINURSO, MONUC, NAM, OAPEC, OAS (observer), OAU, OIC, OSCE (partner), PCA, UN, UNAMSIL, UNCTAD, UNESCO, UNIDO, UNITAR, UNMIBH, UNMIK, UNMOP, UNOMIG, UNRWA, UNTAET, UPU, WFTU, WHO, WIPO, WMO, WToO, WTrO

POLITICAL PARTIES: NDP—National Democratic Party, Ind—Independents, NWP—New Wafd Party, NPU—National Progressive Unionist Party

NATIONAL ECONOMICS

WORLD GNP RANKING: 38th

GNP PER CAPITA: $1,490

INFLATION: 2.7%

BALANCE OF PAYMENTS (BALANCE OF TRADE): -$971 million

EXCHANGE RATES / U.S. DLR.: 3.890-4.575 EGYPTIAN POUNDS

OFFICIAL CURRENCY: EGYPTIAN POUND

GOVERNMENT SPENDING (% OF GDP)

✈ DEFENSE 3.2%	
📖 EDUCATION 4.8%	
✚ HEALTH 4.6%	

0   5   10   15

NUMBER OF CONFLICTS OVER LAST 25 YEARS

	1	2-5	5+
Violent changes in government	●	○	○
Civil wars	○	○	○
International wars	●	○	○
Foreign intervention	○	○	○

- Compulsory national military service.
- Largest armed forces in Arab world.
- Aside from a local arms industry, the US supplies weapons and training.
- A state of emergency, in force since 1981, has been extended to 2005.

NOTABLE WARS AND INSURGENCIES: President Anwar-al-Sadat assassinated, 1981. Backed Allies in Gulf War 1991

EGYPT, THE ARAB WORLD'S MOST POPULOUS COUNTRY, received nominal independence from British rule in 1922. A monarchy reigned until a military junta seized control in 1952, from which point the country began moving toward a presidential democracy, although it remained under the tight control of President Gemal Abdal-Nasser until 1970. Egypt has been relatively politically stable since World War II, with only three national leaders between 1954 and the early 21st century: Nasser, Anwar Sadat, and Hosni Mubarak.

Under Mubarak, the dominant National Democratic Party (NDP) has retained its grip on the political process by repeatedly extending the state of national emergency that began after Sadat's assassination by Islamic terrorists in 1981. Emergency laws were invoked to justify a ban on religious parties, hitting the Labor Party, an Islamic party that was the NDP's political opponent. But Mubarak did not completely enforce the ban until recently, and has balanced this by allowing the proliferation of other parties and slightly greater freedom of the press.

The president is chief executive and leader of the ruling party, and is nominated by two-thirds of the Majlis al-Shaab, the bicameral People's Assembly legislature, and approved by popular referendum. The president appoints the prime minister, who is head of government, and the cabinet. The People's Assembly approves policies, budget, and development plans, and may vote no-confidence in the prime minister or any cabinet member (but not the president). A no-confidence vote would lead to a referendum and, if it fails, dissolution of the Assembly. The other legislative body, the Majlis al-Shura, has only a consultative role.

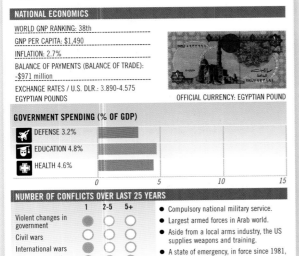

ASSASSINATION TRIAL—MARCH 1982
Lt. Col. Khaled al-Islambouli, a religious extremist, is shown on trial for the assassination of Anwar al-Sadat. Inset: President Anwar al-Sadat in 1978.

HOW THE GOVERNMENT WORKS

LEGISLATIVE BRANCH

Parliament
Bicameral Parliament

People's National Assembly
Composed of 454 members who serve five-year terms: 444 elected by direct popular vote; 10 appointed by president. Half of seats constitutionally reserved for "workers and peasants."

Shura Council
Composed of 264 members who serve six-year terms: 174 elected by direct popular vote; 88 appointed by president. Serves as advisory body.

Regional Governments
Twenty-six governorates overseen by elected local councils.

EXECUTIVE BRANCH

President
Nominated by two-thirds majority vote of parliament, elected to six-year term by national referendum. Serves as head of state.

Prime Minister
Appointed by president. Serves as head of government.

Cabinet
Members appointed by president.

JUDICIAL BRANCH

Supreme Constitutional Court
Rules on constitutionality of laws.

Court of Cassation
Highest court for civil and criminal appeals.

Civil Courts

Criminal Courts

UKRAINE

OFFICIAL NAME: UKRAINE

POLAND · BELARUS
Luts'k · Chornobyl' · Chernihiv
L'viv · Zhytomyr · **KIEV**
SLOVAKIA · Muka-cheve · Kharkiv
HUNGARY · ROMANIA · Kirovohrad · Luhans'k
Zaporizhzhya · Donets'k
MOLDOVA · Mykolayiv · Mariupol'
Supreme Council · Odesa · *Sea of Azov* · RUSSIAN FEDERATION
Sevastopol'
BULGARIA · *Black Sea*
0 · 100 km
0 · 100 miles

POPULATION: 48.4 MILLION	
CAPITAL: KIEV	
AREA: 233,089 SQ. MILES (603,700 SQ. KM)	
INDEPENDENCE: 1991	
CONSTITUTION: 1996	

UKRAINE is Slavic for "border" or "frontier."

RELIGION: Ukrainian Orthodox (Moscow Patriarchate and Kiev Patriarchate), Ukrainian Autocephalous Orthodox, Ukrainian Catholic (Uniate), Protestant, Jewish

ETHNIC GROUPS:
Other 4%
Jewish 1%
Russian 22%
Ukrainian 73%

OFFICIAL LANGUAGE: Ukrainian

REGIONS OR PROVINCES: 24 *oblasti*, one autonomous republic and two municipalities with *oblast* status

DEPENDENT TERRITORIES: None

MEDIA: Regional political differences

SUFFRAGE: 18 years of age; universal

LEGAL SYSTEM: Civil law; no ICJ jurisdiction

WORLD ORGANIZATIONS: BSEC, CCC, CE, CEI, CIS, EAPC, EBRD, ECE, IAEA, IBRD, ICAO, ICRM, IFC, IFRCS, IHO, ILO, IMF, IMO, Interpol, IOC, IOM, ISO, ITU, MONUC, NAM (observer), NSG, OAS (observer), OPCW, OSCE, PCA, PFP, UN, UNAMSIL, UNCTAD, UNESCO, UNIDO, UNIFIL, UNMEE, UNMIBH, UNMIK, UNMOP, UNMOT, UNMOVIC, UPU, WCL, WFTU, WHO, WIPO, WMO, WToO, WTrO (observer), ZC

POLITICAL PARTIES: Agrarian Party, CPU—Communist Party of Ukraine, Democratic Union, Fatherland (Motherland) All Ukrainian Party, FUU—For One Ukraine, PZU—Green Party of Ukraine, YT—Juliya Tymoshenko Election Bloc, Liberal Party, OU—Our Ukraine, Party of Industrialists and Entrepreneurs, Party of Regions, Party of Ukrainian Unity, SelPU—Peasant Party of Ukraine, PDP—People's Democratic Party, Rukh U—People's Movement of Ukraine, Progressive Socialist Party, Reforms Congress, SDPU-O—Social-Democratic Party of Ukraine (United), SPU—Socialist Party of Ukraine, Solidarity, Trudova Ukrayina/Working Ukraine, Rukh K—Ukrainian Popular Movement, Unity, Working Ukraine/Labort Ukraine, Yabluko

NATIONAL ECONOMICS

WORLD GNP RANKING: 55th

GNP PER CAPITA: $700

INFLATION: 22.7%

BALANCE OF PAYMENTS (BALANCE OF TRADE): $1.48 billion

EXCHANGE RATES / U.S. DLR.: 5.435-5.314 HRYVNAS

OFFICIAL CURRENCY: HRYVNA

GOVERNMENT SPENDING (% OF GDP)

✈ DEFENSE 3.4%	
🎓 EDUCATION 4.4%	
✚ HEALTH 2.9%	

0   5   10   15

NUMBER OF CONFLICTS OVER LAST 25 YEARS

	1	2-5	5+
Violent changes in government	○	○	○
Civil wars	○	○	○
International wars	○	○	○
Foreign intervention	○	○	○

- Compulsory national military service to be phased out by 2015.
- Large weapons manufacturing and export sector.
- Ongoing dispute with Romania over territory.
- Signed START-I nuclear disarmament treaty.
- Applied for membership of NATO's Partnerships for Peace in 2002.

NOTABLE WARS AND INSURGENCIES: None

THE FIRST IDENTIFIABLE NOMADIC PEOPLES arrived in Ukraine during the first millennium B.C. and traded with Greek city states along the coast. Waves of invaders passed through the region in the first millennium A.D., but the people that eventually settled were the Slavs. In the 9th century Kiev emerged as the center of a powerful kingdom, but the city was sacked by the Mongols in 1240. In 1667, Poland and Russia split Ukraine between them, and by 1793 the Russian empire had claimed most of the country. Ukraine seized the opportunity presented by World War I and the Bolshevik Revolution to declare independence in 1918, but this was short lived. By 1921, Poland absorbed the western portion of the country, and the remainder became part of the Soviet Union. After the Nazi and Soviet invasions of Poland in 1939, western Ukraine also became part of the Soviet Union. Stalinist measures to suppress Ukrainian national identity and language were so harsh that Ukrainians viewed the Nazi invasion of the Soviet Union in 1941 as liberation. Nazi brutality soon dashed that opinion.

Over the next 50 years, Ukraine's pursuit of its national goals waxed and waned with Soviet liberalism. The 1986 explosion of a Soviet nuclear power plant at Chernobyl, and Soviet attempts to withhold information about the accident proved to be a watershed for some Ukrainians, exposing extensive problems in the Soviet system. Ukraine declared its independence on August 24, 1991 and quickly adopted a multiparty system and legislative protections for minority rights. A new constitution guaranteeing basic human rights and providing for a pluralistic political system was adopted in June 1996, but while Ukraine's first independent elections were orderly, widespread fraud during the 2004 vote led to the "Orange Revolution", in which popular protest forced a repeat of the ballot and a reversed result.

Ukraine patterned its government on the Western model, with three separate branches. Executive powers are vested in a president who is elected by popular vote for a five-year term. The unicameral legislature's powers include enacting legislation, ratifying treaties, impeaching the president under certain circumstances, and approving the budget. The judiciary is autonomous and precedent plays no part in trials, as judges decide cases on their merits within the dictates of codified law.

ISSUES AND CHALLENGES:

- While the constitution guarantees freedom of speech and of the press, authorities sometimes use intimidation to thwart media coverage.
- Ukraine is a country with arbitrarily drawn boundaries that don't heed ethnic ties. Crimea has close ties to Russia and has proposed secession from Ukraine and annexation to Russia.
- The country has considerable environmental problems, especially those arising from the nuclear disaster at Chernobyl and industrial pollution.
- Efforts to foster a market economy have stalled because of weak support from the executive and legislative branches of the government.

HOW THE GOVERNMENT WORKS

LEGISLATIVE BRANCH

Verhovna Rada
(Supreme Council)
Unicameral Parliament
Composed of 450 members elected to four-year terms: 225 by direct popular vote from single-member districts; 225 by proportional representation. Initiates legislation; ratifies treaties; approves budget; declares war; removes prime minister and Cabinet of Ministers with no-confidence vote.

Regional Governments
Twenty-four provinces administered by elected governors and legislatures; one autonomous republic (Crimea).

EXECUTIVE BRANCH

President
Elected to five-year term by direct popular vote. Serves as head of state. Represents nation in foreign affairs; revokes acts of Cabinet; declares national emergencies; dissolves Supreme Council.

Prime minister
Nominated by the president and confirmed by Supreme Council.

Cabinet of ministers
Composed of prime minister, two deputy prime ministers, and 15 ministers; appointed by president, approved by Supreme Council. Oversees government operations.

JUDICIAL BRANCH

Constitutional Court
Rules on constitutionality of laws. Composed of 18 judges appointed to nine-year terms: six by president; six by Supreme Council; six by Congress of Judges.

Supreme Court
Highest court of review and appeal. Judges appointed for life by Supreme Council.

Regional Appellate Courts

Commercial Courts

Local Courts

SOUTH KOREA

OFFICIAL NAME: REPUBLIC OF KOREA

POPULATION: 47.1 MILLION
CAPITAL: SEOUL
AREA: 38,023 SQ. MILES (98,480 SQ. KM)
INDEPENDENCE: 1948
CONSTITUTION: 1948

SOUTH KOREA takes its name from the 10th-century kingdom of Koryo, which united the Korean peninsula.

RELIGION: Mahayana Buddhist 47%, Protestant 38%, Roman Catholic 11%, Confucianist 3%, Other 1%

ETHNIC GROUPS:
Korean 100%

OFFICIAL LANGUAGE: Korean

REGIONS OR PROVINCES: Nine provinces and seven metropolitan cities

DEPENDENT TERRITORIES: None

MEDIA: No political censorship exists in national media

NEWSPAPERS: There are 60 daily newspapers

TV: Seven services: one publicly owned, six independent

RADIO: Nine services: one publicly owned, eight independent

SUFFRAGE: 20 years of age; universal

LEGAL SYSTEM: Chinese and American-European legal traditions; no ICJ jurisdiction

WORLD ORGANIZATIONS: AfDB, APEC, ARF (dialogue partner), AsDB, ASEAN (dialogue partner), Australia Group, BIS, CCC, CP, EBRD, ESCAP, FAO, G-77, IAEA, IBRD, ICAO, ICC, ICFTU, ICRM, IDA, IEA, IEA (observer), IFAD, IFC, IFRCS, IHO, ILO, IMF, IMO, Interpol, IOC, IOM, ISO, ITU, MINURSO, NAM (guest), NEA, NSG, OAS (observer), OECD, OPCW, OSCE (partner), PCA, UN, UNCTAD, UNESCO, UNHCR, UNIDO, UNMOGIP, UNOMIG, UNTAET, UNU, UPU, WCL, WHO, WIPO, WMO, WToO, WTrO, ZC

POLITICAL PARTIES: GNP—Grand National Party, MD—Millennium Democratic Party, ULD—United Liberal Democrats

NATIONAL ECONOMICS

WORLD GNP RANKING: 13th

GNP PER CAPITA: $8,910

INFLATION: 2.3%

BALANCE OF PAYMENTS (BALANCE OF TRADE): $11.4 billion

EXCHANGE RATES / U.S. DLR.: 1265-1314 SOUTH KOREAN WON

OFFICIAL CURRENCY: SOUTH KOREAN WON

GOVERNMENT SPENDING (% OF GDP)

		0	5	10	15
✈	DEFENSE 2.8%				
	EDUCATION 4.1%				
✚	HEALTH 2.4%				

NUMBER OF CONFLICTS OVER LAST 25 YEARS

	1	2-5	5+
Violent changes in government	○	○	○
Civil wars	○	○	○
International wars	○	○	○
Foreign intervention	○	○	○

- Compulsory national military service.
- US provides troops to guard against the ongoing threat from North Korea.
- Border is most heavily defended in world.
- Manufacture of missiles capable of targeting North Korea permitted in 2001.

NOTABLE WARS AND INSURGENCIES: Kwangju uprising 1980. Student protest 1987

WHAT IS KNOWN TODAY AS SOUTH KOREA or the Republic of Korea, has dealt with internal and external conflicts throughout its history. In the early 1900s, it fell into the hands of Japanese totalitarian rule, which lasted until the end of World War II, when the United States and the Soviet Union agreed to split the territory along the 38-degree north latitude line. The south became the Republic of Korea, and the north the Stalinist Democratic People's Republic of Korea. In 1947, the UN organized elections for a unified country, but North Korea refused to comply. When the UN recognized the subsequently elected government of South Korea as the only legitimate one, North Korea invaded the South, starting a three-year war in which China entered on the communist side, and US and UN forces supported the South. Despite four million war dead, the 1953 Armistice left Korea a still-divided land.

DEMILITARIZED ZONE
The DMZ that separates North and South Korea is patrolled by soldiers on both sides, but in April 1996, South Korean soldiers were placed on high alert when North Korean soldiers moved into the village of Panmunjom, in the demilitarized zone, where joint meetings are held.

The First Republic in South Korea began in 1948 under a constitution drawn up after the UN-monitored elections. Syngman Rhee—a Princeton University alumnus and prominent Korean pro-independence leader—became the first president of the nation at the age of 73. In trying to protect the country from the communists of the North, South Korean leaders were forced to maintain a very centralized form of government. However, Rhee had to step down in 1960 in response to pressure to end the authoritarian regime. The Second Republic, though more democratic, lasted less than a year. In 1961, a leader of the opposition, Park Chung Hee, led a military coup establishing the Third Republic and dissolving the National Assembly. He was re-elected in 1963, 1967, and 1971. However, in 1972 he established the Fourth Republic, giving himself more extensive powers. Seven years later he was assassinated by the director of the Korean Central Intelligence Agency (KCIA), and the Fifth Republic was ratified in 1980. It took seven years and many demonstrations demanding the end of authoritarian rule for the country to begin the transition toward democracy under the Sixth Republic.

HOW THE GOVERNMENT WORKS

LEGISLATIVE BRANCH

Kolkhoz
(National Assembly)
Unicameral Parliament
Composed of 273 members who serve four-year terms: 227 elected by direct popular vote; 46 appointed by political parties based on number of seats won in election. (As of 2004, all members will be elected by direct vote.)

Regional Governments
Nine provinces administered by elected governors.

EXECUTIVE BRANCH

President
Elected to single five-year term by direct popular vote. Serves as head of state; commander-in-chief of armed forces. Initiates legislation.

Prime minister
Appointed by president.
Serves as head of government.

State Council
Composed of 20 members appointed by president on advice of prime minister.
Oversees government operations.

JUDICIAL BRANCH

Constitutional Court
Rules on the constitutionality; impeaches president, State Council members and other high officials. Composed of nine judges: three appointed by president; three by National Assembly; three by chief justice.

Supreme Court
Highest court of review and appeal. Justices appointed to six-year terms by president with consent of National Assembly. All but chief justice may be reappointed.

High Courts and Lower Courts
Judges appointed to ten-year terms by Conference of Supreme Court justices and chief justice.

COLOMBIA

OFFICIAL NAME: REPUBLIC OF COLOMBIA

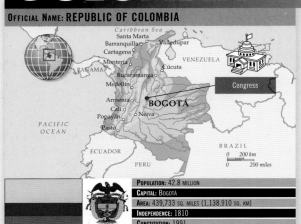

POPULATION: 42.8 MILLION
CAPITAL: BOGOTÁ
AREA: 439,733 SQ. MILES (1,138,910 SQ. KM)
INDEPENDENCE: 1810
CONSTITUTION: 1991

COLOMBIA was named after Christopher Columbus in 1819, the year it first gained independence from Spain.

RELIGION: Roman Catholic 95%, Other 5%

OFFICIAL LANGUAGE: Spanish

REGIONS OR PROVINCES: 32 departments and 1 capital district

DEPENDENT TERRITORIES: None

MEDIA: Partial political censorship exists in national media. The independent press is very small. Journalists have been murdered by paramilitaries and held by guerrillas.

Newspapers: 37 daily newspapers

TV: 3 services: 1 state-owned, 2 independent

Radio: 589 stations: 31 state-owned

SUFFRAGE: 18 years of age; universal

LEGAL SYSTEM: Spanish law; US-based criminal code; accepts ICJ jurisdiction

WORLD ORGANIZATIONS: BCIE, CAN, Caricom (observer), CCC, CDB, ECLAC, FAO, G-3, G-24, G-77, IADB, IAEA, IBRD, ICAO, ICC, ICFTU, ICRM, IDA, IFAD, IFC, IFRCS, IHO, ILO, IMF, IMO, Interpol, IOC, IOM, ISO, ITU, LAES, LAIA, NAM, OAS, OPANAL, OPCW, PCA, RG, UN, UN Security Council (temporary), UNCTAD, UNESCO, UNHCR, UNIDO, UNU, UPU, WCL, WFTU, WHO, WIPO, WMO, WToO, WTrO

POLITICAL PARTIES: PL—Liberal Party, PCC—Colombian Conservative Party, C-Coalition, CR—Radical Change, AL—Liberal Opening, MN—National Movement

ETHNIC GROUPS:

Black Amerindian 3%
Black African 4%
Other 1%
European-African 14%
White 20%
Mestizo 58%

NATIONAL ECONOMICS

WORLD GNP RANKING: 40th

GNP PER CAPITA: $2,020

INFLATION: 9.5%

BALANCE OF PAYMENTS (BALANCE OF TRADE): $41 million

EXCHANGE RATES / U.S. DLR.: 2236-2278 COLOMBIAN PESOS

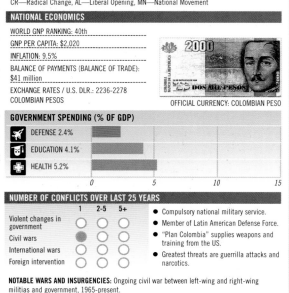

OFFICIAL CURRENCY: COLOMBIAN PESO

GOVERNMENT SPENDING (% OF GDP)

DEFENSE 2.4%
EDUCATION 4.1%
HEALTH 5.2%

0   5   10   15

NUMBER OF CONFLICTS OVER LAST 25 YEARS

	1	2-5	5+
Violent changes in government			
Civil wars			
International wars			
Foreign intervention			

- Compulsory national military service.
- Member of Latin American Defense Force.
- "Plan Colombia" supplies weapons and training from the US.
- Greatest threats are guerrilla attacks and narcotics.

NOTABLE WARS AND INSURGENCIES: Ongoing civil war between left-wing and right-wing militias and government, 1965-present.

COLOMBIA IS ONE OF THE MOST VIOLENT countries in the world. Left-wing guerrillas and paramilitary groups rule large portions of the country. The current violence can be traced to rampant corruption in the government, nurtured in part by the competing Medellín and Cali drug cartels. The cartels control much of Colombia, including some politicians, as well as police and guerrilla groups. Historically, the violence dates back to 19th-century rivalries between the anti-clerical Liberal Party (PL) and the Catholic-aligned Conservative Party (PSC). These rivalries erupted in La Violencia, which lasted from 1948 to 1956, during which 200,000 people were killed. A 1958 agreement between the PL and PSC produced the National Front, which divided Congressional seats evenly and alternated the presidency between the two parties. The agreement curbed violence but stifled debate, leaving the democratic process hamstrung. The election of conservative independent president, Álvaro Uribe Vélez, in 2002 marked the end of the existing two-party system.

In Colombia's presidential democracy, the president serves as chief of state, head of government, commander-in-chief, and head of police, and has the unusual power to invoke a "state of internal commotion," thereby suspending civil rights and legislation. Although the president has more power than the legislative or judicial branches of government, the office's power is limited in comparison with other Latin American countries. The legislative branch features a two-house Congress, which can override a presidential veto with a simple majority in both houses. Congress can initiate, interpret, and repeal laws, and it controls the budget and national spending. Business leaders and the Roman Catholic Church exert considerable influence over economic and social policy.

The 1991 constitution introduced judicial reforms with the ambitious aims of improving efficiency and eliminating corruption. The constitution also increased the autonomy of the attorney general, widening the powers to investigate and prosecute.

ISSUES AND CHALLENGES:

- Between 1986 and 2000, two million people were displaced from their homes through violence, and nearly 3,000 were kidnapped. Twenty mayoral candidates and 20 mayors were killed. Bringing the violence to an end and gaining control over the competing factions depend in part on the success of Plan Colombia, initiated in the late 1990s. This ambitious plan, which is heavily dependent on foreign aid, especially from the US, covers economic, fiscal and judicial reforms. It also involves counter-narcotics activities and the negotiation of peace with guerrillas, including the Revolutionary Armed Forces of Colombia (FARC), the largest of the active guerrilla groups. Reforms carried out under Plan Colombia have included the installation of justices of the peace and local *casas de justicia* (judicial offices), giving people access to legal remedies previously absent.

HOW THE GOVERNMENT WORKS

LEGISLATIVE BRANCH

Congreso
(Congress)
Bicameral Parliament

Senado
(Senate)
Composed of 102 members directly elected to four-year terms by proportional representation; two seats for indigenous representatives. Ratifies declarations of war; selects attorney general; impeaches president, attorney general, and Supreme Court judges.

Cámara de Representantes
(House of Representatives)
161 members elected to four-year terms by popular vote; five seats for ethnic minorities. Initiates tax bills; selects comptroller-general; supervises budget and treasury.

Regional Governments
Thirty-two departments administered by elected legislatures and governors elected to single three-year terms.

EXECUTIVE BRANCH

President
Elected to single four-year term by direct popular vote. Serves as head of state and government; commander-in-chief of armed forces. Vetoes bills; issues decrees; appoints and dismisses government officials without Parliament's approval; invokes "states of internal commotion" and suspends civil liberties; negotiates treaties.

Vice President
Elected on presidential ticket to four-year term.

Cabinet
Members appointed by president. Oversees government operations.

JUDICIAL BRANCH

Constitutional Court
Rules on constitutionality of laws. Composed of eight judges nominated by president, appointed to eight-year terms by Senate.

Supreme Court of Justice
Highest court of review and appeal. Tries impeachment charges. Judges appointed to eight-year terms by Supreme Council of the Judiciary.

Council of State
Rules on executive decrees and administrative matters. Judges appointed to eight-year terms by Supreme Council of the Judiciary.

Lower Courts

ARGENTINA

OFFICIAL NAME: REPUBLIC OF ARGENTINA

POPULATION: 37.5 MILLION
CAPITAL: BUENOS AIRES
AREA: 1,068,296 SQ. MILES (2,766,887 SQ. KM)
INDEPENDENCE: 1816
CONSTITUTION: 1853

ARGENTINA is derived from *argentum*, Latin for "silver".

RELIGION: Roman Catholic 90%, Protestant 2%, Jewish 2%, Other 6%

OFFICIAL LANGUAGE: Spanish

REGIONS OR PROVINCES: 23 provinces, 1 autonomous city

DEPENDENT TERRITORIES: None

MEDIA: No political censorship exists in the national media

Newspapers: There are 181 daily newspapers

TV: 44 stations, 29 independent

Radio: 122 stations: 37 state-controlled

SUFFRAGE: 18 years of age; universal

LEGAL SYSTEM: West European and US legal traditions; no ICJ jurisdiction

WORLD ORGANIZATIONS: AfDB, Australia Group, BCIE, BIS, CCC, ECLAC, FAO, G-6, G-15, G-19, G-24, G-77, IADB, IAEA, IBRD, ICAO, ICC, ICFTU, ICRM, IDA, IFAD, IFC, IFRCS, IHO, ILO, IMF, IMO, Interpol, IOC, IOM, ISO, ITU, LAES, LAIA, Mercosur, MINURSO, MIPONUH, MTCR, NSG, OAS, OPANAL, OPCW, PCA, RG, UN, UNCTAD, UNESCO, UNFICYP, UNHCR, UNIDO, UNIKOM, UNMEE, UNMIBH, UNMIK, UNMOP, UNMOVIC, UNTSO, UNU, UPU, WCL, WFTU, WHO, WIPO, WMO, WToO, WTrO, ZC

POLITICAL PARTIES: PJ—Justicialist Party (Peronists) Alliance—Alliance for Work, Justice and Education (Radical Civic Union-UCR and National Solidarity Front Alliance-FREPASO) ARI— Alternative for a Republic of Equals, AR—Action for the Republic

ETHNIC GROUPS:

Amerindian 1%
Mestizo 14%
Indo-European 85%

NATIONAL ECONOMICS

WORLD GNP RANKING: 17th

GNP PER CAPITA: $7,460

INFLATION: -0.9%

BALANCE OF PAYMENTS (BALANCE OF TRADE): -$8.9 billion

EXCHANGE RATES / U.S. DLR.: 0.9984-1 ARGENTINE PESOS

OFFICIAL CURRENCY: ARGENTINE PESO

GOVERNMENT SPENDING (% OF GDP)

DEFENSE 1.7%
EDUCATION 3.5%
HEALTH 2.4%

| | 0 | 5 | 10 | 15 |

NUMBER OF CONFLICTS OVER LAST 25 YEARS

	1	2-5	5+
Violent changes in government	○	○	○
Civil wars	●	○	○
International wars	○	○	○
Foreign intervention	○	○	○

- No compulsory national military service.
- Soldiers have been deployed in UN peacekeeping missions.
- Assists in defense of Mercosur.
- US provides military supplies.

NOTABLE WARS AND INSURGENCIES: "Dirty War" 1976-1983. Falklands War 1982

AFTER WINNING INDEPENDENCE from Spain in 1816, Argentina established a constitutional democracy with a representational political system. A military coup in 1930 marked the beginning of long periods of military authoritarian rule, including the presidency of Colonel Juan Domingo Perón, a charismatic labor leader who advocated an intermediary position between communism and capitalism. Perón ruled from 1943 until his overthrow in 1955, after which he went into exile. He briefly ruled again from 1973 until his death in 1974, when his wife "Isabelita" took over. A military junta seized control in 1976, beginning a regime infamous for severe human rights violations against its leftist opponents, many thousands of whom became known as the *desaparecidos,* or "disappeared." Following an unsuccessful attempt to seize sovereignty of the Falkland Islands (Islas Malvinas) from Britain in 1982, Argentina returned to democracy in 1983.

Two political parties have historically dominated: the leftist Justicialist, or Peronist, party and the Radical Civic Union (UCR). FREPASO, a four-party alliance, and the Alliance for Work, Justice, and Education—an alliance of UCR and FREPASO— have been successful in recent elections. The Roman Catholic Church and military have strong political influence. In 2001, following riots arising from a severe economic crisis, the president, vice-president, and Cabinet resigned. Several individuals assumed the presidency in the ensuing weeks, some for only hours. In January 2002, the Senate selected a president— the fifth in twelve days—and a tenuous peace was restored.

Although the country has three ostensibly separate branches of government, the presidency is much the strongest.

LEOPOLDO GALTIERI'S FUNERAL—JANUARY 13, 2003
Former dictator, General Galtieri, responsible for the 1982 Falklands War, as well as the disappearance of thousands of people during the "Dirty War", is buried in Buenos Aires.

Duties in the National Congress are split between the Chamber of Deputies, which can impeach members of the executive branch, and the Senate, which can authorize the president to declare a state of siege, approve nominations for public positions, and try those impeached by the Chamber of Deputies.

HOW THE GOVERNMENT WORKS

LEGISLATIVE BRANCH

Congreso Nacional
(National Congress)
Bicameral Parliament

Senado
Senate
Comprises 72 members elected to six-year terms by direct popular vote; three members per province and federal district. Confirms presidential appointments; tries impeachment charges.

Cámara de Diputados
(Chamber of Deputies)
Comprises 257 members directly elected to four-year terms by proportional representation. Initiates impeachment of president, vice-president, ministers, and Supreme Court justices.

Regional Governments
Twenty-three provinces administered by elected governors and legislatures.

EXECUTIVE BRANCH

President
Elected to four-year term by direct popular vote; limit of two consecutive terms. Serves as head of state and government; commander-in-chief of armed forces. Initiates and vetoes bills; enacts laws by decree and suspends civil liberties during emergencies.

Vice-president
Elected on presidential ticket to four-year term by direct popular vote; limit of two consecutive terms.

Cabinet
Members appointed by president. Oversees government operations; presided over by president.

JUDICIAL BRANCH

Supreme Court
Highest court of review and appeal; rules on constitutionality of laws. Composed of nine justices appointed for life by president, confirmed by Senate.

Federal Appeals Courts
Judges appointed for life by president on advice of Magistrates' Council

Courts of First Instance
Judges appointed for life by president on advice of Magistrates' Council

Provincial Courts

TANZANIA

OFFICIAL NAME: UNITED REPUBLIC OF TANZANIA

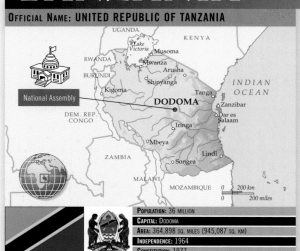

National Assembly

DODOMA

POPULATION: 36 MILLION
CAPITAL: DODOMA
AREA: 364,898 SQ. MILES (945,087 SQ. KM)
INDEPENDENCE: 1964
CONSTITUTION: 1977

TANZANIA is derived from "Tanganyika" and "Zanzibar," the two lands that merged to form the republic in 1964.

RELIGION: Muslim 33%, Christian 33%, Traditional beliefs 30%, Other 4%

OFFICIAL LANGUAGES: English and Swahili

REGIONS OR PROVINCES: 25 regions

DEPENDENT TERRITORIES: None

MEDIA: Partial political censorship exists in national media

NEWSPAPERS: There are 9 daily newspapers

TV: 3 independent services

RADIO: 5 services: 2 state-owned, 3 independent

SUFFRAGE: 18 years of age; universal

LEGAL SYSTEM: English common law; no ICJ jurisdiction

WORLD ORGANIZATIONS: ACP, AfDB, C, CCC, EADB, ECA, FAO, G-6, G-77, IAEA, IBRD, ICAO, ICC, ICFTU, ICRM, IDA, IFAD, IFC, IFRCS, ILO, IMF, IMO, Interpol, IOC, IOM, ISO, ITU, NAM, OAU, OPCW, SADC, UN, UNAMSIL, UNCTAD, UNESCO, UNHCR, UNIDO, UNMEE, UPU, WFTU, WHO, WIPO, WMO, WToO, WTrO

POLITICAL PARTIES: CCM—Revolutionary Party of Tanzania, CUF—Civic United Front, TLP—Tanzania Labor Party, Chadema—Party for Democracy and Progress

ETHNIC GROUPS

Other 1%

African (from over 120 Bantu groups) 99%

NATIONAL ECONOMICS

WORLD GNP RANKING: 88th

GNP PER CAPITA: $270

INFLATION: 5.9%

BALANCE OF PAYMENTS (BALANCE OF TRADE): -$517 million

EXCHANGE RATES / U.S. DLR.: 805-917 TANZANIAN SHILLINGS

OFFICIAL CURRENCY: TANZANIAN SHILLING

GOVERNMENT SPENDING (% OF GDP)

		0	5	10	15
DEFENSE 1.8%					
EDUCATION 2.1%					
HEALTH 1.3%					

NUMBER OF CONFLICTS OVER LAST 25 YEARS

	1	2-5	5+
Violent changes in government	○	○	○
Civil wars	○	○	○
International wars	●	○	○
Foreign intervention	○	○	○

- Compulsory national military service.
- Armed forces linked to ruling party.
- Large reservist force.
- Separatists pose a threat from Zanzibar.

NOTABLE WARS AND INSURGENCIES: Ugandan-Tanzanian War 1978-1979

RANKED BY THE United Nations as one of the poorest nations in the world, the United Republic of Tanzania represents the uneasy union in 1964 of Tanganyika and Zanzibar after the two countries obtained their independence from Great Britain. At the same time, their two main political parties—the Tanganyika African National Union TANU and the Africo-Shirazi Party ASP—merged to form the CCM under the chairmanship of Julius Nyurere, the beloved founding father of Tanzania. In the late 1980s and early 1990s, the government came under severe pressure owing to mismanagement of the public sector, corruption, an inefficient legal system and ambivalence toward human rights. In 1992 a new constitution replaced the socialist one-party government of Julius Nyerere with a multi-party democracy, ruled by a president elected by popular vote every five years.

The president presides over a cabinet composed of two vice-presidents and 27 ministers, a unicameral National Assembly, a judicial system headed by a national Court of Appeals, and a small military. Although the 275-member National Assembly can in theory override the president with a two-thirds majority vote, it actually functions more as a forum for debate on policies initiated by the president. The National Assembly has authority over mainland and foreign affairs, whereas the Zanzibar House of Representatives is responsible for legislation pertaining to the islands.

BURUNDI REFUGEES
Soldiers guard refugees as they listen to former South African President Nelson Mandela give a speech at the Ngara camp in Tanzania.

Despite the emergence of more than a dozen competing political parties, the CCM has remained dominant, with a large majority in the National Assembly and regional and local cells. Nyerere's socialist policy of ujaama, familyhood, remains the official ideology of the CCM and the force behind the cooperative rural development initiatives begun in the 1960s, demonstrating the strength of Nyerere's influence and popularity, which continued until his death in 1999. One of the government's most pressing concerns has been the integration of the governments of Tanzania and Zanzibar, the latter of which has been slow to relinquish its autonomy. Pressures for secession led to an outbreak of violence following the elections in 2000. Socio-economic reforms aimed at relieving poverty are the government's top priority.

HOW THE GOVERNMENT WORKS

LEGISLATIVE BRANCH
Bunge
(National Assembly)
Unicameral Parliament
Composed of 295 members who serve five-year terms: 181 elected by direct popular vote from mainland; 50 elected from Zanzibar; 48 appointed women; 10 appointed by president; five elected from Zanzibar House of Representatives; attorney general. Passes laws for mainland and foreign affairs; overrides vetoes by two-thirds majority vote.

Regional Governments
Islands of Zanzibar have an elected president, who serves a five-year term, and an 81-member House of Representatives (50 elected, 10 appointed by president, 15 reserved for women, 5 ex-officio, and attorney general), serving five terms.

EXECUTIVE BRANCH
President
Elected to five-year term by direct popular vote. Serves as head of state and government; commander-in-chief of armed forces. Signs and vetoes bills.

Two Vice-presidents
Appointed by president. First vice-president must be Zanzibar's president if Tanzania's president is from mainland. Second vice-president serves as prime minister and government's leader in parliament.

Cabinet
Composed of members of parliament, appointed by president. Oversees government operations.

JUDICIAL BRANCH
Court of Appeals
Highest court of review and appeal; rules on constitutionality of laws. Composed of five judges appointed by president.

High Court
Hears civil and criminal cases; holds regular sessions in all regions. Composed of 29 judges appointed by president.

District Courts

Magistrates' Courts

KENYA

OFFICIAL NAME: REPUBLIC OF KENYA

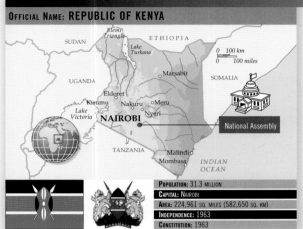

POPULATION:	31.3 MILLION
CAPITAL:	NAIROBI
AREA:	224,961 SQ. MILES (582,650 SQ. KM)
INDEPENDENCE:	1963
CONSTITUTION:	1963

KENYA takes its name from Mount Kenya, also called Kirinyaga or Kere-Nyaga, the "mountain of whiteness".

RELIGION: Christian 60%, Traditional beliefs 25%, Muslim 6%, Other 9%

OFFICIAL LANGUAGES: Kiswahili and English

REGIONS OR PROVINCES: 7 provinces and 1 area

DEPENDENT TERRITORIES: None

MEDIA: Total political censorship exists in national media

NEWSPAPERS: There are 6 daily newspapers

TV: 6 services: 1 state-controlled

RADIO: 9 services: 1 state-controlled

SUFFRAGE: 18 years of age; universal

LEGAL SYSTEM: Tribal and Shari'a (Islamic) law; English common law; accepts ICJ jurisdiction

WORLD ORGANIZATIONS: ACP, AfDB, C, CCC, EADB, ECA, FAO, G-15, G-77, IAEA, IBRD, ICAO, ICFTU, ICRM, IDA, IFAD, IFC, IFRCS, IGAD, ILO, IMF, IMO, Interpol, IOC, IOM, ISO, ITU, MINURSO, MONUC, NAM, OAU, OPCW, UN, UNAMSIL, UNCTAD, UNESCO, UNIDO, UNIKOM, UNMEE, UNMIBH, UNMIK, UNMOP, UNU, UPU, WHO, WIPO, WMO, WToO, WTrO

POLITICAL PARTIES: KANU—Kenya African National Union, DP—Democratic Party, NDP—National Development Party, FORD-K—Forum for the Restoration of Democracy-Kenya, SDP—Social Democratic Party, Saf—Safina, Others include FORF-People, Kenya Social Congress, Shirikisho, FORF-Asili

ETHNIC GROUPS

- Kamba 11%
- Kalenjin 11%
- Luo 13%
- Luhya 14%
- Kikuyu 21%
- Other 30%

NATIONAL ECONOMICS

WORLD GNP RANKING: 82nd

GNP PER CAPITA: $350

INFLATION: 5.9%

BALANCE OF PAYMENTS (BALANCE OF TRADE): -$238 million

EXCHANGE RATES / U.S. DLR.: 78.05.-78.60 KENYA SHILLINGS

OFFICIAL CURRENCY: KENYA SHILLING

GOVERNMENT SPENDING (% OF GDP)

- DEFENSE 2.9%
- EDUCATION 6.6%
- HEALTH 2.4%

0   5   10   15

NUMBER OF CONFLICTS OVER LAST 25 YEARS

	1	2-5	5+
Violent changes in government	○	○	○
Civil wars	●	○	○
International wars	○	○	○
Foreign intervention	○	○	○

- No compulsory national military service.
- Greatest threats are Somali civil war, Burundi and Democratic Republic of the Congo.
- Soldiers deployed in Rift Valley.
- UK and US provide military assistance.

NOTABLE WARS AND INSURGENCIES: Tribal violence in West 1992

THE REPUBLIC OF KENYA is poised for change. In December 2002, Mwai Kibaki of the newcomer National Rainbow Coalition (NARC) won the election, defeating the powerful KANU party and replacing Daniel arap Moi as president of Kenya. Moi had ruled since the death in 1978 of the liberation hero, Jomo Kenyatta, who had assumed the presidency when Kenya won its independence from Great Britain in 1963. Moi's tenure as president was marred by accusations of graft and corruption and outbreaks of ethnic violence. Under his leadership, the nation suffered a declining economy due to decreased tourism following the bombing of the US embassy in 1998, poverty exacerbated by drought, one of the highest population growth rates in the world, and the withdrawal of international aid due to allegations of human rights violations and election fraud. The country officially had only one party, the Kenyan African Nationalist Union (KANU) until 1991, when Moi acceded to pressures and allowed multiparty elections for the first time. Until the victory by NARC, the main political parties besides KANU had been the Forum for Restoration of Democracy-Kenya (FORD-Kenya), the Socialist Democratic Party, and the National Development Party. These and 14 other parties and pressure groups representing Kenya's diverse ethnic make-up organized to form NARC.

Although the country's government is fashioned after the British parliamentary system, the president and executive branch have much more authority. The president, who is chief of state and head of the government, appoints the cabinet members, civil servants, military officers and others. He has the power to dissolve Parliament, call elections, and declare war. Since 1988, all legislation has been drafted and introduced by the government.

Despite its troubled history, Kenya has strengths, including a strong tourist industry, and two important agricultural crops—coffee and tea. If Kibaki can reduce corruption in government and business, capitalize on Kenya's economic strengths, and recapture the trust and support of international leaders, Kenya may well emerge as one of the more stable and prosperous African states.

ISSUES AND CHALLENGES:

- There is a high mortality rate due to the AIDS epidemic, but Kenya also has one of the highest population growth rates in the world.

- A weak economy and infrastructure are a problem, but the government is seeking to overcome these with foreign investment incentives and privatization initiatives.

- Increasing crime and ethnic strife and land disputes that frequently erupt in violence hinder development.

- The country has a small ruling elite and strong class divisions.

- Accusations of human rights violations have resulted in a loss of aid from international sources.

HOW THE GOVERNMENT WORKS

LEGISLATIVE BRANCH

Bunge
(National Assembly)
Unicameral Parliament
Composed of 224 members who serve five-year terms: 210 elected by direct popular vote from single-member districts; 12 appointed by president; speaker and attorney-general serve as ex-officio members. May vote to dissolve itself.

Regional Governments
Sixty-nine rural districts, each headed by commissioner appointed by president.

EXECUTIVE BRANCH

President
Elected to five-year term by direct popular vote; must be parliament member. Serves as head of state and government; commander-in-chief of armed forces. May dissolve parliament at any time.

Vice-president
Parliament member appointed by president. Fills vacant presidency for up to 90 days while successor is elected.

Cabinet
Composed of parliament members appointed by president. Oversees government operations; introduces bills in parliament.

JUDICIAL BRANCH

Court of Appeals
Highest court of appeal in civil and criminal cases. Judges appointed and dismissed by president.

High Court
Hears civil and criminal cases; supervises lower courts. Composed of 30 judges appointed and dismissed by president.

Magistrates' Courts

Kadhi (Muslim) Courts

PERU

OFFICIAL NAME: REPUBLIC OF PERU

PACIFIC OCEAN
ECUADOR
COLOMBIA
Iquitos
Piura
Chiclayo
BRAZIL
Trujillo
Pucallpa
Chimbote
Huánuco
LIMA
Huancayo
Cusco
Ayacucho
Ica
Puno
BOLIVIA
Arequipa
Tacna
CHILE

Congress of the Republic

0 200 km
0 200 miles

POPULATION: 26.1 MILLION
CAPITAL: LIMA
AREA: 496,223 SQ. MILES (1,285,200 SQ. KM)
INDEPENDENCE: 1821
CONSTITUTION: 1993

PERU is derived from a Quechua Indian word that means "land of abundance", referring to the Inca wealth.

RELIGION: Roman Catholic 95%, Other 5%

OFFICIAL LANGUAGES: Spanish and Quechua

REGIONS OR PROVINCES: 24 departments and one constitutional province

DEPENDENT TERRITORIES: None

MEDIA: No political censorship exists in national media

NEWSPAPERS: There are 74 daily newspapers

TV: 11 services: one state-owned, ten independent

RADIO: Three state-owned, and many independent services

SUFFRAGE: 18 years of age; universal

LEGAL SYSTEM: Civil law; no ICJ jurisdiction

WORLD ORGANIZATIONS: ABEDA, APEC, CAN, CCC, ECLAC, FAO, G-15, G-19, G-24, G-77, IADB, IAEA, IBRD, ICAO, ICC, ICFTU, ICRM, IDA, IFAD, IFC, IFRCS, IHO, ILO, IMF, IMO, Interpol, IOC, IOM, ISO (correspondent), ITU, LAES, LAIA, MONUC, NAM, OAS, OPANAL, OPCW, PCA, RG, UN, UNCTAD, UNESCO, UNIDO, UNMEE, UPU, WCL, WFTU, WHO, WIPO, WMO, WToO, WTrO

POLITICAL PARTIES: PP—Peru Posible, APRA—American Popular Revolutionary Alliance, NU—National Unity, FIM—Independent Moralizing Front, UPP—Union for Peru, SP—Somos Peru

ETHNIC GROUPS:

- Other 2%
- White 12%
- Amerindian 54%
- Mistizo 32%

NATIONAL ECONOMICS

WORLD GNP RANKING: 47th

GNP PER CAPITA: $2,080

INFLATION: 3.8%

BALANCE OF PAYMENTS (BALANCE OF TRADE): -$1.63 billion

EXCHANGE RATES / U.S. DLR.: 3.527-3.444 NUEVO SOLES

OFFICIAL CURRENCY: NUEVO SOL

GOVERNMENT SPENDING (% OF GDP)

- ✈ DEFENSE 1.3%
- 📖 EDUCATION 3.2%
- ✚ HEALTH 2.4%

0   5   10   15

NUMBER OF CONFLICTS OVER LAST 25 YEARS

	1	2-5	5+
Violent changes in government	○	○	○
Civil wars	○	●	○
International wars	○	●	○
Foreign intervention	○	○	○

- Compulsory national military service.
- Border security poses the biggest defense issue.
- Terrorism during 2002 blamed on guerrillas and Montesinos sympathizers.

NOTABLE WARS AND INSURGENCIES: Shining Path rebellion 1980-2000. Ecuadorean-Peruvian border wars 1981 and 1995

ONCE THE SEAT OF POWER of the mighty Inca Empire, Peru has been in a constant state of emergency and attempted reform since 1980, when a sustained campaign of guerrilla violence began. Although it has technically been a democracy since independence from Spain in 1824, Peru has functioned under military, authoritarian rule for most of the past century.

The *Sendero Luminoso* (Shining Path), a Maoist group that takes its name from a phrase of Peruvian political thinker Mariategui, who called Marxism the "shining path to the future," has led a peasant guerrilla revolt in Peru, resulting in up to 12,000 deaths. It has earned a reputation as the most dangerous and violent terrorist group in the world. Unlike other Latin American guerrilla groups that have depended on funding from Cuba or other communist nations, the Shining Path is self-financed through contributions from middle-class radicals and crime, and a "war tax" on businesses and individuals.

Independent candidate Alberto Fujimori defied Peru's tradition of control by large parties and won the presidency in 1990. He promised fiscal austerity and an end to both the Shining Path and the Tupac Amaru Revolutionary Movement (MRTA)—the other leftist guerrilla group that has terrorized the country. Fujimori staged a "self coup" *(autogolpe)* in 1992, disbanding the bicameral Congress, reorganizing the judiciary, and increasing the power of the National Intelligence Service (secret police) and military. Although he acceded to demands for congressional elections, these were dominated by two pro-Fujimori parties, ensuring him full support.

ISSUES AND CHALLENGES:

- One of the most serious problems facing Peru has been the activities of guerrilla groups, such as the *Sendero Luminoso*, or Shining Path, whose aggressive indoctrination program and recruitment among young teens ensures a steady flow of members. The arrest and imprisonment of key leaders during Fujimori's presidency greatly reduced the number and virulence of attacks, especially in urban areas, but there are signs of re-emergence. Another group, the Tupac Amaru Revolutionary Movement (MRTA) depends heavily on kidnapping for ransom.

The new unicameral Congress of the Republic drafted a new constitution. It gives the president powers including the ability to enact legislation by decree; set tariffs and establish a budget unilaterally; direct foreign policy; grant pardons and commute sentences; and announce a state of emergency or state of siege. Presidentially appointed ministers are legally accountable for any presidential actions they countersign and for any violations of the constitution by the executive branch, but the president is not. However, Congress can dismiss the president with a simple majority. It did so in 2000, after Fujimori lost popularity due to slowed economic growth, increased authoritarianism, and allegations of widespread corruption.

HOW THE GOVERNMENT WORKS

LEGISLATIVE BRANCH

Congreso de la República
(Congress of the Republic)
Unicameral Parliament
Composed of 120 members elected to five-year terms by direct popular vote from 25 districts. Passes laws, ratifies treaties; authorizes government loans; approves budget; overrides presidential vetoes.

Regional Governments
193 provinces administered by elected mayors and councils.

EXECUTIVE BRANCH

President
Five-year term by direct popular vote; two consecutive term limit. Head of state and government; commander-in-chief of armed forces. Issues decrees; vetoes legislation; declares states of emergency; suspends civil liberties.

Two Vice-presidents
Elected by direct popular vote. First vice-president replaces president if he dies, resigns or is removed from office.

Prime minister
Appointed by president. Coordinates Council of Ministers.

Council of Ministers
Appointed by president. Approves presidential decrees and draft bills sent to Congress.

JUDICIAL BRANCH

Constitutional Tribunal
Rules on constitutionality of laws, individual rights, inter-governmental disputes. Composed of seven magistrates elected to five-year terms by two-thirds majority vote of Congress.

Supreme Court of Justice
Highest court of review and appeal. Composed of 13 judges appointed by National Council of the Judiciary.

Superior Courts
Hear lower-court appeals.

Courts of First Instance
Hear civil and criminal cases.

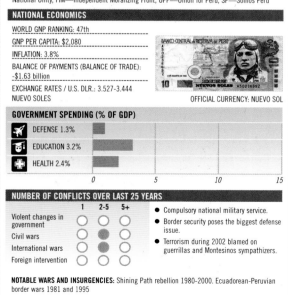

UZBEKISTAN

OFFICIAL NAME: REPUBLIC OF UZBEKISTAN

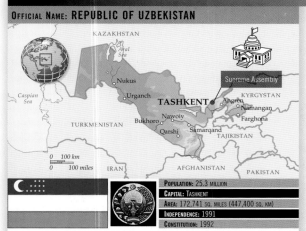

POPULATION: 25.3 MILLION
CAPITAL: TASHKENT
AREA: 172,741 SQ. MILES (447,400 SQ. KM)
INDEPENDENCE: 1991
CONSTITUTION: 1992

UZBEKISTAN is an Arabic word for "land of the Uzbeks". Uzbek comes from the Turkish meaning "genuine man".

RELIGION: Muslim 88% (mostly Sunnis), Eastern Orthodox 9%, Other 3%

OFFICIAL LANGUAGE: Uzbek

REGIONS OR PROVINCES: 12 provinces, one autonomous republic and one city

DEPENDENT TERRITORIES: None

MEDIA: Political censorship exists in national media

NEWSPAPERS: There are three daily newspapers

TV: Two state-controlled services

RADIO: One state-controlled service broadcasting in many languages

SUFFRAGE: 18 years of age; universal

LEGAL SYSTEM: Soviet legal traditions; no ICJ jurisdiction

WORLD ORGANIZATIONS: AsDB, CCC, CIS, EAPC, EBRD, ECE, ECO, ESCAP, FAO, IAEA, IBRD, ICAO, ICRM, IDA, IFC, IFRCS, ILO, IMF, Interpol, IOC, ISO, ITU, NAM, OIC, OPCW, OSCE, PFP, UN, UNCTAD, UNESCO, UNIDO, UPU, WFTU, WHO, WIPO, WMO, WToO, WTrO (observer)

POLITICAL PARTIES: Adolat (Justice) Social Democratic Party, MTP—Democratic National Rebirth Party (Milly Tiklanish), NDP—People's Democratic Party (formerly Communist Party), Self-Sacrificers Party or Fidokorlar National Democratic Party

ETHNIC GROUPS:

- Tajik 5%
- Kazakh 4%
- Russian 8%
- Other 12%
- Uzbek 71%

NATIONAL ECONOMICS

WORLD GNP RANKING: 89th

GNP PER CAPITA: $360

INFLATION: 40.0%

BALANCE OF PAYMENTS (BALANCE OF TRADE): $184 million

EXCHANGE RATES / U.S. DLR.: 322.8–686.9 SOM

OFFICIAL CURRENCY: SOM

GOVERNMENT SPENDING (% OF GDP)

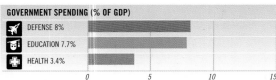

- DEFENSE 8%
- EDUCATION 7.7%
- HEALTH 3.4%

0   5   10   15

NUMBER OF CONFLICTS OVER LAST 25 YEARS

	1	2-5	5+
Violent changes in government	○	○	○
Civil wars	○	○	○
International wars	○	○	○
Foreign intervention	●	○	○

- Compulsory national military service.
- Restructuring of military underway.
- Border is mined to prevent invasion.
- Threats from Islamic militants.
- Accepts nuclear Non-Proliferation Treaty.
- US Defense Threat Reduction Agency operations in west.

NOTABLE WARS AND INSURGENCIES: Islamist militancy 2000

UZBEKISTAN CORRESPONDS ROUGHLY to the ancient Persian province of Sogdiana, conquered in the 4th century B.C. by Alexander the Great. Modern Uzbekistan came into existence as a Soviet republic in 1924, and for several decades the Soviets reaped the economic advantages of its production of cotton and natural resources. It was one of the poorest republics in the Soviet Union. Today it is Central Asia's most populous country, led since 1990 by President Islam Karimov, who came to power a year before Uzbekistan's independence from the Soviet Union. Karimov's incumbency paved the way for his election after independence, with 85 percent of the vote. He remains the country's primary political figure. The 1992 constitution was amended to extend his term of office, and in 2002 the unicameral Supreme Assembly decided to keep Karimov in power for another five years, and also decided to introduce a second legislative chamber. This second chamber could prove to be a vehicle for starting a movement toward democracy.

Uzbekistan's constitution calls for a presidential democracy, with power divided among the three branches of government. However, little has really changed since the Soviet era. International observers believe that Karimov has near-absolute authority and runs the country with scant regard for the other branches. Neither elections nor constitutional referenda have met basic international democratic standards. Karimov enjoys minimal overt opposition, retaining control over the internal police and the military, repressing dissent—such as the 1992 student riots—and requiring political parties to receive government approval before they can participate in politics. Several opposition parties persecuted in the 1990s, and most opposition is now underground. Since bomb attacks by Islamic fundamentalists in 1999, the government has dealt harshly with suspected Islamic extremists, and in 2005 its brutal treatment of the residents of Andijan caused international outcry and stirred wider unrest.

NEGLECT AND DISREPAIR
The decorative ceramic tiles of the Shah-I-Zinda Mosque in Samarqand, Uzbekistan—an Islamic stronghold—show years of neglect.

HOW THE GOVERNMENT WORKS

LEGISLATIVE BRANCH
Oliry Majlis
(Supreme Assembly)
Unicameral Parliament
Composed of 250 members elected to five-year terms by direct popular vote from single-member districts. Meets twice annually. Initiates and passes legislation; confirms presidential appointees.

Regional Governments
Twelve provinces administered by elected councils and governors appointed by president.

EXECUTIVE BRANCH
President
Elected to seven-year term by direct popular vote. Serves as head of state. Initiates and approves legislation; sets government policy; appoints top national and regional officials.

Prime Minister
Appointed by the president. Serves as head of government.

Council of Ministers
Appointed by the president. Chaired by prime minister; oversees government operations.

JUDICIAL BRANCH
Supreme Court
Highest court of review and appeal. Rules on constitutionality of laws. Composed of judges nominated by president and confirmed by parliament.

Regional Courts
Economic Court

VENEZUELA

OFFICIAL NAME: BOLIVARIAN REPUBLIC OF VENEZUELA

POPULATION: 24.6 MILLION	
CAPITAL: CARACAS	
AREA: 352,143 SQ. MILES (912,050 SQ. KM)	
INDEPENDENCE: 1811	
CONSTITUTION: 1999	

VENEZUELA was named "little Venice" by the Europeans who discovered it, after seeing the natives' stilt houses.

RELIGION: Roman Catholic 89%, Protestant and other 11%

OFFICIAL LANGUAGE: Spanish

REGIONS OR PROVINCES: 23 states, 1 federal district, and 1 federal dependency

DEPENDENT TERRITORIES: None

MEDIA: Partial political censorship exists in national media

NEWSPAPERS: There are 86 daily newspapers

TV: 8 services: 2 state-owned, 6 independent

RADIO: 1 state-owned, 500 independent stations

SUFFRAGE: 18 years of age; universal

LEGAL SYSTEM: Civil law; no ICJ jurisdiction

WORLD ORGANIZATIONS: CAN, Caricom (observer), CCC, CDB, ECLAC, FAO, G-3, G-15, G-19, G-24, G-77, IADB, IAEA, IBRD, ICAO, ICC, ICFTU, ICRM, IFAD, IFC, IFRCS, IHO, ILO, IMF, IMO, Interpol, IOC, IOM, ISO, ITU, LAES, LAIA, NAM, OAS, OPANAL, OPCW, OPEC, PCA, RG, UN, UNCTAD, UNESCO, UNHCR, UNIDO, UNIKOM, UNU, UPU, WCL, WFTU, WHO, WIPO, WMO, WToO, WTrO

POLITICAL PARTIES: MVR—Fifth Republic Movement, AD—Democratic Action, PRVZL—Project Venezuela, MAS—Movement toward Socialism, COPE!—Social Christian Party, PP—Patriotic Front composed of the MVR, the MAS and some smaller parties

ETHNIC GROUPS:

- Amerindian 2%
- Black 9%
- White 20%
- Mestizo 69%

NATIONAL ECONOMICS

WORLD GNP RANKING: 36th

GNP PER CAPITA: $4,310

INFLATION: 16.2%

BALANCE OF PAYMENTS (BALANCE OF TRADE): $13.2 billion

EXCHANGE RATES / U.S. DLR.: 699.8-757.5 BOLIVARES

OFFICIAL CURRENCY: BOLIVAR

GOVERNMENT SPENDING (% OF GDP)

- ✈ DEFENSE 1.5%
- 🎓 EDUCATION 5.2%
- ✚ HEALTH 2.6%

0   5   10   15

NUMBER OF CONFLICTS OVER LAST 25 YEARS

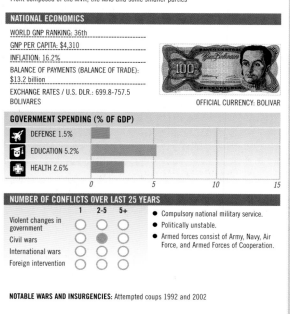

	1	2-5	5+
Violent changes in government	○	○	○
Civil wars	○	●	○
International wars	○	○	○
Foreign intervention	○	○	○

- Compulsory national military service.
- Politically unstable.
- Armed forces consist of Army, Navy, Air Force, and Armed Forces of Cooperation.

NOTABLE WARS AND INSURGENCIES: Attempted coups 1992 and 2002

VENEZUELA HAS STRUGGLED OVER THE PAST DECADE to maintain itself as a democracy in the face of political upheaval. Its first became a democracy in 1958 after a civilian-military coup and the signing of the Pact of Punto Fijo. This set up a presidential system founded on compromise and conciliation, and was followed in 1961 by a constitution that established mechanisms for governing in ways acceptable to all major political interests. The executive branch, for example, was to negotiate with opposition parties, business leaders, labor, the military, and others before introducing bills into Congress, where they were to be promptly approved.

Venezuela today has a multiparty system—as many as seven parties have held a significant number of congressional seats.

The president, as the national executive and head of state, has the right to restrict or suspend constitutional guarantees, but only with the approval of the National Assembly—a unicameral legislature, which in 2000 replaced the former bicameral parliament in accordance with the new consitution of 1999. There is no vice-president. The judicial system is undergoing reforms aimed at boosting efficiency and rooting out corruption. Reforms include instituting jury trials, allowing oral presentations, and appointing judges with less regard for party affiliation.

PROTESTS—DECEMBER 4, 2002
Many thousands across Venezuela, some wearing masks showing Hugo Chávez with donkey ears, marched in protest against the Chávez government, calling for a general strike and the ousting of the leftist government.

Oil-rich Venezuela has been racked by social inequality and political turmoil. In 1992, loyalist troops put down two coup attempts by mid-level military officers. In 1993, President Carlos Andrés Pérez was removed on corruption charges, and the following year civil liberties were temporarily suspended. In 1998, Hugo Chávez, a 1992 coup plotter, was elected president. A military coup replaced him for one day in April 2002, but foreign and domestic protests reinstalled him. However, his subsequent populist policies and increasingly authoritarian rule have touched off violent protests.

HOW THE GOVERNMENT WORKS

LEGISLATIVE BRANCH
Asamblea Nacional
(National Assembly)
Unicameral Parliament
Composed of 165 members elected to five-year terms by direct popular vote and proportional representation; three-term limit; three seats reserved for indigenous peoples.

Regional Governments
Twenty-three states administered by elected governors and assemblies.

EXECUTIVE BRANCH
President,
Elected to six-year term by direct popular vote, two consecutive term limit. Serves as head of state. Initiates legislation; may return bills to Parliament.

Vice-president
Appointed by president.

Cabinet
Members appointed by president with consent of Parliament. Oversees government operations.

JUDICIAL BRANCH
Supreme Tribunal of Justice,
Highest court of review and appeal; rules on constitutionality of laws. Composed of justices appointed to twelve-year terms by Parliament.

District Courts
Courts of First Instance
Municipal Courts

GHANA

OFFICIAL NAME: REPUBLIC OF GHANA

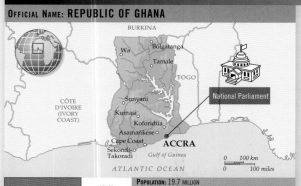

POPULATION: 19.7 MILLION	
CAPITAL: ACCRA	
AREA: 92,100 SQ. MILES (238,540 SQ. KM)	
INDEPENDENCE: 1957	
CONSTITUTION: 1992	

GHANA is named after the ancient African kingdom of Ghana that flourished in the 13th century, 500 miles (800 km) northwest of present-day Ghana.

RELIGION: Christian 43%, Traditional beliefs 38%, Muslim 11%, Other 8%

OFFICIAL LANGUAGE: English

REGIONS OR PROVINCES: 10 regions

DEPENDENT TERRITORIES: None

MEDIA: No political censorship exists in national media

NEWSPAPERS: There are 2 daily newspapers

TV: 1 state-controlled service

RADIO: 1 state-controlled service

SUFFRAGE: 18 years of age; universal

LEGAL SYSTEM: Customary and English common law; no ICJ jurisdiction

WORLD ORGANIZATIONS: ABEDA, ACP, AfDB, C, CCC, ECA, ECOWAS, FAO, G-24, G-77, IAEA, IBRD, ICAO, ICC, ICFTU, ICRM, IDA, IFAD, IFC, IFRCS, ILO, IMF, IMO, Interpol, IOC, IOM (observer), ISO, ITU, MINURSO, MONUC, NAM, OAS (observer), OAU, OPCW, UN, UNAMSIL, UNCTAD, UNESCO, UNIDO, UNIFIL, UNIKOM, UNITAR, UNMEE, UNMIBH, UNMIK, UNMOP, UNMOT, UNU, UPU, WCL, WFTU, WHO, WIPO, WMO, WToO, WTrO

POLITICAL PARTIES: NPP—New Patriotic Party, NDC—National Democratic Congress, Ind—Independents, PNC—People's National Convention, PCP—People's Convention Party

ETHNIC GROUPS:

European and other 1.5%

African (major tribes; Akan, Moshi-Dagomba, Ewe, Ga, Gurma, and Yoruba) 98.5%

NATIONAL ECONOMICS

WORLD GNP RANKING: 101st

GNP PER CAPITA: $340

INFLATION: 25.2%

BALANCE OF PAYMENTS (BALANCE OF TRADE): -$413 million

EXCHANGE RATES / U.S. DLR.: 7275-7400 CEDIS

OFFICIAL CURRENCY: CEDI

GOVERNMENT SPENDING (% OF GDP)

✈	DEFENSE	0.9%
🎓	EDUCATION	4%
✚	HEALTH	1.7%

0   5   10   15

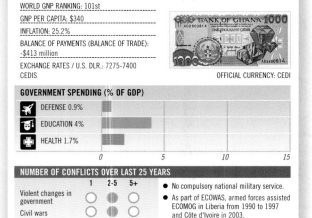

NUMBER OF CONFLICTS OVER LAST 25 YEARS

	1	2-5	5+
Violent changes in government	○	●	○
Civil wars	○	●	○
International wars	○	○	○
Foreign intervention	○	○	○

- No compulsory national military service.
- As part of ECOWAS, armed forces assisted ECOMOG in Liberia from 1990 to 1997 and Côte d'Ivoire in 2003.
- Troops participate in UN peacekeeping missions in Afghanistan, Lebanon, Pakistan and Rwanda.
- Military aid is provided by the West.

NOTABLE WARS AND INSURGENCIES: Military coups 1979 (Acheampong ousted) and 1981 (Limann ousted). Ethnic violence in the north

GHANA ACHIEVED INDEPENDENCE from Great Britain in 1957 under Kwame Nkrumah. Independence brought together two lands as one nation: the British-administered portion of Togoland, and the British Gold Coast colony. Political history since self-rule began has proved less united, featuring sporadic democratic government punctuated by several military coups and regimes.

Following a 1964 constitutional referendum Ghana became a single-party state, suffering military coups in 1966, 1972, 1979 and again in 1981—after which opposition parties were banned, and the constitution suspended. Devaluation of the currency and the government's inability to prevent spiralling inflation provoked growing public discontent that ultimately led to another military coup in 1972 under Colonel I.K. Acheampong. Promising reform, Acheampong began a program of nationalization. Unsuccessful in his goals, he was ousted in 1979 by yet another coup. The present Fourth Republic government began in 1992, when democracy was reinstated under Jerry Rawlings after a decade of military rule. Rawlings won the presidency again in 1996, but was constitutionally prevented from being re-elected in 2000.

Although the political system includes a judicial branch, only the legislature and the executive branches operate according to formal guidelines. Checks and balances exist to prevent either branch from assuming absolute authority. All legislation must receive final approval from both the president and Parliament before becoming law. Furthermore, while the constitution of 1992 provides the president with two separate advisory councils—the Council of State and the National Security Council—each of the president's appointments to the councils must be approved by Parliament. The relationship of the judiciary to the other branches of government is precarious. Ghana has a formal judicial system. Its independence, however, is severely curtailed by the government, which often resorts to ad hoc tribunals to administer justice swiftly rather than permit lengthy legal proceedings.

Like many of its neighbors in West Africa, Ghana has an extremely diverse population. While tensions are rare, ethnicity does largely determine voter allegiance and electoral patterns throughout the country.

ISSUES AND CHALLENGES:

- The stability of democracy in Ghana traditionally reflects the state of the economy. Recent economic downturns may threaten the Fourth Republic.

- Ghana is both a producer of illegal drugs (cannabis) for the world market and a transit hub for narcotics intended for the Western market.

- Foreign investment generally focuses only on gold mining.

- The mining, farming, and timber industries have created an ecological and environmental disaster, destroying 70 percent of the forests.

HOW THE GOVERNMENT WORKS

LEGISLATIVE BRANCH

National Parliament
Unicameral Parliament
Composed of 200 members elected to four-year terms by direct popular vote. Meets at least once annually. Passes laws; approves budget; amends constitution; ratifies treaties; confirms presidential appointments; overrides vetoes.

Regional Governments
Ten regions administered by coordinating councils.

EXECUTIVE BRANCH

President
Elected to four-year term by direct popular vote. Serves as head of state and government; commander-in-chief of armed forces. Appoints top government officials; grants pardons; negotiate treaties; vetoes bills.

Vice-president
Elected to four-year term by direct popular vote.

Council of Ministers
Composed of president, vice-president and between ten and 19 ministers of state. Sets government policy; presided over by president.

JUDICIAL BRANCH

Supreme Court
Highest court of review and appeal. Composed of chief justice and nine other judges appointed to serve to age 70 by president, confirmed by Parliament.

Court of Appeal
Hears lower-court appeals. Composed of ten judges appointed to serve to age 70 by president on advice of Judicial Council.

High Court
Hears civil and criminal cases. Composed of 20 judges appointed to serve to age 65 by president on advice of Judicial Council.

Regional Tribunals

SRI LANKA

OFFICIAL NAME: **DEMOCRATIC SOCIALIST REPUBLIC OF SRI LANKA**

POPULATION:	19.1 MILLION
CAPITAL:	COLOMBO
AREA:	25,332 SQ. MILES (65,610 SQ. KM)
INDEPENDENCE:	1948
CONSTITUTION:	1978

SRI LANKA is translated as "sri" meaning "venerable" and "lanka" meaning "island".

RELIGION: Buddhist 70%, Hindu 15%, Christian 8%, Muslim 7%

OFFICIAL LANGUAGES: Sinhala, Tamil, and English

REGIONS OR PROVINCES: 9 provinces

DEPENDENT TERRITORIES: None

MEDIA: Partial political censorship exists in national media

Newspapers: There are 13 daily newspapers

TV: 4 independent services

Radio: 5 services: 1 state-owned, 4 independent

SUFFRAGE: 18 years of age; universal

LEGAL SYSTEM: Customary and Shari'a (Islamic) law; English common law; Roman-Dutch and Sinhalese legal traditions; no ICJ jurisdiction

WORLD ORGANIZATIONS: AsDB, C, CCC, CP, ESCAP, FAO, G-15, G-24, G-77, IAEA, IBRD, ICAO, ICC, ICFTU, ICRM, IDA, IFAD, IFC, IFRCS, IHO, ILO, IMF, IMO, Interpol, IOC, IOM, ISO, ITU, NAM, OAS (observer), OPCW, PCA, SAARC, UN, UNCTAD, UNESCO, UNIDO, UNU, UPU, WCL, WFTU, WHO, WIPO, WMO, WToO, WTrO

POLITICAL PARTIES: UNP—United National Party, PA—People's Alliance dominated by the Sri Lanka Freedom Party-SLFP, JVP—People's Liberation Front, TULF—Tamil United Liberation Front, SLMC—Sri Lanka Muslim Congress, EPDP—Eelam People's Democratic Party, DPLF—Democratic People's Liberation Front

ETHNIC GROUPS:

Burghur, Malay, and Vedda 1%

Moor 7%

Tamil 18%

Sinhalese 74%

NATIONAL ECONOMICS

WORLD GNP RANKING: 73rd

GNP PER CAPITA: $850

INFLATION: 6.2%

BALANCE OF PAYMENTS (BALANCE OF TRADE): -$1.04 billion

EXCHANGE RATES / U.S. DLR.: 82.70-93.16 SRI LANKA RUPEES

OFFICIAL CURRENCY: SRI LANKA RUPEE

GOVERNMENT SPENDING (% OF GDP)

- ✈ DEFENSE 5.3%
- 🎓 EDUCATION 3.4%
- ✚ HEALTH 1.7%

0   5   10   15

NUMBER OF CONFLICTS OVER LAST 25 YEARS

	1	2-5	5+
Violent changes in government		●	○
Civil wars	●	○	○
International wars	○	○	○
Foreign intervention	●	○	○

- ● No compulsory national military service.
- ● Recruitment drive and modernization of armed forces in process.
- ● Tamil Tigers are a reduced threat to peace following cease-fire.

NOTABLE WARS AND INSURGENCIES: Civil war against Tamil Tiger rebels 1983-2002

FORMERLY A BRITISH COLONIAL POSSESSION CALLED CEYLON, the island of Sri Lanka gained independence in 1948. It changed its name officially to Sri Lanka in 1972, but the political structure of the current government comes from the Second Republican constitution of 1978, which divided the colonial-style government into executive, legislative, and judicial branches.

Sri Lanka is a presidential democracy, so the majority of power is concentrated in the executive branch. The president is elected by the people to a six-year term, and has considerable veto power over the legislature as well as the final word on most matters of national policy. Aside from the power vested in the presidency, the executive branch also administers local government throughout the island's 257 regional councils.

The seat of the legislative branch rests in the National State Assembly, or Jathika Rajya Shabhawa, whose 225 members are also elected by the people to six-year terms. While the Assembly primarily enacts laws and controls public finances, it is also important to the executive branch, as the president appoints the prime minister and cabinet members from its ranks.

The complicated judicial branch is an amalgam of many legal systems. The primary courts, magistrates' courts, and district courts regulate the judicial system at local levels, while the High Courts, the Court of Appeal, and the Supreme Court administer justice and protect the rights of citizens nationally.

TAMIL TIGERS

Members of the Liberation Tigers of Tamil Eelam armed with rocket-propelled grenades demonstrate their strength in the north of the island.

Since 1983, ethnic tensions between the government and the Tamil minority have erupted into a civil war that has claimed nearly 60,000 lives. The main opposition to the government comes from the Liberation Tigers of Tamil Eelam (LTTE), which fights for an independent Tamil state. In December 2002, the government and Tamil minority agreed to a power-sharing arrangement based on a federal system of government.

HOW THE GOVERNMENT WORKS

LEGISLATIVE BRANCH
Jathika Rajya Shabhawa
(National State Assembly)
Unicameral Parliament
Composed of 225 members elected to six-year terms by direct popular vote. Enacts laws; controls public finances; removes prime minister and cabinet with no-confidence vote; removes president with two-thirds majority vote and Supreme Court consent.

Regional Governments
Nine provinces administered by governors appointed by president and elected local councils.

EXECUTIVE BRANCH
President
Elected to six-year term by direct popular vote. Serves as head of state and government; commander-in-chief of armed forces. Presides over cabinet; summons, suspends and dissolves parliament; calls for referenda; declares states of emergency.

Prime Minister
Leader of parliament's majority party or coalition; appointed by president.

Cabinet
Composed of parliament members; appointed by president, approved by parliament. Oversees government operations.

JUDICIAL BRANCH
Supreme Court
Highest court of appeal for civil and criminal cases; Composed of chief justice and 6 to 10 judges appointed to serve to age 65 by president.

Court of Appeal
Hears lower-court appeals. President and 6 to 11 judges appointed to serve to age 63 by president.

High Courts
Hear serious crimes, civil commercial cases, magistrates' and small-claims appeals. Judges appointed by president.

District Courts
Hear first-instance civil cases; serve as family courts.

Magistrates' Courts

Small Claims Courts

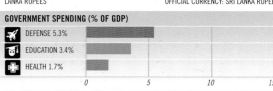

MADAGASCAR

OFFICIAL NAME: REPUBLIC OF MADAGASCAR

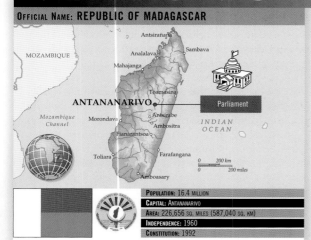

ONCE A POPULAR HAUNT OF PIRATES, Madagascar has been valued for its strategic location in the Indian Ocean since Arabs established trading posts there in the seventh century. British influence began in 1817, with a treaty between the British governor of Mauritius and the Malagasy ruler that extended British military and financial assistance to Madagascar. In 1885, Britain allowed France to make the country a protectorate in exchange for control over part of what is now Tanzania. With military force, the French abolished the Malagasy monarchy and took absolute control of Madagascar in 1896. During World War II, Madagascar was controlled by the Vichy government, then the British, before being returned to the French. Nationalist uprisings that began in the late 1940s culminated in the proclamation of the Republic of Madagascar, an autonomous state within the French community, in 1958. After a two-year period of provisional government, full independence was achieved.

From 1975 until recent times, one man has dominated Madagascan politics—Didier Ratsiraka. His reign lasted until 1993 when he was ousted in elections, but he regained his position as president in 1997. Defeated again in 2001, this time by the opposition leader, Ravalomanana, Ratsiraka began a power struggle that was finally settled in June of 2002 with Ravalomanana taking the presidency.

The constitution mandates three separate and independent branches of government. The president holds the reins of the executive branch, selecting the prime minister and the Council of Ministers—both are responsible to the president. The 1998 constitution provides for a bicameral parliament composed of the National Assembly and the Senate. The National Assembly and the prime minister share the power to initiate legislation. The National Assembly may censure the prime minister and Council of Ministers, requiring their resignations, and impeach the president. The president may dissolve the National Assembly. The Malagasy Senate, comprising both elected and appointed members, represents Madagascar's six autonomous provinces and fulfills an advisory function. Madagascar's legal system is a mix of French civil law and traditional Malagasy law.

ISSUES AND CHALLENGES:

- Chronic malnutrition, malaria infections of epidemic proportions, and three percent annual population growth tax the underfunded health facilities provided free of charge by the state.

- Madagascar lacks self-sufficiency in production of rice, a food staple.

- Long-standing tensions exist between the mostly Catholic masses and the largely Protestant Merina elite.

- Vanilla exports are threatened by less expensive sources.

- An illicit producer of cannabis—used mostly for domestic consumption—Madagascar is also a transshipment point for heroin.

POPULATION: 16.4 MILLION
CAPITAL: ANTANANARIVO
AREA: 226,656 SQ. MILES (587,040 SQ. KM)
INDEPENDENCE: 1960
CONSTITUTION: 1992

MADAGASCAR may owe its name to Marco Polo who called it Madeigascar or Mogelasio in his writings, probably confusing it with Mogadishu in present day Somalia.

RELIGION: Traditional beliefs 52%, Christian (mainly Roman Catholic) 41%, Muslim 7%

OFFICIAL LANGUAGE: French and Malagasy

REGIONS OR PROVINCES: 6 provinces

DEPENDENT TERRITORIES: None

MEDIA: Partial political censorship

Newspapers: There are 5 daily newspapers

TV: 1 state-owned service

RADIO: 1 state-owned service, many independent

SUFFRAGE: 18 years of age; universal

LEGAL SYSTEM: Local traditions and French law; accepts ICJ jurisdiction

WORLD ORGANIZATIONS: ACCT, ACP, AfDB, CCC, ECA, FAO, G-77, IAEA, IBRD, ICAO, ICFTU, ICRM, IDA, IFAD, IFC, IFRCS, ILO, IMF, IMO, InOC, Interpol, IOC, IOM, ISO (correspondent), ITU, NAM, OAU, UN, UNCTAD, UNESCO, UNHCR, UNIDO, UPU, WCL, WFTU, WHO, WIPO, WMO, WToO, WTrO

POLITICAL PARTIES: Arema—Association for the Rebirth of Madagascar, Ind—Independents, L-F—Leader-Torch (Fanilo), AVI—"People are Judged by the work they do," RPSD—Rally for Socialism and Democracy, MFM—Militant Party for the Development of Madagascar

ETHNIC GROUPS:

Betsileo 12%
Other 1%
Betsimisaraka 15%
Other Malay 46%
Merina 26%

NATIONAL ECONOMICS

WORLD GNP RANKING: 120th

GNP PER CAPITA: $250

INFLATION: 12%

BALANCE OF PAYMENTS (BALANCE OF TRADE): -$260 million

EXCHANGE RATES / U.S. DLR.: 6220-6370 MALAGASY FRANCS

OFFICIAL CURRENCY: MALAGASY FRANC

GOVERNMENT SPENDING (% OF GDP)

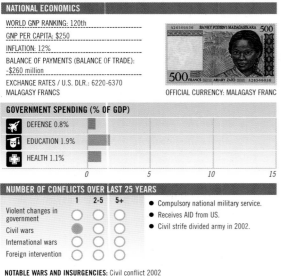

- DEFENSE 0.8%
- EDUCATION 1.9%
- HEALTH 1.1%

0   5   10   15

NUMBER OF CONFLICTS OVER LAST 25 YEARS

	1	2-5	5+
Violent changes in government	○	○	○
Civil wars	●	○	○
International wars	○	○	○
Foreign intervention	○	○	○

- Compulsory national military service.
- Receives AID from US.
- Civil strife divided army in 2002.

NOTABLE WARS AND INSURGENCIES: Civil conflict 2002

HOW THE GOVERNMENT WORKS

LEGISLATIVE BRANCH

Parliament
Bicameral

Assemblée Nationale
(National Assembly)
Composed of 150 members elected to five-year terms by direct popular vote. Meets twice annually. Adopts budget; removes prime minister and Council of Ministers with no-confidence vote; impeaches president.

Senate
Composed of 90 members who serve six-year terms: 60 elected by regional assemblies; 30 appointed by president.

Regional Governments
Six provinces administered by elected governors and legislative councils.

EXECUTIVE BRANCH

President
Elected to five-year term by direct popular vote; two-term limit. Serves as head of state. Introduces bills; promulgates laws; dissolves parliament; presides over Council of Ministers; declares states of emergency.

Prime Minister
Appointed by president, approved by parliament. Serves as head of government. Initiates and executes laws; appoints civil and military officials.

Council of Ministers
Appointed by prime minister. Oversees government operations; answers to president.

JUDICIAL BRANCH

Constitutional Court
Rules on constitutionality of laws; decides election and inter-governmental disputes. Composed of 9 judges appointed to single six-year terms: 3 by president on advice of Council of Ministers; 3 by Superior Council of Magistrates; 2 by National Assembly; 1 by Senate

Supreme Court
Highest court of review and appeal; supervises judiciary and lower courts.

High Court of Justice
Hears charges against president and high national and state officials.

Courts of Appeal

Local Courts

KAZAKHSTAN

OFFICIAL NAME: REPUBLIC OF KAZAKHSTAN

POPULATION: 16.1 MILLION
CAPITAL: ASTANA
AREA: 1,049,150 SQ. MILES (2,717,300 SQ. KM)
INDEPENDENCE: 1991
CONSTITUTION: 1993

KAZAKHSTAN comes from the Arabic word for "land of the Kazakhs". Kazakh comes from the Turkic meaning "someone independent and free".

RELIGION: Muslim (mainly Sunni) 50%, Russian Orthodox 13%, Protestant 1%, Other 36%,

OFFICIAL LANGUAGE: Kazakh

REGIONS OR PROVINCES: 14 provinces and 3 cities

DEPENDENT TERRITORIES: None

MEDIA: Total political censorship exists in national media

Newspapers: There are 5 principal daily newspapers and over 400 others registered

TV: 3 services: 1 state-owned, 2 independent

Radio: 1 state-owned service, several private stations

SUFFRAGE: 18 years of age; universal

LEGAL SYSTEM: Civil law; no ICJ jurisdiction

WORLD ORGANIZATIONS: AsDB, CCC, CIS, EAPC, EBRD, ECE, ECO, ESCAP, FAO, IAEA, IBRD, ICAO, IDA, IDB, IFAD, IFC, IFRCS (associate), ILO, IMF, IMO, Interpol, IOC, IOM (observer), ISO, ITU, NAM (observer), OAS (observer), OIC, OPCW, OSCE, PFP, UN, UNCTAD, UNESCO, UNIDO, UPU, WCL, WFTU, WHO, WIPO, WMO, WToO, WTrO (observer)

POLITICAL PARTIES: Otan—Fatherland Republic Party of Kazakhstan, CPK—Civil Party of Kazakhstan, AP—Agrarian Party, CP—Communist Party of Kazakhstan

ETHNIC GROUPS:
- German 2%
- Ukrainian 4%
- Tatar 2%
- Other 9%
- Russian 30%
- Kazakh 53%

NATIONAL ECONOMICS

WORLD GNP RANKING: 68th

GNP PER CAPITA: $1,260

INFLATION: 13.2%

BALANCE OF PAYMENTS (BALANCE OF TRADE): $1.07bn

EXCHANGE RATES / U.S. DLR.: 145.56-150.90 TENGE

OFFICIAL CURRENCY: TENGE

GOVERNMENT SPENDING (% OF GDP)

- DEFENSE 2%
- EDUCATION 4.4%
- HEALTH 2.7%

(scale: 0, 5, 10, 15)

NUMBER OF CONFLICTS OVER LAST 25 YEARS

	1	2-5	5+
Violent changes in government	○	○	○
Civil wars	○	○	○
International wars	○	○	○
Foreign intervention	○	○	○

- Plans to phase out compulsory national military service by 2004.
- Ratified START-I nuclear reduction treaty.
- Accepts nuclear Non-Proliferation Treaty.
- The US supplied aid in return for destruction of nuclear weapons.

NOTABLE WARS AND INSURGENCIES: None

COLONIZED BY CZARIST RUSSIA in the 1800s and later ruled as part of the Soviet Union, Kazakhstan was the last of the former communist republics to declare independence at the end of the Cold War. Today, Kazakhstan rules itself with a democratic government headed by a strong presidency.

Nomadic tribes occupied Kazakhstan for centuries before the Mongols invaded in the 13th century and established administrative districts to govern the territory. Among the nomadic peoples, the Kazakhs emerged as the dominant clan and developed a common culture and language. Later, the Russian Empire took control through treaties and land seizures, but uprisings by the Kazakhs persisted until Czarist rule collapsed with the Bolshevik Revolution. Fighting between pro- and anti-Bolshevik factions dominated Kazakhstan's brief interlude of independence before the country fell under Soviet control in 1920 and then experienced decades of rule as a USSR republic. Under Stalin's Soviet regime, thousands of victims of communist purges were exiled to Kazakhstan's prisons.

ISSUES AND CHALLENGES:

- Nazarbayev's broadening the scope of presidential authority has received domestic and international criticism.

- Collapse of the Soviet economy adversely affected Kazakhstan by increasing unemployment and inflation.

- Two major ecological disasters threaten Kazakhstan's environment: the shrinking of the Aral Sea and the radioactive contamination of the Semipalatinsk nuclear testing facility.

- An ill equipped and poorly funded health system contributes to a high infant mortality rate and lack of coverage in rural areas.

By the mid-1980s, demands for economic and political reforms erupted into mass demonstrations by young ethnic Kazakhs that were put down by Soviet troops. Nevertheless, unrest continued to deepen, leading Kazakhstan to declare sovereignty as a USSR republic and then finally full independence after the 1991 attempted coup in Moscow against Gorbachev. The constitution it subsequently adopted established an executive branch led by a president with considerable powers and a prime minister who chairs a Council of Ministers that oversees government operations. The legislature is bicameral, with an upper house representing regions and regional governments and a lower house the people.

In power since 1989 as head of the Kazakh Communist Party, Nursultan Nazarbayev was elected president in 1991 and re-elected in 1999. Since taking leadership, he has centralized power in the executive branch while pursuing market-oriented policies. Traditionally of little importance, political parties have emerged as important power centers in Kazakh politics since the creation in 1999 of 10 seats in the Parliament's upper house for party-list votes.

HOW THE GOVERNMENT WORKS

LEGISLATIVE BRANCH

Parliament
Bicameral Parliament

Senat
(Senate)
Composed of 39 members who serve six-year terms: 2 each selected by elected assemblies from 16 principal administrative divisions; 7 appointed by president.

Majlis
(Assembly)
Composed of 77 members directly elected to five-year terms; 67 by popular vote from single-member districts; 10 by proportional representation.

Regional Governments
14 provinces administered by governors appointed by president and elected councils.

EXECUTIVE BRANCH

President
Elected to seven-year term by direct popular vote. Serves as head of state; commander-in-chief of armed forces. Proposes and vetoes bills; issues decrees; initiates constitutional amendments; calls referenda; dissolves parliament; negotiates treaties.

Prime Minister
Appointed by president. Serves as head of government; chairs cabinet.

Council of Ministers
Composed of 4 deputy prime ministers, 14 ministers; all appointed by president. Oversees government operations.

JUDICIAL BRANCH

Supreme Court of Kazakhstan
Highest court of review and appeal; rules on constitutionality of laws; original jurisdiction in some cases. Composed of 44 judges appointed to fixed terms by president.

District Courts

Courts of First Instance

Specialized Courts

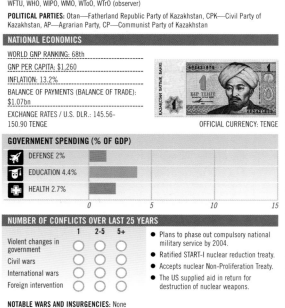

CHILE

OFFICIAL NAME: REPUBLIC OF CHILE

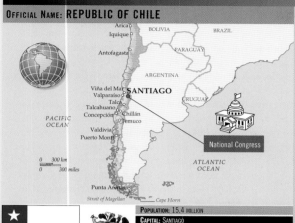

POPULATION:	15.4 MILLION
CAPITAL:	SANTIAGO
AREA:	292,258 SQ. MILES (756,950 SQ. KM)
INDEPENDENCE:	1810
CONSTITUTION:	1980

CHILE has many postulated derivations, including the Mapuche "cold" or Aymará "where the land ends".

RELIGION: Roman Catholic 80%, Other and non-religious 20%

OFFICIAL LANGUAGE: Spanish

REGIONS OR PROVINCES: 13 regions

DEPENDENT TERRITORIES: None

MEDIA: No political censorship exists in media

Newspapers: There are 52 daily newspapers

TV: 1 state-owned services, many independent

Radio: 1 state-owned service, 1046 independent

SUFFRAGE: 18 years of age; universal and compulsory

LEGAL SYSTEM: Spanish law with Austrian and French influences; no ICJ jurisdiction

WORLD ORGANIZATIONS: APEC, CCC, ECLAC, FAO, G-15, G-77, IADB, IAEA, IBRD, ICAO, ICC, ICFTU, ICRM, IDA, IFAD, IFC. IFRCS, IHO, ILO, IMF, IMO, Interpol, IOC, IOM, ISO, ITU, LAES, LAIA, Mercosur (associate), NAM, OAS, OPANAL, OPCW, PCA, RG, UN, UNCTAD, UNESCO, UNHCR, UNIDO, UNITAR, UNMIBH, UNMOGIP, UNTAET, UNTSO, UNU, UPU, WCL, WFTU, WHO, WIPO, WMO, WToO, WTrO

POLITICAL PARTIES: CPD—Concertación-Coalition of Parties for Democracy (Christian Democratic Party—PDC, Party for Democracy—PPD, and Socialist Party of Chile—PS), APC—Alliance for Chile (Independent Democratic Union—UDI, and National Renewal Party—RN), Ind—Independents

ETHNIC GROUPS:

Amerindian 10%

Mixed and European 90%

NATIONAL ECONOMICS

WORLD GNP RANKING: 44th

GNP PER CAPITA: $4,590

INFLATION: 3.8%

BALANCE OF PAYMENTS (BALANCE OF TRADE):-$991 million

EXCHANGE RATES / U.S. DLR.: 573.75-661.15 CHILEAN PESOS

OFFICIAL CURRENCY: CHILEAN PESO

GOVERNMENT SPENDING (% OF GDP)

✈	DEFENSE	3.4%
🎓	EDUCATION	3.7%
➕	HEALTH	2.7%

0   5   10   15

NUMBER OF CONFLICTS OVER LAST 25 YEARS

	1	2-5	5+
Violent changes in government	○	○	○
Civil wars	○	○	○
International wars	○	○	○
Foreign intervention	○	○	○

- Compulsory national military service.
- Many officers still face human rights charges committed under Pinochet.
- Plans to modernize the air force and navy.
- Equipment purchase are partially funded by copper exports.

NOTABLE WARS AND INSURGENCIES: None

CHILE'S DEMOCRATIC TRADITION REACHES BACK to the constitution of 1833, adopted after winning independence from Spain in 1818. Yet it wasn't until the early 20th century that Chilean politics, freed from the country's socially stratified colonial past, embraced the common citizen through vigorous political parties. By mid-century, the Chilean electorate was equally divided among left, center, and right parties, giving centrists substantial leverage to build coalitions. As the left wing began to doubt the benefits of joining coalitions, ideological splits between left and right grew sharper, and there was little room for compromise.

The final split came in 1970, when Salvador Allende, a perennial leftist candidate, was elected president with 36.6 percent of the popular vote. Allende took the country down the "Chilean Road to Socialism," but his policies led to spiraling inflation (1,000 percent a year), economic chaos, and ideological gridlock that made government virtually impossible. In 1973, a military coup ousted the Allende regime and installed General Augusto Pinochet as president. Pinochet outlawed leftist (and eventually all) political parties, and the military regime tortured, killed, and "disappeared," members of all left-wing political parties. Pinochet's 1980 constitution contained a 1989 deadline for returning to civilian democracy, and a well-orchestrated, broad-based campaign voted him out in a 1988 plebiscite. Since then, the constitution has been reformed to create a more democratic state, though the Pinochet influence remains. The president has strong powers with the authority to appoint senators and judges and to force action on legislation within 30 days. He may call special sessions of congress, decree certain laws, and, after leaving the presidency, serve as a senator for life.

ANTI-PINOCHET PROTESTORS IN LONDON—2000

Demonstrators demanding Pinochet's extradition to Spain to face human rights charges show pictures of some those who disappeared under his regime. Inset: Pinochet, who underwent medical tests to determine if he was fit to stand trial.

HOW THE GOVERNMENT WORKS

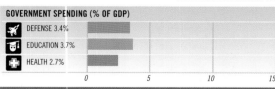

LEGISLATIVE BRANCH

Congreso Nacional
(National Congress)
Bicameral Parliament

Senado
(Senate)
48 members who serve eight-year terms: 38 elected by direct popular vote; 4 appointed by National Security Council; 3 by Supreme Court; 2 by president; former President Frei senator-for-life. Tries impeachment charges.

Cámara de Diputados
(Chamber of Deputies)
120 members; four-year terms by direct popular vote. Adopts accords; impeaches president, ministers, governors, judges.

Regional Governments
13 regions administered by "intendentes" appointed by president; provinces overseen by governors.

EXECUTIVE BRANCH

President
Elected to six-year term by direct popular vote; no immediate re-election. Serves as head of state and government. Calls parliament into special session; vetoes bills; enacts some laws by decree; calls referenda; declares states of emergency.

Cabinet
Composed of 21 members appointed by president without parliament's approval. Oversees government operations.

JUDICIAL BRANCH

Supreme Court
Highest court of review and appeal. Composed of 17 justices nominated by Supreme Court, appointed to serve to age 75 by president.

Appellate Courts
Judges appointed by president.

Local Courts
Judges appointed by president.

CAMEROON

OFFICIAL NAME: REPUBLIC OF CAMEROON

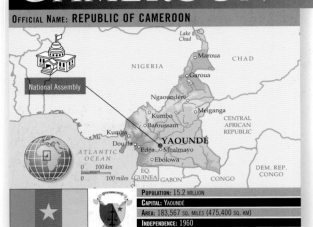

NIGERIA
Lake Chad
Maroua
CHAD
National Assembly
Garoua
Ngaoundéré
Meiganga
Kumbo
Bafoussam
CENTRAL
AFRICAN
REPUBLIC
Kumba
Douala
YAOUNDÉ
ATLANTIC
OCEAN
Edéa
Mbalmayo
Ebolowa
EQ.
GUINEA
GABON
DEM. REP.
CONGO
CONGO
0 100 km
0 100 miles

POPULATION: 15.2 million
CAPITAL: Yaoundé
AREA: 183,567 SQ. MILES (475,400 SQ. KM)
INDEPENDENCE: 1960
CONSTITUTION: 1972

CAMEROON derives its name from Rio de Camarões, or River of Prawns, the name given to the Wouri River.

RELIGION: Roman Catholic 35% Traditional beliefs 25%, Muslim 22%, Protestant 18%

OFFICIAL LANGUAGES: French and English

REGIONS OR PROVINCES: 10 provinces

DEPENDENT TERRITORIES: None

MEDIA: Total political censorship exists in national media

NEWSPAPERS: There are 3 daily newspapers

TV: 1 state-owned service

RADIO: 1 state-owned service

SUFFRAGE: 20 years of age; universal

LEGAL SYSTEM: Common law and French legal traditions; accepts ICJ jurisdiction

WORLD ORGANIZATIONS: ACCT, ACP, AfDB, BDEAC, C, CCC, CEEAC, CEMAC, ECA, FAO, FZ, G-19, G-77, IAEA, IBRD, ICAO, ICC, ICFTU, ICRM, IDA, IDB, IFAD, IFC, IFRCS, ILO, IMF, IMO, Interpol, IOC, ISO (correspondent), ITU, MONUC, NAM, OAU, OIC, OPCW, PCA, UN, UN Security Council (temporary), UNCTAD, UNESCO, UNIDO, UNITAR, UNMIK, UPU, WCL, WFTU, WHO, WIPO, WMO, WToO, WTrO

POLITICAL PARTIES: RDPC—Cameroon People's Democratic Rally, SDF—Social Democratic Front, CDU—Cameroon Democratic Union

ETHNIC GROUPS:

Other African 13%
Non-African less than 1%
Cameroon Highlanders 31%
Eastern Nigritic 7%
North-western Bantu 8%
Fulani 10%
Kirdi 11%
Equatorial Bantu 19%

NATIONAL ECONOMICS

WORLD GNP RANKING: 90th

GNP PER CAPITA: $580

INFLATION: 5.3%

BALANCE OF PAYMENTS (BALANCE OF TRADE): -$153 million

EXCHANGE RATES / U.S. DLR.: 698.7–736.7 CFA FRANCS

OFFICIAL CURRENCY: CFA FRANC

GOVERNMENT SPENDING (% OF GDP)

DEFENSE 1.4%
EDUCATION 2.6%
HEALTH 1%

0   5   10   15

NUMBER OF CONFLICTS OVER LAST 25 YEARS

	1	2-5	5+
Violent changes in government	○	○	○
Civil wars	●	○	○
International wars	○	○	○
Foreign intervention	○	○	○

- No compulsory national military service.
- Territorial dispute with Nigeria over Bakassi Peninsula.
- Dependent on France to provide military training and equipment.

NOTABLE WARS AND INSURGENCIES: Palace Guard revolt 1984.

THE ORIGINS OF CAMEROON AS A COUNTRY lie in German colonization, which began in 1884. After Germany's defeat in World War I, however, the area was divided into two trust territories administered separately by the British and the French. Present-day Cameroon is a product of the union between French Cameroon, which became independent in 1960, and the southern portion of British Cameroon. The northern portion joined Nigeria. The two united in 1961 under a federal system of government, but this was abolished in 1972. Cameroon faces the challenges posed not only by a diverse population of 230 ethnic groups, but also by a potent rift in the Anglophone and Francophone communities.

Following independence, President Ahmadou Ahidjo established an essentially single-party system, remnants of which still affect the current political environment. Democratic reforms in 1990 legalized the formation of multiple parties; however, each subsequent election has only returned the dominant party, the Rassemblement Démocratique du Peuple Camerounais (RDPC), or Cameroon People's Democratic Rally, to power. The elections are widely believed to have been fraudulent by the international community and reform activists. Cameroon has only had two presidents since independence—Ahmadou Ahidjo until 1982 when he retired, and Paul Biya, who had been the prime minister prior to his election.

Nearly all of the political power in Cameroon is vested in the executive branch. Ultimately, the president controls almost every facet of political life, from overseeing the activity of the extensive executive bureaucracy to dictating state policy. Aside from controlling the armed forces, the president also directs international affairs and makes all judicial, political, and military appointments. Furthermore, the President exercises enormous influence in the national legislature and may, for example, initiate legislation, require alterations in legislation that he opposes, and call special sessions of the National Assembly. In fact, executive neglect is a significant reason as to why the Senate—which was to be created under the constitution of 1996—has never appeared.

ISSUES AND CHALLENGES:

- The English-speaking community is politically outspoken, with small factions demanding independence.

- Cameroon has political disputes with virtually all of its neighbors concerning the delimitation of borders and economic zones. Its most virulent dispute is with Nigeria, which at times erupts into armed conflict.

- Accusations of corruption in the government are widespread.

- Lack of funds has forced the nation to cease several development projects.

- Deficient infrastructure hinders the expansion of the country's potentially lucrative oil industry.

HOW THE GOVERNMENT WORKS

LEGISLATIVE BRANCH

Assemblée Nationale (National Assembly) Bicameral Parliament*
Composed of 180 members elected to five-year terms by direct popular vote. Meets three times annually. Initiates and passes bills; approves budget; amends constitution.

Senate
*100-member chamber mandated by 1996 constitution but yet to be established.

Regional Governments
Ten provinces overseen by administrators appointed by president.

EXECUTIVE BRANCH

President
Elected to seven-year term by direct popular vote; two-term limit. Serves as head of state; commander-in-chief of armed forces. Initiates bills; appoints senior government officials; controls state expenditure; declares states of emergency; spends profits of state-owned companies.

Prime Minister
Appointed by president. Serves as head of government.

Council of Ministers
Members appointed by president on advice of prime minister. Presided over by president; Oversees government operations.

JUDICIAL BRANCH

Constitutional Council
Rules on constitutionality of laws. Comprises 11 members appointed to single nine-year terms by president on advice of Parliament and Higher Judicial Council (which oversees the judiciary).

Supreme Court
Highest court of review and appeal; rules administrative and election disputes. Justices appointed by president.

High Court of Justice
Composed of nine justices, six reserve justices; elected by Parliament.

Traditional Courts
Adjudicate domestic, property and probate cases.

ECUADOR

OFFICIAL NAME: REPUBLIC OF ECUADOR

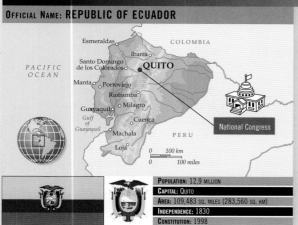

National Congress

POPULATION: 12.9 MILLION
CAPITAL: Quito
AREA: 109,483 SQ. MILES (283,560 SQ. KM)
INDEPENDENCE: 1830
CONSTITUTION: 1998

ECUADOR lies on the equator and its name is simply the Spanish for "equator".

RELIGION: Roman Catholic 93%, Protestant, Jewish, Other 7%

OFFICIAL LANGUAGE: Spanish

REGIONS OR PROVINCES: 22 provinces, (includes Galápagos Islands)

DEPENDENT TERRITORIES: None

MEDIA: Partial political censorship exists in national media.

NEWSPAPERS: There are 29 daily newspapers

TV: 67 independent services

RADIO: 1 state-owned, 320 independent stations

SUFFRAGE: 18 years of age; universal, compulsory for literate persons ages 18-65, optional for other eligible voters

LEGAL SYSTEM: Civil law; no ICJ jurisdiction

WORLD ORGANIZATIONS: CAN, CCC, ECLAC, FAO, G-77, IADB, IAEA, IBRD, ICAO, ICC, ICFTU, ICRM, IDA, IFAD, IFC, IFRCS, IHO, ILO, IMF, IMO, Interpol, IOC, IOM, ISO, ITU, LAES, LAIA, NAM, OAS, OPANAL, OPCW, PCA, RG, UN, UNCTAD, UNESCO, UNIDO, UPU, WCL, WFTU, WHO, WIPO, WMO, WToO, WTrO

POLITICAL PARTIES: DP—Popular Democracy, PSC—Social Christian Party, PRE—Ecuadorean Roldosist Party, ID—Democratic Left NMN-PP—New Country Pachakutik Movement, FRA—Alfarist Radical Front

ETHNIC GROUPS:

- Spanish and Others 7%
- Black 3%
- Amerindian 25%
- Mestizo 65%

NATIONAL ECONOMICS

WORLD GNP RANKING: 74th

GNP PER CAPITA: $1,210

INFLATION: 96.1%

BALANCE OF PAYMENTS (BALANCE OF TRADE): $928 million

EXCHANGE RATES / U.S. DLR.: Currency is US DOLLAR

OFFICIAL CURRENCY: US DOLLAR

GOVERNMENT SPENDING (% OF GDP)

		0	5	10	15
✈	DEFENSE 1.6%				
✚	EDUCATION 3.5%				
✚	HEALTH 1.7%				

NUMBER OF CONFLICTS OVER LAST 25 YEARS

	1	2-5	5+
Violent changes in government	○	○	○
Civil wars	○	○	○
International wars	○	●	○
Foreign intervention	○	○	○

- ● Compulsory national military service.
- ● Army partially funded by oil revenues.
- ● Security threat along the Colombian border.
- ● 56-year border dispute with Peru resolved in 1998.

NOTABLE WARS AND INSURGENCIES: Ecuadorean-Peruvian border wars 1981 and 1995

ECUADOR'S HISTORY IS FRAUGHT with political turmoil. Conquered by the Incas in the 15th century, Ecuador was taken by the Spanish in 1533. By 1822, along with Colombia and Venezuela, it had become a part of the Republic of Gran Colombia. Upon the latter's collapse in 1830, Ecuador became an independent republic. Power has shifted between civilian and military rule, with conflicts arising from regional and class differences, and since 1830 there have been 19 constitutions. These problems have been compounded by others created by the discovery of oil in the late 20th century.

For much of the 1930s and 1940s, one man dominated politics: five-times president, José Velasco Ibarra. In the 12 years that followed his rule, Ecuador saw democratic and free elections in which three different men took office before democracy was once again interrupted by a number of military coups. Although Ecuador returned to civilian rule in the 1970s, indigenous Ecuadoreans and dissident military officers staged a coup in January 2000, replacing then-president Mahuad with Vice-president Gustavo Noboa, who was declared president the following day. The current presidential democracy is fragile, Noboa having been narrowly beaten in the January 2003 elections by Lucio Gutiérrez.

ISSUES AND CHALLENGES:

- ● Income distribution is one of the greatest problems facing Ecuador. Approximately 80 percent of the nation's wealth belongs to 20 percent of the population, and an estimated two million people live in extreme poverty, unable to meet even basic nutritional needs.
- ● Rising unemployment and depreciation of the currency, which led to the adoption of the dollar in 2000, have exacerbated the country's economic woes. The resulting unrest and rising crime rates threaten the stability of the democracy, already marked by allegations of mismanagement and corruption.

Major political parties are split on ideological grounds that date back to the 19th century and reinforce regional tensions. The Conservative Party (CP), the oldest party, is aligned with the landowning elite, the Roman Catholic church, and the state. The Radical Liberal Party (PLR), formed in the early 1900s, serves the interests of coastal commerce and finance, and favors anti-clericalism and decentralization. Both parties have declined in influence as numerous splinter groups have emerged, including the Roldosist Party (PRE), a populist party with no clear ideological position; the centrist Popular Democracy party, which has gained a stronghold in the National Congress; and the right-wing Social Christian Party (PSC), which advocates a free-market economy.

The constitution of 1998 was intended to combat government corruption and give more autonomy to the judicial system. Provincial governors wield considerable influence nationally, especially those from Quito and Guayaquil.

HOW THE GOVERNMENT WORKS

LEGISLATIVE BRANCH

Congreso Nacional (National Congress) Unicameral Parliament
Composed of 121 members: 100 elected to two-year terms from provinces by direct popular vote; 21 directly elected nationally to four-year terms. Leadership posts rotate between two major parties every two years.

Regional Governments
Twenty-two provinces administered by governors appointed by president.

EXECUTIVE BRANCH

President
Elected to four-year term by direct popular vote; no consecutive re-election. Serves as head of state and government.

Vice-president
Elected on presidential ticket to four-year term by direct popular vote; no consecutive re-election.

Cabinet
Appointed by president. Oversees government operations.

JUDICIAL BRANCH

National Council of the Judiciary
Administers judiciary; disciplines lower-court judges. Composed of Supreme Court chief justice and seven members appointed to renewable six-year terms by Supreme Court.

Constitutional Court
Rules on constitutionality of laws. Judges appointed to renewable four-year terms by National Congress.

Supreme Court
Highest court of review and appeal. Justices appointed for life by two-thirds vote of Supreme Court.

Superior Courts

Criminal Courts

Civil Courts

GUATEMALA

OFFICIAL NAME: REPUBLIC OF GUATEMALA

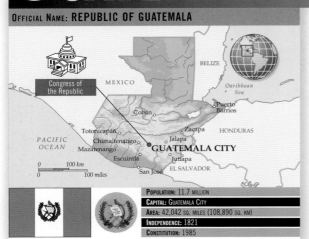

Congress of the Republic

POPULATION: 11.7 MILLION
CAPITAL: GUATEMALA CITY
AREA: 42,042 SQ. MILES (108,890 SQ. KM)
INDEPENDENCE: 1821
CONSTITUTION: 1985

GUATEMALA comes from either "Quauhtemallan"—land of trees, or "Guhatezmalha"—mountain of vomiting water.

RELIGION: Roman Catholic 80%, Protestant 5%, indigenous Mayan beliefs 5%.

OFFICIAL LANGUAGE: Spanish

REGIONS OR PROVINCES: 22 departments

DEPENDENT TERRITORIES: None

MEDIA: Partial political censorship exists in national media

Newspapers: There are 7 daily newspapers

TV: 5 services: 1 state-owned, 4 independent

Radio: 85 stations: 5 state-owned, 80 independent

ETHNIC GROUPS:

Other 10%
Mestizo 30%
Amerindian 60%

SUFFRAGE: 18 years of age; universal (active duty members of the armed forces are not permitted to vote)

LEGAL SYSTEM: Civil law; no ICJ jurisdiction

WORLD ORGANIZATIONS: BCIE, CACM, CCC, ECLAC, FAO, G-24, G-77, IADB, IAEA, IBRD, ICAO, ICFTU, ICRM, IDA, IFAD, IFC, IFRCS, IHO, ILO, IMF, IMO, Interpol, IOC, IOM, ISO (correspondent), ITU, LAES, LAIA (observer), NAM, OAS, OPANAL, OPCW (signatory), PCA, RG, UN, UNCTAD, UNESCO, UNIDO, UNU, UPU, WCL, WFTU, WHO, WIPO, WMO, WToO, WTrO

POLITICAL PARTIES: FRG—Guatemalan Republican Front, PAN—National Advancement Party, NNA—New Nation Alliance

NATIONAL ECONOMICS

WORLD GNP RANKING: 67th

GNP PER CAPITA: $1,680

INFLATION: 6.0%

BALANCE OF PAYMENTS (BALANCE OF TRADE): -$1.05 billion

EXCHANGE RATES / U.S. DLR: 7.782-7.910 QUETZALES

OFFICIAL CURRENCY: QUETZAL

GOVERNMENT SPENDING (% OF GDP)

DEFENSE 0.8%
EDUCATION 2%
HEALTH 2.1%

| | 0 | 5 | 10 | 15 |

NUMBER OF CONFLICTS OVER LAST 25 YEARS

	1	2-5	5+
Violent changes in government	○	●	○
Civil wars	●	○	○
International wars	○	○	○
Foreign intervention	○	○	○

- Compulsory national military service.
- Military aid and equipment supplied by US, Israel, Taiwan, Spain and France.
- Member of Central American Defense Council (CONDECA).
- Armed forces limited to external defense unless ordered by president.

NOTABLE WARS AND INSURGENCIES: Civil war 1961-1996. Coups 1982-1983

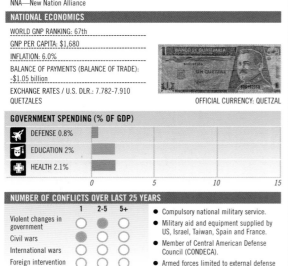

HOME OF THE MAYAN PEOPLE, Guatemala was conquered by the Spanish in 1523. Independence in 1821 was followed by a brief interlude as part of the Mexican Republic, and later as a part of the federation of the United Provinces of Central America. In the last half of the 20th century, Guatemalan politics were marked by frequent bouts of military control and repression, several coups, four constitutions, and a 36-year civil war. A lack of separation of powers among the three branches of the Guatemalan government resulted in a blurring of roles, with the executive, and especially the military, influencing judicial functions and decisions. However, the 1983 coup brought gradual democratic reform, embodied in the 1985 constitution which separates the three branches of government and guarantees their independence (in practice the military and president remain very influential). This was followed by the election of a civilian president, the participation for the first time of a party of the ideological left in 1995, and the end of the guerrilla war in 1996. Concurrently, however, the country endured continued political corruption, acts of violence by the military, and a failed self-coup, by President Jorge Serrano Elías in 1993.

Guatemala is a presidential democracy. Under constitutional changes made in 1994, the president is the chief of state and head of government. The president and vice-president are elected by popular vote, and the president appoints members of the Council of Ministers. The vice-president presides over the Congreso de la República, or National Congress, which is elected by proportional represen-tation. The size of the Congress was reduced from 116 to 80 members in 1994, then increased to 113 in 1999, and was again to grow by 12 to 15 seats in the 2003 election. The extreme-right populist Guatemalan Republican Front won 56% of the vote in the 1999 election, overtaking the previously ruling center-right National Advancement Party (PAN).

The Corte Suprema de Justicia, or Supreme Court of Justice, is the highest court. Its president also supervises trial judges around the country. The Constitutional Court, rules on constitutionality of laws and regulations.

ISSUES AND CHALLENGES:

- Non-voting is punishable by a small fine, but the penalty is seldom imposed.

- Illiterate citizens are not required to vote. The Guatemalan literacy rate is about 69 percent for citizens over 15 years of age, one of the lowest in Latin America.

- Efraín Ríos Montt, military ruler from 1982 to 1986, was elected president of the Congress in 2001, despite being investigated by a Spanish court on charges of genocide.

- A "truth commission" report in 1999 found the military and its allies guilty of 95 percent of human rights violations in the civil war, which claimed 200,000 lives, mostly civilians, making it the longest and costliest civil war in modern Central American history.

HOW THE GOVERNMENT WORKS

LEGISLATIVE BRANCH

Congreso de la República
(Congress of the Republic)
Unicameral Parliament
Composed of 113 members elected to four-year terms by direct popular vote, proportional representation.

Regional Governments
Twenty-two departments administered by governors appointed by president, 331 municipalities with elected mayors and city councils.

EXECUTIVE BRANCH

President
Elected to single four-year term by direct popular vote. Serves as head of state and government.

Vice-president
Elected to single four-year term by direct popular vote; may run for president after four-year interval. Presides over parliament.

Council of Ministers
Members appointed by president. Oversees government operations.

JUDICIAL BRANCH

Constitutional Court
Rules on constitutionality of laws. Composed of five judges elected to five-year terms by parliament.

Supreme Court of Justice
Highest court of review and appeal. Composed of 13 judges elected to five-year terms by parliament from nominees of bar association, law school deans, and appellate judges.

MALAWI

OFFICIAL NAME: **REPUBLIC OF MALAWI**

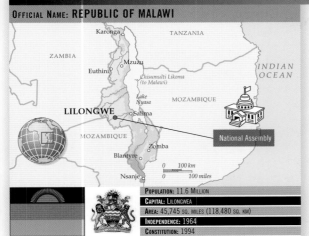

LILONGWE

POPULATION:	11.6 MILLION
CAPITAL:	LILONGWEA
AREA:	45,745 SQ. MILES (118,480 SQ. KM)
INDEPENDENCE:	1964
CONSTITUTION:	1994

MALAWI takes its name from the Marawi or Maravi kingdom—a confederacy of states established in the area in the 1500s.

RELIGION: Protestant 55%, Roman Catholic 20%, Muslim 20%, Traditional beliefs 5%

OFFICIAL LANGUAGE: English

REGIONS OR PROVINCES: 27 districts

DEPENDENT TERRITORIES: None

MEDIA: Partial political censorship exists in national media

Newspapers: There are 5 daily newspapers. Violence against the staff of privately owned newspapers causes concern.

TV: 1 service

Radio: 1 state-owned service

SUFFRAGE: 18 years of age; universal

LEGAL SYSTEM: Customary and English common law; accepts ICJ jurisdiction

WORLD ORGANIZATIONS: ACP, AfDB, C, CCC, ECA, FAO, G-77, IBRD, ICAO, ICFTU, ICRM, IDA, IFAD, IFC, IFRCS, ILO, IMF, IMO, Interpol, IOC, ISO (correspondent), ITU, MONUC, NAM, OAU, OPCW, SADC, UN, UNCTAD, UNESCO, UNIDO, UNMIK, UPU, WFTU, WHO, WIPO, WMO, WToO, WTrO

POLITICAL PARTIES: UDF—United Democratic Front, MCP—Malawi Congress Party, AFORD—Alliance for Democracy, Ind—Independents

ETHNIC GROUPS:

Other 1%

Bantu 99%

NATIONAL ECONOMICS

WORLD GNP RANKING: 140th

GNP PER CAPITA: $170

INFLATION: 29.5%

BALANCE OF PAYMENTS (BALANCE OF TRADE): -$523 million

EXCHANGE RATES / U.S. DLR.: 80.40-67.01 MALAWI KWACHA

OFFICIAL CURRENCY: MALAWI KWACHA

GOVERNMENT SPENDING (% OF GDP)

		0	5	10	15
✈	DEFENSE 1.8%				
🎓	EDUCATION 4.6%				
✚	HEALTH 2.8%				

NUMBER OF CONFLICTS OVER LAST 25 YEARS

	1	2-5	5+
Violent changes in government	○	○	○
Civil wars	○	○	○
International wars	○	○	○
Foreign intervention	○	○	○

- No compulsory national military service.
- Extremely successful program of accepting and repatriating Mozambican refugees.
- Dependent on international aid for refugees.
- Border dispute over Lake Malawi with Tanzania.

NOTABLE WARS AND INSURGENCIES: None

A DENSELY POPULATED sub-Saharan country, Malawi is a multiparty democracy and a rarity in Africa—a nation free of ethnic strife, with most of its citizens of Bantu descent. Scottish missionary David Livingstone reached Lake Malawi (now Lake Nyasa) in 1859, initiating sustained Western contact; Scottish Presbyterian missionaries and traders soon followed. British control began with the creation of the Nyasaland Protectorate in 1891 and continued through the mid-20th century despite Malawian efforts toward independence. Desire for independence increased when Nyasaland was grouped with Northern and Southern Rhodesia to form the Federation of Rhodesia and Nyasaland in 1953. The federation's dissolution in December 1963 left Malawi an independent nation; a constitution adopted in 1965 mandated a one-party system.

Hastings Banda was elected the country's first president in 1965 and was declared president for life in 1971. Banda's autocratic regime took a harsh stance against dissent, and in 1992 the government's reputation for human rights violations brought a halt to foreign aid. Malawians voted for a democracy in a 1993 referendum. Free elections the following year ended Banda's presidency. Bakili Muluzi of the United Democratic Front (UDF) was elected, while the UDF won 82 of the 177 seats and formed a coalition government with the Alliance for Democracy, which was disbanded in 1996. Democratic elections held in 1999 re-elected Muluzi to the presidency.

The country's constitution vests executive power in a president who is popularly elected. A vice-president is elected with the president, but the president may select a second vice-president. The president's role as both chief of state and head of government, as well as his powers to veto any bill passed by the unicameral National Assembly and to dissolve that body, make the executive branch dominant. Malawi has yet to create the 80-seat Senate provided for in the constitution. The constitution calls for an independent judiciary that is similar to that in England.

ISSUES AND CHALLENGES:

- Malawi must rely on imports for all fuel products and much of its consumer goods and food.
- Only a small, elite portion of the population enjoys financial wealth.
- Dependence on agricultural exports makes the country's economy vulnerable to market fluctuations and the ravages of weather.
- Environmental concerns include land degradation and water pollution from agricultural runoff, industry, and sewerage.
- Lack of skilled labor and a deteriorating infrastructure hobble economic development.
- Unresolved dispute with Tanzania over the boundary in Lake Nyasa (Lake Malawi) and the Songwe River remain.

HOW THE GOVERNMENT WORKS

LEGISLATIVE BRANCH

National Assembly
Unicameral Parliament
Composed of 193 members elected to five-year terms by direct popular vote from single-member districts. Amends constitution by two-thirds majority vote.

Regional Governments
Three regions administered by appointed ministers. Twenty-seven districts overseen by elected local councils supervised by Ministry of Local Government.

EXECUTIVE BRANCH

President
Elected to five-year term by direct popular vote. Serves as head of state and government. Assents to or rejects bills; dissolves parliament; calls new elections.

Vice-president
Elected on presidential ticket to five-year term. President also may appoint second vice-president from different party.

Cabinet
Composed of 46 members, including from parliament; appointed by president. Oversees government operations.

JUDICIAL BRANCH

Supreme Court of Appeal
Highest court of review and appeal. Chief justice appointed by president.

High Court
Hears civil and criminal cases. Composed of chief justice and five other judges.

Magistrates' Courts
Hear civil and criminal cases at local level.

GREECE

OFFICIAL NAME: HELLENIC REPUBLIC

Parliament of Greece

POPULATION: 10.6 MILLION	
CAPITAL: ATHENS	
AREA: 50,942 SQ. MILES (131,940 SQ. KM)	
INDEPENDENCE: 1829	
CONSTITUTION: 1975	

GREECE comes from the Latin "Groecia" or in Greek "Graikoi," describing those from Hellas, "land of light".

RELIGION: Greek Orthodox 98%, Other 2%

OFFICIAL LANGUAGE: Greek

REGIONS OR PROVINCES: 51 prefectures and one autonomous region

DEPENDENT TERRITORIES: None

MEDIA: No political censorship exists in national media

Newspapers: There are 122 daily newspapers

TV: 18 services: one state-owned, 17 independent. Many private TV and radio networks evolved after the state broadcasting monopoly ended in 1990

Radio: Two services: one state-owned, one independent

SUFFRAGE: 18 years of age; universal and compulsory

LEGAL SYSTEM: Roman law; accepts ICJ jurisdiction

WORLD ORGANIZATIONS: Australia Group, BIS, BSEC, CCC, CE, CERN, EAPC, EBRD, ECE, EIB, EMU, EU, FAO, G-6, IAEA, IBRD, ICAO, ICC, ICFTU, ICRM, IDA, IEA, IFAD, IFC, IFRCS, IHO, ILO, IMF, IMO, Interpol, IOC, IOM, ISO, ITU, MINURSO, NAM (guest), NATO, NEA, NSG, OAS (observer), OECD, OPCW, OSCE, PCA, UN, UNCTAD, UNESCO, UNHCR, UNIDO, UNIKOM, UNMEE, UNMIBH, UNMIK, UNOMIG, UPU, WEU, WFTU, WHO, WIPO, WMO, WToO, WTrO, ZC

POLITICAL PARTIES: PASOK—Pan-Hellenic Socialist Movement, ND—New Democracy, KKE—Communist Party of Greece, Synaspismos—Left Coalition

ETHNIC GROUPS:

Other 2%

Greek 98%

WORLD GNP RANKING: 30th

GNP PER CAPITA: $11,960

INFLATION: 3.2%

BALANCE OF PAYMENTS (BALANCE OF TRADE): -$9.82 billion

EXCHANGE RATES / U.S. DLR.: 1.0651-1.1231 EUROS

5 EURO

OFFICIAL CURRENCY: EURO

GOVERNMENT SPENDING (% OF GDP)

✈ DEFENSE 4.9%	
EDUCATION 3.1%	
✚ HEALTH 4.7%	

0   5   10   15

NUMBER OF CONFLICTS OVER LAST 25 YEARS

	1	2-5	5+
Violent changes in government	○	○	○
Civil wars	○	○	○
International wars	○	○	○
Foreign intervention	○	○	○

- Compulsory national military service.
- Tensions with Macedonia over its name, the same as a Greek province.
- Border disputes with Turkey over Aegean Sea.
- Signed cooperation agreements with Israel and Egypt.
- US maintains military bases in Greece.

NOTABLE WARS AND INSURGENCIES: Left-wing terror group November 17 active from 1975—leading members arrested in 2002

ANCIENT GREECE WAS THE BIRTHPLACE of political democracy, a fact which the Hellenic people held onto through centuries of subsequent occupation. Modern Greece began its fight for independence in 1821 with the Greek War of Independence, which culminated in it breaking free from the moribund Ottoman Empire. Under pressure from England, France and Russia, independence was granted in 1830 under the leadership of the Bavarian prince Otto, despite the Turks' attempts to reclaim land lost in the decade-long conflict. Thirty years later, Otto was replaced by George I, King of the Hellenes.

In the modern era, the country has been a presidential democracy only since 1974. Under the 1975 constitution, the president is the chief executive. But as in many European nations, the president is more of a figurehead than a vital policy maker. Constitutional revisions in 1986 shifted many powers to the prime minister and Parliament. The president negotiates treaties, but these require parliamentary approval. The president can appoint the prime minister, but must choose the leader of the majority party, if one exists. The president can return bills to Parliament for reconsideration, but this veto can be overridden by a majority vote. By contrast, the prime minister is a strong head of government. Until illness led to his resignation and death in 1996, Andreas Papandreou made the most of the role—powers that include selecting the cabinet, controlling the bureaucracy, and formulating policy.

The unicameral parliament shares legislative responsibility with cabinet ministers. In practice, Parliament simply approves or rejects proposed bills, although it can vote no-confidence in cabinet ministers, forcing the resignation of the minister, or the government. But Greek election procedures make it likely that one party has a majority, or plurality, making no-confidence votes unlikely and providing greater stability than many governments in the region can claim. In the 2000 election, the Papandreou-founded Pan Hellenic Socialist Movement (PASOK) won 53 percent of the Greek Parliament's seats. The judiciary includes a Supreme Judicial Court, the ultimate decider of appeals, and a Special Supreme Tribunal, which resolves election disputes between courts.

ISSUES AND CHALLENGES:

- Greece has a strongly centralized administrative governmental system, despite efforts of the European Union, to which it belongs, to devolve member nations' power to elected regional or local officials.

- Although Greece formerly recognized the Former Yugoslav Republic of Macedonia in 1995, relations remain strained, with fears that Macedonia might wish to absorb the Greek province of Macedonia into a "Greater Macedonia".

- High interest rates and a bureaucratic banking system have discouraged private initiative.

HOW THE GOVERNMENT WORKS

LEGISLATIVE BRANCH

Vouli ton Ellinon
(Parliament of Greece)
Unicameral Parliament
Composed of 300 members who serve four-year terms: 288 elected by direct popular vote to single-member districts; 12 directly elected nationally by proportional; representation. Passes laws; overrides vetoes; ratifies treaties; votes no-confidence in prime minister and cabinet.

Regional Governments
Thirteen regions administered by governors appointed by minister of interior; 51 prefectures each headed by prefect elected by direct popular vote.

EXECUTIVE BRANCH

President
Elected to five-year term by parliament; two-term limit. Serves as head of state; commander-in-chief of armed forces. Represents nation in international affairs; negotiates treaties; declares war with parliament's consent; vetoes bills.

Prime minister
Leader of parliament's majority party or coalition appointed by president. Serves as head of government. Countersigns presidential acts; dismisses ministers.

Cabinet
Members appointed by president on advice of prime minister. Oversees government operations; introduces bills in parliament.

JUDICIAL BRANCH

Supreme Judicial Court
Highest court of review and appeal. Judges appointed for life by president on advice of special councils of judges.

Council of State
Rules on constitutionality of laws, legality of government acts.

Comptrollers' Council
Oversees government accounts; combats government fraud.

Special Supreme Court
Resolves disputes between courts; decides elections cases.

ZAMBIA

OFFICIAL NAME: REPUBLIC OF ZAMBIA

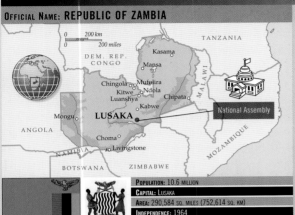

POPULATION: 10.6 MILLION	
CAPITAL: LUSAKA	
AREA: 290,584 SQ. MILES (752,614 SQ. KM)	
INDEPENDENCE: 1964	
CONSTITUTION: 1991	

ZAMBIA is derived from the Zambezi River flowing along its southern border, which means "great river".

RELIGION: Christian 50%-75%, Muslim and Hindu 24%-49%, indigenous beliefs 1%

OFFICIAL LANGUAGE: English

REGIONS OR PROVINCES: Nine provinces

DEPENDENT TERRITORIES: None

MEDIA: Broadcasting is dominated by the government

Newspapers: There are three daily newspapers

TV: One state-controlled, one educational service

Radio: 4 services: One state-controlled

SUFFRAGE: Eight years of age; universal

LEGAL SYSTEM: Customary and English common law; no ICJ jurisdiction

ETHNIC GROUPS:

- European 1.1%
- Other 0.2%
- African 98.7%

WORLD ORGANIZATIONS: ACP, AfDB, C, CCC, ECA, FAO, G-19, G-77, IAEA, IBRD, ICAO, ICFTU, ICRM, IDA, IFAD, IFC, IFRCS, ILO, IMF, Interpol, IOC, IOM, ITU, MONUC, NAM, OAU, OPCW, PCA, SADC, UN, UNAMSIL, UNCTAD, UNESCO, UNIDO, UNMEE, UNMIK, UPU, WHO, WIPO, WMO, WToO, WTrO

POLITICAL PARTIES: AZ—Agenda for Zambia, FDD—Forum for Democracy and Development, HP—Heritage Party, LPF—Liberal Progressive Front, MMD—Movement for Multiparty Democracy, NCC—National Citizens Coalition, NLD—National Leadership for Development, NP—National Party, PF—Patriotic Front, ZRP—Zambian Republican Party, SDP—Social Democratic Party, UNIP—United National Independence Party, UPND—United Party for National Development

NATIONAL ECONOMICS

WORLD GNP RANKING: 131st

GNP PER CAPITA: $300

INFLATION: 27.3%

BALANCE OF PAYMENTS (BALANCE OF TRADE): -$269 million

EXCHANGE RATES / U.S. DLR.: 4500-3810 ZAMBIAN KWACHA

OFFICIAL CURRENCY: ZAMBIAN KWACHA

GOVERNMENT SPENDING (% OF GDP)

DEFENSE 1.8%		
EDUCATION 2.3%		
HEALTH 3.6%		

0   5   10   15

NUMBER OF CONFLICTS OVER LAST 25 YEARS

	1	2-5	5+
Violent changes in government	○	○	○
Civil wars	○	○	○
International wars	○	○	○
Foreign intervention	○	○	○

- No compulsory national military service.
- National Defense Force tasked with internal security.
- Zambian National Service maintains public works projects.
- The major security threat is along the Angolan border.

NOTABLE WARS AND INSURGENCIES: None

ISSUES AND CHALLENGES:

- Transportation difficulties caused by inadequate railroads and roads, and high debt hinder the economy.

- Measures to curb triple-digit inflation resulted in high social welfare costs.

- One of the world's poorest nations, Zambia's social indicators continue to decline—the standard of living is lower than at independence and life expectancy at birth is only thirty-seven years.

- The economy lacks diversification; despite dwindling reserves, copper represents 90 percent of the country's export revenue.

LANDLOCKED ZAMBIA had only occasional contact with Europeans until the mid-19th century, when it experienced a wave of European explorers, missionaries, and traders. Cecil Rhodes, representing British commercial and political interests, obtained mineral rights from tribal chiefs in 1888; later that year, Zambia (then Northern Rhodesia) and Zimbabwe (then Southern Rhodesia) were declared a British sphere of influence. Northern Rhodesia was proclaimed a British protectorate in 1924, and was joined with Southern Rhodesia and Nyasaland (now Malawi) as the Federation of Rhodesia and Nyasaland in 1953. After much turmoil over African determination for self-governance, a two-stage election in 1962 resulted in an African majority in the legislature. Subsequent legislative resolutions called for the secession of Northern Rhodesia from the federation, complete self-governance under a new constitution, and a new legislature based on a wider, more democratic franchise. The federation was dissolved on December 31, 1963, and Northern Rhodesia gained independence on October 24, 1964, becoming the Republic of Zambia.

A constitution proposed in August 1973 called for a single-party democracy with three separate governmental branches. In elections later that year, Kenneth Kaunda—the leader of the United National Independence Party (UNIP) and the fight for independence—was elected president. In December 1990, after an attempted coup and riots, Kaunda signed legislation ending single-party rule. A new constitution, adopted in 1991, enlarged the unicameral National Assembly. Kaunda was ousted in the multiparty elections that followed, bringing to an end nearly two decades of rule.

The Zambian president is vested with extensive powers that include presiding over the cabinet, initiating or vetoing legislation, establishing or dissolving ministries (with legislative approval), and immunity from criminal prosecution for acts committed while in office. Rounding out the executive branch are the vice president, and the cabinet, which formulates policy and answers to the National Assembly legislature.

HOW THE GOVERNMENT WORKS

LEGISLATIVE BRANCH

National Assembly
Unicameral Parliament
Composed of 150 members elected to five-year terms: 142 elected by direct popular vote; 8 appointed by president. Meets at least once annually. Initiates and passes bills; amends constitution; enacts taxes.

Regional Governments
Nine provinces each administered by appointed deputy minister. 55 districts.

EXECUTIVE BRANCH

President
Elected by five-year term by direct popular vote; two-term limit. Serves as head of state and government; commander-in-chief of armed forces. Initiates bills; signs laws; appoints ambassadors; negotiates treaties; grants pardons.

Vice President
Appointed and dismissed by president.

Cabinet
Composed president, vice-president, secretary of state, 24 parliament members, appointed by president. Formulates policy; oversees government operations; presided over by president.

JUDICIAL BRANCH

Supreme Court
Highest court of review and appeal. Composed of five judges appointed by president, approved by parliament.

High Court
Hears civil and criminal cases; unlimited jurisdiction. Judges appointed by president, approved by parliament.

Magistrates courts

Local Courts

SENEGAL

OFFICIAL NAME: REPUBLIC OF SENEGAL

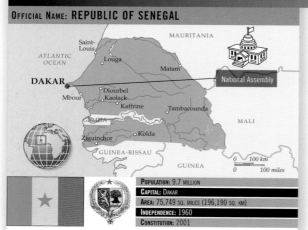

POPULATION: 9.7 MILLION
CAPITAL: DAKAR
AREA: 75,749 SQ. MILES (196,190 SQ. KM)
INDEPENDENCE: 1960
CONSTITUTION: 2001

SENEGAL is named after the Senegal River which the Portuguese sailed in the mid 1400s.

RELIGION: Sunni Muslim 90%, Christian (mainly Roman Catholic) 5%, Traditional beliefs 5%

OFFICIAL LANGUAGE: French

REGIONS OR PROVINCES: 10 regions

DEPENDENT TERRITORIES: None

MEDIA: Partial political censorship exists in national media

NEWSPAPERS: 8 daily newspapers

TV: 2 services: 1 state-owned, 1 private

RADIO: 5 services: 1 state-owned, 4 independent

SUFFRAGE: 18 years of age; universal

LEGAL SYSTEM: French law; accepts ICJ jurisdiction

WORLD ORGANIZATIONS: ACCT, ACP, AfDB, CCC, ECA, ECOWAS, FAO, FZ, G-15, G-77, IAEA, IBRD, ICAO, ICC, ICFTU, ICRM, IDA, IDB, IFAD, IFC, IFRCS, ILO, IMF, IMO, Interpol, IOC, IOM, ITU, MIPONUH, MONUC, NAM, OAU, OIC, OPCW, PCA, UN, UNCTAD, UNESCO, UNIDO, UNIKOM, UNMIBH, UNMIK, UNMOVIC, UPU, WADB (regional), WAEMU, WCL, WFTU, WHO, WIPO, WMO, WToO, WTrO

POLITICAL PARTIES: SC—Sopi (Change) coalition (led by the Senegalese Democratic Party-PDS), AFP—Alliance of Progress Forces, PS—Senegalese Socialist Party, URD—Union for Party for Democracy and Socialism.

ETHNIC GROUPS:

Mandinka 3%
Soninke 1%
European and Lebanese 1%
Jola 4%
Other 9%
Serer 15%
Wolof 4%
Pular 24%

NATIONAL ECONOMICS

WORLD GNP RANKING: 114th

GNP PER CAPITA: $490

INFLATION: 0.7%

BALANCE OF PAYMENTS (BALANCE OF TRADE): -$310 million

EXCHANGE RATES / U.S. DLR.: 698.7-736.7 CFA FRANCS

OFFICIAL CURRENCY: CFA FRANC

GOVERNMENT SPENDING (% OF GDP)

✈ DEFENSE 1.2%		
📖 EDUCATION 3.5%		
✚ HEALTH 2.6%		

0   5   10   15

NUMBER OF CONFLICTS OVER LAST 25 YEARS

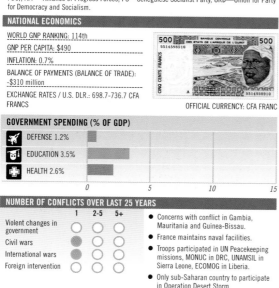

	1	2-5	5+
Violent changes in government	○	○	○
Civil wars	●	○	○
International wars	●	○	○
Foreign intervention	○	○	○

- Concerns with conflict in Gambia, Mauritania and Guinea-Bissau.
- France maintains naval facilities.
- Troops participated in UN Peacekeeping missions, MONUC in DRC, UNAMSIL in Sierra Leone, ECOMOG in Liberia.
- Only sub-Saharan country to participate in Operation Desert Storm.

NOTABLE WARS AND INSURGENCIES: Casamance Secession 1989-present. Senegal-Mauritania Border War 1989-1991

UNLIKE MANY OF ITS WEST AFRICAN neighbours, Senegal has enjoyed a relatively peaceful and stable political history, both before and since independence from France in 1960. Prior to independence, Senegal and the French Soudan merged to form the Mali Federation. After independence, the federation broke up, and the French Soudan became the present-day Republic of Mali. During its colonial period, the capital Dakar served as the administrative center for French-owned West Africa. Previously, Senegal had been the seat of three powerful medieval empires based on the trans-Sahara trade route. This history of political stability and economic prosperity resonates today, as Senegal remains one of the few modern African states that has never experienced a violent transfer of political power or a military coup. Senegalese politics have evolved peacefully since independence from single-party rule into today's multiparty presidential democracy. Amendments to the constitution in 1974 and 1976 increased the number of legal political parties until legal statutes restricting the number of parties were abolished a few years later. In 1981, Senegal's first president, Léopold Senghor, became the first leader in post-colonial Africa to leave power peacefully, albeit to a successor of his own choosing, Abdou Diouf. Presidential power changed hands again in the 2000 elections, which were deemed fair and democratic.

Continued political stability derives largely from economic prosperity vis-à-vis other countries in the region. Senegal has a solid infrastructure, which subsequently supports a strong industrial sector. The information technology sector boomed after the country achieved full Internet connectivity in 1996. Senegal has since had the confidence of the international financial community. This is reflected in its being the first country in West Africa to acquire an international credit rating.

Senegal enjoys a relatively tension-free, multi-ethnic society, another factor that distinguishes it from nearly every other country on the African continent. Rather than dwell on ethnic self-determination, the Senegalese government focused early on building a sense of national identity, which is reflected by a political system now based more on political philosophies than ethnic identities.

ISSUES AND CHALLENGES:

- Separatist groups in the south continuously disrupt free trade along the border with Guinea-Bissau.

- Senegal is a transport point for South Asian heroin intended for the Western markets.

- Senegal has been accused of illicitly cultivating cannabis for the world market.

- Nearly half of Senegal's population is urban, and the country suffers from chronic urban problems such as drug addiction, unemployment, juvenile delinquency and union militancy.

- Illiteracy is Senegal's major educational problem: only 37 percent of the population can read.

HOW THE GOVERNMENT WORKS

LEGISLATIVE BRANCH

Assemblée Nationale (National Assembly) Unicameral Parliament
Composed of 120 members elected to five-year terms by direct popular vote. Meets twice annually for two-month sessions.
Initiates bills; debates budget.

Regional Governments
Ten regions administered by elected assemblies and governors appointed by president.

EXECUTIVE BRANCH

President
Elected to five-year term by direct popular vote; two-term limit.
Serves as head of state; commander-in-chief of armed forces.
Appoints diplomats; negotiates treaties; declares states of emergency; initiates bills; issues decrees.

Prime Minister
Appointed by president. Serves as head of government. Presides over Council of Ministers; answers to president.

Council of Ministers
Members appointed by prime minister on advice of president.
Oversees government operations.

JUDICIAL BRANCH

Constitutional Council
Rules on constitutionality of laws. Composed of senior magistrates and eminent academics and attorneys appointed by president.

The Supreme Court
Highest court of review and appeal. Composed of 10 justices appointed by president.

The High Court of Justice
Hears impeachment charges against president and ministers. Composed of two justices and ten members of National Assembly.

Supreme Court of Appeal
Hears lower-court appeals.

Courts of Assize
Hear felony cases; juries instead of judges render verdicts.

Petty Courts

TUNISIA

OFFICIAL NAME: REPUBLIC OF TUNISIA

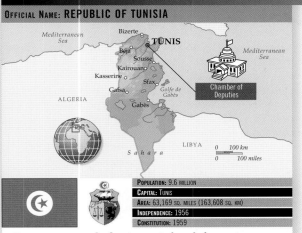

POPULATION: 9.6 MILLION	
CAPITAL: TUNIS	
AREA: 63,169 SQ. MILES (163,608 SQ. KM)	
INDEPENDENCE: 1956	
CONSTITUTION: 1959	

TUNISIA is named after its capital and the ancient Libyan settlement of Tunis.

RELIGION: Muslim (mainly Sunni) 98%, Jewish 1%, Christian 1%

OFFICIAL LANGUAGE: Arabic

REGIONS OR PROVINCES: 23 governorates

DEPENDENT TERRITORIES: None

MEDIA: Significant political censorship exists in national media

NEWSPAPERS: There are 8 daily newspapers

TV: 2 state-owned services

RADIO: 1 state-owned service

SUFFRAGE: 20 years of age; universal

LEGAL SYSTEM: Shari'a (Islamic) and French law; no ICJ jurisdiction

WORLD ORGANIZATIONS: ABEDA, ACCT, AfDB, AFESD, AL, AMF, AMU, BSEC (observer), CCC, ECA, FAO, G-77, IAEA, IBRD, ICAO, ICC, ICFTU, ICRM, IDA, IDB, IFAD, IFC, IFRCS, IHO, ILO, IMF, IMO, Interpol, IOC, IOM, ISO, ITU, MIPONUH, MONUC, NAM, OAS (observer), OAU, OIC, OPCW, OSCE (partner), UN, UNCTAD, UNESCO, UNHCR, UNIDO, UNMEE, UNMIK, UPU, WFTU, WHO, WIPO, WMO, WToO, WTrO

POLITICAL PARTIES: RCD—Constitutional Democracy Rally, MDS—Movement of Social Democrats, PUP—Popular Unity Party, UDU—Unionist Democratic Union, MR—Movement for Renewal, SLP—Social Liberal Party

ETHNIC GROUPS:

European 1%   Other 1%

Arab and Berber 98%

NATIONAL ECONOMICS

WORLD GNP RANKING: 62nd

GNP PER CAPITA: $2,100

INFLATION: 2.9%

BALANCE OF PAYMENTS (BALANCE OF TRADE): -$821 million

EXCHANGE RATES / U.S. DLR.: 1.384-1.461 TUNISIAN DINARS

OFFICIAL CURRENCY: TUNISIAN DINAR

GOVERNMENT SPENDING (% OF GDP)

✈	DEFENSE	1.7%
🎓	EDUCATION	7.6%
✚	HEALTH	2.2%

0   5   10   15

NUMBER OF CONFLICTS OVER LAST 25 YEARS

	1	2-5	5+
Violent changes in government	●	○	○
Civil wars	○	○	○
International wars	○	○	○
Foreign intervention	○	○	○

- Compulsory national military service.
- Military plays an active role in politics.
- US and France supply equipment and training.
- Security threats on border with Algeria.

NOTABLE WARS AND INSURGENCIES: Coup 1987

WITH ITS PROMINENT POSITION in the southern Mediterranean, Tunisia has long been a land of conflict and contrast. Like many of its Arab neighbors, the region endured a history dominated by invasion and conquest, coming for centuries under the rule of foreign empires, including the Carthaginian, Roman, Arab Muslim, Byzantine, Ottoman and French, until it gained independence as modern Tunisia in 1956. Unlike its neighbors, however, the contrasts that arose from centuries of turmoil have not hindered Tunisia from developing into a prosperous and stable nation.

On independence, Habib Bourguiba, the leader of the independence movement, was elected president. He was deposed in 1987 by Zine el-Abedine Ben Ali. The party that has dominated politics for much of Tunisia's history is the Socialist Destourian Party.

The majority of power in Tunisia rests in the president and his party, the Constitutional Democratic Rally (RCD), which has existed under different names since 1920. Traditionally, the executive branch wields great power over the legislature and judiciary. For example, though the legislative Chamber of Deputies has the power to override presidential decisions or a presidential veto, RCD dominance in the Chamber virtually eliminates that possibility, and presidential appointments to the judiciary strengthen the latter's allegiance. However, the government remains the most vibrant democracy in the Arab world, with opposition parties officially encouraged, though restrictions on press freedom still exist in practice and the Internet is heavily censored.

At the heart of every contrast in Tunisia is geography. The country is split between a fertile, lucrative, coastal region and the arid sands of the northern Sahara. The agricultural and tourist industries in the coastal regions complement the oil-producing south, which in turn creates a prosperous economic environment. Economic and political stability has produced a society that suffers from far less turmoil from Islamic fundamentalism than any other Arab nation, though critics do question the government's overt repression of fundamentalist activity. Most notably, however, women are afforded many more social rights than in any other Arab country.

ISSUES AND CHALLENGES:

- Islamic fundamentalism is a constant concern in Tunisia, and the government closely monitors fundamentalist movements in neighboring Algeria and Libya.
- Tunisia supported Iraq in the 1991 Gulf War, which complicated diplomatic ties and froze aid packages from countries such as Kuwait and Saudi Arabia.
- As in many Saharan countries, desertification is an increasing threat to the agricultural sector.
- State-sponsored harassment of Islamic fundamentalists has promted increasing criticism from human rights activists.

HOW THE GOVERNMENT WORKS

LEGISLATIVE BRANCH

Majlis al-Nuwaab
(Chamber of Deputies)
Unicameral Parliament
Composed of 182 members who serve five-year terms: 148 elected by direct popular vote; 34 appointed by opposition parties on proportional basis. Debates national policy; reviews and passes bills proposed by president; overrides vetoes by two-thirds majority vote; no power to impeach president.

Regional Governments
Twenty-three governorates administered by governors appointed by president.

EXECUTIVE BRANCH

President
Elected to five-year term by direct popular vote; two-term limit. Serves as head of state; commander-in-chief of armed forces. Initiates and vetoes bills; rules by decree when Parliament is out of session; declares states of emergency.

Prime Minister
Appointed by president. Serves as head of government.

Council of State
Appointed by president. Oversees government operations; answers to president.

JUDICIAL BRANCH

Higher Council of the Judiciary
Supervises appointment, promotion, and discipline of judges. Presided over by president; members elected by judges from within their ranks.

Constitutional Court
Examines bills proposed by president. No power to rule on constitutionality of laws.

Court of Cassation
Highest court of review and appeals; rules only on points of law, not facts. Composed of judges appointed by president.

Courts of Appeal

Courts of First Instance

Magistrates' Courts

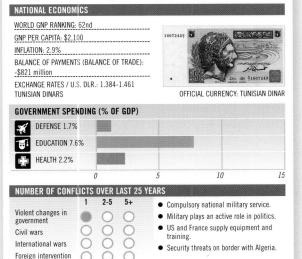

BOLIVIA

OFFICIAL NAME: REPUBLIC OF BOLIVIA

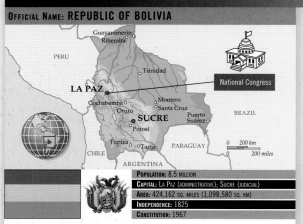

POPULATION: 8.5 MILLION

CAPITAL: LA PAZ (ADMINISTRATIVE); SUCRE (JUDICIAL)

AREA: 424,162 SQ. MILES (1,098,580 SQ. KM)

INDEPENDENCE: 1825

CONSTITUTION: 1967

BOLIVIA was named after Simón Bolívar, the hero of the country's revolution that brought independence.

RELIGION: Roman Catholic 93%, Other 7%

OFFICIAL LANGUAGES: Spanish, Quechua, and Aymará

REGIONS OR PROVINCES: 9 departments

DEPENDENT TERRITORIES: None

MEDIA: No political censorship exists in national media

Newspapers: There are 18 daily newspapers

TV: 1 state-owned service with 9 stations, 36 independent stations

Radio: 1 state-owned service, 145 independent stations

SUFFRAGE: 18 years of age (married); 21 years of age (single); universal and compulsory

LEGAL SYSTEM: French and Spanish law; no ICJ jurisdiction

WORLD ORGANIZATIONS: CCC, ECLAC, FAO, G-77, IADB, IAEA, IBRD, ICAO, ICRM, IDA, IFAD, IFC, IFRCS, ILO, IMF, IMO, Interpol, IOC, IOM, ISO (correspondent), ITU, LAES, LAIA, Mercosur (associate), MONUC, NAM, OAS, OPANAL, OPCW, PCA, RG, UN, UNAMSIL, UNCTAD, UNESCO, UNIDO, UNTAET, UPU, WCL, WFTU, WHO, WIPO, WMO, WToO, WTrO

POLITICAL PARTIES: MNR—Nationalist Revolutionary Movement, MAS—Movement for Socialism, MIR—Movement of the Revolutionary Left, NFR—New Republican Force, MIP—Pachakuti Indigenous Movement, UCS—Union for Civic Solidarity, AND—Nationalist Democratic Action, PS—Socialist Party

ETHNIC GROUPS:

Other 8%
Quechua 37%
European 10%
Mixed 13%
Aymara 32%

NATIONAL ECONOMICS

WORLD GNP RANKING: 93rd

GNP PER CAPITA: $990

INFLATION: 4.6%

BALANCE OF PAYMENTS (BALANCE OF TRADE): -$464 million

EXCHANGE RATES / U.S. DLR.: 6.36-6.82 BOLIVIANOS

OFFICIAL CURRENCY: BOLIVIANO

GOVERNMENT SPENDING (% OF GDP)

		0	5	10	15
✈	DEFENSE 1.4%				
🎓	EDUCATION 4.9%				
✚	HEALTH 4.1%				

NUMBER OF CONFLICTS OVER LAST 25 YEARS

	1	2-5	5+
Violent changes in government	○	○	○
Civil wars	○	○	○
International wars	○	○	○
Foreign intervention	○	○	○

- Compulsory national military service.
- US is largest supplier of military equipment.
- Army is major recipient of defense spending.
- Tensions over water rights with Chile.

NOTABLE WARS AND INSURGENCIES: None

BOLIVIA, INHABITED BY THE AYMARÁ CIVILIZATION until the late 1400s, was conquered by the Incas and then just 50 years later by the Spanish, who called it Upper Peru. Independence from Spain came in 1825. Bolivia's years of self-rule have been marred by almost 200 coups and counter coups—at least one a year from independence until the early 1980s. Most of the struggles have been among the powerful elite and have led to periods of extreme economic crisis. Income inequality and deep disappointment in the political system remain prominent issues.

A major transition came in 1952, when the Nationalist Revolutionary Movement (MNR) led a successful revolution after its presidential candidate, Víctor Paz Estenssoro, won the 1951 election but was denied the presidency by the military. Nationalizing many of the country's tin mines, Estenssoro was able to bring land reform, education and universal suffrage to Bolivia, but over time the MNR became divided on many of the major issues and Estenssoro's government was overthrown in 1964 in a military coup led by his vice-president, General René Barrientos. Barrientos died in a helicopter accident in 1969. Three different presidents then ruled in a period of less than two years, and General Hugo Bánzer Suárez came to power in 1971. Bánzer's military regime remained in place for seven years until national and international pressure led to new elections, which created even more political turmoil.

In 1982, Bolivia brought an end to its tradition of military takeovers and regimes by honoring the results of elections held two years earlier. Hernán Siles Zuazo's civilian government and the Movement of the Revolutionary Left (MIR), however, led the country to economic disaster; inflation reached 25,000 percent in 1985.

The MNR and MIR parties have alternated in power since 1989, except when Banzer won direct presidential elections as the Nationalist Democratic Action (ADN) candidate in 1997. Poor health forced him to resign in 2001. Gonzalo Sánchez de Lozada of the MNR was elected president in 2002. Interestingly, if a presidential candidate does not secure a simple majority of the popular vote in Bolivia, the Chamber of Deputies legislature makes a selection for the presidency from the top two winning candidates.

ISSUES AND CHALLENGES:

- Many voters are disillusioned with the political process—most politicians are viewed as self-serving and corrupt. Few believe the campaign promises of reform.

- Bolivia has an extremely high rate of child mortality, mostly due to disease that could be prevented by immunization. Almost 40 percent of children below three years of age are considered malnourished.

- Bolivia is one of the poorest countries in South America.

HOW THE GOVERNMENT WORKS

LEGISLATIVE BRANCH

Congreso Nacional
(National Congress)
Bicameral Parliament
Passes laws; approves budget; ratifies treaties; overrides vetoes; elects president when no candidate wins absolute majority of popular vote.

Cámara de Senadores
(Chamber of Senators)
Composed of 27 members elected to five-year terms by direct popular vote.

Cámara de Diputados
(Chamber of Deputies)
Composed of 130 members elected to five-year terms by direct popular vote and proportional representation.

Regional Governments
Nine departments administered by officials appointed by central government.

EXECUTIVE BRANCH

President
Elected to five-year term by direct popular vote, no consecutive re-election. Serves as head of state and government. Directs foreign and economic policies; declares states of siege; legislates by decree; vetoes bills (though veto can be overridden by parliament),

Vice-president
Elected to five-year term by direct popular vote. Serves as president of Parliament.

Cabinet
Composed of 13 members; appointed by president, presided over by president; oversees government operations.

JUDICIAL BRANCH

Judicial Council
Disciplinary body of judicial branch. Supreme Court president presides. Composed of four councillors elected to ten-year terms by Parliament.

Supreme Court
Highest court of review and appeal. President and 11 ministers appointed to single 10-year terms by Chamber of Deputies on advice of Judicial Council.

District Courts
Judges appointed to six-year terms by Supreme Court.

Superior Courts
Judges nominated to six-year terms by Judicial Council, appointed by Supreme Court.

Lower Courts
Judges serve four-year terms.

DOMINICAN REPUBLIC

OFFICIAL NAME: DOMINICAN REPUBLIC

Monte Cristi · Puerto Plata · ATLANTIC OCEAN
Mao · Santiago · San Francisco de Macorís
La Vega
HAITI
San Juan · SANTO DOMINGO · El Seibo · San Pedro de Macorís
San Cristóbal · La Romana
Barahona
Caribbean Sea
0 50 km
0 50 miles
National Congress

POPULATION: 2 MILLION
CAPITAL: Santo Domingo
AREA: 18,679 SQ. MILES (48,380 SQ. KM)
INDEPENDENCE: 1865
CONSTITUTION: 1966

THE DOMINICAN REPUBLIC was named by Columbus in honor of his father's patron saint, Saint Dominica.

RELIGION: Roman Catholic 92%, Other and non-religious 8%

OFFICIAL LANGUAGE: Spanish

REGIONS OR PROVINCES: 29 provinces and 1 district

DEPENDENT TERRITORIES: None

MEDIA: No political censorship exists in national media

NEWSPAPERS: There are 11 daily newspapers

TV: 7 services: 1 state-owned, 6 independent

RADIO: 131 services: 1 state-owned, 130 independent

SUFFRAGE: 18 years of age, universal and compulsory; married persons regardless of age; members of the armed forces and police may not vote

LEGAL SYSTEM: French law; accepts ICJ jurisdiction

WORLD ORGANIZATIONS: ACP, Caricom (observer), ECLAC, FAO, G-77, IADB, IAEA, IBRD, ICAO, ICFTU, ICRM, IDA, IFAD, IFC, IFRCS, IHO, ILO, IMF, IMO, Interpol, IOC, IOM, ISO (subscriber), ITU, LAES, LAIA (observer), NAM (observer), OAS, OPANAL, OPCW (signatory), PCA, RG, UN, UNCTAD, UNESCO, UNIDO, UNMIK, UPU, WCL, WFTU, WHO, WIPO, WMO, WToO, WTrO **POLITICAL PARTIES:** PRD—Dominican Revolutionary Party, PLD—Dominican Liberation Party, PRSC—Christian Social Reform Party

ETHNIC GROUPS:
Black 11%
White 16%
Mixed 73%

NATIONAL ECONOMICS

WORLD GNP RANKING: 71st
GNP PER CAPITA: $2,130
INFLATION: 6.5%
BALANCE OF PAYMENTS (BALANCE OF TRADE): -$1.03 billion
EXCHANGE RATES / U.S. DLR.: 16.12-16.4 DOMINICAN REPUBLIC PESOS

OFFICIAL CURRENCY: DOM. REP. PESO

GOVERNMENT SPENDING (% OF GDP)
DEFENSE 0.8%
EDUCATION 2.3%
HEALTH 1.9%
0 5 10 15

NUMBER OF CONFLICTS OVER LAST 25 YEARS

	1	2-5	5+
Violent changes in government	○	○	○
Civil wars	○	○	○
International wars	○	○	○
Foreign intervention	○	○	○

- No compulsory national military service.
- US is largest supplier of military equipment.
- Major threats are contraband and illegal immigrants from Haiti en route to the US.

NOTABLE WARS AND INSURGENCIES: None

THE DOMINICAN REPUBLIC OCCUPIES TWO-THIRDS of the island of Hispaniola ("Little Spain"). The remaining third of the island belongs to the Republic of Haiti. While approximately 73 percent of the population is of mixed race and controls most commercial activity, the white Spanish-speaking minority owns much of the land.

The political history of the Caribbean nation of the Dominican Republic has been marked by great instability, and its democratic ideals interrupted many times over the years by military coups, revolutions, dictatorships, foreign invasions, as well as serious economic crises. The Dominican Republic was occupied by Spanish settlers, later by the French, and then by the Haitians, who remained in control of the island until 1844. That year, the Dominican Republic declared independence, but a few years later chose to be administered again by the Spanish Empire. Spanish rule continued until 1865, when independence was re-established.

In 1916, when the Dominican Republic was going through internal political disorder and economic troubles, the United States occupied the island and remained until 1924. Then for six years the country experimented with democracy, but this period also marked the beginning of the political instability. In 1930, one of the major historical figures, army commander Rafael Trujillo, took over the government, and his dictatorship lasted until his assassination by opposition forces in 1961. Trujillo attempted economic development, but also endorsed the suppression of basic human rights. From that time, a few temporary and unsettled governments briefly ruled the Dominican Republic, until 1966, when Joaquín Balaguer won the presidential elections. Losing the election in 1978 he returned to power in 1986, until international pressure following allegations of corrupt elections in 1994 forced new elections in 1996, which were won by Leonel Fernández.

Santo Domingo was the first city in the western hemisphere to be founded by Europeans

Voters are presented with two ballots for each party—one for local offices, and one for the presidency. Ballot papers are color-coded to indicate the party; this practice continues from times when most adult Dominicans were illiterate.

ISSUES AND CHALLENGES:
- The Dominican Republic has been through a vicious cycle of government changes over the years, which to this day has potential to shake the political system. Economic instability, especially since the international financial crisis of the 1970s, forced its governments to take strict measures, but also led to their unpopularity and dismissal. Almost every change led to greater economic decline, corruption, and political volatility, clearly reflected in the many new constitutions—around 30—drafted since the country's independence in the 1865.

HOW THE GOVERNMENT WORKS

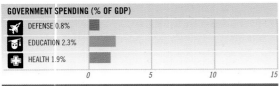

LEGISLATIVE BRANCH
Congresso Nacional
(National Congress)
Bicameral Parliament

Senado
(Senate)
Composed of 30 members elected to four-year terms by direct popular vote: one from each of 29 provinces; one from capital Santo Domingo.

Cámara de Diputados
(Chamber of Deputies)
Composed of 149 members elected to four-year terms by direct popular vote.

Regional Governments
Twenty-nine provinces administered by governors appointed by president; National District of Santo Domingo governed by elected mayor and local council.

EXECUTIVE BRANCH
President
Elected to four-year term by direct popular vote. Serves as head of state and government; commander-in-chief of armed forces and police corps. Initiates bills; proposes budget.

Vice-president
Elected on presidential ticket to four-year term by direct popular vote.

Cabinet
Composed of members appointed by president. Implements laws; oversees government operations.

JUDICIAL BRANCH
Supreme Court
Highest court of review and appeal; initiates judicial bills; appoints lower-court judges. Composed of 11 justices appointed by National Council of Magistrates (which oversees the judiciary)

Courts of Appeal
Land Tribunals
Courts of First Instance

CHAD

OFFICIAL NAME: REPUBLIC OF CHAD

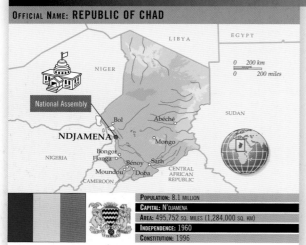

POPULATION: 8.1 MILLION
CAPITAL: N'DJAMENA
AREA: 495,752 SQ. MILES (1,284,000 SQ. KM)
INDEPENDENCE: 1960
CONSTITUTION: 1996

CHAD was named after the lake which forms its southwestern border with Nigeria.

RELIGION: Muslim 50%, Traditional beliefs 43%, Christian 7%

OFFICIAL LANGUAGES: Arabic and French

REGIONS OR PROVINCES: 14 prefectures, to be replaced by 28 departments and 1 city

DEPENDENT TERRITORIES: None

MEDIA: Total political censorship exists in national media. Broadcasting is controlled by the government.

NEWSPAPERS: There are 2 daily newspapers

TV: 1 state-controlled service

RADIO: 8 services; 1 state-controlled, 7 independent

SUFFRAGE: 18 years of age; universal

LEGAL SYSTEM: Customary and French law; no ICJ jurisdiction

ETHNIC GROUPS:
Arab 15%
Tuareg and Toubou 38%
Other 17%
Sara 30%

WORLD ORGANIZATIONS: ACCT, ACP, AfDB, BDEAC, CEEAC, CEMAC, ECA, FAO, FZ, G-77, IBRD, ICAO, ICFTU, ICRM, IDA, IDB, IFAD, IFC, IFRCS, ILO, IMF, Interpol, IOC, ITU, NAM, OAU, OIC, OPCW (signatory), UN, UNCTAD, UNESCO, UNIDO, UPU, WCL, WHO, WIPO, WMO, WToO, WTrO

POLITICAL PARTIES: MPS—Patriotic Salvation Movement, RDP—Rally for Democracy and Progress, FAR—Front of Action Forces for the Republic

NATIONAL ECONOMICS

WORLD GNP RANKING: 143rd

GNP PER CAPITA: $200

INFLATION: 3.8%

BALANCE OF PAYMENTS (BALANCE OF TRADE): -$158 million

EXCHANGE RATES / U.S. DLR.: 698.7–736.7 CFA FRANCS

OFFICIAL CURRENCY: CFA FRANC

GOVERNMENT SPENDING (% OF GDP)

✈ DEFENSE 2.8%	
🎓 EDUCATION 1.7%	
✚ HEALTH 2.3%	

0   5   10   15

NUMBER OF CONFLICTS OVER LAST 25 YEARS

	1	2-5	5+
Violent changes in government			
Civil wars			
International wars			
Foreign intervention			

- Compulsory national military service.
- France supplies military equipment and training.
- Rebels in north are a threat to security, not contained by 2002 peace treaty.

NOTABLE WARS AND INSURGENCIES: Civil war 1979-1982. Libyan invasions of Chad 1979 and 1981. Overt military support from France, Libya, and regional militias during 1980s conflicts. Coups and insurrections

---

CHAD'S RICH HISTORY stretches back centuries to powerful chiefs who ruled the land and its clans of herders and farmers. But its recent history since independence from French colonial rule has been marked by prolonged civil wars. Chad currently is managing a fragile peace among hostile factions under a what is obstensibly a multiparty democracy, though under tight presidential control.

Once part of the ancient kingdoms of Kanem-Bornu and Baguirmi, Chad was overwhelmed by French troops at the turn of the 20th century and incorporated into France's colonial Federation of French Equatorial Africa. Chad began self-rule in 1960, but a tax revolt soon mushroomed into a civil war between Muslims in the north and east, and Christians in the south.

A military coup in 1975 ousted Chad's president, intensifying conflict between regional factions and crippling the national government. International mediation produced the Lagos Accord of 1979, establishing a coalition government balanced among Chad's regions. But the union collapsed amid renewed fighting, ushering in a turbulent period of torture and massacres. Later, Libya entered the strife, sending troops into Chad on behalf of its northern faction. France and Zaire, in response, dispatched their own troops to drive out the Libyans.

By 1990, rivalries among leaders of Chad's government culminated in a military coup by General Idriss Déby, overthrowing the government of President Hissène Habré. True to his promises of multipartyism, political parties were legalized in 1992. In 1996, Déby won election as president in Chad's first multiparty, but widely disputed, election. A successful referendum that year gave Chad a new constitution based on the French model. Under its provisions, Chad's government is composed of an elected president, prime minister and Council of Ministers, a bicameral legislature with a National Assembly and yet-to-be-created Senate, and an independent judiciary. In practice, however, the president holds considerable power over all three branches. Déby retained the presidency in 2001 elections that were marred by claims of fraud and government corruption.

ISSUES AND CHALLENGES:

- Weapon availability is thought to have encouraged the widespread use of guns to solve even minor issues, while armed robbery and vandalism are widespread.

- Chad is highly dependent on aid from France and the World Bank, which has made elementary education a priority. Currently, only 46 percent of children receive any form of schooling.

- While the economy is largely underdeveloped, with limited infrastructure, the recent discovery of oil deposits has presented a huge opportunity for Chad to become a major oil producer.

- A rebellion in the north that began in 1999 remains unresolved, even after a Libyan peace deal in 2002.

HOW THE GOVERNMENT WORKS

LEGISLATIVE BRANCH

National Assembly
Bicameral Parliament
Composed of 155 members elected to four-year terms by direct popular vote. Meets twice annually. Initiates and passes bills; approve prime minister's plan of government; removes prime minister with no-confidence vote; may impeach president for abuses of office.

Senate
Chamber mandated by 1996 constitution but yet to be established.

Regional Governments
Fourteen prefectures administered by governors appointed by president.

EXECUTIVE BRANCH

President
Elected to five-year term by direct popular vote, two-term limit. Serves as head of state; commander-in-chief of armed forces. Initiates and vetoes bills; dissolves Parliament; calls new elections; declares states of emergency.

Prime Minister
Appointed by president. Serves as head of government; chairs Council of Ministers; coordinates economic and social programs.

Council of Ministers
Members appointed by president on advice of prime minister. Oversees government operations.

JUDICIAL BRANCH

Constitutional Council
Rules on constitutionality of laws. Composed of nine judges appointed to nine-year terms by president and Parliament.

High Court of Justice
Tries cases of corruption, drug trafficking, human rights violations, misuse of public funds and treason. Composed of 15 members.

Supreme Court
Highest court of review and appeal. Chief justice, appointed by president, and 15 councillors, appointed by president and National Assembly; all serve for life.

Criminal Courts

Magistrates' Courts

HONDURAS

OFFICIAL NAME: REPUBLIC OF HONDURAS

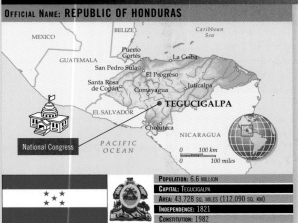

National Congress

TEGUCIGALPA

POPULATION: 6.6 MILLION	
CAPITAL: TEGUCIGALPA	
AREA: 43,728 SQ. MILES (112,090 SQ. KM)	
INDEPENDENCE: 1821	
CONSTITUTION: 1982	

HONDURAS means "depths" in Spanish, which refers to the deep waters off the northern coast.

RELIGION: Roman Catholic 97%, Protestant and Other 3%

OFFICIAL LANGUAGE: Spanish

REGIONS OR PROVINCES: 18 departments

DEPENDENT TERRITORIES: None

MEDIA: Self-censorship, dependence on US sources, corruption, and intimidation guarantee a largely compliant media

NEWSPAPERS: There are 9 daily newspapers

TV: 6 independent services

RADIO: 5 services: 1 state-owned, 4 independent

SUFFRAGE: 18 years of age; universal and compulsory

LEGAL SYSTEM: English common law; Roman and Spanish law; accepts ICJ jurisdiction

WORLD ORGANIZATIONS: BCIE, CACM, ECLAC, FAO, G-77, IADB, IBRD, ICAO, ICFTU, ICRM, IDA, IFAD, IFC, IFRCS, ILO, IMF, IMO, Interpol, IOC, IOM, ISO (subscriber), ITU, LAES, LAIA (observer), MINURSO, NAM, OAS, OPANAL, OPCW (signatory), PCA, RG, UN, UNCTAD, UNESCO, UNIDO, UPU, WCL, WFTU, WHO, WIPO, WMO, WToO, WTrO

POLITICAL PARTIES: PNH—National Party of Honduras, PLH—Liberal Party of Honduras, PDU—Party of Democratic Unification, PINU-SD—Innovation and Unity Party-Social Democracy, PDCH—Honduran Christian Democratic Party

ETHNIC GROUPS:
- Amerindian 4%
- White 1%
- Black African 5%
- Mestizo 90%

NATIONAL ECONOMICS

WORLD GNP RANKING: 107th

GNP PER CAPITA: $860

INFLATION: 11.1%

BALANCE OF PAYMENTS (BALANCE OF TRADE): -$204 million

EXCHANGE RATES / U.S. DLR.: 15.10–15.88 LEMPIRAS

OFFICIAL CURRENCY: LEMPIRA

GOVERNMENT SPENDING (% OF GDP)

- ✈ DEFENSE 1.6%
- 📚 EDUCATION 4%
- ✚ HEALTH 3.9%

0   5   10   15

NUMBER OF CONFLICTS OVER LAST 25 YEARS

	1	2-5	5+
Violent changes in government	○	○	○
Civil wars	◐	○	○
International wars	○	○	○
Foreign intervention	○	○	○

- No compulsory national military service.
- Military not fully staffed since phasing out of conscription.
- Disputes with Belize, El Salvador over territories.

NOTABLE WARS AND INSURGENCIES: Leftist insurgency 1981-1990

LAND OF A ONCE-FLOURISHING MAYAN CIVILIZATION, Honduras in the 20th century struggled through internal rebellions and strained under harsh dictatorships. It now rules itself under a presidential democracy, with its military finally under civilian control.

In the early 1500s, Spain began building settlements along Honduras' coast and ruled the territory for the next three centuries. After independence in 1821, Honduras joined other freed Spanish colonies to form the short-lived United Provinces of Central America. Starting in the 1930s, Honduras was controlled by General Tiburcio Carias Andino. Tied to neighboring dictators and backed by US banana companies, his autocratic rule lasted until 1948. Two subsequent authoritarian regimes ended in a palace coup by military reformists. The 1950s saw attempts to separate the military from politics, but right-wing officers seized the government in a bloody coup in 1963. Mired in corruption, the new regime was soon replaced by more progressive military governments that pursued reforms of the armed forces and built much of present-day Honduras' infrastructure and telecommunications system.

With political instability deepening in El Salvador and Nicaragua, the military hurried plans to return Honduras to civilian rule. General elections were held and in 1982 a new constitution adopted. It established a three-branch system of government: a strong executive branch, headed by an elected president; a unicameral legislature; and an independent judiciary.

Despite civilian rule, the military continued to undermine Honduras' government. Death squads terrorized the populace, murdering many reformers and Liberal Party members. Meanwhile, the use of Honduras by the US to launch air assaults against communist forces in Nicaragua and El Salvador embroiled the nation in the region's civil wars. In 1999, control of the army was put totally into civilian hands, signaling the end of military power in Honduras. Since its new constitution, Honduras has enjoyed six peaceful transfers of power, but still has to deal effectively with gang crime and the murder of street children by death squads.

ISSUES AND CHALLENGES:

- Thousands of Contra fighters left over from US anti-Sandinista campaigns in Nicaragua, coupled with high unemployment, poverty, and unequal wealth distribution, result in outbreaks of violence and a high crime rate. Youth gang culture is a serious problem.

- Slash and burn agricultural methods, unregulated timber, cotton, and cattle industries, inappropriate use of pesticides, and land colonization have adversely affected the environment.

- Political corruption and growing public cynicism may hinder democracy's future stability.

- Poverty and lack of adequate education make industry incapable of competing in global markets.

- The banana industry has not yet recovered from the Hurricane Mitch in 1998, resulting in 5,600 dead and $3 billion-worth of damage.

HOW THE GOVERNMENT WORKS

LEGISLATIVE BRANCH

Congreso Nacional (National Congress) Unicameral Parliament
Composed of 128 members directly elected to four-year terms proportional to the number of votes their party's presidential candidate receives. Each member elected with a substitute to serve out vacated office. Religious leaders, military or police members, public officials and their spouses barred from office.

Regional Governments
Eighteen departments administered by governors appointed by president.

EXECUTIVE BRANCH

President
Elected to four-year term by direct popular vote. Serves as head of state and government. Vetoes bills; calls Parliament into special session; submits budget; negotiates treaties.

Three Vice-presidents
Elected to four-year terms concurrently with president. National Congress elects one to succeed president in case of vacancy.

Cabinet
Composed of 14 members appointed by president. Oversees government operations.

JUDICIAL BRANCH

Supreme Court
Highest Court of review and appeal; has original jurisdiction; rules on constitutionality of laws; appoints lower-court judges and justices of the peace. Comprises nine justices and seven alternatives elected to four-year terms by Parliament.

National Election Tribunal
Oversees electoral process. President chosen by Supreme Court; other members by registered parties.

Courts of Appeal
Hear lower-court appeals.

Courts of First Instance
Hear serious criminal and civil cases.

Justices of the Peace

BENIN

OFFICIAL NAME: REPUBLIC OF BENIN

POPULATION: 6.4 MILLION
CAPITAL: PORTO-NOVO
AREA: 43,483 SQ. MILES (112,620 SQ. KM)
INDEPENDENCE: 1960
CONSTITUTION: 1990

BENIN, formerly known as Dahomey, was renamed in 1974 after the ancient Nigerian kingdom of Benin, which flourished between the 13th and 19th centuries.

RELIGION: Indigenous beliefs 70%, Muslim 15%, Christian 15%

OFFICIAL LANGUAGE: French

REGIONS OR PROVINCES: 12 provinces

DEPENDENT TERRITORIES: None

MEDIA: No political censorship exists in national media.

Newspapers: There are 18 daily newspapers

TV: 5 services: 1 state-owned, 4 independent

Radio: 19 services: 1 state-owned, 18 independent

SUFFRAGE: 18 years of age; universal

LEGAL SYSTEM: Customary law and French civil law; no ICJ jurisdiction

WORLD ORGANIZATIONS: ACP, AfDB, CCC, ECA, ECOWAS, Entente, FAO, FZ, G-77, IAEA, IBRD, ICAO, ICFTU, ICRM, IDA, IDB, IFAD, IFC, IFRCS, ILO, IMF, IMO, Interpol, IOC, IOM, ISO (subscriber), ITU, MIPONUH, MONUC, NAM, OAU, OIC, OPCW, UN, UNCTAD, UNESCO, UNIDO, UNMEE, UNMIK, UPU, WADB (regional), WAEMU, WCL, WFTU, WHO, WIPO, WMO, WToO, WTrO

POLITICAL PARTIES: PRB— Benin Renaissance Party, PRD— Party of Democratic Renewal, FARD—Action Front for Renewal and Development, PSD—Social Democratic Party, MADEP— African Movement for Democracy and Progress, IPD—Impetus for Progress and Democracy

ETHNIC GROUPS:

Other 1%

African (42 ethnic groups, most important being Fon, Adja, Yoruba, and Bariba) 99%

NATIONAL ECONOMICS

WORLD GNP RANKING: 135th

GNP PER CAPITA: $370

INFLATION: 4.2%

BALANCE OF PAYMENTS (BAlANCE OF TRADE): -$168 million

EXCHANGE RATES / U.S. DLR.: 698.7-736.7 CFA FRANCS

OFFICIAL CURRENCY: CFA FRANC

GOVERNMENT SPENDING (% OF GDP)

		0	5	10	15
✈	DEFENSE 1.4%				
	EDUCATION 2.6%				
✚	HEALTH 1.6%				

NUMBER OF CONFLICTS OVER LAST 25 YEARS

	1	2-5	5+
Violent changes in government	○	○	○
Civil wars	○	○	○
International wars	○	○	○
Foreign intervention	○	○	○

- Compulsory national military service.
- Army priority is smuggling along Nigerian border.
- As part of ECOWAS, armed forces assisted ECOMOG in Côte d'Ivoire in 2003.
- Troops participated in UN peacekeeping missions in Liberia, Guinea-Bissau and Togo.

NOTABLE WARS AND INSURGENCIES: None

PRESENT-DAY BENIN CORRESPONDS roughly to the lands of the great kingdom of Dahomey, established in 1625 by the indigenous slave-traders, the Fon. However, by 1900 it had became a colony of France, and in 1958 a self-governing territory, the Republic of Dahomey. The modern state of Benin began on August 1, 1960, when the republic gained full independence from France. Suffering from repeated coups and political fragmentation, the first dozen years of Dahomey were volatile. The turbulence ended on October 26, 1972, when Major Mathieu Kérékou staged the country's last coup, changed the official name to Benin, and instituted a single-party socialist system that was heavily influenced by the Soviet Union. The current political system results from peaceful democratic revolutions in 1989, which coincided with the anti-communist and anti-Soviet uprisings in Eastern Europe and Russia that ended single-party socialist rule in many of those countries as well.

Most political power in Benin rests in the executive branch, and primarily in the offices of the president and Executive Council. Under the president's direction—and with the Council's advice—Council ministries enact national policy and administer the country's 12 provinces.

The legislative branch consists of the Assemblée Nationale, or National Assembly. Common practice in Benin dictates that the Assembly meets for two annual sessions that begin in April and October. At these sessions, members debate policy matters, approve or reject presidential political decisions, and enact domestic legislation. A remarkable aspect of the Assembly is its dedication to multiparty representation, at which it has been largely successful, making Benin unique among West African nations. By early 1996, over 80 political parties were registered in the country, a sharp contrast with the single communist party in 1989. Currently, the two most influential parties are the Party of the Rebirth of Benin (PRB) and the Democratic Renewal Party (PRD).

The country's judicial branch is based on French civil and customary legal systems, which strengthens the nation's cultural and political ties to its most important international benefactor.

ISSUES AND CHALLENGES:

- Based primarily on subsistence agriculture, Benin's economy is underdeveloped. Severe desertification in the north further inhibits economic growth.

- Large-scale smuggling— everything from narcotics to child trafficking—remains a lucrative business in Benin. This has led to a sharp increase in violent crime in recent years.

- Much of Benin's border is not demarcated, and territorial disputes with Niger, Nigeria, Togo, and Burkina Faso frustrate foreign policy.

- A political divide exists between the north and south, reflecting tensions between Muslims and Christians.

HOW THE GOVERNMENT WORKS

LEGISLATIVE BRANCH
Assemblée Nationale
(National Assembly)
Unicameral Parliament
Composed of 83 members elected to four-year terms by direct popular vote.

Regional Governments
Six administrative regions; 12 provinces.

EXECUTIVE BRANCH
President
Elected to five-year term by direct popular vote; two-term limit. Serves as head of state and government.

Prime Minister
Appointed by president.

Executive Council
Composed of 19 members, including president and prime minister; appointed by president, approved by National Assembly.

JUDICIAL BRANCH
Constitutional Court
Rules on constitutionality of laws. Composed of seven members nominated by National Assembly, appointed by president.

Supreme Court
Highest court of review and appeal. Composed of 13 judges: six elected by National Assembly; seven appointed by president.

High Court of Justice
Administers justice on regional and local levels. Composed of all Constitutional Court members (except its president), six deputies, and president of National Assembly.

EL SALVADOR

OFFICIAL NAME: REPUBLIC OF EL SALVADOR

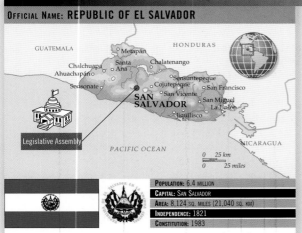

POPULATION: 6.4 MILLION
CAPITAL: SAN SALVADOR
AREA: 8,124 SQ. MILES (21,040 SQ. KM)
INDEPENDENCE: 1821
CONSTITUTION: 1983

EL SALVADOR means "the savior" in Spanish and is literally named for Jesus Christ.

RELIGION: Roman Catholic 80%, Evangelical 18%, Other 2%

OFFICIAL LANGUAGE: Spanish

REGIONS OR PROVINCES: 14 departments

DEPENDENT TERRITORIES: None

MEDIA: Partial political censorship exists in national media

Newspapers: There are 8 daily newspapers

TV: 10 channels: 2 state-owned, 8 independent

Radio: 66 stations: 1 state-owned, 65 independent

SUFFRAGE: 18 years of age; universal

LEGAL SYSTEM: Civil and Roman law; accepts ICJ jurisdiction

WORLD ORGANIZATIONS: BCIE, CACM, ECLAC, FAO, G-77, IADB, IAEA, IBRD, ICAO, ICFTU, ICRM, IDA, IFAD, IFC, IFRCS, ILO, IMF, IMO, Interpol, IOC, IOM, ISO (correspondent), ITU, LAES, LAIA (observer), MINURSO, NAM (observer), OAS, OPANAL, OPCW, PCA, RG, UN, UNCTAD, UNESCO, UNIDO, UPU, WCL, WFTU, WHO, WIPO, WMO, WToO, WTrO

POLITICAL PARTIES: FMLN—Farabundo Martí National Liberation Front, ARENA—Nationalist Republican Alliance, PCN—National Conciliation Party, PDC—Christian Democratic Party, CDU—United Democratic Center

ETHNIC GROUPS:

Amerindian 1%
White 9%
Mestizo 90%

NATIONAL ECONOMICS

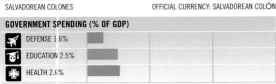

WORLD GNP RANKING: 78th

GNP PER CAPITA: $2,000

INFLATION: 2.3%

BALANCE OF PAYMENTS (BALANCE OF TRADE): -$48 million

EXCHANGE RATES / U.S. DLR.: 8.740-8.747 SALVADOREAN COLONES

OFFICIAL CURRENCY: SALVADOREAN COLÓN

GOVERNMENT SPENDING (% OF GDP)

✈ DEFENSE 1.6%
🎓 EDUCATION 2.5%
✚ HEALTH 2.6%

	0	5	10	15

NUMBER OF CONFLICTS OVER LAST 25 YEARS

	1	2-5	5+
Violent changes in government	●	○	○
Civil wars	●	○	○
International wars	○	○	○
Foreign intervention	●	○	○

- Compulsory national military service.
- Military plays a reduced role in politics and internal security.
- Territorial dispute with Honduras.
- Country recovering from civil war from 1981 to 1992.

NOTABLE WARS AND INSURGENCIES: Coup 1979. Salvadorean Civil War 1981-1992

EL SALVADOR IS POLARIZED BY EXTREME POVERTY AND WEALTH, products of an agricultural economy dominated by a coffee industry historically controlled by an elite few. A 1931 military coup wrested political power from the ruling oligarchy, La Catorce (the Fourteen), ushering in more than 50 years of political rule by a military *caudillo* (chieftain) system and leaving economic control in the hands of a small number of wealthy families. Gross disparities in income resulted in the 1932 revolt led by Agustín Farabundo Martí, which ended with Martí's execution and the massacre of 25,000 indigenous Indians, decimating the Indian population and further polarizing the country. A coup in 1979 by army officers and civilians promising to install democracy did not prevent the eruption of civil war again in 1981, between the Farabundo Martí National Liberation Front (FMLN) guerrillas and the government. This lasted 12 years until the United Nations-brokered peace agreement of 1992. A "Truth Commission" established to investigate the human rights violations of the civil war published its findings in 1993, recommending that those found guilty be removed from office, and as a result, 103 officers were retired.

The executive branch has authority over most political and economic matters of El Salvador. The president, who is chief of state and head of government, selects the Council of Ministers. The Legislative Assembly, elected every three years, has been largely ineffectual due to an even split on legislative issues. Legislative elections held in 2000 replaced the right-wing Nationalist Republican Alliance (ARENA) for the first time with the FMLN—a legal party from 1991—as the largest party in the Parliament. Because of human rights abuses and judicial scandals during the civil war, judicial reform has been a priority. Judicial power is highly concentrated in the Supreme Court. Since the peace settlement, the country has begun a program of reforms that offer hope for stability, despite a fragile economy and uncertain political climate.

By the end of the 20th century, labor was one of El Salvador's biggest exports, as it is in the Philippines, with $1.25 billion a year being sent by emigrants to their families in El Salvador. Remaining is the threat of future uprisings due to continuing hardships and potential resistance to reform from the upper class.

ISSUES AND CHALLENGES:

- Crime is a huge concern for El Salvador. The corrupt judiciary and police force do little to reduce crime.

- Three earthquakes in 2001 devastated both the people and the economy of El Salvador, making it dependent on foreign aid, particularly from the US.

- The health system is woefully inadequate and only the wealthy can afford to travel to the US for treatment.

- Huge disparities are evident between the rich and the poor, with only 20 percent of the population owning nearly 70 percent of the national wealth.

HOW THE GOVERNMENT WORKS

LEGISLATIVE BRANCH
Asamblea Legislativa
(Legislative Assembly)
Unicameral Parliament
Composed of 84 members directly elected to three-year terms by proportional representation.

Regional Governments
Fourteen departments; 262 municipalities administered by elected local councils.

EXECUTIVE BRANCH
President
Elected to single five-year term by absolute majority of direct popular vote. Serves as head of state and government.

Vice-president
Elected on presidential ticket to single five-year term by absolute majority of direct popular vote.

Council of Ministers
Appointed by president. Oversees government operations.

JUDICIAL BRANCH
National Council of Justice
Nominates and evaluates Supreme Court magistrates, lower-court judges, justices of the peace.

Supreme Court
Highest court of review and appeal; rules on constitutionality of laws. Composed of 14 magistrates elected to nine-year staggered terms by two-thirds majority vote of Legislative Assembly.

Courts of Second Instance
Courts of First Instance
Justices of the Peace

PARAGUAY

OFFICIAL NAME: REPUBLIC OF PARAGUAY

BOLIVIA
Pedro Juan Caballero
Concepción
ARGENTINA
ASUNCIÓN
Lambaré
Ciudad del Este
Pilar
Encarnación
BRAZIL
Congress

0 100 km
0 100 miles

POPULATION: 5.6 MILLION
CAPITAL: ASUNCIÓN
AREA: 157,046 SQ. MILES (406,750 SQ. KM)
INDEPENDENCE: 1811
CONSTITUTION: 1992

PARAGUAY is said to derive its name from the Guaraní Indian word meaning "river that gives birth to the sea".

RELIGION: Roman Catholic 90%, Mennonite, and other Protestant 10%

OFFICIAL LANGUAGE: Spanish

REGIONS OR PROVINCES: 17 departments

DEPENDENT TERRITORIES: None

MEDIA: Partial political censorship exists in national media

Newspapers: There are 7 daily newspapers

TV: 4 independent services

Radio: 21 independent services

SUFFRAGE: 18 years of age; universal and compulsory up to age 75

LEGAL SYSTEM: Argentine, French and Roman law; no ICJ jurisdiction

WORLD ORGANIZATIONS: CCC, ECLAC, FAO, G-77, IADB, IAEA, IBRD, ICAO, ICFTU, ICRM, IDA, IFAD, IFC, IFRCS, ILO, IMF, IMO, Interpol, IOC, IOM, ISO (correspondent), ITU, LAES, LAIA, Mercosur, MONUC, NAM (observer), OAS, OPANAL, OPCW, PCA, RG, UN, UNAMSIL, UNCTAD, UNESCO, UNIDO, UNMEE, UPU, WCL, WHO, WIPO, WMO, WToO, WTrO

POLITICAL PARTIES: ANR-PC—National Republican Association-Colorado Party, DA—Democratic Alliance (led by the Authentic Radical Liberal Party-PLRA)

ETHNIC GROUPS:

Other 8%
Amerindian 2%
Mestizo 90%

NATIONAL ECONOMICS

WORLD GNP RANKING: 94th

GNP PER CAPITA: $1,440

INFLATION: 9.0%

BALANCE OF PAYMENTS (BALANCE OF TRADE): -$137 million

EXCHANGE RATES / U.S. DLR.: 3545-4635 GUARANÍES

OFFICIAL CURRENCY: GUARANÍ

GOVERNMENT SPENDING (% OF GDP)

✈ DEFENSE 1.3%		
🎓 EDUCATION 4.5%		
✚ HEALTH 1.7%		

0   5   10   15

NUMBER OF CONFLICTS OVER LAST 25 YEARS

	1	2-5	5+
Violent changes in government	●	○	○
Civil wars	○	○	○
International wars	○	○	○
Foreign intervention	○	○	○

- Compulsory national military service.
- Military tasked with national defense and internal security, assists in presidential programs.
- Tri-border area with Argentina and Brazil provides security and smuggling threat.

NOTABLE WARS AND INSURGENCIES: Coup 1989

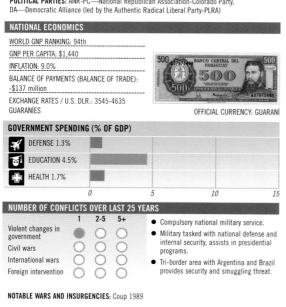

WITH THE ESTABLISHMENT of the capital city in 1537 by Spanish explorer Juan de Salazar, Paraguay became a Spanish colony, which it remained until independence in 1811. Since then, Paraguay has experienced extreme political instability and authoritarianism that ended only in the 1990s. The country's longest dictatorship, and one of the longest in the world, was led by General Alfredo Stroessner. He stayed in power for 35 years, from 1954 to 1989, supported by the military and the powerful political party, the Colorado Party. In 1990, however, Stroessner was ousted in a bloody coup organized by one of his own supporters, General Andrés Rodríguez, who promised to hold open elections in three years. To his surprise, though, Rodríguez lost the popular vote in 1993 to a civilian. The first civilian leader in 40 years, Juan Carlos Wasmosy was also a candidate of the Colorado Party. Internal party power struggles have been constant in Paraguayan politics.

By the next elections, in 1998, another coup was being planned by General Lino Oviedo, one of the presidential candidates. He was arrested and prevented from running, however, when his involvement in the plot was uncovered. A new Colorado Party candidate, Raúl Cubas Grau, won the elections. When, in an appeal case, the Supreme Court upheld Oviedo's earlier guilty sentence, Cubas overturned the judicial decision and refused to send Oviedo back to jail. This led to popular demonstrations against the government and a move in the Senate to impeach Cubas. He resigned the day before the impeachment vote, as it had become clear that the vote would succeed. Both he and Oviedo fled the country, although Oviedo returned in 2000, attempting to overturn a coalition government formed and led by González Macchi. Macchi, in turn, faced impeach-ment by the Senate for corruption and mismanagement, but was cleared of all charges in 2003.

Despite leading to these convoluted events, the constitution of 1992 had set in motion the country's current presidential democracy by providing for a political system divided into three interdependent branches—the executive, legislative, and judicial. This put into practice what had first been codified in the 1967 constitution, but ignored by General Stroessner.

ISSUES AND CHALLENGES:

- Although the last decade has been a much more stable era for Paraguay, its past political instability still has significant influence. The president still holds much more power than any other branches, which means the imbalance of power, though reduced since the last few democratic elections, remains. The president's annual budget is the first priority over any other legislation, and must be debated by both houses within one month; and the Supreme Court tends to avoid political matters.

- The country's political instability is a major deterrent for much-needed foreign investors.

HOW THE GOVERNMENT WORKS

LEGISLATIVE BRANCH

Congreso
(Congress)
Bicameral Parliament

Cámara de Senadores
(Chamber of Senators)
Composed of 45 members directly elected to five-year terms by proportional representation. Ratifies treaties; confirms presidential appointments; passes national defense and expropriation laws.

Cámara de Diputados
(Chamber of Deputies)
Composed of 80 members directly elected to five-year terms by proportional representation. Approves banking, tax and monetary laws; adopts national budget.

Regional Governments
Seventeen departments administered by popularly elected governors and councils.

EXECUTIVE BRANCH

President
Elected to five-year term by direct popular vote. Serves as head of state and government; commander-in-chief of armed forces. Directs foreign policy; prepares national budget; issues decree-laws during recesses of parliament; appoints state general prosecutor.

Vice-president
Elected on presidential ticket to five-year term by direct popular vote.

Council of Ministers
Members appointed by president. Oversees government operations.

JUDICIAL BRANCH

Supreme Court
Highest court of review and appeal. Rules on constitutionality of laws. Composed of 9 justices appointed for life by president, approved by Senate.

Lower Courts

GEORGIA

OFFICIAL NAME: GEORGIA

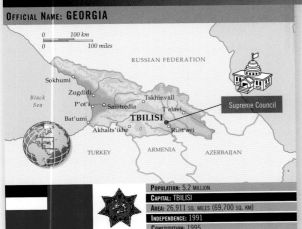

RUSSIAN FEDERATION

Sokhumi

Zugdidi
P'ot'i — Samtredia
Black Sea
Bat'umi
Akhalts'ikhe
T'elavi
Tskhinvali
Rust'avi
TBILISI
Supreme Council

TURKEY   ARMENIA   AZERBAIJAN

POPULATION: 5.2 MILLION	
CAPITAL: TBILISI	
AREA: 26,911 SQ. MILES (69,700 SQ. KM)	
INDEPENDENCE: 1991	
CONSTITUTION: 1995	

GEORGIA is derived from the Arabic word "Kurj" and the Persian word "Gurj", their names for the country.

RELIGION: Georgian Orthodox 65%, Muslim 11%, Russian Orthodox 10%, Armenian Apostolic 8%, Unknown 6%

OFFICIAL LANGUAGE: Georgian; Abkhazian (in Abkhazia)

REGIONS OR PROVINCES: 9 regions, nine cities, and two autonomous republics

DEPENDENT TERRITORIES: None

MEDIA: Partial political censorship exists in national media

Newspapers: Three daily newspapers

TV: 2 services: one state-controlled, one independent

Radio: 1 state-controlled service

SUFFRAGE: 18 years of age; universal

LEGAL SYSTEM: Civil law; accepts ICJ jurisdiction

WORLD ORGANIZATIONS: BSEC, CCC, CE, CIS, EAPC, EBRD, ECE, FAO, IAEA, IBRD, ICAO, ICFTU, IDA, IFAD, IFC, IFRCS, ILO, IMF, IMO, Interpol, IOC, IOM, ITU, OPCW, OSCE, PFP, UN, UNCTAD, UNESCO, UNIDO, UPU, WHO, WIPO, WMO, WToO, WTrO

POLITICAL PARTIES: CUG—Citizens' Union of Georgia, AGUR—All Georgian Union of Revival, ISG—Industry Will Save Georgia, AD—Abkhazian Deputies

ETHNIC GROUPS:

Azeri 6%
Ossetian 3%
Russian 6%
Other 7%
Armenian 8%
Georgian 70%

NATIONAL ECONOMICS

WORLD GNP RANKING: 129th

GNP PER CAPITA: $630

INFLATION: 19.1%

BALANCE OF PAYMENTS (BALANCE OF TRADE): -$162 million

EXCHANGE RATES / U.S. DLR.: 1.960-2.055 LARI

OFFICIAL CURRENCY: LARI

GOVERNMENT SPENDING (% OF GDP)

✈	DEFENSE 2.5%	
	EDUCATION 5.2%	
✚	HEALTH 0.8%	

0   5   10   15

NUMBER OF CONFLICTS OVER LAST 25 YEARS

	1	2-5	5+
Violent changes in government	○	○	○
Civil wars	○	●	○
International wars	○	○	○
Foreign intervention	○	●	○

- Compulsory national military service.
- US provides training for army and secret service.
- Major concern is civil war in Abkhazia, seeking secession.
- Dispute over some boundaries with Russia.

NOTABLE WARS AND INSURGENCIES: Civil wars 1991, 1993-1994. South Ossetian rebellion 1990-1992. Abkhazian rebellion 1992-1993

KNOWN TO THE GREEKS AND ROMANS, who called it Colchis (Kolkheti), the Kingdom of Georgia has been ruled by Persians, Turks, Arabs and Mongols. It became a protectorate of Russia in 1763, and was absorbed fully into the Russian Empire when its monarchy was exiled in 1801. With the collapse of that Empire, Georgia became a republic, experiencing independence briefly between 1918 and 1921, at which point it was occupied by the Red Army. It continued under Soviet rule until the breakup of the USSR in 1991.

Georgia was the second of 15 republics to demand independence from the Soviet Union in that year. It achieved its wish, but has been plagued ever since by economic and political turmoil, including civil war and ethnic disputes involving armed secession attempts by the Abkhazia and South Ossetia regions, and most dramatically the "velvet revolution" of November 2003. Georgia became a presidential democracy under former Soviet foreign minister Eduard Shevardnadze in 1995, when a new constitution replaced the previous cross between a parliamentary and presidential system. Shevardnadze survived two assassination attempts during his presidency, only to be thrown out of office by opposition leader Mikhail Saakashwili, who led a peaceful march on the parliament building after the president had rigged the November 2003 elections. "Velvet" the revolution might have been, but the victors now face the challenge of winning over Moscow.

Under the constitution, a president has considerable powers, including naming and dismissing cabinet ministers, submitting the budget, introducing legislation "out of turn," and, in some instances, suspending regional legislative bodies. The unicameral parliament, the Supreme Council, confirms judicial, military, and executive appointments, ratifies major agreements, and can reject presidential bills. The Shevardnadze-led Citizens' Union of Georgia (CUG) won 56 percent of parliamentary seats in a discredited 1999 election, with the All-Georgian Union of Revival (AGUR) apparently gaining just 24 percent. Whatever the correct figures may have been then, Georgia's political situation now seems more polarized than ever in the light of more recent events.

ISSUES AND CHALLENGES:

- Having thrown the president out of office in 2003, Georgia must rebuild popular trust in the political process, and gain the support of Moscow.

- Georgia has pinned its economic revival on again becoming a transportation corridor for goods between Europe and Asia.

- Russia accuses Georgia of sheltering Chechen insurgents in the Pankisi Gorge and maintains that it should abandon its policies of westernization.

- A UN-brokered peace process begun in mid-2000 stalled over the issue of the future status of Abkhazia.

HOW THE GOVERNMENT WORKS

LEGISLATIVE BRANCH

Umaghiesi Sabcho (Supreme Council)
Unicameral Parliament
Composed of 235 members elected to four-year terms: 85 from single-member districts; 150 by proportional representation. Passes laws; adopts budget; overrides vetoes; confirms appointments; ratifies treaties; impeaches president with two-thirds majority vote and consent of Supreme Court or Constitutional Court.

Regional Governments
Nine regions administered by prefects appointed by president.

EXECUTIVE BRANCH

President
Elected to five-year term by direct popular vote; two-term limit. Serves as head of state and government. Sets parliamentary elections; submits budget; introduces and vetoes bills; chairs National Security Council; appoints senior civil and military officials.

Cabinet of Ministers
Composed of 20 members appointed by president. Oversees government operations; answers to president.

JUDICIAL BRANCH

Constitutional Court
Rules on civil rights and constitutionality of laws. Judges appointed to ten-year terms by president, parliament and Supreme Court.

Supreme Court
Highest court of review and appeal for civil and criminal cases; supervises lower courts. Judges nominated by president, appointed to ten-year terms by parliament.

Lower Courts

NICARAGUA

OFFICIAL NAME: REPUBLIC OF NICARAGUA

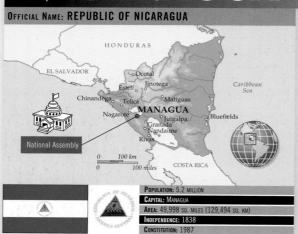

POPULATION:	5.2 MILLION
CAPITAL:	MANAGUA
AREA:	49,998 SQ. MILES (129,494 SQ. KM)
INDEPENDENCE:	1838
CONSTITUTION:	1987

NICARAGUA was named after an Indian chief and his tribe, the Nicarao, that lived in the area when Spanish explorers arrived in the early 1500s.

RELIGION: Roman Catholic 85%, Protestant 10%, Other 5%

OFFICIAL LANGUAGE: Spanish

REGIONS OR PROVINCES: 15 departments and 2 autonomous regions

DEPENDENT TERRITORIES: None

MEDIA: No political censorship exists in national media

Newspapers: There are 8 daily newspapers

TV: 7 services

Radio: 62 stations: 1 state-owned, 61 independent

SUFFRAGE: 16 years of age; universal

LEGAL SYSTEM: Civil law; accepts ICJ jurisdiction

WORLD ORGANIZATIONS: BCIE, CACM, CCC, ECLAC, FAO, G-77, IADB, IAEA, IBRD, ICAO, ICFTU, ICRM, IDA, IFAD, IFC, IFRCS, ILO, IMF, IMO, Interpol, IOC, IOM, ISO (correspondent), ITU, LAES, LAIA (observer), NAM, OAS, OPANAL, OPCW, PCA, RG, UN, UNCTAD, UNESCO, UNHCR, UNIDO, UPU, WCL, WHO, WIPO, WMO, WToO, WTrO

POLITICAL PARTIES: PLC—Liberal Constitutionalist Party, FSLN—Sandinista National Liberation Front, PCN—Conservative Party of Nicaragua

ETHNIC GROUPS:

- Amerindian 5%
- Zambos 4%
- Black 8%
- White 14%
- Mestizo 69%

NATIONAL ECONOMICS

WORLD GNP RANKING: 136th

GNP PER CAPITA: $400

INFLATION: 11.2%

BALANCE OF PAYMENTS (BALANCE OF TRADE): -$505 million

EXCHANGE RATES / U.S. DLR.: 12.90-13.76 CÓRDOBAS ORO

OFFICIAL CURRENCY: CÓRDOBA ORO

GOVERNMENT SPENDING (% OF GDP)

✈	DEFENSE	0.8%
🐾	EDUCATION	4.2%
✚	HEALTH	8.5%

0 5 10 15

NUMBER OF CONFLICTS OVER LAST 25 YEARS

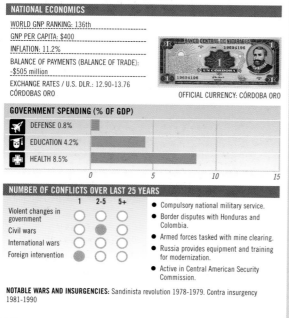

	1	2-5	5+
Violent changes in government	○	○	○
Civil wars	○	○	○
International wars	○	○	○
Foreign intervention	○	○	○

- Compulsory national military service.
- Border disputes with Honduras and Colombia.
- Armed forces tasked with mine clearing.
- Russia provides equipment and training for modernization.
- Active in Central American Security Commission.

NOTABLE WARS AND INSURGENCIES: Sandinista revolution 1978-1979. Contra insurgency 1981-1990

NICARAGUA BECAME independent from Spain in 1821 and an independent republic in 1838, more than 300 years after Hernández de Córdoba had founded the region's first permanent Spanish settlement. Nicaragua has since endured numerous political and economic struggles and civil wars.

Conservatives led the country from 1857 until 1894, when liberal José Santos Zelaya became president. His dictatorship fell with US help in 1909, marking the start of the US's close involvement in the country's history during much of the 20th century. American forces arrived in 1912 to support a conservative government and remained until 1933, except during one nine-month period. The US occupation resulted in years of guerrilla warfare by anti-occupation liberals. One of their most influential leaders was General Augusto César Sandino, from whom the left-wing Sandinistas later took their name. Sandino was assassinated in 1936 and Commander Anastasio Somoza García took power the same year, initiating 44 years of dictatorship and corruption by the Somoza family. In 1978 Anastasio Somoza Debayle, one of Somoza García's sons, was ousted from his second presidency in a revolution led by the Marxist-Leninist Sandinista National Liberation Front (FSLN). Once in power, the FSLN instituted enormous sociopolitical changes, but restricted civil liberties. Eleven years of civil war ensued, with the US suspending aid in 1981 and backing counter-revolutionary Contra forces. The FSLN leader, Daniel Ortega Saavedra, was elected president in 1984.

ALEMÁN TRIAL—FEBRUARY 26, 2003
A sign that reads "Justice for Arnoldo... respect his human rights" during a hearing before the Committee for the Defense of Human Rights and Justice of former president Arnoldo Alemán. Alemán was on trial for fraud and money laundering involving an estimated $100 million.

Hostilities ended in 1990 and free elections were held. The FSLN unexpectedly lost power and Violeta Barrios de Chamorro of the center-right National Opposition Union (UNO) became president. Chamorro made progress toward solidifying democracy, but her coalition did not last long, as its promise of full economic recovery went unfulfilled. The Liberal Constitutionalist Party (PLC) under Arnoldo Alemán won the 1996 and 2001 elections.

HOW THE GOVERNMENT WORKS

LEGISLATIVE BRANCH
Asamblea Nacional
(National Assembly)
Unicameral Parliament
Composed of 93 members directly elected to five-year terms by proportional representation; Overrides presidential vetoes with simple majority vote; amends constitution with 60 percent majority vote.

Regional Governments
Two autonomous regions administered by elected councils; 145 municipalities governed by elected mayors and councils.

EXECUTIVE BRANCH
President
Elected to five-year term by direct popular vote; two-term limit; may not seek immediate reelection. Serves as head of state and government. Vetoes bills; submits budget; appoints ambassadors.

Vice President
Elected on presidential ticket to five-year term by direct popular vote.

Cabinet
Council of Ministers
Composed of 13 members appointed by president. Oversees government operations.

JUDICIAL BRANCH
Supreme Court
Highest court of review and appeal. Composed of 16 judges nominated by president, elected to five-year terms by parliament.

Supreme Electoral Council
Organizes and conducts elections, plebiscites and referendums. Composed of 7 magistrates elected to five-year terms by parliament.

Civil Courts

Criminal Courts

KYRGYZSTAN

OFFICIAL NAME: KYRGYZ REPUBLIC

KAZAKHSTAN
CHINA
BISHKEK Tokmak Karakol
Talas Kara-Balta
Naryn
Dzhalal-Abad
UZBEKISTAN Osh
Sulyukta CHINA
TAJIKISTAN

Supreme Council

0 100 km
0 100 miles

POPULATION: 5 MILLION
CAPITAL: BISHKEK
AREA: 76,641 SQ. MILES (198,500 SQ. KM)
INDEPENDENCE: 1991
CONSTITUTION: 1993

KYRGYZSTAN is Arabic for "land of the Kyrgyz", while Kyrgz itself comes from the Turkic "kyrg" meaning 40 and "yz" meaning tribes.

RELIGION: Muslim 75%, Russian Orthodox 20%, Other 5%

OFFICIAL LANGUAGES: Kyrgyz and Russian

REGIONS OR PROVINCES: 7 provinces and 1 city

DEPENDENT TERRITORIES: None

MEDIA: Partial political censorship exists in national media

Newspapers: There are 4 daily newspapers

TV: 1 state-owned service

Radio: 4 services: 1 state-owned, 3 independent

SUFFRAGE: 18 years of age; universal

LEGAL SYSTEM: Civil law; no ICJ jurisdiction

WORLD ORGANIZATIONS: AsDB, CCC, CIS, EAPC, EBRD, ECE, ECO, ESCAP, FAO, IBRD, ICAO, ICRM, IDA, IDB, IFAD, IFC, IFRCS, ILO, IMF, Interpol, IOC, IOM, ISO (correspondent), ITU, NAM (observer), OIC, OPCW (signatory), OSCE, PCA, PFP, UN, UNAMSIL, UNCTAD, UNESCO, UNIDO, UNMIK, UPU, WFTU, WHO, WIPO, WMO, WToO, WTrO

POLITICAL PARTIES: Party of Communists of Krygyzstan, Union of Democratic Forces

Ethnic groups:

- Kyrgyz 57%
- Russian 19%
- Uzbek 13%
- Other 7%
- Ukrainian 2%
- Tatar 2%

NATIONAL ECONOMICS

WORLD GNP RANKING: 148th

GNP PER CAPITA: $270

INFLATION: 18.7%

BALANCE OF PAYMENTS (BALANCE OF TRADE) -$77 million

EXCHANGE RATES / U.S. DLR.: 48.24-47.72 SOMS

КЫРГЫЗ БАНКЫ
1 БИР СОМ
OFFICIAL CURRENCY: SOM

GOVERNMENT SPENDING (% OF GDP)

✈ DEFENSE	2.4%
🎓 EDUCATION	5.4%
✚ HEALTH	2.2%

0   5   10   15

NUMBER OF CONFLICTS OVER LAST 25 YEARS

	1	2-5	5+
Violent changes in government		○	○
Civil wars	●	○	○
International wars	○	○	○
Foreign intervention	●	○	○

- Compulsory national military service.
- Army was established in 1992.
- Defense treaty with five CIS nations.
- Border disputes with Uzbekistan and Tajikistan.

NOTABLE WARS AND INSURGENCIES: Islamist militancy 2000

FOLLOWING RECENT DISCOVERIES, the Kyrgyz people can now be traced back to the start of the second century B.C., when they were living in northeastern Mongolia. Under Mongol rule, the Kyrgyz migrated south, settling in the mountainous area of Kyrgyzstan during the 15th and 16th centuries. The Central Asian territory of Kyrgyzstan was annexed by the Russian Empire in 1864, but not without numerous revolts and some Kyrgyz fleeing to Afghanistan. Incorporated into the Soviet Union in 1918, Kyrgyzstan became the Kyrgyz Autonomous Soviet Socialist Republic in 1926, and the Kyrgyz Soviet Socialist Republic in 1936. As the Soviet Union collapsed, the Kyrgyz Republic gained independence in 1991. Hopes for democracy initially ran high, but were thwarted by election fraud and corruption.

Askar Akayev was appointed president in 1990, during the waning Soviet era. His presidency was confirmed in the first elections after independence, held in October 1991, and he was re-elected in 1995 and 2000, after the Constitutional Court brushed aside objections to his serving a third term. The 1993 constitution granted the president broad powers, but Akayev has resorted to extra-constitutional measures to amend the document in his favor, casting doubt on its legitimacy. Akayev used government resources to engineer his re-election, and engineered referenda in 1996 and 2003 to extend his powers still further. Matters came to a head in 2005 when accusations of vote-rigging in the parliamentary elections triggered a popular uprising. Akayev fled into exile, and new elections were held in July 2005.

In an effort to decrease Russian (long associated with Soviet) influence, the government has been striving to replace Russian place names with Kyrgyz words, and the Russian language, which dominated previously, with the Kyrgyz language. These and similar measures, along with the increasing Islamization of politics, have led to the emigration of large numbers of highly skilled Russians and other Europeans. As a result, the language replacement program was scaled back in 1994. In 2001, the legislature made Russian an official language, with status equal to that of Kyrgyz.

ISSUES AND CHALLENGES:

- The Kyrgyz economy is in need of revival, but reform has been slow amid mounting political and ethnic tensions, government repression of the opposition, and the country's widespread poverty. The West has provided much-needed funds and expertise for the struggling nation. However, it remains to be seen whether political and economic changes will come.

- Environmental issues include industrial pollution and soil salination, a result of excessive irrigation of cotton crops.

- The country is trying to reduce its over-dependence on the Russian Federation for trade and supplies.

HOW THE GOVERNMENT WORKS

LEGISLATIVE BRANCH

Jogorku Kenesh
Bicameral Parliament

Assembly of People's Representatives
Upper House
Composed of 70 members elected to five-year terms by direct popular vote. Meets several times annually; confirms presidential appointments.

Legislative Assembly
Lower House
Composed of 35 members elected to five-year terms by direct popular vote. Meets year-round; primary lawmaking body.

Regional Governments
Seven provinces administered by governors appointed by president and advisory assemblies.

EXECUTIVE BRANCH

President
Elected for five-year term by direct popular vote; two consecutive term limit. Serves as head of state. Sets domestic and foreign policy; appoints senior officials; declares war; dissolves parliament; calls new elections; initiates constitutional amendments; calls referenda.

Prime Minister
Appointed by president. Serves as head of government.

Council of Ministers
Members appointed by president on advice of prime minister. Oversees government operations.

JUDICIAL BRANCH

Constitutional Court
Rules on constitutionality of laws. Judges nominated by president; appointed to 15-year terms by Assembly of People's Representatives.

Supreme Court
Highest court of review and appeal. Judges nominated by president, appointed to 10-year terms by Assembly of People's Representatives.

Higher Court of Arbitration
Oversees regional courts of arbitration for property disputes.

Lower Courts

COSTA RICA

OFFICIAL NAME: REPUBLIC OF COSTA RICA

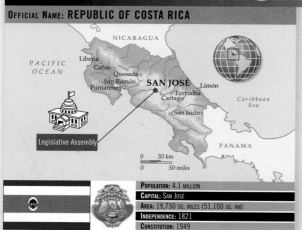

POPULATION: 4.1 MILLION
CAPITAL: SAN JOSÉ
AREA: 19,730 SQ. MILES (51,100 SQ. KM)
INDEPENDENCE: 1821
CONSTITUTION: 1949

COSTA RICA was named "rich coast" by the Spanish, who had heard rumors of gold deposits there.

RELIGION: Roman Catholic 76%, Other (including Protestant) 24%

OFFICIAL LANGUAGE: Spanish

REGIONS OR PROVINCES: 7 provinces

DEPENDENT TERRITORIES: None

MEDIA: No political censorship exists in the national media though it is dominated by conservative opinion.

Newspapers: There are 8 daily newspapers

TV: 8 stations: 1 state-owned, 7 independent

Radio: State-owned and independent stations

SUFFRAGE: 18 years of age; universal and compulsory

LEGAL SYSTEM: Spanish law; accepts ICJ jurisdiction

WORLD ORGANIZATIONS: BCIE, CACM, ECLAC, FAO, G-77, IADB, IAEA, IBRD, ICAO, ICFTU, ICRM, IDA, IFAD, IFC, IFRCS, ILO, IMF, IMO, Interpol, IOC, IOM, ISO, ITU, LAES, LAIA (observer), NAM (observer), OAS, OPANAL, OPCW, PCA, RG, UN, UNCTAD, UNESCO, UNIDO, UNU, UPU, WCL, WFTU, WHO, WIPO, WMO, WToO, WTrO

POLITICAL PARTIES: PUSC— Social Christian Unity Party, PLN—National Liberation Party, PRC—Costa Rican Renewal Party, ML—Liberty Movement, PAC—Citizens' Action Party

ETHNIC GROUPS:

Amerindian 1%
Chinese 1%
Other 1%
Black 3%
White (including Mestizo) 94%

NATIONAL ECONOMICS

WORLD GNP RANKING: 76nd

GNP PER CAPITA: $3,810

INFLATION: 11.0%

BALANCE OF PAYMENTS (BALANCE OF TRADE): -$650 million

EXCHANGE RATES / U.S. DLR.: 317.5-341.3 COSTA RICAN CÓLONES

OFFICIAL CURRENCY: COSTA RICAN COLÓN

GOVERNMENT SPENDING (% OF GDP)

DEFENSE 0.8%
EDUCATION 6%
HEALTH 5.2%

| | 0 | 5 | 10 | 15 |

NUMBER OF CONFLICTS OVER LAST 25 YEARS

	1	2-5	5+
Violent changes in government	○	○	○
Civil wars	○	○	○
International wars	○	○	○
Foreign intervention	○	○	○

- No compulsory national military service.
- Army was abolished in 1948. Costa Rica constitutionally prohibited from having army in 1949.
- Illegal immigrants pose a security threat to the Civil Guard and police.

NOTABLE WARS AND INSURGENCIES: None

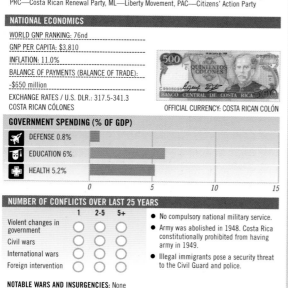

THE REPUBLIC OF COSTA RICA is one of the most stable and democratic countries in Latin America, and has a 90 percent literacy rate. Unlike most other Central American countries, a majority of the population is European, descended from Spanish settlers. The land was first explored by Christopher Columbus in 1502 on his final journey to the New World, Costa Rica was settled in 1522 and for the next three hundred years was ruled by Spain as part of the Captaincy General of Guatemala. The nation gained independence from Spain in 1821 forming a federation with other Central American provinces. In 1838, Costa Rica withdrew from the federation and became a separate republic.

Only two periods of unrest and dictatorship have disrupted the current peaceful democracy that began in 1899 with the first free elections. The first was the dictatorship of Federico Tinoco from 1917 to 1919, and the second, the 44-day civil war of 1948 led by José María Figueres Ferrer ("Don Pepe",) that erupted as a result of disputed elections. The war left more than 2,000 Costa Ricans dead, but the most significant outcome was the constitutional prohibition of a standing military force in Costa Rica, which established the country as a neutral state and has enabled it to use financial resources for public benefit that would otherwise have gone to the military. Costa Rica's traditions of democracy, social welfare and regional peace-making have given it considerable international influence. Figueres was elected president in the first elections held in 1953, and since then there have been 13 presidential elections, with the most recent held in 2002.

Every four years, Costa Ricans elect their president directly through a national, compulsory secret ballot. Elections are generally considered free and fair. The president, a strong executive, and the deputies of the Legislative Assembly cannot serve two consecutive terms, although deputies are permitted to run again after skipping one term. Although minor parties exist, the country's politics have primarily been dominated by two major parties: the National Liberation Party (PLN) and the Social Christian Unity Party (PUSC), both of which have close ties to banana and coffee growers.

ISSUES AND CHALLENGES:

- High domestic debt, for which one controversial solution is selling nationalized institutions, though attempts to partially privatize telecommunications and electricity generation in 2000 led to disturbances.

- Increasing dissatisfaction with political system. Many people support the creation of a third party and advocate writing a new constitution.

- Inequitable distribution of wealth: plantation owners control most of the wealth of the country, while one-fifth of the population is estimated to live in poverty.

HOW THE GOVERNMENT WORKS

LEGISLATIVE BRANCH

Asamblea Legislativa
(Legislative Assembly)
Unicameral Parliament
Composed of 57 members elected to four-year terms by direct popular vote. Must sit out one term before seeking re-election. Passes laws; approves budget; overrides presidential vetoes; amends constitution with two-thirds majority vote.

Regional Governments
Seven provinces administered by governors appointed by president.

EXECUTIVE BRANCH

President
Elected to single four-year term by direct popular vote. Serves as head of state and government. Vetoes bills except budget. Appoints and dismisses ministers without parliament's approval.

Two Vice-presidents
Elected on presidential ticket to single four-year terms by direct popular vote.

Cabinet
Composed of 15 members, including one vice-president; appointed by president. Oversees government operations.

JUDICIAL BRANCH

Supreme Court of Justice
Highest court of review and appeal; rules on constitutionality of laws; selects lower-court judges and magistrates. Composed of 22 members elected to renewable 8-year terms by parliament. Divided into four chambers.

Sala 1
Rules on commercial, civil and family cases.

Sala 2
Rules on labor cases.

Sala 3
Rules on criminal cases.

Sala 4
Rules on constitutional issues; presidential decrees, habeas corpus warrants.

URUGUAY

OFFICIAL NAME: EASTERN REPUBLIC OF URUGUAY

POPULATION: 3.4 MILLION
CAPITAL: MONTEVIDEO
AREA: 68,039 SQ. MILES (176,220 SQ. KM)
INDEPENDENCE: 1828
CONSTITUTION: 1966

URUGUAY was first called the "Banda Oriental de Rio Uruguay" or "Eastern Shore of the Uruguay River".

RELIGION: Roman Catholic 66%, Protestant 2%, Jewish 1%, Non-religious or other 31%

OFFICIAL LANGUAGE: Spanish

REGIONS OR PROVINCES: 19 departments

DEPENDENT TERRITORIES: None

MEDIA: The press is relatively free

Newspapers: There are 36 daily newspapers

TV: 4 services: 1 state-owned, 3 independent

Radio: 6 services: 1 state-owned, 5 independent

SUFFRAGE: 18 years of age; universal and compulsory

LEGAL SYSTEM: Spanish law; accepts ICJ jurisdiction

WORLD ORGANIZATIONS: CCC, ECLAC, FAO, G-77, IADB, IAEA, IBRD, ICAO, ICC, ICRM, IFAD, IFC, IFRCS, IHO, ILO, IMF, IMO, Interpol, IOC, IOM, ISO, ITU, LAES, LAIA, Mercosur, MINURSO, MONUC, NAM (observer), OAS, OPANAL, OPCW, PCA, RG, UN, UNAMSIL, UNCTAD, UNESCO, UNIDO, UNIKOM, UNMEE, UNMOGIP, UNMOT, UNOMIG, UNTAET, UPU, WCL, WFTU, WHO, WIPO, WMO, WToO, WTrO

POLITICAL PARTIES: PC—Colorado Party (Colorados), PN—National Party (Blancos), NE—New Sector/Space Coalition (Nuevo Espacio), EPFA—Progressive Encounter/Broad Front Coalition (Encuentro Progresista/Frente Amplio)

ETHNIC GROUPS:

- Mestizo 6%
- Black 4%
- White 90%

NATIONAL ECONOMICS

WORLD GNP RANKING: 63rd

GNP PER CAPITA: $6,000

INFLATION: 4.8%

BALANCE OF PAYMENTS (BALANCE OF TRADE): -$593 million

EXCHANGE RATES / U.S. DLR.: 12.51-14.77 URUGUAYAN PESOS

OFFICIAL CURRENCY: URUGUAYAN PESO

GOVERNMENT SPENDING (% OF GDP)

DEFENSE 2.6%	
EDUCATION 2.5%	
HEALTH 1.9%	

0   5   10   15

NUMBER OF CONFLICTS OVER LAST 25 YEARS

	1	2-5	5+
Violent changes in government	○	○	○
Civil wars	○	○	○
International wars	○	○	○
Foreign intervention	○	○	○

- No compulsory national military service.
- US supplies military equipment.
- Troops participate in 11 UN peacekeeping missions worldwide.

NOTABLE WARS AND INSURGENCIES: None

FIRST DISCOVERED BY THE SPANISH IN 1516, Uruguay became the center of a territorial battle between Spain, which had colonized the area north of the river Plate, and Portugal, which had established a colony at nearby Colonia del Sacramento. After gaining independence in 1828, Uruguay underwent a period of long, destructive civil wars. However, from the turn of the 20th century it gained a reputation as the most liberal and politically stable country in South America. This lasted until the mid-1960s, a remarkable era of peace and prosperity that allowed Uruguay to develop extensive social programs and encourage an active civil society. But the economic downturn of the late 1960s fostered a violent Marxist rebel group known as the Tupamaros, which eventually forced the military to seize control of the government in 1973. The country was returned to civilian control in 1985, but the sociopolitical legacy of military dictatorship remains a critical issue in today's multiparty democracy.

In 1997, Uruguayans ratified a new constitution to simplify the convoluted electoral system and promote voter participation in the democratic process. The new constitution also increased the political power of the executive branch vis-à-vis the bicameral Asamblea General, or General Assembly, legislature. This and the 1986 mandate that returned control of the military to the presidency make the president the most influential political figure in Uruguay.

Nevertheless, Uruguay retains a tradition of having the strongest legislative leadership and most effective multiparty system in Latin America. Perhaps the General Assembly's most influential roles in the national political environment are the appointment of Supreme Court justices and maintenance of the electoral system, both of which give the legislative branch a great deal of power.

Among the many political parties in Uruguay, the most prominent and popular are the Colorado Party (PC), National Party (PN), and Progressive Broad Front (EPFA). The most contested issues in the General Assembly revolve around the severe economic crisis in 2002 in neighboring Argentina, which inevitably affects Uruguay, and resolution of possible crimes against humanity committed by the military during its rule.

ISSUES AND CHALLENGES:

- Uruguay's economy depends heavily on markets in Brazil and Argentina. Recent economic crashes in both those countries have complicated diplomatic relations, as Uruguay seeks stronger ties with the USA to resolve its own economic downturn.

- Sluggish growth between 2000 and 2003 make it difficult for Uruguay to meet fiscal targets set by the IMF in order to continue receiving aid.

- Uruguay maintains an uncontested dispute with Brazil regarding sovereignty of islands located in the River Quarai (or Río Cuareim) and the Arroio Invernada.

HOW THE GOVERNMENT WORKS

LEGISLATIVE BRANCH

Asamblea General
(General Assembly)
Bicameral Parliament

Camara de Senadores
(Chamber of Senators)
Composed of 31 members elected to five-year terms by direct popular vote.

Camara de Representantes
(Chamber of Representatives)
Composed of 99 members elected to five-year terms by direct popular vote from Uruguay's 19 departments; each department represented by at least two members.

Regional Governments
Nineteen departments administered by elected governors.

EXECUTIVE BRANCH

President
Elected to five-year term by absolute majority of direct popular vote; no consecutive re-election. Serves as head of state and government; commander-in-chief of armed forces.

Vice-president
Elected on presidential ticket to five-year term by direct popular vote. Presides over parliament; chairs cabinet.

Council of Ministers
Composed of 13 members appointed by president, approved by parliament. Oversees government operations.

JUDICIAL BRANCH

Supreme Court
Highest court of review and appeal. Rules on constitutionality of laws; appoints appellate court judges, nominates lower-court judges. Judges nominated by president, elected to 10-year terms by parliament.

Appellate Court

Lower Courts

Military Tribunals

CONGO

OFFICIAL NAME: REPUBLIC OF THE CONGO

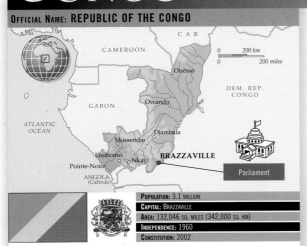

POPULATION: 3.1 MILLION
CAPITAL: BRAZZAVILLE
AREA: 132,046 SQ. MILES (342,000 SQ. KM)
INDEPENDENCE: 1960
CONSTITUTION: 2002

CONGO is named after the ancient Kongo Kingdom, located on the Congo River, and derived from the Bantu word "kong," or mountains.

RELIGION: Christian 50%, Animist 48%, Muslim 2%

OFFICIAL LANGUAGE: French

REGIONS OR PROVINCES: Nine regions and one commune

DEPENDENT TERRITORIES: None

MEDIA: Partial political censorship exists in national media

Newspapers: There are 64 daily newspapers

TV: One state-controlled service

Radio: Four state-controlled services

SUFFRAGE: 18 years of age; universal

LEGAL SYSTEM: Customary and French law; no ICJ jurisdiction

WORLD ORGANIZATIONS: ACCT, ACP, AfDB, BDEAC, CCC, CEEAC, CEMAC, ECA, FAO, FZ, G-77, IBRD, ICAO, ICFTU, ICRM, IDA, IFAD, IFC, IFRCS, ILO, IMF, IMO, Interpol, IOC, IOM, ITU, NAM, OAU, OPCW (signatory), UN, UNCTAD, UNESCO, UNIDO, UPU, WCL, WFTU, WHO, WIPO, WMO, WToO, WTrO

POLITICAL PARTIES: PCT—Congolese Labor Party, UDR—Union for Democracy and the Republic, UPADS—Pan-African Union for Social Democracy

ETHNIC GROUPS:

Other 3%
Mbochi 12%
Bakongo 48%
Teke 17%
Sangha 20%

NATIONAL ECONOMICS

WORLD GNP RANKING: 141st

GNP PER CAPITA: $570

INFLATION: -0.9%

BALANCE OF PAYMENTS (BALANCE OF TRADE): -$252 million

EXCHANGE RATES / U.S. DLR.: 698.7-736.7 CFA FRANCS

OFFICIAL CURRENCY: CFA FRANC

GOVERNMENT SPENDING (% OF GDP)

		0	5	10	15
✈	DEFENSE 2.5%				
	EDUCATION 4.7%				
✚	HEALTH 2%				

NUMBER OF CONFLICTS OVER LAST 25 YEARS

	1	2-5	5+
Violent changes in government	●	○	○
Civil wars	○	●	○
International wars	○	○	○
Foreign intervention	○	○	○

● No compulsory national military service.
● Internal tensions exist between the south and north of the country.
● Security is threatened by instability in Democratic Republic of Congo and Angola.

NOTABLE WARS AND INSURGENCIES: Civil War 1997–1999, 2002–2003

LIKE MANY OF ITS NEIGHBORS in formerly French-controlled West Africa, Congo has endured consistent post-independence political fragmentation punctuated with violent rebellions and civil wars. The country gained independence from France in 1960, after falling under French sovereignty between 1880–83. The first president, Fulbert Youlou, ruled for three years before being overthrown in a three-day uprising, known as "Les Trois Glorieuses". Several unstable governments followed Youlou's until 1968, when Captain Marien Ngouabi staged a military coup, installed himself as president, and established the leftist Congolese Worker's Party (PCT) as the country's sole political party. Although Ngouabi was assassinated in 1977, Marxist rule continued until 1990, when the PCT abandoned its Marxist ideology in favor of a multiparty democracy, which it had implemented by 1992.

A new democratic constitution was ratified later that year, but the subsequent elections swept the PCT and President Sassou-Nguesso from power. Unwilling to accept defeat, the PCT initiated a decade of severe political turmoil, military intervention, and bloody conflict. A fragile cease-fire was obtained in 1999. A 2002 constitution granted a majority of political power to the president. Although the new government seems to provide a degree of stability, occasional violence persists outside Brazzaville.

The volatility that plagues the political environment extends to the social situation. Congo contains one of the most factious tribal environments in Africa, the most significant tensions existing between the northern Bakongo people and the prosperous southern Mbochi. Furthermore, the political instability of the country's neighbors—especially the Democratic Republic of Congo, and Angola—produces mass refugee movements and incites further unrest. The persistent violent conflict in this part of Africa has led to a proliferation of small arms throughout Congo, which is generally accepted as the primary cause of a soaring crime rate. The continuous threat of violence also deters direct foreign investment and aid programs, as well as preventing the country from fully realizing the potential of its oil reserves, its most lucrative economic asset.

ISSUES AND CHALLENGES:

● A decade of violence and political instability has left Congo's civil society in disarray. The French-instituted health care system has all but collapsed, and a majority of the remaining schools are now administered from Paris.

● Congo's economy is over-dependent on oil, and diversifying the economic base is a critical concern.

● The country's large bureaucracy and refugee population place heavy strains on the meager economy.

● In the past, Congo has been used as a depository for toxic waste from Western countries.

HOW THE GOVERNMENT WORKS

LEGISLATIVE BRANCH
Transitional Constituent Assembly
Unicameral Parliament
Composed of 300 members appointed by president.

Regional Governments
Ten provinces administered by governors appointed by president.

EXECUTIVE BRANCH
President
Elected to seven-year term by direct popular vote. Serves as head of state and government; commander-in-chief of armed forces. Rules by decree with few checks on power.

National Executive Council
Composed of 25 members appointed by president. Presided over by president; oversees government operations.

JUDICIAL BRANCH
Military Tribunals
Rule on civilian and military cases; no appeal of verdicts is allowed. Presided over by military judge.

PANAMA

OFFICIAL NAME: REPUBLIC OF PANAMA

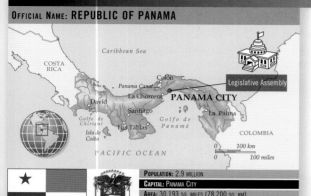

POPULATION: 2.9 MILLION	
CAPITAL: PANAMA CITY	
AREA: 30,193 SQ. MILES (78,200 SQ. KM)	
INDEPENDENCE: 1903	
CONSTITUTION: 1972	

PANAMA is a Cueva Indian word meaning "place of abundance of fish".

RELIGION: Roman Catholic 85%, Protestant 15%

OFFICIAL LANGUAGE: Spanish

REGIONS OR PROVINCES: 9 provinces and 1 territory

DEPENDENT TERRITORIES: None

MEDIA: Partial political censorship exists in national media. A more independent press has emerged since Noriega's overthrow.

Newspapers: There are 8 daily newspapers

TV: 5 independent services

Radio: 1 state-owned service, over 200 independent stations

SUFFRAGE: 18 years of age; universal and compulsory

LEGAL SYSTEM: Civil law; accepts ICJ jurisdiction

WORLD ORGANIZATIONS: CCC, ECLAC, FAO, G-77, IADB, IAEA, IBRD, ICAO, ICFTU, ICRM, IDA, IFAD, IFC, IFRCS, ILO, IMF, IMO, Interpol, IOC, IOM, ISO (correspondent), ITU, LAES, LAIA (observer), NAM, OAS, OPANAL, OPCW, PCA, RG, UN, UNCTAD, UNESCO, UNIDO, UPU, WCL, WFTU, WHO, WIPO, WMO, WToO, WTrO

POLITICAL PARTIES: NN—New Nation (comprises the Democratic Revolutionary Party (PRD), the Solidarity Party, the National Liberal Party and the Papa Egoro Movement), UP—Union for Panama (comprises the Arnulfisto Party (PA) MOLIRENA, the Party for Democratic Change, and MORENA), AO—Action for the Opposition (comprises the Christian Democratic Party, the Liberal Party, the Popular Nationalist Party, and the Civil Renovation Party

ETHNIC GROUPS:
- Asian 4%
- Other 2%
- Amerindian 8%
- Black 12%
- White 14%
- Mestizo 60%

NATIONAL ECONOMICS

WORLD GNP RANKING: 87th

GNP PER CAPITA: $3,260

INFLATION: 1.4%

BALANCE OF PAYMENTS (BALANCE OF TRADE): -$927 million

EXCHANGE RATES / U.S. DLR.: 1 BALBOA

OFFICIAL CURRENCY: BALBOA

GOVERNMENT SPENDING (% OF GDP)

- DEFENSE 1.3%
- EDUCATION 5.1%
- HEALTH 4.9%

`0    5    10    15`

NUMBER OF CONFLICTS OVER LAST 25 YEARS

	1	2-5	5+
Violent changes in government	○	○	○
Civil wars	○	○	○
International wars	●	○	○
Foreign intervention	●	○	○

- No compulsory national military service.
- US removed military bases when Canal Zone reverted in 1999.
- Military was abolished in 1994, replaced by Panamanian Public Force.

NOTABLE WARS AND INSURGENCIES: US invasion 1989

ITS NARROW SHAPE AND ITS LOCATION between the Pacific Ocean and Caribbean Sea have made Panama strategically important to other countries since 16th-century Spain used it as a shortcut for transporting Inca gold to Spain. Panama became part of Colombia in 1821, but in the late 1800s, the United States grew interested in maximizing Panama's potential as a shortcut by dredging a canal across the isthmus. The plan sparked a US-supported revolt against Colombia and Panamanian independence in 1903. The interocean Panama Canal, controlled by the US, was completed in 1914.

An elite minority ruled from independence until a military coup in 1968. General Omar Torrijos Herrera ruled until his death in 1981 in a plane crash. Colonel Manuel Antonio Noriega seized full control of the country by 1983, ruling through figurehead presidents throughout the 1980s. The US invaded Panama in December 1989 after Noriega (now General) was declared president. Panama subsequently declared itself to be in a state of war with the US. The US arrested Noriega on narcotics charges in January 1990 and returned Panama to civilian rule. Panama has since conducted open elections and made progress toward a stable, representative democracy. Proponents say a new constitution is required to move the country further forward.

DISGRACED PRESIDENT

General Manuel Antonio Noriega— indicted in US courts for drug trafficking in 1988 and captured by the US military in 1989. He was sentenced in 1992 to 40 years' imprisonment.

The president has unusual powers, including responsibility for initiating most legislation and sole authority for appointing and removing ministers. Authority is checked, however, by the Legislative Assembly, which can impeach the president, introduce legislation, approve treaties, and declare war.

Post-Noriega governments have struggled with corruption allegations, economic reform, high unemployment, and Panama's large foreign debt. Panama elected its first woman president, Mireya Moscoso, in 1999, the same year it received full control of the Panama Canal Zone from the US.

HOW THE GOVERNMENT WORKS

LEGISLATIVE BRANCH

Asamblea Legislativa (Legislative Assembly) Unicameral Parliament

Composed of 72 members who serve five-year terms: elected by proportional representation in urban districts, elected by direct popular vote in rural districts. Passes laws; overrides vetoes with two-thirds majority vote; ratifies treaties; declares war; decrees amnesty for political offenses; approves budget; impeaches president and Supreme Court justices.

Regional Governments

Nine provinces administered by governors appointed by president; municipalities overseen by elected mayors and councils.

EXECUTIVE BRANCH

President

Elected to single five-year term by direct popular vote. Serves as head of state and government. Initiates bills; appoints and removes government ministers; appoints one of three Electoral Tribunal members; conducts foreign relations; vetoes bills.

First and Second Vice-presidents

Elected on presidential ticket to single five-year term by direct popular vote.

Cabinet Council

Composed of president, vice-presidents, 12 government ministers. Issues states of emergency decrees; suspends constitutional guarantees; oversees national finances.

JUDICIAL BRANCH

Supreme Court

Highest court of review and appeal. Divided into civil, criminal and administrative chambers; rules on constitutionality of laws. Composed of 9 justices nominated to ten-year terms by Cabinet Council, confirmed by parliament.

Superior Courts

District Courts

Municipal Courts

NAMIBIA

OFFICIAL NAME: REPUBLIC OF NAMIBIA

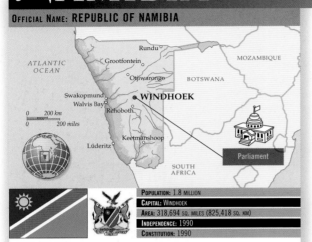

POPULATION: 1.8 million
CAPITAL: WINDHOEK
AREA: 318,694 SQ. MILES (825,418 SQ. KM)
INDEPENDENCE: 1990
CONSTITUTION: 1990

NAMIBIA is derived from "namib" which means "an area where there is nothing" in the local Nama language.

RELIGION: Christian 80%-90% (Lutheran 50% at least), indigenous beliefs 10%-20%

OFFICIAL LANGUAGE: English

REGIONS OR PROVINCES: 13 regions

DEPENDENT TERRITORIES: None

MEDIA: Partial political censorship exists in national media

NEWSPAPERS: There are 4 daily newspapers

TV: 2 independent services

RADIO: 5 independent services

SUFFRAGE: 18 years of age; universal

LEGAL SYSTEM: Roman-Dutch law; no ICJ jurisdiction

WORLD ORGANIZATIONS: ACP, AfDB, C, CCC, ECA, FAO, G-77, IAEA, IBRD, ICAO, ICFTU, ICRM, IFAD, IFC, IFRCS, ILO, IMF, IMO, Interpol, IOC, IOM (observer), ISO (correspondent), ITU, NAM, OAU, OPCW, SACU, SADC, UN, UNCTAD, UNESCO, UNHCR, UNIDO, UNMEE, UPU, WCL, WHO, WIPO, WMO, WToO, WTrO

POLITICAL PARTIES: SWAPO—South West Africa People's Organization, CoD—Congress of Democrats, DTA—Democratic Turnhall Alliance, UDF—United Democratic Front, MAG—Monitor Action Group

ETHNIC GROUPS:

- Ovambo 50%
- Other tribes 16%
- Kavango 9%
- Other 9%
- Damara 8%
- Herero 8%

NATIONAL ECONOMICS

WORLD GNP RANKING: 126th

GNP PER CAPITA: $2,030

INFLATION: 8.6%

BALANCE OF PAYMENTS (BALANCE OF TRADE): $162 million

EXCHANGE RATES / U.S. DLR.: 7.570-11.995 NAMIBIAN DOLLARS

OFFICIAL CURRENCY: NAMIBIAN DOLLAR

GOVERNMENT SPENDING (% OF GDP)

- ✈ DEFENSE 3.6%
- 📖 EDUCATION 8.1%
- ✚ HEALTH 3.3%

(scale: 0, 5, 10, 15)

NUMBER OF CONFLICTS OVER LAST 25 YEARS

	1	2-5	5+
Violent changes in government			
Civil wars	●		
International wars		●	
Foreign intervention	●		

- No compulsory national military service.
- Troops began a withdrawal from a peacekeeping presence in DRC in 2001.
- Border control agreement with Angola.
- Poaching by foreign fishing trawlers is an issue.

NOTABLE WARS AND INSURGENCIES: War of Independence 1966-1988. Involved in DRC

NAMIBIA HAD A LONG AND VIOLENT PATH to independence. Germany annexed Namibia in 1883, bringing much of the prime farmland under white German control. During World War I, South Africa occupied what was then known as South West Africa. After the war, the League of Nations handed the mandate for the territory to South Africa, giving it full power of administration and legislation in 1920. When the League of Nations became the United Nations in 1946, South Africa refused to cede control. The mandate was revoked in 1966, and in the same year, the South West Africa People's Organization (SWAPO), based on Marxist principles, began a guerrilla campaign from Zambia and later from Angola aided by Cuba, with the intention of taking control of South West Africa. The war between SWAPO and South Africa persisted beyond a 1988 peace agreement despite numerous attempts by the United Nations and the Western Contact Group, consisting of Canada, France, Germany, the UK, and the US, to organize elections for an independent Namibia. After 11 years of negotiations, South Africa agreed to withdraw its troops in accordance with a UN peace plan that included Cuba's withdrawal from Angola.

The transition to independence officially began on April 1, 1989 but was marred by further violence when SWAPO disobeyed the terms of the agreement and began moving troops into position to establish a military presence. South African and local police countered these movements resulting in bloodshed.

The period of transition to independence involved the repeal of apartheid policies discriminating against the black majority. With a 98 percent turnout, SWAPO won the first elections with a large majority, making its leader, Sam Nujoma, president. Since independence, SWAPO has been the ruling party, controlling most of the government posts. President Nujoma served a total of three terms before stepping aside for Hifikepunye Pohamba, who won a landslide election victory in November 2004.

ISSUES AND CHALLENGES:

- High unemployment, approaching 40 percent of the population, is causing a rising incidence of crime, as well as growing disparities between income levels.

- Namibia is heavily dependent on South Africa for the majority of its imports, and for both passage and purchase of its exports. Through fishing and mining resources there is much opportunity for seeking other trade partners.

- Namibia is concerned by its environmental issues, becoming the first country in the world to incorporate the protection of the environment into its constitution—protecting approximately 14 percent of the land, including most of the Namib Desert coastal strip.

- Namibia and Botswana are working to resolve disputes along the Caprivi Strip. Botswana residents protest Namibia's planned construction of the Okavango hydroelectric dam on Popa Falls.

HOW THE GOVERNMENT WORKS

LEGISLATIVE BRANCH

Parliament
(National Assembly)
Bicameral Parliament
Composed of 72 members elected to five-year terms by direct popular vote. President may appoint six additional non-voting members. Initiates and passes laws; adopts budget; questions government ministers.

National Council
Composed of 26 members who serve six-year terms: 2 each elected from 13 regional councils. Serves as advisory body; may reject bills.

Regional Governments
Thirteen regions administered by elected councils.

EXECUTIVE BRANCH

President
Elected to five-year term by absolute majority of direct popular vote; two-term limit. Serves as head of state; commander-in-chief of armed forces. Vetoes bills; declares national emergencies.

Prime Minister
Appointed by president. Serves as head of government.

Cabinet
Composed of president, prime minister, deputy prime minister, 20 parliament members; appointed by president. Oversees government operations.

JUDICIAL BRANCH

Judicial Service Commission
Recommends judicial appointments and disciplinary actions. Composed of Supreme Court chief justice, attorney general, judge appointed by president, two legal professionals.

Supreme Court
Highest court of review and appeal. Judges appointed by president on advice of Judicial Service Commission.

High Court
Civil and criminal cases. Judges appointed by president on advice of Judicial Service Commission.

Lower Courts
Presided over by magistrates.

BOTSWANA

OFFICIAL NAME: REPUBLIC OF BOTSWANA

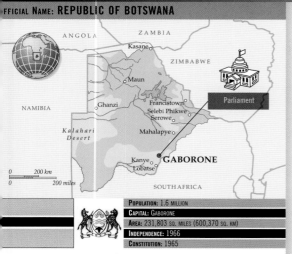

POPULATION: 1.6 MILLION
CAPITAL: GABORONE
AREA: 231,803 SQ. MILES (600,370 SQ. KM)
INDEPENDENCE: 1966
CONSTITUTION: 1965

BOTSWANA is named after the dominant ethnic group, the Tswana, also known as the Batswana.

RELIGION: Indigenous beliefs 85%, Christian 15%

OFFICIAL LANGUAGE: English

REGIONS OR PROVINCES: 9 districts

DEPENDENT TERRITORIES: None

MEDIA: No political censorship exists in national media.

NEWSPAPERS: There is 1 daily newspaper. The government bias in this newspaper is offset by the many journals

TV: 1 state-owned service

RADIO: 3 services: 1 state-owned, 2 independent

SUFFRAGE: 18 years of age; universal

LEGAL SYSTEM: Customary law and Roman-Dutch legal traditions; no ICJ jurisdiction

WORLD ORGANIZATIONS: ACP, AfDB, C, CCC, ECA, FAO, G-77, IBRD, ICAO, ICFTU, ICRM, IDA, IFAD, IFC, IFRCS, ILO, IMF, Interpol, IOC, ISO, ITU, NAM, OAU, OPCW, SACU, SADC, UN, UNCTAD, UNESCO, UNIDO, UPU, WFTU, WHO, WIPO, WMO, WToO, WTrO

POLITICAL PARTIES: BDP—Botswana Democratic Party, BNF—Botswana National Front, BCP—Botswana Congress Party

ETHNIC GROUPS:

Other 2%

Tswana 98%

NATIONAL ECONOMICS

WORLD GNP RANKING: 109th

GNP PER CAPITA: $3,300

INFLATION: 8.6%

BALANCE OF PAYMENTS (BALANCE OF TRADE): $517 million

EXCHANGE RATES / U.S. DLR.: 5.37–7.02 PULA

OFFICIAL CURRENCY: PULA

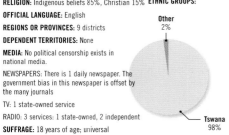

GOVERNMENT SPENDING (% of GDP)

✈ DEFENSE 5.5%		
🎓 EDUCATION 9.1%		
✚ HEALTH 2.5%		

0   5   10   15

NUMBER OF CONFLICTS OVER LAST 25 YEARS

	1	2-5	5+
Violent changes in government	○	○	○
Civil wars	○	○	○
International wars	○	○	○
Foreign intervention	○	○	○

- No compulsory national military service.
- Reformation and modernization of military began in 2000.
- Women have been permitted to enlist since 2000.
- US provides training for Botswana Defense Force.

NOTABLE WARS AND INSURGENCIES: None

BOTSWANA IS CONSIDERED A POLITICAL SUCCESS STORY, its stable government contrasting with the instability of many of Africa's postcolonial countries. Botswana was formed by the United Kingdom as the Bechuanaland Protectorate in 1885 to thwart territorial designs by colonists from neighboring South Africa and what is now Zimbabwe. The northern part of Bechuanaland became Botswana upon independence in 1966, while the southern section became part of the Northwest Province of South Africa. The leader of the independence movement, Seretse Khama, was elected the first president. He was re-elected twice before dying in office in 1980.

This presidential democracy features a particularly strong president. The president is elected by the National Assembly, or lower legislative house. The president serves as both chief of state and head of the government—unlike in countries such as Guinea, where the roles are split between the president and prime minister. Since independence, Botswana has had only three presidents, but a two-term limit came into effect in 1999. The president names a cabinet and a vice-president, has limited veto power over legislation, and can declare war and sign treaties.

The president can also summon or dissolve the National Assembly at any time. The assembly functions like the British House of Commons. The president and National Assembly must consult with Parliament's upper House of Chiefs on tribal and customary matters. Botswana is considered a multiparty democracy, but the Botswana Democratic Party (BDP) has ruled since independence. In the 1999 elections, the BDP won 33 of 40 available seats in the National Assembly. Its rival party, the Botswana National Front (BNF), took six seats. A third party, the Botswana Congress Party (BCP), took one. The BDP also holds all four of the assembly's appointed seats. The independent judiciary draws on both English and Roman-Dutch law, prevalent in the nearby Cape Province of South Africa. The judiciary includes a Court of Appeal, the ultimate appellate body; a High Court, which has unlimited jurisdiction to try all civil and criminal cases and review lower-court decisions; and district magistrates' courts.

ISSUES AND CHALLENGES:

- The official opposition party, the BNF, has proposed that the president be popularly elected, but the governing BDP has been reluctant to accept the suggestion.

- Although some BDP members have been tainted by scandals, Berlin-based Transparency International in 1999 ranked Botswana as the least corrupt country in sub-Saharan Africa.

- Over the years, New York-based Freedom House has given Botswana high marks for its human rights and civic culture.

- Botswana leads the world in the adult HIV/AIDS infection rate—about 39 percent at recent count, well ahead of Swaziland and Zimbabwe, at more than 25 percent.

HOW THE GOVERNMENT WORKS

LEGISLATIVE BRANCH

Parliament
Bicameral

House of Chiefs
Composed of 15 members: 8 chiefs of Batswana tribe's principal subgroups; 4 elected by subchiefs; 3 selected by other 12 members. Serves as advisory body; reviews bills on tribal affairs.

National Assembly
Composed of 46 members who serve five-year terms: 40 elected by direct popular vote from single-member districts; 4 appointed by majority party; president; attorney general.

Regional governments
Nine districts administered by local councils and commissioners appointed by central government; municipalities overseen by elected councils.

EXECUTIVE BRANCH

President
Elected to five-year term by parliament following legislative elections; two-term limit. Serves as head of state and government; commander-in-chief of armed forces.

Vice-president
Appointed by president.

Cabinet
Composed of parliament members appointed by president. Oversees government operations; answers to parliament.

JUDICIAL BRANCH

Court of Appeal
Hears lower-court appeals. Composed of 5 judges appointed by president on advice of Judicial Service Commission.

High Court
Hears civil and criminal cases. Judges appointed by president on advice of Judicial Service Commission.

Magistrates' Courts

Traditional Courts

GUINEA-BISSAU

OFFICIAL NAME: REPUBLIC OF GUINEA-BISSAU

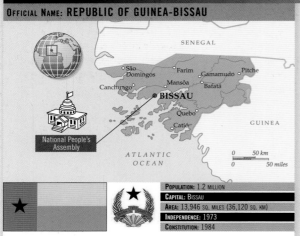

POPULATION: 1.2 MILLION	
CAPITAL: BISSAU	
AREA: 13,946 SQ. MILES (36,120 SQ. KM)	
INDEPENDENCE: 1973	
CONSTITUTION: 1984	

GUINEA-BISSAU, like Guinea, is derived from the Berber word, "aguinaw" or "gnawa" both meaning "black man".

RELIGION: Indigenous beliefs 52%, Muslim 40%, Christian 8%

OFFICIAL LANGUAGE: Portuguese

REGIONS OR PROVINCES: 9 regions

DEPENDENT TERRITORIES: None

MEDIA: Partial political censorship exists in national media

Newspapers: There is 1 daily newspaper

TV: 1 state-owned service

Radio: 3 services: 1 state-owned, 2 independent

SUFFRAGE: 18 years of age; universal

LEGAL SYSTEM: Tribal and customary law; accepts ICJ jurisdiction

WORLD ORGANIZATIONS: ACCT, ACP, AfDB, ECA, ECOWAS, FAO, FZ, G-77, IBRD, ICAO, ICFTU, ICRM, IDA, IDB, IFAD, IFC, IFRCS, ILO, IMF, IMO, Interpol, IOC, IOM, ITU, NAM, OAU, OIC, OPCW (signatory), UN, UNCTAD, UNESCO, UNIDO, UPU, WADB (regional), WAEMU, WFTU, WHO, WIPO, WMO, WToO, WTrO

POLITICAL PARTIES: PRS—Party for Social Renewal, RGB—Guinea-Bissau Resistance, PAIGSC—African Party for the Independence of Guinea and Cape Verde, AD—Alliance for Democracy

ETHNIC GROUPS:

European and Mulatto less than 1%

African (including Balanta, Fula, Manjaca, Mandinga, Papel) 99%

NATIONAL ECONOMICS

WORLD GNP RANKING: 183rd

GNP PER CAPITA: $180

INFLATION: 8.6%

BALANCE OF PAYMENTS (BALANCE OF TRADE) -$27 million

EXCHANGE RATES / U.S. DLR.: 698.7-736.7 CFA FRANCS

OFFICIAL CURRENCY: CFA FRANC

GOVERNMENT SPENDING (% OF GDP)

	0	5	10	15
✈ DEFENSE 1.7%				
🎓 EDUCATION (N/A)				
✚ HEALTH 4%				

NUMBER OF CONFLICTS OVER LAST 25 YEARS

	1	2-5	5+
Violent changes in government	●	○	○
Civil wars	○	●	○
International wars	○	○	○
Foreign intervention	●	○	○

- Compulsory national military service.
- Tensions exists with Sierra Leone and Liberia.
- ECOWAS has intervened to maintain order following coups and rebellions.

NOTABLE WARS AND INSURGENCIES: Military coup in 1980. Civil war 1998-1999

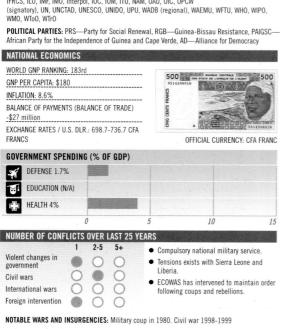

ONE OF THE FIRST AREAS on the African continent explored by the Portuguese in the 15th century, Guinea-Bissau became a territory of Portugal, as did the islands of Cape Verde. Together they fought for the same ideal—independence from Portugal. In 1956, the African Party for the Independence of Guinea and Cape Verde (PAIGC) was formed, an underground independence movement that started an armed rebellion against Portuguese troops in 1961.

Guinea-Bissau has followed a path similar to that of fellow fledgling African democracies including the Central African Republic and Guinea: independence, from Portugal in 1974 after a long liberation war; single-party rule, until 1994; several attempted or successful military coups, between 1980 and 1999; a disputed election, in 1994; frequent constitutional changes (a new constitution in 1984, amended twice in 1991, twice in 1993, and once in 1996); and continued political unrest.

With the advent of full-blown multiparty politics by 1994, the constitution mandated for the first time that the president be elected by universal suffrage, rather than by the legislative branch. But executive powers, including the position of commander-in-chief and the right to appoint a prime minister as head of the government, remained in the president's hands. Following an army rebellion in 1998 and subsequent fighting between presidential and army loyalists, a national unity government was formed, only to be overthrown in 1999. Fresh elections were held for the National People's Assembly, or Assembleia Nacional Popular, and won by the Party for Social Renewal (PRS). PRS candidate Kumba Yala was elected president in 2000, but was removed for inept government in another coup in September 2003. The military then installed a 2-year civilian transitional government.

The post-1990 constitution reduced both the powers and size of the Assembly. The PRS won 37 percent of the Assembly's seats in the 1999 election, but not far behind were Guinea-Bissau Resistance (RGB), with 27 percent, and the African Party for the Independence of Guinea and Cape Verde (PAIGC)—the sole political party until 1994—with 24 percent. The Supremo Tribunal de Justiça, or Supreme Court, is the country's final court of appeals.

ISSUES AND CHALLENGES:

- Guinea-Bissau is one of the ten poorest countries in the world and one of the least developed. The crippled economy, devastated by civil war and the military's bent for governmental meddling, complicate the country's transition to democracy.

- The ethnic character of the country's parties has kept its politics uncertain and allowed the army to play a central role.

- The health system is one of the worst in the world, leading to a high infant mortality rate and an average life expectancy of 45 years.

- About 70 percent of the population are unable to meet their basic needs.

HOW THE GOVERNMENT WORKS

LEGISLATIVE BRANCH

Assembleia Nacional Popular (National People's Assembly) Unicameral Parliament
Composed of 102 members directly elected to four-year terms by proportional representation.

Regional Governments
Eight regions and capital Bissau administered by state committees and elected councils.

EXECUTIVE BRANCH

President
Elected to four-year term by direct popular vote. Serves as head of state; commander-in-chief of armed forces.

Prime Minister
Appointed by president on advice of parliament's party leaders. Serves as head of government.

Council of State
Members appointed by president. Oversees government operations; presided over by president.

JUDICIAL BRANCH

Supreme Court
Highest court of review and appeal for civil and criminal cases. Composed of 9 judges appointed by president.

Regional Courts
Hear felony cases and civil cases valued over $1,000; rules on Sectoral Court appeals.

Sectoral Courts
Hear misdemeanor criminal cases and civil cases under $1,000.

CYPRUS

OFFICIAL NAME: REPUBLIC OF CYPRUS

Turkish Republic of Northern Cyprus
(only recognised by Turkey)
Dipkarpaz (Rizokarpaso)
Lapta (Lapithos)
Girne (Kyrenia)
Çayirova (Ayios)
Güzelyurt (Morphou)
Değirmenlik (Kythrea)
Famagusta Bay
NICOSIA
Gazimağusa (Famagusta)
Ayia Napa
Mediterranean Sea
Larnaca
Sovereign Base Area (to UK)
Paphos
Limassol
Sovereign Base Area (to UK)
Akrotiri
House of Representatives

0   25 km
0   25 miles

POPULATION: 790,000
CAPITAL: NICOSIA
AREA: 3,571 SQ. MILES (9,250 SQ. KM)
INDEPENDENCE: 1960
CONSTITUTION: 1960

CYPRUS is thought to be named after the locally occurring herb, "kupros", or in Greek "Cerastes", which means "the horned".

RELIGION: Greek Orthodox 78%, Muslim 18%, Maronite, Armenian Apostolic, and other 4%

OFFICIAL LANGUAGES: Greek and Turkish

REGIONS OR PROVINCES: 6 districts

DEPENDENT TERRITORIES: None

MEDIA: No political censorship exists in national media

Newspapers: There are 9 daily newspapers

TV: 6 services: 1 state-controlled, 5 independent

Radio: 5 services: 1 state-controlled, 4 independent

SUFFRAGE: 18 years of age; universal

LEGAL SYSTEM: Common and civil law; accepts ICJ jurisdiction

WORLD ORGANIZATIONS: Australia Group, C, CCC, CE, EBRD, ECE, EU, FAO, G-77, IAEA, IBRD, ICAO, ICC, ICFTU, IDA, IFAD, IFC, IFRCS (associate), IHO, ILO, IMF, IMO, Interpol, IOC, IOM, ISO, ITU, NAM, NSG, OAS (observer), OPCW, OSCE, PCA, UN, UNCTAD, UNESCO, UNIDO, UPU, WCL, WFTU, WHO, WIPO, WMO, WToO, WTrO

POLITICAL PARTIES: AKEL—Progressive Party of the Working People, DISY—Democratic Rally, DIKO—Democratic Party, KISOS—Movement of Social Democrats

ETHNIC GROUPS:

Other 5%
Turkish 18%
Greek 77%

NATIONAL ECONOMICS

WORLD GNP RANKING: 86th

GNP PER CAPITA: $12,370

INFLATION: 4.1%

BALANCE OF PAYMENTS (BALANCE OF TRADE): -$456 million

EXCHANGE RATES / U.S. DLR.: 0.6116-0.6461 CYPRUS POUNDS

OFFICIAL CURRENCY: CYPRUS POUND

GOVERNMENT SPENDING (% OF GDP)

DEFENSE 4.8%
EDUCATION 4.5%
HEALTH 6.3%

0   5   10   15

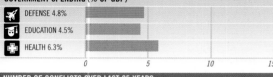

NUMBER OF CONFLICTS OVER LAST 25 YEARS

	1	2-5	5+
Violent changes in government	○	○	○
Civil wars	○	○	○
International wars	○	○	○
Foreign intervention	◐	○	○

- Compulsory national military service.
- UN have performed a peacekeeping mission since 1974.
- Britain maintains two military bases.
- Talks in 2003 regarding reunification did not reached agreement.

NOTABLE WARS AND INSURGENCIES: UN mission (UNFICYP) patrolling the Green Line

---

FOR ALMOST 30 YEARS, UN peacekeeping forces have maintained a buffer zone between the Greek Cypriot Republic of Cyprus in the south of the island and the self-proclaimed Turkish Republic of Northern Cyprus. Trouble between the two communities dates to Cyprus's independence from Britain in 1960. Violence erupted in 1974 when the military junta in Athens sponsored a coup against Archbishop Makarios, the charismatic Greek president of Cyprus, because he had apparently abandoned the policy of enosis (the reunion of Cyprus with Greece). The Turkish government in Ankara seized the northern third of the island to protect the Turkish Cypriot population; Greek Cypriots fled south while Turkish Cypriots went north. The UN is sponsoring ongoing negotiations to try to resolve the standoff.

BUFFER ZONE
A sign warns of mines in the United Nations-controlled area of Cyprus.
Inset: A UN soldier guards the Greek side of the buffer zone that divides the Turkish sector in the north of the island from the Greek south.

The government of the Republic of Cyprus is the internationally recognized authority on the island. The Turkish Cypriots' independent republic, recognized only by Turkey, has its own constitution, democratic elections, and government. The official Cypriot government is a presidential democracy. The president is both head of state and head of government and appoints the Council of Ministers, which shares executive power with the president. There is no vice-president or prime minister because the country's post-independence constitution stipulates that Turkish Cypriots must hold these posts. While the search for a solution to the island's seemingly hopeless situation continues, the original constitution of 1960 remains in place.

The unicameral House of Representatives initiates and passes legislation, though the president can veto bills related to foreign affairs, security, and defense. The constitution recognizes the legislature's independence, and the president has no authority to dissolve the House. The judiciary consists of assize courts, which cover criminal cases, and district courts, which handle both criminal and civil matters. The Supreme Court is the appeal court for all criminal and civil cases and rules on all constitutional disputes.

HOW THE GOVERNMENT WORKS

LEGISLATIVE BRANCH

Vouli Antiprosopon
(House of Representatives)
Unicameral Parliament
Composed of 80 members elected to five-year terms by direct popular vote; 56 seats reserved for Greek Cypriots; 24 seats for Turkish Cypriots.

Regional Governments
Six districts administered by officers appointed by Ministry of Interior.

EXECUTIVE BRANCH

President
Elected to five-year term by direct popular vote. Serves as head of state and government. Appoints attorney general and senior government officials; grants pardons and clemency. Vetoes foreign affairs, security and defense bills.

Prime Minister
Position is constitutionally reserved for Turkish Cypriot.

Council of Ministers
Members appointed by president. Sets policy; oversees government operations; presided over by president.

JUDICIAL BRANCH

Supreme Court
Highest court of review and appeal for civil and criminal cases. Rules on constitutionality of laws. Composed of 10 judges appointed by president.

Supreme Council of Judicature
Appoints, promotes, transfers, disciplines and dismisses all lower-court judges and judicial officers. Composed of attorney general, Supreme Court justices, member of Cypriot bar.

Assize courts
Hear criminal cases.

District Courts
Hear civil and criminal cases.

GUYANA

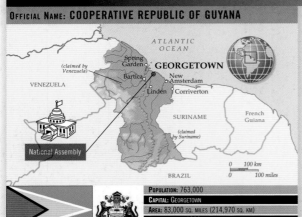

POPULATION: 763,000
CAPITAL: GEORGETOWN
AREA: 83,000 SQ. MILES (214,970 SQ. KM)
INDEPENDENCE: 1966
CONSTITUTION: 1966

GUYANA is derived from an American Indian word "Guiana" that means "the land of many waters".

RELIGION: Christian 50%, Hindu 35%, Muslim 10%, Other 5%

OFFICIAL LANGUAGE: English

REGIONS OR PROVINCES: 10 regions

DEPENDENT TERRITORIES: None

MEDIA: No political censorship exists in national media

Newspapers: There are 2 daily newspapers

TV: 16 services: 1 state-owned, 15 independent

Radio: 1 state-owned service

SUFFRAGE: 18 years of age; universal

LEGAL SYSTEM: English common law with Roman-Dutch influences; no ICJ jurisdiction

WORLD ORGANIZATIONS: ACP, C, Caricom, CCC, CDB, ECLAC, FAO, G-77, IADB, IBRD, ICAO, ICFTU, ICRM, IDA, IFAD, IFC, IFRCS, ILO, IMF, IMO, Interpol, IOC, ISO (subscriber), ITU, LAES, NAM, OAS, OIC, OPANAL, OPCW, PCA, RG, UN, UNCTAD, UNESCO, UNIDO, UPU, WCL, WFTU, WHO, WIPO, WMO, WTrO

POLITICAL PARTIES: PPP-CIVIC—People's Progressive Party-CIVIC, PNC—People's National Congress, GAP-WPA—Guyana Action Party-Working People's Alliance, ROAR—Rise, Organize and Rebuild, TUF—The United Force

ETHNIC GROUPS:
- Other 4%
- Amerindian 4%
- European and Chinese 2%
- East Indian 52%
- Black African 38%

NATIONAL ECONOMICS

WORLD GNP RANKING: 163rd

GNP PER CAPITA: $860

INFLATION: 6.1%

BALANCE OF PAYMENTS (BALANCE OF TRADE): -$117 million

EXCHANGE RATES / U.S. DLR.: 180.5 GUYANA DOLLARS

OFFICIAL CURRENCY: GUYANA DOLLAR

GOVERNMENT SPENDING (% OF GDP)

- ✈ DEFENSE 0.8%
- 📚 EDUCATION 5%
- ✚ HEALTH 4.5%

(scale 0 – 5 – 10 – 15)

NUMBER OF CONFLICTS OVER LAST 25 YEARS

	1	2-5	5+
Violent changes in government	○	○	○
Civil wars	○	●	○
International wars	○	○	○
Foreign intervention	○	○	○

- No compulsory national military service.
- Border dispute with Venezuela.
- US and UK are major suppliers of funding and training for military.

NOTABLE WARS AND INSURGENCIES: Political violence 1998-1999, 2001

ORIGINALLY THREE DUTCH COLONIES—Essequibo, Demerara and Berbice—the area that now makes up the Cooperative Republic of Guyana was ceded to Britain in 1814, and called the British Guiana. The Guyanese gained independence in 1966. Guyana, the only English-speaking nation in South America, is now a presidential democracy.

The first elections, held in 1953, were won by the People's Progressive Party (PPP) under Marxist Cheddi Jagan. However, within five months, the United Kingdom suspended parliament, believing Jagan had plans for a communist Guyana. In 1955, the coalition People's Progressive Party (PPP) split along racial and ideological lines into Afro-Guyanese and Indo-Guyanese factions. Politics have since been primarily based on ethnicity, with the largely Afro-Guyanese People's National Congress (PNC) dominating from 1964 to 1992. Forbes Burnham, who initially ruled Guyana as prime minister alongside Cheddi Jagan, took complete control in 1964. Burnham's rise to power as an autocratic leader came after he forged an alliance with the minor United Force Party. Through constitutional changes, he became president in 1980. Burnham's controversial rule, under which two major political figures were assassinated, human rights were suppressed and electoral fraud was widespread, came to an end with his death in 1985. Jagan and the PPP won the presidency in 1992 in what is widely considered Guyana's first legitimate election since independence. Jagan, changing his Marxist views, adopted free-market reforms. After he died in office in 1997, his widow, Janet, succeeded him as president—an event which was violently contested by the PNC. She resigned in 1999. The PPP remains in power, and violence erupts sporadically between PPP and PNC supporters.

Under Forbes Burnham, Guyana's 1980 constitution turned a largely ceremonial post into a powerful presidency. It vested the powers of head of state, chief executive, and commander-in-chief of the armed forces in a single elected position. The prime minister was made subordinate to the president. The constitution allows for multiple opposition parties, but their leaders have not always been afforded freedom of expression.

ISSUES AND CHALLENGES:

- Tensions between the Afro-Guyanese PNC and the Indo-Guyanese PPP often manifest themselves violently. Political instability has sapped investor confidence.
- Largely dependent on mineral resources for exports, Guyana is vulnerable to fluctuations in world commodity prices.
- The country is one of the poorest in the Western Hemisphere.
- Guyana's largely ineffectual police force has been strongly criticized for corruption.

HOW THE GOVERNMENT WORKS

LEGISLATIVE BRANCH
National Assembly
Unicameral Parliament
Composed of 65 members who serve five-year terms: 53 directly elected by proportional representation; 10 by regional councils: 2 by National Congress of Local Democratic Organs. Passes bills and constitutional amendments; overrides vetoes; removes president with two-thirds majority vote for violating constitution, three-fourths majority vote for gross misconduct.

Regional Governments
10 regions governed by elected regional councils; local communities administered by village or city councils.

EXECUTIVE BRANCH
President
Elected to five-year term by parliament's majority party following legislative elections; two-term limit. Serves as head of state; commander-in-chief of armed forces. Vetoes bills; approves constitutional amendments; dissolves parliament and regional councils; calls new elections.

Prime Minister
Member of parliament; appointed by president. Head of government.

Council of Ministers
Composed of members, including prime minister, appointed by president. Oversees government operations.

JUDICIAL BRANCH
Supreme Court of Judicature
Comprises Court of Appeal and High Court. High Court chancellor, Court of Appeal chief justice and chief magistrate appointed by Judicial Service Commission; other judges appointed by president.

Magistrates' Courts
Hear criminal cases and civil suits involving small claims in each region.

SURINAME

OFFICIAL NAME: REPUBLIC OF SURINAME

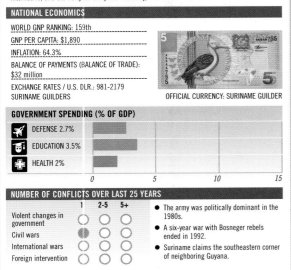

POPULATION: 419,000
CAPITAL: PARAMARIBO
AREA: 63,039 SQ. MILES (163,271 SQ. KM)
INDEPENDENCE: 1975
CONSTITUTION: 1987

SURINAME derives its name from the indigenous Surinen people.

RELIGION: Hindu 27%, Muslim 20%, Roman Catholic 23%, Protestant 25% (predominantly Moravian), Indigenous beliefs 5%

OFFICIAL LANGUAGE: Dutch

REGIONS OR PROVINCES: 10 districts

DEPENDENT TERRITORIES: None

MEDIA: No political censorship in national media

NEWSPAPERS: There are 2 daily newspapers

TV: 2 state-owned services

RADIO: 10 services: 1 state-owned, 9 independent

SUFFRAGE: 18 years of age; universal

LEGAL SYSTEM: Dutch and French legal traditions; accepts ICJ jurisdiction

WORLD ORGANIZATIONS: ACP, Caricom, ECLAC, FAO, G-77, IADB, IBRD, ICAO, ICFTU, ICRM, IDB, IFAD, IFRCS, IHO, ILO, IMF, IMO, Interpol, IOC, ITU, LAES, NAM, OAS, OIC, OPANAL, OPCW, PCA, UN, UNCTAD, UNESCO, UNIDO, UPU, WCL, WHO, WIPO, WMO, WTrO

POLITICAL PARTIES: NF—New Front for Democracy and Development (includes the Suriname National Party, the Progressive Reform Party, and the Suriname Labor Party, and Pertjajah Luhur), MC—Millennium Combination (includes the National Democratic Party (NDP), the Democratic Alternative, and the Party for Unity and Harmony) DNP 2000—Democratic National Platform 2000

ETHNIC GROUPS:

- Other 5%
- Black 9%
- South Asian 34%
- Javanese 18%
- Creole 34%

NATIONAL ECONOMICS

WORLD GNP RANKING:	159th
GNP PER CAPITA:	$1,890
INFLATION:	64.3%
BALANCE OF PAYMENTS (BALANCE OF TRADE):	$32 million
EXCHANGE RATES / U.S. DLR.:	981-2179 SURINAME GUILDERS

OFFICIAL CURRENCY: SURINAME GUILDER

GOVERNMENT SPENDING (% OF GDP)

- ✈ DEFENSE 2.7%
- 🎓 EDUCATION 3.5%
- ✚ HEALTH 2%

0   5   10   15

NUMBER OF CONFLICTS OVER LAST 25 YEARS

	1	2-5	5+	
Violent changes in government	○	○	○	• The army was politically dominant in the 1980s.
Civil wars	◐	○	○	• A six-year war with Bosneger rebels ended in 1992.
International wars	○	○	○	• Suriname claims the southeastern corner of neighboring Guyana.
Foreign intervention	○	○	○	

NOTABLE WARS AND INSURGENCIES: SLA guerrilla war 1986-1992

THE WORLD BANK RANKS Suriname as one of the most resource-rich countries in the world, yet the per capita income is one of the lowest in the Western Hemisphere due to political corruption, mismanagement, and ethnic conflict between the Hindu, Creole, and black communities. A six-year insurgency by black bosneger rebels lasted until 1992. Located on the north coast of South America on the Guyana Plateau, Suriname was ruled by the Dutch for over 300 years. It achieved independence in 1975, and Surinamese were awarded Dutch citizenship. Since then around one-third of the population have taken advantage of this to emigrate to the Netherlands.

Since 1975 the country has struggled through various civil administrations, interrupted by military coups: that led by Desi Bouterse in 1982 resulted in his military dictatorship until 1988. Yielding to demands for a return to democracy, Bouterse implemented a new constitution in 1987, establishing free elections and a civil government. His influence remains significant and his New Democratic Party held power between 1996 and 2000, bracketed by multi-ethnic governments headed by the New Front alliance.

The country's four leading political parties all represent specific ethnic interests. Historically, these four parties and other smaller parties have formed strategic alliances to increase their strength, a practice called consociationalism. The New Front for Democracy and Development for example, is an alliance of the National Party of Suriname (NPS)—which represents the Creole population—the Indonesian Party of High Ideals (KTPI), and the Progressive Reform Party (VHP) of the Hindus.

The president is responsible for the armed forces and foreign affairs, while the vice-president functions as prime minister, chairing the Council of Ministers. The National Assembly elects the president and vice-president, but if a two-thirds majority is not achieved in two ballots, the vote is taken by the People's Assembly, which is composed of the National Assembly and members of district and department councils, and a simple majority determines the winner. The judicial system consists of the High Court of Justice, which has limited power, and lower courts, where most cases are decided.

ISSUES AND CHALLENGES:

- Accounting for 65 percent of export reserves, the supply of bauxite is threatened by decreasing reserves and world prices.

- A preferential agreement with the EU to supply bananas has ended, damaging the banana industry.

- Dependent on economic aid from the Netherlands, Suriname needs major economic reform to become self-sufficient.

HOW THE GOVERNMENT WORKS

LEGISLATIVE BRANCH

National Assembly
Unicameral Parliament
Composed of 51 members directly elected to five-year terms by proportional representation.

People's Assembly
Composed of members of National Assembly, district councils and department councils. Convenes on request of National Assembly or to resolve presidential elections, dismissal of president or constitutional matters regarding Assembly members' powers.

Regional Governments
Ten districts each administered by commissioner appointed by president and elected district councils. Districts are subdivided into departments, also with elected councils.

EXECUTIVE BRANCH

President
Elected to five-year term by two-thirds vote of National Assembly or, if parliament cannot agree, by People's Assembly. Serves as head of state and government.

Vice-president
Elected to five-year term by simple majority of National Assembly. Chairs Council of Ministers as prime minister.

Council of Ministers
Appointed by president; responsible to National Assembly

State Advisory Council
Composed of 15 seats allotted proportionally to all political parties in National Assembly. Chaired by president; advises on national policy.

JUDICIAL BRANCH

High Court of Justice
Supervises lower Magistrates' Courts, settlement of all lawsuits and initiatives of attorney general. Justices appointed for life by president on advice of National Assembly, State Advisory Council, and National Order of Private Attorneys.

Magistrates' Courts

ANGOLA

OFFICIAL NAME: REPUBLIC OF ANGOLA

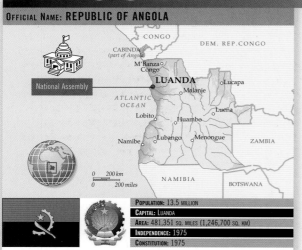

POPULATION: 13.5 MILLION
CAPITAL: LUANDA
AREA: 481,351 SQ. MILES (1,246,700 SQ. KM)
INDEPENDENCE: 1975
CONSTITUTION: 1975

ANGOLA is named after the king of the Quimbundos Kingdom, "Ngola", who ruled over the region in 1483.

RELIGION: Indigenous beliefs 47%, Roman Catholic 38%, Protestant 15%

OFFICIAL LANGUAGE: Portuguese

REGIONS OR PROVINCES: 18 provinces

DEPENDENT TERRITORIES: None

MEDIA: Total political censorship exists in national media

Newspapers: There are 2 daily newspapers

TV: 1 state-controlled service

Radio: 3 services: 1 state-owned, 2 independent

SUFFRAGE: 18 years of age; universal

LEGAL SYSTEM: Customary and Portuguese law; no ICJ jurisdiction

WORLD ORGANIZATIONS: ACP, AfDB, CCC, CEEAC, ECA, FAO, G-77, IAEA, IBRD, ICAO, ICFTU, ICRM, IDA, IFAD, IFC, IFRCS, ILO, IMF, IMO, Interpol, IOC, IOM, ITU, NAM, OAS (observer), OAU, SADC, UN, UNCTAD, UNESCO, UNIDO, UPU, WFTU, WHO, WIPO, WMO, WToO, WTrO

POLITICAL PARTIES: MPLA-PT—Popular Movement for the Liberation of Angola-Workers' Party, UNITA—National Union for the Total Independence of Angola, PRS—Social Renovated Party, FNLA—Angolan National Liberation Front, PLD—Liberal Democratic Party

ETHNIC GROUPS:

- Bakongo 13%
- Ovimbundu 37%
- Other 25%
- Kimbundu 25%

NATIONAL ECONOMICS

WORLD GNP RANKING: 121st

GNP PER CAPITA: $290

INFLATION: 325%

NATIONAL DEBT BALANCE OF PAYMENTS: -$4 million

EXCHANGE RATES / U.S. DLR.: 16.70-31.86 READJUSTED KWANZA

OFFICIAL CURRENCY: READJUSTED KWANZA

GOVERNMENT SPENDING (% OF GDP)

- DEFENSE 19.2%
- EDUCATION 2.6%
- HEALTH 1.6%

| | 0 | 5 | 10 | 15 |

NUMBER OF CONFLICTS OVER LAST 25 YEARS

	1	2-5	5+
Violent changes in government	○	○	○
Civil wars	●	○	○
International wars	●	○	○
Foreign intervention	○	●	○

- No compulsory national military service.
- Spillover fighting from Zambia threatens border security.
- Agreed to ratify the Ottawa Treaty requiring landmine elimination.
- Civil war cease-fire has led to demobilization of 80,000 troops.

NOTABLE WARS AND INSURGENCIES: Angolan civil war 1975-2000. South African and Cuban interventions. UN peacekeeping mission (UNAVEM). Intervened in Democratic Republic of Congo

CIVIL WAR AND ETHNIC STRIFE HAVE RAGED almost constantly in Angola both before and since its independence from Portugal in 1975. The two primary combatants, the legitimate Popular Liberation Movement of Angola (MPLA) and the rebel National Union for the Total Independence of Angola (UNITA), have fought a bloody and savage conflict based on hostilities that predate independence. A coup in 1974 established a military government, but as their coalition broke down, civil war broke out again. With the two groups supported by international forces—MPLA by Cuba and UNITA by South Africa—the MPLA seized Luanda and declared independence in 1975, but the civil war continued undiminished until 1989. The Bicesse Accord signed in 1991 proposed a democratic Angola under the supervision of the United Nations. However, when Jonas Savimbi, leader of UNITA, lost the first elections in 1992, he declared them fraudulent, returning Angola to war. Another attempt at peace, made in 1994, had failed by 1998.

As a result of the war, the formal political, economic, and social institutions that existed before independence have all but collapsed. The official structure of the government is based on a republican system of democracy. In reality, the president and the president's party dominate politics and exert considerable influence on the legislature and judiciary. However, the rural interior of the country is ethnically linked and loyal to UNITA. Subsequently, the formal government controls no more than 90 percent of the country, which disrupts its efficacy as a governing institution.

Examples of the effect of the continual warfare are many. Although oil-rich, Angola suffers constant disruptions in production that prevent full development of the industry. Throughout the country, the astronomical number of land mines—estimated near ten million—deters farmers from plowing their fields, paralyzing any possible agricultural base for the economy. The social toll of the conflict is devastating: The health-care system cannot cope with the volume of war casualties.

Although Angola's future seems bleak, the assassination of longtime UNITA leader Jonas Savimbi by government forces in February 2002 led to peace talks that produced a signed cease-fire agreement in April 2002.

ISSUES AND CHALLENGES:

- Angola's population has more amputees than any other in the world, nearly all of which are caused by encounters with landmines.
- The crime rate in Angola is very high. Murder, smuggling, poaching, and theft are common occurrences.
- The international community placed severe restrictions on the diamond trade—a major source of revenue—because of concerns that the proceeds funded violent militia groups.
- Owing to increased fighting, the UN canceled aid in 1999, placing a further strain on social welfare.

HOW THE GOVERNMENT WORKS

LEGISLATIVE BRANCH

Assembleia Nacional (National Assembly) Unicameral Parliament
Composed of 223 members directly elected to four-year terms by proportional representation. Meets twice annually. Approves national budget; enacts laws.

Regional Governments
Eighteen provinces administered by governors appointed by president and elected assemblies.

EXECUTIVE BRANCH

President
Elected to six-year term by direct popular vote; two-term limit. Serves as head of state and government; commander-in-chief of armed forces. Issues decrees; declares war with parliament's approval; grants pardons; announces general elections; calls special sessions of parliament.

Prime Minister
Appointed by president.

Council of Ministers
Composed of 29 members appointed by president. Oversees government operations; presided over by president.

JUDICIAL BRANCH

Constitutional Court
Mandated by 1992 constitution to rule on constitutionality of laws and court decisions. Yet to be established. Seven members are to be appointed: 3 by president; 3 by parliament; 1 by Supreme Court.

Supreme Court
Highest court of review and appeal. Justice appointed by president.

Provincial Courts

Municipal Courts

ZIMBABWE

OFFICIAL NAME: REPUBLIC OF ZIMBABWE

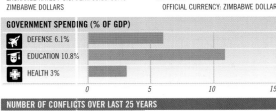

| POPULATION: 12.9 MILLION |
| CAPITAL: HARARE |
| AREA: 150,803 SQ. MILES (390,580 SQ. KM) |
| INDEPENDENCE: 1980 |
| CONSTITUTION: 1979 |

ZIMBABWE means "dwelling place of a chief" or "great stone building" in the indigenous Shona language.

RELIGION: Syncretic (blend of Christian and traditional beliefs) 50%, Christian 25%, Traditional beliefs 24%, Other 1%

OFFICIAL LANGUAGE: English

REGIONS OR PROVINCES: 8 provinces and 2 cities with provincial status

DEPENDENT TERRITORIES: None

MEDIA: Total political censorship exists in national media

Newspapers: There are 3 daily newspapers

TV: 1 state-controlled service

Radio: 1 state-controlled service

SUFFRAGE: 18 years of age; universal

LEGAL SYSTEM: English common law; Roman-Dutch legal traditions; no ICJ jurisdiction

WORLD ORGANIZATIONS: ACP, AfDB, C, CCC, ECA, FAO, G-15, G-77, IAEA, IBRD, ICAO, ICFTU, ICRM, IDA, IFAD, IFC, IFRCS, ILO, IMF, Interpol, IOC, IOM (observer), ISO, ITU, NAM, OAU, OPCW, PCA, SADC, UN, UNCTAD, UNESCO, UNIDO, UNMIK, UPU, WCL, WFTU, WHO, WIPO, WMO, WToO, WTrO

POLITICAL PARTIES: MDC—Movement for Democratic Change, United Parties, ZANU-Ndonga—Zimbabwe African National Union-Ndonga, ZANU-PF—Zimbabwe African National Union-Patriotic Front, ZAPU—Zimbabwe African Peoples Union

ETHNIC GROUPS:

- White 1%
- Asian 1%
- Other African 11%
- Shona 71%
- Ndebele 16%

NATIONAL ECONOMICS

WORLD GNP RANKING: 105th

GNP PER CAPITA: $460

INFLATION: 58.5%

NATIONAL DEBT BALANCE OF PAYMENTS: -$425 million

EXCHANGE RATES / U.S. DLR.: 55.10-55.45 ZIMBABWE DOLLARS

OFFICIAL CURRENCY: ZIMBABWE DOLLAR

GOVERNMENT SPENDING (% OF GDP)

- DEFENSE 6.1%
- EDUCATION 10.8%
- HEALTH 3%

0 5 10 15

NUMBER OF CONFLICTS OVER LAST 25 YEARS

	1	2-5	5+
Violent changes in government	○	○	○
Civil wars	◐	○	○
International wars	◐	○	○
Foreign intervention	○	○	○

- No compulsory national military service.
- Troops remain in Democratic Republic of Congo despite Lusaka Peace Accord.
- Renegade war veterans seizing land are a threat.
- Temporarily suspended by Commonwealth.

NOTABLE WARS AND INSURGENCIES: Involved in Democratic Republic of Congo. Civil strife since 2000

ROBERT MUGABE OF THE LEFT-WING Zimbabwe African National Union—Patriotic Front (ZANU-PF) has ruled Zimbabwe since independence in 1980, first as prime minister and then as executive president since 1987. Formerly the British colony of Southern Rhodesia, Zimbabwe was unilaterally declared independent in 1965 by white-supremacist prime minister, Ian Smith. A guerrilla war against Smith's minority-rule government, UN sanctions, and pressure from Great Britain ultimately resulted in a plan for democratic self-rule in 1979. ZANU-PF won the first post-independence elections and has held power ever since. Mugabe envisioned creating a one-party socialist state, but abandoned the scheme in 1991. The multiparty system envisaged upon independence has not materialized.

Mugabe risks losing support because of government corruption, allegations of election fraud, and growing criticism for fascist tactics—including arrests of journalists, unusual reversals of judicial rulings, and violent occupation of white-owned farms. Constitutional amendments strengthened Mugabe's authority, giving him control over the executive and legislative branches, abolishing Parliament's upper chamber. Mugabe's primary opponent is Morgan Tsvangirai, who heads the Movement for Democratic Change (MDC).

RALLY IN KADOMA—JUNE 16, 2000
Nearly 12,000 people, including many of the war veterans responsible for the recent illegal farm occupations, gather to hear Robert Mugabe speaking at a pre-election rally.

According to the constitution, the executive president fills the role of president and prime minister and is elected by popular majority vote for six-year terms. The unicameral House of Assembly has 150 members, serving five-year terms. One hundred and twenty are elected, eight are appointed by the president, 12 are governors (also appointed by the president), and 10 ex-officio members are traditional chiefs. The Chief Justice of the Supreme Court, appointed by the president on the recommendation of the Judicial Service Commission, heads the judiciary. The judicial branch includes the Supreme Court, the High Court, and lower courts as established by the House of Assembly.

HOW THE GOVERNMENT WORKS

LEGISLATIVE BRANCH

National Assembly
Unicameral Parliament
Composed of 150 members who serve five-year terms: 120 elected by direct popular vote; 12 appointed by the president, 10 traditional chiefs chosen by their peers; 8 provincial governors. Passes laws; amends constitution with two-thirds majority vote. Votes no-confidence in government by two-thirds majority.

Regional Governments
Eight provinces administered by governors appointed by president.

EXECUTIVE BRANCH

President
Elected to six-year term by direct popular vote. Serves as head of state and government; commander-in-chief of armed forces. Negotiates treaties; appoints ambassadors; proclaims martial law; declares war; assents to bills; dissolves parliament.

Two Vice-presidents
Appointed by president. Assist president in executive duties.

Cabinet
Members appointed by president, includes vice-presidents. Oversees government operations. Answers to parliament.

JUDICIAL BRANCH

Supreme Court
Highest court of review and appeal. Judges appointed to serve to age 65 by president on advice of Judicial Service Commission.

High Court
Hears civil and criminal cases. Composed of 23 judges appointed to serve to age 65 by president on advice of Judicial Service Commission.

Magistrates' Courts
Adjudicate criminal cases

Village and Community Courts
Adjudicate civil and minor criminal cases.

BELARUS

OFFICIAL NAME: REPUBLIC OF BELARUS

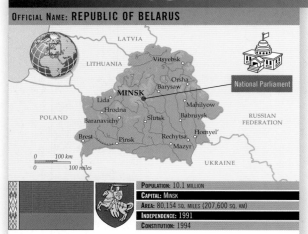

LATVIA
LITHUANIA
Vitsyebsk
Orsha
Barysaw
Lida
MINSK
Hrodna
Mahilyow
POLAND
Baranavichy
Slutsk
Babruysk
RUSSIAN FEDERATION
Brest
Pinsk
Rechytsa
Homyel'
Mazyr
UKRAINE
National Parliament

0 100 km
0 100 miles

POPULATION: 10.1 MILLION	
CAPITAL: MINSK	
AREA: 80,154 SQ. MILES (207,600 SQ. KM)	
INDEPENDENCE: 1991	
CONSTITUTION: 1994	

BELARUS means "white Ruthenia" or "white Rusynia", white being the color traditionally associated with freedom in Slavic culture.

RELIGION: Russian Orthodox 60%, Roman Catholic 8%, Other (including Muslim, Jewish and Protestant) 32%

OFFICIAL LANGUAGES: Belarussian and Russian

REGIONS OR PROVINCES: 6 regions and 1 municipality

DEPENDENT TERRITORIES: None

MEDIA: Total political censorship exists in national media

Newspapers: There are 20 daily newspapers, mostly published in Russian, while weekly papers tend to be published in Belarussian

TV: 1 state-controlled service; several small independent stations

Radio: 1 state-controlled service; some independent stations

SUFFRAGE: 18 years of age; universal

LEGAL SYSTEM: Civil law; no ICJ jurisdiction

WORLD ORGANIZATIONS: CCC, CEI, CIS, EAPC, EBRD, ECE, IAEA, IBRD, ICAO, ICRM, IFC, IFRCS, ILO, IMF, Interpol, IOC, IOM (observer), ISO, ITU, NAM, NSG, OPCW, OSCE, PCA, PFP, UN, UNCTAD, UNESCO, UNIDO, UPU, WFTU, WHO, WIPO, WMO, WTrO (observer)

POLITICAL PARTIES: PKB—Party of Communists of Belarus, Ind—Independents

ETHNIC GROUPS:

Ukrainian 3%
Polish 4%
Other 2%
Russian 13%
Belarussian 78%

NATIONAL ECONOMICS

WORLD GNP RANKING: 60th

GNP PER CAPITA: $2,870

INFLATION: 168.6%

BALANCE OF PAYMENTS (BALANCE OF TRADE): -$162 million

EXCHANGE RATES / U.S. DLR.: 1218-1603 BELARUSSIAN ROUBLES

OFFICIAL CURRENCY: BELARUSSIAN ROUBLE

GOVERNMENT SPENDING (% OF GDP)

✈ DEFENSE 4%		
📚 EDUCATION 5.6%		
✚ HEALTH 4.6%		

0   5   10   15

NUMBER OF CONFLICTS OVER LAST 25 YEARS

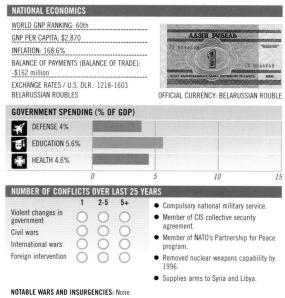

	1	2-5	5+
Violent changes in government	○	○	○
Civil wars	○	○	○
International wars	○	○	○
Foreign intervention	○	○	○

- Compulsory national military service.
- Member of CIS collective security agreement.
- Member of NATO's Partnership for Peace program.
- Removed nuclear weapons capability by 1996.
- Supplies arms to Syria and Libya.

NOTABLE WARS AND INSURGENCIES: None

DEVASTATED BY THE NAZIS IN WORLD WAR II, Belarus only reluctantly severed ties with Moscow when the Soviet Union collapsed in 1991 and has since sought reunification with Russia. Belarus has been widely criticized for being the slowest former Soviet republic by far to carry out political reform. The country is ostensibly a democracy. But in many ways, under Alyaksandr Lukashenka, elected president in 1994, it has been a dictatorship. The 1994 constitution made the president a national figurehead with only weak duties, such as suggesting legislation. A prime minister was to head the government, proposing policies and running the bureaucracy. But Lukashenka increased presidential power considerably, calling for referenda in 1995 and 1996, by which he gained public support for a stronger presidency and a new constitution that lengthened his term of office until 2001. The constitution also further strengthened his power by giving him control of a new upper house of parliament, the Council of the Republic, whose members are named by the president or his subordinates. The Council, in turn, can reject bills passed by the lower House of Representatives. The House can "consider" legislation proposed by the president or motions of no confidence in the executive. The Constitutional Court and Election Commission ruled that the 1996 referendum was illegal, but Lukashenka ignored them.

Deputies who opposed the referendum results refused to sit in the new parliament, creating an illegal opposition "shadow" government. And while local governments are, in theory, autonomous, Lukashenka disbanded them, placing the regions under hand-picked administrators. He thereby created a line of command from the president to the regions. In

CHERNOBYL 14TH ANNIVERSARY—APRIL 26, 2000
Mourning on the anniversary of the Chernobyl nuclear power plant disaster. The explosion in the fourth reactor spread a radioactive cloud over Belarus, Ukraine, Russia and Western Europe.

practice, the parliament, mostly Lukashenka loyalists and institutionally weak, has been largely a rubber stamp. A clampdown on opponents invalidated parliamentary elections in 2000 and 2001. Observers condemned the president's re-election in 2001 as flawed.

HOW THE GOVERNMENT WORKS

LEGISLATIVE BRANCH

Natsionalnoye Sobranie
(National Parliament)
Bicameral Parliament

Soviet Respubliki
(Council of the Republic)
Composed of 64 members who serve four-year terms: 56 elected by regional councils; eight appointed by president. Approves or rejects bills from House; impeaches president.

Palata Pretsaviteley
(House of Representatives)
110 members elected to four-year terms by direct popular vote from single-member districts. Initiates legislation; considers bills from president.

Regional Governments
Six regions governed by local administrators appointed by central government.

EXECUTIVE BRANCH

President
Elected to five-year term by direct popular vote. Serves as head of state; commander-in-chief of armed forces; chair of National Security Council. Proposes, signs and vetoes bills; dissolves parliament.

Prime Minister
Appointed by president. Serves as head of government. Coordinates government ministries.

Council of Ministers
Composed of 26 members appointed by president. Oversees government operations.

JUDICIAL BRANCH

Constitutional Court
Rules on constitutionality of laws. Composed of 12 judges appointed to 11-year terms: six by president; six by Council of the Republic.

Supreme Court
Highest court of review and appeal. Composed of 15 judges appointed by president, approved by Council of the Republic.

Lower Courts

TAJIKISTAN

OFFICIAL NAME: REPUBLIC OF TAJIKISTAN

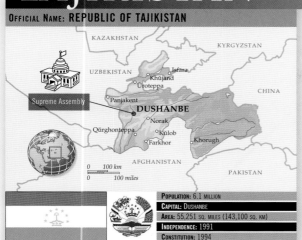

POPULATION: 6.1 MILLION
CAPITAL: DUSHANBE
AREA: 55,251 SQ. MILES (143,100 SQ. KM)
INDEPENDENCE: 1991
CONSTITUTION: 1994

TAJIKISTAN is Persian for "land of the Tajiks", while Tajik itself comes from the Persian "taj" meaning crown and "ik" meaning head.

RELIGION: Sunni Muslim 80%, Shi'a Muslim 5%, Other 15%

OFFICIAL LANGUAGE: Tajik

REGIONS OR PROVINCES: 2 provinces and 1 autonomous province

DEPENDENT TERRITORIES: None

MEDIA: Total political censorship exists in national media

Newspapers: There are 3 daily newspapers

TV: 3 state-controlled services

Radio: 1 state-controlled service

SUFFRAGE: 18 years of age; universal

LEGAL SYSTEM: Civil law; no ICJ jurisdiction

WORLD ORGANIZATIONS: AsDB, CCC, CIS, EAPC, EBRD, ECE, ECO, ESCAP, FAO, IAEA, IBRD, ICAO, ICRM, IDA, IDB, IFAD, IFC, IFRCS, ILO, IMF, IOC, IOM, ITU, OIC, OPCW, OSCE, UN, UNCTAD, UNESCO, UNIDO, UPU, WFTU, WHO, WIPO, WMO, WTrO (observer)

POLITICAL PARTIES: PDPT—People's Democratic Party of Tajikistan, CPT—Communist Party of Tajikistan, IRP—Islamic Revival Party

ETHNIC GROUPS:

- Other 7%
- Russian 3%
- Uzbek 25%
- Tajik 65%

NATIONAL ECONOMICS

WORLD GNP RANKING: 151st

GNP PER CAPITA: $180

INFLATION: 33.0%

BALANCE OF PAYMENTS (BALANCE OF TRADE) -$61 million

EXCHANGE RATES / U.S. DLR.: 2.40-2.55 SOMONI

OFFICIAL CURRENCY: SOMONI

GOVERNMENT SPENDING (% OF GDP)

- ✈ DEFENSE 6.5%
- 🎓 EDUCATION 2.2%
- ✚ HEALTH 5.2%

0   5   10   15

NUMBER OF CONFLICTS OVER LAST 25 YEARS

	1	2-5	5+
Violent changes in government	○	○	○
Civil wars	○	●	○
International wars	○	○	○
Foreign intervention	○	●	○

- Compulsory national military service.
- Russia is main source of military assistance.
- Greatest security threat is Afghanistan border, secured by 20,000 peacekeepers.
- Member of NATO's Partnership for Peace program.
- Border dispute with Kyrgyzstan.

NOTABLE WARS AND INSURGENCIES: Civil war 1992-1994. Islamist militancy 2000

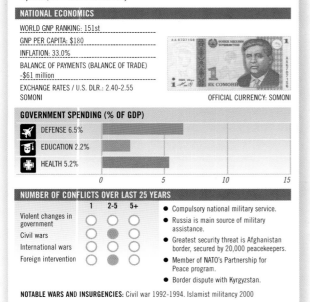

THE LAND THAT IS NOW TAJIKISTAN came under control of the Russian Empire in the 19th century, and under Soviet authority in 1924. The Soviet Union created Tajikistan and neighboring Uzbekistan from an area whose people had considered themselves a single, if diverse, nationality. The country achieved independence in 1991. Civil war immediately followed, between communist government forces and the Islamist coalition United Tajik Opposition (UTO), killing more than 50,000 people and lasting until peace talks began in 1994. Imomali Rakhmanov, who came to power in 1992, was elected Tajikistan's first president in 1994 in elections largely regarded as fraudulent, and was returned to office by voters in 1999. The constitution of Tajikistan also was approved in 1994. The first elections for the national legislature, or Supreme Assembly, were held in 1995, but without opposition participation.

United Nations intervention finally brought about a signed peace agreement in 1997, establishing the Commission of National Reconciliation that guaranteed equal governmental representation for both sides. Rakhmanov still abides by the agreement, maintaining a number of UTO members in senior government positions.

However, after many years of communist leadership and internal power struggles, Tajikistan operates under a presidential regime that is still not fully implemented. Since the agreement ending civil war, elections for both the presidency and for seats in the bicameral Supreme Assembly have been viewed as peaceful but also as flawed by international standards. A balance of power among the three branches of government has not been achieved. According to the constitution, the executive branch has significantly more power than either the legislative or the judicial. The president, for instance, can declare a state of emergency and extend it for up to three months. The office also holds the power to appoint all the judges, which limits the independence of the judiciary called for in the constitution, and to select the governors of all local governments, who answer directly to the president.

ISSUES AND CHALLENGES:

- Even though Tajikistan has achieved some level of stability, its proximity to Afghanistan and its terrorist bases has the potential to create new political turmoil and chaos, as it threatens the order of a nation that is still very frail both politically and economically. The advance of Taliban forces in the region has brought many refugees into Tajikistan.

- Drug trafficking has increased, among other things, the likelihood of crime and the spread of diseases including HIV infection.

- Demand for Tajikistan's most significant resource, uranium, has dropped since the end of the Cold War, while its presence now poses a security risk from terrorist groups.

HOW THE GOVERNMENT WORKS

LEGISLATIVE BRANCH

Majlisi Oli
(Supreme Assembly)
Bicameral Parliament

Majlisi Milliy
(National Assembly)
Composed of 33 members who serve five-year terms: 25 selected by local deputies; eight appointed by president.

Majlisi Namoyandagon
(Assembly of Representatives)
Composed of 63 members elected to five-year terms by direct popular vote.

Regional Governments
Four provinces administered by elected councils and governors appointed by president.

EXECUTIVE BRANCH

President
Elected to seven-year term by absolute majority of direct popular vote; two-term limit. Serves as head of state; chairs parliament. Cancels decrees of parliament; declares states of emergency.

Prime Minister
Appointed by president, confirmed by parliament. Serves as head of government.

Council of Ministers
Composed of 14 senior ministers and 19 advisers, appointed by president. Oversees government operations; chaired by prime minister.

JUDICIAL BRANCH

Constitutional Court
Rules on constitutionality of laws; decides intergovernmental disputes. Judges appointed by president, confirmed by parliament.

Supreme Court
Highest court of review and appeal. Judges appointed by president, confirmed by parliament.

High Economic Court
Judges appointed by president, confirmed by parliament.

Lower courts
Judges appointed by president on advice of minister of justice.

TURKMENISTAN

OFFICIAL NAME: TURKMENISTAN

POPULATION: 4.8 MILLION	
CAPITAL: ASHGABAT	
AREA: 188,455 SQ. MILES (488,100 SQ. KM)	
INDEPENDENCE: 1991	
CONSTITUTION: 1992	

TURKMENISTAN is Arabic for "land of the Turkmen", while Turkmen itself comes from the Turkic "men" meaning "I", thus "I am a Turk".

RELIGION: Sunni Muslim 87%, Eastern Orthodox 11%, Other 2%

OFFICIAL LANGUAGE: Turkmen

REGIONS OR PROVINCES: 5 provinces

DEPENDENT TERRITORIES: None

MEDIA: Total political censorship exists in national media

Newspapers: There are 2 daily newspapers

TV: 1 state-controlled service

Radio: 1 state-controlled service

SUFFRAGE: 18 years of age; universal

LEGAL SYSTEM: Civil law; no ICJ jurisdiction

WORLD ORGANIZATIONS: AsDB, CCC, CIS, EAPC, EBRD, ECE, ECO, ESCAP, FAO, IBRD, ICAO, ICRM, IDB, IFC, IFRCS, ILO, IMF, IMO, IOC, IOM (observer), ISO (correspondent), ITU, NAM, OIC, OPCW, OSCE, PFP, UN, UNCTAD, UNESCO, UNIDO, UPU, WFTU, WHO, WIPO, WMO, WToO, WTrO (observer)

POLITICAL PARTIES: DPT—Democratic Party of Turkmenistan

ETHNIC GROUPS:

- Other 5.1%
- Kazakh 2%
- Russian 6.7%
- Uzbek 9.2%
- Turkmen 77%

NATIONAL ECONOMICS

WORLD GNP RANKING: 119th

GNP PER CAPITA: $750

INFLATION: 14.0%

BALANCE OF PAYMENTS (BALANCE OF TRADE): $412 million

EXCHANGE RATES / U.S. DLR.: 5200 MANATS

OFFICIAL CURRENCY: MANAT

GOVERNMENT SPENDING (% OF GDP)

		0	5	10	15
✈	DEFENSE 4%				
	EDUCATION 4.5%				
✚	HEALTH 4.1%				

NUMBER OF CONFLICTS OVER LAST 25 YEARS

	1	2-5	5+
Violent changes in government	○	○	○
Civil wars	○	○	○
International wars	○	○	○
Foreign intervention	○	○	○

- Compulsory national military service.
- Declaration of "permanent neutrality" recognized by UN in 1995.
- Russia supplies most defense needs.
- Pilots are trained in Pakistan.
- Intra-tribal conflicts are an issue.

NOTABLE WARS AND INSURGENCIES: None

TURKMENISTAN WAS OVERRUN by many of the great conquerors of antiquity—Alexander the Great, the Parthians, the Arabs, the Turkish Seljuks, and the Mongols of Genghis Khan. In the late 19th century it was acquired by czarist Russia. Turkmenistan currently operates, in theory, as a democracy under a presidential regime. In reality, government and politics have changed little since the former Soviet republic gained independence in 1991 after the collapse of the Soviet Union. President Saparmurad Niyazov holds power today with the same authoritarianism he exercised as president of the Turkmen Soviet Socialist Republic. The US-based human rights group Freedom House consistently gives Turkmenistan its lowest rating each year for political rights and civil liberties.

Niyazov became the first president of the new republic, elected without opposition since opposition parties and candidates are forbidden, and remains in power to the present. He serves as both chief of state and head of the government. The 1992 constitution calls for presidential elections every five years, but the Parliament, on the advice of the People's Council—also indirectly controlled by the president—extended Niyazov's term to a term for life in 1999. In 1995, Turkmenistan's declaration of "permanent neutrality" was recognized by the United Nations.

Niyazov in effect controls all three branches of government. Although some of its members are elected, the legislative branch merely advises the president. Most members are from the Democratic Party of Turkmenistan (DPT). Supreme Court judges are not only appointed by the president but can be removed by the president at any time. The constitution provides for freedom of the press and religion, but the government maintains absolute control of all media and restricts all forms of religious expression.

Renaming himself Turkmenbashi—"Head of the Turkmen" or "Father of all Turkmen"—Saparmurad Niyazov has encouraged a personality cult to develop around him. Numerous city streets and buildings have been renamed after him, and statues of the president have been erected throughout the capital city of Ashgabat. Niyazov reportedly renamed the days of the week and months of the year after national symbols or heroes.

ISSUES AND CHALLENGES:

- Although the constitution provides for freedom of religion and press, the government maintains absolute control over both. All religious groups must register by meeting specified criteria. If they are unable to register, they are prohibited from congregating.
- Corruption is rife throughout the government.
- Business opportunities are limited, as most industry and services are government-controlled or owned.
- While Turkmenistan wishes to encourage investment and establish relations with Iran and Turkey, it is wary of Islamic fundamentalism.

HOW THE GOVERNMENT WORKS

LEGISLATIVE BRANCH

Milli Majlis
(Parliament)
Unicameral Parliament
50 members elected to five-year terms. Passes bills; votes of no-confidence.

Halk Maslahaty
(People's Council)
110 members who serve five-year terms: 50 Parliament members, 50 elected members, 10 appointed regional leaders, Supreme Court justices and Cabinet ministers as ex-officio members. Chaired by president; advises on domestic and foreign policy; amends constitution and laws.

Council of Elders
Senior tribal and regional leaders appointed/chaired by president.

Regional Governments
Five provinces administered by governors appointed by president and elected councils.

EXECUTIVE BRANCH

President
Elected to five-year term by direct popular vote; term extended for life by People's Council in 1999. Serves as head of state and government; commander-in-chief of armed forces. Creates laws though edicts; appoints and removes state prosecutors and judges; dissolves Parliament after two no-confidence votes within an 18-month period.

Cabinet
Appointed by president, approved by Parliament. Oversees government operations; chaired by president.

JUDICIAL BRANCH

Supreme Court
Highest court of review. Hears criminal, civil and military cases. Composed of 22 judges appointed to five-year terms by president.

Supreme Economic Court
Hears commercial and taxation cases. Judges appointed by president.

Courts of Appeal
One in each of the provinces and one in the capital. Judges appointed by president.

District Courts
Operate in the provinces and some cities. Appointed by procurator general.

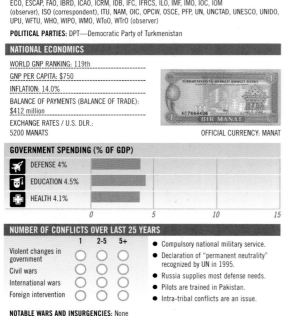

TOGO

OFFICIAL NAME: **REPUBLIC OF TOGO**

POPULATION: 4.7 MILLION	
CAPITAL: LOMÉ	
AREA: 21,924 SQ. MILES (56,785 SQ. KM)	
INDEPENDENCE: 1960	
CONSTITUTION: 1992	

TOGO means "over there", a reference to when German explorers asked the local people the name of the land they could see over the lagoon.

RELIGION: Traditional beliefs 50%, Christian 35%, Muslim 15%

OFFICIAL LANGUAGE: French

REGIONS OR PROVINCES: 5 regions

DEPENDENT TERRITORIES: None

MEDIA: Total political censorship exists in national media

Newspapers: There are 2 daily newspapers

TV: 1 state-owned service

Radio: 3 services: 1 state-owned, 2 independent

SUFFRAGE: universal adult

LEGAL SYSTEM: French law; accepts ICJ jurisdiction

WORLD ORGANIZATIONS: ACCT, ACP, AfDB, CCC, ECA, ECOWAS, Entente, FAO, FZ, G-77, IBRD, ICAO, ICC, ICFTU, ICRM, IDA, IDB, IFAD, IFC, IFRCS, ILO, IMF, IMO, Interpol, IOC, ITU, MIPONUH, NAM, OAU, OIC, OPCW, UN, UNCTAD, UNESCO, UNIDO, UPU, WADB (regional), WAEMU, WCL, WFTU, WHO, WIPO, WMO, WToO, WTrO

POLITICAL PARTIES: RPT—Rally of the Togolese People, Ind—Independents

ETHNIC GROUPS:

Other
1%

African
(37 tribes; largest and most important are Ewe, Mina, and Kabre)
99%

NATIONAL ECONOMICS

WORLD GNP RANKING: 149th

GNP PER CAPITA: $290

INFLATION: 1,9%

BALANCE OF PAYMENTS (BALANCE OF TRADE): -$106 million

EXCHANGE RATES / U.S. DLR.: 698.7-736.7 CFA FRANCS

OFFICIAL CURRENCY: CFA FRANC

GOVERNMENT SPENDING (% OF GDP)

- DEFENSE 2%
- EDUCATION 4.5%
- HEALTH 1.3%

```
0        5        10        15
```

NUMBER OF CONFLICTS OVER LAST 25 YEARS

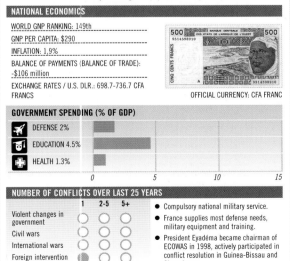

	1	2-5	5+
Violent changes in government	○	○	○
Civil wars	○	○	○
International wars	○	○	○
Foreign intervention	◐	○	○

- Compulsory national military service.
- France supplies most defense needs, military equipment and training.
- President Eyadéma became chairman of ECOWAS in 1998, actively participated in conflict resolution in Guinea-Bissau and Sierra Leone.

NOTABLE WARS AND INSURGENCIES: French help quash attempted coup 1985

ALTHOUGH TOGO RATIFIED a new constitution in 1993 that converted the state into a multiparty republic, most political power lies in the Rally of the Togolese People (RPT) party. General Gnassingbé Eyadéma, the founder of the RPT, has held power continuously as president since he led a bloodless coup in 1967. Bowing to an increasingly influential pro-democracy movement within the country, the government instituted multiparty elections in 1993. However, Eyadéma won each subsequent election by landslide margins. Generally, fewer than 40 percent of eligible voters cast ballots. Opposition groups consistently accuse the government of electoral irregularities and voter intimidation. Subsequently, Togo's election process has faced increased scrutiny from the international community. Meanwhile, the country, which claims to be in transition to democracy, seems to regress further into a military autocracy.

Prior to the constitution of 1993, the National Assembly held little, if any, power that the president could not overrule. The new constitution provides for significantly more authority for the legislature, but 95 percent of the Assembly is composed of the RPT, which diligently carries out Eyadéma's agenda. Contributing to the RPT's dominance of the National Assembly is the fact that the country's main opposition parties—especially the Action Committee for Renewal (CAR) and the Union of Forces of Change—boycott elections, claiming electoral fraud.

SUMMIT—FEBRUARY 19, 2003

The president of Togo, Gnassingbé Eyadéma, meets with his counterpart, the president of France, Jacques Chirac at the Elysée Palace in Paris before the start of the 22nd Franco-African summit.

The judiciary is a four-tiered system. The highest authority on legal matters is the Constitutional Court, which consists of seven members, under which is a Supreme Court, two Courts of Appeals, and numerous tribunals for civil, criminal, commercial, juvenile, state security, and misuse of funds cases.

HOW THE GOVERNMENT WORKS

LEGISLATIVE BRANCH

National Assembly
Unicameral Parliament
Composed of 81 members elected to five-year terms by direct popular vote.

Regional Governments
Five regions: 30 prefectures.

EXECUTIVE BRANCH

President
Elected to five-year term by direct popular vote. Serves as head of state; commander-in-chief of armed forces. Initiates bills; dissolves parliament; appoints government officials; controls national and local budgets.

Prime Minister
Member of parliament's majority party or coalition; appointed by president. Serves as head of government.

Council of Ministers
Appointed by president on advice of prime minister. Oversees government operations.

JUDICIAL BRANCH

Constitutional Court
Rules on constitutionality of laws. Composed of seven judges appointed by president, approved by Judicial Council.

Supreme Court
Split into judicial and administrative chambers. Judges appointed by president, approved by Judicial Council.

Courts of Appeal
Two courts: for criminal cases; for civil and commercial cases.

High Court of Justice
Hears charges against president and Supreme Court judges. Comprises president, presidents of Supreme Court's two chambers, four legislators elected by parliament.

Local Tribunals

COMOROS

OFFICIAL NAME: FEDERAL ISLAMIC REPUBLIC OF THE COMOROS

POPULATION: 727,000
CAPITAL: MORONI
AREA: 838 SQ. MILES (2,170 SQ. KM)
INDEPENDENCE: 1975
CONSTITUTION: 2001

COMOROS as a word is derived from the Arabic word "kamar" or "kumr" which means "moon", and was first used by the French colonialists.

RELIGION: Muslim (mainly Sunni) 98%, Roman Catholic 1%, Other 1%

OFFICIAL LANGUAGES: Arabic, French, and Comoran

REGIONS OR PROVINCES: 3 islands; 4 municipalities

DEPENDENT TERRITORIES: None

MEDIA: Partial political censorship exists in national media

Newspapers: There are 2 weekly newspapers

TV: No TV service

Radio: 1 state-controlled service, some independent services

SUFFRAGE: 18 years of age; universal

LEGAL SYSTEM: Shari'a (Islamic) and French law; no ICJ jurisdiction

WORLD ORGANIZATIONS: ACCT, ACP, AfDB, AFESD, AL, CCC, ECA, FAO, FZ, G-77, IBRD, ICAO, ICRM, IDA, IDB, IFAD, IFC, IFRCS (associate), ILO, IMF, IMO, InOC, Interpol, IOC, ISO (subscriber), ITU, NAM, OAU, OIC, OPCW (signatory), UN, UNCTAD, UNESCO, UNIDO, UPU, WHO, WMO, WTrO (applicant)

POLITICAL PARTIES: RND—National Rally for Development, FNJ—National Front for Justice, Ind—Independent

ETHNIC GROUPS:

Other 3%

Comoran 97%

NATIONAL ECONOMICS

WORLD GNP RANKING: 183rd

GNP PER CAPITA: $380

INFLATION: 3.5%

BALANCE OF PAYMENTS (BALANCE OF TRADE): -$1 million

EXCHANGE RATES / U.S. DLR.: 528-558 COMOROS FRANCS

OFFICIAL CURRENCY: COMOROS FRANC

GOVERNMENT SPENDING (% OF GDP)

	0	5	10	15
DEFENSE (N/A)				
EDUCATION 4.2%				
HEALTH 4.9%				

NUMBER OF CONFLICTS OVER LAST 25 YEARS

	1	2-5	5+
Violent changes in government	○	○	●
Civil wars	○	●	○
International wars	○	○	○
Foreign intervention	○	●	○

- No compulsory national military service.
- Funding for security provided by France and South Africa.
- Defense Treaty with France for provision of training and air and-naval support.
- France maintains troops and a military base.

NOTABLE WARS AND INSURGENCIES: Coups in 1989, 1995, 1999 and 2001. Anjouan separatist conflict

THE COMOROS CONSISTS OF THREE MAIN ISLANDS—Grande Comore, Anjouan, and Mohéli—and several islets that operate under a unified presidential regime. After reaching an agreement with France, which had previously controlled the territory, the islands of the Comoros became independent in 1975 through a Comoran parliamentary resolution. A fourth larger island, Mayotte, chose to remain under the administration of France.

Comoros' history since independence has been marked by political instability, assassination, betrayal, election fraud and government corruption, all reflected in 19 successful and failed coups to date. The nation's first president, Ahmed Abdallah, was overthrown in 1975—the same year the country gained independence—in a coup aided by French mercenaries, who three years later helped to return Abdallah to power. Mercenaries assassinated Abdallah in 1989. Saïd Mohamed Djohar won presidential elections in 1990 but was assassinated in 1995. Mohamed Taki Abdoulkarim became president in 1996. His inability to reach consensus with the islands' leadership, and the country's economic decline, made him generally unpopular, and he was viewed as yet another dictator. By 1997, the islands of Anjouan and Mohéli had declared their independence. Abdoulkarim died of a heart attack in 1998. Colonel Azali Assoumani led a coup a year later that overthrew the interim government, and declared himself president. Azali assumed both executive and legislative powers, but nominated a civilian as prime minister and started drafting a new constitution to reduce national and international criticism. Azali resigned for a few months in 2002 to run in presidential elections. Although he won 75 percent of the popular vote, voter turnout was low, which undermined his victory.

Shortly thereafter, the three main islands became politically unified as the Union of Comoros, a confederation that gives each island equal status and permits the election of its own president and legislature. The elected presidents rotate the presidency of the union every four years, with the federal president having responsibility over the country as a whole.

ISSUES AND CHALLENGES:

- With most farmers practicing subsistence farming, the government needs to import nearly half of the country's food needs.

- Infrastructure is inadequate and limited. Together with the political instability, this prevents investment and the growth of the potentially lucrative tourist industry. Rival militias, particularly on recently-independent Anjouan Island have contributed to a feeling of political instability.

- The Comoros are dependent on aid from France, the EU, the UN and the World Bank, which together provide 40 percent of the country's GDP.

HOW THE GOVERNMENT WORKS

LEGISLATIVE BRANCH

Parliament
Bicameral Parliament

Senate
Composed of 15 members who serve five-year terms: five from each island; chosen by Electoral College.

Assemblée Féderale
(Federal Assembly)
Composed of 42 members elected to five-year terms by direct popular vote from single-member districts.

Regional Governments
Three largest islands administered by an elected president and councils.

EXECUTIVE BRANCH

President
Elected to four-year term by direct popular vote; two-term limit. Serves as head of state and government; commander-in-chief of armed forces.

Prime Minister
Member of parliament's majority party or coalition; appointed by president.

Council of Government
Composed of island governors and members appointed by president. Oversees government operations.

JUDICIAL BRANCH

Supreme Court
Highest court of review and appeal. Rules on constitutionality of laws; supervises presidential elections. Composed of seven judges: two appointed by president; two elected by Federal Assembly; one each appointed by councils of three islands.

Superior Court

Lower Courts

Religious Courts

DJIBOUTI

OFFICIAL NAME: REPUBLIC OF DJIBOUTI

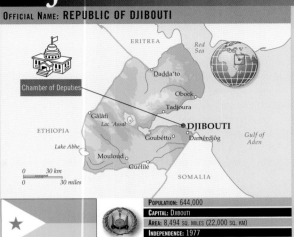

Chamber of Deputies

ERITREA
Red Sea
Dadda'to
Obock
Tadjoura
Galâfi
Lac 'Assal
ETHIOPIA
DJIBOUTI
Goubétto
Damêrdjôg
Gulf of Aden
Lake Abhe
Mouloud
Guêlilé
SOMALIA

0   30 km
0   30 miles

POPULATION: 644,000
CAPITAL: DJIBOUTI
AREA: 8,494 SQ. MILES (22,000 SQ. KM)
INDEPENDENCE: 1977
CONSTITUTION: 1992

DJIBOUTI, previously known as the Territory of the Afars and Issas, was renamed Djibouti after the port city by the same name.

RELIGION: Muslim 94%. Christian 6%

OFFICIAL LANGUAGES: Arabic and French

REGIONS OR PROVINCES: 5 districts

DEPENDENT TERRITORIES: None

MEDIA: Total political censorship exists in national media

Newspapers: There are no daily newspapers

TV: 1 state-controlled service

Radio: 1 state-controlled service

SUFFRAGE: 18 years of age; universal adult

LEGAL SYSTEM: Shari'a (Islamic) and French law; traditional practices; no ICJ jurisdiction

WORLD ORGANIZATIONS: ACCT, ACP, AfDB, AFESD, AL, AMF, ECA, FAO, G-77, IBRD, ICAO, ICFTU, ICRM, IDA, IDB, IFAD, IFC, IFRCS, IGAD, ILO, IMF, IMO, Interpol, IOC, ITU, NAM, OAU, OIC, OPCW (signatory), UN, UNCTAD, UNESCO, UNIDO, UPU, WFTU, WHO, WMO, WToO, WTrO

POLITICAL PARTIES: RPP-FRUD—Alliance of the Popular Rally for Progress (RPP) and the Front for Restoration of Unity and Democracy (FRUD)

ETHNIC GROUPS:

Other 5%
Afar 35%
Issa 60%

NATIONAL ECONOMICS

WORLD GNP RANKING: 169th

GNP PER CAPITA: $880

INFLATION: 2.0%

BALANCE OF PAYMENTS (BALANCE OF TRADE): -$14 million

EXCHANGE RATES / U.S. DLR.: 174.8-170.0 DJIBOUTI FRANCS

OFFICIAL CURRENCY: DJIBOUTI FRANC

GOVERNMENT SPENDING (% OF GDP)

DEFENSE 5%		
EDUCATION 2.9%		
HEALTH 5.4%		

0   5   10   15

NUMBER OF CONFLICTS OVER LAST 25 YEARS

	1	2-5	5+
Violent changes in government	○	○	○
Civil wars	○	●	○
International wars	○	○	○
Foreign intervention	○	○	○

- No compulsory national military service.
- Size of army is undisclosed.
- France maintains a military presence.
- Afar secessionism remains an issue.

NOTABLE WARS AND INSURGENCIES: Civil war 1989, 1991-2000

AN ANCIENT HOMELAND of nomadic herders and traders, Djibouti is finally enjoying domestic peace after the strife that marred its first years of self-government. For more than a century from the 1880s, the French ruled Djibouti, calling it French Somaliland and later the Territory of the Afars and Issas for the land's two main ethnic groups. After independence in 1977, Djibouti began self-rule with a government balanced between the Issas, a Somali clan, which comprises approximately half of the population and is concentrated in the south, and the Afar people, who constitute about 35 percent of the population and occupy the northern and western lands. But the arrangement deteriorated into a bankrupting, decade-long civil war between the government and a predominantly Afar rebel group, the Front for Restoration of Unity and Democracy. Although one faction of the rebels made its peace with the government early in the war, a final peace accord ending all violence was not reached until 2001.

Modeled after the French presidential system, Djibouti's multiparty government today is composed of an elected president, prime minister, Council of Deputies, unicameral Parliament and judiciary. The constitution officially recognizes four political parties, which vie for the presidency and legislative seats: the Popular Rally for Progress, the Front for the Restoration of Unity and Democracy, the Party of Democratic Renewal, and the National Democratic Party. Djibouti's judicial system is based on a mixture of French civil law, Shari'a (Islamic) law, and traditional practices. In cases involving Muslim personal law, religious judges, called qadis, make their rulings according to Islamic legal principles. France maintains one of its largest overseas military bases in Djibouti and still wields considerable influence in the country's affairs. Meanwhile, Djibouti society remains sharply divided between its clans and ethnic groups. The dominance of Djibouti's government and civil service by the Issas continues to spark resentment among the Afars. Complaints are common against government interference in the judiciary.

> The region was one of the first points of contact for early Muslim traders crossing the Red Sea.

ISSUES AND CHALLENGES:

- Minimal natural resources, poor rainfall and soil fertility, and lack of a skilled workforce severely limit the nation's growth.

- Poverty is widespread, with 50 percent of Djibouti's population unemployed and between 45 and 70 percent living below the poverty line.

- Less than 40 percent of Djibouti children attend school, making investment in educational institutions a critical government priority.

- The crushing influx of more than 100,000 refugees from wars in nearby Somalia and Ethiopia has strained Djibouti government resources.

HOW THE GOVERNMENT WORKS

LEGISLATIVE BRANCH

Chambre des Députés
(Chamber of Deputies)
Unicameral Parliament
Composed of 65 members elected to five-year terms by direct popular vote.

Regional Governments
Five districts.

EXECUTIVE BRANCH

President
Elected to six-year term by direct popular vote; two-term limit. Serves as head of state; commander-in-chief of the military.

Prime Minister
Appointed by president. Serves as head of government; chairs Council of Deputies.

Council of Deputies
Composed of 16 members, including the prime minister; appointed by president. Oversees government operations; answers to president.

JUDICIAL BRANCH

Constitutional Council
Rules on constitutionality of laws. Composed of six members appointed to nine-year terms: two by president; two by parliament; two by Superior Council of Justices.

Supreme Court
Highest court of review and appeal. Composed of five justices appointed for life by president.

Superior Appeals Court
Hears criminal cases. Composed of three justices appointed for life by president.

Courts of First Instance
Hear civil cases. Composed of 12 justices appointed for life by president.

EQUATORIAL GUINEA

OFFICIAL NAME: REPUBLIC OF EQUATORIAL GUINEA

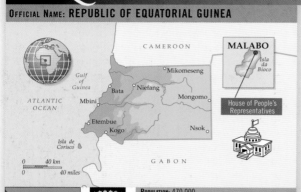

CAMEROON

MALABO

Isla da Bioco

Mikomeseng

Gulf of Guinea

Bata   Niefang

Mbini   Mongomo

ATLANTIC OCEAN

House of People's Representatives

Etembue

Kogo   Nsok

Isla de Corisco

GABON

0   40 km
0   40 miles

POPULATION: 470,000	
CAPITAL: MALABO	
AREA: 10,830 SQ. MILES (28,051 SQ. KM)	
INDEPENDENCE: 1968	
CONSTITUTION: 1991	

EQUATORIAL GUINEA's name is derived from the fact that it is located on the equator, and from the Berber word "aquinaw" meaning black man.

RELIGION: Roman Catholic 90%, Other 10%

OFFICIAL LANGUAGES: Spanish and French

REGIONS OR PROVINCES: 7 provinces

DEPENDENT TERRITORIES: None

MEDIA: Total political censorship exists in national media

Newspapers: There is no regular daily press

TV: 1 state-owned service

Radio: 3 services: 1 state-owned, 2 independent

SUFFRAGE: 18 years of age; universal adult

LEGAL SYSTEM: Tribal custom and Spanish law; no ICJ jurisdiction

WORLD ORGANIZATIONS: ACCT, ACP, AfDB, BDEAC, CEEAC, CEMAC, ECA, FAO, FZ, G-77, IBRD, ICAO, ICRM, IDA, IFAD, IFC, IFRCS, ILO, IMF, IMO, Interpol, IOC, ITU, NAM, OAS (observer), OAU, OPCW, UN, UNCTAD, UNESCO, UNIDO, UPU, WHO, WIPO, WToO, WTrO (applicant)

POLITICAL PARTIES: PDGE—Equatorial Guinea Democratic Party, UP—Popular Union, CDS—Convergence for Social Democracy

ETHNIC GROUPS:

Bubi 4%

Other 11%

Fang 85%

NATIONAL ECONOMICS

WORLD GNP RANKING: 175th

GNP PER CAPITA: $800

INFLATION: 6.0%

BALANCE OF PAYMENTS (BALANCE OF TRADE): -$344 million

EXCHANGE RATES / U.S. DLR.: 698.7-736.7 CFA FRANCS

OFFICIAL CURRENCY: CFA FRANC

GOVERNMENT SPENDING (% OF GDP)

DEFENSE 1.7%

EDUCATION 1.7%

HEALTH 4.2%

0   5   10   15

NUMBER OF CONFLICTS OVER LAST 25 YEARS

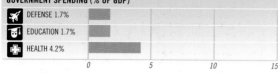

	1	2-5	5+
Violent changes in government			
Civil wars			
International wars			
Foreign intervention			

- No compulsory national military service.
- Military tasked with internal security.
- US, China, and Ukraine supply equipment.
- Heavily dependent on international financial aid for maintenance of equipment, and training.

NOTABLE WARS AND INSURGENCIES: Military coup 1979. Separatists on Bioko 1998

THE COUNTRY OF EQUATORIAL GUINEA comprises the island of Bioko (formerly Fernando Po), some smaller islands, and an enclave on the African coast (formerly known as Río Muni). After about 100 years of of mostly Spanish rule, Equatorial Guinea gained its independence in 1968 and Francisco Macías Nguema was elected president. Within four years, Macías had eliminated all opposition and taken complete control of the government, naming himself president-for-life. Under his brutal, authoritarian regime, up to one-third of the country's population was killed or exiled, religion and education suppressed, and infrastructure neglected, while the economy collapsed. In 1979, Macías' nephew, Teodoro Obiang Nguema Mbasogo, overthrew the government, had his uncle arrested and executed, and assumed the presidency. President Obiang set up the office of prime minister and a legislature—the House of People's Representatives—but neither could function without the president's approval or direction. The party he set up, the Equatorial Guinea Democratic Party, benefits from heavy government funding.

The country holds multiparty elections according to its 1991 constitution, but opposition groups and international observers declare them to be neither free nor fair. In 1996, Obiang was the the only candidate standing. Obiang's party, the Democratic Party of Equatorial Guinea (PDGE), has received overwhelming support in every poll. In protest against widespread irregularities in the 1999 legislative elections, representatives of the Joint Opposition Party (POC) refused to take their seats in the House. The opposition boycotted local elections in 2000. In 2002, rumors of that there had been a plot to overthrow the government in 1997 led to a wave of arrests, including those of several key opposition figures. The country's judiciary also has significant problems. The Supreme Tribunal consists of the president's advisers rather than independent judges; the lower courts operate in an ad hoc manner, with no established procedures and few experienced judicial personnel. Although Obiang has not repeated the worst abuses and atrocities of the Macías years, human rights organizations still list Equatorial Guinea as having one of the world's most repressive regimes.

ISSUES AND CHALLENGES:

- The Fang ethnic group constitutes the majority of the population and dominates politics and business in Equatorial Guinea. Both the Macías and Obiang regimes, dominated by Fang, have particularly oppressed the Bubi people of Bioko Island. When oil was discovered off the coast of Bioko in the mid-1990s, this revitalized the Movement for the Self-Determination of Bioko Island (MAIB) but also caused a harsh crack-down on the group. At least eight MAIB prisoners have died in custody, apparently as a result of torture and lack of medical care.

- The government faces the arduous task of improving the economy which is struggling to recover after the Macías era.

HOW THE GOVERNMENT WORKS

LEGISLATIVE BRANCH
Cámara de Representantes del Pueblo
(House of People's Representatives)
Unicameral Parliament
Composed of 80 members elected to five-year terms by direct popular vote.

Regional governments
Seven provinces administered by governors appointed by president.

EXECUTIVE BRANCH
President
Elected to seven-year term by direct popular vote. Serves as head of state; commander-in-chief of armed forces; minister of defense. Makes laws by decree; dissolves parliament; negotiates and ratify treaties; calls legislative elections.

Prime Minister
Appointed by president.
Serves as head of government. Coordinates domestic affairs.

Cabinet
Council of Ministers
Members appointed by president. Oversees government operations.

JUDICIAL BRANCH
Supreme Tribunal
Highest judicial body; rules by traditional law and national statutes. Composed of president and presidential judicial advisers.

Appeals Courts

Local Magistrates

UGANDA

OFFICIAL NAME: REPUBLIC OF UGANDA

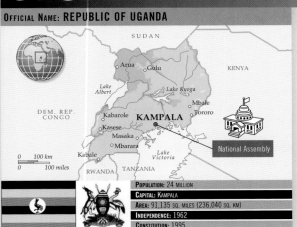

POPULATION: 24 MILLION
CAPITAL: KAMPALA
AREA: 91,135 SQ. MILES (236,040 SQ. KM)
INDEPENDENCE: 1962
CONSTITUTION: 1995

UGANDA's name is derived from the predominant ethnic group, the Buganda. Legend refers to the king as a man called Uganda.

RELIGION: Roman Catholic 33%, Protestant 33%, Traditional beliefs 18%, Muslim (mainly Sunni) 16%.

OFFICIAL LANGUAGE: English

REGIONS OR PROVINCES: 56 districts

DEPENDENT TERRITORIES: None

MEDIA: Partial political censorship exists in national media

NEWSPAPERS: There are 5 daily newspapers

TV: 2 services: 1 state-controlled, 1 independent

RADIO: 4 services: 1 state-controlled, 3 independent

SUFFRAGE: 18 years of age; universal

LEGAL SYSTEM: Customary and English common law; accepts ICJ jurisdiction

WORLD ORGANIZATIONS: ACP, AfDB, C, CCC, EADB, ECA, FAO, G-77, IAEA, IBRD, ICAO, ICFTU, ICRM, IDA, IDB, IFAD, IFC, IFRCS, IGAD, ILO, IMF, Interpol, IOC, IOM, ISO (correspondent), ITU, NAM, OAU, OIC, OPCW, PCA, UN, UNCTAD, UNESCO, UNHCR, UNIDO, UPU, WFTU, WHO, WIPO, WMO, WToO, WTrO

POLITICAL PARTIES: No political parties, elections take place on a non-party basis

ETHNIC GROUPS:
- Bantu tribes 50%
- Other 45%
- Sudanese 5%

NATIONAL ECONOMICS

WORLD GNP RANKING: 100th

GNP PER CAPITA: $300

INFLATION: 2.8%

BALANCE OF PAYMENTS (BALANCE OF TRADE): -$860 million

EXCHANGE RATES / U.S. DLR.: 1767.5-1727.5 NEW UGANDA SHILLINGS

OFFICIAL CURRENCY: NEW UGANDA SHILLING

GOVERNMENT SPENDING (% OF GDP)

		0	5	10	15
✈	DEFENSE 3%				
	EDUCATION 1.6%				
✚	HEALTH 1.9%				

NUMBER OF CONFLICTS OVER LAST 25 YEARS

	1	2-5	5+
Violent changes in government	○	●	○
Civil wars	○	●	○
International wars	○	●	○
Foreign intervention	○	○	○

- No compulsory national military service.
- US military training assistance was terminated in 2000 following Democratic Republic Congo and Rwandan incursions.
- Ethnic groups continue fighting in Great Lakes region.
- Sudanese refugees are an issue.

NOTABLE WARS AND INSURGENCIES: Ugandan-Tanzanian War 1978-1979. War in the Bush 1981-1986. Civil War 1986-1995. Coups 1980, 1985 and 1986. LRA insurgency 1995-present. Involved in Democratic Republic of Congo.

A BRITISH PROTECTORATE FROM 1894, the Republic of Uganda became an independent state in 1962 and a republic five years later. Its political history since independence has been marked by dictatorship, military coups, bloodshed, and power struggles. Milton Obote, an important figure in the nation's early political period and the first prime minister under President Benedicto Kiwanuka, seized control of the government in 1966. Obote was ousted in 1971 by Major General Idi Amin Dada, the military commander who had helped put him in power. The dictatorial regime of Idi Amin from 1971 to 1979 was responsible for the deaths of an estimated 300,000 people, expelled all Asians who were not Ugandan citizens, and seized their businesses. Amin was forced to flee Uganda in 1979 after a failed incursion into Tanzania; elections in 1980 returned Obote to the presidency. His government, also responsible for significant human rights abuses, remained in power until yet another military coup in 1985. Rebel forces led by Yoweri Kaguta Museveni seized control of Uganda in 1986 and installed Museveni as president.

Museveni continues to dominate the politics of Uganda. He has created a "non-party democracy"— political parties are represented in Uganda's structural system, but are banned from campaigning. Legislative candidates run as individuals, which weakens their power and strengthens that of Museveni, who says a multiparty system would lead to ethnic and religious divisions, a major problem in Ugandan politics. The opposition argues that a non-party system means a one-party system, which favors only Museveni himself. Ugandans sided with Museveni in a 2000 referendum, however, voting down a multiparty system.

Predictably, the executive branch is the strongest in the country's government. It is run by the president and his government, consisting mainly of a prime minister and a cabinet. Without a party system or strong coalitions, there is little consensus and negotiation. Thus, the nonexistence of a balance of power creates great political instability and helps strengthen Museveni's dictatorship, even though he was elected by popular vote.

ISSUES AND CHALLENGES:

- Erratic economic management has reduced Uganda to one of the world's poorest and least-developed countries. Since the Idi Amin regime expelled the large Asian population engaged in trade, industry and other professions, the economy has never fully recovered. The government has a goal of reducing poverty to less than 10 percent by 2017. However, the country still faces great extremes between the poor and the rich, which contributes to Uganda's political instability.

- The ongoing wars in Sudan, the Democratic Republic of Congo and Rwanda have flooded Uganda with refugees.

HOW THE GOVERNMENT WORKS

LEGISLATIVE BRANCH

National Assembly
Unicameral Parliament
Composed of 292 members who serve five-year terms: 214 elected by direct popular vote; 68 selected by women, army, disabled, youth and labor special interest groups; 10 appointed by Uganda People's Defense Forces.

Regional Governments
56 districts overseen by appointed administrators; towns and villages governed by elected councils.

EXECUTIVE BRANCH

President
Five-year term by direct popular vote. Head of state and government; commander-in-chief of military. Initiates and gives assent to bills; appoints ambassadors; negotiates treaties; declares war and states of emergency.

Vice-president
Appointed by president, confirmed with simple majority vote of parliament. Assists in supervising cabinet.

Prime Minister
Appointed by president. Assists in supervising cabinet.

Cabinet
Parliament members, appointed by president, confirmed by parliament. National policy; oversees government operations; presided over by president.

JUDICIAL BRANCH

Supreme Court
Highest court of review and appeal. Composed of three judges appointed for life by president.

Court of Appeal
Hears High Court appeals; interprets constitution. Judges appointed for life by president.

High Court
Hears criminal and civil cases; rules on election disputes. Composed of 20 judges appointed for life by president.

Magistrates' Courts

MICRONESIA

OFFICIAL NAME: FEDERATED STATES OF MICRONESIA

POPULATION: 133,000	
CAPITAL: PALIKIR (POHNPEI ISLAND)	
AREA: 271 SQ. MILES (702 SQ. KM)	
INDEPENDENCE: 1986	
CONSTITUTION: 1979	

MICRONESIA as a word translates to "small islands". The world was coined by Europeans from the Ancient Greek in the 19th century.

RELIGION: Roman Catholic 50%, Protestant 48%, Other 2%

OFFICIAL LANGUAGE: English

REGIONS OR PROVINCES: 4 states

DEPENDENT TERRITORIES: None

MEDIA: No political censorship exists in national media

Newspapers: There are no daily newspapers

TV: 4 services: 1 state-owned, 3 independent

Radio: 1 state-owned service

SUFFRAGE: 18 years of age; universal

LEGAL SYSTEM: Common and customary law; Trust Territory laws; no ICJ jurisdiction

WORLD ORGANIZATIONS: ACP, AsDB, ESCAP, G-77, IBRD, ICAO, IDA, IFC, IFRCS (associate), IMF, IOC, ITU, OPCW, Sparteca, SPC, SPF, UN, UNCTAD, UNESCO, WHO, WMO

POLITICAL PARTIES: No formal political parties

ETHNIC GROUPS:

Micronesian 100%

NATIONAL ECONOMICS

WORLD GNP RANKING: 179th

GNP PER CAPITA: $2,110

INFLATION: 2.6%

BALANCE OF PAYMENTS (BALANCE OF TRADE): $67 million

EXCHANGE RATES / U.S. DLR.: Currency is US DOLLAR

OFFICIAL CURRENCY: US DOLLAR

GOVERNMENT SPENDING (% OF GDP)

✈ DEFENSE (N/A)	
📖 EDUCATION (N/A)	
✚ HEALTH 7.4%	

0 5 10 15

NUMBER OF CONFLICTS OVER LAST 25 YEARS

	1	2-5	5+
Violent changes in government	○	○	○
Civil wars	○	○	○
International wars	○	○	○
Foreign intervention	○	○	○

- No compulsory national military service.
- US provides all defense and security needs under Compact of Free Association.
- US used airstrips during the Vietnam War.

NOTABLE WARS AND INSURGENCIES: None

THE FEDERATED STATES OF MICRONESIA comprise four of the five island groups belonging to the Caroline Islands located in the Pacific Ocean: Pohnpei, Chuuk, Kosrae and Yap. The four states—each with its own ethnic language—consist of a total of 607 islands. Palau, the fifth island group, chose to become an independent state.

First annexed by Spain in 1874, Micronesia was sold to Germany and occupied by Japan, before becoming a United Nations Trust Territory of the Pacific under the administration of the USA in 1945. In 1979, as the Federated States of Micronesia (FSM), the islands adopted a constitution. The signing of the Compact of Free Association with the US in 1982 ultimately led to independence in 1986 and the trusteeship was officially terminated four years later. Under this Compact, the US provides defense and financial assistance. A new agreement, negotiated in 2002, provides ongoing assistance for a further 20 years, while also establishing a trust fund to eliminate the need for future US grants.

The president and vice-president are elected by Congress from among the four at-large members, which means that they both always come from different states. On assuming their posts, they are required to resign their seats in Congress, which are then filled by a special election. Most presidents manage only one term in office. The incumbent, Jospeh J. Urusemal, was elected in May 2003. Other members of Congress are elected by popular vote at state level, with electoral districts being reapportioned every ten years. There are no political parties. Each state has its own constitution and an elected governor and a lieutenant governor—only Chuuk has a bicameral legislature. These state governments differ considerably in structure from one another and perform most major governmental functions, barring defense and foreign affairs. Together with the federal government they employ almost one half of working-age Micronesians. Traditional chiefs still maintain a key role in the political system. The Faichuk Islands, in the western corner of Chuuk Lagoon, have pressed for the status of a full state, or even independence, complaining of long-term economic neglect.

ISSUES AND CHALLENGES:

- There is an overdependence on imports and foreign aid, particularly from the US under the Compact of Free Association. The US provides nearly $US 100 million a year, and is responsible for all defense and security issues. The future of the FSM is uncertain, as the government is one of few employers who pay monetary wages, and the economy is based on agriculture and fishing which has been depleted by overfishing.

- A shortage of safe water has led to health risks from cholera, while diabetes and drug abuse are growing health concerns. Most Micronesians have no running water or electricity.

- Widespread unemployment and a high rate of emigration, particularly to the US, are depleting the nation.

HOW THE GOVERNMENT WORKS

LEGISLATIVE BRANCH

National Congress
Unicameral Parliament
Composed of 14 members: six from Chuuk; four from Pohnpei; two from Yap; two from Kosrae. One at-large member from each state elected to four-year term by direct popular vote; ten directly elected to two-year terms from single-member districts based on population.

Regional Governments
State Level: four states overseen by governors elected to four-year terms by direct popular vote. Elected unicameral legislatures in Kosrae, Pohnpei, Yap; elected bicameral legislature in Chuuk. Only Yap has a constitutional council of traditional leaders, who are mainly advisory but with power to veto legislation.

EXECUTIVE BRANCH

President
Elected to four-year term by parliament from among its four at-large members; two-term limit; must relinquish seat in parliament. Serves as head of state and government.

Vice-president
Elected to four-year term by parliament from among its four at-large members; two-term limit. Must relinquish seat in parliament and be from different state than president.

Cabinet
Members appointed by president.

JUDICIAL BRANCH

Supreme Court
Highest trial and appellate court. Composed of chief justice and three judges appointed for life by president, confirmed by two-thirds majority vote of parliament.

State Level Courts
Only Yap has municipal courts where presiding judges are leaders in councils of traditional leaders.

KIRIBATI

OFFICIAL NAME: REPUBLIC OF KIRIBATI

PACIFIC OCEAN

Tungaru (Gilbert Islands)

BAIRIKI — Tarawa

Banaba (Ocean I.)

Phoenix Islands

Line Islands

Kiritimati

Millennium Island

Great House of Assembly

0   600 km
0   600 miles

POPULATION:	92,000
CAPITAL:	BAIRIKI (TARAWA ATOLL)
AREA:	277 SQ. MILES (717 SQ.KM)
INDEPENDENCE:	1979
CONSTITUTION:	1979

KIRIBATI, formerly the Gilbert Islands named after Thomas Gilbert, the explorer who discovered them in 1788, adopted the local pronounciation (kee-ree-bus) in 1979.

RELIGION: Roman Catholic 53%, Kiribati Protestant Church 39%, Other 8%

OFFICIAL LANGUAGE: English

REGIONS OR PROVINCES: 3 units subdivided into 6 districts

DEPENDENT TERRITORIES: None

MEDIA: No political censorship exists in national media

Newspapers: There are no daily newspapers

TV: 1 independent service

Radio: 1 independent service

SUFFRAGE: 18 years of age; universal

LEGAL SYSTEM: Customary and English common law; no ICJ jurisdiction

WORLD ORGANIZATIONS: ACP, AsDB, C, ESCAP, FAO, IBRD, ICAO, ICFTU, ICRM, IDA, IFC, IFRCS, ILO, IMF, ITU, OPCW, Sparteca, SPC, SPF, UN, UNESCO, UPU, WHO, WTrO (applicant)

POLITICAL PARTIES: Ind—Independents, MTM—Maneaban Te Mauri (Protect the Maneaba), BTK—Boutokaan Te Koaua (Pillars of Truth)

ETHNIC GROUPS:

Other 4%

Micronesian 96%

NATIONAL ECONOMICS

WORLD GNP RANKING:	188th
GNP PER CAPITA:	$950
INFLATION:	2.0%
BALANCE OF PAYMENTS (BALANCE OF TRADE):	$1 million
EXCHANGE RATES / U.S. DLR.:	1.7997-1.9535 AUSTRALIAN DOLLARS

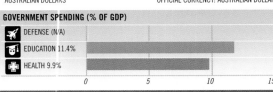

OFFICIAL CURRENCY: AUSTRALIAN DOLLAR

GOVERNMENT SPENDING (% OF GDP)

DEFENSE (N/A)

EDUCATION 11.4%

HEALTH 9.9%

0   5   10   15

NUMBER OF CONFLICTS OVER LAST 25 YEARS

	1	2-5	5+
Violent changes in government	○	○	○
Civil wars	○	○	○
International wars	○	○	○
Foreign intervention	○	○	○

- No compulsory national military service.
- No armed forces.
- Australia and New Zealand provide all defense and security needs, including anti-submarine patrols.

NOTABLE WARS AND INSURGENCIES: None

KIRIBATI CONSISTS OF three groups of South Pacific coral atolls—16 in the Tungaru group, eight Phoenix Islands, eight of the 11 Line Islands (the other three belong to the US), and one volcanic island—Banaba. First encountered by Spanish explorers in 1606, the islands of Kiribati became a British protectorate in 1892 under the name of the Gilbert and Ellice Islands, and then a British colony from 1916 to 1942. As with many Pacific islands, they were occupied by Japan during World War II, plunging the islands into the war between the US and Japan.

A legislative council was set up in 1963 and self-rule granted in 1971. Over the next two years, a governor was appointed to take the place of the British High Commissioner and an elected House of Assembly replaced the legislative council. In 1975 the Ellice Islands separated and became independent as Tuvalu. Full independence from the UK was achieved in 1979, with Kiribati, as the remaining islands now renamed themselves, continued as a member of the British Commonwealth. A treaty of friendship led to the US relinquishing all claims to the Phoenix Islands and eight of the Line Islands.

I-Kiribati politics is still dominated by traditional chiefs. The head of government is the president (beretitenti–berestens) who is directly elected. There are no formal political parties, but some associations of politicians originally formed for elections have proven durable. Some are now known by name.

No-confidence votes in the president are used with relative frequency to change the head of state. This coupled to the weak party political system leads to a certain air of chaos in the National Assembly. Elections in late 2002 were won by the opposition BTK grouping, leading to seven months of uneasy political cohabitation with President Teburoro Tiito, who was backed by MTM. Though Tiito was reelected in February 2003, he was finally ousted by BTK in a vote of no confidence in March. Just two months later MTM regained its parliamentary majority in early legislative elections, but failed to prevent the election of Anote Tong (supported by BTK) as president in July.

ISSUES AND CHALLENGES:

- Population growth over 2 percent has resulted in overcrowding and lagoon pollution on the main island of Tarawa. Resettlement programs to the Phoenix Islands and Line Islands and began in 1995 and 1998 respectively.

- The low-lying islands are threatened by rising sea levels, which cause coastal erosion and damage to coral reefs. The UN has predicted that Kiribati, barely two meters above sea level, could disappear in the 21st century. Two uninhabited islands have already disappeared.

- Kiribati is one of the poorest countries in the Pacific. Natural resources are lacking, with limited land, infertile soil and agriculture limited to subsistence production.

HOW THE GOVERNMENT WORKS

LEGISLATIVE BRANCH
Maneaba Ni Maungatabu
(Great House of Assembly)
Unicameral Parliament
Composed of 42 members who serve four-year terms: 39 elected by direct popular vote from 23 districts; one appointed to represent Banaba Island; attorney general; speaker elected by Maneaba from outside of its membership. Removes president with no-confidence vote.

Regional Governments
The six districts are administered by 21 local government councils (one for each inhabited island), members elected to three-year terms. Parliament members serve ex officio in their own districts.

EXECUTIVE BRANCH
President
Nominated by parliament from among its members; elected to four-year term by direct popular vote; three-term limit. Serves as head of state and government. Appoints attorney general.

Vice-president
Appointed by president.

Cabinet
Composed of vice-president, attorney general, ten parliament members; appointed by president. Oversees government operations.

JUDICIAL BRANCH
Privy Council in London
Final tribunal for appeals.

Court of Appeals
Hears appeals of High Court decisions. Judges appointed by president.

High Court
Hears civil and criminal cases. Judges appointed by president, chief justice with advice of Cabinet.

Magistrates' Courts,
26 courts; magistrates appointed by president.

PALAU

OFFICIAL NAME: REPUBLIC OF PALAU

POPULATION: 19,100	
CAPITAL: KOROR	
AREA: 177 SQ. MILES (458 SQ. KM)	
INDEPENDENCE: 1994	
CONSTITUTION: 1981	

PALAU ("island") is thought to have been discovered when the English ship, the Antelope, under Captain Henry Wilson, was shipwrecked on a reef in 1783.

RELIGION: Christian 66%, Modekngei 34%

OFFICIAL LANGUAGES: Palauan and English

REGIONS OR PROVINCES: 16 states

DEPENDENT TERRITORIES: None

MEDIA: No political censorship exists in national media

NEWSPAPERS: There are no daily newspapers

TV: 2 services: 1 limited independent, 1 state-owned

RADIO: 3 radio stations

SUFFRAGE: 18 years of age; universal

LEGAL SYSTEM: Common and customary laws; Trust Territory laws; no ICJ jurisdiction

WORLD ORGANIZATIONS: ACP, ESCAP, FAO, IBRD, ICAO, ICRM, IDA, IFC, IFRCS, IMF, IOC, Sparteca, SPC, SPF, UN, UNCTAD, UNESCO, WHO

POLITICAL PARTIES: No political parties

ETHNIC GROUPS:

- White 2%
- Asian 28%
- Palauan 70%

NATIONAL ECONOMICS

WORLD GNP RANKING: 189th

GNP PER CAPITA: $5,000

INFLATION: 3.0%

BALANCE OF PAYMENTS (BALANCE OF TRADE): $17.2 billion

EXCHANGE RATES / U.S. DLR.: Currency is US DOLLAR

OFFICIAL CURRENCY: US DOLLAR

GOVERNMENT SPENDING (% OF GDP)

	0	5	10	15
✈ DEFENSE (N/A)				
📖 EDUCATION (N/A)				
✚ HEALTH 6%				

NUMBER OF CONFLICTS OVER LAST 25 YEARS

	1	2-5	5+
Violent changes in government	○	○	○
Civil wars	○	○	○
International wars	○	○	○
Foreign intervention	○	○	○

- No compulsory national military service.
- No armed forces.
- US provides all defense and security needs under Compact of Free Association.

NOTABLE WARS AND INSURGENCIES: None

OF THE MORE THAN 300 ISLETS constituting Palau, only nine are inhabited and more than 70 percent of the population lives in the capital city of Koror on Koror Island. Settled in 2000-1000 B.C. by peoples from Indonesia, New Guinea and the Philippines, Palau was discovered by Spain, sold to Germany, controlled by Japan after World War I and administered by the US as a Trust Territory of the Pacific Islands after World War II. In 1979, four Trust Territories of the Caroline Islands became the Federated States of Micronesia. Palau, though part of the same island group, chose instead to approve a new constitution and become an autonomous republic in 1981. The provisions of the Compact of Free Association with the US, drawn up in 1982, conflicted, however, with Palau's constitution that banned nuclear weapons and military bases. The passage to full independence was therefore obstructed. However, after a series of referenda and an amendment to the constitution, voters approved the Compact in 1993, so allowing military facilities in return for $700 million over 15 years. The acceptance of the Compact finally permitted Palau, known locally as Belau, to emerge from trusteeship to become an independent nation in 1994.

Early political history had violent beginnings. Haruo Remelik, the first president elected to lead the new republic, was assassinated in 1985, and a minister of state was later found guilty of the crime. Just three years later, after allegedly shooting at the home of the speaker of the House of Delegates, the assistant to President Lazarus Salii was jailed. A few months later Salii himself was accused of bribery and committed suicide. Stability followed and in 2001, after a successful run as vice-president for eight years, Tommy Remengesau Jr., was elected as the new president. He has promised to reduce dependence on US financial aid by encouraging tourism.

Each of the 16 states maintains its own governor and legislature on a local level, as well as electing one member of the 16-member House of Representatives. They also elect their highest-ranking traditional chiefs to the Council of Chiefs that advises the president on traditional matters. For purposes of the tribal system, Palau is divided into two regions, Eoueldaob and Badeldaob, which are ruled by two chiefs, the Ibedul and the Reklai respectively.

ISSUES AND CHALLENGES:

- Palau is heavily dependent on foreign aid, which makes up nearly 30 percent of the GDP. The largest donors are the US and Japan.

- In 1998, Senate-proposed legislation permitting offshore investments raised fears of possible money laundering.

- Sand and coral dredging, inadequate facilities for the disposal of waste, and illegal fishing practices threaten the ecosystem.

- Health care is basic, and many of the inhabitants on the outermost islands have access only to traditional healers.

HOW THE GOVERNMENT WORKS

LEGISLATIVE BRANCH

Palau National Congress
Bicameral Parliament

Olbiil Era Kelulau
(House of Delegates)
16 members, one representing each state (single-seat constituencies), elected to four-year term by popular vote.

Senate
Nine senators, elected to four-year term by popular vote, proportional. Only non-partisans elected, no parties exist.

Regional Governments
Sixteen states administered by elected governors and legislatures.

EXECUTIVE BRANCH

President
Head of state and head of government elected to four-year term by popular vote, separate ticket from vice-president.

Vice-president
Elected to four-year term by popular vote, separate ticket from president.

Cabinet
Eight ministers.

Council of Chiefs
Composed of highest chiefs from each of 16 states. Advises president on traditional laws and customs.

JUDICIAL BRANCH

Supreme Court
Highest court of review and appeal. Divided into trial and appellate chambers.

National Court

Court of Common Pleas

Land Court

NAURU

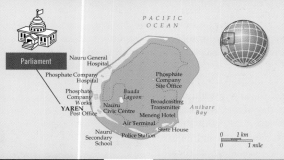

OFFICIAL NAME: REPUBLIC OF NAURU

PACIFIC OCEAN

Parliament
Nauru General Hospital
Phosphate Company Hospital
Phosphate Company Works
YAREN
Nauru Post Office
Buada Lagoon
Nauru Civic Centre
Phosphate Company Site Office
Broadcasting Transmitter
Meneng Hotel
Air Terminal
State House
Nauru Secondary School
Police Station
Anibare Bay

0   1 km
0   1 mile

POPULATION: 11,800	
CAPITAL: NO OFFICIAL CAPITAL	
AREA: 8.1 SQ. MILES (21.9 SQ. KM)	
INDEPENDENCE: 1968	
CONSTITUTION: 1968	

NAURU is the only country in the world that has no capital, the government operates from the Yaren District.

RELIGION: Protestant 66%, Roman Catholic 34%

OFFICIAL LANGUAGE: Nauruan

REGIONS OR PROVINCES: 14 districts

DEPENDENT TERRITORIES: None

MEDIA: No political censorship exists in national media

NEWSPAPERS: There are no daily newspapers

TV: 1 state-owned service

RADIO: 1 state-owned service

SUFFRAGE: 20 years of age; universal and compulsory

LEGAL SYSTEM: English common law; accepts ICJ jurisdiction

WORLD ORGANIZATIONS: ACP, AsDB, C, ESCAP, FAO, ICAO, Interpol, IOC, ITU, OPCW, Sparteca, SPC, SPF, UN, UNESCO, UPU, WHO

POLITICAL PARTIES: All members elected as independents

ETHNIC GROUPS:

- European 5%
- Chinese and Vietnamese 8%
- Other Pacific islanders 25%
- Nauruan 62%

NATIONAL ECONOMICS

WORLD GNP RANKING: 190th

GNP PER CAPITA: $7,270

INFLATION: -3.6%

BALANCE OF PAYMENTS (BALANCE OF TRADE): Not available

EXCHANGE RATES / U.S. DLR.: 1.7997-1.9535 AUSTRALIAN DOLLARS

OFFICIAL CURRENCY: AUSTRALIAN DOLLAR

GOVERNMENT SPENDING (% OF GDP)

		0	5	10	15
✈	DEFENSE (N/A)				
🎓	EDUCATION (N/A)				
✚	HEALTH 5%				

NUMBER OF CONFLICTS OVER LAST 25 YEARS

	1	2-5	5+
Violent changes in government	○	○	○
Civil wars	○	○	○
International wars	○	○	○
Foreign intervention	○	○	○

- No compulsory national military service.
- No armed forces.
- Australia provides all defense and security needs.

NOTABLE WARS AND INSURGENCIES: None

NAMED THE PLEASANT ISLAND by the British explorer, John Fearn, who discovered it in 1798, Nauru is one of only three phosphate islands in the western Pacific Ocean—the others being Banaba in Kiribati and Maketea in French Polynesia. Intertribal animosity on the island led to near continual warfare, and had reduced the population to just 900 people by 1888 when Germany formally annexed the island. Germany ruled for nearly three decades and first discovered the phosphate reserves. For the twenty years following World War I, ownership of Nauru passed to Australia under the League of Nations, with the UK and New Zealand as co-trustees. Japan seized control during World War II, relocating much of the population to Micronesia before Nauru became a United Nations Trust Territory, once again administered by Australia. In 1970 Nauru obtained control of the phosphate and in 1989 sued Australia in the International Court of Justice for compensation for past exploitation of the reserves. The case was settled out of court for a sum of $79 million, but economic mismanagement has brought near financial catastrophe. A trust fund, to which receipts are diverted, will ultimately support Nauru once the phosphate reserves are depleted, but other sources of income including tourism are now being encouraged.

Nauru is the world's smallest republic 8.1 sq. miles (21 sq. km)

Self-government came two years before the country's independence in 1968, with Nauru remaining a member of the Commonwealth. As with other small Pacific nations such as Tuvalu, Nauru has no direct representation during Commonwealth meetings of heads of government.

The first president elected after independence, Hammer DeRoburt, held non-consecutive terms of office for 19 years between 1968 and 1989. Subsequent economic uncertainty has had a direct impact on the political environment, with no-confidence votes ejecting most presidents long before their terms were complete. In 1997 a staggering four presidents were elected and dismissed.

ISSUES AND CHALLENGES:

- The phosphate industry has given Nauru one of the highest per capita incomes in the world, but the high standard of living has been blamed for above-average obesity levels and the related incidence of diabetes, which affects more than one-third of all Nauruans.

- Phosphate mining has devastated the environment, destroying some 80 percent of the ecosystem. Rehabilitation projects have become a priority as phosphate reserves are running out, and an uncertain economic future faces Nauru.

- Nuclear tests performed by the French government in the Pacific are also a concern.

HOW THE GOVERNMENT WORKS

LEGISLATIVE BRANCH

Parliament
Unicameral Parliament
Eighteen members for three-year term unless Parliament is dissolved earlier. Elected from eight constituencies where they stand as independents: seven elect two members each, one elects four members. Speaker, once chosen, cannot be a member of parliament.

EXECUTIVE BRANCH

President
Head of state and head of government. Elected by Parliament from among its members. Can be removed by a vote of no confidence.

Cabinet
Four or five ministers. Appointed by president. Responsible to Parliament. Can be removed by a vote of no confidence.

JUDICIAL BRANCH

Supreme Court
Rules on all constitutional issues. Chief justice and judges appointed by president; must be a barrister or solicitor of five years' standing, must retire at 65.

Appellate Court
Two judges. Decisions can be appealed in Australian High Court.

District Court
Headed by a resident magistrate. Appointed by president in consultation with chief justice of Supreme Court; must be a barrister or solicitor of five years' standing.

Family Court
Headed by a resident magistrate.

TUVALU

OFFICIAL NAME: **TUVALU**

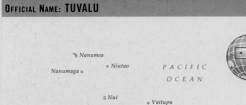

TUVALU CONSISTS OF FIVE CORAL ATOLLS AND FOUR REEF ISLANDS located midway between Australia and Hawaii. Not only one of the most isolated states in the world, it is also one of the least visited with fewer than 1000 tourists annually. While much of the population survives by subsistence farming and fishing, a unique form of revenue was realized in 2000—the sale of the country's Internet domain name, ".tv".

Inhabited by Samoans and Tongans since the 14th century, the islands were first discovered by Europeans in 1765. Formerly the Ellice Islands, they were ruled by the United Kingdom as a British protectorate from 1892 to 1915, and later together with the Gilbert Islands of Kiribati as a colony until 1974. Cultural differences between the Polynesians of the Ellice Islands and the Micronesians of the Gilbert Islands resulted in a vote for separation, which paved the way for independence in 1978. A poll in 1986 as to whether Tuvalu should become a republic was only supported by one atoll, while the decision to remove the Union Jack from the flag in 1995 was reversed in 1997, when the old flag was readopted.

Following independence, two men—Tomasi Puapua and Bikenibeu Paeniu—dominated the political scene. Puapua is the longest-serving prime minister to date (1981-1989) and has been governor-general since 1998, while Paeniu held the position of prime minister for nearly two terms before a vote of no confidence led to his early dismissal in 1999.

Defections within parliament are unrestricted and in 2001 resulted in the collapse of the government, ousting the then prime minister, Faimalaga Luka, after only a few months in office. From late 2000 through late 2002, following the death of Prime Minister Ionatana, economic pressures led to the removal of four prime ministers from office. However, since the change to a monetary economy indications are that political stability should follow. In spite of this, the government is still the main provider of salaried employment, while most Tuvaluans rely on subsistence farming and fishing.

ISSUES AND CHALLENGES:

- With few natural water resources and undrinkable groundwater, catchment systems and desalination plants supply water needs.

- Global warming and rising sea levels threaten the inhabited islands, none of which is more than 15 feet (five meters) above sea level. Both Australia and New Zealand have been asked to assist refugees should the islands become submerged, and the governor-general has addressed the UN encouraging countries to ratify and implement the Kyoto Protocol.

- Crown of Thorns starfish that feed primarily on coral are causing damage to the coral reefs of Tuvalu.

- Many Tuvaluans are migrant laborers working on the phosphate mines of Nauru, but declining resources are forcing their return.

- Little revenue beyond the sale of the Internet domain, fees paid for fishing rights, and a trust fund established in 1987 by Australia, New Zealand, and the UK.

POPULATION:	11,300
CAPITAL:	FONGAFALE
AREA:	10 SQ. MILES (26 SQ. KM)
INDEPENDENCE:	1978
CONSTITUTION:	1978

TUVALU means "group of eight," which refers to the original eight inhabited islands. Nine are now inhabited, as indicated by the nine stars on the flag.

RELIGION: Church of Tuvalu 97%, Seventh-day Adventist 1%, Baha'i 1%, Other 1%

OFFICIAL LANGUAGE: English

REGIONS OR PROVINCES: None

DEPENDENT TERRITORIES: None

MEDIA: No political censorship exists in national media

NEWSPAPERS: There are no daily newspapers

TV: No TV service

RADIO: One state-owned service

SUFFRAGE: 18 years of age; universal

LEGAL SYSTEM: Tribal and customary law; English common law; no ICJ jurisdiction

WORLD ORGANIZATIONS: ACP, AsDB, C, ESCAP, IFRCS (associate), ITU, Sparteca, SPC, SPF, UN, UNCTAD, UNESCO, UPU, WHO, WTrO (applicant)

POLITICAL PARTIES: No political parties

ETHNIC GROUPS:

Micronesian 4%

Polynesian 96%

NATIONAL ECONOMICS

WORLD GNP RANKING:	192nd
GNP PER CAPITA:	US$330
INFLATION:	7%
BALANCE OF PAYMENTS (BALANCE OF TRADE):	Not available
EXCHANGE RATES / U.S. DLR:	1.7997-1.9535 AUSTRALIAN DOLLARS

OFFICIAL CURRENCY: AUSTRALIAN DOLLAR

GOVERNMENT SPENDING (% OF GDP)

DEFENSE (N/A)	
EDUCATION (N/A)	
HEALTH 5.9%	

0   5   10   15

NUMBER OF CONFLICTS OVER LAST 25 YEARS

	1	2-5	5+
Violent changes in government	○	○	○
Civil wars	○	○	○
International wars	○	○	○
Foreign intervention	○	○	○

- No compulsory national military service.
- No armed forces.
- A police force is tasked with internal security.

NOTABLE WARS AND INSURGENCIES: None

HOW THE GOVERNMENT WORKS

LEGISLATIVE BRANCH

Parliament
Unicameral Parliament

Fale I Fono
(House of Assembly)
Composed of 15 members elected to four-year terms by direct popular vote. Debates and passes laws; removes prime minister with no-confidence vote.

Regional Governments
Eight main inhabited atolls, each administered by council composed of six members elected to four-year terms.

EXECUTIVE BRANCH

Governor-General
Appointed by British monarch on advice of prime minister and parliament. Serves as head of state. Dissolves parliament.

Prime Minister
Elected by parliament from among members. Serves as head of government.

Deputy Prime Minister
Elected by parliament from among members.

Cabinet
Composed of prime minister and up to four additional members; appointed by governor-general on advice of prime minister. Oversees government operations.

JUDICIAL BRANCH

High Court
Highest island court. Hears lower-court appeals; rulings may be appealed to Court of Appeal in Fiji. Chief justice must be solicitor or barrister qualified to practice law in Tuvalu.

Magistrates' Court
Hears appeals from lower courts.

Island Courts
Eight panels each composed of three lay magistrates, one for each main inhabited island.

Land Courts
Adjudicate land rights, probate and adoption matters. Composed of 6 judges.

SINGLE-PARTY
RULE

GOVERNMENT WITHOUT OPPOSITION

UNDER SINGLE-PARTY RULE, only one political party is constitutionally allowed to govern. Elections may take place under this system, but the candidates will all be from the same party. It is not the same as military rule, theocracy, or monarchy, but is often imposed by such forms of dictatorship. Conversely a dictator may emerge from a system of single-party rule. When Adolf Hitler became chancellor of Germany in 1933, he instituted single-party rule by the Nazi party as Benito Mussolini had done for the Fascist party in Italy in the 1920s. Francisco Franco emerged triumphant from the Spanish Civil War as a military ruler and his government represented single-party rule until his death. The most obvious examples of single-party rule are communist nations. Cuba's leader, Fidel Castro, overthrew the military dictator Fulgencio Batista only to evolve into a single-party ruler himself. Vietnam's wartime leader Ho Chi Minh professed democratic ideals to free his country from the Japanese, the French, and the Americans, but ultimately imposed single-party communism on the Democratic People's Republic of Vietnam. In post-World War II China, what began as Mao Zedong's defeat of the Nationalist forces yielded more than half a century of single-party communist rule. North Korea followed a similar path under Kim Il Sung. Some nations declare themselves democracies but are, in effect, single-party states.

SINGLE-PARTY RULERS

Clockwise from top left: Haile Selassie, emperor of Ethiopia, whose attempts to modernize his country after World War II never achieved democratic rule, but who remains revered by some; Mao Zedong, creator of the People's Republic of China in 1949, its first Chairman, and potent ideologue; Fidel Castro, who imposed communist rule in Cuba in 1959 and who remains in power, despite US arttempts to destabilize him; Francisco Franco, whose right-wing Falange party controlled Spain from 1939 to 1975; Kim Jong Il, North Korea's communist leader; Pol Pot leader of the murderous Khmer Rouge regime in Cambodia (1975-1979), and who evaded capture until the end of the century; Vladimir Ilich Lenin, Bolshevik leader and founder of the USSR; Idi Amin, president of Uganda (1971-1979); Joseph Stalin, who shaped the USSR following the death of Lenin in 1924 until his own death in 1953; Benito Mussolini, creator of Italy's Fascist party and ruler of Italy from 1922 to 1943; Saddam Hussein, whose Ba'ath Party ruled Iraq from 1968 until 2003, when his regime was toppled by the US-led invasion; Hafez al-Assad, Syrian president (1971-2000); Muammar al-Qaddafi, Libyan leader since he came to power in a coup in 1969; Adolf Hitler, dictator, whose Nazi Party controlled every aspect of German life from 1933 to 1945, when his suicide in a bunker helped bring World War II to an end.

CHINA

CHINESE FLAG
Adopted on Oct 1, 1949. Red is the traditional color of the revolution, the large star—the Communist Party, the small stars—the people.

GREAT WALL OF CHINA
Most of the present wall—once over 4,000 miles (6,400 km) long—was built under the Ming dynasty (1368–1644) as a defence against the Mongols.

UNREST LEADING TO THE CHINESE REVOLUTION IN 1911 and to the eventual establishment by the communists of the People's Republic of China in 1949, began to burgeon in the 19th century, when the actions of aggressive Western powers added to the problems confronting the ruling Qing dynasty.

The legitimacy of the Qing dynasty (1644-1911) established by the previously nomadic Manchus had always been in question. It was the last of a long line of ruling dynasties which, beginning with the Shang in around 1600 B.C., had developed a great civilization. Under the Qing, the Chinese Empire had expanded to its largest extent ever, but the government was corrupt and unable to respond adequately to the challenges it faced from foreign powers. Consequently, China was defeated by Britain in the Opium War of 1840-1842—sparked off by China's attempt to stop the British sale of opium to the

Chinese—by France in 1885, and by Japan in 1895. The superior military forces of Britain, France, the United States, Russia, and others forcibly gained concessions and commercial privileges. China lost control over all its major ports, vassal states such as Annam (now Vietnam), and parts of its empire. The island of Hong Kong was ceded to Britain in 1842, and Taiwan to Japan in 1895.

Meanwhile, the Taiping Rebellion in 1851, and other internal rebellions, laid bare the Qing dynasty's weakness. So, too, did the Boxer Rebellion (1899-1901)—an attempt to drive foreign missionaries out of China,

H O W   T H E   G O V

COMMUNIST PARTY STRUCTURE

▶ **POLITBURO STANDING COMMITTEE**
The Standing Committee of the party's Political Bureau (Politburo), an elite group that defines the Chinese regime's goals and develops government policy. A maximum of nine members permitted. Members in 2003 included the party's general secretary and the state's president, vice-president, and premier.

▶ **POLITBURO**
Political Bureau, semi-elite group that sets overall policy for China. Usually 22 to 24 members, including members of Standing Committee.

▶ **CENTRAL COMMITTEE**
Elected by National Party Congress, has 198 members. Endorses policy initiatives presented to government. Elects Politburo, Secretariat, Central Military Commission (CMC), and Disciplinary Inspection Commission (DIC).

▶ **NATIONAL PARTY CONGRESS**
Theoretically, National Party Congress (NPC)—with more than 2,000 delegates—is party's highest body, but it meets only once every five years. Elects Central Committee and debates CCP policy issues.

STATE STRUCTURE

LEGISLATIVE BRANCH

NATIONAL PEOPLE'S CONGRESS

Unicameral legislative body, largely symbolic, considered highest state power, mostly rubber-stamps CCP-drafted measures, but has become somewhat more independent recently; more than 2,000 members; elected every five years by People's Congresses in the provinces, municipalities and regions, as well as by People's Liberation Army units. Holds annual meetings with little say in policy-making, approves budget, amends constitution, elects high-ranking officials. Most members are also CCP members.

▶ **NPC STANDING COMMITTEE**
Meets more frequently than the NPC, has about 160 members and can enact and amend some laws, but it still mainly approves party-written legislation. Proposes constitutional amendments.

EXECUTIVE BRANCH

PRESIDENT

Chief of state, elected by National People's Congress to a five-year term, confirming CCP selection; is limited to two terms. Typically is also general secretary of CCP; may be chairman of CCP Central Military Commission as well. Issues pardons, declares war, and nominates premier.

▶ **VICE-PRESIDENT**

▶ **PREMIER**
Head of government, elected by NPC. Leads State Council.

▶ **STATE COUNCIL**
Appointed by NPC to which it is responsible, consists of premier, vice-premiers, state councilors, ministers of ministries and commissions, auditor-general, secretary-general; determines responsibilities of ministers.

 REGIONAL AND LOCAL GOVERNMENTS
▶ People's Congresses at city, municipal, and provincial level elected by lower level People's Congresses; report to Central Government
▶ People's Congresses at lower levels elected by constituents
▶ Elected mayors and governors

*Every communist must grasp the truth,
"Political power grows out of the barrel of a gun."*
—Mao Zedong, November 1938

provoking offended nations to send military forces to crush the rebellion. Attempts at reform were too late and too little, whetting dissidents' appetite for more rebellion. The bureaucratic dynasty was unable to respond, plagued by massive social strife and economic stagnation.

In 1911 a Nationalist revolution, led by Sun Yat-sen, resulted in the collapse of the Qing dynasty. Sun Yat-sen became provisional president in 1912, but he then stood aside to allow Yuan-shikai, an imperial general, to head the new government. Sun's new political party, the Kuomintang (KMT), won a majority of the seats in Parliament in a 1913 election. But Yuan died in 1916, and the next decade was marked by rebellions and further political chaos, with Sun's forces waging inconclusive battles for control of

China with numerous warlords. Unable to get help from the Western democracies, in 1921 Sun turned to the Soviet Union, which persuaded him to ally with the new and small Communist Party (CCP). Sun died in 1925, and the leadership of the KMT fell to Chiang Kai-shek, who launched a series of military campaigns against the communists, finally confining them in 1936 to a small area in the north. In the years 1937-1945 there was some cooperation between the communists and Kuomintang in the war against Japan, but in 1945 civil war broke out once again. It ended in 1949 with victory for the communists under Mao Zedong.

CHAIRMAN MAO ZEDONG (1893-1976)
From 1949, communist China was built almost entirely on Mao's vision of a socialist state—a vision that he pursued ruthlessly.

NMENT WORKS

▶ SECRETARIAT
CCP's administrative unit, or "inner cabinet." Carries out daily work of Central Committee and Politburo, working through departments such as the Department for Propaganda. Has overlapping membership with Politburo, carries out party's policy decisions. General secretary, its head, is party leader.

▶ DISCIPLINE INSPECTION COMMISSION
Concerned with checking that party rules are maintained and party policies are properly implemented. Investigates corruption in the party.

▶ CENTRAL MILITARY COMMISSION
Chairmanship of Central Military Commission (CMC) is usually given to the most powerful CCP person. By 2003, three men—Mao Zedong, Deng Xiaoping, and Jiang Zemin—had chaired the CMC for all but four years of the republic's history. Oversees People's Liberation Army (PLA) through the PLA's General Political Department. Determines policies for counterpart Central Military Commission under the government's State Council; leadership is identical for both commissions. Most party CMC members are military officers.

⚖ JUDICIAL BRANCH

SUPREME PEOPLE'S COURT
Judge-president appointed by NPC, limited to two terms; other judges appointed by Standing Committee of National People's Congress. Court is ultimate appellate court, but court powers in China are subordinate to state and CCP goals; criminal, civil, and economic divisions.

▶ SUPREME PEOPLE'S PROCURATORATE
Responsible for seeing that courts conform with lawful procedure.

▶ LOWER PEOPLE'S COURTS
Three courts—Higher People's Courts, Intermediate People's Courts, and Basic People's Courts; lower-level procuratorates; divisions for civil, criminal, administrative, and economic cases.

▶ SPECIAL PEOPLE'S COURTS
Comprise Military Courts hearing criminal military cases.

OPENING OF THE NATIONAL PEOPLE'S CONGRESS
Military police march in front of the Great Hall before the opening of the 11-day congress in March 2002.

ELECTORAL SYSTEM
The Communist Party provides most candidate lists, and little voter choice is offered. Direct elections are held for town, city district, township, county, city, and municipal district People's Congresses. For provincial People's Congresses and the NPC, deputies elect deputies for the next highest level. At or below county level, more competitive elections are held, in which more candidates than positions are offered.

CHINESE COMMUNIST PARTY

THE PARTY SYSTEM

The Russian Revolution of 1917 led to an upsurge of interest in communism among Chinese intellectuals. Members of the May Fourth Movement of 1917–1921 began to view Soviet Russia as a model for China to adopt, and in 1921 the Chinese Communist Party (CCP) was founded. A period in which links were forged between the CCP and the nationalist Kuomintang (KMT) came to an end in the mid-1920s, and mutual hostility between the two parties led to civil war in the 1930s. Interrupted by the war against Japan (1937–1945), the civil war was resumed in 1945 and continued until 1949 when the Kuomintang withdrew to Taiwan and the communists proclaimed the new People's Republic of China.

Under the leadership of Mao Zedong, far-reaching reforms were introduced, including wholesale urban and rural collectivization, and a massive programme of industrialization. A state constitution was created, giving China a Soviet-style regime. In the early 1960s, state president Liu Shaoqi and his protégé, CCP General Secretary Deng Xiaoping, took over the party's direction, adopting pragmatic economic policies at odds with Mao's vision. Mao retaliated, launching a political attack in 1966 and again in 1976. On both occasions, Deng was dismissed from his posts, but after Mao's death in 1976, Deng was able to reassert his pragmatic leadership.

Under Deng, economic growth was the main priority, to be brought about by the modernization of industry, agriculture, science and technology, and the army in China's "second revolution". From 1978, state ownership and planning was reduced, communes were abolished, and citizens given the right to undertake capitalist ventures and trade. Socialism remains the theoretical goal of the Chinese regime, but Marxist ideology has given way considerably to a market-based economy. In 2001, President Jiang Zemin, in a move criticized by hard-line communists, said that private entrepreneurs should be allowed to join the CCP, and the party began to recruit businessmen. Transfer of much of the huge state economic system into private

THE 16TH CONGRESS OF THE CCP
The National Party Congress votes, in November 2002, to continue the emphasis on economic development begun by the late Deng Xiaoping. Entrepreneurs, professionals, and others will be recruited for party membership.

Sun Yat-sen

Chiang Kai-shek and Chang Haush-liang

Civil War KMT soldier

Mao leads peasant uprising

The Long March

China enters the Korean War

BRIEF CHRONOLOGY OF THE CHINESE COMMUNIST PARTY

1911 *Revolution in which Sun Yat-sen spearheads overthrow of the Qing dynasty and creation of a republic. From 1917 he creates a united Nationalist Party (Kuomintang), forms a government in the south, and battles against northern warlords for control of the republic.*

May 4, 1919 *Students in Beijing demonstrate against agreement of Chinese government to transfer of former German concessions to Japan, sparking off further protests and stimulating growth of Communist Party (CCP).*

July 20, 1921 *The CCP holds its founding meeting, with 12 Chinese, including Mao Zedong, and two Russians present.*

1927 *Following period of cooperation between the KMT and CCP in early 1920s, KMT leader Chiang Kai-shek sets out to destroy the communists. Defeats peasant uprising organized by Mao in province of Hunan.*

1931 *Mao becomes chairman of Council of People's Commissars, but KMT military campaign forces him to lead majority of communist Red Army on Long March (1934-1935) to Shensi in north. During Long March, Mao emerges as the effective leader of CCP.*

1937 *War with Japan leads to suspension of civil war between communists and KMT. Communists win support for their stand against Japan.*

1945 *Civil war is resumed. It ends in 1949 with the Kuomintang being defeated and driven out of mainland China to Taiwan.*

October 1, 1949 *The People's Republic of China is founded, with Mao as chairman. Basic reforms, such as nationalization of industry, introduced.*

November 26, 1950 *China enters Korean War, with troops crossing Yalu Jiang River into North Korea, opposing advancing UN (mostly US) forces.*

1953 *First Five-Year plan to industrialize China is launched. Wholesale urban and rural collectivization is undertaken with help from Soviet Union.*

1958 *Mao's second programme to tranform China's economy—the Great Leap Forward—requires collectives to build and run small-scale iron and steel foundries. It leads to mass starvation and withdrawal of Soviet aid. In 1959 Mao is replaced as chairman of the Republic, but he continues in his role as chairman of the CCP.*

"THE LITTLE RED BOOK"
Containing quotes from Mao, the book was given to participants in the Cultural Revolution.

CHINA

ownership has challenged the ability of the CCP to monopolize power. Economic decentralization has also increased the authority of local officials, where some measure of democracy has begun to develop. The provinces, especially those in the southeast, are acting increasingly independently of Beijing. Party control is tightest in government offices, and considerably looser in rural areas, where most people live. In 1999, a few provinces introduced direct elections for neighborhood leaders and the practice has begun to spread. Openly attacking the communists or forming a rival party is still not allowed, however, and directly elected village chiefs and committee leaders must follow the orders of neighborhood CCP secretaries. Two "special administrative regions" have a unique semi-independent status and enjoy a high degree of autonomy. These are Hong Kong, which reverted from British rule to Chinese sovereignty in 1997, and Macao, which reverted from Portuguese rule in 1999.

As younger, reform-minded leaders began their rise to top positions in the 1980s, the new pragmatic leadership adopted economic,

THE MEANING OF MAO

Mao Zedong overcame foes from abroad, enemies inside China, and rivals within the Communist Party to emerge as the father of the modern communist People's Republic of China. He helped the nation overcome centuries of bowing to other countries, using Marxist-Leninist (and Maoist) ideology to build China's might. An avid swimmer, Mao told swimming companions not to think about obstacles in the water, lest they sink—just keep on stroking. He was politically unsinkable, rebuffing challenges as he took charge of the infant CCP, regrouping the party when it was on the run, and turning a chaotic revolutionary China into a single-minded communist state. He said in 1950, "Communism is not love. Communism is a hammer which we use to crush the enemy." Later, until his death, Mao kept rebounding from setbacks, amid a growing clash between his rigid communist goals and the pragmatic economic ideas of his eventual successors.

legal, and other modest political reforms. Students began staging demonstrations in which they protested against the slow pace of reform, culminating in mass protests in May 1989 in Beijing's Tiananmen Square. The Chinese authorities' brutal suppression of the demonstrators made international headlines and was a blatant example of China's violations of the basic human rights of many of its citizens. Fostered by the CCP

authorities' belief that the totalitarian regime must exert a strong grip over its people in order to maintain power and stability, the violations have drawn widespread and worldwide condemnation. In 2002, China released many political and religious prisoners and agreed to work with United Nations experts on such issues as torture and arbitrary detention, but there has been little progress on those promises.

The Cultural Revolution   **Deng given forced labor**   **Funeral of Chairman Mao**   **Fifty-year celebration**   **Tiananmen massacre**   **China joins WTO**

1966 *The Great Proletarian Cultural Revolution is launched by Mao, appealing to the masses over the heads of economic-pragmatist members of the government who have taken control of the party—in particular, President Liu Shaoqi. Anarchy reigns as the Revolution's leaders encourage rampant violence, and party leaders as high as CCP General Secretary Deng Xiaoping are purged and humiliated. In the forefront of the revolution are the Red Guards—young people recruited by Mao to spread his teachings and attack "old" ideas. On August 18, a million Red Guards march through Beijing's streets, destroying "feudal" symbols, abusing people, pillaging houses and museums and destroying temples.*

1969 *Deng is sent to do manual labor for three years at a tractor repair plant, but is later reinstalled in office. He undergoes a second, brief purge in 1976.*

1974-1976 *The Gang of Four, Mao's wife and three associates, used the media to discredit the economic pragmatists. They were arrested and put on trial in 1980-1981.*

September 9, 1976 *Mao's death ends his reign of over 40 years as leader of the CCP, but does not resolve the battle for succession.*

May 4, 1989 *In the Tiananmen Square massacre, the party brutally suppresses students who protest about the slow pace of reform.*

July 1, 1997 *Hong Kong reverts to Chinese sovereignty as a special administrative region. The trade and financial center has been a British colony*

since 1842, with the mainland territory held under a lease since 1898

October 1, 1999 *The 50th anniversary of the founding of the People's Republic of China by the Communist Party is celebrated.*

December 11, 2001 *China becomes the 143rd member of the World Trade Organization, ending a 15-year quest to join in face of much opposition. Entry into the WTO signals recognition of China's importance as one of the world's largest and fastest-growing economies.*

CELEBRATIONS IN 1997
Hong Kong officially becomes part of the Chinese Communist nation.

EXECUTIVE BRANCH

ZHOU ENLAI (1898-1976)
A founder of the CCP and the steadiest of modern-China's leaders, Zhou was Mao's lieutenant for half a century and the government's premier for 27 years. He backed Deng's economic pragmatism.

MAO ZEDONG (1893–1976)
Founder of the People's Republic in 1949 and China's foremost communist theorist, Mao ruled as a ruthless dictator for 27 years.

SUN YAT-SEN (1866-1925)
Heralded as the founder of the modern China, the former doctor led the 1911 Revolution. He briefly headed the new republic and struggled to unify a divided post-dynasty China.

CHIANG KAI-SHEK (1887–1975)
Sun's successor as head of the Kuomintang, and effective head of the Nationalist Republic (1928–1949), Chiang led the KMT in a long civil war with the communists that ended with his defeat in 1949.

DENG XIAOPING (1904–1997)
Deng initiated economic reforms that charted a capitalistic course for China, resulting in one of the world's largest economies. As father of this "second revolution," Deng also ended the Maoist emphasis on a single, prominent and revered national leader.

THE PRESIDENT

Under China's present constitution, drawn up in 1982, there is an executive branch headed by the president as chief of state, with a premier and Cabinet who run the government. The Communist Party, however, has its own version of most government bodies, and CCP officials and units are the architects of policy decisions, with the government counterparts mainly confirming and carrying out these decisions. The task is made easier by the fact that party membership is a prerequisite for most senior party and state positions alike, and usually, the members of both the CCP and state bodies are the same. For example, the CCP's Central Military Commission has the same leaders as the CMC under the government's State Council (the Cabinet), and the CCP version is the only meaningful overseer of the Chinese military. The president names the members of the State Council, but the party elite agrees on many, if not all, members in advance. To keep a tight grip on the government, the party leaders also hold top state posts. The CCP chairman until 1982, and the party's general secretary since then, has usually been China's real leader and, typically, also the president. This approach was begun by Mao Zedong himself, who also headed the People's Liberation Army. An exception was Deng Xiaoping, who never formally headed either the CCP or the government, wanting to downplay his personal role in running the country. He continued, however, to exert strong rule even after relinquishing the posts he did hold. The most notable government premier was Zhou Enlai, who held the post from 1949 until his death in 1976.

THE CABINET OF COMMUNIST CHINA

The State Council, or Cabinet, is the top executive apparatus of the government, drafting legislative bills and preparing the economic plan and budget. The Council's makeup was changed in 1998, to include some 28 ministries, commissions, a state bank, and an auditing office, along with numerous administrations, councils, and other agencies.

AGRICULTURE
In charge of rural economic development and fisheries and controlling animal and plant disease.

CIVIL AFFAIRS
Sets policies in regard to a range of issues, including care of older people, the relief of poverty, and voting at local level.

COMMERCE
Formulates policies and rules for international trade and for improving the operation of the domestic market system.

CONSTRUCTION
Devises strategies for urban and village planning, housing, real estate, and the building industry.

CULTURE
Oversees literary, art and other cultural undertakings, including experimental forms and construction of cultural facilities.

EDUCATION
Drafts policies and guidelines for education, plans for educational reform and language-related work.

FINANCE
Exerts macro-control over economy and issues regulations for the state's taxation, spending, and other financial activities.

FOREIGN AFFAIRS
Promulgates policies and decisions covering foreign policy, relating, in part, to the UN and treaties.

HEALTH
Drafts health laws and regulations and health plans, and organizes prevention and cure of serious diseases.

INFORMATION INDUSTRY
Issues regulations governing electronics and information, telecommunications and software industries.

JUSTICE
Supervises the criminal punishment system, guides the work of lawyers and others, and helps draft new laws.

LABOR & SOCIAL SECURITY
Formulates policies and guidelines for labor and the social security system.

KEY LEADERS OF CHINA

These people were leaders of China both before and after the 1911 Revolution, which ended centuries of imperial rule. The majority contributed to the development of today's Communist Party-run state with growing capitalistic tendencies, but still near-dictatorial political rule.

DOWAGER EMPRESS TZU HSI
1861–1889, 1898–908
Mother of the only son of Emperor Hsien Feng, she ruled as regent after the emperor's death and ordered the Boxer Rebellion (1899–1901).

SUN YAT-SEN
1911–1925
Known as the Father of the Nation, he spearheaded the 1911 Revolution and founded the Kuomintang Party (1919 to 1925). First president of the Republic of China, in 1923 he developed a philosophy called the Three Principles of the People.

CHIANG KAI-SHEK
1925–1949
Head of the Kuomintang from 1925 and of the Republic from 1928 to 1949, when he retreated to Taiwan and became the island's president.

MAO ZEDONG
1949–1976
A founder member of the CCP, he established the People's Republic of China in 1949 and became its chairman as well as being chairman of the CCP.

ZHOU ENLAI
1949–1976
Premier of the People's Republic from 1949 until his death, he kept China together during the Cultural Revolution of 1966–1969.

CHINA

FORMER HEADS OF STATE
Three of China's key leaders, Deng Xiaoping, Mao Zedong, and Jiang Zemin, have been immortalized in these sculptures that are on exhibition in Beijing.

US PRESIDENT'S HISTORIC VISIT
In his "ice-breaking" 1972 visit to Beijing, US President Richard Nixon and First Lady Pat Nixon, inspect the troops with Premier Zhou Enlai.

MILITARY WELCOME
A formal military guard holds a welcoming ceremony for heads of state visiting China.

GREAT HALL
Chinese soldiers provide security at the opening of the People's Consultative Conference, prior to the opening of the 16th National Congress of the Communist Party of China in 2002.

"All diplomacy is a continuation of war by other means."
—Zhou Enlai, Premier (1954)

THE NATIONAL PARTY CONGRESS

The nominally most powerful party organ is the National Party Congress, a large body which delegates the authority to set policy to the CCP Central Committee and its members. The real political power lies in the Politburo and the Politburo Standing Committee, whose members are China's top political leaders. New party and state constitutions in 1982 abolished the post of party chairman and restored the post of president of the republic, giving added weight to government functions and some balance to the authoritative party

structure. The party constitution made the general secretary the party's key official, while expanding the base of political authority to include the Politburo's Standing Committee, the general secretary, and the chairman of the Central Military Commission. The premier serves on the Standing Committee, which thus includes representatives of the party, the military, and the government in its ranks. While past succession has been dictated by death or political agitation, China experienced its most orderly change of leadership in 80 years at the recent 16th National Party

Congress in 2002. Hu Jintao was elected general secretary, and in 2003, president. Though it was widely anticipated that he would open the party to more democratic processes internally, he said nothing about any political reforms in a July 1, 2003 speech on the 82nd anniversary of the CCP's founding.

OVERLEAF: GREAT HALL, BEIJING
Home to the Chinese legislature, Beijing's Great Hall accommodates the members of the 16th National People's Congress in 2002. During this meeting, Hu Jintao was appointed as general secretary.

LAND RESOURCES
Oversees use of land, mineral reserves, and marine resources; manages oceanic and mapping agencies.

NATIONAL AUDITING OFFICE
Conducts or supervises wide range of central or provincial auditing, mainly of state-owned enterprises.

NATIONAL DEFENSE
In charge of organizing the armed forces, including armaments and military personnel training.

PEOPLE'S BANK OF CHINA
The country's central bank exercises macro control of the monetary sector and national treasury.

PERSONNEL
Oversees salaries, policies and regulations relating to government personnel, and reform of that system.

PUBLIC SECURITY
As the top Armed Police organ, coordinates security. This includes overseeing border defense and road-traffic safety.

RAILWAYS
Develops railway-industry strategy and rules, directs railway construction and standardizes the railway transport market.

SCIENCE & TECHNOLOGY
Proposes policies for using science and technology to promote economic and social development in China.

STATE SECURITY
Directs counter-espionage; combats criminal acts endangering China's security, and fosters citizens' loyalty.

SUPERVISION
Oversees the government cadre to ensure that state policies are followed, deciding officials' appointment and removal.

TRANSPORTATION
Formulates regulations and development plans; ensures equal competition for highway and waterway transportation.

WATER RESOURCES
Develops conservation plans and exercises unified management for water resources.

STATE DEVELOPMENT & REFORM COMMISSION
Develops economic and social policies to improve socialist market system.

STATE COMMISSION OF ETHNIC AFFAIRS
Improves legal systems, and guarantees rights for ethnic minorities, while safeguarding state integrity.

NATIONAL DEFENSE SCIENCE, TECHNOLOGY & INDUSTRY
Uses science and technology for national defense.

STATE POPULATION & FAMILY PLANNING COMMISSION
Oversees state population and family planning policies to meet state targets.

DENG XIAOPING
1961–1976
Having held various CCP and state posts, including that of deputy premier three times, he became chairman of the CCP and leader of the People's Republic of China. Forced from his post twice by Mao, he criticized the Cultural Revolution. His policies made China one of the fastest growing economies.

HUA GUOFENG
1976–1981
Chairman of the CCP and premier of the PRC, he was Mao's chosen successor but was ousted by Deng.

HU YAOBANG
1981–1987
Chairman and general secretary of the CCP, he worked to reform China. He was ousted after student protests.

ZHAO ZIYANG,
1987–1989
Premier of the PRC, and general secretary (1987-1989), he was replaced after protests at Tiananmen Square.

JIANG ZEMIN
1989–2002
General Secretary of the CCP (1989-2002), he maintained economic growth, and led China to WTO membership.

HU JINTAO
2002 –
General Secretary of the CCP (2002-), he was named by Deng as being a core 4th-generation leader.

LEGISLATIVE AND JUDICIAL BRANCH

"All cases handled by the people's courts, except for those involving special circumstances as specified by law, shall be heard in public. The accused has the right of defense." —Constitution of China

OPENING CEREMONY
During the opening proceedings of the National People's Congress in March 2003, Chinese delegates stand to sing the "March of the Volunteers," the Chinese national anthem.

LEGISLATIVE BRANCH

The highest organ of the Chinese state under the 1982 constitution is the National People's Congress, elected by local People's Congresses and the armed forces; with nearly 70 percent of its delegates CCP members. Meeting once a year, it acts on State Council legislative proposals, but actually serves primarily as a rubber stamp for CCP-drafted legislation. Its Standing Committee meets every two months, but also serves mainly to carry out the blueprints devised by the CCP.

The Congress ostensibly elects the state's president and vice-president, chairman of the Central Military Commission, and president of the Supreme People's Court, but in doing so it merely confirms party selections. The more-powerful large legislative-type group is the CCP's National Party Congress, which meets every five years, and held its 16th meeting in 2002. It has more than 2,000 members, whose role is to debate policy. However, because of its size and infrequent meetings, it is more a vehicle for announcing political decisions than a means for initiating policy. The smaller party units, topped by the Politburo's Standing Committee, make the country's real political decisions.

This situation began to change in the 1990s as a result of political reforms instituted in the early 1980s. The 1982 constitution, for example, placed less emphasis on the role of the Party Congress in legislative policy, and allowed more serious review of government programs by the state's National People's Congress. In a notable 1999 incident the Congress delayed passing a law that instituted an unpopular fuel tax. It has been given greater leeway to draft laws in certain areas, including human rights. "No" votes of the People's Congress are on the increase—on one occasion a nominee for chief prosecutor received only 65 percent "yes" votes. The Congress's finance committee has also grilled some State Council ministers. Many attribute the NPC's small, but growing, independence to the leadership of Qiao Shi as chairman of the Standing Committee. He failed to win re-election to the Politburo in 1997.

JUDICIAL BRANCH

The Chinese constitution provides for an independent judiciary, but court powers are subordinate to state and Communist Party goals, and the CCP and the government frequently interfere in the judicial process, directing verdicts in many political cases. The

THE GREAT HALL INTERIOR
A member of the National People's Congress surveys the 10,000-seat Great Auditorium in the Great Hall, with its magnificent illuminated ceiling.

EXTERIOR OF THE GREAT HALL, BEIJING
Built in 1959, the legislative assembly hall is located in Tiananmen Square, scene of the 1989 student protests.

highest court, the Supreme People's Court in Beijing, is the final court of appeal, although its rulings can be overturned by the National People's Congress Standing Committee. Under the 1982 constitution, there is a four-level court system, from the Supreme People's Court down through provincial, intermediate and local-level courts, plus special courts. The military courts are under the Ministry of National Defense, and try all treason and espionage cases.

A parallel hierarchy of people's procuratorates, topped by the Supreme People's Procuratorate, is intended to ensure that courts conform with lawful procedure and serve as the state's prosecutors in criminal trials. In contrast with the Western system, in which the judge is an impartial referee between contending attorneys, trials are conducted in an inquisitorial manner, with both judges and "assessors" appointed by the court for their expertise, actively questioning witnesses.

Between an anti-rightist campaign in 1957 and legal reforms in 1979, the courts were viewed by the more left-wing Chinese officials as troublesome and unreliable, so the courts played a small role in the judicial system. Most judicial functions were handled by other party or government organs. But in 1979, the National People's Congress, which appoints members of the Supreme People's Court and oversees it, set about restoring the court-based system. Since 1980, China has been slowly developing a criminal code, and the 1982 constitution enumerated fundamental rights, including freedom of speech, as long as the exercise of these rights does not infringe upon the interests of the state. Attempts by dissidents in the 1990s to use the legal system to seek recourse for government misconduct, and to push for more rigorous enforcement of existing rights, met with some limited success. Reports show, however, that in 2001 there were numerous executions that were carried out after summary trials, without due process or meaningful appeal.

CHINA

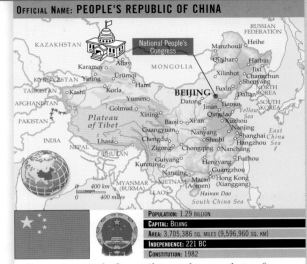

POPULATION: 1.29 BILLION	
CAPITAL: BEIJING	
AREA: 3,705,386 SQ. MILES (9,596,960 SQ. KM)	
INDEPENDENCE: 221 BC	
CONSTITUTION: 1982	

CHINA is named after a Chinese dynasty dating from the 3rd century B.C.—the "Qin" or "Chin" dynasty.

RELIGION: Non-religious 59%, Traditional beliefs 20%, Buddhist 6%, Muslim 2%, Other 13%

OFFICIAL LANGUAGE: Mandarin

REGIONS OR PROVINCES: 23 provinces, 5 autonomous regions and 4 municipalities

DEPENDENT TERRITORIES: None

MEDIA: Total political censorship in national media

Newspapers: There are 39 major daily newspapers

TV: 1 state-owned service

Radio: 2 state-owned services

SUFFRAGE: 18 years of age; universal

LEGAL SYSTEM: Customary and civil law; no ICJ jurisdiction

WORLD ORGANIZATIONS: AfDB, APEC, ARF (dialogue partner), AsDB, ASEAN (dialogue partner), BIS, CCC, CDB, ESCAP, FAO, G-77, IAEA,IBRD, ICAO, ICC, ICRM, IDA, IFAD, IFC, IFRCS, IHO, ILO, IMF, IMO, Interpol, IOC, IOM (observer), ISO, ITU, LAIA (observer), MINURSO, MONUC, NAM (observer), OPCW, PCA, UN, UN Security Council, UNAMSIL, UNCTAD, UNESCO, UNHCR, UNIDO, UNIKOM, UNITAR, UNMEE, UNMIBH, UNMOVIC, UNTSO, UNU, UPU, WHO, WIPO, WMO, WToO, WTrO

POLITICAL PARTIES: CCP—Communist Party of China

ETHNIC GROUPS:

Han 93%, Other 5%, Hui 1%, Zhaung 1%

NATIONAL ECONOMICS

WORLD GNP RANKING: 7th

GNP PER CAPITA: $840

INFLATION: 0.3%

BALANCE OF PAYMENTS (BALANCE OF TRADE): $20.5 billion

EXCHANGE RATES / U.S. DLR.: 8.2774-8.2766 YUAN

OFFICIAL CURRENCY: YUAN

GOVERNMENT SPENDING (% OF GDP)

✈	DEFENSE	5.3%
📖	EDUCATION	2.3%
✚	HEALTH	2.1%

Scale: 0 — 5 — 10 — 15

NUMBER OF CONFLICTS OVER LAST 25 YEARS

	1	2-5	5+
Violent changes in government	○	○	○
Civil wars	○	○	○
International wars	◉	○	○
Foreign intervention	○	○	○

- Compulsory national military service.
- Large weapons industry, including nuclear weapons capability.
- People's Liberation Army, linked to CCP, reduced in size.

NOTABLE WARS AND INSURGENCIES: Sino-Vietnamese War 1979

THE MANY FACES OF COMMUNISM

Communism, marked by authoritarian rule and a centrally managed economy, took hold not in the industrial Western countries as predicted by Karl Marx, but instead, in peasant-predominant Russia, a nation ruled for centuries by despotic czars. It spread to other peasant-based countries with their own histories of imperial or dictatorial rule, such as China and Cuba, and was exported to many East European, Asian, African, and Latin American nations, mainly by the Soviet Union. After being adopted in about 20 nations, communism has collapsed in most of them, spurred on by the demise of the chief sponsor, the USSR. Five communist states with regimes originally based on Marxist doctrine are left—China, North Korea, Vietnam, Laos, and Cuba.

Many communist governments—present and past—have common characteristics: leaders retain control with ruthless totalitarianism, a single party sets the rules, and the economy is tightly run by the party-led regime. Despite common traits at the onset, there have been many significant differences as well. While heavy-handed leadership seemed necessary to keep most communist regimes in power—notably in China, Cuba, North Korea, and Romania, Marxist regimes in Chile and Nicaragua operated democratically before being ousted. Hungary, while still a communist state, organized competitive parliamentary elections in 1985. When Lenin and Stalin ruled, dissidence was not tolerated and purges were prevalent, but when USSR leaders allowed more freedom, the result was the end of communist rule—not only in the Soviet Union, but also in Soviet-bloc countries throughout Eastern Europe and Asia. Some regimes, like Cuba, maintained close ties with their mentor, the Soviet Union, while others broke away in defiance—most notably China, Cambodia, Yugoslavia, and North Korea.

Rule by a single strong leader was commonplace, but it has not always prevailed. In Vietnam, Ho Chi Minh's primary role was to win

the long struggle for independence and control of the north and south alike. The Vietnamese Communist Party has followed collective leadership and consensual rule between factions since the 1950s. Leaders often hold several top jobs to ensure control of the country—Fidel Castro holds four such posts, chairing the Cuban legislature's Council of State, and heading the state, the military, and the party. The Marxist nations were, and are, ruled by one party, but some nominally allow other parties. Membership in the ruling party has been only a small part of the population—ranging from 0.1 percent in Kampuchea to 15.6 percent in North Korea. The Communist Party has exerted direct or indirect control over the government, with the party having the real power.

Reforms to regimes present a mixed picture. Political reform was difficult to fend off in many countries, including the USSR and Eastern Europe—so much so that it led to the collapse of communist rule itself. Not so in China, North Korea, and Cuba, where the party leaders have successfully resisted any substantial political reform. Top party officials in China worry that more reform could open the floodgates for a Soviet-style demise of the communist regime, though capitalistic changes have put the Chinese economy in much better shape than that of the former USSR. The economies of communist countries suffered so many disasters, including devastating famines in China, North Korea, the USSR, Cambodia, and Ethiopia—caused partly by property confiscation and collectivization—that the leaders began to adopt, in varying degrees, methods of once-vilified capitalism. From the early years, and until its demise in 1991, the Soviet Union vacillated between a centrally managed economy and some capitalistic forays. Vietnam and Laos have recently encouraged private-sector activity, Cuba somewhat less so. But China has gone far in invigorating its economy through promotion of entrepreneurship on a major scale.

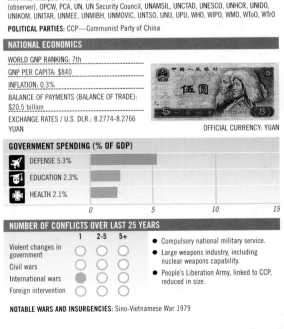

GORBECHEV AND CASTRO
The last Soviet Communist chief, Mikhail Gorbachev and the long-reigning (since 1959) Cuban Communist leader, Fidel Castro walking together in Cuba in 1989.

VIETNAM

OFFICIAL NAME: SOCIALIST REPUBLIC OF VIETNAM

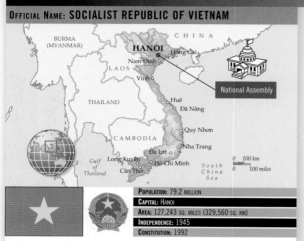

POPULATION: 79.2 MILLION
CAPITAL: HANOI
AREA: 127,243 SQ. MILES (329,560 SQ. KM)
INDEPENDENCE: 1945
CONSTITUTION: 1992

VIETNAM ("southern land"), was so named in 1802 by Nguyen Anh, the first emperor of the Nguyen dynasty.

RELIGION: Buddhist 55%, Christian (mainly Roman Catholic) 7%, Other and non-religious 38%,

OFFICIAL LANGUAGE: Vietnamese

REGIONS OR PROVINCES: 58 provinces and three municipalities

DEPENDENT TERRITORIES: None

MEDIA: Total political censorship exists in national media

NEWSPAPERS: There are ten daily newspapers

TV: One state-owned service with 53 provincial stations

RADIO: One state-owned service with more than 5,000 local stations

SUFFRAGE: 18 years of age; universal

LEGAL SYSTEM: French law; Communist legal traditions; no ICJ jurisdiction

WORLD ORGANIZATIONS: ACCT, APEC, ARF, AsDB, ASEAN, CCC, ESCAP, FAO, G-77, IAEA, IBRD, ICAO, ICRM, IDA, IFAD, IFC, IFRCS, ILO, IMF, IMO, Interpol, IOC, IOM (observer), ISO, ITU, NAM, OPCW, UN, UNCTAD, UNESCO, UNIDO, UPU, WCL, WFTU, WHO, WIPO, WMO, WToO, WTrO (observer)

POLITICAL PARTIES: The sole permitted political grouping is the Vietnamese Fatherland Front—VFF, which is dominated by the Communist Party of Vietnam (CPV)

ETHNIC GROUPS:

Other 6%
Chinese 4%
Thai 2%
Vietnamese 88%

NATIONAL ECONOMICS

WORLD GNP RANKING: 58th

GNP PER CAPITA: $390

INFLATION: -0.6%

BALANCE OF PAYMENTS (BALANCE OF TRADE): $507 million

EXCHANGE RATES / U.S. DLR.: 14.514-15.083 DÔNG

OFFICIAL CURRENCY: DÔNG

GOVERNMENT SPENDING (% OF GDP)

DEFENSE 3%
EDUCATION 3%
HEALTH 0.8%

0   5   10   15

NUMBER OF CONFLICTS OVER LAST 25 YEARS

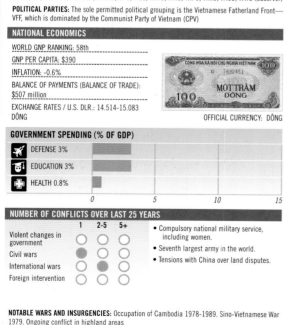

	1	2-5	5+
Violent changes in government			
Civil wars			
International wars			
Foreign intervention			

- Compulsory national military service, including women.
- Seventh largest army in the world.
- Tensions with China over land disputes.

NOTABLE WARS AND INSURGENCIES: Occupation of Cambodia 1978-1989. Sino-Vietnamese War 1979. Ongoing conflict in highland areas

VIETNAM BECAME A FRENCH COLONY in 1883, having been an independent kingdom for most of the previous 1,000 years, and ruled by China for 1,000 years prior to that. Communist leader Ho Chi Minh declared the country independent from France on September 2, 1945, naming it the Democratic Republic of Vietnam, but France refused to relinquish control. After an eight-year guerrilla war, the parties signed the Geneva Agreement in July 1954 to cease hostilities and divide Vietnam temporarily at the seventeenth parallel, creating a communist north and non-communist south. One stipulation of the agreement was that elections for a unified government would swiftly be held. However, the south refused reunification plans, declaring itself the Republic of Vietnam in October 1955, armed by the US. In response, Northern Vietnam encouraged the Viet Cong, a communist guerrilla network in southern Vietnam, to begin an armed campaign against anti-reunification sympathizers. After nearly two decades of fighting that eventually saw US forces sucked into a prolonged and damaging jungle war alongside its allies in the south, North Vietnam seized control of the south in 1976 and created a single Communist Party-dominated republic. This was soon followed by the occupation of Cambodia between 1978 and 1989, and renewed conflict with China during the same period.

Government policy falls under the control of the Politburo, headed by the party's secretary-general, and with policy enforced by the Secretariat. The most recent constitution, approved in April 1992, created the executive offices of president as head of state, and prime minister as head of government. Attendance at Cabinet and legislative committee meetings allows the president to mediate between executive and legislative branches, and to approve appointments in both. To prevent local officials from blocking national programs, the constitution gives the prime minister the power to appoint deputy prime ministers and ministers, dismiss People's Committee leaders, and reject ministerial and committee decisions—provided the legislature approves. In recent years, the unicameral National Assembly has become more potent, while remaining firmly under party control.

ISSUES AND CHALLENGES:

- The major issue facing the the single-party Socialist Republic of Vietnam is moving to a market economy without political liberalization (the regime's policy of *roi moi*, or "renovation"). There is a fear that privatization and competition could undermine the power of the Communist Party of Vietnam (CPV).

- An agreement signed in 1999 with China resolved most of their border disputes, but disagreement remains over the ownership of the Spratly Islands in the South China Sea.

- Environmentally, Vietnam still suffers the consequences of the Vietnam War, which contaminated more than half of its forests.

HOW THE GOVERNMENT WORKS

LEGISLATIVE BRANCH
Quoc-Hoi
(National Assembly)
Unicameral Parliament
Composed of 498 members elected to five-year terms by direct popular vote. Meets twice annually for seven-to-ten-week sessions. Oversees all government functions; passes and amends bills presented by executive branch; amends constitution.

Regional Governments
Fifty-eight provinces administered by elected people's councils.

EXECUTIVE BRANCH
President
Elected to five-year term by National Assembly from among its members. Head of state; commander-in-chief of military.

Prime minister
National Assembly member appointed by president. Serves as head of government.

Politburo
Composed of 15 members elected by the Communist Party. Directed by nine-member Secretariat drawn from Politburo. Sets government policy; oversees implementation.

Cabinet
35 members; appointed by president on advice of prime minister, approved by National Assembly. Oversees government operations.

JUDICIAL BRANCH
Supreme People's Court
Highest judicial authority; oversees local courts; supervises military tribunals.
Chief justice elected to five-year term by National Assembly on advice of president.

Local People's Courts
Adjudicate civil and criminal cases.

SYRIA

OFFICIAL NAME: SYRIAN ARAB REPUBLIC

![map of Syria]

People's Council

POPULATION: 16.6 Million	
CAPITAL: Damascus	
AREA: 71,498 SQ. MILES (184,180 SQ. KM)	
INDEPENDENCE: 1946	
CONSTITUTION: 1973	

SYRIA is said to have been named after Assur, a city on the Tigris River, and means "the water bank."

RELIGION: Sunni Muslim 74%, Other Muslim 16%, Christian 10%

OFFICIAL LANGUAGE: Arabic

REGIONS OR PROVINCES: 13 provinces; city of Damascus

DEPENDENT TERRITORIES: None

MEDIA: Total political censorship exists in national media

NEWSPAPERS: There are 10 daily newspapers

TV: One state-controlled service

RADIO: One state-controlled service; independent music stations were permitted from 2002

SUFFRAGE: 18 years of age; universal

LEGAL SYSTEM: Shari'a (Islamic) and civil law; no ICJ jurisdiction

WORLD ORGANIZATIONS: AFESD, AL, AMF, CAEU, CCC, ESCWA, FAO, G-24, G-77, IAEA, IBRD, ICAO, ICC, ICRM, IDA, IDB, IFAD, IFC, IFRCS, IHO, ILO, IMF, IMO, Interpol, IOC, ISO, ITU, NAM, OAPEC, OIC, UN, UN Security Council (temporary), UNCTAD, UNESCO, UNIDO, UNRWA, UPU, WFTU, WHO, WMO, WToO

POLITICAL PARTIES: Ba'ath Party—Members of the National Progressive Front (allies of the Ba'ath Party), Other Ba'ath—Parties Allied to the Ba'ath Party

ETHNIC GROUPS:

Kurdish 6%
Other 3%
Armenian, Turkmen, Circassian 2%
Arab 89%

NATIONAL ECONOMICS

WORLD GNP RANKING: 75th

GNP PER CAPITA: $940

INFLATION: -0.4%

BALANCE OF PAYMENTS (BALANCE OF TRADE): $1.06 billion

EXCHANGE RATES / U.S. DLR.: 53.5-45.9 SYRIAN POUNDS

OFFICIAL CURRENCY: SYRIAN POUND

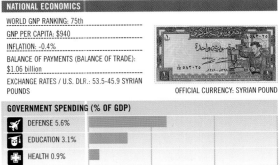

GOVERNMENT SPENDING (% OF GDP)

DEFENSE 5.6%	
EDUCATION 3.1%	
HEALTH 0.9%	

0   5   10   15

NUMBER OF CONFLICTS OVER LAST 25 YEARS

	1	2-5	5+
Violent changes in government	○	○	○
Civil wars	●	○	○
International wars	○	○	○
Foreign intervention	○	○	○

- Compulsory national military service.
- Ongoing tensions with Israel, particularly over Golan Heights.
- Equipment supplied by former Soviet Union.
- Alleged to have weapons of mass destruction.
- Former province held by Turkey remains an issue.

NOTABLE WARS AND INSURGENCIES: Muslim Brotherhood militancy 1965-1985

SYRIA GAINED FULL INDEPENDENCE FROM FRANCE in 1946, after which numerous coups left the country politically unstable. Four years after the 1954 coup, in which then-president Adib Shishakli—himself empowered by a coup—was overthrown, Syria merged with Egypt to form the United Arab Republic until 1961. In 1963 the Ba'athist military junta seized power, and has deployed a mix of economic liberalization and repression to hold power ever since, despite internal power battles among radical factions. The rise of Hafez al-Assad, following a bloodless "corrective" coup on November 13, 1970, brought relative stability to the country.

Ba'ath Party goals include Arab unity, and secularism. While the country's pan-Arabist focus faded after the failure of the short-lived union with Egypt, Syria has had a history of conflict with Israel, to which it lost the Golan Heights in the 1967 war. Syria has backed attacks on Israel from nearby Lebanon, which many Arabs believe forms part of a Greater Syria, along with Palestine, and Jordan. The party is dominated by the minority Alawi sect, fostering resentment among the large Sunni majority in the population. In 1982, Islamic militants belonging to the Muslim Brotherhood, denounced government corruption, calling for democracy and an end to secularism, but were crushed in an army-led massacre. The secular regime has used a network of security and intelligence agencies to retain its grip on power in the face of a rise in Islamic fundamentalism.

While the National Progressive Front is a five-party coalition, Syria is in fact a single-party state, and military power has shaped the Ba'athist political hierarchy. The 1973 constitution grants extensive powers to a Muslim president, who is elected for a seven-year term after nomination by the People's Assembly, the 250-member unicameral People's Council. Hafez al-Assad ruled as president for 30 years until his death in 2000—the longest tenure in modern Syrian history. After Assad's death, parliament amended the constitution, lowering the mandatory minimum age of the president to 34, thereby making it possible for Assad's son, Bashar, to run unopposed.

ISSUES AND CHALLENGES:

- Many of the population see Lebanon, Jordan, and Palestine as Greater Syria, leading to allegations of support for terrorism.
- Unresolved hostilities with Israel require significant spending on military capabilities.
- One in five people is employed by the government in inefficient state-controlled businesses.
- The increasing economic power of the urban merchant and business class is widening the gap between rich and poor.
- Lack of political liberalization.
- Sunni majority (74 percent of the population) resentment with the ruling Alawi minority.

HOW THE GOVERNMENT WORKS

LEGISLATIVE BRANCH

Majlis al shaab
(People's Council)
Unicameral Parliament
Composed of 250 members elected to four-year terms by direct popular vote. Passes bills; approves budget; debates government policies; ratifies treaties; can vote no confidence in prime minister and Council of Ministers, but cannot remove them.

Regional Governments
Thirteen provinces and city of Damascus administered by elected councils and governors nominated by minister of interior, appointed by Council of Ministers.

EXECUTIVE BRANCH

President
Elected to seven-year term by direct popular vote. Must be Muslim. Serves as head of state; commander-in-chief of armed forces; secretary-general of Ba'ath Party. Issues laws with consent of People's Council; amends constitution; appoints civil and military officials; declares war; dissolves People's Council.

Three Vice-presidents
Appointed by president.

Prime minister
Appointed by president.
Serves as head of government.

Council of Ministers
Members appointed by president.
Oversees government operations.

JUDICIAL BRANCH

Supreme Constitutional Court
Rules on constitutionality of laws; decides election disputes. Judges appointed to four-year terms by president.

High Judicial Council
Oversees operations of judiciary; appoints transfers, dismisses lower-court judges. Members appointed by president.

Court of Cassation
Highest court of review and appeal.

Courts of Appeal

Magistrates' Courts

State Security Courts

NORTH KOREA

NORTH KOREAN FLAG
Adopted on September 8, 1948, the blue symbolizes desire for peace; the red, revolutionary struggle; and the white, purity; the red star shows people building socialism under Communist Party leadership.

STATUE OF KIM IL SUNG
Mansudae Grand Monument on Mount Paekto, overlooking Pyongyang, one of 70 North Korean statues of the "Eternal President."

SINCE BEING FREED FROM JAPANESE CONTROL by the Soviet Union when World War II ended, North Korea became one of the harshest Stalinist-brand dictatorships in history, under the ironhanded leadership of Kim Il Sung who ruled for nearly 50 years between 1948 and 1994.

When Kim Il Sung died in 1994 his son and chosen successor Kim Jong Il became the "Dear Leader," taking charge of the country in what has been called an unprecedented Communist hereditary "monarchy". Four years later, the dead Kim Il Sung was declared to be the "President for Eternity," and a new constitution abolished the post of president.

The Korean peninsula had been dominated by its more powerful neighbors for centuries, coming under Japanese rule by 1910. In 1945, Korea was divided between Soviet-led communist rule in the north and a US-backed government in South Korea, in the same way that Germany was at the end of World War II. Kim Il Sung was a Korean army officer who had fled, along with other guerrillas, to the Soviet Union during the war. He returned to

Korea in 1945, where the Soviet occupation forces called him a Japan-fighting hero, and installed him as North Korea's ruler. North Korea invaded South Korea in 1950, but was repelled by the US and other United Nations troops.

Known formally as the Democratic People's Republic of Korea, the country is run by Kim Jong Il and, like other communist states, a single legal party—the three million-strong Korean Workers' Party (KWP). Although the political system originally was patterned after the Soviet model, Kim espoused chuch'e, or "national self reliance," applying principles of Marxism and Leninism in a North Korean manner, to move away from political dependence on any other nation, including the Soviet Union. Kim Il Sung used that

HOW THE GOVERNM

LEGISLATIVE BRANCH

CONGRESS

Congress has had little in the way of meaningful power since Kim Jong Il declared himself sole executive ruler, and his late father president in perpetuity.

▶ **SUPREME PEOPLE'S ASSEMBLY**
The unicameral legislative body consists of 687 members, elected for five-year terms by direct popular vote, as a slate of unopposed candidates selected by the Korean Workers Party. Nominal powers include enacting laws, amending the constitution, and approving the budget and economic plans. But the Assembly has usually rubber-stamped KWP and executive-branch legislative decisions. The SPA has met only infrequently since Kim Il Sung's death in 1994, including a session to ratify the 1998 constitution. An SPA Presidium functions in the intervals between SPA meetings.

SUPREME PEOPLE'S ASSEMBLY
At the opening of the Assembly in Pyongyang, deputies raise their party membership certificates.

REGIONAL POWERS
▶ Provincial People's Assemblies
▶ Local People's Committees
▶ Local Administrative Committees

EXECUTIVE BRANCH

GENERAL SECRETARY

Head of state; combines powers of Chairman of the National Defense Commission, Commander in Chief of the Army and General Secretary of the Korean Workers Party; issues legislation through executive-branch offices, which is confirmed by the SPA.

▶ **PRESIDENT OF SUPREME PEOPLE'S ASSEMBLY PRESIDIUM**
Titular head of state; represents state; chairs Central People's Committee, a supra-cabinet, and State Administration Council, the Cabinet; guides work of the SPA's Presidium when SPA isn't in session; two vice-presidents and two honorary vice-presidents.

▶ **PREMIER**
Head of government; elected by the SPA; chairs Central People's Committee and State Administration Council, the Cabinet; assisted by three vice-premiers.

KIM IL SUNG SQUARE
One million people gather to support North Korea's withdrawl from the Nuclear Non-Proliferation Treaty in 2003.

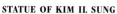

> *"If one knows oneself, one becomes a revolutionary, if one does not know oneself, one becomes a slave."*
> —Kim Jong Il, General Secretary

concept as one weapon as he systematically purged his opposition. After his death, his son took the country's helm, becoming the top legislator, and securing the top posts. In 1998 the NDC was declared by the nominal legislature, the Supreme People's Assembly, "the highest office of state". Since Kim Il Sung's death, the SPA itself and the executive-branch's Central People's Committee have met infrequently, and the KWP has not held a congress since 1980. Under Kim Jong Il, North Korea has taunted the international community by violating nuclear-weapons freeze agreements and threatening to test or export nuclear weapons, prompting observers to speculate that this may have been another attempt to extort aid for an economy in shambles. United States president, George W. Bush, in early 2002 called North Korea part of an "axis of evil".

"THE GREAT LEADER" KIM IL SUNG *(1912-1994)*
A guerrilla fighter against Japan, Sung led Korea for 50 years, purging political competitors and building a Stalinist-brand personality cult.

OFFICIAL NAME: DEMOCRATIC PEOPLE'S REPUBLIC OF KOREA

POPULATION: 22.4 MILLION	
CAPITAL: PYONGYANG	
AREA: 46,540 SQ. MILES (120,540 SQ. KM)	
INDEPENDENCE: 1948	
CONSTITUTION: 1948	

NORTH KOREA takes it name from the kingdom of Koryo, which was established in the 10th century and expanded to encompass the entire Korean peninsula.

RELIGION: Under strict state control. Mostly traditionally Buddhist and Confucianist, some Christian and Chondogyo or the Religion of the Heavenly Way, which is peculiar to Korea

OFFICIAL LANGUAGE: Korean

REGIONS OR PROVINCES: 9 provinces and 4 cities

DEPENDENT TERRITORIES: None

MEDIA: Total political censorship exists in national media

Newspapers: There are 5 daily newspapers

TV: 1 state-controlled service. Television consists mainly of musical shows praising Kim Il Sung and Kim Jong Il and anti-American tirades directed against the Korean War.

Radio: 1 state-controlled service

SUFFRAGE: 17 years of age; universal

LEGAL SYSTEM: German law; Communist and Japanese legal traditions; no ICJ jurisdiction

WORLD ORGANIZATIONS: ARF (dialogue partner), ESCAP, FAO, G-77, ICAO, ICRM, IFAD, IFRCS, IHO, IMO, IOC, ISO, ITU, NAM, UN, UNCTAD, UNESCO, UNIDO, UPU, WFTU, WHO, WIPO, WMO, WToO

POLITICAL PARTIES: DFRF—Democratic Front for the Reunification of the Fatherland

ETHNIC GROUPS:

Korean 100%

NATIONAL ECONOMICS

WORLD GNP RANKING: 77th

GNP PER CAPITA: $573

INFLATION: Not available

BALANCE OF PAYMENTS (BALANCE OF TRADE): Not available

EXCHANGE RATES / U.S. DLR.: 2.2 NORTH KOREAN WON

OFFICIAL CURRENCY: NORTH KOREAN WON

GOVERNMENT SPENDING (% OF GDP)

		0	5	10	15
DEFENSE 13.9%					
EDUCATION (N/A)					
HEALTH 3%					

NUMBER OF CONFLICTS OVER LAST 25 YEARS

	1	2-5	5+
Violent changes in government	○	○	○
Civil wars	○	○	○
International wars	○	○	○
Foreign intervention	○	○	○

- Compulsory national military service.
- Designated part of "axis of evil" by US.
- Nuclear weapons program.
- Manufactures and exports missiles.

NOTABLE WARS AND INSURGENCIES: None

AN INHERITED DICTATORSHIP

Kim Il Sung took Stalinist tyranny to another level. But his son Kim Jong Il, has spent billions of dollars on huge monuments to deify his father, and himself. After Kim Il Sung's death in 1994 and his elevation to "President for Eternity" the post of president was abolished. Instead, Kim Jong Il became the country's de facto paramount leader, cementing his power by being elected general secretary of the Korean Workers Party in 1997, and by having his chairmanship of the National Defense Commission declared the rank of highest post in the state.

⚖ JUDICIAL BRANCH

CENTRAL COURT

The supreme court with its judges elected by the SPA to four-year terms. It is accountable to the SPA or SPA Presidium, and thus is under the control of the state and KWP. The Central Court supervises all courts' trial activities.

▸ **PROCURATOR GENERAL**
A public procurator, named by the Central Procurator's Office, ensures that all courts and citizens conform with central decisions.

▸ **LOWER COURTS**
Provincial, municipal and county-level courts and special courts hear civil and criminal cases in their jurisdiction; judges appointed by local people's assembly.

ELECTORAL SYSTEM

With top leadership positions appointed by the Supreme National Assembly or its Presidium, it is only at local level that citizens can participate. Worthy candidates, who have shown party loyalty, are appointed to the local People's Assembly. These deputies are able to elect other local-level positions.

CUBA

Official Name: REPUBLIC OF CUBA

HAVANA
(La Habana)

ATLANTIC OCEAN

BAHAMAS

National Assembly of People's Power

Pinar del Río · Colón · Santa Clara
Cienfuegos · Camagüey
Archipiélago de los Canarreos · Las Tunas · Holguín · Guantánamo
GUANTÁNAMO BAY (to USA)

Caribbean Sea

HAITI · DOMINICAN REPUBLIC

JAMAICA

Straits of Florida

0   100 km
0   100 miles

POPULATION:	11.2 MILLION
CAPITAL:	HAVANA
AREA:	42,803 SQ. MILES (110,860 SQ. KM)
INDEPENDENCE:	1902
CONSTITUTION:	1976

CUBA as a word means "district", "territory" or "province", coming from the Taino Indian *cubanacan* which means "center place".

RELIGION: Non-religious 49%, Roman Catholic 40%, Atheist 6%, Protestant 1%, Other 4%

OFFICIAL LANGUAGE: Spanish

REGIONS OR PROVINCES: 14 provinces and 1 special municipality

DEPENDENT TERRITORIES: None

MEDIA: Total political censorship exists in national media

NEWSPAPERS: There are 17 regional daily newspapers

TV: 1 state-owned service

RADIO: 1 state-owned service

SUFFRAGE: 16 years of age; universal

LEGAL SYSTEM: Spanish and US law; Communist legal traditions; no ICJ jurisdiction

WORLD ORGANIZATIONS: CCC, ECLAC, FAO, G-77, IAEA, ICAO, ICC, ICRM, IFAD, IFRCS, IHO, ILO, IMO, Interpol, IOC, IOM (observer), ISO, ITU, LAES, LAIA, NAM, OAS (excluded from formal participation since 1962), OPCW, PCA, UN, UNCTAD, UNESCO, UNIDO, UPU, WCL, WFTU, WHO, WIPO, WMO, WToO, WTrO

POLITICAL PARTIES: PCC—Cuban Communist Party

ETHNIC GROUPS:

Black 12%
European-African 22%
White 66%

NATIONAL ECONOMICS

WORLD GNP RANKING: 70th

GNP PER CAPITA: $1,650

INFLATION: 0.3%

BALANCE OF PAYMENTS (BALANCE OF TRADE): In deficit

EXCHANGE RATES / U.S. DLR.: 21.00 CUBAN PESOS

OFFICIAL CURRENCY: CUBAN PESO

GOVERNMENT SPENDING (% OF GDP)

✈ DEFENSE 4.5%	
📖 EDUCATION 6.7%	
✚ HEALTH 6.4%	

0   5   10   15

NUMBER OF CONFLICTS OVER LAST 25 YEARS

	1	2-5	5+
Violent changes in government	○	○	○
Civil wars	○	○	○
International wars	○	○	○
Foreign intervention	○	○	○

- Compulsory national military service.
- Russia is major supplier of weapons.
- Guantánamo Bay is a US military base for prisoners of terrorism war.
- Designated part of "axis of evil" by US.

NOTABLE WARS AND INSURGENCIES: None

CUBA REMAINS ONE of just a few countries where the Communist Party is the only legal political party, but its future after leader Fidel Castro's death is uncertain. Until Castro's rebel forces overthrew the Batista military dictatorship in 1959, the United States exerted tremendous social and economic influence in Cuba. After taking power, Castro's revolutionary government confiscated $1 billion in US assets and nationalized all property, establishing a command economy, and provoking a US trade embargo. The Communist Party immediately recognized Castro's government, which remained allied with the Soviet Union until the USSR's collapse in 1991. The loss of economic support, and a precipitous drop in sugar production, thrust Cuba into recession.

Cuba's president has absolute power. The executive branch consists of the president, vice-president, and Council of Ministers, selected in part for their loyalty to the Cuban Communist Party (PCC). Members of the National Assembly of the People's Power, mostly elites, are elected for five-year terms from a "unity slate" approved by the PCC. The real power of the Assembly rests with the Council of State, an executive subcommittee that functions in secret. Although the Assembly is charged with enacting legislation, opposition to legislation introduced by the executive branch does not occur. The judicial system is under the authority of the Assembly. Lower courts try criminal cases, but there is no protection for citizens accused of political crimes. Opposition to the state is prohibited.

PEASANT MILITIA REVIEW
Cuba's long serving president, Fidel Castro, speaks with fellow revolutionary Major Ernesto "Che" Guevara on August 22, 1960 at a parade at the San Julián Base in Cuba.

Signs of growing discontent began to emerge in the late 1990s, along with higher visibility for the Roman Catholic Church. The free use of American dollars and limited opportunities for individual entrepreneurship have boosted the economy, but it is doubtful whether the Council of State will allow the "dollar economy" to continue unabated.

HOW THE GOVERNMENT WORKS

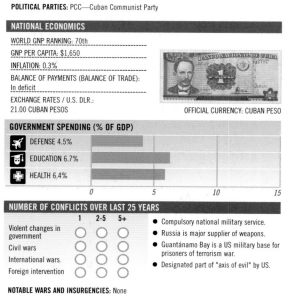

LEGISLATIVE BRANCH
Asamblea Nacional del Poder Popular
(National Assembly of the People's Power)
Unicameral Parliament
Composed of 609 members elected to five-year terms by direct popular vote from Communist Party's candidates slate. Approves budget; amends constitution; declares war; elects attorney general.

Council of State
Composed of 31 National Assembly members; presided over by president and vice-president. Meets as Assembly's executive committee during legislative recesses. Issues decrees, removes ministers; instructs courts; orders mobilization.

Regional Governments
Fourteen provinces governed by elected assemblies.

EXECUTIVE BRANCH
President
Elected by Parliament. Serves as head of state and government; commander-in-chief of armed forces; secretary of Communist Party.

Vice-president
Elected by Parliament. Minister of armed forces; vice-chair of Council of Ministers.

Council of Ministers
Members nominated by Council of State, appointed by National Assembly. Chaired by president; oversees government operations and state-controlled economy; conducts foreign relations and trade; drafts bills; maintains internal security.

JUDICIAL BRANCH
People's Supreme Court
Highest judicial body. Judges elected by Parliament.

Municipal Courts
Provincial Courts
Military Courts
Labor Councils

LIBYA

OFFICIAL NAME: GREAT SOCIALIST PEOPLE'S LIBYAN ARAB JAMAHIRIYAH

POPULATION: 5.4 MILLION
CAPITAL: TRIPOLI
AREA: 679,358 SQ. MILES (1,759,540 SQ. KM)
INDEPENDENCE: 1951
CONSTITUTION: 1969

LIBYA is derived from a Greek word that was used to describe all of North Africa, except the area of Egypt.

RELIGION: Muslim (mainly Sunni) 97%, Other 3%

OFFICIAL LANGUAGE: Arabic

REGIONS OR PROVINCES: 25 municipalities

DEPENDENT TERRITORIES: None

MEDIA: Total political censorship exists in national media

NEWSPAPERS: There are 3 daily newspapers

TV: 1 state-controlled service. Satellite TV and the Internet are widely available, but heavily censored.

RADIO: 2 services: 1 state-controlled, 1 independent

SUFFRAGE: 18 years of age; universal and compulsory

LEGAL SYSTEM: Shari'a (Islamic) and Italian law; no ICJ jurisdiction

WORLD ORGANIZATIONS: ABEDA, AfDB, AFESD, AL, AMF, AMU, CAEU, CCC, ECA, FAO, G-77, IAEA, IBRD, ICAO, ICRM, IDA, IDB, IFAD, IFC, IFRCS, ILO, IMF, IMO, Interpol, IOC, ISO, ITU, NAM, OAPEC, OAU, OIC, OPEC, PCA, UN, UNCTAD, UNESCO, UNIDO, UPU, WFTU, WHO, WIPO, WMO, WToO

POLITICAL PARTIES: None

ETHNIC GROUPS:

Other 5%

Arab and Berber 95%

NATIONAL ECONOMICS

WORLD GNP RANKING: 59th

GNP PER CAPITA: $5,220

INFLATION: 18.5%

BALANCE OF PAYMENTS (BALANCE OF TRADE): $1.48 billion

EXCHANGE RATES / U.S. DLR.: 0.5423-0.6416 LIBYAN DINARS

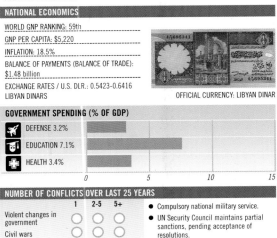

OFFICIAL CURRENCY: LIBYAN DINAR

GOVERNMENT SPENDING (% OF GDP)

- DEFENSE 3.2%
- EDUCATION 7.1%
- HEALTH 3.4%

0   5   10   15

NUMBER OF CONFLICTS OVER LAST 25 YEARS

	1	2-5	5+
Violent changes in government	○	○	○
Civil wars	○	○	○
International wars	○	●	○
Foreign intervention	○	○	

- Compulsory national military service.
- UN Security Council maintains partial sanctions, pending acceptance of resolutions.
- Designated part of "axis of evil" by US.
- Border disputes with Niger and Algeria.

NOTABLE WARS AND INSURGENCIES: Invasion of Chad 1979 and 1981. US attacks on Libyan targets 1981 and 1986

FORMED OUT OF THREE former Ottoman provinces—Cyrenaica, Fezzan, and Tripolitania—Libya has endured centuries of foreign control, a legacy that has fundamentally shaped the current government. A United Nations plan established the territory as an independent monarchy in 1951 after 40 years of Italian occupation. It was the first former European possession in Africa to come to independence through the intervention of the UN. King Idris I, emir of the province of Cyrenaica—who had led the independence movement—became king of the new monarchy.

Guided by the slogan, "Freedom, socialism, and unity," Colonel Mu'ammar al-Gaddafi's Revolutionary Command Council (RCC) rose to power in a coup in September 1969, abolishing the monarchy and renaming the country the Great Socialist People's Libyan Arab Jamahiriyah. Gaddafi's government practices a unique blend of repression and liberal concessions for Libyans. Proclaimed to be a *jamahiriyah*, a state of the masses, the government is in fact a military dictatorship that bans political organizing and dissent. Despite Gaddafi's stringent controls, the system nevertheless has given Libya an unprecedented level of representative government.

Libya has been subject to harsh international criticism over its past sponsorship of terrorism, its repression of dissidents, and the overall nature of the Gaddafi regime. In recent years, it has sought to create a more positive image, turning over two men charged with the 1988 bombing of a passenger jet over Lockerbie, Scotland. Although US President Bush included Libya in his 2002 "axis of evil" speech, negotiations with European governments led the country to renounce its pursuit of weapons of mass destruction in 2003. This new attitude has been rewarded by the lifting of sanctions and an influx of western investment.

The RCC was officially abolished in 1977, but Gaddafi and other former RCC members continue to wield supreme authority. Although he holds no official title, Gaddafi is Libya's de facto chief of state. The government operates under the 1969 Constitutional Proclamation and the "Green Book," Gaddafi's political manifesto of socialism, Islam, and his own distinct philosophy. The Proclamation was supposed to be replaced by a permanent constitution upon conclusion of the "revolution," but this has never occurred.

ISSUES AND CHALLENGES:

- Libya is overly dependent on its oil reserves, sales of which account for 95 percent of export earnings. As an oil-exporting nation Libya is unable to receive foreign aid, in spite of its developing nation status.

- Corruption, mismanagement of the economy and links to terrorism have all contributed to the state of the economy and a high rate of inflation.

- Mostly desert, Libya is forced to import most of its food needs and water is limited.

HOW THE GOVERNMENT WORKS

LEGISLATIVE BRANCH

General People's Congress
Unicameral Parliament
Composed of 750 members: includes chairpersons of local people's congresses and municipal people's congresses, and also representatives of university student unions, the national federation of unions and professional associations. Meets once annually. Discusses and ratifies government plans, policies and programs.

Regional Governments
Twenty-five municipalities governed by elected legislative assemblies.

EXECUTIVE BRANCH

Mu'ammar al-Gaddafi
De facto head of state; commander-in-chief of armed forces. Technically elected by General People's Congress. Enacts laws by decree and proclamation.

General Secretary
Elected by General People's Congress. Serves as head of state.

General Secretariat
Composed of general secretary, staff and advisors. Controls government operations and activities of General People's Congress.

General People's Committee
Twenty secretaries appointed to three-year terms by General Secretariat.

JUDICIAL BRANCH

Supreme Court:
Highest judicial body; divided into five chambers: administrative, civil and commercial, constitutional, criminal and personal matters. Composed of 25 judges appointed by General People's Congress on advice of general secretary.

Appeals Courts
Hear Court of First Instance appeals; tries felony and high crimes cases.

Shari'a Court of Appeals
Hears cases involving Islamic code.

Courts of First Instance
Hear appeals from Partial Courts.

Partial Courts
Hear cases in villages and towns.

LAOS

OFFICIAL NAME: LAO PEOPLE'S DEMOCRATIC REPUBLIC

CHINA
MYANMAR (BURMA)
Phôngsali
VIETNAM
Houayxay
Xam Nua
Louangphabang
Xaignabouli
Xiangkhoang
Pakxan
VIENTIANE
National Assembly
Thakhek
Khanthabouli
THAILAND
Muang Khôngxédôn
Salavan
Pakxé
VIETNAM
CAMBODIA

0   100 km
0   100 miles

POPULATION: 5.4 MILLION
CAPITAL: VIENTIANE
AREA: 91,428 SQ. MILES (236,799 SQ. KM)
INDEPENDENCE: 1949
CONSTITUTION: 1991

Laos is named after the Lao people. The country's ancient name, Lan Xang, meant "land of a million elephants".

RELIGION: Buddhist 85%, Other (including animist) 15%

OFFICIAL LANGUAGE: Lao

REGIONS OR PROVINCES: 16 provinces, 1 municipality and 1 special zone

DEPENDENT TERRITORIES: None

MEDIA: Total political censorship exists in national media

Newspapers: There are 3 daily newspapers

TV: 2 state-owned services

Radio: 2 services: 1 fully state-owned, 1 30% state-owned

SUFFRAGE: 18 years of age; universal

LEGAL SYSTEM: Customary and French law; socialist legal traditions; no ICJ jurisdiction

WORLD ORGANIZATIONS: ACCT, ARF, AsDB, ASEAN, CP, ESCAP, FAO, G-77, IBRD, ICAO, ICRM, IDA, IFAD, IFC, IFRCS, ILO, IMF, Interpol, IOC, ITU, NAM, OPCW, PCA, UN, UNCTAD, UNESCO, UNIDO, UPU, WFTU, WHO, WIPO, WMO, WToO, WTrO (observer)

POLITICAL PARTIES: LPRP—Lao People's Revolutionary Party (the sole legal political party)

ETHNIC GROUPS:

Lao Soung 9%
Ethnic Vietnamese/ Chinese 1%
Lao Theung 22%
Lao Loum 68%

NATIONAL ECONOMICS

WORLD GNP RANKING: 144th

GNP PER CAPITA: $290

INFLATION: 25.1%

BALANCE OF PAYMENTS (BALANCE OF TRADE):- $121m

EXCHANGE RATES / U.S. DLR: 7600 NEW KIPS

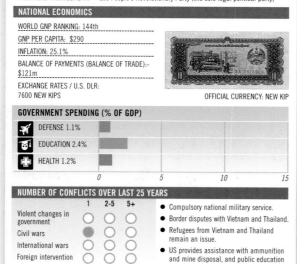

OFFICIAL CURRENCY: NEW KIP

GOVERNMENT SPENDING (% OF GDP)

DEFENSE 1.1%
EDUCATION 2.4%
HEALTH 1.2%

0   5   10   15

NUMBER OF CONFLICTS OVER LAST 25 YEARS

	1	2-5	5+
Violent changes in government	○	○	○
Civil wars	●	○	○
International wars	○	○	○
Foreign intervention	○	○	○

- Compulsory national military service.
- Border disputes with Vietnam and Thailand.
- Refugees from Vietnam and Thailand remain an issue.
- US provides assistance with ammunition and mine disposal, and public education regarding these.

NOTABLE WARS AND INSURGENCIES: Hmong guerrilla war 1977-1992

THE RECORDED HISTORY OF THE LAO PEOPLE begins with the Kingdom of Lan Xang, founded in the 14th century. The kingdom was divided into the principalities of Luang Prabang, Vien Chan (Vientiane), and Champassak in the 18th century, then fell under under Siamese rule. A French territory from 1907, Laos was occupied by the Japanese during World War II and briefly formed an independent government in 1945. Laos gained independence from France in 1949, only to embark on two decades of civil war between the communist Pathet Lao and royalist forces. A coup in 1975 ended the reign of King Savangvatthana and 600 years of monarchy, and the Lao People's Revolutionary Party (LPRP) took power. The LPRP is the only legal political party—an offshoot of Ho Chi Minh's Indochina Communist Party, founded in Vietnam in 1930. Laos has remained a communist stronghold ever since.

Moves toward a free market and political reform have met with limited success. A gradual return to private enterprise and the easing of foreign investment laws were among market reforms begun in 1986, and the 1990s saw the transfer of LPRP power to a younger generation, accompanied by an increase in political protests. Laos became a full member of the Association of Southeast Asian Nations (ASEAN) in 1997, improving relations with former adversaries, such as Thailand and China. Included on the United Nations' list of "Least Developed Nations," Laos receives one of the highest levels of outside aid in the developing world. In general, economic changes have not led to political change. The LPRP, the military, and the executive branch of the government are closely connected and dominate every level of politics, controlling the media and forbidding criticism of the party. With an ethnically diverse population, Laos has seen little national integration, and the dominant Buddhist religion, to which many LPRP leaders belong, is unlikely to serve as a vehicle for political dissent.

Laos adopted a constitution in 1991, enabling the formation of a National Assembly. Even so, almost all government decisions are taken by the nine-member Politburo, 49-member Central Committee, and the Council of Ministers.

ISSUES AND CHALLENGES:

- Considered one of the least developed economies in the world, many people in Laos are still subsistence farmers, and the government has been criticized for inefficient use of aid received. Infrastructure is inadequate and although adult education is on the increase, most workers are unskilled.

- Although the US provides funding to replace poppies with other crops in the northeastern provinces, Laos remains the third-largest opium producer in the world.

- Opportunities to export resources including gas deposits and oil have gone largely unexploited.

HOW THE GOVERNMENT WORKS

LEGISLATIVE BRANCH
Saphathaeng Xat (National Assembly)
Unicameral Parliament
Composed of 109 members elected to five-year terms by direct popular vote. Debates and ratifies bills, development plans, and budgets presented by executive branch.

Regional Governments
Sixteen provinces administered by governors appointed by central government; districts and villages overseen by appointed chiefs.

EXECUTIVE BRANCH
Politburo
Nine members elected by 49-member Central Committee of LPRP. Formulates and controls party and government policies and operations.

President
Elected by two-thirds majority vote of parliament. Head of state; commander-in-chief of armed forces. Issues decrees; promotes judicial and military officials.

Prime Minister
Appointed to five-year term by president, confirmed by parliament. Head of government.

Council of Ministers
Appointed by president, confirmed by National Assembly. Oversees government operations; drafts laws; sets budget.

JUDICIAL BRANCH
People's Supreme Court
Highest judicial authority. Judges appointed by parliament.

Provincial Courts

District Courts

TRANSITIONAL
RULE

THE BIRTH AND REBIRTH OF NATIONS

TRANSITIONAL RULE DESCRIBES a temporary regime in a nation undergoing governmental crisis, whether caused by war, civil unrest, governmental corruption, or some other disaster. Some transitional governments serve while nations are forming or are in the process of drafting a constitution. The United States operated under the Articles of Confederation until the constitution was adopted in 1789. David Ben Gurion was chairman of the Executive Jewish Agency for Palestine as an interim step to the creation of modern Israel. Yasser Arafat led the Palestine Liberation Organization from 1968 to 2004 in what he hoped to be a transition to a Palestinian state. Recovery from war often entails transitional government, as was the case after World War II when military rule by the Allies was temporarily imposed. After coalition forces ended Taliban rule in Afghanistan in 1999, President Hamid Karzai established a transitional government in Kabul to work toward reconstruction. After the 2003 war in Iraq, US-led coalition forces set up temporary military rule in Baghdad under General Jay Garner, though he was quickly replaced. Often, the UN and other supranational organizations play a role. For example, the human rights record of Liberian President Charles Taylor, who seized power in 1989, led to his condemnation by Human Rights Watch, Amnesty International, and other organizations. In 2003 Taylor was finally forced into exile and replaced by a transitional government.

TRANSITIONAL RULERS

Clockwise from top left: Simón Bolívar, "liberator" of much of Spanish South America in the early 19th century; David Ben Gurion, Jewish leader prior to the founding of the state of Israel, then its first prime minister; Douglas MacArthur, US general who administered postwar Japan; Ernesto "Che" Guevara, right-hand man to Fidel Castro in the reorganization of Cuba following the 1959 revolution; Jay Garner, head of the interim military administration in Iraq, 2003; Giuseppe Garibaldi, conqueror and temporary "dictator" of Sicily and Naples in 1860, before his conquests were added to the Kingdom of Italy; Napoleon Bonaparte, general, who in 1799 took power from the Directory in revolutionary France; Yasser Arafat, leader of the PLO 1968–2004; Queen Elizabeth II, whose position as head of state provided continuity as many British Commonwealth countries gained independence in the 1950s and 1960s; Kemal Atatürk, creator of modern Turkey following the defeat of the Ottoman Empire in World War I; Gamal Abdel Nasser, effective ruler of Egypt following a military coup in 1952; Jan Smuts, who tried to reconcile Boer and British interests after the South African War of 1889–1902; King Juan Carlos I, who acceded to the Spanish throne to ensure stability on the death of the dictator General Franco in 1975; Hamid Karzai, president of Afghanistan's transitional post-Taliban government.

IRAQ

IRAQ IS THE SITE of one of the world's oldest civilizations—Mesopotamia—dating back over 5,000 years. From the mid-7th century it was at the heart of a powerful Arab Muslim empire, but it became part of the Turkish Ottoman Empire in the 16th century and then a British mandate in 1916. It gained its independence—as a monarchy—in 1932.

Recent Iraqi history falls into four periods: the British mandate and the monarchy, 1920-1958; military rule, 1958-1968; Ba'ath Party rule, culminating in Saddam Hussein's reign, 1968-2003; and post-Hussein reconstruction. During World War I, when the Ottoman Empire was allied with Germany, the British occupied the three provinces of Mosul, Baghdad, and Basra. A tribal revolt, fueled by Arab nationalism, then forced the issue of independence, and in 1921, a constitutional monarchy was installed. King Faisal from Saudi Arabia and a stranger to Iraqi culture, struggled to balance British demands and those of Iraqi nationalists. In 1958, Iraq's military, toppled the monarchy. Britain had failed because it had relied solely on the educated Sunni population and had failed to embrace the Kurds or the rural

FALL OF A REGIME
A US Marine in Baghdad holds a poster of the fallen leader of Iraq, in April 2003, shortly before the end of the war.

THE GOVERNMENT IN

THE ROAD TO WAR

In January 2002, Iraq was described by US President Bush as part of an "axis of evil" threatening world peace. That September, Saddam agreed to the "unconditional" return of UN weapons inspectors, who arrived in November to resume a search for weapons of mass destruction suspended for four years. On December 7, the Iraqis handed over a 12,000-page dossier on its weapons to the UN, with a declaration that no such weapons now existed. Both the US and Britain rejected the dossier as misleading, and began to build up their forces in the Persian Gulf region.

In February 2003, US secretary of state Colin Powell and the UN weapons inspectors report gave conflicting reports on Iraqi efforts to disarm. The UN became divided over whether this was the right time to go to war, and in early March, France, Germany, Russia, and China made clear their opposition to any

UN security council resolution authorizing military action. The American and British governments then took the decision to go to war without UN backing. On March 20 the US launched its first air attack on Baghdad, opening a war in which US and British troops met with surprisingly little resistance from Iraqi forces. By April 9, US troops had taken control of Baghdad, and on April 15, following the fall of Tikrit, the US declared that major fighting in Iraq was at an end.

RECONSTRUCTION

While the US and Britain had succeeded in getting rid of Saddam Hussein's regime, they failed to capture Saddam for a further eight months. Dissolving the Iraqi armed forces ceated massive unemployment, and the occupying forces struggled to bring law and order to the country and re-establish basic services. A US temporary government—the

Coalition Provisional Authority—was set up in May 2003. This appointed the 25-member Iraqi Governing Council, which began meeting in July with the purpose of naming ministers and creating a committee to draft Iraq's constitution. Progress was slow, and the insurgency amongst Saddam loyalists and Islamic radicals showed no signs of abating, but in January 20005, elections for a Transitional National Assembly attracted a huge turnout despite calls for a Sunni boycott. With a cabinet representing all Iraq's ethnic groups, the Assembly will approve the new constitution and pave the way for full elections.

> *"We are not intimidated by the size of the armies, or the type of hardware the US has brought."*
> —*Saddam Hussein, former president of Iraq*

Shi'ite shaikhs, who represented the majority. For the next decade, military governments flirted with socialism, communism, and pan-Arab nationalism while tightening Iraq's control over its oil. The 1967 Arab defeat by Israel weakened the government and the Arab Socialist Ba'ath Party took power, with Ahmad Hassan al-Bakr as president. The Ba'athists outlawed all other political parties, suppressed a Kurdish rebellion, and undertook nationalization, irrigation, and agrarian initiatives. Saddam Hussein, vice-chairman of the Revolutionary Command Council, consolidated his power among Sunnis, installing relatives throughout the party apparatus and secret police. In 1979, al-Bakr resigned, and Saddam became president, creating a Stalin-like regime—rule through fear and execution. Building up Iraq's military and weapons, Saddam invaded Iran in 1980. He emerged victorious in 1988, but with millions dead and a war debt of over $50 billion. In 1990, Iraq invaded Kuwait, and would not be persuaded to withdraw by

CABINET MEETING
Saddam Hussein meets with the top leaders of the Iraqi armed forces in a military cabinet meeting in December 1998.

a worldwide trade embargo. A US-led 28-member UN coalition evicted Iraqi forces in a four-month war that destroyed much of Iraq's military and civilian infrastructure. The UN demanded disarmament; when Saddam refused, it imposed economic sanctions. In 1998, Hussein expelled UN weapons inspectors. In 2003, stating that Hussein was rebuilding his arsenals and arming terrorists, a US coalition invaded Iraq, deposing Saddam's regime.

T R A N S I T I O N

ISSUES AND CHALLENGES

Law and order, and basic services, such as water and electricity, still need to be properly restored, and the high level of unemployment reduced. US forces were ill-prepared for peacekeeping and have faced mounting postwar guerrilla resistance, leading to mounting casualties. Oil revenues that were intended to pay for the reconstruction of Iraq have declined, at least partly as a result of guerrilla attacks on oil wells and pipes. Some way has to be found of uniting the Iraqis——who are divided along traditional Kurdish, Sunni Muslim, and Shi'ite Muslim lines——and of creating democratic, Iraqi-controlled institutions. There is, however, a possibility that democracy could result in a return to Ba'athism or the rise of Shi'ite fundamentalism.

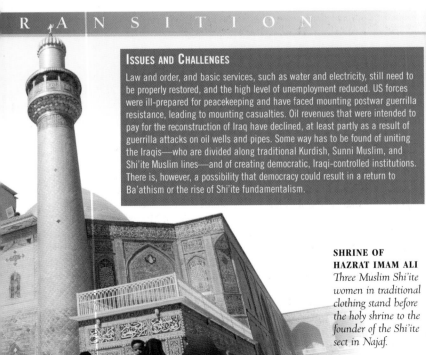

SHRINE OF HAZRAT IMAM ALI
Three Muslim Shi'ite women in traditional clothing stand before the holy shrine to the founder of the Shi'ite sect in Najaf.

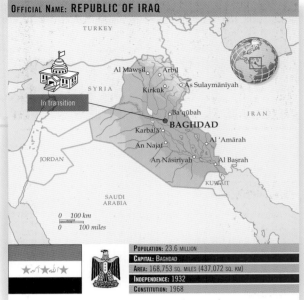

OFFICIAL NAME: REPUBLIC OF IRAQ

In transition

POPULATION: 23.6 MILLION	
CAPITAL: BAGHDAD	
AREA: 168,753 SQ. MILES (437,072 SQ. KM)	
INDEPENDENCE: 1932	
CONSTITUTION: 1968	

IRAQ is thought to come from either a phrase meaning "a well-rooted country" or the ancient Semitic word, *uruk*, which means "the place between the rivers", referring to the Tigris and the Euphrates Rivers between which it lies.

RELIGION: Shi'ite Muslim 62%, Sunni Muslim 33%, Other (including Christian) 5%

OFFICIAL LANGUAGE: Arabic

REGIONS OR PROVINCES: 18 provinces

DEPENDENT TERRITORIES: None

MEDIA: Total political censorship exists in national media

Newspapers: The 9 daily newspapers are all state-controlled

TV: 1 state-controlled service

Radio: 1 state-controlled service

SUFFRAGE: 18 years of age; universal

LEGAL SYSTEM: Shari'a (Islamic) law; new legal system under US occupation force; no ICJ jurisdiction

WORLD ORGANIZATIONS: ABEDA, ACC, AFESD, AL, AMF, CAEU, CCC, EAPC, ESCWA, FAO, G-19, G-77, IAEA, IBRD, ICAO, ICRM, IDA, IDB, IFAD, IFC, IFRCS, ILO, IMF, IMO, Interpol, IOC, ISO, ITU, NAM, OAPEC, OIC, OPEC, PCA, UN, UNCTAD, UNESCO, UNIDO, UPU, WFTU, WHO, WIPO, WMO, WToO

POLITICAL PARTIES: Hussein's National Assembly was composed of Ba'athists and their allies

ETHNIC GROUPS:
- Persian 3%
- Turkman 2%
- Kurdish 16%
- Arab 79%

NATIONAL ECONOMICS

WORLD GNP RANKING: 64th

GNP PER CAPITA: $950

INFLATION: 100%

BALANCE OF PAYMENTS (BALANCE OF TRADE): Not available

EXCHANGE RATES / U.S. DLR.: 0.3124-0.3110 IRAQI DINARS

OFFICIAL CURRENCY: IRAQI DINAR

GOVERNMENT SPENDING (% OF GDP)

	0	5	10	15
✈ DEFENSE 9.7%				
📖 EDUCATION 5.1%				
✚ HEALTH 3.8%				

NUMBER OF CONFLICTS OVER LAST 25 YEARS

	1	2-5	5+
Violent changes in government	●	○	○
Civil wars	○	●	○
International wars	○	●	○
Foreign intervention	○	●	○

- Iraqi Army and Ministry of Defense dissolved in May 2003.
- New Iraqi Army created in August 2003, to be trained and equipped by late 2004.
- Ongoing sporadic violence against US troops.

NOTABLE WARS AND INSURGENCIES: Kurdistan movement 1979-1995. Iran-Iraq War 1980-1988. Gulf War 1990-1991. Shi'ite and Kurd rebellions 1991-1995. Air strikes 1991-2003. US-led invasion 2003

AFGHANISTAN

OFFICIAL NAME: ISLAMIC STATE OF AFGHANISTAN

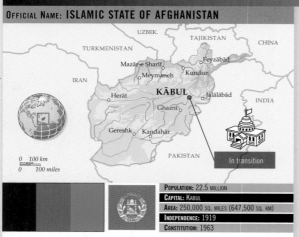

POPULATION: 22.5 MILLION
CAPITAL: KABUL
AREA: 250,000 SQ. MILES (647,500 SQ. KM)
INDEPENDENCE: 1919
CONSTITUTION: 1963

AFGHANISTAN is first recorded in the 3rd century A.D. as a regional name in the Sassanian (Persian) empire.

RELIGION: Sunni Muslim 84%, Shi'a Muslim 15%, Other 1%

OFFICIAL LANGUAGES: Pashtu and Dari

REGIONS OR PROVINCES: 32 provinces

DEPENDENT TERRITORIES: None

MEDIA: Partial political censorship exists in the national media

NEWSPAPERS: There are several daily newspapers. Rural Afghan factions run newspapers

TV: One state-owned service

RADIO: One state-owned service and several independent stations

SUFFRAGE: None; previously males 15-50 years of age

LEGAL SYSTEM: New judicial system under Bonn Agreement; based on Afghan traditions and Shari'a (Islamic) law; no ICJ jurisdiction

WORLD ORGANIZATIONS: AsDB, CP, ECO, ESCAP, FAO, G-77, IAEA, IBRD, ICAO, ICRM, IDA, IDB, IFAD, IFC, IFRCS, ILO, IMF, IOC (suspended), IOM (observer), ITU, NAM, OIC, OPCW (signatory), UN, UNCTAD, UNESCO, UNIDO, UPU, WFTU, WHO, WMO, WToO

POLITICAL PARTIES: The three main groups represented in the Afghan Interim Authority (AIA) are: the Northern Alliance, the Rome Group and the Peshawar Group

ETHNIC GROUPS:

- Other 3%
- Uzbek and Turkmen 15%
- Pashtun 38%
- Hazara 19%
- Tajik 25%

NATIONAL ECONOMICS

WORLD GNP RANKING: 104th

GNP PER CAPITA: $270

INFLATION: 56.7%

BALANCE OF PAYMENTS (BALANCE OF TRADE): -$143 million

EXCHANGE RATES / U.S. DLR.: 4750 AFGHANIS

OFFICIAL CURRENCY: AFGHANI

GOVERNMENT SPENDING (% OF GDP)

✈ DEFENSE 13%	
📖 EDUCATION 2%	
✚ HEALTH 1.6%	

0   5   10   15

NUMBER OF CONFLICTS OVER LAST 25 YEARS

	1	2-5	5+
Violent changes in government	●	○	○
Civil wars	●	○	○
International wars	○	○	○
Foreign intervention	●	○	○

- Compulsory national military service.
- US war on terrorism removed Taliban government.
- NATO commands a peacekeeping mission, the International Security and Assistance Force (ISAF).
- New national army is currently in training.
- Retains a significant number of missiles.

NOTABLE WARS AND INSURGENCIES: Civil war 1973-1996. Soviet occupation 1979-1988. US-led war on terrorism 2001

ALL SEMBLANCE OF LAW and institutional order in Afghanistan was eroded under continuous military conflict after 1979, when Soviet military forces invaded it to bolster the Marxist government that had seized power a year earlier. Shortly after the invasion, the Soviets became engaged in a protracted military conflict with anti-communist Mujahidin forces composed of various Afghan ethnic groups and foreign Islamic militants— supplied by external sources such as the United States and Saudi Arabia. Ten years after the invasion began, the Mujahidin forced the Soviets to withdraw from Afghanistan, leaving behind a devastated economic infrastructure and political chaos.

MEETING – JUNE 11, 2002
Loya Jirga (grand council) delegates meet in Kabul. The council elected Hamid Karzai, the interim leader, to head a new transitional government that would rule the country for the next 18 months.

The Mujahidin attempted to establish a legitimate government and create a national political system. However, they soon splintered, with competing factions fighting for political and military dominance. Infighting gave rise to an anarchic political environment of local government by warlords. The chaos gave rise to the country's most potent political force, the Taliban, a hard-line Islamic fundamentalist group that seized power in 1996 and instituted a repressive regime.

In late 2001, the United States-led "War on Terror" toppled the Taliban and forced most of its members to flee the country. United Nations-led negotiations established an Afghan Interim Authority (AIA) consisting of a Supreme Court, a president, and a grand council, or Loya Jirga. In 2004, the authority adopted a new constitution, leading to presidential elections in the autumn of that year.

Two decades of warfare decimated economic and political resources, as well as the transportation and communication infrastructure. Afghanistan as a political entity must be completely rebuilt. Major challenges will be establishing political control throughout the country, placating ethnic factions, rebuilding infrastructure, instituting national health and educational systems, repatriating millions of Afghan refugees, and re-establishing international diplomatic ties severed by the Taliban.

HOW THE GOVERNMENT WORKS

LEGISLATIVE BRANCH
Non-functioning since June 1993.

EXECUTIVE BRANCH
Transitional Authority
Composed of 30 appointed members. Formed in December 2001 by prominent Afghans under United Nations auspices to create new government following the fall of the Taliban regime.

President
Appointed by Transitional Authority. Serves as head of state and government.

Four Vice-presidents
Appointed by Transitional Authority.

Cabinet
Composed of 30 Transitional Authority members. Oversees government operations; advises president.

JUDICIAL BRANCH
Supreme Court
Highest judicial authority. Judges appointed by Transitional Authority.

SOMALIA

OFFICIAL NAME: SOMALIA

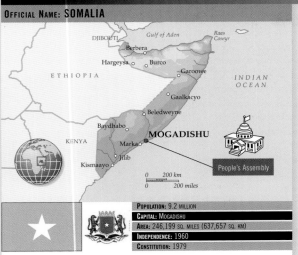

POPULATION: 9.2 MILLION
CAPITAL: MOGADISHU
AREA: 246,199 SQ. MILES (637,657 SQ. KM)
INDEPENDENCE: 1960
CONSTITUTION: 1979

SOMALIA means "land of the Somali" from the Arabic as-Sumal. The Ancient Egyptians called it the Land of Punt.

RELIGION: Sunni Muslim 98%, Christian 2%

OFFICIAL LANGUAGES: Arabic and Somali

REGIONS OR PROVINCES: 18 regions

DEPENDENT TERRITORIES: None

MEDIA: Total political censorship exists in national media

NEWSPAPERS: There are five daily newspapers

TV: Two services: limited to the Mogadishu area

RADIO: 11 services: mostly political or religious

SUFFRAGE: 18 years of age; universal

LEGAL SYSTEM: Shari'a (Islamic) law; accepts ICJ jurisdiction

WORLD ORGANIZATIONS: ACP, AfDB, AFESD, AL, AMF, CAEU, ECA, FAO, G-77, IBRD, ICAO, ICRM, IDA, IDB, IFAD, IFC, IFRCS, IGAD, ILO, IMF, IMO, Interpol, IOC, IOM (observer), ITU, NAM, OAU, OIC, UN, UNCTAD, UNESCO, UNHCR, UNIDO, UPU, WFTU, WHO, WIPO, WMO, WTrO (observer)

POLITICAL PARTIES: None

ETHNIC GROUPS:

Bantu and other non-Somali 15%

Somali 85%

NATIONAL ECONOMICS

WORLD GNP RANKING: 157th

GNP PER CAPITA: $100

INFLATION: Over 100%

BALANCE OF PAYMENTS (BALANCE OF TRADE): -$157 million

EXCHANGE RATES / U.S. DLR.: 2620 SOMALI SHILLINGS

OFFICIAL CURRENCY: SOMALI SHILLING

GOVERNMENT SPENDING (% OF GDP)

		0	5	10	15
✈ DEFENSE 4.5%					
📖 EDUCATION 0.4%					
✚ HEALTH 0.6%					

NUMBER OF CONFLICTS OVER LAST 25 YEARS

	1	2-5	5+
Violent changes in government	●	○	○
Civil wars	○	○	●
International wars	○	●	○
Foreign intervention	○	○	●

- No compulsory national military service.
- Armed forces collapsed with government.
- Major enlistment drive for new national army underway.
- Thought to have terrorist training camps.
- Thousands of militia with varying levels of training and equipment.

NOTABLE WARS AND INSURGENCIES: SDDF Insurgency 1978-1986. Ethiopian-Somali Border Clash 1982. Civil war and conflict 1982-present. US intervention 1992-1995. UN Intervention (UNOSOM)

THE SOMALI DEMOCRATIC REPUBLIC, one of the world's poorest and least developed countries, has no recognized, functioning central government. Located on the easternmost edge of Africa, Somalia lies on the Indian Ocean, sharing the Horn of Africa with Ethiopia and Djibouti. In 1960, the UN Trust Territory of Somalia (formerly an Italian colony) and the British Protectorate of Somaliland merged after gaining independence. In a 1969 military coup, dictator Muhummad Siad Barre seized control. Pursuing an ill-guided scheme of divide and conquer, he armed opposing clans until his government collapsed in 1991, after which he fled the country.

Since the dictatorship's fall, seven of Somalia's 18 regions have seceded—as the Republic of Somaliland in the north and as the Republic of Puntland next to it. Both have established governments and attained some stability, although neither is recognized by any other country. Somalia set up a three-year Transitional National Government (TNG), based in Mogadishu, in 2000. A 245-member interim parliament, selected that year, elected a president from 20 candidates. No formal judiciary exists and a new constitution has yet to be drafted. Islamic courts operate in Mogadishu; elsewhere, clan elders control the judicial system based on Shari'a—Islamic law. Numerous peacemaking and humanitarian interventions have failed, including one by United Task Force (UNITAF) troops in 1992. Later taken over by the UN as the United Nations Operation in Somalia (UNOSOM), this international effort was ultimately abandoned because of the high number of casualties and Somalis' disenchantment with both the US and UN. On the TNG's expiry in 2004, a new interim parliament was set up in Kenya and, under a fresh president, has renewed efforts to unite and rebuild Somali.

Several Islamic groups in Somalia seek the establishment of an Islamic state. Al-Ittihad al-Islami has used violence to achieve its goals, claiming responsibility for a number of terrorist attacks. These and other terrorist offensives worldwide have renewed the interest of the United States, which has applied sanctions to two of the country's Islamic groups.

ISSUES AND CHALLENGES:

- Mass starvation is the major issue facing most Somali people. This has been exacerbated by the withdrawal of UN and US humanitarian support and periods of drought. Most necessities are in short supply.

- While resources exist in the form of minerals and oil, these remain unexploited because of constant warfare.

- Owing to the non-existence of a central government, anarchy reigns in Somalia, with armed clans and bandits filling the vacuum.

- The country remains under the watchful eye of the United States because of suspected links with terrorist networks, including al-Qaida.

HOW THE GOVERNMENT WORKS

LEGISLATIVE BRANCH

Transitional National Assembly
Unicameral Parliament
Composed of 245 members appointed by Somali clans.
Formed in August 2000 to draft new national constitution and hold elections.

Regional Governments
Eighteen regions.

EXECUTIVE BRANCH

President
Appointed to three-year term by Transitional National Assembly.
Serves as head of state.

Prime minister
Appointed by Transitional National Assembly.
Serves as head of government.

Cabinet
Composed of 31 members, appointed by prime minister and Transitional National Assembly.

JUDICIAL BRANCH

No official government courts.
Most regions adjudicate disputes and criminal cases with Shari'a Islamic law or traditional clan-based arbitration.

RWANDA

OFFICIAL NAME: REPUBLIC OF RWANDA

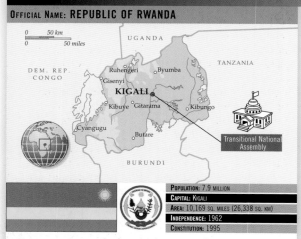

POPULATION: 7.9 MILLION	
CAPITAL: KIGALI	
AREA: 10,169 SQ. MILES (26,338 SQ. KM)	
INDEPENDENCE: 1962	
CONSTITUTION: 1995	

RWANDA is named after the language "kinyarwanda" which is spoken by the majority of the population.

RELIGION: Roman Catholic 56.5%, Protestant 26%, Adventist 11.1%, Muslim 4.6%, Indigenous beliefs 0.1%, None 1.7%

OFFICIAL LANGUAGES: French, English, and Kinyarwandan

REGIONS OR PROVINCES: 12 prefectures

DEPENDENT TERRITORIES: None

MEDIA: Total political censorship exists in national media

Newspapers: There is 1 daily newspaper

TV: 1 state-controlled service

Radio: 2 services: 1 state-controlled, 1 independent

SUFFRAGE: 18 years of age; universal adult

LEGAL SYSTEM: Customary law; Belgian and German law; no ICJ jurisdiction

WORLD ORGANIZATIONS: ACCT, ACP, AfDB, CCC, CEEAC, CEPGL, ECA, FAO, G-77, IBRD, ICAO, ICFTU, ICRM, IDA, IFAD, IFC, IFRCS, ILO, IMF, Interpol, IOC, IOM (observer), ISO (correspondent), ITU, NAM, OAU, OPCW (signatory), UN, UNCTAD, UNESCO, UNIDO, UPU, WCL, WHO, WIPO, WMO, WToO, WTrO

POLITICAL PARTIES: MRND—National Republican Movement for Development and Democracy

ETHNIC GROUPS:

Tutsi 9%
Other (including Twa) 1%
Hutu 90%

NATIONAL ECONOMICS

WORLD GNP RANKING: 138th

GNP PER CAPITA: $230

INFLATION: 4.3%

BALANCE OF PAYMENTS (BALANCE OF TRADE): -$7 million

EXCHANGE RATES / U.S. DLR.: 359.0-452.9 RWANDA FRANCS

OFFICIAL CURRENCY: RWANDA FRANC

GOVERNMENT SPENDING (% OF GDP)

DEFENSE 4.7%	
EDUCATION 1.8%	
HEALTH 2%	

0   5   10   15

NUMBER OF CONFLICTS OVER LAST 25 YEARS

	1	2-5	5+
Violent changes in government	●		
Civil wars		●	
International wars	●		
Foreign intervention	●		

- No compulsory national military service.
- War crimes tribunal was established to try cases of genocide.
- Instability along Democratic Republic of Congo and Burundi borders.
- Tensions with Uganda over troop presence in Democratic Republic of Congo.
- Attempting to demobilize troops.

NOTABLE WARS AND INSURGENCIES: Coup 1980. Tutsi insurgency 1990-1991. Genocide of Tutsis in 1994. Involved in civil war in Democratic Republic of Congo 1996-2002

SINCE RWANDA GAINED INDEPENDENCE from Belgium in 1962, politics have been dominated by tensions between two main ethnic groups, the Hutu and the Tutsi, who have struggled for centuries for control over the region. The property-owning Tutsi ruled for 500 years, causing intense resentment among the Hutu majority until a 1959 revolt caused a power reversal. A continuous cycle of warfare ensued, culminating in unprecedented violence in the 1990s that killed or displaced several hundred thousand Rwandans, leaving the government in shambles.

The 1993 Arusha Peace Accord, prompted after the civil war of 1990 by the Tutsi-led Rwandan Patriotic Front (FPR), provided a glimmer of hope for a democratic integration of opposing voices in a new transitional government. However, disputes quickly arose over the government's composition. Peace was shattered in April 1994, when President Juvenal Habyarimana was killed in an attack on his airplane, sparking an all-out war by Hutu militias on Tutsi and moderate Hutu civilians. An estimated 800,000 Rwandans were killed, while thousands were forced into exile. The economy and fragile democratic initiatives collapsed as much of the international community watched in silence.

The FPR gradually regained control. On July 19, 1994, it adopted the constitution of June 18, 1991, named a Hutu as president, and formed a coalition government based on the Arusha Accord and democratic ideals. Meanwhile, an estimated two million Hutu fled to neighboring countries, fearing Tutsi retribution. Disarming remaining Hutu militants, refurbishing a broken economy, addressing a growing AIDS epidemic, and reintegrating more than two million refugees are problems that continue to challenge the shaky republic. A United Nations war crimes tribunal established in 1995 continues to try the many people accused of genocide. In May 2003 Rwandans overwhelmingly approved a new constitution that led to the first multiparty presidential and parliamentary elections since the 1960s.

MASSACRE—DECEMBER 20, 1997
The bodies of Hutu rebels within the Bigogwe military base near Gisenyi, are passed by Rwandan soldiers. At least 50 people—mostly Hutu rebels—were killed in a battle with the army near two Tutsi refugee camps.

HOW THE GOVERNMENT WORKS

LEGISLATIVE BRANCH
Assemblée Nationale de Transition
(Transitional National Assembly) Unicameral Parliament
Composed of 74 members appointed by their parties under power-sharing Arusha Peace Accord.

Regional Governments
Twelve prefectures.

EXECUTIVE BRANCH
President
Elected to five-year term by direct popular vote. Serves as head of state. Presides over Council of Ministers.

Prime Minister
Appointed by president. Head of government.

Council of Ministers
Appointed by president on advice of national unity government's party leaders. Responsible for national affairs.

JUDICIAL BRANCH
Supreme Court

Constitutional Court
Council of State
Court of Appeals

BURUNDI

OFFICIAL NAME: REPUBLIC OF BURUNDI

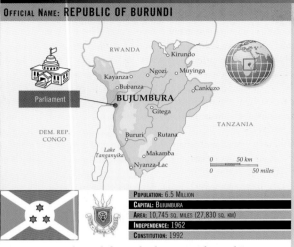

PARLIAMENT

BUJUMBURA

POPULATION: 6.5 MILLION
CAPITAL: BUJUMBURA
AREA: 10,745 SQ. MILES (27,830 SQ. KM)
INDEPENDENCE: 1962
CONSTITUTION: 1992

BURUNDI is derived from the language "kirundi", or "rundi" for short, that is spoken in the country.

RELIGION: Christian 67% (Roman Catholic 62%, Protestant 5%), Indigenous beliefs 23%, Muslim 10%

OFFICIAL LANGUAGES: French and Kirundi

REGIONS OR PROVINCES: 16 provinces

DEPENDENT TERRITORIES: None

MEDIA: Total political censorship exists in national media

Newspapers: There are no daily newspapers

TV: 1 state-controlled service

Radio: 1 state-controlled service, 2 independent stations

SUFFRAGE: 18 years of age; universal adult

LEGAL SYSTEM: Customary law and Belgian-German legal traditions; no ICJ jurisdiction

WORLD ORGANIZATIONS: ACCT, ACP, AfDB, CCC, CEEAC, CEPGL, ECA, FAO, G-77, IBRD, ICAO, ICRM, IDA, IFAD, IFC, IFRCS, ILO, IMF, Interpol, IOC, ITU, NAM, OAU, OPCW, UN, UNCTAD, UNESCO, UNIDO, UPU, WHO, WIPO, WMO, WToO, WTrO

POLITICAL PARTIES: Frodebu—Front for Democracy in Burundi, UPRONA—Union for National Progress

ETHNIC GROUPS:

Tutsi 14%
Twa 1%
Hutu 85%

NATIONAL ECONOMICS

WORLD GNP RANKING: 161th

GNP PER CAPITA: $110

INFLATION: 24.3%

BALANCE OF PAYMENTS (BALANCE OF TRADE): - $49 million

EXCHANGE RATES / U.S. DLR.: 780.4-864.0 BURUNDI FRANCS

OFFICIAL CURRENCY: BURUNDI FRANC

GOVERNMENT SPENDING (% OF GDP)

✈ DEFENSE 5.6%				
🎓 EDUCATION 3.9%				
✚ HEALTH 0.6%				
0	5	10	15	

NUMBER OF CONFLICTS OVER LAST 25 YEARS

	1	2-5	5+
Violent changes in government	○	●	○
Civil wars	○	●	○
International wars	●	○	○
Foreign intervention	○	○	○

• No compulsory national military service.
• Tutsi controlled army.
• Hutu and Tutsi tensions undermine peace.
• Significant numbers of child soldiers, being addressed by UNICEF program.

NOTABLE WARS AND INSURGENCIES: Coups 1987, 1993 and 1996. Ongoing interethnic violence between Hutus and Tutsis. Involvement in Democratic Republic of Congo in 1998

BURUNDI EMERGED FROM COLONIAL RULE IN 1962, but tribal strife, coups, assassinations, and massacres have dominated its decades of independence. Landlocked, Burundi is located on the Nile-Congo watershed, just south of the equator. The one-time African kingdom is struggling to construct a civil society under a tenuous peace accord and transitional government.

Home to the Hutu and Tutsi peoples, Burundi historically was ruled by a Tutsi monarchy. Migrating southward they asserted themselves over the indigenous Bantu people, the Hutu, that they found living in the area of modern-day Burundi. By the 20th century, the kingdom had become part of German East Africa. Following World War I, the League of Nations designated Burundi and neighbouring Rwanda a UN mandated territory under Belgian administration.

Burundi entered its first legislative elections in 1961 with the formation of two competing political parties: the Belgian-supported Christian Democratic Party and the Union for National Progress, led by Tutsi Prince Louis Rwagasore. The Tutsi party won at the polls, but Rwagasore was assassinated. An attempt to install a constitutional monarchy balanced between Hutus and Tutsis failed with the assassination of the Hutu prime minister and subsequent Hutu revolts, a series of coups and repressive military regimes, and a Hutu-Tutsi civil war in the 1980s killing more than 150,000 people.

Despite a multi-ethnic government, a new constitution and elections in the early 1990s, the assassination of the first Hutu president by the Tutsi-controlled military again plunged Burundi into civil war. The deaths of the presidents of both Burundi and Rwanda in a 1994 plane crash intensified fighting in Burundi and touched off a wave of genocide in Rwanda. Yet another Burundi coup brought international condemnation and regional mediations that produced the Arusha Peace Accords in 2000. The pact established a three-year multi-ethnic transitional government, but rebel Hutu factions refused to join the government until the main FDD group agreed a ceasefire in 2003. With demobilisation and disarmament finally underway, a new constitution paving the way for democratic elections, won popular approval in 2005.

ISSUES AND CHALLENGES:

• Continued fighting among Hutu and Tutsi leaves little prospect for political stability.

• Flight of thousands of refugees and a high birth rate leaves Burundi without adequate labor force and places pressure on its economy.

• Deforestation and severe soil erosion threaten Burundi's ecology and agriculture. Tree-planting initiatives and ecological education programs are in effect.

• While most Burundians live at the level of subsistence farming, Tutsi control the wealth and comprise the political and business elite.

HOW THE GOVERNMENT WORKS

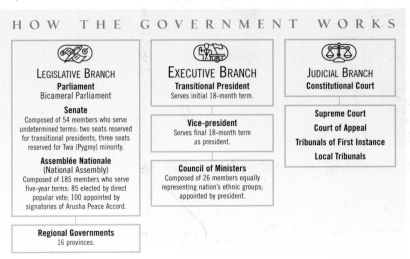

LEGISLATIVE BRANCH
Parliament
Bicameral Parliament

Senate
Composed of 54 members who serve undetermined terms: two seats reserved for transitional presidents, three seats reserved for Twa (Pygmy) minority.

Assemblée Nationale
(National Assembly)
Composed of 185 members who serve five-year terms: 85 elected by direct popular vote; 100 appointed by signatories of Arusha Peace Accord.

Regional Governments
16 provinces.

EXECUTIVE BRANCH
Transitional President
Serves initial 18-month term.

Vice-president
Serves final 18-month term as president.

Council of Ministers
Composed of 26 members equally representing nation's ethnic groups; appointed by president.

JUDICIAL BRANCH
Constitutional Court

Supreme Court
Court of Appeal
Tribunals of First Instance
Local Tribunals

ERITREA

OFFICIAL NAME: STATE OF ERITREA

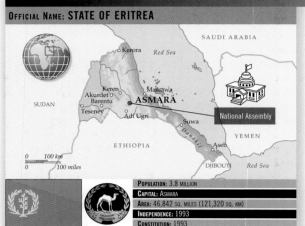

SAUDI ARABIA

Red Sea

Kerora

Keren
Akurdet
Barentu
Teseney
Adi Ugri

Massawa

ASMARA

National Assembly

SUDAN

Suwa

Danakil

YEMEN

ETHIOPIA

Aseb

DJIBOUTI   Red Sea

0   100 km
0   100 miles

| POPULATION: 3.8 MILLION |
| CAPITAL: ASMARA |
| AREA: 46,842 SQ. MILES (121,320 SQ. KM) |
| INDEPENDENCE: 1993 |
| CONSTITUTION: 1993 |

ERITREA is derived from the Latin "Mare Erythraeum" meaning "red sea" which Italy used to describe its colonies located on the Red Sea.

RELIGION: Muslim 45%, Christian 45%, Other 10%

OFFICIAL LANGUAGE: Tigrinya

REGIONS OR PROVINCES: 6 regions

DEPENDENT TERRITORIES: None

MEDIA: Total political censorship exists in national media

NEWSPAPERS: One newspaper is published every 3 days in English, Tigrinya, and Arabic. Independent newspapers are not encouraged.

TV: 1 state-controlled service

RADIO: 1 state-controlled service

SUFFRAGE: 18 years of age; universal

LEGAL SYSTEM: Customary and Shari'a (Islamic) law; Ethiopian legal traditions; no ICJ jurisdiction

WORLD ORGANIZATIONS: ACP, AfDB, CCC, ECA, FAO, IBRD, ICAO, ICFTU, IDA, IFAD, IFC, IFRCS (associate), IGAD, ILO, IMF, IMO, Interpol, IOC, ITU, NAM, OAU, OPCW, PCA, UN, UNCTAD, UNESCO, UNIDO, UPU, WFTU, WHO, WIPO, WMO, WToO

POLITICAL PARTIES: PFDJ—People's Front for Democracy and Justice

ETHNIC GROUPS:

Afar 4%
Saho 3%
Other 3%
Ethnic Tigrinya 50%
Tigre and Kunama 40%

NATIONAL ECONOMICS

WORLD GNP RANKING: 162nd

GNP PER CAPITA: $170

INFLATION: 14.0%

BALANCE OF PAYMENTS (BALANCE OF TRADE): -$208 million

EXCHANGE RATES / U.S. DLR.: 10.2-13.55 NAKFA

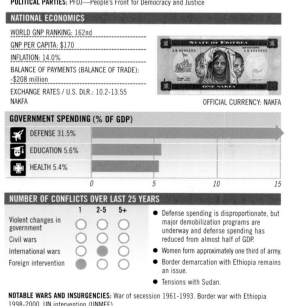

STATE OF ERITREA
A 8 4045550   A 8 4045550
ONE NAKFA

OFFICIAL CURRENCY: NAKFA

GOVERNMENT SPENDING (% OF GDP)

DEFENSE 31.5%
EDUCATION 5.6%
HEALTH 5.4%

0   5   10   15

NUMBER OF CONFLICTS OVER LAST 25 YEARS

	1	2-5	5+
Violent changes in government	○	○	○
Civil wars	○	○	○
International wars	○	●	○
Foreign intervention	●	○	○

● Defense spending is disproportionate, but major demobilization programs are underway and defense spending has reduced from almost half of GDP.

● Women form approximately one third of army.

● Border demarcation with Ethiopia remains an issue.

● Tensions with Sudan.

NOTABLE WARS AND INSURGENCIES: War of secession 1961-1993. Border war with Ethiopia 1998-2000. UN intervention (UNMEE)

AN ITALIAN COLONY FROM 1885, Eritrea became a federated part of Ethiopia in 1952. Haile Selassie's dissolution of the Eritrean parliament in 1962 triggered a 30-year war of independence led by the Eritrean People's Liberation Front (EPLF). It was the EPLF that dominated the provisional government established in 1991 at the end of the war. In 1993, the Eritrean people voted for independence and a transition to democracy and democratic institutions, including a constitution, elections, political parties, and a free press.

The EPLF's strong organization and morale helped stabilize the emerging nation. During the war, the party created viable social, medical, and economic institutions behind the front lines. This experience was essential to its successful exercise of political control as the provisional government. During the transition, the hegemony of the EPLF—renamed the Popular Front for Democracy and Justice (PFDJ)—helped make Eritrea one of East Africa's more peaceful countries.

However, the PFDJ's pervasive control has slowed progress toward democracy. The only president since independence has been PFDJ chairman Issaias Afewerki. Half of the National Assembly is made up of appointed members from the PFDJ, and the body meets infrequently. The president and the appointed State Council, or cabinet, run daily business otherwise. A 1997 constitution was ratified but has not been implemented. The judiciary is nominally independent, but its president was detained in 2001 for protesting government interference. Even PFDJ members have been punished for dissent. After criticizing the government's autocratic style in an open letter in 2001, 11 party dissidents were detained without charges and held incommunicado. The independent press was shut down, and journalists were similarly detained in the crackdown that followed. More than 300 people remained in prison without charges in May 2003. Alongside political tension, there is the potential for religious strife, but Afwerki, a Christian himself, has been careful to include Muslims in his transitional State Council.

Eritrea spends the highest percentage of its GDP on defense—more than any nation in the world

ISSUES AND CHALLENGES:

● War and continuing tension with Ethiopia have set back development. Massawa port was heavily bombed in the 1998–2000 conflict.

● Rebuilding economic and energy infrastructure.

● Reintegrating about 750,000 refugees from the Sudan, Western Europe, and the United States.

● Redeploying over 85,000 fighters to productive, peace-time activity.

● Achieving food self-sufficiency in the face of erratic rain, locust plagues, and widespread soil erosion.

● Resolving border disputes, and defining its relationship, with Ethiopia.

HOW THE GOVERNMENT WORKS

LEGISLATIVE BRANCH
Baito
(National Assembly)
Unicameral Parliament
Composed of 150 members who serve terms of undetermined length: 75 elected by direct popular vote; 75 central committee members of People's Front for Democracy and Justice. Sets and regulates government's internal and external policies; approves budget; ratifies presidential appointments.

Regional Governments
Six regions administered by local assemblies appointed by Eritrean People's Liberation Front.

EXECUTIVE BRANCH
President
Elected by National Assembly. Serves as head of state and government; commander-in-chief of armed forces. Presides over parliament and State Council; nominates heads of ministries, authorities, commissions and offices.

State Council
Composed of 17 members appointed by president. Implements government policies and laws; answers to National Assembly.

JUDICIAL BRANCH
Supreme Court

Regional Courts
District Courts
Village Courts
Military Courts

LIBERIA

OFFICIAL NAME: REPUBLIC OF LIBERIA

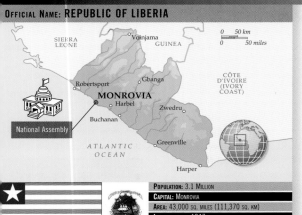

National Assembly

LIBERIA is derived from the Latin word "liber", and means "land of the free" referring to the liberated American slaves who founded it.

POPULATION: 3.1 Million
CAPITAL: Monrovia
AREA: 43,000 SQ. MILES (111,370 SQ. KM)
INDEPENDENCE: 1847
CONSTITUTION: 1986

RELIGION: Indigenous beliefs 40%, Christian 40%, Muslim 20%

OFFICIAL LANGUAGE: English

REGIONS OR PROVINCES: 13 counties

DEPENDENT TERRITORIES: None

MEDIA: Total political censorship exists in national media

Newspapers: There are 7 daily newspapers

TV: 2 services

Radio: 6 services: 1 state-owned, 5 independent

SUFFRAGE: 18 years of age; universal

LEGAL SYSTEM: Tribal-based customary law; American legal traditions; accepts ICJ jurisdiction

WORLD ORGANIZATIONS: ACP, AfDB, CCC, ECA, ECOWAS, FAO, G-77, IAEA, IBRD, ICAO, ICFTU, ICRM, IDA, IFAD, IFC, IFRCS, ILO, IMF, IMO, Interpol, IOC, IOM, ITU, NAM, OAU, OPCW (signatory), UN, UNCTAD, UNESCO, UNIDO, UPU, WCL, WFTU, WHO, WIPO, WMO

POLITICAL PARTIES: NPP—National Patriotic Party, UP—Unity Party, ALCP—All Liberia Coalition Party, LAP—Liberia Action Party

ETHNIC GROUPS:

Americo-Liberians 5%

Indigenous tribes (16 main groups) 95%

NATIONAL ECONOMICS

WORLD GNP RANKING: 153th

GNP PER CAPITA: $330

INFLATION: 5.0%

BALANCE OF PAYMENTS (BALANCE OF TRADE): -$145 million

EXCHANGE RATES / U.S. DLR.: 1 LIBERIAN DOLLAR

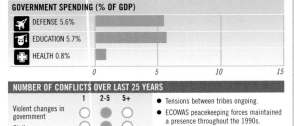

OFFICIAL CURRENCY: LIBERIAN DOLLAR

GOVERNMENT SPENDING (% OF GDP)

✈ DEFENSE 5.6%		
🎓 EDUCATION 5.7%		
✚ HEALTH 0.8%		

0   5   10   15

NUMBER OF CONFLICTS OVER LAST 25 YEARS

	1	2-5	5+
Violent changes in government	○	●	○
Civil wars	○	●	○
International wars	○	●	○
Foreign intervention	○	●	○

● Tensions between tribes ongoing.
● ECOWAS peacekeeping forces maintained a presence throughout the 1990s.
● Instability along borders with Sierra Leone, Guinea and Cote d'Ivoire.

NOTABLE WARS AND INSURGENCIES: Coup 1980. Civil war 1989-1995 and 1997-2003. Economic Community of West African States (ECOWAS) peacekeeping force (mainly Nigerian) 1990-1997. ECOWAS and US peacekeepers 2003

LIKE ITS NEIGHBOR SIERRA LEONE, LIBERIA was created as a refuge for slaves freed from bondage in North America. And like that of Sierra Leone, Liberia's recent history has been marred by civil war and seemingly insurmountable political challenges. First discovered by Portuguese explorers in 1461, who named it the Grain Coast after the abundant pepper grains, Liberia remained uncolonized until 1820 when the first freed slaves established Monrovia. From 1847 to 1980, Liberia was organized as a republic on US lines, despite incursions by local African tribes and the expansionist moves of colonialists. It maintained a largely peaceful existence, ruled as a one-party state by the Americo-Liberian True Whig Party (TWP). The first president was Joseph Jenkins Roberts, born in Norfolk, Virginia.

In April 1980, Samuel K. Doe led a coup that eventually established a military regime, which lasted until Doe's assassination in 1990 by rebels of Charles Taylor's National Patriotic Front of Liberia (NPFL). Political instability and fragmentation immediately aggravated ethnic tensions and plunged the country into a bloody civil war in which many factions fought one another simultaneously. Peace agreements in 1996 ended seven years of armed conflict and restored free and open elections to establish a republican government, again based on the American system. The NPFL, the largest armed group of the civil war, was voted into power with 80 percent of the ballot and with Charles Taylor as president. Political instability continued, however, and armed rebellion resumed on a large scale in 2000.

In 2003, ECOWAS and US peacekeepers arrived and strong international pressure forced Taylor, who had been accused of war crimes, into exile. A transitional government was installed under Gyude Bryant, a businessman who professes political neutrality. He has been leader of the Liberia Action Party since 1992 and was a strong critic of both Doe and Taylor during their tenure of power.

Liberia faces huge challenges. Aside from pacifying and integrating warring ethnic factions, the government must rebuild infrastructure and social services. Perhaps most important, Liberia must convince the international community of its dedication to peace—at home and in the region—to attract renewed foreign aid.

ISSUES AND CHALLENGES:

● Liberia's natural resources, including diamonds and iron ore, are generally underexploited. Diamond's are subject to smuggling while world iron prices are too low to make the necessary investment worthwhile.

● Internal security has displaced thousands and wiped out investor confidence.

● International aid is vital to securing the country's future.

● Armed insurgents need to be disarmed and demobilized to provide lasting security.

HOW THE GOVERNMENT WORKS

LEGISLATIVE BRANCH

National Assembly
Bicameral Parliament

Senate
Composed of 26 members elected to nine-year terms by direct popular vote: two each from 13 counties.

House of Representatives
Composed of 64 members directly elected to six-year terms by proportional representation.

Regional Governments
Thirteen counties administered by local councils and superintendents appointed by president; towns overseen by chiefs.

EXECUTIVE BRANCH

President
Elected to six-year term by direct popular vote. Serves as head of state and government; commander-in-chief of armed forces. Signs and vetoes bills.

Cabinet
Composed of 16 members appointed by president, approved by the Senate. Oversees government operations.

JUDICIAL BRANCH

The Supreme Court
Highest court of review and appeal. Comprises five justices appointed by president, approved by Senate.

Magistrates' Courts
Judges appointed by president, approved by Senate.

Circuit Courts
Judges appointed by president, approved by Senate.

BAHRAIN

OFFICIAL NAME: STATE OF BAHRAIN

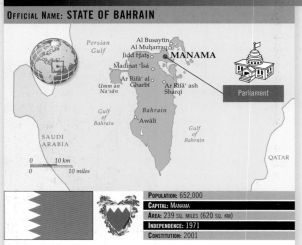

Persian Gulf
Al Busaytin
Al Muharraq
Jidd Hafs
MANAMA
Madinat 'Isa
Ar Rifa' al Gharbi
Umm an Na'san
Ar Rifa' ash Sharqi
Gulf of Bahrain
Bahrain
Awali
SAUDI ARABIA
Gulf of Bahrain
QATAR

Parliament

0   10 km
0   10 miles

POPULATION: 652,000	
CAPITAL: MANAMA	
AREA: 239 SQ. MILES (620 SQ. KM)	
INDEPENDENCE: 1971	
CONSTITUTION: 2001	

BAHRAIN is derived from an Arabic word that means "the two seas".

RELIGION: Shi'a Muslim 70%, Sunni Muslim 30%

OFFICIAL LANGUAGE: Arabic

REGIONS OR PROVINCES: 12 municipalities

DEPENDENT TERRITORIES: None

MEDIA: Total political censorship exists in national media

Newspapers: There are 5 daily newspapers

TV: 1 state-owned service

Radio: 2 services: 1 state-owned, 1 independent

SUFFRAGE: None

LEGAL SYSTEM: Shari'a (Islamic) and English common law; no ICJ jurisdiction

WORLD ORGANIZATIONS: ABEDA, AFESD, AL, AMF, CCC, ESCWA, FAO, G-77, GCC, IBRD, ICAO, ICC, ICRM, IDB, IFC, IFRCS, IHO, ILO, IMF, IMO, Interpol, IOC, ISO (correspondent), ITU, NAM, OAPEC, OIC, OPCW, UN, UNCTAD, UNESCO, UNIDO, UPU, WFTU, WHO, WIPO, WMO, WToO, WTrO

POLITICAL PARTIES: Political parties are prohibited but politically oriented nongovernmental organizations are allowed

ETHNIC GROUPS:

Other Arab 4%
European 2%
Iranian, Indian, Pakistani 24%
Bahraini 70%

NATIONAL ECONOMICS

WORLD GNP RANKING: 110th	
GNP PER CAPITA: $7,640	
INFLATION: -0.4%	
BALANCE OF PAYMENTS (BALANCE OF TRADE): $113 million	
EXCHANGE RATES / U.S. DLR.: 0.3770-0.3771 BAHRAINI DINARS	

OFFICIAL CURRENCY: BAHRAINI DINAR

GOVERNMENT SPENDING (% OF GDP)

- DEFENSE 6.4%
- EDUCATION 4.4%
- HEALTH 2.6%

0   5   10   15

NUMBER OF CONFLICTS OVER LAST 25 YEARS

	1	2-5	5+
Violent changes in government	○	○	○
Civil wars	○	○	○
International wars	○	○	○
Foreign intervention	○	○	○

- No compulsory national military service.
- Provided assistance in war on terrorism.
- US maintains a naval and air force base.
- Signed Defense Cooperation Agreement with US.
- Ongoing tensions with Iran.

NOTABLE WARS AND INSURGENCIES: None

AN ISLAND NATION SITUATED IN THE PERSIAN GULF, Bahrain is ruled by the al-Khalifa family, which has dominated government and politics since 1783, even under the period of under British rule from 1861 until independence in 1971. While 70 percent of the population is Shi'a Muslim, the remaining 30 percent Sunni Muslim minority forms the elite. Sunnis are employed in most of the business and government jobs, while the generally poorer Shi'a tend to hold the more menial positions. The disparity caused sporadic outbursts of protest and general unrest throughout the second half of the 20th century.

A surge of conflicts starting in 1991 appeared to have mainly sectarian overtones, but in fact were rooted in both the economic situation among Shi'a workers calling for a more equitable society, and the demands of the educated class for restoration of the short-lived elected parliament which had been dissolved in 1975. This wave of unrest was marked by increased violence and by intensified resistance from protesters in 1994, when key Shi'a leaders opposed to the regime were arrested. Shaikh Hamad—amir since 1999—has responded with positive reforms in recent years and supported the economic liberalization begun by his father.

The amir functions as head of state and commander-in-chief of the armed forces, but has been advised by a Consultative Council since 1993. A charter of political reforms was approved by the council in 2000, and was supported by a popular referendum in 2001. Also in 2001, the State Security Law was repealed, indicating an end to the imprisonment of political dissidents—mainly Shi'a Muslims. As a direct result of the charter, Bahrain was declared a constitutional monarchy in 2002, leading to elections for a 40-member Council of Deputies that included a dozen Shi'a. Other political reforms have been put in place to encourage foreign investment and support the private sector.

> Bahrain is the smallest and most densely populated Arab state.

ELECTIONS—OCTOBER 2003
The poster shows a candidate running for the first parliamentary elections to be held since 1975. Below: A woman casts her vote at a polling station. This is the first time women have been allowed to vote and run in elections.

HOW THE GOVERNMENT WORKS

LEGISLATIVE BRANCH

Parliament
Bicameral

Consultative Council
Composed of 40 members appointed by amir. Discusses social, educational, health and cultural issues; advises Cabinet on policy.

House of Deputies
Composed of 40 members elected to four-year terms by direct popular vote.

Regional Governments
Five governorates administered jointly by governors appointed by amir and minister of state for municipalities and the environment.

EXECUTIVE BRANCH

Amir
Position is hereditary.
Serves as head of state; commander-in-chief of armed forces.

Prime Minister
Appointed by amir.
Serves as head of government.

Cabinet
Appointed by amir.

JUDICIAL BRANCH

Supreme Judicial Council
Established by amir to regulate nation's religious and civil courts.

MALDIVES

OFFICIAL NAME: REPUBLIC OF MALDIVES

FOR CENTURIES, THE MALDIVES WERE RULED as an Islamic sultanate. Today, the nation of some 1,190 coral islands—of which only 200 are inhabited—located in the Indian Ocean southwest of India, has fashioned a government that seeks to blend democratic institutions with Islamic principles. The first settlers are thought to have arrived from southern India and Sri Lanka. By the 12th century, sailors from East Africa and Arab countries brought their culture, language, and religion to the Maldives. Before the century's close, most Maldivians had converted from Buddhism to Sunni Islam.

After seven decades as a British protectorate, the Maldives secured independence in 1965 and replaced the sultan with a president—Ibrahim Nasir, who ruled for two terms from 1968 to 1978, a cabinet, a unicameral legislature, and a judiciary. Islam remains the strictly enforced national religion. Constitutionally, the president is "the supreme authority to propagate the tenets of Islam." Moreover, judges interpret and apply the shari'a in the adjudication of civil and criminal cases. Trials are conducted and verdicts rendered by judges instead of citizen juries. Criminal sentences can range from flogging and banishment to remote islands to fines, house arrest, and imprisonment.

Politics and government in the Maldives are dominated by a small elite of influential families and powerful clans. There are no organized political parties, and elections for the legislature and presidency are nonpartisan. Candidates run as independents and campaign on their connections and personal qualifications.

Charges of nepotism and corruption have been common in recent years, and several coups have been attempted since independence, including one in 1988, when the Maldives called on nearby India for troops to quell the uprising. A younger generation continues to press for reforms, but proposals for liberalization have been largely rejected by the entrenched ruling class and President Maumoon Abdul Gayoon.. However, internal and international pressures finally led to the announcement of a democratic, multi-party system in 2005.

ISSUES AND CHALLENGES:

- The lack of skilled Maldivian workers remains a stubborn obstacle to the nation's economic growth.

- With 80 percent of Maldives' low-lying countryside just one meter or less above sea level, erosion and rising ocean levels from global warming are a growing worry.

- Protection of the Maldives' fragile environment, especially its coastlines and coral reefs, is an ongoing challenge for maintaining the nation's dominant fisheries and tourism industries.

- Narrowing the wide standard-of-living gap between residents of the prosperous main island of Male' and those living on the Maldives' undeveloped outer atolls will require substantial investments in education and infrastructure construction.

MALDIVES means "thousand islands" and is derived from the Sanskrit words "mal" which means thousand and "diva" meaning island.

POPULATION: 300,000
CAPITAL: MALÉ
AREA: 116 SQ. MILES (300 SQ. KM)
INDEPENDENCE: 1965
CONSTITUTION: 1998

RELIGION: Sunni Muslim 100%

OFFICIAL LANGUAGE: Dhivehi

REGIONS OR PROVINCES: 19 atolls and 1 other first-order administrative division

DEPENDENT TERRITORIES: None

MEDIA: There is a marked degree of press self-censorship; in the past, journalists have been imprisoned. An internet cafe opened in 1998.

NEWSPAPERS: There are 3 daily newspapers

TV: 1 state-owned service

RADIO: 2 services

SUFFRAGE: 21 years of age; universal

LEGAL SYSTEM: Shari'a (Islamic) and English common law; no ICJ jurisdiction

WORLD ORGANIZATIONS: AsDB, C, CCC, CP, ESCAP, FAO, G-77, IBRD, ICAO, IDA, IDB, IFAD, IFC, IMF, IMO, Interpol, IOC, ITU, NAM, OIC, OPCW, SAARC, UN, UNCTAD, UNESCO, UNIDO, UPU, WHO, WMO, WToO, WTrO

POLITICAL PARTIES: None

ETHNIC GROUPS:

Mixed Arab, Sinhalese, Malay 100%

NATIONAL ECONOMICS

WORLD GNP RANKING: 170th

GNP PER CAPITA: $1,960

INFLATION: -1.1%

BALANCE OF PAYMENTS (BALANCE OF TRADE): -$60 million

EXCHANGE RATES / U.S. DLR.: 11.77 RUFIYAA

OFFICIAL CURRENCY: RUFIYAA

GOVERNMENT SPENDING (% OF GDP)

DEFENSE	9.5%	
EDUCATION	6.4%	
HEALTH	3.7%	

0   5   10   15

NUMBER OF CONFLICTS OVER LAST 25 YEARS

	1	2-5	5+
Violent changes in government	○	○	○
Civil wars	○	○	○
International wars	○	○	○
Foreign intervention	●	○	○

- No compulsory national military service.
- Concerns with Islamist militants.
- India has provided military assistance.
- Generally non-aligned.
- National Security Service maintains security.

NOTABLE WARS AND INSURGENCIES: India helped to suppress coup 1988

HOW THE GOVERNMENT WORKS

LEGISLATIVE BRANCH

Majlis
(People's Council)
Unicameral Parliament
Composed of 50 members who serve five-year terms: 42 elected by direct popular vote; eight appointed by president.

Regional Governments
Nineteen atolls each administered by chief appointed by president.

EXECUTIVE BRANCH

President
Nominated by secret ballot by parliament, elected to five-year term by popular vote in national referendum. Serves as head of state and government; commander-in-chief of armed forces. Oversees treasury and monetary authority; grants pardons; signs or vetoes bills; overturns High Court rulings.

Cabinet of Ministers
Composed of 24 members appointed by president. Oversees government operations; answers to parliament.

JUDICIAL BRANCH

High Court of the Maldives
Highest court of review and appeal. Composed of three justices appointed by president.

Civil Court
Criminal Court
Family and Juvenile Court

GLOSSARY OF POLITICAL TERMS

Amir (Emir) The ruler of a Muslim state, or a person in high office, as in *amir al-hajj*, "leader of the pilgrimage." It is also used to denote a male descendant of the Prophet Muhammad.

Anarchy A belief in the liberation of the individual from the bonds of governmental authority. The movement, strong in the 19th century, often resorted to violence. It went into decline after World War II.

Apartheid Policy in which the peoples of South Africa were divided into four racial groups, then forced into segregation under the control of the white racial group. The system was enforced by the government between the years 1948 and 1989.

Appellate A court of law that has the power to review the decisions of a lower court.

Apportionment The basis on which voters are represented in their legislatures. Generally, votes are apportioned according to constituency boundaries.

Autocracy A form of government that is absolute and above the control of law. Unlimited power is invested in one person.

Autonomy Self-government, used generally to describe the degree of political independence possessed by a minority group.

Balance of payments The difference over a specified period of time between the funds received by a country and those that the country pays. It includes the balance of trade.

Balance of trade The difference over a specified period of time between the value of the imports and exports of a country.

Bilateralism An agreement that affects reciprocally two groups, states or nations.

Bipartisan Represents, or is composed of, members of two political groups, holding views shared by both parties or members of both parties.

Cabinet In the UK, a body consisting of the prime minister and senior ministers who formulate government policy. In the US, a body consisting of the heads of the executive departments of government, who advise the president.

Capitalism The economic process is entrusted to private initiative for private profit, so the means of production—land, mines and industry—are controlled by individuals or private corporations.

Cassation In law, quashing, annulling, or reversing a decision. In France, the Court of Cassation is the name of the court of appeal.

Centralization The concentration of administrative authority under one central control.

Chief of State The formal head of a national state, as distinguished from the head of government.

City-state A self-governing city, often allowing government through the assembled body of its citizens. Favored in Ancient Greece and medieval Europe.

Coalition An alliance or temporary union for joint action by various powers or states, or the union in a single government of distinct parties.

Cold War The period between 1945 and 1989 of intense hostility between the Western and Soviet blocs, a conflict characterized by threats, obstruction and propaganda yet with little direct military violence.

Collectivism A belief that gives priority to the community and its rights over those of the individual, leading to a political theory that land and the means of production be owned by the community or central government for the benefit of the people as a whole.

Colonial A state with the characteristics of a colony, an area or people dependent on an external power. In American history, relates to that period when the 13 colonies were still under British control

Common law The unwritten law of England, based on ancient and universal usage, embodied in commentaries, precedent and reported cases.

Commonwealth A loose association or federation of autonomous states under a common allegiance, specifically an association of Britain and independent states that were its former colonies.

Communism A system that denies private ownership, claiming the right of the state to own, and to control through the equitable division of labor, all means of production, distribution and consumption. It was the ideology of the Soviet Union.

Constituency A body of voters who elect a representative member of a public body; the electoral district in which the voters reside.

Constitution The system of principles that defines the legislative, judicial and executive powers of a state or nation.

Council of Ministers A group of senior government ministers who advise the head of government or head of state.

Coup Abbreviation of *coup d'état*, meaning a change of government through violent or illegal means, often by the military.

Court of Appeal The court ruling on appeals against the decisions of lower courts.

Court of first instance The court in which legal proceedings are started.

Customary Law Old, continually practised customs given, by common consent, legal authority.

Decentralization To distribute administrative authority away from a central control point.

De facto A matter of fact, recognizing the reality of existence, possession or force.

De Jure By right, according to law.

Dependent territories Non-sovereign states, often former colonies, under the protection of another state, usually the previous colonial power.

Dependency A state or nation subordinate to another.

Despotism The absolute rule of a country, often associated with a tyrannical leader, or despot.

Dictatorship Government by an absolute ruler (dictator) who has seized power through un-constitutional means, or takes power in times of national emergency.

Direct elections The votes of the people made without modification by other layers of officialdom or the intervention of any representative.

Due Process Legal proceedings carried out in accordance with established rules and proceedings.

Dynasty A powerful group or family that maintains its position over successive generations.

Executive Those who carry out, but do not formulate, laws, decrees, and judicial sentences.

Fascism A belligerent nationalist movement led by Mussolini in Italy in the early 20th century. Depending on rule by dictatorship, the nation was believed superior to others, war was glorified and power-politics ensured oppressive measures for "the benefit of the people." The term is now associated with any form of right-wing, repressive nationalism.

Federal A form of government in which two or more states accept a political unity and shared responsibilities, while each state retains other levels of independent power and authority. The US has a federal form of government.

Feudalism A system, common in medieval Europe, Russia and parts of Asia in which the division and tenure of land into feuds or fiefs were made in exchange for military duties demanded by a monarch or superior ruler. Land owners were served, and their land was worked, by serfs with few rights to choose their employment, leave the feud or own land . Feudalism survived in Russia until 1918 and in Japan the system was finally abolished in 1871.

Fiefdom Formerly referred to a feudal estate and its owner, but now used to denote an illicit control of political, personal power over a geographic area, tribe, community, group or company. Somali warlords are described as running their own fiefdoms.

Filibuster To practise obstruction or delaying tactics in a legislative assembly.

First-Past-The-Post System / Winner takes all An electoral system in which the candidate with a simple majority wins.

Globalization An intense, aggressive pursuit, and extension of trade across international borders, perceived either as a system disdainful of, or even destructive toward local custom and practise, or as a force distributing wealth and modernity across the globe.

GDP Total value of domestic goods and services, but excluding foreign assets or investments produced in a country within a specified time, usually a year.

GNP Total value, including foreign assets and investments, of goods and services produced by a country within a specified time, usually a year.

Governorates The counties or provinces forming administrative units in Egypt and other states of the Middle East.

Guerrilla A combatant who is part of an irregular fighting unit, often participating in an irregular war aiming to achieve political objectives but sometimes formed to fight an invader with superior arms and regular forces.

Head of Government The leader of the government.

Head of State The titular head of state, such as a monarch, but not the leader or head of government.

Hegemony The leadership or predominance of one state over others, usually within a confederacy of states.

Imperialism Government by an emperor or empress, but also applied to the extension of political and economic power leading to the dominance of one nation over other territories and nations.

Inauguration introduce into office with ceremony, as can be seen at the start of a presidential term in the United States.

Indirectly elected Chosen to office not by those to be represented but by others, possibly using methods neither open nor honest.

Inflation A substantial and continuing rise in the level of prices, caused by an increase in the supply of money and credit, or a rapid growth in the economy

Interim Used in financial context, something given or announced part way through the financial year; also, denotes temporary or provisional conditions.

Investiture A formal ceremony confirming or establishing an honour or office on someone.

Isolationism A national policy of withdrawal from foreign affairs, trade or imports.

Judicial review A court investigation and judgement, often into public or political events.

Junta A political group or committee that takes political control, generally after a revolution or coup.

Jurisprudence The science and philosophy of law.

Legislature The ruling body, historically made up of selected officials but in modern democracies the elected government granted the power to make and enact laws.

Liberal Describes one who is not narrow in opinion or judgement, and who challenges orthodox views. Politically, this translates into the belief that liberty and human rights are the responsibility of the state.

Mandate The authority given by the electorate to the party with the majority vote. Also, under the League of Nations, the act of entrusting the control and protection of one state or territory to another, so that before the World War II the territory of Palestine was under the mandate of Britain.

Militarism A high regard for military virtues, and a belief that military efficiency should be of paramount interest to the state. Carried to extremes, may regard military action as superior to diplomatic methods.

Multilateralism The participation of more than two groups in reaching mutually acceptable aims or cooperating in shared political actions.

Nationalism Love of, and loyalty to one's nation, which when given intense political expression may be interpreted as xenophobic, racist or fascist.

Nation-state An area defined by its borders or coastline, the inhabitants assuming a common culture and language, and having the right to govern and defend itself.

Nepotism The habit of the governing class to favour its relatives with honor and and to employ family members in preference to other candidates, even when these are better qualified.

Oligarchy A state, corporation, or place controlled by a small group, often a family, which uses its power for the purpose of self-advancement.

Opposition The main political party opposing the administration of the party in government.

Plebiscite A direct vote of the electors of a state or district on a matter of public importance, although result of the vote does not always force a binding decision

Pluralism A society made up of diverse groups, each maintaining their own cultures under the governing umbrella of one civilization

Plurality The holding of two or more offices by one person. Also, in the US the right to give more than one vote, or to count the votes of more than one constituency. Allowed when an inconclusive result is found in the votes of one of the constituencies.

Plutocracy Government controlled by wealth or a wealthy elite.

Polity A country or state in which the government is perceived as a civil, politically organised unit.

Popular vote When the result of voting in, or for the legislature is suited to the taste, needs, means or understanding of the general public and so greeted with satisfaction.

Privatization A policy in which the state reverts or transfers nationally owned services or the means of production and distribution to private or corporate ownership.

Proletariat The class of laboring wage earners who have no assets in property or capital. The ideas behind Marx's philosophy, collectivism, and communism, aimed to improve the condition of this class by eliminating those who did own land and money.

Propaganda The deliberate and systematic spread of information, or suppression of information, to spread a particular doctrine or political ideal. In the Roman Catholic Church, a committee of Cardinals charged with the care of missionaries abroad.

Proportional representation An electoral system where the number of votes won, not by a single representative, but by a political party, are counted and the count determines the number of party representatives returned to the government.

Protectorate A territory or country, generally inhabited by a vulnerable people, that is seized by, or placed under the protection of a superior power. Some colonies, such as the former Bechuanaland now Botswana, were designated as Protectorates under the British Empire.

Proxy The authority, usually written in a document giving an individual or official the freedom to act as a substitute for another person. May be used to vote, substitute for bride or groom in a marriage ceremony or to control financial affairs of another person. Historically, members of the British House of Lords were allowed to vote by proxy.

uestion time Time allotted in the UK House of ommons during which the prime minister or another inister is questioned on policy or matters of public ncern by members of the House. Modern practice nds to use this time to pit the leader of the pposition against the prime minister.

uorum The minimum number of members of a dy that must assemble together before the oceedings or any decisions can be considered nstitutionally valid.

eapportionment In the US, a change in the oportional distribution of seats in the legislative body, pecially in the House of Representatives, on the basis population, a system considered by the European nion during successive phases of its growth.

ecession A period of reduced economic activity d prosperity.

eferendum A vote open to every voter on a single sue or question opened by the legislature metimes as the result of public demand. The vote binding on the legislature.

eform The legislative body which undertakes to end a faulty piece of legislature, a corrupt or pressive practice, or institute or ensure the removal abuse or wrongdoing.

epublic A state in which government and supreme wer rests with the people, their attitudes and needs pressed through their elected representatives. This es not allow for an hereditary rule.r

evolution A fundamental change of government, ought about by those who live under that vernment. It is a sudden, complete and often olent overthrow of the established institutions to be placed by a new ruler or form of government.

un-off election A last and final contest to decide a evious inconclusive contes.t

anctions An economic withdrawal and, sometimes ilitary action undertaken to threaten and compel a tion to comply with widely accepted moral andards or international law. Trade and cultural nctions helped to erode the apartheid system that ce prevailed in South Africa.

ecession The act of seceding or withdrawing rmally from an alliance, a federation, a political or ligious group. The attempted secession of 11 uthern States from the United States of America d to the American Civil War (1861-1865.

ecular State When the government and legal stem is separated from control of the priests or the ligious establishment. The state's values are based systems and a morality not overtly drawn from ligious examples. After the Revolution of 1789 ance was declared a secular state, despite the eep, abiding faith of the populace and the power ey believed resided in the Church. Communist ates are also typically secular.

enate The upper and smaller division of the gislature, forming an assembly that is given high uthority to scrutinise legislation and inhibit the power the lower, larger house. An elected senate is part of e system in the United States, France, Italy and her democracies.

eparation of powers To divide the areas of uthority between church and state, or between the mestic and federal areas of power in a mmonwealth, union or federation of states.

haikh (Sheikh) An Arab leader who is head of a family clan;lso a general title of respect among Arabs.

ocialism A system that believed the state should wn services and the means of production and stribution, in order to ensure the welfare of the ople. In Europe, this was achieved by consent and nctioned within a controlled capitalism. ommunism, which held a similar philosophy elieved in the violent overthrow of all capitalist ements within the economy.

Sovereign state When the state enjoys autonomous power, and no other state plays any part in its government.

Stagflation A state of affairs in which inflation in the economy is accompanied by zero growth in a country's industrial production. The word is coined from stagnation and inflation.

Statute Any law passed by the legislature and becoming part of the permanent rules guiding society. Also applies to the rules and laws governing an institute such as a university.

Stonewall In a political context, to block off questions and requests by giving evasive replies. In parliament, to obstruct or delay parliamentary debate and proceedings.

Suffrage The right to vote in political elections. Historically, suffrage was given first to wealthy males, then later all adult males and, after a determined struggle women won their right to vote.

Theocracy When a people or nation recognize God or a deity as their ruler and the king as God's representative. God's laws form the statute book for the kingdom and these are administered by priests or a religious caste who are perceived as His agents.

Totalitarianism A system that tolerates no rival loyalties or parties within the state. Individuals are secondary to the needs of society, and all means of production and distribution are controlled by the state. Until its collapse in 1992, the Soviet Union had lived with this system for most of the 20th century.

Trust Territory A dependent territory that has been placed for reasons of its own security or advancement, or by its own request under an administrative authority by the United Nations.

Unilateralism A decision or action taken by one member of a political association made up two or more states. The dissenting member acts alone and risks losing its place within the association. Rhodesia, an African colony of the British Empire suffered sanctions and triggered a civil war within her own borders when in the 1970s she made a Unilateral Declaration of Independence from Britain.

Universal suffrage When all adult citizens or subjects have the right to vote in an election. Modern democracies have universal suffrage.

Veto The right formally invested in a person or constitutional body to declare decisions made by others to be be overruled. These powers are often invested in the chief executive, such as the President of the United States who can prevent permanently or temporarily the enactment of measures passed by the Congress. Also, the United Nations has a right of veto built into its decision-making process.

Vote of confidence / No confidence Usually a vote taken in parliament or by the relevant legislative body that expresses belief and confidence or lack of it in the governing body, and can precipitate a constitutional crisis, or lead to new elections.

Whip An important member of a particular party in Parliament whose duty it is to ensure that all party members attend the occasion of an important division, or vote in the House. The term is derived from the action described in hunting terms of "whipping in" when strong and decisive action is needed from the horses and first came into use in England in1828. It is a serious transgression to defy the party whips.

COUNTRY INDEX

PICTURE CREDITS

The publisher would like to thank the following for their kind permission to reproduce their photographs:

Page position abbreviations key
t=top, b=below, r=right, l=left, c=center, a=above, f=far, t/l = timeline positions left to right, bbr = box bottom row, btr = box top row

Picture Agency Abbreviations key
Alamy = Alamy Images; AA&A = Ancient Art & Architecture; AP = Associated Press; BAL = Bridgeman Art Library, London & New York; Bett = Bettmann; DK=DK Images; Getty = Getty; Hulton = Hulton Archive/Getty; M.E.P.L = Mary Evans Picture Library; RF = RF

1 Corbis/Bett; **2-3** Getty/AFP; **10** AA&A (t/l l-r 3); The Art Archive/Egyptian Museum Cairo/G. Dagli Orti (t/l l-r 4), National Museum Karachi/G. Dagli Orti (ccl); Corbis/A. de Luca (t/l l-r 8), Arte & Immagini srl (t/l l-r 6), (t/l l-r 7), A. Hornak (bl), O. Lang (cb), Diego Lezama Orezzoli (fbla), G. Dagli Orti (cl), (crb), (t/l l-r 2), (t/l l-r 5), R. Wood (cra); DK/British Museum (ccr); M.E.P.L (t/l l-r 1); Getty/H. Sitton (cr); **11** Alamy/Popperfoto (t/l l-r 2); Robert Harding World Imagery (cb); AA&A; The Art Archive (cr), British Library (t/l l-r 7); BAL/Museo Archeologico Nazionale, Naples, Italy (t/l l-r 1); Corbis/A. de Luca (t/l l-r 4), Bett (t/l l-r 5), (t/l l-r 8), (t/l l-r 9), L. Hebberd (c), Historical Picture Archive (ccr), N. Wheeler (cbl), A. Woolfitt (crb); M.E.P.L (t/l l-r 6); **12** The Art Archive (t/l l-r 5); Corbis/Bett (t/l l-r 1), (t/l l-r 2), (t/l l-r 4), (t/l l-r 6), C. Gerstenberg (t/l l-r 3), D. & J. Heaton (cbl); Lucidio Studio Inc. (cl), C. & J. Lenars (cbr), (ccl), (ccr); RF/Sharok Hatami (crb); **13** The Art Archive (t/l l-r 4), Topkapi Museum Istanbul/G. Dagli Orti (t/l l-r 2); BAL/National Palace Museum, Taipei, Taiwan (t/l l-r 3); Corbis/Archivo Iconografico, S.A (t/l l-r 1), Bett (t/l l-r 5), (t/l l-r 6), Burstein Collection (c), Osborne (c); DK/National Maritime Museum (clb); **14** Corbis (t/l l-r 11), Archivo Iconografico, S.A (cbr), (t/l l-r 3), (t/l l-r 6), Asian Art & Archaeology, Inc (cr), Bett (cb), (cbl), (t/l l-r 1), (t/l l-r 12), (t/l l-r 2), (t/l l-r 5), (t/l l-r 8), S. Bianchetti (t/l l-r 4), Christie's Images (c), Hulton-Deutsch Collection (t/l l-r 7), G. Dagli Orti (crb); M.E.P.L (cl), (t/l l-r 9); Hulton/Stock Montage (t/l l-r 10); **15** Corbis (tc), (t/l l-r 1), (t/l l-r 10), (t/l l-r 5), Bett (cl) (t/l l-r 3), (t/l l-r 4), (t/l l-r 6), (t/l l-r 7), (t/l l-r 9), L. Gubb (t/l l-r 12), Hulton-Deutsch Collection (bc), (ccr), (t/l l-r 8), F. G. Mayer (cra), W. McNamee (br), P. Turnley (cr), (t/l l-r 11), B. A. Vikander (cbl); Hulton/Express Collection (ccl); Keystone Collection (cbr); PA Photos/EPA (crb); **16:** NASA (17); **18:** Corbis/Bett (cbl), Hulton-Deutsch Collection (cbl); **18-19** UN/DPI Photo/Susan B. Markisz; **19** Corbis/Hulton-Deutsch Collection (tr), J. Langevin (crb), C. Newton/The Military Picture Library (tcr); Hulton/UN/DPI Photo/Milton Grant (br); **20-21** RF/Vidal; **21:** Getty/G. Vanderelst (tc); Reuters/B. Yip (cra); **22:** Corbis/Y. Khaldei (cl); **22-23** Corbis/Bett (b), (t); **23** Corbis/D. Bartruff (tr), (cra); PA Photos/EPA (cr); **24** AP/J. Jones (bbr l-r 3), Karim (bbr l-r 4), S. Plunkett (btr l-r 4); Corbis/B. Collier Photos (bbr l-r 1), C. Collins (bbr l-r 2), A. Griffiths Belt (btr l-r 5), A. Pizzoli (bbr l-r 5), J. Roininen (btr l-r 3), L. Skoogfors (btr l-r 2); Reuters/STR (btr l-r 1); UN/DPI Photo/United Nations (btr l-r 5); **25** Corbis (btr l-r 3), B. Collier Photos (box: middle row), F. Origlia; Getty/AFP (tr), (bbr l-r 1), (btr l-r 2), (btr l-r 1), (btr l-r 3); Reuters/A. Hashisho (btr l-r 2); **26** Corbis/D. Cattani (br), P. Corral V (tc), V. Moos (bcr); Getty/AFP (bcl); **27** AP/P. Aneli (tr); Corbis/B. Bisson (bcl), R. Klune (br), R. Essel NYC (cr), V. Streano (bl); Reuters/STR (cr); **30** Getty/P. Le Segretain (cl); **31:** AP (br); Corbis/Archivo Iconografico, S.A. (bc), Bett (tl), (tr), (cla), (tcl), (tcr), Christie's Images (bcl), R. de la Harpe/Gallo Images (bl), G. Dagli Orti (tc); Hulton/Archive Photos (cra), (crb), S. Arnold (bl), Stock Montage (br); **32** AP/J. Bounhar (ca); **33** AP/B. Joshi; **37** AFP News Agency; **38-39** Corbis/A. Maher; **44** AP (tr); **46** AP/V. Thian (tr); Corbis/M. Attar (car); **48** Getty/AFP; **49** Corbis/Archivo Iconografico, S.A (crb), (cl); Arte & Immagini srl (cra), (clb), (cr), Bett (bc), (bcl), Burstein Collection (bc), A. de Luca (tr), F. G. Mayer (bcr), M. Nicholson (tcr), V. Rastelli (tc), R. Wood (tr), (bl); **50** AP/STR (clb), V. Salemi (br); Getty/AFP (bl); **51:** Corbis/Bett (tl); **52-53** Corbis/Bett; **54** Corbis/D. Lees; **55** Alamy/Popperfoto (br); **55** AP/Itsuo Inouye (bl); Corbis/Archivo Iconografico, S.A (bc), Bett (tl), (tc), (cra), (cb), (bcr), (tcr), B. Gentile (c), S. Vannini (cla); Getty/AFP (clb), Timelife (bl); **56** Corbis/A. Thévenart (cra); J. Szenes (cb); Getty/P. Bronstein (bl); Reuters/M. Khursheed (tr); **56-57** Reuters/M. Khursheed (b); **57** Corbis (c); **59** Getty/AFP (tr); **61** Corbis (tr), (crb), (bc), (tcl), (tcr), Archivo Iconografico, S.A. (clb), Bett (tr), (cla), S. Bianchetti (br), Christie's Images (bcl), L. Gubb (bl), O. Franken (cra), G. Dagli Orti (tc), P. Turnley (br); **62** Corbis/K. Baldev (br), G. Rowell (bl); Lonely Planet Images/P. Horton (bl); **62-63** Corbis/Y. Arthus-Bertrand; **63** Corbis/Hulton-Deutsch Collection (tr); Getty/Timelife (tl); RF/Sipa

Press (cb); **64** Reuters/A. Dave (acr); **66** AP/Imperial Household Agency (cb); Corbis/Bett (cra), J. F. Raga (cla), Yamaguchi Herbie (b); Getty (bl); **67** AP/Tsugufumi Matsumoto (cbl); Corbis/Bett (tc); Kyodo News (br); **68** AP (tr); Corbis/Bett (tl), (br), (bcl), (tcl), (tcr); Hulton/Topical Press Agency (bcr); **69** AP/Imperial Household Agency, HO (tl), Itsuo Inouye (cra), Tsugufumi Matsumoto (cal), E. Sugita (tcr); Corbis/Bett (br), (bcr), J. Ficara (tcl), M. S. Yamashita (cal); Hulton (bl), Keystone Collection (bcl); **70-71** AP/Itsuo Inouye; **72** Getty (tc), AFP (tr), Koichi Kamoshida (c) Pool Photo; **72-73** Kyodo News (tl); **73** Corbis/Hulton-Deutsch Collection (c); Getty/AFP (tc); Kyodo News (clb); **74** AP/Itsuo Inouye (bc), Tsugufumi Matsumoto (bl); Corbis/Bett (cal); Hulton/Keystone Collection (c); Kyodo News (tr); **74-75** Uniphoto/Kyodo; **75** AP/Tsugufumi Matsumoto (bc); Getty/AFP (bl); Kyodo News (ca); **76** AP/F. Reiss (clb); Corbis/Telepress Syndicate Agency (bl), O. Thierry (cb); **77** Corbis/Bett (cra), F. Frei, Tuncay Erol (crb) **78** AP/J. Finck (br), M. Schreiber (fbr); Corbis (tcl), Bett (bl), (bc), (bcl), O. Franken (bcr), Hulton-Deutsch Collection (bl), R. Maass (tr); Hulton (tl), Keystone Collection (tcr); **79** AP/ J. Finck (br), F. Reiss (tl), (tc), M. Schreiber (cla); Corbis/Bett (bl), (bc), (bcl), (bcr), B. Regis (br); RF/Action Press (tl); **80** Corbis/Bett (bc), B. Regis (cr), G. Schmid (tc); Getty/AFP (tr); **80-81** Alamy/R. Richardson (t); **81** Corbis/Bett (tr); Getty/AFP (bl); Picture Alliance/DPA/Fotroreport/Stephanie Pilick (cb); Reuters/STF (tl); **82** Corbis/D. Bartruff (tr), Bett (bl), B. Regis (bc); **82-83** Tuncay Erol; **83** AP/W. Rothermel (cl); Getty/AFP (bc); **84** Getty/AFP (cr); **85** Getty/AFP (tr); **86** Corbis (c), Bett (bl), B. Thomas (c); **86-87** Corbis/J. Horner (b); **87** Corbis/Bett (tl); PA Photos/M. Fearn (cb); **88** Alamy/Popperfoto (btr l-r 2); Corbis/Hulton-Deutsch Collection (tl), (btr l-r 1), (tcl), (tcr), F. G. Mayer (btr l-r 5), P. Turnley (tr); DK/S. Oliver (c); M.E.P.L (bbr l-r 3), (bbr l-r 1), (bbr l-r 3), (btr l-r 2), (btr l-r 4); Hulton (btr l-r 4); **89** Alamy/Popperfoto (bbr l-r 1), (bbr l-r 3), (bbr l-r 5); Corbis (cra), Bett (btr l-r 5), Hulton-Deutsch Collection (bbr l-r 2), A. Nogues (bbr l-r 6), R. T. Nowitz (tr); DK/S. Oliver (tcl), Wallace Collection (tr); **90** Corbis/Bett (tc); Hulton (clb); Terry Moore (bcl); **90-91** Getty/V.C.L; **91** Corbis (cla), A. Woolfitt (cr), (bc); RF (tc); **92-93** Getty/S. Touhig; **94** AP/L. Buller (bc), J. Parkin (cla); Corbis/R. Olivier (bl); PA Photos/M. Keene (tr), M. Fearn (br); **94-95** PA Photos/J. Stillwell; **95** AP/J. Arzt (c); Corbis/F. Shamim (bc); **96** Corbis/Bett (tr), O. Franco (bc), P. Turnley (bl), L. Williams (cla); Getty/AFP (cr), (cb); **97** Corbis/Bett (tc); Reuters/Vatican (bl); **98** Corbis/C. O'Rear (bl), R. de la Harpe/Gallo Images (cl); **98** Getty/AFP (tr); Silva Joao/Corbis Sygma (c); **98-99** Corbis/L. Hebberd (b); **100** Corbis (cla), Bett (br); Getty/AFP (bl); **100-101** Corbis/R. Manent; **101** Agencia Efe, S.a/S. Barrenechea (br); AP/P. White (ccb); Corbis/Bett (tr); Getty/AFP; **102** Getty/AFP; **103** Getty/AFP; **104** Corbis/B. Thomas (c), P. A. Souders (br); Reproduction authorised by the Library of Parliament/S. Fenn (bl); **104-105** Getty/S. Schulhof; **105** Corbis/Bett (tl); Reuters (br); RF/Action Press (clb) **106** AP/E. Draper (cl); Corbis (bcr), Bett (bl), (br), (bcl); Getty/AFP (bl); **107** Corbis (tr), Bett (bfl), Canada Wide (br), C. J. Morris (br); Getty/S. Best (cl); **108-109** Getty/Y. Marcoux; **110** Reuters/J. Young (c); **111** AP/Teh Eng Koon (cr); **112** Auspics (bl); Corbis/R. Ressmeyer (cla), B. Thomas (c); M.E.P.L (tr); **112-113** Corbis/P. A. Souders (b); **113** Corbis/Penny Tweedie (cr); Getty/AFP (tr), (cb); **114** Corbis/Bett (br), Hulton-Deutsch Collection (bl) M.E.P.L; Getty/AFP (c); Hulton/Topical Press Agency (bcr); Reuters/M. Baker (cl); **115** Corbis/T. Graham (bc), (br), P. A. Souders (cl); Getty/AFP (bl), (tl); **116** AP; **119** AP/G. Cornier; **129** AP/H. Delic; **133** AP/J. Cogill; **161** AP/C. Dharapak; **163** AP/B. Linsley; **164** AFP News Agency (c); AP/J. Dabaghian (bl); **164-165** Corbis/R. Holmes; **165** AP/F. Mori (c); Corbis/Archivo Iconografico, S.A. (tl), Dovic Muriel (bl), Swim Ink (tr); **166** The Art Archive/Musée Carnavalet Paris/G. Dagli Orti (bbr l-r 7); Corbis (bbr l-r 2), (btr l-r 4), Archivo Iconografico, S.A (c), Bett (tl), (bbr l-r 11), (btr l-r 3), (btr l-r 5), S. Bianchetti (btr l-r 2), L. de Selva (btr l-r 6), C. Hellier (bbr l-r 8), Hulton-Deutsch Collection (bbr l-r 5), A. Meyer (btr l-r 1); M.E.P.L (btr l-r 10), (bbr l-r 9); Hulton/Archive Photos (btr l-r 3), Keystone Collection (tc), (tr); **167** AP/P. Kovarik (cla), F. Mori (tcl); Corbis/Archivo Iconografico, S.A (btr l-r 2), (btr l-r 3), (btr l-r 5), Y. Arthus-Bertrand (tr), Bett (bx top: l-r 1), (bx top: l-r 4), Hulton-Deutsch Collection (bbr l-r 2), (bbr l-r 3), (bbr l-r 7), P. Turnley (bbr l-r 11), (bbr l-r 9); Hulton (bbr l-r 1), (bbr l-r 10), Keystone Collection (bbr l-r 5), (bbr l-r 4), (bbr l-r 6), (bbr l-r 8); Reuters (btr l-r 4); U.S Embassy of France/Ministry of Foreign Affairs (tr); **168** Corbis/Y. Arthus-Bertrand (tl), J-B. Vernier (br); J. Donoso (tc), O. Franken (tcr); **168-169** Corbis/M. Southern/Eye Ubiquitous; **169** AP/J. Brinon (bl); Corbis/P. Almasy (tl), Mathilde de L'Ecotais (tl), O. Thierry (bc); **170-171** Corbis/J-B. Vernier; **172** AP/APTV (br); Corbis/Bett (bl), W. Kaehler (cr), A. Nogues (clb); **173** Corbis/A. Nogues (tl), R. Holmes (cl); **176** AP/V. Ghirda; **189** Corbis/A. Gyori (tr); **193** AP/H. Pustina; **195** AP/G. Baker; **196** Popperfoto (cra); **199** AP/D. Alangkara (tr); **201** Getty/AFP (tr); **204** Corbis/Brooks Kraft (bl), Christie's Images (tr); **204-205** National Geographic Image

Collection/R. Nowitz; **205** Corbis/Bett (tr), O. Franken (br); **206** Corbis (tr), (bbr l-r 5), (bbr l-r 8), Bett (tc), (btr l-r 3), (btr l-r 4), W. McNamee (tcr), T. Stanley (tl); Library Of Congress, Washington, D.C : (bbr l-r 1), (bbr l-r 10), (bbr l-r 11), (bbr l-r 2), (bbr l-r 3), (bbr l-r 4), (bbr l-r 5), (bbr l-r 7), (bbr l-r 9), (btr l-r 10), (btr l-r 2), (btr l-r 5), (btr l-r 6), (btr l-r 7), (btr l-r 8), (btr l-r 9); National Gallery Of Art, Washington DC/Stuart Gilbert (btr l-r 1); **207** Corbis (tcl), G. Smith (tl); Getty/J. Chiasson/Liaison (bbr l-r 11); Library Of Congress, Washington, D.C : all images in timeline box (except fbr); Harry Truman Library (cla), White House Collection, Copyright White House Historical Association (cra); John & Jan Zweifel, Orlando, Florida (tr), (cca); **208-209** Getty/P. Morse/White House; **209** Corbis/D. Bartruff (tcr), Brooks Kraft (tcl); Getty/AFP (cl), (bl); One Mile Up, Inc. (cla); Reuters/L. Downing (tl); **211** Corbis/W. McNamee (c), John Springer Collection (bc); One Mile Up, Inc. (clb); Reuters (cr); United States Senate (c); **212** Corbis/Bett (c), (br); Collection of the Supreme Court of the United States/F. Jantzen (tl), (ca); **212-213** Collection of the Supreme Court of the United States/F. Jantzen; **213** Corbis/Bett (bc), T. Wright (bl); Getty/A. Michaels (tr); United States Supreme Court (c); **214** Duke University (tc); Mark Thiessen (tr); Harry Truman Library/Independence MO ©1948, Washington Post. Reprinted with Permission (tl); **214-215** Richard Solomon © C.F. Payne, 2000 (c); **215** ©2000 Mike Collins, Taterbrains.com (clb); Duke University (ftl); University of Oklahoma/Political Communication Centre (tl); Mark Thiessen (tcl); United States Senate/U.S Senate Collection, Centre for Legislative Archives (bcr); **216** Corbis/S. Maze (bl); Getty/J. Edwards (tr), A. Caulfield (cla); RF/BBY (crb); **216-217** Corbis/J. Waterlow/Eye Ubiquitous (b); **217** National Geographic Image Collection/M. Nichols (c); **218** AP/O. Nikishin (tl); Corbis/P. Turnley (tr); Getty/K. Zavrahzin/Liason Agency (c); Russian Information Department (tcl); **218-219** Russian Information Department (b); **219** AP (cb); Getty/J. Lamb (tl); **220** AP (bcr); Corbis (tl), Bett (br), (bcl), (tcl), W. McNamee (tcr), Sygma (bl), P. Turnley (tr); Novosti (ccl); **221** AP (br), (tcl), ITAR-TASS/Presidential Press Service (cla), M. Japaridze (tl), (tr), D. Mills (tc); Corbis/Bett (bl), (bcl), (fbl), P. Turnley (cra), (bcr); Getty/K. Zavrazhin/Liaison Agency (fbr); **222** AP/Maxim Marmur (222-223); **224** AP/D. Brauchli (tr), Maxim Marmur (tl); Corbis/Sygma (tr); Getty/AFP (br); Russian Information Department (clb); **225** Corbis/K. Georges (bc); DK/C. Orr (cl); Reuters (cra); Russian Information Department (bcl); **226** Getty/AFP (cl); **227** Getty/AFP (cla), (c); **228** Corbis (tr), R. Ressmeyer (c); Getty/AF (crb); **228-229** Getty/Photodisc; **229** Corbis/D. Lehman (tc); **230** R. Marquez; **231** AP/Foley (tr); Corbis/Hulton-Deutsch Collection (bl); **233** AP/Yonhap; **239** Corbis/F. Venturi; **240** AP/E. Felix; **242** Popperfoto; **262** AP/E. Felix; **267** AP/C. Guardia; **271** Corbis/P. Blakely (tr), (tcr); **275** Popperfoto; **276** Popperfoto; **279** AP/F. Guillot; **289** Alamy/Popperfoto (cla); Corbis/L. Aigner (tl), Bett (ctr), (bcr); R. Rudman (tr), Rykoff Collection (bc), D. Turnley (tc), P. Turnley (clb), (bl); Hulton/Keystone Collection (br); RF/Sipa Press (cra), (bcl); **290** Corbis/D. Conger (tr); **290-291** AP/Xinhua, Fan Rujun (c); **291** AP (br); Corbis/Bett (tr); **292** AP (fcr), E. Hoshiko (bc), Xinhua, Yao Dawei (tr Corbis/Bett (c); Hulton (cl), Central Press (ccl), (fcl), Three Lions Collection (c); **293** AP (cl), Chien-min Chung (cr), K. Mayama (bc) J. Widener (ccr), Xinhua News Agency (ccl); Corbis/Bett (tr); Getty/AFP (fcl), P. Rogers (fcr); **294** Corbis (bc), (tcl), Bett (tc), (tr), (bl), (br), Hulton-Deutsch Collection (tl), (bcl), Webistan (br); **295** AP (ca), E. Hoshiko (tr), B. Marquez (br), Xinhua (fbl); Corbis (cla), Bett (bl), P. Blakely (tr), J. Langevin (bcr); Getty (bcl), M. Wilson (fbr); Reuters/Guang Niu (c); **296-297** AP/E. Hoshiko; **298** Corbis/J. Sohm/ChromoSohm Inc. (b); Reuters/W. Chu (c), Chien-Min Chung (tl); **299** Corbis/E. Ciol (tc), Swim Ink (tcl), P. Turnley (c); Getty/AFP (tfl); **302** AP/A. Zemlianichenko (bcr), Chien-min Chung (cla), Korea News Service (cl); **302-303** AP/Xinhua/Gong Yidong (b); **303** Corbis (acl); **304** Corbis/Bett; **307** Corbis/L. Addario (tr), L. Aigner (bl), Bett (bl) (tc), (clb), (crb), (bcl), (tcl), C. Bowe (cla), Hulton-Deutsch Collection (cra), (bcr), P. Turnley (br); RF/Sipa Press (cr); **308** Corbis/S. Sherbell (c); Reuters/O. Popov (tr); **308-309** Corbis/M. Attar; **309** Corbis/Sygma (c); **310** AP/N. Behring-Chisolm; **312** AP/B. Linsley; **316** AP/M. Sezer (tr), (cr).

All other images © DK Images. For further information see: www.dkimages.com

New Earth Media would also like to thank the following for their assistance in the production of the book:

Embassies of the world, with special thanks to the Japanese embassy, Spanish embassy, French embassy and the Russian Information Department in Washington D.C. In the United States, the US Supreme Court, the US Senate, the US House of Representatives, the US Treasury Department, the CIA, and the US Department of State. Also the United Nations, the European Union, the UK Houses of Parliament, the Canadian Library of Parliament, and the Library of Congress. Thanks also to Yoshi Tadokoro at Kyodo News, Paul Howalt for icon design, and Ron Wise for supplying many of the official currency images.